LEARNSMART ADVANTAGE

LearnSmart®

LearnSmart, the most widely used adaptive learning resource, is proven to improve grades. By focusing each student on the most important information they need to learn, LearnSmart personalizes the learning experience so they can study as efficiently as possible.

SmartBook®

SmartBook—an extension of LearnSmart—is an adaptive eBook that helps students focus their study time more effectively. As students read, SmartBook assesses comprehension and dynamically highlights where they need to study more.

EASY TO USE

Learning Management System Integration

McGraw-Hill Campus is a one-stop teaching and learning experience available to use with any learning management system. McGraw-Hill Campus provides single sign-on to faculty and students for all McGraw-Hill material and technology from within the school website. McGraw-Hill Campus also allows instructors instant access to all supplements and teaching materials for all McGraw-Hill products.

Blackboard users also benefit from McGraw-Hill's industry-leading integration, providing single sign-on to access all Connect assignments and automatic feeding of assignment results to the Blackboard grade book.

POWERFUL REPORTING

Connect generates comprehensive reports and graphs that provide instructors with an instant view of the performance of individual students, a specific section, or multiple sections. Since all content is mapped to learning objectives, Connect reporting is ideal for accreditation or other administrative documentation.

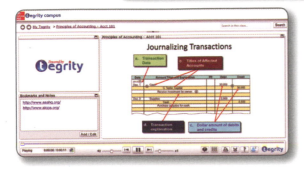

Tegrity

Make your classes available anytime, anywhere. With simple, one-click recording, students can search for a word or phrase and be taken to the exact place in your lecture that they need to review.

MANAGERIAL ECONOMICS

Foundations of Business Analysis and Strategy

MANAGERIAL ECONOMICS: FOUNDATIONS OF BUSINESS ANALYSIS AND STRATEGY, TWELFTH EDITION

Published by McGraw-Hill Education, 2 Penn Plaza, New York, NY 10121. Copyright © 2016 by McGraw-Hill Education. All rights reserved. Printed in the United States of America. Previous editions © 2013, 2011, and 2008. No part of this publication may be reproduced or distributed in any form or by any means, or stored in a database or retrieval system, without the prior written consent of McGraw-Hill Education, including, but not limited to, in any network or other electronic storage or transmission, or broadcast for distance learning.

Some ancillaries, including electronic and print components, may not be available to customers outside the United States.

This book is printed on acid-free paper.

1 2 3 4 5 6 7 8 9 0 DOC/DOC 1 0 9 8 7 6 5

ISBN   978-0-07-802190-9
MHID   0-07-802190-1

Senior Vice President, Products & Markets: *Kurt L. Strand*
Vice President, General Manager, Products & Markets: *Marty Lange*
Vice President, Content Design & Delivery: *Kimberly Meriwether David*
Managing Director: *James Heine*
Senior Brand Manager: *Katie Hoenicke*
Director, Product Development: *Rose Koos*
Senior Product Developer: *Christina Kouvelis*
Product Developer: *Sarah Otterness*
Marketing Manager: *Virgil Lloyd*
Director, Content Design & Delivery: *Linda Avenarius*
Program Manager: *Faye M. Herrig*
Content Project Managers: *Kelly Hart, Kristin Bradley, Karen Jozefowicz*
Buyer: *Susan K. Culbertson*
Design: *Studio Montage, St. Louis, MO*
Content Licensing Specialist: *Beth Thole*
Cover Image: *McGraw-Hill Education*
Compositor: *MPS Limited*
Printer: *R. R. Donnelley*

All credits appearing on page or at the end of the book are considered to be an extension of the copyright page.

Library of Congress Cataloging-in-Publication Data

Cataloging-in-Publication Data has been requested from the Library of Congress.

The Internet addresses listed in the text were accurate at the time of publication. The inclusion of a website does not indicate an endorsement by the authors or McGraw-Hill Education, and McGraw-Hill Education does not guarantee the accuracy of the information presented at these sites.

www.mheducation.com/highered

MANAGERIAL ECONOMICS

Foundations of Business Analysis and Strategy

TWELFTH EDITION

Christopher R. Thomas

University of South Florida

S. Charles Maurice

Texas A&M University
Late Professor Emeritus

The McGraw-Hill Economics Series

To Shelly and Brooke

ABOUT THE AUTHORS

Christopher R. Thomas

Christopher R. Thomas is associate professor of economics at University of South Florida (USF), where he has spent the past 33 years and held the Exide Professorship of Sustainable Enterprise from 2004 through 2010. He worked for two years as an energy economist at Oak Ridge National Laboratory before joining the faculty at USF in 1982. He now teaches managerial economics to undergraduates and to MBA students in both traditional and executive formats. Professor Thomas has published numerous articles on government regulation of industry and antitrust issues and is coeditor of the *Oxford Handbook in Managerial Economics*. Professor Thomas lives with his wife in Brooksville, Florida, where he enjoys photography and playing golf and tennis.

S. Charles Maurice

Chuck Maurice was professor emeritus of economics at Texas A&M University. He spent 30 years in the Department of Economics at Texas A&M, where he served as department head from 1977 through 1981 and held the Rex B. Grey University Professorship of Free Enterprise from 1981 through 1985. Professor Maurice published numerous articles on microeconomic theory in the top economic journals. He co-wrote two scholarly books on natural resource depletion: *The Doomsday Myth* and *The Economics of Mineral Extraction*. He also wrote with Charles Ferguson, and later, Owen Phillips, the widely used intermediate-level microeconomics textbook *Economic Analysis,* which was published from 1971 to 1996. Professor Maurice retired to Gainesville, Florida, where he lived until his death in the spring of 1999.

PREFACE

WHY MANAGERIAL ECONOMICS?

Over the past 40 years, the growing influence of microeconomics and industrial organization economics in every field of business analysis has transformed the role of managerial economics in business school curricula. Economists have understood for some time that every modern course in business strategy and organizational architecture must draw from key areas of advancement in microeconomics and industrial organization. While many business schools have been quick to adopt "strategy" as a fundamental theme in their curricula, this new emphasis on strategy too often falls on the shoulders of a single, one-semester course in business strategy. In a single course, it is extremely difficult, if not impossible, to teach business students managerial economics *and* cover all of the valuable topics in business strategy and organization. In any case, a thorough foundation in managerial economics is required in order to *understand* how to use the many new and important developments in microeconomics and industrial organization.

The objective of *Managerial Economics,* then, is to teach and apply the foundation topics in microeconomics and industrial organization essential for making both the day-to-day business decisions that maximize profit as well as the strategic decisions designed to create and protect profit in the long run. In so doing, we believe *Managerial Economics* helps business students become architects of business tactics and strategy instead of middle managers who plod along the beaten path of others.

PEDAGOGICAL HIGHLIGHTS

The Twelfth Edition of *Managerial Economics* maintains all the pedagogical features that have made previous editions successful. These features follow.

Emphasis on the Economic Way of Thinking

The primary goal of this book has always been, and continues to be, to teach students the economic way of thinking about business decisions and strategy. *Managerial Economics* develops critical thinking skills and provides students with a logical way of analyzing both the routine decisions of managing the daily operations of a business as well as the longer-run strategic plans that seek to manipulate the actions and reactions of rival firms.

Easy to Learn and Teach From

Managerial Economics is a self-contained textbook that requires no previous training in economics. While maintaining a rigorous style, this book is designed to be one of the easiest books in managerial economics from which to teach *and* learn. Rather than parading students quickly through every interesting or new topic in microeconomics and industrial organization, *Managerial Economics* instead carefully develops and applies the most *useful* concepts for business decision making and strategic planning.

Dual Sets of End-of-Chapter Questions

To promote the development of analytical and critical thinking skills, which most students probably do not know how to accomplish on their own, two different kinds of problem sets are provided for each chapter. Much like the pedagogy in mathematics textbooks, which employ both "exercises" and "word problems," *Managerial Economics* provides both Technical Problems and Applied Problems.

- **Technical Problems**—Each section of a chapter is linked (by an icon in the margin)

Now try Technical Problem 3.

to one or more Technical Problems specifically designed to build and reinforce a particular skill. The Technical Problems provide a step-by-step guide for students to follow in developing the analytical skills set forth in each chapter. The answers to all of the Technical Problems are provided to instructors via Create or McGraw-Hill Connect®. The narrow focus of each Technical Problem accomplishes two things: (1) It encourages students to master concepts by taking small "bites" instead of trying to "gulp" the whole chapter at once, and (2) It allows students to pinpoint any areas of confusion so that interaction with the instructor—in the classroom or in the office—will be more productive. When students finish working the Technical Problems, they will have practiced all of the technical skills required to tackle the Applied Problems.

- **Applied Problems**—Following the Technical Problems, each chapter has a set of Applied Problems that serve to build critical thinking skills as well as business decision-making skills. These problems, much like the "word problems" in a math textbook, are a mix of stylized business situations and real-world problems taken from *Bloomberg Businessweek, The Economist, Forbes, The Wall Street Journal,* and other business news publications. Business students frequently find classroom discussion of the Applied Problems among the most valuable lessons of their entire business training. Answers to Applied Problems are available in the *Instructor's Manual*.

The clarity of exposition, coupled with the integrated, step-by-step process of the Technical Problems, allows students to learn most of the technical skills before coming to class. To the extent that technical skills are indeed mastered before class, instructors can spend more time in class showing students how to *apply* the economic way of thinking to business decision making.

Flexible Mathematical Rigor

Starting with only basic algebra and graph-reading skills, all other analytical tools employed in the book are developed within the text itself.

While calculus is not a part of any chapter, instructors wishing to teach a calculus-based course can do so by using the Mathematical Appendices at the end of most chapters. The Mathematical Appendices employ calculus to analyze the key topics covered in the chapter. Most appendices have a set of Mathematical Exercises that requires calculus to solve, and the answers to the Mathematical Exercises are available in the *Instructor's Manual*. A short tutorial, titled "Brief Review of Derivatives and Optimization" is provided via the instructor resource material available through McGraw-Hill Connect®. This six-page review covers the concept of a derivative, the rules for taking derivatives, unconstrained optimization, and constrained optimization.

Self-Contained Empirical Analysis

The Twelfth Edition continues to offer a self-contained treatment of statistical estimation of demand, production, and cost functions. While this text avoids advanced topics in econometrics and strives to teach students only the fundamental statistical concepts needed to estimate demand, production, and cost, the explanations of statistical procedures nonetheless maintain the rigor found in the rest of the book. For those instructors who do not wish to include empirical analysis in their courses, the empirical content can be skipped with no loss of continuity.

Wide Audience

Managerial Economics is appropriate for undergraduate courses in managerial economics and introductory business strategy courses. At the MBA and Executive MBA level, this book works well for "boot camp" or "toolkit" courses in managerial economics, and can also be used as a supplemental text for business strategy and organizational architecture courses. The self-contained nature of the book is especially valuable in night classes, online courses, and Executive MBA courses where students typically have a somewhat limited opportunity to meet with instructors for help outside class.

SUPPLEMENTS

The following ancillaries are available for quick download and convenient access via the Instructor Resource material available through McGraw-Hill Connect®.

Online Appendices and Web Chapter

The *Online Appendices* cover topics that may interest a somewhat narrower group of students and instructors. The following Online Appendices are available:

- Substitution and Income Effects of a Price Change
- Estimating and Forecasting Industry Demand for Price-Taking Firms
- Linear Programming
- Pricing Multiple Products Related in Production

A *Web Chapter* is also available, which, like the appendices, covers a special interest topic. Unlike the appendices, the *Web Chapter* is more robust in length and contains all the elements of a chapter, including, a summary, Technical Problems, and Applied Problems. The following Web Chapter is available:

- The Investment Decision

Test Bank

The *Test Bank* offers well over 1,500 multiple-choice and fill-in-the-blank questions categorized by level of difficulty, AACSB learning categories, Bloom's taxonomy, and topic.

Computerized Test Bank

McGraw-Hill's EZ Test is a flexible and easy-to-use electronic testing program that allows you to create tests from book-specific items. It accommodates a wide range of question types and you can add your own questions. Multiple versions of the test can be created and any test can be exported for use with course management systems. *EZ Test Online* gives you a place to administer your EZ Test-created exams and quizzes online. Additionally, you can access the test bank through McGraw-Hill Connect®.

Instructor's Manual

Written by the author, the *Instructor's Manual* contains Answers to the end-of-chapter Applied Problems and the Mathematical Exercises. Beginning with this Twelfth Edition, the Homework Exercises section moves from the *Student Workbook* to the *Instructor's Manual*. Instructors can assign any or all of these Homework Exercises to students for extra practice. Since the students do not have access to the answers, the Homework Exercises provide an additional set of problems for grading beyond those already available in the Test Bank. In contrast to the Test Bank questions, Homework Exercises are not multiple-choice questions and are designed to look very similar to Technical and Applied Problems found in the textbook.

Duplicate Technical Problems with Answers

For this Twelfth Edition, an entire set of new, duplicate Technical Problems with answers is available to instructors. This additional set of Technical Problems is designed to offer matching problems that instructors can choose to use as additional exercises, as homework assignments, or as exam questions. Students do not have access to either the questions or the answers, and the decision to make answers available to students is the instructor's decision to make. These additional Technical Problems can be accessed by instructors through McGraw-Hill Connect®.

PowerPoint Presentations

PowerPoint Presentations created by Victoria Perk contain animated figures and tables presented in each chapter to make presentations flow in a step-by-step fashion. You can edit, print, or rearrange the slides to fit the needs of your course.

DIGITAL SOLUTIONS

McGraw-Hill Connect®

McGraw-Hill's Connect® is an online assessment solution that connects students with the tools and resources they'll need to achieve success.

Mcgraw-Hill's Connect Features

Connect allows faculty to create and deliver exams easily with selectable test bank items. Instructors can also build their own questions into the system for homework or practice. Other features include:

- **Instructor Library**—The Connect Instructor Library is your repository for additional resources to improve student engagement in and out of class. You can select and use any asset that enhances your lecture. The Connect Instructor Library includes all of the instructor supplements for this text.
- **Student Resources**—The Web Chapter and Online Appendices are available to students via the Student Resource Library.
- **Student Progress Tracking**—Connect keeps instructors informed about how each student, section, and class is performing, allowing for more productive use of lecture and office hours. The progress-tracking function enables you to:
  - View scored work immediately and track individual or group performance with assignment and grade reports.

- Access an instant view of student or class performance relative to learning objectives.
- Collect data and generate reports required by many accreditation organizations, such as AACSB.

- **Diagnostic and Adaptive Learning of Concepts**—LearnSmart and SmartBook offer the first and only adaptive reading experience designed to change the way students read and learn.

LEARNSMART®

Students want to make the best use of their study time. The LearnSmart adaptive self-study technology within Connect provides students with a seamless combination of practice, assessment, and remediation for every concept in the textbook. LearnSmart's intelligent software adapts to every student response and automatically delivers concepts that advance students' understanding while reducing time devoted to the concepts already mastered. The result for every student is the fastest path to mastery of the chapter concepts. LearnSmart:

- Applies an intelligent concept engine to identify the relationships between concepts and to serve new concepts to each student only when he or she is ready.
- Adapts automatically to each student, so students spend less time on the topics they understand and practice more those they have yet to master.
- Provides continual reinforcement and remediation, but gives only as much guidance as students need.
- Integrates diagnostics as part of the learning experience.
- Enables you to assess which concepts students have efficiently learned on their own, thus freeing class time for more applications and discussion.

▌SMARTBOOK®

SmartBook is an extension of LearnSmart–an adaptive eBook that helps students focus their study time more effectively. As students read, SmartBook assesses comprehension and dynamically highlights where they need to study more.

For more information about Connect, go to **connect. mheducation.com,** or contact your local McGraw-Hill sales representative.

McGraw-Hill's Customer Experience Group

We understand that getting the most from your new technology can be challenging. That's why our services don't stop after you purchase our products. You can e-mail our Product Specialists 24 hours a day to get product-training online. Or you can search our knowledge bank of Frequently Asked Questions on our support website. For Customer Support, call **800-331-5094,** or visit **www.mhhe. com/support**.

create™

McGraw-Hill Create™ is a self-service website that allows you to create customized course materials using McGraw-Hill's comprehensive, cross-disciplinary content and digital products. You can even access third-party content such as readings, articles, cases, videos, and more. Arrange the content you've selected to match the scope and sequence of your course. Personalize your book with a cover design and choose the best format for your students–eBook, color print, or black-and-white print. And, when you are done, you'll receive a PDF review copy in just minutes!

NEW FEATURES IN THE TWELFTH EDITION

As with every new edition, I have made a number of revisions to the text by adding new Illustrations, updating and improving topic coverage as needed, and developing a few more Technical and Applied Problems. In this Twelfth Edition, I retired two Illustrations: Illustration 1.3, "Is Baseball Going Broke? Accounting Profits vs. Market Values" and Illustration 2.2, "Do Buyers Really Bid Up Prices?" These retired Illustrations, along with all the other retired Illustrations from past editions, can still be accessed through the Student Library via McGraw-Hill Connect. Five Illustrations are new for this edition:

- Illustration 1.3, "How Do You Value a Golf Course? Estimating the Market Price of a Business"
- Illustration 2.2, "Effects of Changes in Determinants of Supply"
- Illustration 6.1, "$P \times Q$ Measures More Than Just Business's Total Revenue"
- Illustration 12.2, "Diamonds Are Forever— Entry Barriers Are Not"
- Illustration 14.1, "Greyhound Ditches Uniform Pricing for Dynamic Pricing"

In addition to these new Illustrations, Illustration 7.3, "Forecasting New-Home Sales: A Time-Series Forecast" is completely revised using the most recent data for new-home sales. The following recaps the major chapter-by-chapter changes:

- In Chapter 1, the discussion of problems arising from the separation of ownership and control of businesses is revised and updated to more carefully address the concepts of conflicting goals and monitoring problems associated with hidden actions and moral hazard. The presentation of this topic is now more consistent with the modern treatment of incomplete contracts and incomplete information. I chose to not draw the distinction between adverse selection and moral hazard because the outcome of adverse selection in the context of owners and managers is ultimately just the moral hazard: the manager with unknowable and hidden "bad" traits will make non-value-maximizing decisions. While principal–agent problems and corporate control mechanisms are fascinating and complex, coverage in the Twelfth Edition is brief and fundamental, yet still complete enough to stir the interest of better students who may wish to pursue advanced elective courses in business strategy and organization.

- Also new in Chapter 1, Illustration 1.3 examines a "real-world" rule-of-thumb approach to valuing a business's future stream of expected profit, one that is reportedly used by real estate brokers who specialize in selling golf courses. They simplify the valuation process by treating the purchase of a golf course as buying this year's profit in perpetuity. Although this rule of thumb is no doubt too simplistic, students find the simple technique of dividing the single-period profit by the risk-adjusted discount rate to be "useful." Illustration 1.3 discusses the circumstances under which we can reasonably expect to find an equivalence between this simple rule of thumb and the textbook computation of the present value of the stream of future expected profits. To accommodate the students' interest in this topic, I have extended the Mathematical Appendix in Chapter 1 to cover computing present value of a perpetuity along with a quantitative problem that applies this technique.

- Also included in new Illustration 1.3 is a brief explanation of the concept of "enterprise value" (EV), a term now widely used in business publications and investment blogs. EV is promoted as a convenient way to relate the present value of expected profits to the market price paid for a firm. To compute the firm's EV, the transacted market price of a firm is adjusted for the firm's capital structure by subtracting from market price the value of any cash balances the firm may possess and adding the value of any debt obligations that would need to be settled by the firm's buyer at the time of purchase: enterprise value = market price of firm − cash + debt.

- In Chapter 2, a new Illustration 2.2 does for supply what Illustration 2.1 does for demand—it gives students some more examples of variables that shift the supply curve. Illustration 2.2 reinforces the idea that supply curve shifts should be viewed as horizontal shifts in supply, rather than "up" or "down" shifts. Chapter 2 also adopts a rather minor change in notation that should be mentioned here to head off any confusion that might arise. The notation for the expected price of a good in the future is modified slightly to clear up any possible confusion that buyers' expectations of future prices are somehow equivalent to sellers' expectations of future prices. This edition no longer uses P_e to denote *both* demand-and supply-side effects of expected price. Following the convention already adopted in past editions, the subscript for the demand-side variable is henceforth denoted with uppercase E (P_E) and the supply-side variable continues to be denoted with lowercase e (P_e). As a consequence of this change, P_E no longer denotes equilibrium price. $\overline{P}$ now denotes equilibrium price and $\overline{Q}$ denotes equilibrium quantity.

- In Chapter 6, new Illustration 6.1, "$P \times Q$ Measures More Than Just Business's Total Revenue," reminds students that total revenue also measures the total expenditure by consumers on a good or service. The Illustration then shows how to employ demand elasticity to predict the effect of price changes on *consumer expenditures*, which, of course, is the same as predicting the effect of price changes on *total revenue*. Illustration 6.1 can seem obvious or even trivial to instructors, but students often see it clarifying the simple idea.

- In Chapter 7, as previously mentioned, I have updated Illustration 7.3, "Forecasting New-Home Sales: A Time-Series Forecast," by collecting the new-home sales data covering the 36-month period January 2012–December 2014.

Using the latest data, the seasonal dummy variable regression and forecasting model works quite well again to illustrate the power of this rather simple method of capturing seasonal buying patterns on monthly sales of new homes.

- One new Technical Problem is added to both Chapters 11 and 12, and two new Applied Problems have been added to Chapter 12, along with new Illustration 12.2, "Diamonds Are Forever—Entry Barriers Are Not." The new Illustration examines the nature of entry barriers in the New York City taxi cab market and explains how these barriers are now disappearing as a result of new smartphone app-based car services supplied by Uber, Lyft, and Gett.

- Finally, in Chapter 14, new Illustration 14.1, "Greyhound Ditches Uniform Pricing for Dynamic Pricing," discusses the value to Greyhound Bus Company of moving away from uniform pricing to a form of price discrimination called *dynamic pricing*. Although neither the illustration nor the text attempts to model dynamic pricing, students can nonetheless see how Greyhound can profit from charging different prices at different times for the same bus trip.

In addition to the changes in the textbook, the Twelfth Edition also improves the Supplements, which are available to students and instructors via McGraw-Hill Connect. Possibly the most useful of these improvements is the significant expansion in the number of problems available in the Homework Exercises supplement, which as previously noted is now located in the *Instructors' Manual*.

As always, I continue to rely heavily on suggestions for improvement from both students and instructors. I encourage you to contact me directly (crthomas1@usf.edu) with any thoughts you may have for improving the textbook or the accompanying supplements.

A WORD TO STUDENTS

One of the primary objectives in writing this book is to provide you, the student, with a book that enhances your learning experience in managerial economics. However, the degree of success you achieve in your managerial economics course will depend, in large measure, on the effectiveness of your study techniques. I would like to offer you this one tip on studying: Emphasize *active* study techniques rather than *passive* study techniques. Passive study techniques are the kinds of study routines that do not require you to "dig out" the logic for yourself. Some examples of *passive* study activities include reading the text, reviewing class notes, and listening to lectures. These are "passive" in nature because the authors of your textbook or your instructor are providing the analytical guidance and logic for you. You are simply following someone else's reasoning process, working your mind only hard enough to follow along with the authors or instructor. Passive techniques do not cause your brain to "burn" new neural pathways or networks. Generally speaking, students gravitate toward passive study methods, because they are easier and less exhausting than active study methods.

Active study techniques require you to think and reason for yourself. For example, when you close your book, put aside your lecture notes, and try to explain a concept to yourself—perhaps sketching a graph or developing your own numerical example. Only then are you forcing your brain to "burn" a logical path of neurons that will make sense to you later. The better you can explain the "how" and "why" of key concepts and principles in this book, the more thorough will be your understanding and the better you will perform on exams. Of course, some passive study is necessary to become familiar with the material, but genuine understanding and the ability to use the decision-making skills of managerial economics require emphasis on active, rather than passive, study techniques.

ACKNOWLEDGMENTS

Many of the best ideas for improving a textbook come from colleagues, adopters, reviewers, and students. This revision was no exception.

As always, I am grateful to the entire editorial and production team at McGraw-Hill for their considerable help making this revision possible. I would like especially to thank Christina Kouvelis and Sarah Otterness for their thoroughness and good cheer with the substantial editorial work required to complete successfully this Twelfth Edition. Dheeraj Chahal deserves appreciation for his wonderful job managing the process of compositing this book.

I also received numerous comments from my colleagues and adopters that helped improve the topic coverage and as well as some details of exposition. Comments from Professor Yu Leng at Shanghai Jiaotong University were especially helpful. And I would like to thank Ilya Malkov, one of my best economics students, for his willingness to proof read and check the solutions to the many new Technical Problems introduced in this edition.

Finally, I wish to thank my wife and daughter, Shelly and Brooke, for all their love and support during this project. They too are very much part of the team that makes this book possible.

Christopher R. Thomas
Tampa, Florida

BRIEF CONTENTS

CONTENTS

ILLUSTRATIONS IN THE TWELFTH EDITION

Chapter 1

Managers, Profits, and Markets

After reading this chapter, you will be able to:

1.1 Understand why managerial economics relies on microeconomics and industrial organization to analyze business practices and design business strategies.

1.2 Explain the difference between economic and accounting profit and relate economic profit to the value of the firm.

1.3 Describe how separation of ownership and management can lead to a principal–agent problem when goals of owners and managers are not aligned and monitoring managers is costly or impossible for owners.

1.4 Explain the difference between price-taking and price-setting firms and discuss the characteristics of the four market structures.

1.5 Discuss the primary opportunities and threats presented by the globalization of markets in business.

Student of managerial economics: Will I ever use this?
Professor: Only if your career is successful.

Success in the business world, no matter how you slice it, means winning in the marketplace. From CEOs of large corporations to managers of small, privately held companies—and even nonprofit institutions such as hospitals and universities—managers of any of these kinds of organizations cannot expect to make successful business decisions without a clear understanding of how market forces create both opportunities and constraints for business enterprises. Business publications such as *The Wall Street Journal,*

Bloomberg Businessweek, The Economist, Harvard Business Review, Forbes, and *Fortune* regularly cover the many stories of brilliant and disastrous business decisions and strategies made by executive managers. Although luck often plays a role in the outcome of these stories, the manager's understanding—or lack of understanding—of fundamental economic relations usually accounts for the difference between success and failure in business decisions. While economic analysis is not the only tool used by successful managers, it is a powerful and essential tool. Our primary goal in this text is to show you how business managers can use economic concepts and analysis to make decisions and design strategies that will achieve the firm's primary goal, which is usually the maximization of profit.

Publishers roll out dozens of new books and articles each year touting the latest strategy *du jour* from one of the year's most "insightful" business gurus. The never-ending parade of new business "strategies," buzzwords, and anecdotes might lead you to believe that successful managers must constantly replace outdated analytical methods with the latest fad in business decision making. While it is certainly true that managers must constantly be aware of new developments in the marketplace, a clear understanding of the economic way of thinking about business decision making is a valuable and timeless tool for analyzing business practices and strategies. Managerial economics addresses the larger economic and market forces that shape both day-to-day business practices, as well as strategies for sustaining the long-run profitability of firms. Instead of presenting cookbook formulas, the economic way of thinking develops a systematic, logical approach to understanding business decisions and strategies—both today's and tomorrow's.

While this text focuses on making the most profitable business decisions, the principles and techniques set forth also offer valuable advice for managers of nonprofit organizations such as charitable foundations, universities, hospitals, and government agencies. The manager of a hospital's indigent-care facility, for example, may wish to minimize the cost of treating a community's indigent patients while maintaining a satisfactory level of care. A university president, facing a strict budget set by the state board of regents, may want to enroll and teach as many students as possible subject to meeting the state-imposed budget constraint. Although profit maximization is the primary objective addressed in this text, the economic way of thinking about business decisions and strategies provides *all* managers with a powerful and indispensible set of tools and insights for furthering the goals of their firms or organizations.

1.1 THE ECONOMIC WAY OF THINKING ABOUT BUSINESS PRACTICES AND STRATEGY

Because this text relies primarily on economic theory to explain how to make more profitable business decisions, we want to explain briefly how and why economic theory is valuable in learning how to run a business. Managerial economics applies the most useful concepts and theories from two closely related areas of economics— microeconomics and industrial organization—to create a systematic, logical way of analyzing business practices and tactics designed to get the most profit, as well as formulating strategies for sustaining or protecting these profits in the long run.

Economic Theory Simplifies Complexity

No doubt you have heard statements such as "That's OK in theory, but what about the real world?" or "I don't want ivory-tower theorizing; I want a practical solution." Practical solutions to challenging real-world problems are seldom found in cookbook formulas, superficial rules of thumb, or simple guidelines and anecdotes. Profitable solutions generally require that people understand how the real world functions, which is often far too complex to comprehend without making the simplifying assumptions used in theories. Theory allows people to gain insights into complicated problems using simplifying assumptions to make sense out of confusion, to turn complexity into relative simplicity. By abstracting away from the irrelevant, managers can use the economic way of thinking about business problems to make predictions and explanations that are valid in the real world, even though the theory may ignore many of the actual characteristics of the real world. And, as we like to remind students, if it doesn't work in theory or concept, it is highly unlikely to work in practice.

Using economic theory is in many ways like using a road map. A road map abstracts away from nonessential items and concentrates on what is relevant for the task at hand. Suppose you want to drive from Dallas to Memphis. Having never made this trip, you need to have a map. So, you log on to the Internet and go to Google maps, where you get to choose either a satellite view of the region between Dallas and Memphis or a simple street view. The satellite view is an exact representation of the real world; it shows every road, tree, building, cow, and river between Dallas and Memphis. While the satellite view is certainly fascinating to look at, its inclusion of every geographic detail makes it inferior to the much simpler street view in its ability to guide you to Memphis. The simpler street view is better suited to guide you because it abstracts from reality by eliminating irrelevant information and showing only the important roads between Dallas and Memphis. As such, the (abstract) street view gives a much clearer picture of how to get to Memphis than the (real-world) satellite view. Likewise, the economic approach to understanding business reduces business problems to their most essential components.

The Roles of Microeconomics and Industrial Organization

microeconomics
The study of individual behavior of consumers, business firms, and markets, and it contributes to our understanding of business practices and tactics.

As we mentioned previously, managerial economics draws on two closely related areas of economic theory: microeconomics and industrial organization. If you have taken a basic course in economics, you will recall that **microeconomics** is the study and analysis of the behavior of individual segments of the economy: individual consumers, workers and owners of resources, individual firms, industries, and markets for goods and services. As a necessary means for addressing the behavior of rational individuals (both consumers and producers), microeconomics develops a number of foundation concepts and optimization techniques that explain the everyday business decisions managers must routinely make in running a business. These decisions involve such things as choosing the profit-maximizing production level, deciding how much of the various productive inputs to purchase in order to produce the chosen output level at lowest total cost,

ILLUSTRATION 1.1

Managerial Economics
The Right ℞ for Doctors

A number of universities offer MBA programs designed specifically for medical doctors. The majority of the doctors enrolled in these specialized programs are seeking to develop the business-decision-making skills they need to manage private and public medical clinics and hospitals.

Doctors are understandably most interested in courses that will quickly teach them practical business skills. In managerial economics, they have found many valuable tools for business decision making and have been quick to apply the principles and tools of managerial economics to a variety of business problems in medicine. Some of the more interesting of these applications, all of which are topics you will learn about in this text, are discussed here:

- *Irrelevance of fixed costs in decision making:* Nearly all the physicians admitted to making some decisions based on fixed costs. A director of a radiation oncology department complained that many of her hospital's administrative costs are included as part of the incremental costs of treating additional patients. While the hospital prided itself in moving toward a marginal cost pricing structure for services, the accounting department's calculation of marginal cost was inflated by fixed administrative costs.

- *Price discrimination:* A doctor specializing in vasectomies wanted to increase revenue by engaging in price discrimination. After a lengthy discussion about the legality of charging different prices for medical services, he decided to promote his vasectomy clinic by placing a $40-off coupon in the local newspaper's TV guide. He believes that only lower income patients will clip the coupon and pay the lower price.

- *Advertising dilemma:* After a class discussion on the advertising dilemma in oligopoly markets, a doctor who specializes in LASIK eye surgery expressed her relief that none of the other three LASIK surgeons in her small town had shown any interest in advertising their services. She decided it would not be wise for her to begin running radio ads.

- *Linear trend forecasting:* Several physicians used linear trend analysis to forecast patient load. An administrator of a hospital's emergency room services found that using "day-of-week" dummy variables, he could offer hospital administrators statistical evidence—instead of his casual observation—that certain days of the week tend to be (statistically) significantly busier than others.

- *Strategic entry deterrence:* A doctor in New Orleans decided to open new clinics in Baton Rouge and Morgan City. No other clinics like his are currently operating in these two cities. In order to discourage other doctors from opening similar clinics, he plans to price his services just slightly above average total cost but significantly below the price that would maximize profit under monopoly.

- *Profit maximization vs. revenue maximization:* A doctor with a 25 percent ownership interest in a pharmaceutical supply firm realized during class that his sales manager is probably selling too many units because the manager's compensation is based substantially on commissions. The doctor plans to recommend raising drug prices to sell fewer units and to begin paying the sales manager a percentage of profit.

- *Economies of scale and scope:* Hospital managers perceive the current trend toward "managed care" to be forcing hospitals to reduce costs without reducing quality. Economies of scale and scope, to the extent that such economies exist, offer an attractive solution to the need for cost reduction. Hospital administrators in the class were especially interested in empirical methods of measuring economies of scale in order to plan for future expansion or contraction.

- *Cost-minimizing input combination:* One doctor who owns and manages a chain of walk-in clinics decided to reduce the employment of MDs and increase the employment of RNs on the basis of classroom discussion of cost minimization. Apparently, for many of the procedures performed at the clinic, experienced nurses can perform the medical tasks approximately as well as the physicians, as long as the nurses are supervised by MDs. The doctor-manager reasoned that even though MDs have higher marginal products than RNs, the marginal product per dollar spent on RNs exceeded the marginal product per dollar spent on MDs.

Business publications report that doctors with MBA degrees are becoming increasingly powerful in the medical profession as hospitals, health maintenance organizations, and other types of health care clinics hire them to manage the business aspect of health care. Some doctors, as well as the American Medical Association, are opposed to blending business and medical values. Given the nature of the applications of managerial economics cited here, it appears that a course in managerial economics offers doctors insights into the business of medicine that they would not usually get in medical school. Many doctors think this knowledge is good medicine.

choosing how much to spend on advertising, allocating production between two or more manufacturing plants located in different places, and setting the profit-maximizing price(s) for the good(s) the firm sells.

These routine business decisions, made under the prevailing market conditions, are sometimes referred to as *business practices or tactics* to distinguish them from *strategic decisions,* which involve business moves designed intentionally to influence the behavior of rival firms. In other words, the firm's **management team** makes many decisions about **business practices** or **tactics** to create the greatest possible profit for the specific business environment faced by the firm. Because business practices typically involve maximizing or minimizing something, the field of microeconomics can be extremely helpful in understanding how to make these operating decisions. As we will stress throughout this book, microeconomics, with its emphasis on maximizing and minimizing processes, provides a kind of all-purpose, Swiss army knife for explaining how to make the most profitable business decisions. Once you get the hang of this approach, you will see that managerial economics is really just a series of repeated applications of a general method of reasoning known as "marginal analysis." In Chapter 3, we will explain and illustrate the powerful logic of marginal analysis. Economists like to say that marginal analysis provides "the key to the kingdom of microeconomics." Given the central role of microeconomics in managerial economics, we can safely tell you that marginal analysis also provides "the key to the kingdom of *managerial* economics."

While microeconomics serves as our "Swiss army knife" for explaining most business practices, a specialized branch of microeconomics, known as *industrial organization,* gives us an additional, complementary tool for business analysis. **Industrial organization,** which focuses specifically on the behavior and structure of firms and industries, supplies considerable insight into the nature, motivation, and consequences of strategic actions firms may wish to undertake. Many of the most important developments in business analysis and strategic thinking over the past 30 years flow directly from advances in the theory of industrial organization. Most of the discussion in this text about strategic decision making can be attributed to these advances in the field of industrial organization.

business practices or **tactics**
Routine business decisions managers must make to earn the greatest profit under the prevailing market conditions facing the firm.

industrial organization
Branch of microeconomics focusing on the behavior and structure of firms and industries.

FIGURE 1.1
Economic Forces That Promote Long-Run Profitability

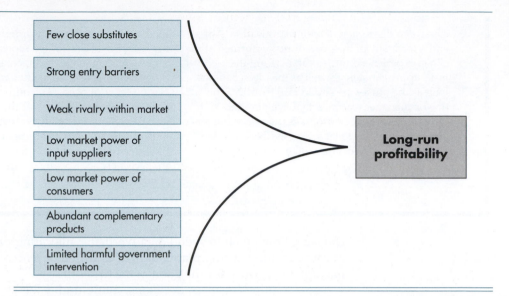

| Few close substitutes |
| Strong entry barriers |
| Weak rivalry within market |
| Low market power of input suppliers |
| Low market power of consumers |
| Abundant complementary products |
| Limited harmful government intervention |

→ **Long-run profitability**

strategic decisions
Business actions taken to alter market conditions and behavior of rivals in ways that increase and/or protect the strategic firm's profit.

Strategic decisions differ from routine business practices and tactics because strategic decisions do not accept the existing conditions of competition as fixed, but rather attempt to shape or alter the circumstances under which a firm competes with its rivals. In so doing, strategic decisions can create greater profits and, in some cases, protect and sustain the profits into the future. While common business practices and tactical decisions are necessary for keeping organizations moving toward their goals—usually profit-maximization—strategic decisions are, in a sense, "optional" actions managers might be able to undertake should circumstances arise making a strategy suitable and likely to succeed. In Chapter 13, we will show you how to apply a variety of concepts from game theory and industrial organization to design strategic moves to make more profit.

With its emphasis on noncooperative game theory and the behavior of firms when rivals are few in number, industrial organization concepts now play a central role in every modern course in business strategy. Business strategists rely heavily on the field of industrial organization to identify and examine the economic forces that influence the long-run profitability of businesses. Figure 1.1 shows a list of economic forces that determine the *level* of profit a firm can expect to earn in the long run and the *durability* of long-run profits.[1] As a business or economics major, you may wish to take an entire course in industrial organization to learn about these forces. In this book, we will cover most of these factors in varying degrees of detail. We are confident that when you finish this course, you will agree that

[1]Michael Porter, in his book *Competitive Strategy*, New York: Free Press, 1980, examines the first five forces in Figure 1.1. His pioneering work, called "Five Forces Analysis," remains a widely studied framework in business strategy courses. More recently, Adam Brandenburger and Barry Nalebuff have added complementarity of products and inputs to the list of economic forces affecting long-run profitability. See their book, *Co-Opetition*, New York: Doubleday, 1996.

managerial economics covers a wide range of important business decisions and offers a powerful, indispensable view of the business world.

1.2 MEASURING AND MAXIMIZING ECONOMIC PROFIT

As mentioned previously, the primary purpose of this text is to show managers how to make decisions that will generate the most profit for their businesses. Profit serves as the score in the "game" of business. It's the amount by which revenues exceed costs. And when costs exceed revenues, the resulting negative profits, or losses, signal owners in no uncertain terms that they are reducing their wealth by owning and running unprofitable businesses. The success of managers' decisions is judged according to a single overriding concern: Are managers' decisions creating higher or lower profits? Managers who can make the largest possible profits not only enrich the owners of firms—and managers are often part or full owners of firms they manage—but they also create for themselves a reputation for profitable decision making that can be worth millions of dollars in executive compensation. Thus, it is crucial for managers to understand how the "score" is calculated and how to achieve the highest possible score without getting sidetracked by issues that don't affect the score. It is essential that managers never forget that the goal of the firm is to maximize economic profits. Nothing else matters in the world of business as much as profit does because the value of a business and the wealth of its owners are determined solely by the amount of profits the firm can earn.

After hearing so much news about scandals over financial reporting errors, as well as several spectacular cases of management and accounting fraud—think Enron, WorldCom, and MF Global—you probably won't be surprised when we explain in this section why "profits" reported in corporate financial statements generally overstate the profitability of firms. The tendency for overstating profits examined in this section, however, has nothing to do with accounting mistakes or fraud. Indeed, the reason accounting reports of profit (which accountants may call net income, net earnings, or net profit, depending on the circumstances) poorly reflect the actual profitability of firms can be explained by examining the generally accepted accounting practices set forth by professional accounting associations subject to approval from government agencies. Before we can explain why financial accounting procedures overstate business profitability, we must first show you how to measure the economic costs businesses incur when using resources to produce goods or services.

Economic Cost of Using Resources

As you know, businesses produce the goods or services they sell using a variety of resources or productive inputs. Many kinds of labor services and capital equipment inputs may be employed along with land, buildings, raw materials, energy, financial resources, and managerial talent. The economic cost of using resources to produce a good or service is the *opportunity cost* to the owners of the firm using those resources. The **opportunity cost** of using any kind of resource is what the owners of a business must give up to use the resource.

opportunity cost
What a firm's owners give up to use resources to produce goods or services.

market-supplied resources
Resources owned by others and hired, rented, or leased in resource markets.

owner-supplied resources
Resources owned and used by a firm.

total economic cost
Sum of opportunity costs of market-supplied resources plus opportunity costs of owner-supplied resources.

explicit costs
Monetary opportunity costs of using market-supplied resources.

implicit costs
Nonmonetary opportunity costs of using owner-supplied resources.

equity capital
Money provided to businesses by the owners.

The method of measuring opportunity costs differs for various kinds of inputs used by businesses. Businesses utilize two kinds of inputs or resources. One of these categories is **market-supplied resources,** which are resources owned by others and hired, rented, or leased by the firm. Examples of resources purchased from others include labor services of skilled and unskilled workers, raw materials purchased in resource markets from commercial suppliers, and capital equipment rented or leased from equipment suppliers. The other category of resources is **owner-supplied resources.** The three most important types of owner-supplied resources are money provided to the business by its owners, time and labor services provided by the firm's owners, and any land, buildings, or capital equipment owned and used by the firm.

Businesses incur opportunity costs for *both* categories of resources used. Thus, the **total economic cost** of resources used in production is the sum of the opportunity costs of market-supplied resources and the opportunity costs of owner-supplied resources. Total economic cost, then, represents the opportunity cost of all resources used by a firm to produce goods or services.

The opportunity costs of using *market-supplied* resources are the out-of-pocket monetary payments made to the owners of resources. The monetary payments made for market-supplied inputs are also known as **explicit costs.** For example, one of the resources Apple Inc. needs to manufacture its iMac computer is an Intel Core i7 microprocessor chip. This chip is manufactured by Intel Corp., and Apple can purchase one for $310. Thus, Apple's opportunity cost to obtain the computer chip is $310, the monetary payment to the owner of the input. We want to emphasize here that explicit costs are indeed opportunity costs; specifically, it's the amount of money sacrificed by firm owners to get market-supplied resources.

In contrast to explicit costs of using market-supplied resources, there are no out-of-pocket monetary or cash payments made for using owner-supplied resources. The opportunity cost of using an *owner-supplied* resource is the best return the owners of the firm could have received had they taken their own resource to market instead of using it themselves. These nonmonetary opportunity costs of using a firm's own resources are called **implicit costs** because the firm makes no monetary payment to use its own resources. Even though firms do not make explicit monetary payments for using owner-supplied inputs, the opportunity costs of using such inputs are not zero. The opportunity cost is only equal to zero if the market value of the resource is zero, that is, if no other firm would be willing to pay anything for the use of the resource.

Even though businesses incur numerous kinds of implicit costs, we will focus our attention here on the three most important types of implicit costs mentioned earlier: (1) the opportunity cost of cash provided to a firm by its owners, which accountants refer to as **equity capital;** (2) the opportunity cost of using land or capital owned by the firm; and (3) the opportunity cost of the owner's time spent managing the firm or working for the firm in some other capacity. For more than 70 years, these implicit costs have been the center of controversy over how accountants should measure the costs of using owner-supplied re-sources. We will have more to say about this issue in our later discussion of measuring business profit, as well as in Illustration 1.2. Let's first look at ex-amples of each of these implicit costs.

ILLUSTRATION 1.2

The Sarbanes-Oxley Act
Will It Close the GAAP between Economic and Accounting Profit?

When Congress passed the Sarbanes-Oxley Act (2002), it gave the federal government substantial new authority to regulate the auditing of corporate financial statements with the aim of reducing fraudu-lent reports of accounting profits. Although Sarbanes-Oxley primarily focuses on detecting and preventing fraud via improved auditing, the act also rekindled interest in a long-standing conceptual disagreement between economists and accountants concerning how to properly measure profits. As we have emphasized in this chapter, accountants follow reporting rules known as generally accepted accounting principles, or GAAP, which do not allow most kinds of implicit costs of owner-supplied resources to be deducted from revenues. Failure to deduct these implicit costs causes accounting measures of profit—referred to on finan-cial statements variously as net earnings, earnings af-ter tax, net income, operating profit, and net profit—to overstate economic profit, because economic profit subtracts all costs of resources used by businesses.

A number of authorities in the fields of finance and accounting believe Sarbanes-Oxley focuses too much attention and regulatory effort on reducing fraud. They believe the most important shortcoming for financial statements stems from accounting rules that poorly measure the profitability of businesses. Robert Bartley, one of several experts who have contributed their opinions on the subject, offered the following observation:

For while there has been some cheating and corner-cutting, the real problem with corporate reporting is con-ceptual. EPS, the familiar earnings per share [accounting profit divided by the number of outstanding shares of common stock], is supposed to measure corporate profit, as determined by GAAP, or generally accepted accounting

principles. But economists have long recognized that profit is . . . by no means the same thing as accounting profit.[a]

This same concern is amplified by G. Bennett Stewart in his commentary on the Sarbanes-Oxley Act:

The real problem [causing the recent accounting scandals] is that earnings and earnings per share (EPS), as measured according to GAAP, are unreliable measures of corporate performance and stock-market value. Accountants simply are not counting what counts or measuring what matters.[b]

We have discussed in this chapter how to measure the implicit costs of several kinds of owner-supplied resources not presently treated as costs under GAAP: the owners' financial capital (i.e., equity capital), physical capital, and land, as well as time spent by owners managing their firms. While all of these types of implicit costs must be treated as costs to bring ac-counting earnings in line with economic profits, it is the opportunity cost of equity capital, according to Stewart, that generates the greatest single distortion in computing accounting profit:

The most noteworthy flaw in GAAP is that no charge is deducted from [revenues] for the cost of providing . . . shareholders with a . . . return on their investment . . . The most significant proposed adjustment of GAAP is to deduct the cost of equity capital from net income [i.e., accounting profit]. Failure to deduct it is a stupendous earnings distortion.[c]

As an example of the magnitude of this distortion, in 2002 the 500 firms that comprise the Standard and Poor's (S&P) stock index employed about $3 trillion of equity capital, which, at a 10 percent annual op-portunity cost of equity capital, represents a resource cost to businesses of $300 billion (0.10 × $3 trillion). To put this cost, which GAAP completely ignores, into perspective, Stewart notes that the sum total of all ac-counting profit for the S&P 500 firms in 2002 was just

(Continued)

$118 billion. After subtracting this opportunity cost of equity capital from aggregate accounting profit, the resulting measure of economic profit reveals that these 500 businesses experienced a loss of $182 billion in 2002. As you can now more fully appreciate, the GAAP between economic and accounting profit creates a sizable distortion that, if corrected, can turn a seemingly profitable business, along with its CEO, into a big loser!

[a]Robert L. Bartley, "Thinking Things Over: Economic vs. Accounting Profit," *The Wall Street Journal*, June 2, 2003, p. A23. Copyright © 2003 Dow Jones & Company, Inc.

[b]G. Bennett Stewart III, "Commentary: Why Smart Managers Do Dumb Things," *The Wall Street Journal*, June 2, 2003, p. A18. Copyright © 2003 Dow Jones & Company.

[c]Ibid.

Initially, and then later as firms grow and mature, owners of businesses—single proprietorships, partnerships, and corporations alike—usually provide some amount of money or cash to get their businesses going and to keep them running. This equity capital is an owner-supplied resource and entails an opportunity cost equal to the best return this money could earn for its owner in some other investment of comparable risk. Suppose, for example, investors use $20 million of their own money to start a firm of their own. Further suppose this group could take the $20 million to the venture capital market and earn a return of 12 percent annually at approximately the same level of risk incurred by using the money in its own business. Thus, the owners sacrifice $2.4 million (= 0.12 × $20 million) annually by providing equity capital to the firm they own. If you don't think this is a real cost, then be sure to read Illustration 1.2.

Now let's illustrate the implicit cost of using land or capital owned by the firm. Consider Alpha Corporation and Beta Corporation, two manufacturing firms that produce a particular good. They are in every way identical, with one exception: The owner of Alpha Corp. rents the building in which the good is produced; the owner of Beta Corp. inherited the building the firm uses and therefore pays no rent. Which firm has the higher costs of production? The costs are the same, even though Beta makes no explicit payment for rent. The reason the costs are the same is that using the building to produce goods costs the owner of Beta the amount of income that could have been earned had the building been leased at the prevailing rent. Because these two buildings are the same, presumably the market rentals would be the same. In other words, Alpha incurred an explicit cost for the use of its building, whereas Beta incurred an implicit cost for the use of its building.[2] Regardless of whether the payment is explicit or implicit, the opportunity cost of using the building resource is the same for both firms.

We should note that the opportunity cost of using owner-supplied inputs may not bear any relation to the amount the firm paid to acquire the input. The opportunity cost reflects the current market value of the resource. If the firm

---

[2]Alternatively, Beta's sacrificed return can be measured as the amount the owner could earn if the resource (the building) were sold and the payment invested at the market rate of interest. The sacrificed interest is the implicit cost when a resource is sold and the proceeds invested. This measure of implicit cost is frequently the same as the forgone rental or lease income, but if they are not equal, the true opportunity cost is the *best* alternative return.

paid $1 million for a plot of land two years ago but the market value of the land has since fallen to $500,000, the implicit cost now is the best return that could be earned if the land is sold for $500,000, not $1 million (which would be impossible under the circumstances), and the proceeds are invested. If the $500,000 could be invested at 6 percent annually, the implicit cost is $30,000 (= $0.06 \times $500,000) per year. You should be careful to note that the implicit cost is *not* what the resource could be sold for ($500,000) but rather it is the best return sacrificed each year ($30,000).

Finally, consider the value of firm owners' time spent managing their own businesses. Presumably, if firm owners aren't managing their businesses or working for their firms in other capacities, they could obtain jobs with some other firms, possibly as managers. The salary that could be earned in an alternative occupation is an implicit cost that should be considered as part of the total cost of production because it is an opportunity cost to these owners. The implicit cost of an owner's time spent managing a firm or working for the firm in some other capacity is frequently, though not always, the same as the payment that would be necessary to hire an equivalent manager or worker if the owner does not work for the firm.

We wish to stress again that, even though no explicit monetary payment is made for the use of owner-supplied resources, $1 worth of implicit costs is no less (and no more) of an opportunity cost of using resources than $1 worth of explicit costs. Consequently, both kinds of opportunity costs, explicit and implicit opportunity costs, are added together to get the total economic cost of resource use. We now summarize this important discussion on measuring the economic costs of using resources in a principle:

Principle   The opportunity cost of using resources is the amount the firm gives up by using these resources. Opportunity costs can be either explicit costs or implicit costs. Explicit costs are the costs of using market-supplied resources, which are the monetary payments to hire, rent, or lease resources owned by others. Implicit costs are the costs of using owner-supplied resources, which are the greatest earnings forgone from using resources owned by the firm in the firm's own production process. Total economic cost is the sum of explicit and implicit costs.

Now try Technical
Problem 1.

Figure 1.2 illustrates the relations set forth in this principle. Now that we have shown you how to measure the cost of using resources, we can explain the difference between economic profit and accounting profit.

Notice to students: The notebooks in the left margin throughout this text are directing you to work the enumerated Technical Problems at the end of the chapter. Be sure to check the answers provided for you at the end of the book *before* proceeding to the next section of a chapter. We have carefully designed the Technical Problems to guide your learning in a step-by-step process.

economic profit
The difference between total revenue and total economic cost.

Economic Profit versus Accounting Profit

Economic profit is the difference between total revenue and total economic cost. Recall from our previous discussion that total economic cost measures the

FIGURE 1.2
Economic Cost of Using Resources

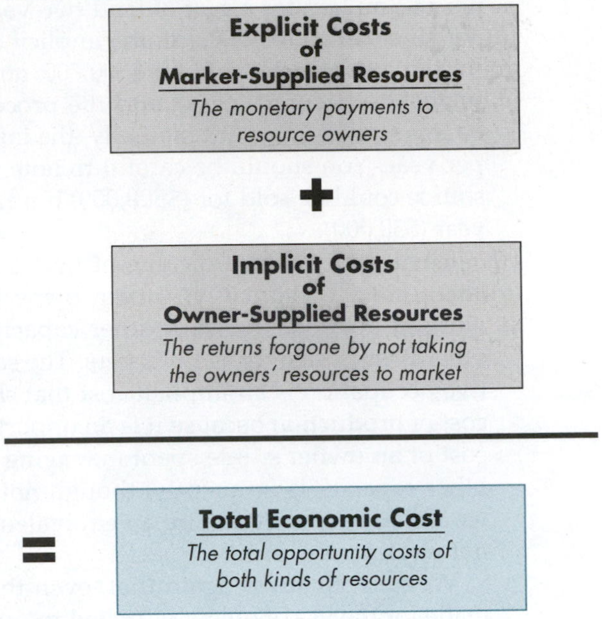

Explicit Costs
of
Market-Supplied Resources
The monetary payments to resource owners

+

Implicit Costs
of
Owner-Supplied Resources
The returns forgone by not taking the owners' resources to market

=

Total Economic Cost
The total opportunity costs of both kinds of resources

opportunity costs of *all* the resources used by the business, both market-supplied and owner-supplied resources, and thus:

$$\text{Economic profit} = \text{Total revenue} - \text{Total economic cost}$$
$$= \text{Total revenue} - \text{Explicit costs} - \text{Implicit costs}$$

Economic profit, when it arises, belongs to the owners of the firm and will increase the wealth of the owners. When revenues fail to cover total economic cost, economic profit is negative, and the loss must be paid for out of the wealth of the owners.

When accountants calculate business profitability for financial reports, they follow a set of rules known as "generally accepted accounting principles" or GAAP. If you have taken courses in accounting, you know that GAAP provides accountants with detailed measurement rules for developing accounting information presented in financial statements, such as balance sheets, cash flow statements, and income statements. The Securities and Exchange Commission (SEC) along with the Financial Accounting Standards Board (FASB), a professional accounting organization, work together to construct the detailed rules of GAAP. To understand the importance of GAAP for our present discussion, you only need to know that GAAP rules do not allow accountants to deduct most types of implicit costs for the purposes of calculating taxable accounting profit.

Accounting profit, then, differs from economic profit because accounting profit does not subtract from total revenue the implicit costs of using resources. **Accounting profit** is the difference between total revenue and explicit costs:

$$\text{Accounting profit} = \text{Total revenue} - \text{Explicit costs}$$

accounting profit
The difference between total revenue and explicit costs.

Depending on the type of financial statement and where it appears in a statement, accounting profit goes by a variety of names such as income, net income, operating income, net profit, earnings, or net earnings.

As you can see, when firms employ owner-supplied resources, the resulting implicit costs are not subtracted from total revenue and the accounting profits reported in financial statements overstate business profitability. All three types of implicit costs discussed earlier are ignored by accountants.[3] We want to stress, however, that when financial accountants omit these implicit costs from financial reports, they are following generally accepted rules set forth by the FASB and SEC. The practice of omitting most kinds of implicit costs, which can be quite large for many firms, is widely recognized by managers, shareholders, government officials, and financial analysts, who make lucrative careers converting the information in financial accounting statements into measures more closely resembling economic profit (see Illustration 1.2).

Business owners, of course, must bear all costs of using resources, both explicit and implicit, regardless of which costs may be deducted for accounting purposes. Because all costs matter to owners of a firm, you should now clearly understand why maximizing economic profit, rather than accounting profit, is the objective of the firm's owners. And, as we explain in the following section, the value of a firm is determined by the amount of economic profit, rather than accounting profit the firm is expected to earn in the current period and all future periods. As you now see, it is economic profit that matters in business decision making, so in the rest of this chapter and in later chapters whenever we refer to "profit," we will mean *economic* profit. We will now summarize the relation between economic and accounting profits in a principle:

Principle Economic profit is the difference between total revenue and total economic cost:

$$\text{Economic profit} = \text{Total revenue} - \text{Total economic cost}$$
$$= \text{Total revenue} - \text{Explicit costs} - \text{Implicit costs}$$

Accounting profit differs from economic profit because accounting profit does not subtract from total revenue the implicit costs of using resources:

$$\text{Accounting profit} = \text{Total revenue} - \text{Explicit costs}$$

Since the owners of firms must cover the costs of all resources used by the firm, maximizing economic profit, rather than accounting profit, is the objective of the firm's owners.

Now try Technical Problem 2.

---

[3]One of the implicit costs that accountants do deduct when computing accounting profit is the cost of depreciation of capital assets, which is the reduction in the value of capital equipment from the ordinary wear and tear of usage. As you may know from taking accounting courses, businesses have several methods to choose from when computing depreciation costs, and some of these methods tend to overstate the actual value of depreciation in the early years of equipment ownership.

Maximizing the Value of the Firm

As we stressed in the preceding discussion and principle, owners of a firm, whether the shareholders of a corporation or the owner of a single proprietorship, are best served by management decisions that seek to maximize the profit of the firm. In general, when managers maximize economic profit, they are also maximizing the value of the firm, which is the price someone will pay for the firm. How much will someone pay for a firm? Suppose you are going to buy a business on January 1 and sell it on December 31. If the firm is going to make an economic profit of $50,000 during the year, you are willing to pay no more than $50,000 (in monthly payments matching the flow of profit) to own the firm for that year. Because other potential buyers are *also* willing to pay up to $50,000, the firm likely sells for very nearly or exactly the amount of the economic profit earned in a year.

value of a firm
The price for which the firm can be sold, which equals the present value of future profits.

When a firm earns a stream of economic profit for a number of years in the future, the **value of a firm**—the price for which it can be sold—is the present value of the future economic profits expected to be generated by the firm:

$$\text{Value of a firm} = \frac{\pi_1}{(1 + r)} + \frac{\pi_2}{(1 + r)^2} + \cdots + \frac{\pi_T}{(1 + r)^T} = \sum_{t=1}^{T} \frac{\pi_t}{(1 + r)^t}$$

risk premium
An increase in the discount rate to compensate investors for uncertainty about future profits.

where π_t is the economic profit expected in period t, r is the risk-adjusted discount rate, and T is the number of years in the life of a firm.[4] Inasmuch as future profit is not known with certainty, the value of a firm is calculated using the profit *expected* to be earned in future periods. The greater the variation in possible future profits, the less a buyer is willing to pay for those risky future profits. The risk associated with not knowing future profits of a firm is accounted for by adding a **risk premium** to the (riskless) discount rate. A risk premium increases the discount rate, thereby decreasing the present value of profit received in the future, in order to compensate investors for the risk of not knowing with certainty the future value of profits. The more uncertain the future profits, the higher the risk-adjusted discount rate used by investors in valuing a firm, and the more heavily future profits will be discounted.

Now try Technical
Problem 3.

> **Principle** The value of a firm is the price for which it can be sold, and that price is equal to the present value of the expected future profits of the firm. The larger (smaller) the risk associated with future profits, the higher (lower) the risk-adjusted discount rate used to compute the value of the firm, and the lower (higher) will be the value of the firm.

---

[4]Because a dollar of profit received in the future is worth less than a dollar received now, multiperiod decision making employs the concept of present value. Present value is the value at the present time of a payment or stream of payments to be received (or paid) some time in the future. The appendix at the end of this chapter reviews the mathematics of present value computations, a topic usually covered in an introductory course in finance or accounting.

ILLUSTRATION 1.3

How Do You Value a Golf Course?
Estimating the Market Price of a Business

Recently golf courses have been raising their membership and green fees, making golf courses more profitable. Not surprisingly, *Golf Digest* reports that prices investors are paying for golf courses are now rising. As we explain in this chapter, the value of any business firm is the price for which the firm can be sold, and this price will reflect the buyer's calculation of the present value of the future profits expected to be generated by the firm.

So, if you wanted to invest in a golf course, how much should you expect to pay to buy one? Because you would be competing with many other investors, you would not expect to pay less than the present value of the golf course's future stream of profits. To help answer this question, *Golf Digest* interviewed Keith Cubba, who is the national director of the golf course group at a large commercial real estate brokerage firm. Based on this interview, *Golf Digest* worked up a valuation of a golf course using a computational technique that is essentially equivalent to the "value of a firm" equation we present on page 14 of this textbook.

Golf Digest begins its computation with a specific annual profit figure, which we will say is $480,000 for this Illustration. *Golf Digest* simplifies its computation in two ways: (1) profit is assumed to be $480,000 in *every* year, and (2) the profit stream continues forever—that is, *T* in our textbook equation is infinity. Then, *Golf Digest* explains that in today's commercial real estate market, investors require a risk-adjusted rate of return equal to about 10 percent annually. The value of this golf course is then calculated by dividing the annual profit by the risk-adjusted rate of return:

$$\text{Value of golf course} = \frac{\pi}{r} = \frac{\$480,000}{0.10} = \$4,800,000$$

As it turns out, $4.8 million is extremely close to the numerical value you would get if you applied the equation we present on page 14 using $480,000 in the numerator for the profit every year over a very long period of time and a risk-adjusted discount rate of 10 percent.[a] Thus, a commercial real estate investor who wishes to earn 10 percent annually by owning this golf course would be willing to pay about $4.8 million to buy it. A more "greedy" investor who requires a return of, say, 16 percent will only be willing to pay $3 million ($480,000/0.16) for the same golf course.

While the valuation analysis in *Golf Digest* is mathematically correct and economically sound, it can be misleading if the specific golf course has additional financial features that cause a buyer to offer a price either higher or lower than the value of the golf course "enterprise" itself. Suppose the golf course has accumulated a cash account of $100,000. Because the buyer of the golf course gets the $100,000 of cash along with the golf course, the buyer would be willing to pay a price for the course that is $100,000 *more* than the present value of the expected stream of profit. Alternatively, suppose the golf course has borrowed money in the past for whatever reason and has $100,000 of debt owed to a bank. At the time of purchase, the buyer of the golf course must pay off the debt to the bank, which *reduces* the price the buyer of the golf course is willing to pay by $100,000. As you can now see, the actual price paid for the golf course may not be equal to the present value of the expected stream of profit if the golf course comes with some amount of cash or debt. Financial economists sometimes refer to the value of the stream of expected profit as the "enterprise value" (EV) of the business. We just call it "the value of the firm" in this textbook.

---

[a] You might be wondering about *Golf Digest's* assumption that a golf course generates a *perpetual* stream of profit (i.e., $T = \infty$). For the golf course in this example, if we let $T = 50$ years in our textbook equation, the value will be $4,759,111, which is just a small deviation from the $4.8 million present value of a perpetual stream of profit. In other words, even if the investor believes the golf course will only generate profit for 50 years, she can still use *Golf Digest's* "perpetuity" formula for the sake of convenience without much worry that she will be overvaluing the present value stream of profit. The nature of this mathematical approximation is also discussed in the Mathematical Appendix at the end of this chapter, "Review of Present Value Calculations."

Source: Peter Finch, "Investors Are Taking a Fresh Look at Golf—and Liking What They See," *Golf Digest*, December 2014, p. 62.

The Equivalence of Value Maximization and Profit Maximization

Owners of a firm want the managers to make business decisions that will maximize the value of the firm, which, as we discussed in the previous subsection, is the sum of the discounted expected profits in current and future periods. As a general rule, then, a manager maximizes the value of the firm by making decisions that maximize expected profit in each period. That is, single-period profit maximization and maximizing the value of the firm are usually equivalent means to the same end: Maximizing profit in each period will result in the maximum value of the firm, and maximizing the value of the firm requires maximizing profit in each period.

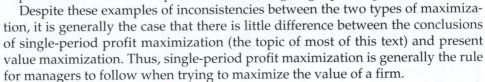

Principle   If cost and revenue conditions in any period are independent of decisions made in other time periods, a manager will maximize the value of a firm (the present value of the firm) by making decisions that maximize profit in every single time period.

The equivalence of single-period profit maximization and maximizing the value of the firm holds only when the revenue and cost conditions in one time period are independent of revenue and costs in future time periods. When today's decisions affect profits in future time periods, price or output decisions that maximize profit in each (single) time period will not maximize the value of the firm. Two examples of these kinds of situations occur when (1) a firm's employees become more productive in future periods by producing more output in earlier periods—a case of learning by doing—and (2) current production has the effect of increasing cost in the future—as in extractive industries such as mining and oil production. Thus, if increasing current output has a positive effect on future revenue and profit, a value-maximizing manager selects an output level that is *greater* than the level that maximizes profit in a single time period. Alternatively, if current production has the effect of increasing cost in the future, maximizing the value of the firm requires a *lower* current output than maximizing single-period profit.

Despite these examples of inconsistencies between the two types of maximization, it is generally the case that there is little difference between the conclusions of single-period profit maximization (the topic of most of this text) and present value maximization. Thus, single-period profit maximization is generally the rule for managers to follow when trying to maximize the value of a firm.

Now try Technical Problem 4.

Some Common Mistakes Managers Make

Taking a course in managerial economics is certainly not a requirement for making successful business decisions. Everyone can name some extraordinarily astute business managers who succeeded in creating and running very profitable firms with little or no formal education in business or economics. Taking this course will not guarantee your success either. Plenty of managers with MBA degrees took courses in managerial economics but nonetheless failed sensationally and ended up getting fired or replaced in hostile takeovers by more profitably managed firms. We firmly believe, however, that a course in managerial economics helps you avoid some of the more common mistakes that have led other managers to fail. As you progress through this book, we will draw your attention at various points along the way to a number of common pitfalls, misconceptions, and even mistakes that real-world managers would do well to avoid.

Although it is too soon for us to demonstrate or prove that certain practices can reduce profit and possibly create losses in some cases—this is only Chapter 1!—we can nonetheless give you a preview of several of the more common mistakes that you will learn to avoid in later chapters. Some of the terms in this brief preview might be unclear to you now, but you can be sure that we will carefully explain things later in the text.

Never increase output simply to reduce average costs Sometimes managers get confused about the role of average or unit cost in decision making. For example, a firm incurs total costs of $100 to produce 20 units. The average or unit cost is $5 for each of the 20 units. Managers may believe, incorrectly, if they can increase output and cause average cost to fall, then profit *must* rise by expanding production. Profit might rise, fall, or stay the same, and the actual change in profit has nothing to do with falling average costs.

As you will learn in Chapter 8, producing and selling more units in the short run can indeed cause unit or average costs to fall as fixed costs of production are spread over a greater number of units. As you will learn in Chapter 9, increasing output in the long run causes average cost to fall when economies of scale are present. However, profit-maximizing firms should never increase production levels simply because average costs can be reduced. As we will show you, it is the *marginal* cost of production—the increment to total cost of producing an extra unit—that matters in decision making. Consequently, a manager who increases or decreases production to reduce unit costs will usually miss the profit-maximizing output level. Quite simply, output or sales expansion decisions should never be made on the basis of what happens to average costs.

Pursuit of market share usually reduces profit Many managers misunderstand the role market share plays in determining profitability. Simply gaining market share does *not* create higher profits. In many situations, if managers add market share by cutting price, the firm's profit actually falls. Illustration 1.4 examines some empirical studies of managers who pursued market share while ignoring profit. You will learn in Chapters 11 and 12 that the best general advice is to ignore market share in business decision making.

We should mention here an important, although rather rare, exception to this rule that will be examined more carefully in Chapter 12: the value of market share when "network effects" are present. Network effects arise when the value each consumer places on your product depends on the number of *other* consumers who also buy your product. Suppose consumers highly value your good because a large number of *other* consumers also buy your good. Under these circumstances, grabbing market share faster than your rivals could give you a dominant position in the market, as consumers switch to your product away from sellers with small market shares. Failing to capture substantial market share might even threaten

ILLUSTRATION 1.4

Managerial Strategy
Maximize Profit or Maximize Market Share?

Although sports and war metaphors are common in business conversation and management seminars, managers may be reducing the value of their firms by placing too much emphasis on beating their competitors out of market share rather than focusing on making the most profit for their shareholders. In a provocative study of managerial strategy, Professors J. Scott Armstrong at the University of Pennsylvania's Wharton School and Fred Collopy at Case Western Reserve University advise CEOs to focus on profits instead of market share. Armstrong and Collopy discovered that, instead of maximizing profit, many managers make decisions with an eye toward performing well relative to their competitors—a decision-making point of view they refer to as "competitor-oriented."

In their nine-year study of more than 1,000 experienced managers, Armstrong and Collopy found that managers are more likely to abandon the goal of profit maximization when they have greater amounts of information about the performance of their rivals. In the study, managers were asked to choose between two pricing plans for a new product—a low-price and a high-price strategy—and were told the five-year present value of expected profits associated with each strategy. The table in the next column presents two of the "treatments" that were administered to different groups of subjects.

The "base" treatment gives the manager no information about how a rival firm will fare under the two plans, while the "beat" treatment allows the manager to know how a decision will affect a rival. In the base treatment, almost all managers, as expected, chose the most profitable strategy (high price). When given information about the rival firm's profit, subjects could see the impact of their decision on their rival, and many managers abandoned profit maximization. In the beat treatment, 60 percent chose not to maximize profit (low price). To address the possibility that the subjects were considering longer-term profits, Armstrong and Collopy changed the payoffs to *20-year* present values. The results were the same.

Armstrong and Collopy believe the abandonment of profit as the firm's objective is a consequence of managers having information about a competitor's

Net Present Value of Expected Profit over Five Years

	Low-price strategy	High-price strategy
Base treatment:		
Your firm	$40 million	$ 80 million
Beat treatment:		
Your firm	40 million	80 million
Rival firm	20 million	160 million

performance. They discovered that exposing managers to techniques that focus on gaining market share increased the proportion of subjects who abandoned profit maximization. When executives take strategic-management courses, they become more likely to make profit-reducing decisions. These results are impressive because they have been repeated in more than 40 experiments with more than 1,000 subjects.

To see if firms that seek to maximize market share (competitor-oriented firms) tend to be less profitable *over the long run* than firms that pursue profit without concern for market share, Armstrong and Collopy tracked the performance of two groups of firms over a 54-year period. The group of firms that made pricing decisions based on competitor-oriented goals, such as increasing market share, were consistently less profitable over the 54-year period than the group that made pricing decisions to increase profit without regard to market share. Furthermore, companies pursuing market share were found to be less likely to survive: "Four of the six companies that focused strictly on market share (Gulf, American Can, Swift, and National Steel) did not survive. All four profit-oriented companies (DuPont, General Electric, Union Carbide, and Alcoa) did."

Armstrong and Collopy conclude that the use of competitor-oriented objectives is detrimental to profitability. To encourage managers to keep their focus on profit and *not* on market share, they offer the following specific advice:

- Do not use market share as an objective.
- Avoid using sports and military analogies because they foster a competitor orientation.

- Do not use management science techniques that are oriented to maximizing market share, such as portfolio planning matrices and experience curve analysis.
- Design information systems to focus attention on the firm's performance, as measured by profits.
- Beware that improvement in the ability to measure market share—specifically through scanner data collected at checkouts—may lead to a stronger focus on market share and less focus on profitability.

In a book about the business strategies of Southwest Airlines, the authors examine the decisions made by the airline's CEO, Herb Kelleher. In a section titled "Say Nuts to Market Share," Kelleher explains the role that market share plays at Southwest Airlines. Kelleher says:

> Market share has nothing to do with profitability . . . Market share says we just want to be big; we don't care if we make money doing it. . . . That is really incongruous if profitability is your purpose.

The book goes on to say that Kelleher believes "confusing the two concepts (increasing profit and increasing market share) has derailed many firms that were otherwise on track in fulfilling their fundamental purpose (maximizing profit and firm value)." Perhaps it was only a coincidence, but we should mention that the value of Southwest Airlines tripled during the early to mid-1990s.

As we emphasize in this chapter, shareholders wish to see the value of their firms maximized. A manager bent on being the biggest airline or biggest auto rental

agency may fail to be the most profitable airline or auto rental agency. As mentioned in our discussion of common management errors, the presence of network effects can make the pursuit of market share a profitable strategy, as we will explain more fully in Chapter 12. In his recent book on market share, Richard Miniter offers this warning on the exceptional case of network effects:

> Every rule has an exception (network effects)—and everyone wants to believe that they are it. Their business is special and unique and therefore profits are not primary for them, but market share is. Too many managers believe that the myth of market share is not myth—for them. In a handful of cases, they're right: Market share is what matters. . . . (In) the majority of cases . . . profit alone should sit on the throne.

We will show you in Chapter 12 how to identify those special few industries when market share matters. As this Illustration stresses, most managers should ignore market share. Between advances in shareholders' willingness and ability to fire CEOs and the active market for corporate control (mergers, acquisitions, and takeovers), a manager who fails to pursue primarily the maximization of profit may have a short career.

Sources: J. Scott Armstrong and Fred Collopy, "Competitor Orientation: Effects of Objectives and Information on Managerial Decisions and Profitability," *Journal of Marketing Research,* May 1996, pp. 188–99; "The Profitability of Winning," *Chief Executive,* June 1, 1994, p. 60; Kevin Freiberg and Jackie Freiberg, *Nuts!: Southwest Airlines' Crazy Recipe for Business and Personal Success* (New York: Broadway Books, 1995), p. 49; Richard Miniter, *The Myth of Market Share* (New York: Crown Business, 2002), p. 139.

your long-run survival in the market. As we will explain fully in Chapter 12, your best move when network effects exist may be to charge a low initial price so that you can dominate the market and charge higher prices in later periods. Again, we must stress that pursuing market share is consistent with profit-maximization only when network effects are present.

Focusing on profit margin won't maximize total profit Profit margin is the difference between the price you charge for each unit and the average cost of producing the units. Suppose you charge $15 per unit, and average or unit cost is $9 per unit. Your profit margin, or average profit per unit, is $6 ($15 − $9) per unit. As we will demonstrate later in Chapters 11 and 12, managers should not make decisions with the primary objective of increasing profit margin because total profit is *not* maximized at the output and price level where profit margin or unit profit is greatest. In later chapters you will learn to ignore profit margin when making pricing and output decisions. As you will see, profit margin is handy for computing the amount of profit a business makes, but profit margin plays no role in making profit-maximizing decisions. This subtle distinction in the proper use of profit margin is not well understood in the business community.

Maximizing total revenue reduces profit You might think if managers have an opportunity to change price or quantity in a way that increases total revenue, they will always wish to do so. As it turns out, increasing revenue does not necessarily increase profit and may even lower profit. You will see that the demand curve facing a firm tells a manager the maximum price a firm can charge to sell various quantities of its product. At any chosen point on demand, total revenue is computed by multiplying price times the quantity demanded. Choosing different points on a firm's demand curve will alter the amount of revenue the firm generates, as well as production costs and the amount of profit left over for the owners. We will show you in Chapters 11 and 12 that the point on a firm's demand curve that maximizes profit will *not* be the price and quantity that maximizes total revenue.[5] General managers have learned that, when the salaries of sales managers are tied to the number of units sold or the dollar amount of revenue generated, sales managers may try to persuade general managers to produce and sell too much product. The result: Revenue goes up, but profit goes down!

Cost-plus pricing formulas don't produce profit-maximizing prices Pricing decisions are probably the most difficult and risky of all the business decisions managers must make. To make matters worse, prices for the same product must routinely be set over and over again as market conditions change month after month and year after year. Of course, some firms produce hundreds, even thousands, of products. So, it's hard to blame managers for trying to find a simple pricing formula requiring nothing more than readily available spreadsheet data. One such pricing formula, cost-plus pricing, is still widely used even though everyone trained in economics and marketing knows that setting prices higher than unit cost by some fixed, arbitrarily determined portion of unit cost almost never works. The unfortunate truth is that cost-plus pricing does not deliver profit-maximizing prices, except by sheer luck.[6] In Chapter 12, we will show you how to set the most profitable prices when everyone pays the same price for the same good—a method

---

[5]In theory, one exception to this rule exists, but it arises very rarely in practice. When a price-setting firm faces marginal costs that are zero, it will maximize profit by maximizing total revenue. We will explain this exception in Chapter 12.

[6]Only when businesses face constant costs can a formula for choosing a profit-maximizing markup on unit cost be contrived. But, this pricing formula is so complicated to apply that it offers no practical advantage over the "marginal revenue equals marginal cost" approach to optimal pricing that you will learn in Chapter 12. We consider this contrived formula to be worthless and do not cover it anywhere in this text.

known as uniform pricing. In Chapter 14, we will show you several advanced pricing techniques, which charge different buyers different prices and generate even more revenue than with uniform prices.

These are just a few of the many mistakes we will teach you how to avoid. Don't be concerned at this point if you're not sure you understand these mistakes—we guarantee you will by the end of the text!

1.3 SEPARATION OF OWNERSHIP AND CONTROL OF THE FIRM

principal–agent relationship
Relationship formed when a business owner (the principal) enters an agreement with an executive manager (the agent) whose job is to formulate and implement tactical and strategic business decisions that will further the objectives of the business owner (the principal).

Business owners frequently choose to delegate control of their businesses to a professional executive or senior manager who will typically be assisted by additional subordinate managers, which creates an executive management team that relieves the owners of management duties. Only in the smallest business organizations—typically sole proprietorships, smaller general partnerships, and family businesses—are you likely to see owners managing their own businesses. The decision to hire professional managers creates a separation between business *ownership* and its *management*. This separation forms a special relationship between business owners and managers known as a *principal–agent relationship*. In this particular type of **principle–agent relationship**, a business owner (the principal) enters an agreement with an executive manager (the agent) whose job is to formulate and implement tactical and strategic business decisions that will further the objectives of the business owner (the principal).[7] The agency "agreement" can, and usually does, take the form of a legal contract to confer some degree of legal enforceability, but it can also be something as simple as an informal agreement settled by a handshake between the owner and manager.

Separating ownership and control of a firm holds the potential to significantly increase a firm's value, especially when it replaces "amateur" owner-managers with more experienced and talented professional business decision makers. In practice, however, some or all of the potential gain to the owners from hiring expert managers can be lost when owners cannot prevent managers from behaving opportunistically by taking self-interested actions that are harmful to the owners. We will now discuss this fundamental problem arising from the separation of ownership and management and examine some ways to solve or at least control the severity of these problems.

The Principal–Agent Problem

A fundamental problem that frequently, but not always, afflicts the principal–agent relationship between business owners and managers occurs when a manager takes an action or makes a decision that advances the interests of the

---

[7]We are employing here a rather specific definition of the principal–agent relationship to focus on the agency relationship between a firm's owners and the firm's executive managers. Business organizations typically form a variety principal–agent relationship in addition to the one between owners and executive managers that we are discussing in this textbook. Several other examples of principal–agent relationships include CEOs and other executive officers (CFO, CIO, and COO), the boards of directors and CEOs, and CEOs and middle managers.

manager but is harmful to the owners because the manager's action reduces the value of the firm. This celebrated problem, which has generated considerable interest and concern among business consultants, economists, and management scholars, is known as the **principal–agent problem**. A principal–agent problem requires the presence of two conditions: (1) the manager's objectives must be different from those of the owner, and (2) the owner must find it too costly or even impossible to monitor the manager's decisions to block any decisions or behavior that would reduce the firm's value.

principal–agent problem
A manager takes an action or makes a decision that advances the interests of the manager but reduces the value of the firm.

Conflicting objectives between owners and managers

In the natural state of affairs between owners and managers, the goals of owners are almost certainly different from the goals of managers, and thus we say that owner and manager goals are *not aligned* or that managers and owners *possess conflicting objectives*. A self-interested owner naturally wants her business run in a way that maximizes the value of her business. A self-interested executive manager—if the penalty is zero or small—will naturally wish to take advantage of opportunities to make decisions or take actions that will promote his well-being even when these decisions also harm the owner of the business.

For example, managers may choose to consume excessive, even lavish perquisites (or perks). It would be an unusual manager indeed who would not like to have the company (i.e., the owners) pay for a lavish office, memberships in exclusive country clubs, extraordinary levels of life and health insurance, a nanny to look after their children, a chauffeured limousine, and, if at all possible, a corporate jet. Although the decision to consume lavish perks is good for the manager, these perks reduce the profitability and value of the firm and thus harm the owners.

Another important example of conflicting goals involves managers who get sidetracked by goals that are inconsistent with value-maximization, such as the pursuit of larger firm *size* or the pursuit of higher market *share*. Studies show that there may be a couple of reasons for this behavior. First, executive managers are notorious for their enormous egos and intense desire to engage in empire building, which they find satisfying even if profit is sacrificed in the process. Second, some executives believe that their future salary and compensation, either at their present job or at their next job, will be richer if the firm they now manage experiences rapid growth in assets, number of employees, or level of sales and revenues relative to their rival firms. As you will learn later in this book, pricing and production decisions focused on creating the biggest, fastest-growing, or relatively largest companies do *not*, as a general rule, maximize profit or the value of the firm. You may recall that American Airlines was the *largest* airline in the United States for many years, but smaller Southwest Airlines was the most *profitable* airline during the same time period. Similarly, the largest car rental agency is usually not the most profitable rental car company, and Samsung's Galaxy S is the market share leader in smartphones but Apple's iPhone 6 has created far more profit for Apple shareholders. Illustration 1.4 examines some of the causes and consequences of managers focusing on maximizing market share instead of economic profit.

Problems with monitoring managers Business owners, recognizing that their interests may diverge from the interests of their managers, can try to bind managers through some form of incentive agreement—typically a legal contract for employment—that is carefully designed using incentives and penalties to force executives to make only decisions that will increase the value of the firm. Let's suppose that a **complete contract**—one that protects owners from every possible deviation by managers from value-maximizing decisions—could in fact be designed by the owners' lawyers. Once this complete contract is signed by the owners and executive manager, the owners then face the costly task of monitoring and enforcing the contract to make sure managers do not shirk, renege, or otherwise underperform when carrying out their contractual responsibilities to maximize the value of the firm.

If monitoring the manager could be accomplished perfectly and at a low cost, then no principle–agent problem would arise because the (hypothetical) complete contract forms an exact alignment of the owners' and manager's objectives, and low-cost monitoring ensures that the contractual alignment of goals is enforced. As you probably guessed, this ideal plan for eliminating the principal–agent problem fails in practice–even if complete contracts could be written—because monitoring managers is usually a costly activity for owners, and thus owners of the firm will not find it in their best interest to perfectly monitor the executive manager. When monitoring costs are significant, as they usually are, managers will be able to undertake some opportunistic actions that further their interests at the expense of the owners.

In more extreme situations, monitoring becomes practically impossible because the manager is able to take **hidden actions** or make hidden decisions that cannot be observed by owners for any economically and legally feasible amount of monitoring effort. Hidden actions can be either good or bad actions from the owners' point of view; that is, a hidden action can either increase or decrease the value of the firm. Because owners do not know whether a hidden action has been taken—either a good one or a bad one—it is impossible for monitoring efforts by owners to block or prevent managers from taking "bad" hidden actions. In this situation, owners' efforts to monitor managers cannot protect owners from a principal–agent problem caused by hidden actions. This particular form of the principal–agent problem is called **moral hazard**. As you can see, moral hazard is both a problem of nonaligned objectives *and* a problem of harmful hidden actions. If either one of these two aspects is missing then there is no moral hazard problem. After all, in the absence of conflicting objectives, managers would make value-maximizing decisions and any hidden actions that might be undertaken would be "good" hidden actions that increase profit rather than "bad" hidden actions that reduce profit.

complete contract
An employment contract that protects owners from every possible deviation by managers from value-maximizing decisions.

hidden actions
Actions or decisions taken by managers that cannot be observed by owners for any feasible amount of monitoring effort.

moral hazard
A situation in which managers take hidden actions that harm the owners of the firm but further the interests of the managers.

Principle   A principal–agent problem arises between a firm's owner and manager when two conditions are met: (1) the objectives of the owner and manager are not aligned, and (2) the owner finds it either too costly or impossible in the case of moral hazard to perfectly monitor the manager to block all management decisions that might be harmful to the owner of the business.

Corporate Control Mechanisms

The discussion of the principle–agent problem is not meant to imply that the owners or shareholders of corporations are completely helpless in the face of managers who aren't doing what owners expect them to do. Rules of corporate governance give shareholders rights that allow them to control managers directly through specific corporate control measures and indirectly through the corporation's board of directors, whose responsibility it is to monitor management. Shareholders themselves, and in partnership with the board of directors, may choose from a variety of mechanisms for controlling agency problems. In addition to these internal governance methods, forces outside the firm can also motivate managers to pursue maximization of the firm's value. We will now review a few of the most important types of these mechanisms for intensifying a manager's desire to maximize profit.

Stockholders often try to resolve or at least reduce the intensity of conflicting objectives between owners and managers by tying managers' compensation to fulfilling the goals of the owner/shareholders. Managers have a greater incentive to make decisions that further the owners' goals when managers themselves are owners. Equity ownership has proven to be one of the most effective mechanisms for taming the principal–agent problem, so much so that a growing number of professional money managers and large institutional investors refuse to invest in firms whose managers hold little or no equity stake in the firms they manage.

The members of the board of directors are agents of the shareholders charged with monitoring the decisions of executive managers. Just as managers are agents for owners, so too are directors, and thus principal–agent problems can arise between directors and shareholders. Many experts in corporate governance believe that the value of the board's monitoring services is enhanced by appointing outsiders—directors not serving on the firm's management team—and by linking directors' compensation to the value of the firm. Although having outsiders on the board and linking board member compensation to firm value are both effective ways to mitigate principal–agent problems, other problems can remain troublesome. Specifically, the effectiveness of a board of directors is undermined when a particular business decision is so complex that the board cannot reliably judge whether the decision furthers shareholder interests or not. And yet another problem arises when CEOs play an important role in the selection of the individual board members. Just how objective will board members be who owe their jobs to the person they are supposed to be monitoring?

Another method of creating incentives for managers to make value-maximizing decisions involves corporate policy on debt financing. A policy that emphasizes financing corporate investments with debt rather than equity—selling shares of common stock to raise financial capital—can further the interests of shareholders in several ways. First, debt financing makes bankruptcy possible, in that firms cannot go bankrupt if they have no debt.

Thus, managers who value their employment have an additional incentive to increase profitability to lower the probability of bankruptcy. Second, managers face less pressure to generate revenues to cover the cost of investments if the payments are dividends to shareholders, which they can choose to defer or neglect altogether, rather than if the investment payments are installments on a loan. Finally, lending institutions themselves have an incentive to monitor managers of firms that borrow money from them. Banks and other lenders are likely to make it difficult for managers to consume excessive perks or make unprofitable investments.

Looking beyond the *internal* control mechanisms discussed, we should add to our discussion of corporate control mechanisms an important *external* force initiated by parties outside the firm itself—a corporate takeover—that can impose an effective solution to the principal–agent problem between shareholders and managers. When the value of a firm under its present management is less than what it would be with a different management team, a profit opportunity arises for outside investors to acquire stock and take control of the underperforming firm and then replace the existing management team with a new and presumably more profitable set of managers. If the new owners are indeed able to increase profit, the firm will become more valuable and the raiders will be rewarded by higher stock prices.

Even though Hollywood movies have portrayed corporate takeovers as greedy maneuvers aimed only at making corporate raiders rich, most economists believe that takeovers can serve as a check on the power of opportunistic managers who exploit principal–agent problems. Takeovers create a market for corporate control of publicly traded businesses that can help resolve the conflict between managers and shareholders caused by separation of ownership and management: managers know they must maximize the value of their firms or else face a takeover and lose their jobs to new management.

1.4 MARKET STRUCTURE AND MANAGERIAL DECISION MAKING

As we have mentioned, managers cannot expect to succeed without understanding how market forces shape the firm's ability to earn profit. A particularly important aspect of managerial decision making is the pricing decision. The structure of the market in which the firm operates can limit the ability of a manager to raise the price of the firm's product without losing a substantial amount, possibly even all, of its sales.

Not all managers have the power to set the price of the firm's product. In some industries, each firm in the industry makes up a relatively small portion of total sales and produces a product that is identical to the output produced by all the rest of the firms in the industry. The price of the good in such a situation is not determined by any one firm or manager but, rather, by the impersonal forces of the marketplace—the intersection of market demand and supply, as you will see in the next chapter. If a manager attempts to raise the price above the

price-taker
A firm that cannot set the price of the product it sells, since price is determined strictly by the market forces of demand and supply.

market-determined price, the firm loses all its sales to the other firms in the industry. After all, buyers do not care from whom they buy this identical product, and they would be unwilling to pay more than the going market price for the product. In such a situation, the firm is a **price-taker** and cannot set the price of the product it sells. We will discuss price-taking firms in detail in Chapter 11, and you will see that the demand curve facing a price-taking firm is horizontal at the price determined by market forces.

price-setting firm
A firm that can raise its price without losing all of its sales.

In contrast to managers of price-taking firms, the manager of a **price-setting firm** does set the price of the product. A price-setting firm has the ability to raise its price without losing all sales because the product is somehow differentiated from rivals' products or perhaps because the geographic market area in which the product is sold has only one, or just a few, sellers of the product. At higher prices the firm sells less of its product, and at lower prices the firm sells more of its product. The ability to raise price without losing all sales is called **market power,** a subject we will examine more thoroughly in Chapters 13 and 14. Before we discuss some of the differing market structures to be analyzed in later chapters of this text, we first want you to consider the fundamental nature and purpose of a market.

market power
A firm's ability to raise price without losing all sales.

What Is a Market?

market
Any arrangement through which buyers and sellers exchange anything of value.

A **market** is any arrangement through which buyers and sellers exchange final goods or services, resources used for production, or, in general, anything of value. The arrangement may be a location and time, such as a commercial bank from 9 a.m. until 6 p.m. on weekdays only, an agricultural produce market every first Tuesday of the month, a trading "pit" at a commodity exchange during trading hours, or even the parking lot of a stadium an hour before game time when ticket scalpers sometimes show up to sell tickets to sporting events. An arrangement may also be something other than a physical location and time, such as a classified ad in a newspaper or a website on the Internet. You should view the concept of a market quite broadly, particularly because advances in technology create new ways of bringing buyers and sellers together.

Markets are arrangements that reduce the cost of making transactions. Buyers wishing to purchase something must spend valuable time and other resources finding sellers, gathering information about prices and qualities, and ultimately making the purchase itself. Sellers wishing to sell something must spend valuable resources locating buyers (or pay a fee to sales agents to do so), gathering information about potential buyers (e.g., verifying creditworthiness or legal entitlement to buy), and finally closing the deal. These costs of making a transaction happen, which are additional costs of doing business over and above the price paid, are known as **transaction costs**. Buyers and sellers use markets to facilitate exchange because markets lower the transaction costs for both parties. To understand the meaning of this seemingly abstract point, consider two alternative ways of selling a used car that you own. One way to

transaction costs
Costs of making a transaction happen, other than the price of the good or service itself.

find a buyer for your car is to canvass your neighborhood, knocking on doors until you find a person willing to pay a price you are willing to accept. This will likely require a lot of your time and perhaps even involve buying a new pair of shoes. Alternatively, you could run an advertisement in the local newspaper describing your car and stating the price you are willing to accept for it. This method of selling the car involves a market—the newspaper ad. Even though you must pay a fee to run the ad, you choose to use this market because the transaction costs will be lower by advertising in the newspaper than by searching door to door.

Different Market Structures

market structure
Market characteristics that determine the economic environment in which a firm operates.

Market structure is a set of market characteristics that determines the economic environment in which a firm operates. As we now explain, the structure of a market governs the degree of pricing power possessed by a manager, both in the short run and in the long run. The list of economic characteristics needed to describe a market is actually rather short:

- *The number and size of the firms operating in the market:* A manager's ability to raise the price of the firm's product without losing most, if not all, of its buyers depends in part on the number and size of sellers in a market. If there are a large number of sellers with each producing just a small fraction of the total sales in a market, no single firm can influence market price by changing its production level. Alternatively, when the total output of a market is produced by one or a few firms with relatively large market shares, a single firm can cause the price to rise by restricting its output and to fall by increasing its output, as long as no other firm in the market decides to prevent the price from changing by suitably adjusting its own output level.

- *The degree of product differentiation among competing producers:* If sellers all produce products that consumers perceive to be identical, then buyers will never need to pay even a penny more for a particular firm's product than the price charged by the rest of the firms. By differentiating a product either through real differences in product design or through advertised image, a firm may be able to raise its price above its rivals' prices if consumers find the product differences sufficiently desirable to pay the higher price.

- *The likelihood of new firms entering a market when incumbent firms are earning economic profits:* When firms in a market earn economic profits, other firms will learn of this return in excess of opportunity costs and will try to enter the market. Once enough firms enter a market, price will be bid down sufficiently to eliminate any economic profit. Even firms with some degree of market power cannot keep prices higher than opportunity costs for long periods when entry is relatively easy.

Microeconomists have analyzed firms operating in a number of different market structures. Not surprisingly, economists have names for these market structures: perfect competition, monopoly, monopolistic competition, and oligopoly. Although each of these market structures is examined in detail later in this text, we briefly discuss each one now to show you how market structure shapes a manager's pricing decisions.

In *perfect competition,* a large number of relatively small firms sell an undifferentiated product in a market with no barriers to the entry of new firms. Managers of firms operating in perfectly competitive markets are price-takers with no market power. At the price determined entirely by the market forces of demand and supply, they decide how much to produce in order to maximize profit. In the absence of entry barriers, any economic profit earned at the market-determined price will vanish as new firms enter and drive the price down to the average cost of production. Many of the markets for agricultural goods and other commodities traded on national and international exchanges closely match the characteristics of perfect competition.

In a *monopoly* market, a single firm, protected by some kind of barrier to entry, produces a product for which no close substitutes are available. A monopoly is a price-setting firm. The degree of market power enjoyed by the monopoly is determined by the ability of consumers to find imperfect substitutes for the monopolist's product. The higher the price charged by the monopolist, the more willing are consumers to buy other products. The existence of a barrier to entry allows a monopolist to raise its price without concern that economic profit will attract new firms. As you will see in Chapter 12, examples of true monopolies are rare.

In markets characterized by *monopolistic competition,* a large number of firms that are small relative to the total size of the market produce differentiated products without the protection of barriers to entry. The only difference between perfect competition and monopolistic competition is the product differentiation that gives monopolistic competitors some degree of market power; they are price-setters rather than price-takers. As in perfectly competitive markets, the absence of entry barriers ensures that any economic profit will eventually be bid away by new entrants. The toothpaste market provides one example of monopolistic competition. The many brands and kinds of toothpaste are close, but not perfect, substitutes. Toothpaste manufacturers differentiate their toothpastes by using different flavorings, abrasives, whiteners, fluoride levels, and other ingredients, along with a substantial amount of advertising designed to create brand loyalty.

In each of the three market structures discussed here, managers do not need to consider the reaction of rival firms to a price change. A monopolist has no rivals; a monopolistic competitor is small enough relative to the total market that its price changes will not usually cause rival firms to retaliate with price changes of their own; and, of course, a perfectly competitive firm is a price-taker and would not change its price from the market-determined price. In contrast, in the case of an *oligopoly* market, just a few firms produce most or all of the market output, so any one firm's pricing policy will have a significant effect on the sales of other firms in the market. This interdependence of oligopoly firms means that actions by any one firm in the market will have an effect on the sales and profits of the other firms. As you will see in Chapter 13, the strategic decision making in oligopoly markets is the most complex of all decision-making situations.

Globalization of Markets

globalization of markets
Economic integration of markets located in nations around the world.

For the past quarter century, businesses around the world have experienced a surge in the **globalization of markets,** a phrase that generally refers to increasing economic integration of markets located in nations throughout the world. Market integration takes place when goods, services, and resources (particularly people and money) flow freely across national borders. Despite excitement in the business press over the present wave of globalization, the process of integrating markets is not a new phenomenon, but rather it is an ongoing process that may advance for some period of time and then suffer setbacks. The last significant wave of globalization lasted from the late 1800s to the start of World War I. During that period, expansion of railroads and the emergence of steamships enabled both a great migration of labor resources from Europe to the United States as well as a surge in the flow of goods between regional and international markets. Even though some governments and some citizens oppose international economic integration, as evidenced by a number of antiglobalization protests, most economists believe the freer flow of resources and products can raise standards of living in rich and poor nations alike.

The movement toward global markets over the last 25 years can be traced to several developments. During this period North American, European, and Latin American nations successfully negotiated numerous bilateral and multilateral trade agreements, eliminating many restrictions to trade flows among those nations. And, during this time, 11 European nations agreed to adopt a single currency—the euro—to stimulate trade on the continent by eliminating the use of assorted currencies that tends to impede cross-border flows of resources, goods, and services. Adding to the momentum for globalization, the Information Age rapidly revolutionized electronic communication, making it possible to buy and sell goods and services over a worldwide Internet. As noted in Illustration 1.5, Microsoft Office software has become something of an international language for businesses, as companies around the world communicate using *Excel* spreadsheets and documents created in Word and PowerPoint. All of these developments contributed to reducing the transaction costs of bringing buyers and sellers in different nations together for the purpose of doing business.

As you can see from this discussion, globalization of markets provides managers with an opportunity to sell more goods and services to foreign buyers and to find new and cheaper sources of labor, capital, and raw material inputs in other countries, but along with these benefits comes the threat of intensified competition by foreign businesses. This trend toward economic integration of markets changes the way managers must view the structure of the markets in which they sell their products or services, as well as the ways they choose to organize production. Throughout the text, we will point out some of the opportunities and challenges of globalization of markets.

ILLUSTRATION 1.5

Internet Spurs Globalization of Services

Antiglobalization protestors in Seattle, Washington, D.C., Quebec, and Genoa have criticized multinational corporations—as well as their governments, the World Trade Organization, the International Monetary Fund, and the World Bank—for moving manufacturing operations to countries with low wages. While the protestors express deep concern that workers in poorer countries will be "exploited" by multinational corporations and be forced to work in sweatshops for "unfair" wages, the more basic fear among protestors seems to be an understandable concern that they will lose their jobs as manufacturing moves to other countries.

Douglas Lavin, in *The Wall Street Journal*, explains that antiglobalization protestors have overlooked a more significant shift in services: "Thanks largely to the fact that a decent education, Microsoft Office, and the Internet are all as useful in Manila as in Minneapolis, the service sector has gone (global)." The worldwide Internet now makes possible for services what railroads and steamships made possible for manufactured goods: Services can be produced anywhere in the world and "delivered" digitally via terrestrial, broadband, fiber-optic cables, or high-capacity satellites in geosynchronous orbits to end users most anywhere in the world. Every imaginable kind of service is now experiencing globalization: from accounting services, claims processing, credit evaluation, and answering customer service questions on 1-800 telephone numbers to data entry, software coding, and even gambling. Businesses in the United States, Britain, Spain, Hong Kong, and France currently lead the way in outsourcing services to workers in other countries, such as India, the Philippines, Jamaica, Ghana, Hungary, and the Czech Republic.

As Lavin emphasizes in his article, the Internet "explosion" coupled with vast improvements in telecommunications technology enabled the service sector to join the process of globalization. Because many Third World nations can afford the infrastructure investments required to access the Internet—even when better roads and bridges may be too costly—Lavin predicts globalization of the service sector could create a significant improvement in living standards in poorer nations. Furthermore, by providing multinational corporations with the ability to buy inexpensive services, globalization tends to increase productivity, which tends to push wages up in the home countries of these corporations. Although protestors may argue globalization harms the poor, Lavin reminds us that the thousands of people now working as accountants for Arthur Andersen in the Philippines and as engineers for Cisco in India are thrilled to trade their education and skills on the Internet, and they are no longer poor.

Economists have long recognized that when two parties voluntarily engage in trade, both parties gain. Globalization of services made possible by the Internet provides an opportunity for such trades: Businesses can reduce their costs, and hundreds of thousands of workers in low-income nations can earn higher wages.

Source: Douglas Lavin, "Globalization Goes Upscale," in *The Wall Street Journal*, February 1, 2002, p. A 21.

1.5 SUMMARY

- Managerial economics applies the most useful concepts and theories from microeconomics and industrial organization to create a systematic, logical way of analyzing business practices and tactics designed to maximize profit, as well as formulating strategies for sustaining or protecting these profits in the long run. Marginal analysis provides the foundation for understanding the everyday business decisions managers routinely make in running a business. Such decisions are frequently referred to as business practices or tactics. Strategic decisions differ from routine business practices or tactics because strategic decisions seek to alter the conditions under which a firm competes with its rivals in ways that will increase and/or protect the firm's long-run profit. Industrial organization identifies seven economic forces that promote long-run profitability: few close substitutes, strong entry barriers, weak rivalry within markets, low market power of input suppliers, low market power of consumers, abundant complementary products, and limited harmful government intervention. (*LO1*)

- The economic cost of using resources to produce a good or service is the opportunity cost to the owners of the firm using those resources. The opportunity cost of using any kind of resource is what the owners of the firm must give up to use the resource. Total economic cost is the sum of the opportunity costs of market-supplied resources (explicit costs) plus the opportunity costs of owner-supplied resources (implicit costs). Economic profit is the difference between total revenue and total economic cost. Accounting profit differs from economic profit because accounting profit does not subtract the implicit costs of using resources from total revenue. The value of a firm is the price for which it can be sold, and that price is equal to the present value of the expected future profit of the firm. The risk associated with not knowing future profits of a firm requires adding a risk premium to the discount rate used for calculating the present value of the firm's future profits. The larger (smaller) the risk associated with future profits, the higher (lower) the risk premium used to compute the value of the firm, and the lower (higher) the value of the firm will be. (*LO2*)

- The decision to hire professional managers to run a business creates a separation between business ownership and its management, forming a principal–agent relationship: a business owner (the principal) contracts with a manager (the agent) to perform tasks designed to further the objectives or goals of the owner. With the separation of ownership and management, a principal–agent *problem* can arise because owners cannot be certain that managers are making decisions to maximize the value of the firm. A principal–agent problem requires the presence of two conditions: (1) manager and owner objectives are not aligned, and (2) the owner finds it either too costly or impossible to monitor the actions and decisions of the manager to ensure these decisions will maximize the firm's value. Monitoring managers becomes an impossible task when managers are able to take hidden actions that cannot be observed by owners. A moral hazard is present if the hidden actions harm owners while benefitting the managers— perhaps by reducing their work effort, by taking excessive perks, or by pursuing goals other than profit maximization. Moral hazard is both a problem of nonaligned objectives and a problem of harmful hidden actions; if either one of these two aspects is missing there is no moral hazard problem. The shareholder owners of a public corporation can control or mitigate agency problems by (1) requiring managers to hold an equity stake the firm, (2) increasing the number of outsiders serving on the company's board of directors, and (3) financing corporate investments with debt instead of equity. In addition to these internal corporate control measures, corporate takeovers, which originate outside the firm, can also effectively motivate managers to make value-maximizing decisions. (*LO3*)

- A price-taking firm cannot set the price of the product it sells because price is determined strictly by the market forces of demand and supply. A price-setting firm sets the price of its product because it possesses some degree of market power, which is the ability to raise price without losing all sales. A market is any arrangement that enables buyers and sellers to exchange goods and services, usually for money payments. Markets exist to reduce transaction costs, which are the costs of making a transaction. Market structure is a set of characteristics that determines the economic environment in which a firm operates: (1) the number and size of firms operating in the market, (2) the degree of product differentiation, and (3) the likelihood of new firms entering. Markets may be structured as one of four types: perfect competition, monopoly, monopolistic competition, and oligopoly. (*LO4*)

- Globalization of markets, which is the process of integrating markets located in nations around the world, is not a new phenomenon but rather an ongoing historical process that brings opportunities and challenges to business managers. Globalization provides managers with an opportunity to sell more goods and services to foreign buyers and to find new and cheaper sources of labor, capital, and raw material inputs in other countries, but along with these benefits comes the threat of intensified competition by foreign businesses. (*LO5*)

KEY TERMS

accounting profit	industrial organization	price-setting firm
business practices or tactics	market	price-taker
complete contract	market power	principal–agent problem
economic profit	market structure	principal–agent relationship
equity capital	market-supplied resources	risk premium
explicit costs	microeconomics	strategic decisions
globalization of markets	moral hazard	total economic cost
hidden actions	opportunity cost	transaction costs
implicit costs	owner-supplied resources	value of a firm

TECHNICAL PROBLEMS*

1. For each one of the costs below, explain whether the resource cost is explicit or implicit, and give the annual opportunity cost for each one. Assume the owner of the business can invest money and earn 10 percent annually.

   a. A computer server to run the firm's network is leased for $6,000 per year.

   b. The owner starts the business using $50,000 of cash from a personal savings account.

   c. A building for the business was purchased for $18 million three years ago but is now worth $30 million.

   d. Computer programmers cost $50 per hour. The firm will hire 100,000 hours of programmer services this year.

   e. The firm owns a 1975 model Clarke-Owens garbage incinerator, which it uses to dispose of paper and cardboard waste. Even though this type of incinerator is now illegal to use for environmental reasons, the firm can continue to use it because it's exempt under a "grandfather" clause in the law. However, the exemption only applies to the current owner for use until it wears out or is replaced. (*Note:* The owner offered to give the incinerator to the Smithsonian Institute as a charitable gift, but managers at the Smithsonian turned it down.)

2. During a year of operation, a firm collects $175,000 in revenue and spends $80,000 on raw materials, labor expense, utilities, and rent. The owners of the firm have provided $500,000 of their own money to the firm instead of investing the money and earning a 14 percent annual rate of return.

   a. The explicit costs of the firm are $_____. The implicit costs are $_____. Total economic cost is $_____.

   b. The firm earns economic profit of $_____.

   c. The firm's accounting profit is $_____.

   d. If the owners could earn 20 percent annually on the money they have invested in the firm, the economic profit of the firm would be _____.

***Notice to students:** The Technical Problems throughout this book have been carefully designed to guide your learning in a step-by-step process. You should work the Technical Problems as indicated by the icons in the left margin, which direct you to the specific problems for that particular section of a chapter, before proceeding to the remaining sections of the chapter.

3. Over the next three years, a firm is expected to earn economic profits of $120,000 in the first year, $140,000 in the second year, and $100,000 in the third year. After the end of the third year, the firm will go out of business.

   a. If the risk-adjusted discount rate is 10 percent for each of the next three years, the value of the firm is $_____. The firm can be sold today for a price of $_____.

   b. If the risk-adjusted discount rate is 8 percent for each of the next three years, the value of the firm is $_____. The firm can be sold today for a price of $_____.

4. Fill in the blanks:

   a. Managers will maximize the values of firms by making decisions that maximize _____ in every single time period, so long as cost and revenue conditions in each period are _____.

   b. When current output has the effect of increasing future costs, the level of output that maximizes the value of the firm will be _____ (smaller, larger) than the level of output that maximizes profit in a single period.

   c. When current output has a positive effect on future profit, the level of output that maximizes the value of the firm will be _____ (smaller, larger) than the level of output that maximizes profit in the current period.

APPLIED PROBLEMS

1. Some managers are known for their reliance on "practical" decision-making rules and processes, and they can be quite skeptical of decision rules that seem too theoretical to be useful in practice. While it may be true that some theoretical methods in economics can be rather limited in their practical usefulness, there is an important corollary to keep in mind: "If it doesn't work in theory, then it won't work in practice." Explain the meaning of this corollary and give a real-world example (*Hint:* see "Some Common Mistakes Managers Make").

2. At the beginning of the year, an audio engineer quit his job and gave up a salary of $175,000 per year in order to start his own business, Sound Devices, Inc. The new company builds, installs, and maintains custom audio equipment for businesses that require high-quality audio systems. A partial income statement for the first year of operation for Sound Devices, Inc., is shown below:

Revenues	
Revenue from sales of product and services	$970,000
Operating costs and expenses	
Cost of products and services sold	355,000
Selling expenses	155,000
Administrative expenses	45,000
Total operating costs and expenses	$555,000
Income from operations	$415,000
Interest expense (bank loan)	45,000
Legal expenses	28,000
Corporate income tax payments	165,000
Net income	$177,000

To get started, the owner of Sound Devices spent $100,000 of his personal savings to pay for some of the capital equipment used in the business. During the first year of operation, the owner of Sound Devices could have earned a 15 percent return by investing in stocks of other new businesses with risk levels similar to the risk level at Sound Devices.

a. What are the total explicit, total implicit, and total economic costs for the year?

b. What is accounting profit?

c. What is economic profit?

d. Given your answer in part *c,* evaluate the owner's decision to leave his job to start Sound Devices.

3. A doctor spent two weeks doing charity medical work in Mexico. In calculating her taxable income for the year, her accountant deducted as business expenses her round-trip airline ticket, meals, and a hotel bill for the two-week stay. She was surprised to learn that the accountant, following IRS rules, could not deduct as a cost of the trip the $8,000 of income she lost by being absent from her medical practice for two weeks. She asked the accountant, "Since lost income is not deductible as an expense, should I ignore it when I make my decision next year to go to Mexico for charity work?" Can you give the doctor some advice on decision making?

4. When Burton Cummings graduated with honors from the Canadian Trucking Academy, his father gave him a $350,000 tractor-trailer rig. Recently, Burton was boasting to some fellow truckers that his revenues were typically $25,000 per month, while his operating costs (fuel, maintenance, and depreciation) amounted to only $18,000 per month. Tractor-trailer rigs identical to Burton's rig rent for $15,000 per month. If Burton was driving trucks for one of the competing trucking firms, he would earn $5,000 per month.

a. How much are Burton Cummings's explicit costs per month? How much are his implicit costs per month?

b. What is the dollar amount of the opportunity cost of the resources used by Burton Cummings each month?

c. Burton is proud of the fact that he is generating a net cash flow of $7,000 (= $25,000 − $18,000) per month, since he would be earning only $5,000 per month if he were working for a trucking firm. What advice would you give Burton Cummings?

5. Explain why it would cost Rafael Nadal or Venus Williams more to leave the professional tennis tour and open a tennis shop than it would for the coach of a university tennis team to do so.

6. An article in *The Wall Street Journal* discusses a trend among some large U.S. corporations to base the compensation of outside members of their boards of directors partly on the performance of the corporation. "This growing practice more closely aligns the director to the company. [Some] companies link certain stock or stock-option grants for directors to improved financial performance, using a measure such as annual return on equity."

How would such a linkage tend to reduce the agency problem between managers and shareholders as a whole? Why could directors be more efficient than shareholders at improving managerial performance and changing their incentives?

7. An article in *The Wall Street Journal* reported that large hotel chains, such as Marriott, are tending to reduce the number of hotels that they franchise to outside owners and increase the number the chain owns and manages itself. Some chains are requiring private owners or franchisees to make upgrades in their hotels, but they are having a difficult time enforcing the policy. Marriott says this upgrading is important because "we've built our name on quality."

      a. Explain the nature of the agency problem facing Marriott.

      b. Why would Marriott worry about the quality of the hotels it doesn't own but franchises?

      c. Why would a chain such as Marriott tend to own its hotels in resort areas, such as national parks, where there is little repeat business, and franchise hotels in downtown areas, where there is a lot of repeat business? Think of the reputation effect and the incentive of franchises to maintain quality.

8. *Fortune* magazine reported that SkyWest, an independent regional airline, negotiated a financial arrangement with Delta and United to provide regional jet service for the two major airlines. For its part of the deal, SkyWest agreed to paint its jets the colors of Delta Connection and United Express and to fly routes specified by the two airlines. In return, Delta and United agreed to pay SkyWest a predetermined profit margin and to cover most of the regional airline's costs. *Fortune* explained that while the deal limited the amount of profit SkyWest could earn, it also insulated the smaller airline from volatility in earnings since Delta and United covered SkyWest's fuel costs, increased its load factor (the percentage of seats occupied), and managed its ticket prices.

    Fortune suggested that Wall Street liked the deal because SkyWest's market valuation increased from $143 million to $1.1 billion after it began its service with the two major airlines. Explain carefully how this arrangement with Delta and United could have caused the value of SkyWest to increase dramatically even though it limited the amount of profit SkyWest could earn.

▣ MATHEMATICAL APPENDIX   Review of Present Value Calculations

The concept of present value is a tool used to determine the value of a firm, which is the present value of expected future profits to be earned. This short presentation provides you with the basic computational skills needed to calculate the present value of a stream of expected profit to be received in future periods.

Present Value of a Single Payment in the Future

The payment you would accept today rather than wait for a payment (or stream of payments) to be received in the future is called the *present value* (*PV*) of that future payment (or stream of payments). Suppose, for example, that a trustworthy person promises to pay you $100 a year from now. Even though you are sure you will get the $100 in a year, a dollar now is worth more than a dollar a year from now. How much money would you accept now rather than wait one year for a guaranteed payment of $100? Because of the time value of money, you will be willing to accept less than $100; that is, the present value of a $100 payment one year from now is *less* than $100. The process of calculating present value is sometimes referred to as *discounting* since the present value of a payment is less than the dollar amount of the future payment.

To properly discount the $100 future payment, you must first determine the opportunity cost of waiting for your money. Suppose that, at no risk, you could earn a return of 6 percent by investing the money over a one-year period. This 6 percent return is called the *risk-free discount rate* since it determines the rate at which you will discount future dollars to determine their present value, assuming you bear no risk of receiving less than the promised amount. In Web Chapter 1, The Investment Decision, we will show you how to determine the appropriate risk premium to add to the risk-free discount rate when the future payment involves a degree of risk. For now, you need not be concerned about adjusting for risk.

Given that you can earn 6 percent (with no risk) on your money, how much money do you need now—let's denote this amount as $X—in order to have exactly $100 a year from now? Since $X(1.06)$ is the value of $X in one year, set this future value equal to $100:

$$\$X(1.06) = \$100$$

It follows that the amount you must invest today ($X) is $94.34 (= $100/1.06) in order to have $100 in a year.

Thus, the present value of $100 to be received in one year is $94.34 now. In other words, you would accept $94.34 now, which will grow to $100 in one year at a 6 percent annual discount rate.

Now suppose that the $100 payment comes not after one year but after two years. Investing $X at 6 percent would yield $X(1.06)$ at the end of year 1 and $[\$X(1.06)](1.06) = \$X(1.06)^2$ at the end of year 2. For an investment to be worth $100 in two years,

$$\$X(1.06)^2 = \$100$$

The amount you must invest today in order to have $100 at the end of two years is $89 [= \$100/(1.06)^2]$. Thus, the present value of $100 in two years with a discount rate of 6 percent is $89.

Clearly a pattern is emerging: The present value of $100 in one year at 6 percent is

$$PV = \frac{\$100}{(1.06)} = \$94.34$$

The present value of $100 in two years at 6 percent is

$$PV = \frac{\$100}{(1.06)^2} = \$89$$

Therefore, the present value of $100 to be received in t years (t being any number of years) with a discount rate of 6 percent is

$$PV = \frac{\$100}{(1.06)^t}$$

This relation can be made even more general to determine the present value of some amount of profit, π, to be received in t years at a discount rate of r. Also note that if the discount rate is 6 percent, for example, r is expressed as 0.06, the decimal equivalent of 6 percent.

Relation   The present value (PV) of $\$\pi$ to be received in t years at a discount rate of r is

$$PV = \frac{\$\pi}{(1 + r)^t}$$

As illustrated above, the present value of a profit flow declines the further in the future it is to be received—for example, the present value of $100 at 6 percent was $94.34 in one year and only $89 in two years. As should be evident from the more general statement of present value, the present value of a profit flow is inversely related to the discount

rate—for example, the present value of $100 to be received in two years is $89 with a discount rate of 6 percent but only $85.73 [= \$100/(1.08)^2] with a discount rate of 8 percent.

Relation   There is an inverse relation between the present value of a profit flow and the time to maturity. The present value of a profit flow to be received in t years is greater than that for the same profit flow to be received in $t + i$ years. There is an inverse relation between the present value of a profit flow and the discount rate.

Present Value of a Stream of Profits

So far we have considered the present value of a single profit payment. We now extend present value analysis to consider the value of a stream of profit payments in the future. Suppose your trustworthy friend promises to pay you $100 in one year and $100 in two years. Using 6 percent as the risk-free discount rate for the first year, the present value of the first payment would be

$$PV = \frac{\$100}{(1.06)} = \$94.34$$

At the 6 percent discount rate, the present value of the second payment would be

$$PV = \frac{\$100}{(1.06)^2} = \$89$$

Thus, the present value of the two-period stream of profit payments is

$$PV = \frac{\$100}{(1.06)} + \frac{\$100}{(1.06)^2} = \$94.34 + \$89 = \$183.34$$

From the preceding, you should be able to see that the present value of a stream of profit payments is equal to the sum of the present values of the profit flows. We can state this more precisely in the following:

Relation   The present value of a stream of profit payments, where $\$\pi_t$ is the cash flow received or paid in period t, is given by

$$PV = \frac{\$\pi_1}{(1 + r)} + \frac{\$\pi_2}{(1 + r)^2} + \frac{\$\pi_3}{(1 + r)^3} + \cdots + \frac{\$\pi_T}{(1 + r)^T}$$

$$= \sum_{t=1}^{T} \frac{\$\pi_t}{(1 + r)^t}$$

where r is the discount rate, and T is the life span of the stream of profit payments.

In the special case for which the profit in each of the T time periods is exactly the same amount, the present value of this stream of constant profit payments can be expressed as

$$PV = \$\pi \times \left(\frac{1 - \frac{1}{(1+r)T}}{r} \right)$$

where the same $\$\pi$ payment is received for T time periods.

In some instances, a firm can be thought of as earning a stream of constant profit payments forever, that is, the firm generates a perpetual flow of $\$\pi$ in every time period forever. Letting $T = \infty$ in the above expression, you can see that the present value simplifies to

$$PV = \$\pi \times \left(\frac{1}{r} \right) = \frac{\$\pi}{r}$$

For example, if a firm wins a perpetual government contract paying $60,000 of profit every year forever—only government agencies would do such a thing—the present value of this stream of profit payments discounted at 6 percent is $1,000,000 (= $60,000/.06). While you might find an infinite time span to be rather farfetched for real-world financial analysis, let's suppose the $60,000 payment lasts for only 100 years, which is still a long time. Setting $T = 100$ in the previous expression (with $\pi = \$60,000$ and $r = .06$), the present value is just a small amount less than $1 million; it is approximately $997,000. As you can see, when T is a large number the easiest way to compute the approximate present value is simply to divide the constant profit payment by the discount rate.

MATHEMATICAL EXERCISES

1. Using a discount rate of 6.5 percent, calculate the present value of a $1,000 profit payment to be received at the end of
   a. One year
   b. Two years
   c. Three years

2. What is the present value of a firm with a five-year life span that earns the following stream of expected profit? (Treat all profits as being received at year-end.) Use a risk-adjusted discount rate of 12 percent.

Year	Expected profit
1	$10,000
2	20,000
3	50,000
4	75,000
5	50,000

3. Suppose that in their divorce settlement, Ashton Kutcher offers Demi Moore $10 million spread evenly over 10 years, but she instead demands $5 million now. If the appropriate discount rate is 8 percent, which alternative is better for Ashton and which for Demi? What if the discount rate is 20 percent?

4. You are considering the purchase of a piece of land that can be leased to the government for 100 years. The annual lease payment is $20,000 and the appropriate discount rate for your situation is 4 percent. What is the (approximate) present value of this stream of constant lease payments?

Chapter 2

Demand, Supply, and Market Equilibrium

After reading this chapter, you will be able to:

2.1 Identify demand functions and distinguish between a change in demand and a change in quantity demanded.

2.2 Identify supply functions and distinguish between a change in supply and a change in quantity supplied.

2.3 Explain why market equilibrium occurs at the price for which quantity demanded equals quantity supplied.

2.4 Measure gains from market exchange using consumer surplus, producer surplus, and social surplus.

2.5 Predict the impact on equilibrium price and quantity of shifts in demand or supply.

2.6 Examine the impact of government-imposed price ceilings and price floors.

Successful managers must be able to accurately predict the prices and production levels of the goods and resources relevant to their businesses. Executive managers at Intel, for example, must plan production of their semiconductor chips many months ahead of buyers' orders. Semiconductor profits depend critically on understanding the market forces affecting both the demand and supply conditions that will ultimately determine the price of Intel's chips and the number of chips they must produce to meet demand. Intel's semiconductor chips will end up in everything from Dell and Mac computers to automobiles, cell phones, and jet aircraft control and navigation systems. Intel faces many competing chip manufacturers in these various markets, so the production planners at Intel cannot make the best decisions without accurate estimates of the prices their chips will fetch in the market and the number of chips they will need to produce. If Intel produces too many semiconductor chips, it will lose money on excessive inventory costs and on the price cuts necessary to unload the excess chips. If Intel produces too few chips, it will miss out on sales as buyers turn to its competitors to fill their orders. And the likelihood of producing the wrong number of semiconductor chips is high if Intel is unable to correctly forecast the prices of its chips.

Supply and demand analysis is one of the most powerful tools of economics for analyzing the way market forces determine prices and output levels in competitive markets. As you will see in this chapter, supply and demand analysis is reasonably simple to learn. And, it is widely used by highly experienced—and well-paid—market analysts and forecasters.

This chapter focuses primarily on the way markets for consumer goods and services function, although the basic concepts apply also to markets for resources, such as labor, land, raw materials, energy, and capital equipment. Supply and demand analysis applies principally to markets characterized by many buyers and sellers in which a homogeneous or relatively nondifferentiated good or service is sold. As we stated in the previous chapter, such markets are called competitive markets. In competitive markets, individual firms are price-takers because prices are determined by the impersonal forces of the marketplace—demand and supply.

We begin the analysis of competitive markets by describing the buyer side of the market—called the *demand side* of the market. Next we describe the seller side—called the *supply side*. We then combine the demand side with the supply side to show how prices and quantities sold are determined in a market. Finally, we show how forces on the demand side or the supply side of the market can change and thereby affect the price and quantity sold in a market.

2.1 DEMAND

quantity demanded
The amount of a good or service consumers are willing and able to purchase during a given period of time (week, month, etc.).

The amount of a good or service that consumers in a market are willing and able to purchase during a given period of time (e.g., a week, a month) is called **quantity demanded.** Although economists emphasize the importance of price in purchasing decisions, as we will do, they also recognize that a multitude of factors other than price affect the amount of a good or service people will purchase. However, to simplify market analysis and make it manageable, economists ignore the many factors that have an insignificant effect on purchases and concentrate only on the most important factors. Indeed, only six factors are considered sufficiently important to be included in most studies of market demand.

This section develops three types of demand relations: (1) *general demand functions*, which show how quantity demanded is related to product price and five other factors that affect demand, (2) *direct demand functions*, which show the relation between quantity demanded and the price of the product when all other variables affecting demand are held constant at specific values, and (3) *inverse demand functions*, which give the maximum prices buyers are willing to pay to obtain various amounts of product. As you will see in this chapter, direct demand functions are derived from general demand functions, and inverse demand curves are derived from direct demand curves. Traditionally, economists have referred to direct demand functions simply as *demand functions* or *demand*. We shall follow this tradition.

The General Demand Function: $Q_d = f(P, M, P_R, \mathcal{T}, P_E, N)$

The six principal variables that influence the quantity demanded of a good or service are (1) the price of the good or service, (2) the incomes of consumers, (3) the prices of related goods and services, (4) the tastes or preference patterns of consumers, (5) the expected price of the product in future periods, and (6) the number of consumers in the market. The relation between quantity demanded and these six factors is referred to as the **general demand function** and is expressed as follows:

general demand function
The relation between quantity demanded and the six factors that affect quantity demanded: $Q_d = f(P, M, P_R, \mathcal{T}, P_E, N)$.

$$Q_d = f(P, M, P_R, \mathcal{T}, P_E, N)$$

where f means "is a function of" or "depends on," and

Q_d = quantity demanded of the good or service
P = price of the good or service
M = consumers' income (generally per capita)
P_R = price of related goods or services
$\mathcal{T}$ = taste patterns of consumers
P_E = expected price of the good in some future period
N = number of consumers in the market

The general demand function shows how all six variables *jointly* determine the quantity demanded. In order to discuss the *individual* effect that any one of these six variables has on Q_d, we must explain how changing just that one variable *by itself* influences Q_d. Isolating the individual effect of a single variable requires that all other variables that affect Q_d be held constant. Thus whenever we speak of the effect that a particular variable has on quantity demanded, we mean the individual effect *holding all other variables constant.*

We now discuss each of the six variables to show how they are related to the amount of a good or service consumers buy. We begin by discussing the effect of changing the *price* of a good while holding the other five variables constant. As you would expect, consumers are willing and able to buy more of a good the lower the price of the good and will buy less of a good the higher the price of the good. Price and quantity demanded are negatively (inversely) related because when the price of a good rises, consumers tend to shift from that good to other goods that are now relatively cheaper. Conversely, when the price of a good falls, consumers tend to purchase more of that good and less of other goods that are now relatively more expensive. Price and quantity demanded are inversely related when all other factors are held constant. This relation between price and quantity demanded is so important that we discuss it in more detail later in this chapter and again in Chapter 5.

Next, we consider changes in *income,* again holding constant the rest of the variables that influence consumers. An increase in income can cause the amount of a commodity consumers purchase either to increase or to decrease. If an increase in income causes consumers to demand more of a good, when all other variables

normal good

A good or service for which an increase (decrease) in income causes consumers to demand more (less) of the good, holding all other variables in the general demand function constant.

inferior good

A good or service for which an increase (decrease) in income causes consumers to demand less (more) of the good, all other factors held constant.

substitutes

Two goods are substitutes if an increase (decrease) in the price of one of the goods causes consumers to demand more (less) of the other good, holding all other factors constant.

complements

Two goods are complements if an increase (decrease) in the price of one of the goods causes consumers to demand less (more) of the other good, all other things held constant.

in the general demand function are held constant, we refer to such a commodity as a **normal good**. A good is also a normal good if a decrease in income causes consumers to demand less of the good, all other things held constant. There are some goods and services for which an increase in income would reduce consumer demand, other variables held constant. This type of commodity is referred to as an **inferior good.** In the case of inferior goods, rising income causes consumers to demand *less* of the good, and falling income causes consumers to demand *more* of the good. Some examples of goods and services that might be inferior include mobile homes, shoe repair services, generic food products, and used cars.

Commodities may be *related in consumption* in either of two ways: as substitutes or as complements. In general, goods are *substitutes* if one good can be used in the place of the other; an example might be Toyotas and Chryslers. If two goods are substitutes, an increase in the price of one good will increase the demand for the other good. If the price of Toyotas rises while the price of Chryslers remains constant, we would expect consumers to purchase more Chryslers—holding all other factors constant. If an increase in the price of a related good causes consumers to demand more of a good, then the two goods are **substitutes.** Similarly, two goods are substitutes if a decrease in the price of one of the goods causes consumers to demand less of the other good, all other things constant.

Goods are said to be *complements* if they are used in conjunction with each other. Examples might be iPods and music, lettuce and salad dressing, or baseball games and hot dogs. A decrease in the price of tickets to the baseball game will increase the quantity of tickets demanded, and thus increase the demand for hot dogs at the game, all else constant. If the demand for one good increases when the price of a related good decreases, the two goods are **complements.** Similarly, two goods are complements if an increase in the price of one of the goods causes consumers to demand less of the other good, all other things constant.[1]

A change in consumer tastes can change demand for a good or service. Obviously, taste changes could either increase or decrease consumer demand. While consumer tastes are not directly measurable (as are the other variables in the general demand function), you may wish to view the variable $\mathcal{T}$ as an index of consumer tastes; $\mathcal{T}$ takes on larger values as consumers perceive a good becoming higher in quality, more fashionable, more healthful, or more desirable in any way. A decrease in $\mathcal{T}$ corresponds to a change in consumer tastes away from a good or service as consumers perceive falling quality, or displeasing appearance, or diminished healthfulness. Consequently, when all other variables in the general demand function are held constant, a movement in consumer tastes toward a good or service will increase demand and a movement in consumer tastes away from a good will decrease demand for the good. A change in consumer tastes or preferences occurs when, for example, the *New England Journal of Medicine*

---

[1]Not all commodities are either substitutes or complements in consumption. Many commodities are essentially independent. For example, we would not expect the price of lettuce to significantly influence the demand for automobiles. Thus, we can treat these commodities as independent and ignore the price of lettuce when evaluating the demand for automobiles.

publishes research findings that show a higher incidence of brain cancer among people who regularly use cell phones. This causes the demand for cell phones to decrease (the taste index $\mathcal{T}$ declines), all other factors remaining constant.

Expectations of consumers also influence consumers' decisions to purchase goods and services. More specifically, consumers' expectations about the future price of a commodity can change their current purchasing decisions. If consumers expect the price to be higher in a future period, demand will probably rise in the current period. On the other hand, expectations of a price decline in the future will cause some purchases to be postponed—thus demand in the current period will fall. An example of this can be seen in the automobile industry. Automakers often announce price increases for the next year's models several months before the cars are available in showrooms in order to stimulate demand for the current year's cars.

Finally, an increase in the number of consumers in the market will increase the demand for a good, and a decrease in the number of consumers will decrease the demand for a good, all other factors held constant. In markets that experience a growth in the number of buyers—such as the health care industry as the population matures or Florida during the tourist season—we would expect demand to increase.

The general demand function just set forth is expressed in the most general mathematical form. Economists and market researchers often express the general demand function in a more specific mathematical form in order to show more precisely the relation between quantity demanded and some of the more important variables that affect demand. They frequently express the general demand function in a linear functional form. The following equation is an example of a linear form of the general demand function:

$$Q_d = a + bP + cM + dP_R + e\mathcal{T} + fP_E + gN$$

where Q_d, P, M, P_R, $\mathcal{T}$, P_E, and N are as defined above, and a, b, c, d, e, f, and g are parameters.

The intercept parameter a shows the value of Q_d when the variables P, M, P_R, $\mathcal{T}$, P_E, and N are all simultaneously equal to zero. The other parameters, b, c, d, e, f, and g, are called **slope parameters:** They measure the effect on quantity demanded of changing one of the variables P, M, P_R, $\mathcal{T}$, P_E, or N while holding the rest of these variables constant. The slope parameter b, for example, measures the change in quantity demanded per unit change in price; that is, $b = \Delta Q_d / \Delta P$.[2] As stressed earlier, Q_d and P are inversely related, and b is negative because ΔQ_d and ΔP have opposite algebraic signs.

The slope parameter c measures the effect on the amount purchased of a one-unit change in income ($c = \Delta Q_d / \Delta M$). For normal goods, sales increase when income rises, so c is positive. If the good is inferior, sales decrease when income rises, so c is negative. The parameter d measures the change in the amount consumers want to buy per unit change in P_R ($d = \Delta Q_d / \Delta P_R$). If an increase in P_R causes sales to

slope parameters
Parameters in a linear function that measure the effect on the dependent variable (Q_d) of changing one of the independent variables (P, M, P_R, $\mathcal{T}$, P_E, and N) while holding the rest of these variables constant.

---

[2]The symbol "Δ" means "change in." Thus, if quantity demanded rises (falls), then ΔQ_d is positive (negative). Similarly, if price rises (falls), ΔP is positive (negative). In general, the ratio of the change in Y divided by the change in X ($\Delta Y / \Delta X$) measures the change in Y per unit change in X.

TABLE 2.1

Summary of the General (Linear) Demand Function
$Q_d = a + bP + cM + dP_R + e\mathcal{T} + fP_E + gN$

Variable	Relation to quantity demanded	Sign of slope parameter
P	Inverse	$b = \Delta Q_d / \Delta P$ is negative
M	Direct for normal goods	$c = \Delta Q_d / \Delta M$ is positive
	Inverse for inferior goods	$c = \Delta Q_d / \Delta M$ is negative
P_R	Direct for substitute goods	$d = \Delta Q_d / \Delta P_R$ is positive
	Inverse for complement goods	$d = \Delta Q_d / \Delta P_R$ is negative
$\mathcal{T}$	Direct	$e = \Delta Q_d / \Delta \mathcal{T}$ is positive
P_E	Direct	$f = \Delta Q_d / \Delta P_E$ is positive
N	Direct	$g = \Delta Q_d / \Delta N$ is positive

rise, the goods are substitutes and d is positive. If an increase in P_R causes sales to fall, the two goods are complements and d is negative. Since $\mathcal{T}$, P_E, and N are each directly related to the amount purchased, the parameters e, f, and g are all positive.[3]

> **Relation** When the general demand function is expressed in linear form:
>
> $$Q_d = a + bP + cM + dP_R + e\mathcal{T} + fP_E + gN$$
>
> the slope parameters (b, c, d, e, f, and g) measure the effect on the amount of the good purchased of changing one of the variables (P, M, P_R, $\mathcal{T}$, P_E, and N) while holding the rest of the variables constant. For example, $b\,(= \Delta Q_d / \Delta P)$ measures the change in quantity demanded per unit change in price holding M, P_R, $\mathcal{T}$, P_E, and N constant. When the slope parameter of a specific variable is positive (negative) in sign, quantity demanded is directly (inversely) related to that variable.

Table 2.1 summarizes this discussion of the general demand function. Each of the six factors that affect quantity demanded is listed, and the table shows whether the quantity demanded varies directly or inversely with each variable and gives the sign of the slope parameters. Again let us stress that these relations are in the context of all other things being equal. An increase in the price of the commodity will lead to a decrease in quantity demanded as long as the other variables—income, the price of related commodities, consumer tastes, price expectations, and the number of customers—remain constant.

A general demand function always includes price as a variable but may not always include every one of the other five variables shown in Table 2.1. Market analysts sometimes omit consumer tastes and price expectations, since these variables may not be important in every situation. The number of customers may also be disregarded in formulating a general demand equation when the number of consumers in a particular market does not change. For example, the demand for city water is not likely to depend on consumer tastes, since fashion generally plays no role in determining water usage, and city water

---

[3]Since consumer tastes are not directly measurable as are the other variables, you may wish to view $\mathcal{T}$ as an index of consumer tastes that ranges in value from 0, if consumers think a product is worthless, to 10 if they think the product is extremely desirable. In this case, the parameter e shows the effect on quantity of a one-unit change in the taste index ($\mathcal{T}$), and e is positive.

should be tasteless! Price expectations are also unlikely to affect municipal water demand. In January, people don't drink more or less water—or bathe more or less frequently—because they expect the price of city water to be lower or higher in February. Furthermore, in a small town that experiences only an inconsequential change in the number of residents, N does not play an important role in determining the variation in Q_d and need not be included in the general demand function. For these reasons, the general linear demand function can sometimes be simplified to include just three variables from Table 2.1:

$$Q_d = a + bP + cM + dP_R$$

Although it is not always appropriate to use this simplified version of the general demand function, the three-variable demand function does provide a reasonable model of consumer demand in many applications.

Direct Demand Functions: $Q_d = f(P)$

The relation between price and quantity demanded per period of time, when all other factors that affect consumer demand are held constant, is called a **direct demand function** or simply **demand.** Demand gives, for various prices of a good, the corresponding quantities that consumers are willing and able to purchase at each of those prices, all other things held constant. The "other things" that are held constant for a specific demand function are the five variables other than price that can affect demand. A demand function can be expressed as an equation, a schedule or table, or a graph. We begin with a demand equation.

A direct demand function can be expressed in the most general form as the equation

$$Q_d = f(P)$$

which means that the quantity demanded is a function of (i.e., depends on) the price of the good, holding all other variables constant. A direct demand function is obtained by holding all the variables in the general demand function constant except price. For example, using a three-variable demand function,

$$Q_d = f(P, \overline{M}, \overline{P}_R) = f(P)$$

where the bar over the variables M and P_R means that those variables are held constant at some specified amount no matter what value the product price takes.

Now try Technical Problem 1.

direct demand function
A table, a graph, or an equation that shows how quantity demanded is related to product price, holding constant the five other variables that influence demand: $Q_d = f(P)$.

> ☐ **Relation** A direct demand function (also called "demand") expresses quantity demanded as a function of product price only: $Q_d = f(P)$. Demand functions—whether expressed as equations, tables, or graphs—give the quantity demanded at various prices, holding constant the effects of income, price of related goods, consumer tastes, expected price, and the number of consumers. Demand functions are derived from general demand functions by holding all the variables in the general demand function constant except price.

To illustrate the derivation of a direct demand function from the general demand function, suppose the general demand function is

$$Q_d = 3{,}200 - 10P + 0.05M - 24P_R$$

To derive a demand function, $Q_d = f(P)$, the variables M and P_R must be assigned specific (fixed) values. Suppose consumer income is $60,000 and the price of a related good is $200. To find the demand function, the fixed values of M and P_R are substituted into the general demand function

$$Q_d = 3,200 - 10P + 0.05(60,000) - 24(200)$$
$$= 3,200 - 10P + 3,000 - 4,800$$
$$= 1,400 - 10P$$

Thus the direct demand function is expressed in the form of a linear demand equation, $Q_d = 1,400 - 10P$. The intercept parameter, 1,400, is the amount of the good consumers would demand if price is zero. The slope of this demand function ($= \Delta Q_d / \Delta P$) is -10 and indicates that a $1 increase in price causes quantity demanded to decrease by 10 units. Although not all demand functions are linear, you will see later in the text that the linear form is a frequently used specification for estimating and forecasting demand functions.

This linear demand equation satisfies all the conditions set forth in the definition of demand. All variables other than product price are held constant—income at $60,000 and the price of a related good at $200. At each price, the equation gives the amount that consumers would purchase at that price. For example, if price is $60,

$$Q_d = 1,400 - (10 \times \$60) = 800$$

or if price is $40,

$$Q_d = 1,400 - (10 \times \$40) = 1,000$$

demand schedule
A table showing a list of possible product prices and the corresponding quantities demanded.

A **demand schedule** (or table) shows a list of several prices and the quantity demanded per period of time at each of the prices, again holding all variables other than price constant. Seven prices and their corresponding quantities demanded are shown in Table 2.2. Each of the seven combinations of price and quantity demanded is derived from the demand function exactly as shown above.

TABLE 2.2

The Demand Schedule for the Demand Function
$D_0: Q_d = 1,400 - 10P$

Price	Quantity demanded
$140	0
120	200
100	400
80	600
60	800
40	1,000
20	1,200

FIGURE 2.1

A Demand Curve:
$Q_d = 1,400 - 10P$

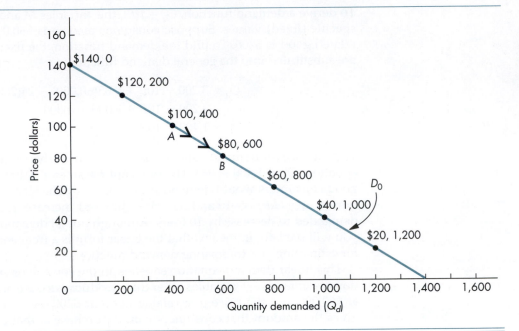

demand curve

A graph showing the relation between quantity demanded and price when all other variables influencing quantity demanded are held constant.

As noted, the final method of showing a demand function is a graph. A graphical demand function is called a **demand curve**. The seven price and quantity demanded combinations in Table 2.2 are plotted in Figure 2.1, and these points are connected with the straight line D_0, which is the demand curve associated with the demand equation $Q_d = 1,400 - 10P$. This demand curve meets the specifications of the definition of demand. All variables other than price are held constant. The demand curve D_0 gives the value of quantity demanded (on the horizontal axis) for every value of price (on the vertical axis).

You may recall from high school algebra that mathematical convention calls for plotting the dependent variable (Q_d) on the vertical axis and the independent variable (P) on the horizontal axis. More than a century ago, however, Alfred Marshall, a famous economist and author of an influential economics textbook, decided to counter this mathematical tradition by plotting all monetary variables—such as prices, revenues, and costs—on the vertical axis. This switch is now an established tradition among economists. We mention here the matter of reversing axes only to make sure that you do not let this minor quirk distract you; it is the only meaningless matter we address here!

inverse demand function

The demand function when price is expressed as a function of quantity demanded: $P = f(Q_d)$.

Inverse Demand Functions: $P = f(Q_d)$

In some situations, it is quite useful to express price as a function of quantity demanded. This form of demand is called the **inverse demand function** because it is the mathematical inverse of the direct demand function. For example, consider the direct demand equation for D_0 in Figure 2.1: $Q_d = 1,400 - 10P$. Solving this direct demand equation for P gives the inverse demand equation: $P = 140 - 1/10Q_d$.[4]

By switching the Q_d and P axes as mentioned above, the graph of demand in Figure 2.1 is, mathematically speaking, a graph of the *inverse* demand function. As you can see in the figure, the vertical intercept is 140, indicating that at a price of $140—frequently called the "choke" price—consumers will demand zero units of the good. The horizontal intercept is 1,400, which is the maximum amount of the good buyers will take when the good is given away ($P = 0$). The slope of the graphed inverse demand is $-1/10$, indicating that if quantity demanded rises by one unit, price must fall 1/10 of a dollar (or 10 cents). This inverse demand, as you can see in the figure, yields price-quantity combinations identical to those given by the direct demand equation, $Q_d = 1,400 - 10P$. In other words, the demand relation shown in Table 2.2 is identically depicted by either a direct or inverse form of the demand equation.

Although demand is generally interpreted as indicating the amount that consumers will buy at each price, sometimes managers and market researchers wish to know the highest price that can be charged for any given amount of the product. As it turns out, every point on a demand curve can be interpreted in either of two ways: (1) the maximum amount of a good that will be purchased if a given price is charged or (2) the maximum price that consumers will pay for a specific amount of a good. Consider, for example, point A ($100, 400) on the demand curve in Figure 2.1. If the price of the good is $100, the maximum amount consumers will purchase is 400 units. Equivalently, $100 is the highest price that consumers can be charged in order to sell a total of 400 units. This price, $100, is called the "demand price" for 400 units, and every price along a demand curve is called the **demand price** for the corresponding quantity on the horizontal axis. Thus the inverse demand function gives the demand price for any specific quantity of the product or service. Later, in section 2.4, we will explain why demand price can also be interpreted as the *economic value* of any specific unit of a product, because, as you now understand from this discussion, demand price is the maximum amount consumers are willing to pay for the good.

demand price
The maximum price consumers will pay for a specific amount of a good or service.

Now try Technical Problems 2–3.

law of demand
Quantity demanded increases when price falls, and quantity demanded decreases when price rises, other things held constant.

Movements along Demand

Before moving on to an analysis of changes in the variables that are held constant when deriving a demand function, we want to reemphasize the relation between price and quantity demanded, which was discussed earlier in this chapter. In the demand equation, the parameter on price is negative; in the demand schedule, price and quantity demanded are inversely related; and in the graph, the demand curve is negatively sloped. This inverse relation between price and quantity demanded is not simply a characteristic of the specific demand function discussed here. This inverse relation is so pervasive that economists refer to it as the **law of demand.** The law of demand states that quantity demanded increases when

---

[4]Recall from high school algebra that the "inverse" of a direct function $Y = f(X)$ is the function $X = f(Y)$, which gives X as a function of Y, and the same pairs of Y and X values that satisfy the direct function $Y = f(Y)$ also satisfy the inverse function $X = f(Y)$. For example, if the direct equation is $Y = 10 - 2X$, then the inverse function, $X = 5 - (1/2)Y$, is found by solving algebraically for X in terms of Y.

price falls and quantity demanded decreases when price rises, other things held constant.

Economists refer to the inverse relation between price and quantity demanded as a law, not because this relation has been proved mathematically but because examples to the contrary have never been observed. If you have doubts about the validity of the law of demand, try to think of any goods or services that you would buy more of if the price were higher, other things being equal. Or can you imagine someone going to the grocery store expecting to buy one six-pack of Pepsi for $2.50, then noticing that the price is $5, and deciding to buy two or three six-packs? You don't see stores advertising higher prices when they want to increase sales or get rid of unwanted inventory.

change in quantity demanded

A movement along a given demand curve that occurs when the price of the good changes, all else constant.

Once a direct demand function, $Q_d = f(P)$, is derived from a general demand function, a **change in quantity demanded** can be caused only by a change in price. The other five variables that influence demand in the general demand function (M, P_R, $\mathcal{T}$, P_E, and N) are fixed in value for any particular demand equation. A change in price is represented on a graph by a movement along a fixed demand curve. In Figure 2.1, if price falls from $100 to $80 (and the other variables remain constant), a change in quantity demanded from 400 to 600 units occurs and is illustrated by a movement along D_0 from point A to point B.

▢ **Relation** For a demand function $Q_d = f(P)$, a change in price causes a change in quantity demanded. The other five variables that influence demand in the general demand function (M, P_R, $\mathcal{T}$, P_E, and N) are fixed at specific values for any particular demand equation. On a graph, a change in price causes a movement along a demand curve from one price to another price.

Shifts in Demand

When any one of the five variables held constant when deriving a direct demand function from the general demand relation changes value, a new demand function results, causing the entire demand curve to *shift* to a new location. To illustrate this extremely important concept, we will show how a change in one of these five variables, such as income, affects a demand schedule.

We begin with the demand schedule from Table 2.2, which is reproduced in columns 1 and 2 of Table 2.3. Recall that the quantities demanded for various product prices were obtained by holding all variables except price constant in the

TABLE 2.3
Three Demand Schedules

(1) Price	(2) D_0: $Q_d = 1,400 - 10P$ Quantity demanded ($M = \$60,000$)	(3) D_1: $Q_d = 1,600 - 10P$ Quantity demanded ($M = \$64,000$)	(4) D_2: $Q_d = 1,000 - 10P$ Quantity demanded ($M = \$52,000$)
$140	0	200	0
120	200	400	0
100	400	600	0
80	600	800	200
60	800	1,000	400
40	1,000	1,200	600
20	1,200	1,400	800

ILLUSTRATION 2.1

Effects of Changes in Determinants of Demand

Much of the discussion of demand in this chapter focuses on understanding the effects of changes in the demand-shifting variables, and the consequent effects of these demand shifts on prices and sales. Some actual examples of these effects should illustrate and reinforce this theoretical analysis.

Changes in Income (M)

As China's economy booms, personal incomes are rising sharply. U.S. and European corporations selling normal goods (e.g., earthmovers, cellular phones, soft drinks, and cognac) are taking advantage of increased demand by Chinese consumers. Even demand for luxury goods (e.g., French-style manors, in-home movie theaters, Bentley automobiles, Louis Vuitton handbags, and jewelry by Cartier) is booming in China. With 12 percent of total world demand for all luxury goods, China could soon pass the United States and Japan to become the world's largest market for luxury goods.

Changes in the Price of Related Goods (P_R)

Falling prices of *new* cars is knocking down demand for *used* cars. Prices for new cars of all makes and models have been falling for the past several years, as dealers have been offering various kinds of incentives to new-car buyers that effectively lower new-car prices. Since used cars are a substitute good for new cars, it is no surprise that falling new-car prices have cut the demand for used cars, as car buyers are attracted away from used cars into lower priced new cars.

Changes in Taste ($\mathcal{T}$)

Breakthroughs in technology, especially in the consumer electronics sector, cause consumers' tastes to change rather quickly, causing demand for the "old" technology goods to dry up and demand for the "new" technology to flourish. In a rare case of consumer tastes reversing to the "old" technology, the demand for vinyl LP record albums sharply increased in 2014.[b] Younger music consumers in the United States are now hip to the idea of "dropping a needle into the groove" to get a superior audio quality that digital music cannot duplicate. This phenomenon has now spread well beyond audiophiles playing their old Beatle albums. Now younger music fans, especially indie-rock fans, are demanding more vinyl albums by new and old artists alike. Sales of vinyl albums were up nearly 50 percent in 2014. This increase in demand for the "old" technology caused by a change in the tastes of a growing number of consumers is still a small share of total demand for music. The convenience of digital music ensures its dominance, at least until digital music becomes an "old" technology and consumer tastes change once again.

Changes in Price Expectations of Consumers (P_E)

For those goods and services that consumers can postpone purchasing, the current demand will be sensitive to buyers' perceptions about future price levels. The housing market is a particularly good example of the importance of price expectations in determining the level of current demand. In the early phase of the collapse of housing prices in Florida, sellers of new homes found it very difficult to sell new homes, even though prices were falling. Potential buyers of new homes, seeing rapidly falling prices, expected even lower prices if they postponed purchasing. Jack Fess, sales manager of a large residential home builder in Florida, summarized the problem in this way: "Closing a deal on a new house is really tough these days when you have to tell the buyer, 'You better buy this house today because if you wait the price is only going to go *down*.'"[a] As home prices continue falling, a point will eventually be reached where buyers no longer believe prices will fall further, and falling price expectations will quit pushing housing demand leftward.

Changes in the Number of Buyers (N)

As the proportion of older Americans rises, the number of people needing health care services is rising sharply, causing demand for every kind of health care service to shift rightward. Demographers predicted this current increase in elderly patients as the unavoidable consequence of the post-World War II baby boom.

These illustrations should give you some idea of the way that changes in the determinants of demand actually shift the demand for goods and services and how such shifts affect the price and sales of the products. They should also give you an insight into how managers can forecast and react to such changes in a manner that furthers the goals of the organization.

[a]Personal conversation with Jack Fess, July 1, 2007.
[b]Neil Shah, "The Biggest Music Comeback of 2014: Vinyl Records," *The Wall Street Journal*, December 11, 2014, p. B1.

FIGURE 2.2
Shifts in Demand

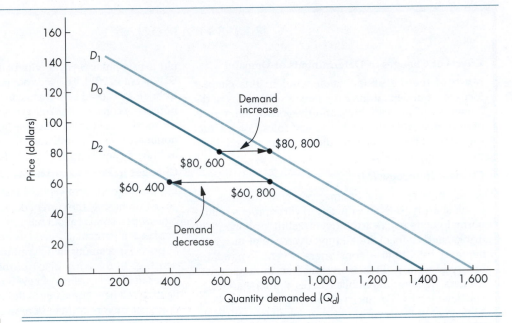

---

increase in demand
A change in the demand function that causes an increase in quantity demanded at every price and is reflected by a rightward shift in the demand curve.

decrease in demand
A change in the demand function that causes a decrease in quantity demanded at every price and is reflected by a leftward shift in the demand curve.

determinants of demand
Variables that change the quantity demanded at each price and that determine where the demand curve is located: M, P_R, $\mathcal{T}$, P_E, and N.

change in demand
A shift in demand, either leftward or rightward, that occurs only when one of the five determinants of demand changes.

general demand function. If income increases from $60,000 to $64,000, quantity demanded increases *at each and every price,* as shown in column 3. When the price is $60, for example, consumers will buy 800 units if their income is $60,000 but will buy 1,000 units if their income is $64,000. In Figure 2.2, D_0 is the demand curve associated with an income level of $60,000, and D_1 is the demand curve after income rises to $64,000. Since the increase in income caused quantity demanded to increase *at every price,* the demand curve shifts to the right from D_0 to D_1 in Figure 2.2. Everywhere along D_1 quantity demanded is greater than along D_0 for equal prices. This change in the demand function is called an **increase in demand.**

A **decrease in demand** occurs when a change in one or more of the variables M, P_R, $\mathcal{T}$, P_E, or N causes the quantity demanded to decrease at every price and the demand curve shifts to the left. Column 4 in Table 2.3 illustrates a decrease in demand caused by income falling to $52,000. At every price, quantity demanded in column 4 is less than quantity demanded when income is either $60,000 or $64,000 (columns 2 and 3, respectively, in Table 2.3). The demand curve in Figure 2.2 when income is $52,000 is D_2, which lies to the left of D_0 and D_1.

While we have illustrated shifts in demand caused by changes in income, a change in any one of the five variables that are held constant when deriving a demand function will cause a shift in demand. These five variables—M, P_R, $\mathcal{T}$, P_E, and N—are called the **determinants of demand** because they determine where the demand curve is located. A **change in demand** occurs when one or more of the determinants of demand change. Think of M, P_R, $\mathcal{T}$, P_E, and N as the five "demand-shifting" variables. The demand curve shifts to a new location only when one or more of these demand-shifting variables changes.

Relation An increase in demand means that, at each price, more is demanded; a decrease in demand means that, at each price, less is demanded. Demand changes, or shifts, when one of the determinants of demand changes. These determinants of demand are income, prices of related goods, consumer tastes, expected future price, and the number of consumers.

The shifts in demand illustrated in Figure 2.2 were derived mathematically from the general demand function. Recall that the demand function D_0 ($Q_d = 1,400 - 10P$) was derived from the general demand function

$$Q_d = 3,200 - 10P + 0.05M - 24P_R$$

where income and the price of a related good were held constant at values of $M = \$60,000$ and $P_R = \$200$. When income increases from \$60,000 to \$64,000, the new demand equation at this higher income is found by substituting $M = \$64,000$ into the general demand function and solving for the new demand function

$$D_1: Q_d = 3,200 - 10P + (0.05 \times 64,000) - 4,800$$
$$= 1,600 - 10P$$

In Figure 2.2, this demand function is shown by the demand curve D_1. At every price, quantity demanded increases by 200 units ($1,600 = 1,400 + 200$). Each of the quantities in column 3 of Table 2.2 was calculated from the new demand equation $Q_d = 1,600 - 10P$. As you can see, every quantity in column 3 is 200 units larger than the corresponding quantity in column 2. Thus the increase in income has caused an increase in demand.

When income falls from \$60,000 to \$52,000, demand shifts from D_0 to D_2. We leave the derivation of the demand function for D_2 as an exercise. The procedure, however, is identical to the process set forth above.

From the preceding discussion, you may have noticed that the direction in which demand shifts when one of the five demand determinants changes depends on the sign of the slope parameter on that variable in the general demand function. The increase in income caused quantity demanded to rise for all prices because $\Delta Q_d/\Delta M$ ($= +0.05$) is positive, which indicates that a \$1 increase in income causes a 0.05-unit increase in quantity demanded at every price level. Since income increased by \$4,000 in this example, quantity demanded increases by 200 units ($= 4,000 \times 0.05$). Thus when the slope parameter on M is positive in the general demand function, an increase in income causes an increase in demand. As explained earlier, when income and quantity demanded are positively related *in the general demand function,* the good is a normal good. If the parameter on M is negative, an increase in income causes a decrease in demand, and the good is an inferior good.[5] Table 2.4 summarizes for all five determinants of demand the relations between the signs of the slope

Now try Technical Problems 4–6.

[5]It is only correct to speak of a change in income affecting *quantity demanded* when referring to the general demand function. Once income has been held constant to derive a direct demand function, a change in income causes a change in demand (a shift in the demand curve), not a change in quantity demanded. The same distinction holds for the other determinants of demand P_R, $\mathcal{T}$, P_E, and N.

TABLE 2.4
Summary of Demand Shifts

Determinants of demand	Demand increases[a]	Demand decreases[b]	Sign of slope parameter[c]
1. Income (M)			
Normal good	M rises	M falls	$c > 0$
Inferior good	M falls	M rises	$c < 0$
2. Price of related good (P_R)			
Substitute good	P_R rises	P_R falls	$d > 0$
Complement good	P_R falls	P_R rises	$d < 0$
3. Consumer tastes ($\mathcal{T}$)	$\mathcal{T}$ rises	$\mathcal{T}$ falls	$e > 0$
4. Expected price (P_E)	P_E rises	P_E falls	$f > 0$
5. Number of consumers (N)	N rises	N falls	$g > 0$

[a]Demand increases when the demand curve shifts rightward.
[b]Demand decreases when the demand curve shifts leftward.
[c]This column gives the sign of the corresponding slope parameter in the general demand function.

parameters and the directions in which demand curves shift when each one of the determinants changes.

As you may also have noticed from the previous discussion, as shown in Figure 2.2, our demand curves shift parallel to one another. These parallel shifts in demand are strictly the result of our decision to illustrate demand curves using *linear* general demand functions. In the next section, you will also see *linear* supply curves, which result in parallel shifts in supply. In the real-world, demand and supply curves are seldom perfectly linear and shifts are seldom parallel. Nonetheless, linear curves and parallel shifts provide the easiest way to learn the basics of demand and supply analysis. And, in many cases, real-world curves can be closely approximated by linear functions. We must warn you, however, that if you draw demand shifts (or supply shifts) that are not parallel, the new demand curve (or supply curve) must *not* cross the original demand curve (or supply curve). To see why, suppose in Figure 2.2 we had mistakenly constructed D_1 to cross D_0 from above at $100—this is *not* shown in the figure—then at prices above $100 demand would have increased and at prices below $100 demand would have decreased. Obviously, this would not represent either an increase in demand or a decrease in demand because quantity demanded must either be larger at every price or smaller at every price, respectively.

2.2 SUPPLY

quantity supplied
The amount of a good or service offered for sale during a given period of time (week, month, etc.).

The amount of a good or service offered for sale in a market during a given period of time (e.g., a week, a month) is called **quantity supplied,** which we will denote as Q_s. The amount of a good or service offered for sale depends on an extremely large number of variables. As in the case of demand, economists ignore all the relatively unimportant variables in order to concentrate on those variables that have the greatest effect on quantity supplied. In general, economists assume that the quantity of a good offered for sale depends on six major variables:

1. The price of the good itself.
2. The prices of the inputs used to produce the good.
3. The prices of goods related in production.
4. The level of available technology.
5. The expectations of the producers concerning the future price of the good.
6. The number of firms or the amount of productive capacity in the industry.

The General Supply Function: $Q_s = f(P, P_I, P_r, T, P_e, F)$

general supply function
The relation between quantity supplied and the six factors that jointly affect quantity supplied: $Q_s = f(P, P_I, P_r, T, P_e, F)$.

The **general supply function** shows how all six of these variables *jointly* determine the quantity supplied. The general supply function is expressed mathematically as

$$Q_s = f(P, P_I, P_r, T, P_e, F)$$

The quantity of a good or service offered for sale (Q_s) is determined not only by the price of the good or service (P) but also by the prices of the inputs used in production (P_I), the prices of goods that are related in production (P_r), the level of available technology (T), the expectations of producers concerning the future price of the good (P_e), and the number of firms or amount of productive capacity in the industry (F).

Now we consider how each of the six variables is related to the quantity of a good or service firms produce. We begin by discussing the effect of a change in the price of a good while holding the other five variables constant. Typically, the higher the price of the product, the greater the quantity firms wish to produce and sell, all other things being equal. Conversely, the lower the price, the smaller the quantity firms will wish to produce and sell. Producers are motivated by higher prices to produce and sell more, while lower prices tend to discourage production. Thus price and quantity supplied are, in general, directly related.

An increase in the price of one or more of the inputs used to produce the product will obviously increase the cost of production. If the cost rises, the good becomes less profitable and producers will want to supply a smaller quantity at each price. Conversely, a decrease in the price of one or more of the inputs used to produce the product will decrease the cost of production. When cost falls, the good becomes more profitable and producers will want to supply a larger amount at each price. Therefore, an increase in the price of an input causes a decrease in production, while a decrease in the price of an input causes an increase in production.

substitutes in production
Goods for which an increase in the price of one good relative to the price of another good causes producers to increase production of the now higher priced good and decrease production of the other good.

Changes in the prices of goods that are related in production may affect producers in either one of two ways, depending on whether the goods are substitutes or complements in production. Two goods, X and Y, are **substitutes in production** if an increase in the price of good X relative to good Y causes producers to increase

complements in production
Goods for which an increase in the price of one good, relative to the price of another good, causes producers to increase production of both goods.

technology
The state of knowledge concerning the combination of resources to produce goods and services.

production of good X and decrease production of good Y. For example, if the price of corn increases while the price of wheat remains the same, some farmers may change from growing wheat to growing corn, and less wheat will be supplied. In the case of manufactured goods, firms can switch resources from the production of one good to the production of a substitute (in production) commodity when the price of the substitute rises. Alternatively, two goods, X and Y, are **complements in production** if an increase in the price of good X causes producers to supply more of good Y. For example, crude oil and natural gas often occur in the same oil field, making natural gas a by-product of producing crude oil, or vice versa. If the price of crude oil rises, petroleum firms produce more oil, so the output of natural gas also increases. Other examples of complements in production include nickel and copper (which occur in the same deposit), beef and leather hides, and bacon and pork chops.

Next, we consider changes in the level of available technology. **Technology** is the state of knowledge concerning how to combine resources to produce goods and services. An improvement in technology generally results in one or more of the inputs used in making the good to be more productive. As we will show you in Chapters 8 and 9, increased productivity allows firms to make more of a good or service with the same amount of inputs or the same output with fewer inputs. In either case, the cost of producing a given level of output falls when firms use better technology, which would lower the costs of production, increase profit, and increase the supply of the good to the market, all other things remaining the same.

A firm's decision about its level of production depends not only on the current price of the good but also upon the firm's *expectation* about the future price of the good. If firms expect the price of a good they produce to rise in the future, they may withhold some of the good, thereby reducing supply of the good in the current period.

Finally, if the number of firms in the industry increases or if the *productive capacity* of existing firms increases, more of the good or service will be supplied at each price. For example, the supply of air travel between New York and Hong Kong increases when either more airlines begin servicing this route or when the firms currently servicing the route increase their capacities to fly passengers by adding more jets to service their New York–Hong Kong route. Conversely, a decrease in the number of firms in the industry or a decrease in the productive capacity of existing firms decreases the supply of the good, all other things remaining constant. As another example, suppose a freeze in Florida decreases the number of firms by destroying entirely some citrus growers. Alternatively, it might leave the number of growers unchanged but decrease productive capacity by killing a portion of each grower's trees. In either situation, the supply of fruit decreases. Thus changes in the number of firms in the industry or changes in the amount of productive capacity in the industry are represented in the supply function by changes in F.

As in the case of demand, economists often find it useful to express the general supply function in linear functional form

$$Q_s = h + kP + lP_I + mP_r + nT + rP_e + sF$$

where Q_s, P, P_I, P_r, T, P_e, and F are as defined earlier, h is an intercept parameter, and k, l, m, n, r, and s are slope parameters. Table 2.5 summarizes this discussion of the general supply function. Each of the six factors that affect production is listed along with the relation to quantity supplied (direct or inverse). Let us again stress that, just as in the case of demand, these relations are in the context of all other things being equal.

Direct Supply Functions: $Q_s = f(P)$

direct supply function
A table, a graph, or an equation that shows how quantity supplied is related to product price, holding constant the five other variables that influence supply: $Q_s = f(P)$.

Just as demand functions are derived from the general demand function, *direct supply functions* are derived from the general supply function. A **direct supply function** (also called simply "supply") shows the relation between Q_s and P holding the **determinants of supply** (P_I, P_r, T, P_e, and F) constant:

$$Q_s = f(P, \overline{P}_I, \overline{P}_r, \overline{T}, \overline{P}_e, \overline{F}) = f(P)$$

where the bar means the determinants of supply are held constant at some specified value. Once a direct supply function $Q_s = f(P)$ is derived from a general supply function, a **change in quantity supplied** can be caused only by a change in price.

determinants of supply
Variables that cause a change in supply (i.e., a ▢ shift in the supply curve).

change in quantity supplied
A movement along a given supply curve that occurs when the price of a good changes, all else constant.

> **Relation**   A direct supply function expresses quantity supplied as a function of product price only: $Q_s = f(P)$. Supply functions give the quantity supplied for various prices, holding constant the effects of input prices, prices of goods related in production, the state of technology, expected price, and the number of firms in the industry. Supply functions are derived from general supply functions by holding all the variables in the general supply function constant except price.

To illustrate the derivation of a supply function from the general supply function, suppose the general supply function is

$$Q_s = 100 + 20P - 10P_I + 20F$$

Technology, the prices of goods related in production, and the expected price of the product in the future have been omitted to simplify this illustration. Suppose the price of an important input is $100, and there are currently 25 firms in the

TABLE 2.5

Summary of the General (Linear) Supply Function
$Q_s = h + kP + lP_I + mP_r + nT + rP_e + sF$

Variable	Relation to quantity supplied	Sign of slope parameter
P	Direct	$k = \Delta Q_s/\Delta P$ is positive
P_I	Inverse	$l = Q_s/\Delta P_I$ is negative
P_r	Inverse for substitutes in production (wheat and corn)	$m = \Delta Q_s/\Delta P_r$ is negative
	Direct for complements in production (oil and gas)	$m = \Delta Q_s/\Delta P_r$ is positive
T	Direct	$n = \Delta Q_s/\Delta T$ is positive
P_e	Inverse	$r = \Delta Q_s/\Delta P_e$ is negative
F	Direct	$s = \Delta Q_s/\Delta F$ is positive

industry producing the product. To find the supply function, the fixed values of P_I and F are substituted into the general supply function:

$$Q_s = 100 + 20P - 10(\$100) + 20(25)$$
$$= -400 + 20P$$

The linear supply function gives the quantity supplied for various product prices, holding constant the other variables that affect supply. For example, if the price of the product is $40,

$$Q_s = -400 + 20(\$40) = 400$$

or if the price is $100,

$$Q_s = -400 + 20(\$100) = 1{,}600$$

supply schedule
A table showing a list of possible product prices and the corresponding quantities supplied.

A **supply schedule** (or table) shows a list of several prices and the quantity supplied at each of the prices, again holding all variables other than price constant. Table 2.6 shows seven prices and their corresponding quantities supplied. Each of the seven price–quantity-supplied combinations is derived, as shown earlier, from the supply equation $Q_s = -400 + 20P$, which was derived from the general supply function by setting $P_I = \$100$ and $F = 25$. Figure 2.3 graphs the **supply curve** associated with this supply equation and supply schedule.

supply curve
A graph showing the relation between quantity supplied and price, when all other variables influencing quantity supplied are held constant.

Inverse Supply Functions: $P = f(Q_s)$

inverse supply function
The supply function when price is expressed as a function of quantity supplied: $P = f(Q_s)$.

Notice in Figure 2.3 that price is shown on the vertical axis and quantity on the horizontal axis as with demand curves. Thus the equation plotted in the figure is the inverse of the supply equation and is called the **inverse supply function:** $P = 20 + 1/20Q$. The slope of this inverse supply equation graphed in Figure 2.3 is $\Delta P/\Delta Q_s$, which equals $1/20$ and is the reciprocal of the slope parameter $k\ (= \Delta Q_s/\Delta P = 20)$.

As your intuition tells you, producers usually quit producing if price falls below some minimum level. You can think of $20 in Figure 2.3 as the lowest price for which production will occur. Mathematically speaking, we might say the supply equation describes supply only over the range of prices $20 or greater ($P \geq \$20$). We will show in later chapters how to find the price level below which production ceases.

TABLE 2.6

The Supply Schedule for the Supply Function S_0: $Q_s = -400 + 20P$

Price	Quantity supplied
$140	2,400
120	2,000
100	1,600
80	1,200
60	800
40	400
20	0

FIGURE 2.3
A Supply Curve:
$Q_s = -400 + 20P$

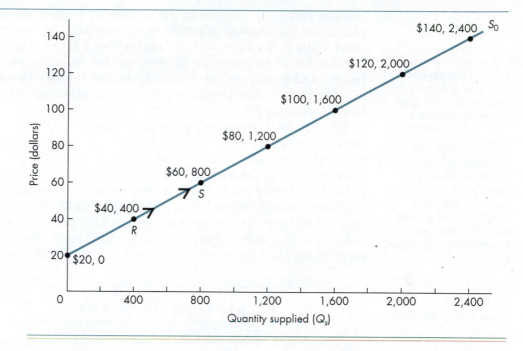

Any particular combination of price and quantity supplied on a supply curve can be interpreted in either of two equivalent ways. A point on the supply schedule indicates either (1) the maximum amount of a good or service that will be offered for sale at a specific price or (2) the minimum price necessary to induce producers to offer a given quantity for sale. This minimum price is sometimes referred to as the **supply price** for that level of output.

As in the case of a demand function, once a direct supply equation, $Q_s = f(P)$, is derived from a general supply function, a change in quantity supplied can be caused only by a change in price. A change in quantity supplied represents a movement along a given supply curve. Consider the supply curve S_0 in Figure 2.3. If product price rises from \$40 to \$60, the quantity supplied increases from 400 to 800 units, a movement from point R to point S along the supply curve S_0.

supply price
The minimum price necessary to induce producers to offer a given quantity for sale.

> **Relation** For a supply function $Q_s = f(P)$, a change in price causes a change in quantity supplied. The other five variables that affect supply in the general supply function (P_I, P_r, T, P_e, F) are fixed in value for any particular supply function. On a graph, a change in price causes a movement along a supply curve from one price to another price.

Now try Technical Problems 7–8.

Shifts in Supply

As we differentiate between a change in quantity demanded because of a change in price and a shift in demand because of a change in one of the determinants of demand, we must make the same distinction with supply. A shift in supply occurs only when one of the five determinants of supply (P_I, P_r, T, P_e, F)

increase in supply
A change in the supply function that causes an increase in quantity supplied at every price, and is reflected by a rightward shift in the supply curve.

decrease in supply
A change in the supply function that causes a decrease in quantity supplied at every price, and is reflected by a leftward shift in the supply curve.

changes value. An increase in the number of firms in the industry, for example, causes the quantity supplied to increase at every price so that the supply curve shifts to the right, and this circumstance is called an **increase in supply.** A decrease in the number of firms in the industry causes a **decrease in supply,** and the supply curve shifts to the left. We can illustrate shifts in supply by examining the effect on the supply function of changes in the values of the determinants of supply.

Table 2.6 is reproduced in columns 1 and 2 of Table 2.7. If the price of the input falls to $60, the new supply function is $Q_s = 20P$, and the quantity supplied increases *at each and every price*, as shown in column 3. This new supply curve when the price of the input falls to $60 is shown as S_1 in Figure 2.4 and lies to the right of S_0 at every price. Thus the decrease in P_I causes the supply curve to shift rightward, illustrating an increase in supply. To illustrate a decrease in supply, suppose the price of the input remains at $100 but the number of firms in the industry decreases to 10 firms. The supply function is now $Q_s = -700 + 20P$, and quantity supplied decreases *at every price*, as shown in column 4. The new supply

TABLE 2.7

Three Supply Schedules

(1) Price	(2) $S_0: Q_s = -400 + 20P$ Quantity supplied ($P_I = \$100$, $F = 25$)	(3) $S_1: Q_s = 20P$ Quantity supplied ($P_I = \$60$, $F = 25$)	(4) $S_2: Q_s = -700 + 20P$ Quantity supplied ($P_I = \$100$, $F = 10$)
$140	2,400	2,800	2,100
120	2,000	2,400	1,700
100	1,600	2,000	1,300
80	1,200	1,600	900
60	800	1,200	500
40	400	800	100
20	0	400	0

FIGURE 2.4

Shifts in Supply

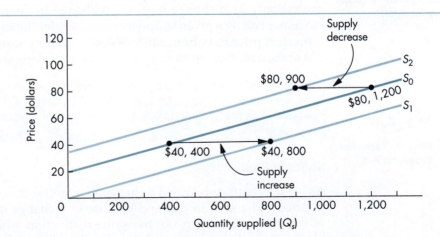

TABLE 2.8
Summary of Supply Shifts

Determinants of supply	Supply increases[a]	Supply decreases[b]	Sign of slope parameter[c]
1. Price of inputs (P_I)	P_I falls	P_I rises	$l < 0$
2. Price of goods related in production (P_r)			
Substitute good	P_r falls	P_r rises	$m < 0$
Complement good	P_r rises	P_r falls	$m > 0$
3. State of technology (T)	T rises	T falls	$n > 0$
4. Expected price (P_e)	P_e falls	P_e rises	$r < 0$
5. Number of firms or productive capacity in industry (F)	F rises	F falls	$s > 0$

[a]Supply increases when the supply curve shifts rightward.
[b]Supply decreases when the supply curve shifts leftward.
[c]This column gives the sign of the corresponding slope parameter in the general supply function.

curve in Figure 2.4, S_2, lies to the left of S_0 at every price. Thus the decrease in the number of firms causes a decrease in supply, which is represented by a leftward shift in the supply curve. You can think of P_I, P_r, T, P_e, and F as the five "supply-shifting" variables. Table 2.8 summarizes this discussion of shifts in supply.

Now try Technical Problems 9–11.

Relation An increase in supply means that, at each price, more of the good is supplied; a decrease in supply means that, at each price, less is supplied. Supply changes (or shifts) when one of the determinants of supply changes. These determinants of supply are the price of inputs, the price of goods related in production, the state of technology, the expected price in the future, and the number of firms or the amount of productive capacity in the industry.

ILLUSTRATION 2.2

Effects of Changes in Determinants of Supply

In this Illustration, we present more examples of changes in supply-shifting variables that are taken from a number of recent events in real-world markets. These examples further reinforce our theoretical discussion about how shifts in the supply curve are caused by changes in the five supply determinants: input prices, technology, prices of goods related in supply, producers' expectations about future prices, and the number of firms or productive capacity in the industry. Always remember to shift the supply curve *horizontally* (not vertically): either leftward for a decrease in supply or rightward for an increase in supply.

Changes in Input Prices (P_I)

U.S. candy makers are cutting production levels in their domestic plants, causing a decrease or leftward shift in the supply of candy manufactured in the United States. The cause of the decrease in the U.S. candy supply can be directly attributed to federal government price supports for sugar that are designed to keep sugar prices artificially high in the United States to protect American sugar growers' profits. Congressional protection of beet and cane sugar growers represents a particularly egregious example of an interest group receiving valuable benefits from government regulation at the expense of the general public. By propping up sugar prices in the United States—about 14 percent higher than the unregulated price of sugar

(Continued)

in the world markets—federal government policy significantly increases the price of a key input for candy makers. As predicted by economic theory, the higher sugar (input) price is reducing the amount of candy produced by manufacturing plants located in the United States And, not surprisingly, U.S. companies are globalizing their candy manufacturing by opening new production plants worldwide, specifically in countries where sugar can be purchased at the lower price in the unregulated global sugar market. As we noted in our Chapter 1 discussion of globalization, one of the primary advantages that globalization of markets offers to managers is the opportunity to reduce production costs by purchasing raw materials from other countries. In this case, managers of candy firms must move their entire production facility into a foreign country to get the lower sugar prices available outside the regulatory authority of Congress. According to Erick Atkinson, the president of Jelly Bean Candy Co., "it's a damn shame," because there are now 60 jobs in Thailand that had previously been located in Lufkin, Texas.[a]

Changes in the Price of Goods Related in Production (P_r)

When two goods are related in production—the two goods are produced using some of the same important resources—a decrease in the price of one good can cause the supply of the other good to shift either rightward or leftward, depending on whether the two goods are related in production as substitutes (rightward shift) or complements (leftward shift). A recent example of *substitutes* in production follows from the increase in soybean supply caused by the falling price of corn. When the demand for the gasoline additive called ethanol dropped sharply (ethanol is made from corn), the price of corn fell sharply as less corn was needed for ethanol production. Facing lower corn prices, Midwest farmers planted less corn and more of other crops, especially more soybeans. Thus, a fall in corn prices caused an increase in the supply of soybeans because either corn or soybeans can be grown on farmland in the Midwest using mostly the same kind of farming equipment and labor resources. We should stress here that corn and soybeans are not *demand*-side substitutes, but rather *supply*-side substitutes because consumers

don't eat more soybeans when the price of corn goes up, as they would if soybeans and corn were indeed substitutes in consumption.

Changes in Technology (T)

Improvements in available technology make at least one of the inputs more productive, and this boost in productivity increases supply by shifting supply rightward. One of the most promising new technologies for the 21st century is *additive manufacturing (AM)* if you're an engineer, or *3D printing* if you're not an engineer. Additive manufacturing starts with a computer-aided design (CAD) file that contains three-dimensional engineering design information for a desired component. Using the CAD file, an AM machine constructs a physical replica of the component by depositing and bonding successive layers of raw material—typically sand, plastic, metal, or glass—to create a fully functional and durable component. AM technology has many thousands of applications in manufacturing and offers tremendous productivity gains in producing parts for everything from aerospace, aircraft, automobiles, to industrial equipment, medical devices, and toy manufacturing. We expect that supply curves for many goods will shift rightward as this new AM technology becomes widely applied.

Changes in Price Expectations of Producers (P_e)

For any particular price, the amount of output producers are willing to supply *today* depends not only on the current price of the good, but current supply also depends on the price producers expect in the future. For example, when events occurring in the current time period cause an *increase* in what sellers believe will be the future price of their good, then sellers will have an incentive to move some of their supply from the current time period to the future time period. Turkey, which supplies more than 70 percent of the world's hazelnuts, experienced an unexpected frost in 2014. The frost killed nearly 30 percent of Turkey's crop of hazelnuts, causing hazelnut prices to double immediately as the current supply of hazelnuts fell dramatically. The decrease in the 2014 supply was reported to be especially severe because, unlike less severe frosts in other years, the 2014 frost harmed *future* hazelnut crops by disrupting the winter pollination of hazelnut flowers.[b] As a consequence, hazelnut farmers worldwide—including farmers who had no frost damage at all—changed their expectations about the price of hazelnuts in 2015. They now expected prices to be much higher in 2015. This upward revision in farmers' beliefs about 2015 prices caused many farmers to hold in inventory some hazelnuts that would otherwise have been sold in 2014. This upward revision in expected price pushed current hazelnut supply even further to the left in 2014. The *current* decrease in hazelnut supply brought by the frost would have been less severe if farmers had not revised upward their forecasts about *future* hazelnut prices.

Changes in Number of Firms or Amount of Productive Capacity (F)

Anything that changes either the number of firms in an industry or the capacity of those firms to produce the good or service will cause the supply curve to shift in response. Mother Nature is frequently the cause of changes in the supply of goods and services. Unseasonably warm winter weather recently created a surge in the number of large lobsters in the Atlantic Ocean. This lobster population boom caused a significant increase or rightward shift in the supply of lobsters as lobster catchers began finding more lobsters in their traps. In other words, with the same number of lobster catchers and lobster pots (i.e., lobster traps), the growing population of lobsters caused an increase in the productive capacity of the existing resources being employed in the lobster industry.

These illustrations should reinforce your understanding of the underlying determinants of supply as the examples in Illustration 2.1 did for demand. As you learn in this chapter, the essential skill for doing demand and supply analysis of real-world markets is the ability to identify correctly all of the underlying demand- and supply-shifters that are working to cause market prices and quantities to move higher or lower.

[a]Alexandra Wexler, "Cheaper Sugar Sends Candy Makers Abroad," *The Wall Street Journal,* October 21, 2013, p. A8.

[b]Huileng Tan and Alexandra Wexler, "Hazelnuts Stir Trouble in the Land of Sweets," *The Wall Street Journal,* December 5, 2014, p. B1.

2.3 MARKET EQUILIBRIUM

market equilibrium
A situation in which, at the prevailing price, consumers can buy all of a good they wish and producers can sell all of the good they wish. The price at which $Q_d = Q_s$.

equilibrium price
The price at which $Q_d = Q_s$.

equilibrium quantity
The amount of a good bought and sold in market equilibrium.

Demand and supply provide an analytical framework for the analysis of the behavior of buyers and sellers in markets. Demand shows how buyers respond to changes in price and other variables that determine quantities buyers are willing and able to purchase. Supply shows how sellers respond to changes in price and other variables that determine quantities offered for sale. The interaction of buyers and sellers in the marketplace leads to **market equilibrium.** Market equilibrium is a situation in which, *at the prevailing price,* consumers can buy all of a good they wish and producers can sell all of the good they wish. In other words, equilibrium occurs when price is at a level for which quantity demanded equals quantity supplied. In equilibrium, the price is called **equilibrium price** and the quantity sold is called **equilibrium quantity.**

To illustrate how market equilibrium is achieved, we can use the demand and supply schedules set forth in the preceding sections. Table 2.9 shows both the demand schedule for D_0 (given in Table 2.2) and the supply schedule for S_0 (given in Table 2.6). As the table shows, equilibrium in the market occurs when price is $60 and both quantity demanded and quantity supplied are equal to 800 units. At every price above $60, quantity supplied is greater than quantity demanded.

TABLE 2.9
Market Equilibrium

(1) Price	(2) S_0 Quantity supplied $Q_s = -400 + 20P$	(3) D_0 Quantity demanded $Q_d = 1,400 - 10P$	(4) Excess supply (+) or excess demand (−) $Q_s - Q_d$
$140	2,400	0	+2,400
120	2,000	200	+1,800
100	1,600	400	+1,200
80	1,200	600	+600
60	800	800	0
40	400	1,000	−600
20	0	1,200	−1,200

excess supply (surplus)
Exists when quantity supplied exceeds quantity demanded.

excess demand (shortage)
Exists when quantity demanded exceeds quantity supplied.

market clearing price
The price of a good at which buyers can purchase all they want and sellers can sell all they want at that price. This is another name for the equilibrium price.

Excess supply or a **surplus** exists when the quantity supplied exceeds the quantity demanded. The first four entries in column 4 of Table 2.9 show the excess supply or surplus at each price above $60. At every price below $60, quantity supplied is less than quantity demanded. A situation in which quantity demanded exceeds quantity supplied is called **excess demand** or a **shortage.** The last two entries in column 4 of the table show the excess demand or shortage at each price below the $60 equilibrium price. Excess demand and excess supply equal zero only in equilibrium. In equilibrium the market "clears" in the sense that buyers can purchase all they want and sellers can sell all they want at the equilibrium price. Because of this clearing of the market, equilibrium price is sometimes called the **market clearing price.**

Before moving on to a graphical analysis of equilibrium, we want to reinforce the concepts illustrated in Table 2.9 by using the demand and supply functions from which the table was derived. To this end, recall that the demand equation is $Q_d = 1,400 - 10P$ and the supply equation is $Q_s = -400 + 20P$. Since equilibrium requires that $Q_d = Q_s$, in equilibrium,

$$1,400 - 10P = -400 + 20P$$

Solving this equation for equilibrium price,

$$1,800 = 30P$$
$$P = \$60$$

At the market clearing price of $60,

$$Q_d = 1,400 - 10(60) = 800$$
$$Q_s = -400 + 20(60) = 800$$

As expected, these mathematically derived results are identical to those presented in Table 2.9.

According to Table 2.9, when price is $80, there is a surplus of 600 units. Using the demand and supply equations, when $P = 80$,

$$Q_d = 1,400 - 10(80) = 600$$
$$Q_s = -400 + 20(80) = 1,200$$

Therefore, when price is $80,

$$Q_s - Q_d = 1,200 - 600 = 600$$

which is the result shown in column 4.

To express the equilibrium solution graphically, Figure 2.5 shows the demand curve D_0 and the supply curve S_0 associated with the schedules in Table 2.9. These are also the demand and supply curves previously shown in Figures 2.1 and 2.3. Clearly, $60 and 800 units are the equilibrium price and quantity at point A in Figure 2.5. Only at a price of $60 does quantity demanded equal quantity supplied.

Market forces will drive price toward $60. If price is $80, producers want to supply 1,200 units while consumers only demand 600 units. An excess supply of 600 units develops. Producers must lower price in order to keep from accumulating unwanted inventories. At any price above $60, excess supply results, and producers will lower price.

If price is $40, consumers are willing and able to purchase 1,000 units, while producers offer only 400 units for sale. An excess demand of 600 units results. Since their demands are not satisfied, consumers bid the price up. Any price below $60 leads to an excess demand, and the shortage induces consumers to bid up the price.

Given no outside influences that prevent price from being bid up or down, an equilibrium price and quantity are attained. This equilibrium price is

FIGURE 2.5

Market Equilibrium

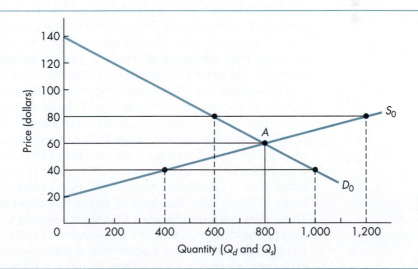

the price that clears the market; both excess demand and excess supply are zero in equilibrium. Equilibrium is attained in the market because of the following:

□   **Principle**   The equilibrium price is that price at which quantity demanded is equal to quantity supplied. When the current price is above the equilibrium price, quantity supplied exceeds quantity demanded. The resulting excess supply induces sellers to reduce price in order to sell the surplus. If the current price is below equilibrium, quantity demanded exceeds quantity supplied. The resulting excess demand causes the unsatisfied consumers to bid up price. Since prices below equilibrium are bid up by consumers and prices above equilibrium are lowered by producers, the market will converge to the equilibrium price–quantity combination.

It is crucial for you to understand that in the analysis of demand and supply there will never be either a permanent shortage or a permanent surplus as long as price is allowed to adjust freely to the equilibrium level. In other words, assuming that market price adjusts *quickly* to the equilibrium level, surpluses or shortages do not occur in free markets. In the absence of impediments to the adjustment of prices (such as government-imposed price ceilings or floors), the market is always assumed to clear. This assumption greatly simplifies demand and supply analysis. Indeed, how many instances of surpluses or shortages have you seen in markets where prices can adjust freely? The duration of any surplus or shortage is generally short enough that we can reasonably ignore the adjustment period for purposes of demand and supply analysis.

Now try Technical Problems 12–13.

2.4 MEASURING THE VALUE OF MARKET EXCHANGE

Now that we have explained why market equilibrium occurs at the intersection of demand and supply curves, we can use demand and supply curves to measure the net gain created by voluntary exchange between the buyers and sellers in markets. Markets arise because buyers and sellers find it mutually beneficial to meet for the purpose of voluntary exchange: buyers bring money to market to exchange for the commodities that sellers bring to market to trade for money. In free-market exchange between buyers and sellers, no government agency or labor union forces consumers to pay for the goods they want or coerces producers to sell their goods.

Throughout time, in societies everywhere, markets have formed for the mutual benefit of consumers and producers. Indeed, history has recorded that even "primitive" warring tribes regularly scheduled days of peace for the sole purpose of allowing voluntary exchange between combatants. In a more contemporary example of the value of markets, you may have read in the newspaper that your local NFL football team has raised the price of season tickets to $1,200, causing many fans to complain about "high" ticket prices. Then, with their next breath, many of these same fans rushed to the box office and purchased season tickets. These fans voluntarily traded $1,200 for a season ticket, and the team owner voluntarily sold them a seat for the season. In spite of the complaining, both the ticket-buying fans and the ticket-selling team owner mutually benefited from the exchange, otherwise these tickets would not have been bought or sold! Clearly, the market for NFL football tickets creates value for those individuals in society—both fans and owners—who voluntarily choose to participate in this market.[6] Indeed, every market where there is voluntary exchange creates value for all the buyers and sellers trading in that market.

Consumer Surplus

economic value
The maximum amount any buyer in the market is willing to pay for the unit, which is measured by the demand price for the unit of the good.

Typically, consumers value the goods they purchase by an amount that exceeds the purchase price of the goods. For any unit of a good or service, the **economic value** of that unit is simply the maximum amount some buyer is willing to pay for the unit. For example, professional real estate agents frequently must remind people who are selling their homes that the value of their property is only as high as some buyer in the market is willing and able to pay, regardless of how much the current owner paid for the home or how much was spent sprucing up the home. Recall that earlier in this chapter we explained that *demand prices*—the prices associated with various quantities along the demand curve—give the maximum price for which each unit can be sold. Thus the economic value of a specific unit of a good or service equals the demand price for the unit, because this price is the maximum amount any buyer is willing and able to pay for the unit:

Economic value of a particular unit = Demand price for the unit
= Maximum amount buyers are willing to pay

Fortunately for consumers, they almost never have to pay the maximum amount they are willing to pay. They instead must pay the *market price*, which is lower than the maximum amount consumers are willing to pay (except for the last unit sold in market equilibrium). The difference between the economic value of a good and the price of the good is the net gain to the consumer, and this difference is called **consumer surplus.** To illustrate this concept numerically, suppose you would be willing to pay as much as $2,000 for a 40-yard-line NFL season ticket rather than stay at home and watch the game on your high-definition television. By purchasing a season ticket at the price of $1,200, you enjoy a net gain or consumer surplus equal to $800. In this way, consumer surplus for each season ticket sold is measured by the difference between the value of the ticket—measured by the ticket's demand price—and the market price paid for season tickets.

consumer surplus
The difference between the economic value of a good (its demand price) and the market price the consumer must pay.

Figure 2.6 illustrates how to measure consumer surplus for the 400th unit of a good using the demand and supply curves developed previously. Recall from our discussion about inverse demand functions that the demand price for 400 units, which is $100 in Figure 2.6, gives the maximum price for which a *total* of 400 units

---

[6]As you probably know, prices of NFL season tickets are not determined by the market forces of demand and supply. NFL ticket prices are instead set by individual price-setting team owners (i.e., they possess some degree of market power). Even though this chapter focuses on price-taking firms, the concepts of consumer, producer, and social surplus developed in this section can be applied to markets in which firms are either price-takers or price-setters.

FIGURE 2.6

Measuring the Value of Market Exchange

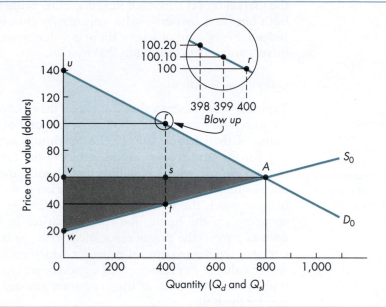

can be sold (see point r). But, as we just mentioned, the demand price of $100 also represents the maximum amount for which the 400*th* unit of the good can be sold. Notice in the blow up at point r that the consumer who is just willing to buy the 400th unit at $100 would not buy the 400th unit for even a penny more than $100. It follows from this reasoning that the demand price of $100 measures the economic value of the 400th unit, *not* the value of 400 units. You can now see that the consumer surplus for the 400th unit equals $40 (= $100 − $60), which is the difference between the demand price (or economic value) of the 400th unit and the market price (at point A). In Figure 2.6, consumer surplus of the 400th unit is the distance between points r and s.

To measure the *total* consumer surplus for all 400 units—instead of the consumer surplus for the single 400th unit—the vertical distance between demand and market price must be summed for all 400 units. Total consumer surplus for 400 units is equal to the area below demand and above market price over the output range 0 to 400 units. In Figure 2.6, total consumer surplus for 400 units is measured by the area bounded by the trapezoid *uvsr*. One way to compute the area of trapezoid *uvsr* is to multiply the length of its base (the distance between v and s) by the average height of its two sides (*uv* and *rs*): 400 × (($80 + $40)/2) = $24,000. Of course you can also divide the trapezoid into a triangle and a rectangle, and then you can add the two areas to get total consumer surplus. Either way, the total consumer surplus when 400 units are purchased is $24,000.

Now let's measure total consumer surplus in market equilibrium. At point A in Figure 2.6, 800 units are bought and sold at the market-clearing price of $60. The area of the red-shaded triangle *uvA* in Figure 2.6 gives the total consumer surplus in market equilibrium. The area of this triangle is $32,000 (= 0.5 × 800 × $80). Thus, $32,000 measures the net gain to all the consumers who voluntarily buy 800 units from producers at $60 per unit. If the government decided for some reason to outlaw completely the consumption of this good, and if all consumers complied with the consumption ban, then the market would disappear, and consumers would be $32,000 worse off by losing the opportunity to buy this good.

Producer Surplus

producer surplus
For each unit supplied, the difference between market price and the minimum price producers would accept to supply the unit (its supply price).

Next we consider the net gain to producers who supply consumers with the goods and services they demand. Producers typically receive more than the minimum payment necessary to induce them to supply their product. For each unit supplied, the difference between the market price received and the minimum price producers would accept to supply the unit is called **producer surplus.** In Figure 2.6, let's consider the producer surplus for the 400th unit supplied when market price is $60. Recall from our previous discussion about inverse supply functions that the *supply price*, which is $40 for the 400th unit, gives the minimum payment required by the suppliers to produce and sell the 400th unit. The producer surplus generated by the production and sale of the 400th unit is the vertical distance between points s and t, which is $20 (= $60 − $40). The total producer surplus for 400 units is the sum of the producer surplus of each of the 400 units. Thus, total producer surplus for 400 units is the area below market price and above supply over the output range 0 to 400. In Figure 2.6, total producer surplus for 400 units is measured by the area of the trapezoid *vwts*. By multiplying the base *vs* (= 400) times the average height of the two parallel sides *vw* ($40) and *st* ($20), you can verify that the area of trapezoid *vwts* is $12,000 [= 400 × ($40 + $20)/2].

Now let's measure the total producer surplus in market equilibrium. At point A, total producer surplus is equal to the area of the gray-shaded triangle *vwA*. Thus, total producer surplus in equilibrium is $16,000 (= 0.5 × 800 × $40). By doing business in this market, producers experience a net gain of $16,000.

Social Surplus

social surplus
The sum of consumer surplus and producer surplus, which is the area below demand and above supply over the range of output produced and consumed.

The net gain to society as a whole from any specific level of output can be found by adding total consumer surplus and total producer surplus generated at that specific level of output. This sum is known as **social surplus.**

At market equilibrium point A in Figure 2.6, social surplus equals $48,000 (= $32,000 + $16,000). As you can now see, the value of social surplus in equilibrium provides a dollar measure of the gain to society from having voluntary exchange between buyers and sellers in this market. In Chapters 12 and 14, we will examine pricing strategies used by firms with market power to transform, as much as possible, consumer surplus into producer surplus. In Chapter 16, we will explain the circumstances under which social surplus is maximized by letting market forces determine the prices at which market exchange takes place.

Now try Technical Problem 14.

2.5 CHANGES IN MARKET EQUILIBRIUM

qualitative forecast
A forecast that predicts only the direction in which an economic variable will move.

quantitative forecast
A forecast that predicts both the direction and the magnitude of the change in an economic variable.

If demand and supply never changed, equilibrium price and quantity would remain the same forever, or at least for a very long time, and market analysis would be extremely uninteresting and totally useless for managers. In reality, the variables held constant when deriving demand and supply curves do change. Consequently, demand and supply curves shift, and equilibrium price and quantity change. Using demand and supply, managers may make either qualitative forecasts or quantitative forecasts. A **qualitative forecast** predicts only the *direction* in which an economic variable, such as price or quantity, will move. A **quantitative forecast** predicts both the *direction* and the *magnitude* of the change in an economic variable.

For instance, if you read in *The Wall Street Journal* that Congress is considering a tax cut, demand and supply analysis enables you to forecast whether the price and sales of a particular product will increase or decrease. If you forecast that price will rise and sales will fall, you have made a qualitative forecast about price and quantity. Alternatively, you may have sufficient data on the exact nature of demand and supply to be able to predict that price will rise by $1.10 and sales will fall by 7,000 units. This is a quantitative forecast. Obviously, a manager would get more information from a quantitative forecast than from a qualitative forecast. But managers may not always have sufficient data to make quantitative forecasts. In many instances, just being able to predict correctly whether price will rise or fall can be extremely valuable to a manager.

Thus an important function and challenging task for managers is predicting the effect, especially the effect on market price, of specific changes in the variables that determine the position of demand and supply curves. We will first discuss the process of adjustment when something causes demand to change while supply remains constant, then the process when supply changes while demand remains constant.

Changes in Demand (Supply Constant)

To illustrate the effects of changes in demand when supply remains constant, we have reproduced D_0 and S_0 in Figure 2.7. Equilibrium occurs at $60 and 800 units, shown as point A in the figure. The demand curve D_1, showing an increase in demand, and the demand curve D_2, showing a decrease in demand, are reproduced from Figure 2.2. Recall that the shift from D_0 to D_1 was caused by an increase in income. The shift from D_0 to D_2 resulted from the decrease in income.

Begin in equilibrium at point A. Now let demand increase to D_1 as shown. At the original $60 price, consumers now demand a' units with the new demand. Since firms are still willing to supply only 800 units at $60, a shortage of $a' - 800$ units results. As described in section 2.3, the shortage causes the price to rise to a new equilibrium, point B, where quantity demanded equals quantity supplied. As you can see by comparing old equilibrium point A to new equilibrium point B, the increase in demand increases both equilibrium price and quantity.

To illustrate the effect of a decrease in demand, supply held constant, we return to the original equilibrium at point A in the figure. Now we decrease the

FIGURE

FIGURE 2.7

Demand Shifts (Supply Constant)

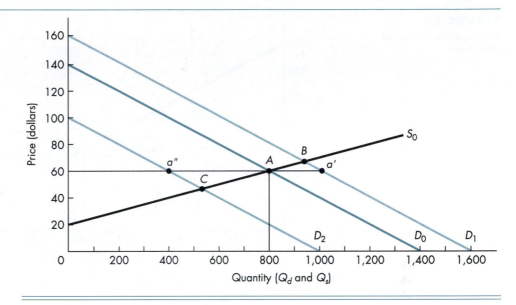

demand to D_2. At the original equilibrium price of $60, firms still want to supply 800 units, but now consumers want to purchase only a'' units. Thus, there is a surplus of $A - a''$ units. As already explained, a surplus causes price to fall. The market returns to equilibrium only when the price decreases to point C. Therefore the decrease in demand decreases both equilibrium price and quantity (compare points A and C). We have now established the following principle:

Principle When demand increases and supply is constant, equilibrium price and quantity both rise. When demand decreases and supply is constant, equilibrium price and quantity both fall.

Changes in Supply (Demand Constant)

To illustrate the effects of changes in supply when demand remains constant, we reproduce D_0 and S_0 in Figure 2.8. The supply curve S_1, showing an increase in supply, and the supply curve S_2, showing a decrease in supply, are reproduced from Figure 2.4. Recall that the shift from S_0 to S_1 was caused by a decrease in the price of an input. The shift from S_0 to S_2 resulted from a decrease in the number of firms in the industry.

Begin in equilibrium at point A. Let supply first increase to S_1 as shown. At the original $60 price consumers still want to purchase 800 units, but sellers now wish to sell a' units, causing a surplus or excess supply of $a' - 800$ units. The surplus causes price to fall, which induces sellers to supply less and buyers to demand more. Price continues to fall until the new equilibrium is attained at point B. As you can see by comparing the initial equilibrium point A in Figure 2.8 to the new equilibrium point B, when supply increases and demand remains constant, equilibrium price will fall and equilibrium quantity will increase.

FIGURE 2.8

Supply Shifts (Demand Constant)

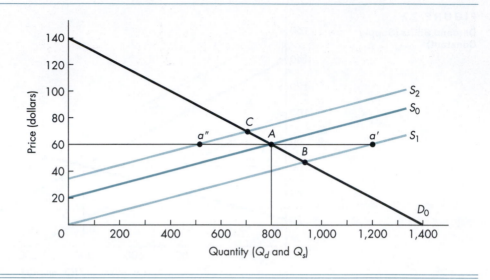

To demonstrate the effect of a supply decrease, we return to the original input price to obtain the original supply curve S_0 and the original equilibrium at point A. Let the number of firms in the industry decrease, causing supply to shift from S_0 to S_2 in Figure 2.8. At the original $60 price, consumers still want to buy 800 units, but now sellers wish to sell only a'' units, as shown in the figure. This leads to a shortage or excess demand of $a'' - A$ units. Shortages cause price to rise. The increase in price induces sellers to supply more and buyers to demand less, thereby reducing the shortage. Price will continue to increase until it attains the new equilibrium at point C. Therefore, when supply decreases while demand remains constant, price will rise and quantity sold will decrease. We have now established the following principle:

Principle When supply increases and demand is constant, equilibrium price falls and equilibrium quantity rises. When supply decreases and demand is constant, equilibrium price rises and equilibrium quantity falls.

Now try Technical Problem 15.

indeterminate
Term referring to the unpredictable change in either equilibrium price or quantity when the direction of change depends upon the relative magnitudes of the shifts in the demand and supply curves.

Simultaneous Shifts in Both Demand and Supply

To this point, we have examined changes in demand or supply holding the other curve constant. In both cases, the effect on equilibrium price and quantity can be predicted. In situations involving *both* a shift in demand *and* a shift in supply, it is possible to predict either the direction in which price changes or the direction in which quantity changes, *but not both*. When it is not possible to predict the direction of change in a variable, the change in that variable is said to be **indeterminate.** The change in either equilibrium price or quantity will be indeterminate when the direction of change depends upon the relative magnitudes of the shifts in the demand and supply curves.

ILLUSTRATION 2.3

Are U.S. Natural Gas Markets "Out of Whack"?

In this Illustration we will show you how to use demand and supply analysis to explain a situation in the U.S. market for natural gas that is confusing to several news analysts at *The Wall Street Journal*. In a recent article, *The Wall Street Journal* reported that the market for natural gas in the United States is "out of whack" because natural gas prices are falling sharply while, at the same time, production of natural gas is also rising.[a] And to further befuddle matters, gas supply appears to be headed for even larger expansion in the next couple of years. In well-functioning markets—that is, ones not "out of whack"—why would the supply of natural gas keep increasing when natural gas prices are falling? Are the "laws of supply and demand" broken in this industry?

We can apply the principles of demand and supply analysis presented in this chapter to explain rather convincingly that natural gas markets are in fact behaving quite predictably, and we can do this using just the facts reported in *The Wall Street Journal* article. Let's begin by examining the market forces causing the "supply glut" of natural gas. The reporters identify three factors causing the "whacked-out" behavior of suppliers. First, high prices for crude oil have stimulated production of crude oil, and this increases supply of natural gas because natural gas is frequently found in the same well as crude oil. Second, natural gas wells also contain large amounts of a valuable chemical used to make plastics called ethane, and ethane prices are rising. Third, U.S. energy suppliers recently began using a new, highly productive technology for exploring and drilling for crude oil and natural gas known as hydraulic fracturing, or "fracking."

As you know from our discussion of supply shifts, all three of these forces cause the U.S. supply of natural gas to shift rightward. The first two of these three factors are simply reductions in the prices of goods related in production (P_r): (1) a rise in the price of crude oil increases the supply of the complementary good natural gas, and (2) a rise in the price of ethane increases the supply of the complementary good natural gas. The third factor is a change in technology (T), which lowers the cost of supplying natural gas and causes the supply of natural gas to shift rightward.

In the figure below, all three factors work to shift the supply of natural gas rightward as indicated by the increase in supply from S_0 to S_1. As supply increases, the equilibrium price of natural gas falls and the equilibrium quantity of natural gas increases as the point of equilibrium moves from A to B. Apparently, *The Wall Street Journal* reporters were expecting the natural gas market to move down supply curve S_0, which would have matched their (mistaken) belief that natural gas production should be declining as market price falls. As you know from this chapter, they forgot to shift the supply curve for natural gas in response to the three supply-side factors that are working together to increase natural gas supplies in the United States. These forces show no immediate signs of reversing, and until they do, or until some other demand or supply forces emerge to counteract them, supply prices will continue to fall and gas production will continue to rise. As you can see, there is nothing "whacked out" about this supply and demand story.

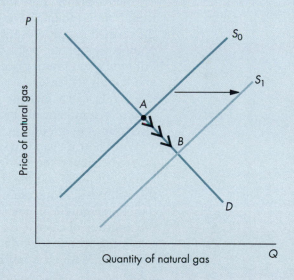

[a]See Russell Gold, Daniel Gilbert, and Ryan Dezember, "Glut Hits Natural-Gas Prices," *The Wall Street Journal*, January 12, 2012, p. A1.

FIGURE 2.9

**Shifts in Both Demand
and Supply:**
Demand and Supply
Both Increase

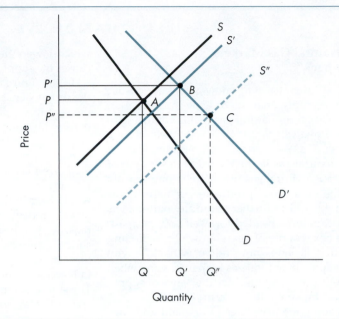

In Figure 2.9, *D* and *S* are, respectively, demand and supply, and equilibrium price and quantity are *P* and *Q* (point *A*). Suppose demand increases to *D'* and supply increases to *S'*. Equilibrium quantity increases to *Q'*, and equilibrium price rises from *P* to *P'* (point *B*). Suppose, however, that supply had increased even more to the dashed supply *S"* so that the new equilibrium occurs at point *C* instead of at point *B*. Comparing point *A* to point *C*, equilibrium quantity still increases (*Q* to *Q"*), but now equilibrium price *decreases* from *P* to *P"*. In the case where both demand and supply increase, a *small* increase in supply relative to demand causes price to rise, while a *large* increase in supply relative to demand causes price to fall. In the case of a simultaneous increase in both demand and supply, equilibrium output always increases, but the change in equilibrium price is indeterminate.

When both demand and supply shift together, either (1) the change in quantity can be predicted and the change in price is indeterminate or (2) the change in quantity is indeterminate and the change in price can be predicted. Figure 2.10 summarizes the four possible outcomes when demand and supply both shift. In each of the four panels in Figure 2.10, point *C* shows an alternative point of equilibrium that reverses the direction of change in one of the variables, price or quantity. You should use the reasoning process set forth above to verify the conclusions presented for each of the four cases. We have established the following principle:

Principle When demand and supply both shift simultaneously, if the change in quantity (price) can be predicted, the change in price (quantity) is indeterminate. The change in equilibrium quantity or price is indeterminate when the variable can either rise or fall depending upon the relative magnitudes by which demand and supply shift.

FIGURE 2.10

Summary of Simultaneous Shifts in Demand and Supply:
The Four Possible Cases

Panel A — Demand increases and supply increases

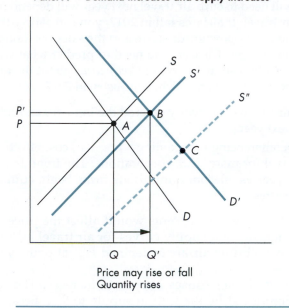

Price may rise or fall
Quantity rises

Panel B — Demand decreases and supply increases

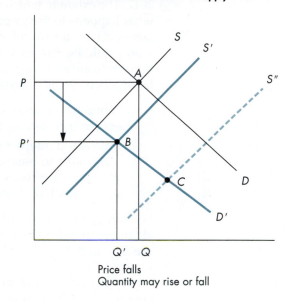

Price falls
Quantity may rise or fall

Panel C — Demand increases and supply decreases

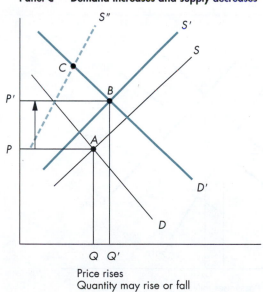

Price rises
Quantity may rise or fall

Panel D — Demand decreases and supply decreases

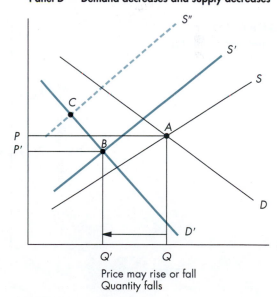

Price may rise or fall
Quantity falls

Predicting the Direction of Change in Airfares: A Qualitative Analysis

Suppose in 2016 you manage the travel department for a large U.S. corporation and your sales force makes heavy use of air travel to call on customers. The president of the corporation wants you to reduce travel expenditures next year in 2017. The extent to which you will need to curb air travel next year will depend on what happens to the price of air travel. If airfares fall in 2017, you can satisfy the wants of both the president, who wants expenditures cut, and the sales personnel, who would be hurt by travel restrictions. Clearly, you need to predict what will happen to airfares. You have recently read in *The Wall Street Journal* about the following two events that you expect will affect the airline industry in 2017:

1. A number of new, small airlines have recently entered the industry and others are expected to enter next year.
2. Broadband Internet videoconferencing is becoming a popular, cost-effective alternative to business travel for many U.S. corporations. The trend is expected to accelerate next year as telecommunications firms begin cutting prices on teleconferencing rates.

We can use Figure 2.11 to analyze how these events would affect the price of air travel in 2017. The current demand and supply curves for air travel in 2016 are D_{2016} and S_{2016}. The current equilibrium airfare is denoted P_{2016} at point A in Figure 2.11.

An increase in the number of airlines causes supply to increase. The increase in supply is shown in Figure 2.11 by the shift in supply to S_{2017}. Because videoconferencing and air travel are substitutes, a reduction in the price of

FIGURE 2.11

Demand and Supply for Air Travel

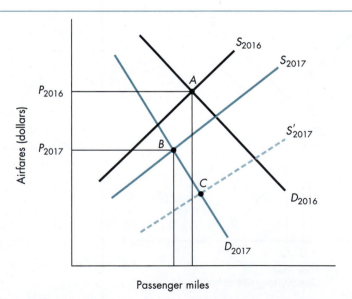

videoconferencing causes a decrease in demand. The decrease in demand is shown in Figure 2.11 by the shift in demand to D_{2017}. Thus, you must analyze a situation in which demand and supply shift simultaneously. The decrease in demand combined with the increase in supply leads you to predict a fall in airfares to point *B* in Figure 2.11. Although you can predict that airfares will definitely fall when demand decreases and supply increases, you cannot predict whether equilibrium quantity will rise or fall in this situation (supply could instead shift to S'_{2017} in Figure 2.11). The change in quantity is indeterminate. The predicted fall in airfares is good news for you but bad news for the financially troubled airline industry.

This analysis of the air travel market is an example of qualitative analysis. You predicted only the *direction* of the price change, not the magnitude of the change. Managers are certainly interested in whether price will increase or decrease. They are also interested in *how much* price will increase or decrease. Determining how much price will rise involves quantitative analysis. To carry out quantitative analysis, either you must be given the exact specification of the market demand and supply equations or you must estimate them from market data. In later chapters we will show you how to estimate demand and supply from market data. We will look now at an example of quantitative analysis where the demand and supply equations have already been estimated for you.

Now try Technical Problem 16.

Advertising and the Price of Milk: A Quantitative Analysis

The American Dairy Association estimates next year's demand and supply functions for milk in the United States will be

$$Q_d = 410 - 25P$$
$$Q_s = -40 + 20P$$

where quantity demanded and quantity supplied are measured in billions of pounds of milk per year, and price is the wholesale price measured in dollars per hundred pounds of milk. First, we predict the price and quantity of milk next year. The market clearing price is easily determined by setting quantity demanded equal to quantity supplied and solving algebraically for equilibrium price

$$Q_d = Q_s$$
$$410 - 25P = -40 + 20P$$
$$450 = 45P$$
$$10 = \overline{P}$$

Thus, the predicted equilibrium price of milk next year is $10 per hundred pounds. The predicted equilibrium output of milk is determined by substituting the market price of $10 into either the demand or the supply function to get $\overline{Q}$

$$Q_d = Q_s = \overline{Q}$$
$$410 - (25 \times 10) = -40 + (20 \times 10) = 160$$

Thus, the equilibrium output of milk is predicted to be 160 billion pounds next year.

Even though that's a lot of milk, the American Dairy Association plans to begin a nationwide advertising campaign to promote milk by informing consumers of the nutritional benefits of milk—lots of calcium and vitamin D. The association estimates the advertising campaign will increase demand to

$$Q_d = 500 - 25P$$

Assuming supply is unaffected by the advertising, you would obviously predict the market price of milk will rise as a result of the advertising and the resulting increase in demand. However, to determine the actual market-clearing price, you must equate the new quantity demanded with the quantity supplied

$$500 - 25P = -40 + 20P$$
$$\overline{P} = 12$$

The price of milk will increase to $12 per hundred pounds with the advertising campaign. Consequently, the prediction is that the national advertising campaign will increase the market price of milk by $2 per hundred pounds. To make a quantitative forecast about the impact of the ads on the level of milk sales, you simply substitute the new market price of $12 into either the demand or the supply function to obtain the new $\overline{Q}$

$$Q_d = Q_s = \overline{Q}$$
$$500 - (25 \times 12) = -40 + (20 \times 12) = 200$$

Now try Technical Problem 17.

This is an example of a quantitative forecast since the forecast involves both the magnitude and the direction of change in price and quantity.

2.6 CEILING AND FLOOR PRICES

Shortages and surpluses *can* occur after a shift in demand or supply, but as we have stressed, these shortages and surpluses are sufficiently short in duration that they can reasonably be ignored in demand and supply analysis. In other words, markets are assumed to adjust fairly rapidly, and we concern ourselves only with the comparison of equilibriums before and after a shift in supply or demand. There are, however, some types of shortages and surpluses that market forces do not eliminate. These are more permanent in nature and result from government interferences with the market mechanism, which prevent prices from freely moving up or down to clear the market.

Typically these more permanent shortages and surpluses are caused by government imposing legal restrictions on the movement of prices. Shortages and surpluses can be created simply by legislating a price below or above equilibrium. Governments have decided in the past, and will surely decide in the future, that the price of a particular commodity is "too high" or "too low" and will proceed to set a "fair price." Without evaluating the desirability of such interference, we can use demand and supply curves to analyze the economic effects of these two types of interference: the setting of minimum and maximum prices.

FIGURE 2.12

Ceiling and Floor Prices

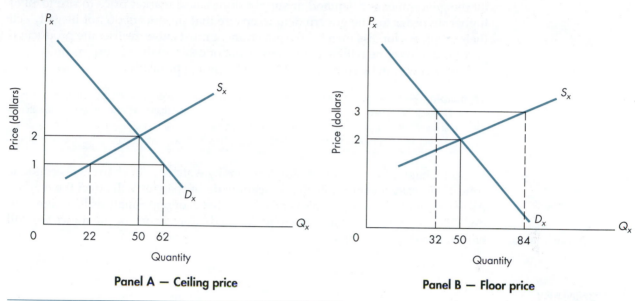

Panel A — Ceiling price

Panel B — Floor price

ceiling price
The maximum price the government permits sellers to charge for a good. When this price is below equilibrium, a shortage occurs.

If the government imposes a maximum price, or **ceiling price,** on a good, the effect is a shortage of that good. In Panel A of Figure 2.12, a ceiling price of $1 is set on some good X. No one can legally sell X for more than $1, and $1 is less than the equilibrium (market clearing) price of $2. At the ceiling price of $1, the maximum amount that producers are willing to supply is 22 units. At $1, consumers wish to purchase 62 units. A shortage of 40 units results from the imposition of the $1 price ceiling. Market forces will not be permitted to bid up the price to eliminate the shortage because producers cannot sell the good for more than $1. This type of shortage will continue until government eliminates the price ceiling or until shifts in either supply or demand cause the equilibrium price to fall to $1 or lower. It is worth noting that "black" (illegal) markets usually arise in such cases. Some consumers are willing to pay more than $1 for good X rather than do without it, and some producers are willing to sell good X for more than $1 rather than forgo the extra sales. In most cases the law is not a sufficient deterrent to the illegal trade of a good at prices above the ceiling.

floor price
The minimum price the government permits sellers to charge for a good. When this price is above equilibrium, a surplus occurs.

Alternatively, the government may believe that the suppliers of the good are not earning as much income as they deserve and, therefore, sets a minimum price or **floor price.** You can see the results of such actions in Panel B of Figure 2.12. Dissatisfied with the equilibrium price of $2 and equilibrium quantity of 50, the government sets a minimum price of $3. Since the government cannot repeal the law of demand, consumers reduce the amount they purchase to 32 units. Producers, of course, are going to increase their production of X to 84 units in response to the

$3 price. Now a surplus of 52 units exists. Because the government is not allowing the price of X to fall, this surplus is going to continue until it is either eliminated by the government or demand or supply shifts cause market price to rise to $3 or higher. In order for the government to ensure that producers do not illegally sell their surpluses for less than $3, the government must either restrict the production of X to 32 units or be willing to buy (and store or destroy) the 52 surplus units.

This section can be summarized by the following principle:

> **Principle**   When the government sets a ceiling price below the equilibrium price, a shortage or excess demand results because consumers wish to buy more units of the good than producers are willing to sell at the ceiling price. If the government sets a floor price above the equilibrium price, a surplus or excess supply results because producers offer for sale more units of the good than buyers wish to consume at the floor price.

Now try Technical Problems 18–19.

For managers to make successful decisions by watching for changes in economic conditions, they must be able to predict how these changes will affect the market. As we hope you have seen, this is precisely what economic analysis is designed to do. This ability to use economics to make predictions is one of the topics we will emphasize throughout the text.

2.7 SUMMARY

- The amount of a good or service consumers are willing and able to purchase is called quantity demanded. Six variables influence quantity demanded: (1) price of the good, (2) income of consumers, (3) prices of related goods, (4) consumer tastes, (5) expected future price of the good, and (6) number of consumers in the market. The direct demand function (or simply "demand") shows the relation between price and quantity demanded when all other factors affecting consumer demand are held constant. The law of demand states that quantity demanded increases (decreases) when price falls (rises), other things held constant. A change in a good's own price causes a change in quantity demanded, which is represented by a movement along the demand curve. When there is a change in income, price of a related good, consumer tastes, expected price, or number of consumers, a "change in demand" occurs and the demand curve shifts rightward or leftward. An increase (decrease) in demand occurs when demand shifts rightward (leftward). (LO1)

- Quantity supplied of a good depends on six factors: (1) price of the good, (2) price of inputs used in production, (3) prices of goods related in production, (4) level of available technology, (5) expectations of producers concerning the future price of the good, and (6) number of firms or amount of productive capacity in the industry.

The direct supply function (or simply "supply") gives the quantity supplied at various prices when all other factors affecting supply are held constant. Only when the good's own price changes does quantity supplied change, causing a movement along the supply curve. When any of the five determinants of supply change—input prices, prices of goods related in production, technology, expected price, or number of firms—a change in supply occurs and the supply curve shifts rightward or leftward. Increasing (decreasing) price causes quantity supplied to increase (decrease), which is represented by upward (downward) movement along a supply curve. (LO2)

- Equilibrium price and quantity are determined by the intersection of demand and supply curves. At the point of intersection, quantity demanded equals quantity supplied, and the market clears. At the market clearing price, there is no excess demand (shortage) and no excess supply (surplus). (LO3)

- Consumer surplus arises because the equilibrium price consumers pay is less than the value they place on the units they purchase. Total consumer surplus from market exchange is measured by the area under demand above market price up to the equilibrium quantity. Producer surplus arises because equilibrium price is greater than the minimum price producers would be willing to accept to produce. Total producer surplus is equal to the area below market price and above supply up to the equilibrium quantity. Social surplus is the sum of consumer surplus and producer surplus. (*LO4*)

■ When demand increases (decreases), supply remaining constant, equilibrium price and quantity both rise (fall). When supply increases (decreases), demand remaining constant, equilibrium price falls (rises) and equilibrium quantity rises (falls). When both supply and demand shift simultaneously, it is possible to predict either the direction in which price changes or the direction in which quantity changes, but not both. The change in equilibrium quantity or price is said to be indeterminate when the direction of change depends upon the relative magnitudes by which demand and supply shift. The four possible cases are summarized in Figure 2.10. (*LO5*)

■ When government sets a ceiling price below equilibrium price, a shortage results because consumers wish to buy more of the good than producers are willing to sell at the ceiling price. If government sets a floor price above equilibrium price, a surplus results because producers supply more units of the good than buyers demand at the floor price. (*LO6*)

KEY TERMS

ceiling price	economic value	market equilibrium
change in demand	equilibrium price	normal good
change in quantity demanded	equilibrium quantity	producer surplus
change in quantity supplied	excess demand (shortage)	qualitative forecast
complements	excess supply (surplus)	quantitative forecast
complements in production	floor price	quantity demanded
consumer surplus	general demand function	quantity supplied
decrease in demand	general supply function	slope parameters
decrease in supply	increase in demand	social surplus
demand curve	increase in supply	substitutes
demand price	indeterminate	substitutes in production
demand schedule	inferior good	supply curve
determinants of demand	inverse demand function	supply price
determinants of supply	inverse supply function	supply schedule
direct demand function	law of demand	technology
direct supply function	market clearing price	

TECHNICAL PROBLEMS

1. The general demand function for good *A* is

$$Q_d = 600 - 4P_A - 0.03M - 12P_B + 15\mathcal{T} + 6P_E + 1.5N$$

where Q_d = quantity demanded of good *A* each month, P_A = price of good *A*, M = average household income, P_B = price of related good *B*, $\mathcal{T}$ = a consumer taste index ranging in value from 0 to 10 (the highest rating), P_E = price consumers expect to pay next month for good *A*, and N = number of buyers in the market for good *A*.

a. Interpret the intercept parameter in the general demand function.

b. What is the value of the slope parameter for the price of good *A*? Does it have the correct algebraic sign? Why?

c. Interpret the slope parameter for income. Is good *A* normal or inferior? Explain.

d. Are goods *A* and *B* substitutes or complements? Explain. Interpret the slope parameter for the price of good *B*.

  e. Are the algebraic signs on the slope parameters for $\mathcal{T}$, $P_{E'}$ and N correct? Explain.

  f. Calculate the quantity demanded of good A when $P_A = \$5$, $M = \$25{,}000$, $P_B = \$40$, $\mathcal{T} = 6.5$, $P_E = \$5.25$, and $N = 2{,}000$.

2. Consider the general demand function:

$$Q_d = 8{,}000 - 16P + 0.75M + 30P_R$$

  a. Derive the equation for the demand function when $M = \$30{,}000$ and $P_R = \$50$.

  b. Interpret the intercept and slope parameters of the demand function derived in part *a.*

  c. Sketch a graph of the demand function in part *a.* Where does the demand function intersect the quantity-demanded axis? Where does it intersect the price axis?

  d. Using the demand function from part *a,* calculate the quantity demanded when the price of the good is \$1,000 and when the price is \$1,500.

  e. Derive the inverse of the demand function in part *a.* Using the inverse demand function, calculate the demand price for 24,000 units of the good. Give an interpretation of this demand price.

3. The demand curve for good X passes through the point $P = \$2$ and $Q_d = 35$. Give two interpretations of this point on the demand curve.

4. Recall that the general demand function for the demand curves in Figure 2.2 is

$$Q_d = 3{,}200 - 10P + 0.05M + 24P_R$$

Derive the demand function for D_2 in Figure 2.2. Recall that for D_2 income is \$52,000 and the price of the related good is \$200.

5. Using a graph, explain carefully the difference between a movement along a demand curve and a shift in the demand curve.

6. What happens to *demand* when the following changes occur?

  a. The price of the commodity falls.

  b. Income increases and the commodity is normal.

  c. Income increases and the commodity is inferior.

  d. The price of a substitute good increases.

  e. The price of a substitute good decreases.

  f. The price of a complement good increases.

  g. The price of a complement good decreases.

7. Consider the general supply function:

$$Q_s = 60 + 5P - 12P_I + 10F$$

where Q_s = quantity supplied, P = price of the commodity, P_I = price of a key input in the production process, and F = number of firms producing the commodity.

  a. Interpret the slope parameters on P, P_I, and F.

  b. Derive the equation for the supply function when $P_I = \$90$ and $F = 20$.

  c. Sketch a graph of the supply function in part *b.* At what price does the supply curve intersect the price axis? Give an interpretation of the price intercept of this supply curve.

  d. Using the supply function from part *b,* calculate the quantity supplied when the price of the commodity is \$300 and \$500.

e. Derive the inverse of the supply function in part b. Using the inverse supply function, calculate the supply price for 680 units of the commodity. Give an interpretation of this supply price.

8. Suppose the supply curve for good X passes through the point $P = \$25$, $Q_s = 500$. Give two interpretations of this point on the supply curve.

9. The following general supply function shows the quantity of good X that producers offer for sale (Q_s):

$$Q_s = 19 + 20P_x - 10P_l + 6T - 32P_r - 20P_e + 5F$$

where P_x is the price of X, P_l is the price of labor, T is an index measuring the level of technology, P_r is the price of a good R that is related in production, P_e is the expected future price of good X, and F is the number of firms in the industry.

a. Determine the equation of the supply curve for X when $P_l = 8$, $T = 4$, $P_r = 4$, $P_e = 5$, and $F = 47$. Plot this supply curve on a graph.

b. Suppose the price of labor increases from 8 to 9. Find the equation of the new supply curve. Plot the new supply curve on a graph.

c. Is the good related in production a complement or a substitute in production? Explain.

d. What is the correct way to interpret each of the coefficients in the general supply function given above?

10. Using a graph, explain carefully the difference between a movement along a supply curve and a shift in the supply curve.

11. Other things remaining the same, what would happen to the *supply* of a particular commodity if the following changes occur?

a. The price of the commodity decreases.

b. A technological breakthrough enables the good to be produced at a significantly lower cost.

c. The prices of inputs used to produce the commodity increase.

d. The price of a commodity that is a substitute in production decreases.

e. The managers of firms that produce the good expect the price of the good to rise in the near future.

f. Firms in the industry purchase more plant and equipment, increasing the productive capacity in the industry.

12. The following table presents the demand and supply schedules for apartments in a small U.S. city:

Monthly rental rate (dollars per month)	Quantity demanded (number of units per month)	Quantity supplied (number of units per month)
$300	130,000	35,000
350	115,000	37,000
400	100,000	41,000
450	80,000	45,000
500	72,000	52,000
550	60,000	60,000
600	55,000	70,000
650	48,000	75,000

a. If the monthly rental rate is $600, excess _____ of _____ apartments per month will occur and rental rates can be expected to _____.

b. If the monthly rental rate is $350, excess _____ of _____ apartments per month will occur and rental rates can be expected to _____.

c. The equilibrium or market clearing rental rate is $_____ per month.

d. The equilibrium number of apartments rented is _____ per month.

13. Suppose that the demand and supply functions for good X are

$$Q_d = 50 - 8P$$
$$Q_s = -17.5 + 10P$$

a. What are the equilibrium price and quantity?

b. What is the market outcome if price is $2.75? What do you expect to happen? Why?

c. What is the market outcome if price is $4.25? What do you expect to happen? Why?

d. What happens to equilibrium price and quantity if the demand function becomes $Q_d = 59 - 8P$?

e. What happens to equilibrium price and quantity if the supply function becomes $Q_s = -40 + 10P$ (demand is $Q_d = 50 - 8P$)?

14. Use the linear demand and supply curves shown below to answer the following questions:

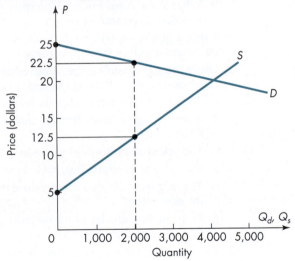

a. The market or equilibrium price is $_____.

b. The economic value of the 2,000th unit is $_____, and the minimum price producers will accept to produce this unit is $_____.

c. When 2,000 units are produced and consumed, total consumer surplus is $_____, and total producer surplus is $_____.

d. At the market price in part a, the net gain to consumers when 2,000 units are purchased is $_____.

e. At the market price in part a, the net gain to producers when they supply 2,000 units is $_____.

f. The net gain to society when 2,000 units are produced and consumed at the market price is $_____, which is called _____.

g. In market equilibrium, total consumer surplus is $_____, and the total producer surplus is $_____.

h. The net gain to society created by this market is $_____.

15. Determine the effect upon equilibrium price and quantity sold if the following changes occur in a particular market:

a. Consumers' income increases and the good is normal.

b. The price of a substitute good (in consumption) increases.

c. The price of a substitute good (in production) increases.

d. The price of a complement good (in consumption) increases.

e. The price of inputs used to produce the good increases.

f. Consumers expect that the price of the good will increase in the near future.

g. It is widely publicized that consumption of the good is hazardous to health.

h. Cost-reducing technological change takes place in the industry.

16. Suppose that a pair of events from Technical Problem 15 occur simultaneously. For each of the pairs of events indicated below, perform a qualitative analysis to predict the direction of change in either the equilibrium price or the equilibrium quantity. Explain why the change in one of these two variables is indeterminate.

a. Both a and h in Technical Problem 15 occur simultaneously.

b. Both d and e in Technical Problem 15 occur simultaneously.

c. Both d and h in Technical Problem 15 occur simultaneously.

d. Both f and c in Technical Problem 15 occur simultaneously.

17. Suppose that the general demand function for good X is

$$Q_d = 60 - 2P_x + 0.01M + 7P_R$$

where

Q_d = quantity of X demanded
P_x = price of X
M = (average) consumer income
P_R = price of a related good R

a. Is good X normal or inferior? Explain.

b. Are goods X and R substitutes or complements? Explain.

Suppose that M = $40,000 and P_R = $20.

c. What is the demand function for good X?

Suppose the supply function is

$$Q_s = -600 + 10P_x$$

d. What are the equilibrium price and quantity?

e. What happens to equilibrium price and quantity if other things remain the same as in part d but income increases to $52,000?

f. What happens to equilibrium price and quantity if other things remain the same as in part d but the price of good R decreases to $14?

g. What happens to equilibrium price and quantity if other things remain the same, income and the price of the related goods are at their original levels, and supply shifts to $Q_s = -360 + 10P_x$?

18. In Technical Problem 12, suppose the city council decides rents are too high and imposes a rent ceiling of $400.

   a. The ceiling on rent causes a _____ of _____ apartments per month.

   b. How many *more* renters would have found an apartment in this city if the ceiling had not been imposed?

   Suppose that instead of imposing a ceiling price, the city council places a floor price of $600 on rental rates.

   c. The floor price on rent causes a _____ of _____ apartments per month.

19. Use the following graph to answer these questions.

   a. What are the equilibrium price and quantity?

   b. What is the effect of a ceiling price of $40?

   c. What is the effect of a floor price of $50? A floor price of $70?

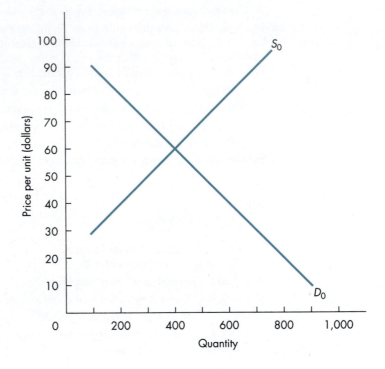

APPLIED PROBLEMS

1. Suppose you are the manager of a California winery. How would you expect the following events to affect the price you receive for a bottle of wine?

   a. The price of comparable French wines decreases.

   b. One hundred new wineries open in California.

   c. The unemployment rate in the United States decreases.

   d. The price of cheese increases.

    e. The price of a glass bottle increases significantly due to new government antishatter regulations.

    f. Researchers discover a new wine-making technology that reduces production costs.

    g. The price of wine vinegar, which is made from the leftover grape mash, increases.

    h. The average age of consumers increases, and older people drink less wine.

2. Florida Citrus Mutual, an agricultural cooperative association for citrus growers in Florida, needs to predict what will happen to the price and output of Florida oranges under the conditions below. What are your predictions? For each part, sketch a graph showing the appropriate demand and supply analysis.

    a. A major freeze destroys a large number of the orange trees in Florida.

    b. The scientists in the agricultural extension service of the University of Florida discover a way to double the number of oranges produced by each orange tree.

    c. The American Medical Association announces that drinking orange juice can reduce the risk of heart attack.

    d. The price of Florida grapefruit falls.

3. Evaluate the following statements using graphical analysis. Provide a brief narrative explanation of your graph to support your evaluation. Make sure the axes and curves in your graphs are properly labeled.

    a. "When demand for home heating oil increases, a shortage of heating oil will occur."

    b. "A decrease in the supply of random access memory (RAM) chips for personal computers causes a shortage of RAM chips."

4. Rising jet fuel prices recently led most major U.S. airlines to raise fares by approximately 15 percent. Explain how this substantial increase in airfares would affect the following:

    a. The demand for air travel.

    b. The demand for hotels.

    c. The demand for rental cars.

    d. The supply of overnight mail.

5. The famous Swedish economist Assar Lindbeck remarked in his book on rent controls, "Rent control appears to be the most efficient technique presently known to destroy a city—except for bombing." Rent controls place price ceilings on rents at levels below equilibrium rental rates for the stated purpose of making housing more affordable for low-income families. Using demand and supply analysis, answer the following questions:

    a. How does imposing rent controls affect the number of housing units available to low-income families?

    b. Under rent controls, can all low-income families get rent-controlled housing?

    c. Who gains from rent controls? Who loses?

    d. Why would Professor Lindbeck think rent controls are destructive?

    e. Can you think of an alternative policy to make plenty of housing available to low-income families that would not be subject to the problems of rent controls?

6. Suppose you are a stock market analyst specializing in the stocks of theme parks, and you are examining Disneyland's stock. *The Wall Street Journal* reports that tourism has slowed down in the United States. At Six Flags Magic Mountain in Valencia, California, a new Viper roller coaster is now operating and another new ride, Psyclone, will be opening this year. Using demand and supply analysis, predict the impact of these

events on ticket prices and attendance at Disneyland. As reported in *The Wall Street Journal*, Disneyland slashed ticket prices and admitted that attendance was somewhat lower. Is this consistent with your prediction using demand and supply analysis? In light of the fact that both price and output were falling at Disneyland, is the law of demand being violated in the world of fantasy?

7. California voters, in an attempt to halt the rapid increase in the state's automobile insurance rates, approved Proposition 103. The measure proposes to roll back auto insurance rates by 20 percent and freeze them for at least a year. Using a graph, show the impact of Proposition 103 on the market for automobile insurance in California. As the costs of providing insurance continue to rise, what do you predict will happen over time in the California market for auto insurance? How would your prediction change if Proposition 103 is defeated?

8. Construct a graph showing equilibrium in the market for movie tickets. Label both axes and denote the initial equilibrium price and quantity as P_0 and Q_0. For each of the following events, draw an appropriate new supply or demand curve for movies, and predict the impact of the event on the market price of a movie ticket and the number of tickets sold in the new equilibrium situation:

   a. Movie theaters double the price of soft drinks and popcorn.

   b. A national video rental chain cuts its rental rate by 25 percent.

   c. Cable television begins offering pay-per-view movies.

   d. The screenwriters' guild ends a 10-month strike.

   e. Kodak reduces the price it charges Hollywood producers for motion picture film.

9. An article in *Bloomberg Businessweek* reported the discovery of a new processing technology that makes it economically feasible to turn natural gas into a liquid petroleum that yields superclean gasoline, diesel fuel, or any other product derived from crude oil. This discovery represents 770 billion barrels of oil equivalent, "enough to slake the world's thirst for oil for 29 years."

   a. Using demand and supply analysis, explain why this new process will *not* cause a surplus of crude oil. If no surplus is created, then what will be the impact of this process on the market for crude oil?

   b. Had this process *not* been discovered, explain why we still would have had "enough" crude oil to meet the growing worldwide demand for crude oil.

10. Firewood prices in places from northern California to Boston and suburban New Jersey have remained steady even though the supply of firewood has been diminished by environmental restrictions on cutting. *The Wall Street Journal* reports that sales of gas fireplaces are outpacing sales of wood-burning hearths and that "people are burning less and less wood." Use supply and demand analysis to show why firewood prices are not rising while the quantity of firewood burned is declining. (*Hint:* Allow for simultaneous shifts in the demand and supply of firewood.)

11. *Bloomberg Businessweek* recently declared, "We have entered the Age of the Internet," and observed that when markets for goods or services gain access to the Internet, more consumers and more businesses participate in the market.* Use supply and demand analysis to predict the effect of e-commerce on equilibrium output and equilibrium price of products gaining a presence on the Internet.

---

*"The Internet Economy: the World's Next Growth Engine", BusinessWeek, October 4, 1999.

12. The world market for newly smelted primary aluminum (i.e., excluding scrap or recycled sources) recently experienced a period of rising inventories and falling prices. *The Wall Street Journal* reported that Russian smelter Rusal, the world's largest aluminum producer, expected primary aluminum ingot prices would need to fall even further before worldwide inventory accumulation could stabilize. Suppose the demand for primary aluminum can be represented by the equation $Q_d = 124 - 0.025\,P$ (Q_d is the annual worldwide quantity demanded in millions of metric tons of new aluminum, P is the dollar price of new aluminum per ton). Further suppose the world supply of aluminum is $Q_s = -50 + 0.025\,P$ (Q_s is the annual worldwide quantity supplied in millions of metric tons of new aluminum, P is the dollar price of new aluminum per ton).

   a. At the time of Rusal's concern, primary aluminum prices were relatively high at $3,600 per ton. At this price, calculate the *monthly* rate of inventory growth in the global aluminum market using the given demand and supply equations for the world aluminum market.

   b. Rusal believed the price of aluminum would fall because of the growing accumulation of inventories worldwide. Evaluate Rusal's prediction by using the demand and supply equations provided to make a prediction about the movement of world aluminum price.

3

Marginal Analysis for Optimal Decisions

After reading this chapter, you will be able to:

3.1 Define several key concepts and terminology.

3.2 Use marginal analysis to find optimal activity levels in unconstrained maximization problems and explain why sunk costs, fixed costs, and average costs are irrelevant for decision making.

3.3 Employ marginal analysis to find the optimal levels of two or more activities in constrained maximization and minimization problems.

Making optimal decisions about the levels of various business activities is an essential skill for all managers, one that requires managers to analyze benefits and costs to make the best possible decision under a given set of circumstances. When Ford Motor Company began producing a redesigned and reengineered Explorer, Ford's CEO decided that the first 5,000 units rolling off assembly lines would not be delivered immediately to Ford dealer showrooms, even as potential buyers waited anxiously to get the new model. Instead, all of the new vehicles were parked in lots outside factories while quality control engineers examined 100 of them for defects in assembly and workmanship. The intense, 24-hour-a-day inspection process continued for three months, delaying the launch of the highly profitable new Explorer. While no one could blame Ford's executives for wanting to minimize costly product recalls, many auto industry analysts, car buyers, and owners of Ford dealerships nonetheless thought Ford was undertaking too much quality control. Ford's CEO assured his critics that choosing to add three months of quality control measures was optimal, or best, under the circumstances. Apparently, he believed the benefit of engaging in three months of quality control effort (the savings attributable to preventing vehicle recalls) outweighed the cost of the additional quality control measures (the loss and delay of profit as 5,000 new Explorers spent three months in factory parking lots).

As you can see, Ford's CEO, weighing costs and benefits, made a critical decision that three months, rather than two months or four months, and a sample of 100 vehicles, rather than 50 vehicles or 300 vehicles, were the optimal or best levels of these two quality control decisions for launching the redesigned Explorer. We don't have enough information about Ford's costs and benefits of quality control to tell you whether the CEO succeeded in making the optimal decision for Ford. We can, however, tell you that one year later *Consumer Reports* still ranked the overall reliability of Ford automobiles dead last and Ford had a new CEO. Perhaps more quality control effort would have been optimal.

A manager's decision is optimal if it leads to the best outcome under a given set of circumstances. Finding the best solution involves applying the fundamental principles of optimization theory developed in this chapter. These analytical principles, which economists refer to as "marginal analysis," turn out to be nothing more than a formal presentation of commonsense ideas you already apply, probably without knowing it, in your everyday life. Marginal analysis supplies the fundamental logic for making optimal decisions. Managers benefit from understanding marginal analysis because it enables them to make better decisions while avoiding some rather common errors in business decision making.

The idea behind marginal analysis is this: When a manager contemplates whether a particular business activity needs adjusting, either more or less, to reach the best value, the manager needs to estimate how changing the activity will affect both the benefits the firm receives from engaging in the activity and the costs the firm incurs from engaging in the activity. If changing the activity level causes benefits to rise by more than costs rise, or, alternatively, costs to fall by more than benefits fall, then the net benefit the firm receives from the activity will rise. The manager should continue adjusting the activity level until no further net gains are possible, which means the activity has reached its optimal value or level.

As mentioned in Chapter 1, managers face two general types of decisions: routine business practice or tactical decisions and strategic decisions that can alter the firm's competitive environment. Marginal analysis builds the essential foundation for making everyday business decisions, such as choosing the number of workers to hire, the amount of output to produce, the amount to spend on advertising, and so on. While strategic decision making relies heavily on concepts from game theory, strategic analysis nevertheless depends indirectly on optimal decision making as the means for computing or forecasting the payoffs under various strategy options.

3.1 CONCEPTS AND TERMINOLOGY

objective function
The function the decision maker seeks to maximize or minimize.

Optimizing behavior on the part of a decision maker involves trying to maximize or minimize an *objective function*. For a manager of a firm, the **objective function** is usually profit, which is to be maximized. For a consumer, the objective function is the satisfaction derived from consumption of goods, which is to be maximized.

For a city manager seeking to provide adequate law enforcement services, the objective function might be cost, which is to be minimized. For the manager of the marketing division of a large corporation, the objective function is usually sales, which are to be maximized. The objective function measures whatever it is that the particular decision maker wishes to either maximize or minimize.

maximization problem
An optimization problem that involves maximizing the objective function.

minimization problem
An optimization problem that involves minimizing the objective function.

activities or choice variables
Variables that determine the value of the objective function.

discrete choice variables
A choice variable that can take only specific integer values.

continuous choice variables
A choice variable that can take any value between two end points.

unconstrained optimization
An optimization problem in which the decision maker can choose the level of activity from an unrestricted set of values.

constrained optimization
An optimization problem in which the decision maker chooses values for the choice variables from a restricted set of values.

If the decision maker seeks to maximize an objective function, the optimization problem is called a **maximization problem.** Alternatively, if the objective function is to be minimized, the optimization problem is called a **minimization problem.** As a general rule, when the objective function measures a benefit, the decision maker seeks to maximize this benefit and is solving a maximization problem. When the objective function measures a cost, the decision maker seeks to minimize this cost and is solving a minimization problem.

The value of the objective function is determined by the level of one or more **activities** or **choice variables.** For example, the value of profit depends on the number of units of output produced and sold. The production of units of the good is the activity that determines the value of the objective function, which in this case is profit. The decision maker controls the value of the objective function by choosing the levels of the activities or choice variables.

The choice variables in the optimization problems discussed in this text will at times vary *discretely* and at other times vary *continuously*. A **discrete choice variable** can take on only specified integer values, such as 1, 2, 3, . . . , or 10, 20, 30, . . . Examples of discrete choice variables arise when benefit and cost data are presented in a table, where each row represents one value of the choice variable. In this text, all examples of discrete choice variables will be presented in tables. A **continuous choice variable** can take on any value between two end points. For example, a continuous variable that can vary between 0 and 10 can take on the value 2, 2.345, 7.9, 8.999, or any one of the infinite number of values between the two limits. Examples of continuous choice variables are usually presented graphically but are sometimes shown by equations. As it turns out, the optimization rules differ only slightly in the discrete and continuous cases.

In addition to being categorized as either maximization or minimization problems, optimization problems are also categorized according to whether the decision maker can choose the values of the choice variables in the objective function from an unconstrained or constrained set of values. **Unconstrained optimization** problems occur when a decision maker can choose *any* level of activity he or she wishes in order to maximize the objective function. In this chapter, we show how to solve only unconstrained *maximization* problems since all the *unconstrained* decision problems we address in this text are maximization problems. **Constrained optimization** problems involve choosing the levels of two or more activities that maximize or minimize the objective function subject to an additional requirement or constraint that restricts the values of *A* and *B* that can be chosen. An example of such a constraint arises when the total cost of the chosen activity levels must equal a specified constraint on cost. In this text, we examine both constrained maximization and constrained minimization problems.

marginal analysis
Analytical technique for solving optimization problems that involves changing values of choice variables by small amounts to see if the objective function can be further improved.

Now try Technical Problem 1.

As we show later in this chapter, the constrained maximization and the constrained minimization problems have one simple rule for the solution. Therefore, you will only have one rule to learn for all constrained optimization problems.

Even though there are a huge number of possible maximizing or minimizing decisions, you will see that all optimization problems can be solved using the single analytical technique, mentioned at the beginning of this chapter: *marginal analysis*. **Marginal analysis** involves changing the value(s) of the choice variable(s) by a small amount to see if the objective function can be further increased (in the case of maximization problems) or further decreased (in the case of minimization problems). If so, the manager continues to make incremental adjustments in the choice variables until no further improvements are possible. Marginal analysis leads to two simple rules for solving optimization problems, one for unconstrained decisions and one for constrained decisions. We turn first to the unconstrained decision.

3.2 UNCONSTRAINED MAXIMIZATION

net benefit
The objective function to be maximized:
$NB = TB - TC$.

Any activity that decision makers might wish to undertake will generate both benefits and costs. Consequently, decision makers will want to choose the level of activity to obtain the maximum possible *net benefit* from the activity, where the **net benefit** (NB) associated with a specific amount of activity (A) is the difference between total benefit (TB) and total cost (TC) for the activity

$$NB = TB - TC$$

Net benefit, then, serves as the objective function to be maximized, and the amount of activity, A, represents the choice variable. Furthermore, decision makers can choose *any* level of activity they wish, from zero to infinity, in either discrete or continuous units. Thus, we are studying *unconstrained* maximization in this section.

The Optimal Level of Activity (A*)

We begin the analysis of unconstrained maximization with a rather typical set of total benefit and total cost curves for some activity, A, as shown in Panel A of Figure 3.1. Total benefit increases with higher levels of activity up to 1,000 units of activity (point G); then total benefit falls beyond this point. Total cost begins at a value of zero and rises continuously as activity increases. These "typical" curves allow us to derive general rules for finding the best solution to all such unconstrained problems, even though specific problems encountered in later chapters sometimes involve benefit and cost curves with shapes that differ somewhat from those shown in Panel A. For example, total benefit curves can be linear. Total cost curves can be linear or even S-shaped. And, as you will see in later chapters, total cost curves can include fixed costs when they take positive values at zero units of activity. In all of these variations, however, the rules for making the best decisions do not change. By learning how to solve the optimization problem as set forth in Figure 3.1, you will be prepared to solve all variations of these problems that come later in the text.

FIGURE 3.1
The Optimal Level of Activity

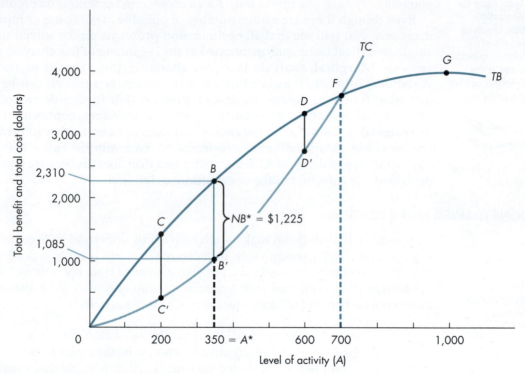

Panel A — Total benefit and total cost curves

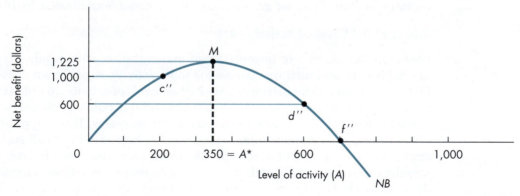

Panel B — Net benefit curve

ILLUSTRATION 3.1

Is Cost–Benefit Analysis Really Useful?

We have extolled the usefulness of marginal analysis in optimal decision making—often referred to as *cost–benefit analysis*—in business decision making as well as decision making in everyday life. This process involves weighing the marginal benefits and marginal costs of an activity while ignoring all previously incurred or sunk costs. The principal rule is to increase the level of an activity if marginal benefits exceed marginal costs and decrease the level if marginal costs exceed marginal benefits. This simple rule, however, flies in the face of many honored traditional principles such as "Never give up" or "Anything worth doing is worth doing well" or "Waste not, want not." So you might wonder if cost–benefit analysis is as useful as we have said it is.

It is, at least according to an article in *The Wall Street Journal* entitled "Economic Perspective Produces Steady Yields." In this article, a University of Michigan research team concludes, "Cost–benefit analysis pays off in everyday living." This team quizzed some of the university's seniors and faculty members on such questions as how often they walk out on a bad movie, refuse to finish a bad novel, start over on a weak term paper, or abandon a research project that no longer looks promising. They believe that people who cut their losses this way are following sound economic rules: calculating the net benefits of alternative courses of action, writing off past costs that can't be recovered, and weighing the opportunity to use future time and effort more profitably elsewhere.[a]

The findings: Among faculty members, those who use cost–benefit reasoning in this fashion had higher salaries relative to their age and departments. Economists were more likely to apply the approach than professors of humanities or biology. Among students, those who have learned to use cost–benefit analysis frequently are apt to have far better grades than their SAT scores would have predicted. The more economics courses the students had taken, the more likely they were to apply cost–benefit analysis outside the classroom. The director of the University of Michigan study did concede that for many Americans cost–benefit rules often appear to conflict with traditional principles such as those we previously mentioned. Notwithstanding these probable conflicts, the study provides evidence that decision makers can indeed prosper by following the logic of marginal analysis and cost–benefit analysis.

[a] "Economic Perspective Produces Steady Yield," *The Wall Street Journal*, March 31, 1992.

---

optimal level of activity
The level of activity that maximizes net benefit (A^*).

The level of activity that maximizes net benefit is called the **optimal level of activity,** which we distinguish from other levels of activity with an asterisk: A^*. In Panel A of Figure 3.1, net benefit at any particular level of activity is measured by the vertical distance between the total benefit and total cost curves. At 200 units of activity, for example, net benefit equals the length of line segment CC', which happens to be \$1,000 as shown in Panel B at point c''. Panel B of Figure 3.1 shows the net benefit curve associated with the TB and TC curves in Panel A. As you can see from examining the net benefit curve in Panel B, the optimal level of activity, A^*, is 350 units, where NB reaches its maximum value. At 350 units in Panel A, the vertical distance between TB and TC is maximized, and this maximum distance is \$1,225 ($= NB^*$).[1]

---

[1] You might, at first, have thought the optimal activity level was 700 units since two curves in Panel A of Figure 3.1 intersect at point F, and this situation frequently identifies "correct" answers in economics. But, as you can see in Panel B, choosing 700 units of activity creates no more net benefit than choosing to do nothing at all (i.e., choosing $A = 0$) because total benefit equals total cost at both zero and 700 units of activity.

Two important observations can now be made about A^* in unconstrained maximization problems. First, the optimal level of activity does not generally result in maximization of *total* benefits. In Panel A of Figure 3.1, you can see that total benefit is still rising at the optimal point B. As we will demonstrate later in this book, for one of the most important applications of this technique, profit maximization, the optimal level of production occurs at a point where revenues are not maximized. This outcome can confuse managers, especially ones who believe any decision that increases revenue should be undertaken. We will have much more to say about this later in the text. Second, the optimal level of activity in an unconstrained maximization problem does not result in minimization of total cost. In Panel A, you can easily verify that total cost isn't minimized at A^* but rather at zero units of activity.

Finding A^* in Figure 3.1 seems easy enough. A decision maker starts with the total benefit and total cost curves in Panel A and subtracts the total cost curve from the total benefit curve to construct the net benefit curve in Panel B. Then, the decision maker chooses the value of A corresponding to the peak of the net benefit curve. You might reasonably wonder why we are going to develop an alternative method, marginal analysis, for making optimal decisions. Perhaps the most important reason for learning how to use marginal analysis is that economists regard marginal analysis as "the central organizing principle of economic theory."[2] The graphical derivation of net benefit shown in Figure 3.1 serves only to *define* and *describe* the optimal level of activity; it does not explain *why* net benefit rises, falls, or reaches its peak. Marginal analysis, by focusing only on the changes in total benefits and total costs, provides a simple and complete explanation of the underlying forces causing net benefit to change. Understanding precisely what causes net benefit to improve makes it possible to develop simple rules for deciding when an activity needs to be increased, decreased, or left at its current level.

We are also going to show that using marginal analysis to make optimal decisions ensures that you will not consider irrelevant information about such things as fixed costs, sunk costs, or average costs in the decision-making process. As you will see shortly, decision makers using marginal analysis can reach the optimal activity level using only information about the benefits and costs *at the margin*. For this reason, marginal analysis requires less information than would be needed to construct TB, TC, and NB curves for all possible activity levels, as shown in Figure 3.1. There is no need to gather and process information for levels of activity that will never be chosen on the way to reaching A^*. For example, if the decision maker is currently at 199 units of activity in Figure 3.1, information about benefits and costs is only needed for activity levels from 200 to 351 units. The optimal level of activity can be found without any information about benefits or costs below 200 units or above 351 units.

Now try Technical Problem 2.

[2]See Robert B. Ekelund, Jr., and Robert F. Hébert, *A History of Economic Theory and Method,* 4th ed. (New York: McGraw-Hill, 1997), p. 264.

Marginal Benefit and Marginal Cost

marginal benefit (*MB*)
The change in total benefit caused by an incremental change in the level of an activity.

marginal cost (*MC*)
The change in total cost caused by an incremental change in the level of an activity.

In order to understand and use marginal analysis, you must understand the two key components of this methodology: *marginal benefit* and *marginal cost.* **Marginal benefit (*MB*)** is the change in total benefit caused by an incremental change in the level of an activity. Similarly, **marginal cost (*MC*)** is the change in total cost caused by an incremental change in activity. Dictionaries typically define "incremental" to mean "a small positive or negative change in a variable." You can think of "small" or "incremental" changes in activity to be any change that is small *relative* to the total level of activity. In most applications it is convenient to interpret an incremental change as a one-unit change. In some decisions, however, it may be impractical or even impossible to make changes as small as one-unit. This causes no problem for applying marginal analysis as long as the activity can be adjusted in relatively small increments. We should also mention that "small" refers only to the change in *activity level*; "small" doesn't apply to the resulting changes in total benefit or total cost, which can be any size.

Marginal benefit and marginal cost can be expressed mathematically as

$$MB = \frac{\text{Change in total benefit}}{\text{Change in activity}} = \frac{\Delta TB}{\Delta A}$$

and

$$MC = \frac{\text{Change in total cost}}{\text{Change in activity}} = \frac{\Delta TC}{\Delta A}$$

where the symbol "Δ" means "the change in" and A denotes the level of an activity. Since "marginal" variables measure rates of change in corresponding "total" variables, marginal benefit and marginal cost are also *slopes* of total benefit and total cost curves, respectively.

The two panels in Figure 3.2 show how the total curves in Figure 3.1 are related to their respective marginal curves. Panel A in Figure 3.2 illustrates the procedure for measuring slopes of total curves at various points or levels of activity. Recall from your high school math classes or a pre-calculus course in college that the slope of a curve at any particular point can be measured by first constructing a line tangent to the curve at the point of measure and then computing the slope of this tangent line by dividing the "rise" by the "run" of the tangent line.[3] Consider, for example, the slope of *TB* at point *C* in Panel A. The tangent line at point *C* rises by 640 units (dollars) over a 100-unit run, and total benefit's slope at point *C* is $6.40 (= $640/100). Thus the marginal benefit of the 200th unit of activity is

---

[3]When a line is tangent to a curve, it touches the curve at only one point. For smooth, continuous curves, only one line can be drawn tangent to the curve at a single point. Consequently, the slope of a curve at a point is unique and equal to the slope of the tangent line at that point. The algebraic sign of the slope indicates whether the variables on the vertical and horizontal axes are directly related (a positive algebraic slope) or inversely related (a negative algebraic slope). For a concise review of measuring and interpreting slopes of curves, see "Review of Fundamental Mathematics" in the *Student Workbook* that accompanies this text.

FIGURE 3.2
Relating Marginals to Totals

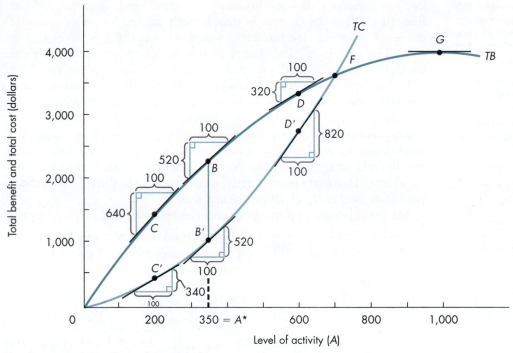

Panel A — Measuring slopes along TB and TC

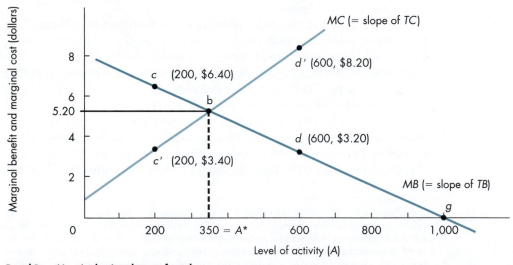

Panel B — Marginals give slopes of totals

$6.40, which means adding the 200th unit of activity (going from 199 to 200 units) causes total benefit to rise by $6.40.[4]

You should understand that the value of marginal benefit also tells you that subtracting the 200th unit (going from 200 to 199 units) causes total benefit to *fall* by $6.40. Because the slope of *TB* at point *C* is $6.40 per unit change in activity, marginal benefit at point *c* in Panel B is $6.40. You can verify that the same relation holds for the rest of the points shown on total benefit (*B*, *D*, and *G*), as well as for the points shown on total cost (*C'*, *B'*, and *D'*). We summarize this important discussion in a principle:

Principle Marginal benefit (marginal cost) is the change in total benefit (total cost) per unit change in the level of activity. The marginal benefit (marginal cost) of a particular unit of activity can be measured by the slope of the line tangent to the total benefit (total cost) curve at that point of activity.

At this point, you might be concerned that constructing tangent lines and measuring slopes of the tangent lines presents a tedious and imprecise method of finding marginal benefit and marginal cost curves. As you will see, the marginal benefit and marginal cost curves used in later chapters are obtained without drawing tangent lines. It is quite useful, nonetheless, for you to be able to visualize a series of tangent lines along total benefit and total cost curves in order to see why marginal benefit and marginal cost curves, respectively, are rising, falling, or even flat. Even if you don't know the *numerical* values of the slopes at points *C*, *B*, *D*, and *F* in Figure 3.2, you can still determine that marginal benefit in Panel B must slope downward because, as you can tell by looking, the tangent lines along *TB* get flatter (slopes get smaller) as the activity increases. Marginal cost, on the other hand, must be increasing in Panel B because, as you can tell by looking, its tangent lines get steeper (slope is getting larger) as the activity increases.

Finding Optimal Activity Levels with Marginal Analysis

As we stated earlier, the method of marginal analysis involves comparing marginal benefit and marginal cost to see if net benefit can be increased by making an incremental change in activity level. We can now demonstrate exactly how this works using the marginal benefit and marginal cost curves in Panel B of Figure 3.2. Let's suppose the decision maker is currently undertaking 199 units of activity in Panel B and wants to decide whether an incremental change in activity can cause net benefit to rise. Adding the 200th unit of activity will cause both total benefit and total cost to rise. As you can tell from points *c* and *c'* in Panel B, *TB* increases by more than *TC* increases ($6.40 is a larger increase than $3.40). Consequently, increasing activity from 199 to 200 units will cause net benefit to rise by

---

[4]When interpreting numerical values for marginal benefit and marginal cost, remember that the values refer to a particular unit of activity. In this example, marginal benefit equals $6.40 for the 200th unit. Strictly speaking, it is incorrect, and sometimes confusing, to say "marginal cost is $6.40 for 200 units." At 200 units of activity, the marginal benefit is $6.40 *for the last unit of activity undertaken* (i.e., the 200th unit).

FIGURE 3.3

Using Marginal Analysis to Find A^*

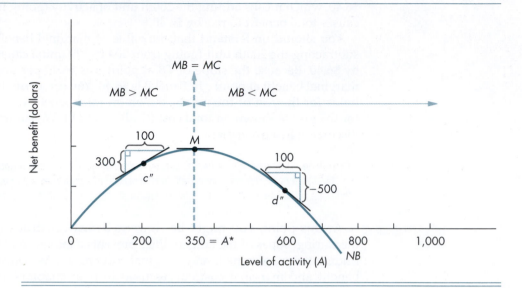

$3 (= \$6.40 - \$3.40)$. Notice in Figure 3.3 that, at 200 units of activity (point c''), net benefit is rising at a rate of $3 (= \$300/100)$ per unit increase in activity, as it must since MB equals \$6.40 and MC equals \$3.40.

After increasing the activity to 200 units, the decision maker then reevaluates benefits and costs at the margin to see whether another incremental increase in activity is warranted. In this situation, for the 201st unit of activity, the decision maker once again discovers that MB is greater than MC, which indicates the activity should be further increased. This incremental adjustment process continues until marginal benefit and marginal cost are exactly equal at point M ($A^* = 350$). As a practical matter, the decision maker can make a single adjustment to reach equilibrium, jumping from 199 units to 350 units in one adjustment of A, or make a series of smaller adjustments until MB equals MC at 350 units of activity. In any case, the number of adjustments made to reach A^* does not, of course, alter the optimal decision or the value of net benefit at its maximum point.

Now let's start from a position of too much activity instead of beginning with too little activity. Suppose the decision maker begins at 600 units of activity, which you can tell is too much activity by looking at the NB curve (in either Figure 3.1 or 3.3). Subtracting the 600th unit of activity will cause both total benefit and total cost to fall. As you can tell from points d and d' in Panel B of Figure 3.2, TC decreases by more than TB decreases (\$8.20 is a larger decrease than \$3.20). Consequently, reducing activity from 600 to 599 units will cause net benefit to rise by $5 (= \$8.20 - \$3.20)$. You can now verify in Figure 3.3 that at 600 units of activity (point d'') net benefit is rising at a rate of \$5 per unit *decrease* in activity. Because MC is still greater than MB at 599 units, the decision maker would continue reducing activity until MB exactly equals MC at 350 units (point M).

TABLE 3.1
Marginal Analysis Decision Rules

	$MB > MC$	$MB < MC$
Increase activity	NB rises	NB falls
Decrease activity	NB falls	NB rises

Table 3.1 summarizes the logic of marginal analysis by presenting the relation between marginal benefit, marginal cost, and net benefit set forth in the previous discussion and shown in Figure 3.3. We now summarize in the following principle the logic of marginal analysis for unconstrained maximization problems in which the choice variable is continuous:

Principle If, at a given level of activity, a small increase or decrease in activity causes net benefit to increase, then this level of the activity is not optimal. The activity must then be increased (if marginal benefit exceeds marginal cost) or decreased (if marginal cost exceeds marginal benefit) to reach the highest net benefit. The optimal level of the activity—the level that maximizes net benefit—is attained when no further increases in net benefit are possible for any changes in the activity, which occurs at the activity level for which marginal benefit equals marginal cost: $MB = MC$.

While the preceding discussion of unconstrained optimization has allowed only one activity or choice variable to influence net benefit, sometimes managers will need to choose the levels of two or more variables. As it turns out, when decision makers wish to maximize the net benefit from several activities, precisely the same principle applies: The firm maximizes net benefit when the marginal benefit from each activity equals the marginal cost of that activity. The problem is somewhat more complicated mathematically because the manager will have to equate marginal benefits and marginal costs for all of the activities *simultaneously*. For example, if the decision maker chooses the levels of two activities A and B to maximize net benefit, then the values for A and B must satisfy two conditions at once: $MB_A = MC_A$ and $MB_B = MC_B$. As it happens in this text, all the unconstrained maximization problems involve just one choice variable or activity.

Now try Technical Problems 3–5.

Maximization with Discrete Choice Variables

In the preceding analysis, the choice variable or activity level was a continuous variable. When a choice variable can vary only discretely, the logic of marginal analysis applies in exactly the same manner as when the choice variable is continuous. However, when choice variables are discrete, decision makers will not usually be able to adjust the level of activity to the point where marginal benefit exactly equals marginal cost. To make optimal decisions for discrete choice variables, decision makers must increase activity until the *last* level of activity is reached for which marginal benefit exceeds marginal cost. We can explain this rule for discrete choice variables by referring to Table 3.2, which shows a schedule of total benefits and total costs for various levels of some activity, A, expressed in integers between 0 and 8.

TABLE 3.2

Optimization with a Discrete Choice Variable

(1) Level of activity (A)	(2) Total benefit of activity (TB)	(3) Total cost of activity (TC)	(4) Net benefit of activity (NB)	(5) Marginal benefit (MB)	(6) Marginal cost (MC)
0	$ 0	$ 0	$ 0	—	—
1	16	2	14	16	2
2	30	6	24	14	4
3	40	11	29	10	5
4	48	20	28	8	9
5	54	30	24	6	10
6	58	45	13	4	15
7	61	61	0	3	16
8	63	80	−17	2	19

Let's suppose the decision maker is currently doing none of the activities and wants to decide whether to undertake the first unit of activity. The marginal benefit of the first unit of the activity is $16, and the marginal cost is $2. Undertaking the first unit of activity adds $16 to total benefit and only $2 to total cost, so net benefit rises by $14 (from $0 to $14). The decision maker would choose to undertake the first unit of activity to gain a higher net benefit. Applying this reasoning to the second and third units of activity leads again to a decision to undertake more activity. Beyond the third unit, however, marginal cost exceeds marginal benefit for additional units of activity, so no further increase beyond three units of activity will add to net benefit. As you can see, the optimal level of the activity is three units because the net benefit associated with three units ($29) is higher than for any other level of activity. These results are summarized in the following principle:

> **Principle** When a decision maker faces an unconstrained maximization problem and must choose among discrete levels of an activity, the activity should be increased if $MB > MC$ and decreased if $MB < MC$. The optimal level of activity is reached—net benefit is maximized—when the level of activity is the last level for which marginal benefit exceeds marginal cost.

Before moving ahead, we would like to point out that this principle *cannot* be interpreted to mean "choose the activity level where MB and MC are as close to equal as possible." To see why this interpretation can lead to the wrong decision, consider the fourth unit of activity in Table 3.2. At four units of activity, MB (= $8) is much closer to equality with MC (= $9) than at the optimal level of activity, where MB (= $10) is $5 larger than MC (= $5). Now you can see why the rule for discrete choice variables cannot be interpreted to mean "get MB as close to MC as possible."

Now try Technical Problem 6.

Sunk Costs, Fixed Costs, and Average Costs Are Irrelevant

sunk costs
Costs that have previously been paid and cannot be recovered.

In our discussion of optimization problems, we never mentioned sunk costs or fixed costs. **Sunk costs** are costs that have previously been paid and cannot be recovered. **Fixed costs** are costs that are constant and must be paid no matter what level of an activity is chosen. Such costs are totally irrelevant in decision making. They either have already been paid and cannot be recovered, as in the case of sunk costs, or must be paid no matter what a manager or any other decision maker decides to do, as in the case of fixed costs. In either case, the *only* relevant decision variables—marginal cost and marginal revenue—are in no way affected by the levels of either sunk or fixed costs.

fixed costs
Costs are constant and must be paid no matter what level of the activity is chosen.

Suppose you head your company's advertising department and you have just paid $2 million to an advertising firm for developing and producing a 30-second television ad, which you plan to air next quarter on broadcast television networks nationwide. The $2 million one-time payment gives your company full ownership of the 30-second ad, and your company can run the ad as many times as it wishes without making any further payments to the advertising firm for its use. Under these circumstances, the $2 million payment is a sunk cost because it has already been paid and cannot be recovered, even if your firm decides not to use the ad after all.

To decide how many times to run the ad next quarter, you call a meeting of your company's advertising department. At the meeting, the company's media buyer informs you that 30-second television spots during *American Idol* will cost $250,000 per spot. The marketing research experts at the meeting predict that the 24th time the ad runs it will generate $270,000 of additional sales, while running it a 25th time will increase sales by $210,000. Using the logic of marginal analysis, the marketing team decides running the new ad 24 times next quarter is optimal because the 24th showing of the ad is the last showing for which the marginal benefit exceeds the marginal cost of showing the ad:

$$MB = \$270,000 > 250,000 = MC$$

It would be a mistake to go beyond 24 showings because the 25th showing would decrease net benefit; the change in net benefit would be −$40,000 (= $210,000 − $250,000).

Two days after this meeting, you learn about a serious accounting error: Your company actually paid $3 million to the advertising firm for developing and producing your company's new television ad, not $2 million as originally reported. As you consider how to handle this new information, you realize that you don't need to call another meeting of the marketing department to reconsider its decision about running the ad 24 times next quarter. Because the amount paid to the advertising firm is a sunk cost, it doesn't affect either the marginal benefit or the marginal cost of running the ad one more time. The optimal number of times to run the ad is 24 times no matter how much the company paid in the past to obtain the ad.

Converting this example to a fixed cost, suppose that two days after your meeting you find out that, instead of making a sunk payment to buy the ad, your company instead decided to sign a 30-month contract leasing the rights to use the television ad for a monthly lease payment of $10,000. This amount is a fixed payment in each of the 30 months and must be paid no matter how many times your company decides to run the ad, even if it chooses never to run the ad. Do you need to call another meeting of the marketing department to recalculate the optimal number of times to run the ad during *American Idol*? As before, no new decision needs to be made. Because the fixed monthly loan payment does not change the predicted gain in sales (*MB*) or the extra cost of running the ad (*MC*), the optimal number of times to run the ad remains 24 times.

While you should now understand that things over which you have no control should not affect decisions, some economic experiments do, surprisingly, find that many people fail to ignore fixed or sunk costs when making decisions. They say things such as, "I've already got so much invested in this project, I have to go on with it." As you are aware, they should weigh the costs and benefits of going on before doing so. Then, if the benefits are greater than the *additional* costs, they should go on; if the *additional* costs are greater than the benefits, they should not go on. As Illustration 3.1 shows, failing to ignore fixed or sunk costs is a bad policy even in everyday decision making.

Another type of cost that should be ignored in finding the optimal level of an activity is the *average* or *unit cost* of the activity. **Average (or unit) cost** is the cost per unit of activity, computed by dividing total cost by the number of units of activity. In order to make optimal decisions, decision makers should not be concerned about whether their decision will push average costs up or down. The reason for ignoring average cost is quite simple: The impact on net benefit of making an incremental change in activity depends only on *marginal* benefit and *marginal* cost ($\Delta NB = MB - MC$), not on *average* benefit or *average* cost. In other words, optimal decisions are made at the margin, not "on the average."

To illustrate this point, consider the decision in Table 3.2 once again. The average cost of two units of activity is $3 (= $6/2) and average cost for three units of activity is $3.67 (= $11/3). Recall from our earlier discussion, the decision to undertake the third unit of activity is made because the marginal benefit exceeds the marginal cost ($10 > $5), and net benefit rises. It is completely irrelevant that the average cost of three units of activity is higher than the average cost of two units of activity. Alternatively, a decision maker should not decrease activity from three units to two units just to achieve a reduction in average cost from $3.67 to $3 per unit of activity; such a decision would cause net benefit to fall from $29 to $24. The following principle summarizes the role of sunk, fixed, and average costs in making optimal decisions:

average (unit) cost
Cost per unit of activity computed by dividing total cost by the number of units of activity.

Now try Technical Problem 7.

> **Principle**   Decision makers wishing to maximize the net benefit of an activity should ignore any sunk costs, any fixed costs, and the average costs associated with the activity because none of these costs affect the marginal cost of the activity and so are irrelevant for making optimal decisions.

3.3 CONSTRAINED OPTIMIZATION

On many occasions a manager will face situations in which the choice of activity levels is constrained by the circumstances surrounding the maximization or minimization problem. These constrained optimization problems can be solved, as in the case of unconstrained maximization, using the logic of marginal analysis. As noted in Section 3.1, even though constrained optimization problems can be either maximization or minimization problems, the optimization rule is the same for both types.

A crucial concept for solving constrained optimization problems is the concept of marginal benefit per dollar spent on an activity. Before you can understand how to solve constrained optimization problems, you must first understand how to interpret the ratio of the marginal benefit of an activity divided by the price of the activity.

Marginal Benefit per Dollar Spent on an Activity

Retailers frequently advertise that their products give "more value for your money." People don't usually interpret this as meaning the best product in its class or the one with the highest value. Neither do they interpret it as meaning the cheapest. The advertiser wants to get across the message that customers will get more for their money or more value for each dollar spent on the product. When product rating services (such as *Consumer Reports*) rate a product a "best buy," they don't mean it is the best product or the cheapest; they mean that consumers will get more value per dollar spent on that product. When firms want to fill a position, they don't necessarily hire the person who would be the most productive in the job—that person may cost too much. Neither do they necessarily hire the person who would work for the lowest wages—that person may not be very productive. They want the employee who can do the job and give the highest productivity for the wages paid.

In these examples, phrases such as "most value for your money," "best buy," and "greatest bang per buck" mean that a particular activity yields the highest marginal benefit per dollar spent. To illustrate this concept, suppose you are the office manager for an expanding law firm and you find that you need an extra copy machine in the office—the one copier you have is being overworked. You shop around and find three brands of office copy machines (brands *A*, *B*, and *C*) that have virtually identical features. The three brands do differ, however, in price and in the number of copies the machines will make before they wear out. Brand *A*'s copy machine costs $2,500 and will produce about 500,000 copies before it wears out. The marginal benefit of this machine is 500,000 ($MB_A = 500,000$) since the machine provides the law office with the ability to produce 500,000 additional copies. To find the marginal benefit *per dollar spent* on copy machine *A*, marginal benefit is divided by price ($P_A = 2,500$):

$$MB_A/P_A = 500,000 \text{ copies}/2,500 \text{ dollars}$$
$$= 200 \text{ copies}/\text{dollar}$$

You get 200 copies for each of the dollars spent to purchase copy machine A.

Now compare machine A with machine B, which will produce 600,000 copies and costs $4,000. The marginal benefit is greater, but so is the price. To determine how "good a deal" you get with machine B, compute the marginal benefit per dollar spent on machine B:

$$MB_B/P_B = 600,000 \text{ copies}/4,000 \text{ dollars}$$
$$= 150 \text{ copies}/\text{dollar}$$

Even though machine B provides a higher marginal benefit, its marginal benefit per dollar spent is lower than that for machine A. Machine A is a better deal than machine B because it yields higher marginal benefit per dollar. The third copy machine produces 580,000 copies over its useful life and costs $2,600. Machine C is neither the best machine (580,000 < 600,000 copies) nor is it the cheapest machine ($2,600 > $2,500), but of the three machines, machine C provides the greatest marginal benefit per dollar spent:

$$MB_C/P_C = 580,000 \text{ copies}/2,600 \text{ dollars}$$
$$= 223 \text{ copies}/\text{dollar}$$

On a bang per buck basis, you would rank machine C first, machine A second, and machine B third.

When choosing among different activities, a decision maker compares the marginal benefits per dollar spent on each of the activities. Marginal benefit (the "bang"), *by itself,* does not provide sufficient information for decision-making purposes. Price (the "buck"), *by itself,* does not provide sufficient information for making decisions. It is marginal benefit per dollar spent (the "bang per buck") that matters in decision making.

Now try Technical
Problem 8.

Constrained Maximization

In the general constrained maximization problem, a manager must choose the levels of two or more activities in order to maximize a total benefit (objective) function subject to a constraint in the form of a budget that restricts the amount that can be spent.[5] Consider a situation in which there are two activities, A and B. Each unit of activity A costs $4 to undertake, and each unit of activity B costs $2 to undertake. The manager faces a constraint that allows a total expenditure of only $100 on activities A and B combined. The manager wishes to allocate $100 between activities A and B so that the combined total benefit from both activities is maximized.

The manager is currently choosing 20 units of activity A and 10 units of activity B. The constraint is met for the combination $20A$ and $10B$ since ($4 × 20) + ($2 × 10) = $100. For this combination of activities, suppose that the marginal benefit of

---

[5]It may look like constrained maximization problems no longer use net benefit as the objective function to be maximized. Note, however, that maximizing total benefit while total cost must remain constant in order to meet a budget constraint does indeed result in the maximum possible amount of net benefit for a given level of total cost.

the last unit of activity A is 40 units of additional benefit and the marginal benefit of the last unit of B is 10 units of additional benefit. In this situation, the marginal benefit per dollar spent on activity A exceeds the marginal benefit per dollar spent on activity B:

$$\frac{MB_A}{P_A} = \frac{40}{4} = 10 > 5 = \frac{10}{2} = \frac{MB_B}{P_B}$$

Spending an additional dollar on activity A increases total benefit by 10 units, while spending an additional dollar on activity B increases total benefit by 5 units. Because the marginal benefit per dollar spent is greater for activity A, it provides "more bang per buck" or is a better deal at this combination of activities.

To take advantage of this fact, the manager can increase activity A by one unit and decrease activity B by two units (now, $A = 21$ and $B = 8$). This combination of activities still costs $100 [($4 \times 21) + ($2 \times 8) = $100]$. Purchasing one more unit of activity A causes total benefit to rise by 40 units, while purchasing two less units of activity B causes total benefit to fall by 20 units. The combined total benefit from activities A and B *rises* by 20 units ($= 40 - 20$) *and* the new combination of activities ($A = 21$ and $B = 8$) costs the same amount, $100, as the old combination. Total benefit rises without spending any more than $100 on the activities.

Naturally, the manager will continue to increase spending on activity A and reduce spending on activity B as long as MB_A/P_A exceeds MB_B/P_B. In most situations, the marginal benefit of an activity declines as the activity increases.[6] Consequently, as activity A is increased, MB_A gets smaller. As activity B is decreased, MB_B gets larger. Thus as spending on A rises and spending on B falls, MB_A/P_A falls and MB_B/P_B rises. A point is eventually reached at which activity A is no longer a better deal than activity B; that is, MB_A/P_A equals MB_B/P_B. At this point, total benefit is maximized subject to the constraint that only $100 is spent on the two activities.

If the original allocation of spending on activities A and B had been one, where

$$\frac{MB_A}{P_A} < \frac{MB_B}{P_B}$$

the manager would recognize that activity B is the better deal. In this case, total benefit could be increased by spending more on activity B and less on activity A while maintaining the $100 budget. Activity B would be increased by two units for every one-unit decrease in activity A (in order to satisfy the

---

[6]Decreasing marginal benefit is quite common. As you drink several cans of Coke in succession, you get ever smaller amounts of additional satisfaction from successive cans. As you continue studying for an exam, each additional hour of study increases your expected exam grade by ever smaller amounts. In such cases, marginal benefit is inversely related to the level of the activity. Increasing the activity causes marginal benefit to fall, and decreasing the activity level causes marginal benefit to rise.

$100 spending constraint) until the marginal benefit per dollar spent is equal for both activities:

$$\frac{MB_A}{P_A} = \frac{MB_B}{P_B}$$

If there are more than two activities in the objective function, the condition is expanded to require that the marginal benefit per dollar spent be equal for all activities.

Now try Technical
Problems 9–10.

Principle To maximize total benefits subject to a constraint on the levels of activities, choose the level of each activity so that the marginal benefit per dollar spent is equal for all activities

$$\frac{MB_A}{P_A} = \frac{MB_B}{P_B} = \frac{MB_C}{P_C} = \cdots = \frac{MB_Z}{P_Z}$$

and at the same time, the chosen level of activities must also satisfy the constraint.

Optimal Advertising Expenditures: An Example of Constrained Maximization

To illustrate how a firm can use the technique of constrained maximization to allocate its advertising budget, suppose a manager of a small retail firm wants to maximize the effectiveness (in total sales) of the firm's weekly advertising budget of $2,000. The manager has the option of advertising on the local television station or on the local AM radio station. As a class project, a marketing class at a nearby college estimated the impact on the retailer's sales of varying levels of advertising in the two different media. The manager wants to maximize the number of units sold; thus the total benefit is measured by the total number of units sold. The estimates of the *increases* in weekly sales (the marginal benefits) from increasing the levels of advertising on television and radio are given in columns 2 and 4 below:

(1) Number of ads	(2) MB_{TV}	(3) $\dfrac{MB_{TV}}{P_{TV}}$	(4) MB_{radio}	(5) $\dfrac{MB_{radio}}{P_{radio}}$
1	400	1.0	360	1.2
2	300	0.75	270	0.9
3	280	0.7	240	0.8
4	260	0.65	225	0.75
5	240	0.6	150	0.5
6	200	0.5	120	0.4

Television ads are more "powerful" than radio ads in the sense that the marginal benefits from additional TV ads tend to be larger than those for more radio ads. However, since the manager is constrained by the limited advertising budget, the relevant measure is not simply marginal benefit but, rather, marginal benefit per dollar spent on advertising. The price of television ads is $400 per ad, and the price of radio ads is $300 per ad. Although the first TV ad dominates the first radio ad in terms of its marginal benefit (increased sales), the marginal benefit per dollar's worth of expenditure for the first radio ad is greater than that for the first television ad:

	Marginal benefit/price	
	Television	Radio
Ad 1	400/400 = 1.00	360/300 = 1.2

This indicates that sales rise by 1 unit per dollar spent on the first television ad and 1.2 units on the first radio ad. Therefore, when the manager is allocating the budget, the first ad she selects will be a radio ad—the activity with the larger marginal benefit per dollar spent. Following the same rule and using the MB/P values in columns 3 and 5 above, the $2,000 advertising budget would be allocated as follows:

Decision	MB/P	Ranking of MB/P	Cumulative expenditures
Buy radio ad 1	360/300 = 1.20	1	$ 300
Buy TV ad 1	400/400 = 1.00	2	700
Buy radio ad 2	270/300 = 0.90	3	1,000
Buy radio ad 3	240/300 = 0.80	4	1,300
Buy TV ad 2	300/400 = 0.75⎤		1,700
Buy radio ad 4	225/300 = 0.75⎦	5 (tie)	2,000

By selecting two television ads and four radio ads, the manager of the firm has maximized sales subject to the constraint that only $2,000 can be spent on advertising activity. Note that for the optimal levels of television and radio ads (two TV and four radio):

$$\frac{MB_{TV}}{P_{TV}} = \frac{MB_{radio}}{P_{radio}} = 0.75$$

Now try Technical Problems 11–12.

The fact that the preceding application used artificially simplistic numbers shouldn't make you think that the problem is artificial. If we add a few zeros to the prices of TV and radio ads, we have the real-world situation faced by advertisers.

Constrained Minimization

Constrained minimization problems involve minimizing a total cost function (the objective function) subject to a constraint that the levels of activities be chosen such that a given level of total benefit is achieved. Consider a manager who must minimize the total cost of two activities, A and B, subject to the constraint that 3,000 units of benefit are to be generated by those activities. The price of activity A is $5 per unit and the price of activity B is $20 per unit. Suppose the manager is currently using 100 units of activity A and 60 units of activity B and this combination of activity generates total benefit equal to 3,000. At this combination of activities, the marginal benefit of the last unit of activity A is 30 and the marginal benefit of

ILLUSTRATION 3.2

Seattle Seahawks Win on "Bang Per Buck" Defense

Behind every professional sports team, a team of business decision makers is constantly at work—there is no off-season for the business team—trying to figure out how to put together the most profitable team of players. In the NFL, the team-building process is a *constrained* optimization problem because the football league imposes restrictions on the amount each team can spend on players in a season, as well as the number of players the team can carry on its roster. Currently, NFL teams are limited to 53 players and a salary cap of $85 million per season. While teams can, and do, structure cash bonuses to players in ways that allow them to exceed the salary caps in any single year, the NFL spending constraint nonetheless restricts the total amount a team can spend on its players. Based on what you have learned in this chapter about constrained optimization, it should come as no surprise to you that, in the business of sports, finding and keeping players who can deliver the greatest bang for the buck may be the most important game a team must play. History has shown that most teams making it to the Super Bowl have played the "bang for the buck" game very well.

To see how personnel directors of NFL teams follow the principles of constrained maximization in choosing their teams' rosters, we can look at the story of the Seattle Seahawks, who played (and lost to) the Pittsburgh Steelers in Super Bowl XL. According to a recent article in *The Wall Street Journal*, the Seahawks' personnel director, Tim Ruskell, who enjoyed wide acclaim for building the highly regarded defenses at Tampa Bay and Atlanta, faced a particularly harsh salary-cap constraint in Seattle for the 2005 football season. The Seahawks' salary cap in 2005 was penalized by $18 million of "dead money"—the term used for money paid by previous contract to players no longer on the team—so Ruskell began with only $67 million to spend on players. Making matters even worse for the team's chief business decision maker was the fact that Seattle had signed giant contracts, even by NFL standards, to keep its biggest stars on offense. Obviously, this left Ruskell with very little money to spend on building the Seahawks' defense. Compared with its Super Bowl rival, Seattle spent $11 million less on defense than did the Steelers. Ruskell's strategy for hiring defensive players, then, had to be extremely effective if Seattle was to have any chance of going to the Super Bowl in 2005.

The way that Ruskell built Seattle's defense, subject to a very tight spending constraint, drew high praise from others in the league: "They did it (built a defense) without breaking the bank at Monte Carlo, and I think that's extremely impressive," remarked Gil Brandt, a former personnel director for the Dallas Cowboys.[a] As you know from our discussion in this chapter, Ruskell must have been very successful at finding defensive players who could deliver the highest possible marginal benefits per dollar spent. To accomplish this, he recruited only inexpensive draft picks and young free agents, who were also likely to play with "exuberance" and perform defensive tasks well enough to get to the Super Bowl. We must stress that Ruskell's strategy depended crucially on *both* the numerator and denominator in the *MB/MC* ratio. He understood that simply hiring the cheapest players would not produce a Super Bowl team. Team scouts had to find players who would also deliver high marginal benefits to the team's defensive squad by making lots of tackles and intercepting lots of passes. Perhaps the best example of Ruskell's success at getting the most "bang for the buck" in 2005 was Lofa Tatapu, a rookie linebacker. Tatapu, who was thought by many team scouts to be too small to be a great linebacker, became a star defensive player for Seattle and cost the team only $230,000—one-tenth the amount paid on average for linebackers in the NFL.

As you can see from this Illustration, making optimal constrained maximization decisions in practice takes not only skill and experience, it sometimes involves a bit of luck! History shows, however, that NFL personnel directors who spend their salary caps to get either the very best players (the greatest bang) or the very cheapest players (the smallest buck), don't usually make it to the Super Bowl. Thus, on Super Bowl game day, fans can generally expect to see the two NFL teams with the highest overall MB/MC ratios. Of course *winning* the Super Bowl is just a betting matter.

[a]Gil Brandt as quoted in Walker, "Holding the Line."

the last unit of activity B is 60. In this situation, the marginal benefit per dollar spent on activity A exceeds the marginal benefit per dollar spent on activity B:

$$\frac{MB_A}{P_A} = \frac{30}{5} = 6 > 3 = \frac{60}{20} = \frac{MB_B}{P_B}$$

Because the marginal benefit per dollar spent is greater for activity A than for activity B, activity A gives "more for the money."

To take advantage of activity A, the manager can reduce activity B by one unit, causing total benefit to fall by 60 units and reducing cost by \$20. To hold total benefit constant, the 60 units of lost benefit can be made up by increasing activity A by two units with a marginal benefit of 30 each. The two additional units of activity A cause total cost to rise by \$10. By reducing activity B by one unit and increasing activity A by two units, the manager *reduces* total cost by \$10 (= \$20 − \$10) without reducing total benefit.

As long as $MB_A/P_A > MB_B/P_B$, the manager will continue to increase activity A and decrease activity B at the rate that holds TB constant until

$$\frac{MB_A}{P_A} = \frac{MB_B}{P_B}$$

If there are more than two activities in the objective function, the condition is expanded to require that the marginal benefit per dollar spent be equal for all activities.

Principle   In order to minimize total costs subject to a constraint on the levels of activities, choose the level of each activity so that the marginal benefit per dollar spent is equal for all activities

$$\frac{MB_A}{P_A} = \frac{MB_B}{P_B} = \frac{MB_C}{P_C} = \cdots = \frac{MB_Z}{P_Z}$$

and at the same time, the chosen level of activities must also satisfy the constraint.

Now try Technical Problem 13.

As you can see, this is the same condition that must be met in the case of constrained maximization.

3.4 SUMMARY

- Formulating an optimization problem involves specifying three things: (1) the objective function to be either maximized or minimized, (2) the activities or choice variables that determine the value of the objective function, and (3) any constraints that may restrict the range of values that the choice variables may take. Choice variables determine the value of the objective function and may be either discrete or continuous. A discrete choice variable can take on only specified integer values. A continuous choice variable can take on any value between two end points. Marginal analysis is an analytical technique for solving optimization problems by changing the value of a choice variable by a small

amount to see if the objective function can be further increased (in the case of maximization problems) or further decreased (in the case of minimization problems). (*LO1*)

- Net benefit from an activity (NB) is the difference between total benefit (TB) and total cost (TC) for the activity: $NB = TB - TC$. The net benefit function is the objective function to be maximized in unconstrained maximization problems. The optimal level of the activity, A^*, is the level of activity that maximizes net benefit. Marginal benefit (marginal cost) is the change in total benefit (total cost) per unit change in the level of activity. The marginal benefit (marginal cost) of a particular unit of activity can be measured by the slope of the line tangent to the total benefit (total cost) curve at that point of activity. The optimal level of the activity is attained when no further increases in net benefit are possible for any changes in the activity. This point occurs at the activity level for which marginal benefit equals marginal cost: $MB = MC$. Sunk costs are costs that have previously been paid and cannot be recovered. Fixed costs are costs that are constant and must be paid no matter what level of activity is chosen. Average (or unit) cost is the cost per unit of activity. Decision makers should ignore any sunk costs, any fixed costs, and the average costs associated with the activity because they are irrelevant for making optimal decisions. (LO2)

■ The ratio of marginal benefit divided by the price of an activity (MB/P) tells the decision maker the additional benefit of that activity per additional dollar spent on that activity, sometimes referred to informally as "bang per buck." In constrained optimization problems, the ratios of marginal benefits to prices of the various activities are used by decision makers to determine how to allocate a fixed number of dollars among activities. To maximize or minimize an objective function subject to a constraint, the ratios of the marginal benefit to price must be equal for all activities. (LO3)

KEY TERMS

activities or choice variables

average (unit) cost

constrained optimization

continuous choice variables

discrete choice variables

fixed costs

marginal analysis

marginal benefit (MB)

marginal cost (MC)

maximization problem

minimization problem

net benefit

objective function

optimal level of activity

sunk costs

unconstrained optimization

TECHNICAL PROBLEMS

1. For each of the following decision-making problems, determine whether the problem involves constrained or unconstrained optimization; what the objective function is and, for each constrained problem, what the constraint is; and what the choice variables are.

   a. We have received a foundation grant to purchase new PCs for the staff. You decide what PCs to buy.

   b. We aren't earning enough profits. Your job is to redesign our advertising program and decide how much TV, direct-mail, and magazine advertising to use. Whatever we are doing now isn't working very well.

   c. We have to meet a production quota but think we are going to spend too much doing so. Your job is to reallocate the machinery, the number of workers, and the raw materials needed to meet the quota.

2. Refer to Figure 3.2 and answer the following questions:

   a. At 600 units of activity, marginal benefit is _____ (rising, constant, positive, negative) because the tangent line at D is sloping _____ (downward, upward).

   b. The marginal benefit of the 600th unit of activity is $_____. Explain how this value of marginal benefit can be computed.

   c. At 600 units of activity, decreasing the activity by one unit causes total benefit to _____ (increase, decrease) by $_____. At point D, total benefit changes at a rate _____ times as much as activity changes, and TB and A are moving in the _____ (same, opposite) direction, which means TB and A are _____ (directly, inversely) related.

   d. At 1,000 units of activity, marginal benefit is _____. Why?

   e. The marginal cost of the 600th unit of activity is $ _____. Explain how this value of marginal cost can be computed.

f. At 600 units of activity, decreasing the activity by one unit causes total cost to _____ (increase, decrease) by $_____. At point D', total cost changes at a rate _____ times as much as activity changes, and TC and A are moving in the _____ (same, opposite) direction, which means TC and A are _____ (directly, inversely) related.

g. Visually, the tangent line at point D appears to be _____ (flatter, steeper) than the tangent line at point D', which means that _____ (NB, TB, TC, MB, MC) is larger than _____ (NB, TB, TC, MB, MC).

h. Because point D lies above point D', _____ (NB, TB, TC, MB, MC) is larger than _____ (NB, TB, TC, MB, MC), which means that _____ (NB, TB, TC, MB, MC) is _____ (rising, falling, constant, positive, negative, zero).

3. Fill in the blanks below. In an unconstrained maximization problem:

a. An activity should be increased if _____ exceeds _____.

b. An activity should be decreased if _____ exceeds _____.

c. The optimal level of activity occurs at the activity level for which _____ equals _____.

d. At the optimal level of activity, _____ is maximized, and the slope of _____ equals the slope of _____.

e. If total cost is falling faster than total benefit is falling, the activity should be _____.

f. If total benefit is rising at the same rate that total cost is rising, the decision maker should _____.

g. If net benefit is rising, then total benefit must be rising at a rate _____ (greater than, less than, equal to) the rate at which total cost is _____ (rising, falling).

4. Use the graph below to answer the following questions:

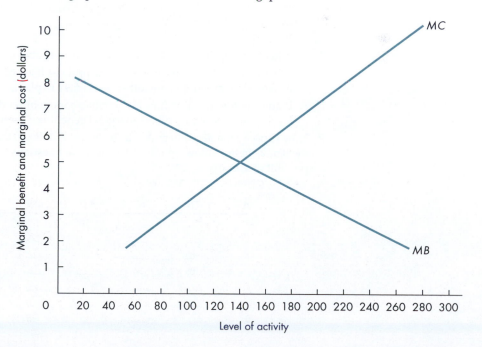

a. At 60 units of the activity, marginal benefit is $_____ and marginal cost is $_____.

b. Adding the 60th unit of the activity causes net benefit to _____ (increase, decrease) by $_____.

c. At 220 units of the activity, marginal benefit is $_____ and marginal cost is $_____.

d. Subtracting the 220th unit of the activity causes net benefit to _____ (increase, decrease) by $_____.

e. The optimal level of the activity is _____ units. At the optimal level of the activity, marginal benefit is $_____ and marginal cost is $_____.

5. Fill in the blanks in the following statement:

If marginal benefit exceeds marginal cost, then increasing the level of activity by one unit _____ (increases, decreases) _____ (total, marginal, net) benefit by more than it _____ (increases, decreases) _____ (total, marginal) cost. Therefore, _____ (increasing, decreasing) the level of activity by one unit must increase net benefit. The manager should continue to _____ (increase, decrease) the level of activity until marginal benefit and marginal cost are _____ (zero, equal).

6. Fill in the blanks in the following table to answer the questions below.

A	TB	TC	NB	MB	MC
0	$ 0	$__	$ 0		
1	__	__	27	$35	$__
2	65	__	__	__	10
3	85	30	__	__	__
4	__	__	51	__	14
5	__	60	__	8	__
6	__	__	__	5	20

a. What is the optimal level of activity in the table above?

b. What is the value of net benefit at the optimal level of activity? Can net benefit be increased by moving to any other level of A? Explain.

c. Using the numerical values in the table, comment on the statement, "The optimal level of activity occurs where marginal benefit is closest to marginal cost."

7. Now suppose the decision maker in Technical Problem 6 faces a fixed cost of $24. Fill in the blanks in the following table to answer the questions below. AC is the average cost per unit of activity.

A	TB	TC	NB	MB	MC	AC
0	$ 0	__	−$24			
1	__	__	3	$35	$__	$32
2	65	__	__	__	10	__
3	85	54	__	__	__	__
4	__	__	27	__	14	__
5	__	__	__	8	__	16.80
6	__	__	__	5	20	__

    a. How does adding $24 of fixed costs affect total cost? Net benefit?

    b. How does adding $24 of fixed cost affect marginal cost?

    c. Compared to A^* in Technical Problem 6, does adding $24 of fixed cost change the optimal level of activity? Why or why not?

    d. What advice can you give decision makers about the role of fixed costs in finding A^*?

    e. What level of activity minimizes average cost per unit of activity? Is this level also the optimal level of activity? Should it be? Explain.

    f. Suppose a government agency requires payment of a one-time, nonrefundable license fee of $100 to engage in activity A, and this license fee was paid last month. What kind of cost is this? How does this cost affect the decision maker's choice of activity level now? Explain.

8. You are interviewing three people for one sales job. On the basis of your experience and insight, you believe Jane can sell 600 units a day, Joe can sell 450 units a day, and Joan can sell 400 units a day. The daily salary each person is asking is as follows: Jane, $200; Joe, $150; and Joan, $100. How would you rank the three applicants?

9. Fill in the blanks. When choosing the levels of two activities, A and B, in order to maximize total benefits within a given budget:

    a. If at the given levels of A and B, MB/P of A is _____ MB/P of B, increasing A and decreasing B while holding expenditure constant will increase total benefits.

    b. If at the given levels of A and B, MB/P of A is _____ MB/P of B, increasing B and decreasing A while holding expenditure constant will increase total benefits.

    c. The optimal levels of A and B are the levels at which _____ equals _____.

10. A decision maker is choosing the levels of two activities, A and B, so as to maximize total benefits under a given budget. The prices and marginal benefits of the last units of A and B are denoted P_A, P_B, MB_A, and MB_B.

    a. If $P_A = \$20$, $P_B = \$15$, $MB_A = 400$, and $MB_B = 600$, what should the decision maker do?

    b. If $P_A = \$20$, $P_B = \$30$, $MB_A = 200$, and $MB_B = 300$, what should the decision maker do?

    c. If $P_A = \$20$, $P_B = \$40$, $MB_A = 300$, and $MB_B = 400$, how many units of A can be obtained if B is reduced by one unit? How much will benefits increase if this exchange is made?

    d. If the substitution in part *c* continues to equilibrium and MB_A falls to 250, what will MB_B be?

11. A decision maker wishes to maximize the total benefit associated with three activities, X, Y, and Z. The price per unit of activities X, Y, and Z is $1, $2, and $3, respectively. The following table gives the ratio of the marginal benefit to the price of the activities for various levels of each activity:

Level of activity	$\dfrac{MB_x}{P_x}$	$\dfrac{MB_y}{P_y}$	$\dfrac{MB_z}{P_z}$
1	10	22	14
2	9	18	12
3	8	12	10
4	7	10	9
5	6	6	8
6	5	4	6
7	4	2	4
8	3	1	2

a. If the decision maker chooses to use one unit of X, one unit of Y, and one unit of Z, the total benefit that results is $_____.

b. For the fourth unit of activity Y, each dollar spent increases total benefit by $_____. The fourth unit of activity Y increases total benefit by $_____.

c. Suppose the decision maker can spend a total of only $18 on the three activities. What is the optimal level of X, Y, and Z? Why is this combination optimal? Why is the combination 2X, 2Y, and 4Z not optimal?

d. Now suppose the decision maker has $33 to spend on the three activities. What is the optimal level of X, Y, and Z? If the decision maker has $35 to spend, what is the optimal combination? Explain.

12. Suppose a firm is considering two different activities, X and Y, which yield the total benefits presented in the schedule below. The price of X is $2 per unit, and the price of Y is $10 per unit.

Level of activity	Total benefit of activity X (TB_X)	Total benefit of activity Y (TB_Y)
0	$ 0	$ 0
1	30	100
2	54	190
3	72	270
4	84	340
5	92	400
6	98	450

a. The firm places a budget constraint of $26 on expenditures on activities X and Y. What are the levels of X and Y that maximize total benefit subject to the budget constraint?

b. What is the total benefit associated with the optimal levels of X and Y in part a?

c. Now let the budget constraint increase to $58. What are the optimal levels of X and Y now? What is the total benefit when the budget constraint is $58?

13. a. If, in a constrained minimization problem, $P_A = \$10$, $P_B = \$10$, $MB_A = 600$, and $MB_B = 300$ and one unit of B is taken away, how many units of A must be added to keep benefits constant?

b. If the substitution in part a continues to equilibrium, what will be the equilibrium relation between MB_A and MB_B?

APPLIED PROBLEMS

1. Using optimization theory, analyze the following quotations:

a. "The optimal number of traffic deaths in the United States is zero."

b. "Any pollution is too much pollution."

c. "We cannot pull U.S. troops out of Afghanistan. We have committed so much already."

d. "If Congress cuts out the International Space Station (ISS), we will have wasted all the resources that we have already spent on it. Therefore, we must continue funding the ISS."

e. "Since JetGreen Airways has experienced a 25 percent increase in its insurance premiums, the airline should increase the number of passengers it serves next quarter in order to spread the increase in premiums over a larger number of tickets."

2. Appalachian Coal Mining believes that it can increase labor productivity and, therefore, net revenue by reducing air pollution in its mines. It estimates that the marginal cost function for reducing pollution by installing additional capital equipment is

$$MC = 40P$$

where P represents a reduction of one unit of pollution in the mines. It also feels that for every unit of pollution reduction the marginal increase in revenue (MR) is

$$MR = 1,000 - 10P$$

How much pollution reduction should Appalachian Coal Mining undertake?

3. Two partners who own Progressive Business Solutions, which currently operates out of an office in a small town near Boston, just discovered a vacancy in an office building in downtown Boston. One of the partners favors moving downtown because she believes the additional business gained by moving downtown will exceed the higher rent at the downtown location plus the cost of making the move. The other partner at PBS opposes moving downtown. He argues, "We have already paid for office stationery, business cards, and a large sign that cannot be moved or sold. We have spent so much on our current office that we can't afford to waste this money by moving now." Evaluate the second partner's advice not to move downtown.

4. Twentyfirst Century Electronics has discovered a theft problem at its warehouse and has decided to hire security guards. The firm wants to hire the optimal number of security guards. The following table shows how the number of security guards affects the number of radios stolen per week.

Number of security guards	Number of radios stolen per week
0	50
1	30
2	20
3	14
4	8
5	6

a. If each security guard is paid $200 a week and the cost of a stolen radio is $25, how many security guards should the firm hire?

b. If the cost of a stolen radio is $25, what is the most the firm would be willing to pay to hire the first security guard?

c. If each security guard is paid $200 a week and the cost of a stolen radio is $50, how many security guards should the firm hire?

5. U.S. Supreme Court Justice Stephen Breyer's book *Breaking the Vicious Circle: Toward Effective Risk Regulation* examines government's role in controlling and managing the health risks society faces from exposure to environmental pollution. One major problem examined in the book is the cleanup of hazardous waste sites. Justice Breyer was extremely critical of policymakers who wish to see waste sites 100 percent clean.

    a. Explain, using the theory of optimization and a graph, the circumstances under which a waste site could be made "too clean." (Good answers are dispassionate and employ economic analysis.)

    b. Justice Breyer believes that society can enjoy virtually all the health benefits of cleaning up a waste site for only a "small fraction" of the total cost of completely cleaning a site. Using graphical analysis, illustrate this situation. (*Hint:* Draw *MB* and *MC* curves with shapes that specifically illustrate this situation.)

6. In Illustration 3.1, we noted that the rule for maximization set forth in the text contradicts some honored traditional principles such as "Never give up," "Anything worth doing is worth doing well," or "Waste not, want not." Explain the contradiction for each of these rules.

7. Janice Waller, the manager of the customer service department at First Bank of Jefferson County, can hire employees with a high school diploma for $20,000 annually and employees with a bachelor's degree for $30,000. She wants to maximize the number of customers served, given a fixed payroll. The following table shows how the total number of customers served varies with the number of employees:

Number of employees	Total number of customers served	
	High school diploma	Bachelor's degree
1	120	100
2	220	190
3	300	270
4	370	330
5	430	380
6	470	410

    a. If Ms. Waller has a payroll of $160,000, how should she allocate this budget in order to maximize the number of customers served?

    b. If she has a budget of $150,000 and currently hires three people with high school diplomas and three with bachelor's degrees, is she making the correct decision? Why or why not? If not, what should she do? (Assume she can hire part-time workers.)

    c. If her budget is increased to $240,000, how should she allocate this budget?

8. Bavarian Crystal Works designs and produces lead crystal wine decanters for export to international markets. The production manager of Bavarian Crystal Works estimates total and marginal production costs to be

$$TC = 10,000 + 40Q + 0.0025Q^2$$

and

$$MC = 40 + 0.005Q$$

where costs are measured in U.S. dollars and Q is the number of wine decanters produced annually. Because Bavarian Crystal Works is only one of many crystal producers in the world market, it can sell as many of the decanters as it wishes for $70 apiece. Total and marginal revenue are

$$TR = 70Q \quad \text{and} \quad MR = 70$$

where revenues are measured in U.S. dollars and Q is annual decanter production.

a. What is the optimal level of production of wine decanters? What is the marginal revenue from the last wine decanter sold?

b. What are the total revenue, total cost, and net benefit (profit) from selling the optimal number of wine decanters?

c. At the optimal level of production of decanters, an extra decanter can be sold for $70, thereby increasing total revenue by $70. Why does the manager of this firm *not* produce and sell one more unit?

9. Joy Land Toys, a toy manufacturer, is experiencing quality problems on its assembly line. The marketing division estimates that each defective toy that leaves the plant costs the firm $10, on average, for replacement or repair. The engineering department recommends hiring quality inspectors to sample for defective toys. In this way many quality problems can be caught and prevented before shipping. After visiting other companies, a management team derives the following schedule showing the approximate number of defective toys that would be produced for several levels of inspection:

Number of inspectors	Average number of defective toys (per day)
0	92
1	62
2	42
3	27
4	17
5	10
6	5

The daily wage of inspectors is $70.

a. How many inspectors should the firm hire?

b. What would your answer to *a* be if the wage rate is $90?

c. What if the average cost of a defective toy is $5 and the wage rate of inspectors is $70?

⊡ **MATHEMATICAL APPENDIX**   **A Brief Presentation of Optimization Theory**

Theory of Unconstrained Maximization

This section sets forth a mathematical analysis of unconstrained maximization. We begin with a single-variable problem in its most general form. An activity, the level of which is denoted as x, generates both benefits and costs. The total benefit function is $B(x)$ and the total cost function is $C(x)$. The objective is to maximize net benefit, NB, defined as the difference between total benefit and total cost. Net benefit is itself a function of the level of activity and can be expressed as

(1) $$NB = NB(x) = B(x) - C(x)$$

The necessary condition for maximization of net benefit is that the derivative of NB with respect to x equal zero

(2) $$\frac{dNB(x)}{dx} = \frac{dB(x)}{dx} - \frac{dC(x)}{dx} = 0$$

Equation (2) can then be solved for the optimal level of x, denoted x^*. Net benefit is maximized when

(3) $$\frac{dB(x)}{dx} = \frac{dC(x)}{dx}$$

Since dB/dx is the change in total benefit with respect to the level of activity, this term is marginal benefit. Similarly for cost, dC/dx is the change in total cost with respect to the level of activity, and this term is marginal cost. Thus, net benefit is maximized at the level of activity where marginal benefit equals marginal cost.

This unconstrained optimization problem can be easily expanded to more than one choice variable or kind of activity. To this end, let total benefit and total cost be functions of two different activities, denoted by x and y. The net benefit function with two activities is expressed as

(4) $$NB = NB(x, y) = B(x, y) - C(x, y)$$

Maximization of net benefit when there are two activities affecting benefit and cost requires both of the partial derivatives of NB with respect to each of the activities to be equal to zero:

(5a) $$\frac{\partial NB(x, y)}{\partial x} = \frac{\partial B(x, y)}{\partial x} - \frac{\partial C(x, y)}{\partial x} = 0$$

(5b) $$\frac{\partial NB(x, y)}{\partial y} = \frac{\partial B(x, y)}{\partial y} - \frac{\partial C(x, y)}{\partial y} = 0$$

Equations (5a) and (5b) can be solved simultaneously for the optimal levels of the variables, x^* and y^*. Maximization of net benefit thus requires

(6a) $$\frac{\partial B}{\partial x} = \frac{\partial C}{\partial x}$$

and

(6b) $$\frac{\partial B}{\partial y} = \frac{\partial C}{\partial y}$$

For each activity, the marginal benefit of the activity equals the marginal cost of the activity. The problem can be expanded to any number of choice variables with the same results.

Turning now to a mathematical example, consider the following specific form of the total benefit and total cost functions:

(7) $$B(x) = ax - bx^2$$

and

(8) $$C(x) = cx - dx^2 + ex^3$$

where the parameters, a, b, c, d, and e are all positive.

Now the net benefit function can be expressed as

(9) $$NB = NB(x) = B(x) - C(x)$$
$$= ax - bx^2 - cx + dx^2 - ex^3$$

To find the optimal value of x, take the derivative of the net benefit function with respect to x and set it equal to zero:

(10) $$\frac{dNB}{dx} = a - 2bx - c + 2dx - 3ex^2$$
$$= (a - c) - 2(b - d)x - 3ex^2 = 0$$

This quadratic equation can be solved using the quadratic formula or by factoring.[a]

Suppose the values of the parameters are $a = 60$, $b = 0.5$, $c = 24$, $d = 2$, and $e = 1$. The net benefit function is

(11) $$NB = NB(x) = 60x - 0.5x^2 - 24x + 2x^2 - x^3$$

Now take the derivative of NB [or substitute parameter values into equation (10)] to find the condition for optimization:

(12) $$(60 - 24) - 2(0.5 - 2)x - 3(1)x^2 = 36 + 3x - 3x^2 = 0$$

This equation can be factored: $(12 - 3x)(3 + x) = 0$. The solutions are $x = 4$, $x = -3$. (*Note:* The quadratic equation can also be used to find the solutions.) The value of x that maximizes net benefit is $x^* = 4$.[b] To find the optimal, or maximum, value of net benefit, substitute $x^* = 4$ into equation (11) to obtain

$$NB^* = 60(4) - 0.5(4)^2 - 24(4) + 2(4)^2 - (4)^3 = 104$$

Theory of Constrained Maximization

In a constrained maximization problem, a decision maker determines the level of the activities, or choice variables, in order to obtain the most benefit under a given cost constraint. In a constrained minimization problem, a decision maker determines the levels of the choice variables in order to obtain the lowest cost of achieving

---

[a]The solution to a quadratic equation yields two values for x. The maximization, rather than minimization, solution is the value of x at which the second-order condition is met:

$$\frac{d^2NB}{dx^2} = -2(b - d) - 6ex < 0$$

[b]This value of x is the one that satisfies the second-order condition for a maximum in the preceding footnote:

$$\frac{d^2NB}{dx^2} = -2(-1.5) - 6(1)(4) = -21 < 0$$

a given level of benefit. As we showed in the text, the solutions to the two types of problems are the same. We first consider constrained maximization.

Constrained optimization

We first assume a general total benefit function with two choice variables, the levels of which are denoted x and y: $B(x, y)$. The partial derivatives of this function represent the marginal benefit for each activity:

$$MB_x = \frac{\partial B(x, y)}{\partial x} \quad \text{and} \quad MB_y = \frac{\partial B(x, y)}{\partial y}$$

The constraint is that the total cost function must equal a specified level of cost, denoted as $\overline{C}$:

$$(13) \qquad C(x, y) = P_x x + P_y y = \overline{C}$$

where P_x and P_y are the prices of x and y. Now the Lagrangian function to be maximized can be written as

$$(14) \qquad \mathcal{L} = B(x, y) + \lambda(\overline{C} - P_x x - P_y y)$$

where λ is the Lagrangian multiplier. The first-order condition for a maximum requires the partial derivatives of the Lagrangian with respect to the variables x, y, and λ to be zero:

$$(14a) \qquad \frac{\partial \mathcal{L}}{\partial x} = \frac{\partial B}{\partial x} - \lambda P_x = 0$$

$$(14b) \qquad \frac{\partial \mathcal{L}}{\partial y} = \frac{\partial B}{\partial y} - \lambda P_y = 0$$

$$(14c) \qquad \frac{\partial \mathcal{L}}{\partial \lambda} = \overline{C} - P_x x - P_y y = 0$$

Notice that satisfaction of the first-order condition (14c) requires that the cost constraint be met.

Rearranging the first two equations (14a) and (14b):

$$\frac{\partial B}{\partial x} = \lambda P_x \quad \text{or} \quad \frac{MB_x}{P_x} = \lambda$$

$$\frac{\partial B}{\partial y} = \lambda P_y \quad \text{or} \quad \frac{MB_y}{P_y} = \lambda$$

It therefore follows that the levels of x and y must be chosen so that

$$(15) \qquad \frac{MB_x}{P_x} = \frac{MB_y}{P_y}$$

The marginal benefits per dollar spent on the last units of x and y must be equal.

The three equations in (14) can be solved for the equilibrium values x^*, y^*, and λ^* by substitution or by Cramer's rule. Therefore, x^* and y^* give the values of the choice variables that yield the maximum benefit possible at the given level of cost.

Constrained minimization

For the constrained minimization problem, we want to choose the levels of two activities, x and y, to obtain a given level of benefit at the lowest possible cost. Therefore, the problem is to minimize $C = P_x x + P_y y$, subject to $B = B(x, y)$, where $\overline{B}$ is the specified level of benefit. The Lagrangian function is

$$(16) \qquad \mathcal{L} = P_x x + P_y y + \lambda[\overline{B} - B(x, y)]$$

The first-order conditions are

$$\frac{\partial \mathcal{L}}{\partial x} = P_x - \lambda \frac{\partial B}{\partial x} = 0$$

$$(17) \qquad \frac{\partial \mathcal{L}}{\partial y} = P_y - \lambda \frac{\partial B}{\partial y} = 0$$

$$\frac{\partial \mathcal{L}}{\partial \lambda} = [\overline{B} - B(x, y)] = 0$$

As in the constrained maximization problem, the first two equations can be rearranged to obtain

$$(18) \qquad \frac{\partial B}{\partial x} = \frac{1}{\lambda} P_x \quad \text{or} \quad \frac{MB_x}{P_x} = \frac{1}{\lambda}$$

$$\frac{\partial B}{\partial y} = \frac{1}{\lambda} P_y \quad \text{or} \quad \frac{MB_y}{P_y} = \frac{1}{\lambda}$$

Once again the marginal benefits per dollar spent on the last units of x and y must be the same, because, from (18),

$$\frac{MB_x}{P_x} = \frac{MB_y}{P_y}$$

The three equations in (17) can be solved for the equilibrium values x^*, y^*, and λ^* by substitution or by Cramer's rule. These are the values of the choice variables that attain the lowest cost of reaching the given level of benefit.

MATHEMATICAL EXERCISES

1. Assume the only choice variable is x. The total benefit function is $B(x) = 170x - x^2$, and the cost function is $C(x) = 100 - 10x + 2x^2$.

   a. What are the marginal benefit and marginal cost functions?

   b. Set up the net benefit function and then determine the level of x that maximizes net benefit.

   c. What is the maximum level of net benefit?

2. The only choice variable is x. The total benefit function is $B(x) = 100x - 2x^2$, and the total cost function is $C(x) = \frac{1}{3}x^3 - 6x^2 + 52x + 80$.

   a. What are the marginal benefit and marginal cost functions?

   b. Set up the net benefit function and then determine the level of x that maximizes net benefit. (Use the positive value of x.)

   c. What is the maximum level of net benefit?

3. A decision maker wishes to maximize total benefit, $B = 3x + xy + y$, subject to the cost constraint, $\overline{C} = 4x + 2y = 70$. Set up the Lagrangian and then determine the values of x and y at the maximum level of benefit, given the constraint. What are the maximum benefits?

4. A decision maker wishes to minimize the cost of producing a given level of total benefit, $B = 288$. The cost function is $C = 6x + 3y$ and the total benefit function is $B = xy$. Set up the Lagrangian and then determine levels of x and y at the minimum level of cost. What is the minimum value of cost?

5. In Figure 3.1, the total benefit and total cost curves are represented by the following mathematical functions:

$$TB = TB(A) = 8A - 0.004A^2$$

and

$$TC = TC(A) = A + 0.006A^2$$

   a. Find the marginal benefit function. Verify that points c, b, and d in Figure 3.2 lie on the marginal benefit curve.

   b. Find the marginal cost function. Verify that points c', b, and d' in Figure 3.2 lie on the marginal cost curve.

   c. Derive the net benefit function. Verify the slopes of net benefit at points M, c'', and d'' in Figure 3.3.

   d. Find the optimal level of activity and the maximum value of net benefit. Does your answer match Figure 3.3?

Chapter 4

Basic Estimation Techniques

After reading this chapter, you will be able to:

4.1 Set up and interpret simple linear regression equations.

4.2 Estimate intercept and slope parameters of a regression line using the method of least-squares.

4.3 Determine whether estimated parameters are statistically significant using either t-tests or p-values associated with parameter estimates.

4.4 Evaluate how well a regression equation "fits" the data by examining the R^2 statistic and test for statistical significance of the whole regression equation using an F-test.

4.5 Set up and interpret multiple regression models that use more than one explanatory variable.

4.6 Use linear regression techniques to estimate the parameters of two common nonlinear models: quadratic and log-linear regression models.

To implement the various techniques discussed in this text, managers must be able to determine the mathematical relation between the economic variables that make up the various functions used in managerial economics: demand functions, production functions, cost functions, and others. For example, managers often must determine the total cost of producing various levels of output. As you will see in Chapter 10, the relation between total cost (C) and quantity (Q) can be specified as

$$C = a + bQ + cQ^2 + dQ^3$$

where a, b, c, and d are the *parameters* of the cost equation. **Parameters** are coefficients in an equation that determine the exact mathematical relation among the variables in the equation. Once the numerical values of the parameters are

parameters
The coefficients in an equation that determine the exact mathematical relation among the variables.

determined, the manager then knows the quantitative relation between output and total cost. For example, suppose the values of the parameters of the cost equation are determined to be $a = 1{,}262$, $b = 1.0$, $c = -0.03$, and $d = 0.005$. The cost equation can now be expressed as

$$C = 1{,}262 + 1.0Q - 0.03Q^2 + 0.005Q^3$$

This equation can be used to compute the total cost of producing various levels of output. If, for example, the manager wishes to produce 30 units of output, the total cost can be calculated as

$$C = 1{,}262 + 30 - 0.03(30)^2 + 0.005(30)^3 = \$1{,}400$$

Thus for the cost function to be useful for decision making, the manager must know the numerical values of the parameters.

The process of finding estimates of the numerical values of the parameters of an equation is called **parameter estimation.** Although there are several techniques for estimating parameters, the values of the parameters are often obtained by using a technique called **regression analysis.** Regression analysis uses data on economic variables to determine a mathematical equation that describes the relation between the economic variables. Regression analysis involves both the estimation of parameter values and testing for statistical significance.

In this chapter, we will set forth the *basics* of regression analysis. We want to stress that throughout the discussion of regression analysis, in this chapter and the chapters that follow, we are not as much interested in your knowing the ways the various statistics are calculated as we are in your knowing how these statistics can be interpreted and used. We will often rely on intuitive explanations, leaving formal derivations for the appendixes at the end of the chapter.

4.1 THE SIMPLE LINEAR REGRESSION MODEL

Regression analysis is a technique used to determine the mathematical relation between a **dependent variable** and one or more **explanatory variables.** The explanatory variables are the economic variables that are thought to affect the value of the dependent variable. In the *simple linear regression model,* the dependent variable Y is related to only *one* explanatory variable X, and the relation between Y and X is linear

$$Y = a + bX$$

This is the equation for a straight line, with X plotted along the horizontal axis and Y along the vertical axis. The parameter a is called the **intercept parameter** because it gives the value of Y at the point where the regression line crosses the Y-axis. (X is equal to 0 at this point.) The parameter b is called the **slope parameter** because it gives the slope of the regression line. The slope of a line measures the rate of change in Y as X changes ($\Delta Y/\Delta X$); it is therefore the change in Y per unit change in X.

Note that Y and X are linearly related in the regression model; that is, the effect of a change in X on the value of Y is constant. More specifically, a one-unit

parameter estimation
The process of finding estimates of the numerical values of the parameters of an equation.

regression analysis
A statistical technique for estimating the parameters of an equation and testing for statistical significance.

dependent variable
The variable whose variation is to be explained.

explanatory variables
The variables that are thought to cause the dependent variable to take on different values.

intercept parameter
The parameter that gives the value of Y at the point where the regression line crosses the Y-axis.

slope parameter
The slope of the regression line, $b = \Delta Y/\Delta X$, or the change in Y associated with a one-unit change in X.

change in X causes Y to change by a constant b units. The simple regression model is based on a linear relation between Y and X, in large part because estimating the parameters of a linear model is relatively simple statistically. As it turns out, assuming a linear relation is not overly restrictive. For one thing, many variables are actually linearly related or very nearly linearly related. For those cases where Y and X are instead related in a curvilinear fashion, you will see that a simple transformation of the variables often makes it possible to model nonlinear relations within the framework of the linear regression model. You will see how to make these simple transformations later in this chapter.

A Hypothetical Regression Model

true (or actual) relation
The true or actual underlying relation between Y and X that is unknown to the researcher but is to be discovered by analyzing the sample data.

To illustrate the simple regression model, consider a statistical problem facing the Tampa Bay Travel Agents' Association. The association wishes to determine the mathematical relation between the dollar volume of sales of travel packages (S) and the level of expenditures on newspaper advertising (A) for travel agents located in the Tampa–St. Petersburg metropolitan area. Suppose that the **true** (or **actual**) **relation** between sales and advertising expenditures is

$$S = 10,000 + 5A$$

where S measures monthly sales in dollars and A measures monthly advertising expenditures in dollars. The true relation between sales and advertising is unknown to the analyst; it must be "discovered" by analyzing data on sales and advertising. Researchers are never able to know with certainty the exact nature of the underlying mathematical relation between the dependent variable and the explanatory variable, but regression analysis does provide a method for estimating the true relation.

Figure 4.1 shows the true or actual relation between sales and advertising expenditures. If an agency chooses to spend nothing on newspaper advertising, its sales are expected to be $10,000 per month. If an agency spends $3,000 monthly on ads, it can expect sales of $25,000 (= $10,000 + 5 \times 3,000$). Because $\Delta S/\Delta A = 5$, for every $1 of additional expenditure on advertising, the travel agency can expect a $5 increase in sales. For example, increasing outlays from $3,000 to $4,000 per month causes expected monthly sales to rise from $25,000 to $30,000, as shown in Figure 4.1.

The Random Error Term

The regression equation (or line) shows the level of expected sales for each level of advertising expenditure. As noted, if a travel agency spends $3,000 monthly on ads, it can expect on average to have sales of $25,000. We should stress that $25,000 should be interpreted not as the exact level of sales that a firm will experience when advertising expenditures are $3,000 but only as an average level. To illustrate this point, suppose that three travel agencies in the Tampa–St. Petersburg area each spend exactly $3,000 on advertising. Will all three of these firms experience sales of precisely $25,000? This is *not* likely. While each of these three firms spends exactly the same amount on advertising, each firm experiences certain *random*

FIGURE 4.1

The True Regression Line: Relating Sales and Advertising Expenditures

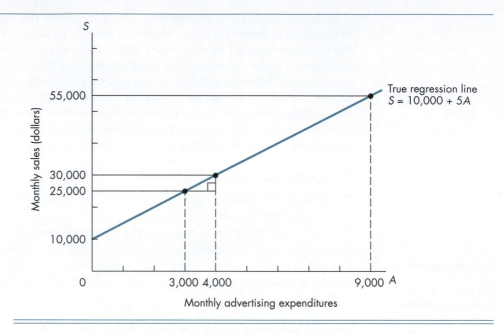

effects that are peculiar to that firm. These random effects cause the sales of the various firms to deviate from the expected $25,000 level of sales.

Table 4.1 illustrates the impact of random effects on the actual level of sales achieved. Each of the three firms in Table 4.1 spent $3,000 on advertising in the month of January. According to the true regression equation, each of these travel agencies would be expected to have sales of $25,000 in January. As it turns out, the manager of the Tampa Travel Agency used the advertising agency owned and managed by her brother, who gave better than usual service. This travel agency actually sold $30,000 worth of travel packages in January—$5,000 more than the expected or average level of sales. The manager of Buccaneer Travel Service was on a ski vacation in early January and did not start spending money on advertising until the middle of January. Buccaneer Travel Service's sales were only $21,000—$4,000 less than the regression line predicted. In January, nothing unusual happened to Happy Getaway Tours, and its sales of $25,000 exactly matched what the average travel agency in Tampa would be expected to sell when it spends $3,000 on advertising.

TABLE 4.1

The Impact of Random Effects on January Sales

Firm	Advertising expenditure	Actual sales	Expected sales	Random effect
Tampa Travel Agency	$3,000	$30,000	$25,000	$5,000
Buccaneer Travel Service	3,000	21,000	25,000	−4,000
Happy Getaway Tours	3,000	25,000	25,000	0

Because of these random effects, the level of sales for a firm cannot be *exactly* predicted. The regression equation shows only the *average* or *expected* level of sales when a firm spends a given amount on advertising. The exact level of sales for any particular travel agency (such as the *i*th agency) can be expressed as

$$S_i = 10,000 + 5A_i + e_i$$

where S_i and A_i are, respectively, the sales and advertising levels of the *i*th agency and e_i is the random effect experienced by the *i*th travel agency. Since e_i measures the amount by which the *actual* level of sales differs from the average level of sales, e_i is called an *error term*, or a *random error*. The **random error term** captures the effects of all the minor, unpredictable factors that cannot reasonably be included in the model as explanatory variables.

random error term
An unobservable term added to a regression model to capture the effects of all the minor, unpredictable factors that affect Y but cannot reasonably be included as explanatory variables.

Because the *true* regression line is unknown, the first task of regression analysis is to obtain estimates of *a* and *b*. To do this, data on monthly sales and advertising expenditures must be collected from Tampa Bay–area travel agents. Using these data, a regression line is then fitted. Before turning to the task of fitting a regression line to the data points in a sample, we summarize the simple regression model in the following statistical relation:

Now try Technical Problem 1.

> **Relation**   The simple linear regression model relates a dependent variable Y to a single independent explanatory variable X in a linear equation called the true regression line
>
> $$Y = a + bX$$
>
> where *a* is the Y-intercept, and *b* is the slope of the regression line $(\Delta Y / \Delta X)$. The regression line shows the average or expected value of Y for each level of the explanatory variable X.

4.2 FITTING A REGRESSION LINE

The purpose of regression analysis is twofold: (1) to estimate the parameters (*a* and *b*) of the true regression line and (2) to test whether the estimated values of the parameters are statistically significant. (We will discuss the meaning of statistical significance later.) We turn now to the first task—the estimation of *a* and *b*. You will see that estimating *a* and *b* is equivalent to fitting a straight line through a scatter of data points plotted on a graph. Regression analysis provides a way of finding the line that "best fits" the scatter of data points.

time-series
A data set in which the data for the dependent and explanatory variables are collected over time for a specific firm.

To estimate the parameters of the regression equation, an analyst first collects data on the dependent and explanatory variables. The data can be collected over time for a specific firm (or a specific industry); this type of data set is called a **time-series.** Alternatively, the data can be collected from several different firms or industries at a given time; this type of data set is called a **cross-sectional** data set. No matter how the data are collected, the result is a scatter of data points (called a **scatter diagram**) through which a regression line can be fitted.

cross-sectional
A data set in which the data on the dependent and explanatory variables are collected from many different firms or industries at a given point in time.

scatter diagram
A graph of the data points in a sample.

To show how the parameters are estimated, we refer once again to the Tampa Bay Travel Agents' Association. Suppose the association asks seven agencies

TABLE 4.2

Sales and Advertising Expenditures for a Sample of Seven Travel Agencies

Firm	Sales	Advertising expenditure
A	$15,000	$2,000
B	30,000	2,000
C	30,000	5,000
D	25,000	3,000
E	55,000	9,000
F	45,000	8,000
G	60,000	7,000

population regression line

The equation or line representing the true (or actual) underlying relation between the dependent variable and the explanatory variable(s).

sample regression line

The line that best fits the scatter of data points in the sample and provides an estimate of the population regression line.

(out of the total 475 agencies located in the Tampa–St. Petersburg area) for data on their sales and advertising expenditures during the month of January. These data (a cross-sectional data set) are presented in Table 4.2 and are plotted in a scatter diagram in Figure 4.2. Each dot in the figure refers to a specific sales–expenditure combination in the table. Even though the data points do not lie on a straight line—recall that random errors prevent this—the data points seem to indicate that a positive relation exists between sales and advertising. The higher the level of advertising, the higher (on average) the level of sales. The objective of regression analysis is to find the straight line that best fits the scatter of data points. Since fitting a line through a scatter of data points simply involves choosing values of the parameters a and b, fitting a regression line and estimation of parameters are conceptually the same thing.

The association wants to use the data in the sample to estimate the true regression line, also called the **population regression line.** The line that best fits the data in the sample is called the **sample regression line.** Since the sample

FIGURE 4.2

The Sample Regression Line: Relating Sales and Advertising Expenditures

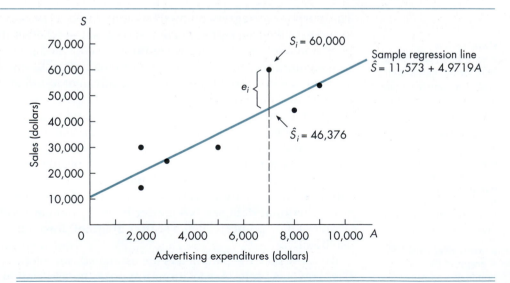

contains information on only seven out of the total 475 travel agencies, it is highly unlikely that the sample regression line will be exactly the same as the true regression line. The sample regression line is only an estimate of the true regression line. Naturally, the larger the size of the sample, the more accurately the sample regression line will estimate the true regression line.

In Figure 4.2, the sample regression line that best fits the seven sample data points presented in Table 4.2 is given by

$$\hat{S} = 11{,}573 + 4.9719A$$

method of least-squares
A method of estimating the parameters of a linear regression equation by finding the line that minimizes the sum of the squared distances from each sample data point to the sample regression line.

where $\hat{S}$ is called the fitted or predicted value of S. Regression analysis uses the **method of least-squares** to find the sample regression line that best fits the data in the sample. The principle of least-squares is based on the idea that the sample regression line that is most likely to match the *true* regression line is the line that minimizes the sum of the squared distances from each sample data point to the *sample* regression line.

fitted or predicted value
The predicted value of Y (denoted $\hat{Y}$) associated with a particular value of X, which is obtained by substituting that value of X into the sample regression equation.

Look at the sample data point for advertising expenditures of $7,000 and sales of $60,000 in Figure 4.2. The sample regression equation indicates that advertising expenditures of $7,000 will result in $46,376 ($= 11{,}573 + 4.9719 \times 7{,}000$) of sales. The value $46,376 is called the **fitted** or **predicted value** of sales, which we denote as $\hat{S}_i$. The difference between the actual value of sales and the fitted (predicted) value, $S_i - \hat{S}_i$, is called the **residual** and is equal to the vertical distance between the data point and the fitted regression line (denoted e_i in Figure 4.2). The residual for the data point at ($7,000, $60,000) is $13,624 ($= \$60{,}000 - \$46{,}376$). Regression analysis selects the straight line (i.e., chooses a and b) to minimize the sum of the squared residuals (Σe_i^2), which is why it is often referred to as least-squares analysis.

residual
The difference between the actual value of Y and the fitted (or predicted) value of Y: $Y_i - \hat{Y}_i$.

We are not concerned with teaching you the details involved in computing the least-squares estimates of a and b, since computers are almost always used in regression analysis for this purpose. Nevertheless, it might be informative for you to see how the computer can calculate estimates of a and b. The formulas by which the estimates of a and b are computed are frequently called **estimators.** The formulas the computer uses for computing the least-squares estimates of a and b (denoted $\hat{a}$ and $\hat{b}$ to indicate that these are **estimates** and not the true values) are

estimators
The formulas by which the estimates of parameters are computed.

estimates
The estimated values of parameters obtained by substituting sample data into estimators.

$$\hat{b} = \frac{\Sigma(X_i - \overline{X})(Y_i - \overline{Y})}{\Sigma(X_i - \overline{X})^2}$$

and

$$\hat{a} = \overline{Y} - b\overline{X}$$

where $\overline{Y}$ and $\overline{X}$ are, respectively, the sample means of the dependent variable and independent variable, and X_i and Y_i are the observed values for the ith observation. Fortunately, these computations will be done for you by a computer.

TABLE 4.3

Examples of Printouts for Regression Analysis

DEPENDENT VARIABLE: S		R-SQUARE	F-RATIO	P-VALUE ON F
OBSERVATIONS: 7		0.7652	16.30	0.0100

VARIABLE	PARAMETER ESTIMATE	STANDARD ERROR	T-RATIO	P-VALUE
INTERCEPT	11573.0	7150.83	1.62	0.1665
A	4.97191	1.23154	4.04	0.0100

Panel A—"Generic" style

	A	B	C	D	E	F	G
1	SUMMARY OUTPUT						
2							
3	*Regression Statistics*						
4	Multiple R	0.8748					
5	R Square	0.7652					
6	Adjusted R Square	0.7183					
7	Standard Error	8782.6438					
8	Observations	7					
9							
10	ANOVA						
11		*df*	*SS*	*MS*	*F*	*Significance F*	
12	Regression	1	1257182986	1257182986	16.30	0.0100	
13	Residual	5	385674157.3	77134831.46			
14	Total	6	1642857143				
15							
16		*Coefficients*	*Standard Error*	*t Stat*	*P-value*	*Lower 95%*	*Upper 95%*
17	Intercept	11573.0	7150.83	1.62	0.1665	-6808.7222	29954.7896
18	A	4.97191	1.23154	4.04	0.0100	1.8061	8.1377

Panel B—*Microsoft Excel*

We can now summarize least-squares estimation with the following statistical relation:

Relation Estimating the parameters of the true regression line is equivalent to fitting a line through a scatter diagram of the sample data points. The sample regression line, which is found using the method of least-squares, is the line that best fits the sample

$$\hat{Y} = \hat{a} + \hat{b}X$$

where $\hat{a}$ and $\hat{b}$ are the least-squares estimates of the true (population) parameters a and b. The sample regression line estimates the true regression line.

Many computer software programs can compute the least-squares estimates for linear regression analysis, along with a variety of associated statistics for assessing the performance of the regression model, some of which we will explain to you in this chapter. Table 4.3 shows two versions of computer regression printouts for the regression analysis of the seven travel agencies presented in Table 4.2. In each panel, the parameter estimates for a and b are highlighted in color. Panel A shows a typical or "generic" regression printout, and we will use this simplified format throughout this book. Panel B shows the same regression analysis, as it looks when performed using Microsoft's *Excel* software to perform regression analysis. As you can see, cells B17 and B18 give $\hat{a}$ and $\hat{b}$, respectively. We want to emphasize that we do *not* intend to teach you how to use *all* of the statistics provided by these regression software packages. You must take one or two statistics courses to become proficient in regression analysis. In this textbook, we are attempting only to introduce you to basic estimation techniques and procedures.

We now turn to the task of testing hypotheses about the true values of a and b—which are unknown to the researcher—using the information contained in the sample. These tests involve determining whether the dependent variable is truly related to the independent variable or whether the relation as estimated from the sample data is due only to the randomness of the sample.

Now try Technical Problem 2.

4.3 TESTING FOR STATISTICAL SIGNIFICANCE

statistically significant
There is sufficient evidence from the sample to indicate that the true value of the coefficient is not 0.

Once the parameters of an equation are estimated, the analyst must address the question of whether the parameter estimates ($\hat{a}$ and $\hat{b}$) are significantly different from 0. If the estimated coefficient is far enough away from 0—either sufficiently greater than 0 (a positive estimate) or sufficiently less than 0 (a negative estimate)—the estimated coefficient is said to be **statistically significant.** The question of statistical significance arises because the estimates are themselves random variables. The parameter estimates are random because they are calculated using values of Y and X that are collected in a random fashion (remember, the sample is a random sample). Because the values of the parameters are *estimates* of the true parameter values, the estimates are rarely equal to the true parameter values. In other words, the estimates calculated by the computer are almost always going to be either too large or too small.

hypothesis testing
A statistical technique for making a probabilistic statement about the true value of a parameter.

Because the estimated values of the parameters ($\hat{a}$ and $\hat{b}$) are unlikely to be the true values (a and b), it is possible that a parameter could truly be equal to 0 even though the computer calculates a parameter estimate that is not equal to 0. Fortunately, statistical techniques exist that provide a tool for making probabilistic statements about the true values of the parameters. This tool is called **hypothesis testing.**

To understand fully the concept of hypothesis testing, you would need to take at least one course, and probably two, in statistics. In this text we intend only to motivate through intuition the *necessity* and *process* of performing a test of statistical significance. Our primary emphasis will be to show you how to test the hypothesis that Y is truly related to X. If Y is indeed related to X, the true value of the slope parameter b will be either a positive or a negative number. (Remember, if $b = \Delta Y / \Delta X = 0$, no change in Y occurs when X changes.) Thus, the explanatory variable X has a statistically significant effect on the dependent variable Y when $b \neq 0$.[1]

---

[1]Testing for statistical significance of the intercept parameter a is typically of secondary importance to testing for significance of the slope parameters. As you will see, it is the slope parameters rather than the intercept parameter that provide the most essential information for managerial decision making. Nevertheless, it is customary to test the intercept parameter for statistical significance in exactly the same manner as the slope parameter is tested.

Now try Technical
Problem 3.

We will now discuss the procedure for testing for statistical significance by describing how to measure the accuracy, or precision, of an estimate. Then we will introduce and explain a statistical test (called a t-test) that can be used to make a probabilistic statement about whether Y is truly related to the explanatory variable X—that is, whether the true value of the parameter b is zero.

The Relative Frequency Distribution for $\hat{b}$

As noted, the necessity of testing for statistical significance arises because the analyst does not know the true values of a and b—they are estimated from a random sample of observations on Y and X. Consider again the relation between sales of travel packages and advertising expenditures estimated in the previous section. The least-squares estimate of the slope parameter b from the sample of seven travel agencies shown in Table 4.2 is 4.9719. Suppose you collected a new sample by randomly selecting seven other travel agencies and use their sales and advertising expenditures to estimate b. The estimate for b will probably not equal 4.9719 for the second sample. Remember, $\hat{b}$ is computed using the values of S and A in the sample. Because of randomness in sampling, different samples generally result in different values of S and A, and thus different estimates of b. Therefore, $\hat{b}$ is a random variable—its value varies in repeated samples.

relative frequency distribution
The distribution (and relative frequency) of values $\hat{b}$ can take because observations on Y and X come from a random sample.

The relative frequency with which $\hat{b}$ takes on different values provides information about the *accuracy* of the parameter estimates. Even though researchers seldom have the luxury of taking repeated samples, statisticians have been able to determine theoretically the **relative frequency distribution** of values that $\hat{b}$ would take in repeated samples. This distribution is also called the probability density function, or pdf, by statisticians. Figure 4.3 shows the relative frequency distribution for $\hat{b}$, *when the true value of* b *is equal to 5.*

FIGURE 4.3

Relative Frequency Distribution for $\hat{b}$ When $b = 5$

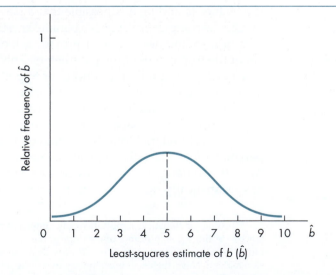

Notice that the distribution of values that $\hat{b}$ might take in various samples is centered around the true value of 5. Even though the probability of drawing a sample for which $\hat{b}$ exactly equals 5 is extremely small, the average (mean or expected) value of all possible values of $\hat{b}$ is 5. The estimator $\hat{b}$ is said to be an **unbiased estimator** if the average (mean or expected) value of the estimator is equal to the true value of the parameter. Statisticians have demonstrated that the least-squares estimators of a and b ($\hat{a}$ and $\hat{b}$) are unbiased estimators in a wide variety of statistical circumstances. Unbiasedness does not mean that any one estimate equals the true parameter value. Unbiasedness means only that, in repeated samples, the estimates tend to be centered around the true value.

unbiased estimator
An estimator that produces estimates of a parameter that are on average equal to the true value of the parameter.

The smaller the dispersion of $\hat{b}$ around the true value, the more likely it is that an estimate of $\hat{b}$ is close to the true value. In other words, the smaller the variance of the distribution of $\hat{b}$, the more accurate estimates are likely to be. Not surprisingly, the variance of the estimate of b plays an important role in the determination of statistical significance. The square root of the variance of $\hat{b}$ is called the *standard error of the estimate*, which we will denote $S_{\hat{b}}$.[2] All computer regression routines compute standard errors for the parameter estimates.

The Concept of a *t*-Ratio

When we regressed sales on advertising expenditures for the seven travel agencies in Table 4.2, we obtained an estimate of b equal to 4.9719. Because 4.9719 is not equal to 0, this seems to suggest that the level of advertising does indeed affect sales. (Remember that if $b = 0$, there is no relation between sales and advertising.) As explained earlier, the estimate of b calculated using a random sample may take on a range of values. Even though 4.9719 is greater than 0, it is possible that the true value of b is 0. In other words, the analyst runs some risk that the true value of b is 0 even when $\hat{b}$ is not calculated to be 0.

The probability of drawing a sample for which the estimate of b is much larger than 0 is very small when the true value of b is actually 0. How large does $\hat{b}$ have to be for an analyst to be quite sure that b is not really 0 (i.e., advertising does play a significant role in determining sales)? The answer to this question is obtained by performing a hypothesis test. The hypothesis that one normally tests is that $b = 0$. Statisticians use a **t-test** to make a probabilistic statement about the likelihood that the true parameter value b is not equal to 0. Using the t-test, it is possible to determine statistically how large $\hat{b}$ must be in order to conclude that b is not equal to 0.

t-test
A statistical test used to test the hypothesis that the true value of a parameter is equal to 0 ($b = 0$).

To perform a t-test for statistical significance, we form what statisticians call a **t-ratio**:

t-ratio
The ratio of an estimated regression parameter divided by the standard error of the estimate.

$$t = \frac{\hat{b}}{S_{\hat{b}}}$$

where $\hat{b}$ is the least-squares estimate of b and $S_{\hat{b}}$ is the standard error of the estimate, both of which are calculated by the computer. The numerical value of the t-ratio is called a **t-statistic**.

t-statistic
The numerical value of the t-ratio.

[2]More correctly, the standard error of the estimate is the square root of the *estimated* variance of $\hat{b}$.

By combining information about the size of $\hat{b}$ (in the numerator) and the accuracy or precision of the estimate (in the denominator), the t-ratio indicates how much confidence one can have that the true value of b is actually larger than (significantly different from) 0. The larger the absolute value of the t-ratio, the more confident one can be that the true value of b is not 0. To show why this is true, we must examine both the numerator and the denominator of the t-ratio. Consider the numerator when the estimate $\hat{b}$ is positive. When b is actually 0, drawing a random sample that will produce an estimate of b that is much larger than 0 is unlikely. Thus the larger the numerator of the t-ratio, the less likely it is that b really does equal 0. Turning now to the denominator of the t-ratio, recall that $S_{\hat{b}}$, the standard error of the estimate, measures the accuracy of the estimate of b. The smaller the standard error of $\hat{b}$ (and thus the more accurate $\hat{b}$ is), the smaller the error in estimation is likely to be. Consequently, the farther from 0 $\hat{b}$ is (i.e., the larger the numerator) and the smaller the standard error of the estimate (i.e., the smaller the denominator), the larger the t-ratio, and the more sure we are that the true value of b is greater than 0.

Now consider the situation when the estimate $\hat{b}$ is negative (e.g., if we had estimated the relation between profits and shoplifting). In this case we would be more certain that b was really negative if the t-ratio had a more negative magnitude. Regardless of whether $\hat{b}$ is positive or negative, the following important statistical relation is established:

Now try Technical Problem 4.

> **Relation** The larger the absolute value of $\hat{b}/S_{\hat{b}}$ (the t-ratio), the more probable it is that the true value of b is not equal to 0.

Performing a t-Test for Statistical Significance

The t-statistic is used to test the hypothesis that the true value of b equals 0. If the calculated t-statistic or t-ratio is greater than the **critical value of t** (to be explained later), then the hypothesis that $b = 0$ is rejected in favor of the alternative hypothesis that $b \neq 0$. When the calculated t-statistic exceeds the critical value of t, b is significantly different from 0, or, equivalently, b is statistically significant. If the hypothesis that $b = 0$ cannot be rejected, then the sample data are indicating that X, the explanatory variable for which b is the coefficient, is not related to the dependent variable Y ($\Delta Y/\Delta X = 0$). Only when a parameter estimate is statistically significant should the associated explanatory variable be included in the regression equation.

critical value of t
The value that the t-statistic must exceed in order to reject the hypothesis that $b = 0$.

Type I error
Error in which a parameter estimate is found to be statistically significant when it is not.

Although performing a t-test is the correct way to assess the statistical significance of a parameter estimate, there is always some risk that the t-test will indicate $b \neq 0$ when in fact $b = 0$. Statisticians refer to this kind of mistake as a **Type I error**—finding a parameter estimate to be significant when it is not.[3] The probability of making a Type I error when performing a t-test is referred to

---

[3]Statisticians also recognize the possibility of committing a Type II error, which occurs when an analyst *fails* to find a parameter estimate to be statistically significant when it *truly* is significant. In your statistics class you will study both types of errors, Type I and Type II. Because it is usually impossible to determine the probability of committing a Type II error, tests for statistical significance typically consider only the possibility of committing a Type I error.

level of significance
The probability of finding the parameter to be statistically significant when in fact it is not.

as the **level of significance** of the *t*-test. The level of significance associated with a *t*-test is the probability that the test will indicate $b \neq 0$ when in fact $b = 0$. Stated differently, the significance level is the probability of finding the parameter to be statistically significant when in fact it is not. As we are about to show you, an analyst can control or select the level of significance for a *t*-test. Traditionally, either a 0.01, 0.02, 0.05, or 0.10 level of significance is selected, which reflects the analyst's willingness to tolerate at most a 1, 2, 5, or 10 percent probability of finding a parameter to be significant when it is not. In practice, however, the significance level tends to be chosen arbitrarily. We will return to the problem of selecting the appropriate level of significance later in this discussion of *t*-tests.

level of confidence
The probability of correctly failing to reject the true hypothesis that $b = 0$; equals one minus the level of significance.

A concept closely related to the level of significance is the level of confidence. The **level of confidence** equals one minus the level of significance, and thus gives the probability that you will *not* make a Type I error. The confidence level is the probability a *t*-test will *correctly* find no relation between Y and X (i.e., $b = 0$). The lower the level of significance, the greater the level of confidence. If the level of significance chosen for conducting a *t*-test is 0.05 (5 percent), then the level of confidence for the test is 0.95 (95 percent), and you can be 95 percent confident that the *t*-test will correctly indicate lack of significance. The levels of significance and confidence provide the same information, only in slightly different ways: The significance level gives the probability of making a Type I error, while the confidence level gives the probability of *not* making a Type I error. A 5 percent level of significance and a 95 percent level of confidence mean the same thing.

Relation In testing for statistical significance, the level of significance chosen for the test determines the probability of committing a Type I error, which is the mistake of finding a parameter to be significant when it is not truly significant. The level of confidence for a test is the probability of not committing a Type I error. The lower (higher) the significance level of a test, the higher (lower) the level of confidence for the test.

The *t*-test is simple to perform. First, calculate the *t*-statistic (*t*-ratio) from the parameter estimate and its standard error, both of which are calculated by the computer. (In most statistical software, the *t*-ratio is also calculated by the computer.) Next, find the appropriate critical value of *t* for the chosen level of significance. (Critical values of *t* are provided in a *t*-table at the end of this book, along with explanatory text.) The critical value of *t* is defined by the level of significance and the appropriate degrees of freedom. The **degrees of freedom** for a *t*-test are equal to $n - k$, where n is the number of observations in the sample and k is the number of parameters estimated.[4] (In the advertising example, there are $7 - 2 = 5$ degrees of freedom, since we have seven observations and estimated two parameters, a and b.)

degrees of freedom
The number of observations in the sample minus the number of parameters being estimated by the regression analysis $(n - k)$.

Once the critical value of *t* is found for, say, the 5 percent level of significance or 95 percent level of confidence, the absolute value of the calculated *t*-statistic

---

[4]Occasionally you may find other statistics books (or *t*-tables in other books) that define k as the "number of explanatory variables" rather than the "number of parameters estimated," as we have done in this text. When k is not defined to include the estimated intercept parameter, then the number of degrees of freedom must be calculated as $n - (k + 1)$. No matter how k is defined, the degrees of freedom for the *t*-test are always equal to the number of observations minus the number of parameters estimated.

is compared with the critical value of t. If the absolute value of the t-statistic is greater than the critical value of t, we say that, at the 95 percent confidence level, the estimated parameter is (statistically) significantly different from zero. If the absolute value of the calculated t-statistic is less than the critical value of t, the estimated value of b cannot be treated as being significantly different from 0 and X plays no statistically significant role in determining the value of Y.

Returning to the advertising example, we now test to see if 4.9719, the estimated value of b, is significantly different from 0. The standard error of $\hat{b}$, which is calculated by the computer, is equal to 1.23. Thus the t-statistic is equal to 4.04 (= 4.9719/1.23). Next we compare 4.04 to the critical value of t, using a 5 percent significance level (a 95 percent confidence level). As noted, there are 5 degrees of freedom. If you turn to the table of critical t-values at the end of the text, you will find that the critical value of t for 5 degrees of freedom and a 0.05 level of significance is 2.571. Because 4.04 is larger than 2.571, we reject the hypothesis that b is 0 and can now say that 4.9719 ($\hat{b}$) is significantly different from 0. This means that advertising expenditure is a statistically significant variable in determining the level of sales. If 4.04 had been less than the critical value, we would not have been able to reject the hypothesis that b is 0 and we would not have been able to conclude that advertising plays a significant role in determining the level of sales.

The procedure for testing for statistical significance of a parameter estimate is summarized in the following statistical principle:

> **Principle**   To test for statistical significance of a parameter estimate $\hat{b}$, compute the t-ratio
>
> $$t = \frac{\hat{b}}{S_{\hat{b}}}$$
>
> where $S_{\hat{b}}$ is the standard error of the estimate $\hat{b}$. Next, for the chosen level of significance, find the critical t-value in the t-table at the end of the text. Choose the critical t-value with $n - k$ degrees of freedom for the chosen level of significance. If the absolute value of the t-ratio is greater (less) than the critical t-value, then $\hat{b}$ is (is not) statistically significant.

Using *p*-Values to Determine Statistical Significance

Using a t-test to determine whether a parameter estimate is statistically significant requires that you select a level of significance at which to perform the test. In most of the situations facing a manager, choosing the significance level for the test involves making an arbitrary decision. We will now show you an alternative method of assessing the statistical significance of parameter estimates that does not require that you "preselect" a level of significance (or, equivalently, the level of confidence) or use a t-table to find a critical t-value. With this alternative method, the *exact degree* of statistical significance is determined by answering the question, "Given the t-ratio calculated for $\hat{b}$, what would be the lowest level of significance—or the highest level of confidence—that would allow the hypothesis $b = 0$ to be rejected in favor of the alternative hypothesis $b \neq 0$?"

Consider the t-test for the parameter estimate 4.9719. In the previous section, the effect of advertising (A) on sales (S) was found to be statistically significant because the calculated *t*-ratio 4.04 exceeded 2.571, the critical *t*-value for a 5 percent level of significance (a 95 percent level of confidence). A *t*-ratio *only* as large as 2.571 would be sufficient to achieve a 5 percent level of significance that $b \neq 0$. The calculated *t*-ratio 4.04 is much larger than the critical *t* for the 5 percent significance level. This means a significance level *lower* than 5 percent (or a confidence level *higher* than 95 percent) would still allow one to reject the hypothesis of no significance ($b = 0$). What is the lowest level of significance or, equivalently, the greatest level of confidence that permits rejecting the hypothesis that $b = 0$ when the computer calculates a *t*-ratio of 4.04? The answer is given by the *p-value* for 4.04, which most statistical software, and even spreadsheets, can calculate.

p-value
The exact level of significance for a test statistic, which is the probability of finding significance when none exists.

The **p-value** associated with a calculated *t*-ratio gives the *exact* level of significance for a *t*-ratio associated with a parameter estimate.[5] In other words, the *p*-value gives the exact probability of committing a Type I error—finding significance when none exists—if you conclude that $b \neq 0$ on the basis of the *t*-ratio calculated by the computer. One minus the *p*-value is the exact degree of confidence that can be assigned to a particular parameter estimate.

The *p*-value for the calculated *t*-ratio 4.04 (= 4.9719/1.23) is 0.010. A *p*-value of 0.010 means that the exact level of significance for a *t*-ratio of 4.04 is 1 percent and the exact level of confidence is 99 percent. Rather than saying *b* is statistically significant at the 5 percent level of significance (or the 95 percent level of confidence), using the *p*-value we can make a more precise, and stronger, statement: $\hat{b}$ is statistically significant at exactly the 1 percent level of significance. In other words, at the 99 percent confidence level advertising affects sales ($b \neq 0$); that is, there is only a 1 percent chance that advertising does *not* affect sales.

While *t*-tests are the traditional means of assessing statistical significance, most computer software packages now routinely print the *p*-values associated with *t*-ratios. Rather than preselecting a level of significance (or level of confidence) for *t*-tests, it is now customary to report the *p*-values associated with the estimated parameters—usually along with standard errors and *t*-ratios—and let the users of the statistical estimations decide whether the level of significance is acceptably low or the level of confidence is acceptably high.

> **Relation** The exact level of significance associated with a *t*-statistic, its *p*-value, gives the exact (or minimum) probability of committing a Type I error—finding significance when none exists—if you conclude that $b \neq 0$ on the basis of the *t*-ratio calculated by the computer. One minus the *p*-value is the exact degree of confidence that can be assigned to a particular parameter estimate.

Now try Technical Problem 5.

4.4 EVALUATION OF THE REGRESSION EQUATION

Once the individual parameter estimates $\hat{a}$ and $\hat{b}$ have been tested for statistical significance using *t*-tests, researchers often wish to evaluate the *complete* estimated regression equation, $Y = \hat{a} + \hat{b}X$. Evaluation of the regression equation involves determining how well the estimated regression equation "explains" the variation

---

[5]Although this section discusses *t*-statistics, a *p*-value can be computed for any test statistic, and it gives the exact significance level for the associated test statistic.

in Y. Two statistics are frequently employed to evaluate the overall acceptability of a regression equation. The first is called the *coefficient of determination*, normally denoted as "R^2" and pronounced "R-square." The second is the *F-statistic*, which is used to test whether the *overall* equation is statistically significant.

The Coefficient of Determination (R^2)

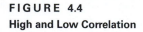

coefficient of determination (R^2)
The fraction of total variation in the dependent variable explained by the regression equation.

The **coefficient of determination (R^2)** measures the fraction of the total variation in the dependent variable that is explained by the regression equation. In terms of the example used earlier, it is the fraction of the variation in sales that is explained by variation in advertising expenditures. Therefore, the value of R^2 can range from 0 (the regression equation explains none of the variation in Y) to 1 (the regression equation explains all the variation in Y). While the R^2 is printed out as a decimal value by most computers, the R^2 is often spoken of in terms of a percentage. For example, if the calculated R^2 is 0.7542, we could say that approximately 75 percent of the variation in Y is explained by the model.

If the value of R^2 is high, there is high correlation between the dependent and independent variables; if it is low, there is low correlation. For example, in Figure 4.4, Panel A, the observations in the scatter diagram all lie rather close to the regression line. Because the deviations from the line are small, the correlation between X and Y is high and the value of R^2 will be high. In the extreme case when all of the observations lie on a straight line, R^2 will be equal to 1. In Panel B, the observations are scattered widely around the regression line. The correlation between X and Y in this case is much less than that in Panel A, so the value of R^2 is rather small.

We must caution you that high correlation between two variables (or even a statistically significant regression coefficient) does not necessarily mean the

FIGURE 4.4
High and Low Correlation

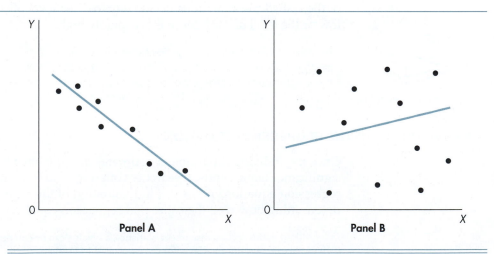

variation in the dependent variable Y is *caused by* the variation in the independent variable X. It might be the case that variation in Y is caused by variation in Z, but X happens to be correlated to Z. Thus, Y and X will be correlated even though variation in X does not cause Y to vary. A high R^2 does not prove that Y and X are causally related, only that Y and X are correlated. We summarize this discussion with a statistical relation:

> **Relation**   The coefficient of determination (R^2) measures the fraction of the total variation in Y that is explained by the variation in X. R^2 ranges in value from 0 (the regression explains none of the variation in Y) to 1 (the regression explains all the variation in Y). A high R^2 indicates Y and X are highly correlated and the scatter diagram tightly fits the sample regression line.

The *F*-Statistic

F-statistic
A statistic used to test whether the overall regression equation is statistically significant.

Although the R^2 is a widely used statistic, it is subjective in the sense of how much explained variation—explained by the regression equation—is enough to view the equation as being statistically significant. An alternative is the **F-statistic.** In very general terms, this statistic provides a measure of the ratio of explained variation (in the dependent variable) to unexplained variation. To test whether the overall equation is significant, this statistic is compared with a critical F-value obtained from an F-table (at the end of this text). The critical F-value is identified by two separate degrees of freedom and the significance level. The first of the degrees of freedom is $k - 1$ (i.e., the number of independent variables) and the second is $n - k$. If the value for the calculated F-statistic exceeds the critical F-value, the regression equation is statistically significant at the specified significance level. The discussion of the F-statistic is summarized in a statistical relation:

> **Relation**   The F-statistic is used to test whether the regression equation as a whole explains a significant amount of the variation in Y. The test involves comparing the F-statistic to the critical F-value with $k - 1$ and $n - k$ degrees of freedom and the chosen level of significance. If the F-statistic exceeds the critical F-value, the regression equation is statistically significant.

Rather than performing an F-test, which requires that you select arbitrarily a significance or confidence level, you may wish to report the exact level of significance for the F-statistic. The p-value for the F-statistic gives the exact level of significance for the regression equation as a whole. One minus the p-value is the exact level of confidence associated with the computed F-statistic.

All the statistics you will need to analyze a regression—the coefficient estimates, the standard errors, the t-ratios, R^2, the F-statistic, and the p-value—are automatically calculated and printed by most available regression programs. As mentioned earlier, our objective is not that you understand how these statistics are calculated. Rather, we want you to know how to set up a regression and interpret the results. We now provide you with a hypothetical example of a regression analysis that might be performed by a manager of a firm.

Controlling Product Quality at SLM: A Regression Example

Specialty Lens Manufacturing (SLM) produces contact lenses for patients who are unable to wear standard contact lenses. These specialty contact lenses must meet extraordinarily strict standards. The production process is not perfect, however, and some lenses have slight flaws. Patients receiving flawed lenses almost always detect the flaws, and the lenses are returned to SLM for replacement. Returned lenses are costly, in terms of both redundant production costs and diminished corporate reputation for SLM. Every week SLM produces 2,400 lenses, and inspectors using high-powered microscopes have time to examine only a fraction of the lenses before they are shipped to doctors.

Management at SLM decided to measure the effectiveness of its inspection process using regression analysis. During a 22-week time period, SLM collected data each week on the number of lenses produced that week that were later returned by doctors because of flaws (F) and the number of hours spent that week examining lenses (H). The manager estimated the regression equation

$$F = a + bH$$

using the 22 weekly observations on F and H. The computer printed out the following output:

DEPENDENT VARIABLE: F		R-SQUARE	F-RATIO	P-VALUE ON F
OBSERVATIONS: 22		0.4527	16.54	0.001
VARIABLE	PARAMETER ESTIMATE	STANDARD ERROR	T-RATIO	P-VALUE
INTERCEPT	90.0	28.13	3.20	0.004
H	−0.80	0.32	−2.50	0.021

As expected, $\hat{a}$ is positive and $\hat{b}$ is negative. If no inspection is done ($H = 0$), SLM's management expects 90 lenses from each week's production to be returned as defective. The estimate of b ($\hat{b} = \Delta F/\Delta H = -0.80$) indicates that each additional hour per week spent inspecting lenses will decrease the number of flawed lenses by 0.8. Thus it takes 10 extra hours of inspection to find eight more flawed lenses.

To determine if the parameter estimates $\hat{a}$ and $\hat{b}$ are significantly different from zero, the manager can conduct a t-test on each estimated parameter. The t-ratios for $\hat{a}$ and $\hat{b}$ are 3.20 and −2.50, respectively:

$$t_{\hat{a}} = 90.0/28.13 = 3.20 \quad \text{and} \quad t_{\hat{b}} = -0.80/0.32 = -2.50$$

The critical t-value is found in the table at the end of the book. There are 22 observations and two parameters, so the degrees of freedom are $n - k = 22 - 2 = 20$. Choosing the 5 percent level of significance (a 95 percent level of confidence), the critical t-value is 2.086. Because the absolute values of $t_{\hat{a}}$ and $t_{\hat{b}}$ both exceed 2.086, both $\hat{a}$ and $\hat{b}$ are statistically significant at the 5 percent significance level.

ILLUSTRATION 4.1

R&D Expenditures and the Value of the Firm

To determine how much to spend on research and development (R&D) activities, a manager may wish to know how R&D expenditures affect the value of the firm. To investigate the relation between the value of a firm and the amount the firm spends on R&D, Wallin and Gilman[a] used simple regression analysis to estimate the model

$$V = a + bR$$

where the value of the firm (V) is measured by the price-to-earnings ratio, and the level of expenditures on R&D (R) is measured by R&D expenditures as a percentage of the firm's total sales.

Wallin and Gilman collected a cross-sectional data set on the 20 firms with the largest R&D expenditures in the 1981–1982 time period. The computer output from a regression program and a scatter diagram showing the 20 data points with the sample regression line are presented here:

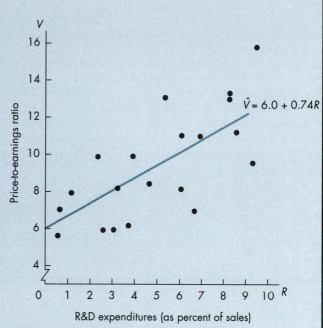

$\hat{V} = 6.0 + 0.74R$

DEPENDENT VARIABLE:	V	R-SQUARE	F-RATIO	P-VALUE ON F	
OBSERVATIONS:	20	0.5274	20.090	0.0003	

VARIABLE	PARAMETER ESTIMATE	STANDARD ERROR	T-RATIO	P-VALUE
INTERCEPT	6.00	0.917	6.54	0.0001
R	0.74	0.165	4.48	0.0003

First, we test to see if the estimate of a is statistically significant. To test for statistical significance, use the t-ratio for $\hat{a}$, which the computer has calculated for you as the ratio of the parameter estimate to its standard error:

$$t_{\hat{a}} = \frac{6.00}{0.917} = 6.54$$

and compare this value with the critical value of t. We use a 5 percent significance level (a 95 percent confidence level). Because there are 20 observations and two parameters are estimated, there are $20 - 2 = 18$ degrees of freedom. The table at the end of the text (critical t-values) gives us a critical value of 2.101. The calculated t-value for $\hat{a}$ is larger than 2.101, so we conclude that $\hat{a}$ is significantly different from 0. The p-value for $\hat{a}$ is so small (0.0001) that the probability of finding significance when none exists is virtually 0. In this case, the selection of a 5 percent significance level greatly underestimates the exact degree of significance associated with the estimate of a. The estimated value of a suggests that firms that spend nothing on R&D, on average, have price-to-earnings ratios of 6.

The estimate of b (0.74) is positive, which suggests V and R are directly related. The calculated t-ratio is 4.48, which is greater than the critical value of t. The p-value for $\hat{b}$ indicates the significance level of the t-test could

(*Continued*)

have been set as low as 0.0003, or 0.03 percent, and the hypothesis that $b = 0$ could be rejected. In other words, with a t-statistic equal to 4.48, the probability of incorrectly concluding that R&D expenditures significantly affect the value of a firm is just 0.03 percent. Or stated equivalently in terms of a confidence level, we can be 99.97 percent confident that the t-test would *not* indicate statistical significance if none existed. The value of $\hat{b}$ implies that if a firm increases R&D expenditures by 1 percent (of sales), the firm can expect its value (as measured by the P/E ratio) to rise by 0.74.

The R^2 for the regression equation indicates that about 53 percent of the total variation in the value of a firm is explained by the regression equation; that is, 53 percent of the variation in V is explained by the variation in R. The regression equation leaves 47 percent of the variation in the value of the firm unexplained.

The F-ratio is used to test for significance of the entire equation. To determine the critical value of F (with a 5 percent significance level), it is necessary to determine the degrees of freedom. In this case, $k - 1 = 2 - 1 = 1$ and $n - k = 20 - 2 = 18$ degrees of freedom. In the table of values of the F-statistic at the end of the text, you can look down the $k - 1 = 1$ column until you get to the 18th row ($n - k = 18$) and read the value 4.41. Since the calculated F-value (20.090) exceeds 4.41, the regression equation is significant at the 5 percent significance level. In fact, the F-value of 20.090 is much larger than the critical F-value for a 5 percent level of significance, suggesting that the exact level of significance will be much lower than 0.05. The p-value for the F-statistic, 0.0003, confirms that the exact significance level is much smaller than 0.05.

[a]C. Wallin and J. Gilman, "Determining the Optimal Level for R&D Spending," *Research Management* 14, no. 5 (Sep./Oct. 1986), pp. 19–24.

Source: Adapted from a regression problem presented in Terry Sincich, *A Course in Modern Business Statistics* (Dellen/Macmillan, 1994), p. 432.

Instead of performing a t-test at a fixed level of significance, the manager could assess the significance of the parameter estimates by examining the p-values for $\hat{a}$ and $\hat{b}$. The exact level of significance for $\hat{a}$ is 0.004, or 0.4 percent, which indicates that the t-statistic of 3.20 is just large enough to reject the hypothesis that $\hat{a}$ is 0 at a significance level of 0.004 (or a confidence level of 0.996). The p-value for $\hat{a}$ is so small that the manager almost certainly has avoided committing a Type I error (finding statistical significance where there is none). The exact level of significance for $\hat{b}$ is 0.021, or 2.1 percent. For both parameter estimates, the p-values provide a stronger assessment of statistical significance than could be established by satisfying the requirements of a t-test performed at a 5 percent level of significance.

Overall, because $R^2 = 0.4527$, the equation explains about 45 percent of the total variation in the dependent variable (F), with 55 percent of the variation in F remaining unexplained. To test for significance of the entire equation, the manager could use an F-test. The critical F-value is obtained from the table at the end of the book. Since $k - 1 = 2 - 1 = 1$, and $n - k = 22 - 2 = 20$, the critical F-value at the 5 percent significance level is 4.35. The F-statistic calculated by the computer, 16.54, exceeds 4.35, and the entire equation is statistically significant. The p-value for the F-statistic shows that the exact level of significance for the entire equation is 0.001, or 0.1 percent (a 99.9 percent level of confidence).

Using the estimated equation, $\hat{F} = 90.0 - 0.80H$, the manager can estimate the number of flawed lenses that will be shipped for various hours of weekly inspection. For example, if inspectors spend 60 hours per week examining lenses, SLM can expect 42 ($= 90 - 0.8 \times 60$) of the lenses shipped to be flawed.

Now try Technical Problems 6–7.

4.5 MULTIPLE REGRESSION

So far we have discussed simple regressions involving a linear relation between the dependent variable Y and a *single* explanatory variable X. In many problems, however, the variation in Y depends on more than one explanatory variable. There may be quite a few variables needed to explain adequately the variation in the dependent variable. **Multiple regression models** use two or more explanatory variables to explain the variation in the dependent variable. In this section, we will show how to use and interpret multiple regression models.

multiple regression models
Regression models that use more than one explanatory variable to explain the variation in the dependent variable.

The Multiple Regression Model

A typical multiple regression equation might take the form

$$Y = a + bX + cW + dZ$$

In this equation, Y is the dependent variable; a is the intercept parameter; X, W, and Z are the explanatory variables; and b, c, and d are the slope parameters for each of these explanatory variables.

As in simple regression, the slope parameters b, c, and d measure the change in Y associated with a one-unit change in one of the explanatory variables, holding the rest of the explanatory variables constant. If, for example, $c = 3$, then a one-unit increase in W results in a three-unit increase in Y, holding X and Z constant.

Estimation of the parameters of a multiple regression equation is accomplished by finding a linear equation that best fits the data. As in simple regression, a computer is used to obtain the parameter estimates, their individual standard errors, the F-statistic, the R^2, and the p-values. The statistical significance of the individual parameters and of the equation as a whole can be determined by t-tests and an F-test, respectively.[6] The R^2 is interpreted as the fraction of the variation in Y explained by the *entire set* of explanatory variables taken together. Indeed, the only real complication introduced by multiple regression is that there are more t-tests to perform. Although (as you may know from courses in statistics) the *calculation* of the parameter estimates becomes much more difficult as additional independent variables are added, the manner in which they are *interpreted* does not change. Illustration 4.2 provides an example of multiple regression.

Now try Technical Problems 8–9.

4.6 NONLINEAR REGRESSION ANALYSIS

While linear regression models can be applied to a wide variety of economic relations, there are also many economic relations that are nonlinear in nature. Nonlinear regression models are used when the underlying relation between Y and X plots as a curve, rather than a straight line. An analyst generally chooses a nonlinear regression model when the scatter diagram shows a curvilinear pattern.

---

[6]When the p-value for a parameter estimate is not small enough to meet the researcher's tolerance for risk of committing a Type I error, the associated explanatory variable is typically dropped from the regression equation. A new equation is estimated with only the explanatory variables that have sufficiently small p-values.

In some cases, economic theory will strongly suggest that Y and X are related in a nonlinear fashion, and the analyst can expect to see a curvilinear pattern in the scatter of data points. Later in this text, we will introduce you to several important economic relations that are nonlinear in nature. You will need to know how to estimate the parameters of a nonlinear economic relation using the techniques of regression analysis.

In this section, we will show you two forms of nonlinear regression models for which the parameters can be estimated using *linear* regression analysis. The trick to using *linear* regression to estimate the parameters in *nonlinear* models is to transform the nonlinear relation into one that is linear and can be estimated by the techniques of least-squares. Two extremely useful forms of nonlinear models that you will encounter later in the text are (1) quadratic regression models and (2) log-linear regression models. As you will see, using either one of these two nonlinear models does not complicate the analysis much at all.

Quadratic Regression Models

quadratic regression model
A nonlinear regression model of the form $Y = a + bX + cX^2$.

One of the most useful nonlinear forms for managerial economics is the **quadratic regression model,** which can be expressed as

$$Y = a + bX + cX^2$$

In a number of situations involving production and cost relations examined later in this book, the theoretical relations between economic variables will graph as either a ∪-shaped or an inverted-∪-shaped curve. You may recall from your high school algebra class that quadratic functions have graphs that are either ∪- or ∩-shaped, depending on the signs of b and c. If b is negative and c is positive, the quadratic function is ∪-shaped. If b is positive and c is negative, the quadratic function is ∩-shaped. Thus, a ∪-shaped quadratic equation ($b < 0$ and $c > 0$) is appropriate when as X increases, Y first falls, eventually reaches a minimum, and then rises thereafter. Alternatively, an inverted-∪-shaped quadratic equation ($b > 0$ and $c < 0$) is appropriate if as X increases, Y first rises, eventually reaches a peak, and then falls thereafter.

To estimate the three parameters of the quadratic relation (a, b, and c), the equation must be transformed into a linear form that can be estimated using linear regression analysis. This task is accomplished by creating a new variable Z, defined as $Z = X^2$, then substituting Z for X^2 to transform the quadratic model into a linear model:

$$Y = a + bX + cX^2$$
$$= a + bX + cZ$$

The slope parameter for Z (c) is identical to the slope parameter for X^2 (c).

This simple transformation is accomplished by having the computer create a new variable Z by squaring the values of X for each observation. You then regress Y on X and Z. The computer will generate an intercept parameter estimate ($\hat{a}$), a slope parameter estimate for $X(\hat{b})$, and a slope parameter estimate for $Z(\hat{c})$. The

ILLUSTRATION 4.2

Do Auto Insurance Premiums Really Vary with Costs?

In an article examining the effect of Proposition 103 on auto insurance rates in California, Benjamin Zycher noted that an adult male with no citations or at-fault accidents who lived in Hollywood could expect to pay an annual insurance premium of $1,817. The same adult male driver would have to pay only $862 if he lived in Monrovia, only $697 in San Diego, and only $581 in San Jose. Zycher explains that this variability in premiums exists because insurers obviously determine premiums by considering the individual's driving record, type of car, sex, age, and various other factors that are "statistically significant predictors of an individual driver's future losses."

Also important in the determination of insurance premiums is the geographic location of the driver's residence. Future losses are likely to be smaller in rural areas compared with urban areas because of lower vehicle densities, reduced theft, smaller repair costs, and so on. Using data on bodily injury premiums for 20 California counties, we investigated the relation between insurance premiums and two explanatory variables: the number of claims and the average dollar cost of a claim in the various counties. Specifically, we wanted to determine if the variation in premiums across counties can be adequately explained by cost differences across the counties.

Using the data shown in the accompanying table, we estimated the following multiple regression equation:

$$P = a + b_1N + b_2C$$

where P is the average bodily injury premium paid per auto, N is the number of claims per thousand insured vehicles, and C is the average dollar amount of each bodily injury claim. The computer output for this multiple regression equation is given on the next page.

There is evidence from these parameter estimates that bodily injury premiums in a particular county are positively related to both the number of

Bodily Injury in California: Claims, Costs, and Premiums

Country	Claims[a] (N)	Cost[b] (C)	Annual premium[c] (P)
Los Angeles	23.9	$10,197	$319.04
Orange	19.5	9,270	255.00
Ventura	16.7	9,665	225.51
San Francisco	16.3	8,705	208.95
Riverside	15.2	8,888	200.13
San Bernardino	15.6	8,631	196.22
San Diego	16.0	8,330	191.80
Alameda	14.4	8,654	191.46
Marin	13.0	8,516	190.78
San Mateo	14.1	7,738	189.01
Sacramento	15.3	7,881	181.42
Santa Clara	14.4	7,723	179.74
Contra Costa	13.2	8,702	177.92
Santa Barbara	10.7	9,077	176.65
Sonoma	10.6	9,873	171.38
Fresno	14.7	7,842	168.11
Kern	11.9	7,717	160.97
Humboldt	12.2	7,798	151.02
Butte	11.1	8,783	129.84
Shasta	9.7	9,803	126.34

[a]Per thousand insured vehicles.
[b]Average per claim.
[c]Average premium income per insured auto.
Source: Western Insurance Information Service.

claims in that county and the average cost of those claims. Specifically, an additional claim per thousand vehicles in a county ($\Delta N = 1$) tends to increase yearly premiums by $11.32. A $1,000 increase in the average cost of claims in a county ($\Delta C = 1,000$) tends to increase premiums by about $11 annually. The intercept in this regression has no meaningful interpretation.

The p-values for the individual parameter estimates indicate that all estimates are significant at less than the 0.05 level. You can confirm this by performing t-tests at the 5 percent significance level on each of the three estimated parameters.

(Continued)

DEPENDENT VARIABLE: P	R-SQUARE	F-RATIO	P-VALUE ON F
OBSERVATIONS: 20	0.9116	87.659	0.0001

VARIABLE	PARAMETER ESTIMATE	STANDARD ERROR	T-RATIO	P-VALUE
INTERCEPT	−74.139	34.612	−2.14	0.0470
N	11.320	0.953	11.88	0.0001
C	0.01155	0.004	2.87	0.0107

Notice also that the R^2 is 0.9116, indicating that 91 percent of the variation in premiums is explained by variables N and C. The p-value on the F-ratio also provides more statistical evidence that the relation between the dependent variable P and the explanatory variables N and C is quite strong. The critical F-value for $F_{2,17}$ at a 5 percent level of significance is 3.59. Because the F-statistic exceeds this value by a large amount, the regression equation is statistically significant at a level below 0.01 percent.

It is interesting to note how well the level of premiums can be explained using only two explanatory variables. Indeed, this regression analysis supports Benjamin Zycher's claim that the substantial statewide variation in California auto insurance premiums can be attributed to geographic differences in the costs incurred by insurers.

Source: Benjamin Zycher, "Automobile Insurance Regulation, Direct Democracy, and the Interests of Consumers," *Regulation*, Summer 1990.

estimated slope parameter for Z is $\hat{c}$, which, of course, is the slope parameter on X^2. We illustrate this procedure with an example.

Figure 4.5 on page 145 shows a scatter diagram for 12 observations on Y and X (shown by the table in the figure). When we look at the scatter of data points, it is clear that fitting a straight line through the data points would produce a "poor" fit but fitting a U-shaped curve will produce a much better fit. To estimate the parameters of a quadratic regression equation, a new variable Z ($= X^2$) is generated on the computer. The actual data used in the regression are presented in Figure 4.5. The computer printout from the regression of Y on X and Z is shown here:

DEPENDENT VARIABLE: Y	R-SQUARE	F-RATIO	P-VALUE ON F
OBSERVATIONS: 12	0.7542	13.80	0.0018

VARIABLE	PARAMETER ESTIMATE	STANDARD ERROR	T-RATIO	P-VALUE
INTERCEPT	140.08	16.80	8.34	0.0001
X	−19.51	4.05	−4.82	0.0010
Z	1.01	0.20	5.05	0.0006

FIGURE 4.5
A Quadratic Regression Equation

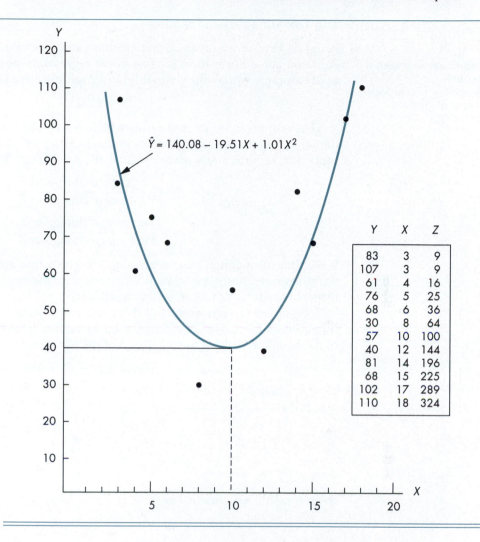

$$\hat{Y} = 140.08 - 19.51X + 1.01X^2$$

Y	X	Z
83	3	9
107	3	9
61	4	16
76	5	25
68	6	36
30	8	64
57	10	100
40	12	144
81	14	196
68	15	225
102	17	289
110	18	324

Thus, the estimated quadratic regression equation is

$$\hat{Y} = 140.08 - 19.51X + 1.01X^2$$

The estimated slope parameter for Z is 1.01. As explained above, 1.01 is also the slope parameter estimate for X^2. The estimated equation can be used to estimate the value of Y for any particular value of X. For example, if X is equal to 10, the quadratic regression equation predicts that Y will be equal to 45.98 ($= 140.08 - 19.51 \times 10 + 1.01 \times 10^2$). In any multiple regression equation, the estimated parameters are tested for statistical significance by performing the usual t-tests as discussed above.

Now try Technical Problem 10.

Log-Linear Regression Models

log-linear regression model
A nonlinear regression model of the form $Y = aX^bZ^c$.

Another kind of nonlinear equation that can be estimated by transforming the equation into a linear form is a **log-linear regression model** in which Y is related to one or more explanatory variables in a multiplicative fashion

$$Y = aX^bZ^c$$

This nonlinear functional form, which we employ in Chapter 7 to estimate demand functions and in the appendix to Chapter 10 to estimate production functions, is particularly useful because the parameters b and c are elasticities

$$b = \frac{\text{Percentage change in } Y}{\text{Percentage change in } X}$$

$$c = \frac{\text{Percentage change in } Y}{\text{Percentage change in } Z}$$

Using this form of nonlinear regression, the elasticities are estimated directly: The parameter estimates associated with each explanatory variable are elasticities. (The parameter a, however, is not an elasticity.)

To estimate the parameters of this nonlinear equation, it must be transformed into a linear form. This is accomplished by taking *natural logarithms* of both sides of the equation. Taking the logarithm of the function $Y = aX^bZ^c$ results in

$$\ln Y = (\ln a) + b(\ln X) + c(\ln Z)$$

So, if we define

$$Y' = \ln Y$$
$$X' = \ln X$$
$$Z' = \ln Z$$
$$a' = \ln a$$

the regression equation is linear

$$Y' = a' + bX' + cZ'$$

Once estimates have been obtained, tests for statistical significance and evaluation of the equation are done precisely as we described earlier. The only difference is that the intercept parameter estimate provided by the computer is not a; rather it is equal to $\ln a$. To obtain the parameter estimate for a, we must take the antilog of the parameter estimate $\hat{a}'$:

$$\text{antilog } (\hat{a}') = e^{a'}$$

The antilog of a number can be found using the "e^x" key on most hand calculators. We illustrate the log-linear regression model with an example.

Panel A of Figure 4.6 shows a scatter diagram of 12 observations on Y and X. The scatter diagram in Panel A suggests that a curvilinear model will fit these data better than a linear model. Suppose we use a log-linear model with one

FIGURE 4.6

A Log-Linear Regression Equation

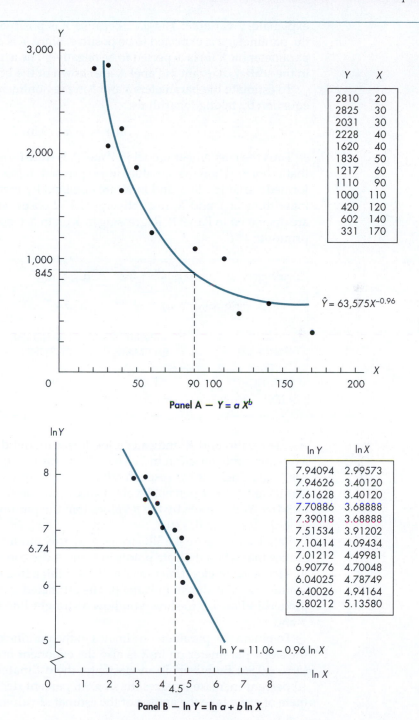

Y	X
2810	20
2825	30
2031	30
2228	40
1620	40
1836	50
1217	60
1110	90
1000	110
420	120
602	140
331	170

$\hat{Y} = 63{,}575 X^{-0.96}$

Panel A — $Y = a\,X^b$

ln Y	ln X
7.94094	2.99573
7.94626	3.40120
7.61628	3.40120
7.70886	3.68888
7.39018	3.68888
7.51534	3.91202
7.10414	4.09434
7.01212	4.49981
6.90776	4.70048
6.04025	4.78749
6.40026	4.94164
5.80212	5.13580

$\ln Y = 11.06 - 0.96 \ln X$

Panel B — $\ln Y = \ln a + b \ln X$

explanatory variable: $Y = aX^b$. Because Y is positive at all points in the sample, the parameter a is expected to be positive. Since Y is decreasing as X increases, the parameter on $\overline{X}$ (b) is expected to be negative. The actual values of Y and X plotted in the scatter diagram in Panel A are shown in the box in Panel A.

To estimate the parameters a and b in the nonlinear equation, we transform the equation by taking logarithms:

$$\ln Y = \ln a + b \ln X$$

Thus the curvilinear model in Panel A is transformed into an equivalent model that is linear when the variables are expressed in logarithms. In Panel B, the transformed variables, $\ln Y$ and $\ln X$, are obtained by instructing the computer to take logarithms of Y and X, respectively. The 12 observations, in terms of logarithms, are displayed in Panel B. Regressing $\ln Y$ on $\ln X$ results in the following computer printout:

DEPENDENT VARIABLE:	LNY	R-SQUARE	F-RATIO	P-VALUE ON F
OBSERVATIONS:	12	0.8750	70.0	0.0001

VARIABLE	PARAMETER ESTIMATE	STANDARD ERROR	T-RATIO	P-VALUE
INTERCEPT	11.06	0.48	23.04	0.0001
LNX	−0.96	0.11	−8.73	0.0001

As the F-ratio and R^2 indicate, a log-linear model does a quite reasonable job of explaining the variation in Y. The t-ratios for the intercept and slope parameters are 23.04 and −8.73, respectively. Both parameter estimates are statistically significant at the 1 percent level because both t-statistics exceed the critical t-value of 3.169. You can see by the p-values that the parameter estimates are significant at levels less than 0.0001.

Panel B of Figure 4.6 illustrates why this model is called a log-linear model. Notice that when the data points in Panel A are converted to logarithms ($\ln Y$ and $\ln X$), the *natural logarithms* of Y and X exhibit a linear relation, as indicated by the scatter diagram shown in Panel B. The estimated log-linear regression equation is plotted in Panel B to show you how a straight line fits the natural logarithms of Y and X.

To obtain the parameter estimates in the nonlinear equation $Y = aX^b$, note that the slope parameter on $\ln X$ is also the exponent on X in the nonlinear equation ($\hat{b} = -0.96$) Because b is an elasticity, the estimated elasticity is −0.96. Thus, a 10 percent increase in X results in a 9.6 percent decrease in Y. To obtain an estimate of a, we take the antilog of the estimated value of the intercept parameter

$$\hat{a} = \text{antilog } (11.06) = e^{11.06} = 63,575$$

Now try Technical
Problem 11.

To show that the two models are mathematically equivalent, we have calculated the predicted value of ln Y when ln X is equal to 4.5. Using the estimated log-linear regression equation, we find that when ln $X = 4.5$, ln $Y = 6.74$ [$= 11.06 - 0.96(4.5)$]. Taking antilogs of ln Y and ln X, we get the point $X = 90$ and $Y = 845$ [$= 63{,}575(90)^{-0.96}$]. Thus, the two equations are equivalent representations of the mathematical relation between Y and X.

We hope you have seen from this brief overview that regression analysis is extremely useful because it offers managers a way of estimating the functions they need for managerial decision making. We say much more about specific applications of regression analysis in later chapters, but at this point we want you simply to understand that regression techniques are actually used in managerial decision making.

4.7 SUMMARY

■ A simple linear regression model relates a dependent variable Y to a single independent (or explanatory) variable X in a linear fashion: $Y = a + bX$. The intercept parameter a gives the value of Y at the point where the regression line crosses the Y-axis, which is the value of Y when X is zero. The slope parameter b gives the change in Y associated with a one-unit change in X ($b = \Delta Y/\Delta X$). Since the variation in Y is affected not only by variation in X, but also by various random effects as well, the actual value of Y cannot be predicted exactly. The regression equation is correctly interpreted as providing the average value, or the expected value, of Y for a given value of X. (LO1)

■ Parameter estimates are obtained by choosing values of a and b that create the best-fitting line that passes through the scatter diagram of the sample data points. This method of estimating a and b is the method of least-squares, and the estimated regression line, $\hat{Y} = \hat{a} + \hat{b}X$, is the sample regression line, which estimates the true or population regression line. Many computer software programs, including Microsoft's Excel spreadsheet, can compute least-squares estimates of regression parameters. (LO2)

■ If an estimated coefficient is far enough away from 0, it is said to be statistically significant. The question of statistical significance arises because the estimates $\hat{a}$ and $\hat{b}$ do not, in general, equal the true values of a and b. The estimator of a parameter is unbiased if the expected value of the associated relative frequency distribution is equal to the true value of the parameter. Although the method of least-squares can produce unbiased estimates of a and b, it is necessary to test the

parameter estimates for statistical significance. In testing for statistical significance, the level of significance chosen for the test determines the probability of committing a Type I error, which is the mistake of finding a parameter to be significant when it is not truly significant. To test for statistical significance of a parameter estimate $\hat{b}$, compute the t-ratio, which is equal to $\hat{b}$ divided by the standard error of the estimate $\hat{b}$. If the absolute value of the t-ratio is greater (less) than the critical t-value, then $\hat{b}$ is (is not) statistically significant. As an alternative to a t-test, p-values can be used to determine statistical significance. The exact level of significance associated with a t-statistic, called its p-value, gives the exact (or minimum) probability of committing a Type I error—finding significance when none exists—if you conclude that $b \neq 0$ on the basis of the t-ratio calculated by the computer. (LO3)

■ The coefficient of determination R^2 measures the percentage of the total variation in the dependent variable that is explained by the regression equation. The value of R^2 ranges from 0 to 1. A high R^2 indicates Y and X are highly correlated and the scatter diagram tightly fits the sample regression line. The F-statistic is used to test whether the regression equation as a whole explains a significant amount of the variation in Y. The test involves comparing the F-statistic to the critical F-value with $k - 1$ and $n - k$ degrees of freedom and the chosen level of significance. If the F-statistic exceeds the critical F-value, the regression equation is statistically significant. (LO4)

■ Multiple regression uses more than one explanatory variable to explain the variation in the dependent variable. The coefficient for each of the explanatory variables measures the change in Y associated with a one-unit change in that explanatory variable. (*LO5*)

- Two types of nonlinear models can be easily transformed into linear models that can be estimated using linear regression analysis. These are quadratic regression models and log-linear regression models. Quadratic regression models are appropriate when the curve fitting the scatter plot is either $\cup$-shaped or $\cap$-shaped. A quadratic equation, $Y = a + bX + cX^2$, can be transformed into a linear form by computing a new variable $Z = X^2$, which is then substituted for X^2 in the regression. Then, the regression equation to be estimated is $Y = a + bX + cZ$. Log-linear regression models are appropriate when the relation is in multiplicative exponential form $Y = aX^bZ^c$. The equation is transformed by taking natural logarithms: $\ln Y = \ln a + b \ln X + c \ln Z$. The coefficients b and c are elasticities. (*LO6*)

KEY TERMS

coefficient of determination (R^2)	level of significance	sample regression line
critical value of t	log-linear regression model	scatter diagram
cross-sectional	method of least-squares	slope parameter
degrees of freedom	multiple regression models	statistically significant
dependent variable	parameter estimation	time-series
estimates	parameters	t-ratio
estimators	population regression line	true (or actual) relation
explanatory variables	p-value	t-statistic
fitted or predicted value	quadratic regression model	t-test
F-statistic	random error term	Type I error
hypothesis testing	regression analysis	unbiased estimator
intercept parameter	relative frequency distribution	
level of confidence	residual	

TECHNICAL PROBLEMS

1. A simple linear regression equation relates R and W as follows:

$$R = a + bW$$

   a. The explanatory variable is _____, and the dependent variable is _____.
   b. The slope parameter is _____, and the intercept parameter is _____.
   c. When W is zero, R equals _____.
   d. For each one unit increase in W, the change in R is _____ units.

2. Regression analysis is often referred to as least-squares regression. Why is this name appropriate?

3. Regression analysis involves estimating the values of parameters and testing the estimated parameters for significance. Why must parameter estimates be tested for statistical significance?

4. Evaluate the following statements:

   a. "The smaller the standard error of the estimate, $S_{\hat{b}}$, the more accurate the parameter estimate."

b. "If $\hat{b}$ is an unbiased estimate of b, then $\hat{b}$ equals b."

c. "The more precise the estimate of $\hat{b}$ (i.e., the smaller the standard error of $\hat{b}$), the higher the t-ratio."

5. The linear regression in problem 1 is estimated using 26 observations on R and W. The least-squares estimate of b is 40.495, and the standard error of the estimate is 16.250. Perform a t-test for statistical significance at the 5 percent level of significance.

a. There are _____ degrees of freedom for the t-test.

b. The value of the t-statistic is _____. The critical t-value for the test is _____.

c. Is $\hat{b}$ statistically significant? Explain.

d. The p-value for the t-statistic is _____. (*Hint:* In this problem, the t-table provides the answer.) The p-value gives the probability of rejecting the hypothesis that _____ ($b = 0$, $b \neq 0$) when b is truly equal to _____. The confidence level for the test is _____ percent.

e. What does it mean to say an estimated parameter is statistically significant at the 5 percent significance level?

f. What does it mean to say an estimated parameter is statistically significant at the 95 percent confidence level?

g. How does the level of significance differ from the level of confidence?

6. Ten data points on Y and X are employed to estimate the parameters in the linear relation $Y = a + bX$. The computer output from the regression analysis is the following:

DEPENDENT VARIABLE: Y	R-SQUARE	F-RATIO	P-VALUE ON F
OBSERVATIONS: 10	0.5223	8.747	0.0187

VARIABLE	PARAMETER ESTIMATE	STANDARD ERROR	T-RATIO	P-VALUE
INTERCEPT	800.0	189.125	4.23	0.0029
X	−2.50	0.850	−2.94	0.0187

a. What is the equation of the sample regression line?

b. Test the intercept and slope estimates for statistical significance at the 1 percent significance level. Explain how you performed this test, and present your results.

c. Interpret the p-values for the parameter estimates.

d. Test the overall equation for statistical significance at the 1 percent significance level. Explain how you performed this test, and present your results. Interpret the p-value for the F-statistic.

e. If X equals 140, what is the fitted (or predicted) value of Y?

f. What fraction of the total variation in Y is explained by the regression?

7. A simple linear regression equation, $Y = a + bX$, is estimated by a computer program, which produces the following output:

DEPENDENT VARIABLE: Y	R-SQUARE	F-RATIO	P-VALUE ON F		
OBSERVATIONS: 25	0.7482	68.351	0.00001		
VARIABLE	PARAMETER ESTIMATE	STANDARD ERROR	T-RATIO	P-VALUE	
INTERCEPT	325.24	125.09	2.60	0.0160	
X	0.8057	0.2898	2.78	0.0106	

    a. How many degrees of freedom does this regression analysis have?

    b. What is the critical value of t at the 5 percent level of significance?

    c. Test to see if the estimates of a and b are statistically significant.

    d. Discuss the p-values for the estimates of a and b.

    e. How much of the total variation in Y is explained by this regression equation? How much of the total variation in Y is unexplained by this regression equation?

    f. What is the critical value of the F-statistic at a 5 percent level of significance? Is the overall regression equation statistically significant?

    g. If X equals 100, what value do you expect Y will take? If X equals 0?

8. Evaluate each of the following statements:

    a. "In a multiple regression model, the coefficients on the explanatory variables measure the percent of the total variation in the dependent variable Y explained by that explanatory variable."

    b. "The more degrees of freedom in the regression, the more likely it is that a given t-ratio exceeds the critical t-value."

    c. "The coefficient of determination (R^2) can be exactly equal to one only when the sample regression line passes through each and every data point."

9. A multiple regression model, $R = a + bW + cX + dZ$, is estimated by a computer package, which produces the following output:

DEPENDENT VARIABLE: R	R-SQUARE	F-RATIO	P-VALUE ON F		
OBSERVATIONS: 34	0.3179	4.660	0.00865		
VARIABLE	PARAMETER ESTIMATE	STANDARD ERROR	T-RATIO	P-VALUE	
INTERCEPT	12.6	8.34	1.51	0.1413	
W	22.0	3.61	6.09	0.0001	
X	−4.1	1.65	−2.48	0.0188	
Z	16.3	4.45	3.66	0.0010	

    a. How many degrees of freedom does this regression analysis have?

    b. What is the critical value of t at the 2 percent level of significance?

c. Test to see if the estimates of $a, b, c,$ and d are statistically significant at the 2 percent significance level. What are the exact levels of significance for each of the parameter estimates?

d. How much of the total variation in R is explained by this regression equation? How much of the total variation in R is unexplained by this regression equation?

e. What is the critical value of the F-statistic at the 1 percent level of significance? Is the overall regression equation statistically significant at the 1 percent level of significance? What is the exact level of significance for the F-statistic?

f. If W equals 10, X equals 5, and Z equals 30, what value do you predict R will take? If $W, X,$ and Z are all equal to 0?

10. Eighteen data points on M and X are used to estimate the quadratic regression model $M = a + bX + cX^2$. A new variable, Z, is created to transform the regression into a linear form. The computer output from this regression is

DEPENDENT VARIABLE:	M	R-SQUARE	F-RATIO	P-VALUE ON F
OBSERVATIONS:	18	0.6713	15.32	0.0002

VARIABLE	PARAMETER ESTIMATE	STANDARD ERROR	T-RATIO	P-VALUE
INTERCEPT	290.0630	53.991	5.37	0.0001
X	−5.8401	2.1973	−2.66	0.0179
Z	0.07126	0.01967	3.62	0.0025

a. What is the variable Z equal to?

b. Write the estimated quadratic relation between M and X.

c. Test each of the three estimated parameters for statistical significance at the 2 percent level of significance. Show how you performed these tests and present the results.

d. Interpret the p-value for $\hat{c}$.

e. What is the predicted value of M when X is 300?

11. Suppose Y is related to R and S in the following nonlinear way:

$$Y = aR^bS^c$$

a. How can this nonlinear equation be transformed into a linear form that can be analyzed by using multiple regression analysis?

Sixty-three observations are used to obtain the following regression results:

DEPENDENT VARIABLE:	LNY	R-SQUARE	F-RATIO	P-VALUE ON F
OBSERVATIONS:	63	0.8151	132.22	0.0001

VARIABLE	PARAMETER ESTIMATE	STANDARD ERROR	T-RATIO	P-VALUE
INTERCEPT	−1.386	0.83	−1.67	0.1002
LNR	0.452	0.175	2.58	0.0123
LNS	0.30	0.098	3.06	0.0033

b. Test each estimated coefficient for statistical significance at the 5 percent level of significance. What are the exact significance levels for each of the estimated coefficients?

c. Test the overall equation for statistical significance at the 5 percent level of significance. Interpret the p-value on the F-statistic.

d. How well does this nonlinear model fit the data?

e. Using the estimated value of the intercept, compute an estimate of a.

f. If $R = 200$ and $S = 1,500$, compute the expected value of Y.

g. What is the estimated elasticity of R? Of S?

APPLIED PROBLEMS

1. The director of marketing at Vanguard Corporation believes that sales of the company's Bright Side laundry detergent (S) are related to Vanguard's own advertising expenditure (A), as well as the combined advertising expenditures of its three biggest rival detergents (R). The marketing director collects 36 weekly observations on S, A, and R to estimate the following multiple regression equation:

$$S = a + bA + cR$$

where S, A, and R are measured in dollars per week. Vanguard's marketing director is comfortable using parameter estimates that are statistically significant at the 10 percent level or better.

a. What sign does the marketing director expect a, b, and c to have?

b. Interpret the coefficients a, b, and c.

The regression output from the computer is as follows:

DEPENDENT VARIABLE:	S	R-SQUARE	F-RATIO	P-VALUE ON F
OBSERVATIONS:	36	0.2247	4.781	0.0150

VARIABLE	PARAMETER ESTIMATE	STANDARD ERROR	T-RATIO	P-VALUE
INTERCEPT	175086.0	63821.0	2.74	0.0098
A	0.8550	0.3250	2.63	0.0128
R	−0.284	0.164	−1.73	0.0927

c. Does Vanguard's advertising expenditure have a statistically significant effect on the sales of Bright Side detergent? Explain, using the appropriate p-value.

d. Does advertising by its three largest rivals affect sales of Bright Side detergent in a statistically significant way? Explain, using the appropriate p-value.

e. What fraction of the total variation in sales of Bright Side remains unexplained? What can the marketing director do to increase the explanatory power of the sales equation? What other explanatory variables might be added to this equation?

f. What is the expected level of sales each week when Vanguard spends $40,000 per week and the combined advertising expenditures for the three rivals are $100,000 per week?

2. In his analysis of California's Proposition 103 (see Illustration 4.2), Benjamin Zycher notes that one of the most important provisions of this proposition is eliminating the practice by insurance companies of basing premiums (in part) on the geographic location of drivers. Prohibiting the use of geographic location to assess the risk of a driver creates a substantial implicit subsidy from low-loss counties to high-loss counties, such as Los Angeles, Orange, and San Francisco counties. Zycher hypothesizes that the percent of voters favoring Proposition 103 in a given county (V) is inversely related to the (average) percentage change in auto premiums (P) that the proposition confers upon the drivers of that county.

The data in the table below were presented by Zycher to support his contention that V and P are inversely related:

County	Percent for Proposition 103 (V)	Change in average premium (P)
Los Angeles	62.8	−21.4
Orange	51.7	−8.2
San Francisco	65.2	−0.9
Alameda	58.9	+8.0
Marin	53.5	+9.1
Santa Clara	51.0	+11.8
San Mateo	52.8	+12.6
Santa Cruz	54.2	+13.0
Ventura	44.8	+1.4
San Diego	44.1	+10.7
Monterey	41.6	+15.3
Sacramento	39.3	+16.0
Tulare	28.7	+23.3
Sutter	32.3	+37.1
Lassen	29.9	+46.5
Siskiyou	29.9	+49.8
Modoc	23.2	+57.6

Sources: California Department of Insurance and Office of the California Secretary of State.

Using the data in the table, we estimated the regression equation

$$V = a + bP$$

to see if voting behavior is related to the change in auto insurance premiums in a statistically significant way. Here is the regression output from the computer:

DEPENDENT VARIABLE: V	R-SQUARE	F-RATIO	P-VALUE ON F
OBSERVATIONS: 17	0.7399	42.674	0.0001

VARIABLE	PARAMETER ESTIMATE	STANDARD ERROR	T-RATIO	P-VALUE
INTERCEPT	53.682	2.112	25.42	0.0001
P	−0.528	0.081	−6.52	0.0001

a. Does this regression equation provide evidence of a statistically significant relation between voter support for Proposition 103 in a county and changes in average auto premiums affected by Proposition 103 in that county? Perform an *F*-test at the 95 percent level of confidence.

b. Test the intercept estimate for significance at the 95 percent confidence level. If Proposition 103 has no impact on auto insurance premiums in any given county, what percent of voters do you expect will vote for the proposition?

c. Test the slope estimate for significance at the 95 percent confidence level. If *P* increases by 10 percent, by what percent does the vote for Proposition 103 decline?

3. A security analyst specializing in the stocks of the motion picture industry wishes to examine the relation between the number of movie theater tickets sold in December and the annual level of earnings in the motion picture industry. Time-series data for the last 15 years are used to estimate the regression model

$$E = a + bN$$

where *E* is total earnings of the motion picture industry measured in dollars per year and *N* is the number of tickets sold in December. The regression output is as follows:

DEPENDENT VARIABLE: E		R-SQUARE	F-RATIO	P-VALUE ON F
OBSERVATIONS: 15		0.8311	63.96	0.0001
VARIABLE	PARAMETER ESTIMATE	STANDARD ERROR	T-RATIO	P-VALUE
INTERCEPT	25042000.0	20131000.0	1.24	0.2369
N	32.31	8.54	3.78	0.0023

a. How well do movie ticket sales in December explain the level of earnings for the entire year? Present statistical evidence to support your answer.

b. On average, what effect does a 100,000-ticket increase in December sales have on the annual earnings in the movie industry?

c. Sales of movie tickets in December are expected to be approximately 950,000. According to this regression analysis, what do you expect earnings for the year to be?

4. The manager of Collins Import Autos believes the number of cars sold in a day (*Q*) depends on two factors: (1) the number of hours the dealership is open (*H*) and (2) the number of salespersons working that day (*S*). After collecting data for two months (53 days), the manager estimates the following log-linear model:

$$Q = aH^bS^c$$

a. Explain how to transform this log-linear model into a linear form that can be estimated using multiple regression analysis.

The computer output for the multiple regression analysis is shown below:

DEPENDENT VARIABLE:	LNQ	R-SQUARE	F-RATIO	P-VALUE ON F
OBSERVATIONS: 53		0.5452	29.97	0.0001

VARIABLE	PARAMETER ESTIMATE	STANDARD ERROR	T-RATIO	P-VALUE
INTERCEPT	0.9162	0.2413	3.80	0.0004
LNH	0.3517	0.1021	3.44	0.0012
LNS	0.2550	0.0785	3.25	0.0021

b. How do you interpret coefficients b and c? If the dealership increases the number of salespersons by 20 percent, what will be the percentage increase in daily sales?

c. Test the overall model for statistical significance at the 5 percent significance level.

d. What percent of the total variation in daily auto sales is explained by this equation? What could you suggest to increase this percentage?

e. Test the intercept for statistical significance at the 5 percent level of significance. If H and S both equal 0, are sales expected to be 0? Explain why or why not.

f. Test the estimated coefficient b for statistical significance. If the dealership decreases its hours of operation by 10 percent, what is the expected impact on daily sales?

□ **STATISTICAL APPENDIX**

Multicollinearity

When using regression analysis, we assume that the explanatory (the right-hand side) variables are linearly independent of one another. If this assumption is violated, we have the problem of *multicollinearity*. Under normal circumstances, multicollinearity will result in the estimated standard errors being larger than their true values. This means, then, that if multicollinearity exists, finding statistical significance will be more difficult. More specifically, if moderate multicollinearity is present, the estimate of the coefficient, $\hat{b}$, will be unbiased but the estimated standard error, $S_{\hat{b}}$, will be increased. Thus the t-coefficient, $t = \hat{b}/S_{\hat{b}}$, will be reduced, and it will be more difficult to find statistical significance.

Multicollinearity is not unusual. The question is what to do about it. As a general rule, the answer is *nothing*. To illustrate, consider the following function that denotes some true relation:

$$Y = a + bX + cZ$$

Problems Encountered in Regression Analysis

If X and Z are not linearly independent—if X and Z are collinear—the standard errors of the estimates for b and c will be increased. Shouldn't we just drop one? Not in the normal instance. If Z is an important explanatory variable, the exclusion of Z would be a *specification error* and would result in biased estimates of the coefficients— a much more severe problem.

Heteroscedasticity

The problem of *heteroscedasticity* is encountered when the variance of the error term is not constant. It can be encountered when there exists some relation between the error term and one or more of the explanatory variables— for example, when there exists a positive relation between X and the errors (i.e., large errors are associated with large values of X).

In such a case, the estimated parameters are still unbiased, but the standard errors of the coefficients are biased, so the calculated t-ratios are unreliable. This problem, most normally encountered in cross-section studies, sometimes can be corrected by performing a transformation on the data or equation. Otherwise, it becomes necessary to employ a technique called weighted least-squares estimation.

Autocorrelation

The problem of *autocorrelation*, associated with time-series data, occurs when the errors are not independent over time. For example, it could be the case that a high error in one period tends to promote a high error in the following period.

With autocorrelation (sometimes referred to as *serial correlation*) the estimated parameters are unbiased, but the standard errors are again biased, resulting in unreliability of the calculated t-ratios. Tests for determining if autocorrelation is present (most notably the Durbin-Watson test) are included in most of the available regression packages. Furthermore, most packages also include techniques for estimating an equation in the presence of autocorrelation.

Chapter 5

Theory of Consumer Behavior

After reading this chapter, you will be able to:

5.1 Explain the concept of utility and the basic assumptions underlying consumer preferences.

5.2 Define the concept of indifference curves and explain the properties of indifference curves and indifference maps.

5.3 Construct a consumer's budget line and explain how to rotate or shift the budget line when either prices or income change.

5.4 Derive and interpret the equilibrium conditions for an individual consumer to be maximizing utility subject to a budget constraint.

5.5 Use indifference curves to derive a demand curve for an individual consumer and construct a market demand curve by horizontally summing individual demand curves.

5.6 Define a corner solution and explain the condition that creates a corner solution.

Understanding consumer behavior is the first step in making profitable pricing, advertising, product design, and production decisions. Firms spend a great deal of time and money trying to estimate and forecast the demand for their products. Obtaining accurate estimates of demand requires more than a superficial understanding of the underpinnings of demand functions. A manager's need for practical analysis of demand, both estimation of demand and demand forecasting, requires an economic model of consumer behavior to guide the analysis.

When you finish this chapter, you will have a solid understanding of why consumers choose to purchase one bundle of products rather than some other bundle. As you continue your study of business, you will discover that the theory of consumer behavior is an important tool in other business courses you will take, particularly in marketing. You will see its value for managerial economics in the next two chapters when we examine demand elasticities in Chapter 6 and when we show you how to estimate and forecast consumer demand in Chapter 7.

5.1 BASIC ASSUMPTIONS OF CONSUMER THEORY

As with all economic models, the theory of consumer behavior employs some simplifying assumptions that allow us to focus on the fundamental determinants of consumer behavior and to abstract away from the less important aspects of the consumer's decision process. Consumer behavior is modeled directly from the theory of constrained maximization described in Chapter 3. We begin this section with a short discussion of the specific form of the consumer's optimizing decision. Then we will explore the nature of consumer preferences for goods or services.

The Consumer's Optimization Problem

As a basic premise for analyzing consumer behavior, we will assume that all individuals make consumption decisions with the goal of maximizing their total satisfaction from consuming various goods and services, subject to the constraint that their spending on goods exactly equals their incomes. Few, if any, people have incomes sufficient to buy as much as they desire of every good or service, so choices must be made about how to spend their limited incomes. To keep the income constraint as simple as possible, we will not allow consumers either to spend less than their incomes (i.e., no saving is allowed) or to spend more than their incomes (i.e., no borrowing is allowed). While it is not particularly difficult to allow saving and borrowing in our model, doing so would not change any of the conclusions that we will reach.

The basic model of consumer theory seeks to explain how consumers make their purchasing decisions when they are *completely informed* about all things that matter. Specifically, buyers are assumed to know the full range of products and services available, as well as the capacity of each product to provide utility. We also assume they know the price of each good and their incomes during the time period in question. Admittedly, to assume perfect knowledge is an abstraction from reality, but assuming complete information does not distort the relevant aspects of real-world consumer decisions.

Properties of Consumer Preferences

Consumer theory requires that consumers be able to rank (or to order) various combinations of goods and services according to the level of satisfaction associated with each combination. Such combinations of goods or services are called **consumption bundles**. Figure 5.1 shows a number of typical consumption bundles for two goods, X and Y. Bundle A consists of 10 units of good X and 60 units of good Y, bundle B consists of 20X and 40Y, bundle C consists of 40X and

consumption bundle
A particular combination of specific quantities of goods or services.

FIGURE 5.1

Typical Consumption Bundles for Two Goods, *X* and *Y*

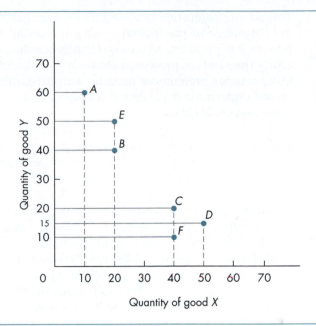

20*Y*, and so on. Two important assumptions must be made about how people rank bundles of goods: consumer preferences must be *complete* and *transitive*.

Complete preference ordering For any given pair of consumption bundles, consumers must be able to rank the bundles according to the level of satisfaction they would enjoy from consuming the bundles. A consumption bundle would be ranked higher (i.e., preferred) to another bundle if the preferred bundle yields more satisfaction than the other, less-preferred bundle. Or, if the two bundles yield exactly the same level of satisfaction, the consumer would be indifferent between the two bundles and would give the two bundles the same ranking. When a consumer can rank all conceivable bundles of commodities, the consumer's preferences are said to be **complete**.

complete
Consumers are able to rank all conceivable bundles of commodities.

For example, a consumer who is confronted with bundles *A* and *B* in Figure 5.1 must be able to make one of the following three possible responses:

1. I prefer bundle *A* to bundle *B* (denoted as *A* > *B*).
2. I prefer bundle *B* to bundle *A* (denoted as *B* > *A*).
3. I am indifferent between bundles *A* and *B* (denoted as *A* ~ *B*).

The consumer's preferences are complete if the consumer can do this for every possible pair of consumption bundles. Completeness of the preference ordering is essential for our model, because consumers would not be able to identify the most satisfying bundle without a complete ranking of all possible consumption bundles.

transitive
Consumer preferences are transitive if $A > B$, and $B > C$, then it follows that $A > C$.

Transitive preference ordering Consumer preferences are **transitive** when they are consistent in the following way. If bundle A is preferred to bundle B, and bundle B is preferred to bundle C, then bundle A *must* be preferred to bundle C. Using the symbols presented above: If $A > B$, and $B > C$, then it follows that $A > C$. Consumer preferences must be transitive, otherwise inconsistent preferences would undermine the ability of consumer theory to explain or predict the bundles consumers will choose.

To see why transitivity is necessary, let's suppose a Walmart shopper can purchase any one of three bundles of goods, A, B, or C, each of which costs exactly the same amount. Furthermore, suppose the consumer's preferences violate the transitivity property in the following way: $A > B$, $B > C$, but, in violation of transitivity, $C > A$. Under this preference ranking, the shopper will be unable to make up his mind about which of these three bundles he would prefer to buy. Suppose, for some reason, he places bundle A in his basket and heads for the checkout line. On his way to check out, he realizes that bundle C should be in his basket, not bundle A because he believes C is more satisfying than A. After putting bundle A back on the shelf and placing bundle C in his basket, he heads back to the checkout line. But, once again, he decides along the way that he has the wrong bundle, because bundle B is more satisfying than bundle C. So, he grabs bundle B to replace bundle C. Of course, as you clearly see, he will now want to switch *back to the original bundle A* because bundle A is more satisfying than bundle B. This process would go on forever—or at least until Walmart closes or store security cameras detect his odd behavior!

More is preferred to less (nonsatiation) Completeness and transitivity are the only absolutely necessary assumptions for consumer theory. However, we are going to adopt one more assumption that will keep matters as simple as possible. We are going to assume that consumers always prefer to have more of a good rather than less of the good. We do recognize that people may consume so much of something that they become satiated with it and do not want any more. However, no one would intentionally purchase so much of a good that they would be happier to have less of it.

Now try Technical Problems 1–2.

The Utility Function

utility
Benefits consumers obtain from the goods and services they consume.

Utility is the name economists give to the benefits consumers obtain from the goods and services they consume. While utility implies usefulness, many of the products most of us consume may not be particularly useful. Nonetheless, we will follow tradition and refer to the benefits obtained from goods and services as utility.

Settling on a name for the benefits does not solve the problem of how to measure these benefits from consumption. Who could say how many units of benefit, or how much utility, they receive from consuming an ice cream cone or a pizza or from going to the dentist? After all, it is not possible to plug a "utility meter" into a consumer's ear and measure the amount of utility generated by consuming some good or service. And even if we could measure utility, what units or denomination would we use? In class, we have used terms such as "utils," which is too serious; "globs," which is too frivolous; "bushels," which is too precise; and others we need not mention. Over time, we have settled on the phrase "units of utility," which is certainly pedestrian and dull, but it seems as good a name as any.

utility function
An equation that shows an individual's perception of the level of utility that would be attained from consuming each conceivable bundle of goods: $U = f(X, Y)$.

Consumer preferences can be represented as a **utility function**. A utility function shows an individual's perception of the level of utility that would be attained from consuming each conceivable bundle or combination of goods and services. A simple form of a utility function for a person who consumes only two goods, X and Y, might be

$$U = f(X, Y)$$

where X and Y are, respectively, the amounts of goods X and Y consumed, f means "a function of" or "depends on," and U is the amount of utility the person receives from each combination of X and Y. Thus, utility depends on the quantities consumed of X and Y.

The actual numbers assigned to the levels of utility are arbitrary. We need only say that if a consumer prefers one combination of goods, say, $20X$ and $30Y$, to some other combination, say, $15X$ and $32Y$, the amount of utility derived from the first bundle is greater than the amount from the second

$$U = f(20,30) > U = f(15,32)$$

5.2 INDIFFERENCE CURVES

indifference curve
A set of points representing different bundles of goods and services, each of which yields the same level of total utility.

A fundamental tool for analyzing consumer behavior is an **indifference curve**, which is a set of points representing different combinations of goods and services, each of which provides an individual with the same level of utility. Therefore, the consumer is indifferent among all combinations of goods shown on an indifference curve—hence the name.

Figure 5.2 shows a representative indifference curve with the typically assumed shape. All combinations of goods X and Y along indifference curve I yield the consumer the same level of utility. In other words, the consumer is indifferent among all points, such as point A, with 10 units of X and 60 units of Y; point B, with $20X$ and $40Y$; point C, with $40X$ and $20Y$; and so on. At any point on I, it is possible to take away some amount of X and add some amount of Y and leave the consumer with the same level of utility. Conversely, we can add X and take away just enough Y to make the consumer indifferent between the two combinations.

Indifference curves are downward sloping. Because the consumer obtains utility from both goods, when more X is added, some Y must be taken away in order to maintain the same level of utility. Consequently, indifference curves must be downward sloping.

Indifference curves are convex. A convex shape means that as consumption of X is increased relative to consumption of Y, the consumer is willing to accept a smaller

FIGURE 5.2

A Typical Indifference Curve

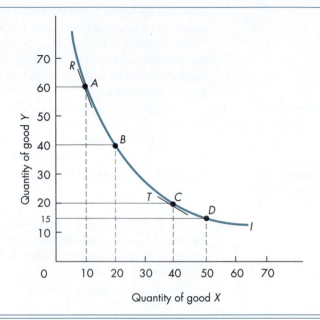

reduction in Y for an equal increase in X in order to stay at the same level of utility. This property is apparent in Figure 5.2. Begin at point A, with 10 units of X and 60 units of Y. In order to increase the consumption of X by 10 units, to 20, the consumer is willing to reduce the consumption of Y by 20 units, to 40. Given indifference curve I, the consumer will be indifferent between the two combinations represented by A and B. Next begin at C, with $40X$ and $20Y$. From this point, to gain an additional 10 units of X (move to point D), the consumer is willing to give up only 5 units of Y, much less than the 20 units willingly given up to obtain 10 more units at point A. The convexity of indifference curves implies a diminishing marginal rate of substitution, to which we now turn.

Marginal Rate of Substitution

marginal rate of substitution (MRS)
A measure of the number of units of Y that must be given up per unit of X added so as to maintain a constant level of utility.

The **marginal rate of substitution (MRS)** measures the number of units of Y that must be given up per unit of X added so as to maintain a constant level of utility. Returning to Figure 5.2, you can see that the consumer is indifferent between combinations A (10X and 60Y) and B (20X and 40Y). Thus, the rate at which the consumer is willing to substitute is

$$\frac{\Delta Y}{\Delta X} = \frac{60 - 40}{10 - 20} = -\frac{20}{10} = -2$$

The marginal rate of substitution is 2, meaning that the consumer is willing to give up two units of Y for each unit of X added. Because it would be cumbersome to have the minus sign on the right side of the equation, the marginal rate of substitution is defined as

$$MRS = -\frac{\Delta Y}{\Delta X} = 2$$

For the movement from C to D along I, the marginal rate of substitution is

$$MRS = -\frac{\Delta Y}{\Delta X} = -\frac{(20 - 15)}{(40 - 50)} = \frac{5}{10} = \frac{1}{2}$$

In this case the consumer is willing to give up only ½ unit of Y per additional unit of X added.

Therefore, the marginal rate of substitution diminishes along an indifference curve. When consumers have a small amount of X relative to Y, they are willing to give up a lot of Y to gain another unit of X. When they have less Y relative to X, they are willing to give up less Y in order to gain another unit of X.

We have, thus far, calculated the marginal rate of substitution for relatively large changes in the quantities of the two goods: that is, over *intervals* along an indifference curve. In Figure 5.2, the *MRS* over the interval from A to B is 2, and the *MRS* over the interval from C to D is 1/2. Now consider measuring the *MRS* at a *point* on an indifference curve; that is, let the changes in X and Y along the indifference curve be extremely small. The marginal rate of substitution at a point can be closely approximated by (the absolute value of) the slope of a line tangent to the indifference curve at the point. For example, consider point C in Figure 5.3. A line tangent to indifference curve I at point C, TT', has a slope of −0.75 ($\Delta Y/\Delta X = -600/800$). The (absolute value of the) slope of the tangent line gives a good *estimate* of the amount of Y that must be given up to keep utility constant when one more unit of X is consumed. Suppose the consumer moves along the indifference curve by adding

FIGURE 5.3

The Slope of an Indifference Curve and the *MRS*

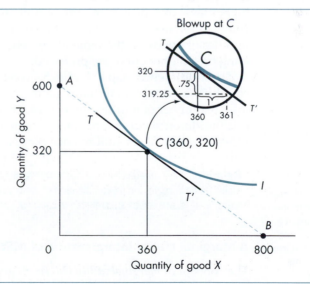

one more unit of X, from 360 to 361 units. Using the slope of the tangent line as an approximation, the change in Y needed to keep utility constant is -0.75; in other words, a one-unit increase in X requires a 0.75-unit decrease in Y to remain indifferent. But as the blowup in Figure 5.3 shows, if the movement is along the indifference curve, only a little *less* than 0.75 unit of Y must be sacrificed to remain indifferent. Nevertheless, the (absolute value of the) slope of the tangent line is a fairly close approximation of the exact *MRS*. As the changes in X and Y become smaller and smaller, the (absolute value of the) tangent line becomes a better and better approximation of the *MRS* at that point.

In Figure 5.2, the (absolute values of the) slopes of tangent lines R and T give the marginal rates of substitution at points A and C, respectively. When we look at these tangents, it is easy to see that the (absolute value of the) slope of the indifference curve, and hence the *MRS*, decreases as X increases and Y decreases along the indifference curve. This results from the assumption that indifference curves are convex.

Now try Technical
Problems 3–4.

> **Relation** Indifference curves are negatively sloped and convex. Moving along an indifference curve, when the consumption of one good is increased, consumption of the other good is necessarily reduced by the amount required to maintain a constant level of utility. For a unit increase (decrease) in X, the marginal rate of substitution measures the decrease (increase) in Y needed to keep utility constant $(MRS = -\Delta Y/\Delta X)$. For very small changes in X, the marginal rate of substitution is the negative of the slope of the indifference curve at a point. The marginal rate of substitution decreases as the consumer moves down an indifference curve.

Indifference Maps

An indifference map is made up of two or more indifference curves. Figure 5.4 shows a typical indifference map, with four indifference curves, *I, II, III,* and *IV*. Any indifference curve lying above and to the right of another represents a higher level of utility. Thus, any combination of X and Y on *IV* is preferred to any combination on *III*, any combination on *III* is preferred to any on *II*, and so on. All bundles of goods on the same indifference curve are equivalent; all combinations lying on a higher curve are preferred.

The indifference map in Figure 5.4 consists of only four indifference curves. We could have drawn many, many more. In fact, the X–Y space actually contains an infinite number of indifference curves. Each point in the space lies on one and only one indifference curve. That is, the same combination of goods cannot give two levels of utility. Thus, indifference curves cannot intersect.

marginal utility
The addition to total utility that is attributable to the addition of one unit of a good to the current rate of consumption, holding constant the amounts of all other goods consumed.

> **Relation** An indifference map consists of several indifference curves. The higher (or further to the right) an indifference curve, the greater the level of utility associated with the curve. Combinations of goods on higher indifference curves are preferred to combinations on lower curves.

A Marginal Utility Interpretation of *MRS*

The concept of *marginal utility* (*MU*) can give additional insight into the properties of indifference curves, particularly the slope of indifference curves. **Marginal utility**

FIGURE 5.4
Indifference Map

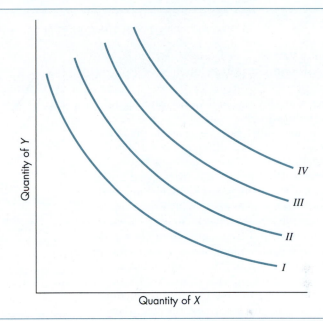

is the addition to total utility that is attributable to consuming one more unit of a good, holding constant the amounts of all other goods consumed. Thus marginal utility of good X equals $\Delta U / \Delta X$, where X is the quantity of the good. Economists typically assume that as the consumption of a good increases, the marginal utility from an additional unit of the good diminishes. While diminishing marginal utility cannot be proved theoretically, falling marginal utility appears to characterize the pattern of consumption for most people with most goods.

Just imagine how you feel about the soft drinks you consume at a football game on a hot day. The first soft drink boosts your utility by a substantial amount. The second soft drink does taste good, and it increases your utility, but the increase in utility is not as great as it was for the first soft drink. So while the marginal utility of the second soft drink is positive, it is smaller than the marginal utility of the first soft drink. Similarly, the third and fourth soft drinks also make you feel better (i.e., increase your utility), but by successively smaller amounts.

The change in total utility that results when both X and Y change by small amounts is related to the marginal utilities of X and Y as

$$\Delta U = (MU_x \times \Delta X) + (MU_y \times \Delta Y)$$

where MU_x and MU_y are the marginal utilities of X and Y, respectively. To illustrate this relation, suppose a consumer increases consumption of X by 2 units ($\Delta X = 2$) and decreases consumption of Y by 1 unit ($\Delta Y = -1$). Further suppose

ILLUSTRATION 5.1

Fly Fast or Fly Far:
Analyzing MRS for Corporate Jets

When Cessna Aircraft Corp. and Gulfstream Aircraft, Inc., each introduced new business jets—the Cessna Citation X and the Gulfstream V—analysts predicted that the success of the two different aircraft would reveal the relative importance to business buyers of speed and range. The Citation X, with a speed up to 600 miles per hour, was the fastest civilian plane short of the Concord. The Gulfstream V, with a range up to 7,500 miles, was the longest-range business jet. Cessna boasted that its jet could fly moguls from New York to California for breakfast, then back to New Jersey in time for cocktails. Gulfstream cited its jet's ability to fly 14 hours nonstop, from California to Spain or India.

Industry analysts differed in their predictions about the success in the market of the two planes. Some predicted consumers would value the range of Gulfstream more; others said that Cessna's speed would prevail. Obviously the Gulfstream also flies pretty fast, and the Cessna also flies pretty far, but the two manufacturers chose to emphasize different features. In terms of indifference curves, Cessna viewed the indifference map of corporate jet buyers as being something like the curves shown in Panel A of the graph in the next column. It believed that consumers would be willing to trade-off a lot of range for more speed. In this case, the marginal rate of substitution between range and speed is high. Gulfstream viewed the indifference map as being like the curves shown in Panel B. That is, consumers would not be willing to trade-off as much range for more speed. In this view, the marginal rate of substitution between range and speed is low.

A great deal of money rode on these decisions, since the startup cost of a new airplane is very high and it often takes the market a long time to render a verdict. A Canadian firm planning to introduce a competitor to the Gulfstream estimated that its startup costs would be about $1 billion (U.S.).

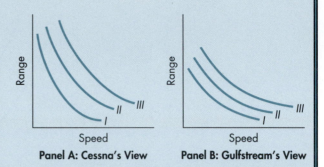

Panel A: Cessna's View   **Panel B: Gulfstream's View**

This situation illustrates the importance of predicting trade-offs in business decision making. Products have many different characteristics. Managers making long-range decisions often try to determine the relative values that consumers place on these different characteristics, and one product generally cannot incorporate all the desirable characteristics.

For example, an ice cream manufacturer must decide how much fat to put into a new product. Fat makes ice cream taste good, but for dietary reasons many consumers value low-fat, low-cholesterol food. The manufacturer must evaluate consumer trade-offs between taste and health. Automobile manufacturers must predict the willingness of consumers to trade-off performance, styling, and reliability in their cars. According to some observers, U.S. auto manufacturers made the wrong decision several years ago when they emphasized size and style over reliability. As it turned out, consumers valued reliability more than the U.S. automakers had predicted, and the firms subsequently lost considerable sales to foreign producers.

It is not the actual estimation and graphing of indifference curves that is useful to decision makers. It is the *concept* of these curves that is useful. All products have some substitutes, and consumers are willing to trade one product for another at some rate. The important thing is estimating the rate at which they are willing to make the trade-off.

the marginal utility of X is 25 for each additional unit of X, and the marginal utility of Y is 10. The amount by which utility changes is computed as

$$\Delta U = (25 \times 2) + (10 \times -1) = 40$$

Consuming 2 more X and 1 less Y causes total utility to rise by 40 units of utility.

For points on a given indifference curve, all combinations of goods yield the same level of utility, so ΔU is 0 for all changes in X and Y that would keep the consumer on the same indifference curve. From the above equation, if $\Delta U = 0$, it follows that

$$\Delta U = 0 = (MU_x \times \Delta X) + (MU_y \times \Delta Y)$$

Therefore, solving for $-\Delta Y / \Delta X$,

$$-\frac{\Delta Y}{\Delta X} = \frac{MU_x}{MU_y}$$

where $-\Delta Y/\Delta X$ is the negative of the slope of the indifference curve, or the marginal rate of substitution. Thus, the marginal rate of substitution can be interpreted as the ratio of the marginal utility of X divided by the marginal utility of Y

Now try Technical Problem 5.

$$MRS = \frac{MU_x}{MU_y}$$

5.3 THE CONSUMER'S BUDGET CONSTRAINT

If consumers had unlimited incomes or if goods were free, there would be no problem of economizing. People could buy whatever they wanted and would have no problem of choice. But this is not generally the case. Consumers are constrained as to what bundles of goods they can purchase based on the market-determined prices of the goods and on their incomes. We now turn to an analysis of the income constraint faced by consumers.

Budget Lines

Consumers normally have limited incomes and goods are not free. Their problem is how to spend the limited income in a way that gives the maximum possible utility. The constraint faced by consumers can be illustrated graphically.

Suppose the consumer has a fixed income of $1,000, which is the maximum amount that can be spent on the two goods in a given period. For simplicity, assume the entire income is spent on X and Y. If the price of X is $5 per unit and the price of Y is $10 per unit, the amount spent on X ($5 \times X$) plus the amount spent on Y ($10 \times Y$) must equal the $1,000 income

$$\$5X + \$10Y = \$1,000$$

Alternatively, solving for Y in terms of X,

$$Y = \frac{\$1,000}{\$10} - \frac{\$5}{\$10}X = 100 - \frac{1}{2}X$$

FIGURE 5.5

A Consumer's Budget Constraint

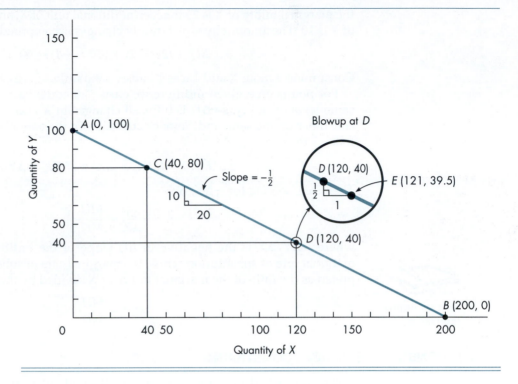

budget line

The line showing all bundles of goods that can be purchased at given prices if the entire income is spent.

The graph of this equation, shown in Figure 5.5, is a straight line called the *budget line*. A **budget line** is the set of all combinations or bundles of goods that can be purchased at given prices *if the entire income is spent.* Bundles costing less than $1,000 lie below *AB*. All bundles above budget line *AB* cost more than $1,000. Thus, the budget line divides the commodity space into the set of attainable bundles and the set of unattainable bundles.

To purchase any one of the bundles of *X* and *Y* on the budget line *AB* in Figure 5.5, the consumer spends exactly $1,000. If the consumer decides to spend all $1,000 on good *Y* and spend nothing on good *X*, 100 (= $1,000/$10) units of *Y* can be purchased (point *A* in Figure 5.5). If the consumer spends all $1,000 on *X* and buys no *Y*, 200 (= $1,000/$5) units of *X* can be purchased (point *B*). In Figure 5.5, consumption bundles *C*, with 40*X* and 80*Y*, and *D*, with 120*X* and 40*Y*, represent two other combinations of goods *X* and *Y* that can be purchased by spending exactly $1,000, because (80 × $10) + (40 × $5) = $1,000 and (40 × $10) + (120 × $5) = $1,000.

The slope of the budget line, −1/2 (= $\Delta Y/\Delta X$), indicates the amount of *Y* that must be given up if one more unit of *X* is purchased. For every additional unit of *X* purchased, the consumer must spend $5 more on good *X*. To continue meeting the budget constraint, $5 less must be spent on good *Y*; thus the consumer must give up 1/2 unit of *Y*. To illustrate this point, suppose the consumer is currently purchasing bundle D but wishes to move to bundle E, which is composed of 1 more unit of X and 1/2 unit less of Y (see the blowup in Figure 5.5). Bundles D and E both cost $1,000 to purchase, but the consumer must trade-off 1/2 unit of good Y for the extra unit of good X in bundle E.

The rate at which the consumer can trade-off Y for one more unit of X is equal to the price of good X (here $5) divided by the price of good Y (here $10); that is,

$$\text{Slope of the budget line} = -P_x/P_y$$

where P_x and P_y are the prices of goods X and Y, respectively. In Figure 5.5, the slope of the budget line is $-1/2$, which equals $-\$5/\$10$.

The relation between income (M) and the amount of goods X and Y that can be purchased can be expressed as

$$M = P_x X + P_y Y$$

This equation can also be written in the form of a straight line:

$$Y = \frac{M}{P_y} - \frac{P_x}{P_y} X$$

The first term, M/P_y, gives the amount of Y the consumer can buy if no X is purchased. As noted, $-P_x/P_y$ is the slope of the budget line and indicates how much Y must be given up for an additional unit of X.

The general form of a typical budget line is shown in Figure 5.6. The line AB shows all combinations of X and Y that can be purchased with the given

FIGURE 5.6
A Typical Budget Line

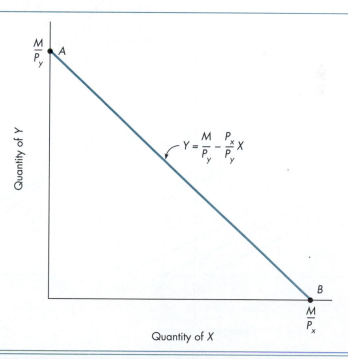

$$Y = \frac{M}{P_y} - \frac{P_x}{P_y} X$$

Quantity of Y

Quantity of X

income (M) and given prices of the goods (P_x and P_y). The intercept on the Y-axis, A, is M/P_y; the horizontal intercept, B, is M/P_x. The slope of the budget line is $-P_x/P_y$.

Shifting the Budget Line

If income (M) or the price ratio (P_x/P_y) changes, the budget line must change. Panel A of Figure 5.7 shows the effect of changes in income. Begin with the original budget line shown in Figure 5.5, AB, which corresponds to $1,000 income and prices of X and Y of $5 and $10, respectively. Next, let income increase to $1,200, holding the prices of X and Y constant. Because the prices do not change, the slope of the budget line remains the same ($-1/2$). But since income increases, the vertical intercept (M/P_y) increases (shifts upward) to 120 (= $1,200/$10). That is, if the consumer now spends the entire income on good Y, 20 more units of Y can be purchased than was previously the case. The horizontal intercept (M/P_x) also increases, to 240 (= $1,200/$5). The result of an increase in income is, therefore, a parallel shift in the budget line from AB to RN. The increase in income increases the set of combinations of the goods that can be purchased.

Alternatively, begin once more with budget line AB and then let income decrease to $800. In this case the set of possible combinations of goods decreases. The vertical and horizontal intercepts decrease to 80 (= $800/$10) and 160 (= $800/$5), respectively, causing a parallel shift in the budget line to FZ, with intercepts of 80 and 160. The decrease in income shrinks the set of consumption bundles that can be purchased.

Panel B shows the effect of changes in the price of good X. Begin as before with the original budget line AB and then let the price of X fall from $5 to $4 per unit. Since M/P_y does not change, the vertical intercept remains at A (100 units of Y). However, when P_x decreases, the absolute value of the slope (P_x/P_y) falls to 4/10

FIGURE 5.7
Shifting Budget Lines

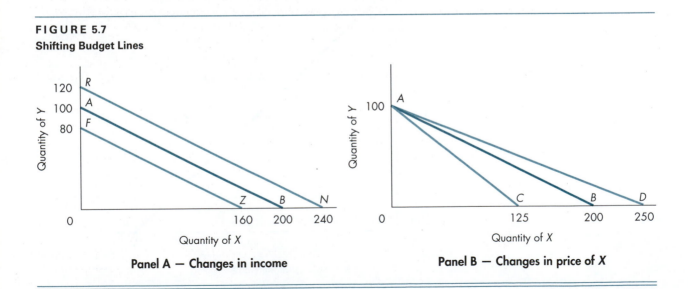

Panel A — Changes in income

Panel B — Changes in price of X

(= \$4/\$10). In this case, the budget line becomes less steep. After the price of X falls, more X can be purchased if the entire income is spent on X. Thus the horizontal intercept increases from 200 to 250 units of X (= \$1,000/\$4). In Panel B, the budget line pivots (or rotates) from AB to AD.

An increase in the price of good X to \$8 causes the budget line to pivot backward, from AB to AC. The intercept on the horizontal axis decreases to 125 (= \$1,000/\$8). When P_x increases to \$8, the absolute value of the slope of the line, P_x/P_y, increases to 8/10 (= \$8/\$10). The budget line becomes steeper when P_x rises, while the vertical intercept remains constant.

Now try Technical
Problem 6.

Relation   An increase (decrease) in income causes a parallel outward (inward) shift in the budget line. An increase (decrease) in the price of X causes the budget line to pivot inward (outward) around the original vertical intercept.

5.4 UTILITY MAXIMIZATION

Now we have all the tools needed to analyze consumer choice. The budget line shows all bundles of commodities that are available to the consumer, given the limited income and market-determined prices. The indifference map shows the preference ordering of all conceivable bundles of goods.

Maximizing Utility Subject to a Limited Income

We will illustrate the maximization process graphically with an example. Joan Johnson is an overworked, underpaid management trainee. Johnson's monthly food budget is \$400, which, because she works such long hours, is spent only on pizzas and burgers. The price of a pizza is \$8, and the price of a burger is \$4. Johnson's task is to determine the combination of pizzas and burgers that yields the highest level of utility possible from the \$400 food budget at the given prices.

The maximization process is shown graphically in Figure 5.8. Indifference curves I through IV represent a portion of Johnson's indifference map between pizzas, plotted along the vertical axis, and burgers, plotted along the horizontal axis. Her budget line, from 50 pizzas to 100 burgers, shows all combinations of the two fast foods that Johnson can consume during a month. If she spends the entire \$400 on pizzas at \$8 each, she can consume 50 pizzas. If she spends the entire \$400 on burgers at \$4 each, she can consume 100 burgers. Or she can consume any other combination on the line. The absolute value of the slope of the budget line is the price of burgers divided by the price of pizzas, or $P_B/P_P =$ \$4/\$8 = 1/2. This indicates that to consume one additional \$4 burger, Johnson must give up half of an \$8 pizza. Alternatively, 1 more pizza can be bought at a cost of 2 burgers.

As is clear from the graph, the highest possible level of utility is reached when Johnson purchases 30 pizzas and 40 burgers a month. This combination is represented by point E, at which the budget line is tangent to indifference curve III.

FIGURE 5.8

Constrained Utility Maximization

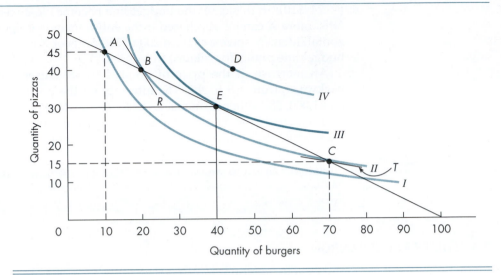

Many other combinations of the two fast foods, such as 40 pizzas and 45 burgers at point *D* on indifference curve *IV*, are preferable to the combination at *E*, but these other combinations cannot be purchased at the given prices and the $400 income. For example, 40 pizzas and 45 burgers would cost $500. All such bundles lie outside Johnson's budget constraint.

Johnson can purchase many combinations along her budget line other than the one at point *E*. These other combinations all lie on lower indifference curves and are therefore less preferred. Consider the combination at point *A*, consisting of 45 pizzas and 10 burgers. This combination can be purchased with the $400 income but, because it is on indifference curve *I*, it clearly gives a lower level of utility than combination *E* on indifference curve *III*. If Johnson is consuming the combination at point *A*, she can increase the number of burgers, decrease the number of pizzas at the rate of 1 more burger for 1/2 less pizza, and move down the budget line. This substitution leads to higher and higher levels of utility—for example, 40 pizzas and 20 burgers (combination *B*) are on indifference curve *II* and therefore provide more utility than combination *A* on curve *I*. Johnson should not stop at *B*. She should continue substituting pizzas for burgers until point *E* on curve *III* is attained. Thus, every combination on the budget line above point *E* represents a lower level of utility than can be attained by consuming 30 pizzas and 40 burgers.

Alternatively, suppose Johnson is consuming 15 pizzas and 70 burgers—combination *C*. This combination is on indifference curve *II*, which is below *III* and therefore represents a lower level of utility than combination *E*. Johnson can increase the number of pizzas and decrease the number of burgers at the rate of 1/2 of a pizza for every burger given up and can move to higher indifference curves. She should continue substituting pizzas for burgers until combination *E* is reached. Thus every combination on the budget line below E represents a lower level of utility than is attainable with 30 pizzas and 40 burgers.

By elimination, we have shown that every other combination on the budget line yields less utility than combination E. Thus utility is maximized with the given income and prices when Johnson consumes at point E, the point at which the budget line is tangent to indifference curve *III*, the highest attainable indifference curve. It therefore follows that the highest attainable level of utility is reached by consuming the combination at which the marginal rate of substitution (the absolute value of the slope of the indifference curve) equals the price ratio (the absolute value of the slope of the budget line).

We can use this relation between the *MRS* and the price ratio to provide more insight into why every other combination on the budget line yields less utility than the combination at point E. Consider again the combination at B, with 40 pizzas and 20 burgers. At this combination, the *MRS* (the absolute value of the slope of indifference curve *II*) is greater than the absolute value of the slope of the budget line, $P_B/P_P = 1/2$. Suppose the *MRS* at B is 2 (the slope of tangent R equals 2). This means that Johnson, in order to obtain 1 more burger, is *just willing* to exchange 2 pizzas. Exchanging 2 pizzas for 1 more burger leaves Johnson at the same level of utility—she is made no better and no worse off by this exchange. If Johnson could get 1 burger and give up *less* than 2 pizzas, she would be better off. Since burgers cost only half as much as pizzas, the market allows Johnson to obtain 1 more burger while only giving up half a pizza. Giving up half a pizza to get 1 more burger is a much more favorable exchange rate than the exchange rate she is just willing to make (giving up 2 pizzas for 1 burger). Thus Johnson moves to a higher indifference curve by trading only half a pizza for an additional burger.

As you can see, at every other combination on the budget line above E, the absolute value of the slope of the indifference curve—the *MRS*—must be greater than the absolute value of the slope of the budget line. Therefore, at each of these combinations, Johnson, by the same argument, can raise her utility by adding a burger and giving up less pizza than she would be willing to give up in order to gain the additional burger. Thus all combinations above E, at which the *MRS* is greater than 1/2, leads to less utility than combination E.

At any combination on the budget line below E, the *MRS* is obviously less than the price ratio. Suppose the *MRS* at combination C is 1/10 (the absolute value of the slope of tangent T equals 1/10), meaning that Johnson is just willing to give up 10 burgers in order to obtain an additional pizza. Because the absolute value of the slope of the budget line is 1/2, she can obtain the additional pizza by giving up only 2 burgers. She clearly becomes better off by sacrificing the 2 burgers for the additional pizza.

At every point on the budget line below E, the *MRS* is less than 1/2, and Johnson can obtain the additional pizza by giving up fewer burgers than the amount she is just willing to give up. Thus she should continue reducing the number of burgers and increasing the number of pizzas until utility is maximized at E with 30 pizzas and 40 burgers. Again we have shown that all combinations other than E yield less utility from the given income.

The marginal rate of substitution is the rate at which the consumer is *willing* to substitute one good for another. The price ratio is the rate at which the consumer is *able* to substitute one good for another in the market. Thus the optimal combination of goods occurs where the rate at which the consumer is willing to substitute equals the rate at which he or she is able to substitute. We can summarize the concept of consumer utility maximization with the following:

Now try Technical
Problems 7–9.

> **Principle** A consumer maximizes utility subject to a limited income at the combination of goods for which the indifference curve is just tangent to the budget line. At this combination, the marginal rate of substitution (the absolute value of the slope of the indifference curve) is equal to the price ratio (the absolute value of the slope of the budget line):
>
> $$-\frac{\Delta Y}{\Delta X} \; MRS = \frac{P_x}{P_Y}$$

Marginal Utility Interpretation of Consumer Optimization

Recall from Chapter 3 that a decision maker attains the highest level of benefits possible within a given cost constraint when the marginal benefit per dollar spent on each activity is equal across all activities and the cost constraint is met.

A consumer attains the highest level of utility from a given income when the marginal rate of substitution for any two goods is equal to the ratio of the prices of the two goods: $MRS = P_x/P_y$. Since the marginal rate of substitution is equal to the ratio of the marginal utilities of the two goods, utility-maximization occurs when the entire income is spent and

$$MRS = \frac{MU_x}{MU_y} = \frac{P_x}{P_y}$$

or, by rearranging this equation,

$$\frac{MU_x}{P_x} = \frac{MU_y}{P_y}$$

The second expression means that marginal utility per dollar spent on the last unit of good X equals marginal utility per dollar spent on the last unit of good Y.

To see why marginal utilities per dollar spent must be equal for the last unit consumed of both goods, suppose the condition did not hold and

$$\frac{MU_x}{P_x} < \frac{MU_y}{P_y}$$

Because the marginal utility per dollar spent on good X is less than the marginal utility per dollar spent on Y, the consumer should take dollars away from X and spend them on Y. As long as the inequality holds, the lost utility from each dollar taken away from X is less than the added utility from each additional dollar spent on Y, and the consumer continues to substitute Y for X. As the consumption of X decreases, the marginal utility of X rises. As Y increases, its marginal utility declines. The consumer continues substituting until MU_x/P_x equals MU_y/P_y.

ILLUSTRATION 5.2

Information Matters

In the theory of consumer behavior presented in this chapter, we assume consumers possess all the important information necessary to successfully make utility-maximizing choices facing budget constraints that limit their attainable sets of consumption bundles. Specifically, we assume consumers can rank order all possible bundles of goods or services to know whether bundle *A* is preferred to *B*, *B* is preferred to *A*, or *A* and *B* are equally satisfying. Obviously, this requires a vast knowledge of all available goods and services, including knowledge about tangible and intangible properties that create utility for each good or service. Consumer theory also assumes each consumer knows his or her budget constraint and the market prices of all goods and services. The actual choices consumers make will depend on the amount and quality of information they possess and also on their ability to process the information they possess.

Not surprisingly, most businesses understand the importance of managing the flow of information consumers use to make their buying decisions. In the Information Age, the tactics businesses employ to supply information to consumers about product availability, characteristics, and prices have become a central focus of research and experimentation in the field of marketing. Making sure your potential buyers know your product exists and where it can be purchased ranks as the first objective of consumer information management. Simply advertising a product through traditional print and media outlets may not be sufficient to compete in today's digital information world.

When Microsoft rolled out its Windows Phone known as "Mango," Microsoft's CEO admitted that sales of its smartphone were disappointing. The primary reason he gave for the weak sales was that "45 percent of smartphone customers (were) still not aware of Windows Phone 7," even though Microsoft spent millions on advertising Mango. Part of the problem for Microsoft was that its competition from Apple's iPhone and Google's Android devices overwhelmed Microsoft's strategy of relying almost exclusively on print advertising methods. In the past, print and television advertising "carried the load" for delivering product information to potential buyers. Recently, however, a new source of information for shoppers has become a powerful platform for supplying and shaping the information buyers use in decision making, one that businesses can use both to enhance the effectiveness of traditional advertising and even replace it in some cases.

As you may have guessed, consumers now rely heavily on a variety of digital communication channels to get always-on access to product information. With widespread availability of mobile technology, buyers can now connect to information networks instantly, anytime and anywhere. Consumer product and service information comes over the Internet from numerous sources: branded websites; user-generated content distributed through social networks such as Facebook, LinkedIn, and Twitter; web-based communities dedicated to specific product groups or industries; and even blogs giving answers to questions submitted online. Managing your product's presence online and in the blogosphere is the cutting edge of marketing science, creating a new set of marketing skills and tools.

As an example of the growing importance of digital communication channels and diminishing relative importance of traditional advertising, the pharmaceutical industry has completely changed its consumer marketing strategies. Pharmaceutical companies service two kinds of buyers: practicing physicians who write prescriptions for patients and consumers who seek out particular medical treatments on their own. A recent article in *Pharmaceutical Executive* makes the case for using "digital and mobile technologies to make medical information available at the point of care." Over 75 percent of doctors in the United States own an iPhone, iPad, or iPod, and 60 percent of physicians rely on social media discussions for health information. In order to ensure that information about drugs is timely and relevant—new reviews of pharmaceutical research and legal cases emerge on a week-by-week basis—pharmaceutical companies

(Continued)

are granting highly trained marketing teams greater authority to quickly respond online, either directly or through social networking channels, to customer inquiries about the latest reports, reviews, and studies concerning the companies' drugs.

Although the assumption of perfectly informed consumers currently serves as a necessary simplifying assumption in consumer theory, the emerging field of consumer information management (CIM) coupled with the digital information revolution may eventually make the "perfect information" assumption a reality. Perhaps the next step in the implementation of modern technology to consumer decisions will involve individual consumers undergoing brain scans to download their preferences to their portable iBuy devices, and letting the iBuys

collect online all the necessary information for the artificial intelligence software to display the consumer's optimal consumption bundle. While we cannot be certain that consumers will ever have such a gadget as the iBuy, we are certain that any software which eventually comes along to make optimal consumer purchasing decisions will be programmed to compute and compare MU/P for hundreds of thousands of goods and services. If you plan to be the person who writes this algorithm for the iBuy, you should make sure you understand the consumer theory set forth in this chapter.

Sources: Nicholas Kolakowski, "Microsoft Rolls Out Windows Phone 'Mango'," *eWeek*, October 3, 2011, p. 16; "Understanding the New Consumer Mind-Set," *Pharmaceutical Executive*, August, 2011, pp. 1–4.

A numerical example should make this concept more concrete: Suppose a customer with an income of $140 is spending it all on 20 units of X priced at $4 each and 30 units of Y priced at $2 each: ($4 × 20) + ($2 × 30) = $140. Further suppose that the marginal utility of the last unit of X is 20 and the marginal utility of the last unit of Y is 16. The ratio of marginal utilities per dollar spent on X and Y is

$$\frac{MU_x}{P_x} = \frac{20}{4} = 5 < 8 = \frac{16}{2} = \frac{MU_y}{P_y}$$

The consumer should reallocate spending on X and Y because it is possible to increase utility while still spending only $140. To see how this can be done, let the consumer spend one more dollar on Y. Buying another dollar's worth of good Y causes utility to increase by 8 units. In order to stay within the $140 budget, the consumer must also reduce spending on good X by one dollar. Spending $1 less on good X causes utility to fall by 5 units. Because the consumer loses 5 units of utility from reduced consumption of good X but gains 8 units of utility from the increased consumption of good Y, the consumer experiences a net gain in utility of 3 units while still spending only $140. The consumer should continue transferring dollars from X to Y as long as $MU_x/P_x < MU_y/P_y$. Because MU_x increases as less X is purchased and MU_y decreases as more Y is purchased, the consumer will achieve utility maximization when $MU_x/P_x = MU_y/P_y$, and no further changes should be made.

Alternatively, when

$$\frac{MU_x}{P_x} > \frac{MU_y}{P_y}$$

Now try Technical Problem 10.

the marginal utility per dollar spent on X is greater than the marginal utility per dollar spent on Y. The consumer should take dollars away from Y and buy additional X, continuing to substitute until the equality holds.

☐ **Principle** To obtain maximum satisfaction from a limited income, a consumer allocates income so that the marginal utility per dollar spent on each good is the same for all commodities purchased, and all income is spent.

Thus far, for graphical purposes, we have assumed that the consumer purchases only two goods. The analysis is easily extended, although not graphically, to any number of goods. Because the aforementioned equilibrium conditions must apply to *any* two goods in a consumer's consumption bundle, they must apply to all goods in the bundle. Therefore, if a consumer purchases N goods, $X_1, X_2, X_3, \ldots, X_N$ with prices $P_1, P_2, P_3, \ldots, P_N$ from a given income M, utility maximization requires

$$P_1 X_1 + P_2 X_2 + P_3 X_3 + \cdots + P_N X_N = M$$

and

$$MRS = \frac{P_j}{P_i}$$

for any two goods, X_i and X_j. Alternatively, in terms of marginal utilities per dollar spent,

$$\frac{MU_1}{P_1} = \frac{MU_2}{P_2} = \frac{MU_3}{P_3} = \cdots = \frac{MU_N}{P_N}$$

In this way the maximization principle is expanded to cover any number of goods.

Finding the Optimal Bundle of Hot Dogs and Cokes

The following numerical example will illustrate the points made in this section. Suppose you attend the afternoon baseball game and have only $40 to spend on hot dogs and Cokes. You missed lunch, and $40 is not going to be enough money to buy all the Cokes and hot dogs you would want to consume. The only rational thing to do is to maximize your utility subject to your $40 budget constraint.

On the back of your baseball program you make a list of the marginal utility you expect to receive from various levels of hot dog and Coke consumption. You then divide the marginal utilities by the prices of hot dogs and Cokes, $5 and $4, respectively. The back of your baseball program looks like the table below.

Units per game	Marginal utility of hot dogs (MU_H)	$\frac{MU_H}{P_H}$	Marginal utility of Cokes (MU_C)	$\frac{MU_C}{P_C}$
1	40	8	120	30
2	30	6	80	20
3	25	5	40	10
4	20	4	32	8
5	15	3	16	4
6	10	2	8	2

Using this information, you can now figure out how to get the most satisfaction from consuming hot dogs and Cokes, given your budget constraint. Should you buy a Coke or a hot dog first? The first unit of Coke increases total utility by 30 units for each dollar spent (on the first Coke), while the first hot dog increases total utility by only 8 units per dollar spent (on the first hot dog). You buy the first Coke and have $36 left. After finishing the first Coke, you consider whether to buy the first hot dog or the second Coke. Because $8 (= MU_H/P_H) < 20(= MU_C/P_C)$, you buy the second Coke and have $32 left. Using similar reasoning, you buy the third Coke.

The fourth Coke and the first hot dog both increase total utility by 8 units per dollar spent. You buy both of them and note that the marginal utilities per dollar spent both equal 8. This is not yet optimal, however, because you have spent only $21 (1 hot dog and 4 Cokes). You continue using marginal analysis until you end up buying 4 hot dogs and 5 Cokes, at which $MU_H/P_H = 4 = MU_C/P_C$. You have spent the entire $40 on the 4 hot dogs and 5 Cokes. No other combination of Cokes and hot dogs that you could have purchased for $40 would have yielded more total utility.

Now try Technical Problem 11.

5.5 INDIVIDUAL DEMAND AND MARKET DEMAND CURVES

We can now use the theory of consumer utility maximization to derive a demand curve for an individual consumer and, by aggregating individual demand curves, we can derive market demand curves.

An Individual Consumer's Demand Curve

We can use Figure 5.9 to show how an individual consumer's demand curve is obtained. Begin with income of $1,000 and prices of good X and good Y both equal to $10. The corresponding budget line is given by budget line 1, from $100Y$ to $100X$, in the upper panel of the figure. The consumer maximizes utility where budget line 1 is tangent to indifference curve I, consuming 50 units of X. Thus when income is $1,000, one point on this consumer's demand for X is $10 and 50 units of X. This point is illustrated on the price–quantity graph in the lower panel of Figure 5.9.

Following the definition of demand, we hold income and the price of the other good Y constant, while letting the price of X fall from $10 to $8. The new budget line is budget line 2. Because income and the price of Y remain constant, the vertical intercept does not change, but because the price of X has fallen, the budget line must pivot outward along the X-axis. The new X-intercept for budget line 2 is 125 (= $1,000/$8). With this new budget line, the consumer now maximizes utility where budget line 2 is tangent to indifference curve II, consuming 65 units of X. Thus another point on the demand schedule in the lower panel must be $8 and 65 units of X.

Next, letting the price of X fall again, this time to $5, the new budget line is budget line 3. At the price $5, the consumer chooses 90 units of X, another point on this consumer's demand curve. Thus we have derived the following demand schedule for good X:

Price	Quantity demanded
$10	50
8	65
5	90

FIGURE 5.9
Deriving a Demand Curve

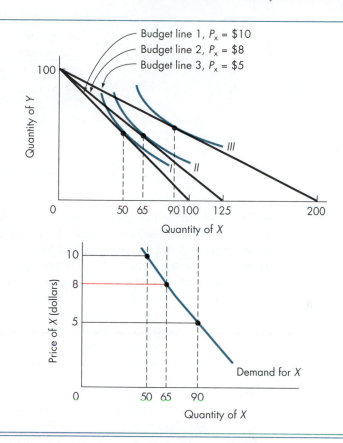

This schedule, with other points so generated, is graphed as a demand curve in price–quantity space in the lower part of Figure 5.9. This demand curve is downward-sloping. As the price of X falls, the quantity of X the consumer is willing and able to purchase increases, following the rule of demand. Furthermore, we followed the definition of demand, holding income and the price of the other good (goods) constant. Thus an individual's demand for a good is derived from a series of utility-maximizing points. We used only three such points, but we could easily have used more in order to obtain more points on the demand curve.

Now try Technical Problem 12.

market demand
A list of prices and the quantities consumers are willing and able to purchase at each price in the list, other things being held constant.

Principle The demand curve of an individual for a specific commodity relates utility-maximizing quantities purchased to market prices, holding constant income and the prices of all other goods. The slope of the demand curve illustrates the law of demand: Quantity demanded varies inversely with price.

Market Demand and Marginal Benefit

Managers are typically more interested in market demand for a product than in the demand of an individual consumer. Recall that in Chapter 2 we defined **market demand** as a list of prices and the corresponding quantity consumers are

TABLE 5.1

Aggregating Individual Demands

Price	Quantity demanded			Market demand
	Consumer 1	Consumer 2	Consumer 3	
$6	3	0	0	3
5	5	1	0	6
4	8	3	1	12
3	10	5	4	19
2	12	7	6	25
1	13	10	8	31

willing and able to purchase at each price in the list, holding constant income, the prices of other goods, tastes, price expectations, and the number of consumers. When deriving individual demand in this chapter, we pivoted the budget line around the vertical intercept, therefore holding income and the prices of other goods constant. Because the indifference curves remained constant, tasteswere unchanged.

Thus, the discussion here conforms to the conditions of market demand. To obtain the market demand function, we need only to aggregate the individual demand functions of all potential customers in the market. We will now demonstrate this aggregation process, which is frequently called *horizontal summation* because the aggregation of numerical values takes place along the horizontal axis.

Suppose there are only three individuals in the market for a particular commodity. In Table 5.1, the quantities demanded by each consumer at each price in column 1 are shown in columns 2, 3, and 4. Column 5 shows the sum of these quantities demanded at each price and is therefore the market demand. Because the demand for each consumer is negatively sloped, market demand is negatively sloped also. Quantity demanded is inversely related to price.

Figure 5.10 shows graphically how a market demand curve can be derived from the individual demand curves. The individual demands of consumers 1, 2, and 3 from Table 5.1 are shown graphically as D_1, D_2, and D_3, respectively. The market demand curve D_M is simply the sum of the quantities demanded at each price. At $6, consumer 1 demands 3 units. Because the others demand nothing, 3 is the quantity demanded by the market. At every other price, D_M is the horizontal summation of the quantities demanded by the three consumers. And if other consumers came into the market, their demand curves would be added to D_M to obtain the new market demand.

Relation   The market demand curve is the horizontal summation of the demand curves of all consumers in the market. It therefore shows how much all consumers demand at each price over the relevant range of prices.

As explained in Chapter 2, the market demand curve gives *demand prices* for any quantity demanded of the good. Because the demand price for a specific quantity

FIGURE 5.10

Derivation of Market Demand

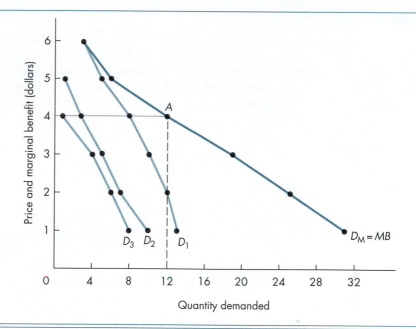

demanded is the maximum price consumers will pay for that unit of a good, demand price measures, in dollars, the *economic value* or benefit to consumers of that unit. Thus, for any particular quantity demanded, the price on the vertical axis of the market demand curve measures two things: (1) the maximum price consumers will pay to buy that quantity of the good, and (2) the dollar value of the benefit to buyers of that particular unit of the good. A market demand curve, then, gives the marginal benefit (value) individuals place on the last unit consumed.

In Figure 5.10, we denote the dual roles of market demand by labeling market demand both as "D_M" and as "MB." Consider point A, which shows $4 is the maximum price for which 12 units can be sold in this market of three individual buyers. The marginal benefit for every buyer in this market is $4 for the last unit purchased. Specifically, consumer 1 values the eighth unit he consumes at $4, consumer 2 values the third unit she consumes at $4, and consumer 3 values the first unit he consumes at $4. Clearly, when buyers in this market purchase 12 units at a price of $4, the marginal benefit of the last unit consumed is $4 for everyone in this market. Demand prices along market demand curves, then, measure the marginal benefit or value of the last unit consumed for every individual consumer in society.

Now try Technical Problem 13.

Relation   The demand prices at various quantities along a market demand curve give the marginal benefit (value) of the last unit consumed for every buyer in the market, and thus market demand can be interpreted as the marginal benefit curve for a good.

5.6 CORNER SOLUTIONS

corner solution

The utility-maximizing bundle lies at one of the endpoints of the budget line and the consumer chooses to consume zero units of a good.

Thus far in this chapter we have discussed only the solution to the consumer's optimization problem in which the consumer chooses to purchase some positive amount of *both* X and Y. In many circumstances, however, consumers spend their entire budget and choose to purchase none of some specific good. This outcome is called a **corner solution** because the utility-maximizing consumption bundle lies at one of the corners formed at one of the endpoints where the budget line meets the Y-axis (zero X is consumed) or the X-axis (zero Y is consumed).

Let's consider a corner solution in which the consumer chooses to purchase none of good X. This situation arises when the price of good X is sufficiently high relative to the marginal utility of X that the consumer optimally decides not to purchase any units of X, even though the consumer does find X satisfying (i.e., MU_x is positive) and can afford to purchase some X within the budget constraint. You can certainly think of many goods like this in your own budget. For example, you might love freshly squeezed orange juice and be able to pay $8 for a quart of fresh-squeezed juice, and yet you optimally choose not to buy even a single quart of fresh-squeezed orange juice. And there are many other grocery items that never end up in your basket, not because you can't afford them or because they taste bad, but because you can get more total utility by spending your limited income on other goods that give you greater additional satisfaction per dollar.

Figure 5.11 shows a corner solution in which the consumer spends her entire budget on good Y and buys none of good X. The consumer faces budget constraint

FIGURE 5.11
Corner Solution: X* = 0

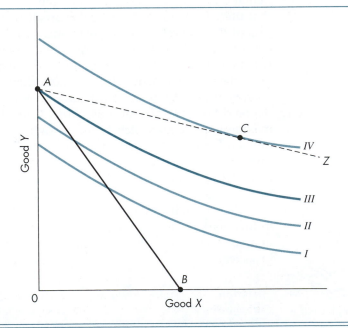

AB, and the highest utility she can attain is on indifference curve *III* at point *A*. Even though she can afford to buy good *X*, and good *X* gives her satisfaction, she nonetheless chooses to buy zero *X* (i.e., *X** = 0) and spend her entire budget on good *Y*. The reason for a corner solution can be seen by examining *MU/P* for *X* and *Y*. At point *A*, you can see the slope of indifference curve *III* is smaller in absolute value than the slope of the budget line: $MRS < P_x/P_y$. Thus, in terms of marginal utilities per dollar spent on *X* and *Y*

$$\frac{MU_x}{P_x} < \frac{MU_y}{P_y}$$

Even when the consumer spends all of her income on *Y*, the marginal utility per dollar spent on good *X* delivers less "bang per buck" than the last dollar spent on good *Y*. Notice that for a sufficiently large decrease in the price of *X* relative to the price of *Y* (say, to a price ratio depicted by budget line *Az*), the budget line could become tangent to some indifference curve at a point where both *X* and *Y* are bought: point *C* on indifference curve *IV*. Hence, the consumer will purchase a positive amount of *X* if the relative price of *X* decreases sufficiently.

In general, a corner solution, in which the consumer purchases none of some good *X*, results when

$$\frac{MU_x}{P_x} < \frac{MU_i}{P_i} = \cdots = \frac{MU_j}{P_j}$$

Now try Technical Problem 14.

for all goods *i*, *j*, etc. where the *i*th and *j*th goods are purchased in positive amounts. The consumer spends all of her income, yet the marginal utility per dollar spent on *X* is less than the marginal utility per dollar spent on any other good that is purchased. This is usually what we mean when we say we "cannot afford" something.

5.7 SUMMARY

- The basic premise for analyzing consumer behavior is that all individuals make consumption decisions with the goal of maximizing their total satisfaction from consuming various goods and services, subject to the constraint that their spending on goods exactly equals their incomes. Basic consumer theory treats buyers as if they are completely informed about all things that matter to consumers: the range of products available, the prices of all products, the capacity of products to satisfy, and their incomes. Consumer preferences are assumed to possess several properties: consumer preferences are complete, consumer preferences are transitive, and consumers always prefer more of a good to less of the good. The benefit consumers obtain from the goods and services they consume is called *utility*, and the utility function shows an individual's

perception of the level of utility from consuming each conceivable bundle of goods. Indifference curves provide a means of depicting graphically the preferences of a consumer. *(LO1)*

- An indifference curve is a set of points representing different bundles of goods and services, each of which yields the same level of total utility. Indifference curves are downward sloping and convex. The marginal rate of substitution, which is the absolute value of the slope of the indifference curve, diminishes as the consumer moves downward along an indifference curve. Marginal utility is the addition to total utility attributable to adding one unit of a good, holding constant the amounts of all other goods consumed. The *MRS* shows the rate at which one good can be substituted for another while keeping utility constant, and can be interpreted as the ratio of the marginal utility of X divided by the marginal utility of Y. An indifference map consists of several indifference curves, and the higher an indifference curve is on the map, the greater the level of utility associated with the curve. (LO2)

■ The consumer's budget line shows the set of all consumption bundles that can be purchased at a given set of prices and income if the entire income is spent. When income increases (decreases), the budget line shifts outward away from (inward toward) the origin and remains parallel to the original budget line. If the price of X increases (decreases), the budget line will pivot around the fixed vertical intercept and get steeper (flatter). (LO3)

■ A consumer maximizes utility subject to a limited money income at the combination of goods for which the indifference curve is just tangent to the budget line. At this combination, the MRS (absolute value of the slope of the indifference curve) is equal to the price ratio (absolute value of the slope of the budget line). Alternatively, and equivalently, the consumer allocates money income so that the marginal utility per dollar spent on each good is the same for all commodities purchased and all income is spent. (LO4)

■ An individual consumer's demand curve relates utility-maximizing quantities to market prices, holding constant money income and the prices of all other goods. The slope of the demand curve illustrates the law of demand: quantity demanded varies inversely with price. Market demand is a list of prices and the quantities consumers are willing and able to purchase at each price in the list, other things being held constant. Market demand is derived by horizontally summing the demand curves for all the individuals in the market. The demand prices at various quantities along a market demand curve give the marginal benefit (value) of the last unit consumed for every buyer in the market, and thus market demand can be interpreted as the marginal benefit curve for a good. (LO5)

■ When a consumer spends her entire budget and chooses to purchase none of a specific good, this outcome is called a *corner solution* because the utility-maximizing consumption bundle lies at one of the corners formed by the endpoints of the budget line. Corner solutions occur for good X when the consumer spends all of her income, yet the marginal utility per dollar spent on X is less than the marginal utility per dollar spent on any other good that is purchased. This is usually what we mean when we say we "cannot afford something." (LO6)

KEY TERMS

budget line
complete
consumption bundle
corner solution

indifference curve
marginal rate of substitution (MRS)
marginal utility
market demand

transitive
utility
utility function

TECHNICAL PROBLEMS

1. Answer the following questions about consumer preferences:
   a. If Julie prefers Diet Coke to Diet Pepsi and Diet Pepsi to regular Pepsi but is indifferent between Diet Coke and Classic Coke, what are her preferences between Classic Coke and regular Pepsi?
   b. If James purchases a Ford Mustang rather than a Ferrari, what are his preferences between the two cars?
   c. If Julie purchases a Ferrari rather than a Ford Mustang, what are her preferences between the two cars?
   d. James and Jane are having a soft drink together. Coke and Pepsi are the same price. If James orders a Pepsi and Jane orders a Coke, what are the preferences of each between the two colas?

2. Answer each part of this question using the consumption bundles shown in Figure 5.1. Assume a consumer has complete and transitive preferences for goods X and Y and does not experience satiation for any bundle given in Figure 5.1.

   a. In a comparison of bundles A and D, this consumer could rationally make which of the following statements: I prefer A to D, I prefer D to A, or I am indifferent between A and D?

   b. If this consumer is indifferent between bundles A and B, then bundle E must be _____ (less, more, equally) preferred to bundle A. Explain your answer.

   c. Bundle C must be _____ (less, more, equally) preferred to bundle F. Explain your answer.

   d. Bundle F must be _____ (less, more, equally) preferred to bundle D. Explain your answer.

3. Suppose that two units of X and eight units of Y give a consumer the same utility as four units of X and two units of Y. Over this range:

   a. What is the marginal rate of substitution over this range of consumption?

   b. If the consumer obtains one more unit of X, how many units of Y must be given up in order to keep utility constant?

   c. If the consumer obtains one more unit of Y, how many units of X must be given up in order to keep utility constant?

4. Use the graph below of a consumer's indifference curve to answer the questions:

   a. What is the MRS between A and B?

   b. What is the MRS between B and C?

   c. What is the MRS at B?

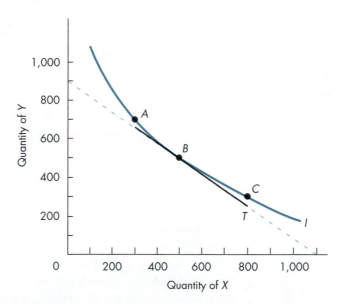

5. A consumer buys only two goods, X and Y.

   a. If the MRS between X and Y is 2 and the marginal utility of X is 20, what is the marginal utility of Y?

    b. If the *MRS* between *X* and *Y* is 3 and the marginal utility of *Y* is 3, what is the marginal utility of *X*?

    c. If a consumer moves downward along an indifference curve, what happens to the marginal utilities of *X* and *Y*? What happens to the *MRS*?

6. Use the figure below to answer the following questions:

    a. The equation of budget line *LZ* is *Y* = _____ − _____ *X*.

    b. The equation of budget line *LR* is *Y* = _____ − _____ *X*.

    c. The equation of budget line *KZ* is *Y* = _____ − _____ *X*.

    d. The equation of budget line *MN* is *Y* = _____ − _____ *X*.

    e. If the relevant budget line is *LR* and the consumer's income is $200, what are the prices of *X* and *Y*? At the same income, if the budget line is *LZ*, what are the prices of *X* and *Y*?

    f. If the budget line is *MN*, P_y = $40, and P_x = $20, what is income? At the same prices, if the budget line is *KZ*, what is income?

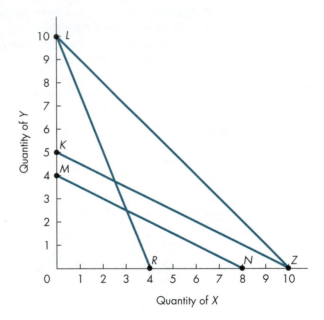

7. Suppose a consumer has the indifference map shown below. The relevant budget line is *LZ*. The price of good *Y* is $10.

    a. What is the consumer's income?

    b. What is the price of *X*?

    c. Write the equation for the budget line *LZ*.

    d. What combination of *X* and *Y* will the consumer choose? Why?

    e. What is the marginal rate of substitution at this combination?

    f. Explain in terms of the *MRS* why the consumer would not choose combinations designated by *A* or *B*.

g. Suppose the budget line pivots to *LM*, income remaining constant. What is the new price of *X*? What combination of *X* and *Y* is now chosen?

h. What is the new *MRS*?

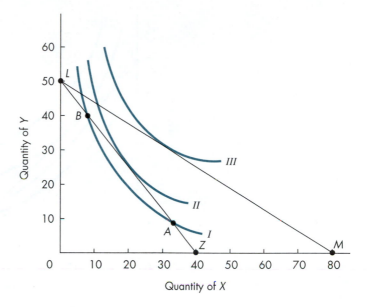

8. Suppose that the marginal rate of substitution is 2, the price of *X* is $3, and the price of *Y* is $1.

a. If the consumer obtains 1 more unit of *X*, how many units of *Y* must be given up in order to keep utility constant?

b. If the consumer obtains 1 more unit of *Y*, how many units of *X* must be given up in order to keep utility constant?

c. What is the rate at which the consumer is *willing* to substitute *X* for *Y*?

d. What is the rate at which the consumer is *able* to substitute *X* for *Y*?

e. Is the consumer making the utility-maximizing choice? Why or why not? If not, what should the consumer do? Explain.

9. The following graph shows a portion of a consumer's indifference map. The consumer faces the budget line *LZ*, and the price of *X* is $20.

a. The consumer's income = $_____.

b. The price of *Y* is $_____.

c. The equation for the budget line *LZ* is _____.

d. What combination of *X* and *Y* does the consumer choose? Why?

e. The marginal rate of substitution for this combination is _____.

f. Explain in terms of *MRS* why the consumer does not choose either combination *A* or *B*.

g. What combination is chosen if the budget line is *MZ*?

h. What is the price of *Y*?

i. What is the price of X?

j. What is the MRS in equilibrium?

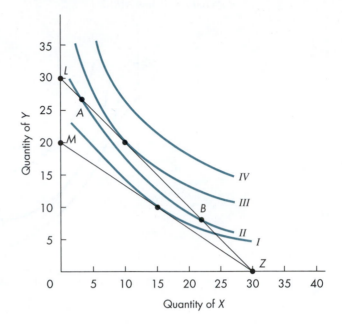

10. Sally purchases only pasta and salad with her income of $160 a month. Each month she buys 10 pasta dinners at $6 each and 20 salads at $5 each. The marginal utility of the last unit of each is 30. What should Sally do? Explain.

11. Assume that an individual consumes three goods, X, Y, and Z. The marginal utility (assumed measurable) of each good is independent of the rate of consumption of other goods. The prices of X, Y, and Z are, respectively, $1, $3, and $5. The total income of the consumer is $65, and the marginal utility schedule is as follows:

Units of good	Marginal utility of X (units)	Marginal utility of Y (units)	Marginal utility of Z (units)
1	12	60	70
2	11	55	60
3	10	48	50
4	9	40	40
5	8	32	30
6	7	24	25
7	6	21	18
8	5	18	10
9	4	15	3
10	3	12	1

a. Given a $65 income, how much of each good should the consumer purchase to maximize utility?

b. Suppose income falls to $43 with the same set of prices; what combination will the consumer choose?

c. Let income fall to $38; let the price of X rise to $5 while the prices of Y and Z remain at $3 and $5. How does the consumer allocate income now? What would you say if the consumer maintained that X is not purchased because he or she could no longer afford it?

12. The following graph shows a portion of a consumer's indifference map and three budget lines. The consumer has an income of $1,000.

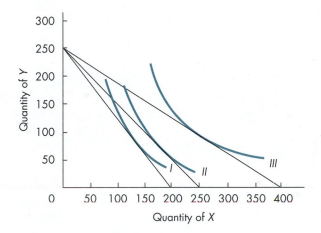

What is the price of Y? What are three price–quantity combinations on this consumer's demand curve?

13. Suppose there are only three consumers in the market for a particular good. The quantities demanded by each consumer at each price between $1 and $9 are shown in the following table:

| Price of X | Quantity demanded | | | Market demand |
	Consumer 1	Consumer 2	Consumer 3	
$9	0	5	10	_____
8	0	10	20	_____
7	10	15	30	_____
6	20	20	40	_____
5	30	25	50	_____
4	40	30	60	_____
3	50	35	70	_____
2	60	40	80	_____
1	70	45	90	_____

a. Using the following axes, draw the demand curve for each of the three consumers. Label the three curves D_1, D_2, and D_3, respectively.

b. Fill in the blanks in the table for the market quantity demanded at each price.

c. Construct the market demand curve in the graph, and label it D_M.

d. Construct the marginal benefit curve in the graph, and label it *MB*.
e. What is the marginal benefit of the 180th unit?
f. Is the marginal benefit the same for all consumers when 180 units are consumed? Explain.

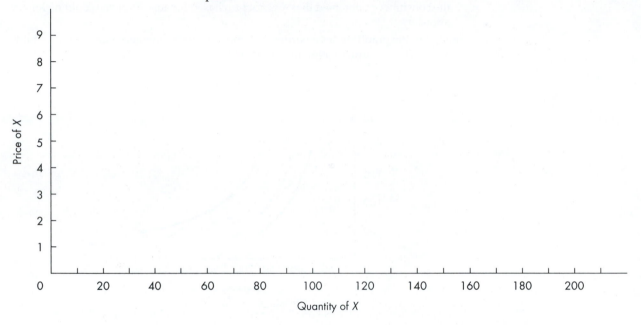

14. A consumer has the indifference map shown below. The market prices of *X* and *Y* are $24 and $8, respectively. The consumer has $120 to spend on goods *X* and *Y*.

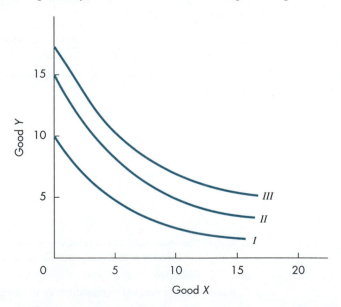

a. Construct the consumer's budget line and find the utility-maximizing consumption bundle. Label this bundle "E". Bundle E is composed of _____ units of X and _____ units of Y.

b. For bundle E, the marginal rate of substitution is _____ (greater than, less than, equal to) the slope of the budget line (in absolute value). The ratio MU/P for good X is _____ (greater than, less than, equal to) the ratio MU/P for good Y.

c. Bundle E _____ (is, is not) a corner solution.

   Now suppose the consumer's income and the price of Y remain the same, but the price of X decreases to $8.

d. Construct the new budget line and find the new utility-maximizing consumption bundle. Label this bundle "N". Bundle N is composed of _____ units of X and _____ units of Y.

e. For bundle N, the marginal rate of substitution is _____ (greater than, less than, equal to) the slope of the budget line (in absolute value). The ratio MU/P for good X is _____ (greater than, less than, equal to) the ratio MU/P for good Y.

f. Bundle N _____ (is, is not) a corner solution.

APPLIED PROBLEMS

1. Bridget has a limited income and consumes only wine and cheese; her current consumption choice is four bottles of wine and 10 pounds of cheese. The price of wine is $10 per bottle, and the price of cheese is $4 per pound. The last bottle of wine added 50 units to Bridget's utility, while the last pound of cheese added 40 units.

   a. Is Bridget making the utility-maximizing choice? Why or why not?

   b. If not, what should she do instead? Why?

2. Suppose Bill is on a low-carbohydrate diet. He can eat only three foods: Rice Krispies, cottage cheese, and popcorn. The marginal utilities for each food are tabulated below. Bill is allowed only 167 grams of carbohydrates daily. Rice Krispies, cottage cheese, and popcorn provide 25, 6, and 10 grams of carbohydrates per cup, respectively. Referring to the accompanying table, respond to the following questions:

Units of food (cups/day)	Marginal utility of Rice Krispies	Marginal utility of cottage cheese	Marginal utility of popcorn
1	175	72	90
2	150	66	80
3	125	60	70
4	100	54	60
5	75	48	50
6	50	36	40
7	25	30	30
8	25	18	20

   a. Given that Bill can consume only 167 grams of carbohydrates daily, how many cups of each food will he consume daily? Show your work.

   b. Suppose Bill's doctor tells him to further reduce his carbohydrate intake to 126 grams per day. What combination will he consume?

3. Increasingly, employees are being allowed to choose benefit packages from a menu of items. For instance, workers may be given a package of benefits that includes basic and optional items. Basics might include modest medical coverage, life insurance equal to a year's salary, vacation time based on length of service, and some retirement pay. But then employees can use credits to choose among such additional benefits as full medical coverage, dental and eye care, more vacation time, additional disability income, and higher company payments to the retirement fund. How do you think flexible benefit packages would affect an employee's choice between higher wages and more benefits?

4. The owner–manager of Good Guys Enterprises obtains utility from income (profit) and from having the firm behave in a socially conscious manner, such as making charitable contributions or civic expenditures. Can you set up the problem and derive the optimization conditions if the owner–manager wishes to obtain a specific level of utility at the lowest possible cost? Do these conditions differ from the utility-maximizing conditions?

5. In terms of the consumer theory set forth in this chapter, can you explain the meaning of the following statements?

   a. "I think you get more for your money from Nike than from Reebok."

   b. "I wanted to buy a Porsche Boxster rather than a Chevy Camaro, but it just wasn't worth it."

   c. "I'd like to go to Mexico over spring break, but I just can't afford it," said Don. Jill asked, "Don't you have enough money in your account?" Don replied, "Yeah, but I can't afford to go."

   d. "I'll have to flip a coin to decide whether to buy chocolate chip or vanilla fudge ice cream."

6. The Air Force awarded a $93 billion (or more) contract to a group led by Lockheed, Boeing, and General Dynamics to build the new fighter plane for the 21st century, the YF-22 Lightning 2. A group headed by Northrop and McDonnell Douglas, which had spent more than $1 billion on development for their alternative YF-23, lost out on the contract. That evening on CNN's *Crossfire,* the Secretary of Defense explained that the Lockheed group got the contract because their "quality for the price per plane was higher." He didn't elaborate. In terms of the theory set forth in this chapter, did he mean

   a. The Lockheed quality was higher?

   b. The Lockheed price was lower?

   If neither, what did he mean?

▣ MATHEMATICAL APPENDIX   A Brief Presentation of Consumer Theory

This appendix provides a mathematical analysis of the theory of consumer behavior and the derivation of demand functions from a consumer's utility-maximization conditions.

The Relation between the Marginal Rate of Substitution and Marginal Utility

A consumer has a general utility function with two goods of

$$U = U(X, Y)$$

The marginal utilities are defined as

$$MU_x = \partial U/\partial X \quad \text{and} \quad MU_y = \partial U/\partial Y$$

The marginal rate of substitution (*MRS*), showing the rate at which the consumer is willing to substitute one good for the other while holding utility constant, is

$$MRS = -dY/dX$$

The minus sign is included to keep *MRS* positive because $dY/dX < 0$ along an indifference curve.

To derive the relation between *MRS* and marginal utilities, take the total differential of the utility function and set $dU = 0$ to hold utility constant along a given indifference curve:

$$(1) \qquad dU = \frac{\partial U}{\partial X} dX + \frac{\partial U}{\partial Y} dY = 0$$

Solving equation (1) for $MRS = -dY/dX$,

$$MRS = -\frac{\partial Y}{\partial X} = \frac{\partial U/\partial X}{\partial U/\partial Y} = \frac{MU_x}{MU_y}$$

Because MU_x decreases and MU_y increases as X increases and Y decreases when moving downward along an indifference curve, the indifference curve is convex; that is, $-d^2Y/dX^2 < 0$.

Utility Maximization Subject to an Income Constraint

We now derive mathematically the consumer's utility-maximizing conditions.

The consumer maximizes utility

$$U = U(X, Y)$$

subject to an income (budget) constraint

$$M = P_x X + P_y Y$$

The Lagrangian function to be maximized is

$$\lambda = U(X, Y) + \lambda(M - P_x X - P_y Y)$$

where P_x and P_y are the prices of goods X and Y, M is income, and λ is the Lagrangian multiplier. Maximization of the function with respect to the levels of X and Y requires the following first-order conditions:

$$(2a) \qquad \frac{\partial \lambda}{\partial X} = \frac{\partial U}{\partial X} - \lambda P_x = 0$$

$$(2b) \qquad \frac{\partial \lambda}{\partial Y} = \frac{\partial U}{\partial Y} - \lambda P_y = 0$$

Setting $\partial \mathcal{L}/\partial \lambda$ equal to zero forces the budget constraint to be met:

$$(3) \qquad M = P_x X - P_y Y = 0$$

Combining equations (2a) and (2b), the necessary conditions for maximizing utility subject to the budget constraint are

$$(4) \qquad \frac{\partial U/\partial X}{\partial U/\partial Y} = P_x/P_y$$

Note that $\partial U/\partial X$ and $\partial U/\partial Y$ are the marginal utilities of the two goods; their ratio is the marginal rate of substitution. The ratio P_x/P_y is the absolute value of the slope of the budget line. Hence, the necessary condition for income-constrained utility maximization is that the marginal rate of substitution between the two commodities be equal to the ratio of their prices. That is, from equation (4),

$$\frac{\partial U/\partial X}{\partial U/\partial Y} = \frac{MU_x}{MU_y} = \frac{P_x}{P_y}$$

or

$$(5) \qquad \frac{MU_x}{P_x} = \frac{MU_y}{P_y}$$

The marginal utilities per dollar spent on the last units of X and Y are equal.

Derivation of the Consumer's Demand Function

The optimization conditions shown in equations (2) and (3) form a system of three equations that can be solved for the optimal values of λ^*, X^*, and Y^* in terms of the parameters M, P_x, and P_y. The demand functions from this solution are

$$X^* = X^*(M, P_x, P_y)$$

$$(6) \qquad \text{and}$$

$$Y^* = Y^*(M, P_x, P_y)$$

These demands are functions of the good's own price, the price of the related good, and income, as discussed in this chapter and in Chapter 2. To conform to the law of demand,

$$\frac{\partial X^*}{\partial P_x} < 0 \qquad \text{and} \qquad \frac{\partial Y^*}{\partial P_y} < 0$$

The derivatives $\frac{\partial X^*}{\partial P_x}$, $\frac{\partial X^*}{\partial M}$, $\frac{\partial Y^*}{\partial P_y}$, and $\frac{\partial Y^*}{\partial M}$ can be of any sign, although $\frac{\partial X^*}{\partial M}$ and $\frac{\partial Y^*}{\partial M}$ cannot both be negative. That is, both goods cannot be inferior because more income would lead to less expenditure, which violates the assumptions of consumer theory.

MATHEMATICAL EXERCISES

1. Assume a consumer with the utility function

$$U = U(X, Y) = X^2Y^2$$

and the typical budget constraint

$$M = P_xX + P_yY$$

   a. Set up the constrained maximization problem and derive the first-order conditions.
   b. Derive the consumer's demand for X and Y in terms of the parameters.

2. Assume a consumer with the utility function

$$U = U(X, Y) = (X + 2)(Y + 1)$$

   and the budget constraint ($M = 95$, $P_x = 10$, and $P_y = 5$)

$$95 = 10X + 5Y$$

   a. Set up the constrained maximization problem, and derive the first-order conditions.
   b. Find the amounts of goods X and Y the consumer will purchase in equilibrium.

ONLINE APPENDIX 1: Substitution and Income Effects of a Price Change

This appendix can be found online via McGraw-Hill *Connect®* or *Create*™. For more information, refer to the Preface.

Chapter 6

Elasticity and Demand

After reading this chapter, you will be able to:

6.1 Define price elasticity of demand and use it to predict changes in quantity demanded and changes in the price of a good.

6.2 Explain the role price elasticity plays in determining how a change in price affects total revenue.

6.3 List and explain several factors that affect price elasticity of demand.

6.4 Calculate price elasticity over an interval along a demand curve and at a point on a demand curve.

6.5 Relate marginal revenue to total revenue and demand elasticity and write the marginal revenue equation for linear inverse demand functions.

6.6 Define and compute the income elasticity of demand and the cross-price elasticity of demand.

Most managers agree that the toughest decision they face is the decision to raise or lower the price of their firms' products. When Walt Disney Company decided to raise ticket prices at its theme parks in Anaheim, California, and Orlando, Florida, the price hike caused attendance at the Disney parks to fall. The price increase was a success, however, because it boosted Disney's revenue: the price of a ticket multiplied by the number of tickets sold. For Disney, the higher ticket price more than offset the smaller number of tickets purchased, and revenue increased. You might be surprised to learn that price increases do not always increase a firm's revenue. For example, suppose just one gasoline producer, ExxonMobil, were to increase the price of its brand of gasoline while rival gasoline producers left their gasoline prices unchanged. ExxonMobil would likely experience falling revenue, even though it increased its price, because many ExxonMobil customers would switch to one of the many other brands of gasoline. In this situation, the reduced amount of gasoline sold would more than offset the higher price of gasoline, and ExxonMobil would find its revenue falling.

When managers *lower* price to attract more buyers, revenues may either rise or fall, again depending upon how responsive consumers are to a price reduction. For example, in an unsuccessful marketing strategy, called "Campaign 55," McDonald's Corporation lowered the price of its Big Mac and Quarter Pounders to 55 cents in an effort to increase revenue. The price reduction resulted in *lower* revenue, and McDonald's abandoned the low-price strategy for all but its breakfast meals—lower prices did increase breakfast revenues. Obviously, managers need to know how a price increase or decrease is going to affect the quantity sold and the revenue of the firm. In this chapter, you will learn how to use the concept of price elasticity to predict how revenue will be affected by a change in the price of the product. You can easily understand why managers of price-setting firms find this chapter to be particularly useful; they can use knowledge about demand elasticities to help them make better decisions about raising or lowering prices. And, even for managers of price-taking firms (i.e., firms in competitive markets where prices are determined by the intersection of market demand and supply), knowledge of price elasticity of industry demand can help managers predict the effect of changes in market price on total industry sales and total consumer expenditures in the industry.

Managers recognize that quantity demanded and price are inversely related. When they are making pricing decisions, as you saw in the examples of Disney, ExxonMobil, and McDonald's, it is even more important for managers to know *by how much* sales will change for a given change in price. A 10 percent decrease in price that leads to a 2 percent increase in quantity demanded differs greatly in effect from a 10 percent decrease in price that causes a 50 percent increase in quantity demanded. There is a substantial difference in the effect on total revenue between these two responses to a change in price. Certainly, when making pricing decisions, managers should have a good idea about how responsive consumers will be to any price changes and whether revenues will rise or fall.

The majority of this chapter is devoted to the concept of *price elasticity of demand,* a measure of the responsiveness of quantity demanded to a change in price along a demand curve and an indicator of the effect of a price change on total consumer expenditure on a product. The concept of price elasticity provides managers, economists, and policymakers with a framework for understanding why consumers in some markets are extremely responsive to changes in price while consumers in other markets are not. This understanding is useful in many types of managerial decisions.

We will begin by defining the price elasticity of demand and then show how to use price elasticities to find the percentage changes in price or quantity that result from movements along a demand curve. Next, the relation between elasticity and the total revenue received by firms from the sale of a product is examined in detail. Then we discuss three factors that determine the degree of responsiveness of consumers, and hence the price elasticity of demand. We also show how to compute the elasticity of demand either over an interval or at a point on demand. Then we examine the concept of marginal revenue and demonstrate the relation among demand, marginal revenue, and elasticity. The last section of this chapter introduces two other important elasticities: income and cross-price elasticities.

6.1 THE PRICE ELASTICITY OF DEMAND

As noted earlier, price elasticity of demand measures the responsiveness or sensitivity of consumers to changes in the price of a good or service. We will begin this section by presenting a formal (mathematical) definition of price elasticity and then show how price elasticity can be used to predict the change in sales when price rises or falls or to predict the percentage reduction in price needed to stimulate sales by a given percentage amount.

price elasticity of demand (E)
The percentage change in quantity demanded, divided by the percentage change in price. E is always a negative number because P and Q are inversely related.

Consumer responsiveness to a price change is measured by the **price elasticity of demand (E),** defined as

$$E = \frac{\%\Delta Q}{\%\Delta P} = \frac{\text{Percentage change in quantity demanded}}{\text{Percentage change in price}}$$

Because price and quantity demanded are inversely related by the law of demand, the numerator and denominator always have opposite algebraic signs, and the price elasticity is always negative. The price elasticity is calculated for movements along a given demand curve (or function) as price changes and all other factors affecting quantity demanded are held constant. Suppose a 10 percent price decrease ($\%\Delta P = -10\%$) causes consumers to increase their purchases by 30 percent ($\%\Delta Q = +30\%$). The price elasticity is equal to -3 ($= +30\%/-10\%$) in this case. In contrast, if the 10 percent decrease in price causes only a 5 percent increase in sales, the price elasticity would equal -0.5 ($= +5\%/-10\%$). Clearly, the smaller (absolute) value of E indicates less sensitivity on the part of consumers to a change in price.

elastic
Segment of demand for which $|E| > 1$.

When a change in price causes consumers to respond so strongly that the percentage by which they adjust their consumption (in absolute value) *exceeds* the percentage change in price (in absolute value), demand is said to be **elastic** over that price interval. In mathematical terms, demand is elastic when $|\%\Delta Q|$ exceeds $|\%\Delta P|$, and thus $|E|$ is greater than 1. When a change in price causes consumers to respond so weakly that the percentage by which they adjust their consumption (in absolute value) is *less than* the percentage change in price (in absolute value), demand is said to be **inelastic** over that price interval. In other words, demand is inelastic when the numerator (in absolute value) is smaller than the denominator (in absolute value), and thus $|E|$ is less than 1. In the special instance in which the percentage change in quantity (in absolute value) *just equals* the percentage change in price (in absolute value), demand is said to be **unitary elastic,** and $|E|$ is equal to 1. Table 6.1 summarizes this discussion.

inelastic
Segment of demand for which $|E| < 1$.

unitary elastic
Segment of demand for which $|E| = 1$.

TABLE 6.1	Elasticity	Responsiveness	$|E|$
Price Elasticity of Demand (E), $E = \dfrac{\%\Delta Q}{\%\Delta P}$	Elastic	$|\%\Delta Q| > |\%\Delta P|$	$|E| > 1$
	Unitary elastic	$|\%\Delta Q| = |\%\Delta P|$	$|E| = 1$
	Inelastic	$|\%\Delta Q| < |\%\Delta P|$	$|E| < 1$

Note: The symbol "| |" denotes the absolute value.

Predicting the Percentage Change in Quantity Demanded

Suppose a manager knows the price elasticity of demand for a company's product is equal to -2.5 over the range of prices currently being considered by the firm's marketing department. The manager is considering decreasing price by 8 percent and wishes to predict the percentage by which quantity demanded will increase. From the definition of price elasticity, it follows that

$$-2.5 = \frac{\%\Delta Q}{-8\%}$$

so, with a bit of algebraic manipulation, $\%\Delta Q = +20\%$ ($= -2.5 \times -8\%$). Thus, the manager can increase sales by 20 percent by lowering price 8 percent. As we mentioned in the introduction, price elasticity information about industry demand can also help price-taking managers make predictions about industry- or market-level changes. For example, suppose an increase in industry supply is expected to cause market price to fall by 8 percent, and the price elasticity of *industry* demand is equal to -2.5 for the segment of demand over which supply shifts. Using the same algebraic steps just shown, total industry output is predicted to increase by 20 percent in this case.

Predicting the Percentage Change in Price

Suppose a manager of a different firm faces a price elasticity equal to -0.5 over the range of prices the firm would consider charging for its product. This manager wishes to stimulate sales by 15 percent. The manager is willing to lower price to accomplish the increase in sales but needs to know the percentage amount by which price must be lowered to obtain the 15 percent increase in sales. Again using the definition of price elasticity of demand, it follows that

$$-0.5 = \frac{+15\%}{\%\Delta P}$$

so, after some algebraic manipulation, $\%\Delta P = -30\%$ ($= 15\%/-0.5$). Thus, this manager must lower price by 30 percent to increase sales by 15 percent. As we explained in the case of predicting percentage changes in quantity demanded, elasticity of industry demand can also be used to make predictions about changes in market-determined prices. For example, suppose an increase in industry supply is expected to cause market output to rise by 15 percent, and the price elasticity of *industry* demand is equal to -0.5 for the portion of demand over which supply shifts. Following the algebraic steps shown above, market price is predicted to fall by 30 percent. As you can see, the techniques for predicting percentage changes in quantity demanded and price can be applied to both individual firm demand curves or industry demand curves.

As you can see, the concept of elasticity is rather simple. Price elasticity is nothing more than a mathematical measure of how sensitive quantity demanded is to changes in price. We will now apply the concept of price elasticity to a crucial question facing managers. How does a change in the price of the firm's product affect the total revenue received?

Now try Technical Problems 1–2.

6.2 PRICE ELASTICITY AND TOTAL REVENUE

total revenue (*TR*)
The total amount paid to producers for a good or service (*TR* = *P* × *Q*).

Managers of firms, as well as industry analysts, government policymakers, and academic researchers, are frequently interested in how total revenue changes when there is a movement along the demand curve. **Total revenue (*TR*),** which also equals the total expenditure by consumers on the commodity, is simply the price of the commodity times quantity demanded, or

$$TR = P \times Q$$

As we have emphasized, price and quantity demanded move in opposite directions along a demand curve: If price rises, quantity falls; if price falls, quantity rises. The change in price and the change in quantity have opposite effects on total revenue. The relative strengths of these two effects will determine the overall effect on *TR*. We will now examine these two effects, called the price effect and the quantity effect, along with the price elasticity of demand to establish the relation between changes in price and total revenue.

Price Elasticity and Changes in Total Revenue

price effect
The effect on total revenue of changing price, holding output constant.

When a manager raises the price of a product, the increase in price, by itself, would increase total revenue if the quantity sold remained constant. Conversely, when a manager lowers price, the decrease in price would decrease total revenue if the quantity sold remained constant. This effect on total revenue of changing price, for a given level of output, is called the **price effect.** When price changes, the quantity sold does not remain constant; it moves in the opposite direction of price. When quantity increases in response to a decrease in price, the increase in quantity, by itself, would increase total revenue if the price of the product remained constant. Alternatively, when quantity falls after a price increase, the reduction in quantity, by itself, would decrease total revenue if product price remained constant. The effect on total revenue of changing the quantity sold, for a given price level, is called the **quantity effect.** The price and quantity effects always push total revenue in opposite directions. Total revenue moves in the direction of the stronger of the two effects. If the two effects are equally strong, no change in total revenue can occur.

quantity effect
The effect on total revenue of changing output, holding price constant.

Suppose a manager increases price, causing quantity to decrease. The price effect, represented below by an upward arrow above *P*, and the quantity effect, represented by a downward arrow above *Q*, show how the change in *TR* is affected by opposing forces

$$\overset{\uparrow}{} \quad \overset{\downarrow}{}$$
$$TR = P \times Q$$

To determine the direction of movement in *TR*, information about the relative strengths of the price effect and output effect must be known. The elasticity of demand tells a manager which effect, if either, is dominant.

If demand is elastic, |*E*| is greater than 1, the percentage change in *Q* (in absolute value) is greater than the percentage change in *P* (in absolute value), and the quantity effect dominates the price effect. To better see how the dominance of the quantity effect determines the direction in which TR moves, you can represent the dominance of the quantity effect by drawing the arrow above Q longer than the arrow above P. The direction of the dominant effect—the quantity effect here—tells a manager that TR will fall when price rises and demand is elastic:

$$\downarrow \quad \uparrow \quad \downarrow$$
$$TR = P \times Q$$

If a manager *decreases* price when demand is elastic, the arrows in this diagram reverse directions. The arrow above Q is still the longer arrow because the quantity effect always dominates the price effect when demand is elastic.

Now consider a price increase when demand is *inelastic*. When demand is inelastic, $|E|$ is less than 1, the percentage change in Q (in absolute value) is less than the percentage change in P (in absolute value), and the price effect dominates the quantity effect. The dominant price effect can be represented by an upward arrow above P that is longer than the downward arrow above Q. The direction of the dominant effect tells the manager that TR will rise when price rises and demand is inelastic

$$\uparrow \quad \uparrow \quad \downarrow$$
$$TR = P \times Q$$

When a manager decreases price and demand is inelastic, the arrows in this diagram would reverse directions. A downward arrow above P would be a long arrow because the price effect always dominates the quantity effect when demand is inelastic.

When demand is unitary elastic, $|E|$ is equal to 1, and neither the price effect nor the quantity effect dominates. The two effects exactly offset each other, so price changes have no effect on total revenue when demand is unitary elastic.

Relation The effect of a change in price on total revenue ($TR = P \times Q$) is determined by the price elasticity of demand. When demand is elastic (inelastic), the quantity (price) effect dominates. Total revenue always moves in the same direction as the variable (P or Q) having the dominant effect. When demand is unitary elastic, neither effect dominates, and changes in price leave total revenue unchanged.

Table 6.2 summarizes the relation between price changes and revenue changes under the three price elasticity conditions.

TABLE 6.2		Elastic $|\%\Delta Q| > |\%\Delta P|$ Q-effect dominates	Unitary elastic $|\%\Delta Q| = |\%\Delta P|$ No dominant effect	Inelastic $|\%\Delta Q| < |\%\Delta P|$ P-effect dominates
Relations between Price Elasticity and Total Revenue (TR)	Price rises	*TR* falls	No change in *TR*	*TR* rises
	Price falls	*TR* rises	No change in *TR*	*TR* falls

Changing Price at Borderline Video Emporium: A Numerical Example

The manager at Borderline Video Emporium faces the demand curve for Blu-ray DVD discs shown in Figure 6.1. At the current price of $18 per DVD Borderline can sell 600 DVDs each week. The manager can lower price to $16 per DVD and increase sales to 800 DVDs per week. In Panel A of Figure 6.1, over the interval *a* to *b* on demand curve *D* the price elasticity is equal to −2.43. (You will learn how to make this calculation in Section 6.4.) Because the demand for Blu-ray DVDs is elastic over this range of prices (|−2.43| > 1), the manager knows the quantity effect dominates the price effect. Lowering price from $18 to $16 results in an increase in the quantity of DVDs sold, so the manager knows that total revenue, which always moves in the direction of the dominant effect, must increase.

To verify that revenue indeed rises when the manager at Borderline lowers the price over an elastic region of demand, you can calculate total revenue at the two prices, $18 and $16

Point *a*: $TR = \$18 \times 600 = \$10,800$
Point *b*: $TR = \$16 \times 800 = \$12,800$

FIGURE 6.1

Changes in Total Revenue of Borderline Video Emporium

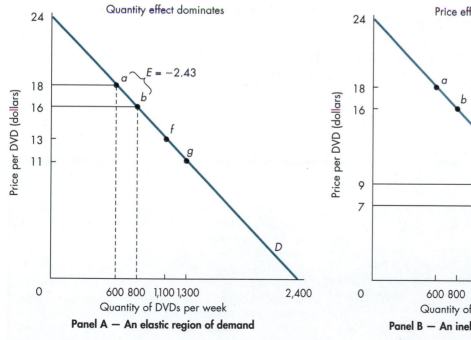

Panel A — An elastic region of demand

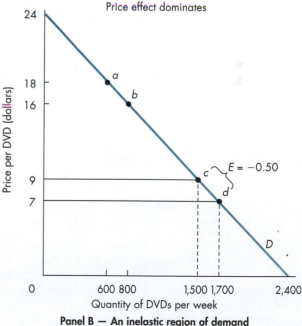

Panel B — An inelastic region of demand

Total revenue rises by $2,000 (= 12,800 − 10,800) when price is reduced over this elastic region of demand. Although Borderline earns less revenue on each DVD sold, the number of DVDs sold each week rises enough to more than offset the downward price effect, causing total revenue to rise.

Now suppose the manager at Borderline is charging just $9 per compact disc and sells 1,500 DVDs per week (see Panel B). The manager can lower price to $7 per disc and increase sales to 1,700 DVDs per week. Over the interval *c* to *d* on demand curve *D*, the elasticity of demand equals −0.50. Over this range of prices for DVDs, the demand is inelastic ($|-0.50| < 1$), and Borderline's manager knows the price effect dominates the quantity effect. If the manager lowers price from $9 to $7, total revenue, which always moves in the direction of the dominant effect, must decrease.

To verify that revenue falls when the manager at Borderline lowers price over an inelastic region of demand, you can calculate total revenue at the two prices, $9 and $7

$$\text{Point } c: TR = \$9 \times 1,500 = \$13,500$$
$$\text{Point } d: TR = \$7 \times 1,700 = \$11,900$$

Total revenue falls by $1,600 ($\Delta TR = \$11,900 − \$13,500 = −\$1,600$). Total revenue always falls when price is reduced over an inelastic region of demand. Borderline again earns less revenue on each DVD sold, but the number of DVDs sold each week does not increase enough to offset the downward price effect and total revenue falls.

If the manager decreases (or increases) the price of Blu-ray DVDs over a unitary-elastic region of demand, total revenue does not change. You should verify that demand is unitary elastic over the interval *f* to *g* in Panel A of Figure 6.1.

Note in Figure 6.1 that demand is elastic over the $16 to $18 price range but inelastic over the $7 to $9 price range. In general, the elasticity of demand varies along any particular demand curve, even one that is linear. It is usually incorrect to say a demand curve is either elastic or inelastic. You can say only that a demand curve is elastic or inelastic over a particular price range. For example, it is correct to say that demand curve *D* in Figure 6.1 is elastic over the $16 to $18 price range and inelastic over the $7 to $9 price range.

Now try Technical Problems 3–5.

ILLUSTRATION 6.1

P × Q Measures More Than Just Business' Total Revenue

As you know from our explanation in Section 6.2, demand elasticity provides the essential piece of information needed to predict how total revenue changes—increases, decreases, or stays the same—when the price of a good or service changes. We mention in that discussion that price multiplied by quantity can also mea-

sure the amount spent by consumers who buy *Q* units of the good at price *P*. In other words, total revenue for a business is exactly equal to the total expenditure by consumers.

While business owners and managers focus on *P × Q* as measuring their revenue for the purpose of computing their business profit, politicians and government policymakers frequently view *P × Q* as measuring the "burden" on consumers buying the good or service. And thus policymakers can use the price elasticity of demand to predict how price changes are likely to affect the total amount spent by consumers to buy a product. For example, policymakers believe raising taxes on cigarettes causes cigarette prices to rise and, by the law of demand, will reduce the quantity of cigarettes purchased and improve smokers' health. Unfortunately, however, the demand for cigarettes remains "stubbornly inelastic," and this causes total expenditure on cigarettes by smokers to rise substantially with higher taxes on cigarettes. Critics of higher cigarette taxes point out that, with the cigarette tax increases, smokers' health probably deteriorates even more rapidly because smokers will only decrease the number of cigarettes they smoke by a small amount; they will simply spend more income to buy the cigarettes, leaving less money for other, more healthful grocery items. Policymakers sometimes defend the higher taxes by (perversely and correctly) noting that further cigarette price hikes will eventually move smokers into the elastic region of their demand curves so that higher prices would then cause significant declines in the quantity demanded and reduce the amount spent on cigarettes. Although we cannot dispute the analytical conclusion that cigarette demand will become elastic if only the price is high enough, getting to that price point on cigarette demand is very likely to take a lot more income out of smokers' pockets before we see any decline in spending on cigarettes.

Another example demonstrating the usefulness of interpreting $P \times Q$ as a measure of total consumer spending, rather than as a measure of total revenue, involves the "taxi cab" fare war going on in Manhattan. The current price war in Manhattan was sparked by the entry of new "car-service" firms such as Gett, Lyft, and Uber that pick up riders who use their smartphones to "hail" cab rides.[a] Before these new competitors entered the market in Manhattan, taxi cab fares were high enough to be positioned in the *elastic* region of the demand for car rides. The price elasticity of demand is important in this situation because, for now, drivers at the new companies are not complaining about falling fares. Their incomes are rising, measured by multiplying the cab fare times the number of rides (i.e., $P \times Q$) because demand is elastic at the current fares. And, with rising incomes for their drivers, Gett, Lyft, and Uber are able to expand the number of cars servicing Manhattan. Of course, if cab fares continue falling, eventually demand will become inelastic and driver incomes, $P \times Q$, will decline. At that point, car drivers will not be so happy with the fare war!

[a]These new car-service companies are not legally defined as "taxi cabs" and therefore they cannot legally pick up riders on the street who hail with a hand raised. Nonetheless, riders view hailing one of these "app car-service" rides with their smartphones as nearly identical to hailing by hand a yellow taxi cab.
Source: Anne Kadet, "Car-App Car Services Compete for Passengers with Low Fares," *The Wall Street Journal*, October 10, 2014.

6.3 FACTORS AFFECTING PRICE ELASTICITY OF DEMAND

Price elasticity of demand plays such an important role in business decision making that managers should understand not only how to use the concept to obtain information about the demand for the products they sell, but also how to recognize the factors that affect price elasticity. We will now discuss the three factors that make the demand for some products more elastic than the demand for other products.

Availability of Substitutes

The availability of substitutes is by far the most important determinant of price elasticity of demand. The better the substitutes for a given good or service, the more elastic the demand for that good or service. When the price of a good rises, consumers will substantially reduce consumption of that good if they perceive that close substitutes are readily available. Naturally, consumers will be less responsive to a price increase if they perceive that only poor substitutes are available.

Some goods for which demand is rather elastic include fruit, corporate jets, and life insurance. Alternatively, goods for which consumers perceive few or no good substitutes have low price elasticities of demand. Wheat, salt, and gasoline tend to have low price elasticities because there are only poor substitutes available—for instance, corn, pepper, and diesel fuel, respectively.

The definition of the market for a good greatly affects the number of substitutes and thus the good's price elasticity of demand. For example, if all the grocery stores in a city raised the price of milk by 50 cents per gallon, total sales of milk would undoubtedly fall—but probably not by much. If, on the other hand, only the Food King chain of stores raised price by 50 cents, the sales of Food King milk would probably fall substantially. There are many good substitutes for Food King milk, but there are not nearly as many substitutes for milk in general.

Percentage of Consumer's Budget

The percentage of the consumer's budget that is spent on the commodity is also important in the determination of price elasticity. All other things equal, we would expect the price elasticity to be directly related to the percentage of consumers' budgets spent on the good. For example, the demand for refrigerators is probably more price elastic than the demand for toasters because the expenditure required to purchase a refrigerator would make up a larger percentage of the budget of a "typical" consumer.

Time Period of Adjustment

The length of the time period used in measuring the price elasticity affects the magnitude of price elasticity. In general, the longer the time period of measurement, the larger (the more elastic) the price elasticity will be (in absolute value). This relation is the result of consumers' having more time to adjust to the price change.

Consider, again, the way consumers would adjust to an increase in the price of milk. Suppose the dairy farmers' association is able to convince all producers of milk nationwide to raise their milk prices by 15 percent. During the first week the price increase takes effect, consumers come to the stores with their grocery lists already made up. Shoppers notice the higher price of milk but have already planned their meals for the week. Even though a few of the shoppers will react immediately to the higher milk prices and reduce the amount of milk they purchase, many shoppers will go ahead and buy the same amount of milk as they purchased the week before. If the dairy association collects sales data and measures the price elasticity of demand for milk after the first week of the price hike, they will be happy to see that the 15 percent increase in the price of milk caused only a modest reduction in milk sales.

Over the coming weeks, however, consumers begin looking for ways to consume less milk. They substitute foods that have similar nutritional composition to milk; consumption of cheese, eggs, and yogurt all increase. Some consumers will even switch to powdered milk for some of their less urgent milk needs—perhaps to feed the cat or to use in cooking. Six months after the price increase, the dairy association again measures the price elasticity of milk. Now the price elasticity of demand is probably much larger in absolute value (more elastic) because it is measured over a six-month time period instead of a one-week time period.

For most goods and services, given a longer time period to adjust, the demand for the commodity exhibits more responsiveness to changes in price—the demand becomes more elastic. Of course, we can treat the effect of time on elasticity within the framework of the effect of available substitutes. The greater the time period available for consumer adjustment, the more substitutes become available and economically feasible. As we stressed earlier, the more available are substitutes, the more elastic is demand.

Now try Technical Problem 6.

6.4 CALCULATING PRICE ELASTICITY OF DEMAND

As noted at the beginning of the chapter, the price elasticity of demand is equal to the ratio of the percentage change in quantity demanded divided by the percentage change in price. When calculating the value of E, it is convenient to avoid computing percentage changes by using a simpler formula for computing elasticity that can be obtained through the following algebraic operations

$$E = \frac{\%\Delta Q}{\%\Delta P} = \frac{\frac{\Delta Q}{Q} \times 100}{\frac{\Delta P}{P} \times 100}$$

$$= \frac{\Delta Q}{\Delta P} \times \frac{P}{Q}$$

Thus, price elasticity can be calculated by multiplying the slope of demand ($\Delta Q/\Delta P$) times the ratio of price divided by quantity (P/Q), which avoids making tedious percentage change computations. The computation of E, while involving the rather simple mathematical formula derived here, is complicated somewhat by the fact that elasticity can be measured either (1) over an interval (or arc) along demand or (2) at a specific point on the demand curve. In either case, E still measures the sensitivity of consumers to changes in the price of the commodity.

The choice of whether to measure demand elasticity at a point or over an interval of demand depends on the length of demand over which E is measured. If the change in price is relatively small, a point measure is generally suitable. Alternatively, when the price change spans a sizable arc along the demand curve, the interval measurement of elasticity provides a better measure of consumer responsiveness than the point measure. As you will see shortly, point elasticities are more easily computed than interval elasticities. We begin with a discussion of how to calculate elasticity of demand over an interval.

interval (or arc) elasticity
Price elasticity calculated over an interval of a demand curve:

$E = \frac{\Delta Q}{\Delta P} \times \frac{\text{Average } P}{\text{Average } Q}$

Computation of Elasticity over an Interval

When elasticity is calculated over an interval of a demand curve (either a linear or a curvilinear demand), the elasticity is called an **interval (or arc) elasticity**. To measure E over an arc or interval of demand, the simplified formula presented earlier—slope of demand multiplied by the ratio of P divided by Q—needs to be modified slightly. The modification only requires that the *average values* of P and Q over the interval be used:

$$E = \frac{\Delta Q}{\Delta P} \times \frac{\text{Average } P}{\text{Average } Q}$$

Recall from our previous discussion of Figure 6.1 that we did not show you how to compute the two values of the interval elasticities given in Figure 6.1. You can now make these computations for the intervals of demand *ab* and *cd* using the above formula for interval price elasticities (notice that *average* values for P and Q are used):

$$E_{ab} = \frac{+200}{-2} \times \frac{17}{700} = -2.43$$

$$E_{cd} = \frac{+200}{-2} \times \frac{8}{1600} = -0.5$$

Now try Technical Problem 7.

Relation   When calculating the price elasticity of demand over an interval of demand, use the interval or arc elasticity formula:

$$E = \frac{\Delta Q}{\Delta P} \times \frac{\text{Average } P}{\text{Average } Q}$$

Computation of Elasticity at a Point

point elasticity
A measurement of demand elasticity calculated at a point on a demand curve rather than over an interval.

As we explained previously, it is appropriate to measure elasticity at a point on a demand curve rather than over an interval when the price change covers only a small interval of demand. Elasticity computed at a point on demand is called **point elasticity** of demand. Computing the price elasticity at a point on demand is accomplished by multiplying the slope of demand ($\Delta Q/\Delta P$), computed *at the point of measure,* by the ratio P/Q, computed using the values of P and Q at the point of measure. To show you how this is done, we can compute the *point* elasticities in Figure 6.1 when Borderline Music Emporium charges $18 and $16 per compact disc at points a and b, respectively. Notice that the value of $\Delta Q/\Delta P$ for the linear demand in Figure 6.1 is -100 ($= +2400/-24$) at every point along D, so the two point elasticities are computed as

$$E_a = -100 \times \frac{18}{600} = -3$$

$$E_b = -100 \times \frac{16}{800} = -2$$

Relation   When calculating the price elasticity of demand at a point on demand, multiply the slope of demand ($\Delta Q/\Delta P$), computed at the point of measure, by the ratio P/Q, computed using the values of P and Q at the point of measure.

ILLUSTRATION 6.2

Texas Calculates Price Elasticity

In addition to its regular license plates, the state of Texas, as do other states, sells personalized or "vanity" license plates. To raise additional revenue, the state will sell a vehicle owner a license plate saying whatever the owner wants as long as it uses six letters (or numbers), no one else has the same license as the one requested, and it isn't obscene. For this service, the state charges a higher price than the price for standard licenses.

Many people are willing to pay the higher price rather than display a license of the standard form, such as 387 BRC. For example, an ophthalmologist announces his practice with the license MYOPIA. Others tell their personalities with COZY-1 and ALL MAN.

When Texas decided to increase the price for vanity plates from $25 to $75, a Houston newspaper reported that sales of these plates fell from 150,000 down to 60,000 vanity plates. As it turned out, demand was rather inelastic over this range. As you can calculate using the interval method, the price elasticity was −0.86. The newspaper reported that vanity plate revenue *rose* after the price increase ($3.75 million to $4.5 million), which would be expected for a price increase when demand is inelastic.

But the newspaper quoted the assistant director of the Texas Division of Motor Vehicles as saying, "Since the demand dropped[a] the state didn't make money from the higher fees, so the price for next year's personalized plates will be $40." If the objective of the state is to make money from these licenses and if the numbers in the article are correct, this is the wrong thing to do. It's hard to see how the state lost money by increasing the price from $25 to $75—the revenue increased and the cost of producing plates must have

decreased because fewer were produced. So the move from $25 to $75 was the right move.

Moreover, let's suppose that the price elasticity between $75 and $40 is approximately equal to the value calculated for the movement from $25 to $75 (−0.86). We can use this estimate to calculate what happens to revenue if the state drops the price to $40. We must first find what the new quantity demanded will be at $40. Using the arc elasticity formula and the price elasticity of −0.86,

$$E = \frac{\Delta Q}{\Delta P} \times \frac{\text{Average } P}{\text{Average } Q}$$
$$= \frac{60,000 - Q}{75 - 40} \times \frac{(75 + 40)/2}{(60,000 + Q)/2} = -0.86$$

where Q is the new quantity demanded. Solving this equation for Q, the estimated sales are 102,000 (rounded) at a price of $40. With this quantity demanded and price, total revenue would be $4,080,000, representing a decrease of $420,000 from the revenue at $75 a plate. If the state's objective is to raise revenue by selling vanity plates, it should increase rather than decrease price.

This Illustration actually makes two points. First, even decision makers in organizations that are not run for profit, such as government agencies, should be able to use economic analysis. Second, managers whose firms are in business to make a profit should make an effort to know (or at least have a good approximation for) the elasticity of demand for the products they sell. Only with this information will they know what price to charge.

[a]It was, of course, quantity demanded that decreased, not demand.

Source: Adapted from Barbara Boughton, "A License for Vanity," *Houston Post*, October 19, 1986, pp. 1G, 10G.

Point elasticity when demand is linear Consider a general linear demand function of three variables—price (P), income (M), and the price of a related good (P_R)

$$Q = a + bP + cM + dP_R$$

Suppose income and the price of the related good take on specific values of $\overline{M}$ and $\overline{P_R}$, respectively. Recall from Chapter 2 when values of the demand determinants ($\overline{M}$ and $\overline{P_R}$ in this case) are held constant, they become part of the constant term in the direct demand function:

$$Q = a' + bP$$

where $a' = a + c\overline{M} + d\overline{P_R}$. The slope parameter b, of course, measures the rate of change in quantity demanded per unit change in price: $b = \Delta Q/\Delta P$. Thus price elasticity at a point on a linear demand curve can be calculated as

$$E = b\frac{P}{Q}$$

where P and Q are the values of price and quantity at the point of measure. For example, let's compute the elasticity of demand for Borderline Music at a price of $9 per CD (see point c in Panel B of Figure 6.1). You can verify for yourself that the equation for the direct demand function is $Q = 2,400 - 100P$, so $b = -100$ and

$$E = -100\frac{9}{1,500} = -\frac{3}{5} = -0.6$$

Even though multiplying b by the ratio P/Q is rather simple, there happens to be an even easier formula for computing point price elasticities of demand. This alternative point elasticity formula is

$$E = \frac{P}{P - A}$$

where P is the price at the point on demand where elasticity is to be measured, and A is the price-intercept of demand.[1] Note that, for the linear demand equation $Q = a' + bP$, the price intercept A is $-a'/b$. In Figure 6.1, let us apply this alternative formula to calculate again the elasticity at point c ($P = \$9$). In this case, the price-intercept A is $24, so the elasticity is

$$E = \frac{9}{9 - 24} = -0.6$$

which is exactly equal to the value obtained previously by multiplying the slope of demand by the ratio P/Q. We must stress that, because the two formulas $b\frac{P}{Q}$ and $\frac{P}{P - A}$ are mathematically equivalent, they always yield identical values for point price elasticities.

---

[1] This alternative formula for computing price elasticity is derived in the mathematical appendix for this chapter.

Now try Technical
Problems 8–9.

Relation For linear demand functions $Q = a' + bP$, the price elasticity of demand can be computed using either of two equivalent formulas:

$$E = b\frac{P}{Q} = \frac{P}{P-A}$$

where P and Q are the values of price and quantity demanded at the point of measure on demand, and $A\,(= -a'/b)$ is the price-intercept of demand.

Point elasticity when demand is curvilinear When demand is curvilinear, the formula $E = \frac{\Delta Q}{\Delta P} \times \frac{P}{Q}$ can be used for computing point elasticity simply by substituting the slope of the *curved* demand at the point of measure for the value of $\Delta Q/\Delta P$ in the formula. This can be accomplished by measuring the slope of the tangent line at the point of measure. Figure 6.2 illustrates this procedure.

In Figure 6.2, let us measure elasticity at a price of $100 on demand curve D. We first construct the tangent line T at point R. By the "rise over run" method, the slope of T equals $-4/3\,(= -140/105)$. Of course, because P is on the vertical axis and Q is on the horizontal axis, the slope of tangent line T gives $\Delta P/\Delta Q$ not $\Delta Q/\Delta P$. This is easily fixed by taking the inverse of the slope of tangent line T to get $\Delta Q/\Delta P = -3/4$. At point R price elasticity is calculated using $-3/4$ for the slope of demand and using $100 and 30 for P and Q, respectively

$$E_R = \frac{\Delta Q}{\Delta P} \times \frac{P}{Q} = -\frac{3}{4} \times \frac{100}{30} = -2.5$$

FIGURE 6.2

Calculating Point Elasticity for Curvilinear Demand

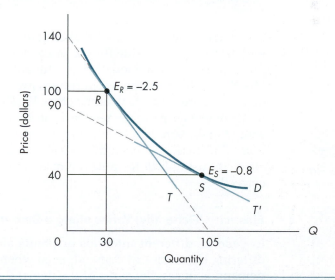

As it turns out, the alternative formula $E = P/(P - A)$ for computing point elasticity on *linear* demands can also be used for computing point elasticities on *curvilinear* demands. To do so, the price-intercept of the tangent line T serves as the value of A in the formula. As an example, we can recalculate elasticity at point R in Figure 6.2 using the formula $E = P/(P - A)$. The price-intercept of tangent line T is \$140

$$E_R = \frac{P}{P - A} = \frac{100}{100 - 140} = -2.5$$

As expected, -2.5 is the same value for E_R obtained earlier.

Since the formula $E = P/(P - A)$ doesn't require the slope of demand or the value of Q, it can be used to compute E in situations like point S in Figure 6.2 where the available information is insufficient to be able to multiply slope by the P/Q ratio. Just substitute the price-intercept of T' (= \$90) into the formula $E = P/(P - A)$ to get the elasticity at point S

$$E_S = \frac{P}{P - A} = \frac{40}{40 - 90} = -0.8$$

> **Relation** For curvilinear demand functions, the price elasticity at a point can be computed using either of two equivalent formulas:
>
> $$E = \frac{\Delta Q}{\Delta P} \times \frac{P}{Q} = \frac{P}{P - A}$$
>
> where $\Delta Q/\Delta P$ is the slope of the curved demand at the point of measure (which is the inverse of the slope of the tangent line at the point of measure), P and Q are the values of price and quantity demanded at the point of measure, and A is the price-intercept of the tangent line extended to cross the price-axis.

We have now established that both formulas for computing point elasticities will give the same value for the price elasticity of demand whether demand is linear or curvilinear. Nonetheless, students frequently ask which formula is the "best" one. Because the two formulas give identical values for E, neither one is better or more accurate than the other. We should remind you, however, that you may not always have the required information to compute E both ways, so you should make sure you know both methods. (Recall the situation in Figure 6.2 at point S.) Of course, when it is possible to do so, we recommend computing the elasticity using *both* formulas to make sure your price elasticity calculation is correct!

Now try Technical Problem 10.

Elasticity (Generally) Varies along a Demand Curve

In general, different intervals or points along the same demand curve have differing elasticities of demand, even when the demand curve is linear. When demand is linear, the slope of the demand curve is constant. Even though the *absolute* rate at which quantity demanded changes as price changes ($\Delta Q/\Delta P$) remains constant, the *proportional* rate of change in Q as P changes (%ΔQ/%ΔP) varies along a linear demand curve. To see why, we can examine the basic formula for elasticity, $E = \dfrac{\Delta Q}{\Delta P} \times \dfrac{P}{Q}$. Moving along a linear demand does not cause the term $\Delta Q/\Delta P$ to change, but elasticity does vary because the ratio P/Q changes. Moving down demand, by reducing price and selling more output, causes the term P/Q to decrease which reduces the absolute value of E. And, of course, moving up a linear demand, by increasing price and selling less output, causes P/Q and $|E|$ to increase. Thus, P and $|E|$ vary directly along a *linear* demand curve.

For movements along a *curved* demand, both the slope and the ratio P/Q vary continuously along demand. For this reason, elasticity generally varies along curvilinear demands, but there is no general rule about the relation between price and elasticity as there is for linear demand.

As it turns out, there is an exception to the general rule that elasticity varies along curvilinear demands. A special kind of curvilinear demand function exists for which the demand elasticity is constant for all points on demand. When demand takes the form $Q = aP^b$, the elasticity is constant along the demand curve and equal to b.[2] Consequently, no calculation of elasticity is required, and the price elasticity is simply the value of the exponent on price, b. The absolute value of b can be greater than, less than, or equal to 1, so that this form of demand can be elastic, inelastic, or unitary elastic at all points on the demand curve. As we will show you in the next chapter, this kind of demand function can be useful in statistical demand estimation and forecasting.

Figure 6.3 shows a constant elasticity of demand function, $Q = aP^b$, with the values of a and b equal to 100,000 and -1.5, respectively. Notice that price elasticity equals -1.5 at both points U and V where prices are \$20 and \$40, respectively

$$E_U = \frac{P}{P - A} = \frac{20}{20 - 33.33} = -1.5$$

$$E_V = \frac{P}{P - A} = \frac{40}{40 - 66.67} = -1.5$$

Clearly, you never need to compute the price elasticity of demand for this kind of demand curve because E *is* the value of the exponent on price (b).

Now try Technical Problem 11.

Relation In general, the price elasticity of demand varies along a demand curve. For linear demand curves, price and $|E|$ vary directly: The higher (lower) the price, the more (less) elastic is demand. For a curvilinear demand, there is no general rule about the relation between price and elasticity, except for the special case of $Q = aP^b$, which has a constant price elasticity (equal to b) for all prices.

---

[2]See the appendix at the end of this chapter for a mathematical proof of this result.

FIGURE 6.3

Constant Elasticity of Demand

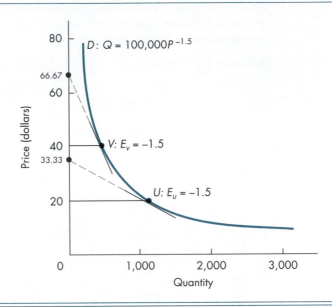

6.5 MARGINAL REVENUE, DEMAND, AND PRICE ELASTICITY

The responsiveness of consumers to changes in the price of a good must be considered by managers of price-setting firms when making pricing and output decisions. The price elasticity of demand gives managers essential information about how total revenue will be affected by a change in price. As it turns out, an equally important concept for pricing and output decisions is *marginal revenue.* **Marginal revenue (MR)** is the addition to total revenue attributable to selling one additional unit of output:

marginal revenue (MR)
The addition to total revenue attributable to selling one additional unit of output; the slope of total revenue.

$$MR = \Delta TR / \Delta Q$$

Because marginal revenue measures the rate of change in total revenue as quantity changes, *MR* is the slope of the *TR* curve. Marginal revenue is related to price elasticity because marginal revenue, like price elasticity, involves changes in total revenue caused by movements along a demand curve.

Marginal Revenue and Demand

As noted, marginal revenue is related to the way changes in price and output affect total revenue along a demand curve. To see the relation between marginal revenue and price, consider the following numerical example. The demand schedule for a product is presented in columns 1 and 2 of Table 6.3. Price times quantity gives the total revenue obtainable at each level of sales, shown in column 3.

Marginal revenue, shown in column 4, indicates the change in total revenue from an additional unit of sales. Note that marginal revenue equals price only

TABLE 6.3

Demand and Marginal Revenue

	(1) Unit sales	(2) Price	(3) Total revenue	(4) Marginal revenue ($\Delta TR/\Delta Q$)
	0	$4.50	$ 0	—
	1	4.00	4.00	$4.00
	2	3.50	7.00	3.00
	3	3.10	9.30	2.30
	4	2.80	11.20	1.90
	5	2.40	12.00	0.80
	6	2.00	12.00	0
	7	1.50	10.50	−1.50

for the first unit sold. For the first unit sold, total revenue is the demand price for 1 unit. The first unit sold adds $4—the price of the first unit—to total revenue, and the marginal revenue of the first unit sold equals $4; that is, $MR = P$ for the first unit. If 2 units are sold, the second unit should contribute $3.50 (the price of the second unit) to total revenue. But total revenue for 2 units is only $7, indicating that the second unit adds only $3 (= $7 − $4) to total revenue. Thus the marginal revenue of the second unit is not equal to price, as it was for the first unit. Indeed, examining columns 2 and 4 in Table 6.3 indicates that $MR < P$ for all but the first unit sold.

Marginal revenue is less than price ($MR < P$) for all but the first unit sold because price must be lowered in order to sell more units. Not only is price lowered on the marginal (additional) unit sold, but price is also lowered for all the *inframarginal units* sold. The **inframarginal units** are those units that could have been sold at a higher price had the firm not lowered price to sell the marginal unit. Marginal revenue for any output level can be expressed as

inframarginal units
Units of output that could have been sold at a higher price had a firm not lowered its price to sell the marginal unit.

$$MR = \text{Price} - \frac{\text{Revenue lost by lowering price}}{\text{on the inframarginal units}}$$

The second unit of output sells for $3.50. By itself, the second unit contributes $3.50 to total revenue. But marginal revenue is not equal to $3.50 for the second unit because to sell the second unit, price on the first unit is lowered from $4 to $3.50. In other words, the first unit is an inframarginal unit, and the $0.50 lost on the first unit must be subtracted from the price. The net effect on total revenue of selling the second unit is $3 (= $3.50 − $0.50), the same value as shown in column 4 of Table 6.3.

If the firm is currently selling 2 units and wishes to sell 3 units, it must lower price from $3.50 to $3.10. The third unit increases total revenue by its price, $3.10. To sell the third unit, the firm must lower price on the 2 units that could have been sold for $3.50 if only 2 units were offered for sale. The revenue lost on the 2 inframarginal units is $0.80 (= $0.40 × 2). Thus the marginal revenue of the third unit is \$2.30 (= \$3.10 − \$0.80), and marginal revenue is less than the price of the third unit.

It is now easy to see why $P = MR$ for the first unit sold. For the first unit sold, price is not lowered on any inframarginal units. Because price must fall in order to sell additional units, marginal revenue must be less than price at every other level of sales (output).

As shown in column 4, marginal revenue declines for each additional unit sold. Notice that it is positive for each of the first 5 units sold. However, marginal revenue is 0 for the sixth unit sold, and it becomes negative thereafter. That is, the seventh unit sold actually causes total revenue to decline. Marginal revenue is positive when the effect of lowering price on the inframarginal units is less than the revenue contributed by the added sales at the lower price. Marginal revenue is negative when the effect of lowering price on the inframarginal units is greater than the revenue contributed by the added sales at the lower price.

> **Relation** Marginal revenue must be less than price for all units sold after the first, because the price must be lowered to sell more units. When marginal revenue is positive, total revenue increases when quantity increases. When marginal revenue is negative, total revenue decreases when quantity increases. Marginal revenue is equal to 0 when total revenue is maximized.

Figure 6.4 shows graphically the relations among demand, marginal revenue, and total revenue for the demand schedule in Table 6.3. As noted, MR is below price (in Panel A) at every level of output except the first. When total revenue (in Panel B) begins to decrease, marginal revenue becomes negative. Demand and marginal revenue are both negatively sloped.

Sometimes the interval over which marginal revenue is measured is greater than one unit of output. After all, managers don't necessarily increase output by just one unit at a time. Suppose in Table 6.3 that we want to compute marginal revenue when output increases from 2 units to 5 units. Over the interval, the change in total revenue is \$5 (= \$12 − \$7), and the change in output is 3 units. Marginal revenue is \$1.67 (= $\Delta TR/\Delta Q$ = \$5/3) per unit change in output; that is, each of the 3 units contributes (on average) \$1.67 to total revenue. As a general rule, whenever the interval over which marginal revenue is being measured is more than a single unit, divide ΔTR by ΔQ to obtain the marginal revenue for each of the units of output in the interval.

As mentioned in Chapter 2 and as you will see in Chapter 7, *linear* demand equations are frequently employed for purposes of empirical demand estimation and demand forecasting. The relation between a linear demand equation and its marginal revenue function is no different from that set forth in the preceding relation. The case of a linear demand is special because the relation between demand and marginal revenue has some additional properties that do not hold for nonlinear demand curves.

When demand is linear, marginal revenue is linear and lies halfway between demand and the vertical (price) axis. This implies that marginal revenue must be twice as steep as demand, and demand and marginal revenue share the same

FIGURE 6.4

Demand, Marginal Revenue, and Total Revenue

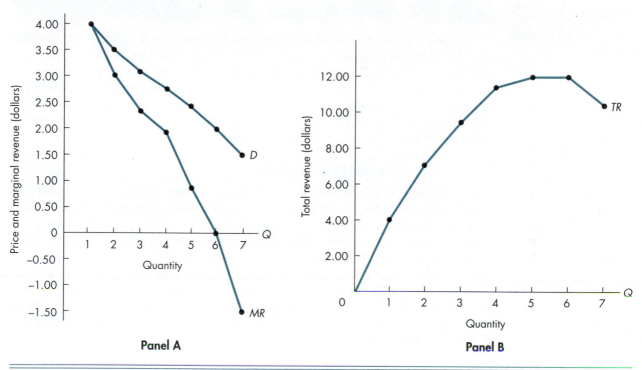

Panel A

Panel B

intercept on the vertical axis. We can explain these additional properties and show how to apply them by returning to the simplified linear demand function ($Q = a + bP + cM + dP_R$) examined earlier in this chapter (and in Chapter 2). Again we hold the values of income and the price of the related good R constant at the specific values $\overline{M}$ and $\overline{P}_R$, respectively. This produces the linear demand equation $Q = a' + bP$, where $a' = a + c\overline{M} + d\overline{P}_R$. Next, we find the inverse demand equation by solving for $P = f(Q)$ as explained in Chapter 2 (you may wish to review Technical Problem 2 in Chapter 2)

$$P = -\frac{a'}{b} + \frac{1}{b}Q$$
$$= A + BQ$$

where $A = -a'/b$ and $B = 1/b$. Since a' is always positive and b is always negative (by the law of demand), it follows that A is always positive and B is always negative: $A > 0$ and $B < 0$. Using the values of A and B from inverse demand, the equation for marginal revenue is $MR = A + 2BQ$. Thus marginal revenue is linear, has the same vertical intercept as inverse demand (A), and is twice as steep as inverse demand ($\Delta MR/\Delta Q = 2B$).

☐ **Relation** When inverse demand is linear, $P = A + BQ (A > 0, B < 0)$, marginal revenue is also linear, intersects the vertical (price) axis at the same point demand does, and is twice as steep as the inverse demand function. The equation of the linear marginal revenue curve is $MR = A + 2BQ$.

Figure 6.5 shows the linear inverse demand curve $P = 6 - 0.05Q$. (Remember that B is negative because P and Q are inversely related.) The associated marginal revenue curve is also linear, intersects the price axis at \$6, and is twice as steep as the demand curve. Because it is twice as steep, marginal revenue intersects the quantity axis at 60 units, which is half the output level for which demand intersects the quantity axis. The equation for marginal revenue has the same vertical intercept but twice the slope: $MR = 6 - 0.10Q$.

Marginal Revenue and Price Elasticity

Using Figure 6.5, we now examine the relation of price elasticity to demand and marginal revenue. Recall that if total revenue increases when price falls and quantity rises, demand is elastic; if total revenue decreases when price falls and quantity rises, demand is inelastic. When marginal revenue is positive in Panel A, from a quantity of 0 to 60, total revenue increases as price declines in Panel B; thus demand is elastic over this range. Conversely, when marginal revenue is negative, at any quantity greater than 60, total revenue declines when price falls; thus demand must be inelastic over this range. Finally, if marginal revenue is 0, at a quantity of 60, total revenue does not change when quantity changes, so the price elasticity of demand is unitary at 60.

FIGURE 6.5
Linear Demand, Marginal Revenue, and Elasticity ($Q = 120 - 20P$)

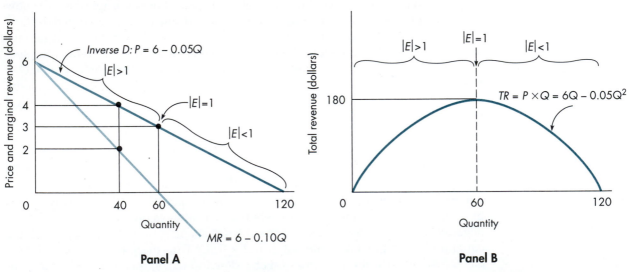

Panel A

Panel B

TABLE 6.4	(1)	(2)	(3)
Marginal Revenue, Total Revenue, and Price Elasticity of Demand	Marginal revenue	Total revenue	Price elasticity of demand
	$MR > 0$	TR increases as Q increases (P decreases)	Elastic ($|E| > 1$)
	$MR = 0$	TR is maximized	Unit elastic ($|E| = 1$)
	$MR < 0$	TR decreases as Q increases (P decreases)	Inelastic ($|E| < 1$)

Except for marginal revenue being linear and twice as steep as demand, all the preceding relations hold for nonlinear demands. Thus, the following relation (also summarized in Table 6.4) holds for all demand curves:

Relation   When MR is positive (negative), total revenue increases (decreases) as quantity increases, and demand is elastic (inelastic). When MR is equal to 0, the price elasticity of demand is unitary.

The relation among marginal revenue, price elasticity of demand, and price at any quantity can be expressed still more precisely. As shown in this chapter's appendix, the relation between marginal revenue, price, and price elasticity, *for linear or curvilinear demands*, is

$$MR = P\left(1 + \frac{1}{E}\right)$$

where E is the price elasticity of demand and P is product price. When demand is elastic ($|E| > 1$), $|1/E|$ is less than 1, $1 + (1/E)$ is positive, and marginal revenue is positive. When demand is inelastic ($|E| < 1$), $|1/E|$ is greater than 1, $1 + (1/E)$ is negative, and marginal revenue is negative. In the case of unitary price elasticity ($E = -1$), $1 + (1/E)$ is 0, and marginal revenue is 0.

To illustrate the relation between MR, P, and E numerically, we calculate marginal revenue at 40 units of output for the demand curve shown in Panel A of Figure 6.5. At 40 units of output, the point elasticity of demand is equal to -2 [$= P/(P - A) = 4/(4 - 6)$]. Using the formula presented above, MR is equal to 2 [$= 4(1 - 1/2)$]. This is the same value for marginal revenue that is obtained by substituting $Q = 40$ into the equation for marginal revenue: $MR = 6 - 0.1(40) = 2$.

Relation   For any demand curve, when demand is elastic ($|E| > 1$), marginal revenue is positive. When demand is inelastic ($|E| < 1$), marginal revenue is negative. When demand is unitary elastic ($|E| = 1$), marginal revenue is 0. For all demand and marginal revenue curves:

$$MR = P\left(1 + \frac{1}{E}\right)$$

where E is the price elasticity of demand.

Now try Technical Problems 12–14.

6.6 OTHER DEMAND ELASTICITIES

Sometimes economists and business decision makers are interested in measuring the sensitivity of consumers to changes in either income or the price of a related good. **Income elasticity** measures the responsiveness of quantity demanded to changes in income, holding all other variables in the general demand function constant. **Cross-price elasticity** measures the responsiveness of quantity demanded to changes in the price of a related good, when all the other variables in the general demand function remain constant. In this section we show how to calculate and interpret these two elasticities.

Income Elasticity (E_M)

As noted, income elasticity measures the responsiveness of quantity purchased when income changes, all else constant. Income elasticity, E_M, is the percentage change in quantity demanded divided by the percentage change in income, holding all other variables in the general demand function constant, including the good's own price:

$$E_M = \frac{\%\Delta Q}{\%\Delta M} = \frac{\Delta Q/Q}{\Delta M/M} = \frac{\Delta Q}{\Delta M} \times \frac{M}{Q}$$

As you can see, the sign of E_M depends on the sign of $\Delta Q/\Delta M$, which may be positive (if the good is normal) or negative (if the good is inferior). Thus if the good is normal, the income elasticity is positive. If the good is inferior, the income elasticity is negative.

Income elasticity, like price elasticity of demand, can be measured either over an interval or at a point on the general demand curve. For the interval measure of income elasticity, compute $\Delta Q/\Delta M$ over the interval and multiply this slope by the ratio of average income divided by average quantity

$$E_M = \frac{\Delta Q}{\Delta M} \times \frac{\text{Average } M}{\text{Average } Q}$$

When the change in income is relatively small, the point measure of income elasticity is calculated by multiplying the slope $\Delta Q/\Delta M$ by the ratio M/Q. For the linear demand function, $Q = a + bP + cM + dP_R$, the point measure of income elasticity is

$$E_M = c\frac{M}{Q}$$

because slope parameter c measures $\Delta Q/\Delta M$, as you learned in Chapter 2.

To illustrate the use of income elasticity, consider Metro Ford, a new-car dealership in Atlanta. The manager of Metro Ford expects average household income in Fulton County to increase from $45,000 to $50,000 annually when the current recession ends, causing an increase in the demand for new cars. At a constant average price of $30,000 per car, the increase in income will cause sales to rise from 800 to 1,400 units per month. Panel A in Figure 6.6 illustrates this situation. The increase in income shifts the demand for new cars rightward—a new car is a normal good. To calculate the income elasticity of demand, we use the arc elasticity method of computing percentage changes over an interval. The income elasticity of demand in Panel A is

$$E_M = \frac{\Delta Q}{\Delta M} \times \frac{\text{Average } M}{\text{Average } Q} = \frac{600}{5,000} \times \frac{47,500}{1,100} = 5.18$$

FIGURE 6.6

Calculating Income Elasticity of Demand

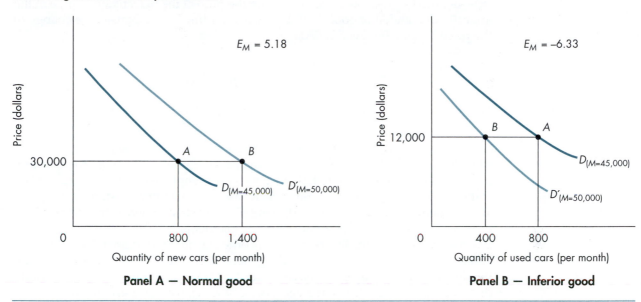

Panel A — Normal good

Panel B — Inferior good

We should mention that the choice of $30,000 as the price at which to measure income elasticity is arbitrary. The manager at Metro Ford probably chose a price of $30,000 as a typical new-car price. Also notice that averages for Q and M are used because the income elasticity is computed for the interval A to B.

Now consider Lemon Motors, a used-car dealership in Atlanta. Panel B in Figure 6.6 depicts the demand for used cars at Lemon Motors. The increase in household income in Fulton County causes a decrease in demand for used cars from D to D'—used cars are assumed to be inferior goods in this example. If used-car prices hold at $12,000, sales at the used-car dealership fall from 800 to 400 units per month. Again using the arc method of computing percentage changes, the income elasticity of demand is

$$E_M = \frac{\Delta Q}{\Delta M} \times \frac{\text{Average } M}{\text{Average } Q} = \frac{-400}{5,000} \times \frac{47,500}{600} = -6.33$$

As expected, the income elasticity is negative for an inferior good.

◻ **Relation** The income elasticity measures the responsiveness of consumers to changes in income when the price of the good and all other determinants of demand are held constant. The income elasticity is positive (negative) for normal (inferior) goods.

Cross-Price Elasticity (E_{XR})

The cross-price elasticity of a good, as already noted, measures the responsiveness of quantity demanded of one good to changes in the price of a related good R, when all the other variables in the general demand function remain constant. The cross-price elasticity between the good in question (X) and another good (R)—denoted E_{XR}—is calculated by taking the ratio of the percentage change in the quantity demanded of good X ($\%\Delta Q_X$) and dividing by the percentage change in the price of the other good R ($\%\Delta P_R$)

$$E_{XR} = \frac{\%\Delta Q_X}{\%\Delta P_R} = \frac{\Delta Q_X / Q_X}{\Delta P_R / P_R} = \frac{\Delta Q_X}{\Delta P_R} \times \frac{P_R}{Q_X}$$

Note that the sign of E_{XR} depends on the sign of $\Delta Q_X / \Delta P_R$, which can be positive or negative. Recall from Chapter 2 that if an increase in the price of one good causes the quantity purchased of another good to increase, the goods are substitutes (i.e., $\Delta Q_X / \Delta P_R > 0$). If the rise in the price of one good causes the quantity purchased of another good to fall, the goods are complements (i.e., $\Delta Q_X / \Delta P_R < 0$). If there is no change in the quantity purchased of the other good, the two goods are independent (i.e., $\Delta Q_X / \Delta P_R = 0$). Thus E_{XR} is positive when X and R are substitutes; E_{XR} is negative when X and R are complements.[3]

Cross-price elasticity, like price and income elasticities of demand, can be measured over intervals or at points on the general demand curve. As before, to obtain the interval measure of elasticity, compute $\Delta Q / \Delta P_R$ over the interval and multiply this slope times the ratio of average price of the related good divided by average quantity:

$$E_{XR} = \frac{\Delta Q}{\Delta P_R} \times \frac{\text{Average } P_R}{\text{Average } Q}$$

When the change in the price of the related good is relatively small, the point measure of E_{XR} is calculated by multiplying the slope $\Delta Q / \Delta P_R$ by the ratio P_R / Q. For the linear demand function, $Q = a + bP + cM + dP_R$, the point measure of E_{XR} is

$$E_{XR} = d\frac{P_R}{Q}$$

because, as explained in Chapter 2, d measures $\Delta Q / \Delta P_R$.

Suppose the general manager of the Tampa Bay Buccaneers is studying the demand for Buccaneer football tickets. Of particular concern is the sensitivity of Buccaneer fans to the price of Tampa Bay Lightning tickets (P_L)—Tampa's hockey team—and the price of parking for football games at Raymond James Stadium (P_p), a substitute good and a complementary good, respectively, for Buccaneer football fans. The Bucs' general manager has learned that the owner of the Lightning plans to cut its already "low" ticket price of $45 per hockey game by 5 percent. After the Buccaneers became Super Bowl champions in 2003, general seating ticket

---

[3]We should note that the cross-price elasticity of X for R need not equal the cross-price elasticity of R for X, although the two will generally have the same signs.

prices (P) were raised to $75 per game. Since the Super Bowl victory, average household income has stagnated at $50,000 ($M$). So, rather than raise ticket prices any further at this time, the general manager plans to increase parking fees by 10 percent (currently $15 per vehicle), unless, of course, ticket demand turns out to be quite sensitive to parking fees.

The Buccaneer general manager obtains from a consulting firm the following statistically estimated demand for tickets in the general seating areas, which excludes club and luxury seating:

$$Q = 49{,}800 - 750P + 0.85M + 400P_L - 625P_P$$

The general manager decides to calculate the cross-price elasticities for hockey tickets and parking fees, E_{XL} and E_{XP}, respectively, at the point on demand corresponding to the current values of the demand variables: $P = \$75$, $M = \$50{,}000$, $P_L = \$45$, and $P_P = \$15$. The estimated quantity demanded of Buccaneer football tickets in the general seating areas is 44,675 [$= 49{,}800 - (750 \times 75) + (0.85 \times 50{,}000) + (400 \times 45) - (625 \times 15)$]. The cross-price elasticity of Buccaneer ticket demand with respect to Lightning ticket prices (E_{XL}) can be calculated as follows:

$$E_{XL} = \frac{\Delta Q}{\Delta P_L} \times \frac{P_L}{Q} = 400\frac{45}{44{,}675} = 0.40$$

Note that the cross-price elasticity between Buccaneer and Lightning tickets is positive (for substitutes) but rather small, indicating football and hockey are rather weak substitutes in Tampa. Similarly, the cross-price elasticity of Buccaneer ticket demand with respect to parking fees (E_{XP}) is computed as

$$E_{XP} = \frac{\Delta Q}{\Delta P_P} \times \frac{P_P}{Q} = -625\frac{15}{44{,}675} = -0.21$$

The cross-price elasticity between football and parking is negative (as expected for complements) but small, indicating that Buccaneer fans are not particularly responsive to changes in the price of parking.

With such small absolute values of the cross-price elasticities, the Buccaneers' general manager can reasonably conclude that falling hockey ticket prices and rising parking fees are not likely to have much effect on demand for general seating football tickets. More precisely, the 5 percent drop in Lightning ticket prices is likely to cause only a 2 percent ($= 5\% \times 0.40$) decrease in the quantity of Bucs tickets sold, and the 10 percent increase in parking fees is predicted to decrease ticket sales by just 2.1 percent ($= 10\% \times -0.21$).

Relation The cross-price elasticity measures the responsiveness of the quantity demanded of one good when the price of another good changes, holding the price of the good and all other determinants of demand constant. Cross-price elasticity is positive (negative) when the two goods are substitutes (complements).

ILLUSTRATION 6.3

Empirical Elasticities of Demand

When we use the appropriate data and statistical techniques, it is possible to estimate price, income, and cross-price elasticities from actual demand schedules. We have collected a sample of estimated demand elasticities from a variety of sources and present them in the accompanying table. In the chapter on empirical demand functions, we will show how to estimate actual demand elasticities.

Looking at the price elasticities presented in the table, note that the demand for some basic agricultural products such as butter, chicken, pork, and eggs is inelastic. Fruit, for which consumers can find many substitutes, has a much more elastic demand than chicken, pork, or eggs. Whether ground into hamburger or cut into steaks, beef is usually more expensive than the other two basic meats, chicken and pork. Because beef represents a larger fraction of households' grocery bill, consumers are more sensitive to change in beef prices than to changes in chicken prices. And, because steaks are more expensive than ground beef, consumers will be more sensitive to steak prices. Apparently consumers of beer, wine, and cigarettes can find few substitutes for these items since the demand elasticities are quite inelastic for all three. Demand for clothing, something most of us are unwilling to go without, is inelastic. A recent study found that buyers of dynamic random access memory (DRAM) chips are so insensitive to price changes that it estimated demand to be perfectly inelastic for DRAM chips! We do not wish to dispute the results of this study, but we suspect the demand for DRAM chips is perfectly inelastic only for a very narrow range of prices. As prices for bandwidth decline, Internet service providers (ISPs) apparently gobble up bandwidth to transmit data between different countries on fiber-optic cables. For any particular type and brand of ready-to-eat cereal, consumers can find plenty of readily available substitutes. Consequently, the demand for raisin bran cereal is rather large for both leading brands. Another factor affecting price elasticity is the length of time consumers have to adjust to a price change. For example, electricity demand is more price-responsive in the long run than in the short run. It is interesting that gasoline demand is inelastic in the short run but elastic in the long run.

Normal goods have positive income elasticities of demand (E_M), and inferior goods have negative income elasticities. Ground beef and potatoes are inferior goods since E_M is negative. Steaks are more strongly normal than chicken or pork, indicating that a given percentage increase in income causes over a fourfold (fivefold) increase in steak consumption than chicken (pork) consumption. Wine is more strongly normal than beer. The high income elasticity of demand for foreign travel indicates that consumer demand for foreign travel is quite responsive to changes in income. Life insurance is a normal good for both Japanese and Americans, but Japanese demand for life insurance is nearly twice as sensitive to changes in income as U.S. demand for life insurance.

We explained in the text that cross-price elasticities are positive for substitutes and negative for complements. All four pairs of goods in the table are substitutes ($E_{XY} > 0$). Steaks and chicken are weak substitutes, while margarine and butter seem to be rather strong substitutes. Beer and wine drinkers substitute between the two alcoholic beverages but apparently not with much enthusiasm. The extremely low cross-price elasticity of demand between Kellogg's and Post brands of raisin bran cereal suggests that buyers of Kellogg's brand possess strong brand-loyalty and are quite unwilling to switch to the Post brand.

Table of Empirical Elasticities of Demand

Price elasticities of demand (E):

Butter	−0.24
Chicken	−0.30
Pork	−0.77
Eggs	−0.26
Beef (ground)	−1.01
Beef (steaks)	−1.15
Fruit	−3.02
Beer	−0.20
Wine	−0.67
Cigarettes	−0.51
Clothing	−0.62
Taxi cabs New York City	−0.22
Dynamic Random Access Memory (DRAM) chips	−0.0
Transnational fiber-optic bandwidth	−2.0

Kellogg's Raisin Bran	−2.06
Post Raisin Bran	−2.03
Electricity (short run)	−0.28
Electricity (long run)	−0.90
Gasoline (short run)	−0.43
Gasoline (long run)	−1.50
Income elasticities of demand (E_M):	
Beef (ground)	−0.19
Beef (steaks)	1.87
Chicken	0.42
Pork	0.34
Potatoes	−0.81
Beer	0.76
Wine	1.72
Life insurance in Japan	2.99
Life insurance in United States	1.65
Cross-price elasticities of demand (E_{XR}):	
Beef (steaks) and chicken	0.24
Margarine and butter	1.53
Beer and wine	0.56
Kellogg's Raisin Bran and Post Raisin Bran	0.01

Sources: For price, cross-price, and income elasticities for agricultural products, see Dale Heien, "The Structure of Food Demand: Interrelatedness and Duality," *American Journal of Agricultural Economics*, May 1982; and K. S. Huang, "A Complete System of U.S. Demand for Food," *Technical Bul-* *letin* No. 1821, Economic Research Service, U.S. Department of Agriculture, September 1993. For cigarettes price elasticity, see Frank Chaloupka, "Rational Addictive Behavior and Cigarette Smoking," *Journal of Political Economy*, August 1991. For clothing price elasticities, see Richard Blundell, Panos Pashardes, and Guglielmo Weber, "What Do We Learn about Consumer Demand Patterns from Micro Data," *American Economic Review*, June 1993. For alcohol elasticities, see Jon Nelson, "Broadcast Advertising and U.S. Demand for Alcoholic Beverages," *Southern Economic Journal*, April 1999. For cereal elasticities, see A. Nevo, "Mergers with Differentiated Products: The Case of the Ready to Eat Cereals Industry," *RAND Journal of Economics*, Autumn 2000. For short-run and long-run gasoline and electricity elasticities, see Robert Archibald and Robert Gillingham, "An Analysis of Short-Run Consumer Demand for Gasoline Using Household Survey Data," *Review of Economics and Statistics*, November 1980; and Chris King and Sanjoy Chatterjee, "Predicting California Demand Response: How Do Customers React to Hourly Prices?" *Public Utilities Fortnightly* 141, no. 13 (July 1, 2003). For income elasticity of demand for electricity, see Cheng Hsiao and Dean Mountain, "Estimating the Short-Run Income Elasticity of Demand for Electricity by Using Cross-Sectional Categorized Data," *Journal of the American Statistical Association*, June 1985. For the price elasticity of fiber-optic bandwidth, see the editorial "Fear of Fiber-Optic Glut May be Misguided," *Lightwave* 17, no. 9 (August 2000). Life insurance elasticities can be found in Dai I. Chi, "Japan: Life, But Not as We Know It," *Euromoney*, October 1998. For the price elasticity of DRAM chips, see Jim Handy, "Has the Market Perked Up Yet?" *Electronics Times*, June 5, 2000. For taxi cab elasticity, see Bruce Schaller, "Elasticities for Taxicab Fares and Service Availability," *Transportation* 26 (1999).

6.7 SUMMARY

- Price elasticity of demand, E, measures responsiveness or sensitivity of consumers to changes in the price of a good by taking the ratio of the percentage change in quantity demanded to the percentage change in the price of the good: $E = \%\Delta Q_d/\%\Delta P$. The larger the absolute value of E, the more sensitive buyers will be to a change in price. Demand is elastic when $|E| > 1$, demand is inelastic when $|E| < 1$, and demand is unitary elastic when $|E| = 1$. If price elasticity is known, the percentage change in quantity demanded can be predicted for a given percentage change in price: $\%\Delta Q_d = \%\Delta P \times E$. And the percentage change in price required for a given change in quantity demanded can be predicted when E is known: $\%\Delta P = \%\Delta Q_d \div E$. (LO1)

- The effect of changing price on total revenue is determined by the price elasticity of demand. When demand is elastic (inelastic), the quantity (price) effect dominates. Total revenue always moves in the same direction as the variable, price or quantity, having the dominant effect. When demand is unitary elastic, neither effect dominates, and changes in price leave total revenue unchanged. (LO2)

- Several factors affect the elasticity of demand for a good: (1) the better and more numerous the substitutes for a good, the more elastic is the demand for the good; (2) the greater the percentage of the consumers' budgets spent on the good, the more elastic is demand; and (3) the longer the time period consumers have to adjust to price changes, the more responsive they will be and the more elastic is demand. (*LO3*)

■ When calculating E over an interval of demand, use the interval or arc elasticity formula: multiply slope of demand, $\Delta Q/\Delta P$, times the ratio Average P/Average Q. When calculating E at a point on demand, multiply the slope of demand, computed at the point of measure, times the ratio P/Q, computed using the values of P and Q at the point of measure. When demand is linear, $Q = a' + bP$, the point elasticity can be computed using either of two equivalent formulas: $E = b(P/Q)$ or $E = P/(P - A)$, where P and Q are the values of price and quantity demanded at the point of measure along demand, and A $(= -a'/b)$ is the price-intercept of demand. For curvilinear demand functions, the point elasticity is computed using the formula $E = P/(P - A)$ and A is the price-intercept of the tangent line extended from the point on demand to cross the price-axis. In general, E varies along a demand curve, and for linear demand curves, price and $|E|$ vary directly: the higher (lower) the price, the more (less) elastic is demand. (*LO4*)

■ Marginal revenue, MR, is the change in total revenue per unit change in output. Marginal revenue is 0 when total revenue is maximized. When inverse demand is linear, $P = A + BQ$, MR is also linear, intersects the vertical (price) axis at the same point demand does, and is twice as steep as the inverse demand function: $MR = A + 2BQ$. When MR is positive (negative), total revenue increases (decreases) as quantity increases, and demand is elastic (inelastic). When MR is 0, the price elasticity of demand is unitary and total revenue is maximized. For any demand curve, when demand is elastic (inelastic), MR is positive (negative). When demand is unitary elastic, MR is 0. For all demand curves, $MR = P[1 + (1/E)]$. (*LO5*)

■ Income elasticity, E_M, measures the responsiveness of quantity demanded to changes in income, holding the price of the good and all other demand determinants constant: $E_M = \%\Delta Q_d/\%\Delta M$. Income elasticity is positive (negative) if the good is normal (inferior). Cross-price elasticity, E_{XY}, measures the responsiveness of quantity demanded of good X to changes in the price of related good Y, holding the price of good X and all other demand determinants for good X constant: $E_{XY} = \%\Delta Q_X/\%\Delta P_Y$. Cross-price elasticity is positive (negative) when the two goods are substitutes (complements). (*LO6*)

KEY TERMS

cross-price elasticity (E_{XR})	interval (or arc) elasticity	quantity effect
elastic	marginal revenue (MR)	total revenue
income elasticity (E_M)	point elasticity	unitary elastic
inelastic	price effect	
inframarginal units	price elasticity of demand (E)	

TECHNICAL PROBLEMS

1. Moving along a demand curve, quantity demanded decreases 8 percent when price increases 10 percent.
   a. The price elasticity of demand is calculated to be _____.
   b. Given the price elasticity calculated in part *a*, demand is _____ (elastic, inelastic, unitary elastic) along this portion of the demand curve.
   c. For this interval of demand, the percentage change in quantity in absolute value is _____ (greater than, less than, equal to) the percentage change in price in absolute value.

2. Fill in the blanks:

   a. The price elasticity of demand for a firm's product is equal to −1.5 over the range of prices being considered by the firm's manager. If the manager decreases the price of the product by 6 percent, the manager predicts the quantity demanded will _____ (increase, decrease) by _____ percent.

   b. The price elasticity of demand for an industry's demand curve is equal to −1.5 for the range of prices over which supply increases. If total industry output is expected to increase by 30 percent as a result of the supply increase, managers in this industry should expect the market price of the good to _____ (increase, decrease) by _____ percent.

3. Fill in the blanks:

   a. When demand is elastic, the _____ effect dominates the _____ effect.

   b. When demand is inelastic, the _____ effect dominates the _____ effect.

   c. When demand is unitary elastic, _____ effect dominates.

   d. When a change in price causes a change in quantity demanded, total revenue always moves in the _____ direction as the variable (P or Q) having the _____ effect.

4. Fill in the blanks:

   a. When demand is elastic, an increase in price causes quantity demanded to _____ and total revenue to _____.

   b. When demand is inelastic, a decrease in price causes quantity demanded to _____ and total revenue to _____.

   c. When demand is unitary elastic, an increase in price causes quantity demanded to _____ and total revenue to _____.

   d. If price falls and total revenue falls, demand must be _____.

   e. If price rises and total revenue stays the same, demand must be _____.

   f. If price rises and total revenue rises, demand must be _____.

5. In Panel A of Figure 6.1, verify that demand is unitary elastic over the price range of $11 to $13 without calculating the price elasticity of demand.

6. For each pair of price elasticities, which elasticity (in absolute value) is larger? Why?

   a. The price elasticity for carbonated soft drinks or the price elasticity for Coca-Cola.

   b. The price elasticity for socks (men's or women's) or the price elasticity for business suits (men's or women's).

   c. The price elasticity for electricity in the short run or the price elasticity for electricity in the long run.

7. Use the graph on the next page to answer the following questions:

   a. The interval elasticity of demand over the price range $3 to $5 is _____.

   b. The interval elasticity of demand over the price range $10 to $11 is _____.

   c. The interval elasticity of demand over the price range $5 to $7 is _____.

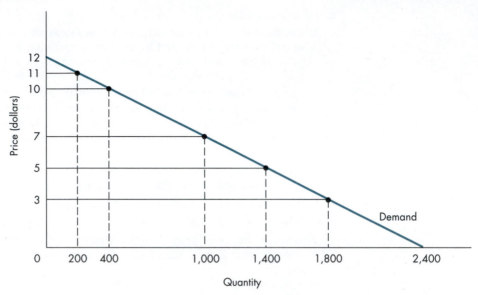

8. *a.* For the linear demand curve in Technical Problem 7, compute the price elasticity at each of the price points given in the following table. Make the elasticity calculations using the two alternative formulas, $E = (\Delta Q/\Delta P) \times (P/Q)$ and $E = P/(P - A)$.

Price point	$E = \dfrac{\Delta Q}{\Delta P} \times \dfrac{P}{Q}$	$E = \dfrac{P}{P - A}$
$ 3	_____	_____
5	_____	_____
7	_____	_____
10	_____	_____
11	_____	_____

b. Which formula is more accurate for computing price elasticities? Explain.

9. Use the linear demand curve shown below to answer the following questions:

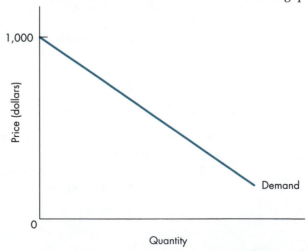

a. The point elasticity of demand at a price of $800 is _____.
b. The point elasticity of demand at a price of $200 is _____.
c. Demand is unitary elastic at a price of $_____.
d. As price rises, |E| _____ (gets larger, gets smaller, stays the same) for a linear demand curve.

10. Use the figure below to answer the following questions:

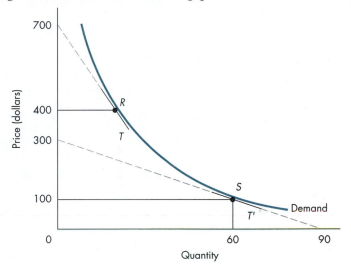

a. Calculate price elasticity at point S using the method $E = \dfrac{\Delta Q}{\Delta P} \times \dfrac{P}{Q}$.
b. Calculate price elasticity at point S using the method $E = \dfrac{P}{P - A}$.
c. Compare the elasticities in parts a and b. Are they equal? Should they be equal?
d. Calculate price elasticity at point R.
e. Which method did you use to compute E in part d, $E = \dfrac{\Delta Q}{\Delta P} \times \dfrac{P}{Q}$ or $E = \dfrac{P}{P - A}$? Why?

11. Suppose the demand for good X is $Q = 20P^{-1}$.
a. When $P = \$1$, total revenue is _____.
b. When $P = \$2$, total revenue is _____.
c. When $P = \$4$, total revenue is _____.
d. The price elasticity of demand is equal to _____ at every price. Why?

12. The figure on the next page shows a linear demand curve. Fill in the blanks a through l as indicated in the figure.

13. For the linear demand curve in Technical Problem 12 (on the next page):
a. Write the equation for the demand curve.
b. Write the equation for the inverse demand curve.
c. Write the equation for the total revenue curve.
d. Write the equation for the marginal revenue curve.
e. Check your answers for Technical Problem 12 using the equations for demand, inverse demand, and marginal revenue, and total revenue.

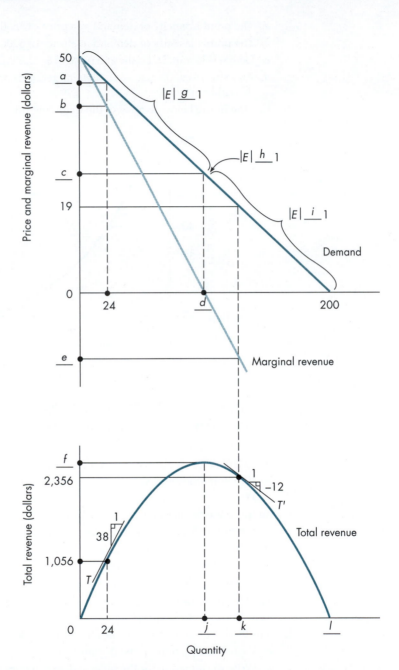

14. Write the equation for the demand curve in the graph for Technical Problem 7. What is the equation for marginal revenue? At what price is demand unitary elastic? At what output is marginal revenue equal to 0?

15. In the following two panels, the demand for good X shifts due to a change in income (Panel A) and a change in the price of a related good Y (Panel B). Holding the price of good X constant at $50, calculate the following elasticities:

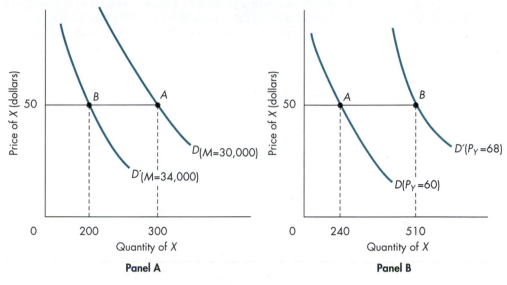

Panel A   **Panel B**

a. Panel A shows how the demand for X shifts when income increases from $30,000 to $34,000. Use the information in Panel A to calculate the income elasticity of demand for X. Is good X normal or inferior?

b. Panel B shows how the demand for X shifts when the price of related good Y increases from $60 to $68. Use the information in Panel B to calculate the cross-price elasticity. Are goods X and Y substitutes or complements?

16. The general linear demand for good X is estimated to be

$$Q = 250,000 - 500P - 1.50M - 240P_R$$

where P is the price of good X, M is average income of consumers who buy good X, and P_R is the price of related good R. The values of P, M, and P_R are expected to be $200, $60,000, and $100, respectively. Use these values at this point on demand to make the following computations.

a. Compute the quantity of good X demanded for the given values of P, M, and P_R.

b. Calculate the price elasticity of demand E. At this point on the demand for X, is demand elastic, inelastic, or unitary elastic? How would increasing the price of X affect total revenue? Explain.

c. Calculate the income elasticity of demand E_M. Is good X normal or inferior? Explain how a 4 percent increase in income would affect demand for X, all other factors affecting the demand for X remaining the same.

d. Calculate the cross-price elasticity E_{XR}. Are the goods X and R substitutes or complements? Explain how a 5 percent decrease in the price of related good R would affect demand for X, all other factors affecting the demand for X remaining the same.

APPLIED PROBLEMS

1. In an article about the financial problems of *USA Today*, *Newsweek* reported that the paper was losing about $20 million a year. A Wall Street analyst said that the paper should raise its price from 50 cents to 75 cents, which he estimated would bring in an additional $65 million a year. The paper's publisher rejected the idea, saying that circulation could drop sharply after a price increase, citing *The Wall Street Journal*'s experience after it increased its price to 75 cents. What implicit assumptions are the publisher and the analyst making about price elasticity?

2. Assume that the demand for cosmetic or plastic surgery is price inelastic. Are the following statements true or false? Explain.

   a. When the price of plastic surgery increases, the number of operations decreases.

   b. The percentage change in the price of plastic surgery is less than the percentage change in quantity demanded.

   c. Changes in the price of plastic surgery do not affect the number of operations.

   d. Quantity demanded is quite responsive to changes in price.

   e. If more plastic surgery is performed, expenditures on plastic surgery will decrease.

   f. The marginal revenue of another operation is negative.

3. What effect, if any, does each of the following events have on the price elasticity of demand for corporate-owned jets?

   a. A decline in corporate earnings causes firms to cut their travel budgets, which in turn causes expenditures on corporate jet travel to become a larger fraction of total spending on corporate travel.

   b. Further deregulation of the commercial airlines industry substantially increases the variety of departure times and destinations offered by commercial airlines.

   c. The cost of manufacturing corporate jets rises.

   d. A new, much more fuel-efficient corporate jet is introduced.

4. Aztec Enterprises depends heavily on advertising to sell its products. Management at Aztec is allowed to spend $2 million monthly on advertising, but no more than this amount. Each month, Aztec spends exactly $2 million on advertising. What is Aztec's elasticity of demand for advertising? Can you write the equation for Aztec's demand for advertising?

5. U.S. cigarette makers face enormous punitive damage penalties after losing a series of class-action lawsuits that heaped penalties amounting to several hundred billion dollars on the tobacco industry. In spite of the huge penalties, *The Wall Street Journal* reported, "The damage (to cigarette makers) is generally under control."[†] What action do you suppose the cigarette companies took to avoid bankruptcy? Why did this action succeed?

6. The price elasticity of demand for imported whiskey is estimated to be −0.20 over a wide interval of prices. The federal government decides to raise the import tariff on foreign whiskey, causing its price to rise by 20 percent. Will sales of whiskey rise or fall, and by what percentage amount?

7. As manager of Citywide Racquet Club, you must determine the best price to charge for locker rentals. Assume that the (marginal) cost of providing lockers is 0. The monthly demand for lockers is estimated to be

$$Q = 100 - 2P$$

[†]Milo Geyelin and Gordon Fairclough, "Tobacco Industry Has Resources For Coping With Huge Jury Award" *The Wall Street Journal*, July 17, 2000.

where P is the monthly rental price and Q is the number of lockers rented per month.

a. What price would you charge?

b. How many lockers are rented monthly at this price?

c. Explain why you chose this price.

8. The demand curve for haircuts at Terry Bernard's Hair Design is

$$P = 20 - 0.20Q$$

where Q is the number of cuts per week and P is the price of a haircut. Terry is considering raising her price above the current price of $15. Terry is unwilling to raise price if the price hike will cause revenues to fall.

a. Should Terry raise the price of haircuts above $15? Why or why not?

b. Suppose demand for Terry's haircuts increases to $P = 40 - 0.40Q$. At a price of $15, should Terry raise the price of her haircuts? Why or why not?

9. Movie attendance dropped 8 percent as ticket prices rose a little more than 5 percent. What is the price elasticity of demand for movie tickets? Could price elasticity be somewhat overestimated from these figures? That is, could other things have changed, accounting for some of the decline in attendance?

10. *The Dallas Morning News* reported the findings of a study by the Department of Transportation that examined the effect on average airfares when new, low-priced carriers, such as Southwest Airlines or Vanguard Airlines, entered one of three city-pair markets: Baltimore–Cleveland, Kansas City–San Francisco, or Baltimore–Providence. Use the following excerpts from the newspaper article to calculate the arc elasticity of demand for each of the three city-pairs. How do the three computed elasticities compare? Based on the computed elasticities, describe travelers' responsiveness to the reductions in airfares.

a. "(In) Baltimore and Cleveland, for example, . . . just 12,790 people flew between those cities in the last three months of 1992, at an average fare of $233. Then Dallas-based Southwest Airlines entered the market. In the last three months of 1996, 115,040 people flew between the cities at an average fare of $66."

b. "(On) the Kansas City–San Francisco connection . . . (during) the last quarter of 1994 some 35,690 people made the trip at an average fare of $165. Two years later, after the arrival of Vanguard Airlines, fares had dropped to an average of $107 and traffic had nearly doubled to 68,100."

c. "On the Baltimore–Providence, R.I., route, where the average fare fell from $196 to $57, . . . the number of passengers carried jumped from 11,960 to 94,116."*

---

*Quotes from various articles by *The Associated Press*, Copyright © 2011.

▣ MATHEMATICAL APPENDIX   Demand Elasticity

The Price Elasticity of Demand

Let the demand function be expressed as $Q = Q(P)$, where the law of demand requires that quantity demanded and price be inversely related: $dQ/dP = Q'(P) < 0$, so the demand curve is downward-sloping. The slope of the demand curve measures the *absolute* rate of change in Q as P changes. The value of the absolute rate of change depends upon the units of measure of both P and Q. A measure

of the *proportional* rate of change is invariant to the units of measure of P and Q. The price elasticity, E, measures the proportional rate of change in quantity demanded as price changes

(1)
$$E = \frac{\frac{dQ}{Q}}{\frac{dP}{P}} = \frac{dQ}{dP}\frac{P}{Q} = Q'(P)\frac{P}{Q}$$

As shown here, the price elasticity can also be expressed as the slope of demand, $Q'(P)$, times a proportionality factor, P/Q. Since the slope of demand is negative and the proportionality factor is always positive, E is always a negative number.

When demand is linear, $Q'(P)$ is constant. E, however, is *not* constant as changes in price cause movements along a linear demand function. Moving down a linear demand, P falls and Q increases, causing the proportionality factor to decrease. Thus, as P decreases, E diminishes in absolute value; that is, $|E|$ decreases.

Price Elasticity and Changes in Total Revenue

In this section it will be useful to employ the inverse demand function, $P = P(Q)$, so that total revenue can be conveniently expressed as a function of Q. Total revenue for a firm is the price of the product times the number of units sold

(2) $\qquad$ Total revenue $= TR = R(Q) = P(Q)Q$

To examine how total revenue changes as sales increase with lower prices, the derivative of total revenue, known as marginal revenue, is defined as

(3) Marginal revenue $= MR = R'(Q) = P(Q) + P'(Q)Q$

where $P'(Q) = dP/dQ < 0$. Marginal revenue is positive, negative, or zero as total revenue is rising, falling, or at its maximum value, respectively.

To derive the relation between price elasticity and changes in total revenue (i.e., marginal revenue), marginal revenue can be expressed as a function of E as follows: First, factor P out of the expression for MR in (3)

(4) $\qquad MR = R'(Q) = P\left(1 + P'(Q)\dfrac{Q}{P}\right)$

Notice that $P'(Q)(Q/P)$ is the inverse of E. Substituting $1/E$ into expression (4) results in a useful relation between MR, P, and E

(5) $\qquad MR = R'(Q) = P\left(1 + \dfrac{1}{E}\right)$

Several important relations can be derived from equation (5):
1. When Q is continuous and $Q > 0$, MR is less than P.[a]
   In the special case of a horizontal demand curve, $E = -\infty$, $MR = P$. You will see this special case in a later chapter.
2. When demand is unitary elastic $(E = -1)$, $MR = 0$ and an infinitesimally small change in Q causes no change in TR. Therefore, TR is at its maximum value when demand is unitary elastic and $MR = 0$.

3. When demand is elastic (inelastic), MR is positive (negative), a decrease in P causes an increase in Q, and total revenue rises (falls).

Linear Demand, Marginal Revenue, and Point Elasticity

Let the straight-line demand be expressed as an inverse demand function

(6) $\qquad P = P(Q) = A + BQ$

where A is the positive price intercept and $B = dP/dQ$ is the negative slope of the inverse demand line. The total revenue received by the firm for a given level of sales Q is

(7) $\quad TR = R(Q) = P(Q)Q = (A + BQ)Q = AQ + BQ^2$

Notice that a linear demand function has a quadratic total revenue function that graphs as a ∩-shaped curve.

Marginal revenue associated with a linear demand function can be found by taking the derivative of total revenue

(8) $\qquad MR = R'(Q) = A + 2BQ$

In absolute value, the slope of MR, $2B$, is twice as great as the slope of inverse demand, B. Both curves have the same vertical intercept A. This relation is shown in Figure 6A.1.

To derive the point price elasticity for a linear demand, it is convenient to employ the demand function expressed as $Q = Q(P)$, rather than the inverse demand in equation (6). The demand function associated with the inverse demand in equation (6) is

(9) $\qquad Q = Q(P) = -\dfrac{A}{B} + \dfrac{1}{B}P = \dfrac{1}{B}(-A + P)$

The slope of the demand function, dQ/dP, is $1/B$. Substituting $1/B$ for dQ/dP and expression (9) for Q in the elasticity equation (1) provides a rather simple algebraic expression for the point elasticity of demand when demand is linear

(10) $\qquad E = \dfrac{1}{B}\dfrac{P}{\frac{1}{B}(-A + P)} = \dfrac{P}{(P - A)}$

---

[a] When quantity is a discrete variable, rather than a continuous variable, $P = MR$ for the first unit sold. For the first unit sold, there are no inframarginal units, so no revenue is lost by lowering price to sell the first unit. After the first unit sold, $P > MR$.

FIGURE 6A.1

Linear Demand and Marginal Revenue

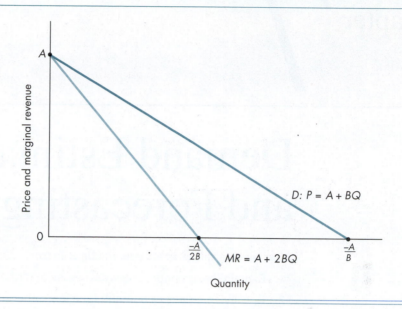

Equation (10) makes it clear that E is not constant for linear demands. The elasticity of demand varies inversely with price along a linear demand curve

(11) $$\frac{dE}{dP} = \frac{-A}{(P-A)^2} < 0$$

As price falls along a linear demand, E gets larger algebraically (i.e., less negative), $|E|$ gets smaller, and demand becomes less elastic. Similarly, as price rises, $|E|$ gets larger and demand becomes more elastic.

The Special Case of Constant Elasticity of Demand: $Q = aP^b$

When demand takes the form $Q = aP^b$, the elasticity of demand is constant and equal to b

(12) $$E = \frac{dQ}{dP} \times \frac{P}{Q} = baP^{b-1}\left(\frac{P}{aP^b}\right) = b$$

For example, when $Q = aP^{-1}$, demand is unitary elastic for all prices.

MATHEMATICAL EXERCISES

1. Consider the linear demand function $Q = 20 - 0.5P$.
   a. Write the inverse demand function.
   b. Write the total revenue function.
   c. Using calculus, find the level of output, Q_{rmax}, where total revenue reaches its maximum value. What price P_{rmax} maximizes total revenue? What is the value of TR at its maximum point?
   d. Write the equation for marginal revenue. Using MR, verify that Q_{rmax} derived in part c maximizes total revenue.
   e. Calculate the point elasticity of demand at P_{rmax}. Does E have the expected value? Explain briefly.
2. Suppose demand takes the form $Q = 36P^{-1}$.
   a. Show that the price elasticity of demand is constant and equal to -1.
   b. Write the total and marginal revenue functions.

7

Demand Estimation and Forecasting

After reading this chapter, you will be able to:

7.1 Explain the strengths and weaknesses of direct methods of demand estimation.

7.2 Specify an empirical demand function, either a linear or nonlinear functional form, and explain the mathematical properties of each type.

7.3 Employ linear regression methodology to estimate the demand function for a single price-setting firm.

7.4 Forecast sales and prices using time-series regression analysis.

7.5 Use dummy variables in time-series demand analysis to account for cyclical or seasonal variation in sales.

7.6 Discuss and explain several important problems that arise when using statistical methods to forecast demand.

Information about demand is essential for making pricing and production decisions. General Motors, Ford, Chrysler, Nissan, and other large automobile manufacturers all use empirical estimates of demand in making decisions about how many units of each model to produce and what prices to charge for different car models. Managers at the national headquarters of Domino's Pizza need to estimate how pizza demand in the United States is affected by a downturn in the economy: Take-out food businesses tend to prosper during recessions. At HCA, Inc., one of the largest hospital operators in the United States, short-run and long-run estimates of patient load (demand) in its various geographic markets are crucial for making expansion plans. Virtually all large electric utilities employ economists and statisticians to estimate current demand for electricity. A knowledge of *future* demand conditions can also be extremely useful to managers of both price-taking and price-setting firms when they are planning production schedules, inventory control, advertising campaigns, output in future periods, and investment, among other things. Many medium- and large-size firms rely on their own forecasting departments to provide forecasts of industry or firm-level demand.

Large business enterprises pioneered the use of empirical demand functions and econometric price forecasts in business pricing decisions. When thousands, even millions, of units are to be priced, managers are understandably uncomfortable making "seat-of-the-pants" guesses about the optimal price to charge. Furthermore, businesses, large and small, know that changing prices is a costly practice. New-price lists must be disseminated both to the salesforce and to customers. Changing prices may give loyal buyers a reason to shop around again. Most managers wish to avoid, or at least reduce, the substantial anxiety that accompanies pricing decisions. Indeed, many managers admit that they avoid, as much as they possibly can, making pricing decisions for fear of making enormously costly mistakes. As a general rule, managers intensely dislike "throwing darts" until they find the right price (the bull's eye); they covet any information or technique of analysis that can help them make profitable pricing decisions. We cannot, in fairness, tell you that econometric analysis and forecasting of demand solves all of management's pricing problems. It can, however, provide managers with valuable information about demand, which should improve any manager's price-setting skills.

Like all tools used in decision making, statistical demand analysis and forecasting has some important limits, which we discuss at the end of this chapter. Profitable pricing decisions require skillful use of both judgment and quantitative analysis. While large firms generally have been more willing to employ statistical demand analysis, significant improvement in the sophistication, availability, and ease of use of econometric software—coupled with falling prices on powerful desktop computers—is now luring more medium- and small-size firms into using statistical demand analysis and forecasting. Some of the latest methods for pricing—known by such buzzwords as demand-based management (DBM), revenue management (RM), yield management, and market segmentation—all require highly accurate statistical estimates of the demand equations for every product and market served by the firm wishing to implement these techniques. Point-of-sale data, which are generated at checkout by laser scans of specially coded price tags, create large-scale data sets that make it possible to estimate and forecast demand much more accurately.

The fundamental building block of statistical demand analysis is the *empirical demand function*. **Empirical demand functions** are demand equations derived from actual market data. From empirical demand functions, managers can get quantitative estimates of the effect on sales of changes in the price of the product, changes in the level of consumer income, and changes in the price of competing products and products that are complements in consumption. As you will see in later chapters, empirical demand functions can be extremely useful in making pricing and production decisions.

We begin our discussion of empirical demand analysis and forecasting with a description of some of the more direct methods of demand estimation: consumer interviews and market studies. We deal rather briefly with these methods, attempting only to point out the strengths and weaknesses in each. Next, we show

empirical demand functions
Demand equations derived from actual market data.

you how to use regression analysis to estimate demand functions and associated demand elasticities: price, income, and cross-price elasticities (Sections 7.2 and 7.3). In general, there are two different statistical situations for estimating demand functions: (1) estimating demand for a competitive price-taking industry or (2) estimating demand for a single firm that possesses some degree of price-setting power. In this chapter and throughout the rest of this text, we will focus on estimating demand for a price-setting firm rather than estimating demand for a price-taking industry because the statistical technique required to properly estimate a price-taking industry demand curve is quite a bit more advanced than the standard regression methodology (as presented in Chapter 4) that can be properly employed to estimate demand for a price-setting firm. For those students who wish to learn how to estimate industry demand (and supply) and how to make price and output forecasts for competitive industries, we provide a thorough presentation of this methodology in Online Appendix 2: Estimating and Forecasting Industry Demand for Price-Taking Firms, which can be found via McGraw-Hill *Connect*®.

In the second part of this chapter (Sections 7.4 and 7.5), we examine one of the most popular and widely used time-series methods for forecasting future prices and sales levels: linear trend forecasting. As you will see, this time-series method of forecasting can be applied to a wide variety of forecasting needs of a business. And, best of all, linear trend forecasting can be accomplished with modest data requirements.

This chapter about demand estimation and forecasting is intended to provide you with an introductory treatment of empirical demand analysis. Although our discussion of statistical demand estimation and statistical demand forecasting is limited to the simpler methods, these methods are widely used in business to analyze and forecast demand. Almost all of the more advanced techniques of empirical demand analysis that you will encounter in your marketing research, business forecasting, advanced statistics, and econometrics courses are extensions of, or related to, the methods we present in this chapter.

7.1 DIRECT METHODS OF DEMAND ESTIMATION

Direct methods of demand estimation are techniques that do not involve regression analysis. After reading about some of these direct methods of estimation, you may get the impression that direct estimation techniques are quite simple and straightforward. This is far from correct. Many of the techniques used in making direct estimates of demand are quite sophisticated and require a great deal of experience and expertise to estimate demand accurately. This section is designed only to give an overview of some of the methods that can be used and is not meant to teach you how to make these types of estimates. Such instruction is left to more advanced marketing courses.

Consumer Interviews

Since consumers themselves should be the most knowledgeable about their individual demand functions for particular commodities, the most straightforward method of demand estimation would be simply to ask potential buyers how much of the commodity they would buy at different prices with alternative values for the determinants of demand (i.e., the price of substitute commodities, the price of complementary commodities, and so on). At the simplest level, this might be accomplished by stopping shoppers and asking them how much of the product they would buy at various prices. At a more sophisticated level, this procedure would entail administering detailed questionnaires to a selected sample of the population by professional interviewers. While this procedure appears very simple, there are several substantial problems. Among these problems are (1) the selection of a representative sample, (2) response bias, and (3) the inability of the respondent to answer accurately. Let's look at each of these problems briefly.

When selecting a sample of the population for a survey, the resulting demand estimation is reliable only if the survey uses a representative sample. A **representative sample** has the same characteristics as the population as a whole. A representative sample is typically obtained by *randomly* selecting members for the sample from the general population. For example, if 52 percent of the population is female, and if 35 percent have annual incomes over $65,000, then a representative sample should have approximately 52 percent females and 35 percent persons with incomes over $65,000. In actuality, it is very difficult to obtain a truly representative sample.

representative sample
A sample, usually drawn randomly, that has characteristics that accurately reflect the population as a whole.

A classic illustration of what can happen if the sample is not random occurred during the presidential campaign of 1948. A survey was performed that predicted an overwhelming victory for Thomas Dewey. In fact, Harry Truman won the election. The problem with the survey was that the sample was drawn from the subscription list of a particular magazine. The subscribers were not representative of the entire population of the United States; they were instead a subgroup of the voting population and had some important characteristics in common. Thus, the biased sample led to biased results. In 1936, in a similar but less celebrated election forecast error, a popular magazine predicted Franklin Roosevelt would lose the election, but it was wrong because the pollsters used a telephone survey and only wealthy people were able to afford phones at that time. Today, election forecasting has become so accurate—in large part due to the advanced sampling techniques now employed by pollsters—that television networks are not allowed to project winners until the polls are all closed on election day.

Another example of a biased sample yielding misleading results occurred at a home-building convention, during which Owens-Corning Fiberglass Corporation commissioned a survey to determine the industry's outlook for future sales. The results were startling. The survey indicated that builders were planning to increase housing starts by an amazing 30 percent. When asked to interpret the bullish forecast, Michael Sumichrast, chief economist for the National Association of Home Builders, replied that "it shows when you ask stupid questions, you get stupid answers." Apparently, the survey did not use a representative sample. As it turns out, the survey was taken only among the builders who attended the convention, and these builders tend to be the larger and more aggressive companies that would naturally be more bullish in their outlook.

response bias
The difference between the response given by an individual to a hypothetical question and the action the individual takes when the situation actually occurs.

A **response bias** can result simply from the fact that those interviewed are giving hypothetical answers to hypothetical questions. The answers do not necessarily reflect what the individual will do; rather, they may reflect intentions or desires. More importantly, however, the responses may be biased by the manner in which the question is asked. In many cases, the questions may be such that the respondents give what they view as a more socially acceptable response, rather than reveal their true preferences.

One example of response bias is found in a survey by an automobile manufacturer taken many years ago—during a time of cheap gasoline. Potential consumers were asked if they would be interested in buying small, economical cars (i.e., fuel-efficient cars) that were not flashy, fast, or showy. A large number of people said they would indeed buy such a car. On the basis of this survey, the manufacturer introduced a small, fuel-efficient car—with disastrous results. Perhaps had the respondents—who indicated that they wanted economy cars—been asked whether their *neighbors* would buy such cars, they might have provided more valid responses. It's easier to say that your neighbor wants a flashy car than to admit that you do. The point is that the wrong question was asked. The way the question was asked induced a response bias.

Past surveys by food manufacturers have yielded bad results because of response bias. The food industry has a lot riding on the claims that people make about what they eat. Food companies have, in the past, conducted their market research by asking people what they eat. On the basis of the results of these surveys, the food manufacturers would develop new products. But, as noted in *The Wall Street Journal,* there is one big problem: "People don't always tell the truth."[1] As Harry Balzer, the vice president of a market research firm, said: "Nobody likes to admit he likes junk food." In other words, a response bias exists in such surveys. Instead of answering truthfully, a consumer is likely to give a socially acceptable answer. Asking a sweets-eater how many Twinkies he eats "is like asking an alcoholic if he drinks much."

Finally, it is quite possible that the respondent is *simply unable to answer accurately the question posed.* Conceptually, the firm performing the survey may want to know about the elasticity of demand for its products. Thus, the firm is interested in the response of consumers to incremental changes in price and some other variable. For example, the firm needs to know how the consumers would react to such things as a 1, 2, or 3 percent increase (or decrease) in price or a 5 percent increase (decrease) in advertising expenditures. Obviously, most people interviewed are not able to answer such questions precisely.

Although the survey technique is plagued with these inherent difficulties, it can still be an extremely valuable tool for a manager to use in quantifying demand. The trick in doing a survey is to avoid the pitfalls, and, as the following discussion indicates, that can be done.

---

[1]Betsy Morris, "Study to Detect True Eating Habits Finds Junk-Food Fans in Health-Food Ranks," *The Wall Street Journal*, February 3, 1984.

Market Studies and Experiments

A somewhat more expensive and difficult technique for estimating demand and demand elasticity is the controlled market study or experiment. The analyst attempts to hold everything constant during the study except for the price of the good.

Those carrying out such market studies normally display the products in several different stores, generally in areas with different characteristics, over a period of time. They make certain that there are always sufficient amounts available in every store at each price to satisfy demand. In this way the effect of changes in supply is removed. There is generally no advertising. During the experiment period, price is changed in relatively small increments over a range, and sales are recorded at each price. In this way, many of the effects of changes in other things can be removed, and a reasonable approximation of the actual demand curve can be estimated.

An example of such an approach is a study conducted by M&M/Mars using 150 stores over a 12-month period to determine the optimal weights for its candy bars.[2] Instead of altering the price from store to store, the company kept price constant and altered the size of the product. As the director of sales development reported, in stores where the size was increased, "sales went up 20 percent to 30 percent almost overnight." As a result, M&M/Mars decided to change much of its product line.

A relatively new technique for estimating demand is the use of experiments performed in a laboratory or in the field. Such experiments are a compromise between market studies and surveys. In some types of laboratory experiments, volunteers are paid to simulate actual buying conditions without going through real markets. Volunteer consumers are given money to go on simulated market trips. The experimenter changes relative prices between trips. After many shopping trips by many consumers an approximation of demand is obtained. The volunteers have the incentive to act as though they are really shopping because there is a probability that they may keep their purchases.

Going a step further, some economists have conducted experiments about consumer behavior—with the help of psychologists—in mental institutions and in drug centers, by setting up token economies (which incidentally are supposed to have therapeutic value). Patients receive tokens for jobs performed. They can exchange these tokens for goods and services. The experimenters can change prices and incomes and thus generate demand curves, the properties of which are compared with the theoretical properties of such curves.

The experimental approach to estimating the demand for products has rapidly moved out of the laboratories to the real-world applications more of interest to Wall Street and Main Street. The rapid growth of microcomputers and cable television systems has made possible market experiments that could only have been dreamed of a decade ago.

Now try Technical Problem 1.

---

[2]See John Koten, "Why Do Hot Dogs Come in Packs of 10 and Buns in 8s or 12s?" *The Wall Street Journal,* September 21, 1984.

7.2 SPECIFICATION OF THE EMPIRICAL DEMAND FUNCTION

Managers can use the techniques of regression analysis outlined in Chapter 4 to obtain estimates of the demand for their firms' products. The theoretical foundation for specifying and analyzing empirical demand functions is provided by the theory of consumer behavior, which was presented in Chapter 5. In this section, we will show you two possible specifications of the demand function to be estimated.

A General Empirical Demand Specification

To estimate a demand function for a product, it is necessary to use a specific functional form. Here we will consider both linear and nonlinear forms. Before proceeding, however, we must simplify the general demand relation. Recall that quantity demanded depends on the price of the product, consumer income, the price of related goods, consumer tastes or preferences, expected price, and the number of buyers. Given the difficulties inherent in quantifying taste and price expectations, we will ignore these variables—as is commonly done in many empirical demand studies—and write the general demand function as

$$Q = f(P, M, P_R, N)$$

where

Q = quantity purchased of a good or service

P = price of the good or service

M = consumers' income

P_R = price(s) of related good(s)

N = number of buyers

While this general demand specification seems rather simple and straightforward, the task of defining and collecting the data for demand estimation requires careful consideration of numerous factors. For example, it is important to recognize the geographic boundaries of the product market. Suppose a firm sells its product only in California. In this case, the consumer income variable (M) should measure the buyers' incomes in the state of California. Using average household income in the United States would be a mistake unless California's household income level matches nationwide income levels and trends. It is also crucial to include the prices of all substitute and complement goods that affect sales of the firm's product in California. Although we will illustrate empirical demand functions using just one related good (either a substitute or a complement), there are often numerous related goods whose prices should be included in the specification of an empirical demand function. Whether the market is growing (or shrinking) in size is another consideration. Researchers frequently include a measure of population in the demand specification as a proxy variable for the number of buyers. As you can see from this brief discussion, defining and collecting data to estimate even a simple general demand function requires careful consideration.

A Linear Empirical Demand Specification

The simplest demand function is one that specifies a linear relation. In linear form, the empirical demand function is specified as

$$Q = a + bP + cM + dP_R + eN$$

In this equation, the parameter b measures the change in quantity demanded that would result from a one-unit change in price. That is, $b = \Delta Q/\Delta P$, which is assumed to be negative. Also,

$$c = \Delta Q/\Delta M \gtrless 0 \text{ if the good is } \begin{cases}\text{normal}\\\text{inferior}\end{cases}$$

and

$$d = \Delta Q/\Delta P_R \gtrless 0 \text{ if commodity } R \text{ is a } \begin{cases}\text{substitute}\\\text{complement}\end{cases}$$

The parameter e measures the change in quantity demanded per one-unit change in the number of buyers; that is, $e = \Delta Q/\Delta N$, which is assumed to be positive. Using the techniques of regression analysis, this linear demand function can be estimated to provide estimates of the parameters a, b, c, d, and e. Then t-tests are performed, or p-values examined, to determine whether these parameters are statistically significant.

As stressed in Chapter 6, elasticities of demand are an important aspect of demand analysis. The elasticities of demand—with respect to price, income, and the prices of related commodities—can be calculated from a linear demand function without much difficulty. From our discussion in Chapter 6, it follows that, for a linear specification, the *estimated* price elasticity of demand is

$$\hat{E} = \hat{b} \times \frac{P}{Q}$$

As you know from the discussion of demand elasticity in Chapter 6, the price elasticity depends on where it is measured along the demand curve (note the P/Q term in the formula). The elasticity should be evaluated at the price and quantity values that correspond to the point on the demand curve being analyzed. In similar manner, the income elasticity may be estimated as

$$\hat{E}_M = \hat{c} \times \frac{M}{Q}$$

Likewise, the estimated cross-price elasticity is

$$\hat{E}_{XR} = \hat{d} \times \frac{P_R}{Q}$$

Now try Technical Problem 2.

where the X in the subscript refers to the good for which demand is being estimated. Note that we denote values of variables and parameters that are statistically estimated (i.e., empirically determined) by placing a "hat" over the variable or parameter. In this discussion, for example, the empirical elasticities are designated as $\hat{E}$, $\hat{E}_M$, and $\hat{E}_{XR}$, while the empirically estimated parameter values are designated by $\hat{a}$, $\hat{b}$, $\hat{c}$, $\hat{d}$, and $\hat{e}$.

A Nonlinear Empirical Demand Specification

The most commonly employed nonlinear demand specification is the log-linear (or constant elasticity) form. A log-linear demand function is written as

$$Q = aP^b M^c P_R^d N^e$$

The obvious potential advantage of this form is that it provides a better estimate if the true demand function is indeed nonlinear. Furthermore, as you may recall from Chapter 4, this specification allows for the direct estimation of the elasticities. Specifically, the value of parameter b measures the price elasticity of demand. Likewise, c and d, respectively, measure the income elasticity and cross-price elasticity of demand.[3]

Now try Technical Problem 3.

As you learned in Chapter 4, to obtain estimates from a log-linear demand function, you must convert it to natural logarithms. Thus, the function to be estimated is linear in the logarithms

$$\ln Q = \ln a + b \ln P + c \ln M + d \ln P_R + e \ln N$$

Choosing a Demand Specification

Although we have presented only two functional forms (linear and log-linear) as possible choices for specifying the empirical demand equation, there are many possible functional forms from which to choose. Unfortunately, the exact functional form of the demand equation generally is not known to the researcher. As noted in Chapter 4, choosing an incorrect functional form of the equation to be estimated results in biased estimates of the parameters of the equation. Selecting the appropriate functional form for the empirical demand equation warrants more than a toss of a coin on the part of the researcher.

In practice, choosing the functional form to use is, to a large degree, a matter of judgment and experience. Nevertheless, there are some things a manager can do to suggest the best choice of functional form. When possible, a manager should consider the functional form used in similar empirical studies of demand. If a linear specification has worked well in the past or has worked well for other products that are similar, specifying a linear demand function may be justified. In some cases a manager may have information or experience that indicates whether the demand function is either linear or curvilinear, and this functional form is then used to estimate the demand equation.

---

[3]The appendix to this chapter shows the derivation of the elasticities associated with the log-linear demand specification.

ILLUSTRATION 7.1

Demand for Imported Goods in Trinidad and Tobago:

A Log-Linear Estimation

Trinidad and Tobago, two small developing countries in the Caribbean, rely heavily on imports from other nations to provide their citizens with consumer and capital goods. Policymakers in these two countries need estimates of the demand for various imported goods to aid them in their trade-related negotiations and to make forecasts of trade balances in Trinidad and Tobago. The price elasticities and income elasticities of demand are of particular interest.

Using data on prices and income, John S. Gafar estimated the demand for imported goods in the two countries, using a log-linear specification of demand.[a] According to Gafar, the two most common functional forms used to estimate import demand are the linear and log-linear forms. As we noted, the choice of functional form is often based on the past experience of experts in a particular area of empirical research. Gafar chose to use the log-linear specification because a number of other import studies "have shown that the log-linear specification is preferable to the linear specification."[b] Gafar noted that he experimented with both the linear and log-linear forms and found the log-linear model had the higher R^2.

In his study, Gafar estimated the demand for imports of eight groups of commodities. The demand for any particular group of imported goods is specified as

$$Q_d = aP^bM^c$$

where Q_d is the quantity of the imported good demanded by Trinidad and Tobago, P is the price of the imported good (relative to the price of a bundle of domestically produced goods), and M is an income variable. Taking natural logarithms of the demand equation results in the following demand equation to be estimated:

$$\ln Q_d = \ln a + b \ln P + c \ln M$$

Recall from the discussion in the text that b is the price elasticity of demand and c is the income elasticity of demand. The sign of $\hat{b}$ is expected to be negative and the sign of $\hat{c}$ can be either positive or negative. The results of estimation are presented in the accompanying table.

Estimated Price and Income Elasticities in Trinidad and Tobago

Product group	Price elasticity estimates ($\hat{b}$)	Income elasticity estimates ($\hat{c}$)
Food	−0.6553	1.6411
Beverages and tobacco	−0.0537[n]	1.8718
Crude materials (except fuel)	−1.3879	4.9619
Animal and vegetable oils and fats	−0.3992	1.8688
Chemicals	−0.7211	2.2711
Manufactured goods	−0.2774[n]	3.2085
Machinery and transport equipment	−0.6159	2.9452
Miscellaneous manufactured articles	−1.4585	4.1997

Only two of the estimated parameters are *not* statistically significant at the 5 percent level of significance (denoted by "n" in the table). Note that all the product groups have the expected sign for $\hat{b}$, except manufactured goods, for which the parameter estimate is not statistically significant. The estimates of $\hat{c}$ suggest that all eight product groups are normal goods ($\hat{c} > 0$). As you can see, with the log-linear specification, it is much easier to estimate demand elasticities than it is with a linear specification.

[a]John S. Gafar, "The Determinants of Import Demand in Trinidad and Tobago: 1967–84," *Applied Economics* 20 (1988).
[b]Ibid.

Sometimes researchers employ a series of regressions to settle on a suitable specification of demand. If the estimated coefficients of the first regression specification have the wrong signs, or if they are not statistically significant, the specification of the model may be wrong. Researchers may then estimate some new specifications, using the same data, to search for a specification that gives significant coefficients with the expected signs.[4]

For the two specifications we have discussed here, a choice between them should consider whether the sample data to be used for estimating demand are best represented by a demand function with varying elasticities (linear demand) or by one with constant elasticity (log-linear demand). When price and quantity observations are spread over a wide range of values, elasticities are more likely to vary, and a linear specification with its varying elasticities is usually a more appropriate specification of demand. Alternatively, if the sample data are clustered over a narrow price (and quantity) range, a constant-elasticity specification of demand, such as a log-linear model, may be a better choice than a linear model. Again we stress that experience in estimating demand functions and additional training in econometric techniques are needed to become skilled at specifying the empirical demand function. We now discuss how to estimate the parameters of the empirical demand function.

7.3 ESTIMATING DEMAND FOR A PRICE-SETTING FIRM

As noted earlier, estimating the parameters of the empirical demand function can be accomplished using regression analysis. However, the method of estimating demand depends on whether the demand to be estimated is a single price-setting *firm's* demand or is a competitive price-taking *industry's* demand. As previously mentioned, estimating industry demand requires more advanced statistical methods than estimating the demand for a single firm;[5] thus we will limit our discussion in this text to estimating demand for a price-setting firm. In this section, we will show you how to use ordinary regression, as set forth in Chapter 4, to estimate a single price-setting firm's demand.

Before discussing an example of how to estimate the demand for a price-setting firm, we give you the following step-by-step guide.

---

[4]In a strict statistical sense, it is incorrect to estimate more than one model specification with the same set of data. This practice is common, however, given the high costs often associated with collecting sample data.

[5]For the least-squares method of estimating the parameters of a regression equation to yield unbiased estimates of the regression parameters, the explanatory variables cannot be correlated with the random error term of the equation. Virtually all the applications covered in this book involve explanatory variables that are not likely to be correlated with the random error term in the equation. There is one important exception, however, and it involves the estimation of industry demand, because the price of the product—an explanatory variable in all demand functions—varies with shifts in both demand and supply. As it turns out, correctly estimating the industry demand for price-taking firms requires the use of a special technique called *two-stage least-squares* (2SLS). Online Topic 1, which can be found through McGraw-Hill *Connect*®, shows you how to use 2SLS to estimate both demand and supply equations for competitive industries and to forecast future industry prices and quantities.

Step 1: Specify the price-setting firm's demand function As discussed previously in Section 7.2, the demand function for the firm is specified by choosing a linear or curvilinear functional form and by deciding which demand-shifting variables to include in the empirical demand equation along with the price of the good or service.

Step 2: Collect data on the variables in the firm's demand function Data must be collected for quantity and price as well as for the demand-shifting variables specified in Step 1.

Step 3: Estimate the price-setting firm's demand The parameters of the firm's demand function can be estimated using the linear regression procedure set forth in Chapter 4. Demand elasticities can then be computed as discussed previously in Section 7.2.

Estimating the Demand for a Pizza Firm: An Example

We will now illustrate how a firm with price-setting power can estimate the demand equation for its output. Consider Checkers Pizza, one of only two home delivery pizza firms serving the Westbury neighborhood of Houston. The manager and owner of Checkers Pizza, Ann Chovie, knows that her customers are rather price-conscious. Pizza buyers in Westbury pay close attention to the price she charges for a home-delivered pizza and the price her competitor, Al's Pizza Oven, charges for a similar home-delivered pizza.

Ann decides to estimate the empirical demand function for her firm's pizza. She collects data on the last 24 months of pizza sales from her own company records. She knows the price she charged for her pizza during that time period, and she also has kept a record of the prices charged at Al's Pizza Oven. Ann is able to obtain average household income figures from the Westbury Small Business Development Center. The only other competitor in the neighborhood is the local branch of McDonald's. Ann is able to find the price of a Big Mac for the last 24 months from advertisements in old newspapers. She adjusts her price and income data for the effects of inflation by deflating the dollar figures, using a deflator she obtained from the *Survey of Current Business*.[6] To measure the number of buyers in the market area (N), Ann collected data on the number of residents in Westbury. As it turned out, the number of residents had not changed during the last 24 months, so Ann dropped N from her specification of demand. The data she collected are presented in the appendix at the end of this chapter.

---

[6]The *Survey of Current Business* can be found at the website for the U.S. Department of Commerce, Bureau of Economic Analysis: *www.bea.gov/scb*. Implicit price deflators are presented quarterly from 1959 to the present in Table C.1, "GDP and Other Major NIPA Aggregates."

ILLUSTRATION 7.2

Estimating the Demand for Corporate Jets

Given the success that many of our former students have experienced in their careers and the success we predict for you, we thought it might be valuable for you to examine the market for corporate aircraft. Rather than dwell on the lackluster piston-driven and turboprop aircraft, we instead focus this illustration on the demand for corporate jets. In a recent empirical study of general aviation aircraft, McDougall and Cho estimated the demand using techniques that are similar to the ones in this chapter.[a] Let's now look at how regression analysis can be used to estimate the demand for corporate jets.

To estimate the demand for corporate jets, McDougall and Cho specified the variables that affect jet aircraft sales and the general demand relation as follows:

$$Q_J = f(P, P_R, M, D)$$

when

Q_J = number of new corporate jets purchased

P = price of a new corporate jet

P_R = price of a used corporate jet

M = income of the buyers

D = so-called dummy variable to account for seasonality of jet sales

Since the market for used jets is extensively used by corporations, the price of used jets (a substitute) is included in the demand equation. We should note that P and P_R are not the actual prices paid for the aircraft but are instead the user costs of an aircraft. A jet aircraft provides many miles of transportation, not all of which are consumed during the first period of ownership. The user cost of a jet measures the cost per mile (or per hour) of operating the jet by spreading the initial purchase price over the lifetime of jet transportation services and adjusting for depreciation in the value of the aircraft.

The income of the buyers (M) is approximated by corporate profit because most buyers of small jet aircraft are corporations. The data used to estimate the demand equation are quarterly observations (1981I–1985III). Many corporations purchase jets at year-end for tax purposes. Consequently, jet sales tend to be higher in the fourth quarter, all else constant, than in the other three quarters of any given year. Adjusting for this pattern of seasonality is accomplished by adding a variable called a "dummy variable," which takes on values of 1 for observations in the fourth quarter and 0 for observations in the other three quarters. In effect, the dummy variable shifts the estimated demand equation rightward during the fourth quarter. A complete explanation of the use of dummy variables to adjust for seasonality in data is presented later in this chapter (Section 7.5).

The following linear model of demand for corporate jets is estimated:

$$Q_J = a + bP + cP_R + dM + eD_4$$

McDougall and Cho estimated this demand equation using least-squares estimation rather than two-stage least-squares because they noted that the supply curve for aircraft is almost perfectly elastic or horizontal. If the supply of jets is horizontal, the supply price of new jets is constant no matter what the level of output. Because the market price of jets is determined by the position of the (horizontal) jet supply curve, and the position of supply is fixed by the exogenous determinants of supply, the price of jets is itself exogenous. If jet price (P) is exogenous, least-squares regression is appropriate. The computer output obtained by McDougall and Cho from estimating this equation is shown on the next page.

Theoretically, the predicted signs of the estimated coefficients are (1) $\hat{b} < 0$ because demand for corporate jets is expected to be downward-sloping; (2) $\hat{c} > 0$ because new and used jets are substitutes; (3) $\hat{d} > 0$ because corporate jets are expected to be normal goods; and (4) $\hat{e} > 0$ because the tax effect at year-end should cause jet demand to increase (shift rightward) during the fourth quarter. All the estimates, except $\hat{d}$, match the expected signs.

The p-values for the individual parameter estimates indicate that all the variables in the model play

DEPENDENT VARIABLE:	QJ	R-SQUARE	F-RATIO	P-VALUE ON F
OBSERVATIONS:	18	0.8623	20.35	0.0001

VARIABLE	PARAMETER ESTIMATE	STANDARD ERROR	T-RATIO	P-VALUE
INTERCEPT	17.33	43.3250	0.40	0.6956
P	−0.00016	0.000041	−3.90	0.0018
PR	0.00050	0.000104	4.81	0.0003
M	−0.85010	0.7266	−1.17	0.2630
D4	31.99	8.7428	3.66	0.0030

a statistically significant role in determining sales of jet aircraft, except corporate profits. The model as a whole does a good job of explaining the variation in sales of corporate jets: 86 percent of this variation is explained by the model ($R^2 = 0.8623$). The F-ratio indicates that the model as a whole is significant at the 0.01 percent level.

McDougall and Cho estimated the price and cross-price elasticities of demand using the values of Q_J, P, and P_R in the third quarter of 1985:

$$E = \hat{b} \frac{P_{1985III}}{Q_{1985III}} = -3.95$$

$$E_{NU} = \hat{c} \frac{P_{R'1985III}}{Q_{1985III}} = 6.41$$

where E_{NU} is the cross-price elasticity between new-jet sales and the price of used jets. The price elasticity estimate suggests that the quantity demanded of new corporate jets is quite responsive to changes in the price of new jets ($|E| > 1$). Furthermore, a 10 percent decrease in the price of used jets is estimated to cause a 64.1 percent decrease in sales of new corporate jets. Given this rather large cross-price elasticity, used jets appear to be viewed by corporations as extremely close substitutes for new jets, and for this reason, we advise all of our managerial economics students to look closely at the used-jet market before buying a new corporate jet.

[a]The empirical results in this illustration are taken from Gerald S. McDougall and Dong W. Cho, "Demand Estimates for New General Aviation Aircraft: A User-Cost Approach," *Applied Economics* 20 (1988).

Since the price of pizza at Checkers Pizza is set by Ann—she possesses a degree of market power—she can estimate the empirical demand equation using linear regression. Ann first estimates the following linear specification of demand using the 24 monthly observations she collected:

$$Q = a + bP + cM + dP_{Al} + eP_{BMac}$$

where

Q = sales of pizza at Checkers Pizza

P = price of a pizza at Checkers Pizza

M = average annual household income in Westbury

P_{Al} = price of a pizza at Al's Pizza Oven

P_{BMac} = price of a Big Mac at McDonald's

The following computer printout shows the results of her least-squares regression:

VARIABLE	DEPENDENT VARIABLE: Q	R-SQUARE	F-RATIO	P-VALUE ON F
	OBSERVATIONS: 24	0.9555	101.90	0.0001

VARIABLE	PARAMETER ESTIMATE	STANDARD ERROR	T-RATIO	P-VALUE
INTERCEPT	1183.80	506.298	2.34	0.0305
P	−213.422	13.4863	−15.83	0.0001
M	0.09109	0.01241	7.34	0.0001
PAL	101.303	38.7478	2.61	0.0171
PBMAC	71.8448	27.0997	2.65	0.0158

Ann tests the four estimated slope parameters ($\hat{b}$, $\hat{c}$, $\hat{d}$, and $\hat{e}$) for statistical significance at the 2 percent level of significance. The critical t-value for 19 degrees of freedom ($n - k = 24 - 5$) at the 2 percent significance level is 2.539. The t-ratios for all four slope parameters exceed 2.539, and thus the coefficients are all statistically significant. She is pleased to see that the model explains about 95.5 percent of the variation in her pizza sales ($R^2 = 0.9555$) and that the model as a whole is highly significant, as indicated by the p-value on the F-statistic of 0.0001.

Ann decides to calculate estimated demand elasticities at values of P, M, P_{Al}, and P_{BMac} that she feels "typify" the pizza market in Westbury for the past 24 months. These values are $P = 9.05$, $M = 26,614$, $P_{Al} = 10.12$, and $P_{BMac} = 1.15$. At this "typical" point on the estimated demand curve, the quantity of pizza demanded is

$$Q = 1,183.80 - 213.422(9.05) + 0.09109(26,614) + 101.303(10.12) + 71.8448(1.15)$$
$$= 2,784.4$$

The elasticities for the linear demand specification are estimated in the now familiar fashion

$$\hat{E} = \hat{b}\,(P/Q) = -213.422(9.05/2,784.4) = -0.694$$
$$\hat{E}_M = \hat{c}(M/Q) = 0.09109(26,614/2,784.4) = 0.871$$
$$\hat{E}_{XAl} = \hat{d}(P_{Al}/Q) = 101.303(10.12/2,784.4) = 0.368$$
$$\hat{E}_{XBMac} = \hat{e}(P_{BMac}/Q) = 71.8448(1.15/2,784.4) = 0.030$$

Ann's estimated elasticities show that she prices her pizzas at a price where demand is inelastic ($|\hat{E}| < 1$). A 10 percent increase in average household income will cause sales to rise by 8.71 percent—pizzas are a normal good in Westbury. The estimated cross-price elasticity $\hat{E}_{XAl}$ suggests that if Al's Pizza Oven raises its pizza price by 10 percent, sales of Checkers' pizzas will increase by 3.68 percent. While the price of a Big Mac does play a statistically significant role in determining sales of Checkers' pizzas, the effect is estimated to be quite small. Indeed, a 10 percent decrease in the price of a Big Mac will decrease sales of Checkers' pizzas only by about one-third of 1 percent (0.30 percent). Apparently families in Westbury aren't very willing to substitute a Big Mac for a home-delivered pizza from Checkers Pizza.

While Ann is satisfied that a linear specification of demand for her firm's pizza does an outstanding job of explaining the variation in her pizza sales, she decides to estimate a nonlinear model just for comparison. Ann chooses a log-linear demand specification of the form

$$Q = aP^b M^c P_{Al}^d P_{BMac}^e$$

which can be transformed (by taking natural logarithms) into the following estimable form:

$$\ln Q = \ln a + b \ln P + c \ln M + d \ln P_{Al} + e \ln P_{BMac}$$

The regression results from the computer are presented here:

DEPENDENT VARIABLE:	LNQ	R-SQUARE	F-RATIO	P-VALUE ON F
OBSERVATIONS:	24	0.9492	88.72	0.0001

VARIABLE	PARAMETER ESTIMATE	STANDARD ERROR	T-RATIO	P-VALUE
INTERCEPT	−0.72517	1.31437	−0.55	0.5876
LNP	−0.66269	0.04477	−14.80	0.0001
LNM	0.87705	0.12943	6.78	0.0001
LNPAL	0.50676	0.14901	3.40	0.0030
LNPBMAC	0.02843	0.01073	2.65	0.0158

While the F-ratio and R^2 for the log-linear model are just slightly smaller than those for the linear specification and the intercept estimate is not statistically significant at any generally used level of significance, the log-linear specification certainly performs well. Recall that the slope parameter estimates in a log-linear model are elasticities. Although the elasticity estimates from the log-linear model come close to the elasticity estimates from the linear model, linear and log-linear specifications may not always produce such similar elasticity estimates. In general, the linear demand is appropriate when elasticities are likely to vary, and a log-linear specification is appropriate when elasticities are constant. In this case, Ann could use either one of the empirical demand functions for business decision making.

Now try Technical Problems 4–5.

7.4 TIME-SERIES FORECASTS OF SALES AND PRICE

As explained in the introduction to this chapter, we will confine our discussion of statistical forecasting methods to time-series models. A *time-series* is simply a time-ordered sequence of observations on a variable. In general,

time-series model
A statistical model that shows how a time-ordered sequence of observations on a variable is generated.

a **time-series model** uses only the time-series history of the variable of interest to predict future values. Time-series models describe the process by which these historical data were generated. Thus to forecast using time-series analysis, it is necessary to specify a mathematical model that represents the generating process. We will first discuss a general forecasting model and then give examples of price and sales forecasts.

Linear Trend Forecasting

A linear trend is the simplest time-series forecasting method. Using this type of model, one could posit that sales or price increase or decrease linearly over time. For example, a firm's sales for the period 2007–2016 are shown by the 10 data points in Figure 7.1. The straight line that best fits the data scatter, calculated using simple regression analysis, is illustrated by the solid line in the figure. The fitted line indicates a positive trend in sales. Assuming that sales in the future will continue to follow the same trend, sales in any future period can be forecast by extending this line and picking the forecast values from this *extrapolated* dashed line for the desired future period. We have illustrated sales forecasts for 2017 and 2022 ($\hat{Q}_{2017}$ and $\hat{Q}_{2022}$) in Figure 7.1.

Summarizing this procedure, we assumed a linear relation between sales and time:

$$\hat{Q}_t = a + bt$$

Using the 10 observations for 2007–2016, we regressed time ($t = 2007, 2008, \ldots ,$ 2016), the independent variable expressed in years, on sales, the dependent variable expressed in dollars, to obtain the estimated trend line:

$$\hat{Q}_t = \hat{a} + \hat{b}t$$

This line best fits the historical data. It is important to test whether there is a statistically significant positive or negative trend in sales. As shown in Chapter 4,

---

FIGURE 7.1

A Linear Trend Forecast

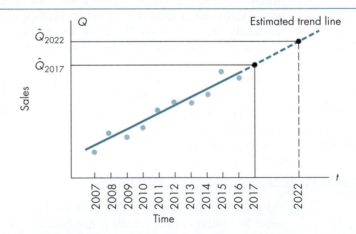

it is easy to determine whether $\hat{b}$ is significantly different from zero either by using a t-test for statistical significance or by examining the p-value for $\hat{b}$. If $\hat{b}$ is positive and statistically significant, sales are trending upward over time. If $\hat{b}$ is negative and statistically significant, sales are trending downward over time. However, if $\hat{b}$ is not statistically significant, one would assume that $b = 0$, and sales are constant over time. That is, there is no relation between sales and time, and any variation in sales is due to random fluctuations.

If the estimation indicates a statistically significant trend, you can then use the estimated trend line to obtain forecasts of future sales. For example, if a manager wanted a forecast for sales in 2017, the manager would simply insert 2017 into the estimated trend line:

$$\hat{Q}_{2017} = \hat{a} + \hat{b} \times (2017)$$

A Sales Forecast for Terminator Pest Control

In January 2016, Arnold Schwartz started Terminator Pest Control, a small pest-control company in Atlanta. Terminator Pest Control serves mainly residential customers citywide. At the end of March 2017, after 15 months of operation, Arnold decides to apply for a business loan from his bank to buy another pest-control truck. The bank is somewhat reluctant to make the loan, citing concern that sales at Terminator Pest Control did not grow significantly over its first 15 months of business. In addition, the bank asks Arnold to provide a forecast of sales for the next three months (April, May, and June).

Arnold decides to do the forecast himself using a time-series model based on past sales figures. He collects the data on sales for the last 15 months—sales are measured as the number of homes serviced during a given month. Because data are collected monthly, Arnold creates a continuous time variable by numbering the months consecutively as January 2016 = 1, February 2016 = 2, and so on. The data for Terminator and a scatter diagram are shown in Figure 7.2.

Arnold estimates the linear trend model

$$Q_t = a + bt$$

and gets the following printout from the computer:

DEPENDENT VARIABLE:	Q	R-SQUARE	F-RATIO	P-VALUE ON F
OBSERVATIONS: 15		0.9231	156.11	0.0001

VARIABLE	PARAMETER ESTIMATE	STANDARD ERROR	T-RATIO	P-VALUE
INTERCEPT	46.57	3.29	14.13	0.0001
T	4.53	0.36	12.49	0.0001

FIGURE 7.2

Forecasting Sales for Terminator Pest Control

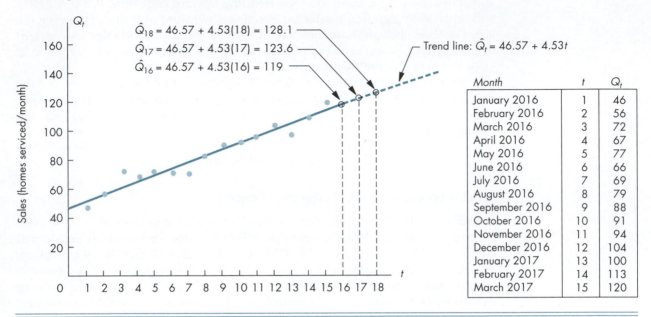

Month	t	Q_t
January 2016	1	46
February 2016	2	56
March 2016	3	72
April 2016	4	67
May 2016	5	77
June 2016	6	66
July 2016	7	69
August 2016	8	79
September 2016	9	88
October 2016	10	91
November 2016	11	94
December 2016	12	104
January 2017	13	100
February 2017	14	113
March 2017	15	120

The t-ratio for the time variable, 12.49, exceeds the critical t of 3.012 for 13 degrees of freedom ($= 15 - 2$) at the 1 percent level of significance. The exact level of significance for the estimate 4.53 is less than 0.0001, as indicated by the p-value. Thus the sales figures for Terminator suggest a statistically significant upward trend in sales. The sales forecasts for April, May, and June of 2017 are

$$\text{April 2017: } \hat{Q}_{16} = 46.57 + (4.53 \times 16) = 119$$

$$\text{May 2017: } \hat{Q}_{17} = 46.57 + (4.53 \times 17) = 123.6$$

$$\text{June 2017: } \hat{Q}_{18} = 46.57 + (4.53 \times 18) = 128.1$$

Now try Technical Problem 6.

The bank decided to make the loan to Terminator Pest Control in light of the statistically significant upward trend in sales and the forecast of higher sales in the three upcoming months.

A Price Forecast for Georgia Lumber Products

Suppose you work for Georgia Lumber Products, a large lumber producer in south Georgia, and your manager wants you to forecast the price of lumber for the next two quarters. Information about the price of a ton of lumber is readily available. Using eight quarterly observations on lumber prices since 2014(III), you estimate a linear trend line for lumber prices through the 2016(II) time period.

Your computer output for the linear time trend model on lumber price looks like the following printout:

DEPENDENT VARIABLE: P		R-SQUARE	F-RATIO	P-VALUE ON F
OBSERVATIONS: 8		0.7673	19.79	0.0043
VARIABLE	PARAMETER ESTIMATE	STANDARD ERROR	T-RATIO	P-VALUE
INTERCEPT	2066.0	794.62	2.60	0.0407
T	25.00	5.62	4.45	0.0043

Both parameter estimates $\hat{a}$ and $\hat{b}$ are significant at the 5 percent significance level because both t-ratios exceed 2.447, the critical t for the 5 percent significance level. (Notice also that both p-values are less than 0.05.) Thus the real (inflation-adjusted) price for a ton of lumber exhibited a statistically significant trend upward since the third quarter of 2014. Lumber prices have risen, on average, $25 per ton each quarter over the range of this sample period (2014 III through 2016 II).

To forecast the price of lumber for the next two quarters, you make the following computations:

$$\hat{P}_{2016\ (III)} = 2066 + (25 \times 9) = \$2,291 \text{ per ton}$$
$$\hat{P}_{2016\ (IV)} = 2066 + (25 \times 10) = \$2,316 \text{ per ton}$$

As you can see by the last two hypothetical examples, the linear trend method of forecasting is a simple procedure for generating forecasts for either sales or price. Indeed, this method can be applied to forecast any economic variable for which a time-series of observations is available.

7.5 SEASONAL (OR CYCLICAL) VARIATION

seasonal or cyclical variation
The regular variation that time-series data frequently exhibit.

Time-series data may frequently exhibit regular, **seasonal,** or **cyclical variation** over time, and the failure to take such regular variations into account when estimating a forecasting equation would bias the forecast. Frequently, when quarterly or monthly sales are being used to forecast sales, seasonal variation may occur—the sales of many products vary systematically by month or by quarter. For example, in the retail clothing business, sales are generally higher before Easter and Christmas. Thus sales would be higher during the second and fourth quarters of the year. Likewise, the sales of hunting equipment would peak during early fall, the third quarter. In such cases, you would definitely wish to incorporate these systematic variations when estimating the equation and forecasting future sales. We now describe the technique most commonly employed to handle cyclical variation.

FIGURE 7.3

Sales with Seasonal Variation

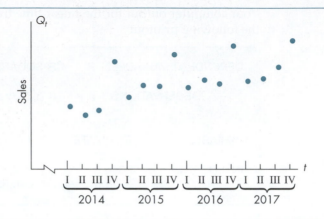

Correcting for Seasonal Variation by Using Dummy Variables

Consider the simplified example of a firm producing and selling a product for which sales are consistently higher in the fourth quarter than in any other quarter. A hypothetical data scatter is presented in Figure 7.3. In each of the four years, the data point in the fourth quarter is much higher than in the other three. While a time trend clearly exists, if the analyst simply regressed sales against time, without accounting for the higher sales in the fourth quarter, too large a trend would be estimated (i.e., the slope would be too large). In essence, there is an upward shift of the trend line in the fourth quarter. Such a relation is presented in Figure 7.4. In the fourth quarter, the intercept is higher than in the other quarters. In other words, a', the intercept of the trend line for the fourth-quarter data points, exceeds a, the intercept of the trend line for the data points in the other quarters. One way of specifying this relation is to define a' as $a' = a + c$, where c is some positive number. Therefore, the regression line we want to estimate will take the form

$$\hat{Q}_t = a + bt + c$$

where $c = 0$ in the first three quarters.

dummy variable
A variable that takes only values of 0 and 1.

To estimate the preceding equation, statisticians use what is commonly referred to as a *dummy variable* in the estimating equation. A **dummy variable** is a variable that can take on only the values of 0 or 1. In this case, we would assign the dummy variable (D) a value of 1 if the sales observation is from the fourth quarter and 0 in the other three quarters. The data are shown in Table 7.1, where Q_t represents the sales figure in the tth period and $D = 1$ for quarter IV and 0 otherwise. Since quarterly data are being used, time is converted into integers to obtain a continuous time variable. Using these data, the following equation is estimated:

$$Q_t = a + bt + cD$$

FIGURE 7.4

The Effect of Seasonal Variation

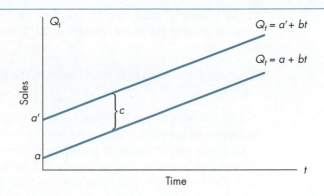

TABLE 7.1

Creating a Dummy Variable

Q_t	t	D
$Q_{2014(I)}$	1	0
$Q_{2014(II)}$	2	0
$Q_{2014(III)}$	3	0
$Q_{2014(IV)}$	4	1
$Q_{2015(I)}$	5	0
$Q_{2015(II)}$	6	0
$Q_{2015(III)}$	7	0
$Q_{2015(IV)}$	8	1
$Q_{2016(I)}$	9	0
$Q_{2016(II)}$	10	0
$Q_{2016(III)}$	11	0
$Q_{2016(IV)}$	12	1
$Q_{2017(I)}$	13	0
$Q_{2017(II)}$	14	0
$Q_{2017(III)}$	15	0
$Q_{2017(IV)}$	16	1

This specification produces two equations like those shown in Figure 7.4. The estimated slope of the two equations would be the same. For quarters I, II, and III the estimated intercept is $\hat{a}$, while for the fourth quarter the estimated intercept is $\hat{a} + \hat{c}$. This estimation really means that for any future period t, the sales forecast would be

$$\hat{Q}_t = \hat{a} + \hat{b}t$$

unless period t occurs in the fourth quarter, in which case the sales forecast would be

$$\hat{Q}_t = \hat{a} + \hat{b}t + \hat{c} = (\hat{a} + \hat{c}) + \hat{b}t$$

For example, referring to the data in Table 7.1, when a manager wishes to forecast sales in the third quarter of 2018, the manager uses the equation

$$\hat{Q}_{2018(III)} = \hat{a} + \hat{b}(19)$$

If a manager wishes to forecast sales in the fourth quarter of 2018, the forecast is

$$\hat{Q}_{2018(IV)} = (\hat{a} + \hat{c}) + \hat{b}(20)$$

In other words, when the forecast is for quarter IV, the forecast equation adds the amount $\hat{c}$ to the sales that would otherwise be forecast.[7]

Going a step further, it could be the case that there exist quarter-to-quarter differences in sales (i.e., in Figure 7.4, there would be four trend lines). In this case, three dummy variables are used: D_1 (equal to 1 in the first quarter and 0 otherwise), D_2 (equal to 1 in the second quarter and 0 otherwise), and D_3 (equal to 1 in the third quarter and 0 otherwise).[8] Then, the manager estimates the equation

$$Q_t = a + bt + c_1 D_1 + c_2 D_2 + c_3 D_3$$

In quarter I the intercept is $a + c_1$, in quarter II it is $a + c_2$, in quarter III it is $a + c_3$, and in quarter IV it is a only.

To obtain a forecast for some future quarter, it is necessary to include the coefficient for the dummy variable for that particular quarter. For example, predictions for the third quarter of a particular year would take the form

$$\hat{Q}_t = \hat{a} + \hat{b}t + \hat{c}_3$$

Perhaps the best way to explain how dummy variables can be used to account for cyclical variation is to provide an example.

The Dummy-Variable Technique: An Example

Jean Reynolds, the sales manager of Statewide Trucking Company, wishes to predict sales for all four quarters of 2019. The sales of Statewide Trucking are subject to seasonal variation and also have a trend over time. Reynolds obtains sales data for 2015–2018 by quarter. The data collected are presented in Table 7.2. Note that because quarterly data are used, time is converted into a continuous variable by numbering quarters consecutively in column 4 of the table.

Reynolds knows, from a college course in managerial economics, that obtaining the desired sales forecast requires that she estimate an equation containing three dummy variables—one less than the number of time periods in the annual cycle. She chooses to estimate the following equation:

$$Q_t = a + bt + c_1 D_1 + c_2 D_2 + c_3 D_3$$

---

[7]Throughout this discussion, we have assumed that trend lines differ only with respect to the intercepts—the slope is the same for all the trend lines. Dummy variables can also be used to reflect differences in slopes. This technique is beyond the scope of this text, and we refer the interested reader to Damodar Gujarati and Dawn Porter, *Basic Econometrics*, 5th ed. (New York: McGraw-Hill, 2009).

[8]Likewise, if there were month-to-month differences, 11 dummy variables would be used to account for the monthly change in the intercept. When using dummy variables, you must always use one less dummy variable than the number of periods being considered.

TABLE 7.2

Quarterly Sales Data for Statewide Trucking Company (2015–2018)

(1) Year	(2) Quarter	(3) Sales	(4) t	(5) D_1	(6) D_2	(7) D_3
2015	I	$72,000	1	1	0	0
	II	87,000	2	0	1	0
	III	87,000	3	0	0	1
	IV	150,000	4	0	0	0
2016	I	82,000	5	1	0	0
	II	98,000	6	0	1	0
	III	94,000	7	0	0	1
	IV	162,000	8	0	0	0
2017	I	97,000	9	1	0	0
	II	105,000	10	0	1	0
	III	109,000	11	0	0	1
	IV	176,000	12	0	0	0
2018	I	105,000	13	1	0	0
	II	121,000	14	0	1	0
	III	119,000	15	0	0	1
	IV	180,000	16	0	0	0

where D_1, D_2, and D_3 are, respectively, dummy variables for quarters I, II, and III. Using the data in Table 7.2, she estimates the preceding equation, and the results of this estimation are shown here:

DEPENDENT VARIABLE: QT	R-SQUARE	F-RATIO	P-VALUE ON F
OBSERVATIONS: 16	0.9965	794.126	0.0001

VARIABLE	PARAMETER ESTIMATE	STANDARD ERROR	T-RATIO	P-VALUE
INTERCEPT	139625.0	1743.6	80.08	0.0001
T	2737.5	129.96	21.06	0.0001
D1	−69788.0	1689.5	−41.31	0.0001
D2	−58775.0	1664.3	−35.32	0.0001
D3	−62013.0	1649.0	−37.61	0.0001

Upon examining the estimation results, Reynolds notes that a positive trend in sales is indicated ($\hat{b} > 0$). To determine whether the trend is statistically significant, either a t-test can be performed on $\hat{b}$ or the p-value for $\hat{b}$ can be assessed for significance. The calculated t-value for $\hat{b}$ is $t_{\hat{b}} = 21.06$. With $16 - 5 = 11$ degrees of freedom, the critical value of t (using a 5 percent significance level) is 2.201. Because $21.06 > 2.201$, $\hat{b}$ is statistically significant. The p-value for b is so small (0.01 percent) that the chance of making a Type I error—incorrectly finding significance—is virtually 0. Thus Reynolds has strong evidence suggesting a positive trend in sales.

Next, Reynolds calculates the estimated intercepts of the trend line for each of the four quarters. In the first quarter,

$$\hat{a} + \hat{c}_1 = 139{,}625 - 69{,}788$$
$$= 69{,}837$$

in the second quarter

$$\hat{a} + \hat{c}_2 = 139{,}625 - 58{,}775$$
$$= 80{,}850$$

in the third quarter

$$\hat{a} + \hat{c}_3 = 139{,}625 - 62{,}013$$
$$= 77{,}612$$

and in the fourth quarter

$$\hat{a} = 139{,}625$$

These estimates indicate that the intercepts, and thus sales, are lower in quarters I, II, and III than in quarter IV. The question that always must be asked is: Are these intercepts *significantly* lower?

To answer this question, Reynolds decides to compare quarters I and IV. In quarter I, the intercept is $\hat{a} + \hat{c}_1$, in quarter IV, it is $\hat{a}$. Hence, if $\hat{a} + \hat{c}$ is significantly lower than $\hat{a}$, it is necessary that $\hat{c}_1$ be significantly less than 0. That is, if

$$\hat{a} + \hat{c}_1 < \hat{a}$$

it follows that $\hat{c}_1$, 0. Reynolds already knows that $\hat{c}_1$ is negative; to determine if it is significantly negative, she can perform a t-test. The calculated value of t for $\hat{c}_1$ is -41.31. Because $|-41.31| > 2.201$, $\hat{c}_1$ is significantly less than 0. This indicates that the intercept—and the sales—in the first quarter are less than that in the fourth. The t-values for $\hat{c}_2$ and $\hat{c}_3$, -35.32 and -37.61, respectively, are both greater (in absolute value) than 2.201 and are significantly negative. Thus the intercepts in the second and third quarters are also significantly less than the intercept in the fourth quarter. Hence, Reynolds has evidence that there is a significant increase in sales in the fourth quarter.

She can now proceed to forecast sales by quarters for 2019. In the first quarter of 2019, $t = 17$, $D_1 = 1$, $D_2 = 0$, and $D_3 = 0$. Therefore, the forecast for sales in the first quarter of 2019 would be

$$\hat{Q}_{2019(I)} = \hat{a} + \hat{b} \times 17 + \hat{c}_1 \times 1 + \hat{c}_2 \times 0 + \hat{c}_3 \times 0$$
$$= \hat{a} + \hat{b} \times 17 + \hat{c}_1$$
$$= 139{,}625 + 2{,}737.5 \times 17 - 69{,}788$$
$$= 116{,}374.5$$

Using precisely the same method, the forecasts for sales in the other three quarters of 2019 are as follows:

$$2019(II): \hat{Q}_{2019(II)} = \hat{a} + \hat{b} \times 18 + \hat{c}_2$$
$$= 139{,}625 + 2{,}737.5 \times 18 - 58{,}775$$
$$= 130{,}125$$

$$2019(III): \hat{Q}_{2019(III)} = \hat{a} + \hat{b} \times 19 + \hat{c}_3$$
$$= 139{,}625 + 2{,}737.5 \times 19 - 62{,}013$$
$$= 129{,}624.5$$

$$2019(IV): \hat{Q}_{2019(IV)} = \hat{a} + \hat{b} \times 20$$
$$= 139{,}625 + 2{,}737.5 \times 20$$
$$= 194{,}375$$

In this example, we have confined our attention to quarterly variation. However, exactly the same techniques can be used for monthly data or any other type of seasonal or cyclical variation. In addition to its application to situations involving seasonal or cyclical variation, the dummy-variable technique can be used to account for changes in sales (or any other economic variable that is being forecast) due to forces such as wars, bad weather, or even strikes at a competitor's production facility. We summarize the dummy-variable technique with the following relation:

Now try Technical Problem 7.

Relation   When seasonal variation causes the intercept of the demand equation to vary systematically from season to season, dummy variables can be added to the estimated forecasting equation to account for the cyclical variation. If there are N seasonal time periods to be accounted for, $N - 1$ dummy variables are added to the demand equation. Each of these dummy variables accounts for one of the seasonal time periods by taking a value of 1 for those observations that occur during that season, and a value of 0 otherwise. Used in this way, dummy variables allow the intercept of the demand equation to vary across seasons.

Before leaving the discussion of time-series models, we should mention that the linear trend model is just one—and probably the simplest—of many different types of time-series models that can be used to forecast economic variables. More advanced time-series models fit cyclical patterns, rather than straight lines, to the scatter of data over time. These techniques, which involve moving-average models, exponential smoothing models, and Box-Jenkins models, go well beyond the scope of a managerial textbook. In fact, you can take entire courses in business forecasting that will teach how to implement some of these more sophisticated time-series forecasting techniques. Sophisticated techniques, however, are frequently not required, or at best, only add minor improvements to linear trend analysis. See Illustration 7.3 for a linear trend forecast of new home sales using actual sales data for the period 2012 to 2014.

ILLUSTRATION 7.3

Forecasting New-Home Sales
A Time Series Forecast

Suppose that in January 2015, the market analyst of a national real estate firm wanted to forecast the total number of new homes that would be sold in the United States in March 2015. Let's examine how this analyst could have used time-series techniques to forecast sales of new homes. The data for the number of new homes sold monthly during the years 2012–2014 are presented in the accompanying table (columns 1–3) and are shown by the solid line (Q_t) in the accompanying graph. These data can be found at the website for the U.S. Department of Housing and Urban Development: *www.census.gov/newhomesales*.

The market analyst forecasted sales using a linear trend, and the following linear specification is estimated:

$$Q_t = a + bt$$

where Q_t is the number of new homes sold in the tth month, and $t = 1, 2, \ldots, 36$. Note that because these are monthly data, the analyst converted time into integers, as shown in column 4 of the table (ignore column 5 for now). When the analyst ran a regression analysis on the 36 time-series observations on new-home sales, it resulted in Computer Output 1 on the following page.

The estimated trend line, $\hat{Q}_t = 31{,}361.9 + 151.609t$, is labeled $\hat{Q}_t$ in the graph.

The estimate of b is positive ($\hat{b} = 151.609$), indicating sales were increasing over the time period 2012–2014. The analyst needs to assess the statistical significance of $\hat{b}$. The p-value for $\hat{b}$ is less than 0.05, which indicates the upward trend in new-home sales over the period 2012–2014 is statistically significant at better than the 5 percent level of significance (to be precise, the 3.83 percent level). Note also that the R^2 indicates the trend line poorly fits the sales data, as can be seen in the graph as well. Only about 12 percent of the total variation in home sales can be explained by the passage of time (t), even though the time trend is statistically significant at better than the 5 percent level. About 88 percent of the variation in sales remains unexplained, which suggests that something more than just the time trend (t) may be needed to explain satisfactorily the variation

Monthly Sales of New Homes in the United States (2012–2014)

(1) Year	(2) Month	(3) Sales	(4) t	(5) D_t
2012	1	23,000	1	0
	2	30,000	2	0
	3	34,000	3	1
	4	34,000	4	1
	5	35,000	5	1
	6	34,000	6	1
	7	33,000	7	1
	8	31,000	8	1
	9	30,000	9	0
	10	29,000	10	0
	11	28,000	11	0
	12	28,000	12	0
2013	1	32,000	13	0
	2	36,000	14	0
	3	41,000	15	1
	4	43,000	16	1
	5	40,000	17	1
	6	43,000	18	1
	7	33,000	19	1
	8	31,000	20	1
	9	31,000	21	0
	10	36,000	22	0
	11	32,000	23	0
	12	31,000	24	0
2014	1	33,000	25	0
	2	35,000	26	0
	3	39,000	27	1
	4	39,000	28	1
	5	43,000	29	1
	6	38,000	30	1
	7	35,000	31	1
	8	36,000	32	1
	9	37,000	33	0
	10	36,000	34	0
	11	31,000	35	0
	12	30,000	36	0

Source: U.S. Department of Housing and Urban Development. Internet site: *www.census.gov/newhomesales*

Computer Output 1

DEPENDENT VARIABLE:	QT	R-SQUARE	F-RATIO	P-VALUE ON F
OBSERVATIONS: 36		0.1202	4.64	0.0383

VARIABLE	PARAMETER ESTIMATE	STANDARD ERROR	T-RATIO	P-VALUE
INTERCEPT	31361.9	1492.59	21.01	0.0001
T	151.609	70.3485	2.16	0.0383

in new-home sales. In a moment, we show that adding seasonality to the trend model can improve matters substantially.

Using the estimated linear trend line, the market analyst can forecast sales for March 2015 ($t = 39$) by substituting the value 39 for t:

$$\hat{Q}_{March2015} = 31{,}361.9 + 151.609 \times 39 = 37{,}275$$

Thus, using linear trend analysis, the number of new homes sold in March 2015 is forecast to be 37,275. The number of homes actually sold in March 2015 turned out to be 45,000. You can verify this figure at the Internet site mentioned above and in the table. The analyst's forecast, using a trend-line technique, underestimates the actual number of homes sold by 17.2 percent [$= (37{,}275 - 45{,}000) \times 100/45{,}000)$], a sizable error.

The market analyst could improve the forecast by modifying the forecast equation to reflect the seasonality of new-home sales: in the spring and summer months, new-home sales tend to be higher than in other months as families try to relocate while

school is out of session. Let's examine how adding a dummy variable to account for this seasonality can substantially improve the market analyst's sale forecast.

To account for the seasonal increase in new-home sales during the spring and summer months (March through August), the analyst can define a dummy variable, D_t, to be equal to 1 when $t = 3, \ldots, 8, 15, \ldots,$ 20, and 27, ..., 32. The dummy variable is equal to zero for all other months. The values of the dummy variable are shown in column 5 of the table. Adding this dummy variable to the trend line results in the following equation to be estimated:

$$Q_t = a + bt + cD_t$$

Again using the sales data for 2012–2014, a regression analysis results in Computer Output 2 below.

As in the first regression when no adjustment was made for seasonality, a statistically significant upward trend in sales is present. The p-value for each of the parameter estimates in the model with a dummy variable is so small that there is less than a 0.01 percent

Computer Output 2

DEPENDENT VARIABLE:	QT	R-SQUARE	F-RATIO	P-VALUE ON F
OBSERVATIONS: 36		0.4935	16.07	0.0001

VARIABLE	PARAMETER ESTIMATE	STANDARD ERROR	T-RATIO	P-VALUE
INTERCEPT	28095.3	1326.76	21.18	0.0001
T	177.449	54.4339	3.26	0.0026
D	5577.12	1130.95	4.93	0.0001

(*Continued*)

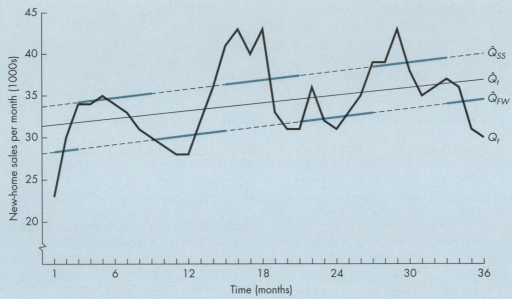

chance of making a Type I error (mistakenly finding significance). Note that after accounting for seasonal variation, the trend line becomes steeper (177.449 > 151.609).

The estimated intercept for the trend line is 28,095.3 for fall and winter months ($D_t = 0$). During the spring and summer buying season, the estimated intercept of the trend line is

$$\hat{a} + \hat{c} = 28{,}095.3 + 5{,}577.12 = 33{,}672.42$$

To check for statistical significance of $\hat{c}$, we note that the p-value for $\hat{c}$ indicates less than a 0.01 percent chance that $c = 0$. Thus the statistical evidence suggests that there is a significant increase in sales of new homes during the spring and summer months. The increase in the average number of new homes sold in March through August compared with September through February is about 5,577 more homes per month. In other words, entering the selling season (March–August) causes sales to spike upward by 5,577 homes per month while continuing to trend upward by 177 units per month.

The estimated trend lines representing the spring and summer months ($\hat{Q}_{SS}$) and the fall and winter months ($\hat{Q}_{FW}$) are shown in the graph. Note that the spring and summer trend line is parallel to the fall and winter line, but the sales intercept is higher during spring and summer months. The estimated trend line for the fall and winter months is the solid portion of the lower trend line. For the spring and summer months, the estimated trend line is the solid portion of the upper trend line. Note how much better the line fits when it is seasonally adjusted. Indeed, the R^2 increased from 0.1202 to 0.4935.

We now determine whether adding the dummy variable improves the accuracy of the market analyst's forecast of sales in March 2015. Using the estimated trend line accounting for seasonal variation in sales, the sales forecast for March 2015 ($t = 39$) is now

$$\hat{Q}_{March2015} = 28{,}095.3 + 177.449 \times 39 + 5{,}577.12 \times 1 = 40{,}592.9$$

As you can see by comparing the two forecasts, this forecast is an improvement over the unadjusted sales forecast. This sales forecast accounting for seasonality underestimates the actual level of sales by only 4,407 homes, or just 9.8 percent [= (40,592.9 − 45,000) × 100/45,000]. Compare this with the previous forecast of 37,275, which underestimated actual sales by 17.2 percent. Accounting for seasonality of new-home sales reduces the forecast error by 43 percent, which is certainly a meaningful improvement in the accuracy of the forecast created by adding the seasonal dummy variable. In order to further improve the accuracy of the forecast, the analyst might try using one of the more complicated time-series techniques that fit cyclical curves to the data, thereby improving the fit (R^2) and the forecast. As already noted, these techniques are well beyond the scope of this text and are not guaranteed to improve forecasts.

7.6 SOME FINAL WARNINGS

We have often heard it said about forecasting that "he who lives by the crystal ball ends up eating ground glass." Although we do not make nearly so dire a judgment, we do feel that you should be aware of the major limitations of and problems inherent in forecasting. Basically, our warnings are concerned with three issues: confidence intervals, specification, and change of structure.

To illustrate the issue of confidence intervals in forecasting, consider once again the simple linear trend model

$$Q_t = a + bt$$

To obtain the prediction model, we must estimate two coefficients a and b. Obviously, we cannot estimate these coefficients with certainty. Indeed, the estimated standard errors reflect the magnitude of uncertainty (i.e., potential error) about the values of the parameters.

In Figure 7.5, we illustrate a situation in which there are observations on sales for periods t_1 through t_n. Due to the manner in which it was calculated,

FIGURE 7.5

Confidence Intervals

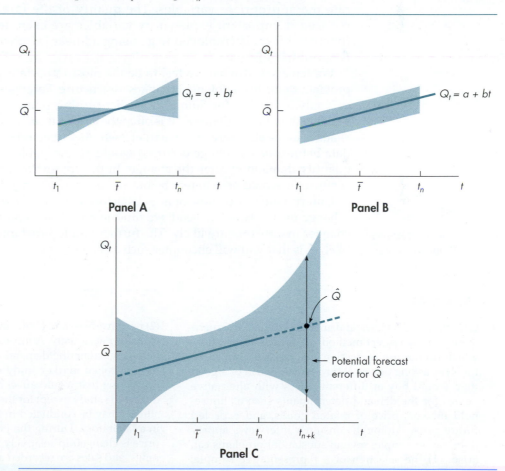

Panel A

Panel B

Panel C

the regression line will pass through the sample mean of the data points $(\overline{Q}, \overline{t})$. In Panel A, we illustrate as the shaded area our confidence region if there exist errors only in the estimation of the slope *b*. In Panel B, the shaded area represents the confidence region if an error exists only in the estimation of the intercept *a*. These two shaded areas are combined in Panel C. As you can see, the further the value of *t* is from the mean value of *t*, the wider the zone of uncertainty becomes.

Now consider what happens when we use the estimated regression line to predict future sales. At a future time period t_{n+k}, the prediction for sales will be a point on the extrapolated regression line (i.e., $\hat{Q}$). However, note what happens to the region of uncertainty about this estimate. The further one forecasts into the future, the wider is this region of uncertainty, and this region increases geometrically rather than arithmetically.

We mentioned the problem of incorrect specification in our discussion of demand estimation, but we feel that it is important enough to deserve another mention here. To generate reliable forecasts, the model used must incorporate the appropriate variables. The quality of the forecast can be severely reduced if important explanatory variables are excluded or if an improper functional form is employed (e.g., using a linear form when a nonlinear form is appropriate).

We have saved what we feel to be the most important problem for last. This problem stems from potential changes in structure. Forecasts are widely, and often correctly, criticized for failing to predict turning points—sharp changes in the variable under consideration. It is often the case that such changes are the result of changes in the structure of the market itself. Any demand relation estimated using data before such a change occurred would be incapable of correctly forecasting quantity demanded after the change. In the context of a demand function, the coefficients would be different before and after the change.

Unfortunately, we know of no satisfactory method of handling this problem of "change in structure." Instead, we must simply leave you with the warning that changes in structure are likely. The further you forecast into the future, the more likely it is that you will encounter such a change.

Now try Technical Problems 8–9.

7.7 SUMMARY

- Consumer interviews and market studies or experiments are two direct methods of demand estimation, which do not use regression analysis. This approach involves asking potential buyers how much of a good they would buy at different prices with alternative values for the demand determinants such as household income, price of related goods, and expected future price. Although consumer interviews appear to be rather simple, several substantial problems can arise: (1) the selection of a representative sample, (2) response bias, and (3) the inability of the respondent to answer accurately. A more costly and difficult technique for estimating demand and demand elasticity is the controlled market study or experiment in which everything that would affect demand is held constant during the study except for the price of the good. These studies may be conducted in the stores themselves or in a laboratory. During the period of the experiment, price is changed in relatively small increments over a range, and sales are recorded at each price. In this way, many of the effects of changes in other things can be removed, and a reasonable approximation of the actual demand curve can be estimated. (*LO1*)

■ Empirical demand functions are demand equations derived from actual market data and are extremely useful in making pricing and production decisions. Two specifications for demand, linear and log-linear, are presented in this chapter. When demand is specified to be linear in form, the coefficients on each of the explanatory variables measure the rate of change in quantity demanded as that explanatory variable changes, holding all other explanatory variables constant. In linear form, the empirical demand function is $Q = a + bP + cM + dP_R$, where Q is the quantity demanded, P is the price of the good or service, M is consumer income, and P_R is the price of some related good R. In the linear form, the expected signs of the coefficients are: (1) b is expected to be negative, (2) if good X is normal (inferior), c is expected to be positive (negative), and (3) if related good R is a substitute (complement), d is expected to be positive (negative). For the linear demand specification, the estimated elasticities of demand are computed as $\hat{E} = \hat{b}$ (P/Q), $\hat{E}_M = \hat{c}(M/Q)$, and $\hat{E}_{XR} = \hat{d}(P_R/Q)$. When demand is specified in log-linear form, the demand function is written as $Q = aP^bM^cP_R^d$. To estimate the log-linear demand function, the demand equation must be converted to logarithms: $\ln Q = \ln a + b \ln P + c \ln M + d \ln P_R$. The demand elasticities are the exponents of the explanatory variables $\hat{E} = \hat{b}$, $\hat{E}_M = \hat{c}$, and $\hat{E}_{XR} = \hat{d}$. (*LO2*)

■ Estimating parameters of an empirical demand function can be accomplished using regression analysis. However, the steps in doing so depend on whether the demand to be estimated is a single price-setting firm's demand or a competitive price-taking industry's demand. Estimating industry demand requires more advanced statistical methods than estimating the demand for a single firm; thus, the discussion in this text is limited to estimating demand for a price-setting firm. The first step to estimating a single price-setting firm's demand is to specify the firm's demand function by choosing a linear or curvilinear functional form and to decide which demand-shifting variables to include

in the empirical demand equation. The second step is to collect data on all the variables in the empirical demand function. In the final step, the parameters of the firm's demand function are estimated using the linear regression procedure presented in Chapter 4. (*LO3*)

■ A time-series model shows how a time-ordered sequence of observations on a variable, such as price or output, is generated. The simplest form of time-series forecasting is linear trend forecasting. In a linear trend model, sales in each time period, Q_t, are assumed to be linearly related to time, t, as $Q_t = a + bt$. Regression analysis is used to estimate the values of a and b. If $b > 0$, sales are increasing over time, and if $b < 0$, sales are decreasing. If $b = 0$, then sales are constant over time. The statistical significance of a trend is determined by testing $\hat{b}$ for statistical significance or by examining the p-value for $\hat{b}$. (*LO4*)

■ Seasonal or cyclical variation can bias the estimation of a and b in linear trend models. To account for seasonal variation in trend analysis, dummy variables are added to the trend equation. Dummy variables serve to shift the trend line up or down according to the particular seasonal pattern encountered. The significance of seasonal behavior is determined by using a t-test or p-value for the estimated coefficient on the dummy variable. When using dummy variables to account for N seasonal time periods, $N-1$ dummy variables are added to the linear trend. Each dummy variable accounts for one of the seasonal time periods. The dummy variable takes a value of 1 for those observations that occur during the season assigned to that dummy variable, and a value of 0 otherwise. (*LO5*)

■ When making forecasts, analysts must recognize the limitations that are inherent in forecasting: (1) the further into the future the forecast is made, the wider the confidence interval or region of uncertainty; (2) if the model is misspecified by either excluding an important variable or by using an inappropriate functional form, then the reliability of the forecast will be reduced; and (3) forecasts are incapable of predicting sharp changes that occur because of structural changes in the market itself. (*LO6*)

KEY TERMS

dummy variable	representative sample	seasonal or cyclical variation
empirical demand functions	response bias	time-series model

TECHNICAL PROBLEMS

1. Cite the three major problems with consumer interviews or surveys and provide an example of each.

2. The estimated market demand for good X is

$$\hat{Q} = 70 - 3.5P - 0.6M + 4P_Z$$

where $\hat{Q}$ is the estimated number of units of good X demanded, P is the price of the good, M is income, and P_Z is the price of related good Z. (All parameter estimates are statistically significant at the 1 percent level.)

 a. Is X a normal or an inferior good? Explain.

 b. Are X and Z substitutes or complements? Explain.

 c. At $P = 10$, $M = 30$, and $P_Z = 6$, compute estimates for the price ($\hat{E}$), income ($\hat{E}_M$), and cross-price elasticities ($\hat{E}_{XZ}$).

3. The empirical demand function for good X is estimated in log-linear form as

$$\ln \hat{Q} = 11.74209 - 1.65 \ln P + 0.8 \ln M - 2.5 \ln P_Y$$

where $\hat{Q}$ is the estimated number of units of good X demanded, P is the price of X, M is income, and P_Y is the price of related good Y. (All parameter estimates are significantly different from 0 at the 5 percent level.)

 a. Is X a normal or an inferior good? Explain.

 b. Are X and Y substitutes or complements? Explain.

 c. Express the empirical demand function in the alternative (nonlogarithmic) form: $\hat{Q} = $ _____.

 d. At $P = 50$, $M = 36,000$, and $P_Y = 25$, what are the estimated price ($\hat{E}$), income ($\hat{E}_M$), and cross-price elasticities ($\hat{E}_{XY}$)? What is the predicted number of units of good X demanded?

4. A linear industry demand function of the form

$$Q = a + bP + cM + dP_R$$

was estimated using regression analysis. The results of this estimation are as follows:

DEPENDENT VARIABLE: Q	R-SQUARE	F-RATIO	P-VALUE ON F
OBSERVATIONS: 24	0.8118	28.75	0.0001

VARIABLE	PARAMETER ESTIMATE	STANDARD ERROR	T-RATIO	P-VALUE
INTERCEPT	68.38	12.65	5.41	0.0001
P	−6.50	3.15	−2.06	0.0492
M	0.13926	0.0131	10.63	0.0001
PR	−10.77	2.45	−4.40	0.0002

 a. Is the sign of $\hat{b}$ as would be predicted theoretically? Why?

 b. What does the sign $\hat{c}$ of imply about the good?

c. What does the sign of $\hat{d}$ imply about the relation between the commodity and the related good R?

d. Are the parameter estimates $\hat{a}, \hat{b}, \hat{c}$, and $\hat{d}$ statistically significant at the 5 percent level of significance?

e. Using the values $P = 225$, $M = 24{,}000$, and $P_R = 60$, calculate estimates of
   (1) The price elasticity of demand ($\hat{E}$).
   (2) The income elasticity of demand ($\hat{E}_M$).
   (3) The cross-price elasticity ($\hat{E}_{XR}$).

5. The following log-linear demand curve for a price-setting firm is estimated using the ordinary least-squares method:

$$Q = aP^b M^c P_R^d$$

Following are the results of this estimation:

DEPENDENT VARIABLE: LNQ		R-SQUARE		F-RATIO	P-VALUE ON F
OBSERVATIONS: 25		0.8587		89.165	0.0001

VARIABLE	PARAMETER ESTIMATE	STANDARD ERROR	T-RATIO	P-VALUE
INTERCEPT	6.77	4.01	1.69	0.0984
LNP	−1.68	0.70	−2.40	0.0207
LNM	−0.82	0.22	−3.73	0.0005
LNPR	1.35	0.75	1.80	0.0787

a. The estimated demand equation can be expressed in natural logarithms as $\ln Q = $ _____.

b. Does the parameter estimate for b have the expected sign? Explain.

c. Given these parameter estimates, is the good a normal or an inferior good? Explain. Is good R a substitute or a complement? Explain.

d. Which of the parameter estimates are statistically significant at the 5 percent level of significance?

e. Find the following estimated elasticities:
   (1) The price elasticity of demand ($\hat{E}$).
   (2) The cross-price elasticity of demand ($\hat{E}_{XR}$).
   (3) The income elasticity of demand ($\hat{E}_M$).

f. A 10 percent decrease in household income, holding all other things constant, will cause quantity demanded to _____ (increase, decrease) by _____ percent.

g. All else constant, a 10 percent increase in price causes quantity demanded to _____ (increase, decrease) by _____ percent.

h. A 5 percent decrease in the price of R, holding all other variables constant, causes quantity demanded to _____ (increase, decrease) by _____ percent.

6. A linear trend equation for sales of the form

$$Q_t = a + bt$$

was estimated for the period 2003–2017 (i.e., t = 2003, 2004, . . . , 2017). The results of the regression are as follows:

DEPENDENT VARIABLE: QT	R-SQUARE	F-RATIO	P-VALUE ON F
OBSERVATIONS: 15	0.6602	25.262	0.0002

VARIABLE	PARAMETER ESTIMATE	STANDARD ERROR	T-RATIO	P-VALUE
INTERCEPT	73.71460	34.08	2.16	0.0498
T	3.7621	0.7490	5.02	0.0002

a. Evaluate the statistical significance of the estimated coefficients. (Use 5 percent for the significance level.) Does this estimation indicate a significant trend?

b. Using this equation, forecast sales in 2018 and 2019.

c. Comment on the precision of these two forecasts.

7. Consider a firm subject to quarter-to-quarter variation in its sales. Suppose that the following equation was estimated using quarterly data for the period 2011–2018 (the time variable goes from 1 to 32). The variables D_1, D_2, and D_3 are, respectively, dummy variables for the first, second, and third quarters (e.g., D_1 is equal to 1 in the first quarter and 0 otherwise).

$$Q_t = a + bt + c_1D_1 + c_2D_2 + c_3D_3$$

The results of the estimation are presented here:

DEPENDENT VARIABLE: QT	R-SQUARE	F-RATIO	P-VALUE ON F
OBSERVATIONS: 32	0.9817	361.133	0.0001

VARIABLE	PARAMETER ESTIMATE	STANDARD ERROR	T-RATIO	P-VALUE
INTERCEPT	51.234	7.16	7.15	0.0001
T	3.127	0.524	5.97	0.0001
D1	−11.716	2.717	−4.31	0.0002
D2	−1.424	0.636	−2.24	0.0985
D3	−17.367	2.112	−8.22	0.0001

a. At the 5 percent level of significance, perform t- and F-tests to check for statistical significance of the coefficients and the equation. Discuss also the significance of the coefficients and equation in terms of p-values.

b. Calculate the intercept in each of the four quarters. What do these values imply?

c. Use this estimated equation to forecast sales in the four quarters of 2019.

8. Describe the major shortcomings of time-series models.

9. In the final section of this chapter we provided warnings about three problems that frequently arise. List, explain, and provide an example of each.

APPLIED PROBLEMS

1. Wilpen Company, a price-setting firm, produces nearly 80 percent of all tennis balls purchased in the United States. Wilpen estimates the U.S. demand for its tennis balls by using the following linear specification:

$$Q = a + bP + cM + dP_R$$

where Q is the number of cans of tennis balls sold quarterly, P is the wholesale price Wilpen charges for a can of tennis balls, M is the consumers' average household income, and P_R is the average price of tennis rackets. The regression results are as follows:

DEPENDENT VARIABLE: Q		R-SQUARE	F-RATIO	P-VALUE ON F
OBSERVATIONS: 20		0.8435	28.75	0.001

VARIABLE	PARAMETER ESTIMATE	STANDARD ERROR	T-RATIO	P-VALUE
INTERCEPT	425120.0	220300.0	1.93	0.0716
P	−37260.6	12587	−22.96	0.0093
M	1.49	0.3651	4.08	0.0009
PR	−1456.0	460.75	−3.16	0.0060

a. Discuss the statistical significance of the parameter estimates $\hat{a}, \hat{b}, \hat{c},$ and $\hat{d}$ using the p-values. Are the signs of $\hat{b}, \hat{c},$ and $\hat{d}$ consistent with the theory of demand?

Wilpen plans to charge a wholesale price of $1.65 per can. The average price of a tennis racket is $110, and consumers' average household income is $24,600.

b. What is the estimated number of cans of tennis balls demanded?

c. At the values of P, M, and P_R given, what are the estimated values of the price ($\hat{E}$), income ($\hat{E}_M$), and cross-price elasticities ($\hat{E}_{XR}$) of demand?

d. What will happen, in percentage terms, to the number of cans of tennis balls demanded if the price of tennis balls decreases 15 percent?

e. What will happen, in percentage terms, to the number of cans of tennis balls demanded if average household income increases by 20 percent?

f. What will happen, in percentage terms, to the number of cans of tennis balls demanded if the average price of tennis rackets increases 25 percent?

2. Cypress River Landscape Supply is a large wholesale supplier of landscaping materials in Georgia. Cypress River's sales vary seasonally; sales tend to be higher in the spring months than in other months.

a. Suppose Cypress River estimates a linear trend *without* accounting for this seasonal variation. What effect would this omission have on the estimated sales trend?

b. Alternatively, suppose there is, in fact, no seasonal pattern to sales, and the trend line is estimated using dummy variables to account for seasonality. What effect would this have on the estimation?

3. Rubax, a U.S. manufacturer of athletic shoes, estimates the following linear trend model for shoe sales:

$$Q_t = a + bt + c_1 D_1 + c_2 D_2 + c_3 D_3$$

where

Q_t = sales of athletic shoes in the tth quarter

$t = 1, 2, \ldots, 28$ [2011(I), 2011(II), ..., 2017(IV)]

D_1 = 1 if t is quarter I (winter); 0 otherwise

D_2 = 1 if t is quarter II (spring); 0 otherwise

D_3 = 1 if t is quarter III (summer); 0 otherwise

The regression analysis produces the following results:

DEPENDENT VARIABLE: QT		R-SQUARE	F-RATIO	P-VALUE ON F
OBSERVATIONS: 28		0.9651	159.01	0.0001

VARIABLE	PARAMETER ESTIMATE	STANDARD ERROR	T-RATIO	P-VALUE
INTERCEPT	184500	10310	17.90	0.0001
T	2100	340	6.18	0.0001
D1	3280	1510	2.17	0.0404
D2	6250	2220	2.82	0.0098
D3	7010	1580	4.44	0.0002

a. Is there sufficient statistical evidence of an upward trend in shoe sales?

b. Do these data indicate a statistically significant seasonal pattern of sales for Rubax shoes? If so, what is the seasonal pattern exhibited by the data?

c. Using the estimated forecast equation, forecast sales of Rubax shoes for 2018(III) and 2019(II).

d. How might you improve this forecast equation?

□ **MATHEMATICAL APPENDIX**   **Empirical Elasticities**

Derivation of Elasticity Estimates for Linear and Log-Linear Demands

As demonstrated in Chapter 6, the price elasticity of demand is

$$E = \frac{\partial Q}{\partial P} \times \frac{Q}{P}$$

With the linear specification of the demand function,

$$Q = a + bP + cM + dP_R$$

the parameter b is an estimate of the partial derivative of quantity demanded with respect to the price of the product,

$$\hat{b} = \text{Estimate of} \left(\frac{\partial Q}{\partial P} \right)$$

Hence for any price–quantity demanded combination (P, Q), the estimated price elasticity of that point on the demand function is

$$\hat{E} = \hat{b} \times \frac{P}{Q}$$

With the log-linear specification of the demand function,

$$Q = aP^b M^c P_R^d$$

the partial derivative of quantity demanded with respect to price is

$$\frac{\partial Q}{\partial P} = baP^{b-1}M^c P_R^d = \frac{bQ}{P}$$

Hence, $\hat{b}$ is an estimate of price elasticity

$$\hat{E} = \frac{\hat{b}Q}{P} \times \frac{P}{Q} = \hat{b}$$

Using the same methodology, estimates of income and cross-price elasticities can be obtained. The estimates are summarized in the following table:

Note that the elasticity estimates from the linear specification depend on the point on the demand curve at which the elasticity estimate is evaluated. In contrast, the log-linear demand curve exhibits constant elasticity estimates.

Elasticity	Definition	Estimate from linear specification	Estimate from log-linear specification
Price	$E = \frac{\partial Q}{\partial P} \times \frac{P}{Q}$	$\hat{b} \times \frac{P}{Q}$	$\hat{b}$
Income	$E_M = \frac{\partial Q}{\partial M} \times \frac{M}{Q}$	$\hat{c} \times \frac{P}{Q}$	$\hat{c}$
Cross-price	$E_{XR} = \frac{\partial Q}{\partial P_R} \times \frac{P_R}{Q}$	$\hat{d} \times \frac{P_R}{Q}$	$\hat{d}$

□ **DATA APPENDIX**   **Data for Checkers Pizza**

Observation	Q	P	M	P_{Al}	P_{BMac}
1	2,659	8.65	25,500	10.55	1.25
2	2,870	8.65	25,600	10.45	1.35
3	2,875	8.65	25,700	10.35	1.55
4	2,849	8.65	25,970	10.30	1.05
5	2,842	8.65	25,970	10.30	0.95
6	2,816	8.65	25,750	10.25	0.95
7	3,039	7.50	25,750	10.25	0.85
8	3,059	7.50	25,950	10.15	1.15
9	3,040	7.50	25,950	10.00	1.25
10	3,090	7.50	26,120	10.00	1.75
11	2,934	8.50	26,120	10.25	1.75
12	2,942	8.50	26,120	10.25	1.85
13	2,834	8.50	26,200	9.75	1.50
14	2,517	9.99	26,350	9.75	1.10
15	2,503	9.99	26,450	9.65	1.05
16	2,502	9.99	26,350	9.60	1.25
17	2,557	9.99	26,850	10.00	0.55
18	2,586	10.25	27,350	10.25	0.55
19	2,623	10.25	27,350	10.20	1.15
20	2,633	10.25	27,950	10.00	1.15
21	2,721	9.75	28,159	10.10	0.55
22	2,729	9.75	28,264	10.10	0.55
23	2,791	9.75	28,444	10.10	1.20
24	2,821	9.75	28,500	10.25	1.20

□ **ONLINE APPENDIX 2: Estimating and Forecasting Industry Demand for Price-Taking Firms**

This appendix can be found online via *Connect*® or *Create*™. For more information, refer to the Preface.

Chapter 8

Production and Cost in the Short Run

After reading this chapter, you will be able to:

8.1 Explain general concepts of production and cost analysis.

8.2 Examine the structure of short-run production based on the relation among total, average, and marginal products.

8.3 Examine the structure of short-run costs using graphs of the total cost curves, average cost curves, and the short-run marginal cost curve.

8.4 Relate short-run costs to the production function using the relations between (i) average variable cost and average product, and (ii) short-run marginal cost and marginal product.

No doubt almost all managers know that profit is determined not only by the revenue a firm generates but also by the costs associated with production of the firm's good or service. Many managers, however, find managing the revenue portion of the profit equation more interesting and exciting than dealing with issues concerning the costs of production. After all, revenue-oriented decisions may involve such tasks as choosing the optimal level and mix of advertising media, determining the price of the product, and making decisions to expand into new geographic markets or new product lines. Even the decision to buy or merge with other firms may be largely motivated by the desire to increase revenues. When revenue-oriented tasks are compared with those involved in production issues—spending time with production engineers discussing productivity levels of workers or the need for more and better capital equipment, searching for lower-cost suppliers of production inputs, adopting new technologies to reduce production costs, and perhaps even engaging in a downsizing plan—it is not surprising that managers may enjoy time spent on revenue decisions more than time spent on production and cost decisions.

As barriers to trade weakened or vanished in the 1990s, the resulting global-ization of markets and heightened competition made it much more difficult to increase profits by charging higher prices. Global competition has intensified the need for managers to increase productivity and reduce costs in order to sat-isfy stockholders' desire for greater profitability. As one management consultant recently interviewed in *The Wall Street Journal* put it, "Cost-cutting has become the holy-grail of corporate management." Managers must understand the funda-mental principles of production and cost to reduce costs successfully. Many costly errors have been made by managers seeking to "reengineer" or "restructure" pro-duction. Most of these errors could have been avoided had the managers pos-sessed an understanding of the fundamentals of production and cost that we will now set forth. This chapter and the next show how the structure of a firm's costs is determined by the nature of the production process that transforms inputs into goods and services and by the prices of the inputs used in producing the goods or services. In Chapter 10, we show you how to employ regression analysis to esti-mate the production and cost functions for a firm.

Managers make production decisions in two different decision-making time frames: short-run production decisions and long-run production decisions. In short-run decision-making situations, a manager must produce with some inputs that are fixed in quantity. In a typical short-run situation, the manager has a fixed amount of plant and equipment with which to produce the firm's output. The manager can change production levels by hiring more or less labor and purchas-ing more or less raw material, but the size of the plant is viewed by the manager as essentially unchangeable or fixed for the purposes of making production deci-sions in the short run.

Long-run decision making concerns the same types of decisions as the short run with one important distinction: A manager can choose to operate in any size plant with any amount of capital equipment. Once a firm builds a new plant or changes the size of an existing plant, the manager is once more in a short-run decision-making framework. Sometimes economists think of the short run as the time period during which production actually takes place and the long run as the planning horizon during which future production will take place. As you will see, the structure of costs differs in rather crucial ways depending on whether production is taking place in the short run or whether the manager is planning for a particular level of production in the long run. This chapter pres-ents the fundamentals of the theory of production and the theory of cost in the short run.

8.1 SOME GENERAL CONCEPTS IN PRODUCTION AND COST

production
The creation of goods and services from inputs or resources.

Production is the creation of goods and services from inputs or resources, such as labor, machinery and other capital equipment, land, raw materials, and so on. Obviously, when a company such as Ford makes a truck or car or when Exxon-Mobil refines a gallon of gasoline, the activity is production. But production goes much further than that. A doctor produces medical services, a teacher produces education, and a singer produces entertainment. So production involves services as well as making the goods people buy. Production is also undertaken by governments and nonprofit organizations. A city police department produces protection, a public school produces education, and a hospital produces health care.

In the following chapters, we will analyze production within the framework of business firms using inputs to produce goods rather than services. It is conceptually easier to visualize the production of cars, trucks, or refrigerators than the production of education, health, or security, which are hard to measure and even harder to define. Nonetheless, throughout the discussion, remember that the concepts developed here apply to services as well as goods and to government production as well as firm production.

Production Functions

A production function is the link between levels of input usage and attainable levels of output. The production function formally describes the relation between physical rates of output and physical rates of input usage. With a given state of technology, the attainable quantity of output depends on the quantities of the various inputs employed in production. A **production function** is a schedule (or table or mathematical equation) showing the maximum amount of output that can be produced from any specified set of inputs, given the existing technology or state of knowledge concerning available production methods.

production function
A schedule (or table or mathematical equation) showing the maximum amount of output that can be produced from any specified set of inputs, given the existing technology.

Many different inputs are used in production. So, in the most general case, we can define maximum output Q to be a function of the level of usage of the various inputs X. That is,

$$Q = f(X_1, X_2, \ldots, X_n)$$

However, in our discussion we will generally restrict attention to the simpler case of a product whose production entails only one or two inputs. We will normally use capital and labor as the two inputs. Hence, the production function we will usually be concerned with is

$$Q = f(L, K)$$

variable proportions production
Production in which a given level of output can be produced with more than one combination of inputs.

where L and K represent, respectively, the amounts of labor and capital used in production. However, we must stress that the principles to be developed apply to situations with more than two inputs and, as well, to inputs other than capital and labor.

For most production functions, the same output can be produced using different combinations of capital and labor. For example, when less labor is used, more capital can be added to reach the same level of production. When input substitution is possible, we call this kind of production **variable proportions production.** In contrast, when there is one, and only one, ratio or mix of inputs that can be used to produce a good, we call this **fixed proportions production.** In this case, when output is expanded, usage of all inputs must be expanded at the same rate to maintain the fixed input ratio. At first glance, this might seem to be the usual condition.

fixed proportions production
Production in which one, and only one, ratio of inputs can be used to produce a good.

However, real-world examples of fixed proportions production are hard to come by. As a consequence, we will concentrate on production with variable proportions throughout this book.

Technical and Economic Efficiency

Production engineers, who are responsible for designing and managing processes for transforming inputs into goods or services, frequently speak of "efficiency" in a way that differs from managers, who are responsible for maximizing the profit generated from producing goods or services. To understand the nature and importance of this difference, we must distinguish between two types of efficiency: *technical efficiency* and *economic efficiency*.

technical efficiency
Producing the maximum output for any given combination of inputs and existing technology.

Technical efficiency is achieved when a firm produces the maximum possible output for a given combination of inputs and existing technology. Since production functions show the *maximum* output possible for any particular combination of inputs, it follows that production functions are derived assuming inputs are going to be employed in a technically efficient way. When a firm is technically efficient, every input is being utilized to the fullest extent possible, and there is no other way to get more output without using more of at least one input. And thus, for a technically efficient firm, reducing the usage of any input will necessarily cause output to fall.

Amergen Inc., a firm manufacturing electric generators, provides an excellent example of how engineers strive to achieve technical efficiency in production. Amergen's assembly-line process begins with workers manually performing five steps before the generator reaches a computer-controlled drill press. Here, the computer-controlled machine drills 36 holes in the generator, and, in doing so, two pounds of iron are removed. Using this procedure, 10 assembly-line workers and one computer-controlled drill press were producing 140 generators each day. Recently, however, a production engineer at Amergen discovered that moving the computer-controlled drill press to the *beginning* of the assembly line, ahead of the five steps performed manually, would save a significant amount of labor energy because each generator would weigh two pounds less as it moves downstream on the assembly line. The production engineer was unable to find any other change that would further increase output. Thus, Amergen's production became technically efficient: 150 generators was the maximum number of generators that could be produced using 10 laborers and one drill press.

economic efficiency
Producing a given level of output at the lowest-possible total cost.

Like the Amergen example above, engineers at most firms focus on ensuring that production takes place in a technically efficient manner. Business managers, however, are not only interested in technical efficiency but also plan to achieve *economic efficiency* in production. **Economic efficiency** is achieved when the firm produces its chosen level of output at the lowest-possible total cost. The reason managers focus on economic efficiency is simple: profit cannot be maximized unless the firm's output is produced at the lowest-possible total cost.

We can now explain the relationship between technical and economic efficiency. When a firm is economically efficient it must also be technically efficient, because minimizing total cost cannot happen if the amount of any input could be reduced without causing output to fall. However, it *is* possible to produce in a technically efficient way without achieving economic efficiency. Typically there are numerous technically efficient input combinations capable of producing any particular output level. While production engineers might be satisfied using any one of the technically efficient combinations of inputs, managers want to use *only* the combination with the lowest total cost—the economically efficient one. The input combination that turns out to be economically efficient depends crucially on the prices of the inputs. For a different set of input prices, a different technically efficient input combination will become the economically efficient one. This point is illustrated in Technical Problem 2 at the end of this chapter.

Now try Technical Problems 1–2.

Inputs in Production

When analyzing a firm's production process and the associated costs of producing the good or service, it is important for tactical decision making and strategic analysis of market competition to distinguish between several major types of inputs: *variable*, *fixed*, or *quasi-fixed*. A **variable input** is one for which the level of usage may be readily varied in order to change the level of output. Many types of labor services as well as raw materials and energy to run production facilities are variable inputs. Payments for variable inputs are called *variable costs*. Producing more output is accomplished by using greater amounts of the variable inputs, and output is reduced by using smaller amounts of the variable inputs. Thus, variable costs are directly related to the level of output.

In contrast to variable inputs, the usage of some inputs remains constant or fixed as the level of output rises or falls. There are two primary reasons why input usage may be fixed as output varies. First, when the cost of adjusting the level of input usage is prohibitively high, a manager will treat the level of usage of that input as fixed at its current level of usage. No matter how much output the firm produces—even when output is zero—the firm uses a constant amount of the input and must pay for the input even if the firm ceases production. This kind of input is called a **fixed input**, and payments for fixed inputs are called *fixed costs*. As an example of a fixed input, consider the number of aircraft operated by a commercial airline. Most airlines choose to lease, rather than buy, the aircraft in their fleets. A Boeing 737 aircraft, one of the most widely used jets, leases for about $400,000 per month, depending on the age of the aircraft and the number of passengers it can carry. Although the lengths of aircraft leases vary, 10-year leases are common for new aircraft. During this 10-year period, it is very costly to break a lease agreement and return a plane. For this reason, airlines almost always continue to pay the $400,000 per-month lease payments when demand for air travel decreases, forcing some of their planes to sit in hangars until demand picks up again. And, when airlines wish to increase the number of planes in their fleets, it can take up to 24 months to lease a new aircraft. Typically, airline managers view aircraft as fixed inputs over a one- to two-year time period.

variable input
Input for which the level of usage may be varied to increase or decrease output.

fixed input
An input for which the level of usage cannot be changed and which must be paid even if no output is produced.

The second reason for input fixity arises when, in order to produce any positive amount of output, a necessary input must be purchased in some fixed size or lump amount. Because of the inherent lumpiness or indivisibility of such inputs, producing the first unit of output requires the firm to pay for an entire "lump" of the indivisible input. Further expansion of output can be accomplished without using any more of the lumpy input. This type of fixed input is called a **quasi-fixed input** to distinguish it from an ordinary fixed input, and payments for quasi-fixed inputs are called *quasi-fixed costs*. Although fixed and quasi-fixed inputs are both used in constant amounts as output varies, fixed inputs must be paid even if output is zero while quasi-fixed inputs need *not* be purchased if output is zero.

Quasi-fixed inputs are rather common in many industries. Consider a broadcast radio station: To broadcast the first minute of radio news and entertainment, one entire radio antenna tower must be purchased and installed. Increasing transmission time from one minute all the way up to 24 hours, seven days a week, still requires only one antenna tower. Or consider a doctor's office: The amount of electricity used for lighting the office and examination rooms does not vary with the number of patients the doctor examines—unless the lights are turned off when examination rooms are empty.

Even though examples can be found in a wide variety of industries, quasi-fixed inputs only play an important role in business strategy when these costs are relatively large in relation to variable costs of production. For the rest of this chapter and most of the remaining chapters in this book, we will largely ignore *quasi*-fixed inputs in our production and cost analysis to avoid any confusion about the nature of fixed costs. Unless we specifically state that an input is a *quasi*-fixed input, we will treat all *fixed* inputs as "ordinary" fixed inputs: a fixed amount of the input is employed for all output levels, and must be paid for even when output is zero. We must, however, discuss quasi-fixed inputs again in Chapter 9. There, we will explain how quasi-fixed inputs can affect the shape of firms' long-run average cost curves, which in turn play a crucial role in determining the number and size of the firms that compete in an industry. And then in Chapters 12 and 13, you will learn about the role quasi-fixed costs play in both a firm's decision to enter a new market and an incumbent firm's ability to strategically deter new firms from entering a market.

quasi-fixed input
A lumpy or indivisible input for which a fixed amount must be used for any positive level of output, and none is purchased when output is zero.

Now try Technical Problem 3.

Short-Run and Long-Run Production Periods

As mentioned in the introduction, economists distinguish between the *short-run* and the *long-run* periods of production. The **short run** refers to the current time span during which one or more inputs are fixed inputs and must be paid whether or not any output is produced. Changes in output during the short-run period must be accomplished exclusively by changes in the use of the variable inputs. The **long run** refers to the time period far enough in the future to allow all *fixed* inputs to become *variable* inputs. Possibly the simplest statement capturing the difference between short-run and long-run production periods is: "Firms operate in the short run and plan for the long run."

short run
Current time span during which at least one input is a fixed input.

long run
Time period far enough in the future to allow all fixed inputs to become variable inputs.

Using the simplified production function discussed previously for a firm using only two inputs, labor (L) and capital (K), we can view the production function $Q = f(L, K)$ as the *long-run* production function, because output in the long run varies by changing the amounts of the variable inputs L and K. Once a firm chooses to purchase and install a particular amount of capital, $\overline{K}$, the firm then begins operating in a short-run situation with the chosen *fixed* amount of capital. The *short-run* production function can be expressed as $Q = f(L, \overline{K})$, where capital is fixed at the current level $\overline{K}$. In the short run, with capital fixed at its current level, output varies *only* as the level of labor usage varies, and we can express the short-run production function more simply as $Q = f(L)$, where we have dropped the term $\overline{K}$ because capital usage cannot vary. The firm will continue to operate with this particular short-run production function until a time in the future is reached when it is possible to choose a different amount of capital. The length of time it takes to make a change in K (i.e., the length of the short-run period) varies widely across firms and industries. Consequently, we cannot give you a particular amount of time for the short-run production period. The short-run period lasts as long as it takes for the firm to be able to change the current levels of usage of its fixed inputs.

Now it should be clear to you why the firm's current short-run production condition is different for *every* possible level of capital the firm might choose in the long run. Simply stated, the long run consists of all possible future short-run situations—one for every level of capital the firm can employ in the future. For this reason, the long-run production period is frequently called the firm's *planning horizon*. A firm's **planning horizon** is the collection of all possible short-run situations the firm can face in the future composed of one short-run situation for every level of capital the firm can choose in the long run.

planning horizon
Set of all possible short-run situations the firm can face in the future.

> **Relation** In the short run at least one input is a fixed input, and in the long run all fixed inputs become variable inputs. The long-run planning horizon is the set of all possible short-run situations from which the firm may choose to operate in the long run.

Now try Technical Problem 4.

In the long run managers will choose the most advantageous (i.e., the optimal) amount of capital based on the price of capital relative to other inputs and the intended output level. However, when production levels or input prices change, a firm may find itself positioned with too much or too little capital in the current short-run period. When the firm has too much or too little capital in the short run, it will be able to reduce total production costs in the future by making long-run adjustments in capital usage. We will have much more to say about restructuring costs in the next chapter.

Sunk Costs versus Avoidable Costs

sunk cost in production
Payment for an input that, once made, cannot be recovered should the firm no longer wish to employ that input. Fixed costs are sunk costs.

We first introduced the concept of sunk costs in Chapter 3 when we developed rules for finding the optimal level of any activity in general. We will now apply the concept of sunk costs to a firm's costs of production and explain how sunk costs differ from *avoidable costs* of production. A **sunk cost in production** is a payment for an input that, once made, cannot be recovered should the firm no longer wish to employ that input. To keep matters clear, you should think of the firm's production occurring over a series of time periods: days, weeks, months, quarters, or years, for example. An input payment made in any particular time period is a sunk cost if that input payment cannot be recovered if it turns out in later time periods the firm no longer needs that input. For this reason, fixed costs are sunk costs of production.

Once a sunk cost is incurred, a manager should ignore the sunk cost for decision-making purposes. After an unrecoverable payment is made, it is irrelevant for all future decisions and is in no way a part of the economic cost of production in *future* time periods. Recall that the economic cost to the owners of a business for using a resource is equal to the opportunity cost to the business owners for using the resource. After a business makes a *sunk* payment for an input, the cost of using the input *thereafter* is zero, because the input cannot be returned for a refund nor can it be sold, rented, or leased to some other business to recover the sunk cost. Under some circumstances, a portion of the payment can be recovered, either as a refund or by renting or subleasing the input to another firm. In that case, only the *nonrecoverable* portion of the input payment is a sunk cost.

An example should be quite helpful here. Suppose that at 8:00 a.m. on January 1, a homebuilder pays $10,000 to a local government agency for an annual, nontransferable building license that permits the firm to build homes from January 1 to December 31. The $10,000 building license is part of the annual total cost of building homes. Although the $10,000 must be paid to start doing business for the year, once the license is paid for on January 1, it then immediately becomes a sunk cost for the rest of that year; there is no opportunity cost for using this *nontransferable* license for the remainder of the year. Thus, after January 1, the opportunity cost of owning this license is zero and should not be considered for decision-making purposes during the rest of the year. We wish to stress here that even though the sunk cost does not matter after January 1 *for decision-making purposes*, it does matter *for computing the annual cost and profit* of the firm: the cost of the license reduces profit by $10,000.

Now let's suppose that on July 1 the builder decides to quit building new homes for the rest of the year. When making the decision to cease production on July 1, the builder should completely ignore the $10,000 sunk cost of the license, because none of the sunk payment can be recovered when deciding to shut down new construction. But consider this twist: What if the local building agency offers a one-time bailout for distressed homebuilders by refunding one-fourth of the annual license fee (i.e., $2,500) at any time during the year for builders that cease production. With this bailout option, the sunk cost of the license drops to $7,500 and the economic cost of using the license for the remainder of the year rises from zero to $2,500.

Avoidable costs are the opposite of sunk costs. An **avoidable cost in production** is an input payment that a firm can recover or avoid paying should the manager no longer wish to use that input. Avoidable costs *do* matter in decision making and should *not* be ignored. In our previous example, when the building agency

avoidable cost in production
Payment for an input that a firm can recover or avoid paying should the firm no longer wish to use that input. Variable costs and quasi-fixed costs are avoidable costs.

TABLE 8.1
Inputs in Production

Input type	Payment	Relation to output	Avoidable or sunk?	Employed in short run (SR) or long run (LR)?
Variable input	Variable cost	Direct	Avoidable	Both *SR* and *LR*
Fixed input	Fixed costs	Constant	Sunk	Only *SR*
Quasi-fixed input	Quasi-fixed cost	Constant	Avoidable	If required: *SR* and *LR*

offered a bailout, $2,500 of the total cost of the building permit became an avoidable cost. The cost of variable inputs and quasi-fixed inputs are always avoidable costs in production.[1] As you will see in upcoming chapters, the distinction between avoidable and sunk costs plays a critical role in decisions about shutting down production, entering new markets, and exiting markets in which the firm currently operates.

This completes our discussion of general production and cost relations. Table 8.1 summarizes the distinguishing characteristics of the three major types of productive inputs. As you can see from the table and our discussion in this section, short-run production always requires *both* variable and fixed inputs, and may sometimes require one or more quasi-fixed inputs. Long-run production employs only avoidable inputs, which includes variable inputs and sometimes quasi-fixed inputs, but never includes fixed inputs.

Now try Technical Problem 5.

8.2 PRODUCTION IN THE SHORT RUN

We begin the analysis of production in the short run with the simplest kind of short-run situation: only *one* variable input and *one* fixed input

$$Q = f(L, \overline{K})$$

The firm has chosen the level of capital (made its investment decision), so capital is fixed in amount. Once the level of capital is fixed, the only way the firm can change its output is by changing the amount of labor it employs.

Total Product

Suppose a firm with a production function of the form $Q = f(L, K)$ can, in the long run, choose levels of both labor and capital between 0 and 10 units. A production function giving the maximum amount of output that can be produced from every possible combination of labor and capital is shown in Table 8.2. For example, from the table, 4 units of labor combined with 3 units of capital can produce a maximum of 325 units of output; 6 labor and 6 capital can produce a maximum of 655 units of output; and so on. Note that with 0 capital, no output can be produced regardless of the level of labor usage. Likewise, with 0 labor, there can be no output.

---

[1]Because quasi-fixed costs are avoidable costs, economists sometimes call the cost of quasi-fixed inputs either "avoidable fixed costs" or "nonsunk fixed costs." We will always use the more traditional name, "quasi-fixed costs."

TABLE 8.2

A Production Function

					Units of capital (K)						
	0	**1**	**2**	**3**	**4**	**5**	**6**	**7**	**8**	**9**	**10**
0	0	0	0	0	0	0	0	0	0	0	0
1	0	25	52	74	90	100	108	114	118	120	121
2	0	55	112	162	198	224	242	252	258	262	264
3	0	83	170	247	303	342	369	384	394	400	403
4	0	108	220	325	400	453	488	511	527	535	540
5	0	125	258	390	478	543	590	631	653	663	670
6	0	137	286	425	523	598	655	704	732	744	753
7	0	141	304	453	559	643	708	766	800	814	825
8	0	143	314	474	587	679	753	818	857	873	885
9	0	141	318	488	609	708	789	861	905	922	935
10	0	137	314	492	617	722	809	887	935	953	967

(Left axis label: Units of labor (L))

Once the level of capital is fixed, the firm is in the short run, and output can be changed only by varying the amount of labor employed. Assume now that the capital stock is fixed at 2 units of capital. The firm is in the short run and can vary output only by varying the usage of labor (the variable input). The column in Table 8.2 under 2 units of capital gives the total output, or total product of labor, for 0 through 10 workers. This column, for which $K = 2$, represents the short-run production function when capital is fixed at 2 units.

These total products are reproduced in column 2 of Table 8.3 for each level of labor usage in column 1. Thus, columns 1 and 2 in Table 8.3 define a production

TABLE 8.3

Total, Average, and Marginal Products of Labor (with capital fixed at 2 units)

(1) Number of workers (L)	(2) Total product (Q)	(3) Average product (AP = Q/L)	(4) Marginal product (MP = ΔQ/ΔL)
0	0	—	—
1	52	52	52
2	112	56	60
3	170	56.7	58
4	220	55	50
5	258	51.6	38
6	286	47.7	28
7	304	43.4	18
8	314	39.3	10
9	318	35.3	4
10	314	31.4	−4

function of the form $Q = f(L, \overline{K})$, where $\overline{K} = 2$. In this example, total product (Q) rises with increases in labor up to a point (9 workers) and then declines. While total product does eventually *fall* as more workers are employed, managers would not (knowingly) hire additional workers if they knew output would fall. In Table 8.3, for example, a manager can hire either 8 workers or 10 workers to produce 314 units of output. Obviously, the economically efficient amount of labor to hire to produce 314 units is 8 workers.

Average and Marginal Products

Average and marginal products are obtained from the production function and may be viewed merely as different ways of looking at the same information. The **average product of labor** (*AP*) is the total product divided by the number of workers

$$AP = Q/L$$

In our example, average product, shown in column 3, first rises, reaches a maximum at 56.7, then declines thereafter.

The **marginal product of labor** (*MP*) is the additional output attributable to using one additional worker with the use of all other inputs fixed (in this case, at 2 units of capital). That is,

$$MP = \Delta Q/\Delta L$$

where Δ means "the change in." The marginal product schedule associated with the production function in Table 8.3 is shown in column 4 of the table. Because no output can be produced with 0 workers, the first worker adds 52 units of output; the second adds 60 units (i.e., increases output from 52 to 112); and so on. Note that increasing the amount of labor from 9 to 10 actually decreases output from 318 to 314. Thus the marginal product of the 10th worker is negative. In this example, marginal product first increases as the amount of labor increases, then decreases, and finally becomes negative. This is a pattern frequently assumed in economic analysis.

In this example, the production function assumes that labor, the variable input, is increased one worker at a time. But we can think of the marginal product of an input when more than 1 unit is added. At a fixed level of capital, suppose that 20 units of labor can produce 100 units of output and that 30 units of labor can produce 200 units of output. In this case, output increases by 100 units as labor increases by 10. Thus

$$MP = \frac{\Delta Q}{\Delta L} = \frac{100}{10} = 10$$

Output increases by 10 units for each additional worker hired.

We might emphasize that we speak of the marginal product of labor, not the marginal product of a particular laborer. We assume that all workers are the same, in the sense that if we reduce the number of workers from 8 to 7 in Table 8.3, total

**average product
of labor (AP)**
Total product (output)
divided by the number
of workers (AP = Q/L).

**marginal product
of labor (MP)**
The additional output
attributable to using one
additional worker with
the use of all other inputs
fixed (MP = ΔQ/ΔL).

FIGURE 8.1

Total, Average, and Marginal Products ($\bar{K} = 2$)

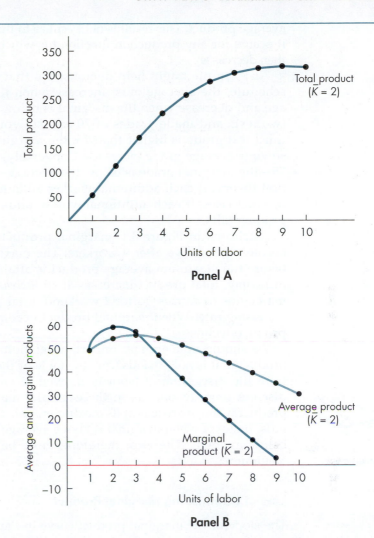

Total product
($\bar{K} = 2$)

Units of labor

Panel A

Average product
($\bar{K} = 2$)

Marginal
product ($\bar{K} = 2$)

Units of labor

Panel B

product falls from 314 to 304 regardless of which of the 8 workers is released. Thus the order of hiring makes no difference; a third worker adds 58 units of output no matter who is hired.

Figure 8.1 shows graphically the relations among the total, average, and marginal products set forth in Table 8.3. In Panel A, total product increases up to 9 workers, then decreases. Panel B incorporates a common assumption made in production theory: Average product first rises then falls. When average product is increasing, marginal product is greater than average product (after the first worker, at which they are equal). When average product is decreasing, marginal product is less than average product. This result is not peculiar to this particular production function; it occurs for any production function for which average product first increases then decreases.

An example might help demonstrate that for any average and marginal schedule, the average must increase when the marginal is above the average and decrease when the marginal is below the average. If you have taken two tests and made grades of 70 and 80, your average grade is 75. If your third test grade is higher than 75, the marginal grade is above the average, so your average grade increases. Conversely, if your third grade is less than 75—the marginal grade is below the average—your average falls. In production theory, if each additional worker adds more than the average, average product rises; if each additional worker adds less than the average, average product falls.

As shown in Figure 8.1, marginal product first increases then decreases, becoming negative after 9 workers. The maximum marginal product occurs before the maximum average product is attained. When marginal product is *increasing*, total product increases at an *increasing* rate. When marginal product begins to *decrease* (after 2 workers), total product begins to increase at a *decreasing* rate. When marginal product becomes negative (10 workers), total product declines.

We should note another important relation between average and marginal product that is not obvious from the table or the graph but does follow directly from the discussion. If labor is allowed to vary continuously rather than in discrete units of one, as in the example, marginal product equals average product when average is at its maximum. This follows because average product must increase when marginal is above average and decrease when marginal is below average. The two, therefore, must be equal when average is at its maximum.

Now try Technical
Problems 6, 7.

Law of Diminishing Marginal Product

law of diminishing marginal product
The principle that as the number of units of the variable input increases, other inputs held constant, a point will be reached beyond which the marginal product decreases.

The slope of the marginal product curve in Panel B of Figure 8.1 illustrates an important principle, the **law of diminishing marginal product**. As the number of units of the variable input increases, other inputs held constant, there exists a point beyond which the marginal product of the variable input declines. When the amount of the variable input is small relative to the fixed inputs, more intensive utilization of fixed inputs by variable inputs may initially increase the marginal product of the variable input as this input is increased. Nonetheless, a point is reached beyond which an increase in the use of the variable input yields progressively less additional output. Each additional unit has, on average, fewer units of the fixed inputs with which to work.

To illustrate the concept of diminishing marginal returns, consider the kitchen at Mel's Hot Dogs, a restaurant that sells hot dogs, french fries, and soft drinks. Mel's kitchen has one gas range for cooking the hot dogs, one deep-fryer for cooking french fries, and one soft-drink dispenser. One cook in the kitchen can prepare 15 meals (consisting of a hot dog, fries, and soft drink) per hour. Two cooks can prepare 35 meals per hour. The marginal product of the second cook is 20 meals per hour, five more than the marginal product of the first cook. One cook possibly concentrates on making fries and soft drinks while the other cook prepares hot dogs. Adding a third cook results in 50 meals per hour being produced, so the marginal product of the third worker is 15 (= 50 − 35) additional meals per hour.

Therefore, after the second cook, the marginal product of additional cooks begins to decline. The fourth cook, for example, can increase the total number of meals prepared to 60 meals per hour—a marginal product of just 10 additional meals. A fifth cook adds only five extra meals per hour, an increase to 65 meals. Even though the third, fourth, and fifth cooks increase the total number of meals prepared each hour, their marginal contribution is diminishing because the amount of space and equipment in the kitchen is fixed (i.e., capital is fixed). Mel could increase the size of the kitchen or add more cooking equipment to increase the productivity of all workers. The point at which diminishing returns set in would then possibly occur at a higher level of employment.

The marginal product of additional cooks can even become negative. For example, adding a sixth cook reduces the number of meals from 65 to 60. The marginal product of the sixth cook is −5. Do not confuse *negative* marginal product with *diminishing* marginal product. Diminishing marginal product sets in with the third cook, but marginal product does not become negative until the sixth cook is hired. Obviously, the manager would not want to hire a sixth cook, because output would fall. The manager would hire the third, or fourth, or fifth cook, even though marginal product is decreasing, if more than 35, 50, or 60 meals must be prepared. As we will demonstrate, managers do in fact employ variable inputs beyond the point of diminishing returns but not to the point of negative marginal product.

The law of diminishing marginal product is a simple statement concerning the relation between marginal product and the rate of production that comes from observing real-world production processes. While the eventual diminishing of marginal product cannot be proved or refuted mathematically, it is worth noting that a contrary observation has never been recorded. That is why the relation is called a law.

Changes in Fixed Inputs

The production function shown in Figure 8.1 and also in Table 8.3 was derived from the production function shown in Table 8.2 by holding the capital stock fixed at 2 units ($\overline{K} = 2$). As can be seen in Table 8.2, when different amounts of capital are used, total product changes for each level of labor usage. Indeed, each column in Table 8.2 represents a different short-run production function, each corresponding to the particular level at which capital stock is fixed. Because the output associated with every level of labor usage changes when capital stock

TABLE 8.4

The Effect of Changes in Capital Stock

L	$\overline{K} = 2$			$\overline{K} = 3$		
	Q	AP	MP	Q	AP	MP
0	0	—	—	0	—	—
1	52	52	52	74	74	74
2	112	56	60	162	81	88
3	170	56.7	58	247	82.3	85
4	220	55	50	325	81.3	78
5	258	51.6	38	390	78	65
6	286	47.7	28	425	70.8	35
7	304	43.4	18	453	64.7	28
8	314	39.3	10	474	59.3	21
9	318	35.3	4	488	54.2	14
10	314	31.4	−4	492	49.2	4

changes, a change in the level of capital causes a *shift* in the total product curve for labor. Because total product changes for every level of labor usage, average product and marginal product of labor also must change at every level of labor usage.

Referring once more to Table 8.2, notice what happens when the capital stock is increased from 2 to 3 units. The total product of 3 workers increases from 170 to 247, as shown in column 3. The average product of three workers increases from 56.7 to 82.3 (= 247/3). The marginal product of the third worker increases from 58 to 85 [$\Delta Q/\Delta L = (247 - 162)/1 = 85$]. Table 8.4 shows the total, average, and marginal product schedules for two levels of capital stock, $\overline{K} = 2$ and $\overline{K} = 3$. As you can see, *TP*, *AP*, and *MP* all increase at each level of labor usage as *K* increases from 2 to 3 units. Figure 8.2 shows how a change in the fixed amount of capital shifts the product curves. In Panel A, increasing $\overline{K}$ causes the total product curve to shift upward, and in Panel B, the increase in $\overline{K}$ causes both *AP* and *MP* to shift upward. Note that the two capital levels in Figure 8.2 represent two of the 10 possible short-run situations (see Table 8.2) comprising the firm's long-run planning horizon.

We are now ready to derive the cost structure of the firm in the short run. For any level of output the manager wishes to produce, the economically efficient amount of labor to combine with the fixed amount of capital is found from the total product curve. In Figure 8.1, if the manager wishes to produce 220 units of output, the amount of labor that will produce 220 units at the lowest total cost is 4 units. The total cost of producing 220 units of output is found by multiplying the price of labor per unit by 4 to get the total expenditure on labor; this amount is then added to the cost of the fixed input. This computation can be done for every level of output to get the short-run total cost of production. We turn now to the costs of production in the short run.

Now try Technical Problem 8.

FIGURE 8.2

Shifts in Total, Average, and Marginal Product Curves

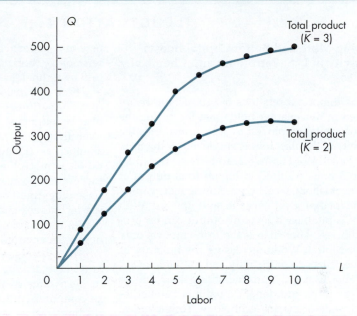

Panel A — Shift in total product when *K* increases

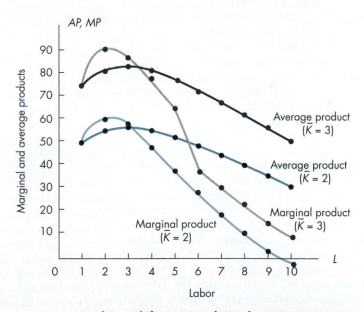

Panel B — Shifts in *MP* and *AP* when *K* increases

ILLUSTRATION 8.1

Employing More and Better Capital Boosts Productivity in U.S. Petroleum and Chemical Industries

One of the important relations of production theory established in this chapter holds that increasing the amount of capital employed by a firm increases the productivity of the *other* inputs employed by the firm. Recall in Panel A of Figure 8.2, an increase in capital from 2 to 3 units resulted in higher total output at every level of labor usage, because using more capital causes the total product curve to shift upward. With 3 units of capital, each level of output can be produced with less labor than if the firm employs only 2 units of capital. While increasing the quantity of capital boosts labor productivity and output at every level of labor usage, the productivity gained will be even greater if the additional capital input embodies advanced, state-of-the-art technology. Technological progress makes newly acquired capital equipment more productive than the firm's existing stock of capital because the older, currently employed capital is designed around less advanced technology. Thus purchasing *better* capital magnifies the increase in productivity that results from having *more* capital. This strategy of combining more and better capital to sharply increase productivity is exactly what has happened in two very important industries: crude oil production and petrochemical refining.

Petroleum-producing firms in the United States are experiencing a period of high productivity in exploration operations (the process of finding underground and undersea oil deposits) and development and production operations (the process of getting the oil to the earth's surface). The amount of new crude oil discovered and produced is increasing rapidly, even as the amount of time, labor, energy, and number of wells drilled have decreased. To achieve the impressive gains in productivity, oil-producing firms in the United States invested heavily during the 1990s in new technologies that promised to lower both the cost of finding oil deposits and the cost of getting oil out of the ground. These new technologies involve adding new and better types of capital to the exploration and production process. Three of the most important

new and better technologies are three-dimensional seismology, horizontal drilling, and new deepwater drilling technologies.

Three-dimensional (3D) views of underground rock formations provide a tremendous advantage over two-dimensional (2D) seismology techniques. Even though 3D seismological analysis costs twice as much as 2D analysis, the success rate in exploration is more than doubled and average costs of exploration decrease more than 20 percent. The 3D seismology method, coupled with horizontal drilling techniques and so-called geosteering drill bits, makes it possible to recover more of the oil in the newly discovered deposits. Deepwater drilling, which on average yields five times as much crude oil as onshore drilling does, is booming now. Advances in deepwater drilling platform technology—such as computer-controlled thrusters using coordinate readings from satellites to keep floating platforms in place—have made deep deposits in the Gulf of Mexico accessible. Some deep deposits in the Gulf of Mexico are as large as some of the oil fields in the Middle East. According to *The Wall Street Journal*, "Reserves at depths approaching a mile or more now represent the biggest single new old resource since the Middle East came on line in the 1930s."[a]

In the petrochemical industry, equally impressive advancements in technology are changing the methods and processes for obtaining fuels and valuable chemicals from crude oil. An article in *Fortune* magazine explains how this is being accomplished: "Instead of highly trained technicians manually monitoring hundreds of complex processes, the work is now done faster, smarter, and more precisely by computer. . . . The result: greater efficiency . . . and significant savings."[b] In one such project, BP (formerly British Petroleum), purchased $75 million of new capital to renovate an old petrochemical plant in Texas City. By adding computer-controlled digital automation to the old plant and equipment, the old plant was transformed into a leading producer of specialty chemicals. Adding more (and better) capital increased the productivity of the other refinery resources, making it possible to decrease the usage of some of these inputs.

According to the article in *Fortune*, overall productivity increased a "steep 55 percent," which allowed BP to relocate 10 percent of the workers at the Texas City plant to other BP refineries, and "the plant now uses 3 percent less electricity and 10 percent less natural gas."

As we explain in this chapter, productivity and costs are inversely related. All of this new and better capital makes the oil patch much more productive, which in turn makes it less costly to secure future energy supplies.

[a]Steve Liesman, "Big Oil Starts to Tap the Vast Reserves That Are Buried Far Below the Waves," *The Wall Street Journal*, July 3, 2000, p. 1.

[b]Gene Bylinsky, "Elite Factories: Two of America's Best Have Found New Life Using Digital Technology," *Fortune*, August 11, 2003.

8.3 SHORT-RUN COSTS OF PRODUCTION

Recall from the discussion of total economic cost of using resources in Chapter 1 that the opportunity cost to the owners of a firm of using resources to produce goods and services is the amount the owners give up by using these resources. We recommend that you take a few minutes before continuing with this section to review Figure 1.2 and the associated principle for measuring the total economic cost of using inputs or resources in the production of goods or services.

As noted in Chapter 1, the opportunity costs of using productive inputs can be either explicit costs or implicit costs. Explicit costs arise when a firm uses resources that it does not own and must therefore purchase in the markets for these resources. Thus the monetary payments to hire, rent, or lease resources owned by others represent the explicit opportunity costs of using market-supplied inputs. Implicit costs are the costs of using any resources the firm owns. The opportunity costs of using owner-supplied resources are the greatest earnings forgone from using resources owned by the firm in the firm's own production process. Even though no explicit monetary payment is made for the use of owner-supplied resources, $1 of implicit costs are no less (and no more) of an opportunity cost of using resources than $1 of explicit costs. Including implicit costs in both personal and business decision making is so important that we offer Illustration 8.2 to reinforce this point.

As explained in Chapter 1 and illustrated in Figure 1.2, total economic cost of using inputs in the production process is the sum of all explicit and implicit costs. Throughout the remainder of this chapter and in later chapters, when we refer to a firm's costs, we include both explicit and implicit costs, even though we will not explicitly divide them into two separate categories. In all cases, "cost" will mean the entire opportunity cost of using resources.

Short-Run Total Costs

total fixed cost (*TFC*)
The total amount paid for fixed inputs. Total fixed cost does not vary with output.

As noted earlier, in the short run the levels of use of some inputs are fixed, and the costs associated with these fixed inputs must be paid regardless of the level of output produced. Other costs vary with the level of output. **Total fixed cost (*TFC*)**

ILLUSTRATION 8.2

Implicit Costs and Household Decision Making

As we explain in the text, the implicit opportunity cost to the firm of using a resource owned by the firm equals the best possible forgone payment the firm could have received if it had rented or leased the resource to another firm or had chosen to sell the resource in the market and invest the returns from the sale rather than retain the input for its own use. Producers decide how much of a resource to use on the basis of the opportunity cost of the resource, regardless of whether that opportunity cost is an explicit cost or an implicit cost. You should not get the impression that opportunity costs, particularly implicit costs, are relevant only to decisions about production. All decision makers, including household decision makers, must consider both explicit and implicit costs to get the most from their limited resources.

Consider homeowners who pay off their mortgages early. Suppose a homeowner wins the state lottery and decides to pay off a $100,000 balance on a home mortgage. After "burning the mortgage," the homeowner no longer must make monthly mortgage payments, an explicit cost of homeownership. Ignoring maintenance costs and changes in the market value of the home, is the cost of owning the home now zero? Certainly not. By using his or her own financial resources to pay off the mortgage, the homeowner must forgo the income that could

have been earned if the $100,000 had been invested elsewhere. If the homeowner could earn 7.5 percent on a certificate of deposit, the implicit cost (opportunity cost) of paying off the mortgage is $7,500 per year. Smart lottery winners do not pay off their mortgages if the interest rate on the mortgage is less than the rate of interest they can earn by putting their money into investments no more risky than homeownership. They do pay off their mortgages if the rate on the mortgage is higher than the rate they can earn by making investments no more risky than homeownership.

Another example of how implicit costs affect decisions made by households involves the story of Jamie Lashbrook, an 11-year-old boy from Brooksville, Florida. Jamie won two tickets to Super Bowl XXV by kicking a field goal before a Tampa Bay Buccaneers game. Jamie quickly discovered that using the two "free" tickets does in fact involve an opportunity cost. Less than one day after winning the tickets, Jamie's father had received more than a dozen requests from people who were willing to pay as much as $1,200 for each ticket. Although the boy *obtained* the tickets at little or no cost, *using* these tickets involved an implicit cost—the payment Jamie could have received if he had sold the tickets in the marketplace rather than using them himself. We don't know if Jamie actually went to the Super Bowl or not, but even this 11-year-old decision maker knew better than to ignore the implicit cost of using a resource.

---

total variable cost (*TVC*)
The amount paid for variable inputs. Total variable cost increases with increases in output.

is the sum of the short-run fixed costs that must be paid regardless of the level of output produced. **Total variable cost (*TVC*)** is the sum of the amounts spent for each of the variable inputs used. Total variable cost increases as output increases. Short-run **total cost (*TC*)**, which also increases as output increases, is the sum of total variable and total fixed cost:

$$TC = TVC + TFC$$

total cost (*TC*)
The sum of total fixed cost and total variable cost. Total cost increases with increases in output ($TC = TFC + TVC$).

To show the relation between output (Q) and total cost in the short run, we present the simplest case. A firm uses two inputs, capital and labor, to produce output. The total fixed cost paid for capital is $6,000 per period. In Table 8.5 column 2, the total fixed cost (*TFC*) for each of 7 possible levels of output is $6,000, including 0 units of output. Column 3 shows the total variable cost (*TVC*) for each level of output. Total variable cost is 0 when output is 0 because the firm hires

TABLE 8.5

Short-Run Total Cost Schedules

(1) Output (Q)	(2) Total fixed cost (TFC)	(3) Total variable cost (TVC)	(4) Total Cost (TC) TC = TFC + TVC
0	$6,000	$ 0	$ 6,000
100	6,000	4,000	10,000
200	6,000	6,000	12,000
300	6,000	9,000	15,000
400	6,000	14,000	20,000
500	6,000	22,000	28,000
600	6,000	34,000	40,000

none of the variable input, labor, if it decides not to produce. As the level of production rises, more labor must be hired, and total variable cost rises, as shown in column 3. Total cost (TC) is obtained by adding total fixed cost and total variable cost. Column 4 in Table 8.5, which shows the total cost of production for various levels of output, is the sum of columns 2 and 3.

Figure 8.3 shows the total cost curves associated with the total cost schedules in Table 8.5. The total-fixed-cost curve is horizontal at $6,000, indicating that TFC is constant for all levels of output. Total variable cost starts at the origin, because the firm incurs no variable costs if production is zero; TVC rises thereafter as output increases, because to produce more the firm must use more resources, thereby increasing cost. Since total cost is the sum of TFC and TVC, the TC

FIGURE 8.3

Total Cost Curves

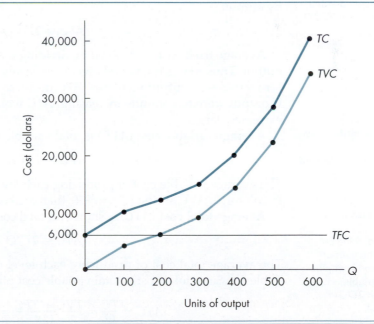

TABLE 8.6

Average and Marginal Cost Schedules

(1) Output (Q)	(2) Average fixed cost (AFC) AFC = TFC/Q	(3) Average variable cost (AVC) AVC = TVC/Q	(4) Average total cost (ATC) ATC = TC/Q	(5) Short-run marginal cost (SMC) SMC = ΔTC/ΔQ
0	—	—	—	—
100	$60	$40	$100	$ 40
200	30	30	60	20
300	20	30	50	30
400	15	35	50	50
500	12	44	56	80
600	10	56.7	66.7	120

curve lies above the *TVC* curve by an amount exactly equal to $6,000 (*TFC*) at each output level. Consequently, *TC* and *TVC* are parallel and have identical shapes.

Average and Marginal Costs

A more useful way of depicting the firm's cost structure is through the behavior of short-run average and marginal costs. Table 8.6 presents the average and marginal costs derived from the total cost schedules in Table 8.5. First, consider average fixed cost, given in column 2. **Average fixed cost (*AFC*)** is total fixed cost divided by output:

average fixed cost (AFC)
Total fixed cost divided by output (*AFC* = *TFC/Q*).

$$AFC = TFC/Q$$

Average fixed cost is obtained by dividing the fixed cost (in this case $6,000) by output. Thus *AFC* is high at relatively low levels of output; because the denominator increases as output increases, *AFC* decreases over the entire range of output. If output were to continue increasing, *AFC* would approach 0 as output became extremely large.

average variable cost (AVC)
Total variable cost divided by output (*AVC* = *TVC/Q*).

Average variable cost (*AVC*) is total variable cost divided by output:

$$AVC = TVC/Q$$

The average variable cost of producing each level of output in Table 8.6 is shown in column 3. *AVC* at first falls to $30, then increases thereafter.

average total cost (ATC)
Total cost divided by output or the sum of average fixed cost plus average variable cost (*ATC* = *TC/Q* = *AVC* + *AFC*).

Average total cost (*ATC*) is short-run total cost divided by output:

$$ATC = TC/Q$$

The average total cost of producing each level of output is given in column 4 of Table 8.6. Since total cost is total variable cost plus total fixed cost,

$$ATC = \frac{TC}{Q} = \frac{TVC + TFC}{Q} = AVC + AFC$$

The average total cost in the table has the same general structure as average variable cost. It first declines, reaches a minimum at $50, then increases thereafter. The minimum ATC is attained at a larger output (between 300 and 400) than that at which AVC attains its minimum (between 200 and 300). This result is not peculiar to the cost schedules in Table 8.6; as we will show later, it follows for all average cost schedules of the general type shown here.

short-run marginal cost (SMC)
The change in either total variable cost or total cost per unit change in output ($\Delta TVC/\Delta Q = \Delta TC/\Delta Q$).

Finally, **short-run marginal cost (SMC)** is defined as the change in either total variable cost or total cost per unit change in output

$$SMC = \frac{\Delta TVC}{\Delta Q} = \frac{\Delta TC}{\Delta Q}$$

The two definitions are the same because when output increases, total cost increases by the same amount as the increase in total variable cost. Thus as $TC = TFC + TVC$,

$$SMC = \frac{\Delta TC}{\Delta Q} = \frac{\Delta TFC}{\Delta Q} + \frac{\Delta TVC}{\Delta Q} = 0 + \frac{\Delta TVC}{\Delta Q} = \frac{\Delta TVC}{\Delta Q}$$

The short-run marginal cost is given in column 5 of Table 8.6. It is the per-unit change in cost resulting from a change in output when the use of the variable input changes. For example, when output increases from 0 to 100, both total and variable costs increase by $4,000. The change in cost per unit of output is, therefore, $4,000 divided by the increase in output, 100, or $40. Thus, the marginal cost over this range is $40. It can be seen that MC first declines, reaches a minimum of $20, then rises. Note that minimum marginal cost is attained at an output (between 100 and 200) below that at which either AVC or ATC attains its minimum. Marginal cost equals AVC and ATC at their respective minimum levels. We will return to the reason for this result later.

The average and marginal cost schedules in columns 3, 4, and 5 are shown graphically in Figure 8.4. Average fixed cost is not graphed because it is a curve that simply declines over the entire range of output and because, as you will see, it is irrelevant for decision making. The curves in Figure 8.4 depict the properties of the cost schedules we have discussed. All three curves decline at first and then rise. Marginal cost equals AVC and ATC at each of their minimum levels. Marginal cost is below AVC and ATC when they are declining and above them when they are increasing. Since AFC decreases over the entire range of output and since $ATC = AVC + AFC$, ATC becomes increasingly close to AVC as output increases. As we show later, these are the general properties of typically assumed average and marginal cost curves.

General Short-Run Average and Marginal Cost Curves

Most of the properties of cost curves set forth thus far in this section were derived by using the specific cost schedules in Tables 8.5 and 8.6. These properties also hold for general cost curves when output and therefore cost vary continuously

FIGURE 8.4

**Average and Marginal
Cost Curves**

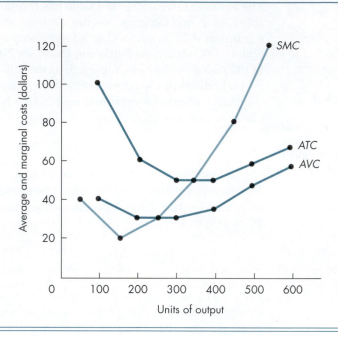

FIGURE 8.5

**Short-Run Average and
Marginal Cost Curves**

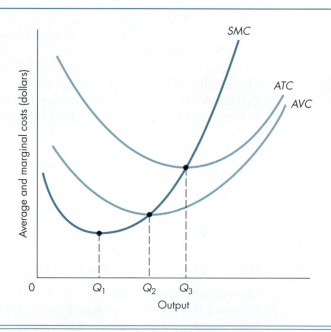

rather than discretely. These typical average and marginal cost curves are shown in Figure 8.5. These curves show the following:

> **Relations**   (1) *AFC* declines continuously, approaching both axes asymptotically (as shown by the decreasing distance between *ATC* and *AVC*). (2) *AVC* first declines, reaches a minimum at Q_2, and rises thereafter. When *AVC* is at its minimum, *SMC* equals *AVC*. (3) *ATC* first declines, reaches a minimum at Q_3, and rises thereafter. When *ATC* is at its minimum, *SMC* equals *ATC*. (4) *SMC* first declines, reaches a minimum at Q_1, and rises thereafter. *SMC* equals both *AVC* and *ATC* when these curves are at their minimum values. Furthermore, *SMC* lies below both *AVC* and *ATC* over the range for which these curves decline; *SMC* lies above them when they are rising.

In general, the reason marginal cost crosses *AVC* and *ATC* at their respective minimum points follows from the definitions of the cost curves. If marginal cost is below average variable cost, each additional unit of output adds less to cost than the average variable cost of that unit. Thus average variable cost must decline over this range. When *SMC* is above *AVC*, each additional unit of output adds more to cost than *AVC*. In this case, *AVC* must rise.

So when *SMC* is less than *AVC*, average variable cost is falling; when *SMC* is greater than *AVC*, average variable cost is rising. Thus *SMC* must equal *AVC* at the minimum point on *AVC*. Exactly the same reasoning can be used to show that *SMC* crosses *ATC* at the minimum point on the latter curve.

Now try Technical Problems 9–10.

8.4 RELATIONS BETWEEN SHORT-RUN COSTS AND PRODUCTION

We will now describe, in some detail, exactly how the short-run cost curves set forth in the preceding section are derived. As you will recall, once the total variable cost (*TVC*) and the total fixed cost (*TFC*) are developed, all the other costs—*TC, ATC, AVC, AFC,* and *SMC*—can be derived directly from the simple formulas that define these costs. Total fixed cost is simply the sum of the payments for the fixed inputs. As we will now show, total variable cost is derived directly from the short-run production function. In addition to deriving *TVC* from the total product curve, we also show how average variable cost can be derived from average product and how marginal cost can be derived from marginal product.

Total Costs and the Short-Run Production Function

We begin with the short-run production function shown in columns 1 and 2 in Table 8.7. If 4 units of labor are employed, the firm can produce (a maximum of) 100 units; if 6 units of labor are employed, the firm's maximum output is 200 units; and so on. (Remember, the production function assumes technical efficiency.) For this example, we assume the wage rate—the price of a unit of labor services (*w*)— is $1,000. Total variable cost for any given level of output is simply the amount of labor employed multiplied by the wage rate

$$TVC = w \times L$$

Column 3 shows the total variable costs associated with the various levels of output. Obviously, *TVC* is derived directly from the short-run production function.

TABLE 8.7

Short-Run Production and Short-Run Total Costs

Short-run production		Short-run total costs		
(1) Labor (L)	(2) Output (Q)	(3) Total variable cost (TVC = wL)	(4) Total fixed cost (TFC = rK)	(5) Total cost (TC = wL + rK)
0	0	0	$6,000	$ 6,000
4	100	$ 4,000	6,000	10,000
6	200	6,000	6,000	12,000
9	300	9,000	6,000	15,000
14	400	14,000	6,000	20,000
22	500	22,000	6,000	28,000
34	600	34,000	6,000	40,000

Note that TVC is derived for a particular wage rate. If the wage rate increases, TVC must increase at each level of output.

To see how total fixed cost is determined, assume that the short-run production function in columns 1 and 2 is derived for a firm using 3 units of capital in the short run ($\bar{K} = 3$) and that capital costs $2,000 per unit to employ. Thus the total fixed cost is

$$TFC = r \times K = \$2,000 \times 3 = \$6,000$$

where r is the price of a unit of capital services. Column 4 shows the total fixed cost for each level of output.

Short-run total cost (TC) is the sum of the total variable cost and total fixed costs of production

$$TC = wL + rK$$

Column 5 in Table 8.7 shows the total cost of producing each level of output in the short run when the firm's level of capital is fixed at three units. Note that these total cost schedules are the same as the ones in Table 8.5. Using the formulas set forth earlier in this chapter, we could easily derive AVC and SMC from the TVC schedule and ATC from the TC schedule. However, we can give you more of an understanding of the reasons for the typical shape of these curves by showing the relation between AVC and AP and SMC and MP, which we discuss next.

Average Variable Cost and Average Product

Table 8.8 reproduces the production function in columns 1 and 2 of Table 8.7. The average product of labor ($AP = Q/L$) is calculated in column 3 of Table 8.8. The relation between AVC and AP can be seen as follows: Consider the 100 units of output that can be produced by 4 workers. The total variable cost of using 4 workers is found by multiplying $1,000—the wage rate—by the 4 workers employed:

$$TVC = \$1,000 \times 4$$

TABLE 8.8

Average and Marginal Relations between Cost and Production

		Short-run production			Short-run costs	
(1)	(2)	(3) AP (Q/L)	(4) MP ($\Delta Q/\Delta L$)		(5) AVC (w/AP)	(6) SMC (w/MP)
Labor	Q					
0	0	—	—		—	—
4	100	25	25		$40	$ 40
6	200	33.33	50		30	20
9	300	33.33	33.33		30	30
14	400	28.57	20		35	50
22	500	22.73	12.50		44	80
34	600	17.65	8.33		56.67	120

The 100 units of output produced by the 4 workers can be found by multiplying 25—the average product—by the 4 workers employed:

$$Q = 25 \times 4$$

Because AVC is TVC divided by Q,

$$AVC = \frac{TVC}{Q} = \frac{\$1,000 \times 4}{25 \times 4} = \frac{\$1,000}{25} = \frac{w}{AP} = \$40$$

From this numerical illustration, you can see that AVC can be calculated as either TVC/Q or w/AP. It is easy to show that this relation holds in general for any production function with one variable input. In general,

$$AVC = \frac{TVC}{Q} = \frac{w \times L}{AP \times L} = \frac{w}{AP}$$

In Table 8.8, column 5 shows the value of average variable cost calculated by dividing $1,000 by average product at each level of output. You should verify that the computation of AVC in Table 8.8 ($AVC = w/AP$) yields the same values for AVC as the values obtained for AVC in Table 8.6 ($AVC = TVC/Q$).

Marginal Cost and Marginal Product

The relation between marginal cost and marginal product is also illustrated in Table 8.8. Column 4 shows the marginal product associated with the additional labor employed to increase production in 100-unit intervals. For example, to increase production from 100 to 200 units, two additional workers are required (an increase from 4 to 6 units of labor), so the marginal product is 50 units per additional worker. The change in total variable cost associated with going from 100 to 200 units of output is $2,000—$1,000 for each of the two extra workers. So,

$$SMC = \frac{\Delta TVC}{\Delta Q} = \frac{\$1,000 \times 2}{50 \times 2} = \frac{w}{MP} = \$20$$

Repeating this calculation for each of the 100-unit increments to output, you can see that the marginal cost at each level of output is the wage rate divided by the marginal product, and this will be true for any production function with one variable input, since

$$SMC = \frac{\Delta TVC}{\Delta Q} = \frac{\Delta(w \times L)}{\Delta Q} = w\frac{\Delta L}{\Delta Q} = \frac{w}{MP}$$

Now try Technical
Problems 11–12.

You can verify that the values for marginal cost calculated as w/MP in Table 8.8 are identical to the values for marginal cost calculated as $\Delta TC/\Delta Q$ in Table 8.6.

The Graphical Relation between *AVC, SMC, AP*, and *MP*

Figure 8.6 illustrates the relation between cost curves and product curves. We have constructed a typical set of product and cost curves in Panels A and B, respectively. Assume the wage rate is $21, and consider first the product and cost curves over the range of labor usage from 0 to 500 units of labor. In Panel A, marginal product lies above average product over this range, so average product is rising. Because marginal cost is inversely related to marginal product ($SMC = w/MP$) and average variable cost is inversely related to average product ($AVC = w/AP$), and because both MP and AP are rising, both SMC and AVC are falling as output rises when labor usage increases (up to points A and B in Panel A). Marginal product reaches a maximum value of 9 at 500 units of labor usage (point A). The level of output that corresponds to using 500 units of labor is found by using the relation $AP = Q/L$. Since $AP = 6.5$ and $L = 500$, Q must be 3,250 ($= 6.5 \times 500$). Thus marginal product reaches its *maximum* value at 3,250 units of output, and, consequently, marginal cost must reach its *minimum* value at 3,250 units of output. At 3,250 units, marginal cost is equal to $2.33 ($= w/MP = $21/9$), and average variable cost is equal to $3.23 ($= w/AP = $21/6.5$). Points A and B in Panel A correspond to points a and b in Panel B of Figure 8.6.

One of the most important relations between production and cost curves in the short run involves the effect of the law of diminishing marginal product on the marginal cost of production. While marginal product generally rises at first, the law of diminishing marginal product states that when capital is fixed, a point will eventually be reached beyond which marginal product must begin to fall. As marginal product begins to fall, marginal cost begins to rise. In Figure 8.6, marginal product begins to fall beyond 500 units of labor (beyond point A in Panel A). Marginal cost begins to rise beyond 3,250 units of output (beyond point a in Panel B).

Consider the range of labor usage between 500 and 800 units of labor. Marginal product is falling, but while marginal product still lies above average product, average product continues to rise up to point C, where $MP = AP$. At point C, average product reaches its maximum value at 800 units of labor. When 800 units of labor are employed, 5,600 units of output are produced ($5,600 = AP \times L = 7 \times 800$). Thus, at 5,600 units of output, marginal cost and average variable cost are both equal to $3

$$SMC = w/MP = \$21/7 = \$3$$

$$AVC = w/AP = \$21/7 = \$3$$

FIGURE 8.6
**Short-Run Production
and Cost Relations**

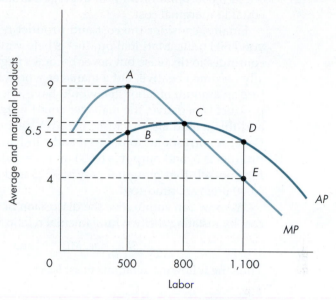

Panel A — Product curves

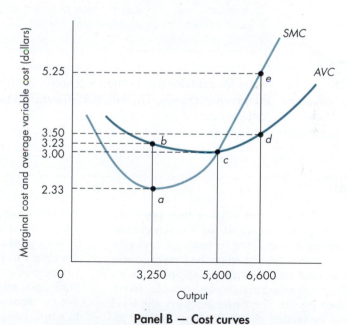

Panel B — Cost curves

So, at 5,600 units of output, average variable cost reaches its minimum and is equal to marginal cost.

Finally, consider the cost and product relations as labor usage increases beyond 800 units. Marginal product is below average product, and average product continues to decrease but never becomes negative. Marginal product will eventually become negative, but a manager who wishes to minimize costs would never hire an amount of labor that would have a negative marginal product. If marginal product is negative, the manager could *increase* output by *decreasing* labor usage, and this would also decrease the firm's expenditure on labor. Points D and E in Panel A correspond to points d and e in Panel B. At 1,100 units of labor, average product is 6, and output is 6,600 units ($= AP \times L = 6 \times 1,100$). You should verify for yourself that marginal cost is $5.25 and average variable cost is $3.50 when 6,600 units are produced.

We now can summarize the discussion of the relation between production and cost by restating the two fundamental relations between product and cost variables

$$SMC = w/MP \qquad \text{and} \qquad AVC = w/AP$$

Thus the following relations must hold:

> **Relations**   When marginal product (average product) is increasing, marginal cost (average variable cost) is decreasing. When marginal product (average product) is decreasing, marginal cost (average variable cost) is increasing. When marginal product equals average product at maximum AP, marginal cost equals average variable cost at minimum AVC.

Now try Technical Problem 13.

As we explained in Section 8.2, when the fixed inputs are allowed to change, all the product curves, TP, AP, and MP, shift. This, of course, will shift the short-run cost curves.

8.5 SUMMARY

■ Technical efficiency occurs when a firm produces the maximum possible output for a given combination of inputs and existing technology, and economic efficiency is achieved when the firm produces its chosen level of output at the lowest-possible total cost. Production inputs can be variable, fixed, or quasi-fixed inputs. For variable inputs, the level of usage can be readily changed. Usage of fixed inputs cannot be changed and must be paid even if no output is produced. Quasi-fixed inputs are lumpy, indivisible inputs for which a fixed amount must be employed for any positive level of output, and none of the input is purchased when output is zero.

The short run refers to the current time span during which one or more inputs are fixed inputs and must be paid whether or not any output is produced, and the long run refers to the period far enough in the future that all fixed inputs become variable inputs. Sunk costs are input payments that, once made, cannot be recovered should the firm no longer wish to employ that input. Sunk costs are irrelevant for future decisions and are not part of economic cost of production in future time periods. Avoidable costs are payments a firm can recover or avoid paying, and thus avoidable costs do matter in decision making. (*LO1*)

- The total product curve shows the short-run production relation $Q = f(L, \overline{K})$ with Q on the vertical axis and L on the horizontal axis. The total product curve gives the economically efficient amount of labor for any output level when capital is fixed at $\overline{K}$ units in the short run. The average product of labor is the total product divided by the number of workers: $AP = Q/L$. The marginal product of labor is the additional output attributable to using one additional worker with the use of capital fixed: $MP = \Delta Q/\Delta L$. The law of diminishing marginal product states that as the number of units of the variable input increases, other inputs held constant, a point will be reached beyond which the marginal product of the variable input declines. When marginal product is greater (less) than average product, average product is increasing (decreasing). When average product is at its maximum, marginal product equals average product. (LO2)

- Short-run total cost, TC, is the sum of total variable cost, TVC, and total fixed cost, TFC: $TC = TVC + TFC$. Average fixed cost, AFC, is TFC divided by output: $AFC = TFC/Q$. Average variable cost, AVC, is TVC divided by output: $AVC = TVC/Q$. Average total cost (ATC) is TC divided by output: $ATC = TC/Q$. Short-run marginal cost, SMC, is the change in either TVC or TC per unit change in output: $SMC = \Delta TVC/\Delta Q = \Delta TC/\Delta Q$. Figure 8.5 shows a typical set of short-run cost curves that are characterized by the following relations. (LO3)

- The link between product curves and cost curves in the short run when one input is variable is reflected in the relations $AVC = w/AP$ and $SMC = w/MP$, where w is the price of the variable input. When MP (AP) is increasing, SMC (AVC) is decreasing. When MP (AP) is decreasing, SMC (AVC) is increasing. When MP equals AP at AP's maximum value, SMC equals AVC at AVC's minimum value. (LO4)

KEY TERMS

average fixed cost (AFC)
average product of labor (AP)
average total cost (ATC)
average variable cost (AVC)
avoidable cost in production
economic efficiency
fixed input
fixed proportions production

law of diminishing marginal product
long run
marginal product of labor (MP)
planning horizon
production
production function
quasi-fixed input
short run

short-run marginal cost (SMC)
sunk cost in production
technical efficiency
total cost (TC)
total fixed cost (TFC)
total variable cost (TVC)
variable input
variable proportions production

TECHNICAL PROBLEMS

1. "When a manager is using a technically efficient input combination, the firm is also producing in an economically efficient manner." Evaluate this statement.
2. A firm plans to produce 1,000 units per day of good X. The firm's production engineer finds two technically efficient processes (i.e., input combinations of labor and capital) to produce 1,000 units per day:

	Process 1	Process 2
Labor	10	8
Capital	20	25

a. If the production function for the existing technology is $Q = f(L, K)$, where Q is the maximum possible output, L is the amount of labor used, and K is the amount of capital used, then $f(10, 20) =$ _____ and $f(8, 25) =$ _____.

b. If the firm must pay $200 per day for a unit of labor and $100 per day for a unit of capital, which process is economically efficient?

c. If the firm must pay $250 per day for a unit of labor and $75 per day for a unit of capital, which process is economically efficient?

d. "No matter what input prices prevail, as long as the firm employs either process 1 or process 2 it will be technically efficient." Evaluate this statement.

3. Jetways Airline flies passengers between New York and Miami, making one round-trip daily using a leased Boeing 737 aircraft. Consider the number of passengers served daily as the output for the airline. Identify each of the following costs as either a variable, a fixed, or a quasi-fixed cost:

a. Cost of in-flight snacks and beverages for passengers.

b. Expenditure on jet fuel.

c. Labor expense for pilots.

d. Monthly lease payment for Boeing 737 during the term of the lease.

e. Monthly fee at two airports for passenger check-in/ticketing counter space (airports charge airlines on a "pay-as-you-go" basis).

4. For each of the following situations, determine whether the manager is concerned with a short-run or a long-run production decision. Explain briefly in each case.

a. A petroleum drilling supervisor on an offshore drilling platform decides to add an extra six-hour shift each day to keep the drill rig running 24 hours per day.

b. The vice president of offshore petroleum drilling operations in the Gulf of Mexico chooses to deploy three more offshore drilling platforms in the Gulf.

c. A manufacturing engineer plans the production schedule for the month.

d. After studying a demographic report on future increases in birthrates, a hospital administrator decides to add a new pediatric wing to the hospital.

5. A start-up biomedical engineering firm has begun manufacturing a drug-coated bimetallic stent, which is a thin wire mesh tube inserted in clogged coronary arteries to prop them open and prevent future heart attacks. Identify the following costs of manufacturing the stents as either sunk or avoidable costs now that the firm has received final approval from the Food and Drug Administration (FDA) and manufacturing is currently in progress:

a. Biomedical research and development costs to design the heart stent.

b. Costs of running clinical trials to win FDA approval to begin making and selling the stent to cardiologists.

c. Labor costs to operate the manufacturing equipment.

d. Cost of the drug, high-grade stainless steel, and titanium used in making the stents.

e. Set-up cost incurred to install the manufacturing equipment and to train workers to operate the equipment.

f. Legal costs of filing a patent application.

6. Fill in the blanks in the following table:

Units of labor	Total product	Average product	Marginal product
1	____	40	____
2	____	____	48
3	138	____	____
4	____	44	____
5	____	____	24
6	210	____	____
7	____	29	____
8	____	____	−27

7. Refer to Table 8.3 and explain precisely why using 10 units of labor and 2 units of capital is not economically efficient.

8. The following table shows the amount of total output produced from various combinations of labor and capital:

Units of labor	Units of capital			
	1	2	3	4
1	50	120	160	180
2	110	260	360	390
3	150	360	510	560
4	170	430	630	690
5	160	480	710	790

   a. Calculate the marginal product and average product of labor when capital is held constant at 2 units. When the average product of labor is increasing, what is the relation between the average product and the marginal product? What about when the average product of labor is decreasing?

   b. Calculate the marginal product of labor for each level of the capital stock. How does the marginal product of the second unit of labor change as the capital stock increases? Why?

9. Fill in the blanks in the following table:

Output	Total cost	Total fixed cost	Total variable cost	Average fixed cost	Average variable cost	Average total cost	Marginal cost
100	260	____	60	____	____	____	____
200	____	____	____	____	____	____	0.30
300	____	____	____	____	0.50	____	____
400	____	____	____	____	____	1.05	____
500	____	____	360	____	____	____	____
600	____	____	____	____	____	____	3.00
700	____	____	____	____	1.60	____	____
800	2,040	____	____	____	____	____	____

10. Assume average variable cost is constant over a range of output. What is marginal cost over this range? What is happening to average total cost over this range?

11. Suppose that a firm is currently employing 20 workers, the only variable input, at a wage rate of $60. The average product of labor is 30, the last worker added 12 units to total output, and total fixed cost is $3,600.

    a. What is marginal cost?

    b. What is average variable cost?

    c. How much output is being produced?

    d. What is average total cost?

    e. Is average variable cost increasing, constant, or decreasing? What about average total cost?

12. The first two columns in the following table give a firm's short-run production function when the only variable input is labor, and capital (the fixed input) is held constant at 5 units. The price of capital is $2,000 per unit, and the price of labor is $500 per unit.

Units of labor	Units of output	Average product	Marginal product	Cost			Average cost			Marginal cost
				Fixed	Variable	Total	Fixed	Variable	Total	
0	0	XX	XX	———	———	———	XX	XX	XX	XX
20	4,000	———	———	———	———	———	———	———	———	———
40	10,000	———	———	———	———	———	———	———	———	———
60	15,000	———	———	———	———	———	———	———	———	———
80	19,400	———	———	———	———	———	———	———	———	———
100	23,000	———	———	———	———	———	———	———	———	———

    a. Complete the table.

    b. What is the relation between average variable cost and marginal cost? Between average total cost and marginal cost?

    c. What is the relation between average product and average variable cost? Between marginal product and marginal cost?

13. Assume that labor—the only variable input of a firm—has the average and marginal product curves shown in the following graph. Labor's wage is $60 per unit.

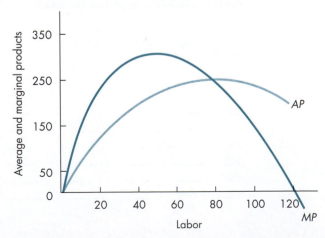

a. When the firm attains minimum average variable cost, how many units of labor is it using?

b. What level of output is associated with minimum average variable cost?

c. What is the average variable cost of producing this output?

d. Suppose the firm is using 100 units of labor. What is output? What is marginal cost? What is average variable cost?

APPLIED PROBLEMS

1. On the first day of the new year to get her business started, the owner/photographer of Exquisite Portraits Inc. paid $200 for business cards, $1,000 for a listing in Yellow Pages, and $250 for an annual business license. She also leased a professional portrait camera and studio lighting equipment by signing an agreement to pay a monthly lease of $1,000 each month for the next 12 months. This lease is ironclad: She must pay for all 12 months and she cannot sublease to anyone else. She rents her office and studio for $1,400 per month that must be paid at the beginning of each month. She does not have a lease on the office/studio, so she can vacate the office/studio at the end of any month should she decide to move to a new location or to go out of business. After she opens the office/studio on the first day of each month, her monthly cost of electricity for lighting the office and running her coffee machine is constant at $45 per month, because she always keeps the lights on in the office and drinks the same amount of coffee no matter how many photos she shoots each month. Additional electricity is required for the portrait studio lights, which varies directly with the number of hours the lights are used each month for photo sessions. Last year, before starting this business, the owner of Exquisite Portraits Inc. earned a salary of $5,000 per month working at a bank. Answer the following questions about the costs for Exquisite Portraits Inc.:

   a. What are monthly fixed costs, quasi-fixed costs, and variable costs for Exquisite Portraits Inc.?

   b. If the owner of Exquisite Portraits Inc. wants to close her studio and go out of business at the end of August, identify her sunk costs and avoidable costs.

   c. At the end of August, what role would the sunk costs play in the owner/photographer's decision to go out of business?

   d. In making her decision to start her own business, would her decision have been more or less difficult to make if sunk costs were zero at Exquisite Portraits? Explain.

2. At a management luncheon, two managers were overheard arguing about the following statement: "A manager should never hire another worker if the new person causes diminishing returns." Is this statement correct? If so, why? If not, explain why not.

3. Engineers at a national research laboratory built a prototype automobile that could be driven 180 miles on a single gallon of unleaded gasoline. They estimated that in mass production the car would cost $60,000 per unit to build. The engineers argued that Congress should force U.S. automakers to build this energy-efficient car.

   a. Is energy efficiency the same thing as economic efficiency? Explain.

   b. Under what circumstances would the energy-efficient automobile described here be economically efficient?

   c. If the goal of society is to get the most benefit from its limited resources, then why not ignore economic efficiency and build the energy-saving automobile?

4. After two quarters of increasing levels of production, the CEO of Canadian Fabrication & Design was upset to learn that, during this time of expansion, productivity of the newly hired sheet metal workers declined with each new worker hired. Believing that the new workers were either lazy or ineffectively supervised (or possibly both), the CEO instructed the shop foreman to "crack down" on the new workers to bring their productivity levels up.

   a. Explain carefully in terms of production theory why it might be that no amount of "cracking down" can increase worker productivity at CF&D.

   b. Provide an alternative to cracking down as a means of increasing the productivity of the sheet metal workers.

5. An article in *BusinessWeek* warned of the dangers of deflation as the collapse of numerous Asian economies was creating worries that Asia might try to "export its way out of trouble" by oversupplying everything from automobiles to semiconductors. Evidence that deflation had become a genuine concern for managers was provided by a statement in the article by John Smith, chairman and CEO of General Motors Corporation: "Fundamentally, something has changed in the economy. In today's age, you cannot get price increases." The article offers the following advice to managers: "Productivity growth lets companies boost profits even as prices fall." Using short-run production and cost theory, comment on this advice.

6. *BusinessWeek*, in an article dealing with management, wrote, "When he took over the furniture factory three years ago . . . [the manager] realized almost immediately that it was throwing away at least $100,000 a year worth of wood scrap. Within a few weeks, he set up a task force of managers and workers to deal with the problem. And within a few months, they reduced the amount of scrap to $7,000 worth [per year]." Was this necessarily an *economically efficient* move?

7. In January 2014, Digital Advantage, an electronics retailer located in Sacramento, plans to open a new store in Tacoma. The CEO expects to sign a 12-month lease on a 10,000 square foot retail store in a newly constructed mall. The lease amount is $144,000 for the year 2014 with an agreement that Digital Advantage will make 12 monthly lease payments of $12,000 on the first day of each month. During the 12-month period of the lease contract, should the manager of Digital Advantage consider the monthly payments of $12,000 avoidable or sunk costs? Why does it matter whether the lease payments are avoidable or sunk costs since, in either case, the lease payment must be paid to prevent immediate eviction from the property?

8. Oversize Transport Inc. supplies custom delivery service for very large construction equipment in the southeast region of the United States. The most common load for the specialty trucker is the Caterpillar model 740 dump truck, which is about 258 feet long. The owner of Oversize Transport, who also drives the firm's single 275-foot long tractor-trailer rig, chooses to lease this huge piece of capital equipment under a five-year contract requiring monthly lease payments of $5,500 per month. Oversize Transport could not service this profitable market with any rig shorter than 275 feet. A typical delivery takes about a day and a half, so Oversize Transport can make at most only 20 deliveries per month with its one tractor-trailer rig. Under what circumstances is the tractor-trailer a fixed input? A quasi-fixed input?

☐ **MATHEMATICAL APPENDIX**

This appendix uses calculus to derive several useful relations in short-run production and cost analysis. We consider only the two-input case; however, all results hold for any number of inputs in production. Define the production function as

$$(1) \qquad Q = f(L, K)$$

where Q is the maximum possible output attainable when L units of labor and K units of capital are employed to produce a good or service. Thus the production function is characterized by technical efficiency. Assume that production requires positive amounts of both inputs:

$$(2) \qquad Q = f(0, K) = f(L, 0) = 0$$

If the usage of either input is zero, output is zero. In the short run, at least one input is fixed. Assume capital is the fixed input. By holding capital constant at $\overline{K}$ units, the short-run production function can be expressed as

$$(3) \qquad Q = f(L, \overline{K}) = g(L)$$

Thus $g(L)$ is the short-run production function when capital is fixed at $\overline{K}$ units.

Average Product and Marginal Product

The relation between average and marginal product plays an important role in understanding the nature of production and the shape of short-run cost curves. Average product is defined as

$$(4) \qquad AP = AP(L) = Q/L$$

and marginal product is defined as the rate of change in output as the variable input labor changes:

$$(5) \qquad MP = MP(L) \frac{dQ}{dL} = \frac{dg(L)}{dL} = g'(L)$$

Recall from this chapter that *when AP is increasing (decreasing), MP is greater (less) than AP. When AP reaches its maximum value, MP = AP.* This relation can be demonstrated by differentiating AP with respect to L to find the condition under which AP increases or decreases:

$$(6) \qquad \frac{d(AP)}{dL} = \frac{d(Q/L)}{dL} = \frac{(dQ/dL)L - Q}{L^2}$$

$$= \frac{1}{L}(MP - AP)$$

Thus the sign of $d(AP)/dL$ is positive (negative) when MP is greater (less) than AP. So AP rises (falls) when MP

is greater (less) than AP. The peak of AP occurs where the slope of AP is zero; that is, $d(AP)/dL$ is zero. Thus the maximum point on AP is reached where $MP = AP$.

The Cost Relations: *ATC, AVC,* and *SMC*

Begin by defining short-run total cost TC to be a function of the level of production, Q:

$$TC = TC(Q) = TVC(Q) + TFC$$

where $TVC(Q)$ is total variable cost and TFC is total fixed cost. Because $dTFC/dQ = 0$, short-run marginal cost is the rate of change in either TC or TVC as output changes:

$$(7) \qquad SMC = \frac{dTC}{dQ} = \frac{dTVC}{dQ}$$

Recall that TC and TVC are parallel, so their slopes are identical at any level of production. Average total cost, ATC, can be expressed as

$$(8) \qquad ATC = ATC(Q) = \frac{TC(Q)}{Q} = \frac{TVC(Q)}{Q} + \frac{TFC}{Q}$$

$$= AVC(Q) + AFC(Q)$$

Note that *average* fixed cost is a function of Q, while *total* fixed cost is not a function of Q.

Recall from this chapter that *when ATC is increasing (decreasing), MC is greater (less) than ATC. When ATC reaches its minimum value, SMC = ATC.* This relation can be demonstrated by differentiating ATC with respect to Q to find the condition under which ATC increases or decreases:

$$\frac{dATC}{dQ} = \frac{d[TVC(Q)/Q + TFC/Q]}{dQ}$$

$$= \frac{\frac{dTVC(Q)}{dQ}Q - TVC \times 1 + 0 \times Q - TFC \times 1}{Q^2}$$

Factoring the term $1/Q$ simplifies the expression:

$$(9) \qquad \frac{dATC}{dQ} = \frac{1}{Q}\left(\frac{dTVC}{dQ} - \frac{TVC}{Q} - \frac{TFC}{Q}\right)$$

$$= \frac{1}{Q}(SMC - AVC - AFC)$$

$$= \frac{1}{Q}(SMC - ATC)$$

Thus the sign of $dATC/dQ$ is positive (negative) when SMC is greater (less) than ATC. The minimum point on ATC occurs where its slope is zero, which is where $SMC = ATC$.

Relations between Production and Cost

The structure of a firm's cost curves is determined by the production function. To show that the shapes of the cost curves are determined by the production function, we now derive the relations between (1) MP and SMC and (2) AP and AVC.

Relation between MP and SMC

Recall that $SMC = dTVC/dQ$. If $TVC = wL$ and w is a constant, SMC can be expressed as

$$(10) \qquad SMC = \frac{d(wL)}{dQ} = w\frac{dL}{dQ} = w\frac{1}{MP} = \frac{w}{MP}$$

SMC and MP are inversely related. As labor productivity rises (falls) in the short run, SMC falls (rises). Over the range of input usage characterized by diminishing returns (MP is falling), marginal cost is rising in the short run.

Relation between AP and AVC

Recall also that $AVC = TVC/Q$. Again substituting wL for TVC:

$$(11) \qquad AVC = \frac{wL}{Q} = w\frac{L}{Q} = w\frac{1}{AP} = \frac{w}{AP}$$

From expression (11), it is clear that when average product is rising (falling), average variable cost is falling (rising). Average variable cost reaches its minimum value where average product reaches its maximum value, which, as we demonstrated above, is where $MP = AP$.

MATHEMATICAL EXERCISES

1. Consider the production function $Q = 20K^{1/2}L^{1/2}$. The firm operates in the short run with 16 units of capital.
    a. The firm's short-run production function is $Q =$ _____.
    b. The average product of labor function is $AP =$ _____.
    c. The marginal product of labor function is $MP =$ _____.
    d. Show that marginal product diminishes for all levels of labor usage.

2. Total cost (TC) and total variable cost (TVC) are parallel, yet average total cost (ATC) and average variable cost (AVC) are not parallel.
    a. Demonstrate mathematically that ATC and AVC are not parallel.
    b. Show mathematically that when both ATC and AVC are falling, ATC falls faster than AVC, and when both are rising, AVC rises faster than ATC.

3. For the short-run production function in exercise 1, let the wage be $20.
    a. Derive $AVC(Q)$.
    b. When 160 units are produced, _____ units of labor are employed, and the average product is _____. Average variable cost is $_____.
    c. Derive $SMC(Q)$.
    d. Using the marginal product (MP) function derived in part c, the marginal product is _____ when 160 units are produced. SMC is $_____. Verify that $SMC(Q)$ evaluated at $Q = 4$ is identical to calculating SMC by using the ratio w/MP.

Chapter 9

Production and Cost in the Long Run

After reading this chapter, you will be able to:

9.1 Graph a typical production isoquant and discuss the properties of isoquants.

9.2 Construct isocost curves for a given level of expenditure on inputs.

9.3 Apply optimization theory to find the optimal input combination.

9.4 Construct the firm's expansion path and show how it relates to the firm's long-run cost structure.

9.5 Calculate long-run total, average, and marginal costs from the firm's expansion path.

9.6 Explain how a variety of forces affects long-run costs: scale, scope, learning, and purchasing economies.

9.7 Show the relation between long-run and short-run cost curves using long-run and short-run expansion paths.

No matter how a firm operates in the short run, its manager can always change things at some point in the future. Economists refer to this future period as the "long run." Managers face a particularly important constraint on the way they can organize production in the short run: The usage of one or more inputs is fixed. Generally the most important type of *fixed* input is the physical capital used in production: machinery, tools, computer hardware, buildings for manufacturing, office space for administrative operations, facilities for storing inventory, and so on. In the long run, managers can choose to operate with whatever amounts and kinds of capital resources they wish. This is the essential feature of long-run analysis of production and cost. In the long run, managers are *not stuck* with too much or too little capital—or any fixed input for that matter. As you will see in this chapter, long-run flexibility in resource usage usually creates an opportunity for firms to reduce their costs in the long run.

Since a long-run analysis of production generates the "best-case" scenario for costs, managers cannot make tactical and strategic decisions in a sensible way unless they possess considerable understanding of the long-run cost structure available to their firms, as well as the long-run costs of any rival firms they might face. As we mentioned in the previous chapter, firms *operate* in the short run and *plan* for the long run. The managers in charge of production operations must have accurate information about the short-run cost measures discussed in Chapter 8, while the executives responsible for long-run planning must look beyond the constraints imposed by the firm's existing short-run configuration of productive inputs to a future situation in which the firm can choose the optimal combination of inputs.

Recently, U.S. auto manufacturers faced historic challenges to their survival, forcing executive management at Ford, Chrysler, and General Motors to examine every possible way of reorganizing production to reduce long-run costs. While short-run costs determined their current levels of profitability—or losses in this case—it was the flexibility of long-run adjustments in the organization of production and structure of costs that offered some promise of a return to profitability and economic survival of American car producers. The outcome for U.S. carmakers depends on many of the issues you will learn about in this chapter: economies of scale, economies of scope, purchasing economies, and learning economies. And, as you will see in later chapters, the responses by rival auto producers—both American and foreign—will depend most importantly on the rivals' *long-run* costs of producing cars, SUVs, and trucks. Corporate decisions concerning such matters as adding new product lines (e.g., hybrids or electric models), dropping current lines (e.g., Pontiac at GM), allowing some divisions to merge, or even, as a last resort, exiting through bankruptcy all require accurate analyses and forecasts of long-run costs.

In this chapter, we analyze the situation in which the fixed inputs in the short run become variable inputs in the long run. In the long run, we will view *all* inputs as variable inputs, a situation that is both more complex and more interesting than production with only one variable input—labor. For clarification and completeness, we should remind you that, unlike fixed inputs, *quasi*-fixed inputs do *not* become variable inputs in the long run. In both the short- and long-run periods, they are indivisible in nature and must be employed in specific lump amounts that do not vary with output—unless output is zero, and then none of the quasi-fixed inputs will be employed or paid. Because the amount of a quasi-fixed input used in the short run is generally the same amount used in the long run, we do not include quasi-fixed inputs as choice variables for long-run production decisions.[1] With this distinction in mind, we can say that *all* inputs are variable in the long run.

---

[1]An exception to this rule occurs when, as output increases, the fixed lump amount of input eventually becomes fully utilized and constrains further increases in output. Then, the firm must add another lump of quasi-fixed input in the long run to allow further expansion of output. This exception is not particularly important because it does not change the principles set forth in this chapter or other chapters in this textbook. Thus, we will continue to assume that when a quasi-fixed input is required, only *one* lump of the input is needed for all positive levels of output.

9.1 PRODUCTION ISOQUANTS

isoquant
A curve showing all possible combinations of inputs physically capable of producing a given fixed level of output.

An important tool of analysis when two inputs are variable is the *production isoquant* or simply *isoquant*. An **isoquant** is a curve showing all possible combinations of the inputs physically capable of producing a given (fixed) level of output. Each point on an isoquant is technically efficient; that is, for each combination on the isoquant, the maximum possible output is that associated with the given isoquant. The concept of an isoquant implies that it is possible to substitute some amount of one input for some of the other, say, labor for capital, while keeping output constant. Therefore, if the two inputs are continuously divisible, as we will assume, there are an infinite number of input combinations capable of producing each level of output.

To understand the concept of an isoquant, return for a moment to Table 8.2 in the preceding chapter. This table shows the maximum output that can be produced by combining different levels of labor and capital. Now note that several levels of output in this table can be produced in two ways. For example, 108 units of output can be produced using either 6 units of capital and 1 worker or 1 unit of capital and 4 workers. Thus, these two combinations of labor and capital are two points on the isoquant associated with 108 units of output. And if we assumed that labor and capital were continuously divisible, there would be many more combinations on this isoquant.

Other input combinations in Table 8.2 that can produce the same level of output are

$$Q = 258: \text{using } K = 2, L = 5 \quad \text{or} \quad K = 8, L = 2$$
$$Q = 400: \text{using } K = 9, L = 3 \quad \text{or} \quad K = 4, L = 4$$
$$Q = 453: \text{using } K = 5, L = 4 \quad \text{or} \quad K = 3, L = 7$$
$$Q = 708: \text{using } K = 6, L = 7 \quad \text{or} \quad K = 5, L = 9$$
$$Q = 753: \text{using } K = 10, L = 6 \quad \text{or} \quad K = 6, L = 8$$

Each pair of combinations of K and L is two of the many combinations associated with each specific level of output. Each demonstrates that it is possible to increase capital and decrease labor (or increase labor and decrease capital) while keeping the level of output constant. For example, if the firm is producing 400 units of output with 9 units of capital and 3 units of labor, it can increase labor by 1, decrease capital by 5, and keep output at 400. Or if it is producing 453 units of output with $K = 3$ and $L = 7$, it can increase K by 2, decrease L by 3, and keep output at 453. Thus an isoquant shows how one input can be substituted for another while keeping the level of output constant.

Characteristics of Isoquants

We now set forth the typically assumed characteristics of isoquants when labor, capital, and output are continuously divisible. Figure 9.1 illustrates three such isoquants. Isoquant Q_1 shows all the combinations of capital and labor that yield 100 units of output. As shown, the firm can produce 100 units of output by using 10 units of capital and 75 of labor, or 50 units of capital and 15 of labor, or any other

FIGURE 9.1

A Typical Isoquant Map

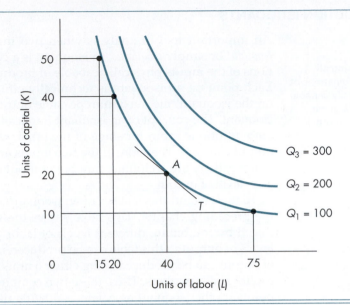

combination of capital and labor on isoquant Q_1. Similarly, isoquant Q_2 shows the various combinations of capital and labor that can be used to produce 200 units of output. And isoquant Q_3 shows all combinations that can produce 300 units of output. Each capital–labor combination can be on only one isoquant. That is, isoquants cannot intersect.

Isoquants Q_1, Q_2, and Q_3 are only three of an infinite number of isoquants that could be drawn. A group of isoquants is called an isoquant map. In an **isoquant map**, all isoquants lying above and to the right of a given isoquant indicate higher levels of output. Thus in Figure 9.1 isoquant Q_2 indicates a higher level of output than isoquant Q_1, and Q_3 indicates a higher level than Q_2.

isoquant map
A graph showing a group of isoquants.

Marginal Rate of Technical Substitution

As depicted in Figure 9.1, isoquants slope downward over the relevant range of production. This negative slope indicates that if the firm decreases the amount of capital employed, more labor must be added to keep the rate of output constant. Or if labor use is decreased, capital usage must be increased to keep output constant. Thus the two inputs can be substituted for one another to maintain a constant level of output. The rate at which one input is substituted for another along an isoquant is called the **marginal rate of technical substitution (MRTS)** and is defined as

marginal rate of technical substitution (MRTS)
The rate at which one input is substituted for another along an isoquant $\left(-\frac{\Delta K}{\Delta L}\right)$.

$$MRTS = -\frac{\Delta K}{\Delta L}$$

The minus sign is added to make MRTS a positive number because $\Delta K/\Delta L$, the slope of the isoquant, is negative.

Over the relevant range of production, the marginal rate of technical substitution diminishes. As more and more labor is substituted for capital while holding output constant, the absolute value of $\Delta K/\Delta L$ decreases. This can be seen in Figure 9.1. If capital is reduced from 50 to 40 (a decrease of 10 units), labor must be increased by 5 units (from 15 to 20) to keep the level of output at 100 units. That is, when capital is plentiful relative to labor, the firm can discharge 10 units of capital but must substitute only 5 units of labor to keep output at 100. The marginal rate of technical substitution in this case is $-\Delta K/\Delta L = -(-10)/5 = 2$, meaning that for every unit of labor added, 2 units of capital can be discharged to keep the level of output constant. However, consider a combination where capital is more scarce and labor more plentiful. For example, if capital is decreased from 20 to 10 (again a decrease of 10 units), labor must be increased by 35 units (from 40 to 75) to keep output at 100 units. In this case the MRTS is 10/35, indicating that for each unit of labor added, capital can be reduced by slightly more than one-quarter of a unit.

As capital decreases and labor increases along an isoquant, the amount of capital that can be discharged for each unit of labor added declines. This relation is seen in Figure 9.1. As the change in labor and the change in capital become extremely small around a point on an isoquant, the absolute value of the slope of a tangent to the isoquant at that point is the MRTS ($-\Delta K/\Delta L$) in the neighborhood of that point. In Figure 9.1, the absolute value of the slope of tangent T to isoquant Q_1 at point A shows the marginal rate of technical substitution at that point. Thus the slope of the isoquant reflects the rate at which labor can be substituted for capital. As you can see, the isoquant becomes less and less steep with movements downward along the isoquant, and thus MRTS declines along an isoquant.

Relation of *MRTS* to Marginal Products

For very small movements along an isoquant, the marginal rate of technical substitution equals the ratio of the marginal products of the two inputs. We will now demonstrate why this comes about.

The level of output, Q, depends on the use of the two inputs, L and K. Since Q is constant along an isoquant, ΔQ must equal zero for any change in L and K that would remain on a given isoquant. Suppose that, at a point on the isoquant, the marginal product of capital (MP_K) is 3 and the marginal product of labor (MP_L) is 6. If we add 1 unit of labor, output would increase by 6 units. To keep Q at the original level, capital must decrease just enough to offset the 6-unit increase in output generated by the increase in labor. Because the marginal product of capital is 3, 2 units of capital must be discharged to reduce output by 6 units. In this case the $MRTS = -\Delta K/\Delta L = -(-2)/1 = 2$, which is exactly equal to $MP_L/MP_K = 6/3 = 2$.

In more general terms, we can say that when L and K are allowed to vary slightly, the change in Q resulting from the change in the two inputs is the marginal product of L times the amount of change in L plus the marginal product of K times its change. Put in equation form

$$\Delta Q = (MP_L)(\Delta L) + (MP_K)(\Delta K)$$

To remain on a given isoquant, it is necessary to set ΔQ equal to 0. Then, solving for the marginal rate of technical substitution yields

$$MRTS = -\frac{\Delta K}{\Delta L} = \frac{MP_L}{MP_K}$$

Using this relation, the reason for diminishing $MRTS$ is easily explained. As additional units of labor are substituted for capital, the marginal product of labor diminishes. Two forces are working to diminish labor's marginal product: (1) Less capital causes a downward shift of the marginal product of labor curve, and (2) more units of the variable input (labor) cause a downward movement along the marginal product curve. Thus, as labor is substituted for capital, the marginal product of labor must decline. For analogous reasons the marginal product of capital increases as less capital and more labor are used. The same two forces are present in this case: a movement along a marginal product curve and a shift in the location of the curve. In this situation, however, both forces work to increase the marginal product of capital. Thus, as labor is substituted for capital, the marginal product of capital increases. Combining these two conditions, as labor is substituted for capital, MP_L decreases and MP_K increases, so MP_L/MP_K will decrease.

Now try Technical Problem 1.

9.2 ISOCOST CURVES

isocost curve
Line that shows the various combinations of inputs that may be purchased for a given level of expenditure at given input prices.

Producers must consider relative input prices to find the least-cost combination of inputs to produce a given level of output. An extremely useful tool for analyzing the cost of purchasing inputs is an *isocost curve*. An **isocost curve** shows all combinations of inputs that may be purchased for a given level of total expenditure at given input prices. As you will see in the next section, isocost curves play a key role in finding the combination of inputs that produces a given output level at the lowest possible total cost.

Characteristics of Isocost Curves

Suppose a manager must pay $25 for each unit of labor services and $50 for each unit of capital services employed. The manager wishes to know what combinations of labor and capital can be purchased for $400 total expenditure on inputs. Figure 9.2 shows the isocost curve for $400 when the price of labor is $25 and the price of capital is $50. Each combination of inputs on this isocost curve costs $400 to purchase. Point A on the isocost curve shows how much capital could be purchased if no labor is employed. Because the price of capital is $50, the manager can spend all $400 on capital alone and purchase 8 units of capital and 0 units of labor. Similarly, point D on the isocost curve gives the maximum amount of labor—16 units—that can be purchased if labor costs $25 per unit and $400 are spent on labor alone. Points B and C also represent input combinations that cost $400. At point B, for example, $300 (= $50 × 6) are spent on capital and $100 (= $25 × 4) are spent on labor, which represents a total cost of $400.

If we continue to denote the quantities of capital and labor by K and L, and denote their respective prices by r and w, total cost, C, is $C = wL + rK$. Total cost is

FIGURE 9.2

An Isocost Curve
(w = $25 and r = $50)

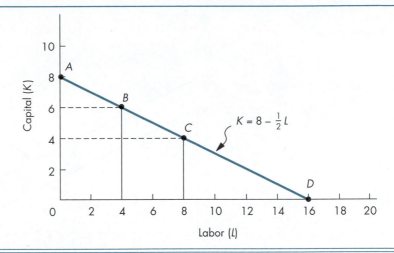

simply the sum of the cost of L units of labor at w dollars per unit and of K units of capital at r dollars per unit:

$$C = wL + rK$$

In this example, the total cost function is $400 = 25L + 50K$. Solving this equation for K, you can see the combinations of K and L that can be chosen: $K = \dfrac{400}{50} - \dfrac{25}{50}L = 8 - \dfrac{1}{2} L$. More generally, if a fixed amount $\overline{C}$ is to be spent, the firm can choose among the combinations given by

$$K = \frac{\overline{C}}{r} - \frac{w}{r}L$$

If $\overline{C}$ is the total amount to be spent on inputs, the most capital that can be purchased (if no labor is purchased) is $\overline{C}/r$ units of capital, and the most labor that can be purchased (if no capital is purchased) is $\overline{C}/w$ units of labor.

The slope of the isocost curve is equal to the negative of the relative input price ratio, $-w/r$. This ratio is important because it tells the manager how much capital must be given up if one more unit of labor is purchased. In the example just given and illustrated in Figure 9.2, $-w/r = -\$25/\$50 = -1/2$. If the manager wishes to purchase 1 more unit of labor at $25, 1/2 unit of capital, which costs $50, must be given up to keep the total cost of the input combination constant. If the price of labor happens to rise to $50 per unit, r remaining constant, the slope of the isocost curve is $-\$50/\$50 = -1$, which means the manager must give up 1 unit of capital for each additional unit of labor purchased to keep total cost constant.

Shifts in Isocost Curves

If the constant level of total cost associated with a particular isocost curve changes, the isocost curve shifts parallel. Figure 9.3 shows how the isocost curve shifts

FIGURE 9.3

Shift in an Isocost Curve

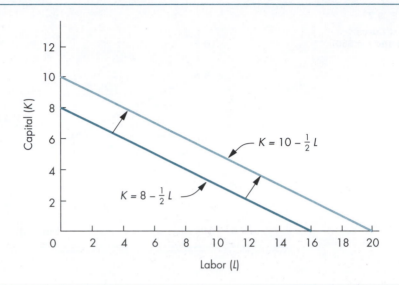

when the total expenditure on resources $(\overline{C})$ increases from \$400 to \$500. The isocost curve shifts out parallel, and the equation for the new isocost curve is

$$K = 10 - \frac{1}{2}L$$

The slope is still $-1/2$ because $-w/r$ does not change. The K-intercept is now 10, indicating that a maximum of 10 units of capital can be purchased if no labor is purchased and \$500 are spent.

In general, an increase in cost, holding input prices constant, leads to a parallel upward shift in the isocost curve. A decrease in cost, holding input prices constant, leads to a parallel downward shift in the isocost curve. An infinite number of isocost curves exist, one for each level of total cost.

Now try Technical
Problem 2.

> **Relation** At constant input prices, w and r for labor and capital, a given expenditure on inputs $(\overline{C})$ will purchase any combination of labor and capital given by the following equation, called an isocost curve:
>
> $$K = \frac{\overline{C}}{r} - \frac{w}{r}L$$

9.3 FINDING THE OPTIMAL COMBINATION OF INPUTS

We have shown that any given level of output can be produced by many combinations of inputs—as illustrated by isoquants. When a manager wishes to produce a given level of output at the lowest possible total cost, the manager chooses the combination on the desired isoquant that costs the least. This is a constrained *minimization* problem that a manager can solve by following the rule for constrained optimization set forth in Chapter 3.

Although managers whose goal is profit maximization are generally and primarily concerned with searching for the least-cost combination of inputs to produce a given (profit-maximizing) output, managers of nonprofit organizations may face an alternative situation. In a nonprofit situation, a manager may have a budget or fixed amount of money available for production and wish to maximize the amount of output that can be produced. As we have shown using isocost curves, there are many different input combinations that can be purchased for a given (or fixed) amount of expenditure on inputs. When a manager wishes to maximize output for a given level of total cost, the manager must choose the input combination on the isocost curve that lies on the highest isoquant. This is a constrained *maximization* problem, and the rule for solving it was set forth in Chapter 3.

Whether the manager is searching for the input combination that minimizes cost for a given level of production or maximizes total production for a given level of expenditure on resources, the optimal combination of inputs to employ is found by using the same rule. We first illustrate the fundamental principles of cost minimization with an output constraint; then we will turn to the case of output maximization given a cost constraint.

Production of a Given Output at Minimum Cost

The principle of minimizing the total cost of producing a given level of output is illustrated in Figure 9.4. The manager wants to produce 10,000 units of output

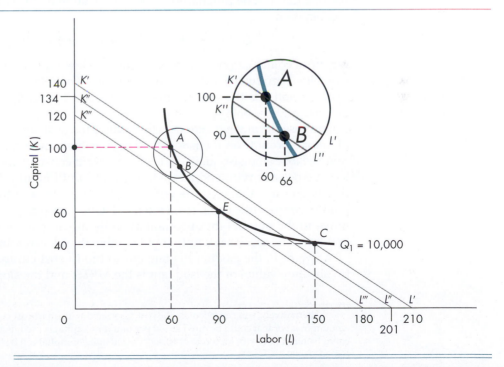

FIGURE 9.4

Optimal Input Combination to Minimize Cost for a Given Output

at the lowest possible total cost. All combinations of labor and capital capable of producing this level of output are shown by isoquant Q_1. The price of labor (w) is $40 per unit, and the price of capital (r) is $60 per unit.

Consider the combination of inputs 60L and 100K, represented by point A on isoquant Q_1. At point A, 10,000 units can be produced at a total cost of $8,400, where the total cost is calculated by adding the total expenditure on labor and the total expenditure on capital:[2]

$$C = wL + rK = (\$40 \times 60) + (\$60 \times 100) = \$8,400$$

The manager can lower the total cost of producing 10,000 units by moving down along the isoquant and purchasing input combination B, because this combination of labor and capital lies on a lower isocost curve ($K''L''$) than input combination A, which lies on $K'L'$. The blowup in Figure 9.4 shows that combination B uses 66L and 90K. Combination B costs $8,040 [= (\$40 \times 66) + (\$60 \times 90)]$. Thus the manager can decrease the total cost of producing 10,000 units by $360 (= \$8,400 - \$8,040)$ by moving from input combination A to input combination B on isoquant Q_1.

Since the manager's objective is to choose the combination of labor and capital on the 10,000-unit isoquant that can be purchased at the lowest possible cost, the manager will continue to move downward along the isoquant until the lowest possible *isocost* curve is reached. Examining Figure 9.4 reveals that the lowest cost of producing 10,000 units of output is attained at point E by using 90 units of labor and 60 units of capital on isocost curve $K'''L'''$, which shows all input combinations that can be purchased for $7,200. Note that at this cost-minimizing input combination

$$C = wL + rK = (\$40 \times 90) + (\$60 \times 60) = \$7,200$$

No input combination on an isocost curve below the one going through point E is capable of producing 10,000 units of output. The total cost associated with input combination E is the lowest possible total cost for producing 10,000 units when $w = \$40$ and $r = \$60$.

Suppose the manager chooses to produce using 40 units of capital and 150 units of labor—point C on the isoquant. The manager could now increase capital and reduce labor along isoquant Q_1, keeping output constant and moving to lower and lower isocost curves, and hence lower costs, until point E is reached. Regardless of whether a manager starts with too much capital and too little labor (such as point A) or too little capital and too much labor (such as point C), the manager can move to the optimal input combination by moving along the isoquant to lower and lower isocost curves until input combination E is reached.

At point E, the isoquant is tangent to the isocost curve. Recall that the slope (in absolute value) of the isoquant is the *MRTS*, and the slope of the isocost curve

---

[2]Alternatively, you can calculate the cost associated with an isocost curve as the maximum amount of labor that could be hired at $40 per unit if no capital is used. For $K'L'$, 210 units of labor could be hired (if $K = 0$) for a cost of $8,400. Or 140 units of capital can be hired at $60 (if $L = 0$) for a cost of $8,400.

(in absolute value) is equal to the relative input price ratio, w/r. Thus, at point E, $MRTS$ equals the ratio of input prices. At the cost-minimizing input combination,

$$MRTS = \frac{w}{r}$$

Now try Technical Problem 3.

To minimize the cost of producing a given level of output, the manager employs the input combination for which $MRTS = w/r$.

The Marginal Product Approach to Cost Minimization

Finding the optimal levels of two activities A and B in a constrained optimization problem involved equating the marginal benefit per dollar spent on each of the activities (MB/P). A manager compares the marginal benefit per dollar spent on each activity to determine which activity is the "better deal": that is, which activity gives the higher marginal benefit per dollar spent. At their optimal levels, both activities are equally good deals $(MB_A/P_A = MB_B/P_B)$ and the constraint is met.

The tangency condition for cost minimization, $MRTS = w/r$, is equivalent to the condition of equal marginal benefit per dollar spent. Recall that $MRTS = MP_L/MP_K$; thus the cost-minimizing condition can be expressed in terms of marginal products

$$MRTS = \frac{MP_L}{MP_K} = \frac{w}{r}$$

After a bit of algebraic manipulation, the optimization condition may be expressed as

$$\frac{MP_L}{w} = \frac{MP_K}{r}$$

The marginal benefits of hiring extra units of labor and capital are the marginal products of labor and capital. Dividing each marginal product by its respective input price tells the manager the additional output that will be forthcoming if one more dollar is spent on that input. Thus, at point E in Figure 9.4, the marginal product per dollar spent on labor is equal to the marginal product per dollar spent on capital, and the constraint is met $(Q = 10,000$ units$)$.

To illustrate how a manager uses information about marginal products and input prices to find the least-cost input combination, we return to point A in Figure 9.4, where $MRTS$ is greater than w/r. Assume that at point A, $MP_L = 160$ and $MP_K = 80$; thus $MRTS = 2$ $(= MP_L/MP_K = 160/80)$. Because the slope of the isocost curve is $2/3$ $(= w/r = 40/60)$, $MRTS$ is greater than w/r, and

$$\frac{MP_L}{w} = \frac{160}{40} = 4 > 1.33 = \frac{80}{60} = \frac{MP_K}{r}$$

The firm should substitute labor, which has the higher marginal product per dollar, for capital, which has the lower marginal product per dollar. For example, an additional unit of labor would increase output by 160 units while increasing labor cost by $40. To keep output constant, 2 units of capital must be released, causing output to fall 160 units (the marginal product of each unit of capital released is 80), but the cost of capital would fall by $120, which is $60 for each of the 2 units of capital released. Output remains constant at 10,000 because the higher output from 1 more unit of labor is just offset by the lower output from two fewer units of capital. However, because labor cost rises by only $40 while capital cost falls by $120, the total cost of producing 10,000 units of output falls by $80 (= $120 − $40).

This example shows that when MP_L/w is greater than MP_K/r, the manager can reduce cost by increasing labor usage while decreasing capital usage just enough to keep output constant. Because $MP_L/w > MP_K/r$ for every input combination along Q_1 from point A to point E, the firm should continue to substitute labor for capital until it reaches point E. As more labor is used, MP_L falls because of diminishing marginal product. As less capital is used, MP_K rises for the same reason. As the manager substitutes labor for capital, $MRTS$ falls until equilibrium is reached.

Now consider point C, where $MRTS$ is less than w/r, and consequently MP_L/w is less than MP_K/r. The marginal product per dollar spent on the last unit of labor is less than the marginal product per dollar spent on the last unit of capital. In this case, the manager can reduce cost by increasing capital usage and decreasing labor usage in such a way as to keep output constant. To see this, assume that at point C, $MP_L = 40$ and $MP_K = 240$, and thus $MRTS = 40/240 = 1/6$, which is less than w/r (= 2/3). If the manager uses one more unit of capital and 6 fewer units of labor, output stays constant while total cost falls by $180. (You should verify this yourself.) The manager can continue moving upward along isoquant Q_1, keeping output constant but reducing cost until point E is reached. As capital is increased and labor decreased, MP_L rises and MP_K falls until, at point E, MP_L/w equals MP_K/r. We have now derived the following:

Principle To produce a given level of output at the lowest possible cost when two inputs (L and K) are variable and the prices of the inputs are, respectively, w and r, a manager chooses the combination of inputs for which

$$MRTS = \frac{MP_L}{MP_K} = \frac{w}{r}$$

which implies that

$$\frac{MP_L}{w} = \frac{MP_K}{r}$$

The isoquant associated with the desired level of output (the slope of which is the $MRTS$) is tangent to the isocost curve (the slope of which is w/r) at the optimal combination of inputs. This optimization condition also means that the marginal product per dollar spent on the last unit of each input is the same.

Now try Technical Problem 4.

Production of Maximum Output with a Given Level of Cost

As discussed earlier, there may be times when managers can spend only a fixed amount on production and wish to attain the highest level of production consistent

FIGURE 9.5

Output Maximization for a Given Level of Cost

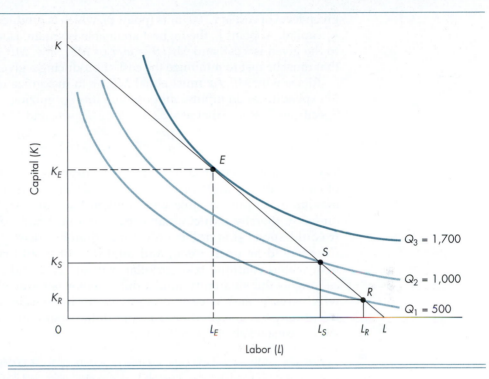

with that amount of expenditure. This is a constrained maximization problem the optimization condition for constrained maximization is the same as that for constrained minimization. In other words, the input combination that maximizes the level of output for a given level of total cost of inputs is that combination for which

$$MRTS = \frac{w}{r} \quad \text{or} \quad \frac{MP_L}{w} = \frac{MP_K}{r}$$

This is the same condition that must be satisfied by the input combination that minimizes the total cost of producing a given output level.

This situation is illustrated in Figure 9.5. The isocost line KL shows all possible combinations of the two inputs that can be purchased for the level of total cost (and input prices) associated with this isocost curve. Suppose the manager chooses point R on the isocost curve and is thus meeting the cost constraint. Although 500 units of output are produced using L_R units of labor and K_R units of capital, the manager could produce more output at no additional cost by using less labor and more capital.

This can be accomplished, for example, by moving up the isocost curve to point S. Point S and point R lie on the same isocost curve and consequently cost the same amount. Point S lies on a higher isoquant, Q_2, allowing the manager to produce 1,000 units without spending any more than the given amount on inputs (represented by isocost curve KL). The highest level of output attainable with the given level of cost is 1,700 units (point E), which is produced by using L_E labor and K_E capital. At point E, the highest attainable isoquant, isoquant Q_3, is just tangent to the given isocost, and $MRTS = w/r$ or $MP_L/w = MP_K/r$, the same conditions that must be met to minimize the cost of producing a given output level.

To see why MP_L/w must equal MP_K/r to maximize output for a given level of expenditures on inputs, suppose that this optimizing condition does not hold. Specifically, assume that $w = \$2$, $r = \$3$, $MP_L = 6$, and $MP_K = 12$, so that

$$\frac{MP_L}{w} = \frac{6}{2} = 3 < 4 = \frac{12}{3} = \frac{MP_K}{r}$$

The last unit of labor adds 3 units of output per dollar spent; the last unit of capital adds 4 units of output per dollar. If the firm wants to produce the maximum output possible with a given level of cost, it could spend \$1 less on labor, thereby reducing labor by half a unit and hence output by 3 units. It could spend this dollar on capital, thereby increasing output by 4 units. Cost would be unchanged, and total output would rise by 1 unit. And the firm would continue taking dollars out of labor and adding them to capital as long as the inequality holds. But as labor is reduced, its marginal product will increase, and as capital is increased, its marginal product will decline. Eventually the marginal product per dollar spent on each input will be equal. We have established the following:

Principle In the case of two variable inputs, labor and capital, the manager of a firm maximizes output for a given level of cost by using the amounts of labor and capital such that the marginal rate of technical substitution ($MRTS$) equals the input price ratio (w/r). In terms of a graph, this condition is equivalent to choosing the input combination where the slope of the given isocost curve equals the slope of the highest attainable isoquant. This output-maximizing condition implies that the marginal product per dollar spent on the last unit of each input is the same.

We have now established that economic efficiency in production occurs when managers choose variable input combinations for which the marginal product per dollar spent on the last unit of each input is the same for all inputs. While we have developed this important principle for the analysis of long-run production, we must mention for completeness that this principle also applies in the short run when two or more inputs are variable.

9.4 OPTIMIZATION AND COST

Using Figure 9.4 we showed how a manager can choose the optimal (least-cost) combination of inputs to produce a given level of output. We also showed how the total cost of producing that level of output is calculated. When the optimal input combination for each possible output level is determined and total cost is calculated for each one of these input combinations, a total cost curve (or schedule) is generated. In this section, we illustrate how any number of optimizing points can be combined into a single graph and how these points are related to the firm's cost structure.

FIGURE 9.6
An Expansion Path

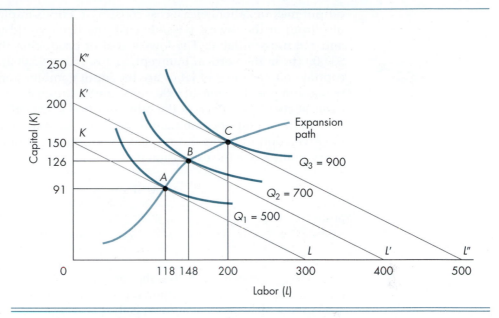

An Expansion Path

In Figure 9.4 we illustrated one optimizing point for a firm. This point shows the optimal (least-cost) combination of inputs for a given level of output. However, as you would expect, there exists an optimal combination of inputs for every level of output the firm might choose to produce. And the proportions in which the inputs are used need not be the same for all levels of output. To examine several optimizing points at once, we use the *expansion path*.

The **expansion path** shows the cost-minimizing input combination for each level of output with the input price ratio held constant. It therefore shows how input usage changes as output changes. Figure 9.6 illustrates the derivation of an expansion path. Isoquants Q_1, Q_2, and Q_3 show, respectively, the input combinations of labor and capital that are capable of producing 500, 700, and 900 units of output. The price of capital (r) is $20 and the price of labor (w) is $10. Thus any isocost curve would have a slope of $10/20 = 1/2$.

The three isocost curves KL, $K'L'$, and $K''L''$, each of which has a slope of $1/2$, represent the minimum costs of producing the three levels of output, 500, 700, and 900 because they are tangent to the respective isoquants. That is, at optimal input combinations A, B, and C, $MRTS = w/r = 1/2$. In the figure, the expansion path connects these optimal points and all other points so generated.

Note that points A, B, and C are also points indicating the combinations of inputs that can produce the maximum output possible at each level of cost given by isocost curves KL, $K'L'$, and $K''L''$. The optimizing condition, as emphasized, is the same for cost minimization with an output constraint and

expansion path
The curve or locus of points that shows the cost-minimizing input combination for each level of output with the input/price ratio held constant.

output maximization with a cost constraint. For example, to produce 500 units of output at the lowest possible cost, the firm would use 91 units of capital and 118 units of labor. The lowest cost of producing this output is therefore $3,000 (from the vertical intercept, $20 × 150 = $3,000). Likewise, 91 units of capital and 118 units of labor are the input combination that can produce the maximum possible output (500 units) under the cost constraint given by $3,000 (isocost curve KL). Each of the other optimal points along the expansion path also shows an input combination that is the cost-minimizing combination for the given output or the output-maximizing combination for the given cost. At every point along the expansion path,

$$MRTS = \frac{MP_L}{MP_K} = \frac{w}{r}$$

and

$$\frac{MP_L}{w} = \frac{MP_K}{r}$$

Therefore, the expansion path is the curve or locus of points along which the marginal rate of technical substitution is constant and equal to the input price ratio. It is a curve with a special feature: It is the curve or locus along which the firm will expand output when input prices are constant.

Now try Technical Problem 5.

Relation The expansion path is the curve along which a firm expands (or contracts) output when input prices remain constant. Each point on the expansion path represents an efficient (least-cost) input combination. Along the expansion path, the marginal rate of technical substitution equals the constant input price ratio. The expansion path indicates how input usage changes when output or cost changes.

The Expansion Path and the Structure of Cost

An important aspect of the expansion path that was implied in this discussion and will be emphasized in the remainder of this chapter is that the expansion path gives the firm its cost structure. The lowest cost of producing any given level of output can be determined from the expansion path. Thus, the structure of the relation between output and cost is determined by the expansion path.

Recall from the discussion of Figure 9.6 that the lowest cost of producing 500 units of output is $3,000, which was calculated as the price of capital, $20, times the vertical intercept of the isocost curve, 150. Alternatively, the cost of producing 500 units can be calculated by multiplying the price of labor by the amount of labor used plus the price of capital by the amount of capital used:

$$wL + rK = (\$10 \times 118) + (\$20 \times 91) = \$3,000$$

Using the same method, we calculate the lowest cost of producing 700 and 900 units of output, respectively, as

$$(\$10 \times 148) + (\$20 \times 126) = \$4,000$$

and

$$(\$10 \times 200) + (\$20 \times 150) = \$5,000$$

Similarly, the sum of the quantities of each input used times the respective input prices gives the minimum cost of producing every level of output along the expansion path. As you will see later in this chapter, this allows the firm to relate its cost to the level of output used.

9.5 LONG-RUN COSTS

Now that we have demonstrated how a manager can find the cost-minimizing input combination when more than one input is variable, we can derive the cost curves facing a manager in the long run. The structure of long-run cost curves is determined by the structure of long-run production, as reflected in the expansion path.

Derivation of Cost Schedules from a Production Function

We begin our discussion with a situation in which the price of labor (w) is $5 per unit and the price of capital (r) is $10 per unit. Figure 9.7 shows a portion of the firm's expansion path. Isoquants Q_1, Q_2, and Q_3 are associated, respectively, with 100, 200, and 300 units of output.

For the given set of input prices, the isocost curve with intercepts of 12 units of capital and 24 units of labor, which clearly has a slope of $-5/10$ ($= -w/r$), shows the least-cost method of producing 100 units of output: Use 10 units of labor and 7 units of capital. If the firm wants to produce 100 units, it spends $50 ($5 × 10) on labor and $70 ($10 × 7) on capital, giving it a total cost of $120.

Similar to the short run, we define **long-run average cost (LAC)** as

long-run average cost (LAC)
Long-run total cost divided by output ($LAC = LTC/Q$).

$$LAC = \frac{\text{Long-run total cost } (LTC)}{\text{Output } (Q)}$$

FIGURE 9.7

Long-Run Expansion Path

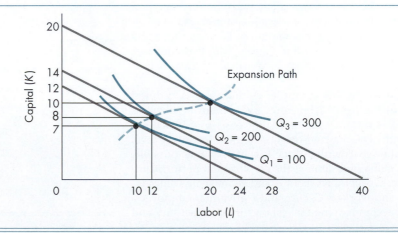

ILLUSTRATION 9.1

Downsizing or Dumbsizing
Optimal Input Choice Should Guide
Restructuring Decisions

One of the most disparaged strategies for cost cutting has been corporate "downsizing" or, synonymously, corporate "restructuring." Managers downsize a firm by permanently laying off a sizable fraction of their workforce, in many cases, using across-the-board layoffs.

If a firm employs more than the efficient amount of labor, reducing the amount of labor employed can lead to lower costs for producing the same amount of output. Business publications have documented dozens of restructuring plans that have failed to realize the promised cost savings. Apparently, a successful restructuring requires more than "meat-ax," across-the-board cutting of labor. *The Wall Street Journal* reported that "despite warnings about downsizing becoming dumbsizing, many companies continue to make flawed decisions—hasty, across-the-board cuts—that come back to haunt them."[a]

The reason that across-the-board cuts in labor do not generally deliver the desired lower costs can be seen by applying the efficiency rule for choosing inputs that we have developed in this chapter. To either minimize the total cost of producing a given level of output or to maximize the output for a given level of cost, managers must base employment decisions on the marginal product per dollar spent on labor, MP/w. Across-the-board downsizing, when no consideration is given to productivity or wages, cannot lead to an efficient reduction in the amount of labor employed by the firm. Workers with the lowest MP/w ratios must be cut first if the manager is to realize the greatest possible cost savings.

Consider this example: A manager is ordered to cut the firm's labor force by as many workers as it takes to lower its total labor costs by $10,000 per month. The manager wishes to meet the lower level of labor costs with as little loss of output as possible. The manager examines the employment performance of six workers: workers A and B are senior employees, and workers C, D, E, and F are junior employees. The accompanying table shows the productivity and wages paid monthly to each of these six workers. The senior workers (A and B) are paid more per month than the junior workers (C, D, E, and F), but the senior workers are more productive than the junior workers. Per dollar spent on wages, each senior worker contributes 0.50 unit of output per month, while each dollar spent on junior workers contributes 0.40 unit per month. Consequently, the senior workers provide the firm with more "bang per buck," even though their wages are higher. The manager, taking an across-the-board approach to cutting workers, could choose to lay off $5,000 worth of labor in each category: lay off worker A and workers C and D. This across-the-board strategy saves the required $10,000, but output falls by 4,500 units per month (= 2,500 + 2 × 1,000). Alternatively, the manager could rank the workers according to the marginal product per dollar spent on each worker. Then, the manager could start by sequentially laying off the workers with the smallest marginal product per dollar spent. This alternative approach would lead the manager to lay off four junior workers. Laying off workers C, D, E, and F saves the required $10,000 but reduces output by 4,000 units per month (= 4 × 1,000). Sequentially laying off the workers that give the least bang for the buck results in a smaller reduction in output while achieving the required labor savings of $10,000.

This illustration shows that restructuring decisions should be made on the basis of the production theory presented in this chapter. Input employment decisions cannot be made efficiently without using

Worker	Marginal product (*MP*)	Wage (*w*)	*MP/w*
A	2,500	$5,000	0.50
B	2,500	$5,000	0.50
C	1,000	$2,500	0.40
D	1,000	$2,500	0.40
E	1,000	$2,500	0.40
F	1,000	$2,500	0.40

information about both the productivity of an input *and* the price of the input. Across-the-board approaches to restructuring cannot, in general, lead to efficient reorganizations because these approaches do not consider information about worker productivity per dollar spent when making the layoff decision. Reducing the amount of labor employed is not "dumbsizing" if a firm is employing more than the efficient amount of labor. *Dumbsizing* occurs only when a manager lays off the wrong workers or too many workers.

[a]Alex Markels and Matt Murray, "Call It Dumbsizing: Why Some Companies Regret Cost-Cutting," *The Wall Street Journal*, May 14, 1996.

long-run marginal cost (LMC)
The change in long-run total cost per unit change in output ($LMC = \Delta LTC/\Delta Q$).

and **long-run marginal cost (LMC)** as

$$LMC = \frac{\Delta LTC}{\Delta Q}$$

Therefore at an output of 100,

$$LAC = \frac{LTC}{Q} = \frac{\$120}{100} = \$1.20$$

Since there are no fixed inputs in the long run, there is no fixed cost when output is 0. Thus the long-run marginal cost of producing the first 100 units is

$$LMC = \frac{\Delta LTC}{\Delta Q} = \frac{\$120 - 0}{100 - 0} = \$1.20$$

The first row of Table 9.1 gives the level of output (100), the least-cost combination of labor and capital that can produce that output, and the long-run total, average, and marginal costs when output is 100 units.

Returning to Figure 9.7, you can see that the least-cost method of producing 200 units of output is to use 12 units of labor and 8 units of capital. Thus producing

TABLE 9.1
Derivation of a Long-Run Cost Schedule

	(1)	(2)	(3)	(4)	(5)	(6)
		Least-cost combination of				
	Output	Labor (units)	Capital (units)	Total cost (*LTC*) ($w = \$5, r = \$10$)	Long-run average cost (*LAC*)	Long-run marginal cost (*LMC*)
	100	10	7	$120	$1.20	$1.20
	200	12	8	140	0.70	0.20
	300	20	10	200	0.67	0.60
	400	30	15	300	0.75	1.00
	500	40	22	420	0.84	1.20
	600	52	30	560	0.93	1.40
	700	60	42	720	1.03	1.60

200 units of output costs $140 (= $5 × 12 + $10 × 8). The average cost is $0.70 (= $140/200) and, because producing the additional 100 units increases total cost from $120 to $140, the marginal cost is $0.20 (= $20/100). These figures are shown in the second row of Table 9.1, and they give additional points on the firm's long-run total, average, and marginal cost curves.

Figure 9.7 shows that the firm will use 20 units of labor and 10 units of capital to produce 300 units of output. Using the same method as before, we calculate total, average, and marginal costs, which are given in row 3 of Table 9.1.

Figure 9.7 shows only three of the possible cost-minimizing choices. But, if we were to go on, we could obtain additional least-cost combinations, and in the same way, we could calculate the total, average, and marginal costs of these other outputs. This information is shown in the last four rows of Table 9.1 for output levels from 400 through 700.

Thus, at the given set of input prices and with the given technology, column 4 shows the long-run total cost schedule, column 5 the long-run average cost schedule, and column 6 the long-run marginal cost schedule. The corresponding long-run total cost curve is given in Figure 9.8, Panel A. This curve shows the least cost at which each quantity of output in Table 9.1 can be produced when no

FIGURE 9.8
Long-Run Total, Average, and Marginal Cost

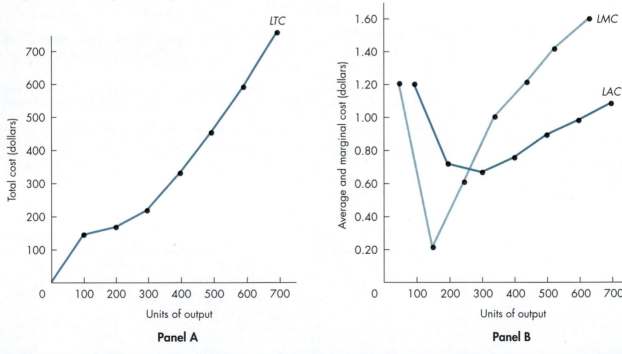

Panel A

Panel B

input is fixed. Its shape depends exclusively on the production function and the input prices.

This curve reflects three of the commonly assumed characteristics of *LTC*. First, because there are no fixed costs, *LTC* is 0 when output is 0. Second, cost and output are directly related; that is, *LTC* has a positive slope. It costs more to produce more, which is to say that resources are scarce or that one never gets something for nothing. Third, *LTC* first increases at a decreasing rate, then increases at an increasing rate. This implies that marginal cost first decreases, then increases.

Turn now to the long-run average and marginal cost curves derived from Table 9.1 and shown in Panel B of Figure 9.8. These curves reflect the characteristics of typical *LAC* and *LMC* curves. They have essentially the same shape as they do in the short run—but, as we shall show below, for different reasons. Long-run average cost first decreases, reaches a minimum (at 300 units of output), then increases. Long-run marginal cost first declines, reaches its minimum at a lower output than that associated with minimum *LAC* (between 100 and 200 units), and then increases thereafter.

In Figure 9.8, marginal cost crosses the average cost curve (*LAC*) at approximately the minimum of average cost. As we will show next, when output and cost are allowed to vary continuously, *LMC* crosses *LAC* at exactly the minimum point on the latter. (It is only approximate in Figure 9.8 because output varies discretely by 100 units in the table.)

The reasoning is the same as that given for short-run average and marginal cost curves. When marginal cost is less than average cost, each additional unit produced adds less than average cost to total cost, so average cost must decrease. When marginal cost is greater than average cost, each additional unit of the good produced adds more than average cost to total cost, so average cost must be increasing over this range of output. Thus marginal cost must be equal to average cost when average cost is at its minimum.

Figure 9.9 shows long-run marginal and average cost curves that reflect the typically assumed characteristics when output and cost can vary continuously.

Now try Technical Problem 6.

Relations   As illustrated in Figure 9.9, (1) long-run average cost, defined as

$$LAC = \frac{LTC}{Q}$$

first declines, reaches a minimum (here at Q_2 units of output), and then increases. (2) When *LAC* is at its minimum, long-run marginal cost, defined as

$$LMC = \frac{\Delta LTC}{\Delta Q}$$

equals *LAC*. (3) *LMC* first declines, reaches a minimum (here at Q_1, less than Q_2), and then increases. *LMC* lies below *LAC* over the range in which *LAC* declines; it lies above *LAC* when *LAC* is rising.

FIGURE 9.9
Long-Run Average and Marginal Cost Curves

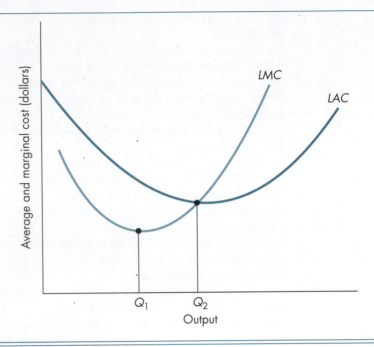

9.6 FORCES AFFECTING LONG-RUN COSTS

As they plan for the future, business owners and managers make every effort to avoid undertaking operations or making strategic plans that will result in losses or negative profits. When managers foresee market conditions that will not generate enough total revenue to cover long-run total costs, they will plan to cease production in the long run and exit the industry by moving the firm's resources to their best alternative use. Similarly, decisions to add new product lines or enter new geographic markets will not be undertaken unless managers are reasonably sure that long-run costs can be paid from revenues generated by entering those new markets. Because the long-run viability of a firm—as well as the number of product lines and geographic markets a firm chooses—depends crucially on the likelihood of covering long-run costs, managers need to understand the various economic forces that can affect long-run costs. We will now examine several important forces that affect the long-run cost structure of firms. While some of these factors cannot be directly controlled by managers, the ability to predict costs in the long run requires an understanding of all forces, internal and external, that affect a firm's long-run costs. Managers who can best forecast future costs are likely to make the most profitable decisions.

economies of scale
Occurs when long-run average cost (*LAC*) falls as output increases.

Economies and Diseconomies of Scale

The shape of a firm's long-run average cost curve (*LAC*) determines the range and strength of *economies* and *diseconomies of scale*. **Economies of scale** occur when

FIGURE 9.10
Economic and Disecomies of Scale.

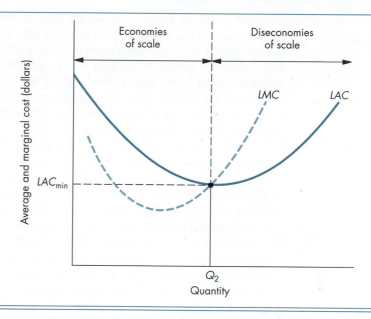

long-run average cost *falls* as output increases. In Figure 9.10, economies of scale exist over the *range* of output from zero up to Q_2 units of output. **Diseconomies of scale** occur when long-run average cost *rises* as output increases. As you can see in the figure, diseconomies of scale set in beyond Q_2 units of output.

The *strength* of scale economies or diseconomies can been seen, respectively, as the *reduction* in unit cost over the range of scale economies or the *increase* in LAC above its minimum value LAC_{min} beyond Q_2. Recall that average cost falls when marginal cost is less than average cost. As you can see in the figure, over the output range from 0 to Q_2, LAC is falling because LMC is less than LAC. Beyond Q_2, LMC is greater than LAC, and LAC is rising.

Reasons for scale economies and diseconomies Before we begin discussing reasons for economies and diseconomies of scale, we need to remind you of two things that cannot be reasons for rising or falling unit costs as quantity increases along the LAC curve: changes in technology and changes in input prices. Recall that both technology and input prices are held constant when deriving expansion paths and long-run cost curves. Consequently, as a firm moves along its LAC curve to larger scales of operation, any economies and diseconomies of scale the firm experiences must be caused by factors other than changing technology or changing input prices. When technology or input prices do change, as we will show you later in this section, the entire LAC curve shifts upward or downward, perhaps even changing shape in ways that will alter the range and strength of existing scale economies and diseconomies.

Probably the most fundamental reason for economies of scale is that larger-scale firms have greater opportunities for **specialization and division of labor**. As an

---

diseconomies of scale
Occurs when long-run average cost (*LAC*) rises as output increases.

Now try Technical Problem 7.

specialization and division of labor
Dividing production into separate tasks allows workers to specialize and become more productive, which lowers unit costs.

example, consider Precision Brakes, a small-scale automobile brake repair shop servicing only a few customers each day and employing just one mechanic. The single mechanic at Precision Brakes must perform every step in each brake repair: moving the car onto a hydraulic lift in a service bay, removing the wheels, removing the worn brake pads and shoes, installing the new parts, replacing the wheels, moving the car off the lift and out of the service bay, and perhaps even processing and collecting a payment from the customer. As the number of customers grows larger at Precision Brakes, the repair shop may wish to increase its scale of operation by hiring more mechanics and adding more service bays. At this larger scale of operation, some mechanics can specialize in lifting the car and removing worn out parts, while others can concentrate on installing the new parts and moving cars off the lifts and out of the service bays. And, a customer service manager would probably process each customer's work order and collect payments. As you can see from this rather straightforward example, large-scale production affords the opportunity for dividing a production process into a number of specialized tasks. Division of labor allows workers to focus on single tasks, which increases worker productivity in each task and brings about very substantial reductions in unit costs.

A second cause of falling unit costs arises when a firm employs one or more quasi-fixed inputs. Recall that quasi-fixed inputs must be used in fixed amounts in both the short run and long run. As output expands, quasi-fixed costs are spread over more units of output causing long-run average cost to fall. The larger the contribution of quasi-fixed costs to overall total costs, the stronger will be the downward pressure on *LAC* as output increases. For example, a natural gas pipeline company experiences particularly strong economies of scale because the quasi-fixed cost of its pipelines and compressor pumps accounts for a very large portion of the total costs of transporting natural gas through pipelines. In contrast, a trucking company can expect to experience only modest scale economies from spreading the quasi-fixed cost of tractor-trailer rigs over more transportation miles, because the variable fuel costs account for the largest portion of trucking costs.

A variety of technological factors constitute a third force contributing to economies of scale. First, when several different machines are required in a production process and each machine produces at a different rate of output, the operation may have to be quite sizable to permit proper meshing of equipment. Suppose only two types of machines are required: one that produces the product and one that packages it. If the first machine can produce 30,000 units per day and the second can package 45,000 units per day, output will have to be 90,000 units per day to fully utilize the capacity of each type of machine: three machines making the good and two machines packaging it. Failure to utilize the full capacity of each machine drives up unit production costs because the firm is paying for some amount of machine capacity it does not need or use.

Another technological factor creating scale economies concerns the costs of capital equipment: The expense of purchasing and installing larger machines is usually proportionately less than for smaller machines. For example, a printing press that can run 200,000 papers per day does not cost 10 times as much as one that can run 20,000 per day—nor does it require 10 times as much building space,

10 times as many people to operate it, and so forth. Again, expanding size or scale of operation tends to reduce unit costs of production.

A final technological matter might be the most important technological factor of all: As the scale of operation expands, there is usually a *qualitative* change in the optimal production process and type of capital equipment employed. For a simple example, consider ditch digging. The smallest scale of operation is one worker and one shovel. But as the scale expands, the firm does not simply continue to add workers and shovels. Beyond a certain point, shovels and most workers are replaced by a modern ditch-digging machine. Furthermore, expansion of scale also permits the introduction of various types of automation devices, all of which tend to reduce the unit cost of production.

You may wonder why the long-run average cost curve would ever rise. After all possible economies of scale have been realized, why doesn't the *LAC* curve become horizontal, never turning up at all? The rising portion of *LAC* is generally attributed to limitations to efficient management and organization of the firm. As the scale of a plant expands beyond a certain point, top management must necessarily delegate responsibility and authority to lower-echelon employees. Contact with the daily routine of operation tends to be lost, and efficiency of operation declines. Furthermore, managing any business entails controlling and coordinating a wide variety of activities: production, distribution, finance, marketing, and so on. To perform these functions efficiently, a manager must have accurate information, as well as efficient monitoring and control systems. Even though information technology continues to improve in dramatic ways, pushing higher the scale at which diseconomies set in, the cost of monitoring and controlling large-scale businesses eventually leads to rising unit costs.

As an organizational plan for avoiding diseconomies, large-scale businesses sometimes divide operations into two or more separate management divisions so that each of the smaller divisions can avoid some or all of the diseconomies of scale. Unfortunately, division managers frequently compete with each other for allocation of scarce corporate resources—such as workers, travel budget, capital outlays, office space, and R & D expenditures. The time and energy spent by division managers trying to influence corporate allocation of resources is costly for division managers, as well as for top-level corporate managers who must evaluate the competing claims of division chiefs for more resources. Overall corporate efficiency is sacrificed when lobbying by division managers results in a misallocation of resources among divisions. Scale diseconomies, then, remain a fact of life for very large-scale enterprises.

Constant costs: Absence of economies and diseconomies of scale In some cases, firms may experience neither economies nor diseconomies of scale, and instead face *constant costs*. When a firm experiences **constant costs** in the long run, its *LAC* curve is flat and equal to its *LMC* curve at all output levels. Figure 9.11 illustrates a firm with constant costs of $20 per unit: Average and marginal costs are both equal to $20 for all output levels. As you can see by the flat *LAC* curve, firms facing constant costs experience neither economies nor diseconomies of scale.

constant costs
Neither economies nor diseconomies of scale occur, thus *LAC* is flat and equal to *LMC* at all output levels.

FIGURE 9.11

The Special Case of Constant Costs: LMC = LAC

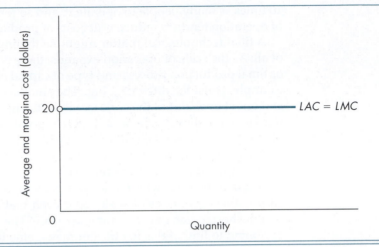

Instances of truly constant costs at all output levels are not common in practice. However, businesses frequently treat their costs as if they are constant even when their costs actually follow the more typical U-shape pattern shown in Figure 9.9. The primary reason for assuming constant costs, when costs are in fact U-shaped, is to simplify cost (and profit) computations in spreadsheets. This simplifying assumption might not adversely affect managerial decision making if marginal and average costs are very nearly equal. However, serious decision errors can occur when *LAC* rises or falls by even modest amounts as quantity rises. In most instances in this textbook, we will assume a representative *LAC*, such as that illustrated earlier in Figure 9.9. Nonetheless, you should be familiar with this special case because many businesses treat their costs as constant.

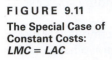

Now try Technical Problem 8.

Minimum efficient scale (*MES*) In many situations, a relatively modest scale of operation may enable a firm to capture all available economies of scale, and diseconomies may not arise until output is very large. Figure 9.12 illustrates such a situation by flattening *LAC* between points *m* and *d* to create a range of output over which *LAC* is constant. Once a firm reaches the scale of operation at point *m* on *LAC*, it will achieve the lowest possible unit costs in the long run, LAC_{min}. The minimum level of output (i.e., scale of operation) that achieves all available economies of scale is called **minimum efficient scale (*MES*)**, which is output level Q_{MES} in Figure 9.12. After a firm reaches minimum efficient scale, it will enjoy the lowest possible unit costs for all output levels up to the point where diseconomies set in at Q_{DIS} in the figure.

minimum efficient scale (*MES*)
Lowest level of output needed to reach minimum long-run average cost.

Firms can face a variety of shapes of *LAC* curves, and the differences in shape can influence long-run managerial decision making. In businesses where economies of scale are negligible, diseconomies may soon become of paramount importance, as *LAC* turns up at a relatively small volume

FIGURE 9.12
Minimum Efficient Scale

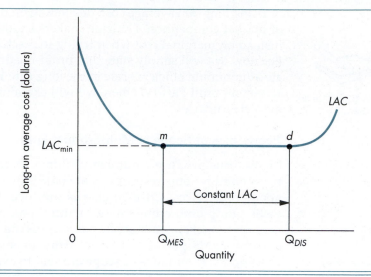

of output. Panel A of Figure 9.13 shows a long-run average cost curve for a firm of this type. Panel B illustrates a situation in which the range and strength of the available scale economies are both substantial. Firms that must have low unit costs to profitably enter or even just to survive in this market will need to operate at a large scale when they face the *LAC* in Panel B. In many real-world situations, Panel C typifies the long-run cost structure: *MES* is reached at a low level of production and then costs remain constant for a wide range of output until eventually diseconomies of scale take over.

Before leaving this discussion of scale economies, we wish to dispel a commonly held notion that *all* firms should plan to operate at minimum efficient scale in the long run. As you will see in Part IV of this book, the long run profit-maximizing output or scale of operation can occur in a region of falling, constant,

FIGURE 9.13
MES* with Various Shapes of *LAC

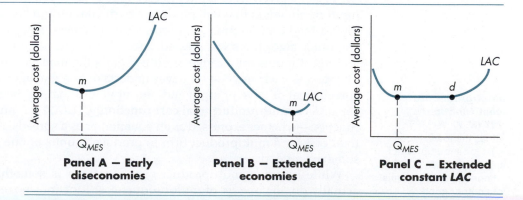

or rising long-run average cost, depending on the shape of *LAC* and the intensity of market competition. Decision makers should ignore average cost and focus instead on marginal cost when trying to reach the optimal level of any activity. For now, we will simply state that profit-maximizing firms do *not* always operate at minimum efficient scale in the long run. We will postpone a more detailed statement until Part IV, where we will examine profit-maximization in various market structures.

Now try Technical Problem 9.

Economies of Scope in Multiproduct Firms

Many firms produce a number of different products. Typically, multiproduct firms employ some resources that contribute to the production of two or more goods or services: Citrus orchards produce both oranges and grapefruit, oil wells pump both crude oil and natural gas, automotive plants produce both cars and trucks, commercial banks provide a variety of financial services, and hospitals perform a wide array of surgical operations and medical procedures. **Economies of scope** are said to exist whenever it is less costly for a multiproduct firm to produce two or more products together than for separate single-product firms to produce *identical* amounts of each product. Economists believe the prevalence of scope economies may be the best explanation for why we observe so many multiproduct firms across most industries and in most countries.

economies of scope
Exist when the joint cost of producing two or more goods is less than the sum of the separate costs of producing the goods.

Multiproduct cost functions and scope economies Thus far, our analysis of production and costs has focused exclusively on single-product firms. We are now going to examine long-run total cost when a firm produces two or more goods or services. Although we will limit our discussion here to just two goods, the analysis applies to any number of products.

A multiproduct total cost function is derived from a *multiproduct expansion path*. To construct a multiproduct expansion path for two goods X and Y, production engineers must work with a more complicated production function—one that gives technically efficient input combinations for various *pairs* of output quantities (X, Y). For a given set of input prices, engineers can find the economically efficient input combination that will produce a particular output combination (X, Y) at the lowest total cost. In practice, production engineers use reasonably complicated computer algorithms to repeatedly search for and identify the efficient combinations of inputs for a range of output pairs the manager may wish to produce. This process, which you will never undertake as a manager, typically results in a spreadsheet or table of input and output values that can be rather easily used to construct a **multiproduct total cost function: $LTC(X, Y)$**. A multiproduct total cost function—whether expressed as an equation or as a spreadsheet—gives the lowest total cost for a multiproduct firm to produce X units of one good and Y units of some other good.

multiproduct total cost function: $LTC(X, Y)$
Gives the lowest total cost for a multiproduct firm to produce X units of one good and Y units of another good.

While deriving multiproduct cost functions is something you will never actually do, the *concept* of multiproduct cost functions nonetheless proves quite useful in defining scope economies and explaining why multiproduct efficiencies arise. Economies of scope exist when

$$LTC(X, Y) < LTC(X, 0) + LTC(0, Y)$$

where $LTC(X,0)$ and $LTC(0,Y)$ are the total costs when *single*-product firms specialize in production of X and Y, respectively. As you can see from this mathematical expression, a multiproduct firm experiencing scope economies can produce goods X and Y together at a lower total cost than two single-product firms, one firm specializing in good X and the other in good Y.

Consider Precision Brakes and Mufflers—formerly our single-product firm known as Precision Brakes—that now operates as a multiservice firm repairing brakes and replacing mufflers. Precision Brakes and Mufflers can perform 4 brake jobs (B) and replace 8 mufflers (M) a day for a total cost of $1,400:

$$LTC(B, M) = LTC(4, 8) = \$1,400$$

A single-service firm specializing in muffler replacement can install 8 replacement mufflers daily at a total cost of $1,000: $LTC(0,8) = \$1,000$. A different single-service firm specializing in brake repair can perform 4 brake jobs daily for a total cost of $600: $LTC(4,0) = \$600$. In this example, a multiproduct firm can perform 4 brake jobs and replace 8 mufflers at lower total cost than two *separate* firms producing the same level of outputs:

$$LTC(4, 8) < LTC(0, 8) + LTC(4, 0)$$
$$\$1,400 < \$1,000 + \$600$$
$$\$1,400 < \$1,600$$

Thus, Precision Brakes and Mufflers experiences economies of scope for this combination of muffler repair services.

An important consequence of scope economies for managerial decision making concerns the incremental or marginal cost of adding new product or service lines: Firms that already produce good X can add production of good Y at lower cost than a specialized, single-product firm can produce Y. You can quickly confirm the validity of this statement by subtracting $LTC(X, 0)$ from both sides of the original mathematical expression for economies of scope:

$$LTC(X, Y) - LTC(X, 0) < LTC(0, Y)$$

The left side of this expression shows the marginal cost of adding Y units at a firm already producing good X, which, in the presence of scope economies, costs less than having a single-product firm produce Y units. To illustrate this point, suppose Precision Brakes, the single-product firm specializing in brake jobs, is performing 4 brake jobs daily. If Precision Brakes wishes to become a multiservice company by adding 8 muffler repairs daily, the marginal or incremental cost to do so is $800:

$$LTC(4, 8) - LTC(4, 0) = \$1,400 - \$600$$
$$= \$800$$

ILLUSTRATION 9.2

Declining Minimum Efficient Scale (*MES*) Changes the Shape of Semiconductor Manufacturing

Even those who know relatively little about computer technology have heard of Moore's Law, which has correctly predicted since 1958 that the number of transistors placed on integrated circuits will double every two years. This exponential growth is expected to continue for another 10 to 15 years. Recently, transistor size has shrunk from 130 nanometers (one nanometer = 1 billionth of a meter) to 90 nanometers, and Intel Corp. is on the verge of bringing online 65-nanometer production technology for its semiconductor chips. The implication of Moore's Law for consumers has been, of course, a tremendous and rapid increase in raw computing power coupled with higher speed, and reduced power consumption.

Unfortunately for the many semiconductor manufacturers—companies like Intel, Samsung, Texas Instruments, Advanced Micro Devices, and Motorola, to name just a few—Moore's Law causes multi*billion* dollar semiconductor fabrication plants to become outdated and virtually useless in as little as five years. When a $5 billion dollar fabrication plant gets amortized over a useful lifespan of only five years, the daily cost of the capital investment is about $3 million *per day*. The only profitable way to operate a semiconductor plant, then, is to produce and sell a very large number of chips to take advantage of the sizable scale economies available to the industry. As you know from our discussion of economies of scale, semiconductor manufacturers must push production quantities at least to the point of minimum efficient scale, or *MES*, to avoid operating at a cost disadvantage.

As technology has continually reduced the size of transistors, the long-run average cost curve has progressively shifted downward and to the right, as shown in the accompanying figure. While falling *LAC* is certainly desirable, chip manufacturers have also experienced rising *MES* with each cycle of shrinking. As you can see in the figure, *MES* increases

from point *a* with 250-nanometer technology to point *d* with the now widespread 90-nanometer technology. Every chip plant—or "fab," as they are called—must churn out ever larger quantities of chips in order to reach *MES* and remain financially viable semiconductor suppliers. Predictably, this expansion of output drives down chip prices and makes it increasingly difficult for fabs to earn a profit making computer chips.

Recently, a team of engineering consultants succeeded in changing the structure of long-run average cost for chipmakers by implementing the lean manufacturing philosophy and rules developed by Toyota Motor Corp. for making its cars. According to the consultants, applying the Toyota Production System (TPS) to chip manufacturing "lowered cycle time in the (plant) by 67 percent, . . . reduced costs by 12 percent, . . . increased the number of products produced by 50 percent, and increased production capacity by 10 percent, all without additional investment." (p. 25)

As a result of applying TPS to chip making, the long-run average cost curve is now lower at all quantities, and it has a range of constant costs beginning at a significantly lower production rate. As shown by LAC_{TPS} in the figure, *LAC* is lower and *MES* is smaller (*MES* falls from Q' to Q_{MES}). The consultants predict the following effects on competition in chip manufacturing caused by reshaping long-run average costs to look like LAC_{TPS}:

The new economics of semiconductor manufacturing now make it possible to produce chips profitably in much smaller volumes. This effect may not be very important for the fabs that make huge numbers of high-performance chips, but then again, that segment will take up a declining share of the total market. This isn't because demand for those chips will shrink. Rather, demand will grow even faster for products that require chips with rapid time-to-market and lower costs . . . (p. 28)

We agree with the technology geeks: The new shape of *LAC* will enhance competition by keeping more semiconductor manufacturers, both large and "small," in the game.

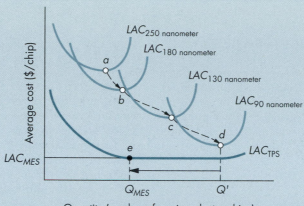

Source: Clayton Christensen, Steven King, Matt Verlinden, and Woodward Yang, "The New Economics of Semiconductor Manufacturing," *IEEE Spectrum*, May 2008, pp. 24–29.

Recall that a single-product firm specializing in muffler repair incurs a total cost of $1,000 to perform 8 muffler repairs: $LTC(0, 8) = \$1,000$, which is more costly than letting a multiproduct firm add 8 muffler repairs a day to its service mix.

As you can see from this example, the existence of economies of scope confers a cost advantage to multiproduct firms compared to single-product producers of the same goods. In product markets where scope economies are strong, managers should expect that new firms entering a market are likely to be multiproduct firms, and existing single-product firms are likely to be targets for acquisition by multiproduct firms.

Now try Technical Problem 10.

Reasons for economies of scope

Economists have identified two situations that give rise to economies of scope. In the first of these situations, economies of scope arise because multiple goods are produced together as *joint products*. Goods are **joint products** if employing resources to produce one good causes one or more other goods to be produced as by-products at little or no additional cost. Frequently, but not always, the joint products come in fixed proportions. One of the classic examples is that of beef carcasses and the leather products produced with hides that are by-products of beef production. Other examples of joint products include wool and mutton, chickens and fertilizer, lumber and saw dust, and crude oil and natural gas. Joint products always lead to economies of scope. However, occurrences of scope economies are much more common than cases of joint products.

A second cause for economies of scope, one more commonplace than joint products, arises when **common or shared inputs** contribute to the production of two or more goods or services. When a common input is purchased to make good X, as long as the common input is not completely used up in

joint products
When production of good X causes one or more other goods to be produced as byproducts at little or no additional cost.

common or shared inputs
Inputs that contribute to the production of two or more goods or services.

ILLUSTRATION 9.3

Scale and Scope Economies in the Real World

Government policymakers, academic economists, and industry analysts all wish to know which industries are subject to economies of scale and economies of scope. In this Illustration, we will briefly summarize some of the empirical estimates of scale and scope economies for two service industries: commercial banking and life insurance.

Commercial Banking

When state legislatures began allowing interstate banking during the 1980s, one of the most controversial outcomes of interstate banking was the widespread consolidation that took place through mergers and acquisitions of local banks by large out-of-state banks. According to Robert Goudreau and Larry Wall, one of the primary incentives for interstate expansion is a desire by banks to exploit economies of scale and scope.[a] To the extent that significant economies of scale exist in banking, large banks will have a cost advantage over small banks. If there are economies of scope in banking, then banks offering more banking services will have lower costs than banks providing a smaller number of services. Thomas Gilligan, Michael Smirlock, and William Marshall examined 714 commercial banks to determine the extent of economies of scale and scope in commercial banking.[b] They concluded that economies of scale in banking are exhausted at relatively low output levels. The long-run average cost curve (LAC) for commercial banks is shaped like LAC in Panel C of Figure 9.13, with minimum efficient scale (MES) occurring at a relatively small scale of operation. Based on these results, small banks do not necessarily suffer a cost disadvantage as they compete with large banks.

Economies of scope also appear to be present for banks producing the traditional set of bank products (i.e., various types of loans and deposits). Given their empirical evidence that economies of scale do not extend over a wide range of output, Gilligan, Smirlock, and Marshall argued that public policymakers should not encourage bank mergers on the basis of cost savings. They also pointed out that government regulations restricting the types of loans and deposits that

a bank may offer can lead to higher costs, given their evidence of economies of scope in banking.

Life Insurance

Life insurance companies offer three main types of services: life insurance policies, financial annuities, and accident and health (A & H) policies. Don Segal used data for approximately 120 insurance companies in the U.S. over the period 1995–1998 to estimate a multiproduct cost function for the three main lines of services offered by multiproduct insurance agencies.[c] He notes "economies of scale and scope may affect managerial decisions regarding the scale and mix of output" (p. 169). According to his findings, insurance companies experience substantial scale economies, as expected, because insurance policies rely on the statistical law of large numbers to pool risks of policyholders. The larger the pool of policyholders, the less risky, and hence less costly, it will be to insure risk. He finds LAC is still falling—but much less sharply—for the largest scale firms, which indicates that MES has not been reached by the largest insurance companies in the United States.

Unfortunately, as Segal points out, managers cannot assume a causal relation holds between firm size and unit costs—a common statistical shortcoming in most empirical studies of scale economies. The problem is this: Either (1) large size causes lower unit costs through scale economies or (2) those firms in the sample that are more efficiently managed and enjoy lower costs of operation will grow faster and end up larger in size than their less efficient rivals. In the second scenario, low costs are correlated with large size even in the absence of scale economies. So, managers of insurance companies—and everyone else for that matter—need to be cautious when interpreting statistical evidence of scale economies.

As for scope economies, the evidence more clearly points to economies of scope: "a joint production of all three lines of business by one firm would be cheaper than the overall cost of producing these products separately" (p. 184). Common inputs for supplying life insurance, annuities, and A&H policies include both the labor and capital inputs, as long as these inputs are not subject to "complete congestion" (i.e., completely exhausted or used up) in the production of any one service line. As you would expect, the actuaries, insurance agents, and managerial and clerical staff who work to supply life insurance policies can also work to provide annuities and A&H policies as well. Both physical capital—office space and equipment—and financial capital—monetary assets held in reserve to pay policy claims—can serve as common inputs for all three lines of insurance services. Segal's multiproduct cost function predicts a significant cost advantage for large, multiservice insurance companies in the United States.

[a]Robert Goudreau and Larry Wall, "Southeastern Interstate Banking and Consolidation: 1984-W," *Economic Review*, Federal Reserve Bank of Atlanta, November/December (1990), pp. 32–41.
[b]Thomas Gilligan, Michael Smirlock, and William Marshall, "Scale and Scope Economies in the Multi-Product Banking Firm," *Journal of Monetary Economics* 13 (1984), pp. 393–405.
[c]Don Segal, "A Multi-Product Cost Study of the U.S. Life Insurance Industry," *Review of Quantitative Finance and Accounting* 20 (2003), pp. 169–186.

producing good X, then it is also available at little or no extra cost to make good Y. Economies of scope arise because the marginal cost of adding good Y by a firm already producing good X—and thus able to use common inputs at very low cost—will be less costly than producing good Y by a single-product firm incurring the full cost of using common inputs. In other words, the cost of the common inputs gets spread over multiple products or services, creating economies of scope.[3]

The common or shared resources that lead to economies of scope may be the inputs used in the manufacture of the product, or in some cases they may involve only the administrative, marketing, and distribution resources of the firm. In our example of Precision Brakes and Mufflers, the hydraulic lift used to raise cars—once it has been purchased and installed for muffler repair—can be used at almost zero marginal cost to lift cars for brake repair. As you might expect, the larger the share of total cost attributable to common inputs, the greater will be the cost-savings from economies of scope. We will now summarize this discussion of economies of scope with the following relations:

Relations   When economies of scope exist: (1) The total cost of producing goods X and Y by a multi-product firm is less than the sum of the costs for specialized, single-product firms to produce these goods: $LTC(X, Y) < LTC(X, 0) + LTC(0, Y)$, and (2) Firms already producing good X can add production of good Y at lower cost than a single-product firm can produce Y: $LTC(X, Y) - LTC(X, 0) < LTC(0, Y)$. Economies of scope arise when firms produce joint products or when firms employ common inputs in production.

[3]We should note that common or shared inputs are typically *quasi-fixed inputs*. Once a fixed-sized lump of common input is purchased to make the first unit of good X, not only can more units of good X be produced without using any more of the common input, but good Y can also be produced without using any more of the common inputs. Of course, in some instances, as production levels of one or both goods increases, the common input may become exhausted or congested, requiring the multiproduct firm to purchase another lump of common input as it expands its scale and/or scope of operation. As in the case of scale economies, scope economies can emerge when quasi-fixed costs (of common inputs) are spread over more units of output, both X and Y.

Purchasing Economies of Scale

As we stressed previously in the discussion of economies of scale, changing input prices cannot be the cause of scale economies or diseconomies because, quite simply, input prices remain constant along any particular *LAC* curve. So what *does* happen to a firm's long-run costs when input prices change? As it turns out, the answer depends on the cause of the input price change. In many instances, managers of individual firms have no control over input prices, as happens when input prices are set by the forces of demand and supply in resource markets. A decrease in the world price of crude oil, for example, causes a petroleum refiner's long-run average cost curve to shift downward at every level of output of refined product. In other cases, managers as a group may influence input prices by expanding an entire industry's production level, which, in turn, significantly increases the demand and prices for some inputs. We will examine this situation in Chapter 11 when we look at the long-run supply curves for increasing-cost industries.

Sometimes, however, a purchasing manager for an individual firm may obtain *lower* input prices as the firm expands its production level. **Purchasing economies of scale** arise when large-scale purchasing of raw materials—or any other input, for that matter—enables large buyers to obtain lower input prices through quantity discounts. At the threshold level of output where a firm buys enough of an input to qualify for quantity discounting, the firm's *LAC* curve shifts downward. Purchasing economies are common for advertising media, some raw materials, and energy supplies.

Figure 9.14 illustrates how purchasing economies can affect a firm's long-run average costs. In this example, the purchasing manager gets a quantity discount

purchasing economies of scale
Large buyers of inputs receive lower input prices through quantity discounts, causing *LAC* to shift downward at the point of discount.

FIGURE 9.14
Purchasing Economies of Scale

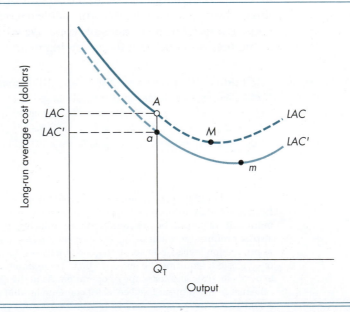

on one or more inputs once the firm's output level reaches a threshold of Q_T units at point A on the original LAC curve. At Q_T units and beyond, the firm's LAC will be lower at every output level, as indicated by LAC' in the figure. Sometimes input suppliers might offer progressively steeper discounts at several higher output levels. As you would expect, this creates multiple downward shifting points along the LAC curve.

Learning or Experience Economies

For many years economists and production engineers have known that certain industries tend to benefit from declining unit costs as the firms gain experience producing certain kinds of manufactured goods (airframes, ships, and computer chips) and even some services (heart surgery and dental procedures). Apparently, workers, managers, engineers, and even input suppliers in these industries "learn by doing" or "learn through experience." As total *cumulative* output increases, **learning or experience economies** cause long-run average cost to fall at every output level.

learning or experience economies
When cumulative output increases, causing workers to become more productive as they learn by doing and *LAC* shifts downward as a result.

Notice that learning economies differ substantially from economies of scale. With scale economies, unit costs falls as a firm increases output, moving rightward and downward along its LAC curve. With learning or experience economies, the entire LAC curve shifts downward at every output as a firm's *accumulated* output grows. The reasons for learning economies also differ from the reasons for scale economies.

The classic explanation for learning economies focuses on labor's ability to learn how to accomplish tasks more efficiently by repeating them many times; that is, learning by doing. However, engineers and managers can also play important roles in making costs fall as cumulative output rises. As experience with production grows, design engineers usually discover ways to make it cheaper to manufacture a product by making changes in specifications for components and relaxing tolerances on fit and finish without reducing product quality. With experience, managers and production engineers will discover new ways to improve factory layout to speed the flow of materials through all stages of production and to reduce input usage and waste. Unfortunately, the gains from learning and experience eventually run out, and then the LAC curve no longer falls with growing cumulative output.

In Figure 9.15, learning by doing increases worker productivity in Panel A, which causes unit costs to fall at every output level in Panel B. In Panel A, average productivity of labor begins at a value of 10 units of output per worker at the time a firm starts producing the good. As output accumulates over time from 0 to 8,000 total units, worker productivity rises from 10 units per worker (point s) to its greatest level at 20 units of output per worker (point l) where no further productivity gains can be obtained through experience alone. Notice that the length of time it takes to accumulate 8,000 units in no way affects the amount by which AP rises. In Panel A, to keep things simple, we are showing *only* the effect of learning on labor productivity. (As labor learns better how to use machines, capital productivity also increases, further contributing to the downward shift of LAC in Panel B.)

FIGURE 9.15
Learning of Experience Economies

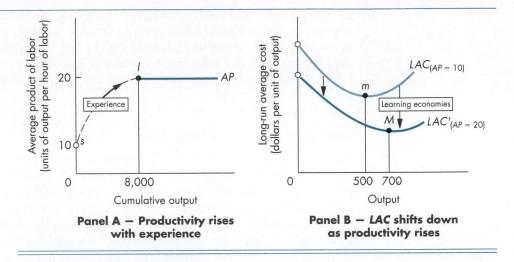

Panel A — Productivity rises with experience

Panel B — LAC shifts down as productivity rises

As a strategic matter, the ability of early entrants in an industry to use learning economies to gain a cost advantage over potential new entrants will depend on how much time start-up firms take going from point s to point l. As we will explain later, faster learning is not necessarily better when entry deterrence is the manager's primary goal. We will have more to say about this matter when we look at strategic barriers to entry in Chapter 12. For now, you can ignore the *speed* at which a firm gains experience. Generally, it is difficult to predict where the new minimum efficient scale (*MES*) will lie once the learning process is completed at point l in the figure. In Panel B, we show *MES* increasing from 500 to 700 units, but *MES* could rise, fall, or stay the same.

As a manager you will almost certainly rely on production engineers to estimate and predict the impact of experience on *LAC* and *MES*. A manager's responsibility is to use this information, which improves your forecasts of future costs, to make the most profitable decisions concerning pricing and output levels in the current period and to plan long-run entry and exit in future periods—topics we will cover in the next two parts of this book.[4]

In this section, we examined a variety of forces affecting the firm's long-run cost structure. While scale, scope, purchasing, and learning economies can all lead to lower total and average costs of supplying goods and services, we must warn you that managers should not increase production levels solely for the purpose of chasing any one of these cost economies. As you will learn in Part IV of this book, where we show you how to make profit-maximizing output and pricing decisions,

---

[4]We have chosen to bypass a quantitative treatment of learning economies in this text largely because engineers and accountants typically do such computations. For those who wish to see some quantitative methods, we recommend James R. Martin's summary of quantitative methodologies for computing the cost savings from learning curves at the following link to the Management and Accounting Web (MAAW): http://maaw.info/LearningCurveSummary.htm.

the optimal positions for businesses don't always require taking full advantage of any scale or scope economies available to the firm. Furthermore, it may not be profitable to expand production to the point where economies arise in purchasing inputs or at a rate that rapidly exploits potential productivity gains from learning by doing. However, as you can now understand, estimating and forecasting long-run cost of production will not be accurate if they overlook these important forces affecting the long-run structure of costs. All of these forces provide firms with an opportunity to reduce costs in the long run in ways that simply are not available in the short run when scale and scope are fixed.

9.7 RELATIONS BETWEEN SHORT-RUN AND LONG-RUN COSTS

Now that you understand how long-run production decisions determine the structure of long-run costs, we can demonstrate more clearly the important relations between short-run and long-run costs. As we explained at the beginning of Chapter 8, the long run or planning horizon is the collection of all possible short-run situations, one for every amount of fixed input that may be chosen in the long-run planning period. For example, in Table 8.2 in Chapter 8, the columns associated with the 10 levels of capital employment each represent a different short-run production function, and, as a group of short-run situations, they comprise the firm's planning horizon. In the first part of this section we will show you how to construct a firm's long-run planning horizon—in the form of its long-run average cost curve (LAC)—from the short-run average total cost (ATC) curves associated with each possible level of capital the firm might choose. Then, in the next part of this section, we will explain how managers can exploit the flexibility of input choice available in long-run decision making to alter the structure of short-run costs in order to reduce production costs (and increase profit).

Long-Run Average Cost as the Planning Horizon

To keep matters simple, we will continue to discuss a firm that employs only two inputs, labor and capital, and capital is the plant size that becomes fixed in the short run (labor is the variable input in the short run). Since the long run is the set of all possible short-run situations, you can think of the long run as a catalog, and each page of the catalog shows a set of short-run cost curves for one of the possible plant sizes. For example, suppose a manager can choose from only three plant sizes, say plants with 10, 30, and 60 units of capital. In this case, the firm's long-run planning horizon is a catalog with three pages: page 1 shows the short-run cost curves when 10 units of capital are employed, page 2 shows the short-run cost curves when 30 units of capital are employed, and page 3 the cost curves for 60 units of capital.

The long-run planning horizon can be constructed by overlaying the cost curves from the three pages of the catalog to form a "group shot" showing all three short-run cost structures in one figure. Figure 9.16 shows the three short-run average total cost (ATC) curves for the three plant sizes that make up the planning horizon in this example: $ATC_{K=10}$, $ATC_{K=30}$, and $ATC_{\overline{K}=60}$. Note that we have omitted the associated AVC and SMC curves to keep the figure as simple as possible.

FIGURE 9.16

**Long-Run Average Cost
(*LAC*) as the Planning
Horizon**

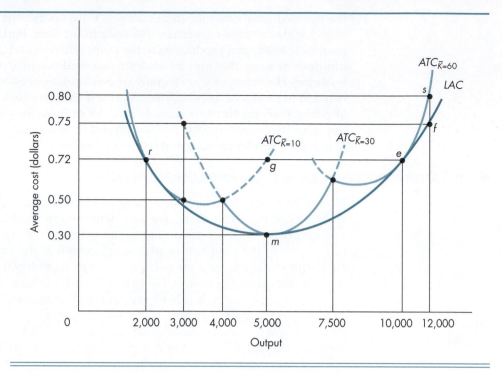

When the firm wishes to produce any output from 0 to 4,000 units, the manager will choose the small plant size with the cost structure given by $ATC_{\bar{K}=10}$ because the average cost, and hence the total cost, of producing each output over this range is lower in a plant with 10 units of capital than in a plant with either 30 units or 60 units of capital. For example, when 3,000 units are produced in the plant with 10 units of capital, average cost is $0.50 and total cost is $1,500, which is better than spending $2,250 (= $0.75 × 3,000) to produce 3,000 units in the medium plant with 30 units of capital. (Note that if the *ATC* curve for the large plant in Figure 9.16 is extended leftward to 3,000 units of production, the average and total cost of producing 3,000 units in a plant with 60 units of capital is higher than both of the other two plant sizes.)

When the firm wishes to produce output levels between 4,000 and 7,500 units, the manager would choose the medium plant size (30 units of capital) because $ATC_{\bar{K}=30}$ lies below both of the other two *ATC* curves for all outputs over this range. Following this same reasoning, the manager would choose the large plant size (60 units of capital) with the cost structure shown by $ATC_{\bar{K}=60}$ for any output greater than 7,500 units of production. In this example, the planning horizon, which is precisely the firm's long-run average cost (*LAC*) curve, is formed by the light-colored, solid portions of the three *ATC* curves shown in Figure 9.16.

Firms can generally choose from many more than three plant sizes. When a very large number of plant sizes can be chosen, the *LAC* curve smoothes out and typically takes a ∪-shape as shown by the dark-colored *LAC* curve in Figure 9.16. The set of all tangency points, such as *r, m,* and *e* in Figure 9.16, form a *lower envelope* of average costs. For this reason, long-run average cost is called an "envelope" curve.

While we chose to present the firm's planning horizon as the envelope of short-run average cost curves, the same relation holds between the short-run and long-run total or marginal cost curves: Long-run cost curves are always comprised of all possible short-run curves (i.e., they are the envelope curves of their short-run counterparts). Now that we have established the relation between short- and long-run costs, we can demonstrate why short-run costs are generally higher than long-run costs.

Now try Technical Problem 11.

Restructuring Short-Run Costs

In the long run, a manager can choose any input combination to produce the desired output level. As we demonstrated earlier in this chapter, the optimal amount of labor and capital for any specific output level is the combination that minimizes the long-run total cost of producing that amount of output. When the firm builds the optimal plant size and employs the optimal amount of labor, the total (and average) cost of producing the intended or planned output will be the same in both the long run and the short run. In other words, long-run and short-run costs are identical when the firm produces the output in the short run for which the fixed plant size (capital input) is optimal. However, if demand or cost conditions change and the manager decides to increase or decrease output in the short run, then the current plant size is no longer optimal. Now the manager will wish to restructure its short-run costs by adjusting plant size to the level that is optimal for the new output level, as soon as the next opportunity for a long-run adjustment arises.

We can demonstrate the gains from restructuring short-run costs by returning to the situation presented in Figure 9.4, which is shown again in Figure 9.17. Recall that the manager wishes to minimize the total cost of producing 10,000 units when the price of labor (*w*) is $40 per unit and the price of capital (*r*) is $60 per unit. As explained previously, the manager finds the optimal (cost-minimizing) input combination at point *E: L** = 90 and *K** = 60. As you also know from our previous discussion, point *E* lies on the expansion path, which we will now refer to as the "long-run" expansion path in this discussion.

We can most easily demonstrate the gains from adjusting plant size (or capital levels) by employing the concept of a *short-run expansion path*. A **short-run expansion path** gives the cost-minimizing (or output-maximizing) input combination for each level of output when capital is fixed at $\overline{K}$ units in the short run. To avoid any confusion in terminology, we must emphasize that the term "expansion path" always refers to a *long-run* expansion path, while an expansion path for the short run, to distinguish it from its long-run counterpart, is always called a *short-run* expansion path.

Suppose the manager wishes to produce 10,000 units. From the planning horizon in Figure 9.16, the manager determines that a plant size of 60 units of capital is the optimal plant to build for short-run production. As explained previously, once the manager builds the production facility with 60 units of capital, the firm

short-run expansion path
Horizontal line showing the cost-minimizing input combinations for various output levels when capital is fixed in the short run.

FIGURE 9.17

Gains from Restructuring Short-Run Costs

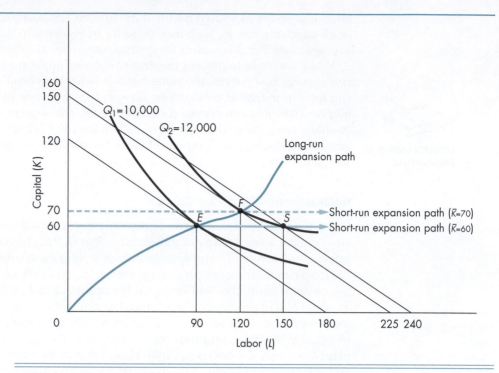

operates with the short-run cost structure given by $ATC_{\bar{K}=60}$. This cost structure corresponds to the firm's short-run expansion path in Figure 9.17, which is a horizontal line at 60 units of capital passing through point E on the long-run expansion path. As long as the firm produces 10,000 units in the short run, all of the firm's inputs are optimally adjusted and its long- and short-run costs are identical: Total cost is $7,200 (= $40 × 90 + $60 × 60) and average cost is $0.72 (= $7,200/10,000). In general, when the firm is producing the output level in the short run using the long-run optimal plant size, ATC and LAC are tangent at that output level. For example, when the firm produces 10,000 units in the short run using 60 units of capital, $ATC_{\bar{K}=60}$ is tangent to LAC at point e.

If the manager decides to increase or decrease output in the short run, short-run production costs will then exceed long-run production costs because input levels will not be at the optimal levels given by the long-run expansion path. For example, if the manager increases output to 12,000 units in the short run, the manager must employ the input combination at point S on the short-run expansion path in Figure 9.17. The short-run total cost of producing 12,000 units is $9,600 (= $40 × 150 + $60 × 60) and average total cost is $0.80 (= $9,600/12,000) at point s in Figure 9.17. Of course, the manager realizes that point F is a less costly input combination for producing 12,000 units, because input combination F lies on a lower isocost line than S. In fact, with input combination F, the total cost of producing 12,000 units is $9,000 (= $40 × 120 + $60 × 70), and average cost is $0.75 (= $9,000/12,000), as shown at point f in Figure 9.16. Short-run costs exceed long-run costs for output levels below 10,000 units as well, because a plant size of 60 units of capital is too big (i.e., larger than the optimal plant size) for every output below point E on the long-run expansion path.

At the next opportunity to adjust plant size, the manager will increase plant size to 70 units, as long as the firm plans to continue producing 12,000 units. Increasing capital to 70 units causes the short-run expansion path to shift upward as shown by the broken horizontal line in Figure 9.17. By restructuring short-run production, the manager reduces the short-run total costs of producing 12,000 units by $600 (= $9,600 − $9,000). As you will see in Part IV, firms can increase their profits—sometimes even convert losses to profits—by adjusting their fixed inputs to create a lower cost structure for short-run production operations. We can now summarize this discussion with the following principle.

Now try Technical Problem 12.

Principle   Because managers have the greatest flexibility to choose inputs in the long run, costs are lower in the long run than in the short run for all output levels except the output level for which the fixed input is at its optimal level. Thus the firm's short-run costs can generally be reduced by adjusting the fixed inputs to their optimal long-run levels when the long-run opportunity to adjust fixed inputs arises.

9.8 SUMMARY

■ In the long run, all fixed inputs become variable inputs and the firm operates with the optimal levels of every input. Isoquants are an important tool of analysis when both labor and capital are variable inputs. An isoquant is a curve showing all possible input combinations capable of producing a given level of output. Isoquants must be downward sloping because if greater amounts of labor are used, then less capital is required to produce a given level of output. The marginal rate of technical substitution, MRTS, is the slope of an isoquant and measures the rate at which the two inputs can be substituted for one another while maintaining a constant level of output. MRTS can be expressed as the ratio of two marginal products, and a minus sign is added to make MRTS a positive number because isoquants are negatively sloped: $MRTS = -(\Delta K/\Delta L) = MP_L/MP_K$. (LO1)

■ Isocost curves show the various combinations of inputs that may be purchased for a given level of expenditure ($\overline{C}$) at given input prices (w and r). The equation of an isocost curve is given by $K = (\overline{C}/r) - (w/r)L$. The slope of an isocost curve is the negative of the input price ratio ($-w/r$). The K-intercept is $\overline{C}/r$, which represents the amount of capital that may be purchased when all $\overline{C}$ dollars are spent on capital (i.e., zero labor is purchased). (LO2)

■ A manager minimizes total cost of producing $\overline{Q}$ units of output by choosing the input combination on isoquant $\overline{Q}$, which is just tangent to an isocost curve. Because the optimal input combination occurs at the point of tangency between the isoquant and an isocost curve, the two slopes are equal in equilibrium. Mathematically, the equilibrium condition may be expressed as $MP_L/MP_K = w/r$ or $MP_L/w = MP_K/r$. In order to maximize output for a given level of expenditure on inputs, a manager must choose the combination of inputs that equates the marginal rate of technical substitution and the input price ratio, which requires choosing an input combination satisfying exactly the same conditions set forth above for minimizing cost. (LO3)

■ The expansion path shows the optimal (or efficient) input combination for every level of output. The expansion path is derived for a specific set of input prices, and along an expansion path the input-price ratio is constant and equal to the marginal rate of technical substitution. Long-run cost curves are derived from the expansion path. The long-run total cost of producing any particular output level, LTC, is the sum of the optimal amounts of labor, L^*, and capital, K^*, multiplied times their respective input prices: $LTC = wL^* + rK^*$. (LO4)

- Long-run average cost, LAC, is defined as $LAC = LTC/Q$ and measures the unit cost of output. Long-run marginal cost, LMC, is defined as $LMC = \Delta LTC/\Delta Q$ and measures the incremental cost of producing another unit. LMC lies below (above) LAC when LAC is falling (rising). LMC equals LAC at LAC's minimum value. (LO5)
- When LAC is decreasing, economies of scale are present, and when LAC is increasing, diseconomies of scale are present. The minimum efficient scale of operation, MES, is the lowest level of output needed to reach the minimum value of long-run average cost. When economies of scope, exist, the total cost of producing goods X and Y by a multiproduct firm is less than the sum of the costs for specialized, singleproduct firms to produce these goods: $LTC(X, Y) < LTC(X, 0) + LTC(0, Y)$. Firms already producing good X can add production of good Y at lower cost than a single-product firm can produce Y: $LTC(X, Y) - LTC(X, 0) < LTC(0, Y)$. Economies of scope arise when firms produce joint products or when firms employ common inputs in production. Purchasing economies of scale arise when large-scale purchasing of inputs enables large buyers to obtain lower input prices through quantity discounts. At the threshold output level where the firm buys enough resource to receive quantity discounting, the LAC curve shifts downward. Learning or experience economies arise when, as cumulative output increases, workers become more productive as they learn by doing. Learning causes the LAC curve to shift downward until all gains from experience have been captured. (LO6)
- The relations between long-run cost and short-run cost can be summarized by the following points: (1) LMC intersects LAC when the latter is at its minimum point, (2) at each output where a particular ATC is tangent to LAC, the relevant SMC equals LMC, and (3) for all ATC curves, the point of tangency with LAC is at an output less (greater) than the output of minimum ATC if the tangency is at an output less (greater) than that associated with minimum LAC. Because managers possess the greatest flexibility in choosing inputs in the long run, long-run costs are lower than short-run costs for all output levels except the output level for which the short-run fixed input is at its optimal level. Unless the firm is operating at the point of intersection between the long-run expansion path and its current short-run expansion path, a firm's short-run costs can be reduced by adjusting the fixed inputs to their optimal long-run levels when the opportunity to adjust fixed inputs arises in the long run. (LO7)

KEY TERMS

common or shared inputs

constant costs

diseconomies of scale

economies of scale

economies of scope

expansion path

isocost curve

isoquant

isoquant map

joint products

learning or experience economies

long-run average cost (LAC)

long-run marginal cost (LMC)

marginal rate of technical
  substitution (MRTS)

minimum efficient scale (MES)

multiproduct total cost function:
  LTC(X,Y)

purchasing economies of scale

short-run expansion path

specialization and division
  of labor

TECHNICAL PROBLEMS

1. The accompanying figure shows the isoquant for producing 1,000 units.

   a. At point A in the figure, the marginal rate of technical substitution (MRTS) is _____.

   b. At point A in the figure, increasing labor usage by 1 unit requires that the manager _____ (increase, decrease) capital usage by (approximately) _____ units to keep the level of production at exactly 1,000 units.

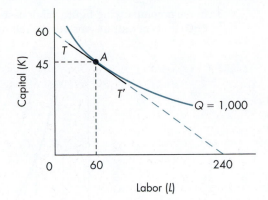

c. If the marginal product of the 45th unit of capital is 80, then the marginal product of the 60th unit of labor is _____.

2. The price of capital is $50 per unit. Use the accompanying figure, which shows an isocost curve, to answer the questions that follow:

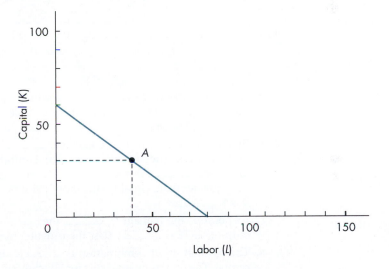

a. The equation for the isocost curve shown in the figure is $K = $ _____. The price of labor is $_____ per unit. The total cost associated with this isocost curve is $_____.

b. Input combination A is _____ units of labor and _____ units of capital. The total cost of input combination A is $_____. Verify that point A satisfies the isocost equation in part a.

c. For the input prices used in parts a and b, construct the isocost curve for input combinations costing $4,500. For the $4,500 isocost curve, the capital intercept is _____ and the labor intercept is _____. The equation of the isocost curve is $K = $ _____. If 40 units of labor are employed, then _____ units of capital can be employed for a total cost of $4,500.

3. In the accompanying figure, labor costs $100 per unit. The manager wants to produce 2,500 units of output. Answer the following questions:

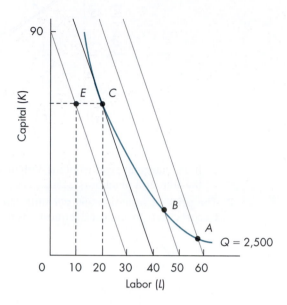

a. At point A, the MRTS is _____ (less than, greater than, equal to) the input price ratio w/r. The total cost of producing 2,500 units with input combination A is $_____. The price of capital is $_____ per unit.

b. By moving from A to B, the manager _____ (decreases, increases) labor usage and _____ (decreases, increases) capital usage. The move from A to B decreases _____ but leaves _____ unchanged. At B, MRTS is _____ (less than, greater than, equal to) the input price ratio w/r. The total cost of producing at B is $_____.

c. At point C, the manager _____ the _____ cost of producing 2,500 units of output. MRTS is _____ (less than, greater than, equal to) the input price ratio w/r.

d. The optimal input combination is _____ units of labor and _____ units of capital. The minimum total cost for which 2,500 units can be produced is $_____.

e. Input combination E costs $_____. Explain why the manager does not choose input combination E.

4. Suppose a firm is currently using 500 laborers and 325 units of capital to produce its product. The wage rate is $25, and the price of capital is $130. The last laborer adds 25 units to total output, while the last unit of capital adds 65 units to total output. Is the manager of this firm making the optimal input choice? Why or why not? If not, what should the manager do?

5. An expansion path can be derived under the assumption either that the manager attempts to produce each output at minimum cost or that the manager attempts to produce the maximum output at each level of cost. The paths are identical in both cases. Explain.

6. The accompanying graph shows five points on a firm's expansion path when the price of labor is $25 per unit and the price of capital is $100 per unit. From this graph, fill in the blanks in the following table:

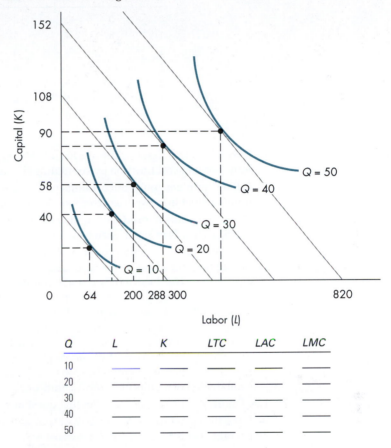

Q	L	K	LTC	LAC	LMC
10	____	____	____	____	____
20	____	____	____	____	____
30	____	____	____	____	____
40	____	____	____	____	____
50	____	____	____	____	____

7. In Technical Problem 6, economies of scale exist over the range of output _____ to _____ units. Diseconomies of scale exist over the range of output _____ to _____ units.

8. For the firm in Figure 9.11 that experiences constant long-run costs, calculate the following costs:

   a. At 200 units of output, long-run average cost is $_____, long-run marginal cost is $_____, and long-run total cost is $_____.

   b. At 500 units of output, long-run average cost is $_____, long-run marginal cost is $_____, and long-run total cost is $_____.

9. In Technical Problem 6, the minimum efficient scale (MES) is _____ units. Is MES also the profit-maximizing level of output in the long run?

10. A firm planning to produce two goods, X and Y, obtains the following spreadsheet showing a portion of the multiproduct expansion path when the firm employs two inputs, L and K:

Multiproduct expansion path				Multiproduct total cost
L	K	X	Y	LTC(X, Y)
0	0	0	0	0
1	6	4	0	___
2	11	8	0	___
1	10	0	6	___
2	25	0	12	___
1	12	4	6	___
2	32	8	12	___

a. If the firm faces input prices of $40 and $80, respectively, for L and K, construct the multiproduct cost function by computing the missing values for LTC(X, Y).

b. If the firm plans to produce 4 units of X and 6 units of Y in the long run, will the multiproduct firm experience economies of scope? Explain.

c. If the firm plans to produce 8 units of X and 12 units of Y in the long run, will the multiproduct firm experience economies of scope? Explain.

d. For a firm that is already producing 4 units of X, the marginal cost of adding 6 units of Y to its production mix is $_____, which is _____ (greater than, less than, equal to) the cost incurred by a single-product firm producing 6 units of Y, which is $_____. Thus, economies of scope _____ (exist, do not exist) for the product combination of 4 units of X and 6 units of Y.

e. For a firm that is already producing 12 units of Y, the marginal cost of adding 8 units of X to its production mix is $_____, which is _____ (greater than, less than, equal to) the cost incurred by a single-product firm producing 8 units of X, which is $_____. Thus, economies of scope _____ (exist, do not exist) for the product combination of 8 units of X and 12 units of Y.

11. Use Figure 9.16 to answer the following questions.

a. If the firm produces 5,000 units of output with a plant using 10 units of capital, the average cost is $_____ and total cost is $_____.

b. If the firm produces 5,000 units of output with a plant using 30 units of capital, the average cost is $_____ and total cost is $_____.

c. In the long-run planning horizon, which plant should the manager choose to produce 5,000 units of output? Why?

12. The figure on the next page shows the long-run and short-run expansion paths as originally illustrated in Figure 9.17. Continue to assume that the price of labor is $40 per unit and the price of capital is $60 per unit. The manager is operating in the short run with 60 units of capital. Suppose the manager wants to produce 8,000 units of output.

a. In the short run, the cost-minimizing input combination is _____ units of labor and _____ units of capital.

b. The short-run total cost of producing 8,000 units is $_____ and ATC is $_____ per unit.

c. If the manager plans to continue producing 8,000 units in the long run, the manager could lower the total cost of producing 8,000 units by $_____ by employing _____ units of labor and _____ units of capital.

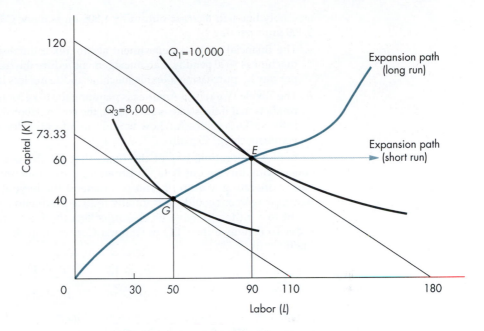

d. Construct the new short-run expansion path once the long-run adjustment in part *c* has been completed.

APPLIED PROBLEMS

1. An airline transportation consultant offers the CEO of BlueStar, a struggling new commercial airline company, the following advice concerning the airline's high operating costs in the current quarter: "You don't have enough aircraft to operate efficiently. However, at some point in the long run, you will have the opportunity to add aircraft to your fleet in order to reduce your *total* costs and still carry the same passenger load." Does this advice make any sense? In the long run, how can BlueStar's *total* costs fall by adding more aircraft to its fleet? Must BlueStar experience economies of scale for the consultant's advice to be correct?

2. The Largo Publishing House uses 400 printers and 200 printing presses to produce books. A printer's wage rate is $20, and the price of a printing press is $5,000. The last printer added 20 books to total output, while the last press added 1,000 books to total output. Is the publishing house making the optimal input choice? Why or why not? If not, how should the manager of Largo Publishing House adjust input usage?

3. How does the theory of efficient production apply to managers of government bureaus or departments that are not run for profit? How about nonprofit clubs that collect just enough dues from their members to cover the cost of operation?

4. The MorTex Company assembles garments entirely by hand even though a textile machine exists that can assemble garments faster than a human can. Workers cost $50 per day, and each additional laborer can produce 200 more units per day (i.e., marginal product is constant and equal to 200). Installation of the first textile machine on the

assembly line will increase output by 1,800 units daily. Currently the firm assembles 5,400 units per day.

a. The financial analysis department at MorTex estimates that the price of a textile machine is $600 per day. Can management reduce the cost of assembling 5,400 units per day by purchasing a textile machine and using less labor? Why or why not?

b. The Textile Workers of America is planning to strike for higher wages. Management predicts that if the strike is successful, the cost of labor will increase to $100 per day. If the strike is successful, how would this affect the decision in part a to purchase a textile machine? Explain.

5. Gamma Corporation, one of the firms that retains you as a financial analyst, is considering buying out Beta Corporation, a small manufacturing firm that is now barely operating at a profit. You recommend the buyout because you believe that new management could substantially reduce production costs, and thereby increase profit to a quite attractive level. You collect the following product information in order to convince the CEO at Gamma Corporation that Beta is indeed operating inefficiently:

$$MP_L = 10 \qquad P_L = \$20$$

$$MP_K = 15 \qquad P_K = \$15$$

Explain how these data provide evidence of inefficiency. How could the new manager of Beta Corporation improve efficiency?

6. We frequently hear the following terms used by businesspersons. What does each mean in economic terminology?

a. Spreading the overhead.

b. A break-even level of production.

c. The efficiency of mass production.

7. The production engineers at Impact Industries have derived the expansion path shown in the following figure. The price of labor is $100 per unit.

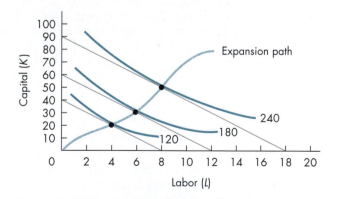

a. What price does Impact Industries pay for capital?

b. If the manager at Impact decides to produce 180 units of output, how much labor and capital should be used in order to minimize total cost?

    c. What is the total cost of producing 120, 180, and 240 units of output in the long run?

    d. Impact Industries originally built the plant (i.e., purchased the amount of capital) designed to produce 180 units optimally. *In the short run with capital fixed,* if the manager decides to expand production to 240 units, what is the amount of labor and capital that will be used? (*Hint:* How must the firm expand output in the short run when capital is fixed?)

    e. Given your answer to part *d,* calculate average variable, average fixed, and average total cost in the short run.

8. Commercial bakeries typically sell a variety of products (breads, rolls, muffins, cakes, etc.) to local grocery stores. There are substantial economies of scale in the production of each one of the bakery products, which makes it cost-effective for bakeries to specialize in the production of just one product. Grocery stores, however, prefer to buy from multiproduct bakeries that sell a full line of bakery products. How might managers organize production to take advantage of the economies of scale and scope in production and marketing that exist in the baking industry?

9. The Qwik Serve Walk-In Clinic always has three MDs and eight RNs working at its 24-hour clinic, which serves customers with minor emergencies and ailments. The clinic has hired an efficiency expert to examine its operations and make suggestions for reducing costs.

    For some of the medical procedures done at the clinic, experienced nurses can perform the medical tasks approximately as well as the physicians can, as long as the nurses are supervised by MDs. Because MDs are more highly trained than nurses, the marginal product of MDs is higher than the marginal product of RNs.

    The manager of the clinic is confused by the efficiency consultant's report because the report recommends using more RNs and fewer MDs to lower the cost of providing a given level of medical services. Under what circumstances would it be economically efficient for this clinic to use more RNs and fewer MDs (given $MP_{MD} > MP_{RN}$)? Explain.

10. Ross Perot added his memorable "insight" to the debate over the North American Free Trade Agreement (NAFTA) when he warned that passage of NAFTA would create a "giant sucking sound" as U.S. employers shipped jobs to Mexico, where wages are lower than wages in the United States. As it turned out, many U.S. firms chose *not* to produce in Mexico despite the much lower wages there. Explain why it may not be economically efficient to move production to foreign countries, even ones with substantially lower wages.

11. Brake repair and muffler repair require many tools and other capital equipment that can be classified as shared or common inputs.

    a. What are some of these shared or common inputs in muffler and brake repair?

    b. Are brake repairs and muffler repairs joint products? Why or why not?

    Firms that produce *only* muffler repair services must spend $900,000 on common inputs used in brake and muffler repair. The marginal cost of muffler repair is $50. The long-run total cost function for a firm specializing in muffler repair is

$$LTC(Q_M) = 900{,}000 + 50Q_M$$

    Firms that produce *only* brake repair services must also spend $900,000 on common inputs used in brake and muffler repair. The marginal cost of brake repair is $50. The long-run total cost function for a firm specializing in brake repair is

$$LTC(Q_B) = 900{,}000 + 60Q_B$$

Firms that do only muffler repair work or only brake repair work can extend their service line to include the other type of repair work by spending $25,000 to train their mechanics to do the new type of repair work and to undertake initial advertising costs to inform consumers of the new service.

c. Write the mathematical expression for the multiproduct long-run total cost function $LTC(Q_M, Q_B)$, which gives the long-run total cost for a repair shop doing Q_M muffler repairs and Q_B brake repairs.

d. A small company, All Brakes and Mufflers, Inc., plans to perform 5,000 muffler repairs and 4,000 brake repairs annually. Use the multiproduct cost function in part c to calculate the long-run total cost for All Brakes and Mufflers to produce this combination of services.

Down the street from All Brakes and Mufflers are two rival firms, Just Brakes Inc. and Just Mufflers Inc., which each specialize in doing only one type of repair work.

e. Just Mufflers, Inc. plans to perform 5,000 muffler repairs annually. Calculate the total costs for Just Mufflers, Inc. to do 5,000 muffler repairs.

f. Just Brakes, Inc. plans to perform 4,000 brake repairs annually. Calculate the total costs for Just Brakes, Inc. to do 4,000 brake repairs.

g. Do you find evidence of economies of scope in brake and muffler repair? Explain why using your answers in parts d, e, and f.

h. What are the implications of your finding in part g for the nature of competition in this brake and muffler repair market? How do you explain the fact that specialty companies like Just Brakes or Just Mufflers sometimes do compete successfully with multiservice rivals that do both brake and muffler repair?

▣ **MATHEMATICAL APPENDIX**   **Production and Cost Relations with Two Variable Inputs**

Cost Minimization

Define a two-input production function as

(1) $$Q = f(L, K)$$

The marginal products of the two inputs are the partial derivatives

$$MP_L = \frac{\partial Q}{\partial L} \quad \text{and} \quad MP_K = \frac{\partial Q}{\partial K}$$

First, let's establish that the slope of an isoquant (in absolute value) equals the ratio of the marginal products. First, take the total differential of the production function:

$$dQ = \frac{\partial f}{\partial L} dL + \frac{\partial f}{\partial K} dK = MP_L dL + MP_K dK$$

Along an isoquant dL and dK must be such that dQ is 0. Thus we next set $dQ = 0$ and solve for the $MRTS$:

$$MP_L dL + MP_K dK = 0$$

$$MP_K dK = -MP_L dL$$

$$MRTS = -\frac{dK}{dL} = \frac{MP_L}{MP_K}$$

Now consider a manager who plans to produce a specific level of output, denoted as $\overline{Q}$. The manager's optimization problem is to choose L and K to minimize the long-run total cost (C) of producing $\overline{Q}$ units of output. Given input prices for L and K, denoted as w and r, respectively, the long-run total cost of employing any input combination (L, K) is $C = wL + rK$. The constrained minimization problem is solved by minimizing the following Lagrangian function:

$$\mathcal{L} = wL + rK + \lambda[\overline{Q} - f(L, K)]$$

where λ is the Lagrangian multiplier. Minimization of the Lagrangian equation, which is a function of three variables L, K, and λ, requires that L, K, and λ be chosen such that the following first-order necessary conditions are satisfied:

(2a) $$\frac{\partial \mathcal{L}}{\partial L} = w - \frac{\partial Q}{\partial L} = 0$$

(2b) $$\frac{\partial \mathcal{L}}{\partial K} = r - \frac{\partial Q}{\partial K} = 0$$

(2c) $$\frac{\partial \mathcal{L}}{\partial \lambda} = \overline{Q} - f(L, K) = 0$$

Combining conditions (2a) and (2b) in ratio form, it follows that the necessary condition for minimizing the cost of producing $\overline{Q}$ units of output is

(3) $\quad \dfrac{w}{r} = \dfrac{\partial Q/\partial L}{\partial Q/\partial K} = \dfrac{MP_L}{MP_K} = MRTS \quad$ or $\quad \dfrac{MP_L}{w} = \dfrac{MP_K}{r}$

Necessary condition (3) for minimization requires that the manager choose an input combination such that the slope of the isocost line is equal to the slope of the isoquant, which is the tangency solution derived in this chapter. Thus conditions (2a) and (2b) require that the manager select input combinations that lie on the expansion path. Alternatively, the conditions for minimization require that the marginal products per dollar spent on each input be equal. Finally, to ensure that $\overline{Q}$ units of output are produced, the manager must not only be on the expansion path but also be on the $\overline{Q}$ isoquant. Necessary condition (2c) forces the manager to be on the $\overline{Q}$ isoquant.

Output Maximization: Duality in Cost and Production

Now let the manager choose L and K to maximize output for a given level of total cost, C. This constrained maximization problem is solved by maximizing the following Lagrangian function:

$$\mathcal{L} = f(L, K) + \lambda(\overline{C} - wL - rK)$$

Maximization of the Lagrangian equation, which is a function of three variables, L, K, and λ, requires that L, K, and λ be chosen so that the following partial derivatives simultaneously equal 0:

(4a) $\quad \dfrac{\partial \mathcal{L}}{\partial L} = \dfrac{\partial Q}{\partial L} - \lambda w = 0$

(4b) $\quad \dfrac{\partial \mathcal{L}}{\partial K} = \dfrac{\partial Q}{\partial K} - \lambda r = 0$

(4c) $\quad \dfrac{\partial \mathcal{L}}{\partial \lambda} = \overline{C} - wL - rK = 0$

Combining conditions (4a) and (4b) in ratio form, it follows that the necessary condition for maximizing output for a given level of cost is the same as that in expression (3), the conditions for cost minimization.

Thus, as we showed in this chapter, both cost minimization or output maximization require that the manager choose the input combination where the isoquant is tangent to the isocost line. Since these two alternative approaches for finding optimal levels of L and K result in identical expansion paths, mathematicians say a *duality* exists in cost and production theory.

The Expansion Path and Efficient Input-Usage Functions

Recall from the chapter that the expansion path is the locus of L and K combinations for which the marginal rate of technical substitution equals the (constant) input price ratio. Thus the expansion path can be expressed as

(5) $\qquad\qquad K^* = K^*(L^*; w, r)$

where K^* and L^* are the efficient levels of input usage for producing various levels of output, *given* fixed input prices w and r. The expansion path in expression (5) is obtained from expression (3) by solving algebraically for K^* in terms of L^*, w, and r. For each value of L^* in (5), there is a single value of K^*.

From the expansion path, it is possible to express the optimal levels of input usage as functions of $\overline{Q}$ given the fixed input prices w and r

(6) $\qquad L^* = L^*(\overline{Q}; w, r)$ and $K^* = K^*(\overline{Q}; w, r)$

To derive efficient input-usage functions, substitute the values of labor and capital (L^*, K^*) that solve firstorder necessary conditions for cost-minimization into expression 2c

(7) $\qquad\qquad \overline{Q} - f(L^*, K^*) = 0$

To find $L^*(\overline{Q}; w, r)$, substitute the expansion path equation (5) into (7) and solve for L^* in terms of $\overline{Q}$, w, and r. To find $K^*(\overline{Q}; w, r)$, substitute the expression $L^*(\overline{Q}; w, r)$ into the expansion path equation (5) to get $K^*(\overline{Q}; w, r)$. The efficient input functions, which are derived from the expansion path, are used to derive the long-run cost functions for a firm. Next we show how this is done for the production function $Q = AL^aK^{1-a}$.

The Expansion Path and Long-Run Costs: $Q = AL^aK^{1-a}$

Let the production function be defined as $Q = AL^aK^{1-a}$, where a is restricted by $0 < a < 1$. Begin by finding the two marginal product functions

(8a) $\qquad MP_L = \dfrac{\partial Q}{\partial L} = aAL^{a-1} K^{1-a}$

(8b) $\qquad MP_K = \dfrac{\partial Q}{\partial K} = (1 - a)AL^a K^{-a}$

MRTS is the ratio of the marginal products:

(9) $\quad MRTS = \dfrac{MP_L}{MP_K} = \dfrac{aAL^{a-1}K^{1-a}}{(1-a)AL^a K^{-a}} = \dfrac{a}{(1-a)}\dfrac{K}{L}$

Since the MRTS is a function of the capital–labor ratio (K/L), the MRTS will be constant along a straight line out of the origin in K–L space. Thus, the expansion path must be linear in this case. (Why?) The expansion path, given fixed input prices w and r, is derived from the tangency condition:

(10) $\quad \dfrac{aK^*}{(1-a)L^*} = \dfrac{w}{r}$

Substituting for K^*, the expansion path is expressed as

(11) $\quad K^* = K^*(L^*; w, r) = \dfrac{w}{r}\dfrac{(1-a)}{a}L^*$

As noted, the expansion path for this production function is a straight line out of the origin: $K^* = mL^*$, where $m = w(1-a)/ra > 0$.

Now we derive the efficient input-usage functions. For L^*, substitute (11) into (2c):

(12) $\quad \overline{Q} - f(L^*, K^*) = \overline{Q} - A(L^*)^a \left(\dfrac{w}{r}\dfrac{1-a}{a}L^*\right)^{1-a} = 0$

Solving implicit function (12) for L^* yields the following efficient usage function for labor:

(13) $\quad L^* = L^*(\overline{Q}; w, r) = \dfrac{\overline{Q}}{A}\left[\dfrac{w(1-a)}{ra}\right]^{-(1-a)}$

To find the efficient usage function for capital, substitute (13) into (11):

(14) $\quad K^* = K^*(\overline{Q}; w, r) = \dfrac{w}{r}\dfrac{1-a}{a}\dfrac{\overline{Q}}{A}\left[\dfrac{w(1-a)}{ra}\right]^{-(1-a)}$

$\qquad = \left(\dfrac{w}{r}\dfrac{1-a}{a}\right)^{1-(1-a)}\dfrac{\overline{Q}}{A}$

$\qquad = \left(\dfrac{w}{r}\dfrac{1-a}{a}\right)^{a}\dfrac{\overline{Q}}{A}$

The efficient input-usage functions (13) and (14) are single-valued functions; that is, for any $\overline{Q}$, there is a single L^* and a single K^*. The long-run cost functions are derived using the efficient input-usage functions for L^* and K^*:

(15) $\quad LTC(Q; w, r) = wL^* + rK^*$

$\qquad = \dfrac{Q}{A}w^a r^{1-a}\left[\left(\dfrac{a}{1-a}\right)^{1-a} + \left(\dfrac{1-a}{a}\right)^a\right]$

(16) $\quad LAC(Q; w, r) = \dfrac{LTC}{Q}$

$\qquad = \dfrac{1}{A}w^a r^{1-a}\left[\left(\dfrac{a}{1-a}\right)^{1-a} + \left(\dfrac{1-a}{a}\right)^a\right]$

(17) $\quad LMC(Q; w, r) = \dfrac{\partial LTC}{\partial Q}$

$\qquad = \dfrac{1}{A}w^a r^{1-a}\left[\left(\dfrac{a}{1-a}\right)^{1-a} + \left(\dfrac{1-a}{a}\right)^a\right]$

Notice that for this production function costs are constant: LAC and LMC are constant (i.e., not functions of Q) and are equal $(LAC = LMC)$.

MATHEMATICAL EXERCISES

1. The production function is $Q = AL^aK^b$, where $a > 0$ and $b > 0$.
   a. The marginal product of labor is $MP_L =$ _____.
   b. The marginal product of capital is $MP_K =$ _____.
   c. The marginal rate of technical substitution is $MRTS =$ _____.
   d. Show that the isoquants for this production function are convex. [*Hint:* Show that MRTS diminishes as L increases. (Why?)]
   e. Derive the equation for the long-run expansion path.
2. For the production function in exercise 1, let the price of labor be w and the price of capital be r.
   a. The efficient usage function for labor is $L^* =$ _____.
   b. The efficient usage function for capital is $K^* =$ _____.
   c. Find the long-run cost functions: LTC, LAC, and LMC.
   d. Show that both LAC and LMC increase at any Q when either w or r increases.

3. The production function for a firm is $Q = 24L^{.5}K^{.5}$. In the short run, the firm has a fixed amount of capital, $\overline{K} = 121$. The price of labor is $10 per unit, and the price of capital is $20 per unit.

    a. The short-run production function is $Q =$ _____.

    b. The marginal product of labor is $MP_L =$ _____. Show that the marginal product of labor diminishes for all levels of labor usage.

    c. Write the equation for the short-run expansion path.

    d. Derive the short-run TVC, TFC, and TC functions.

    e. Derive SMC, AVC, ATC, and AFC.

4. For the production function in exercise 3:

    a. Find the long-run expansion path.

    b. Derive the efficient input-usage functions for labor and capital.

    c. Derive the long-run cost functions: LTC, LAC, and LMC.

    d. Graph the LAC and LMC curves.

    e. What level of output is the minimum efficient scale of production (MES)?

10

Production and Cost Estimation

After reading this chapter, you will be able to:

10.1 Specify and explain the properties of a short-run cubic production function.

10.2 Employ regression analysis to estimate a short-run production function.

10.3 Discuss two important problems concerning the proper measurement of cost: correcting for inflation and measuring economic (opportunity) costs.

10.4 Specify and estimate a short-run cost function using a cubic specification.

$\mathbf{M}$anagers use estimates of production and cost functions to make output, pricing, hiring, and investment decisions. Chapters 8 and 9 set forth the basic theories of production and cost. We will now show you some statistical techniques that can be used to estimate production and cost functions. The focus will be on estimating short-run production functions and short-run cost functions. These are the functions that managers need to make a firm's pricing, output, and hiring decisions. Although long-run production and cost functions can help managers make long-run decisions about investments in plant and equipment, most of the analysis in this text concerns short-run operational decisions. Application of regression analysis to the estimation of short-run production and cost functions is a rather straightforward task. However, because of difficult problems with the data that are required to estimate long-run production and cost functions—as well as the more complex regression equations required—managers typically restrict their use of regression analysis to estimation of short-run production and cost functions.

We begin by showing how to use regression analysis to estimate short-run production functions. The first step in estimating a production function and the associated product curves (such as average product and marginal product) is to specify the **empirical production function,** which is the exact mathematical form of the equation to be estimated. We discuss how to specify a cubic equation to estimate

empirical production function
The mathematical form of the production function to be estimated.

short-run production functions when only one input, labor, is variable. As we will see, the cubic equation has the properties of the theoretical short-run production function discussed in Chapter 8. Next, we explain how to estimate the parameters of the short-run production function and test for statistical significance.

After developing the techniques of empirical production analysis, we turn to estimation of short-run cost equations. The cubic specification is also employed to estimate the short-run cost functions. The analysis of empirical cost functions begins with a brief discussion of some general issues concerning the nature of estimating cost functions, such as adjusting for inflation and measurement of economic cost. We then explain how to estimate the various short-run cost functions derived in Chapter 8: the average variable cost (AVC), marginal cost (SMC), and total variable cost (TVC) curves. Then we demonstrate how to estimate and test the parameters of these cost functions.

We must stress at the outset that the purpose here is not so much to teach you how to do the actual estimations of the functions but, rather, to show how to use and interpret the estimates of production and cost equations. The computer will do the tedious calculations involved with estimation. However, you must tell it what to estimate. Therefore, you should learn how to choose the particular function that is best suited for the purpose at hand.

As already noted, this chapter focuses primarily on short-run production and cost estimation. However, we have set forth the techniques used to estimate long-run production and cost functions in the appendix at the end of this chapter. Once you see that application of regression analysis to short-run functions is rather easy, you may wish to tackle this more difficult appendix treating long-run empirical analysis.

10.1 SPECIFICATION OF THE SHORT-RUN PRODUCTION FUNCTION

Before describing how to estimate short-run production functions, we will first specify an appropriate functional form for the long-run production function. The short-run production function is derived from the long-run production function when holding the levels of some inputs constant. Once the fixed inputs are held constant at some predetermined levels and only one input is allowed to vary, the production equation to be estimated should have the theoretical characteristics set forth in Chapter 8.

In this chapter, we will continue to consider the case of two variable inputs, labor and capital. The most general form of such a production function is

$$Q = f(L, K)$$

long-run production function
A production function in which all inputs are variable.

In this form, the production function can be viewed as a **long-run production function** because both labor (L) and capital (K) are variable inputs. In the short run, when the level of capital usage is fixed at $\overline{K}$, the **short-run production function** is expressed in general form as

short-run production function
A production function in which at least one input is fixed.

$$Q = f(L, \overline{K}) = g(L)$$

The exact mathematical form of this production function is frequently referred to as the *estimable form* of the production function. In general, an *estimable form* of an equation—whether it is a production equation, cost equation, or any other type of equation—is the exact mathematical form of the equation that can be estimated using regression analysis.

A suitable functional form for estimating either a long-run or a short-run production function is the **cubic production function**

cubic production function
A production function of the form $Q = aK^3L^3 + bK^2L^2$.

$$Q = aK^3L^3 + bK^2L^2$$

For this form of the production function, both inputs are required to produce output. If either capital or labor usage equals 0, no output is produced. Furthermore, the cubic production function has convex isoquants, so the marginal rate of technical substitution diminishes as required by the theory of production. (All the mathematical properties of cubic production functions set forth in this chapter are mathematically derived in this chapter's appendix.)

Holding capital constant at $\overline{K}$ units ($K = \overline{K}$), the **short-run cubic production function** is

short-run cubic production function
A production function of the form $Q = AL^3 + BL^2$.

$$Q = a\overline{K}^3L^3 + b\overline{K}^2L^2$$
$$= AL^3 + BL^2$$

where $A = a\overline{K}^3$ and $B = b\overline{K}^2$, and both A and B are constant when $\overline{K}$ is constant. The average and marginal products for the cubic short-run production function are, respectively,

$$AP = \frac{Q}{L} = AL^2 + BL$$

and

$$MP = \frac{\Delta Q}{\Delta L} = 3AL^2 + 2BL$$

As shown in the appendix, for the average and marginal products to first rise, reach a maximum, and then fall, A must be negative and B must be positive. This requires that, in the above production function, $a < 0$ and $b > 0$. It is also shown in the appendix that the level of labor usage beyond which marginal product begins to fall, and diminishing returns set in, is

$$L_m = -\frac{B}{3A}$$

When marginal product equals average product and average product is at its maximum (as discussed in Chapter 8),[1]

$$L_a = -\frac{B}{2A}$$

---

[1] The level of labor usage at which AP reaches its maximum value, L_a, can be found algebraically. First, set AP equal to MP

$$AL^2 + BL = 3AL^2 + 2BL$$

or

$$0 = 2AL^2 + BL$$

Solving for L, the level of labor usage at which average product is maximized is $L_a = -B/2A$.

FIGURE 10.1

Marginal and Average Product Curves for the Short-Run Cubic Production Function:
$Q = AL^3 + BL^2$

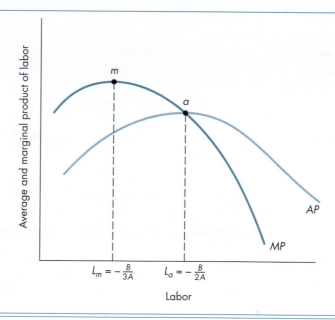

Average and marginal product of labor

m

a

AP

MP

$L_m = -\dfrac{B}{3A}$ $L_a = -\dfrac{B}{2A}$

Labor

Recall that A is negative ($A < 0$) and B is positive ($B > 0$), so both L_m and L_a are positive. These relations are shown in Figure 10.1.

Note that when the fixed level of capital changes, both A ($= a\overline{K}^3$) and B ($= b\overline{K}^2$) change in value and all three product curves (TP, AP, and MP) shift.[2] Also note that once estimates of A and B are obtained for any one of the three product equations (TP, AP, and MP), the other two have also been estimated; that is, A and B are the only two parameters that need to be estimated to get all three equations.

The short-run cubic production function exhibits all the theoretical properties discussed in Chapter 8. Table 10.1 summarizes the cubic specification of the short-run production function.

Now try Technical Problem 1.

10.2 ESTIMATION OF A SHORT-RUN PRODUCTION FUNCTION

Now that we have specified a cubic form for the short-run production function, we can discuss how to estimate this production function. As we see, only the simple techniques of regression analysis presented in Chapter 4 are needed to estimate the cubic production function in the short run when capital is fixed. We illustrate the process of estimating the production function with an example.

---

[2]Recall from Tables 8.2 and 8.3 in Chapter 8 that capital is held constant in any given column. The entire marginal and average product schedules change when capital usage changes.

TABLE 10.1

Summary of the Short-Run Cubic Production Function

	Short-run cubic production function
Total product	$Q = AL^3 + BL^2$
	where $A = a\overline{K}^3$
	$B = b\overline{K}^2$
Average product	$AP = AL^2 + BL$
Marginal product	$MP = 3AL^2 + 2BL$
Diminishing marginal returns	Beginning at $L_m = -\dfrac{B}{3A}$
Diminishing average product	Beginning at $L_a = -\dfrac{B}{2A}$
Restrictions on parameters	$A < 0$
	$B > 0$

Suppose a small plant uses labor with a fixed amount of capital to assemble a product. There are 40 observations on labor usage (hours per day) and output (number of units assembled per day). The manager wishes to estimate the production function and the marginal product of labor. Figure 10.2 presents a scatter diagram of the 40 observations.

The scatter diagram suggests that a cubic specification of short-run production is appropriate because the scatter of data points appears to have an S-shape,

FIGURE 10.2

Scatter Diagram for a Cubic Production Function

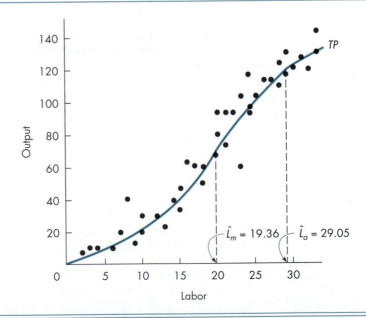

similar to the theoretical total product curve set forth in Chapter 8. For such a curve, the slope first increases and then decreases, indicating that the marginal product of labor first increases, reaches a maximum, and then decreases. Both the marginal product and average product curves should take on the inverted-U-shape described in Chapter 8 and shown in Figure 8.3.

Because it seems appropriate to estimate a cubic production function in this case, we specify the following estimable form

$$Q = AL^3 + BL^2$$

Following the procedure discussed in Chapter 4, we transform the cubic equation into a linear form for estimation

$$Q = AX + BW$$

regression through the origin
A regression in which the intercept term is forced to equal 0.

where $X = L^3$ and $W = L^2$. To correctly estimate the cubic equation, we must account for the fact that the cubic equation does not include an intercept term. In other words, the estimated regression line must pass through the origin; that is, when $L = 0$, $Q = 0$. **Regression through the origin** simply requires that the analyst specify in the computer routine that the intercept term be "suppressed." Most computer programs for regression analysis provide the user with a simple way to suppress the intercept term. After we use a regression routine to estimate a cubic equation for the 40 observations on output and labor usage (and suppressing the intercept), the following computer output is forthcoming:

DEPENDENT VARIABLE:	Q	R-SQUARE	F-RATIO	P-VALUE ON F
OBSERVATIONS:	40	0.9837	1148.83	0.0001

VARIABLE	PARAMETER ESTIMATE	STANDARD ERROR	T-RATIO	P-VALUE
L3	−0.0047	0.0006	−7.833	0.0001
L2	0.2731	0.0182	15.005	0.0001

The F-ratio and the R^2 for the cubic specification are quite good.[3] The critical value of F with $k − 1 = 1$ and $n − k = 38$ degrees of freedom is 4.1 at the 5 percent significance level. The p-values for both estimates $\hat{A}$ and $\hat{B}$ are so small that there is less

---

[3]For purposes of illustration, the hypothetical data used in this example were chosen to fit closely an S-shaped cubic equation. In most real-world applications, you will probably get smaller values for the F-ratio, R^2, and t-statistics.

than a 0.01 percent chance of making a Type I error (mistakenly concluding that $A \neq 0$ and $B \neq 0$). The following parameter estimates are obtained from the printout

$$\hat{A} = -0.0047 \qquad \text{and} \qquad \hat{B} = 0.2731$$

The estimated short-run cubic production function is

$$\hat{Q} = -0.0047L^3 + 0.2731L^2$$

The parameters theoretically have the correct signs: $\hat{A} < 0$ and $\hat{B} > 0$. We must test to see if $\hat{A}$ and $\hat{B}$ are significantly negative and positive, respectively. The computed t-ratios allow us to test for statistical significance

$$t_{\hat{a}} = -7.83 \qquad \text{and} \qquad t_{\hat{b}} = 15.00$$

The absolute values of both t-statistics exceed the critical t-value for 38 degrees of freedom at a 5 percent level of significance (2.021). Hence, $\hat{A}$ is significantly negative and $\hat{B}$ is significantly positive. Both estimates satisfy the theoretical characteristics of a cubic production function.

The estimated marginal product of labor is

$$\widehat{MP} = 3\hat{A}L^2 + 2\hat{B}L$$

$$= 3(-0.0047)L^2 + 2(0.2731)L$$

$$= -0.0141L^2 + 0.5462L$$

The level of labor usage beyond which diminishing returns set in (after MP_L reaches its maximum) is estimated as

$$\hat{L}_m = -\frac{\hat{B}}{3\hat{A}} = \frac{0.2731}{3(-0.0047)} = 19.36$$

Note in Figure 10.2 that $\hat{L}_m$ is at the point where total product no longer increases at an increasing rate but begins increasing at a decreasing rate. The estimated average product of labor is

$$\widehat{AP} = \hat{A}L^2 + \hat{B}L$$

$$= (-0.0047)L^2 + (0.2731)L$$

The maximum average product is attained when $AP = MP$ at the estimated level of labor usage

$$\hat{L}_a = -\frac{\hat{B}}{2\hat{A}} = \frac{0.2731}{2(-0.0047)} = 29.05$$

Now try Technical Problem 2. Maximum AP, as expected, occurs at a higher level of labor usage than maximum MP (see Figure 10.2). The evidence indicates that the cubic estimation of the production function from the data points in Figure 10.2 provides a good fit and has all the desired theoretical properties.

10.3   SHORT-RUN COST ESTIMATION: SOME PROBLEMS WITH MEASURING COST

The techniques of regression analysis can also be used to estimate cost functions. Cost depends on the level of output being produced, as well as the prices of the inputs used in production. This relation can be expressed mathematically as

$$TC = TC(Q; w, r)$$

where we continue to let w denote the price of a unit of labor services and r the price of a unit of capital services. Before describing procedures used in estimating short-run cost functions, we must discuss two important considerations that arise when measuring the cost of production: the problem of inflation and that of measuring economic cost.

When short-run cost functions are being estimated, the data will necessarily be such that the level of usage of one (or more) of the inputs is fixed. In the context of the two-input production function employed in Chapter 8, this restriction could be interpreted to mean that the firm's capital stock is fixed while labor usage is allowed to vary. In most cases, a manager will be using a time-series set of observations on cost, output, and input prices to estimate the short-run cost function. The time period over which the data are collected should be short enough so that at least one input remains fixed. For instance, an analyst might collect monthly observations over a two-year period in which the firm did not change its basic plant (i.e., capital stock). Thus the analyst could obtain 24 observations on cost, output, and input prices. When using a time-series data set of this type, an analyst should be careful to adjust the cost and input price data (which are measured in dollars) for inflation and to make sure the cost data measure economic cost. We now discuss these two possible problems.

Correcting Data for the Effects of Inflation

nominal cost data
Data that have not been corrected for the effects of inflation.

While output is expressed in physical units, cost and input prices are expressed in nominal dollars. Hence, the **nominal cost data** would include the effect of inflation. That is, over time, inflation could cause reported costs to rise, even if output remained constant. Such a situation is depicted in Figure 10.3. As you can see in this figure, estimation based on a data set affected by inflation indicates that cost rises more steeply than it would if inflation did not exist in the data. To accurately measure the real increase in cost caused by increases in output, it is necessary to eliminate the effects of inflation.

deflating
Correcting for the influence of inflation by dividing nominal cost data by an implicit price deflator.

Correcting for the effects of inflation is easily accomplished by **deflating** nominal cost data into constant (or real) dollars by using an *implicit price deflator*. To convert nominal cost into a constant-dollar amount, the nominal cost data are divided by the appropriate price deflator for the period under consideration. Implicit price deflators can be obtained from the *Survey of Current Business*, published by the Bureau of Economic Analysis at the U.S. Department of Commerce (*www.bea.doc.gov*). We will illustrate the process of deflating nominal cost data later in this chapter.

FIGURE 10.3
The Problem of Inflation

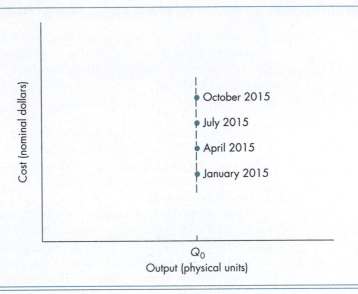

Inflation also can affect input prices, but for short-run cost estimation this is seldom a problem. As long as inflation affects all input prices and cost equally—that is, all input prices and cost rise equiproportionately—the effect of inflation on cost estimation is fully corrected for by deflating nominal cost. For example, if there is a 4 percent increase in cost and in the prices of both labor and capital, deflating cost by 4 percent will remove the effect of inflation, even when the prices of the inputs are not included in the cost equation. Therefore, it is a fairly common practice to omit input prices in short-run cost estimation because the span of the time-series data set is generally short enough that changes in the real input prices do not occur or are quite small. Thus, we will concentrate on showing how to adjust for inflation in the cost data and not be concerned with the effects of inflation on input prices.

Problems Measuring Economic Cost

Another potentially troublesome problem can result from the difference between the accounting definition of cost and the economic definition of cost. As stressed in Chapters 1 and 8, the cost of using resources in production is the opportunity cost of using the resources. Since accounting data are of necessity based on expenditures, opportunity cost may not be reflected in the firm's accounting records. To illustrate this problem, suppose a firm owns its own machinery. The opportunity cost of this equipment is the income that could be derived if the machinery were leased to another firm, but this cost would not be reflected in the accounting data.

In a two-input setting, total cost at a given level of outputs is

$$C = wL + rK$$

The wage rate should reflect the opportunity cost of labor to the firm; so expenditures on labor, wL (including any additional compensation not paid as wages), would reflect opportunity cost. The problem is the calculation of the firm's opportunity cost of capital. The cost of capital, r, must be calculated in such a way that it reflects the **user cost of capital**. User cost includes not only the acquisition cost of a unit of capital but also (1) the return forgone by using the capital rather than renting it, (2) the depreciation charges resulting from the use of the capital, and (3) any capital gains or losses associated with holding the particular type of capital. Likewise, the measurement of the capital stock K must be such that it reflects the stock actually owned by the firm. For example, you might want the capital variable to reflect the fact that a given piece of capital has depreciated physically or embodies a lower technology than a new piece of capital. While these problems are difficult, they are not insurmountable. The main thing to remember is that such opportunity-cost data would be expected to differ greatly from the reported cost figures in accounting data.

user cost of capital
The firm's opportunity cost of using capital.

10.4 ESTIMATION OF A SHORT-RUN COST FUNCTION

As is the case when estimating a production function, specification of an appropriate equation for a cost function must necessarily precede the estimation of the parameters using regression analysis. The specification of an empirical cost equation must ensure that the mathematical properties of the equation reflect the properties and relations described in Chapter 8. Figure 10.4 illustrates again the typically assumed total variable cost, average variable cost, and marginal cost curves.

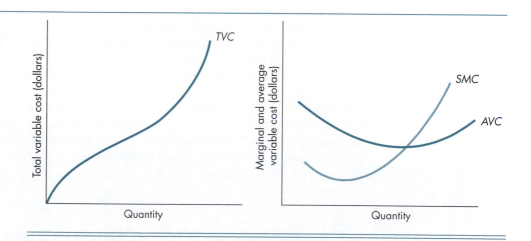

FIGURE 10.4
Typical Short-Run Cost Curves

Estimation of Typical Short-Run Costs

Since the shape of any one of the three cost curves determines the shape of the other two, we begin with the average variable cost curve. Because this curve is U-shaped, we use the following quadratic specification:

$$AVC = a + bQ + cQ^2$$

As explained earlier, input prices are not included as explanatory variables in the cost equation because the input prices (adjusted for inflation) are assumed to be constant over the relatively short time span of the time-series data set. In order for the AVC curve to be U-shaped, a must be positive, b must be negative, and c must be positive; that is, $a > 0$, $b < 0$, and $c > 0$.[4]

Given the specification for average variable cost, the specifications for total variable cost and marginal cost are straightforward if $AVC = TVC/Q$, it follows that

$$TVC = AVC \times Q = (a + bQ + cQ^2)Q = aQ + bQ^2 + cQ^3$$

Note that this equation is a cubic specification of TVC, which conforms to the S-shaped TVC curve in Figure 10.4.

The equation for marginal cost is somewhat more difficult to derive. It can be shown, however, that the marginal cost equation associated with the above TVC equation is

$$SMC = a + 2bQ + 3cQ^2$$

If, as specified for AVC, $a > 0$, $b < 0$, and $c > 0$, the marginal cost curve will also be U-shaped.

Because all three of the cost curves, TVC, AVC, and SMC, employ the same parameters, it is necessary to estimate only one of these functions to obtain estimates of all three. For example, estimation of AVC provides estimates of a, b, and c, which can then be used to generate the marginal and total variable cost functions. The total cost curve is trivial to estimate; simply add the constant fixed cost to total variable cost.

As for the estimation itself, ordinary least-squares estimation of the total (or average) variable cost function is usually sufficient. Once the estimates of a, b, and c are obtained, it is necessary to determine whether the parameter estimates are of the hypothesized signs and statistically significant. The tests for significance are again accomplished by using either t-tests or p-values.

Using the estimates of a total or average variable cost function, we can also obtain an estimate of the output at which average cost is a minimum. Remember that when average variable cost is at its minimum, average variable cost and marginal cost are equal. Thus we can define the minimum of average variable cost as the output at which

$$AVC = SMC$$

---

[4]The appendix to this chapter derives the mathematical properties of a cubic cost function.

TABLE 10.2

Summary of a Cubic Specification for Total Variable Cost

	Cubic total variable cost function
Total variable cost	$TVC = aQ + bQ^2 + cQ^3$
Average variable cost	$AVC = a + bQ + cQ^2$
Marginal cost	$SMC = a + 2bQ + 3cQ^2$
AVC reaches minimum point	$Q_m = -b/2c$
Restrictions on parameters	$a > 0$
	$b < 0$
	$c > 0$

Using the specifications of average variable cost and marginal cost presented earlier, we can write this condition as

$$a + bQ + cQ^2 = a + 2bQ + 3cQ^2$$

or

$$bQ + 2cQ^2 = 0$$

Solving for Q, the level of output at which average variable cost is minimized is

$$Q_m = -b/2c$$

Table 10.2 summarizes the mathematical properties of a cubic specification for total variable cost.

Before estimating a short-run cost function, we want to mention a potential problem that can arise when the data for average variable cost are clustered around the minimum point of the average cost curve, as shown in Figure 10.5. If the average variable cost function is estimated using data points clustered as shown in the figure, the result is that while $\hat{a}$ is positive and $\hat{b}$ is negative, a t-test or a p-value would indicate that $\hat{c}$ is not statistically different from 0. This result does not mean that the average cost curve is not ∪-shaped. The problem

FIGURE 10.5

A Potential Data Problem

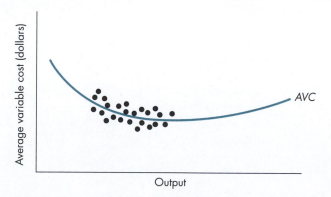

is that because there are no observations for the larger levels of output, the estimation simply cannot determine whether average cost is rising over that range of output.

Estimation of Short-Run Costs at Rockford Enterprises: An Example

In July 2014, the manager at Rockford Enterprises decided to estimate the total variable, average variable, and marginal cost functions for the firm. The capital stock at Rockford has remained unchanged since the second quarter of 2012. The manager collected quarterly observations on cost and output over this period and the resulting data were as follows:

Quarter	Output	Average variable cost ($)
2012 (II)	300	$38.05
2012 (III)	100	39.36
2012 (IV)	150	28.68
2013 (I)	250	28.56
2013 (II)	400	48.03
2013 (III)	200	33.51
2013 (IV)	350	45.32
2014 (I)	450	59.35
2014 (II)	500	66.81

Average variable cost was measured in nominal (i.e., current) dollars, and the cost data were subject to the effects of inflation. Over the period for which cost was to be estimated, costs had increased due to the effects of inflation. The manager's analyst decided to eliminate the influence of inflation by deflating the nominal costs. Recall that such a deflation involves converting nominal cost into constant-dollar cost by dividing the nominal cost by an appropriate price index. The analyst used the implicit price deflator for gross domestic product (GDP) published in the *Survey of Current Business*, which can be found at the website for the Bureau of Economic Analysis (*www.bea.gov/scb*). The following values for the price deflator were used to deflate the nominal cost data:

Quarter	Implicit Price Deflator (2009 = 100)
2012 (II)	109.16
2012 (III)	109.73
2012 (IV)	110.60
2013 (I)	111.54
2013 (II)	112.22
2013 (III)	113.12
2013 (IV)	114.03
2014 (I)	114.95
2014 (II)	115.89

To obtain the average variable cost, measured in constant (2009) dollars, for the 300 units produced in the second quarter of 2012, $38.05 is divided by the implicit price deflator 104.94 (divided by 100), which gives $36.26

$$\$36.26 = \frac{\$38.05}{104.94 \div 100}$$

Note that it is necessary to divide the implicit price deflator by 100 because the price deflators in the *Survey of Current Business* are expressed as percentages. Repeating this computation for each of the average variable cost figures, the manager obtained the following inflation-adjusted cost data:

Quarter	Output	Deflated average variable cost ($)
2012 (II)	300	$36.26
2012 (III)	100	37.33
2012 (IV)	150	27.10
2013 (I)	250	26.89
2013 (II)	400	45.10
2013 (III)	200	31.34
2013 (IV)	350	42.24
2014 (I)	450	55.13
2014 (II)	500	61.73

Given these inflation-adjusted data, the manager estimated the cost functions. As shown above, it is sufficient to estimate any one of the three cost curves to obtain the other two because each cost equation is a function of the same three parameters: a, b, and c. The manager decided to estimate the average variable cost function:

$$AVC = a + bQ + cQ^2$$

and obtained the following printout from the estimation of this equation:

DEPENDENT VARIABLE: AVC		R-SQUARE	F-RATIO	P-VALUE ON F
OBSERVATIONS: 9		0.9382	45.527	0.0002
VARIABLE	PARAMETER ESTIMATE	STANDARD ERROR	T-RATIO	P-VALUE
INTERCEPT	44.473	6.487	6.856	0.0005
Q	−0.143	0.0482	−2.967	0.0254
Q2	0.000362	0.000079	4.582	0.0037

After the estimates were obtained, the manager determined that the estimated coefficients had the theoretically required signs: $\hat{a} > 0$, $\hat{b} < 0$, and $\hat{c} > 0$. To determine whether these coefficients are statistically significant, the *p*-values were examined, and the exact level of significance for each of the estimated coefficients was acceptably low (all the *t*-ratios are significant at better than the 5 percent level of significance).

The estimated average variable cost function for Rockford Enterprises is, therefore,

$$\widehat{AVC} = 44.473 - 0.143Q + 0.000362Q^2$$

which conforms to the shape of the average variable cost curve in Figure 10.4. As emphasized above, the marginal cost and total variable cost equations are easily determined from the estimated parameters of *AVC*, and no further regression analysis is necessary. In this case,

$$\widehat{SMC} = \hat{a} + 2\hat{b}\,Q + 3\hat{c}Q^2$$

$$= 44.473 - 0.286Q + 0.0011Q^2$$

and

$$\widehat{TVC} = \hat{a}Q + \hat{b}Q^2 + \hat{c}Q^3$$

$$= 44.473Q - 0.143Q^2 + 0.000362Q^3$$

To illustrate the use of the estimated cost equations, suppose the manager wishes to calculate the marginal cost, average variable cost, and total variable cost when Rockford is producing 350 units of output. Using the estimated marginal cost equation, the marginal cost associated with 350 units is

$$SMC = 44.473 - 0.286(350) + 0.0011(350)^2$$

$$= 44.473 - 100.10 + 134.75$$

$$= \$79.12$$

Average variable cost for this level of output is

$$AVC = 44.473 - 0.143(350) + 0.000362(350)^2$$

$$= 44.473 - 50.05 + 44.345$$

$$= \$38.77$$

and total variable cost for 350 units of output is

$$TVC = AVC \times Q$$

$$= 38.77 \times 350$$

$$= \$13{,}569$$

The total cost of 350 units of output would, of course, be $13,569 plus fixed cost.

Finally, the output level at which average variable cost is minimized can be computed as

$$Q_m = -b/2c$$

In this example,

$$Q_m = \frac{0.143}{2 \times 0.000362} = 197$$

At Rockford Enterprises, average variable cost reaches its minimum at an output level of 197 units, when

$$AVC = 44.473 - 0.143(197) + 0.000362(197)^2$$

$$= 44.473 - 28.17 + 14.05$$

$$= \$30.35$$

Now try Technical Problem 3.

As you can see from this example, estimation of short-run cost curves is just a straightforward application of cost theory and regression analysis. Many firms do, in fact, use regression analysis to estimate their costs of production.

10.5 SUMMARY

- The first step in estimating a production function and the associated product curve—average product and marginal product—is to specify the empirical production function, which is the exact mathematical form of the equation to be estimated. The most general form of a production function with two variable inputs, labor (L) and capital (K), is $Q = f(L,K)$, and because both L and K are variable inputs, this form of the production function can be viewed as a long-run production function. In the short run when capital is fixed at $\overline{K}$, the short-run production function in general form is $Q = f(L, \overline{K}) = g(L)$. A suitable functional form for estimating either a long-run or a short-run production function is the cubic production function: $Q = aK^3L^3 + bK^2L^2$. Holding capital constant at $\overline{K}$ units, the short-run cubic production function is $Q = a\overline{K}^3L^3 + b\overline{K}^2L^2 = AL^3 + BL^2$, where $A = a\overline{K}^3$ and $B = b\overline{K}^2$. The average and marginal products of labor are, respectively, $AP = Q/L = AL^2 + BL$ and $MP = \Delta Q/\Delta L = 3AL^2 + 2BL$. Marginal product of labor begins to diminish beyond L_m units of labor and average product of labor begins to diminish beyond L_a units of labor, where $L_m = -B/(3A)$ and $L_a = -B/(2A)$. In order to have the necessary properties of a production function, the parameters must satisfy two restrictions: A must be negative ($A < 0$) and B must be positive ($B > 0$). (*LO1*)

- To estimate a cubic short-run production function using linear regression analysis, you must first transform the cubic equation into linear form $Q = AX + BW$, where $X = L^3$ and $W = L^2$. In order to correctly estimate the cubic equation, the estimated regression line must pass through the origin. (*LO2*)

- In most cases, a manager will use a time-series set of observations on cost, output, and input prices to estimate the short-run cost function. The effects of inflation on cost data must be eliminated. To adjust nominal cost figures for inflation, divide each observation by the appropriate price index for that time period. Collecting data may be complicated by the fact that accounting data are based on expenditures and may not include the firm's opportunity cost of using the various inputs. The wage rate should reflect the opportunity cost of labor to the firm, which must include any additional compensation not paid as wages. The user cost of capital includes not only acquisition costs of capital but also (1) the return forgone by using the capital rather than renting it, (2) the depreciation charges resulting from the use of the capital, and (3) any capital gains or losses associated with holding the particular type of capital. (*LO3*)

- A suitable functional form for the short-run cost function is a cubic total variable cost function: $TVC = aQ + bQ^2 + cQ^3$. The average variable cost and marginal cost functions are, respectively, $AVC = a + bQ + cQ^2$ and $SMC = a + 2bQ + 3cQ^2$. Average variable cost reaches its minimum value at $Q_m = -b/2c$. To conform to the theoretical properties of a cost function, the parameters must satisfy the restrictions: $a > 0$, $b < 0$, and $c > 0$. Because all three cost curves (TVC, AVC, and SMC) employ the same parameters, it is only necessary to estimate any one of these functions to obtain estimates of all three curves. (*LO4*)

KEY TERMS

cubic production function	long-run production function	short-run cubic production function
deflating	nominal cost data	short-run production function
empirical production function	regression through the origin	user cost of capital

TECHNICAL PROBLEMS

1. The following cubic equation is a long-run production function for a firm:

$$Q = -0.002K^3L^3 + 6K^2L^2$$

Suppose the firm employs 10 units of capital.

a. What are the equations for the total product, average product, and marginal product of labor curves?

b. At what level of labor usage does the marginal product of labor begin to diminish?

c. Calculate the marginal product and average product of labor when 10 units of labor are being employed.

Now suppose the firm doubles capital usage to 20 units.

d. What are the equations for the total product, average product, and marginal product of labor curves?

e. What happened to the marginal and average product of labor curves when capital usage increased from 10 to 20 units? Calculate the marginal and average products of labor for 10 units of labor now that capital usage is 20 units. Compare your answer to part c. Did the increase in capital usage affect marginal and average product as you expected?

2. A firm estimates its cubic production function of the form

$$Q = AL^3 + BL^2$$

and obtains the following estimation results:

DEPENDENT VARIABLE:	Q	R-SQUARE	F-RATIO	P-VALUE ON F
OBSERVATIONS:	25	0.8457	126.10	0.0001

VARIABLE	PARAMETER ESTIMATE	STANDARD ERROR	T-RATIO	P-VALUE
L3	−0.002	0.0005	−4.00	0.0005
L2	0.400	0.080	5.00	0.0001

a. What are the estimated total, average, and marginal product functions?

b. Are the parameters of the correct sign, and are they significant at the 1 percent level?

c. At what level of labor usage is average product at its maximum?

Now recall the following formulas derived in Chapter 8: $AP = Q/L$, $AVC = w/AP$, and $SMC = w/MP$. Assume that the wage rate for labor (w) is $200.

d. What is output when average product is at its maximum?

    e. At the output level for part *d*, what are average variable cost and marginal cost?

    f. When the rate of labor usage is 120, what is output? What are *AVC* and *SMC* at that output?

    g. Conceptually, how could you derive the relevant cost curves from this estimate of the production functions?

3. Consider estimation of a short-run average variable cost function of the form

$$AVC = a + bQ + cQ^2$$

Using time-series data, the estimation procedure produces the following computer output:

DEPENDENT VARIABLE:	AVC	R-SQUARE	F-RATIO	P-VALUE ON F
OBSERVATIONS:	15	0.4135	4.230	0.0407

VARIABLE	PARAMETER ESTIMATE	STANDARD ERROR	T-RATIO	P-VALUE
INTERCEPT	30.420202	6.465900	4.70	0.0005
Q	−0.079952	0.030780	−2.60	0.0232
Q2	0.000088	0.000032	2.75	0.0176

    a. Do the parameter estimates have the correct signs? Are they statistically significant at the 5 percent level of significance?

    b. At what level of output do you estimate average variable cost reaches its minimum value?

    c. What is the estimated marginal cost curve?

    d. What is the estimated marginal cost when output is 700 units?

    e. What is the estimated average variable cost curve?

    f. What is the estimated average variable cost when output is 700 units?

APPLIED PROBLEMS

1. You are planning to estimate a short-run production function for your firm, and you have collected the following data on labor usage and output:

Labor usage	Output
3	1
7	2
9	3
11	5
17	8
17	10
20	15
24	18
26	22
28	21
30	23

a. Does a cubic equation appear to be a suitable specification, given these data? You may wish to construct a scatter diagram to help you answer this question.

b. Using a computer and software for regression analysis, estimate your firm's short-run production function using the data given here. Do the parameter estimates have the appropriate algebraic signs? Are they statistically significant at the 5 percent level?

c. At what point do you estimate marginal product begins to fall?

d. Calculate estimates of total, average, and marginal products when the firm employs 23 workers.

e. When the firm employs 23 workers, is short-run marginal cost (*SMC*) rising or falling? How can you tell?

2. Dimex Fabrication Co., a small manufacturer of sheet-metal body parts for a major U.S. automaker, estimates its long-run production function to be

$$Q = -0.015625K^3L^3 + 10K^2L^2$$

where Q is the number of body parts produced daily, K is the number of sheet-metal presses in its manufacturing plant, and L is the number of labor-hours per day of sheet-metal workers employed by Dimex. Dimex is currently operating with eight sheet-metal presses.

a. What is the total product function for Dimex? The average product function? The marginal product function?

b. Managers at Dimex can expect the marginal product of additional workers to fall beyond what level of labor employment?

c. Dimex plans to employ 50 workers. Calculate total product, average product, and marginal product.

3. The chief economist for Argus Corporation, a large appliance manufacturer, estimated the firm's short-run cost function for vacuum cleaners using an average variable cost function of the form

$$AVC = a + bQ + cQ^2$$

where AVC = dollars per vacuum cleaner and Q = number of vacuum cleaners produced each month. Total fixed cost each month is $180,000. The following results were obtained:

DEPENDENT VARIABLE:	AVC	R-SQUARE	F-RATIO	P-VALUE ON F
OBSERVATIONS:	19	0.7360	39.428	0.0001

VARIABLE	PARAMETER ESTIMATE	STANDARD ERROR	T-RATIO	P-VALUE
INTERCEPT	191.93	54.65	3.512	0.0029
Q	−0.0305	0.00789	23.866	0.0014
Q2	0.0000024	0.00000098	2.449	0.0262

a. Are the estimates $\hat{a}$, $\hat{b}$, and $\hat{c}$ statistically significant at the 2 percent level of significance?

b. Do the results indicate that the average variable cost curve is U-shaped? How do you know?

c. If Argus Corporation produces 8,000 vacuum cleaners per month, what is the estimated average variable cost? Marginal cost? Total variable cost? Total cost?

d. Answer part c, assuming that Argus produces 10,000 vacuum cleaners monthly.

e. At what level of output will average variable cost be at a minimum? What is minimum average variable cost?

◻ **MATHEMATICAL APPENDIX**   **Empirical Production and Cost Relations**

The Cubic Production Function

In this chapter, the cubic production function was introduced

$$Q = aK^3L^3 + bK^2L^2$$

This functional form is best suited for short-run applications, rather than long-run applications. When capital is fixed ($K = \overline{K}$), the short-run cubic production function is

$$Q = a\overline{K}^3L^3 + b\overline{K}^2L^2$$
$$= AL^3 + BL^2$$

where $A = a\overline{K}^3$ and $B = b\overline{K}^2$. This section of the appendix presents the mathematical properties of the short-run cubic production function.

Input usage

To produce output, some positive amount of labor is required

$$Q(0) = A(0)^3 + B(0)^2 = 0$$

Marginal product

The marginal product function for labor is

$$\frac{dQ}{dL} = Q_L = 3AL^2 + 2BL$$

The slope of marginal product is

$$\frac{d^2Q}{dL^2} = Q_{LL} = 6AL + 2B$$

For marginal product of labor to first rise, then fall, Q_{LL} must first be positive and then negative. Q_{LL} will be positive, then negative (as more labor is used) when A is

negative and B is positive. These are the only restrictions on the short-run cubic production function:

$$A < 0 \quad \text{and} \quad B > 0$$

Marginal product of labor reaches its maximum value at L_m units of labor usage. This occurs when $Q_{LL} = 0$. Setting $Q_{LL} = 0$ and solving for L_m,

$$L_m = -\frac{B}{3A}$$

Average product

The average product function for labor is

$$AP = \frac{Q}{L} = AL^2 + BL$$

Average product reaches its maximum value at L_a units of labor usage. This occurs when $dAP/dL = 2AL + B = 0$. Solving for L_a,

$$L_a = \frac{B}{2A}$$

The Cubic Cost Function

The cubic cost function,

$$TVC = aQ + bQ^2 + cQ^3$$

generates average and marginal cost curves that have the typical U-shapes set forth in Chapter 8. If $AVC = TVC/Q$,

$$AVC = a + bQ + cQ^2$$

The slope of the average variable cost function is

$$\frac{dAVC}{dQ} = b + 2cQ$$

Average variable cost is at its minimum value when $dAVC/dQ = 0$, which occurs when $Q = -b/2c$. To guarantee a minimum, the second derivative,

$$\frac{d^2AVC}{dQ^2} = 2c$$

must be positive, which requires c to be positive.

When $Q = 0$, $AVC = a$, which must be positive. For average variable cost to have a downward-sloping region, b must be negative. Thus the parameter restrictions for a short-run cubic cost function are

$$a > 0, \qquad b < 0, \qquad \text{and} \qquad c > 0$$

The marginal cost function is

$$SMC = \frac{dTVC}{dQ} = a + 2bQ + 3cQ^2$$

The Cobb-Douglas Production Function

In this chapter, we used a cubic specification for estimating the production function. In this appendix, we show you another nonlinear specification of the production function that has been widely used in business economics applications. We will describe the mathematical properties of both the long-run and the short-run Cobb-Douglas production function and explain how to estimate the parameters by using regression analysis. To help you distinguish between the Cobb-Douglas form and the cubic form, we will use Greek letters to represent the parameters of the Cobb-Douglas functions.

The long-run Cobb-Douglas production function: $Q = \gamma K^\alpha L^\beta$

Input Usage
To produce output, both inputs are required

$$Q(0, L) = \gamma 0^\alpha L^\beta = Q(K, 0) = \gamma K^\alpha 0^\beta = 0$$

Marginal Products
The marginal product functions for capital and labor are

$$\frac{\partial Q}{\partial K} = Q_K = \alpha\gamma K^{\alpha-1}L^\beta = \alpha\frac{Q}{K}$$

and

$$\frac{\partial Q}{\partial L} = Q_L = \beta\gamma K^\alpha L^{\beta-1} = \beta\frac{Q}{L}$$

For the marginal products to be positive, α and β must be positive. The second derivatives,

$$\frac{\partial^2 Q}{\partial K^2} = Q_{KK} = \alpha(\alpha - 1)\,\gamma K^{\alpha-2}L^\beta$$

and

$$\frac{\partial^2 Q}{\partial L^2} = Q_{LL} = \beta(\beta - 1)\,\gamma K^\alpha L^{\beta-2}$$

demonstrate that, if the marginal products are diminishing (i.e., Q_{KK} and $Q_{LL} < 0$), α and β must be less than 1.

Marginal Rate of Technical Substitution
From Chapter 9, the MRTS of L for K is Q_L/Q_K. In the context of the Cobb-Douglas function,

$$MRTS = \frac{Q_L}{Q_K} = \frac{\beta}{\alpha}\frac{K}{L}$$

Note first that the MRTS is invariant to output,

$$\frac{\partial MRTS}{\partial Q} = 0$$

Hence, the Cobb-Douglas production is *homothetic*—the production function has a straight-line expansion path and changes in the output level have no effect on relative input usage. Moreover, the MRTS demonstrates that the Cobb-Douglas production function is characterized by convex isoquants. Taking the derivative of the MRTS with respect to L,

$$\frac{\partial MRTS}{\partial L} = -\frac{\beta}{\alpha}\frac{K}{L^2}$$

Hence, the MRTS diminishes as capital is replaced with labor: The isoquants are convex.

Output Elasticities
Output elasticities are defined as

$$E_K = \frac{\partial Q}{\partial K}\frac{K}{Q} = Q_K\frac{K}{Q}$$

and

$$E_L = \frac{\partial Q}{\partial L}\frac{L}{Q} = Q_L\frac{L}{Q}$$

Using the Cobb-Douglas specification,

$$E_K = \left(\alpha\frac{Q}{K}\right)\frac{K}{Q} = \alpha$$

and

$$E_L = \left(\beta\frac{Q}{K}\right)\frac{L}{Q} = \beta$$

The Function Coefficient
Begin with a production function, $Q = Q(K, L)$. Suppose that the levels of usage of both inputs are increased by the same proportion (λ); that is, $Q = Q(\lambda K, \lambda L)$. The definition of the function coefficient($\mathscr{E}$) is

$$\mathscr{E} = \frac{dQ/Q}{d\lambda/\lambda}$$

Take the total differential of the production function

$$dQ = Q_K dK + Q_L dL$$

and rewrite this as

$$dQ = Q_K K \frac{dK}{K} + Q_L L \frac{dL}{L}$$

Because K and L were increased by the same proportion, $dK/K = dL/L = d\lambda/\lambda$. Thus

$$dQ = \frac{d\lambda}{\lambda} (Q_K K + Q_L L)$$

When we use this expression, the function coefficient is

$$\mathcal{E} = Q_K \times \frac{K}{Q} + Q_L \times \frac{L}{Q} = E_K + E_L$$

In the context of the Cobb-Douglas production function, it follows that

$$\mathcal{E} = \alpha + \beta$$

Estimating the long-run Cobb-Douglas production function

The mathematical properties of the Cobb-Douglas production function make it a popular specification for estimating long-run production functions. After converting to natural logarithms, the estimable form of the Cobb-Douglas function ($Q = \gamma K^\alpha L^\beta$) is

$$\ln Q = \ln \gamma + \alpha \ln K + \beta \ln L$$

Recall from the previous discussion that $\hat{\alpha}$ and $\hat{\beta}$ are estimates of the output elasticities of capital and labor, respectively. Recall also that the estimated marginal products,

$$MP_K = \hat{\alpha} \frac{Q}{K} \quad \text{and} \quad MP_L = \hat{\beta} \frac{Q}{L}$$

are significantly positive and decreasing (the desired theoretical property) if the t-tests or p-values on $\hat{\alpha}$ and $\hat{\beta}$ indicate that these coefficients are significantly positive but less than 1 in value.

The function coefficient is estimated as

$$\hat{\xi} = \hat{\alpha} + \hat{\beta}$$

and provides a measure of returns to scale. To determine whether $(\hat{\alpha} + \hat{\beta})$ is significantly greater (less) than 1, a t-test is performed. If $(\hat{\alpha} + \hat{\beta})$ is not significantly greater (less) than 1, we cannot reject the existence of constant returns to scale. To determine whether the sum, $(\hat{\alpha} + \hat{\beta})$, is significantly different from 1, we use the following t-statistic:

$$t_{\hat{\alpha} + \hat{\beta}} = \frac{(\hat{\alpha} + \hat{\beta}) - 1}{S_{\hat{\alpha} + \hat{\beta}}}$$

where the value 1 indicates that we are testing "different from" and $S_{\hat{\alpha} + \hat{\beta}}$ is the estimated standard error of the sum of the estimated coefficients ($\hat{\alpha} + \hat{\beta}$). After calculating this t-statistic, it is compared to the critical t-value from the table. Again note that inasmuch as the calculated t-statistic can be negative (when $\hat{\alpha} + \hat{\beta}$ is less than 1), it is the absolute value of the t-statistic that is compared with the critical t-value. Some statistical software can give p-values for this test.

The only problem in performing this test involves obtaining the estimated standard error of $(\hat{\alpha} + \hat{\beta})$. All regression packages can provide the analyst, upon request, with variances and covariances of the regression coefficients, $\hat{\alpha}$ and $\hat{\beta}$, in a variance–covariance matrix.[a] Traditionally, variances of $\hat{\alpha}$ and $\hat{\beta}$ are denoted as $\text{Var}(\hat{\alpha})$ and $\text{Var}(\hat{\beta})$ and the covariance between $\hat{\alpha}$ and $\hat{\beta}$ as $\text{Cov}(\hat{\alpha}, \hat{\beta})$. As you may remember from a statistics course,

$$\text{Var}(\hat{\alpha} + \hat{\beta}) = \text{Var}(\hat{\alpha}) + \text{Var}(\hat{\beta}) + 2\,\text{Cov}(\hat{\alpha}, \hat{\beta})$$

The estimated standard error of $(\hat{\alpha} + \hat{\beta})$ is

$$S_{\hat{\alpha} + \hat{\beta}} = \sqrt{\text{Var}(\hat{\alpha}) + \text{Var}(\hat{\beta}) + 2\text{Cov}(\hat{\alpha}, \hat{\beta})}$$

The short-run Cobb-Douglas production function

When capital is fixed in the short run at $\overline{K}$, the short-run Cobb-Douglas production function is

$$Q = \gamma \overline{K}^\alpha L^\beta = \delta L^\beta$$

where $\delta = \gamma K^\alpha$. Note that if L is 0, no output is forthcoming. For output to be positive, δ must be positive. The marginal product of labor is

$$Q_L = \delta \beta L^{\beta - 1}$$

For marginal product to be positive, β must be positive. The second derivative

$$Q_{LL} = \beta(\beta - 1)\delta L^{\beta - 2}$$

---

[a]The variance–covariance matrix is a listing (in the form of a matrix on the computer printout) of the estimated variances and covariances of all the estimated coefficients. For example, in the regression of $Y = \hat{\alpha} + \hat{\beta}X$, the variance–covariance matrix provides estimates of $\text{Var}(\hat{\alpha})$, $\text{Var}(\hat{\beta})$, and $\text{Cov}(\hat{\alpha}, \hat{\beta})$. As noted in Chapter 4, the variance of a regression coefficient provides a measure of the dispersion of the variable about its mean. The covariance of the regression coefficients provides information about the joint distribution: that is, the relation between the two regression coefficients.

reveals that if the marginal product of labor is diminishing, β must be less than 1. Thus the restrictions for the Cobb-Douglas production in the short run are

$$\delta > 0 \quad \text{and} \quad 0 < \beta < 1$$

Estimating the short-run Cobb-Douglas production function

As in the case of the long-run Cobb-Douglas production function, the short-run Cobb-Douglas production function must also be transformed into a linear form by converting it to natural logarithms. The equation actually estimated is

$$\ln Q = \tau + \beta \ln L$$

where $\tau = \ln \delta$. Recall that β must be positive for the marginal product of labor to be positive and less than 1 for the marginal product to be decreasing (i.e., $0 < \beta < 1$). It is common practice to test that $\beta > 0$ and $\beta < 1$ using a t-test.

Estimation of a Long-Run Cost Function

Because the general form for the long-run cost function with two inputs is

$$LTC = f(Q, w, r)$$

and because cross-sectional data are generally used for long-run estimation, the empirical specification of a long-run cost function must, as emphasized earlier, include the prices of inputs as explanatory variables. At first glance, it would appear that the solution would be simply to add the input prices as additional explanatory variables in the cost function developed above and express total cost as

$$LTC = aQ + bQ^2 + cQ^3 + dw + er$$

This function, however, fails to satisfy a basic characteristic of cost functions. A total cost function can be written as $LTC = wL + rK$. If both input prices double, holding output constant, input usage will not change but total cost will double. Letting LTC' denote total cost after input prices double,

$$LTC' = (2w)L + (2r)K$$
$$= 2(wL + rK)$$
$$= 2LTC$$

The long-run cost function suggested here does not satisfy this requirement. For a given output, if input prices double,

$$LTC' = aQ + bQ^2 + cQ^3 + d(2w) + e(2r)$$
$$= aQ + bQ^2 + cQ^3 + dw + er + (dw + er)$$
$$= LTC + dw + er$$

and LTC' is not equal to $2LTC$.

Therefore, an alternative form for estimating a long-run cost function must be found. The most commonly employed form is a log-linear specification such as the Cobb-Douglas specifications. With this type of specification, the total cost function is expressed as

$$LTC = \alpha Q^{\beta} w^{\gamma} r^{\delta}$$

Using this functional form, when input prices double while holding output constant

$$LTC' = \alpha Q^{\beta} (2w)^{\gamma} (2r)^{\delta}$$
$$= 2^{(\gamma+\delta)} (\alpha Q^{\beta} w^{\gamma} r^{\delta})$$
$$= 2^{(\gamma+\delta)} LTC$$

If $\gamma + \delta = 1$, doubling input prices indeed doubles the total cost of producing a given level of output—the required characteristic of a cost function. Hence, it is necessary to *impose* this condition on the proposed log-linear cost function by defining δ as $1 - \gamma$; so

$$LTC = \alpha Q^{\beta} w^{\gamma} \gamma^{1-\gamma}$$
$$= \alpha Q^{\beta} w^{\gamma} r^{-\gamma} r$$
$$= \alpha Q^{\beta} (w/r)^{\gamma} r$$

The parameter restrictions are $\alpha > 0$, $\beta > 0$, and $0 < \gamma < 1$, which ensure that total cost is positive and increases when output and input prices increase.

To estimate the above total cost equation, it must be converted to natural logarithms

$$\ln LTC = \ln \alpha + \beta \ln Q + \gamma \ln\left(\frac{w}{r}\right) + 1 \ln r$$

While we can estimate the parameters α, β, and γ, this formulation requires that the coefficient for ln r be *precisely* equal to 1. If we were to estimate this equation, such a value cannot be guaranteed. To impose this condition on the empirical function, we simply move ln r to the left-hand side of the equation to obtain

$$\ln LTC - \ln r = \ln \alpha + \beta \ln Q + \gamma \ln(w/r)$$

which, using the rules of logarithms, can be rewritten as

$$\ln\left(\frac{LTC}{r}\right) = \ln\alpha + \beta \ln Q + \gamma \ln(w/r)$$

This equation is then estimated to obtain an estimate of the long-run cost function.

As noted earlier, the primary use of the long-run cost function is in the firm's investment decision. Therefore, once the previous cost equation is estimated, its most important use is determining the extent of economies of scale. From the discussion of log-linear functions in Chapter 4, the coefficient β indicates the *elasticity of total cost* with respect to output; that is,

$$\beta = \frac{\text{Percentage change in total cost}}{\text{Percentage change in output}}$$

When $\beta > 1$, cost is increasing more than proportionately to output (e.g., if the percentage change in output is 25 percent and the percentage change in cost is 50 percent, β would be equal to 2); therefore long-run average cost would be increasing. Hence if $\beta > 1$, the estimates indicate diseconomies of scale. If $\beta < 1$, total cost increases proportionately less than the increase in output and economies of scale would be indicated. Furthermore, note that the magnitude of the estimate of β indicates the "strength" of the economies or diseconomies of scale. Finally, if $\beta = 1$, there are constant returns to scale. The statistical significance of β is tested in the manner outlined earlier. Table 10A.1 summarizes the mathematical properties of the Cobb-Douglas specification for long-run total cost.

Estimating Long-Run Cost for U.S. Electric Utility Firms

To illustrate the estimation of a long-run cost function, we can use the data in Table 10A.2, which is a sample of 20 privately owned electric utility firms. The data for each firm are:

Output (Q): total generation and transmission of electric power, expressed in millions of kilowatt-hours.

Capital (K): Stock of physical capital held by the firm, expressed in millions of dollars.

Labor (L): Total number of employees, expressed in thousands of workers.

Cost of using capital (r): Estimated user cost of capital, $r = q_K(i + \delta)$, where q_K is the unit acquisition cost of the capital stock, i is the real rate of interest, and δ is the rate of depreciation.

Cost of using labor (w): Average annual payment per worker expressed in thousands of dollars.

As we explained above, the data required for estimation of long-run cost are total cost, output, and the input prices. Because total cost is $C = wL + rK$, we can calculate total cost by using the capital usage, labor usage, and

TABLE 10A.1

Summary of the Cobb-Douglas Specification for Long-Run Total Cost

Long-run total cost	$LTC = \alpha Q^\beta w^\gamma r^{1-\gamma}$
	$= \alpha Q^\beta\left(\frac{w}{r}\right)^\gamma r$
Estimable form	$\ln\left[\frac{LTC}{r}\right] = \ln\alpha + \beta \ln Q + \gamma \ln\left(\frac{w}{r}\right)$
Elasticity of total cost	$\beta = \frac{\%\Delta LTC}{\%\Delta Q}$
If $\begin{cases}\beta<1\\\beta=1\\\beta>1\end{cases}$ there exist $\begin{cases}\text{economies of}\\\text{constant returns to}\\\text{diseconomies of}\end{cases}$ scale	
Restrictions on parameters	$\alpha > 0$
	$\beta > 0$
	$0 < \gamma < 1$

TABLE 10A.2

Sample Data for 20 Private U.S. Electric Utility Firms

Firm	C	Q	K	L	r	w
1	30.8923	4.612	321.502	1.019	0.06903	8.5368
2	58.5825	8.297	544.031	2.118	0.06903	9.9282
3	15.1205	1.820	156.803	0.448	0.06754	10.1116
4	32.8014	5.849	250.441	1.265	0.07919	10.2522
5	22.7768	3.145	247.983	0.603	0.06481	11.1194
6	11.9176	1.381	82.867	0.665	0.06598	9.6992
7	34.4028	5.422	366.062	0.962	0.06754	10.0613
8	47.5209	7.115	485.406	1.435	0.06565	10.9087
9	18.9136	3.052	99.115	0.829	0.10555	10.1954
10	36.0902	4.394	292.016	1.501	0.06572	11.2585
11	3.2401	0.248	21.002	0.145	0.07919	10.8759
12	62.0032	9.699	556.138	2.391	0.06903	9.8758
13	74.7206	14.271	667.397	2.697	0.06789	10.9051
14	96.0053	17.743	998.106	3.625	0.06903	7.4775
15	63.4357	14.956	598.809	3.085	0.06572	7.8062
16	15.9901	3.108	118.349	0.714	0.07919	9.2689
17	42.3249	9.416	423.213	1.733	0.06565	8.3906
18	44.6781	6.857	468.897	1.406	0.06565	9.8826
19	59.2520	9.745	514.037	2.442	0.06860	9.8235
20	38.7337	4.442	236.043	1.497	0.08206	12.9352

input price data presented in Table 10A.2. The function to be estimated is

$$\log (TC/r) = \log \alpha + \beta \log Q + \gamma \log (w/r)$$

The computer output obtained from this estimation is[b]

As we have shown, the coefficient β is of primary importance because it indicates the existence of economies or diseconomies of scale. In our estimation $\beta < 1$, so economies of scale are indicated. However, it is necessary to determine whether this coefficient is statistically

DEPENDENT VAR:	LOG (TC/R)		F-RATIO: 324.328
OBSERVATIONS:	20		R-SQUARE: 0.9745
VARIABLE	PARAMETER ESTIMATE		STANDARD ERROR
INTERCEPT	−0.41600		1.03943
LOG Q	0.83830		0.03315
LOG (W/R)	1.05435		0.20939

[b]A user of this text pointed out a troublesome point in this estimation: In the log-linear specification, both γ and δ would be expected to be between 0 and 1. In this estimation, γ was estimated to be 1.05435 > 1. However, the estimate of γ is not significantly greater than (different from) 1. The t-statistic in this case is

$$t = \frac{1.05435 - 1}{0.20939} = 0.260$$

Clearly 0.260 < 2.110. So, although troublesome, these estimates do not conflict with the required theoretical properties.

significant. Using the methodology described earlier in this chapter, the appropriate test statistic is

$$t_{\hat{\beta}} = \frac{\hat{\beta} - 1}{S_{\hat{\beta}}}$$

$$= \frac{0.83830 - 1}{0.03315}$$

$$= -4.87783$$

We then compare the absolute value of this test statistic with the critical t-value. In this example, since we have $20 - 3 = 17$ degrees of freedom, the critical value of t (at a 95 percent confidence level) is 2.110. Because 4.87783 exceeds 2.110, it follows that $\hat{\beta}$ is statistically significant and that there is indeed evidence of economies of scale.

MATHEMATICAL EXERCISES

1. Why would the restrictions $A > 0$ and $B < 0$ be inappropriate for a short-run cubic production function?

2. For the short-run cubic production function, show that increasing $\overline{K}$ always results in an increase in the level of labor usage at which diminishing returns begin.

3. Consider the Cobb-Douglas production function $Q = 36K^{0.5}L^{1.0}$.
   a. Find the marginal product functions.
   b. Write equations for the $MRTS$ and the output elasticities.
   c. The function coefficient is equal to _____, so the production function is characterized by _____ returns to scale.

4. Let the long-run total cost function be $LTC = (1/12)Qw^{0.5}r^{0.5}$.
   a. Demonstrate that a doubling of input prices causes LTC to double.
   b. Find the elasticity of total cost. This long-run total cost function is characterized by _____ scale.
   c. Let $w = \$16$ and $r = \$25$, and find LMC and LAC. Graph the LMC and LAC curves. Are these curves consistent with part b?
   d. Is your answer to part b consistent with your answer to part d in Mathematical Exercise 4 in Chapter 9?

ONLINE APPENDIX 3: Linear Programming

This appendix can be found online via *Connect*® or *Create*™. For more information, refer to the Preface.

11

Managerial Decisions in Competitive Markets

After reading this chapter, you will be able to:

11.1 Discuss three characteristics of perfectly competitive markets.

11.2 Explain why the demand curve facing a perfectly competitive firm is perfectly elastic and serves as the firm's marginal revenue curve.

11.3 Find short-run profit-maximizing output, derive firm and industry supply curves, and identify the amount of producer surplus earned.

11.4 Explain the characteristics of long-run competitive equilibrium for a firm, derive long-run industry supply curves, and identify economic rent and producer surplus.

11.5 Find the profit-maximizing level of usage of a variable input.

11.6 Employ empirically estimated or forecasted values of market price, average variable cost, and marginal cost to calculate the firm's profit-maximizing output and profit.

Now we are ready to get to the bottom line. Literally. Up to this point in the text, we have developed several tools—optimization theory, demand analysis and forecasting, and production and cost analysis—that you may have found interesting enough as single topics. But now, and for the rest of the text, we bring these tools together to build a framework for making the most important decisions affecting the profitability of the firm: how much to produce and what price to charge. We are going to analyze how managers make price and output decisions to maximize the profit of the firm.

As it turns out, the nature of the price and output decision is strongly influenced by the structure of the market in which the firm sells its product. Recall from Chapter 1 that we discussed the characteristics of several market structures. Market structure determines whether a manager will be a price-setter or a price-taker. The theoretical market structure in which firms take the market price as given is called perfect competition. We begin our discussion of pricing and output decisions by examining how managers of price-taking, perfectly competitive firms should make production decisions to maximize profit. We will develop a number of important ideas that will carry over and apply to managers who are price-setters. For example, we will demonstrate that output decisions should never be based on considerations of fixed costs, that a firm may find it desirable to continue producing even though the firm is losing money, that a manager should not stop hiring labor just because labor productivity begins to fall, and that in the absence of entry barriers a firm can be expected to earn zero economic profit in the long run.

As we begin our discussion of profit maximization for price-taking firms, you may wonder how many managers are really price-takers, rather than price-setters. In a recent survey of one of our executive MBA classes, even we were surprised to find that 34 of the 38 manager-students felt that their firms had little or no control over the price they could charge for their products; their prices were determined by market forces beyond their control. Although the assumptions of perfect competition, to be set forth in the next section, may seem quite narrowly focused, many managers face market conditions that closely approximate the model of perfect competition. And even if you are a manager of a price-setting firm, you will find the analysis of profit maximization under competitive conditions to be a valuable framework for making profitable decisions.

We assume in this chapter and the following four chapters that the goal of the manager is to maximize the firm's profit. It has been suggested that a manager may have other goals: to maximize the firm's sales, or rate of growth of sales; to maximize a firm's market share; to maximize the manager's own utility by using the firm's resources for personal benefit; or to promote the manager's favorite social causes. Such goals can lead to conflicts between owners and managers. It is our goal in this book to show how to make decisions that will make you a more effective manager, which generally means maximizing the profit of the firm. If you choose a different goal, you do so at your own risk.

When we assume that a firm maximizes its profit, we refer to its economic profit. Economic profit (π) is the firm's total revenue minus its total economic cost. Recall from Figure 1.1 that total economic cost is the sum of the explicit costs of using market-supplied resources (monetary payments to outside suppliers of inputs) plus the implicit costs of using owner-supplied resources (best returns forgone by using owners' resources). Thus,

$$\text{Economic profit} = \pi = \text{Total revenue} - \text{Total economic cost}$$
$$= \text{Total revenue} - \text{Explicit costs} - \text{Implicit costs}$$

As you might expect, the manager's profit-maximizing decision is a direct application of the theory of unconstrained maximization, set forth in Chapter 3. Managers of firms that are price-takers look at price and cost conditions to answer three fundamental questions: (1) Should the firm produce or shut down? (2) If the firm produces, what is the optimal level of production? (3) What are the optimal levels of inputs to employ? Because the manager of a perfectly competitive firm takes product price as given, there is obviously no pricing decision.

After briefly setting forth all the characteristics of perfect competition, we first analyze how a manager determines the firm's output or level of production that maximizes profit. We address the short-run decision, when some inputs are fixed, and then the long-run decision, when all inputs are variable. Finally, we discuss how a manager chooses the levels of input usage that maximize profit. We will show that the output and the input decisions each lead to the same results.

11.1 CHARACTERISTICS OF PERFECT COMPETITION

The most important characteristic of perfectly competitive markets is that each firm in a competitive market behaves as a price-taker: Competitive firms take the market price of the product, which is determined by the intersection of supply and demand, as given. This price-taking behavior is the hallmark of a competitive market. In all other market structures—monopoly, monopolistic competition, and oligopoly—firms enjoy some degree of price-setting power. Three characteristics define **perfect competition**:

perfect competition
A market structure that exists when (1) firms are price-takers, (2) all firms produce a homogeneous product, and (3) entry and exit are unrestricted.

1. Perfectly competitive firms are price-takers because each individual firm in the market is so small relative to the total market that it cannot affect the market price of the good or service it produces by changing its output. Of course, if *all* producers act together, changes in quantity will definitely affect market price. But if perfect competition prevails, each producer is so small that individual changes will go unnoticed.

2. All firms produce a homogeneous or perfectly standardized commodity. The product of each firm in a perfectly competitive market is identical to the product of every other firm. This condition ensures that buyers are indifferent as to the firm from which they purchase. Product differences, whether real or imaginary, are precluded under perfect competition.

3. Entry into and exit from perfectly competitive markets are unrestricted. There are no barriers preventing new firms from entering the market, and nothing prevents existing firms from leaving a market.

In spite of the term *competitive*, perfectly competitive firms do not recognize any competitiveness among themselves; that is, no direct competition among firms exists. The theoretical concept of perfect competition is diametrically opposed to the generally accepted concept of competition. Because firms in perfectly competitive markets produce identical products and face a market-determined price, managers of competitive firms have no incentive to "beat their rivals" out of sales because each firm can sell all it wants. And, of course, price-taking firms cannot compete through any kind of pricing tactics.

Markets that do not precisely meet the three conditions set forth for perfect competition frequently come close enough that the firms nonetheless behave as if they are perfect competitors. The managers in the executive MBA class surveyed in the introduction to this chapter do not operate in perfectly competitive markets, but they do face a sufficient number of firms producing nearly identical goods in markets with only weak restrictions on entry, and so view themselves as price-takers. As we will show you in the next section and in the next chapter, the degree of competition faced by managers is reflected in the elasticity of the *firm's* demand. The profit-maximizing decisions developed in this chapter apply even to firms that are not exactly or perfectly competitive.

11.2 DEMAND FACING A PRICE-TAKING FIRM

Suppose you are the owner–manager of a small citrus orchard that specializes in the production of oranges, which your firm then processes to be sold as frozen concentrate. You wish to determine the maximum price you can charge for various levels of output of frozen concentrate; that is, you wish to find the demand schedule facing your firm. After consulting *The Wall Street Journal*, you find that the market-determined price of orange juice concentrate is $1.20 per pound. You have 50,000 pounds of concentrate to sell, which makes your output minuscule compared with the tens of millions of pounds of orange juice concentrate sold in the market as a whole. On top of that, you realize that buyers of orange juice concentrate don't care from whom they buy because all orange juice concentrate is virtually identical (homogeneous).

All at once it hits you like a ton of oranges: You can sell virtually all the orange juice concentrate you wish at the going market price of $1.20 per pound. Even if you increased your output tenfold to 500,000 pounds, you could still find buyers willing to pay you $1.20 per pound for the entire 500,000 pounds because your output, by itself, is not going to affect (shift) market supply in any perceptible way. Indeed, if you lowered the price to sell more oranges, you would be needlessly sacrificing revenue. You also realize that you cannot charge a price higher than $1.20 per pound because buyers will simply buy from one of the thousands of other citrus producers that sell orange juice concentrate identical to your own.

By this reasoning, you realize that the demand curve facing your citrus grove can be drawn as shown in Figure 11.1. The demand for your firm's product is horizontal at a price of $1.20 per pound of orange juice concentrate. The demand

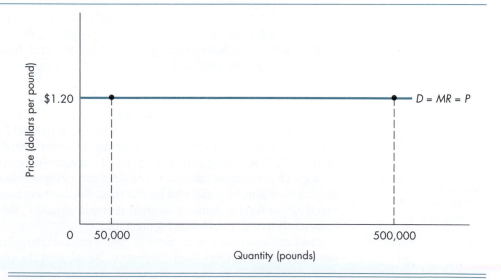

FIGURE 11.1

Demand and Marginal Revenue Facing a Citrus Producer

FIGURE 11.2
Derivation of Demand for a Price-Taking Firm

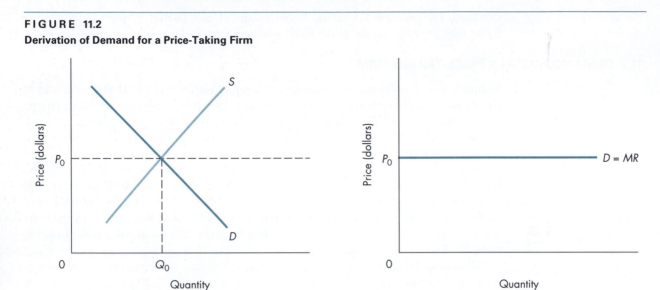

Panel A — Market

Panel B — Demand curve facing a price-taker

price for any level of orange juice concentrate is $1.20, no matter how many pounds you produce. This means that every extra pound sold contributes $1.20 to total revenue, and hence the market price of $1.20 is also the marginal revenue for every pound of orange juice concentrate sold. The demand curve facing the citrus producer is also its marginal revenue curve.

We can generalize this discussion to apply to *any* firm that operates as a price-taker in a competitive market. When a market is characterized by a large number of (relatively) small producers, each producing a homogeneous product, the demand curve facing the manager of each individual firm is horizontal at the price determined by the intersection of the *market* demand and supply curves. In addition, the horizontal demand curve is also the marginal revenue curve facing the manager.

Figure 11.2 illustrates the derivation of demand for a price-taking firm. Note, in the figure, that the *market* demand curve D in Panel A is downward-sloping, which the law of demand always requires of a demand curve. It is the demand curve faced by a single price-taking firm that is horizontal, as shown in Panel B of Figure 11.2. Recall that demand price is the maximum price buyers can be charged for a given amount of the good. The demand price is constant, and equal to P_0, for any level of output produced by the firm. Because each additional unit sold adds exactly P_0 to total revenue, marginal revenue equals P_0 for all output levels for the firm, as shown in Panel B in Figure 11.2.

The horizontal demand curve facing a price-taking firm is frequently called a **perfectly** (or infinitely) **elastic demand**. Recall that the point elasticity of demand

perfectly elastic demand
Horizontal demand facing a single, price-taking firm in a competitive market ($|E| = \infty$).

is measured by $E = P/(P - A)$, where A is the price intercept of the demand curve. Measured at any given price, as demand becomes flatter, $|P - A|$ becomes smaller and $|E|$ becomes larger. In the limit when demand is horizontal, $P - A = 0$, and $|E| = \infty$. Thus, for a horizontal demand, demand is said to be infinitely elastic or perfectly elastic.

Looked at another way, the product sold by a competitive firm has a large number of *perfect* substitutes: the identical (homogeneous) products sold by the other firms in the industry. The better the substitutes for a product, the more elastic the demand for the product. It follows from this relation that a perfectly competitive firm, facing many perfect substitutes, will have a perfectly elastic demand.

Again, we emphasize that the fact that perfectly competitive firms face a perfectly elastic or horizontal demand does not mean that the law of demand does not apply to perfectly competitive markets. It does. The *market demand* for the product is downward-sloping.

Now try Technical Problem 1.

> **Relation** The demand curve facing a competitive price-taking firm is horizontal or perfectly elastic at the price determined by the intersection of the *market* demand and supply curves. Because marginal revenue equals price for a competitive firm, the demand curve is also simultaneously the marginal revenue curve (i.e., $D = MR$). Price-taking firms can sell all they want at the market price. Each additional unit of sales adds to total revenue an amount equal to price.

11.3 PROFIT MAXIMIZATION IN THE SHORT RUN

We now turn to the output decision facing the manager of a price-taking firm operating in a competitive industry in the short run. Recall that the short run is the time period during which a firm employs one or more fixed inputs and any number of variable inputs. The fixed costs are sunk and must be paid even if the firm decides to cease production. The variable costs increase with the level of output and can be avoided if the manager decides to cease production.[1]

shut down
A firm produces zero output in the short run but must still pay for fixed inputs.

A manager must make two decisions in the short run. The first decision is whether to produce or *shut down* during the period. **Shut down** means the manager decides to produce zero output by hiring no variable inputs (and no quasi-fixed inputs, if the firm uses any). When production is zero, the only costs incurred by the firm are the unavoidable fixed costs. To make the decision to produce a positive level of output rather than shut down, the manager considers only the avoidable variable costs that will be incurred if the firm produces some positive quantity of goods or services. As you will see in this section, a manager will choose to produce a positive amount of output *only* if doing so generates enough total revenue to cover the firm's avoidable total variable costs of production.

---

[1]Firms sometimes incur quasi-fixed costs that do not vary with output but can be avoided if the manager decides to cease production in either the short run or long run. When there are quasi-fixed inputs, total avoidable cost is the sum of total variable cost plus total quasi-fixed cost. To keep our discussions as simple as possible throughout this chapter and the rest of the book, we will treat total *variable* cost as the only component of total *avoidable* cost, unless we specifically state the firm employs quasi-fixed inputs.

If the manager makes the first decision to produce rather than shut down, the second decision involves choosing the optimal level of output. Using the terminology presented in Chapter 3, the optimal level of output is the quantity that maximizes the firm's net benefit function, which is economic profit (π). Under some circumstances, which we discuss later, a manager will choose to incur losses (i.e., profit is negative) yet continue to produce rather than shut down. In such a situation, the manager will choose the output that *minimizes* the loss of the firm. Because minimizing a loss is equivalent to maximizing a negative profit, the decision rule for finding the optimal level of production is exactly the same regardless of whether profit is positive or negative. For this reason, we will speak of profit *maximization* even though the rule applies to a firm that is minimizing a loss.

In this section, we first discuss the firm's output decision when it can earn positive economic profit. We apply marginal analysis to find the profit-maximizing output. We then explain the conditions under which the manager should choose to shut down rather than produce. Next, we return to a central theme from Chapter 3: sunk costs, fixed costs, and average costs are irrelevant for making optimal decisions. We then finish this section by deriving the supply curve for a competitive, price-taking firm.

The Output Decision: Earning Positive Economic Profit

Figure 11.3 shows a typical set of short-run cost curves: short-run marginal cost (*SMC*), average total cost (*ATC*), and average variable cost (*AVC*). Average fixed cost is omitted for convenience and because, as we demonstrated in Chapter 3 and show you again in this section, fixed costs are irrelevant for decision-making purposes. Let's suppose the market-determined price, and therefore marginal revenue, is $36 per unit. What level of output should the firm produce to maximize profit?

One of the more common mistakes managers make when choosing a firm's production level is to select the quantity that generates the highest possible *profit margin* for the firm, rather than the maximum profit. **Profit margin** is the difference between price and average total cost, $P - ATC$. When all units of output are sold for the same price, profit margin is equivalent to *average profit*.[2] **Average profit** is simply total profit divided by output, π/Q, and thus measures profit per unit. The equivalence of average profit and profit margin is easy to see with only a bit of algebra

profit margin
The difference between price and average total cost: $P - ATC$.

average profit
Total profit divided by quantity: π/Q. Measures profit per unit and is equivalent to profit margin when all units sell for the same price.

$$\text{Average profit} = \frac{\pi}{Q} = \frac{(P - ATC)Q}{Q}$$

$$= P - ATC = \text{Profit margin}$$

---

[2]The practice of charging the same price for every unit sold is called *uniform pricing*. In Chapter 14, we will examine some pricing techniques that involve charging different prices for different units of the same good or service. In these instances, profit margin will vary for different units sold and thus will not be equivalent to average profit.

FIGURE 11.3

Profit Maximization when P = $36

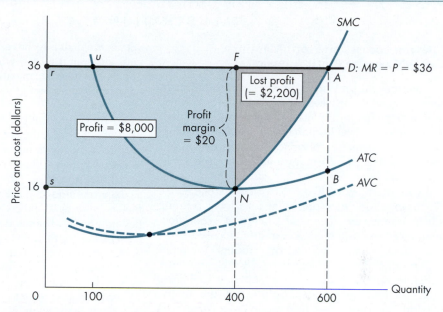

Panel A — Common mistake: maximizing profit margin

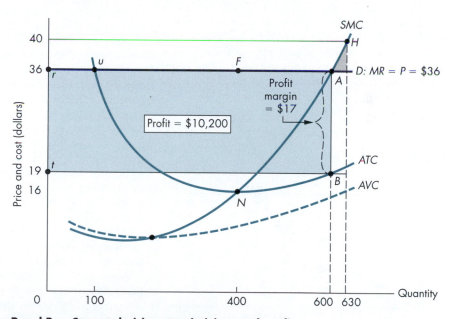

Panel B — Correct decision: maximizing total profit

ILLUSTRATION 11.1

Chevron Focuses on Profit Margin: Can It Maximize Profit Anyway?

We commented previously in this chapter that managers sometimes mistakenly believe that increasing or even maximizing profit margin should be one of their principle objectives in managerial decision making. Perhaps these managers believe maximizing profit and maximizing profit margin are coinciding goals. They certainly are not.

In an interview with *The Wall Street Journal*,[a] Mike Wirth, executive vice president for global refining and marketing operations at Chevron Corporation, announced that Chevron is currently "focused … on being able to widen our (profit) margins" for refining crude oil into gasoline, diesel, jet fuel, and other valuable refined products. As you saw in Figure 11.3, maximizing profit margin—or equivalently, maximizing profit per unit or average profit—is generally inconsistent with the goal of maximizing profit and value of the firm. In this Illustration we will examine Chevron's plans to expand its profit margin to highlight the pitfalls of making managerial decisions based on pushing up *profit margin* rather than pushing up *profit*. While *The Wall Street Journal* article doesn't provide all of the quantitative details we'd like to have, we can nonetheless show you, in general terms, why Chevron's management can choose to either maximize profit margin or maximize profit along with the value of Chevron stock—it cannot do both.

To allow for multiple refined products in the simplest possible way, the nearby graph measures refined output on the horizontal axis as the number of barrels of a *blend* of the various products, such as gasoline, diesel, jet fuel, and so on. Obviously, refineries would not actually combine or "package" gasoline, diesel, and jet fuel in the same 42-gallon barrel, it nonetheless simplifies our graphs of demand and cost to assume that each barrel of output contains portions of every product. Subject to some constraints associated with the petro-chemistry of refining processes, refiners are able to vary their blends of products coming from the crude oil input in a way that maximizes the total revenue generated from selling multiple products. We will not need to worry about how Chevron chooses the optimal blend here; we will just assume the blending decision has been made optimally. Because Chevron Corp. sells its petroleum products in markets that closely resemble perfect competition, the demand for Chevron's refined products is shown in the nearby figure as perfectly elastic (i.e., horizontal). The price per barrel of refined product on the vertical axis equals the number of dollars needed to buy the blend of products found in each barrel, based on the prevailing market-determined prices for gasoline, diesel, jet fuel, etc.[b] The figure also shows a typical set of U-shaped short-run cost curves.

Before Chevron decided to pursue higher refinery profit margins, as stated in *The Wall Street Journal* article, let's suppose Chevron was making its output decision correctly to maximize profit at point *a* where $P = SMC$. At Q^*, Chevron's initial profit margin is equal to the vertical distance between points *a* and *b* in our figure.

Now let's see what happens when Chevron's management decides to increase profit margin, as announced by Mr. Wirth. As a means of achieving higher profit margins, *The Wall Street Journal* reports that Chevron is restructuring its costs by making long-run investments to lower production costs (recall how this works from our discussion of long-run restructuring

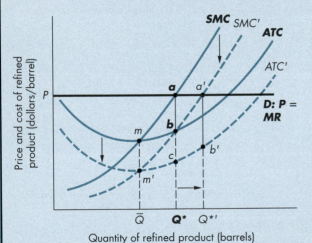

Quantity of refined product (barrels)

Source: Jessica Resnick-Ault, "Chevron Focuses on Refineries," *WSJ.com*, May 13, 2009.

in Chapter 9). Chevron has undertaken "an investment program, that's long overdue" to create cost savings by upgrading its refineries "to extract as much capacity as possible from its refineries." The effort, known as "Reliability Refinery," raised capacity utilization of refinery capital by 6.6 percent, compared to a year ago, and raised throughput by 60,000 barrels per day for the same time period. As you learned in Chapter 8, a rise in productivity of refineries will cause a reduction in production costs at every level of refined output. In the figure, we show the effect of Chevron's Reliability Refinery project by shifting costs downward to ATC' and SMC'.[c]

Now you can clearly see why Chevron cannot maximize *both* profit and the spread between P and ATC. If the company continues to produce Q^* barrels of refined product, profit margin will indeed increase because unit costs are now lower. In the figure, the vertical distance between P and ATC' (distance a to c) is larger than before the Reliability Refinery effort reduced refining costs (distance a to b). Mr. Wirth is correct when he claims that by lowering cost and raising profit margin, Chevron now makes more profit on Q^* units. But herein lies the problem we wish to illustrate: While Chevron has truly succeeded in squeezing more (total) profit out of the same amount of refined product, the company is nonetheless making an error in its output decision by focusing on profit margin. Because of the reduction in marginal production costs, Chevron must increase its output of refined product to make the greatest possible profit—even though increasing output will *lower* its profit margin. As you can see clearly in the nearby figure, the new profit-maximizing quantity occurs at the higher output level, $Q^{*'}$, where $P = SMC'$ at point a'. Profit margin at $Q^{*'}$, which is the distance a' to b', is less than profit margin at Q^*, which is the distance a to c.

Based on *The Wall Street Journal* article, we do not know whether Chevron took advantage of its lower marginal cost to expand output at its refineries. However, it is not farfetched at all to imagine that production managers at Chevron would be unwilling to ramp up output and risk upsetting some other manager at Chevron who sees profit margins getting squeezed as output expands from Q^* to $Q^{*'}$. In fact, if Chevron's management team truly focuses all of its attention on profit margin, as Mr. Wirth

suggests, then managers might even make matters worse by *reducing* output from Q^* to $\overline{Q}$. This would maximize Chevron's profit margin, but reduce its profit and the value of the corporation. Again, we do not have enough information from *The Wall Street Journal* interview to know exactly what decision process was followed at Chevron. However, we know enough to be able to lay out the troubles and pitfalls that Chevron's managers would face if they get sidetracked by concerns over profit margin. The Reliability Refinery project was not a mistake for Chevron; it lowered cost and increased profit. The mistake here, if in fact any mistake was even made, was to let profit margin creep into the output decision.

As you can see from this Illustration and our presentation in Figure 11.3, businesses cannot maximize both (total) profit, $TR - TC$, and profit margin, $P - ATC$, at the same time (i.e., at the same level of output).[d] For this reason, managers should ignore profit margin when making output decisions. We are not aware of any studies or quantitative estimates of corporate value lost by managers who mistakenly try to maximize profit margin, but in view of the seemingly widespread desire by managers to earn higher profit margins, we suspect the cost could be substantial.

[a]This Illustration is based on the online article by Jessica Resnick-Ault, "Chevron Focuses on Refineries," *WSJ.com*, May 13, 2009.

[b]Suppose, for example, each 42-gallon barrel of blend contains 24 gallons of gasoline, 16 gallons of jet fuel, and 2 gallons of worthless gunk. Further suppose market prices for gasoline and jet fuel are, respectively, $3/gallon and $2/gallon. The price for a barrel of this blend of refined products is $104 per barrel, which is the amount of revenue each barrel generates when the gasoline and jet fuel are sold at market prices [i.e., $104 = ($3 \times 24) + ($2 \times 16)$].

[c]Theoretically, the quantity where ATC reaches its minimum value could rise, fall, or stay the same. Strictly for convenience, we shifted ATC down in a way that leaves the minimum point on ATC' unchanged at $\overline{Q}$.

[d]There is only one very narrow exception to this rule: When market price happens to be equal to minimum average total cost, then price also equals marginal cost and profit will be maximized (and equal to zero) at the same output that maximizes profit margin.

This relation between average profit and profit margin also holds in the long run; just substitute LAC for ATC.

The output that maximizes profit margin ($P - ATC$) does not also maximize profit ($TR - TC$), with only one superficial exception.[3] For this reason, profit-maximizing managers should ignore profit margin (or profit per unit) when making their production decisions. Suppose the manager of a firm facing the costs shown in Figure 11.3 chooses to produce only 400 units of output in Panel A, because the manager sees the difference between price and average total cost is maximized at 400 units (i.e., where ATC is minimized). Notice in Panel A that the vertical distance from point F to point N, which measures profit margin (and average profit) at 400 units, is $20 ($36 − $16). By visual inspection, you can verify that $20 must be the *highest* possible profit margin because price is $36 for every unit sold and average total cost reaches its minimum value, $16, at point N.

Let's now compute the profit when the manager mistakenly chooses to produce 400 units. As you can see in Panel A, at 400 units, total revenue is $14,400, which is price times quantity ($36 × 400), and total cost is $6,400, which is average total cost times quantity ($16 × 400). Profit, then, is $8,000 (=$14,400 − $6,400) when the firm produces 400 units and maximizes profit margin.[4] So, what's wrong with making a profit of $8,000?

The answer is simple: This firm could make even more profit—$10,200 to be precise—by producing 600 units, as shown in Panel B. By expanding production from 400 to 600 units, *total* profit (π) rises as profit *margin* falls or, equivalently, as average profit falls. Plenty of highly paid CEOs find this outcome puzzling. Hardly a day passes that you will not see, somewhere in the business news, an executive manager bragging about raising profit margins or promising to do so in the future. We will now clear up this confusion by employing the logic of marginal analysis presented in Chapter 3.

Return to point N in Panel A where the firm is producing and selling 400 units. Let the manager increase production by 1 unit to 401 units. Because this firm is a price-taking firm for which price equals marginal revenue ($P = $36 = MR), selling the 401st unit for $36 causes total revenue to rise by $36. Producing the 401st unit causes total cost to rise by the amount of short-run marginal cost, which is $16 (approximately). By choosing to produce and sell the 401st unit, the manager adds $36 to revenue and adds only $16 to cost, thereby adding $20 to the firm's total profit. By this same reasoning, the manager would continue increasing production as long as MR (or, equivalently, P) is greater than SMC. From 401 units to 600 units at point A, each unit adds to total profit the difference between P and SMC. Thus, output should be increased to 600 units, as shown in Panel B, where $P = MR = SMC = $36. At 600 units, total revenue is $21,600 (=$36 × 600).

---

[3]When market price is exactly equal to minimum average total cost (P = minimum ATC), price also equals marginal cost ($P = SMC$) and *only* at this unique quantity is it possible to maximize both profit margin and total profit.

[4]Notice that total profit can also be calculated by multiplying profit margin (average profit) by quantity: $8,000 = $20 × 400.

Total cost is $11,400 (=$19 × 600). Thus, the maximum possible profit is $10,200 (=$21,600 − $11,400). In Panel A, the gray-shaded area below *MR* and above *SMC* is equal to the value of the *lost* profit when only 400 units are produced instead of 600 units. We can summarize this very important discussion in a principle:

Principle   Managers cannot maximize both profit and profit margin at the same level of output. For this reason, profit margin—or, equivalently, average profit—should be ignored when making profit-maximizing decisions. When a firm can make positive profit in the short run, profit is maximized at the output level where $MR (= P) = SMC$.

This principle applies to choosing the profit-maximizing level of any decision variable: quantity, price, input usage, advertising budget, Research and Development (R&D) spending, and so on.

So far, we have focused our attention on the loss of profit when managers produce *less* than the profit-maximizing amount. Now suppose the manager makes the mistake of supplying *too much* output by producing and selling 630 units in Panel B. As you can see, marginal revenue (price) is now *less* than marginal cost: Price is $36 and marginal cost of the 630th unit is $40 (point *H*). The manager could decrease output by 1 unit and reduce total cost by $40 (the cost of the extra resources needed to produce the 630th unit). The lost sale of the 630th unit would reduce revenue by only $36, so the firm's profit would increase by $4. By the same reasoning, the manager would continue to decrease production as long as *MR* (= *P*) is less than *SMC* (back to point *A*). The gray-shaded area in Panel B is the lost profit from producing 630 units instead of 600 units. It follows from this discussion that the manager maximizes profit by choosing the level of output where *MR* (= *P*) = *SMC*. This rule is, of course, the rule of unconstrained maximization set forth in Chapter 3 (*MB* = *MC*) with profit serving as the net benefit (*TB* − *TC*) to be maximized.

Figure 11.4 shows the total revenue (*TR*), total cost (*TC*), and profit (π) curves for the situation presented in Figure 11.3. Notice in Panel A that *TR* is linear with slope equal to $36 (= *P* = *MR*) because each additional unit sold adds $36 to total revenue. Also note that in Panel B, at 401 units, the slope of the profit curve is $20, which follows from the preceding discussion about producing the 401st unit. At 600 units, the maximum profit is $10,200, which occurs at the peak of the profit curve (point *A'*) where the slope of the profit curve is zero. The points *U* and *V* in Figure 11.4 (100 units and 950 units) are sometimes called **break-even points** because total revenue equals total cost and the firm earns zero profit.

break-even points
Output levels where
P = *ATC* and profit
equals zero: points *U*
and *V* in Figure 11.4.

Because the total cost of producing 600 units ($11,400) includes the opportunity cost of the resources provided by the firm's owners (i.e., the implicit costs), the owners earn $10,200 more than they could have earned if they had instead employed their resources in their best alternative. The $10,200 economic profit, then, is a return to the owners *in excess* of their best alternative use of their resources.

The Output Decision: Operating at a Loss or Shutting Down

Sometimes the price of a competitive firm's product is less the average total cost (*P* < *ATC*) for all output levels. This means that total revenue (*P* × *Q*) will fall

FIGURE 11.4
Profit Maximization when *P* = $36

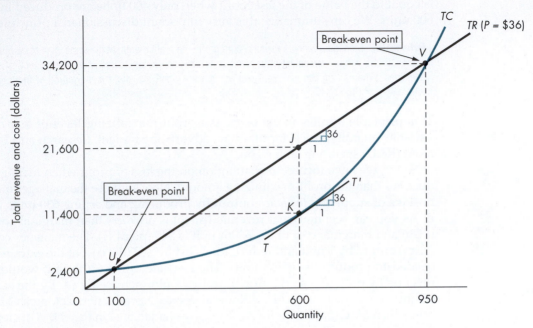

Panel A — Total revenue and total cost

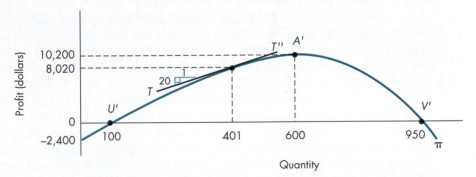

Panel B — The profit curve when price is $36

short of total cost ($ATC \times Q$), and the firm will suffer a loss no matter what output it produces—even if it shuts down and produces nothing. In this situation, the manager must choose an output level—either zero output or a positive output—that will minimize the loss in the short run. Obviously, if a firm shuts down and produces no output it generates no revenue and incurs no avoidable variable costs, but must still pay for its fixed inputs. Thus, a firm that shuts down in the short run loses an amount equal to its fixed costs:

$$\pi = TR - TVC - TFC = 0 - 0 - TFC$$
$$= -TFC$$

Clearly, a manager should only produce a positive output, instead of shutting down, if producing a positive output results in a smaller loss than total fixed cost.

Whenever a firm faces a loss in the short run, the firm's loss is minimized by producing the output where $P = SMC$ (rather than producing nothing at all), as long as its revenue will at least pay all of the avoidable costs incurred, even if revenue cannot also cover the unavoidable fixed costs. As a general rule, managers should produce a positive amount of output only when they expect to generate enough revenue to pay all the costs the firm could avoid by producing nothing at all: Total revenue must cover total avoidable cost.[5] This rule applies in both short-run and long-run production periods. We will now look more closely at the short-run situation and examine the long-run situation later in this chapter.

When total revenue exceeds the firm's total variable costs ($TR > TVC$)—or equivalently, price exceeds average variable cost ($P > AVC$)—the firm takes in enough revenue to pay all its variable costs and has some revenue left over, which it can use to pay a portion of its fixed costs. Therefore, the firm's loss will be less than its total fixed cost when it produces a positive output, which is better than losing the full amount of fixed costs if nothing is produced. Now consider the alternative situation when $P < AVC$, and total revenue does not cover all variable costs. In this situation, the firm would lose more than its fixed costs if it decides to produce, because it loses the portion of its variable costs it cannot cover *plus* all of its fixed costs. As you can see, this is worse than shutting down and losing only the amount of total fixed costs. Thus, firms should shut down and produce nothing when total revenue falls below total variable cost ($TR < TVC$) or, equivalently, when price falls below average variable cost ($P < AVC$).

When price exactly equals average variable cost ($P = AVC$), the loss is the same for either decision, and the manager is indifferent between producing the output where $P = SMC$ or producing no output all. To resolve any confusion over this point of indifference, we will assume managers choose to produce rather than

---

[5]As mentioned in footnote 1, when firms employ quasi-fixed inputs, total avoidable cost includes total variable cost plus total quasi-fixed cost. Thus, firms with quasi-fixed costs should produce, rather than shut down, only when total revenue covers total variable cost plus total quasi-fixed cost. Unless we specifically state that a firm incurs quasi-fixed costs, we will assume that total avoidable cost is identical to total variable cost.

shut down when P exactly equals AVC. We can now summarize the manager's decision to produce or not to produce in the following principle:

□ **Principle** In the short run, the manager of a firm will choose to produce the output where $P =$ SMC, rather than shut down, as long as total revenue is greater than or equal to the firm's total avoidable cost or total variable cost ($TR \geq TVC$). Or, equivalently, a firm should produce as long as price is greater than or equal to average variable cost ($P \geq AVC$). If total revenue cannot cover total avoidable cost, that is, if total revenue is less than total variable cost (or, equivalently, $P < AVC$), the manager will shut down and produce nothing, losing an amount equal to total fixed cost.

Figure 11.5 illustrates the manager's decision to produce or shut down. Suppose the manager faces a price of $10.50. The firm suffers an unavoidable loss in the short run because $10.50 is less than average total cost ($P < ATC$) at every level of output. If the manager does decide to produce, rather than shut down, the firm should produce 300 units where $MR (= P) = SMC = \$10.50$. At 300 units of output, total revenue is $3,150 (= \$10.50 \times 300$), total cost is $5,100 ($17 \times 300$), and the firm earns a (negative) profit equal to –$1,950 (= \$3,150 − \$5,100$). The manager should choose to produce 300 units at a loss of $1,950 only if the firm would lose more than $1,950 by producing nothing.

To compute the total fixed cost (the loss when $Q = 0$), recall that $TFC = AFC \times Q$. Also recall that $AFC = ATC − AVC$. You can see in Figure 11.5 that at 300 units of output $AFC = \$8$ (the distance from G to F, or $17 − \$9$), so $TFC = \$8 \times \$300 = \$2,400$. Clearly, the manager should produce 300 units at a loss of $1,950 rather than produce 0 units (shut down) and lose $2,400.

FIGURE 11.5
Loss Minimization in the Short Run: $P = \$10.50$

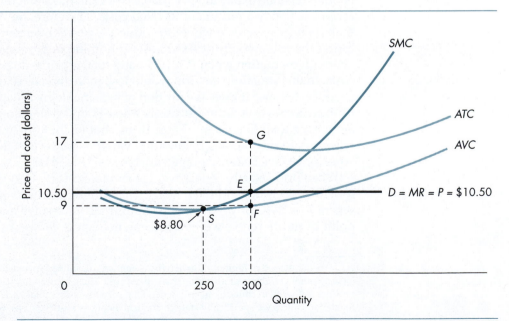

Notice also that, at 300 units, price ($10.50) exceeds average variable cost ($9) by $1.50. Thus, on 300 units of output, the total revenue of $3,150 exceeds the total variable cost of $2,700 (= $9 × 300) by $450 (= $3,150 − $2,700). The $450 revenue left over after paying variable costs can then be applied toward paying a part of the $2,400 fixed cost. The remainder of the fixed costs that are not covered represent the loss to the firm ($1,950 = $2,400 − $450).

As you can now see, when price falls below *minimum* average variable cost, the firm will shut down in the short run. For this reason, minimum average variable cost is called the **shutdown price.** In Figure 11.5, the firm's shutdown price is $8.80 at point S. If price is greater than or equal to $8.80, the firm should produce the output where $P = SMC$. If price falls below $8.80, the firm should shut down.

shutdown price

The price below which a firm shuts down in the short run (minimum *AVC*).

The Irrelevance of Sunk Costs, Fixed Costs, and Average Costs

Recall that decision makers trying to find the optimal level of any activity must compare the activity's marginal benefit to its marginal cost, completely ignoring any sunk costs and fixed costs associated with the activity. Also recall that average costs of an activity do not contribute to finding the optimal level; marginal cost must be employed to find optimal activity levels. We now wish to illustrate the irrelevance of costs other than marginal cost for managers of price-taking firms who wish to find profit-maximizing levels of production in the short run. As you will see in the next chapter, our discussion here also applies to managers of price-setting firms.

Let's begin with sunk costs, which we discussed in Chapters 3 and 8. As you will recall, sunk costs are input payments made in the past that cannot be recovered now or in the future. When we say that sunk costs are irrelevant for decision-making purposes, we do not mean that sunk costs never mattered in *any* decision. In the decisions facing the firm *prior* to making the sunk payment, the manager viewed the now sunk input cost as an *avoidable* cost, and, as such, the input cost was then part of the marginal cost of making a decision. Only after a sunk payment is made, which makes the cost forever unrecoverable, does the payment become irrelevant for current and future decisions. You might wish to review the example presented in Chapter 8 of the sunk license fee incurred by a homebuilder. Once the license fee is paid on January 1, it becomes an irrelevant sunk cost for the rest of the year. In fact, the economic cost of the license for the rest of the year is exactly zero. The sunk cost is now a historical cost that is unrecoverable and thus irrelevant.

In Chapter 3 we also emphasized the irrelevance of average cost for finding optimal activity levels. In the present situation, the irrelevance extends to three average cost measures: average total cost, average variable cost, and average fixed cost. While measures of average cost are certainly useful for computing values of total costs (i.e., multiplying average cost by quantity gives the total cost), the decision rule for finding the optimal quantity of output to produce employs marginal cost ($P = SMC$), not average cost. As we demonstrated in Panel A of Figure 11.3, choosing the output level that minimizes average total cost (ATC) and maximizes profit margin ($P − ATC$) generally fails to maximize profit (π).

While you should now be convinced that *ATC* is best ignored in making output decisions, you might contend that average variable cost, *AVC*, does matter in decision making: The shutdown rule compares price to average variable cost. Doesn't this mean *AVC* matters in making optimal output decisions? Precisely speaking, the shutdown rule only applies to the question of *whether* to produce. The shutdown rule does not contribute to finding the optimal output level when the manager chooses to produce a positive amount. Thus, *AVC does* matter when deciding whether to produce, but *AVC* is irrelevant for finding the (positive) optimal level of output. When firms choose to produce, managers must know *marginal* cost (along with marginal revenue) to find the optimal output level that maximizes profit or minimizes loss.

To provide you with more insight into why fixed costs do not matter in decision making, we remind you that the marginal cost curve is unaffected by changes in fixed cost. Recall from Chapter 8 that the U–shape of the marginal cost curve is determined by the S–shape of the total variable cost curve or the shape of the marginal product curve. In Figure 11.5, for example, any change whatsoever in fixed cost has no effect on the marginal cost curve. If total fixed costs double, *SMC* does not shift or change shape, and marginal revenue still intersects marginal cost at the same level of output. No matter what the level of fixed costs, 300 units is the profit-maximizing (loss-minimizing) level of output when price is $10.50.

To illustrate that fixed costs do not affect the decision to produce or not to produce, we chose five different levels of total fixed costs and examined the shutdown decision for a firm with the *SMC* and *AVC* curves shown in Figure 11.5. Keeping market price at $10.50, Table 11.1 shows all the relevant revenue, cost, and profit information for each of the five levels of fixed cost. First note that the optimal level of production for any of the five levels of fixed cost is 300 units because *SMC* equals $10.50 at 300 units, no matter what the level of fixed costs. In all cases shown in Table 11.1, total revenue is $3,150, total variable cost is $2,700, and, after all variable costs are paid, $450 remains to apply toward the fixed costs.

When fixed cost is only $200, economic profit is positive because revenue exceeds all costs. Obviously the manager chooses to produce and earn a profit, rather than produce nothing and lose the fixed cost. For each of the other four cases, the revenue remaining after paying variable cost is not enough to pay all the fixed cost, and profit is negative. Columns 7 and 8, respectively, show the loss

TABLE 11.1
The Irrelevance of Fixed Costs

(1) Total fixed costs	(2) Price	(3) Output	(4) Total revenue	(5) Total variable costs	(6) Revenue remaining after paying variable costs	(7) Profit (loss) if $Q = 300$	(8) Profit (loss) if $Q = 0$
$ 200	$10.50	300	$3,150	$2,700	$450	$ 250	$ −200
2,400	10.50	300	3,150	2,700	450	−1,950	−2,400
3,000	10.50	300	3,150	2,700	450	−2,550	−3,000
10,000	10.50	300	3,150	2,700	450	−9,550	−10,000
100,000	10.50	300	3,150	2,700	450	−99,550	−100,000

if the firm produces 300 units (where $P = SMC$) and the loss if the firm produces nothing and loses its fixed cost.

Note that in all cases when the firm makes a loss, the loss from producing 300 units is $450 less than the loss if the firm shuts down. No matter how high the total fixed cost, the firm loses $450 less by producing a positive amount of output than by producing nothing (shutting down). The level of fixed cost has no effect on the firm's decision to produce.

We can now summarize the short-run output decision for price-taking firms with a principle:

Now try Technical Problems 2–5.

Principle (1) Average variable cost tells whether to produce; the firm ceases to produce—shuts down— if price falls below minimum *AVC*. (2) Marginal cost tells how much to produce; if $P \geq$ minimum *AVC*, the firm produces the output at which $SMC = P$. (3) Average total cost tells how much profit or loss is made if the firm decides to produce; profit equals the difference between *P* and *ATC* (average profit or profit margin) multiplied by the quantity produced and sold.

Short-Run Supply for the Firm and Industry

Using the concepts developed in the preceding discussion, it is possible to derive the short-run supply curve for an individual firm in a competitive market. Figure 11.6 illustrates the process. In Panel A, points *a*, *b*, and *c* are the profit-maximizing

FIGURE 11.6
Short-Run Firm and Industry Supply

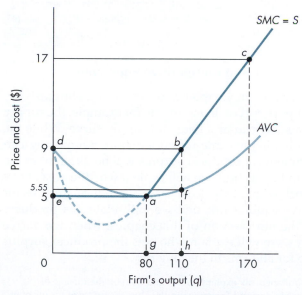

Panel A — Supply curve for the firm

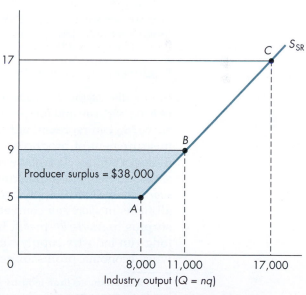

Panel B — Short-run industry supply curve (100 firms with identical costs)

equilibrium points for the firm at prices of $5, $9, and $17, respectively. That is, the marginal cost curve above average variable cost indicates the quantity the firm would be willing and able to supply at each price, which is the definition of supply. Panel A shows 80, 110, and 170 units of output as the quantities supplied when market price is $5, $9, and $17, respectively. For a market price lower than minimum average variable cost, quantity supplied is zero.

As long as input prices remain constant as all firms in the industry vary their production levels, the industry supply curve can be obtained by summing (horizontally) the marginal cost curves of each producer. If, for example, the industry has 100 firms identical to the one shown in Panel A, the industry quantity supplied is 8,000 units at a price of $5, 11,000 units at a price of $9, and 17,000 at a price of $17, as shown in Panel B. The firm's short-run supply, S, is upward-sloping, so supply for a competitive industry, S_{SR}, must also be upward-sloping.[6] Notice that, for any particular level of industry output, the supply prices along the short-run industry supply curve S_{SR} are equal to the marginal cost experienced by every firm in the industry. At point B, for example, $9 is the marginal cost of producing the 11,000th unit. The 11,000th unit produced in this industry is the 110th unit for one of the 100 firms in the industry, and, no matter which firm produced it, the marginal cost of the 110th unit is $9. For this reason, the short-run industry supply curve can also be viewed as the *industry* marginal cost curve.

Relation   The short-run supply curve for an individual price-taking firm is the portion of the firm's marginal cost curve above minimum average variable cost. For market prices less than minimum average variable cost, quantity supplied is zero. The short-run supply curve for a competitive industry can be obtained by horizontally summing the supply curves of all the individual firms in the industry. Short-run industry supply is always upward-sloping, and supply prices along the industry supply curve give the marginal costs of production for every firm contributing to industry supply.

Producer Surplus and Profit in Short-Run Competitive Equilibrium

In our discussion of producer surplus in Chapter 2, we did not distinguish between short-run and long-run supply curves. In Figure 2.6, for example, the supply curve, S_0, can represent either a short-run or a long-run supply curve. While the measurement of producer surplus is the same for either short-run or long-run industry supply curves, the recipients of producer surplus will be different in the short run than in the long run. In this section, we will explain why the area above *short-run* industry supply and below market price measures producer surplus for all firms in *short-run* competitive equilibrium, and we will relate this producer surplus to *short-run* profit. In the next section of this chapter, when we derive long-run industry supply curves, we will explain who gets the producer surplus when economic profits are zero for all firms in the long run.

---

[6]If all producers in an industry simultaneously expand output and thereby their usage of inputs, there may be a noticeable increase in demand for some inputs. Thus the prices of inputs may be bid up, which causes an increase in all firms' cost curves, including marginal cost. Under these circumstances, the industry's short-run supply curve S_{SR} will be somewhat more steeply sloped, and somewhat more inelastic, than when input prices are constant.

As we mentioned previously, producer surplus is equal to the area above supply and below the market price over the range of output supplied for both the short-run and long-run periods of analysis. For each unit supplied, any revenue greater than the supply price (i.e., the minimum price needed to induce producers to supply a unit) represents a net gain from trading with consumers. As we showed you in the derivation of short-run firm and industry supply curves, the supply price for every unit of output equals its short-run marginal cost of production. In Panel A of Figure 11.6, for example, the marginal cost of producing the 110th unit is $9, which is the cost of obtaining the additional variable inputs needed to produce the 110th unit. Obviously, a manager will not supply the 110th unit for any price less than the $9 cost of the variable inputs needed to produce this unit.

By summing the differences between market price and supply price (= SMC) for every unit supplied, total producer surplus for a firm in the short run is equal to the difference between total revenue and total variable cost:

$$\text{Producer surplus} = TR - TVC > \pi$$

Thus producer surplus is greater than short-run economic profit by the amount of total fixed costs ($TR - TVC$).

In Panel A of Figure 11.6, suppose the market price is $9 so that a single firm supplies 110 units. The single firm's total producer surplus is $380, which is the difference between its total revenue and total variable cost at 110 units of output (ignoring 50 cents rounding error)

$$
\begin{aligned}
\text{Producer surplus} &= TR - TVC \\
&= \$9 \times 110 - \$5.55 \times 110 \\
&= \$990 - \$610 \\
&= \$380
\end{aligned}
$$

Or, equivalently, $380 can also be found by computing the area above supply and below market price over the 110 units of output. Because SMC happens to be linear above point a in Figure 11.6, producer surplus can be computed (without resorting to calculus) simply by calculating the area of trapezoid *edba*:[7]

$$
\begin{aligned}
\text{Producer surplus} &= \text{Area of trapezoid edba} \\
&= \text{Height} \times \text{Average base} = (\$9 - \$5) \times \left(\frac{80 + 110}{2}\right) \\
&= \$380
\end{aligned}
$$

For the industry, the total producer surplus is the area above S_{SR} and below $9 in Panel B. Because there are 100 firms in the industry with costs identical to those

---

[7]Notice that trapezoid *edba* is what is left after the area of polygon 0*eabh* (= TVC) is subtracted from the area of rectangle 0*dbh* (= TR). Polygon 0*eabh* is indeed equal to TVC because the area of rectangle 0*eag* gives the TVC of the first 80 units and the area of trapezoid *gabh* (the area under SMC) gives the TVC for the remaining 30 units.

shown in Panel A, the shaded area in Panel B, $38,000, is simply 100 times the producer surplus of a single firm (= 100 × $380).

> **Relation**   Short-run producer surplus is the amount by which total revenue exceeds total variable cost and equals the area above the short-run supply curve below market price over the range of output supplied. Short-run producer surplus exceeds economic profit by the amount of total fixed costs.

This concludes our analysis of a competitive price-taking firm's short-run profit-maximizing output decision. We will now analyze the profit-maximizing output decision of price-taking firms in the long run when all inputs, and therefore all costs, are variable.

11.4 PROFIT MAXIMIZATION IN THE LONG RUN

In the short run, the manager's production decisions are limited because some of the inputs used by the firm are fixed for the short-run period of production. Typically, the key input that a manager views as fixed in the short run is the amount of capital available to the firm in the form of plant or equipment. In the long run, all inputs are variable, and a manager can choose to employ any size plant—amount of capital—required to produce most efficiently the level of output that will maximize profit. The choice of plant size is often referred to as the "scale of operation." The scale of operation may be fixed in the short run, but in the long run it can be altered as economic conditions warrant.

The long run can also be viewed as the planning stage, prior to a firm's entry into an industry. In this stage the firm is trying to decide how large a production facility to construct: that is, the optimal scale of operation. Once the plans have congealed (a particular-size plant is built), the firm operates in a short-run situation. Recall that a fundamental characteristic of perfect competition is unrestricted entry and exit of firms into and out of the industry. As you will see in this section, the entry of new firms, which is possible only in the long run, plays a crucial role in long-run analysis of competitive industries.

Profit-Maximizing Equilibrium for the Firm in the Long Run

Suppose that an entrepreneur is considering entering a competitive industry in which the firms already in the industry are making economic profits. The prospective entrant, knowing the long-run costs and the product price, expects to make an economic profit also. Because all inputs are variable, the entrant can choose the scale or the plant size for the new firm. We examine the decision graphically.

In Figure 11.7, LAC and LMC are the long-run average and marginal cost curves. The firm's perfectly elastic demand D indicates the equilibrium price ($17) and is the same as marginal revenue. As long as price is greater than long-run average cost, the firm can make a profit. Thus, in Figure 11.7, any output between 20 and 290 units yields some economic profit. As mentioned earlier, the points of output B and B' are sometimes called the break-even points. At these two points, price equals long-run average cost and economic profit is 0.

FIGURE 11.7

Profit-Maximizing Equilibrium in the Long Run

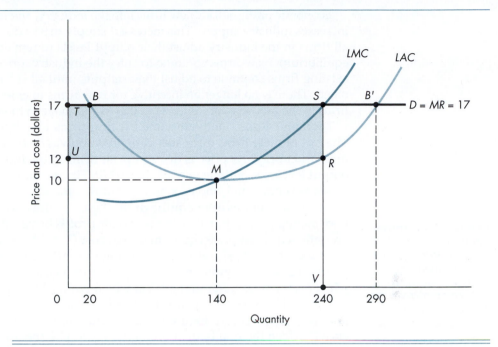

Maximum profit occurs at 240 units of output (point S), where marginal revenue equals long-run marginal cost. The firm would want to select the plant size to produce 240 units of output. Note that the firm, under these circumstances, would not want to produce 140 units of output at point M, the minimum point of long-run average cost. At M, marginal revenue exceeds marginal cost, so the firm can gain by producing more output. As shown in Figure 11.7, at point S total revenue (price times quantity) at 240 units of output is equal to $4,080 (= $17 × 240), which is the area of the rectangle $0TSV$. The total cost (average cost times quantity) is equal to $2,880 (= $12 × 240), which is the area of the rectangle $0URV$. The total profit is $1,200 [= ($17 − $12) × 240], which is the area of the rectangle $UTSR$.

Thus the firm would plan to operate at a scale (or plant size) such that long-run marginal cost equals price. This would be the most profitable situation under the circumstances. But, as we shall show, these circumstances will change. If the firm illustrated in Figure 11.7 is free to enter the industry, so are other prospective entrants. And this entry will drive down the market price. We will now show how this occurs.

Long-Run Competitive Equilibrium for the Industry

While the individual firm is in long-run profit-maximizing equilibrium when $MR = LMC$ (as shown in Figure 11.7), the *industry* will not be in long-run equilibrium until there is no incentive for new firms to enter or incumbent firms to exit. The economic force that induces firms to enter into an industry or that drives firms out of an industry is the existence of economic profits or economic losses, respectively.

Economic profits attract new firms into the industry, and entry of these new firms increases industry supply. This increased supply drives down price. As price falls, all firms in the industry adjust their output levels to remain in profit-maximizing equilibrium. New firms continue to enter the industry, price continues to fall, and existing firms continue to adjust their outputs until all economic profits are eliminated. There is no longer an incentive for new firms to enter, and the owners of all firms in the industry earn only what they could make in their best alternatives.

Economic losses motivate some existing firms to exit, or leave, the industry. The exit of these firms decreases industry supply. The reduction in supply drives up market price. As price is driven up, all firms in the industry must adjust their output levels to continue maximizing profit. Firms continue to exit until economic losses are eliminated, and economic profit is zero.

Long-run competitive equilibrium, then, requires not only that all firms be maximizing profits, but also that economic profits be zero.[8] These two conditions are satisfied when price equals marginal cost ($P = LMC$), so that firms are maximizing profit, and price also equals average cost ($P = LAC$), so that no entry or exit occurs. These two conditions for equilibrium can be satisfied simultaneously only when price equals minimum LAC, at which point $LMC = LAC$.

Figure 11.8 shows a typical firm in long-run competitive equilibrium.[9] The long-run cost curves in Figure 11.8 are similar to those in Figure 11.7. The difference between the two figures is that in Figure 11.7 the *firm* is maximizing profit, but the industry is not yet in 0-profit equilibrium. In Figure 11.8, the firm is maximizing profit (P equals LMC), and the industry is also in long-run competitive equilibrium because economic profit is zero ($P = LAC$).

Long-run equilibrium occurs at a price of $10 and output of 140, at point M. Each (identical) firm in the industry makes neither economic profit nor loss. There is no incentive for further entry because the rate of return in this industry is the normal rate of return, which is equal to the firm's best alternative. For the same reason, there is no incentive for a firm to leave the industry. The number of firms stabilizes, and each firm operates with a plant size represented by short-run marginal and average cost, *SMC* and *ATC*, respectively. We can now summarize long-run competitive equilibrium with a principle:

long-run competitive equilibrium
Condition in which all firms are producing where $P = LMC$ and economic profits are zero ($P = LAC$).

Principle   In long-run competitive equilibrium, all firms are maximizing profit ($P = LMC$), and there is no incentive for firms to enter or exit the industry because economic profit is zero ($P = LAC$). Long-run competitive equilibrium occurs because of the entry of new firms into the industry or the exit of existing firms from the industry. The market adjusts so that $P = LMC = LAC$, which is at the minimum point on LAC.

Now try Technical Problem 6.

[8]Economists, regulators, and policy analysts sometimes refer to the implicit cost of owner-supplied resources as "normal profit." Total economic costs of production equal explicit costs plus normal profit. Thus when economic profit is zero, the owners are making just enough accounting profit (total revenue minus explicit costs) to pay themselves an amount equal to what they could have earned by using their resources in their best alternative use. When economic profit is zero, we can say the firm is earning just a normal profit or normal rate of return.

[9]We will assume that all firms in the industry have identical cost curves. For example, Figures 11.7 and 11.8 show the cost curves of a typical firm. While it is not necessary to assume identical costs for all firms, this assumption substantially simplifies the theoretical analysis without affecting the conclusions.

FIGURE 11.8

Long-Run Equilibrium for a Firm in a Competitive Industry

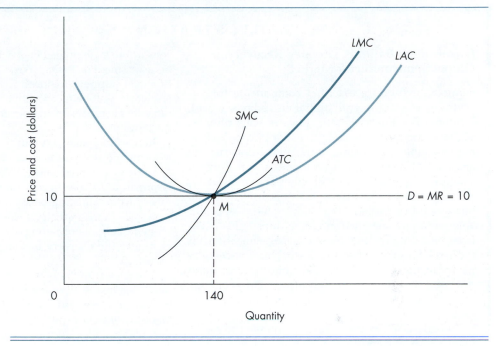

Long-Run Supply for a Perfectly Competitive Industry

In the short run when the amount of capital in an industry is fixed, as well as the number of firms, an increase in price causes industry output to increase. This increase is accomplished by each firm's using its fixed capital more intensively; that is, each firm hires more of the variable inputs to increase output.

In the long run, when entry of new firms is possible, the industry's response to an increase in price takes on a new dimension: The industry's supply adjustment to a change in price is not complete until entry or exit results in zero economic profit. This means that for all points on the long-run industry supply curve, economic profit must be zero.

To derive the industry supply curve in the long run, we must differentiate between two types of industries: (1) an increasing-cost industry and (2) a constant-cost industry. An industry is an **increasing-cost industry** if, as all firms in the industry expand output and thus input usage, the prices of some inputs used in the industry rise. For example, if the personal computer industry expands production by 15 percent, the price of many specialized inputs (such as microprocessor chips, RAM boards, disk drives, and so on) will increase, causing marginal and average cost for all firms to shift upward. An industry is a **constant-cost industry** if, as industry output and input usage increase, all prices

increasing-cost industry
An industry in which input prices rise as all firms in the industry expand output.

constant-cost industry
An industry in which input prices remain constant as all firms in the industry expand output.

ILLUSTRATION 11.2

Government Bailouts Threaten Recovery of Global Semiconductor Market[a]

Semiconductors are essential components for everything electronic and digital in today's world: iPhones, BlackBerrys, MP3 players, cell phones, digital cameras, solid state drives for PCs, as well as new technologies dealing with smart infrastructure and control systems for electric cars. As a real-world example of a nearly perfectly competitive industry, the global semiconductor industry is accustomed to boom-and-bust cycles. After enjoying the most profitable period for memory and logic chips in history—from 2002 until early 2007—the global semiconductor industry found itself saddled with huge excess capacity at the end of 2008. Semiconductor demand dropped sharply, as did chip prices. The economic losses in 2007 and 2008 were the largest in the history of the industry.

In early 2009, as the industry continued to bleed, many CEOs and industry analysts were alarmed by the failure of chipmakers to reign in supply. In past bust cycles, the industry behaved just like the theory of perfect competition predicts: Many chip fabrication companies were forced into bankruptcy and exited the industry and those firms that survived continued to cut production until chip prices climbed back to profitable levels. The bust cycle could be expected to take 6 to 18 months, but it always worked in the past to clear the market of excess capacity.

Some industry analysts worried that the bust of 2007 was somehow different from past downturns, and might not go away on its own. The situation has become "desperate" according to Daniel Heyler, head of global semiconductor research for Merrill Lynch in Hong Kong, in late 2008. A different expert estimated that every chipmaker in Taiwan (25 percent of world chip supply) could shut down and there would still be oversupply.

And so the government bailouts began. China's biggest chipmaker received $170 million. The state of Saxony, Germany, supplied Qimonda with $206 million in support. In Korea, Hynix Semiconductor got close to $600 million in new "loans" from consortium state-owned banks. Bruce Einhorn offered his assessment in *BusinessWeek*: "If others keep giving financial support to local companies, chipmakers elsewhere will be faced with a tough decision: They can either compete on an uneven playing field or cede the terrain."

In this Illustration, we will apply the theory of long-run competitive equilibrium set forth in this chapter to address two questions: (1) What, if anything, went wrong in 2007/2008 to prevent the semiconductor industry from adjusting on its own to end the longest bust cycle in the industry's history? and (2) Will government bailouts of failing chip manufacturers help or hinder the recovery of the global semiconductor industry?

The answer to the first question is "probably nothing." The losses were indeed large and long-lasting because the previous boom period attracted large amounts of new capital in the form of new fabrication plants and foundries. When the bust hit, semiconductor manufacturers had no better choice than to continue producing chips at deeply depressed prices because they could earn enough revenue to cover their (avoidable) variable costs of operation. Unfortunately, chip prices can fall well below average total cost before semiconductor firms will shut down because fixed costs make up a large fraction of total chip cost—up to 70 percent.

Consider the nearby figure showing a typical set of short-run cost curves for a fabrication plant and the firm's demand curve when the market-determined price of a semiconductor wafer is $200 per wafer. In the short run the firm does not shut down, but rather continues to produce at a rate of 2,000 wafers per day to minimize its loss. At 2,000 wafers per day, the average total cost is $500 per unit, so the firm loses $300 on every chip it produces and total losses amount to $600,000 (= $300 × 2,000) per day. While this is certainly a large loss, it is nonetheless a smaller loss than would be incurred in the short run if the wafer plant shut down and lost all of its fixed cost—that is, lost $700,000 (= $350 × 2,000) per day.

Notice the relatively large proportion of fixed costs in the plant's total cost structure, as is typical of semiconductor firms. Total cost is $1 million, which is the sum of its total variable cost ($300,000 per day) plus its total fixed cost ($700,000 per day). As you can see in the figure, fixed costs are so large relative to variable costs that chip prices must fall a long way below minimum *ATC* (the break-even price is $350) before reaching minimum *AVC* (the shutdown price is $135). Because the unprecedented strength of the 2002–2007 boom pushed chip prices to record high levels, it is not surprising that it took longer than usual for prices to fall far enough to warrant shutting down fabrication plants.[b]

Turning to the second question, you can probably see that government bailouts are not necessary to help the *surviving* firms achieve profitability. Although it will take longer than usual for excess capacity to exit the industry, which will lead chip prices up along with profits, there is no particular reason to believe the equilibrating process is not working just fine. If the semiconductor market is indeed moving toward a new long-run equilibrium, then government bailouts will slow, rather than speed, the wringing out of excess capacity. Avi Cohen, chief research analyst at Avian Securities in Boston, makes this point perfectly

well, stating that no one wants "governments rescuing less-competitive companies. The supply never goes away."

As our theory predicted, worldwide sales of semiconductors made a sharp turn around in 2010 with global chip sales rising 32 percent in 2010. Competitive market forces worked in their usual, predictable way to move the semiconductor industry out of its slump into a period of profitability. Had governments held back their subsidies to chip manufacturers in 2008, the recovery might well have started in 2009. In any case, we can be certain that the boom and bust cycle will repeat itself—as long as the global market for semiconductors remains a perfectly competitive industry.

[a]This illustration draws heavily from Bruce Einhorn, "Chipmakers on the Edge," *BusinessWeek*, January 5, 2009, pp. 30–31; and Evan Ramstad, "Memory Chips Signal Sector Getting Set for Recovery," *The Wall Street Journal*, April 27, 2009, p. B1.

[b]Bust periods in the semiconductor business are generally longer than for many other industries because the highly specialized nature of the capital equipment sharply limits the number of alternative uses in other industries. This extends the period of time it takes for capital to move out of semiconductor manufacturing, and lengthens the time to reach a new long-run competitive equilibrium.

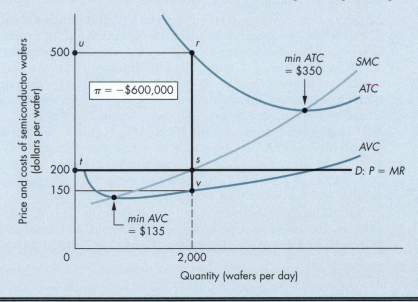

FIGURE 11.9

Long-Run Industry Supply for a Constant-Cost Industry

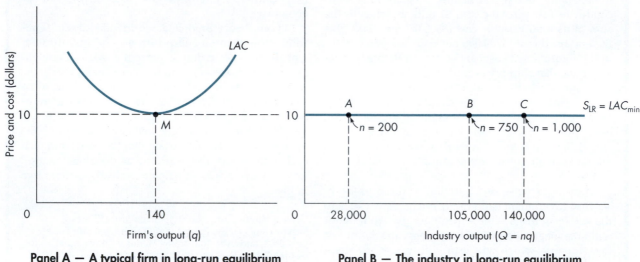

Panel A — A typical firm in long-run equilibrium   Panel B — The industry in long-run equilibrium

of inputs used in the industry remain constant.[10] For example, the rutabaga industry is probably so small that its usage of inputs such as fertilizer, farm labor, and machinery have no effect on the prices of these inputs. This industry is therefore probably a constant-cost industry.

Figure 11.9 shows the relation between a typical firm in a constant-cost industry (Panel A) and the long-run industry supply curve, S_{LR}, for a constant-cost industry (Panel B). Note that the supply price in the long run is constant and equal to $10 for all levels of industry output. This result follows from the long-run equilibrium condition that economic profit must be zero. The long-run supply price, $10, is equal to minimum long-run average cost (LAC_{min}) for every level of output produced by the industry because the entry of new firms always bids price down to the point of zero economic profit (point M in Figure 11.9). Because the industry is a constant-cost industry, expansion of industry output does not cause minimum LAC (point M) to rise. Therefore, long-run supply price is constant and equal to both minimum LAC and LMC. Because supply price is constant, S_{LR} is flat or perfectly elastic for constant-cost industries.

For example, if industry output expands from 28,000 units to 105,000 units through the entry of new firms, each firm (old and new) ends up producing 140 units of output at the minimum LAC (and LMC) of $10. No single firm expands

---

[10]Theoretically it is possible that input prices might fall as industry output rises, in which case there is a decreasing-cost industry. Decreasing-cost industries are so extremely rare that we will not consider them in this text.

FIGURE 11.10

Long-Run Industry Supply for an Increasing-Cost Industry

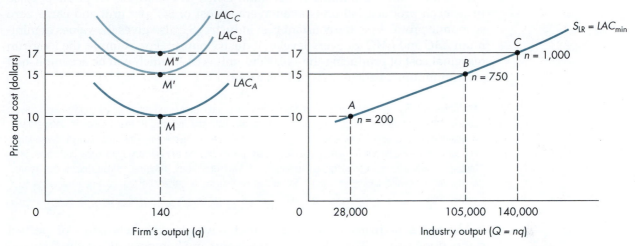

Panel A — A typical firm in long-run equilibrium

Panel B — The industry in long-run equilibrium

output (q) in the long run; industry output ($Q = nq$) expands because there are more firms, each producing 140 units. When the industry produces 28,000, 105,000, and 140,000 units, the industry is in long-run equilibrium with 200, 750, and 1,000 firms, respectively. At point A, for example, 200 firms (n) each produce 140 units (q) for a total industry output (Q) equal to 28,000 units ($= nq = 200 \times 140$). Finally, note that at every point on S_{LR} (A, B, and C, for example), economic profit is zero. Thus, the long-run supply price, $10, gives the minimum long-run average cost and marginal cost for every level of industry output: $P = \$10 = LAC_{min} = LMC$.

Next consider an increasing-cost industry. Figure 11.10 illustrates the relation between a typical firm in an increasing-cost industry (Panel A) and the long-run industry supply curve (Panel B). Because the industry is an increasing-cost industry, as the industry expands output, resource prices rise, causing the long-run average cost in Panel A to shift upward. LAC_A, LAC_B, and LAC_C represent the increasingly higher long-run average costs associated with industry output levels of 28,000, 105,000, and 140,000 units, respectively. For example, when the industry output increases from 28,000 units, produced by 200 firms, to 105,000 units, input prices rise, causing minimum LAC to rise to M' (in Panel A). Each firm in the industry still produces 140 units, but there are now 750 firms producing a total industry output of 105,000 units at an average cost of $15.[11] Just as in the case of a

---

[11]In Figure 11.10 we have assumed that the minimum points on the higher LAC curves, LAC_B and LAC_C, remain at 140 units of output. Actually, M' and M'' could also be at output levels either larger or smaller than 140 units; in this case, we would simply have to adjust the number of firms associated with points B and C in Panel B.

constant-cost industry, economic profit is zero at all points along S_{LR}. And similarly, when industry output increases from 105,000 to 140,000 units, input prices rise further, causing minimum LAC (and LMC) to rise to M''. At point C, 1,000 firms each produce 140 units at an average cost of \$17 per unit and earns zero economic profit. As in the constant-cost industry, S_{LR} also gives the values of minimum LAC and LMC for every level of industry output. For example, the long-run marginal cost of producing the 140,000th unit is \$17, which will be accomplished at a (minimum) average cost of \$17 per unit.

Relations   For both constant-cost and increasing-cost industries, long-run industry supply curves give supply prices for various levels of industry output, allowing the industry to reach long-run competitive equilibrium. Economic profit for every firm in the industry is zero at all points on the long-run industry supply. For both constant-cost and increasing-cost industries, prices on long-run industry supply give both minimum long-run average (LAC_{min}) and long-run marginal cost (LMC) for all firms. Long-run industry supply curves are either flat or upward-sloping according to whether the industry is either constant-cost or increasing-cost, respectively.

Managers of firms in industries that have the characteristics of perfect competition (in particular, low barriers to entry and homogenous product) should expect to see economic profit competed away in the long run by the entry of new firms, regardless of whether constant or increasing costs characterize the industry. Likewise, managers should expect that losses in the short run will be eliminated in the long run as firms exit the industry and the price of the product rises. Managers can also expect to see entry of new firms driving up the prices they pay for inputs if they are operating in an increasing-cost industry that is expanding.

Now try Technical Problems 7–8.

Economic Rent and Producer Surplus in Long-Run Equilibrium

Thus far in our derivation of long-run industry supply curves, we have assumed that all firms possess identical costs of production, and any number of these identical firms can freely enter the market when positive economic profit encourages them to do so. However, firms will experience cost differences when the productive resources they employ vary in quality and, hence, productivity. Such differences in resource productivity result in higher payments to the better resources. These excess payments play an important role in determining who receives the producer surplus when long-run industry supply is upward-sloping. Because no producer surplus is created by constant-cost industries, the discussion in this section applies only when industry supply is upward-sloping.

Firms using relatively higher quality resources will have lower LAC and LMC curves than firms using lower quality resources. Consider the following examples of firms that experience cost advantages because they have access to extraordinarily productive resources. A petroleum firm that owns vast oil deposits located close to the surface of the earth will have much lower costs of production than other oil companies that must pump oil from wells located offshore in very deep water. A firm that holds a patent on a production process for producing a synthetic growth hormone for animal feed will be able to produce the growth hormone more cheaply than firms that must rely on more costly alternative processes. An airline that employs more experienced or talented mechanics will enjoy a maintenance cost advantage over rival airlines that hire less experienced or less talented mechanics.

Even though some firms have lower costs than their rivals, all firms nonetheless earn zero economic profit in long-run competitive equilibrium. This outcome may surprise you because you may think that firms with lower production costs could earn at least some economic profit if their higher-cost rivals are able to break even (earn zero economic profit). For an industry in long-run competitive equilibrium, however, you would be wrong most of the time.

economic rent
A payment to a resource in excess of the resource's opportunity cost.

This rather surprising outcome arises because firms with lower costs will end up paying a premium or additional payment to retain superior resources, which exceeds the price that other firms pay to use ordinary resources. Economists call such additional payments "economic rents." **Economic rent** is a payment to a superior (and thus more productive) resource over and above what the resource could earn in its best alternative employment (its opportunity cost). Other firms, competing for the use of an extraordinarily productive resource, will bid up the economic rent paid by the low-cost firms to the resource owners. Ultimately, economic rents are bid up until the firms using the superior resource earn zero economic profit in long-run competitive equilibrium.[12]

We can best illustrate the concept of economic rent with an example. Suppose that you are an experienced construction supervisor for a builder of medium-priced homes, and you are exceptionally talented at organizing subcontractors: concrete workers, carpenters, bricklayers, plumbers, painters, and so forth. You can build a house in 10 percent less time than the typical experienced construction supervisor in the industry, and this saving of time reduces the cost of constructing a house. Your superior talent effectively reduces annual construction costs by $75,000 compared to the costs of every other builder in the industry. Further assume that an experienced construction supervisor is typically paid $100,000 a year, which is what you are paid.

The home construction industry in your market is in long-run equilibrium, and every other builder in the industry earns zero economic profit. Your firm, however, makes an economic profit of $75,000 a year. You are solely responsible for the $75,000 economic profit, because your firm is identical in every way to every other firm except for your superior skills. You could be the supervisor for any other firm in the market and earn $75,000 economic profit for that firm. You know it and, presumably, the other firms know it also, as does the owner of the firm that employs you.

You know now, and probably would have known anyway, that you should ask for a raise of around $75,000, to a salary of $175,000. You could get a raise of about $75,000 from other firms in the market because, presumably, you could lower their costs as well. Even if you didn't ask your employer for the raise, other

---

[12]Rent also arises in the short run because firms receive a price on some units produced that exceeds the opportunity cost of the additional resources required to produce those units. Rent earned in the short run due to fixed inputs is frequently called "quasi-rent" by economists to differentiate it from economic rent, which is a long-run cost. Because quasi-rent exactly equals producer surplus in the short run, we will refer to short-run quasi-rent as producer surplus in this text.

firms, aware of your ability to lower costs, would try to lure you away by bidding up your salary.

Your employer, and any other employer in the market, really has little choice. A firm could pay you the additional $75,000 and then just break even because all economic profit would go toward your salary. Or your firm could refuse to pay the additional $75,000, causing you to move to another firm or perhaps start your own. Your original employer would find that its costs had increased by $75,000 *after* you left and would consequently earn zero profit. Thus each firm in the market would earn zero profit whether it hires you at $175,000 or not. But because of your superior skills you would earn a premium of $75,000, which is, of course, the economic rent in this example. Note that the other supervisors, who are paid the typical salary of $100,000, are earning zero economic rent.

This same type of analysis holds for any resource that, if compensated at only its opportunity cost, would result in the firm's earning economic profit in long-run competitive equilibrium. The return to that resource will be bid up as in the above example. Therefore, once economic rent is included as a cost to firms using superior resources, their economic profits will be zero. While this example examined rents to superior skills of a manager, resources such as superior land, superior location, superior craftsmanship, or superior capital (that cannot be easily duplicated) can also earn economic rent for their owners.

As mentioned, economic rent plays an important role in understanding the nature of long-run producer surplus. In our discussion of short-run industry supply curves, we showed you that the area above S_{SR} and below market price measures producer surplus in the short run. This surplus area equals the total revenue minus total variable costs of all of the firms in the industry. In the long-run, however, there are no economic profits in equilibrium because all firms face resource costs, including payment of economic rents, exactly equal to their revenues. In what sense, then, can we interpret the area above upward-sloping long-run industry supply and below price as long-run producer surplus?

To answer this question, we have reproduced in Figure 11.11 the demand and supply curves from Figure 2.6. For present purposes, the supply curve is now the industry's long-run supply curve, S_{LR}. At every point along S_{LR}, the firms in the industry are earning zero economic profit. Consequently, the area of long-run producer surplus, triangle vwA, measures the economic rent payments made to superior factors of production. In other words, all producer surplus in the long-run ends up in the pockets of the resource suppliers, and no producer surplus goes to the firms supplying the output in this market. In Figure 11.11, the resource suppliers earn $16,000 of economic rent, while the perfectly competitive output suppliers earn no economic profit whatsoever. We can now summarize the discussion of economic rent and long-run producer surplus in the following principle.

Now try Technical Problem 9.

Principle   Firms that employ exceptionally productive resources earn zero economic profit in long-run competitive equilibrium because the potential economic profit from employing a superior resource is paid to the resource owner as economic rent. In increasing-cost industries, all long-run producer surplus is paid to resource suppliers as economic rent.

FIGURE 11.11

Economic Rent in Long-Run Competitive Equilibrium

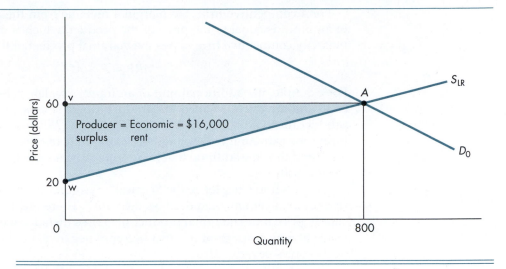

11.5 PROFIT-MAXIMIZING INPUT USAGE

Thus far we have analyzed the firm's profit-maximizing decision in terms of the output decision. But we can also consider profit maximization from the input side. When we determine the profit-maximizing level of output, we implicitly have determined the economically efficient level of input usage of the firm. Recall from Chapters 8 and 9 that the cost function is directly related to the production function. Thus when we determine a unique profit-maximizing level of output, we also determine the cost-minimizing quantity of each input that is used in the production process. It is possible, then, to determine a profit-maximizing output level directly from the input decision.

Marginal Revenue Product and the Hiring Decision

The principle of choosing input usage to maximize profits is simple and follows directly from the theory of unconstrained maximization set forth in Chapter 3. The firm should expand its usage of any input or resource as long as additional units of the input add more to the firm's revenue than to its cost. The firm would not increase the usage of any input if hiring more units increases the firm's cost more than its revenue.

    The additional revenue added by another unit of the input is called the **marginal revenue product (MRP)** of that input and is equal to the marginal revenue from selling the output produced times the marginal product of the input

marginal revenue product (MRP)
($MRP = \Delta TR/\Delta I$)
The additional revenue earned when the firm hires one more unit of the input.

$$MRP = \frac{\Delta TR}{\Delta I} = MR \times MP$$

where I is the level of usage of a particular input.

For a competitive firm, the marginal revenue from the additional production of an input is equal to the price of the product, which *is* marginal revenue for a perfectly competitive firm, times the marginal product of the input

$$MRP = P \times MP$$

For example, if 1 additional unit of an input, say, labor, has a marginal product of 10 and the price at which the product can be sold is \$5, the marginal revenue product for that unit of the input is \$50 (= $P \times MP$ = \$5 × 10). In other words, hiring the extra unit of labor adds 10 extra units of output that can be sold for \$5 each, and thus the addition to total revenue attributable to hiring this extra unit of labor is \$50.

As shown in Chapter 8, the "typical" marginal product curve first increases, reaches a maximum, then declines thereafter. Therefore, the *MRP* curve, which is simply price times marginal product, also rises then declines. At the level of input usage at which marginal product becomes negative, the marginal revenue product becomes negative also.

The quantity of an input a manager chooses to hire depends on the marginal revenue product and the price of the input. Assume that a manager can hire as much of an input as is desired at a constant price—that is, the price that must be paid for the input is the same no matter how much or how little is hired.

A general rule for a continuously variable input is illustrated graphically in Figure 11.12. In this example, labor is the only variable input, and only the decreasing portion of *MRP* is shown. The *MRP* curve is simply the *MP* curve

FIGURE 11.12

Profit-Maximizing Labor Usage

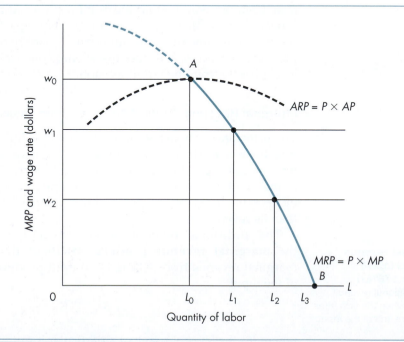

multiplied by the market price of the product produced at each level of labor usage over the relevant range. Therefore, if at a labor usage of $\overline{L}$ the marginal product is $\overline{MP}$, $\overline{MRP} = \overline{P} \times \overline{MP}$, where $\overline{P}$ is product price. This means that the $\overline{L}$th worker adds $\overline{MRP}$ to total revenue. If the wage rate is w_1, the manager would wish to hire L_1 units of labor. The manager would not stop short of L_1, because up to employment level L_1 an additional unit of labor adds more to revenue than to cost. The manager would not hire more than L_1, because beyond L_1 the added cost would exceed the added revenue. If the wage rate falls to w_2, the manager would increase labor usage to L_2 units. Hence, if labor is the firm's only variable input, the manager maximizes profits or minimizes loss by employing the amount of labor for which the marginal revenue product of labor equals the wage rate

$$MRP = w$$

This result holds for any variable input.[13]

> **Principle**   If the *MRP* of an additional unit of a variable input is greater than the price of that input, that unit should be hired. If the *MRP* of an additional unit adds less than its price, that unit should not be hired. If the usage of the variable input varies continuously, the manager should employ the amount of the input at which
>
> $$MRP = \text{Input price}$$

This principle is equivalent to the condition that the profit-maximizing, competitive firm will produce the level of output at which $P = SMC$. Recall from Chapter 8 that cost minimization at any level of output requires that

$$SMC = \frac{w}{MP}$$

Recall also that the profit-maximizing level of output is where

$$P = SMC$$

But, from the cost-minimization condition, when one input is variable,

$$P = SMC = \frac{w}{MP}$$

or

$$P \times MP = w$$

which gives the profit-maximizing level of input usage. Thus the profit-maximizing, output-choice condition, $P = SMC$, is equivalent to the profit-maximizing, input-choice condition, $MRP = w$. Each leads to the same level of output and the same level of input usage.

---

[13]As noted, we did not include the upward-sloping portion of the *MRP* curve because this segment is not relevant to the hiring decision. If the wage equals *MRP* and *MRP* is increasing, the manager could hire additional units, and the marginal revenue product of these inputs would be greater than the wage. Therefore, this level of input use would not be profit-maximizing.

Average Revenue Product and the Shutdown Decision

We now want to be more precise about the range of *MRP* over which a manager would actually operate. Clearly, a manager never hires labor beyond the point at which *MRP* becomes negative: When *MRP* is negative, hiring more labor *decreases* total revenue. Furthermore, we will now demonstrate that a manager shuts down operations (i.e., hires no labor) if the wage rate rises above the *average revenue product* of labor. The **average revenue product (*ARP*)** of labor is the average revenue per worker, *ARP* = *TR/L*, and it is easy to see that *ARP* can be calculated as price times average product:

average revenue product (*ARP*)
The average revenue per worker (*ARP* = *TR/L*).

$$ARP = \frac{TR}{L} = \frac{PQ}{L} = P\frac{Q}{L} = P \times AP$$

To see why a manager shuts down when $w > ARP$, suppose $MRP = w$—as necessary for profit maximization—at a level of labor usage where *ARP* is less than the wage rate

$$w > ARP$$

Substituting *TR/L* for *ARP* into this inequality results in the following expression

$$w > TR/L$$

Now multiply both sides of the inequality by *L*, and you can see that

$$wL > TR \quad \text{or} \quad TVC > TR$$

Thus total variable cost exceeds total revenue when $w > ARP$. From previous analysis, you know that the manager should shut down when total revenue does not cover total variable costs. Therefore, no labor would be hired if the average revenue product is less than the wage rate. In Figure 11.12, the competitive firm shuts down if the wage rate rises above w_0 at point *A*.

In Figure 11.12, the firm's demand for labor is the *MRP* curve over the range of labor usage L_0 to L_3 (between points *A* and *B*). To maximize profit, the manager chooses the level of labor usage for which $MRP = w$. When wages rise above w_0 in Figure 11.12 at the level of labor usage for which $MRP = w$, the wage rate exceeds the average revenue product $(w > ARP)$ and the manager will shut the firm down and hire no labor at all. At all wage rates above point *A*, the firm shuts down. Below point *B*, *MRP* is negative, and the manager would never hire more than L_3 units of labor. We now summarize the discussion in a principle:

Now try Technical Problem 10.

Principle If the price of a single variable input employed by a competitive firm rises above the point of maximum *ARP* $(= P \times AP)$, then the firm minimizes its loss by shutting down and hiring none of the variable input.

Before concluding the discussion of the hiring decision, we should explain that when there is more than one variable input, the firm's hiring decision remains essentially the same as for a single variable input, even though it is more complicated mathematically. For every variable input, the manager maximizes profit by hiring the quantity of the input at which its *MRP* equals its price. If, for example, the firm uses two variable inputs, labor and capital, the manager maximizes profits by using both inputs at such levels that

$$MRP_L = w$$

$$MRP_K = r$$

Because the marginal product of either input shifts according to the level of usage of the other, these conditions must hold *simultaneously*.[14]

11.6 IMPLEMENTING THE PROFIT-MAXIMIZING OUTPUT DECISION

Although it is useful for managers to know the fundamentals of the theory of profit maximization, it is even more useful for them to know how to implement and use the theory to maximize their firms' profits. A manager should be able to use empirical estimates or forecasts of the relevant variables and equations to determine the actual values of the decision variables that maximize the firm's profit. You have spent a lot of time learning the techniques of estimating the various demand, production, and cost functions. Now you will learn how to use these empirical skills to answer an important question facing a manager: How can the theory of profit maximization be used in practice to make profit-maximizing decisions about production?

We will first outline how managers can, in general, determine the optimizing conditions. This outline gives a pattern for situations in which numerical estimates of the variables and equations are available. Then we present an example of how a firm can use this approach to determine the optimal level of output.

General Rules for Implementation

We emphasized that a manager must answer two questions when choosing the level of output that maximizes profit. These two questions and the answers forthcoming from the theoretical analysis are summarized as follows:

1. Should the firm produce or shut down? *Produce as long as the market price is greater than or equal to minimum average variable cost: $P \geq AVC_{min}$. Shut down otherwise.*

2. If production occurs, how much should the firm produce? *Produce the output at which market price (which is marginal revenue) equals marginal cost $P = SMC$.*

---

[14]With a bit of algebra, after substituting the relations $MRP_L = P \times MP_L$ and $MRP_K = P \times MP_K$ into these conditions for profit maximization, it can be shown that the amounts of labor and capital that maximize profit are also economically efficient (lie on the expansion path) because they also meet the condition $w/r = MP_L/MP_K$. While all input combinations that maximize profit lie on the expansion path, only one input combination on the expansion path maximizes profit—the input combination on the isoquant corresponding to the profit-maximizing output.

It follows from these rules that to determine the optimal level of output, a manager must obtain estimates or forecasts of the market price of the good produced by the firm, the firm's average variable cost function, and the firm's marginal cost function. The steps explained next can be followed to find the profit-maximizing rate of production and the level of profit the firm will earn.

Step 1: Forecast the price of the product

To decide whether to produce and how much to produce, a manager must obtain a forecast of the price at which the completed product can be sold. Remember that a perfectly competitive firm does not face a downward-sloping demand curve but simply takes the market price as given. We showed in Chapter 7 how to use two statistical techniques—time-series forecasting and econometric forecasting—to forecast the price of the product.

Step 2: Estimate average variable cost (AVC) and marginal cost (SMC)

As emphasized in Chapter 10, the cubic specification is the appropriate form for estimating a family of short-run cost curves. Thus the manager could estimate the following average variable cost function

$$AVC = a + bQ + cQ^2$$

As demonstrated in Chapter 10, the marginal cost function associated with this average variable cost function is

$$SMC = a + 2bQ + 3cQ^2$$

Step 3: Check the shutdown rule

When P is less than AVC, the firm loses less money by shutting down than it would lose if it produced where $P = SMC$. A manager can determine the price below which a firm should shut down by finding the *minimum* point on the AVC curve, AVC_{min}. As long as price is greater than (or equal to) AVC_{min}, the firm will produce rather than shut down. Recall from Chapter 10 that the average variable cost curve reaches its minimum value at $Q_m = -b/2c$. The minimum value of average variable cost is then determined by substituting Q_m into the AVC function

$$AVC_{min} = a + bQ_m + c(Q_m)^2$$

The firm should produce as long as $P \geq AVC_{min}$. If the forecasted price is greater than (or equal to) minimum average variable cost ($P \geq AVC_{min}$), the firm should produce the output level where $P = SMC$. If the forecasted price is less than the minimum average variable cost ($P < AVC_{min}$), the firm should shut down in the short run, and it loses an amount equal to its total fixed costs.

Step 4: If $P \geq AVC_{min}$, find the output level where $P = SMC$

A perfectly competitive firm should produce the level of output for which $P = SMC$—if $P \geq AVC_{min}$. Thus if the manager decides to produce in the short run, the manager maximizes profit by finding the output level for which $P = SMC$. In the case of a cubic specification for cost, profit maximization or loss minimization requires that

$$P = SMC = a + 2bQ + 3cQ^2$$

Solving this equation for Q^* gives the optimal output level for the firm—unless P is less than AVC, and then the optimal output level is zero.

Step 5: Computation of profit or loss

Once a manager determines how much to produce, the calculation of total profit or loss is straightforward. Profit or loss is equal to total revenue minus total cost. Total revenue for a competitive firm is price times quantity sold. Total cost is the sum of total variable cost and total fixed cost, where total variable cost is average variable cost times the number of units sold. Hence, total profit, denoted as π is

$$
\begin{aligned}
\pi &= TR - TC \\
&= (P \times Q^*) - [(AVC \times Q^*) + TFC] \\
&= (P - AVC)Q^* - TFC
\end{aligned}
$$

If $P < AVC_{min}$, the firm shuts down, and $\pi = -TFC$.

To illustrate how to implement these steps to find the profit-maximizing level of output and to forecast the profit of the firm, we now turn to a hypothetical firm that operates in a perfectly competitive market.

Profit Maximization at Beau Apparel: An Illustration

As an example, we use the output decision facing the manager of Beau Apparel, Inc., a clothing manufacturer that produces moderately priced men's shirts. Beau Apparel is only one of many firms that produce a fairly homogeneous product, and none of the firms in this moderate-price shirt market engages in any significant advertising.

Price forecasts

In mid-December 2015, the manager of Beau Apparel was preparing the firm's production plan for the first quarter of 2016. The manager wanted to obtain a forecast of the wholesale price of shirts for the first quarter of 2016. This price forecast would subsequently be used in making the production decision for Beau Apparel. The manager requests price forecasts from Beau Apparel's Marketing/Forecasting Division. The market researchers, using forecasting techniques similar to those described in Chapter 7, provided the manager with three wholesale price forecasts based on three different assumptions about economic conditions in the first quarter of 2016

High:	$20
Medium:	$15
Low:	$10

Estimation of average variable cost and marginal cost The manager of Beau Apparel chose a cubic specification of short-run cost for estimating the average variable cost and the marginal cost curves. Using time-series data over the six-year time period 2010(I) through 2015(IV), during which Beau Apparel had the same-size plant, the following average variable cost function was estimated

$$AVC = 20 - 0.003Q + 0.00000025Q^2$$

All the estimated coefficients (20, −0.003, and 0.00000025) had the required signs and were statistically significant. The estimated average cost function provided the information needed for making the decision to produce or shut down. We will return to this decision after we discuss how the manager of Beau Apparel estimated the marginal cost function.

As explained in Chapter 10, the parameter estimates for the average variable cost function can be used to obtain the estimated marginal cost function

$$SMC = a + 2bQ + 3cQ^2$$

where a, b, and c are the estimated parameters (coefficients) for the AVC function. The manager used the estimated coefficients of the average variable cost equation to obtain the corresponding marginal cost function. For the estimate of the average variable cost function given above, the corresponding marginal cost function for shirts was

$$SMC = 20 + 2(-0.003)Q + 3(0.00000025)Q^2$$
$$= 20 - 0.006Q + 0.00000075Q^2$$

After obtaining forecasts of price and estimates of the average variable cost and marginal cost curves, the manager was able to answer the two production questions: (1) Should the firm produce or shut down? And (2) if production is warranted, how much should the firm produce? We now can show how the manager of Beau Apparel made these two decisions and calculated the firm's forecasted profit.

The shutdown decision Because the estimated average variable cost function for shirts was

$$AVC = 20 - 0.003Q + 0.00000025Q^2$$

AVC reaches its minimum value at

$$Q_m = \frac{-(-0.003)}{2(0.00000025)} = 6,000$$

Substituting this output level into the estimated average variable cost function, the value of average variable cost at its minimum point is

$$AVC_{min} = 20 - 0.003(6,000) + 0.00000025(6,000)^2 = \$11$$

Thus average variable cost reaches its minimum value of $11 at 6,000 units of output.

The manager of Beau Apparel then compared this minimum average variable cost with the three price forecasts for the first quarter of 2016. For the high forecast, $20,

$$\hat{P}_{2016(I)} = \$20 > \$11 = AVC_{min}$$

so the firm should produce in order to maximize profit or minimize loss. Likewise, with the medium forecast, $15,

$$\hat{P}_{2016(I)} = \$15 > \$11 = AVC_{min}$$

and the firm also should produce. However, if the market-determined price of shirts turned out to be equal to the low forecast, $10, the firm should shut down (produce zero output) because

$$\hat{P}_{2016(I)} = \$10 < \$11 = AVC_{min}$$

In this case, total revenue would not cover all variable costs of production, and the firm would be better off shutting down and losing only its fixed costs. The manager, therefore, must determine only how much output to produce when price is either $20 or $15.

The output decision   Given the estimated marginal cost equation for Beau Apparel, profit maximization or loss minimization requires that

$$P = SMC = 20 - 0.006Q + 0.00000075Q^2$$

The manager first considered the high forecast of wholesale shirt prices. After setting the $20 forecasted price equal to estimated marginal cost, the optimal production of shirts when price is $20 was found by solving

$$20 = 20 - 0.006Q + 0.00000075Q^2$$

Subtracting 20 from both sides of the equation and factoring out a Q term results in the following expression

$$0 = Q(-0.006 + 0.00000075Q)$$

There are two solutions to this equation, since the right-hand side of the equation is 0 if either $Q = 0$ or $Q = 8,000$. Because the manager of Beau Apparel had already determined that price was greater than AVC_{min} and production was warranted, the manager concluded that the profit-maximizing output level was 8,000 units.

Using the medium price forecast of $15, the manager again determined the optimal output by equating the forecasted price to estimated marginal cost

$$15 = 20 - 0.006Q + 0.00000075Q^2$$

or

$$0 = 5 - 0.006Q + 0.00000075Q^2$$

The solution to this equation is not as simple as was the preceding case, because the left-hand side of the equation cannot be factored. To solve a quadratic equation that cannot be factored, the quadratic formula must be used[15]

$$Q = \frac{-(-0.006) \pm \sqrt{(0.006)^2 - 4(5)(0.00000075)}}{2(0.00000075)} = \frac{0.006 \pm 0.004583}{0.0000015}$$

The two solutions for this quadratic equation are $Q = 945$ and $Q = 7,055$.

To determine which solution is optimal, the manager computed the average variable cost for each level of output

$$AVC_{Q=945} = 20 - 0.003(945) + 0.00000025(945)^2 = \$17.39$$

$$AVC_{Q=7,055} = 20 - 0.003(7,055) + 0.00000025(7,055)^2 = \$11.28$$

Because the price forecast of $15 is less than $17.39, the manager would not produce the output level $Q = 945$. If the wholesale price is expected to be $15, the manager would produce 7,055 units, at which AVC is $11.28. We now consider the amount of profit or loss that Beau Apparel would earn at each of the optimal levels of output.

Computation of total profit or loss Total revenue is price times quantity sold. Total cost is the sum of total variable cost and total fixed cost, where total variable cost is average variable cost times the number of units sold. Hence, total profit (loss) is

$$\pi = TR - TC$$
$$= (P \times Q) - [(AVC \times Q) + TFC]$$

The manager expects total fixed costs for the shirt division for 2016(I) to be $30,000. The values for total revenue and total variable cost depend on the price forecast and corresponding optimal output. We now show how the manager of Beau Apparel computed profit or loss for each of the three forecasts of the wholesale price of shirts.

High-price forecast (P = $20) In this case, Beau Apparel's manager determined that the optimal level of production would be 8,000 units. The average variable cost when 8,000 units are produced is

$$AVC_{Q=8,000} = 20 - 0.003(8,000) + 0.00000025(8,000)^2 = \$12$$

Economic profit when price is $20 would be

$$\pi = (\$20 \times 8,000) - [(\$12 \times 8,000) + \$30,000] = \$34,000$$

---

[15]For an equation of the form $A + BX + CX^2 = 0$, the two solutions, X_1 and X_2, are

$$X_1, X_2 = \frac{-B \pm \sqrt{B^2 - 4AC}}{2C}$$

If you are accustomed to the alternative expression of the equation, $AX^2 + BX + C = 0$, then the denominator for the solution is $2A$ (instead of $2C$).

If the price of shirts is $20 per unit in the first quarter of 2016, Beau Apparel should produce 8,000 units to earn a profit of $34,000, which is the maximum profit possible, given this price.

Middle-price forecast (P = 15)   If the price of shirts is $15 in the first quarter of 2016, the optimal level of output is 7,055 units. The average variable cost is

$$AVC_{Q=7,055} = 20 - 0.003(7,055) + 0.00000025(7,055)^2 = \$11.28$$

Economic profit when price is $15 would be

$$\pi = (\$15 \times 7,055) - [(\$11.28 \times 7,055) + \$30,000] = -\$3,755$$

When the price of shirts is $15, the shirt division of Beau Apparel would be expected to suffer a *loss* of $3,755 in the first quarter of 2016. Note that the firm should continue to produce since this is the minimum loss possible when price is $15. If Beau Apparel shut down production when price is $15, the firm would lose an amount equal to the total fixed cost of $30,000—considerably more than the $3,755 the firm loses by producing 7,055 units.

Low-price forecast (P = 10)   At a price of $10 per shirt, the firm would shut down and produce 0 output ($Q = 0$). In this case, economic profit would be equal to $-TFC$:

$$\pi = (\$10 \times 0) - (0 + \$30,000) = -\$30,000$$

Beau Apparel would minimize loss in this situation by producing nothing and losing only its fixed costs of $30,000.

This extended example about Beau Apparel's production decision illustrates how the manager of a firm that sells in a perfectly competitive market can find the optimal level of output. Our purpose in using the three different price forecasts was to illustrate the decision-making rules developed earlier in the chapter, where we showed that a firm makes one of the following choices in the short run:

1. Produce a positive level of output and earn an economic profit (if $P \geq AVC$ and $P > ATC$).
2. Produce a positive level of output and suffer an economic loss less than the amount of total fixed cost (if $AVC \leq P < ATC$).
3. Produce zero output and suffer an economic loss equal to total fixed cost (if $P < AVC$).

The profit-maximizing and loss-minimizing decisions of Beau Apparel are shown graphically in Figure 11.13. The marginal, average variable, and average total cost curves are a graphical representation of those estimated previously. In Panel A, the product price is $20 (= MR). As you can see in the graph, $SMC = \$20$ at 8,000 units of output. At 8,000 units, $AVC = \$12$, as shown, and $AFC = \$30,000/8,000 = \$3.75$. Therefore $ATC = \$12 + \$3.75 = \$15.75$. Profit is $(P - ATC)Q = (\$20 - \$15.75)8,000 = \$34,000$, as derived earlier.

FIGURE 11.13
Profit and Loss at Beau Apparel

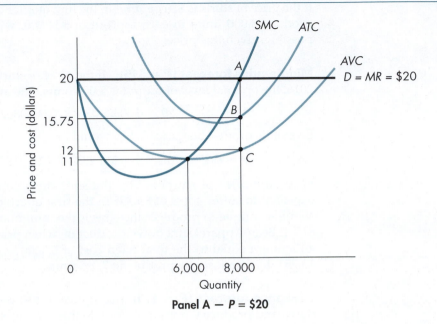

Panel A — P = $20

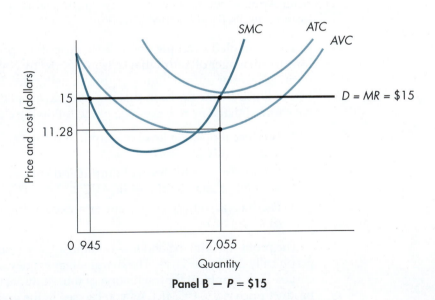

Panel B — P = $15

Panel B illustrates the loss-minimizing situation when $P = MR = \$15$. As shown, $SMC = \$15$ at 945 and 7,055 units of output. The lower output would not be chosen because price is less than average variable cost at this output. Thus the firm produces 7,055 units of output, where AVC is less than 15. As shown in the graph, average total cost is greater than 15 at every level of output, so Beau Apparel cannot make an economic profit. In the figure, at an output of 7,055, average variable cost is 11.28, so total variable cost is $79,580 (= \$11.28 \times 7,055)$. The firm can use its total revenue of $105,825 (= \$15 \times 7,055)$ to pay all its variable cost and use the remainder, $26,245$, to pay part of its fixed cost. Therefore, Beau Apparel loses $3,755 (= \$30,000 - \$26,245)$, the portion of total fixed cost not covered by revenue.

As the figure shows in Panel A, average variable cost reaches its minimum at 6,000 units of output, where $AVC = \$11$. The firm would shut down and produce zero output if price falls below $11.

Now try Technical Problem 11.

11.7 SUMMARY

- Perfect competition occurs when a market possesses these three characteristics: (1) firms are price-takers because each firm is so small relative to the total market output that it cannot affect the market price by changing its output, (2) all firms produce a homogeneous or perfectly standardized commodity, and (3) entry into and exit from the market are unrestricted. (LO1)

- The demand curve for a perfectly competitive firm is perfectly elastic or horizontal at the market-determined equilibrium price, and marginal revenue equals price for a competitive firm. Therefore, the demand curve facing a perfectly competitive firm is also simultaneously the marginal revenue curve: $D = MR$. Price-taking firms can sell all they want at the market price. (LO2)

- Managers make two decisions in the short run: (1) produce or shut down, and (2) if produce, how much to produce. When positive profit is possible, profit is maximized at the output where $P = SMC$. Firms do not shut down as long as total revenue, TR, at least covers total avoidable cost, which in the absence of quasi-fixed costs means $TR \geq TVC$ because avoidable cost is identical to variable cost when no quasi-fixed inputs are employed. (In this textbook, there are no quasi-fixed inputs unless specifically stated otherwise.) If TR cannot cover TVC ($TR < TVC$ or equivalently $P < AVC$), the firm should shut down and produce nothing, losing only its total fixed costs, TFC. When a firm does choose to produce, only marginal cost matters in finding the profit-maximizing output, and so managers must ignore profit margin, fixed costs, sunk costs, and average costs when making their production decisions. The firm's short-run supply curve is the portion of its marginal cost curve above minimum average variable cost. When market price falls below minimum AVC, quantity supplied is zero. The industry's short-run supply curve is derived by horizontally summing supply curves of all firms in the industry. The short-run industry supply is always upward-sloping, and supply prices along the industry supply curve give the marginal costs of production for every firm contributing to industry supply. Short-run producer surplus is the amount by which total revenue exceeds total variable cost and equals the area above the short-run supply curve below market price over the range of output supplied. Short-run producer surplus exceeds economic profit by the amount of total fixed costs. (LO3)

- In long-run competitive equilibrium, all firms are in profit-maximizing equilibrium ($P = LMC$), and there is no incentive for firms to enter or exit the industry because economic profit is zero ($P = LAC$). In long-run competitive equilibrium $P = LMC = LAC$, which is at the minimum point on LAC. The long-run industry supply curves can be either flat for constant cost industries or upward-sloping for increasing cost industries. In constant-cost industries, input prices remain constant as industry output expands, and the minimum point on LAC is unchanged. Because long-run supply price equals minimum LAC, the long-run industry supply curve is perfectly elastic or horizontal. In increasing-cost industries, input prices are bid up as industry output expands, causing minimum LAC and long-run supply price to rise, and thus long-run industry supply curves are upward-sloping. For both constant-cost and increasing-cost industries, economic profit is zero for every firm in the industry at every point on the long-run industry supply curve, and thus long-run supply prices equal both minimum LAC and LMC for all firms in the industry. Economic rent is a payment to the owner of an exceptionally productive resource in excess of the resource's opportunity cost. Firms that employ such superior resources earn only a normal profit in long-run competitive equilibrium because the potential economic profit from employing a superior resource is paid to the resource owner as economic rent. (*LO4*)

■ Choosing either output or input usage leads to the same optimal output decision and profit level, because the profit-maximizing level of input usage produces exactly the output that maximizes profit. Marginal revenue product (*MRP*) of an additional unit of a variable input is the additional revenue from hiring one more unit of the input. For the variable input labor, $MRP = \Delta TR/\Delta L = P \times MP$. When a manager chooses to produce rather than shut down, the optimal level of input usage is found by following this rule: If the marginal revenue product of an additional unit of the input is greater (less) than the price of the input, then that unit should (should not) be hired. If the usage of the variable input varies continuously, the manager should employ the amount of the input at which MRP equals input price. Average revenue product (*ARP*) of labor is the average revenue per worker: $ARP = TR/L$. ARP can be calculated as the product of price times the average product of labor: $ARP = P \times AP$. If the price of a single variable input (i.e., the wage rate for labor) rises above the point of maximum ARP, then the firm minimizes its loss by shutting down and hiring none of the variable input. (*LO5*)

■ Five steps can be employed to find the profit-maximizing rate of production and the level of profit for a competitive firm: (1) forecast the price of the product, (2) estimate average variable cost and marginal cost, (3) check the shutdown rule, (4) if $P \geq AVC_{min}$ find the output level where $P = SMC$, and (5) compute profit or loss. (*LO6*)

KEY TERMS

average profit

average revenue product (*ARP*)

break-even points

constant-cost industry

economic rent

increasing-cost industry

long-run competitive equilibrium

marginal revenue product (*MRP*)

perfect competition

perfectly elastic demand

profit margin

shut down

shutdown price

TECHNICAL PROBLEMS

1. The left-hand side of the following graph shows market demand and supply curves in a competitive market. Draw the demand facing a competitive firm selling in this market on the right-hand graph.

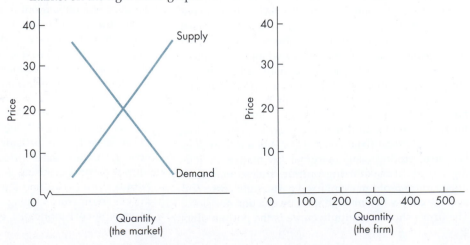

a. What is the firm's demand elasticity at 200 units of output? At 400 units?
b. What is the firm's marginal revenue from selling the 200th unit of output? From the 400th unit?

2. Answer the questions below using the cost curves for the price-taking firm shown in the following graph:

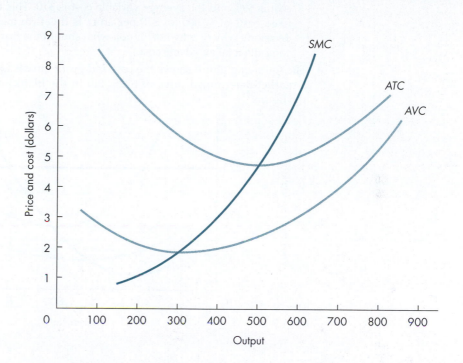

a. If price is $7 per unit of output, draw the marginal revenue curve. The manager should produce _____ units to maximize profit.
b. Because average total cost is $_____ for this output, total cost is $_____.
c. The firm makes a profit of $_____.
d. At _____ units, profit margin (or average profit) is maximized. Why is this output level *different from* the answer to part *a*?
e. Let price fall to $3, and draw the new marginal revenue curve. The manager should now produce _____ units to maximize profit.
f. Total revenue is now $_____ and total cost is $_____. The firm makes a loss of $_____.
g. Total variable cost is $_____, leaving $_____ to apply to fixed cost.
h. If price falls below $_____, the firm will produce zero output. Explain why.

3. a. In a competitive industry, the market-determined price is $12. For a firm currently producing 50 units of output, short-run marginal cost is $15, average total cost is $14, and average variable cost is $7. Is this firm making the profit-maximizing decision? Why or why not? If not, what should the firm do?

b. In a different competitive market, the market-determined price is $25. A firm in this market is producing 10,000 units of output, and, at this output level, the firm's average total cost reaches its minimum value of $25. Is this firm making the profit-maximizing decision? Why or why not? If not, what should the firm do?

c. In yet another competitive industry, the market-determined price is $60. For a firm currently producing 100 units of output, short-run marginal cost is $50, average total cost is $95, and the average variable cost is $10. This firm also incurs total quasi-fixed costs of $7,000 (or $70 per unit). Is this firm making the profit-maximizing decision? Why or why not? If not, what should the firm do? (*Hint:* You will need to compute total avoidable cost.)

4. The following figure shows the cost and profit curves for a price-taking firm facing a market-determined price of $225. Fill in the blanks *a* through *e* as indicated in the figure.

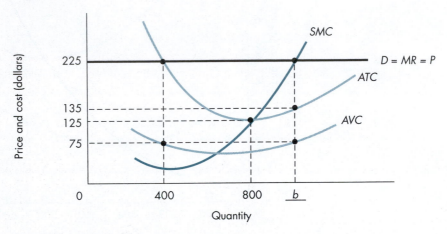

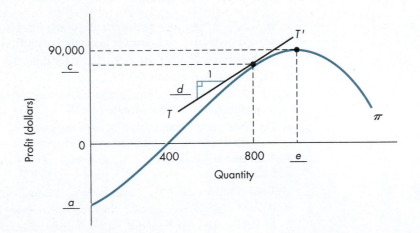

5. A perfectly competitive firm faces a market-determined price of $25 for its product.

(1) Quantity	(2) Total cost	(3) Average total cost	(4) Marginal cost	(5) Marginal revenue	(6) Profit margin	(7)
0	1000					
100	2000					
200	3300					
300	4800					
400	7000					
500	9600					

a. The firm's total costs are given in the schedule above. Fill in columns 3 and 4 for average total cost and marginal cost.

b. Fill in columns 5 and 6 for marginal revenue and profit margin.

c. How much output should the competitive firm produce? Explain.

d. Label column 7 "Total profit" and fill in the values. Is your answer to part c correct? Explain.

e. Suppose the demand for the firm's product decreases and the market price falls to $14. Should the firm shut down? If not, how much output should the firm produce? Explain.

6. The following figure shows long-run average and marginal cost curves for a competitive firm. The price of the product is $40.

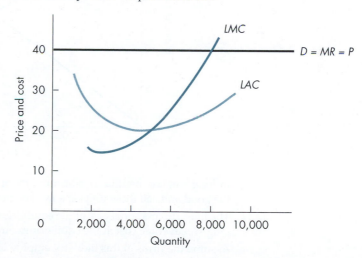

a. How much will the firm produce? What will be its economic profit?

b. When the industry attains long-run competitive equilibrium, what will be the price and the firm's output? What will be the firm's economic profit?

7. Suppose that a competitive industry is in long-run competitive equilibrium. Then the price of a substitute good (in consumption) decreases. What will happen in the short run to
   a. The market demand curve?
   b. The market supply curve?
   c. Market price?
   d. Market output?
   e. The firm's output?
   f. The firm's profit?
   What will happen in the long run?

8. The supply curve for an industry shows the relation between supply price and industry output.
   a. The long-run competitive supply curve for a constant-cost industry is horizontal. Why is supply price constant?
   b. The long-run competitive supply curve for an increasing-cost industry is upward-sloping. Why does supply price increase as industry production rises?

9. The figure on the next page shows a long-run industry supply curve (S_{LR}) and the demand curve (D) facing the competitive industry.

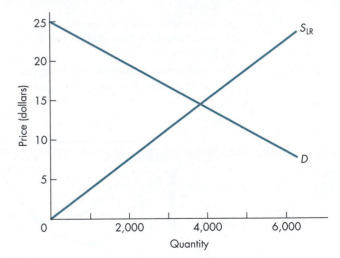

   a. In long-run competitive equilibrium, the industry will produce _____ units of the good and sell these units at a market-clearing price of $_____ per unit.
   b. The long-run marginal cost at the equilibrium output in part a is $_____, and the long-run average cost at the equilibrium output is $_____.
   c. Assume the firms in this industry employ inputs of varying quality and productivity, and respond to this statement: "Even though the firms with the higher quality inputs have lower costs than their rivals, all firms in the industry earn the same amount of economic profit." Is this statement true or false? Explain.
   d. Total producer surplus in long-run competitive equilibrium is $_____ for this industry.

e. Every firm in this industry earns economic profit equal to $\$$_____, and the high-quality resources earn total economic rents equal to $\$$_____.

f. If all resources used by this industry are of equal quality (and equal productivity), what would the long-run industry supply curve look like? How much producer surplus would be generated in equilibrium? How much economic rent would be paid to resources used by the firms?

10. Consider a price-taking firm that has total fixed cost of $50 and faces a market-determined price of $2 per unit for its output. The wage rate is $10 per unit of labor, the only variable input. Using the following table, answer the questions below.

(1) Units of labor	(2) Output	(3) Marginal product	(4) Marginal revenue product	(5) Marginal cost	(6) Profit
1	5	_____	_____	_____	_____
2	15	_____	_____	_____	_____
3	30	_____	_____	_____	_____
4	50	_____	_____	_____	_____
5	65	_____	_____	_____	_____
6	77	_____	_____	_____	_____
7	86	_____	_____	_____	_____
8	94	_____	_____	_____	_____
9	98	_____	_____	_____	_____
10	96	_____	_____	_____	_____

a. Fill in the blanks in column 3 of the table by computing the marginal product of labor for each level of labor usage.

b. Fill in the blanks in column 4 of the table by computing the marginal revenue product for each level of labor usage.

c. How much labor should the manager hire to maximize profit? Why?

d. Fill in the blanks in column 5 of the table by computing marginal cost.

e. How many units of output should the manager produce to maximize profit? Why?

f. Fill in the blanks in column 6 with the profit earned at each level of labor usage.

g. Do your answers to parts c and e maximize profit? Does it matter whether the manager chooses labor usage or chooses output to maximize profit? Why?

h. How much labor should the manager hire when the wage rate is $20? How much profit is earned? Is marginal product greater or less than average product at this level of labor usage? Why does it matter?

11. Suppose that the manager of a firm operating in a competitive market has estimated the firm's average variable cost function to be

$$AVC = 10 - 0.03Q + 0.00005Q^2$$

Total fixed cost is $600.

a. What is the corresponding marginal cost function?

b. At what output is AVC at its minimum?

c. What is the minimum value for AVC?

If the forecasted price of the firm's output is $10 per unit:

d. How much output will the firm produce in the short run?

e. How much profit (loss) will the firm earn?

If the forecasted price is $7 per unit:

f. How much output will the firm produce in the short run?

g. How much profit (loss) will the firm earn?

If the forecasted price is $5 per unit:

h. How much output will the firm produce in the short run?

i How much profit (loss) will the firm earn?

APPLIED PROBLEMS

1. The MidNight Hour, a local nightclub, earned $100,000 in accounting profit last year. This year the owner, who had invested $1 million in the club, decided to close the club. What can you say about economic profit (and the rate of return) in the night-club business?

2. Redstone Clayworks, Inc., a small firm located in Sedona, manufactures clay fire pits that homeowners place on their patios for decoration and light-duty heating. Red-stone is one of 53 firms worldwide supplying clay fire pits to retailers such as Home Depot, Lowe's, Front Gate, and other upscale home product chains. Despite the best marketing efforts of these retailers to differentiate their individual brands of fire pits, consumers don't care much about brands: A clay fire pit is a clay fire pit, regardless of who sells it. The following spreadsheet below provides data on Redstone's costs of production:

(1) Q	(2) TC	(3) TFC	(4) TVC
0	5,000	5,000	0
100	10,000	5,000	5,000
200	18,000	5,000	13,000
300	27,000	5,000	22,000
400	38,000	5,000	33,000
500	50,000	5,000	45,000
600	66,000	5,000	61,000
700	84,000	5,000	79,000
800	104,000	5,000	99,000
900	126,000	5,000	121,000
1,000	150,000	5,000	145,000

a. Create a spreadsheet using Microsoft Excel (or any other spreadsheet software) that matches the one above by entering the output and cost data given above. Then use the appropriate formulas to create four new columns in your spread-sheet for average fixed cost (AFC), average variable cost (AVC), average total cost (ATC), and short-run marginal cost (SMC). [Computation check: At $Q = 400$, $SMC = \$110$].

The world demand and supply curves for clay fire pits intersect at $190 per unit.

b. Use the appropriate formulas to create two more columns in your spreadsheet for total revenue (TR) and marginal revenue (MR). [Computation check: At Q = 400: MR = $190].

c. Use the appropriate formulas to create three more columns in your spreadsheet for profit (PROF), average profit (AVGPROF), and profit margin (PROFMARG). [Computation check: At Q = 400: AVGPROF = $95].

d. If Redstone's manager wishes to minimize average total cost, how many clay fire pits should be produced? How many to maximize profit margin?

e. Redstone's manager is fired, and you are now the manager of Redstone Clayworks. How many fire pits would you choose to produce? Why?

f. Now triple the total fixed costs to $15,000 in your spreadsheet. How does this change your production decision in part e? Explain briefly.

g. Suppose a congressional environmental panel announces that greenhouse gases from clay fire pits are contributing significantly to global warming. The announcement causes worldwide demand for fire pits to shrink substantially, and clay fire pit prices fall to $65 per unit. How does this change your production decision in part e? Explain briefly. [Note: Return total fixed cost to the original level of $5,000.]

3. The manager of All City Realtors wants to hire some real estate agents to specialize in selling housing units acquired by the Resolution Trust Corporation (RTC) in its attempt to bail out the savings and loan industry. The commission paid by the RTC to the company to sell these homes is a flat rate of $2,000 per unit sold, rather than the customary commission that is based on the sale price of a home. The manager estimates the following marginal product schedule for real estate agents dealing in government-owned housing:

Number of real estate agents	Marginal product (number of additional units sold per year)	Marginal revenue product
1	20	_____
2	17	_____
3	15	_____
4	12	_____
5	8	_____
6	4	_____

a. Construct the marginal revenue product schedule by filling in the blanks in the table.

b. If the manager of All City Realtors must pay a wage rate of $32,000 per year to get agents who will specialize in selling RTC housing, how many agents should the manager hire? Why?

c. If the wage rate falls to $18,000 per year, how many agents should the manager hire?

d. Suppose the RTC raises its commission to $3,000 per unit sold. Now what is the marginal revenue product for each real estate agent employed?

e. Now that the RTC is paying $3,000 per unit sold, how many agents should the manager hire if the wage rate is $30,000?

4. HoneyBee Farms, a medium-size producer of honey, operates in a market that fits the competitive market definition relatively well. However, honey farmers are assisted by support prices above the price that would prevail in the absence of controls. The owner of HoneyBee Farms, as well as some other honey producers, complain that they can't make a profit even with these support prices. Explain why. Explain why even higher support prices would not help honey farmers in the long run.

5. Insurance agents receive a commission on the policies they sell. Many states regulate the rates that can be charged for insurance. Would higher or lower rates increase the incomes of agents? Explain, distinguishing between the short run and the long run.

6. If all the assumptions of perfect competition hold, why would firms in such an industry have little incentive to carry out technological change or much research and development? What conditions would encourage research and development in competitive industries?

7. At a recent board meeting, the president and CEO got into a heated argument about whether to shut down the firm's plant in Miami. The Miami plant currently loses $60,000 monthly. The president of the firm argued that the Miami plant should continue to operate, at least until a buyer is found for the production facility. The president's argument was based on the fact that the Miami plant's fixed costs are $68,000 per month. The CEO exploded over this point, castigating the president for considering fixed costs in making the shutdown decision. According to the CEO, "Everyone knows fixed costs don't matter!"

   a. Should the Miami plant be closed or continue to operate at a loss in the short run?

   b. How would you explain to the incorrect party that he or she is wrong?

8. Suppose you own a home remodeling company. You are currently earning short-run profits. The home remodeling industry is an increasing-cost industry. In the long run, what do you expect will happen to

   a. Your firm's costs of production? Explain.

   b. The price you can charge for your remodeling services? Why?

   c. Profits in home remodeling? Why?

9. The New York City Parks Department doubled the annual fee for the hot-dog pushcart that had the exclusive license for the spot just south of the Metropolitan Museum of Art to $288,000. Why would anyone pay almost $300,000 for a pushcart license? Who is obtaining the economic rent for the obviously lucrative pushcart location? How much economic profit is the pushcart owner probably earning?

10. Grocery stores and gasoline stations in a large city would appear to be examples of competitive markets: There are numerous relatively small sellers, each seller is a price-taker, and the products are quite similar.

    a. How could we argue that these markets are *not* competitive?

    b. Could each firm face a demand curve that is *not* perfectly elastic?

    c. How profitable do you expect grocery stores and gasoline stations to be in the long run?

11. During a coffee-room debate among several young MBAs who had recently graduated, one of the young executives flatly stated, "The most this company can lose on its Brazilian division is the amount it has invested (its fixed costs)." Not everyone agreed with this statement. In what sense is this statement correct? Under what circumstances could it be false? Explain.

12. During the summer of 2009 at the European Union's headquarters in Brussels, dairy farmers across Europe protested low milk prices caused by the EU's move away from farm crop subsidy programs toward more heavy reliance on market-determined prices for agricultural products. *The Wall Street Journal* reported that the dairy farmers demanded "a *fair* price for (their) milk, which covers at least (their) production cost and some profit margin." The EU Farm Commissioner responded, "what farmers need to do is produce less."

    a. Although in economics there is no such thing as a "fair" price, how might market-determined prices be considered "fair" in an economic sense?

    b. Why don't dairy farmers take the Commissioner's advice and just produce less milk?

13. EverKleen Pool Services provides weekly swimming pool maintenance in Atlanta. Dozens of firms provide this service. The service is standardized; each company cleans the pool and maintains the proper levels of chemicals in the water. The service is typically sold as a four-month summer contract. The market price for the four-month service contract is $115.

    EverKleen Pool Services has fixed costs of $3,500. The manager of EverKleen has estimated the following marginal cost function for EverKleen, using data for the last two years:

    $$SMC = 125 - 0.42Q + 0.0021Q^2$$

    where *SMC* is measured in dollars and *Q* is the number of pools serviced each summer. Each of the estimated coefficients is statistically significant at the 5 percent level.

    a. Given the estimated marginal cost function, what is the average variable cost function for EverKleen?

    b. At what output level does *AVC* reach its minimum value? What is the value of *AVC* at its minimum point?

    c. Should the manager of EverKleen continue to operate, or should the firm shut down? Explain.

    d. The manager of EverKleen finds two output levels that appear to be optimal. What are these levels of output and which one is actually optimal?

    e. How much profit (or loss) can the manager of EverKleen Pool Services expect to earn?

    f. Suppose EverKleen's fixed costs rise to $4,000. How does this affect the optimal level of output? Explain.

14. Airline industry experts generally believe that because of the "highly competitive" nature of U.S. airline markets, it is usually impossible to pass on higher jet fuel prices to passengers by raising ticket prices.

    a. What factors do you suppose contribute to making U.S. airline markets "highly competitive"?

    b. Accepting the premise that U.S. airline markets are indeed highly competitive, analyze in both the short run and long run the difficulty of raising ticket prices when jet fuel prices rise.

15. Legendary for his business and investment acumen, Warren Buffett is frequently called the "Oracle of Omaha" after his birthplace in Omaha, Nebraska. As one of the world's wealthiest business owner-investors, business executives are always interested in any insight or opinion Mr. Buffett might wish to share. Explain each one of the

following statements made by Warren Buffett. (Quotations from *The Wall Street Journal*, September 23, 2002.)*

a. "You cannot be the high-cost producer in a commodity business."

b. "Sometimes it's not even any good to be the low-cost producer."

_____

* Martha Brannigan, "Airlines to Lobby Government For More Aid as Losses Mount" *The Wall Street Journal*, May 13, 2009.

▣ MATHEMATICAL APPENDIX

This appendix describes a manager's choice of output and input usage to maximize profit for a perfectly competitive firm facing a market-determined price for the product it sells. We examine the decision about the profit-maximizing output level first using the most general cost function and then using a quadratic cost function. Next, we derive the profit-maximizing conditions when the manager chooses the level of usage of first one variable input and then two variable inputs.

The Firm Chooses the Level of Output

Assume that the firm is in the short run, so some costs are fixed. Let the market-determined price be $\overline{P}$. The firm's total revenue is

$$R(Q) = \overline{P}Q$$

The firm's profit function is

(1) $$\pi = \overline{P}Q - TVC(Q) - TFC$$

where $TVC(Q)$ is total variable cost and TFC is total fixed cost.

The first-order condition for a maximum requires

(2) $$\frac{d\pi}{dQ} = \overline{P} - \frac{dTVC}{dQ} = 0$$

The second-order condition for a maximum is that at the equilibrium quantity

(3) $$\frac{d^2\pi}{dQ^2} = -\frac{d^2TVC}{dQ^2} < 0$$

Because, in equation (2), $dTVC/dQ$ is marginal cost (SMC), choosing the quantity of output that maximizes profit requires that price equal marginal cost: $\overline{P} = SMC$. The second-order condition shows that in profit-maximizing equilibrium, marginal cost must be upward-sloping: $d^2TVC/dQ^2 > 0$. Equation (2) can be solved for the profit-maximizing output, Q^*.

Profit Maximization for Price-Taking Firms

If, at Q^*,

$$\pi = \overline{P}Q^* - TVC(Q^*) - TFC > 0$$

the firm makes an economic profit. If

$$\pi = \overline{P}Q^* - TVC(Q^*) - TFC < 0$$

the firm makes a loss. In this case the firm should produce Q^* rather than shutting down when

$$|\overline{P}Q^* - TVC(Q^*) - TFC| < TFC$$

which occurs if, at Q^*, price is greater than average variable cost:

(4) $$\overline{P} > \frac{TVC(Q^*)}{Q^*}$$

The firm loses less than its fixed cost, which is the amount it would lose if it shuts down and produces nothing. If at Q^* price is less than average variable cost, the firm should shut down and produce nothing. It loses all its fixed cost rather than its fixed cost plus the amount of variable cost not covered by revenue.

Because the second-order condition in equation (3) requires that marginal cost be upward-sloping, the firm's short-run supply must be upward-sloping. The higher the price, the greater the equilibrium output at which price equals marginal cost. Since, from equation (4), the firm produces nothing if price falls below minimum average variable cost, the supply is zero at prices below minimum AVC.

For a less general approach, let the total variable cost function be the cubic function

$$TVC(Q) = aQ + bQ^2 + cQ^3$$

where a, b, and c are positive. We continue to assume that the market-determined price is $\overline{P}$. The profit function is

(5) $$\pi = \overline{P}Q - TVC(Q) - TFC$$
$$= \overline{P}Q - aQ + bQ^2 - cQ^3 - TFC$$

For profit maximization, differentiate equation (5) and set the derivative equal to zero:

(6) $$\frac{d\pi}{dQ} = \overline{P} - (a - 2bQ + 3cQ^2) = 0$$

Since $SMC = dTVC(Q)/dQ = a - 2bQ + 3cQ^2$, price equals marginal cost in profit-maximizing equilibrium. The second-order condition for a maximum is

(7) $$\frac{d^2\pi}{dQ^2} = 2b - 6cQ < 0$$

or, solving equation (7) for Q, for a maximum it must be the case that

(8) $$Q > \frac{b}{3c}$$

To obtain the profit-maximizing level of output Q^*, solve the quadratic equation formed from equation (6):

$$(\overline{P} - a) - 2bQ + 3cQ^2 = 0$$

After solving such a quadratic equation, you will get two values for Q^*. The profit-maximizing Q^* will be the one at which the second-order condition in (8) holds, ensuring that this is the value of Q^* at which marginal cost is upward-sloping. This will be the larger of the two solutions. If total revenue exceeds total variable cost, that is, if

$$\overline{P} > AVC(Q^*) = TVC(Q^*)/Q^* = a - bQ^* + cQ^{*2}$$

the firm produces Q^* and profit or loss is

$$\pi = \overline{P}Q^* - aQ^* + bQ^{*2} - cQ^{*3} - TFC$$

If $P < AVC(Q^*) = a - bQ^* + cQ^{*2}$ the firm shuts down, produces nothing, and loses its total fixed cost.

The Firm Chooses Input Usage

First we assume the firm chooses the level of usage of a single variable input, labor (L), to maximize profit. All other inputs ($\overline{K}$) are fixed in amount. The price of the product is $\overline{P}$. Let the production function be as derived for the short run in the Mathematical Appendix to Chapter 8:

$$Q = f(L, \overline{K}) = g(L)$$

The firm chooses L, so the following profit function is maximized:

(9) $$\pi = \overline{P}g(L) - wL - TFC$$

where w is the wage paid to labor and TFC is the fixed payment to the fixed input. Profit maximization requires

(10) $$\frac{d\pi}{dL} = \overline{P}\left(\frac{dQ}{dL}\right) - w = 0$$

Since $dQ/dL = MP_L$ is the marginal product of labor, equation (10) can be expressed as

$$MP_L \times \overline{P} = \text{Marginal revenue product} = w$$

Equation (10) can be solved for L^*, then $Q^* = g(L^*)$.

If, at L^*, $MRP < ARP = \overline{P}g(L^*)/L^*$, total revenue will be greater than total variable cost ($PQ^* > wL^*$) and the firm will produce. Its profit or loss will be

$$\pi = \overline{P}g(L^*) - w - TFC$$

If, however, $MRP = w > \overline{P}Q^*/L^*$, total revenue will be less than total variable cost ($\overline{P}Q^* < wL^*$). In this case the firm would shut down and lose only its total fixed cost, rather than its total fixed cost plus the portion of total variable cost not covered by revenue.

Now assume that the firm uses two variable inputs, L and K, to produce Q and no inputs are fixed. The prices of L and K are, respectively, w and r. The production function is

$$Q = f(L, K)$$

The product price remains $\overline{P}$. The profit function is

$$\pi = \overline{P}f(L, K) - wL - rK$$

Because the firm chooses the levels of L and K to maximize profit, the first-order equilibrium conditions are

(11a) $$\overline{P}\frac{dQ}{dL} - w = 0$$

(11b) $$\overline{P}\frac{dQ}{dK} - r = 0$$

Equations (11a) and (11b) can be solved for the profit-maximizing levels of L^* and K^*; then the optimal level of output is $Q^* = f(L^*, K^*)$. This value of Q^* can be substituted into the profit equation to find the maximum level of profit.

Equations (11a) and (11b) can be rewritten as

(12a) $$\overline{P} \cdot MP_L = MRP_L = w$$

(12b) $$\overline{P} \cdot MP_K = MRP_K = r$$

Thus, in equilibrium, the marginal revenue product of each input equals its price.

Chapter

12

Managerial Decisions for Firms with Market Power

After reading this chapter, you will be able to:

12.1 Define market power and describe how own-price elasticity, cross-price elasticity, and the Lerner index are used to measure market power.

12.2 Explain why barriers to entry are necessary for market power in the long run and discuss the major types of entry barriers.

12.3 Find the profit-maximizing output and price for a monopolist.

12.4 Find the profit-maximizing input usage for a monopolist.

12.5 Find the profit-maximizing price and output under monopolistic competition.

12.6 Employ empirically estimated or forecasted demand, average variable cost, and marginal cost to calculate profit-maximizing output and price for monopolistic or monopolistically competitive firms.

12.7 Select production levels at multiple plants to minimize the total cost of producing a given total output for a firm.

For many years, the "premium" brands of coffee at grocery stores sold for prices very close to the prices of generic "value-brands," and a "coffeehouse" was a roadside establishment serving mostly weary truck drivers. As everyone on the planet knows, Starbucks Corp. changed the commodity-like nature of coffee by successfully creating "grande" cachet with its cappuccinos, lattes, and mochas served in Starbucks cafés designed to look like the coffeehouses in Italy. Although far from being a pure monopolist, Starbucks nonetheless dominated the specialty coffee market for many years. Starbucks enjoyed substantial market power, giving it the ability to price its coffee beans and specialty drinks well above costs and to earn impressive profits for many years. Times have now changed for Starbucks, however, as it finds itself surrounded by rivals offering competing coffee products. Companies such as Second Cup, Dunkin' Donuts, and even McDonald's, attracted by the economic profits in specialty coffees and facing no barriers to entry, have diminished Starbucks' market power and profitability. Even though some market analysts blame management for opening too many Starbucks coffeehouses worldwide, the greater problem was the inability to prevent new firms from entering its profitable niche. As you will learn in this chapter, lasting market power cannot happen without some type of entry barrier.

market power
The ability possessed by all price-setting firms to raise price without losing all sales, which causes the price-setting firm's demand to be downward-sloping.

Market power—something competitive firms don't have—makes long-run economic profit possible. All price-setting firms possess **market power,** which is the ability to raise their prices without losing all their sales.[1] In contrast to the competitive price-taking firms discussed in Chapter 11, price-setting firms do not sell standardized commodities in markets with many other sellers of nearly identical products, and so price-setting firms do not face perfectly elastic (horizontal) demand curves. Because the product is somehow differentiated from rivals' products or perhaps because the geographic market area has only one (or just a few) sellers of the product, firms with market power face downward-sloping demand curves for the products they sell. All firms except price-taking competitors—monopolies, monopolistic competitors, and oligopolies—have some market power.

When firms with market power raise price, even though sales do not fall to zero, sales do, of course, decrease because of the law of demand. The effect of the change in price on the firm's sales depends to a large extent on the amount of its market power, which can differ greatly among firms. Firms with market power range in scope from virtual monopolies with a great deal of latitude over the prices they charge, such as Amgen's Enbrel drug for psoriatic arthritis treatment, to firms with a great deal of competition and only a small amount of market power, such as shoe stores or clothing stores in a large mall.

The primary focus of this chapter is to show how managers of price-setting firms can choose price, output, and input usage in a way that maximizes the firm's profit. For the types of firms discussed in this chapter—firms possessing market power that can set prices without worrying too much about retaliatory responses by any rival firms—the profit-maximizing decision is a straightforward application of the $MR = MC$ rule. However, in the next chapter on oligopoly firms, we will discuss complications that arise for oligopoly managers because their demand and marginal revenue conditions depend critically on the decisions of rival firms.

---

[1]In other courses or in other textbooks, you may see the terms *market power* and *monopoly power* used interchangeably, as if both terms have exactly the same meaning. Strictly speaking, they do not. Throughout this textbook we will always use the term *market power*, rather than *monopoly power*, when we refer to the price-setting power allowing firms to raise price without losing all sales. In Chapter 16 we will explain that monopoly power is a *legal* concept that differs in rather important ways from the *economic* concept of market power.

Understanding the complexities of decision making when rivals can undermine planned price changes will require the tools of strategic decision making presented in the next chapter. Thus, for now, you should understand that decision-making rules presented in this chapter will be much simpler than those in Chapter 13 for oligopoly. The reason for this is that the monopolist has no rival firms to worry about and the monopolistically competitive firm faces only relatively small rivals who can be safely ignored for decision-making purposes.

The first part of this chapter describes some ways of measuring market power that are more precise and concrete than terms such as "great deal" or "limited amount." We then discuss some of the determinants of the market power possessed by a firm and reasons why some firms have much more market power than others.

The major portion of the chapter is devoted to the theory of monopoly. A **monopoly** exists when a firm produces and sells a good or service for which there are no close substitutes and other firms are prevented by some type of entry barrier from entering the market. A monopoly, consequently, has more market power than any other type of firm. Although there are few true monopolies in real-world markets—and most of these are subject to some form of government regulation— many large and small firms possess a considerable amount of market power in the sense of having few close substitutes for the products they sell. The theory of monopoly provides the basic analytical framework for the analysis of how managers of all price-setting firms with market power can make decisions to maximize their profit (except, as mentioned, oligopolistic firms that face a high degree of interdependence).

We end this chapter with a fairly brief analysis of firms selling in markets under conditions of **monopolistic competition**. Under monopolistic competition, the market consists of a large number of relatively small firms that produce similar but slightly differentiated products and therefore have some, but not much, market power. Monopolistic competition is characterized by easy entry into and exit from the market. Most retail and wholesale firms and many small manufacturers are examples of monopolistic competition.

Certainly, monopoly and monopolistic competition are very different market structures, but firms in both of these market structures possess some degree of market power. In both cases, managers employ precisely the same analysis to choose the profit-maximizing point on a downward-sloping demand curve. As we will show you in this chapter, there is virtually no difference between monopoly and monopolistic competition in the short run. And even though the outcomes are somewhat different in the long run for the two structures, it is convenient to examine decision making in both of these kinds of market structures in a single chapter.

monopoly
A firm that produces a good for which there are no close substitutes in a market that other firms are prevented from entering because of a barrier to entry.

monopolistic competition
A market consisting of a large number of firms selling a differentiated product with low barriers to entry.

12.1 MEASUREMENT OF MARKET POWER

Even though we have not set forth a precise way to measure a firm's market power, you have probably figured out that the amount of market power is related to the availability of substitutes. The better the substitutes for the product sold by a firm, the less market power the firm possesses. However, there is no single measurement of market power that is totally acceptable to economists, policymakers, and the courts. Economists have come to rely on several measures of market power. These methods are widely used, frequently in antitrust cases that require objective measurement of market power.

Any of the methods of measuring the market power of a firm will fail to provide an accurate measure of market power if the scope of the market in which the firm competes has not been carefully defined. This section begins by discussing how to determine the proper market definition: identifying the products that compete with one another and the geographic area in which the competition occurs. Then we discuss some measures of market power.

Market Definition

market definition
The identification of the producers and products that compete for consumers in a particular geographic area.

A **market definition** identifies the producers and products or service types that compete in a particular geographic area, which is just large enough to include all competing sellers. As you can see by this definition of a market, properly defining a market requires considering the level of competition in both the product dimension and the geographic dimension of a market. Although the methodology of appropriately defining a market is primarily of interest to firms engaged in federal or state antitrust litigation—specifically cases involving illegal monopolization of a market or the impact of a proposed merger on the merged firm's market power—managers should know how to properly define the firm's market to measure correctly the firm's market power. We will now discuss some guidelines for determining the proper product and geographic dimensions of a market.

A properly defined market should include all the products or services that consumers perceive to be substitutes. A manager who fails to identify all the products that consumers see as substitutes for the firm's product will likely overestimate the firm's market power. The CEO of Coca-Cola would be foolish to view the company as a monopolist in the production of cola soft drinks and expect it to enjoy substantial market power. No doubt Coca-Cola's syrup formula is a closely guarded secret, but most soft-drink consumers consider rival brands of soft drinks, as well as a variety of noncarbonated drinks such as iced tea and Gatorade, as reasonable substitutes for Coca-Cola.

The geographic boundaries of a market should be just large enough to include all firms whose presence limits the ability of other firms to raise price without a substantial loss of sales. Two statistics provide guidelines for delineating the geographic dimensions of a market: (1) the percentage of sales to *buyers* outside the market and (2) the percentage of sales from *sellers* outside the market. Both percentages will be small if the geographic boundary includes all active buyers and sellers. These two guidelines for determining the geographic dimensions of a market are sometimes referred to as LIFO and LOFI: little in from outside and little out from inside.

As mentioned earlier, economists have developed several measures of market power. We will discuss briefly only a few of the more important measures.

Elasticity of Demand

One approach to measuring how much market power a firm possesses is to measure the elasticity of the firm's demand curve. Recall that a firm's ability to raise price without suffering a substantial reduction in unit sales is inversely related to the price elasticity of demand. The less elastic is demand, the smaller the percentage reduction in quantity demanded associated with any particular price increase. The more elastic is demand, the larger the percentage decrease in unit sales associated with a given increase in price. Also recall that the elasticity of demand is greater (i.e., more elastic) the larger the number of substitutes available for a firm's product. As demand becomes less elastic, consumers view the product as having fewer good substitutes.

Although a firm's market power is greater the less elastic its demand, this does not mean a firm with market power chooses to produce on the inelastic portion of its demand. In other words, market power does not imply that a manager produces where $|E| < 1$; rather, the less elastic is demand, the greater the degree of market power. We will demonstrate later in this chapter that a monopolist always chooses to produce and sell on the elastic portion of its demand.

Relation The degree to which a firm possesses market power is inversely related to the elasticity of demand. The less (more) elastic the firm's demand, the greater (less) its degree of market power. The fewer the number of close substitutes consumers can find for a firm's product, the less elastic is demand and the greater the firm's market power. When demand is perfectly elastic (demand is horizontal), the firm possesses no market power.

The Lerner Index

A closely related method of measuring the degree of market power is to measure the extent to which price deviates from the price that would exist under competition. The **Lerner index**, named for Abba Lerner, who popularized this measure, is a ratio that measures the proportionate amount by which price exceeds marginal cost

Lerner index
A ratio that measures the proportionate amount by which price exceeds marginal cost: $\frac{P - MC}{P}$.

$$\text{Lerner index} = \frac{P - MC}{P}$$

Price equals marginal cost when firms are price-takers, so the Lerner index equals zero under competition. The higher the value of the Lerner index, the greater the degree of market power.

The Lerner index can be related to the price elasticity of demand. In profit-maximizing equilibrium, marginal cost equals marginal revenue. Also recall from Chapter 6 that $MR = P(1 + 1/E)$. Thus the Lerner index can be expressed as

$$\text{Lerner index} = \frac{P - MR}{P} = \frac{P - P(1 + 1/E)}{P} = 1 - (1 + 1/E) = -\frac{1}{E}$$

In this form, it is easy to see that the less elastic is demand, the higher the Lerner index and the higher the degree of market power. The Lerner index is consistent with this discussion, showing that market power is inversely related to the elasticity of demand.

Relation The Lerner index, $\frac{P - MC}{P}$, measures the proportionate amount by which price exceeds marginal cost. Under perfect competition, the index is equal to zero, and the index increases in magnitude as market power increases. The Lerner index can be expressed as $-1/E$, which shows that the index, and market power, vary inversely with the elasticity of demand. The lower (higher) the elasticity of demand, the greater (smaller) the Lerner index and the degree of market power.

Cross-Price Elasticity of Demand

An indicator, though not strictly a measure, of market power is the cross-price elasticity of demand. Cross-price elasticity measures the sensitivity of the quantity purchased of one good to a change in the price of another good. It indicates whether two goods are viewed by consumers as substitutes. A large, positive cross-price elasticity means that consumers consider the goods to be readily substitutable. Market power in this case is likely to be weak. If a firm produces a product for which there are no other products with a high (positive) cross-price elasticity, the firm is likely to possess a high degree of market power.

The cross-price elasticity of demand is often used in antitrust cases to help determine whether consumers of a particular firm's product perceive other products to be substitutes for that product. Using cross-price elasticities, antitrust officials try to determine which products compete with one another. For example, antitrust officials might wish to determine the degree of market power enjoyed by Nike brand athletic shoes. Nike Corporation has spent a great deal of money advertising to establish a prominent position in the market for athletic shoes. To determine which other products compete with Nike, the cross-price elasticity of the quantity demanded of Nike shoes with respect to a change in the price of a rival's product can be calculated. Using such cross-price elasticities, antitrust officials can determine whether consumers view Nike as having any real competitors in the market for athletic shoes.

Relation If consumers view two goods to be substitutes, the cross-price elasticity of demand (E_{XY}) is positive. The higher the cross-price elasticity, the greater the perceived substitutability and the smaller the degree of market power possessed by the firms producing the two goods.

These are only a few of the measures of market power. The courts in antitrust cases and the Justice Department in merger and acquisition hearings sometimes use a combination of measures, including concentration ratios and share of the market. It is also not always clear just how high a cross elasticity or how low an elasticity constitutes "too much" market power. If you are ever involved in such a hearing, you should be aware of the problems in measuring market power. Illustration 12.1 shows the difficulty of determining what constitutes a market and what determines the amount of market power.

Now try Technical Problem 1.

12.2 BARRIERS TO ENTRY

Entry or potential entry of new firms into a market can erode the market power of existing firms by increasing the number of substitutes. Therefore, as a general case, a firm can possess a high degree of market power only when strong barriers

ILLUSTRATION 12.1

Monopoly at Microsoft?

Some of the most contentious issues in the recent antitrust case against Microsoft stemmed from the question of whether Microsoft had a monopoly in the market for PC operating systems. And, even if Microsoft did have a monopoly in its Windows operating system, did it have sufficient market power to harm consumers? And, even if Microsoft possessed sufficient market power to harm consumers, would consumers benefit by breaking Microsoft up into two smaller companies? Don't think for a moment that we can answer these questions definitively in a short illustration, or even in a long one for that matter. We can't. But we can illustrate the rich complexities of these interesting questions by surveying the opinions of a number of economists as reported by various business news publications.

Alan Reynolds (Director of Economic Research at the Hudson Institute)

It was routinely reported that Microsoft's Windows software "runs on more than 90 percent of the world's PCs." This fraction would be worrisome if it meant that Microsoft had captured all but 10 percent of the *total market* for operating systems. To evaluate the usefulness of the reported market share, we must consider the market definition employed to make the calculation. As we emphasized in the text, a properly defined market should include all the products that consumers perceive to be substitutes. Reynolds argued that the Department of Justice defined the market for operating systems far too narrowly, and so inflated Windows' share of the operating system market.

The Justice Department defined the market in the Microsoft case to be "single-user computers with Intel microprocessors." Reynolds noted that this narrow definition of the market in which Microsoft competes excludes such competitors as Apple computers because they don't use Intel microprocessors; Sun Microsystems workstations; any operating system used as part of a business network (e.g., Solaris and UNIX); and operating systems used in handheld and subnotebook computers. In short, Reynolds believed

the Justice Department stacked the deck against Microsoft by excluding many genuine competitors of Microsoft's Windows operating system. Reynolds also noted that, in high-tech industries, dominant firms are normal: Quicken has 80 percent of the home-finance software market, Netscape once had 90 percent of the browser market, and Intel has 76 percent of the microprocessor chip market.

Richard Schmalensee (MIT Economist and Expert Witness for Microsoft)

During his testimony as an expert witness for Microsoft, Schmalensee made a particularly insightful point: Microsoft may indeed have owned most of the market for operating systems, but it did not have a high degree of market power and was not a harmful monopoly. Schmalensee calculated that, if Microsoft was indeed a monopolist wielding great market power because it faced little or no competition, the profit-maximizing price for Windows 98 would have been somewhere between $900 and $2,000. The Justice Department's attorney expressed his astonishment over this calculation by asking Schmalensee if he thought a price of $2,000 made sense as the profit-maximizing price for Microsoft to actually charge for Windows. "Of course not, because Microsoft faces significant long-run competition. That's precisely the point." As we explained in the text, the degree of market power a monopolist possesses depends on the availability of close substitutes. Schmalensee explained that not only did Windows 98 face potential competition from new entrants in the future, it also had to compete with two highly successful and widely available rival products: Windows 3.1 and Windows 95. Perhaps a consumer's best protection from the alleged Microsoft monopoly was to own an early version of Windows.

Franklin Fisher (MIT Economist and Expert Witness for Department of Justice)

"Microsoft has engaged in anticompetitive conduct that has no compelling economic justification but for its effect of restricting competition," according to testimony in the case by Franklin Fisher, an expert in antitrust matters pertaining to monopoly practices.[a]

The government introduced into evidence numerous internal Microsoft memos and strategy documents. The language in these documents painted a picture of a firm obsessed with beating its rivals in every way possible. In one e-mail circulated among the top executives at Microsoft on the topic of subverting rival Java software language: "Subversion has always been our best tactic . . . Subversion is almost always a better tactic than a frontal assault. It leaves the competition confused; they don't know what to shoot at anymore." While the tactics employed by Microsoft to beat its rivals do seem ruthless to us, we suspect the same kind of memos would surface if the trial involved Pfizer, Toyota, Bank of America, or any other profit-maximizing firm.

The Economist (Editorial Opinion in the British Business News Magazine)

In an editorial opinion, *The Economist* expressed its concern that many of the high-tech markets in the New Economy experience network externalities, which increase the likelihood that a single firm may dominate a market. Once a dominant firm establishes a large, "installed" base of customers who use its brand of high technology, consumers may become locked in, creating a monopoly by blocking the entry of new firms and new technologies. For antitrust enforcement agencies charged with the duty of preventing new monopolies and breaking up old ones, the continual product improvement and falling computer product prices make it difficult to demonstrate that consumers are harmed by "monopoly abuse" in high-tech markets. Consequently, *The Economist* worried that Microsoft could stifle innovation and inflict serious harm to high-tech consumers and the New Economy.

The Economist, like Franklin Fisher, viewed Microsoft's business behavior as evidence of its intent to use its market power to maintain its market dominance. "An amazing trail of e-mails and management papers has depicted a company ready, it seems, to do almost anything to protect its Windows monopoly . . . When, as in the Microsoft case, a monopolist's conduct seems to be chilling innovation in markets in which the competition is largely defined by innovation, the argument for antitrust intervention is compelling."

Gary Becker (Nobel Prize–Winning Economist at University of Chicago)

The Department of Justice proposed breaking Microsoft into two independent firms: an operating-system company (Windows) and an applications company (MS Office, Internet Explorer, and other Microsoft applications). DOJ believed a breakup was needed to encourage faster technological innovation. Becker saw two problems with the Justice Department's arguments. First, economists are not sure that competition fosters greater rates of innovation than monopoly. Becker referred to the original thinking on this issue by Joseph Schumpeter (1883–1950), who believed that monopoly markets experience higher rates of innovation than competitive ones. Monopolies stimulate more technological innovation, according to Schumpeter, because they don't have to worry about competitors (quickly) imitating their innovations, driving down their profits.

Becker also argued that the Department of Justice has not provided any quantitative evidence that the dominant position held by Microsoft in operating systems had slowed technical progress in the computer-Internet industry:

> The government and its experts cite a few potential innovations that were supposedly discouraged by Microsoft's aggressive behavior. Even if these examples are valid, the government does not consider whether there have been other innovations stimulated by a large market for new software applications made possible by the dominant Windows platform.

Over the last 40 years, enormous technological progress has occurred in the computer-Internet industry. That progress, Becker pointed out, did not slow down as Microsoft built its powerful position in operating systems during the last 20 years of this period. Maybe Microsoft's rivals who complained in court were hoping the Justice Department would *protect* them from competition rather than *promote* competition?

As we told you at the beginning of this Illustration, we wish we could give you the answer to all of these questions, but we can't. Indeed, the answers proved difficult for all involved in this case. Eventually, the trial judge, Judge Thomas Penfield Jackson, found Microsoft guilty of illegal monopolization and ordered Microsoft to be split into two firms. On appeal, the U.S. Appeals

(Continued)

Court reversed the breakup order and removed Judge Jackson from the case. In November 2001, Microsoft and the Justice Department reached a settlement on penalties and remedies that received final approval in November 2002 by the new judge in the case, Judge Colleen Kollar-Kotelly. Clearly, the question of illegal monopolization proved to be quite challenging for all concerned. You should try to reach your own conclusion and discuss your reasoning with classmates and your professor. Now, more than 15 years after settlement, the decision in this landmark antitrust case continues to be debated by antitrust scholars, economists, and lawyers.

[a]Niles Lathem, "Feds Wrapping Up: MIT PROF:MSFT Has Monopoly" *New York Post*, January 6, 1999.

Sources: Alan Reynolds, "U.S. v. Microsoft: The Monopoly Myth," *The Wall Street Journal*, April 4, 1999; "Big Friendly Giant," *The Economist*, January 30, 1999; John R. Wilke and Keithe Perine, "Final Government Witness Testifies Against Microsoft in Antitrust Trial," *The Wall Street Journal*, January 6, 1999; "Lessons from Microsoft," *The Economist*, March 6, 1999; Gary S. Becker, "Uncle Sam Has No Business Busting Up Microsoft," *BusinessWeek*, June 19, 2000; Don Clark, Mark Wigfield, Nick Wingfield, and Rebecca Buckman, "Judge Approves Most of Pact, in Legal Victory for Microsoft," *The Wall Street Journal*, November 1, 2002.

---

strong barrier to entry
A condition that makes it difficult for new firms to enter a market in which economic profits are being earned.

to the entry of new firms exist. A **strong barrier to entry** exists when it is difficult for new firms to enter a market where existing firms are making an economic profit. Strong barriers to entry hinder the introduction of new, substitute products and protect the profits of firms already in the market.

An example of a strong barrier to entry is a cable TV franchise granted by a city government to only one cable company. This fortunate company is protected from other firms' competing away any economic profits and is close to being a monopoly. Note that we said "close" to being a monopoly because the cable company has some outside competition even though it is the only cable company in town. Possible substitutes, though certainly not perfect ones, might be regular broadcast television, satellite dishes, radio, books and magazines, rental movies, and so on. Thus the firm would be a monopoly if the cable TV market is the relevant market but *not* a monopoly if the entertainment market is the relevant market. We should note that in cases in which a government body protects a firm from entry by other firms into a market, it typically regulates the protected firm.

Weak barriers to entry generally exist in most retail markets. Retail stores typically do not have much market power because entry by other firms into the market is easy and there are good substitutes for the products of firms selling in the market. The products are not perfect substitutes, however, because other firms cannot sell identical products in the identical location. Nonetheless, firms can produce close substitutes. Therefore, no retail firm has much market power because it cannot raise its price much above its rivals' without a substantial loss of sales.

In this chapter we will focus on *structural* entry barriers, which are barriers arising from cost and/or demand conditions in the market. Later in Chapter 13 we will examine some *strategic* entry barriers, which are barriers created by altering the way potential rivals view the profitability of entering.

Barriers Created by Government

Possibly the most effective and durable kind of entry barrier is created when a government agency or commission limits the number of firms that can legally operate in a particular market. Typically this is accomplished by requiring firms to hold government-issued licenses or permits in order to legally supply goods or services in a specific market. Then, by strictly limiting the number of these licenses and permits, government can restrict supply in the protected market and effectively keep prices artificially high. The reasons government agencies give for restricting entry into markets frequently emphasize the need for government to promote consumer safety, quality of the environment, working conditions for labor, and employment of efficient production processes and technology. Recognizing that prices are likely to be higher when entry is restricted, government agencies may choose to regulate prices in the industries where licenses impede the entry of new firms.

Some examples of barriers created by government include the Federal Communications Commission (FCC) granting operating licenses to radio and television stations, and local governments granting exclusive franchises for various types of utility services such as electricity, water, cable television, and local telephone service. When government creates a monopoly franchise, such as a public utility, the monopolist is nearly always subject to price regulation by a government agency. In other examples of licensing and permitting—such as barbershops, nail salons, chiropractors, home builders, and taxicabs—a large number of firms will be granted licenses, and government then relies on competition among rival licensees to keep prices "fair" rather than directly regulating prices. As you would expect, when government entry barriers create a high degree of market power, the resulting future stream of protected profit will drive up the price that new firms would be willing to pay for the right to operate in such a market. Illustration 12.2 examines the regulation of taxicabs in New York City to show you how the value of a government license to operate can be undermined by changes in rules that allow new competitors to enter a protected market.

Another potentially effective government barrier to competition lies in the patent laws. These laws make it possible for a person to apply for and obtain the exclusive right to manufacture a specific type of product (a product patent) or to manufacture a good or service by means of a specified process that provides an absolute cost advantage (a process patent). Holding either type of patent, however, does not necessarily create substantial or durable market power because patents do not prevent rival firms from developing closely related substitute goods in the case of *product* patents and developing virtually identical production processes in the case of *process* patents. Many years ago International Business Machines (IBM) possessed the exclusive right to produce its patented personal computer. IBM PCs were the de facto standard for buyers of personal computers, making IBM the

ILLUSTRATION 12.2

Diamonds Are Forever—Entry Barriers Are Not

Since the inception of its medallion program in 1937, New York City has controlled entry into its taxicab market by strictly limiting the number of medallions issued.[a] The taxicab medallion gives the owner the right to operate one taxicab not just for one year but *forever*. In most years the only way for a new taxicab to enter the New York City market is for the new cab owner to buy an existing medallion from another cab owner. The market price of a single taxicab medallion in New York City reached a million dollars a couple of years ago. It is not surprising that the market price of a taxi medallion is high since buyers will rationally bid up medallion prices to levels that are approximately equal to what they estimate the present value to be for the expected stream of future profits from operating a taxicab in New York City forever. Many other large cities around the world have also implemented medallion systems like the one in New York City. Taxicab medallions worldwide are now arguably more valuable than diamonds; but unlike diamonds, medallions are not actually "forever."

Coincidentally, it was in 1938, just a year after New York City created the world's first taxicab medallion system that the famous diamond company De Beers launched its phenomenally successful advertising campaign that originated the expression "diamonds are forever" and perhaps permanently transformed ordinary diamonds into the coveted symbol of eternal love. Critics of taxicab regulation have on occasion likened owning a New York City taxicab medallion to owning a very large diamond. This would be a mistake, however, because over the past year the market price of taxicab medallions in New York dropped about $170,000—even as diamond prices continued to rise. Furthermore, the average prices of medallions dropped 17 percent in Chicago, and 20 percent in Boston, and the medallion price in Philadelphia is now in a free fall with no bottom in sight. After so many years of steady price increases, why are taxi medallion prices falling now?

To see why medallion prices are falling you need to understand that protection "forever" from the entry of more taxicabs into the marketplace lasts only until some clever entrepreneur finds an alternative way to break into the taxicab market without buying a medallion. And this is exactly what is currently happening in taxicab markets around the world.

Taxicabs in large cities have always competed with other kinds of car services. New Yorkers will find bright yellow taxicabs with medallions attached to their hoods competing for passengers with so-called livery cabs (pronounced like "delivery"). Livery cabs are legally distinguished from medallion taxicabs in a number of ways, but two of these distinctions are especially important: (1) livery cab owners are not required to buy medallions, and (2) livery cabs are not allowed to pick up passengers standing on the street who hail for a cab ride with a lifted hand. Only medallion taxicabs can legally pick up street hails. Livery cabs are restricted to serve only passengers who "prearrange" their trips typically through a radio dispatcher. It is this second legal distinction that is now failing to protect medallion owners from competition. Recently, judges and courts have ruled that in addition to using radio dispatch, a trip can also be legally prearranged when the cab is hailed by means of a smartphone application, a process known as "virtual hailing" or "e-hailing."

Now we are seeing a new form of livery cab company emerge. "App-based" car service companies such as Uber, Lyft, and Gett are increasingly taking riders away from medallion cabs because many tech-savvy riders prefer app-based car services for a number of reasons. App-based car services are easy to use: riders e-hail a cab by entering on their smartphones their current location and desired final destination, and then the first app-car driver to arrive gets their business. The fare is automatically charged to the credit card associated with their account, and the rider has the option to rate the driver's service with one to five stars, which of course promotes high-quality service. To make matters even worse for the medallion taxicabs, the app-based car service companies have launched a price war resulting in app-based fares that are sometimes lower than taxicab fares.

As you might have predicted, the owners of taxi medallions are fighting in courts to stop the entry of these app-based car services. Unfortunately for medallion owners, the new technology of smartphone hailing seems unstoppable now, and medallion prices seemed destined to continue falling. Even government barriers to entry are not guaranteed to be "forever." When barriers to entry create a large pool of protected economic profit, it is only a matter of time before new entrants find a way to get in.

[a]The Taxi and Limousine Commission in New York City issued 13,437 taxi medallions, a number that has not changed much at all since 1937.

Sources: Anne Kadet, "Car-App Car Services Compete for Passengers with Low Fares: A Luxury Car Service is Now Cheaper than a Taxi," *The Wall Street Journal*, October 10, 2014; Joshua Brustein, "Uber's Fare War on New York Taxis Puts Million-Dollar Medallions at Risk," *Bloomberg Businessweek.com*, July 7, 2014.

dominant PC manufacturer (but not a pure monopolist). The economic value of IBM's patented PC architecture was rapidly eroded by rival manufacturers of so-called "IBM clones" that employed superficially different circuits that circumvented patent laws and yet operated all software applications just like an IBM PC. As the PC market became saturated with IBM-compatible machines from dozens of rival manufacturers, IBM's profits from PCs declined and eventually IBM quit making personal computers. The patented architecture did not create a durable monopoly position for IBM, but the patents held by IBM certainly slowed the entry of rivals and also gave some buyers a reason to pay the somewhat higher price that IBM could charge.

Economies of Scale

Economies of scale can create a barrier to entry when the long-run average cost curve of a firm decreases over a wide range of output, relative to the demand for the product. Consequently, a new firm that wishes to enter this type of market must enter on a large scale to keep its costs as low as the large-scale firm or firms already operating in the market. The necessity of entering on a large scale is usually not a barrier to entry by itself, but when it is coupled with relatively small product demand, a strong barrier to entry can be created.

Consider an industry where four existing firms each produce about 200,000 units annually to take advantage of substantial economies of scale. At the current price of the product, annual sales are running at about 800,000 units per year. While many entrepreneurs could obtain the financial backing to enter this industry with a large-scale plant capable of producing 200,000 units, there is no room in the industry for a fifth large-scale producer without a significant decline in the price of the product. Even though a fifth firm could enter the industry producing perhaps 50,000 units annually, the per-unit production costs would be much higher than competitors' costs because of the substantial economies of scale. There just isn't room for a new firm to enter this industry on a scale big enough to enjoy costs as low as those of its rivals. In such situations, economies of scale create a barrier to entry.

Essential Input Barriers

An important source of market power, primarily one of historical importance, is a firm's ability to gain control of supplies of essential raw materials. If one firm (or perhaps a few firms) controls all the known supply of a necessary and essential ingredient for a particular product, the firm (or firms) can refuse to sell that ingredient to other firms at a price low enough for them to compete. When no others can produce the product, monopoly results. For many years the Aluminum Company of America (Alcoa) owned almost every source of bauxite, a necessary ingredient in the production of aluminum, in North America. The control of resource supply, coupled with certain patent rights, provided Alcoa with an absolute monopoly in aluminum production. It was only after World War II that

Now try Technical Problem 2.

the federal courts effectively broke Alcoa's monopoly in the aluminum industry. There have been other such historical examples, but at the present time there are few cases of firms with considerable market power because of exclusive control of a raw material.

Brand Loyalties

On the demand side, older firms may have, over time, built up the allegiance of their customers. New firms can find this loyalty difficult to overcome. For example, no one knows what the service or repair policy of a new firm may be. The preference of buyers can also be influenced by a long successful advertising campaign; established brands, for instance, allow customers recourse if the product should be defective or fall short of its advertised promises. Although technical economies of scale may be insignificant, new firms might have considerable difficulty establishing a market organization and overcoming buyer preference for the products of older firms. A classic example of how loyalty preserves monopoly power can be found in the concentrated-lemon-juice market. ReaLemon lemon juice successfully developed such strong brand loyalties among consumers that rival brands evidently could not survive in the market. The situation was so serious that the courts forced ReaLemon to license its name to would-be competitors.

The role of advertising as a barrier to entry has long been a source of controversy. Some argue that advertising acts as a barrier to entry by strengthening buyer preferences for the products of established firms. On the other hand, consider the great difficulty of entering an established industry without access to advertising. A good way for an entrenched monopoly to discourage entry would be to get the government to prohibit advertising. The reputation of the old firm would enable it to continue its dominance. A new firm would have difficulty informing the public about the availability of a new product unless it was able to advertise. Thus advertising may be a way for a new firm to overcome the advantages of established firms. The effect of advertising on entry remains a point of disagreement among economists.

Consumer Lock-In

switching costs
Costs consumers incur when they switch to new or different products or services.

consumer lock-in
High switching costs make previous consumption decisions very costly to change.

For some products or services, consumers may find it costly to switch to another brand—either an existing rival's brand or a new entrant's brand of product or service. Some of the kinds of **switching costs** incurred by consumers include things such as installation or initiation fees, search costs to learn about availability and prices of substitutes, and costs of learning how to use a new or different product or service. When high switching costs make previous consumption decisions so costly to alter that rivals do not believe they can induce many, if any, consumers to change their consumption decisions, then a situation known as **consumer lock-in** results. Consumer lock-in, of course, discourages new firms from entering a profitable market, and thus protects incumbent firms from new competition. High switching costs may arise naturally, or firms may strategically design products and services to have high switching costs to create a consumer lock-in barrier to entry.

While consumer lock-in can certainly create a strong barrier to entry, high monopoly profits nonetheless create a strong incentive for potential entrants to find ways to overcome a lock-in barrier. For example, when Microsoft decided to enter the market for household financial software with its Money program, Quicken had already established a virtual monopoly, and satisfied consumers seemed unwilling to incur the costs of switching from Quicken to Money. Microsoft, however, overcame this consumer lock-in barrier by designing its Money program to accept financial data files stored in Quicken's proprietary format so that switchers would not need to reenter their financial data. Microsoft also employed similar commands for its software and provided specialized help menus for users making the switch from Quicken. Thus, by lowering the switching costs facing consumers, Microsoft overcame a consumer lock-in barrier to entry and successfully ended Quicken's monopoly.

Network Externalities (or Network Effects)

network externalities (or network effects)
When the benefit or utility a consumer derives from consuming a good depends positively on the *number* of other consumers who use the good.

For most goods, the utility you get from consuming the good does not depend on how many other people consume the good. The value or benefit *you* receive is the same whether the good is purchased by 10 other people or 10 million other people. In contrast to this "normal" situation, however, there are a few special goods and services for which your utility varies directly with the total number of consumers of the good. In other words, a larger number of consumers buying a product will enhance the value you get from that product.[2] Such goods are characterized by **network externalities (or network effects)**. Some examples of goods or services believed to experience network effects include cellular phones, Internet access services, computer operating systems (such as Microsoft Windows or Apple OS X), e-mail, job search or dating service companies, and online auction websites (such as eBay).

There are two possible reasons why network externalities arise. First, network externalities are likely to characterize products and services when the usefulness of the product requires connecting consumers. For example, your utility from having a cell phone increases as the number of other people who have cell phones in the cellular network increases. Most people carry a cell phone to make and receive calls to and from many people, so the value of having a cell phone grows with the size of the network of people you can reach. An online dating service will be more valuable to single individuals looking for a companion if the dating service has a large membership. A large electricity

---

[2]It is also possible that a consumer's individual utility might vary *inversely* with the number of other consumers buying a particular good. This situation is sometimes referred to as a "snob effect" or negative network externality. Since negative network effects cannot create entry barriers, we will not analyze snob effects in this text.

transmission grid may be more valuable to individual homeowners than a small grid because a large grid will be more quickly restored to operation should it fail or be knocked out by a natural disaster of any kind (e.g., hurricane, wild fire, flood, etc.) Second, network externalities arise if complementary goods are important to users of the network good. For example, software applications are important complements to computer operating systems. As the number of Apple computer users increases, software companies will write more software for Apple computers, making ownership of Apple computers more satisfying, and in turn increasing demand for Apple computers. Repair service or troubleshooting can be extremely valuable for many products. Consumers may believe that manufacturers will provide better service or phone support when there are many users of a good. A computer "bug" in Microsoft Word is likely to get fixed much sooner than the same bug would be fixed in Corel's WordPerfect because the network of users is larger. And, even if Microsoft is slow to fix bugs, a large network of bloggers who use MS Word can offer free "work-arounds" on the Internet.

Our primary interest in network externalities in this textbook concerns barriers to entry. Network effects can make it difficult for new firms to enter markets where incumbent firms have established a large base or network of buyers. Because the value of the good depends on the number of users, it will be difficult to enter and compete as a small-size firm. Buyers want to be part of the large network of consumers held by the established incumbent.

As you may recall from our discussion in Chapter 1 (and also in Illustration 1.4) of common mistakes managers make, we strongly warned against making decisions for the purpose of gaining market share. As a general rule, maximizing market share is *not* equivalent to maximizing profit and the value of the firm. However, we also pointed out that network externalities can present an exception to this rule. In a network industry, a price cut by Firm A, which causes a number of buyers to switch from rival firms to Firm A, can set in motion a *self-reinforcing* or *snowball process*. The initial gain in Firm A's market share adds to its network size, causing even more buyers to switch from rivals, in turn further increasing Firm A's network size and so on until the market tips all the way to Firm A. In this scenario, the profit-maximizing price is lower than it would be if there were no network externalities. Gaining market share can lead to higher profit under these circumstances.

It follows that when network externalities are significant, an incumbent firm possessing a large number of consumers may enjoy a formidable barrier to entry. Buyers value the incumbent firm's large network and will be reluctant to switch to an entering firm's product for which the network of other consumers is too small to be attractive.

Sunk Costs as a General Barrier to Entry

The last structural barrier to entry we wish to discuss—sunk costs—can be viewed as a general type of entry barrier that can include the other entry barriers we have discussed above. You will find it helpful to think of managers as making two decisions. The first decision is whether to enter the market, and the second decision, if the manager chooses to enter, is how to set price and output to maximize profit in the market after entering. When a firm must incur "setup costs" to enter a market, these costs are sunk costs the firm must pay to enter and must be treated as the costs of entry. In other words, the costs of entering a market are the sunk costs incurred by making the decision to enter a market. These entry costs, because they are sunk costs, are not costs of doing business once a firm is an incumbent firm—that is, after a firm has entered. All sunk costs of entry should be ignored because they do not affect post-entry profit. However, entry costs can serve as a barrier to entry if they are so high that the manager cannot expect to earn enough future profit in the market to make entry worthwhile.

A simple example will be helpful here. Suppose there is a market in which the incumbent firms are making $1,200 of profit each month in long-run equilibrium. You would like to enter this market because after you enter and a new long-run equilibrium is established your firm and the other firms in the market will each earn $1,000 of profit each month. If there are no sunk costs of entry, then you would certainly enter the market. The decision would be an easy one because you could always exit the market if monthly profit later becomes negative. Alternatively, suppose you must incur a lump sum cost of $50,000 to enter and this cost is sunk—you cannot recover any of the $50,000 if you later decide to exit the market. What should you do now that entry is costly? Let's keep things simple and ignore the time value of money (i.e., assume your discount rate is zero). You would choose to enter this market if you were certain the market would last for at least 50 months. As you can see in this simple example, the higher the sunk costs of entry, the greater market profitability must be in order to make entry worthwhile. Thus, high sunk costs relative to the profitability of entry can serve as a barrier to entry.

As you can now see, the other entry barriers discussed previously may require an entering firm to incur some amount of sunk costs to enter the market. Economies of scale *may* create a barrier to entry *if* sunk set-up costs must be incurred to acquire a production facility large enough to give you the same unit costs as incumbent firms. As an example of this, you may need to pay for an environmental impact study before you can build your plant. When access to essential inputs is restricted or when patents, licenses, advertising, switching costs or network externalities exist, a firm that wishes to enter must frequently incur costs to overcome these barriers. If the costs of overcoming a structural barrier are sunk and large relative to the profitability of entering the market, then sunk costs can serve as a barrier to entry.

Despite the existence of barriers to entry, firms can lose and have lost their positions of extensive market power. Even quite strong barriers to entry can be overcome. A monopolist can become complacent in its protected position and allow inefficiencies to enter the production process. This raises the cost, and hence the price, and allows new, more efficient firms to enter the market. Some

Now try Technical Problem 3.

potential entrants are ingenious enough to find ways to lower cost, or (as noted earlier) get around patent protection, or overcome brand loyalty to the established firm. Thus barriers to entry cannot completely protect the established firm with great market power.

12.3 PROFIT MAXIMIZATION UNDER MONOPOLY: OUTPUT AND PRICING DECISIONS

We will now analyze the profit-maximizing decision of firms that are pure monopolies. Keep in mind that the fundamentals of this monopoly decision apply to a large extent to all firms with market power. The manager of a monopoly treats the market demand curve as the firm's demand curve. As was the case for perfect competition, we assume that the manager wishes to maximize profit. Thus the manager of a monopoly firm chooses the point on the market demand curve that maximizes the profit of the firm. While the manager of a monopoly does, in fact, determine the price of the good, price cannot be chosen independent of output. The manager must choose price and output combinations that lie on the market demand curve.

In Figure 12.1, for example, if the manager wishes to charge a price of $14 per unit, the monopoly firm can sell (consumers will buy) only 900 units of the product. Alternatively, if the manager decides to sell 900 units, the highest

FIGURE 12.1

Demand and Marginal Revenue Facing a Monopolist

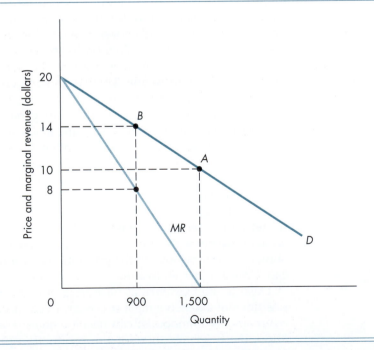

price that can be charged for this output is $14. So, while the monopolist can choose both price and output, the two choices are not independent of one another.

In practice, some monopolists choose price and let market demand determine how many units will be sold, whereas other monopolists choose the level of output to produce and then sell that output at the highest price market demand allows. Consider your electric utility company. Electric utilities set the price of a unit of electricity, say, 10 cents per kilowatt-hour, and then stand ready to supply as many kilowatt-hours as consumers wish to buy at that price. You can be sure that your electric company has estimated its demand function and knows approximately how much electricity will be demanded at various prices.

Alternatively, an automobile manufacturer might decide to produce 300,000 cars of a particular model in a given year. The manufacturer sells these cars at the highest possible price given the existing market demand. Again, you can be sure that the automobile manufacturer has estimated the demand for its cars and knows approximately the average price at which each car can be sold.

Given the demand curve facing a monopolist, choosing price to maximize profit is equivalent to choosing output to maximize profit. To be consistent with our discussion of profit maximization under perfect competition, we will view the monopolist as choosing *output* to maximize profit.

The basic principle of profit maximization—profit is maximized by producing and selling the output at which marginal cost equals marginal revenue—is the same for the monopoly as for the competitive firm. A manager can increase profit by expanding output as long as the marginal revenue from the expansion exceeds the marginal cost of expanding output. A manager would reduce output if marginal revenue is less than marginal cost. The fundamental difference for a monopolist is that marginal revenue is not equal to price.

Principle   A monopolist chooses the point on the market demand curve that maximizes profit. If marginal revenue exceeds marginal cost, a profit-maximizing monopolist increases output. If marginal revenue is less than marginal cost, the monopolist does not produce these additional units.

Demand and Marginal Revenue for a Monopolist

A monopoly, facing a downward-sloping demand, must lower the price in order to sell more. As shown in Figure 12.1 and discussed in Chapter 6, marginal revenue is less than price for every unit sold except the first. You will recall that marginal revenue is the change in the firm's total revenue from an additional unit of sales; symbolically, $MR = \Delta TR/\Delta Q$. In Figure 12.1, if the firm sells 900 units at $14 each, you can see from the marginal revenue curve that the marginal or additional revenue from selling the 900th unit is $8. This means that reducing the price just enough to increase sales from 899 to 900 adds $8 to the firm's revenue, rather than the $14 price at which the 900th unit is sold. The reason is that to sell the 900th unit, the firm must reduce the price on the 899 units it could have sold at the slightly higher price.

Although we set forth a technical analysis of the relation between MR and P in Chapter 6, we can perhaps give you a bit more understanding of why MR is less than P with a hypothetical example. Suppose you manage a small appliance store that has been selling 20 radios a day at $50 apiece. You want to increase your sales of radios, so one day you reduce the price to $49. Sure enough, you sell 21 radios that day at the reduced price. So you sold one more at $49. You check the cash register and compare the receipts with those from previous days. You had been receiving $1,000 (= $50 × 20). Now you see that you have taken in $1,029 (= $49 × 21) from selling radios. Your revenue increased by $29, but what happened to the $49 at which the additional radio was sold? Did someone steal $20 from the register? What happened was that, to sell the 21st radio, you had to take a $1 price reduction on the 20 you could have sold at $50. This $1 price reduction accounts for the "missing" $20.

Figure 12.1 illustrates the relation between demand and marginal revenue for a linear demand curve. When demand is linear, marginal revenue is twice as steep as demand and consequently lies halfway between demand and the vertical axis. When MR is positive, between 0 and 1,500 units, demand is elastic. When MR is negative, above 1,500 units, demand is inelastic. When MR equals 0, at 1,500 units, demand is unitary elastic.

Now try Technical
Problems 4–5.

> **Relation** The market demand curve is the demand curve for the monopolist. Because the monopolist must lower price to sell additional units of output, marginal revenue is less than price for all but the first unit of output sold. When marginal revenue is positive (negative), demand is elastic (inelastic). For a linear market demand, the monopolist's marginal revenue is also linear, with the same vertical intercept as demand, and is twice as steep.

Maximizing Profit at Southwest Leather Designs: An Example

Southwest Leather Designs specializes in the production of fashionable leather belts for women. Southwest's original designs are sometimes imitated by rival leather goods manufacturers, but the Southwest logo is a registered trademark that affords the company some protection from outright counterfeiting of its products. Consequently, Southwest Leather enjoys a degree of market power that would not be present if imitators could make identical copies of its belts, trademark and all.

Table 12.1 presents the demand and cost conditions faced by the manager of Southwest Leather Designs. Columns 1 and 2 give the demand schedule for 1,000 through 9,000 units of output (leather belts) in discrete intervals of 1,000. Column 3 shows the associated total revenue schedule (price times quantity). The total cost of producing each level of output is given in column 4. The manager computes profit or loss from producing and selling each level of output by subtracting total cost from total revenue. Profit is presented in column 7. Examination of the

TABLE 12.1

Profit Maximization for Southwest Leather Designs

(1) Output (Q)	(2) Price (P)	(3) Total revenue (TR = PQ)	(4) Total cost (TC)	(5) Marginal revenue $\left(MR = \dfrac{\Delta TR}{\Delta Q}\right)$	(6) Marginal cost $\left(SMC = \dfrac{\Delta TC}{\Delta Q}\right)$	(7) Profit (π)
0	$40.00	$ 0	$40,000	—	—	$−40,000
1,000	35.00	35,000	42,000	$35.00	$ 2.00	−7,000
2,000	32.50	65,000	43,500	30.00	1.50	21,500
3,000	28.00	84,000	45,500	19.00	2.00	38,500
4,000	25.00	100,000	48,500	16.00	3.00	51,500
5,000	21.50	107,500	52,500	7.50	4.00	55,000
6,000	18.92	113,520	57,500	6.02	5.00	56,020
7,000	17.00	119,000	63,750	5.48	6.25	55,250
8,000	15.35	122,800	73,750	3.80	10.00	49,050
9,000	14.00	126,000	86,250	3.20	12.50	39,750

profit column indicates that the maximum profit ($56,020) occurs when Southwest Leather Designs sells 6,000 belts at a price of $18.92.

The manager of Southwest Leather Designs can reach the same conclusion using the marginal revenue–marginal cost approach. Marginal revenue and marginal cost are shown, respectively, in columns 5 and 6. The marginal revenue from selling additional leather belts exceeds the marginal cost of producing the additional belts until 6,000 units are sold. After 6,000 units the marginal revenue for each of the next 1,000 belts is $5.48 per belt while the marginal cost for each of the next 1,000 belts is $6.25 per belt. Clearly, increasing output and sales from 6,000 to 7,000 belts would lower profit. Thus profit must increase until 6,000 units are produced; then profit decreases thereafter. This is the same solution that was obtained by subtracting total cost from total revenue: An output of 6,000 belts maximizes profit.

The example in Table 12.1 is shown graphically in Figure 12.2. Because marginal revenue and marginal cost are per-unit changes in revenue and cost over discrete changes in output of 1,000 units, we plot these values in the middle of the 1,000-unit interval. For example, marginal revenue for the first 1,000 units sold is $35 per unit for each of these 1,000 units. We plot this value of marginal revenue ($35) at 500 units of output. We do this at all levels of output for both marginal revenue and marginal cost.

In Figure 12.2, marginal revenue equals marginal cost at 6,000 units of output, which, as you saw from the table, is the profit-maximizing level of output. The demand curve shows that the price that Southwest Leather Designs will charge for the 6,000 belts is $18.92.

We turn now from a specific numerical example of profit maximization for a monopolist to a more general graphical analysis of a monopolist in the short run. In this case, we will assume for analytical convenience that output and price are continuously divisible.

Now try Technical Problem 6.

FIGURE 12.2

Profit Maximization for Southwest Leather Designs: Choosing Output

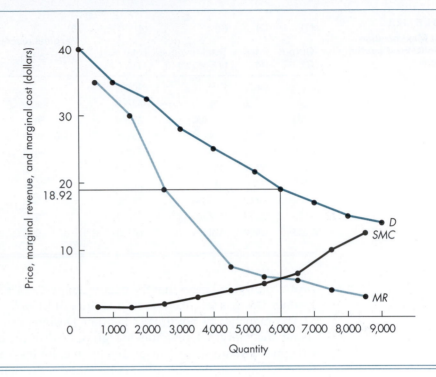

Short-Run Equilibrium: Profit Maximization or Loss Minimization

A monopolist, just as a perfect competitor, attains maximum profit by producing and selling the rate of output for which the positive difference between total revenue and total cost is greatest; or it attains a minimum loss by producing the rate of output for which the negative difference between total revenue and total cost is least. As long as total revenue covers total avoidable cost, this condition occurs when marginal revenue equals marginal cost. As was the case for the perfectly competitive firm, when price is less than average variable cost, the manager shuts down production in the short run.[3] We will first discuss profit maximization and then loss minimization.

The position of short-run equilibrium is easily described graphically. Figure 12.3 shows the relevant cost and revenue curves for a monopolist. Because

_____

[3]When firms employ quasi-fixed inputs, the firm's total avoidable cost will include total variable cost (_TVC_) _and_ total quasi-fixed cost (_TQFC_). Thus, firms with quasi-fixed costs should produce, rather than shut down, only when total revenue covers total variable cost plus total quasi-fixed cost (_TR_ ≥ _TVC_ + _TQFC_) or, equivalently, when price covers average variable cost plus average quasi-fixed cost (_P_ ≥ _AVC_ + _AQFC_). Unless we specifically state that a firm employs quasi-fixed inputs, we will keep matters simple and assume that total _avoidable_ cost is identical to total _variable_ cost (i.e., _TQFC_ = 0). Illustration 12.3 analyzes a firm's pricing decision when quasi-fixed costs are present.

FIGURE 12.3

Short-Run Profit-Maximizing Equilibrium under Monopoly

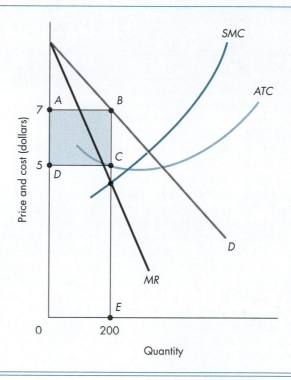

AVC and *AFC* are not necessary for exposition, they are omitted. Note that demand is the downward-sloping market demand curve. Marginal revenue is also downward-sloping and lies below the demand curve everywhere except at the vertical intercept. The short-run cost curves confronting a monopolist are derived in exactly the fashion described in Chapter 8 and have the typically assumed shapes. Figure 12.3 shows a situation in which price exceeds average total cost, and thus the monopolist earns an economic profit.

The monopolist maximizes profit by producing 200 units of output where *MR* = *SMC*. From the demand curve, the monopolist can (and will) charge $7 per unit. Total revenue is $1,400 (= $7 × 200), or the area of the rectangle 0*ABE*. The average total cost of producing 200 units of output is $5. Total cost of producing 200 units is $1,000 (= $5 × 200), or the area of the rectangle 0*DCE*. Economic profit is *TR* minus *TC*, $400 (= $1,400 − $1,000), or the shaded area *ABCD*. Because price is greater than average total cost at the equilibrium output of 200 units, the monopolist earns an economic profit. This need not be the case, however.

People often have the idea that monopoly firms can always make a profit; if the firm is making losses, it can simply raise price until it makes a profit. It is,

ILLUSTRATION 12.3

Quasi-Fixed Costs and Pricing Decisions by Stainless Steel Makers

The CEO of Universal Stainless & Alloy Products Inc., a capital-intensive manufacturer of specialty steel products that possesses some degree of market power (specialty stainless steel is not a homogeneous commodity) raised its prices *twice* over a 30-day period, according to a recent article in *The Wall Street Journal*.[a] According to the CEO, the price hikes were in direct response to *falling* demand for stainless-steel products. Can raising price be the optimal response to falling demand? The short answer: No. In this Illustration we will examine the confusion experienced by Universal and several other stainless-steel makers when they raised their prices to counter falling demand for stainless-steel product.

The source of confusion for the stainless-steel CEOs concerns their apparent misunderstanding of the role fixed costs play in decision making, both fixed and quasi-fixed costs in the stainless-steel industry. As we have stressed in Chapters 3, 11, and again in this chapter, "regular" fixed costs do not matter for decision-making purposes. Managers should never make production or pricing decisions for the purpose of spreading fixed costs over more units of output. Furthermore, the firm's decision to shut down in the short run (or to exit in the long run) is decided by comparing revenue to avoidable costs: When total revenue covers total avoidable costs, keep producing; if not, shut down (or exit in the long run). Fixed costs play no role in the short-run shutdown decision or the pricing and production decisions because they must be paid even if output is zero. In contrast, any *quasi*-fixed costs a firm might incur *do* matter, but only for making the shutdown decision in the short run. As we explained in Chapter 11 and this chapter, because quasi-fixed costs can be avoided if output is zero, the firm's avoidable costs include both variable costs and quasi-fixed costs. Thus, a stainless-steel firm that employs quasi-fixed inputs will produce in the short run only if total revenue covers total avoidable cost, which is the sum of variable costs of production plus the quasi-fixed costs. As you can see, the existence of quasi-fixed costs *increases* the amount of revenue (i.e., raises the shutdown price) that must be reached

to continue producing rather than shut down in the short run.

The *WSJ* article quotes several of the CEOs as they explain their reasoning for raising their specialty steel prices. One stainless-steel executive explains his price hike as follows:

> Unlike (price) increases announced in recent years, this is obviously not driven by increasing global demand, but rather by fixed costs being proportioned across significantly lower demand.

In other words, decreasing demand caused a drop in the quantity of stainless sold, and this reduction in output caused an increase in average fixed costs because there were fewer tons of stainless-steel over which to spread or "proportion" the fixed costs. The figure below shows the demand for a stainless-steel maker that possesses some degree of market power and earns positive profit before falling demand causes a loss. The original demand and marginal revenue conditions, denoted D_A and MR_A, require price to be set at point a on demand in order to maximize profit prior to the decrease in demand ($SMC = MR_A$ at Q_A^*). (Notice that point a lies slightly above ATC, creating a positive profit for the steel firm.) When demand decreases to D_B, which also causes marginal revenue to shift to MR_B, the new optimal price is at point b on D_B ($SMC = MR_B$ at Q_B^*). As you can see, moving from point a to point b *must* reduce total revenue because both price and quantity fall. Even if the firm kept price unchanged after the decline in demand (see point f), total revenue would still decline. In either case, at point f or point b, profit is now negative because price is lower than average total cost.

What should the stainless-steel maker do once demand decreases? At least one mistake, raising the price of stainless-steel, was made, and perhaps a second mistake was made: continuing to produce stainless-steel rather than shutting down operations. Let's first consider the price hike. Raising price after a decrease in demand (i.e., setting price somewhere above point f along D_B), does several undesirable things. Raising price above point f on D_B instead of lowering price to point b only *adds* to the loss of sales when demand for stainless falls. The global recession caused demand for steel to shift leftward, which is something management

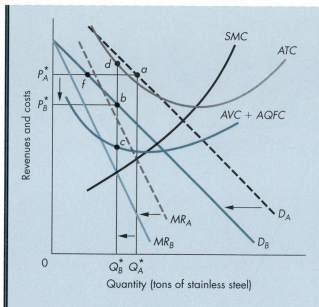

quasi-fixed cost of running the blower is avoidable if the plant shuts down. Unless the now lower total revenue can cover all the variable costs plus the quasi-fixed costs of running the pre-heater, the stainless-steel firm should shut down operation in the short run and lose only its total (unavoidable) fixed cost. According to the article, the stainless-steel makers are continuing to produce in the short run, so we will assume that total revenue is indeed sufficient to cover all avoidable costs. We show this situation in our figure. As you can verify at point b, the new price, P_B^*, is greater than the sum of average variable cost (AVC) plus average quasi-fixed cost ($AQFC$) at point c on the curve labeled "$AVC + AQFC$".

Now we can explain why raising price (incorrectly) *might* also cause the firm to make the wrong shutdown decision. Based on the figure we have constructed, the optimal price exceeds average avoidable cost (i.e., point b lies above point c), so total revenue from selling Q_B^* tons of steel at price P_B^* will indeed cover total avoidable cost. However, because the CEO made the wrong pricing decision by setting price somewhere above point f on D_B, we cannot be sure that total revenue at the *wrong* price will be sufficient to warrant continued production in the short run. While the *WSJ* article does not tell us whether or not the firm's revenue is covering all of its avoidable costs, you can see from this Illustration, nonetheless, how making the wrong pricing decision could cause the firm needlessly to shut down in the short run and lose more than the minimum possible loss.

We can summarize this rather complicated Illustration with two general points. First, as a general rule, when the demand for your product falls, raising price is not the optimal response if profit-maximization is your aim. We cannot help but wonder why the CEO at Universal Stainless & Alloy Products made this decision twice. Perhaps he raised price again after the first price hike failed to raise revenue or reduce average fixed costs. Second, making an incorrect pricing decision by setting price higher than optimal will result in lower total revenue, which could lead the manager mistakenly to shut down.

can do nothing about, but as you can see clearly in the figure, management's decision to raise prices made matters even worse. Not only will there be fewer tons of steel to spread fixed costs over—a completely irrelevant concern in any case—but stainless-steel demand is elastic here and raising price also reduces total revenue! Specifically, by choosing, incorrectly, to set price higher than point f instead of at point b, some total revenue is needlessly sacrificed because demand is elastic at point b (i.e., MR is positive).[b]

On the second issue of shutting down stainless-steel production, the CEO must distinguish between fixed cost and quasi-fixed cost, because stainless-steel production involves substantial quasi-fixed costs. At Universal's facility an enormous blower serves as a pre-heater by blasting 2,300 degree Fahrenheit hot air at the giant ladle holding the molten steel. The pre-heater must continue running even when no steel is being produced to prevent a melt-down of the refractory bricks that heat the ladle and to avoid damage caused by starting and stopping the motors. The cost of running the giant pre-heater is the same whether Universal makes one batch or a dozen batches of steel.

It is clear from this description of stainless-steel production that running the huge blower represents a quasi-fixed cost: A lump amount of "blowing" is needed for the first ton and this amount is constant as more tons are produced. And, in contrast to "regular" fixed costs, the

[a]This Illustration is based on Robert Guy Matthews, "Fixed Costs Chafe at Steel Mills," *The Wall Street Journal,* June 10, 2009, p. B2.
[b]In case you think we have contrived an elastic demand situation at point b, let us remind you that demand can never be inelastic at the profit-maximizing point on demand because SMC cannot be negative and so, where MR and SMC cross, MR cannot be negative (and demand cannot be inelastic) at this point.
Sources: Robert Guy Matthews, "Fixed Costs Chafe at Steel Mills," *The Wall Street Journal,* June 10, 2009, p. B2.

FIGURE 12.4
Short-Run Loss Minimization under Monopoly

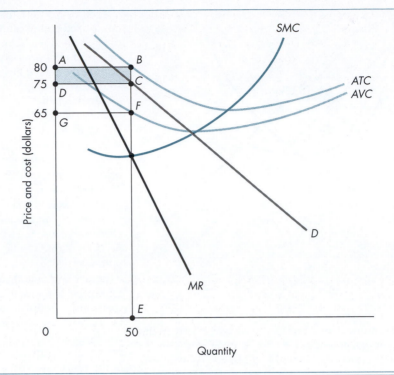

however, a misconception that all monopolies are ensured a profit. Figure 12.4 illustrates a monopolist that makes losses in the short run. Marginal cost equals marginal revenue at 50 units of output, which, from the demand curve, can be sold for $75 each. Total revenue, then, is $3,750 (= $75 × 50), or the area 0DCE. Because average total cost is $80 per unit, total cost is $4,000 (= $80 × 50), or the area 0ABE. Since total cost exceeds total revenue, the firm experiences a loss of $250 (= $4,000 − $3,750), which is the shaded area ABCD.

Note that in Figure 12.4 the monopolist would produce rather than shut down in the short run because total revenue (area 0DCE) exceeds the total variable cost of $3,250 (= $65 × 50), or area 0GFE. After all variable costs have been covered, there is still some revenue, $500 (area GDCF), left over to apply to fixed cost. Since total fixed cost in this example is $750 (= $15 × 50), or area ABFG, the firm loses less by producing 50 units than by shutting down. If the monopolist shuts down, it would, of course, lose its entire fixed cost of $750.

If demand decreases so that it lies below AVC at every level of output and the monopolist could not cover all its variable cost at any price, the firm would shut down and lose only fixed cost. This is exactly the same shutdown rule as that of the perfect competitor.

We should note that a monopolist would never choose a situation in which it was producing and selling an output on the inelastic portion of its demand.

When demand is inelastic, marginal revenue is negative (see Table 6.4). Because marginal cost is always positive, it must equal marginal revenue when the latter is also positive. Thus the monopolist will always be on the elastic portion of demand.

In the short run, the primary difference between a monopoly and a perfect competitor lies in the slope of the demand curve. Either may earn a pure profit; either may incur a loss.

Now try Technical Problems 7–9.

Principle   In the short run, the manager of a monopoly firm will choose to produce the output where $MR = SMC$, rather than shut down, as long as total revenue at least covers the firm's total avoidable cost, which is the firm's total variable cost ($TR \geq TVC$). The price for that output is given by the demand curve. If total revenue cannot cover total avoidable cost, that is, if total revenue is less than total variable cost (or, equivalently, $P < AVC$), the manager will shut down and produce nothing, losing an amount equal to total fixed cost.

Long-Run Equilibrium

A monopoly exists if there is only one firm in the market. Among other things, this statement implies that entry into the market is closed. Thus, if a monopolist earns an economic profit in the short run, no new producer can enter the market in the hope of sharing whatever profit potential exists. Therefore, economic profit is not eliminated in the long run, as was the case under perfect competition. The monopolist, however, will make adjustments in plant size as demand conditions warrant, to maximize profit in the long run.

Clearly, in the long run, a monopolist would choose the plant size designed to produce the quantity at which long-run marginal cost equals marginal revenue. Profit would be equal to the product of output times the difference between price and long-run average cost

$$\pi = P \times Q - LAC \times Q = Q(P - LAC)$$

New entrants cannot come into the industry and compete away profits—entry will not shift the demand curve facing the monopolist.

Demand conditions may change for reasons other than the entry of new firms, and any such change in demand and marginal revenue causes a change in the optimal level of output in both the short run and the long run. Suppose demand does change, due perhaps to a change in consumer income. In the short run, the manager will adjust output to the level where the new marginal revenue curve intersects the short-run marginal cost curve (or it will shut down if $P < AVC$). This short-run adjustment in output is accomplished without the benefit of being able to adjust the size of the plant to its optimal size. Recall from Chapter 9 that the plant size that minimizes the cost of production varies with the level of output. Hence, in the long run, the manager would adjust plant size to the level that minimizes the cost of producing the optimal level of output. If there is no plant size for which long-run average cost is less than price, the monopolist would not operate in the long run and would exit the industry.

FIGURE 12.5
Long-Run Profit Maximization under Monopoly

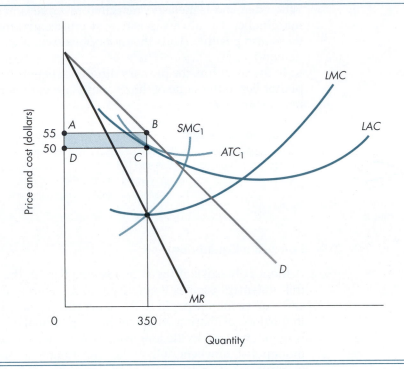

☐ **Principle** The manager of a monopoly firm maximizes profit in the long run by choosing to produce the level of output where marginal revenue equals long-run marginal cost ($MR = LMC$). unless price is less than long-run average cost ($P < LAC$), in which case the firm exits the industry. In the long run, the manager will adjust plant size to the optimal level; that is, the optimal plant is the one with the short-run average cost curve tangent to the long-run average cost at the profit-maximizing output level.

Now try Technical Problem 10.

This principle is illustrated in Figure 12.5. The level of output that maximizes profit in the long run is 350 units, the point at which $MR = LMC$. In the long run, the manager adjusts plant size so that 350 units are produced at the lowest possible total cost. In Figure 12.5, the optimal plant size is the one with short-run average total cost and marginal cost curves labeled ATC_1 and SMC_1, respectively. Thus the average cost of producing 350 units is $50 per unit. The manager will sell the 350 units at a price of $55 to maximize profit. Long-run profit is $1,750 [$= Q \times (P - LAC) = 350 \times (\$55 - \$50)$], or the area $ABCD$. By the now-familiar argument, this is the maximum profit possible under the given revenue and cost conditions.

12.4 PROFIT-MAXIMIZING INPUT USAGE

Thus far we have analyzed monopoly profit maximization in terms of the output decision. As was the case for competition, the manager can also maximize profit by choosing the optimal level of input usage. Choosing the optimal level of input usage results in exactly the same output, price, and profit level as choosing the optimal level of output would. We now discuss the monopoly firm's input decision assuming that there is only one variable input.

The analytical principles underlying the input decision for the manager of a monopoly are the same as those for managers of perfectly competitive firms. But since price does not equal marginal revenue for a monopoly, $P \times MP$ is not the correct measure of the **marginal revenue product** (**MRP**)—the increase in revenue attributable to hiring an additional unit of the variable input. Suppose a monopolist employs an additional unit of labor, which causes output to increase by the amount of the marginal product of labor. To sell this larger output, the manager must reduce the price of the good. Each additional unit adds marginal revenue (MR) to total revenue. Thus the additional unit of labor adds to total revenue an amount equal to marginal revenue times the marginal product of labor

$$MRP = \Delta TR / \Delta L = MR \times MP$$

For example, suppose hiring the 10th unit of labor increases output by 20 units ($MP = 20$). To sell these 20 additional units of output, the monopolist must lower price. Further suppose that marginal revenue is $5 per additional unit. Thus the additional revenue attributable to hiring the 10th unit of labor is the $5 additional revenue received on each of the 20 additional units of output produced and sold, or $100 (= $5 × 20). The marginal revenue product of the 10th unit of labor is $100.

Recall that in the case of perfect competition, marginal revenue product is measured by multiplying price (= MR) by the marginal product of labor. Also recall that MRP for a perfect competitor declines because marginal product declines. For a monopolist, marginal revenue product declines with increases in input usage not only because marginal product declines but also because marginal revenue declines as output is increased.

Figure 12.6 shows the positive portion of MRP below ARP, which is the relevant portion of the MRP curve for a monopolist employing labor as its only variable input. Just as for a perfectly competitive firm, a monopolist shuts down and hires no labor when the wage rate exceeds average revenue product ($w > ARP$) at the level of input usage where $MRP = w$. Suppose the wage rate is $45. To maximize profit, the manager should hire 400 units of labor at a wage rate of $45. To see why this is the optimal level of labor usage, suppose the manager hires only 300 units of labor. Hiring the 301st unit of labor adds slightly less than $58 to total revenue while adding only $45 to total cost. Clearly, hiring the 301st unit increases profit, in this case, $13 (= $58 − $45). The manager should continue to hire additional units of labor until $MRP = w_1 = $45 at point A in Figure 12.6. If the manager mistakenly hired more than 400 units, say, 500 units of labor, the additional revenue from hiring the last unit of labor ($30 for the 500th unit) is less than the additional cost, $45, and profit falls if the 500th worker is hired. Getting rid of the 500th worker lowers cost by $45 but revenue falls by only $30;

marginal revenue product (MRP)
The additional revenue attributable to hiring one additional unit of the input, which is also equal to the product of marginal revenue times marginal product, $MRP = MR \times MP$.

FIGURE 12.6

A Monopoly Firm's Demand for Labor

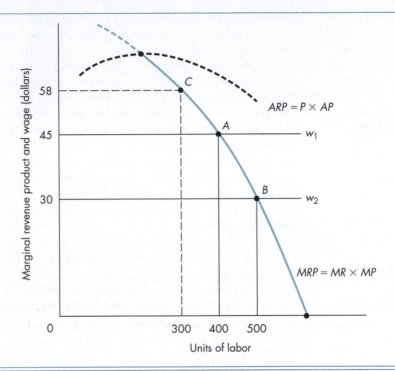

thus, reducing labor by 1 unit increases profit by $15. And each additional 1 unit reduction in labor similarly increases profit until labor usage is reduced down to the 400th worker.

If the wage rate falls to $30 per unit (shown by the horizontal line w_2), the manager should hire 500 units of labor (point B) to maximize monopoly profit. Similarly, at a wage of $58, the manager would hire 300 workers (point C). Thus you can see that, over the relevant range, the *MRP* curve is the monopolist's demand curve for a single variable input.

We now show that a monopolist would never choose a level of variable input usage at which the average revenue product is less than the marginal revenue product ($ARP < MRP$). If, at the level of input usage where $MRP = w$,

$$MRP > ARP$$

then

$$w > PQ/L$$

and

$$wL > PQ$$

which implies that total variable cost exceeds total revenue, and the profit-maximizing monopolist would hire 0 units of the variable input and shut down.

Now try Technical
Problems 11–12.

Principle When producing with a single variable input, a monopolist will maximize profit by employing that amount of the input for which marginal revenue product (MRP) equals the price of the input when input price is given. Consequently, the MRP curve, over the relevant range, is the monopolist's demand curve for the variable input when only one variable input is employed. The relevant range of the MRP curve is the downward-sloping, positive portion of MRP for which $ARP > MRP$.

As for the case of a competitive firm, the manager of a firm with market power that employs two or more variable inputs maximizes profits by choosing input levels so that the marginal revenue product equals the input price for all inputs simultaneously.

Recall that, for a price-taking firm, the profit-maximizing condition that the marginal revenue product of labor equals the wage rate ($MRP = w$) is equivalent to the profit-maximizing condition that product price equals marginal cost ($P = SMC$). By "equivalent" we mean that regardless of whether the manager chooses Q or L to maximize profit, the resulting levels of output, labor usage, and profit are identical. We will now demonstrate that, for a monopolist, the profit-maximizing condition $MRP = w$ is equivalent to the profit-maximizing condition $MR = SMC$.

Suppose the manager of a monopoly firm chooses the level of output to maximize profit. The optimal output for the monopolist is where

$$MR = MC$$

Recall from Chapter 8 that

$$SMC = \frac{w}{MP}$$

where MP is the marginal product of labor and w is its price. Substituting this equation for marginal cost, the profit-maximizing condition $MR = SMC$ can be expressed as

$$MR = \frac{w}{MP}$$

or

$$MR \times MP = w$$

$$MRP = w$$

Thus you can see that the two profit-maximizing rules are equivalent: $MR = MC$ implies $MRP = w$, and vice versa.

Relation For a monopolist, the profit-maximizing condition that the marginal revenue product of the variable input must equal the price of the input ($MRP = w$) is equivalent to the profit-maximizing condition that marginal revenue must equal marginal cost ($MR = MC$). Thus, regardless of whether the manager chooses Q or L to maximize profit, the resulting levels of input usage, output, price, and profit are the same in either case.

12.5 MONOPOLISTIC COMPETITION

As we pointed out at the beginning of this chapter, the general model of monopoly is useful in the analysis of firm behavior in other types of markets in which firms have some degree of market power but are not pure monopolies. Firms in such markets, facing downward-sloping demands, attempt to maximize profit in the same way a monopoly does: by setting $MR = MC$. In these intermediate markets, between firms with the most market power (monopoly) and firms with the least (perfect competition), certain complications arise for the profit-maximizing decision. In this section, we analyze intermediate market structure in which firms have the least market power of all firms that are not perfect competitors: monopolistic competition.

Monopolistically competitive markets are characterized by (1) a large number of relatively small firms; (2) products that are similar to, but somewhat different from, one another; and (3) unrestricted entry and exit of firms into and out of the market. The only difference between monopolistic competition and perfect competition is that under monopolistic competition firms produce a differentiated product. The major difference between monopolistic competition and monopoly is that under monopolistic competition firms can easily enter into and exit out of the market. Thus, as the name implies, monopolistic competition has characteristics of both monopoly and perfect competition.

Product differentiation under monopolistic competition prevents a firm's demand from becoming horizontal. Real or perceived differences between goods, though slight, will make them less than perfect substitutes. For example, gasoline stations in a particular city are good, but not perfect, substitutes for one another. Your car would run on gasoline from any gasoline station, but stations differ in location, and people's tastes differ: Some people prefer BP, some prefer ExxonMobil, some prefer the service at Joe's, others prefer Julie's service. And the differentiating characteristics go on and on. The most important point is that although the products are similar, they are differentiated, causing each firm to have a small amount of market power.

We will first set forth the theory of monopolistic competition in its original form, as developed by Edward Chamberlin in the 1930s.[4] Because each firm in the market sells a slightly differentiated product, it faces a downward-sloping demand curve, which is relatively elastic but not horizontal. Any firm could raise its price slightly without losing all its sales, or it could lower its price slightly without gaining the entire market. Under the original set of assumptions employed by Chamberlin, each firm's output is so small relative to the total sales in the market that the firm believes that its price and output decisions will go unnoticed by other firms in the market. It therefore acts independently.

As you will see, the theory of monopolistic competition is essentially a long-run theory; in the short run, there is virtually no difference between monopolistic

---

[4]E. H. Chamberlin, *The Theory of Monopolistic Competition* (Cambridge, MA: Harvard University Press, 1933).

competition and monopoly. In the long run, because of unrestricted entry into the market, the theory of monopolistic competition closely resembles the theory of perfect competition.

Short-Run Equilibrium

With the given demand, marginal revenue, and cost curves, a monopolistic competitor maximizes profit or minimizes loss by equating marginal revenue and marginal cost. Figure 12.7 illustrates the short-run, profit-maximizing equilibrium for a firm in a monopolistically competitive market. Profit is maximized by producing an output of Q and selling at price P.

In the situation illustrated, the firm will earn an economic profit, shown as the shaded area $PABC$. However, as was the case for perfect competition and monopoly, in the short run the firm could operate with a loss, if the demand curves lies below ATC but above AVC. If the demand curve falls below AVC, the firm would shut down.

In its original form, there appears to be little competition in monopolistic competition as far as the short run is concerned. Indeed Figure 12.7 is identical to one illustrating short-run equilibrium for a monopoly. In the long run, however, a monopoly cannot be maintained if there is unrestricted entry into the market. If firms are earning economic profit in the short run, other firms will enter and

FIGURE 12.7

Short-Run Profit Maximization under Monopolistic Competition

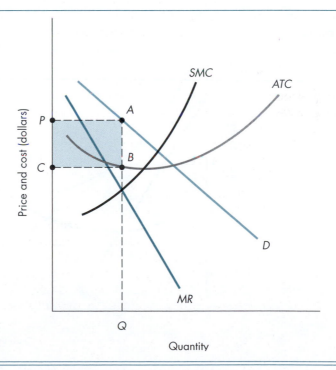

produce the product, and they will continue to enter until all economic profits are eliminated.

Long-Run Equilibrium

While the short-run equilibrium for a firm under monopolistic competition is similar to that under monopoly, the long-run equilibrium is more closely related to the equilibrium position under competition. Because of unrestricted entry, all economic profit must be eliminated in the long run, which occurs at an output at which price equals long-run average cost. This occurs when the firm's demand is tangent to long-run average cost. The only difference between this equilibrium and that for perfect competition is that, for a firm in a monopolistically competitive market, the tangency cannot occur at minimum average cost. Because the demand curve facing the firm is downward-sloping under monopolistic competition, the point of tangency must be on the downward-sloping range of long-run average cost. Thus the long-run equilibrium output under monopolistic competition is less than that forthcoming under perfect competition in the long run.

This long-run result is shown in Figure 12.8. *LAC* and *LMC* are the long-run average and marginal cost curves for a typical monopolistically competitive firm. Suppose that the original demand curve is given by D_m. In this case the

FIGURE 12.8

Long-Run Equilibrium under Monopolistic Competition

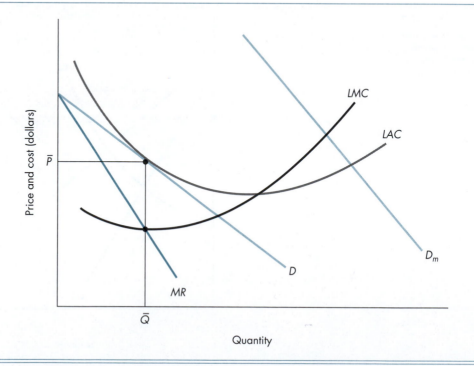

firm would be making substantial economic profits because demand lies above *LAC* over a wide range of output, and if this firm is making profits, potential new entrants would expect that other firms in the market are also earning economic profits. These profits would then attract new firms into the market. Even though the new firms would not sell exactly the same products as existing firms, their products would be very similar. So as new firms enter, the number of substitutes would increase and the demand facing the typical firm would shift backward and probably become more elastic (though not perfectly elastic). Entry will continue as long as there is some economic profit being earned. Thus entry causes each firm's demand curve to shift backward until a demand curve such as *D* in Figure 12.8 is reached. This long-run demand curve, *D*, is tangent to *LAC* at a price of *P* and output of $\overline{Q}$.

In such an equilibrium either an increase or a decrease in price by the firm would lead to losses. No further entry would occur as there are no economic profits to be earned in this market.

If too many firms enter the market, each firm's demand curve would be pushed so far back that demand falls below *LAC*. Firms would be suffering losses and exit would take place. As this happened, the demand curve would be pushed back up to tangency with *LAC*. Free entry and exit under monopolistic competition must lead to a situation where demand is tangent to *LAC*—where price equals average cost—and no economic profit is earned, but the firms do earn a normal profit.

The equilibrium in Figure 12.8 must also be characterized by the intersection of *LMC* and *MR*. Only at output $\overline{Q}$ can the firm avoid a loss, so this output must be optimal. But the optimal output requires that marginal cost equal marginal revenue. Thus at $\overline{Q}$, it must be the case that *MR = LMC*.

Now try Technical Problems 13–14.

> **Relation** Long-run equilibrium in a monopolistically competitive market is attained when the demand curve for each producer is tangent to the long-run average cost curve. Unrestricted entry and exit lead to this equilibrium. At the equilibrium output, price equals long-run average cost and marginal revenue equals long-run marginal cost.

In closing our discussion of monopolistic competition, we briefly mention two points. First, according to the original model as set forth here, firms act independently when making decisions, ignoring the actions of other firms in the market. In reality firms may not act independently when faced with competition from closely related firms, possibly because of proximity; in fact, they may exhibit a great deal of interdependence and intense personal rivalry. We will address this possibility at more length in the next chapter. This change in assumptions will not alter the long-run, zero-profit conclusions of the theory, however.

Short of getting the government to prevent entry, there is nothing firms in a monopolistically competitive market can do about having their profits competed away. Even if the firms were to conspire to fix a price, new firms would enter. Each firm would find its demand decreased and its sales reduced until price equaled average cost and economic profits were zero, although possibly at a higher price than would occur in the absence of the price-fixing agreement.

Second, we have emphasized that, under monopolistic competition, profits are competed away in the long run. This is correct in general. But we do not mean to imply that there is no opportunity for astute managers to postpone this situation to the future by innovative decision making. Firms selling in monopolistically competitive markets can and do advertise and change product quality in an effort to lengthen the time period over which they earn economic profit. Those managers who are successful in their marketing strategy can sometimes earn profit for a long time. Some firms can reduce their cost. However, successful strategies can be imitated by competitors' selling a product that is rather similar. Therefore, under monopolistic competition there is always a strong tendency for economic profit to be eliminated in the long run, no matter what strategies managers undertake.

12.6 IMPLEMENTING THE PROFIT–MAXIMIZING OUTPUT AND PRICING DECISION

Managers of firms that have some control over the price they charge should know the fundamentals of the theory of profit maximization by firms with market power. They should also know how to use empirical estimates of the demand for the firm's product and the cost equations for determining the price and level of output that maximize the firm's profit. This section describes how to use empirical analysis to find that optimal price and output. We devote most of this section to examining the price and output decision for a monopoly. However, as we stressed previously, the decision-making process for a monopoly is applicable to any firm with market power, with perhaps a few modifications for changes in the form of the demand and marginal revenue functions to account for differences in the market structure.

We will first outline how managers can, in general, determine the optimizing conditions. This outline gives a pattern for situations in which numerical estimates of the variables and equations are available. Then we present an example of how a firm can use this approach to determine the optimal level of output.

General Rules for Implementation

A manager must answer two questions when finding the price and output that maximizes profit. These two questions and the answers forthcoming from the theoretical analysis are summarized as follows:

1. Should the firm produce or shut down? *Produce as long as the market price equals or exceeds minimum average variable cost: $P \geq AVC_{min}$. Shut down otherwise.*
2. If production occurs, how much should the firm produce and what price should it charge? *Produce the output at which marginal revenue equals marginal cost—$MR = SMC$—and charge the price from the demand curve for the profit-maximizing output.*

ILLUSTRATION 12.4

Hedging Jet Fuel Prices: Does It Change the Profit-Maximizing Price of a Ticket?

Many companies engage in a financial practice called "hedging" when they use large amounts of a key input and wish to insure against sharp increases in the price of the important input. While the details of creating a hedge involve rather complex financial instruments—derivatives, futures contracts, and call and put options—the fundamental principle of hedging input prices is not difficult to understand as long as you remember that hedging is a form of insurance for protecting the firm from rising input prices. Hedging lowers the cost of *obtaining* an input, but it does not lower the cost of *using* an input.[a] At any point in time, the cost of using an input is whatever the input could be sold for at that time in the input market. Consequently, the input price that matters for making current decisions about price and output is the price of the input when it will be used in production, not the price created by hedging. This distinction is extremely important for managers to understand, and yet, many managers and business analysts are confused about the role of input price hedging in maximizing the profit and value of firms.

Southwest Airlines, for example, has been very aggressive in hedging the price of jet fuel over the past 20 years, and many airline industry analysts believe Southwest's successful jet fuel hedges made it possible for the airline to charge lower airfares than their rivals who were not so active or successful in jet fuel hedging. When a jet fuel hedge works successfully, the savings to Southwest can be substantial. In a typical year, Southwest burns over a billion gallons of jet fuel. In one recent year, when jet fuel prices rose sharply, Southwest's fuel hedges allowed it to buy jet fuel at a price of $1.98 per gallon while rival American Airlines paid $2.74 per gallon for its fuel. As a result of this successful hedging, Southwest's financial statement for the year showed a sizeable profit in the section where it reported earnings on hedging activity. We must emphasize, however, that the hedged price of jet fuel had no impact at all on the *economic profit from flying passengers*. In fact, all airlines incur identical per gallon costs for jet fuel because they all face the same current or spot price in jet fuel markets. For decision-making purposes, Southwest, as well as all other airlines, will not choose to make a flight unless airfare revenues can cover the total (avoidable) variable costs of the flight. The computation of variable fuel costs is done using the spot price of jet fuel at flight time rather than the historic cost of obtaining the jet fuel. Also, when determining air fares, Southwest and all other airlines possessing some degree of market power will follow the $MR = MC$ rule to find the profit-maximizing price on their respective demand curves. For profit-maximizing decisions it is the spot price, not the hedged price, of jet fuel that determines the marginal cost of making a flight. Thus, airfares will not be affected by hedging jet fuel, although successful hedging does increase the portion of the airline's profit attributable to the financial transactions associated with fuel hedging.

As a final cautionary note about hedging input prices, we must stress that not all hedging is successful, because input price changes are typically difficult to predict accurately. Southwest Airlines has on several occasions suffered substantial losses on its jet fuel hedges when crude oil prices fell unexpectedly, causing the price of jet fuel to fall as well.[b] Hedging input prices can add to the value of a firm when input prices rise sharply, but it can also be a burden when input prices fall. Either way, managers wishing to maximize profit from the production of goods and services should always use the actual market price of the input for making output and pricing decisions.

[a]You learned in Chapter 8 that the cost of *using* any input is what the firm gives up to employ the input in its own operation rather than selling, leasing, or renting the input to someone else. Even if the cost of obtaining an input is zero, the cost of using the input is its current market price. Recall from Illustration 8.2 that Jamie Lashbrook *obtained* two Super Bowl tickets for free and he learned that the cost for him to *use* the tickets was equal to $1,200 for each ticket, the amount other sport fans offered to pay him for his two tickets.
[b]In 2008, for example, Southwest Airlines reported a quarterly loss of $247 million on its fuel hedging activity, even as it reported positive profit from airline operations.

It follows from these rules that to determine the optimal price and output, a manager will need estimates or forecasts of the market demand of the good produced by the firm, the inverse demand function, the associated marginal revenue function, the firm's average variable cost function, and the firm's marginal cost function. We now set forth the steps that can be followed to find the profit-maximizing price and output for a firm with market power.

Step 1: Estimate the demand equation

To determine the optimal level of output, the manager must estimate the marginal revenue function. Marginal revenue is derived from the demand equation; thus the manager begins by estimating demand. In the case of a linear demand specification, the empirical demand function facing the monopolist can be written as

$$Q = a + bP + cM + dP_R$$

where Q is output, P is price, M is income, and P_R is the price of a good related in consumption. To obtain the estimated demand curve for the relevant time period, the manager must have forecasts for the values of the exogenous variables, M and P_R, for that time period. Once the empirical demand equation has been estimated, the forecasts of M and P_R (denoted $\hat{M}$ and $\hat{P}_R$) are substituted into the estimated demand equation, and the demand function is expressed as

$$Q = a' + bP$$

where $a' = a + c\hat{M} + d\hat{P}_R$.

Step 2: Find the inverse demand equation

Before we can derive the marginal revenue function from the demand function, the demand function must be expressed so that price is a function of quantity: $P = f(Q)$. This is accomplished by solving for P in the estimated demand equation in step 1

$$P = \frac{-a'}{b} + \frac{1}{b}Q$$
$$= A + BQ$$

where $A = \frac{-a'}{b}$ and $B = \frac{1}{b}$. This form of the demand equation is the *inverse demand function*. Now the demand equation is expressed in a form that makes it possible to solve for marginal revenue in a straightforward manner.

Step 3: Solve for marginal revenue

Now recall that when demand is expressed as $P = A + BQ$, marginal revenue is $MR = A + 2BQ$. Using the inverse demand function, we can write the marginal revenue function as

$$MR = A + 2BQ$$
$$= \frac{-a'}{b} + \frac{2}{b}Q$$

Step 4: Estimate average variable cost (*AVC*) and marginal cost (*SMC*) In Chapter 10 we discussed in detail the empirical techniques for estimating cubic cost functions. There is nothing new or different about estimating *SMC* and *AVC* for a monopoly firm. The usual forms for the *AVC* and *SMC* functions, when *TVC* is specified as a cubic equation, are

$$AVC = a + bQ + cQ^2$$
$$SMC = a + 2bQ + 3cQ^2$$

You may wish to review this step by returning to Chapter 10 or to Chapter 11.

Step 5: Find the output level where *MR* = *SMC* To find the level of output that maximizes profit or minimizes losses, the manager sets marginal revenue equal to marginal cost and solves for *Q*

$$MR = A + 2BQ = a + 2bQ + 3cQ^2 = SMC$$

Solving this equation for Q^* gives the optimal level of output for the firm—unless *P* is less than *AVC*, and then the optimal level of output is zero.

Step 6: Find the optimal price Once the optimal quantity, Q^*, has been found in step 5, the profit-maximizing price is found by substituting Q^* into the inverse demand equation to obtain the optimal price, P^*

$$P^* = A + BQ^*$$

This price and output will be optimal only if price exceeds average variable cost.

Step 7: Check the shutdown rule For any firm, with or without market power, if price is less than average variable cost, the firm will shut down ($Q^* = 0$) because it makes a smaller loss producing nothing than it would lose if it produced any positive amount of output. The manager calculates the average variable cost at Q^* units

$$AVC^* = a + bQ^* + cQ^{*2}$$

If $P^* \geq AVC^*$, then the monopolist produces Q^* units of output and sells each unit of output for P^* dollars. If $P^* < AVC^*$, then the monopolist shuts down in the short run.

Step 8: Computation of profit or loss To compute the profit or loss, the manager makes the same calculation regardless of whether the firm is a monopolist, oligopolist, or perfect competitor. Total profit or loss is

$$\pi^* = TR - TC$$
$$= (P^* \times Q^*) - [(AVC^* \times Q^*) + TFC]$$

Now try Technical
Problem 15.

If $P < AVC$, the firm shuts down, and $\pi = -TFC$.

To illustrate how to implement these steps to find the profit-maximizing price and output level and to forecast profit, we now turn to a hypothetical firm that possesses a degree of market power.

Maximizing Profit at Aztec Electronics: An Example

By virtue of several patents, Aztec Electronics possesses substantial market power in the market for advanced wireless stereo headphones. In December 2015, the manager of Aztec wished to determine the profit-maximizing price and output for its wireless stereo headphones for 2016.

Estimation of demand and marginal revenue The demand for wireless headphones was specified as a linear function of the price of wireless headphones, the income of the buyers, and the price of stereo tuners (a complementary good)

$$Q = f(P, M, P_R)$$

Using data available for the period 2005–2015, a linear form of the demand function was estimated. The resulting estimated demand function was

$$Q = 41{,}000 - 500P + 0.6M - 22.5P_R$$

where output (Q) is measured in units of sales and average annual family income (M) and the two prices (P and P_R) are measured in dollars. Each estimated parameter has the expected sign and is statistically significant at the 5 percent level.

From an economic consulting firm, the manager obtained 2016 forecasts for income and the price of the complementary good (stereo tuners) as, respectively, \$45,000 and \$800. Using these values—$\hat{M} = 45{,}000$ and $\hat{P}_R = 800$—the estimated (forecasted) demand function for 2016 was

$$Q = 41{,}000 - 500P + 0.6(45{,}000) - 22.5(800) = 50{,}000 - 500P$$

The inverse demand function for the estimated (empirical) demand function was obtained by solving for P

$$P = 100 - 0.002Q$$

From the inverse demand function, the manager of Aztec Electronics obtained the estimated marginal revenue function

$$MR = 100 - 0.004Q$$

Figure 12.9 illustrates the estimated linear demand and marginal revenue curves for Aztec Electronics.

Estimation of average variable cost and marginal cost The manager of Aztec Electronics obtained an estimate of the firm's average variable cost function using

FIGURE 12.9

Demand and Marginal Revenue for Aztec Electronics

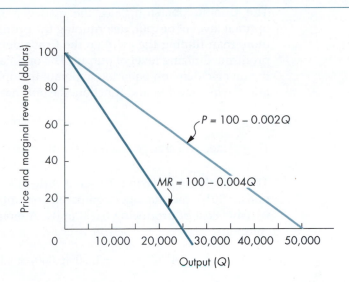

a short-run quadratic specification (as described in Chapter 10). The estimated average variable cost function was

$$AVC = 28 - 0.005Q + 0.000001Q^2$$

For this estimation, AVC was measured in dollar units and Q was measured in units of sales. Given the estimated average variable cost function, the marginal cost function is

$$SMC = 28 - 0.01Q + 0.000003Q^2$$

As you can see, the specification and estimation of cost functions are the same regardless of whether a firm is a price-taker or a price-setter.

The output decision   Once the manager of Aztec obtained estimates of the marginal revenue function and the marginal cost function, the determination of the optimal level of output was accomplished by equating the estimated marginal revenue equation with the estimated marginal cost equation and solving for Q^*. Setting MR equal to SMC results in the following expression

$$100 - 0.004Q = 28 - 0.01Q + 0.000003Q^2$$

Solving this equation for Q, the manager of Aztec finds two solutions: $Q = 6,000$ and $Q = -4,000$. Inasmuch as $Q = -4,000$ is an irrelevant solution—negative outputs are impossible—the optimal level of output is $Q^* = 6,000$. That is, the profit-maximizing (or loss-minimizing) number of wireless stereo headphones to produce and sell in 2016 is 6,000 units—if the firm chooses to produce rather than shut down.

The pricing decision Once the manager of Aztec Electronics has found the optimal level of output, determining the profit-maximizing price is really nothing more than finding the price on the firm's demand curve that corresponds to the profit-maximizing level of output. The optimal output level Q^* is substituted into the inverse demand equation to obtain the optimal price. Substituting $Q^* = 6,000$ into the inverse demand function, the optimal price P^* is

$$P^* = 100 - 0.002(6,000) = \$88$$

Thus Aztec will charge $88 for a set of headphones in 2016.

The shutdown decision To see if Aztec Electronics should shut down production in 2016, the manager compared the optimal price of $88 with the average variable cost of producing 6,000 units. Average variable cost for 6,000 units was computed as

$$AVC^* = 28 - 0.005(6,000) + 0.000001(6,000)^2 = \$34$$

Obviously, $88 is greater than $34; so if these forecasts prove to be correct in 2016, all the variable costs will be covered and the manager should operate the plant rather than shut it down. Note that Aztec's expected total revenue in 2016 was $528,000 (= $88 × 6,000) and estimated total variable cost was $204,000 (= $34 × 6,000). Because total revenue exceeded total variable cost ($TR > TVC$), the manager did not shut down.

Computation of total profit or loss Computation of profit is a straightforward process once the manager has estimated total revenue and all costs. The manager of Aztec has already estimated price and average variable cost for 2016, but total fixed cost is needed to calculate total profit or loss. On the basis of last year's data, the manager of Aztec Electronics estimated that fixed costs would be $270,000 in 2016. The profit was calculated to be

$$\pi = TR - TVC - TFC$$
$$= \$528,000 - \$204,000 - \$270,000$$
$$= \$54,000$$

Figure 12.10 shows the estimated equations for 2016 and the profit-maximizing price and output. At point A, $MR = SMC$, and the profit-maximizing level of output is 6,000 units ($Q^* = 6,000$). At point B, the profit-maximizing price is $88, the price at which 6,000 units can be sold. At point C, ATC is $79, which was calculated as

$$ATC = TC/Q = (\$204,000 + \$270,000)/6,000$$
$$= \$79$$

The total profit earned by Aztec is represented by the area of the shaded rectangle.

FIGURE 12.10

**Profit Maximization at
Aztec Electronics**

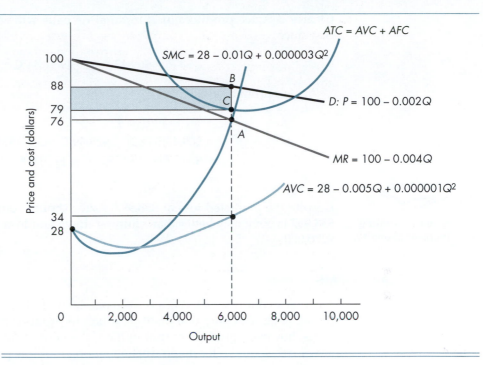

The firm makes a loss   Now suppose that per capita income falls, causing the demand facing Aztec to fall to

$$P = 80 - 0.002Q$$

so marginal revenue is now

$$MR = 80 - 0.004Q$$

Average variable and marginal costs remain constant.

To determine the new level of output under the new estimated demand conditions, the manager equates the new estimated marginal revenue equation with the marginal cost equation and solves for Q^*

$$80 - 0.004Q = 28 - 0.01Q + 0.000003Q^2$$

Again there are two solutions: $Q = -3{,}167$ and $Q = 5{,}283$. Ignoring the negative level of output, the optimal level is $Q^* = 5{,}283$. Substituting this value into the inverse demand function, the optimal price is

$$P^* = 80 - 0.002(5{,}283) = \$69.43$$

To determine whether to produce or shut down under the reduced-demand situation, the manager calculated the average variable cost at the new level of output and compared it with price

$$AVC = 28 - 0.005(5{,}283) + 0.000001(5{,}283)^2 = \$29.49$$

Clearly if Aztec produces in 2016, total revenue will cover all of total variable cost since

$$P = \$69.43 > \$29.49 = AVC$$

Aztec's profit or loss is

$$
\begin{aligned}
\pi &= TR - TVC - TFC \\
&= \$69.43(5{,}283) - \$29.49(5{,}283) - \$270{,}000 \\
&= \$366{,}799 - \$155{,}796 - \$270{,}000 \\
&= -\$58{,}997
\end{aligned}
$$

Now try Technical Problem 16 and 17.

Despite the predicted loss of $58,997, Aztec should continue producing. Losing $58,997 is obviously better than shutting down and losing the entire fixed cost of $270,000.

12.7 MULTIPLANT FIRMS

Thus far in our discussion of profit-maximizing decisions, we have assumed that the manager has only one plant in which to produce the firm's product. Many firms, however, produce output in more than one plant. We will now show you how firms should allocate production among multiple production facilities. Even though our discussion here focuses on a firm with market power, the rule that we develop here applies to all firms, regardless of the degree of market power possessed.

When firms produce in more than one plant, it is likely that the various plants will have different cost conditions. The problem facing the firm is how to allocate the firm's desired level of total production among these plants so that the total cost is minimized.

For simplicity, suppose there are only two plants, A and B, producing the desired total output level (Q_T) of 450 units, but at different marginal costs such that

$$MC_A > MC_B$$

where plant A produces 160 units (Q_A) and plant B produces 290 units (Q_B). In this situation, the manager should transfer output from the higher-cost plant A to the lower-cost plant B. As long as the marginal cost of producing in plant B is lower, total cost of producing Q_T units can be lowered by transferring production. For example, suppose MC_A equals $25 (for the 160th unit at plant A) and MC_B equals $10 (for the 290th unit at plant B). One unit of output taken away from plant A lowers the firm's total cost by $25. Making up the lost unit by producing it at plant B increases total cost only by $10, and 450 units are still produced. As you can see, however, the total cost of producing 450 units falls by $15. The firm would continue taking output away from plant A and increasing the output of plant B, thus lowering total cost, until $MC_A = MC_B$.

This equality would result because MC_A falls as the output of plant A decreases and MC_B rises as the output of plant B increases. Thus we can conclude that marginal costs must be equal for both plants to minimize the total cost of producing 450 units.

> **Principle** For a firm that produces using two plants, A and B, with marginal costs MC_A and MC_B, respectively, the total cost of producing any given level of total output $Q_T (= Q_A + Q_B)$ is minimized when the manager allocates production between the two plants so that the marginal costs are equal: $MC_A = MC_B$.

total marginal cost curve (MC_T)
Horizontal summation of all plants' marginal cost curves, which gives the addition to total cost attributable to increasing total output (Q_T) by one unit.

The total output decision is easily determined. The horizontal summation of all plants' marginal cost curves is the firm's **total marginal cost curve (MC_T)**. This total marginal cost curve is equated to marginal revenue in order to determine the profit-maximizing output and price. This output is divided among the plants so that the marginal cost is equal for all plants.

The two-plant case is illustrated in Figure 12.11. Demand facing the firm is D, and marginal revenue is MR. The marginal cost curves for plants A and B are, respectively, MC_A and MC_B. The total marginal cost curve for the firm is the

FIGURE 12.11
A Multiplant Firm

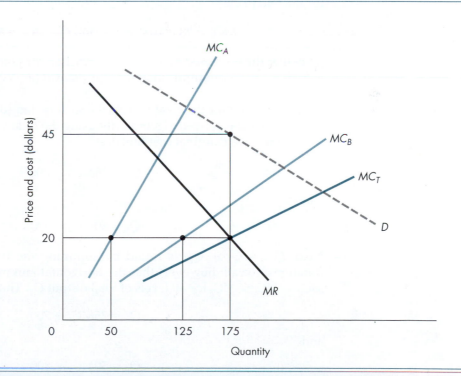

horizontal summation of MC_A and MC_B, labeled MC_T. Profit is maximized at that output level where MC_T equals marginal revenue, at an output of 175 units and a price of \$45. Marginal cost at this output is \$20. Equalization of marginal cost requires that plant A produce 50 units and plant B produce 125 units, which of course sums to 175 as MC_T is the horizontal summation of MC_A and MC_B. This allocation equalizes marginal cost and consequently minimizes the total cost of producing 175 units.

To further illustrate the principle of optimally allocating output in a multiplant situation, we turn now to a numerical illustration. As you will see, the algebra is somewhat more complex than it is for the single-plant case, but the principle is the same: The manager maximizes profit by producing the output level for which marginal revenue equals marginal cost.

Multiplant Production at Mercantile Enterprises

Mercantile Enterprises—a firm with some degree of market power—produces its product in two plants. Hence, when making production decisions, the manager of Mercantile must decide not only how much to produce but also how to allocate the desired production between the two plants.

The production engineering department at Mercantile was able to provide the manager with simple, linear estimates of the incremental (marginal) cost functions for the two plants

$$MC_A = 28 + 0.04Q_A \qquad \text{and} \qquad MC_B = 16 + 0.02Q_B$$

Note that the estimated marginal cost function for plant A (a plant built in 1998) is higher for every output than that for plant B (a plant built in 2005); plant B is more efficient.

The equation for the total marginal cost function (the horizontal sum of MC_A and MC_B) can be derived algebraically using the following procedure. First, solve for both inverse marginal cost functions

$$Q_A = 25MC_A - 700$$

and

$$Q_B = 50MC_B - 800$$

Next, $Q_T \ (= Q_A + Q_B)$ is found by summing the two inverse marginal cost functions. Recall, however, that the horizontal summing process requires that $MC_A = MC_B = MC_T$ for all levels of total output Q_T. Thus it follows that

$$Q_A = 25MC_T - 700$$

and

$$Q_B = 50MC_T - 800$$

FIGURE 12.12

Multiplant Production at Mercantile Enterprises

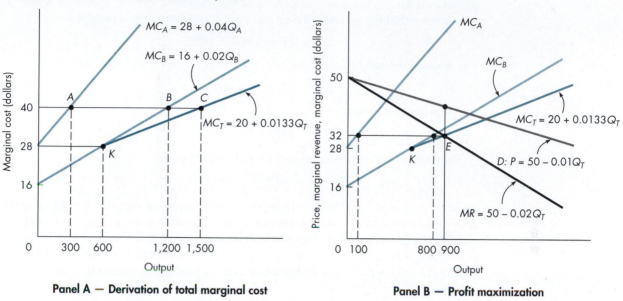

Panel A — Derivation of total marginal cost

Panel B — Profit maximization

Summing the two inverse marginal cost functions results in the inverse *total* marginal cost function

$$Q_T = Q_A + Q_B = 75MC_T - 1{,}500$$

which, after taking the inverse to express marginal cost once again as a function of output, results in the total marginal cost function

$$MC_T = 20 + 0.0133Q_T$$

The marginal cost functions for plants A and B and the associated total marginal cost function are shown in Panel A of Figure 12.12. The process of horizontal summation can be seen by noting that when $MC = \$40$, $Q_A = 300$ units (point A), $Q_B = 1{,}200$ units (point B), and $Q_T = Q_A + Q_B = 1{,}500$ units (point C). Thus, if 1,500 units are to be produced, the manager should allocate production so that 300 units are produced in plant A and 1,200 units are produced in plant B. This allocation of production between the two plants minimizes the total cost of producing a total of 1,500 units.

Note that when Q_T is less than 600 units, plant A is shut down and only plant B is operated. Until Mercantile increases total production to 600 units or more (point K), the marginal cost of producing any output at all in plant A is greater than the marginal cost of producing additional units in plant B. For output levels in the 0 to 600-unit range, MC_B is the relevant total marginal cost curve since $Q_A = 0$. For total output levels greater than 600 units, Mercantile Enterprises will operate *both* plants and MC_T is the total marginal cost function.

Suppose that the estimated demand curve for Mercantile's output is

$$Q_T = 5,000 - 100P$$

The inverse demand function is

$$P = 50 - 0.01Q_T$$

and marginal revenue is

$$MR = 50 - 0.02Q_T$$

Equating marginal revenue and total marginal cost,

$$50 - 0.02Q_T = 20 + 0.0133Q_T$$

and solving for Q_T, the profit-maximizing level of output for Mercantile Enterprises is $Q_T^* = 900$. At this output level, marginal revenue and total marginal cost are both $32 at point E in Panel B of Figure 12.12. To minimize the cost of producing 900 units, the production of the 900 units should be allocated between plants A and B so that the marginal cost of the last unit produced in either plant is $32:

$$MC_A = 28 + 0.04Q_A = 32 \quad \text{and} \quad MC_B = 16 + 0.02Q_B = 32$$

Hence, for plant A, $Q_A^* = 100$, so 100 units will be produced in plant A. For plant B, $Q_B^* = 800$, so 800 units will be produced in plant B.

Now suppose that forecasted demand decreases and a new forecast of the demand for Mercantile's output is

$$Q_T = 4,000 - 100P$$

Given that the corresponding marginal revenue function is

$$MR = 40 - 0.02Q_T$$

the firm's profit-maximizing output (where $MR = MC_T$) declines to 600 units. At this output, marginal revenue and marginal cost are both $28. Equating MC_A and MC_B to $28, the manager found that for plant A, $Q_A^* = 0$, and for plant B, $Q_B^* = 600$. With the new (lower) forecast of demand, plant A will be shut down and all the output will be produced in plant B. As you can verify, if demand declines further, Mercantile would still produce, using only plant B. So for output levels of 600 or fewer units, the total marginal cost function is MC_B.

In effect, the total marginal cost function has a "kink" at point K in the figure. The kink at point K represents the total output level below which the high-cost plant is shut down. A kink occurs when marginal cost in the low-cost plant equals the minimum level of marginal cost in the high-cost plant, thereby making it optimal to begin producing with an additional plant. [The low-cost (high-cost) plant is the plant with lowest (highest) marginal cost at $Q = 0$.] The output at which the kink occurs is found by setting marginal cost in the *low*-cost plant equal to the minimum value of marginal cost in the *high*-cost plant

$$MC_B = 28 = 16 + 0.02Q$$

so the high-cost plant begins operating when Q exceeds 600 units.

The preceding discussion and example show how a manager should allocate production between two plants to minimize the cost of producing the level of output that maximizes profit. The principle of equating marginal costs applies in exactly the same fashion to the case of three or more plants: Marginal cost is the same in all plants that produce. The only complication arises in the derivation of total marginal cost.

Once the total marginal cost function is derived, either by summing the individual plants' marginal cost curves graphically or by solving algebraically, the manager uses the total marginal cost function to find the profit-maximizing level of total output.

Now try Technical Problems 18–20.

> **Principle**   A manager who has *n* plants that can produce output will maximize profit when the firm produces the level of total output and allocates that output among the *n* plants so that
>
> $$MR = MC_T = MC_1 = \cdots = MC_n$$

12.8 SUMMARY

- Market power—something perfectly competitive firms do not possess—is the ability to raise price without losing all sales. Firms with market power face downward-sloping demand curves or, equivalently, price-setting firms possess market power. A monopoly exists when a single firm produces and sells a particular good or service for which there are no good substitutes and new firms are prevented from entering the market. Monopolistic competition arises when the market consists of a large number of relatively small firms that produce similar, but slightly differentiated, products and therefore have some, but not much, market power. Monopolistic competition is characterized by easy entry into and exit from the market. In both market structures, firms can set prices without concern about retaliatory price responses by rival firms: monopolies have no rivals and monopolistically competitive firms view rival firms as relatively small and unimportant. The degree to which a firm possesses market power is inversely related to price elasticity of demand. The less (more) elastic the firm's demand, the greater (less) its degree of market power. The Lerner index measures market power by calculat-

ing the proportionate amount by which price exceeds marginal cost. This ratio is inversely related to the (absolute value of) the elasticity of demand: $(P - MC)/P = -1/E$. When consumers view two goods as substitutes, the cross-price elasticity of demand (E_{XY}) is positive. The larger the cross-price elasticity, the greater the substitutability between two goods, and the smaller the degree of market power possessed by the two firms. (*LO1*)

- A firm can possess a high degree of market power only when strong barriers to the entry of new firms exist. Seven major types of entry barriers are economies of scale, barriers created by government, essential input barriers, brand loyalties, consumer lock-in, network externalities, and sunk costs. (*LO2*)

- In the short run, the manager of a monopoly firm will choose to produce the output where $MR = SMC$, rather than shut down, as long as total revenue at least covers the firm's total avoidable cost, which is the firm's total variable cost ($TR \geq TVC$). The price for that output is given by the demand curve. If total revenue cannot cover total variable cost (or, equivalently, $P < AVC$), the manager will shut down and produce nothing, losing an amount equal to total fixed cost. In the long run, the monop-olist maximizes profit by choosing to produce where $MR = LMC$, unless price is less than long-run aver-age cost ($P < LAC$), in which case the firm exits the industry. (*LO3*)

■ For firms with market power, marginal revenue prod-uct (*MRP*) is equal to marginal revenue times marginal product: $MRP = MR \times MP$. When producing with a single variable input, labor, a firm with market power maximizes profit by employing that amount of labor for which $MRP = w$. The relevant range of the *MRP* curve is the downward sloping, positive portion of *MRP* where $ARP > MRP$. Regardless of whether the manager chooses Q or L to maximize profit, the resulting levels of input usage, output, price, and profit are the same in either case. (*LO4*)

■ Short-run equilibrium under monopolistic competi-tion is exactly the same as for monopoly. Long-run equilibrium in a monopolistically competitive mar-ket is attained when the demand curve for each pro-ducer is tangent to the long-run average cost curve.

Unrestricted entry and exit lead to this equilibrium. At the equilibrium output, price equals long-run average cost, and marginal revenue equals long-run marginal cost. (*LO5*)

■ Eight steps can be employed to find the profit-maximizing price, output, and level of profit for a monopoly or monopolistically competitive firm: (1) estimate the demand equation, (2) find the inverse demand equation, (3) solve for marginal revenue, (4) estimate average variable cost and marginal cost, (5) find the output level where $MR = SMC$, (6) find the profit-maximizing price, (7) check the shutdown rule, and (8) compute profit or loss. (*LO6*)

■ If a firm produces in two plants, *A* and *B*, it should allocate production between the two plants so that $MC_A = MC_B$. The optimal total output for the firm is that output for which $MR = MC_T$. Hence, for profit maximization, the firm should produce the level of total output and allocate this total output between the two plants so that $MR = MC_T = MC_A = MC_B$. (*LO7*)

KEY TERMS

consumer lock-in

Lerner index

marginal revenue product (*MRP*)

market definition

market power

monopolistic competition

monopoly

network externalities
(or network effects)

strong barrier to entry

switching costs

total marginal cost curve (MC_T)

TECHNICAL PROBLEMS

1. Compare the market power of the following pairs of firms. Explain.
   a. Bank of America and the First National Bank of Pecos, Texas.
   b. The "Big Three" U.S. auto manufacturers prior to the early 1970s and the same firms after the early 1970s.
   c. A regional phone company and a regional electric company in the same area.
2. Explain why input barriers to entry have probably declined in importance with the recent expansion of international markets.
3. For each of the following products, could consumer lock-in or network externalities (or both) create a barrier to entry? Explain why or why not.
   a. Toothpaste.
   b. Vinyl LP record albums.

4. Assume a monopoly has the following demand schedule:

Price	Quantity
$20	200
15	300
10	500
5	700

 a. Calculate total revenue at each P and Q combination.
 b. Calculate marginal revenue per unit for each decrease in price.
 c. For the change in price from $20 to $15, is demand elastic or inelastic? How much revenue does the firm lose from reducing the price on the 200 units it could have sold for $20? How much revenue does the firm gain from selling 100 more units at $15? Compare the two changes; then compare these changes with MR.
 d. Answer part c for the price change from $15 to $10.

5. The following graph shows demand and MR for a monopoly:

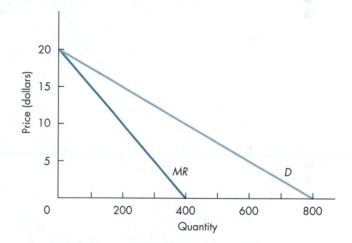

 a. If the firm wants to sell 200 units, what price does it charge?
 b. If the firm charges a price of $15, how much will it sell?
 c. What is MR for parts a and b? Is demand elastic or inelastic?
 d. If the firm charges $10, how much will it sell? What is demand elasticity?

6. A monopolist faces the following demand and cost schedules:

Price	Quantity	Total cost
$20	7	$36
19	8	45
18	9	54
17	10	63
16	11	72
15	12	81

  a. How much output should the monopolist produce?
  b. What price should the firm charge?
  c. What is the maximum amount of profit that this firm can earn?
7. The following graph shows demand, *MR*, and cost curves for a monopoly in the short run:

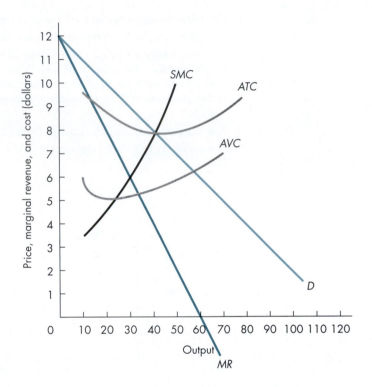

  a. Profit is maximized at a price of $_____.
  b. The profit-maximizing level of output is _____.
  c. At the optimal level of output, total revenue is $_____, total cost is $_____, and profit is $_____.
  d. If the manager mistakenly sets price at $10 and sells 20 units, will profit margin (i.e., *P − ATC*) be larger or smaller than when price is set at the optimal level in part *c*? (*Note*: Average total cost is $8.75 when 20 units are produced.) Using marginal analysis, explain why this happens.
8. Explain why the manager of a profit-maximizing monopoly always produces and sells on the elastic portion of the demand curve. If costs are 0, what output will the manager produce? Explain.
9. The figure below shows demand, marginal revenue, and short-run cost curves for a monopoly:

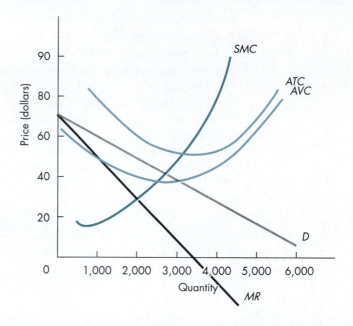

a. How much should the firm produce? What price should it charge?
b. What is the firm's profit (loss)?
c. What is total revenue? What is total variable cost?
d. If the firm shuts down in the short run, how much will it lose?

10. Consider a monopoly firm with the demand and cost curves below. Assume that the firm is operating in the short run with the plant designed to produce 400 units of output optimally.

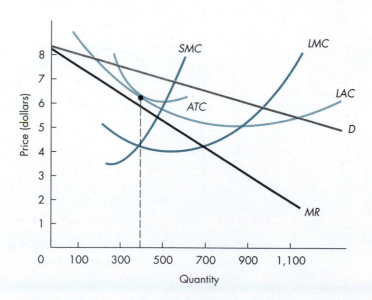

a. What output should be produced?

b. What will be the price?

c. How much profit is made?

d. If the firm can change plant size and move into the long run, what will be output and price?

e. Will profit increase? How do you know?

f. Draw in the new short-run average and marginal cost curves associated with the new plant size.

11. In the following table, columns 1 and 2 make up a portion of the production function of a monopolist using a single variable input, labor. Columns 2 and 3 make up the demand function facing the monopolist over this range of output.

(1) Labor	(2) Quantity	(3) Price
9	50	$21
10	100	20
11	140	19
12	170	18
13	190	17
14	205	16
15	215	15

a. Derive *MP, MR,* and *MRP* over this range.

b. If the wage rate is $60, how much labor would the manager hire? Why? What if the wage falls to $40?

12. The following figure shows the average revenue product and the marginal revenue product of labor for a monopoly:

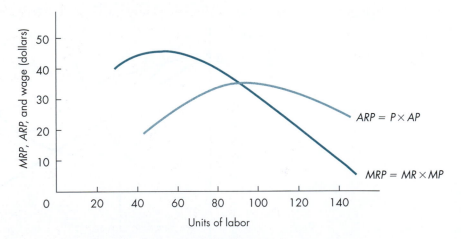

a. If the wage is $20, how much labor would the firm hire?

b. If the wage is $10, how much labor would the firm hire?

c. If the wage is $40, how much labor would the firm hire?

13. Describe the features of monopolistic competition:
    a. How is it similar to monopoly?
    b. How is it similar to perfect competition?
    c. What are the characteristics of short-run equilibrium?
    d. What are the characteristics of long-run equilibrium?
    e. How is long-run equilibrium attained?

14. The following graph shows the long-run average and marginal cost curves for a monopolistically competitive firm:

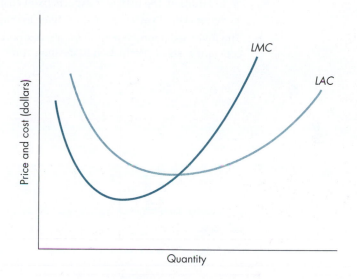

    a. Assume the firm is in the short run and making profits. Draw in the demand and marginal revenue curves. Show output and price.
    b. Now let the firm reach long-run equilibrium. Draw in precisely the new demand and marginal revenue curves. Show output and price.
    c. Why must $MR = LMC$ at *exactly* the same output at which LAC is tangent to demand?
    d. Contrast this firm's output and price in long-run equilibrium with the price and output if this firm was a perfect competitor.

15. The manager of a monopoly firm obtained the following estimate of the demand function for its output:

$$Q = 2,600 - 100P + 0.2M - 500P_R$$

From an econometric forecasting firm, the manager obtained forecasts for the 2017 values of M and P_R as, respectively, $20,000 and $2. For 2017 what is:
    a. The forecasted demand function?
    b. The inverse demand function?
    c. The marginal revenue function?

16. For the firm in problem 15, the manager estimated the average variable cost function as

$$AVC = 20 - 0.07Q + 0.0001Q^2$$

where AVC was measured in dollars per unit and Q is the number of units sold.

a. What is the estimated marginal cost function?
b. What is the optimal level of production in 2017?
c. What is the optimal price in 2017?
d. Check to make sure that the firm should actually produce in the short run rather than shut down.
   In addition, the manager expects fixed costs in 2017 to be $22,500.
e. What is the firm's expected profit or loss in 2017?

17. The inverse demand equation for a monopoly firm is $P = 100 - 2Q$, and the firm faces constant costs of production in the long run with $LAC = LMC = \$20$.

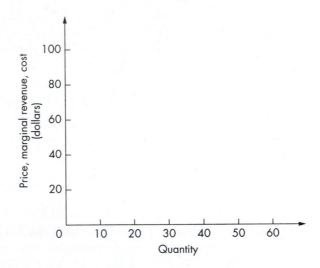

a. On the axes above, construct the demand and cost curves facing the monopoly firm and label the curves D, LAC, and LMC, respectively.
b. On the axes above, construct the marginal revenue curve facing the monopoly firm and label the curve MR.
c. Find the profit-maximizing price and output and label this point on demand A.
d. What is the maximum amount of profit the monopolist can make?
Now suppose the firm's constant costs increase to $40 per unit ($LAC' = LMC' = \$40$).
e. On the axes above, construct the new cost curves facing the monopoly and label the cost curves LAC' and LMC'.
f. Now that costs are higher, should the manager raise or lower price to maximize profit? By how much? Label the new profit-maximizing point on demand B.
g. Now that costs are higher, what is the maximum amount of profit the monopolist can make?

18. In the following graph, D represents the demand for dishwashers facing the Allclean Company. The firm manufactures dishwashers in two plants; MC_1 and MC_2 are their marginal cost curves.

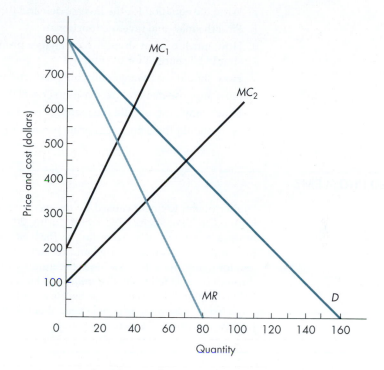

a. How many dishwashers should the firm produce?

b. What price should the firm set?

c. How should the output be allocated between the two plants so as to maximize profit?

19. Consider a firm that is using two plants, A and B, with these MC functions

$$MC_A = 10 + 0.01Q_A \quad \text{and} \quad MC_B = 4 + 0.03Q_B$$

a. Find the inverse marginal cost functions.

b. Set $MC_A = MC_T$ and $MC_B = MC_T$, and find the algebraic sum $Q_A + Q_B = Q_T$.

c. Take the inverse of the horizontal sum in part b to get the total marginal cost (MC_T) expressed as a function of total output (Q_T).

d. Beyond what level of output will the firm use both plants in production? (*Hint:* Find the output level where MC_T kinks.)

e. If the manager of this firm wished to produce 1,400 units at the least possible total cost, should 700 units be produced in each plant? Why or why not? If not, what should the allocation be?

f. Draw a graph of MC_A, MC_B, and MC_T. Check your algebraic derivation of total marginal cost with your graph. Check your answer to part e.

20. Suppose the firm in Technical Problem 19 faces the following demand function:

$$Q = 4{,}000 - 125P$$

a. Write the equation for the inverse demand function.

b. Find the marginal revenue function.

c. How much output should the manager produce to maximize profit? What price should be charged for the output?

d. How should the manager allocate production between plants *A* and *B?*

Now suppose demand decreases to $Q = 800 - 80P$.

e. How many units should the manager produce to maximize profit?

f. How should the manager allocate production between plants *A* and *B?*

APPLIED PROBLEMS

1. Higher unemployment caused by the recession and higher gasoline prices have contributed to a substantial reduction during 2008 in the number of vehicles on roads, bridges, and in tunnels. According to *The Wall Street Journal* (April 28, 2009), the reduction in demand for toll bridge and tunnel crossings created a serious revenue problem for many cities. In New York, the number of vehicles traveling across bridges and through tunnels fell from 23.6 million in January 2008 to 21.9 million in January 2009. "That drop presents a challenge, because road tolls subsidize MTA subways, which are more likely to be used as people get out of their cars."* In an apparent attempt to raise toll revenue, the MTA increased tolls by 10 percent on the nine crossings it controls.

a. Is MTA a monopolist in New York City? Do you think MTA possesses a high degree of market power? Why or why not?

b. If the marginal cost of letting another vehicle cross a bridge or travel through a tunnel is nearly zero, how should the MTA set tolls to maximize profit? To maximize toll revenue? How are these two objectives related?

c. With the decrease in demand for bridge and tunnel crossings, what is the optimal way to adjust tolls: raise tolls, lower tolls, or leave tolls unchanged? Explain carefully?

2. QuadPlex Cinema is the only movie theater in Idaho Falls. The nearest rival movie theater, the Cedar Bluff Twin, is 35 miles away in Pocatello. Thus QuadPlex Cinema possesses a degree of market power. Despite having market power, QuadPlex Cinema is currently suffering losses. In a conversation with the owners of QuadPlex, the manager of the movie theater made the following suggestions: "Since QuadPlex is a local monopoly, we should just increase ticket prices until we make enough profit."

a. Comment on this strategy.

b How might the market power of QuadPlex Cinema be measured?

c. What options should QuadPlex consider in the long run?

3. The *El Dorado Star* is the only newspaper in El Dorado, New Mexico. Certainly, the *Star* competes with *The Wall Street Journal*, *USA Today*, and *The New York Times* for national news reporting, but the *Star* offers readers stories of local interest, such as local news,

---

*Douglas Belkin, "Commutes Speed Up as Fewer Drive" *The Wall Street Journal*, April 28, 2009.

weather, high-school sporting events, and so on. The *El Dorado Star* faces the demand and cost schedules shown in the spreadsheet that follows:

(1) Number of newspapers per day (Q)	(2) Price (P)	(3) Total cost per day (TC)
0	0	$2,000
1,000	$1.50	2,100
2,000	1.25	2,200
3,000	1.00	2,360
4,000	0.85	2,520
5,000	0.75	2,700
6,000	0.65	2,890
7,000	0.50	3,090
8,000	0.35	3,310
9,000	0.10	3,550

a. Create a spreadsheet using Microsoft Excel (or any other spreadsheet software) that matches the one above by entering the output, price, and cost data given.

b. Use the appropriate formulas to create three new columns (4, 5, and 6) in your spreadsheet for total revenue, marginal revenue (MR), and marginal cost (MC), respectively. [Computation check: At $Q = 3,000$, $MR = \$0.50$ and $MC = \$0.16$]. What price should the manager of the *El Dorado Star* charge? How many papers should be sold daily to maximize profit?

c. At the price and output level you answered in part b, is the *El Dorado Star* making the greatest possible amount of total revenue? Is this what you expected? Explain why or why not.

d. Use the appropriate formulas to create two new columns (7 and 8) for total profit and profit margin, respectively. What is the maximum profit the *El Dorado Star* can earn? What is the maximum possible profit margin? Are profit and profit margin maximized at the same point on demand?

e. What is the total fixed cost for the *El Dorado Star*? Create a new spreadsheet in which total fixed cost increases to $5,000. What price should the manager charge? How many papers should be sold in the short run? What should the owners of the *Star* do in the long run?

4. Tots-R-Us operates the only day-care center in an exclusive neighborhood just outside of Washington, D.C. Tots-R-Us is making substantial economic profit, but the owners know that new day-care centers will soon learn of this highly profitable market and attempt to enter the market. The owners decide to begin spending immediately a rather large sum on advertising designed to decrease elasticity. Should they wait until new firms actually enter? Explain how advertising can be employed to allow Tots-R-Us to keep price above average cost without encouraging entry.

5. Antitrust authorities at the Federal Trade Commission are reviewing your company's recent merger with a rival firm. The FTC is concerned that the merger of two rival firms in the same market will increase market power. A hearing is scheduled for your company to present arguments that your firm has not increased its market power through this merger. Can you do this? How? What evidence might you bring to the hearing?

6. You own a small bank in a state that is now considering allowing interstate banking. You oppose interstate banking because it will be possible for the very large money center banks in New York, Chicago, and San Francisco to open branches in your bank's geographic market area. While proponents of interstate banking point to the benefits to consumers of increased competition, you worry that economies of scale might ultimately force your now profitable bank out of business. Explain how economies of scale (if significant economies of scale in fact do exist) could result in your bank being forced out of business in the long run.

7. The Harley-Davidson motorcycle company, which had a copyright on the word "hog," applied for exclusive rights to its engine sound. Why would a company want copyrights on two such mundane things?

8. *The Wall Street Journal* reported that businesses are aggressively pushing consumers to pay bills electronically. Numerous banks dropped their monthly fees for online bill paying, and many merchants are offering incentives for customers to sign up for online bill payment. Aside from the direct cost savings to businesses, such as lower postage and other administrative costs, what other reason might explain business's interest in online bill payment?

9. Even if the firms in a monopolistically competitive market collude successfully and fix price, economic profit will still be competed away if there is unrestricted entry. Explain. Will price be higher or lower under such an agreement in long-run equilibrium than would be the case if firms didn't collude? Explain.

10. The Ali Baba Co. is the only supplier of a particular type of Oriental carpet. The estimated demand for its carpets is

$$Q = 112{,}000 - 500P + 5M$$

where Q = number of carpets, P = price of carpets (dollars per unit), and M = consumers' income per capita. The estimated average variable cost function for Ali Baba's carpets is

$$AVC = 200 - 0.012Q + 0.000002Q^2$$

Consumers' income per capita is expected to be $20,000 and total fixed cost is $100,000.

a. How many carpets should the firm produce to maximize profit?

b. What is the profit-maximizing price of carpets?

c. What is the maximum amount of profit that the firm can earn selling carpets?

d. Answer parts *a* through *c* if consumers' income per capita is expected to be $30,000 instead.

11. Dr. Leona Williams, a well-known plastic surgeon, has a reputation for being one of the best surgeons for reconstructive nose surgery. Dr. Williams enjoys a rather substantial degree of market power in this market. She has estimated demand for her work to be

$$Q = 480 - 0.2P$$

where Q is the number of nose operations performed monthly and P is the price of a nose operation.

a. What is the inverse demand function for Dr. Williams's services?

b. What is the marginal revenue function?

The average variable cost function for reconstructive nose surgery is estimated to be

$$AVC = 2Q^2 - 15Q + 400$$

where AVC is average variable cost (measured in dollars), and Q is the number of operations per month. The doctor's fixed costs each month are $8,000.

    c. If the doctor wishes to maximize her profit, how many nose operations should she perform each month?

    d. What price should Dr. Williams charge to perform a nose operation?

    e. How much profit does she earn each month?

12. A firm with two factories, one in Michigan and one in Texas, has decided that it should produce a total of 500 units to maximize profit. The firm is currently producing 200 units in the Michigan factory and 300 units in the Texas factory. At this allocation between plants, the last unit of output produced in Michigan added $5 to total cost, while the last unit of output produced in Texas added $3 to total cost.

    a. Is the firm maximizing profit? If so, why? If not, what should it do?

    b. If the firm produces 201 units in Michigan and 299 in Texas, what will be the increase (decrease) in the firm's total cost?

13. In a recent "earnings call," a teleconference call to shareholders in which the CEO reports and discusses quarterly earnings per share, Coca-Cola's CEO Muhtar Kent bragged about "winning" market share from rival beverage company PepsiCo. However, rising sugar costs in 2011 are forcing Coke to raise soft drink prices by 3 to 4 percent, and this could undermine Coke's market share gains if Pepsi does not also raise its soft drink prices. *The Wall Street Journal* (April 27, 2011) reports that, in an effort to continue "winning the market share battle," Kent plans to maintain relatively low prices in soft drinks by raising prices disproportionately higher in other categories such as fruit juices and sport drinks. The *WSJ* raises the concern that "winning market share may come at too great a financial cost."** Discuss some reasons why Coke's pricing tactics to win market share could in fact reduce Coke's profit and earnings per share.

14. In a *Wall Street Journal* article titled "Sparing Fliers Even Higher Airfares," Scott McCartney claims that jet fuel hedging by Southwest Airlines resulted in lower airfares for passengers on all airlines: "Without (the fuel hedging) windfall, (Southwest) likely would have had to jack up fares well beyond last year's (fares)."[†] Other airline industry analysts have also claimed that Southwest charges no fee for baggage ("Bags Fly Free") largely because of the airline's success in hedging its fuel costs. Evaluate these two claims. [*Hint*: You should read Illustration 12.4 before you answer this question.]

15. Amtrak, a national passenger railroad heavily subsidized by taxpayers, operates at a huge loss every year. Recently, officials at Amtrak expressed confidence that they can turn things around by "running the railroad like a business." Specifically, Amtrak's managers plan to raise ticket prices to "trim costs and boost revenues." What must be true about Amtrak's demand elasticity for this plan to work? What effect will raising price have on Amtrak's costs?

16. The owners of the Tampa Bay Buccaneers have seen demand for season tickets decline steadily, probably because the team's performance is ranked near the bottom of 32 teams in the National Football League. The team owners are now considering a decrease in season ticket prices. Using graphical analysis, show that when demand decreases for a monopolist, price must be cut to maximize profit.

** John Jannarone, "The Price of Coke's Market Share" *The Wall Street Journal*, April 27, 2011.
[†] Scott McCartney, "Sparing Fliers Even Higher Airfares," *The Wall Street Journal*, June 6, 2006.

⊡ **MATHEMATICAL APPENDIX** **Profit Maximization for a Monopoly**

This appendix describes a manager's choice of output and price or input usage to maximize profit for a monopoly.

The Monopolist Chooses Output and Price

Assume that the firm is in the short run, so some costs are fixed. Let the inverse demand for a monopoly be

$$P = P(Q)$$

so total revenue is

$$R(Q) = P(Q)Q$$

The monopoly profit function is

(1) $$\pi = R(Q) - TVC(Q) - TFC$$

where $TVC(Q)$ is total variable cost and TFC is total fixed cost.

The first-order condition for profit maximization requires

(2) $$d\pi/dQ = dR/dQ - dTVC/dQ = 0$$

The second-order condition for profit maximization is that at the equilibrium quantity

$$d^2\pi/dQ^2 = d^2R/dQ^2 - d^2TVC/dQ^2 < 0$$

Because in equation (2) dR/dQ is marginal revenue and dC/dQ is marginal cost, choosing the quantity of output that maximizes profit requires that marginal revenue equal marginal cost: $MR = SMC$. Solve equation (2) for the equilibrium output Q^* so the equilibrium price is $P^* = P(Q^*)$.

If

$$\pi = P(Q^*)Q^* - TVC(Q^*) - TFC > 0$$

the firm makes an economic profit. If

$$\pi = P(Q^*)Q^* - TVC(Q^*) - TFC < 0$$

the firm makes a loss. In this case the firm should produce Q^* rather than shutting down when

$$|P(Q^*)Q^* - TVC(Q^*) - TFC| \leq TFC$$

which occurs if, at Q^*, price is greater than or equal to average variable cost:

$$P(Q^*) \geq TVC(Q^*)/Q^*$$

The firm loses less than its total fixed cost, which is the amount it would lose if it shuts down and produces nothing. If at Q^* price is less than average variable cost, the firm should shut down and produce nothing. It loses all its fixed cost rather than its fixed cost plus the amount of variable cost not covered by revenue.

We next demonstrate that the profit-maximizing price and quantity must lie on the elastic portion of demand. Because

$$MR = dR/dQ = P(Q) + Q(dP/dQ)$$
$$= P[1 + (Q/P)(dP/dQ)] = P[1 + (1/E)]$$

where E is the elasticity of demand, in equilibrium

(3) $$MR = P[1 + 1/E] = MC$$

Since MC and P must be positive, $(1 + 1/E) > 0$, which, because $E < 0$, requires that E be greater than one in absolute value: $|E| > 1$. Thus in equilibrium P^* and Q^* must lie on the elastic portion of demand.

For a less general approach, assume that the inverse demand function is the linear function:

$$P(Q) = a - bQ$$

where a and b are positive. Let the total variable cost function be the cubic function,

$$TVC(Q) = dQ - eQ^2 + fQ^3$$

where d, e, and f are positive. The profit function is therefore

(4) $$\pi = PQ - TVC(Q) - TFC$$
$$= aQ - bQ^2 - dQ + eQ^2 - fQ^3 - TFC$$

For profit maximization, differentiate (4) and set it equal to 0:

(5) $$d\pi/dQ = (a - 2bQ) - (d - 2eQ + 3fQ^2) = 0$$

Since $MR = a - 2bq$, and $SMC = d - 2eQ + 3fQ^2$, $MR = SMC$ in profit-maximizing equilibrium. The second-order condition for a maximum is

(6) $$d^2\pi/dQ^2 = -2b + 2e - 6fQ < 0$$

or, solving equation (6) for Q, for a maximum, it must be the case that

(7) $$Q > (e - b)/3f$$

To obtain the profit-maximizing level of Q^*, solve the quadratic equation formed from equation (5):

$$(a - d) - (2b + 2e)Q - 3fQ^2 = 0$$

After solving such a quadratic equation, you will obtain two values for Q^*. The profit-maximizing Q^* will be the value at which the second-order condition in (7) holds, ensuring that this is the value of Q^* at which marginal cost crosses marginal revenue from below. This will be the larger of the two solutions in such problems. To obtain the equilibrium price, substitute Q^* into the inverse demand function:

$$P^* = a - bQ^*$$

If the total revenue equals or exceeds total variable cost, that is, if $P(Q^*) \geq TVC(Q^*)/Q^*$, then profit or loss is

$$\pi = aQ^* - bQ^{*2} - dQ^* + eQ^{*2} - fQ^{*3} - TFC$$

The Monopolist Chooses Input Usage

Now we assume that the manager chooses the level of usage of a single variable input, L, in order to maximize profit. All other inputs are fixed in amount. Let the production function be as derived for the short run in the Mathematical Appendix to Chapter 8:

$$Q = f(L, K) = g(L)$$

The inverse demand function is

$$P = P(Q) = P[g(L)]$$

The firm chooses L so that the following profit function is maximized:

(8) $\pi = P[g(L)]g(L) - wL - TFC$

where w is the wage paid to labor and TFC is the fixed payment for the fixed inputs. Profit maximization requires

(9a) $d\pi/dL = (dP/dQ)(dQ/dL)g(L) + P(dQ/dL) - w$

          $= 0$

or

(9b) $(dQ/dL)[(dP/dQ)Q + P] = w$

Because dQ/dL is marginal product and $[(dP/dQ)Q + P]$ is marginal revenue, equation (9b) can be expressed as

$$MP \times MR = \text{Marginal revenue product} = w$$

Equation (9a) or (9b) can be solved for L^*; then $Q^* = g(L^*)$ and $P^* = P(Q^*)$.

If, at L^*, $MRP \leq ARP = P[g(L^*)]/L^*$, the firm will produce and its profit or loss will be

$$\pi = P[g(L^*)]g(L^*) - wL^* - TFC$$

If, however, $MRP = w > P^*Q^*/L^*$, total revenue will be less than total variable cost; that is, $wL^* > P^*Q^*$. In this case the firm would shut down and lose only its total fixed cost, rather than its total fixed cost plus the portion of total variable cost not covered by revenue.

Now assume that the firm uses two variable inputs, L and K, and no inputs are fixed. The prices of L and K are, respectively, w and r. The production function is

$$Q = f(L, K)$$

and the inverse demand function is

$$P = P(Q) = P[f(L, K)]$$

The profit function is now

$$\pi = f(L, K)P[f(L, K)] - wL - rK$$

If the firm chooses the levels of L and K to maximize profit, the first-order equilibrium conditions are

(10a) $P[f(L, K)](\partial Q/\partial L) + Q(dP/dQ)(\partial Q/\partial L) - w = 0$

(10b) $P[f(L, K)](\partial Q/\partial K) + Q(dP/dQ)(\partial Q/\partial K) - r = 0$

Equations (10a) and (10b) can be solved for the optimal levels of L^* and K^*; then the optimal levels of output and price are $Q^* = f(L^*, K^*)$ and $P^* = P[f(L^*, K^*)]$. These values can be substituted into the above profit equation to find the maximum level of profit.

Equations (10a) and (10b) can be rewritten as

(11a) $\partial Q/\partial L(P + QdP/dQ) = MP_L \times MR = MRP_L = w$

(11b) $\partial Q/\partial K(P + QdP/dQ) = MP_K \times MR = MRP_K = r$

Thus in equilibrium the marginal revenue product of each input equals its price.

The Multiplant Firm's Allocation Decision

To maximize profit, a multiplant firm will produce the level of output at which the horizontal sum of each plant's marginal cost equals marginal revenue. Each plant will produce the output at which the marginal costs of all plants are equal.

Assume the firm has two plants, A and B, whose total cost functions are, respectively, $C_A(Q_A)$ and $C_B(Q_B)$. The firm's total revenue function is $R(Q_A + Q_B) = R(Q)$. Thus the firm's profit function is

$$\pi = R(Q) - C_A(Q_A) - C_B(Q_B)$$

Maximizing profit with respect to Q_A and Q_B requires

$$\frac{\partial \pi}{\partial Q_A} = \frac{dR}{dQ} - \frac{dC_A(Q_A)}{dQ_A} = 0$$

$$\frac{\partial \pi}{\partial Q_B} = \frac{dR}{dQ} - \frac{dC_B(Q_B)}{dQ_B} = 0$$

Combining these conditions, profit is maximized when

$$MR = MC_A = MC_B$$

Thus MC must be the same in both plants and also equal to MR.

Chapter 13

Strategic Decision Making in Oligopoly Markets

After reading this chapter, you will be able to:

13.1 Employ concepts of dominant strategies, dominated strategies, Nash equilibrium, and best-response curves to make simultaneous decisions.

13.2 Employ the roll-back method to make sequential decisions, determine existence of first- or second-mover advantages, and employ credible commitments to gain first- or second-mover advantage.

13.3 Understand and explain why cooperation can sometimes be achieved when decisions are repeated over time and discuss four types of facilitating practices for reaching cooperative outcomes.

13.4 Explain why it is difficult, but not impossible, to create strategic barriers to entry by either limit pricing or capacity expansion.

We are now going to address some new types of business decision-making problems that arise when just a few firms produce most or all of the total market output. When the number of firms competing in a market is small, any one firm's pricing policy will have a significant effect on sales of other firms in the market. Indeed, in markets where a relatively small number of firms compete, *every* kind of decision affecting any one firm's profit—such as decisions about pricing, output, and advertising as well as decisions about expanding production facilities or increasing spending on research and development—also affects profits of every other firm in the market. The profit earned by each firm in a market having only a few sellers depends on decisions made by every other firm competing in the same market, and so profits of all firms are interdependent.

Consider these examples of rival firms whose sales, and consequently profits, are interdependent:

- American Airlines might be debating whether to reduce fares on all its European flights this summer. The reductions could substantially increase its profitable vacation-travel business. But if Delta, United, and other large overseas carriers match the reductions, a costly fare war could result, causing losses for all.

- Coca-Cola may be preparing an expensive new advertising campaign. Its advertising agency says the new campaign should be extremely effective. But how will Pepsi react? Will it respond with an even more expensive advertising campaign of its own, or will it continue as is? Pepsi's response will have a huge effect on the profitability of Coca-Cola's decision.

- At a much smaller marketing level, Joe's Pizza Express, a successful local restaurant in the downtown business district, wants to open a new restaurant in a recently developed suburban area. But will Pizza Hut or Domino's also come into the new suburb, which, for the next several years, will probably not be large enough to support more than one pizza place? During this period, Joe could lose a lot of money.

These types of business decisions differ substantially from the decision-making processes developed in previous chapters in which managers took price or demand as given and did not need to consider the reactions of rival managers when making decisions. In these examples, managers must make decisions knowing that their decisions will affect the sales and profitability of their rivals and that their rivals will then react to their decisions. Depending on how their rivals react, their own sales and profitability will then be affected. However, these managers do not know what their rivals will actually do. To make the best decisions, even though they almost never know for sure what their competitors' reactions will be, these managers must "get into the heads" of their rival managers to make predictions or conjectures about their reactions.

Successful managers must learn how to anticipate the actions and reactions of other firms in their markets. In this chapter we will show you how successfully predicting a rival's reaction requires managers to assume their rivals will always make those decisions that are likely to be the most profitable ones for them given the decisions they expect *their* rivals to make. Interdependence, then, requires *strategic behavior*. **Strategic behavior** consists of the actions taken by firms and any actions that firms can convincingly threaten to take, to plan for, and react to, the actions of competitors. Knowing about and anticipating potential moves and countermoves of other firms is of critical importance to managers in markets where firms' sales and profits are interdependent.

Economists generally use the term **oligopoly** in reference to a market in which a few relatively large firms have moderate to substantial market power and, what is more important, they recognize their interdependence. Each firm knows that its actions or changes will have an effect on other firms and that the other firms will, in response, take actions or make changes that will affect its sales. But no firm is really sure how the other firms will react.

strategic behavior
Actions taken by firms to plan for and react to competition from rival firms.

oligopoly
A market consisting of a few relatively large firms, each with a substantial share of the market and all recognize their interdependence.

This scenario applies to the previous example in which American Airlines considered how its rivals would react before it decided to reduce fares. Coca-Cola didn't know what Pepsi would do if it introduced a new advertising campaign or what the effect of Pepsi's reaction would be. The owner of Joe's Pizza Express considered what the large pizza chains would do if Pizza Express entered the new suburb. We will devote this chapter to analyzing how managers of firms operating in oligopoly markets can make decisions when they are uncertain about the reaction of rivals; yet these reactions affect their own sales and profits and so must be considered in reaching decisions. We can now summarize in a principle the problem of interdependence in oligopoly.

> **Principle** Interdependence of firms' profits, the distinguishing characteristic of oligopoly markets, arises when the number of firms in a market is small enough that every firm's price and output decision affects the demand and marginal revenue conditions of every other firm in the market.

The discussion of oligopoly in this chapter is designed to introduce you to and give you some insight into the way managers of firms in oligopoly markets make decisions. As you will see, the study of strategic behavior is similar to the study of players participating in a game of strategy, such as chess, poker, bridge, or checkers. This is why this important area of economic analysis is called "game theory." In this chapter, we will use models of game theory to show how managers of oligopoly firms can try to get into the heads of their rivals to make the most profitable decisions for themselves. You will see that strategic decision making in oligopoly markets frequently results in a situation in which each firm makes the best decision for itself given the decisions it expects its rivals will make, but this kind of "noncooperative" decision making leads to lower profits for all firms. Noncooperative oligopoly outcomes are generally good for consumers but bad for the firms that earn lower profits as a consequence.

We also examine some ways in which cooperative oligopoly decisions may arise. When you finish this chapter, you will understand why oligopoly firms may wish to make decisions cooperatively and how they can sometimes, but certainly not always, achieve cooperation in making decisions. We must warn you at the outset of this chapter that many forms of overt or explicit cooperation, also called "collusion" or "price-fixing" by legal authorities, are illegal in the United States and in many other countries. For example, the CEO of American Airlines could call the CEO of Delta and work out a pricing agreement between the two firms. But such price fixing is illegal in the United States, and business executives have been fined and sent to prison for doing just that. We will show you how cooperative outcomes can sometimes be achieved in oligopoly markets without resorting to illegal practices and why price-fixing agreements generally do not last very long in any case.

Now try Technical Problem 1.

13.1 DECISION MAKING WHEN RIVALS MAKE SIMULTANEOUS DECISIONS

As emphasized in the introduction, the "fewness of firms" in oligopoly markets causes each firm's demand and marginal revenue conditions, and hence each firm's profits, to depend on the pricing decisions, output decisions, expansion decisions, and so forth, of every rival firm in an oligopoly market. The resulting interdependence and strategic behavior make decisions much more complicated and uncertain. To make the best decisions they can when every firm is trying to anticipate the decisions of every other firm, managers must learn to think strategically.

Perhaps you are thinking, "Sure, interdependence complicates decision making and makes it messy. So what do I as a manager do in such situations? How do I go about making strategic decisions?" We can't give you a set of rules to follow. The art of making strategic decisions is learned from experience.

We can, however, introduce you to a tool for thinking about strategic decision making: *game theory*. **Game theory** provides a useful guideline on how to behave in strategic situations involving interdependence. This theory was developed more than 50 years ago to provide a systematic approach to strategic decision making. During the past 25 years, it has become increasingly important to economists for analyzing oligopoly behavior. It is also becoming more useful to managers in making business decisions. Unfortunately, learning the principles of game theory will not guarantee that you will always "win" or make greater profit than your rivals. In the real world of business decision making, your rival managers will also be strategic thinkers who will try to predict your actions, and they will try to counteract your strategic decisions. And, to make winning even less certain, many unpredictable, and even unknown, events are frequently just as important as strategic thinking in determining final outcomes in business. Game theory can only provide you with some general principles or guidelines to follow in strategic situations like those that oligopoly managers face.

You might think of the word *game* as meaning something fun or entertaining to do, but managers may or may not find it fun to play the strategic games that arise in oligopoly. To game theorists—economists who specialize in the study of strategic behavior—a **game** is any decision-making situation in which people compete with each other for the purpose of gaining the greatest individual payoff, rather than group payoff, from playing the game. In the game of oligopoly, the people in the game, often called "players," are the managers of the oligopoly firms. Payoffs in the oligopoly game are the individual profits earned by each firm.

In this section, we will introduce you to strategic thinking by illustrating some of the fundamental principles of strategic decision making that can help you make better decisions in one of the more common kinds of strategic situations managers face: making *simultaneous decisions* about prices, production, advertising levels, product styles, quality, and so on. **Simultaneous decision games** occur in oligopoly markets when managers must make their individual decisions without knowing the decisions of their rivals. Simultaneous decision games can arise when managers make decisions at precisely the same time without knowledge of their rivals' decisions. However, decisions don't have to take place at the same time to be "simultaneous"; it is only necessary for managers not to know

game theory
An analytical guide or tool for making decisions in situations involving interdependence.

game
Any decision-making situation in which people compete with each other for the purpose of gaining the greatest individual payoff.

simultaneous decision games
A situation in which competing firms must make their individual decisions without knowing the decisions of their rivals.

ILLUSTRATION 13.1

How Can Game Theory Be Used in Business Decision Making?
Answers from a Manager

"Game theory is hot . . . it's been used to analyze everything from the baseball strike to auctions at the FCC." So began an article in *The Wall Street Journal* by F. William Barnett.[a]

Barnett points out that game theory helps managers pay attention to interactions with competitors, customers, and suppliers and focus on how near-term actions promote long-term interests by influencing what the players do. After describing a version of the prisoners' dilemma game, he notes that an equilibrium (such as the one we show in cell D of Table 13.1) is unattractive to all players.

Some rules of the road: Examine the number, concentration, and size distribution of the players. For example, industries with four or fewer players have the greatest potential for game theory, because (1) the competitors are large enough to benefit more from an improvement in general industry conditions than they would from improving their position at the expense of others (making the the pie bigger rather than getting a bigger share of a smaller pie) and (2) with fewer competitors it is possible to think through the different combinations of moves and countermoves.

Keep an eye out for strategies inherent in your market share. Small players can take advantage of larger companies, which are more concerned with maintaining the status quo. Barnett's example: Kiwi Airlines, with a small share of the market, was able to cut fares by up to 75 percent between Atlanta and Newark without a significant response from Delta and Continental. But, he notes, large players can create economies of scale or scope, such as frequent-flier programs, that are unattractive to small airlines.

Understand the nature of the buying decision. For example, if there are only a few deals in an industry each year, it is very hard to avoid aggressive competition. Scrutinize your competitors' cost and revenue structures. If competitors have a high proportion of fixed-to-variable cost, they will probably behave more aggressively than those whose production costs are more variable.

Examine the similarity of firms. When competitors have similar cost and revenue structures, they often behave similarly. The challenge is to find prices that create the largest markets, then use nonprice competition—distribution and service. Finally, analyze the nature of demand. The best chances to create value with less aggressive strategies are in markets with stable or moderately growing demand.

Barnett concludes, "Sometimes [game theory] can increase the size of the pie. But for those who misunderstand [the] fundamentals of their industry, game theory is better left to the theorists." As we said earlier, strategic decision making is best learned from experience.

[a]F. William Barnett, "Making Game Theory Work in Practice," *The Wall Street Journal*, February 13, 1995.

what their rivals have decided to do when they make their own decisions. If you have information about what your rival has chosen to do *before* you make your decision, then you are in a *sequential* decision-making game, which we will discuss in the next section of this chapter.

Making decisions without the benefit of knowing what their rivals have decided is, as you might suspect, a rather common, and unpleasant, situation for managers. For example, to meet publishers' deadlines, two competing clothing retailers must decide by Friday, July 1, whether to run expensive full-page ads in local papers for the purpose of notifying buyers of their Fourth of July sales that begin on Monday. Both managers would rather save the expense of advertising because they know buyers expect both stores to have holiday sales and will shop at both stores on the Fourth of July even if no ads are run by either store.

Unless they tell each other—or receive a tipoff from someone working at the newspaper—neither manager will know whether the other has placed an ad until Monday morning, long after they have made their "simultaneous" decisions. As we mentioned earlier, making decisions without knowing what rivals are going to do is quite a common situation for managers. Any of the strategic decisions described at the beginning of this chapter could be a simultaneous decision game.

To introduce you to the concept of oligopoly games, we begin with the grandfather of most economic games. While it doesn't involve oligopoly behavior at all, it is a widely known and widely studied game of simultaneous decision making that captures many of the essential elements of oligopoly decision making. This famous game is known as the *prisoners' dilemma*.

Now try Technical Problem 2.

The Prisoners' Dilemma

The model of the prisoners' dilemma is best illustrated by the story for which it is named. Suppose that a serious crime—say, grand-theft auto—is committed and two suspects, Bill and Jane, are apprehended and questioned by the police. The suspects know that the police do not have enough evidence to make the charges stick unless one of them confesses. If neither suspect confesses to the serious charges, then the police can only convict the suspects on much less serious charges—perhaps, felony vandalism. So the police separate Bill and Jane and make each one an offer that is known to the other. The offer is this: If one suspect confesses to the crime and testifies in court against the other, the one who confesses will receive only a 1-year sentence, while the other (who does not confess) will get 12 years. If both prisoners confess, each receives a 6-year sentence. If neither confesses, both receive 2-year sentences on the minor charges. Thus Bill and Jane each could receive 1 year, 2 years, 6 years, or 12 years, depending on what the other does.

Table 13.1 shows the four possibilities in a table called a *payoff table*. A **payoff table** is a table showing, for every possible combination of actions that players can make, the outcomes or "payoffs" for each player. Each of the four cells in

payoff table
A table showing, for every possible combination of decisions players can make, the outcomes or "payoffs" for each of the players in each decision combination.

TABLE 13.1

The Prisoners' Dilemma: A Dominant Strategy Equilibrium

		Bill	
		Don't confess	Confess
Jane	**Don't confess**	A **2 years,** *2 years*	B **12 years,** *1 year*
	Confess	C **1 year,** *12 years*	D **6 years,** *6 years*

Table 13.1 represents the outcome of one of the four possible combinations of actions that could be taken by Bill and Jane. For example, cells A and D in the payoff table show the payoffs for Bill and Jane if both do not confess or do confess, respectively. Cells B and C show the consequences if one confesses and the other does not. In each cell, the years spent in prison for each one of the two suspects is listed as a pair of numbers separated by a comma. The first number, shown in bold face, gives Jane's prison sentence, and the second number, shown in italics, gives Bill's prison sentence.[1] Both suspects know the payoff table in Table 13.1, and they both know that the other one knows the payoff table. This **common knowledge** of the payoff table plays a crucial role in determining the outcome of a simultaneous decision game. What the suspects don't know, since their decisions are made simultaneously, is what the other has decided to do.

The police have designed the situation so that both Bill and Jane will be induced to confess and both will end up in cell D (excuse the pun). To see this, put yourself into Bill's head and imagine what he must be thinking. Bill knows that Jane must decide between the two actions "confess" and "don't confess." If Jane does not confess ("bless her heart"), Bill receives a lighter sentence by confessing ("sorry Jane, I promise I'll visit you often"). If Jane confesses ("Jane, you dirty rat"), Bill still receives a lighter sentence by confessing: 6 years compared with 12. Therefore, confessing is always better than not confessing for Bill ("Sorry Jane, what did you expect me to do?")—it gives Bill a lighter sentence no matter what Jane does. The only rational thing for Bill to do is confess. The police, of course, counted on Bill thinking rationally, so they are not surprised when he confesses. And they also expect Jane to confess for precisely the same reason: Confessing is the best action Jane can take, no matter what action she predicts Bill will take. So both Bill and Jane will probably confess and end up with sentences of 6 years each.

The prisoners' dilemma illustrates a way of predicting the likely outcome of a strategic game using the concept of a *dominant strategy*. In game theory a **dominant strategy** is a strategy or action that provides the best outcome no matter what decisions rivals decide to make. In the prisoners' dilemma, confessing is a dominant strategy for each suspect. Naturally, rational decision makers should always take the action associated with a dominant strategy, if they have one. This establishes the following principle for strategic decision making.

common knowledge
A situation in which all decision makers know the payoff table, and they believe all other decision makers also know the payoff table.

dominant strategy
A strategy or action that always provides the best outcome no matter what decisions rivals make.

> **Principle** When a dominant strategy exists—an action that always provides a manager with the best outcome no matter what action the manager's rivals choose to take—a rational decision maker always chooses to follow its own dominant strategy and predicts that if its rivals have dominant strategies, they also will choose to follow their dominant strategies.

Finding dominant strategies, especially in larger payoff tables, can sometimes be difficult. A useful method for finding dominant strategies can be easily illustrated using the payoff table for the prisoners' dilemma in Table 13.1. Let's

---

[1]Throughout this chapter, we will follow the convention of listing payoffs to players in each cell of a payoff table as **payoff to row player**, *payoff to column player*.

dominant-strategy equilibrium
Both players have dominant strategies and play them.

begin with Jane: For each *column* (i.e., for each decision Bill could make), find the cell that gives Jane her best payoff and pencil a "*J*" in that cell. Following this procedure for this game, you will mark two *J*'s: one in cell C and one in cell D. Now repeat this process for Bill: For each *row* (i.e., for each decision Jane could make), find the cell that gives Bill's best payoff and pencil a "*B*" in that cell. Following this procedure, you will mark two *B*'s: one in cell B and one in cell D. Since *all J*'s line up in *one* row, that row (**Confess**) is a dominant strategy for Jane. Similarly, Bill possesses a dominant strategy because *all B*'s line up in *one* column (*Confess*).

As you can now see, it is easy, once dominant strategies are discovered, to predict the likely outcome of games in which both players have dominant strategies. Game theorists call such an outcome a **dominant-strategy equilibrium**. When both players have dominant strategies, the outcome of the game can be predicted with a high degree of confidence. The compelling nature of a dominant-strategy equilibrium results from the fact that, when all decision makers have dominant strategies (and know their dominant strategies), managers will be able to predict the actions of their rivals with a great deal of certainty.

An important characteristic of the prisoners' dilemma, and one that makes it valuable for understanding oligopoly outcomes, is that cooperation is unlikely to occur because there is an incentive to cheat. To see this, suppose that, before committing their crime, Bill and Jane make a promise to each other that they will never confess to their crime. Once again let's get into Bill's head to see what he is thinking. Suppose Bill predicts that Jane will keep her promise not to confess ("Jane loves me; she would never break her promise to me"). He then has an incentive to cheat on his promise because he can get out of jail in just one year instead of two years by confessing ("Oh Jane, come on; I promise I'll wait for you"). Alternatively, if you think that it's farfetched for Bill to trust Jane ("Jane *never* loved me the way I loved her"), then suppose Bill predicts Jane will confess. Now his best decision, when he predicts Jane will cheat by confessing, is also to cheat and confess. Without some method of forcing each other to keep their promises not to confess, Bill and Jane will probably both cheat by confessing.

Despite the fact that both suspects choose dominant strategies that are best for them no matter what the other suspect chooses to do, they end up in a cell (cell D) where they are both worse off than if they had cooperated by not confessing. This paradoxical outcome has made the prisoners' dilemma one of the most studied games in economics because it captures the difficult nature of cooperation in oligopoly markets. We now summarize the nature of a prisoners' dilemma.

Relation A prisoners' dilemma arises when all rivals possess dominant strategies, and, in dominant-strategy equilibrium, they are all worse off than if they had cooperated in making their decisions.

As we will explain later in this chapter, managers facing prisoners' dilemma situations may be able to reach cooperative outcomes if, instead of having only one opportunity to make their decisions, they get to repeat their decisions many times in the future. We will save our examination of repeated decisions, as well as a more precise discussion of "cooperation" and "cheating," for Section 13.3. Until then, our discussion will continue examining situations in which managers have only a single opportunity to make their decisions.

Now try Technical Problem 3.

Most strategic situations, in contrast to the prisoners' dilemma game, do not have a dominant-strategy equilibrium. We will now examine some other ways oligopoly managers can make simultaneous decisions when some, or even all, of the firms do not have dominant strategies.

Decisions with One Dominant Strategy

In a prisoners' dilemma situation, all firms have dominant strategies to follow and managers rationally decide to follow their dominant strategies, even though the outcome is not as good as it could be if the firms cooperated in making their decisions. If just one firm possesses a dominant strategy, rival managers know that particular firm will choose its dominant strategy. Knowing what your rival is going to do can tell you much about what you should do. We illustrate the value of knowing what your rival is going to do with the following example.

Pizza Castle and Pizza Palace are located almost side by side across the street from a major university. The products of Castle and Palace are somewhat differentiated, yet their primary means of competition is pricing. For illustrative purposes, suppose each restaurant can choose between only two prices for its pizza: a high price of $10 and a low price of $6. Clearly, the profit for each firm at each of the prices depends greatly on the price charged by the other firm. Once again, you see that profits of oligopolists are interdependent.

Table 13.2 shows the payoff table facing Castle and Palace. If both charge $10, each does quite well, making $1,000 a week profit, as shown in cell A. If both lower their prices to $6, sales increase some; each restaurant will probably maintain its market share; and, because of the lower price, the profit of each falls to $400 a week, as shown in cell D. However, if either firm lowers its price to $6 while the other maintains its price at $10, the firm with the lower price will capture most of

TABLE 13.2

Pizza Pricing: A Single Dominant Strategy

		Palace's price	
		High ($10)	Low ($6)
Castle's price	**High ($10)**	A **$1,000,** *$1,000*	B **$500,** *$1,200*
	Low ($6)	C **$1,200,** *$300*	D **$400,** *$400*

Payoffs in dollars of profit per week.

the other's business. Comparing cells B and C shows that the loss of market share is less serious for Castle when it is underpriced by Palace than the loss of market share for Palace when it is underpriced by Castle: Castle, when underpriced, makes $500 a week, but Palace, when underpriced, makes only $300. The reason for this difference is Castle's policy, which Palace does not believe in, of offering free soft drinks whenever it is underpriced by its rival.

As you can determine from the payoff table in Table 13.2, Castle does *not* have a dominant strategy. However, the manager at Castle sees (as does the manager at Palace) that Palace does have a dominant strategy: price low at $6. Knowing that Palace's manager will rationally choose to set price low at $6, Castle's manager will likely decide to price high at $10 (and give away soft drinks). Thus, cell B is the outcome of the simultaneous decision game. We have established another important principle for making simultaneous decisions.

Now try Technical
Problem 4.

> **Principle**   When a firm does not have a dominant strategy, but at least one of its rivals *does* have a dominant strategy, the firm's manager can predict with confidence that its rivals will follow their dominant strategies. Then, the manager can choose its own best strategy, knowing the actions that will almost certainly be taken by those rivals possessing dominant strategies.

Successive Elimination of Dominated Strategies

dominated strategies
Strategies that would never be chosen no matter what rivals might choose to do.

When deciding what to do in a simultaneous decision situation, managers should eliminate from consideration all **dominated strategies**, strategies that would never be chosen no matter what rivals might choose to do. Using dominated strategies to simplify decision making requires that managers eliminate all dominated strategies that can be identified on a "first-round" of searching and then eliminate any new dominated strategies that reveal themselves after one or more rounds of elimination. Thus, **successive elimination of dominated strategies** is an iterative decision-making process in which managers first eliminate all dominated strategies in the original payoff table. The first round of elimination creates a new payoff table, known as a *reduced* payoff table, which has fewer decisions for the manager to consider. Then, any strategies that become dominated after the first round of elimination are likewise eliminated to create yet another reduced payoff table, which, of course, has still fewer decisions to consider. The process of elimination continues until no dominated strategies remain in the final payoff table.

successive elimination of dominated strategies
An iterative decision-making process in which dominated strategies are eliminated to create a reduced payoff table with fewer decisions for managers to consider.

We can illustrate this elimination procedure by making the pizza pricing problem facing Castle and Palace somewhat more complex. Consider the new, larger payoff table in Table 13.3. Managers at Castle and Palace can now choose high ($10), medium ($8), or low ($6) pizza prices. In the beginning payoff table, shown in Panel A of Table 13.3, no dominant strategy exists for either Castle or Palace. Both managers, however, have dominated strategies in the beginning payoff table that they will never choose. Palace will never choose to price high, since no matter what price it believes Castle might set, a high price is never the best decision for Palace. Similarly, Castle will never believe setting a medium

TABLE 13.3

Pizza Pricing: Successive Elimination of Dominated Strategies

			Palace's price				
		High ($10)		Medium ($8)		Low ($6)	
Castle's price	**High ($10)**	A	$1,000, *$1,000*	B	$900, *$1,100*	C	$500, *$1,200*
	Medium ($8)	D	$1,100, *$400*	E	$800, *$800*	F	$450, *$500*
	Low ($6)	G	$1,200, *$300*	H	$500, *$350*	I	$400, *$400*

Payoffs in dollars of profit per week.

Panel A—Beginning Payoff Table

			Palace's price		
		Medium ($8)		Low ($6)	
Castle's price	**High ($10)**	B	$900, *$1,100*	C	$500, *$1,200*
	Low ($6)	H	$500, *$350*	I	$400, *$400*

Panel B—Reduced Payoff Table

		Palace's price	
		Low ($6)	
Castle's price	**High ($10)**	C	$500, *$1,200*

Panel C—Unique Solution

price is its best solution. Both dominated strategies—high for Palace and medium for Castle—should be removed from the beginning payoff table in Panel A.[2]

After the managers remove the two dominated strategies, the reduced payoff table, shown in Panel B of Table 13.3, has only two rows and two columns. Notice that now, after eliminating dominated strategies, both firms have dominant

___

[2]The procedure we discussed earlier for finding dominant strategies by marking each player's best decision for each decision the rival player might make also identifies *dominated* strategies. For the player whose decisions are listed by rows in the payoff table—call this player "Rowe"—a dominated strategy exists for Rowe if there is a row with no *R*'s marked in that row. Similarly, for the player whose decisions are listed by columns in the payoff table—call this player "Collum"—a dominated strategy exists for Collum if there is a column with no *C*'s marked in that column.

strategies. Castle's dominant strategy is to price high, and Palace's dominant strategy is to price low. Both pizza firms will want to follow their newly discovered dominant strategies, and they end up in the payoff table in cell C with Castle earning $500 of profit a week and Palace earning $1,200 of profit a week. Notice that cell C can also be found by a *second* round of elimination of dominated strategies. In Panel B, Castle's low price and Palace's medium price are both dominated strategies, which, when eliminated, produce the unique solution in Panel C.

We wish we could tell you that every time you can apply successive elimination of dominated strategies, you will discover a pair of dominant strategies. We can, however, tell you that eliminating dominated strategies *always* simplifies a decision-making problem, even when it doesn't completely solve the decision problem as it did for Castle and Palace in Panel C of Table 13.3. We summarize this discussion with the following principle for decision making:

> **Principle** In a simultaneous decision having no dominant-strategy equilibrium, managers can simplify their decisions by eliminating all dominated strategies that may exist. The process of elimination should be repeated until no more dominated strategies turn up.

When it occurs, strategic dominance, whether it takes the form of dominant strategies or dominated strategies, delivers a powerful tool to managers for making simultaneous decisions. Strategically astute managers always search first for dominant strategies, and, if no dominant strategies can be discovered, they next look for dominated strategies. Unfortunately, simultaneous decisions frequently fail to provide managers with either dominant or dominated strategies. In the absence of any form of strategic dominance, managers must use a different, but related, guiding concept for making simultaneous decisions. This concept, known as *Nash equilibrium*, can sometimes, but not always, guide managers in making simultaneous decisions.

Now try Technical
Problems 5–6.

Nash Equilibrium: Making Mutually Best Decisions

When simultaneous decisions cannot be made using the clear and powerful rules of strategic dominance, decision makers must find some other guide for making strategic decisions. We will now discuss an approach frequently employed by game theorists to explain how decision makers can make the best decisions in simultaneous decision situations. This solution to making simultaneous decisions is known as a *Nash equilibrium*, named for the game theorist John F. Nash, who first proposed the solution in the 1940s and whose lifework provided the basis for the movie *A Beautiful Mind.*

The fundamental idea guiding managers to a Nash equilibrium is that managers will choose the strategy that gives them the highest payoff, given what they believe will be the actions of their rivals. To achieve this end, managers must correctly anticipate the actions of rivals. Unless managers correctly predict what their rivals will do, they will make the wrong decisions. So managers will not believe they are making best decisions for themselves unless they also believe they are correctly predicting the actions of their rivals. How, then, can managers correctly predict what their rivals will do so that they can choose the best response to their rivals?

As we mentioned, every rival is trying to accomplish precisely the same thing: Each tries to make the best decision for itself given its beliefs about what the rest of its rivals will do. To accomplish this end, they must believe they are correctly predicting each other's actions; otherwise they will not believe they are making the best decisions for themselves. Strategically thinking managers, however, will not be satisfied that their predictions are correct unless the predicted action for each and every rival would be the best decision for that rival to take based on the rival's own predictions about the actions its rivals will take. This discussion establishes the following relation:

Relation For all firms in an oligopoly market to be predicting correctly each others' decisions—managers cannot make *best* decisions without *correct* predictions—all firms must be choosing individually best actions given the predicted actions of their rivals, which they can then believe are correctly predicted.

It follows, then, that strategically astute managers will search the payoff table for *mutually best decisions:* cells in the payoff table in which all managers are doing the best they can given their beliefs about the other managers' actions. Strategic thinkers realize that only mutually best decisions can result in mutually correct predictions about rival decisions, which, in turn, ensure that the decisions are indeed the best ones to make. This is the subtle and complex nature of a **Nash equilibrium,** which we can now define formally as a set of actions or decisions for which all managers are choosing their best actions given the actions chosen by their rivals. Payoff tables may contain more than one Nash equilibrium cell, and some payoff tables may have no Nash cells. As you will see shortly, the concept of Nash equilibrium is only helpful when payoff tables have exactly one Nash equilibrium cell.

While Nash equilibrium allows all managers to do best for themselves given other managers' own best decisions, we must stress that the managers are not cooperating with each other when they choose a Nash set of actions. The reason they choose a Nash equilibrium is not because they are trying to help each other do their best. They make Nash decisions only because they know they cannot make the best decisions for themselves unless they *correctly* predict the decisions their rivals will make. And, as we explained, unless managers correctly predict what their rivals will do, they will not, individually, make the best decisions for themselves.

We wish to be extremely clear about how you interpret each decision or action associated with a Nash equilibrium cell. In a Nash cell, managers view their own decisions as the actions they should take to achieve their own best outcomes based on the actions they believe or anticipate the others will take to reach their best outcomes. Since the rivals' actions have not yet been taken, they must be regarded as the actions a manager *believes* they will take, *anticipates* they will take, *predicts* they will take, or *expects* them to take. The words *believe, anticipate, predict,* and *expect* all reflect the fundamental problem of simultaneous decisions: Managers

Nash equilibrium
A set of actions for which all managers are choosing their best actions given the actions chosen by their rivals.

cannot know ahead of time what actions rivals will actually take. While this interpretation of decisions in a Nash equilibrium cell is, as we mentioned earlier, a subtle one, you will need to remind yourself of this interpretation throughout most of the rest of this chapter.

Because all decisions are mutually best decisions in Nash equilibrium, no single firm can *unilaterally* (by itself) make a different decision and do better. This property or condition of Nash equilibrium is known as **strategic stability**, and it provides the fundamental reason for believing that strategic decision makers will likely decide on a Nash pair of decisions. If they do not choose a Nash equilibrium set of decisions, then at least one of the managers could choose a different action, without any change in other managers' actions, and do better. When a unilateral change in one firm's decision can make that firm better off, strategically thinking managers cannot reasonably believe or predict the actions of a non-Nash cell will be chosen. In a game with two players, for example, only a Nash equilibrium pair of decisions makes strategic sense for *both* managers. As you can now appreciate, the reason strategically astute managers will likely make Nash decisions is a rather subtle line of reasoning. We can now summarize the case for choosing a Nash equilibrium set of actions in a principle.

strategic stability
In a Nash equilibrium cell, no decision maker can unilaterally change its decision and improve its individual payoff.

> **Principle**   Nash decisions are likely to be chosen because Nash sets of decisions are mutually best and, thus, "strategically stable." No firm can do better unilaterally changing its decision. Non-Nash decisions are unlikely to be chosen because at least one firm can do better by unilaterally changing its action.

Even though strategic stability provides a compelling reason for choosing a Nash equilibrium set of decisions, reaching a Nash equilibrium outcome in practice can be difficult and uncertain. In many strategic decisions, there may be two or more mutually best cells in the payoff table. Managers then must choose from a number of different Nash equilibrium decision sets.[3] Generally, it is so difficult to predict how decision makers choose a single Nash equilibrium cell from multiple Nash equilibria that we cannot give you a guideline, or any kind of rule, for making best decisions when you find multiple sets of mutually best decisions. Once again, we must stress that, in many strategic situations, game theory cannot tell you how to make the best decisions. And, even when game theory can provide rules for making best decisions, the rules only tell you the best decision assuming that your rival views the payoff table exactly as you do and that your rival thinks strategically.

Actual decision outcomes can, and often do, differ from the decisions that would seem to be mutually best for firms because managers may calculate payoffs differently or they may not know with certainty the payoffs in every cell of the payoff table. And, of course, one or more of the decision makers may not

---

[3]Game theorists have shown that, under rather common circumstances and with a modified concept of equilibrium, all simultaneous decision games have at least one Nash equilibrium strategy set. The nature of these circumstances and the extended definition of Nash equilibrium require more discussion than we wish to undertake in this introductory discussion of strategic decision making.

TABLE 13.4

Super Bowl Advertising: A Unique Nash Equilibrium

		Pepsi's budget		
		Low	Medium	High
Coke's budget	**Low**	A $60, $45	B $57.5, $50	C $45, $35
	Medium	D $50, $35	E $65, $30	F $30, $25
	High	G $45, $10	H $60, $20	I $50, $40

Payoffs in millions of dollars of semiannual profit.

recognize the subtle strategic logic of making Nash decisions. Unfortunately, we cannot assure you that every manager making strategic decisions has read and understood this chapter. Strategic errors happen.

Super Bowl Advertising: An Example of Nash Equilibrium

To illustrate the "mutually best" nature of a Nash equilibrium outcome, we will now consider Coke and Pepsi's advertising decision for an upcoming Super Bowl game. As you can see from studying the payoff table in Table 13.4, Coke has found a more effective advertising agency than Pepsi: In every cell, Coke's payoff is greater than Pepsi's payoff. The effect on sales and profit of Super Bowl ads lasts about six months, so payoffs in Table 13.4 reflect profits (in millions of dollars) for the first half of the year, since the Super Bowl game will be played in January.

Even with a better advertising agency, however, Coke does not have a dominant strategy: If Pepsi chooses a low budget, Coke's best choice is a low budget; if Pepsi chooses a medium budget, Coke's best choice is a medium budget; and if Pepsi chooses a high budget, Coke's best choice is a high budget. Also notice that each and every one of Coke's budget actions will be the best action for one of Pepsi's decisions, so Coke does not have any *dominated* strategies either.

Searching across each row in the payoff table, you can verify that Pepsi's best action for each of Coke's actions is *Medium, Low,* or *High* respectively, as Coke chooses **Low, Medium,** or **High** levels of Super Bowl advertising. Since Pepsi does not have one action that is best no matter what Coke does, Pepsi has no dominant strategy. And, since each and every one of Pepsi's three budget choices will be the best action for one of the decisions Coke can make, Pepsi, like Coke, has no *dominated* strategies. Thus there are no dominant or dominated strategies for either Coke or Pepsi.

After examining each cell in the payoff table in Table 13.4, you can confirm that the only Nash equilibrium pair of actions is cell I (**High,** *High*), where Coke earns

$50 million and Pepsi earns $40 million in semiannual profits.[4] Even though this is a mutually best decision for Coke and Pepsi, this unique Nash equilibrium does not provide Coke and Pepsi with the highest possible payoffs. They could both do better than the Nash outcome if they cooperated in making their advertising decisions. In Table 13.4, you can see that Coke and Pepsi could both do better by agreeing to choose low advertising budgets for the Super Bowl. In cell A (**Low,** *Low*), Coke's semiannual profit is $60 million and Pepsi's semiannual profit is $45 million, and both firms are better off than in Nash equilibrium.

Why don't Coke and Pepsi agree to cooperate and choose the decision pair in cell A (**Low,** *Low*), which increases both of their individual profits? You can answer this question quite convincingly by considering the strategic stability property of Nash equilibrium. In cell A, as in every other cell except the Nash cell (**High,** *High*), either Coke or Pepsi, or in some cells, both firms, could increase their profits by changing advertising levels, *even with no change in the other's level of advertising.* In cell A (**Low,** *Low*), both managers know that if Coke decides to go with **Low,** Pepsi can unilaterally improve its profit by increasing its ad budget from *Low* to *Medium* in cell B. So it would be foolish for Coke to believe that Pepsi will decide on a low budget if Pepsi believes Coke will choose a low budget.

As we explained earlier, neither manager can believe that its prediction about a rival's decision will be correct unless the predicted action is the best action the rival can take given the decision of *its* rival. Only decision pairs that are mutually best decisions result in both managers correctly anticipating their rival's decision. Mutually best decisions will also be mutually correct or believable decisions, and mutually correct or believable decisions will also be mutually best decisions.

The strategic stability of a Nash equilibrium pair of decisions is sufficiently compelling as a means of predicting the decisions that managers will make when faced with simultaneous decisions that game theorists expect most managers will choose the Nash decision cell when there is only *one* Nash cell in the payoff table. When payoff tables contain more than one Nash equilibrium cell, no prediction is possible in general.

> **Principle** When managers face a simultaneous decision-making situation possessing a unique Nash equilibrium set of decisions, rivals can be expected to make the decisions leading to the Nash equilibrium. If there are multiple Nash equilibria, there is generally no way to predict the likely outcome.

Before leaving our discussion of Nash equilibrium, we need to explain the relation between dominant-strategy equilibrium and a Nash equilibrium. In a dominant-strategy equilibrium, both firms are making best decisions *no matter what the rival does.* In a Nash equilibrium, both firms are making the best decisions *given*

---

[4]Once again, the procedure we discussed earlier for finding dominant and dominated strategies by marking each player's best decisions also identifies Nash equilibrium pairs of actions. For each column in Table 13.4, find the cell that gives Coke's best payoff and pencil a *C* in that cell. For each row, find the cell that gives Pepsi's best payoff and pencil a *P* in that cell. Following this procedure for Table 13.4 results in *C*'s in cells A, E, and I, and *P*'s in cells B, D, and I. Any cell, such as cell I, with *both a C and a P* in it will be a Nash equilibrium.

the decision they believe their rivals will make. Managers believe rivals choose dominant strategies when they have them, and a dominant-strategy equilibrium is also a Nash equilibrium: Managers believe rivals will choose their dominant strategies. So all dominant-strategy equilibria are also Nash equilibria, but Nash equilibria can, and often do, occur without either dominant or dominated strategies, as we just showed you in the Super Bowl advertising game. You should now be able to show that the dominant-strategy equilibrium in the prisoners' dilemma, cell D in Table 13.1, is a Nash equilibrium by verifying that (**Confess,** *Confess*) allows both suspects to do the best they can given the action they predict the other will take.

Now try Technical Problem 7.

> **Relation**   All dominant-strategy equilibria are also Nash equilibria, but Nash equilibria can occur without either dominant or dominated strategies.

Best-Response Curves and Continuous Decision Choices

Thus far we have assumed that managers face only two or three discrete decision alternatives, with each one represented by a row or column in a payoff table. In many decisions, actions or strategies are continuous decision variables. (Recall the discussion in Chapter 3 of continuous and discrete decision variables.) When managers make pricing decisions, they seldom view the choices as being either "low" or "high" prices. Instead they choose the best price from a continuous range of prices. Economists have developed a tool, called *best-response curves,* to analyze and explain simultaneous decisions when decision choices are continuous rather than discrete. A firm's **best-response curve** indicates the best decision to make (usually the profit-maximizing one) based on, or accounting for, the decision the firm expects its rival will make.

best-response curve
A curve indicating the best decision (usually the profit-maximizing one) given the decision the manager believes a rival will make.

To illustrate the concept of best-response curves, we use an example of two oligopoly airlines that compete with each other through pricing, although we could have chosen an example of output, advertising, product quality, or any other form of nonprice competition. The two airlines, Arrow Airlines and Bravo Airways, are the only airlines offering service to customers traveling between Lincoln, Nebraska, and Colorado Springs, Colorado. Managers at Arrow and Bravo are planning to set their round-trip coach ticket prices for travel during an upcoming four-day period of peak travel demand around Christmas. When prices are set, neither manager will know the price set by the other, so the decision is a simultaneous one.

Product differentiation exists between the two airlines because Arrow has newer, more comfortable jets than Bravo. The following demand functions for Arrow and Bravo are known to both airline managers (airline demand, then, is common knowledge):

$$Q_A = 4,000 - 25P_A + 12P_B$$
$$Q_B = 3,000 - 20P_B + 10P_A$$

where Q_A and Q_B are the total number of round-trip tickets sold and P_A and P_B are the prices charged, respectively, by Arrow and Bravo airlines over the four-day Christmas holiday travel period.

As it turns out, the managers make their pricing decisions several months before Christmas—but they won't be able to change their prices once they are chosen—and thus all of their costs during the Christmas season are variable costs at the time of the pricing decision. To keep matters simple, we will assume long-run costs are constant for airlines—so that marginal costs and average costs are equal—even though we know that airlines don't really experience constant costs.[5] Because Arrow uses newer, more fuel-efficient planes than Bravo, Arrow has lower costs than Bravo

$$LAC_A = LMC_A = \$160$$

$$LAC_B = LMC_B = \$180$$

Arrow incurs, on average, a cost of $160 per round-trip passenger, which is also Arrow's marginal cost of an extra round-trip passenger. Bravo, with its older planes, faces higher average and marginal costs of $180 per round-trip passenger.

To facilitate making simultaneous pricing decisions, each airline needs to know the best price for it to charge for any price it might expect its rival to charge. To fully account for their interdependence when making simultaneous pricing decisions, both managers need to know *both* their own best-response curve as well as the best-response curve of their rival. Managers must have knowledge of both their own and their rival's demand and cost conditions to construct their best-response curves. We will now show you how Arrow can construct its best-response curve, which is a straight line in this example.

Suppose Arrow believes Bravo will set a price of $100. The demand facing Arrow is found by substituting Bravo's price of $100 into Arrow's demand

$$Q_A = 4,000 - 25P_A + 12 \times \$100 = 5,200 - 25P_A$$

Following the steps set forth in Chapter 12 (Section 12.6), Arrow's manager can derive the following inverse demand and marginal revenue functions for Arrow

$$P_A = 208 - 0.04Q_A$$

and

$$MR_A = 208 - 0.08Q_A$$

Then, setting $MR_A = LMC_A$, the manager finds that Arrow's profit-maximizing output when Bravo charges $100 is 600 round-trip tickets

$$208 - 0.08Q_A = 160$$

and

$$Q_A^* = 600$$

---

[5]Carrying one more passenger on a plane requires very little extra fuel and peanuts, so marginal cost is much lower than average cost; indeed marginal cost is virtually zero for additional passengers sitting in otherwise empty seats. Since *LMC* is less than *LAC*, long-run average cost for airlines falls as the number of passengers increases. While allowing average costs to decrease would be more realistic in this airline example, it would only complicate the graphical analysis yet add nothing to your understanding of response curve analysis.

ILLUSTRATION 13.2

Mr. Nash Goes to Hollywood

There's trouble in Hollywood, and big trouble it is. Too many movie stars are becoming members of an elite club that film producers detest. The troublesome club, which some producers have reportedly named the "$25 Million per Movie Club," had just two members in 2000: Mel Gibson and Adam Sandler. The two film producers that paid Gibson and Sandler record-breaking $25 million salaries for single movies, Columbia Pictures and New Line Cinema, wanted to keep this news a secret because, once other producers and actors learn of these deals, many more actors will likely demand and receive entry into "the club." The new benchmark salary for top stars comes at a time when Hollywood's profits are falling sharply. According to market analysts, the primary cause for falling profits in the motion picture industry is soaring costs of production—and actors' salaries make up a large chunk of total production costs. Joe Roth, chairman of Walt Disney Studios, worries that the lack of cooperation in holding the line on salaries "could send the whole thing into chaos," and every big star would gain membership to the $25 Million per Movie Club. And even more worrisome, some producers think a $30 Million per Movie Club might soon open and begin a membership drive.

You might wonder, then, why the four or five largest film studios don't cooperate with one another by holding the line on actors' salaries. After all, film producers don't need to worry that big-name stars will turn down movie roles at the old benchmark of $20 million per film if all producers can agree to pay the same amount for top stars ($20 million per film). Why, then, are all of the Hollywood film producers hiking salaries?

We can answer this question by applying the concept of a prisoners' dilemma to the filmmakers' salary decision to "hold the line" at $20 million per film or to "hike salaries" to $25 million per film. To keep things simple, suppose that there are only two major film producers in Hollywood, New Line Cinema and Columbia Pictures. The two film producers compete to hire the big-name stars in Hollywood whose names can almost guarantee a film will be hugely profitable. Assume Hollywood has only six such big-name stars. Each studio plans to make six films this year, and each film could use one top star who would be paid either $20 million or $25 million, depending on the salary decision made by each studio. Furthermore, assume producers can make their films and earn their entire theater and video revenues in the same year. New Line and Columbia make their salary decisions without knowing the other's decision at the time they make their own decision, so that the situation represents a simultaneous strategic decision.

The payoff table below shows the profit outcomes for each studio for the various decision situations. In cell A, both film producers stick to a $20 million benchmark and end up splitting the talent pool of six top stars: Columbia and New Line each land three of the six big-name stars. They do not plan to cooperate in splitting the stars equally; they just *expect* to get equal shares of the total number when they both pay the same salary. By keeping costs "low" and sharing equally the biggest stars, each studio expects to make $100 million of total profit on its six films this year. In cell D, the producers each decide to hike salaries to $25 million per film and expect to share equally the big stars. Annual profits are just $85 million each because production costs rise by $15 million (= 3 top stars × $5 million salary hike) for each filmmaker.

		New Line Cinema	
		Hold the line ($20M)	Hike salaries ($25M)
Columbia Pictures	**Hold the line ($20M)**	A **$100M,** *$100M*	B **$50M,** *$150M*
	Hike salaries ($25M)	C **$150M,** *$50M*	D **$85M,** *$85M*

Payoffs in millions of dollars of annual profit.

Cells B and C show payoffs when one studio "holds the line" and the other "hikes salaries." The studio hiking salaries expects to attract all six of the top stars, while the studio that holds the line at $20 million per film cannot expect to attract any of the six top stars and will have to hire less-profitable actors. The payoffs in cells B and C reflect the advantage to one studio of getting all the stars ($150 million annual profit) and the disadvantage to the other studio of getting none of the stars ($50 million annual profit).

As we explained in our discussion of prisoners' dilemma games, both Columbia and New Line have dominant strategies: hike salaries. Dominant strategy equilibrium occurs in cell D, which is also strategically stable and is the only Nash equilibrium cell in this strategic game. Notice that when both studios choose their dominant strategies in cell D, they both do worse than they could if they both would decide to hold the line on salaries in cell A. Cell A, however, is not strategically stable because both film studios can unilaterally increase their profits by hiking salaries *if they believe the other studio will hold the line on salaries.* And, as we have stressed throughout this chapter, rational decision makers do not believe it is correct to predict rivals will do anything other than what is best for themselves. Since, in cell A, both film studios are not doing best for themselves given the expected choice of the other studios, cell A would not be chosen by rational decision makers.

The prisoners' dilemma model of making salary decisions provides a rather convincing explanation of what might otherwise seem like an irrational situation in Hollywood: Filmmakers are losing money because of rising production costs, but the film producers continue to hike salaries of top stars. While we cannot confirm the truth of this rumor, we have heard from reliable sources that the secret toast of Hollywood's most highly paid stars is "All hail to Mr. Nash." Film producers have been overheard using a slight variation of this salute.

Source: This Illustration is based on Tom King, "Hollywood Raises Salaries Past the $20-Million Mark," *The Wall Street Journal,* January 7, 2000.

The best price for Arrow to charge when it thinks Bravo is going to charge $100 is found by substituting $Q_A^* = 600$ into the inverse demand, and this price is $184 ($= 208 - 0.04 \times 600$).

This process for finding Arrow's best price when Bravo charges $100, which is illustrated by point *r* in Panel A of Figure 13.1, locates only *one* point (point *R*) on the best-response curve for Arrow Airlines shown in Panel B. By repeating the process for all other prices that Bravo might be expected to charge, Arrow can construct a complete best-response curve. For any price that Bravo might set, Arrow's best-response curve, shown as BR_A in Panel B, gives the price that Arrow should set to maximize Arrow's profit.

You might be concerned, and quite reasonably so, that constructing a best-response curve requires far too much computational effort since the process just discussed, and illustrated in Panel A, must be repeated for *every* price Bravo might choose. Best-response curves, however, are rather easily constructed when demand and marginal cost curves are both linear, as they are in this example, because the best-response curves will be straight lines.[6] Arrow's manager only needs

---

[6]When demand or marginal cost curves, or both, are not linear, calculus can be used to derive mathematical equations for best-response curves. In the appendix to this chapter, we show you how to derive best-response curves by using calculus.

FIGURE 13.1

Deriving the Best-Response Curve for Arrow Airlines

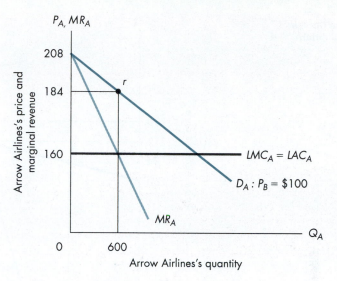

Panel A — Arrow believes P_B = $100

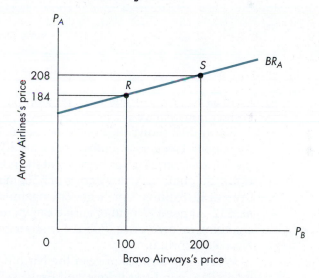

Panel B — Two points on Arrow's best-response curve

to find best prices for *two* of the prices Bravo might set. A straight line passing through these two points will then produce Arrow's entire best-response curve.

To see how this works, suppose now that Bravo is expected to set a price of $200 instead of $100. You can verify for yourself that Arrow's best-response is to set a price of $208. After plotting this best-response point in Panel B, shown

FIGURE 13.2

**Best-Response Curves
and Nash Equilibrium**

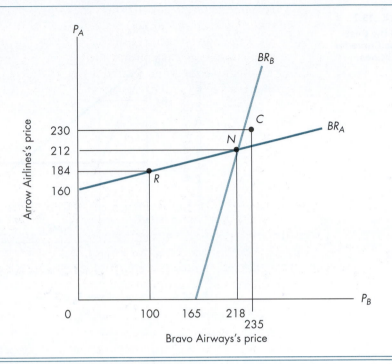

there as point S, a straight line passing through points R and S produces Arrow's best-response curve BR_A.

Figure 13.2 shows the best-response curves for both Arrow Airlines and Bravo Airways. Managers at both airlines are likely to set prices at the intersection of the best-response curves because, at the point of intersection, mutually best prices result. At point N, Arrow's price of $212 maximizes Arrow's profit if Bravo sets its price at $218. Bravo's price of $218 maximizes Bravo's profit if Arrow sets its price at $212. At point N, neither airline can increase its individual profit by unilaterally changing its own price. Point N is strategically stable, and the pair of prices is a Nash equilibrium.

When both airlines price at the Nash point for the Christmas holiday, Arrow sells 1,316 round-trip tickets, and Bravo sells 760 tickets

$$Q_A = 4{,}000 - (25 \times 212) + (12 \times 218) = 1{,}316$$

$$Q_B = 3{,}000 - (20 \times 218) + (10 \times 212) = 760$$

At the Nash prices, Arrow Airlines earns profit of $68,432 [= (212 − 160) × 1,316], and Bravo can expect to earn profit of $28,880 [= (218 − 180) × 760].

Once again, we want to emphasize that the Nash equilibrium at point N is not chosen because the managers are coordinating their pricing in a cooperative way. The prices at point N are chosen because both managers, keenly aware of their interdependence, know that they cannot do the best for themselves individually unless they correctly anticipate the price the other will set. Beliefs about what rivals will charge can only be correct if rivals are also setting their best prices.

While the prices at point N allow each one of the airlines to do the best it can given the price set by its rival, this does *not* mean that no other price pair is better for both airlines. Actually, point N in Figure 13.2 may well be similar to cell D in the prisoners' dilemma. Neither firm is making as much profit as would be possible if both firms *cooperated* and both set higher prices.

To confirm that Arrow and Bravo could both make more profit if they cooperated in setting higher prices, we will let you verify that point C in Figure 13.2, where Arrow's price is $230 and Bravo's price is $235, is a more profitable pair of prices for *both* airlines. Point C is not unique. There are many other price pairs that can increase both firms' profits. The airlines don't end up with one of these better combinations of prices because such price pairs are not strategically stable when firms behave noncooperatively. Neither airline can prevent the other from cheating on a cooperative agreement to set prices at point C. Both airlines have an incentive to cheat on an agreement to set their prices at point C because both airlines can increase their individual profits by unilaterally lowering their own prices.

As we will show you later in this chapter, this is exactly why managers seldom succeed at colluding to set high prices. Unilateral cheating by either firm's secretly lowering its price will increase the profit of the cheating firm—unless, as you will see later, all firms cheat. Once again, you can see the crucial role that interdependence plays in making pricing decisions in oligopoly markets. We can now summarize this section with a principle.

Now try Technical
Problems 8–11.

> **Principle** When decision choices are continuous, best-response curves give managers the profit-maximizing price to set given the price they anticipate their rival will set. A Nash equilibrium occurs at the price pair where the firms' best-response curves intersect.

13.2 STRATEGY WHEN RIVALS MAKE SEQUENTIAL DECISIONS

sequential decisions
When one firm makes its decision first, then a rival firm makes its decision.

In contrast to simultaneous decisions, the natural process of some decisions requires one firm to make a decision, and then a rival firm, *knowing the action taken by the first firm,* makes its decision. Such decisions are called **sequential decisions.** For example, a potential entrant into a market will make its decision to enter or stay out of a market first, and then the incumbent firm (or firms) responds to the entry decision by adjusting prices and outputs to maximize profit given the decision of the potential entrant. In another common kind of sequential decision, one firm makes its pricing, output, or advertising decision ahead of another. The firm making its decision second knows the decision of the first firm. As we will show you in this section, the order of decision making can sometimes, but not always, create an advantage to going first or going second when making sequential decisions.

Even though they are made at different times, sequential decisions nonetheless involve strategic interdependence. Sequential decisions are linked over time: The best decision a manager can make today depends on how rivals will respond tomorrow. Strategically astute managers, then, must think ahead to anticipate their rivals' future decisions. Current decisions are based on what managers believe rivals will likely do in the future. You might say a manager jumps ahead in time and then thinks backward to the present. Making sequential decisions, like making simultaneous decisions, involves getting into the heads of rivals to predict their decisions so that you can make better decisions for yourself. Once again, oligopoly decisions involve strategic interdependence.

Making Sequential Decisions

game tree
A diagram showing the structure and payoff of a sequential decision situation.

decision nodes
Points in a game tree, represented by boxes, where decisions are made.

Sequential decisions can be analyzed using payoff tables, but an easier method, which we will employ here, involves the use of *game trees*. A **game tree** is a diagram showing firms' decisions as **decision nodes** with branches extending from the nodes, one for each action that can be taken at the node. The sequence of decisions usually proceeds from left to right along branches until final payoffs associated with each decision path are reached. Game trees are fairly easy to understand when you have one to look at, so let's look at an example now. Suppose that the pizza pricing decision in Table 13.2 is now a sequential decision. Castle Pizza makes its pricing decision first at decision node 1, and then Palace Pizza makes its pricing decision second at one of the two decision nodes labeled with 2s. Panel A in Figure 13.3 shows the game tree representing the sequential decision.

Castle goes first in this example, as indicated by the leftmost position of decision node 1. Castle can choose either a high price along the top branch or a low price along the bottom branch. Next, Palace makes its decision to go high or low. Since Palace goes second, it knows the pricing decision of Castle. Castle's decision, then, requires two decision nodes, each one labeled 2: one for Palace's decision if Castle prices high and one for Palace's decision if Castle prices low. Payoffs for the four possible decision outcomes are shown at the end of Palace's decision branches. Notice that the payoffs match those shown in the payoff table of Table 13.2.

Castle decides first, so it doesn't know Palace's price when it makes its pricing decision. How should the manager of Castle pizza make its pricing decision? As in simultaneous decisions, the manager of Castle tries to anticipate Palace's decision by assuming Palace will take the action giving Palace the highest payoff. So Castle's manager looks ahead and puts itself in Palace's place: "If I price high, Palace receives its best payoff by pricing low: $1,200 is better than $1,000 for Palace. If I price low, Palace receives its best payoff by pricing low: $400 is better than $300." In this situation, since Palace chooses low no matter what Castle chooses, Palace has a dominant strategy: price low. Panel B in Figure 13.3 shows Palace's best decisions as gray-colored branches.

Knowing that Palace's dominant strategy is low, Castle predicts Palace will price low for either decision Castle might make. Castle's manager, then, should choose to price high and earn $500 because $500 is better than pricing low and earning $400.

FIGURE 13.3
Sequential Pizza Pricing

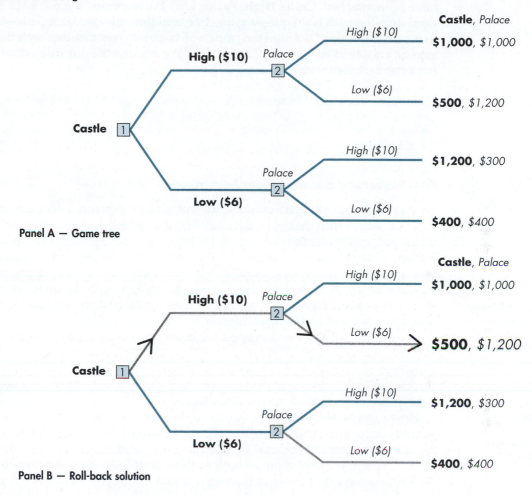

Panel A — Game tree

Panel B — Roll-back solution

roll-back method
Method of finding a
Nash solution to a
sequential decision by
looking ahead to future
decisions to reason
back to the best current
decision. (Also known as
backward induction.)

This process of looking ahead to future decisions to make the best current decision
is called the *backward induction technique* or, more simply, the **roll-back method** of
making sequential decisions.

Notice that the roll-back solution to a sequential decision is a Nash equilibrium: Castle earns the highest payoff, given the (best) decision it predicts Palace
will make, and Palace is making its best decision given the (best) decision Castle
makes. We must stress, however, that Palace, by making its decision last, does not
need to *anticipate* or *predict* Castle's decision; Castle's decision is known with certainty when Palace chooses its price. The complete roll-back solution to the pizza

pricing decision, also referred to as the *equilibrium decision path*, is indicated in Panel B by the unbroken sequence of gray-colored branches on which arrowheads have been attached: Castle **High,** Palace *Low*. Furthermore, the roll-back equilibrium decision path is unique—a game tree contains only one such path—because in moving backward through the game, roll back requires that the *single* best decision be chosen at each node of the game.[7] We summarize our discussion of this important concept with a principle.

> **Principle**   When firms make sequential decisions, managers make best decisions for themselves by working backward through the game tree using the roll-back method. The roll-back method results in a unique path that is also a Nash decision path: Each firm does the best for itself given the best decisions made by its rivals.

First-Mover and Second-Mover Advantages

As you might have already guessed, the outcome of sequential decisions may depend on which firm makes its decision first and which firm goes second. Sometimes you can increase your payoff by making your decision first in order to influence later decisions made by rivals. Letting rivals know with certainty what you are doing—going first usually, but not always, does this—increases your payoff if rivals then choose actions more favorable to you. In such situations, a **first-mover advantage** can be secured by making the first move or taking the first action in a sequential decision situation.

first-mover advantage
A firm can increase its payoff by making its decision first.

In other situations, firms may earn higher payoffs by letting rivals make the first move, committing themselves to a course of action and making that action known to firms making later decisions. When higher payoffs can be earned by reacting to earlier decisions made by rivals, the firm going second in a sequential decision enjoys a **second-mover advantage.**

second-mover advantage
A firm can increase its payoff by making its decision second.

How can you tell whether a sequential decision has a first-mover advantage, a second-mover advantage, or neither type of advantage (the order of decision making doesn't matter either way)? The simplest way, and frequently the only way, is to find the roll-back solution for both sequences. If the payoff increases by being the first-mover, a first-mover advantage exists. If the payoff increases by being the second-mover, a second-mover advantage exists. If the payoffs are unchanged by reversing the order of moves, then, of course, the order doesn't matter. We now illustrate a decision for which a first-mover advantage exists.

Suppose the Brazilian government awards two firms, Motorola and Sony, the exclusive rights to share the market for cellular phone service in Brazil. Motorola and Sony are allowed to service as many customers in Brazil as they wish, but the government sets a ceiling price for cellular service at $800 annually per customer. The two companies know that each plans to charge the maximum price allowed, $800.

---

[7]Game theorists refer to the Nash equilibrium path found by implementing the roll-back method as a *subgame–perfect equilibrium path* because best decisions are made at every node or "subgame" in the game tree.

Motorola and Sony can both provide either *analog* or *digital* cellular phones. Motorola, however, has a cost advantage in analog technology, and Sony has a cost advantage in digital technology. Their annual costs per customer, which remain constant for any number of customers served, are as follows:

	Motorola	Sony
Annual cost of analog service	$250	$400
Annual cost of digital service	$350	$325

Demand forecasters at Motorola and Sony work together to estimate the total demand for cellular phone service in Brazil. They discover that Brazilians do not care which technology they buy, but total sales will suffer if Motorola and Sony do not agree to offer the *same* technology. The desire to have a single technology arises because the two technologies will probably not be compatible: Analog customers and digital customers will not be able to communicate. (Motorola and Sony can solve the compatibility problem, but it will take several years to solve the problem.) Demand estimates show that, at a price of $800 per year, a total of 50,000 Brazilians will sign up for cell phone service if Motorola and Sony provide the same technology, but only 40,000 will sign up at $800 per year if the two firms offer different technologies. Motorola and Sony expect that sales will be evenly divided between them: 25,000 customers each if the same technologies are chosen or 20,000 customers each if they choose different technologies.

You can see from the payoff table in Figure 13.4 that Motorola and Sony both make greater profit if they choose the same technologies than if they choose opposite technologies: Cells A and D are both better than either cell C or B. If the technology decision is made simultaneously, *both* cells A and D are Nash equilibrium cells, and game theory provides no clear way to predict the outcome. Motorola, of course, would like to end up in cell A since it has a cost advantage in analog technology and will sell more analog phone service if Sony also chooses analog. How can Motorola entice Sony to choose analog technology so that the outcome is cell A?

The clever manager at Motorola sees that, if Motorola chooses its (analog) technology first, cell A is the predicted outcome. To see why cell A is the likely outcome, we turn to Panel B, which shows the game tree when Motorola goes first. To find the solution to this sequential game, Motorola's manager applies the roll-back method. First, the manager finds Sony's best decisions at Sony's two decision nodes. At the decision node where Motorola chooses *Digital,* Sony's best decision is **Digital,** which is the outcome in cell D. At the decision node where Motorola chooses *Analog,* Sony's best decision is **Analog,** which is the outcome in cell A. Then, rolling back to Motorola's decision, Motorola knows that if it chooses *Digital,* then it will end up with $11.25 million when Sony makes its best decision, which is to go **Digital.** If Motorola chooses *Analog,* then it will end up with $13.75 million when Sony makes its best decision, which is to go **Analog.** Roll-back analysis indicates Motorola does best, given the choice Sony will later make, by choosing *Analog.* This Nash equilibrium path is shown in Panel B as the gray-colored branches with arrows.

FIGURE 13.4

First-Mover Advantage in Technology Choice

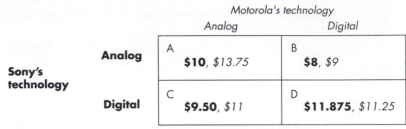

Panel A — Simultaneous technology decision

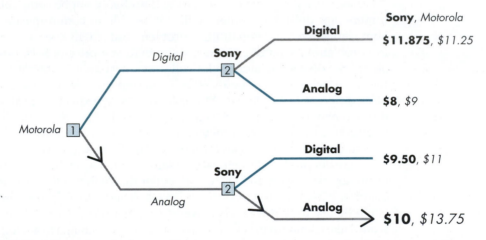

Panel B — Motorola secures a first-mover advantage

To have a first-mover advantage, Motorola must receive a higher payoff when it goes first compared with its payoff when it goes second. In this game, Motorola does indeed experience a first-mover advantage because roll-back analysis shows that Motorola earns only $11.25 million when Sony goes first. (You will verify this in Technical Problem 13.) Thus Motorola gains a first-mover advantage in this game of choosing cellular phone technology. We summarize our discussion of first-mover and second-mover advantage with a relation.

▣ **Relation** To determine whether the order of decision making can confer an advantage when firms make sequential decisions, the roll-back method can be applied to the game trees for each possible sequence of decisions. If the payoff increases by being the first (second) to move, then a first-mover (second-mover) advantage exists. If the payoffs are identical, then order of play confers no advantage.

Now try Technical
Problems 12–13.

As you probably noticed, we did not discuss here *how* Motorola gains the first-mover position in this game of choosing cellular phone technology. Determining which firm goes first (or second) can be quite complex, and difficult to predict, when both firms recognize that going first (or second) confers a first-mover (or second-mover) advantage. We will now examine several strategic moves that firms might employ to alter the structure of a game to their advantage.

Strategic Moves: Commitments, Threats, and Promises

As we have emphasized, strategic decision making requires you to get into the heads of your rivals to anticipate their reactions to your decisions. We now want to take you a step beyond *anticipating* your rivals' reactions to taking actions to *manipulate* your rivals' reactions. We will now examine three kinds of actions managers can take to achieve better outcomes for themselves, usually to the detriment of their rivals. These strategic actions, which game theorists refer to as **strategic moves**, are called *commitments, threats,* and *promises.*

These three strategic moves, which, in most cases, must be made before rivals have made their decisions, may be utilized separately or in combination with each other. Strategic moves will achieve their desired effects only if rivals think the firms making the moves will actually carry out their commitments, threats, or promises. Rivals will ignore strategic moves that are not *credible.* A strategic move is **credible** if, when a firm is called upon to act on the strategic move, it is in the best interest of the firm making the move to carry it out. Making strategic moves credible is not easy, and we cannot give you any specific rules that will work in every situation. We will, however, provide you with the basic ideas for making credible strategic moves in the discussions that follow.[8] We first discuss commitments, which are unconditional strategic moves, and then we turn to threats and promises, which are conditional moves.

Managers make **commitments** by announcing, or demonstrating to rivals in some other way, that they will bind themselves to take a particular action or make a specific decision *no matter what action or decision is taken by its rivals.* Commitments, then, are unconditional actions the committing firms undertake for the purpose of increasing their payoffs. A commitment only works if rivals believe the committing firm has genuinely locked itself into a specific decision or course of action. In other words, commitments, like all strategic moves, must be credible to have strategic value.

Generally, a firm's commitment will not be credible unless it is *irreversible.* If some other decision later becomes the best decision for the committing firm, rivals will expect the committing firm to abandon its commitment if it can. Rivals will

strategic moves
Three kinds of actions that can be used to put rivals at a disadvantage: commitments, threats, or promises.

credible
A strategic move that will be carried out because it is in the best interest of the firm making the move to carry it out.

commitments
Unconditional actions taken for the purpose of increasing payoffs to the committing firms.

---

[8]To get a more thorough and richer development of the practical application of strategic moves to business decision making than is possible in one or two chapters of a textbook, we recommend you read two of our favorite books on the subject: Avinash Dixit and Barry Nalebuff, *Thinking Strategically: The Competitive Edge in Business, Politics, and Everyday Life* (New York: W. W. Norton, 1991); and John MacMillan, *Games, Strategies, and Managers* (New York: Oxford University Press, 1992).

believe a commitment is irreversible only if it would be prohibitively costly, or even impossible, for the committing firm to reverse its action. In short, only *credible* commitments—those that are irreversible—successfully alter rivals' beliefs about the actions the committing firm will take.

To illustrate how credible commitments can improve profitability, suppose that Motorola and Sony make their choices between analog and digital technologies *simultaneously* according to the payoff table shown in Panel A of Figure 13.4. The outcome of the simultaneous game is difficult for either firm to predict since there are *two* Nash equilibrium cells, A and D. The manager of Motorola, however, decides to make a commitment to analog technology *before* the simultaneous decision takes place by building a facility in Brazil specifically designed for manufacturing and servicing *only* analog phones. Both firms know that the cost of converting Motorola's new plant to production of digital cellular phones is enormous. Consequently, Motorola is unlikely to incur the huge costs of converting to digital technology, so Sony views Motorola's action as irreversible. Thus Motorola's strategic move is a *credible* commitment because Sony believes Motorola's action is irreversible.

Notice that Motorola's commitment transforms the *simultaneous* decision situation in Panel A into the *sequential* decision situation shown in Panel B. Motorola, through its use of credible commitment, seizes the first-mover advantage and ensures itself the outcome in cell A. We have now established the following principle.

Principle　Firms make credible commitments by taking unconditional, irreversible actions. Credible commitments give committing firms the first moves in sequential games, and by taking the first actions, committing firms manipulate later decisions their rivals will make in a way that improves their own profitability.

threats
Conditional strategic moves that take the form: "If you do A, I will do B, which is costly to you."

In contrast to commitments, which are unconditional in nature, threats and promises are *conditional* decisions or actions. **Threats**, whether they are made explicitly or tacitly, take the form of a conditional statement, "If you take action *A*, I will take action *B*, which is undesirable or costly to you." The purpose of making threats is to manipulate rivals' beliefs about the likely behavior of the threatening firms in a way that increases payoffs to the threatening firms. For example, firms that are already producing a product or service in a market and earning profits there may try to deter new firms from entering the profitable market by threatening, "If you enter this market, I will then lower my price to make the market unprofitable for you."

Threats do not always succeed in altering the decisions of rivals. For threats to be successful in changing rivals' behavior, rivals must believe the threat will actually be carried out. Following our discussion about credible strategic moves, a threat is credible if, when the firm is called upon to act on the threat, it is in the best interest of the firm making the threat to carry it out.

Consider again the simultaneous technology decision in Panel A of Figure 13.4. Suppose, before the simultaneous decisions are made, Motorola threatens Sony by saying to Sony, "If you choose digital technology for your cellular phones, we will choose analog." In making this threat, Motorola wants Sony to think, "Since Motorola is going to go analog if we choose digital, then we might as well choose analog because cell A is better for us than cell C." Motorola's threat, however, will fail to produce this thinking by Sony. Instead of this reasoning, it is much more likely that Sony will think, "Motorola's threat is not credible: if we choose digital, Motorola's best decision is to choose digital, and so Motorola will not carry out its threat." As you can see, Motorola's threat is ignored and, consequently, has no strategic value. Once again, only credible strategic moves matter.

promises
Conditional strategic moves that take the form: "If you do A, I will do B, which is desirable to you."

Promises, like threats, are also conditional statements that must be credible to affect strategic decisions. Promises take the form of a conditional statement, "If you take action *A*, I will take action *B*, which is desirable or rewarding to you." For example, one rival may promise other rivals that if they do not add to their product some costly improvement that consumers desire, it will not add the costly improvement to its product either. Promises, just like commitments and threats, must be credible to affect the decisions of rivals. We summarize our discussion of strategic moves—commitments, threats, and promises—in a principle.

Principle Managers make strategic moves to manipulate their rivals' decisions for the purpose of increasing their own profits by putting rivals at a strategic disadvantage. Only credible strategic moves matter; rivals ignore any commitments, threats, or promises that will not be carried out should the opportunity to do so arise.

Now try Technical
Problem 14.

We cannot overstate the value of learning to utilize strategic moves in decision making. Stories in the business press about "smart" or "successful" managers quite often are stories about how managers have utilized credible commitments, threats, or promises to secure more profitable outcomes. We will now discuss one of the most important types of strategic moves: moves that deter new rivals from entering markets where economic profits are being earned.

13.3 COOPERATION IN REPEATED STRATEGIC DECISIONS

As you know, oligopolists pursuing their individual gains can, and often do, end up worse off than if they were to cooperate. The situation is analogous to dividing a pie. People are struggling to get a larger share of a pie, but in the struggle some of the pie gets knocked off the table and onto the floor, and they end up sharing a smaller pie. A solution preferred by all participants exists but is difficult to achieve. And, even if the preferred situation is somehow reached, such as the results in cell A in the prisoners' dilemma (Table 13.1) or point C in the airline example (Figure 13.2), rivals have a strong incentive to change their actions, which leads back to the noncooperative Nash equilibrium: cell D in the prisoners' dilemma or point N in the airline example. **Cooperation** occurs, then, when oligopoly firms make individual decisions that make every firm better off than they would be in a noncooperative Nash equilibrium outcome.

cooperation
When firms make decisions that make every firm better off than in a noncooperative Nash equilibrium.

As we have now established, when prisoners' dilemma decisions are made just one time, managers have almost no chance of achieving cooperative outcomes. In many instances, however, decisions concerning pricing, output, advertising, entry, and other such strategic decisions are made repeatedly. Decisions made

TABLE 13.5
A Pricing Dilemma for AMD and Intel

		AMD's price	
		High	Low
Intel's price	**High**	A: Cooperation **$5,** $2.5	B: AMD cheats **$2,** $3
	Low	C: Intel cheats **$6,** $0.5	D: Noncooperation **$3,** $1

Payoffs in millions of dollars of profit per week.

---

repeated decisions
Decisions made over and over again by the same firms.

over and over again by the same firms are called **repeated decisions.** Repeating a strategic decision provides managers with something they do not get in one-time decisions: a chance to punish cheaters. The opportunity to punish cheating in repeated decisions can completely change the outcome of strategic decisions.

One-Time Prisoners' Dilemma Decisions

Prisoners' dilemma scenarios, as we explained previously, always possess a set of decisions for which every firm earns a higher payoff than they can when they each choose to follow their dominant strategies and end up in the noncooperative Nash equilibrium.[9] Cooperation is possible, then, in all prisoners' dilemma decisions.

Cooperation does not happen in one-time prisoners' dilemma situations because cooperative decisions are strategically unstable. If a firm believes its rivals are going to choose the cooperative decision in a simultaneous decision, then the firm can increase its profit by choosing the noncooperative decision. For convenience in discussions concerning cooperation, game theorists call making non-cooperative decisions **cheating.** We must stress, however, that "cheating" does not imply that the oligopoly firms have made any kind of explicit, or even tacit, agreement to cooperate. If a firm's rivals expect that firm to make a cooperative decision, they will have an incentive to cheat by making a noncooperative decision. All oligopoly managers know this and so choose not to cooperate. While the incentive to cheat makes cooperation a strategically unstable outcome in a one-time simultaneous decision, cooperation may arise when decisions are repeated.

cheating
When a manager makes a noncooperative decision.

We can best illustrate the possibility of cooperation, as well as the profit incentive for cheating, with an example of a pricing dilemma. Suppose two firms, Intel and Advanced Micro Devices (AMD), dominate the wholesale market for high-speed microprocessor chips for personal computers. Intel and AMD simultaneously set their chip prices. For now, let us consider this a one-time simultaneous pricing decision, and the prices set by the firms will be valid for a period of one week. (In the next section, we will reconsider this decision when it is repeated every week.) Table 13.5 shows the profit payoffs from setting either high or low

---

[9]To keep things simple, we continue to restrict our discussion to decisions having only one Nash equilibrium. Game theorists so far have been unable to provide much useful guidance for decisions possessing multiple Nash equilibria.

prices for high-speed computer chips. You can verify from the payoff table that a prisoners' dilemma situation exists.

When the semiconductor chip prices are set noncooperatively, as they will be when the pricing decision is made only once, both firms will choose to set low prices and end up in cell D. Setting a low price for computer chips is the dominant strategy for both firms and this leads to the noncooperative Nash equilibrium outcome (cell D). As in every prisoners' dilemma game, both firms can do better by cooperating rather than by choosing their dominant strategy–Nash equilibrium actions. Intel and AMD both can choose high prices for their chips and both can then earn greater profits in cell A than in the noncooperative cell D: Intel earns an additional $2 million ($5 million − $3 million) and AMD earns an additional $1.5 million ($2.5 million − $1 million) through cooperation.

The problem with cooperation, as we have stressed previously, is that the decisions Intel and AMD must make to get to cell A are not strategically stable. Both firms worry that the other will cheat if one of them decides to cooperate and price high. For example, if AMD expects Intel is going to cooperate and set a high price, AMD does better by cheating and setting a low price in cell B: AMD earns $0.5 million more ($3 million − $2.5 million) by cheating than by making the cooperative decision to price high. Similarly, Intel can cheat on AMD in cell C and earn $1 million more ($6 million − $5 million) by cheating than by cooperating.

Suppose the managers at AMD and Intel tell each other that they will set high prices. This is, of course, farfetched since such a conversation is illegal. We are only trying to explain here why such an agreement would not work to achieve cooperation, so we can go ahead with our examination of this hypothetical scenario anyway. If the simultaneous pricing decision is to be made just once, neither firm can believe the other will live up to the agreement. Let us get into the head of AMD's manager to see what she thinks about setting AMD's price high. If AMD cooperates and prices high, it dawns on her that Intel has a good reason to cheat: Intel does better by cheating ($1 million better in cell C than in cell A) when Intel believes AMD will honor the agreement. And furthermore, she thinks, "What's the cost to Intel for cheating?" She won't know if Intel cheated until after they have both set their prices (the prices are set simultaneously). At that point, Intel's manager could care less if he ruins his reputation with her; it's a one-time decision and the game is over. Any hope of reaching a cooperative outcome vanishes when she realizes that Intel's manager must be thinking precisely the same things about her incentive to cheat. There is no way he is going to trust her not to cheat, so she *expects* him to cheat. The best she can do when he cheats is to cheat as well. And so an opportunity to achieve cooperation collapses over worries about cheating.

Even though cooperation is possible in all prisoners' dilemma situations, oligopoly firms have compelling reasons to believe rivals will cheat when the decision is to be made only one time. In these one-time decisions, there is no practical way for firms to make their rivals believe they will not cheat. When there is no tomorrow in decision making, rivals know they have only one chance to get the

Now try Technical
Problem 15.

most for themselves. A decision to cheat seems to be costless to the cheating firm because it expects its rival to cheat no matter what it decides to do. Furthermore, firms don't have to worry about any future costs from their decisions to cheat because they are making one-time decisions. Our discussion of decision making in one-time prisoners' dilemmas establishes the following principle.

> **Principle**   Cooperation is possible in every prisoners' dilemma decision, but cooperation is not strategically stable when the decision is made only once. In one-time prisoners' dilemmas, there can be no future consequences from cheating, so both firms expect the other to cheat, which then makes cheating the best response for each firm.

Punishment for Cheating in Repeated Decisions

punishment for cheating
Making a retaliatory decision that forces rivals to return to a noncooperative Nash outcome.

Punishment for cheating, which cannot be done in a one-time decision, makes cheating costly in repeated decisions. Legal sanctions or monetary fines for cheating are generally illegal in most countries; **punishment for cheating** usually takes the form of a retaliatory decision by the firm doing the punishment that returns the game to a noncooperative Nash decision—the decision everyone wanted to avoid through cooperation.

To illustrate how retaliatory decisions can punish rivals for noncooperative behavior, suppose that AMD and Intel make their pricing decisions repeatedly. AMD and Intel list their wholesale computer chip prices on the Internet every Monday morning, and the managers expect this to go on forever.[10] Table 13.5 shows the weekly payoffs for the repeated pricing decisions, and these payoffs are not expected to change from week to week in this hypothetical example. Further suppose that AMD and Intel have been making, up until now, cooperative weekly pricing decisions in cell A. Now, in the current week—call this week 1—AMD's manager decides to cheat by setting a low price. Thus during week 1, Intel and AMD receive the profit payoffs in cell B of Table 13.5. Intel's manager can punish AMD in the next weekly repetition, which would be week 2, by lowering its price. Notice that AMD cannot avoid getting punished in week 2 should Intel decide to retaliate by pricing low. In week 2, AMD can either price low and end up in cell D or price high and end up in cell C; either decision punishes AMD. Of course we predict AMD would choose to price low in week 2, because cell D minimizes AMD's cost of punishment from Intel's retaliatory price cut.

It follows from the discussion above that Intel can make a *credible* threat in week 1 to punish cheating with a retaliatory price cut in week 2 because cutting price is Intel's best response in week 2 to cheating in week 1. You can see from the payoff table (Table 13.5) that Intel's profit increases by making the retaliatory cut

---

[10]Game theorists have studied a variety of repeated games: games repeated forever and games repeated a fixed or finite number of times. They even distinguish the finite games according to whether players do or do not know when the games will end. These subtle differences are important because they can dramatically affect the possibility of cooperation, and hence, the outcome of repeated games. To keep our discussion as simple and meaningful as possible, we will limit our analysis to situations in which managers believe the decisions will be repeated forever.

from $2 million per week to either $3 million per week or to $6 million per week, depending on AMD's pricing decision in week 2. You can also verify for yourself that AMD can similarly make a credible threat to cut price in retaliation for an episode of cheating by Intel.

In repeated decisions, unlike one-time decisions, cheating can be punished in later rounds of decision making. By making credible threats of punishment, strategically astute managers can sometimes, but not always, achieve cooperation in prisoners' dilemmas. We are now ready to examine how punishment can be used to achieve cooperation in repeated decisions.

Now try Technical
Problems 16–17.

Deciding to Cooperate

Recall from Chapter 1 that managers should make decisions that maximize the (present) value of a firm, which is the sum of the discounted expected profits in current and future periods. The decision to cooperate, which is equivalent to deciding not to cheat, affects a firm's future stream of profits. Consequently, managers must gauge the effect of cheating on the present value of their firm. Cooperation will increase a firm's value if the present value of the costs of cheating exceeds the present value of the benefits from cheating. Alternatively, cheating will increase a firm's value if the present value of the benefits from cheating outweighs the present value of the costs of cheating. When all firms in an oligopoly market choose not to cheat, then cooperation is achieved in the market.

Figure 13.5 shows the stream of future benefits and costs for a firm that cheats for N periods of time before getting caught, after which it is punished by a retaliatory price cut for P periods of time.[11] The benefits from cheating received in each of the N time periods $(B_1, B_2, \ldots, B_N)$ are the gains in profit each period from cheating rather than cooperating: $\pi_{Cheat} - \pi_{Cooperate}$. For simplicity, we assume the payoffs, and hence the benefits and costs of cheating, are constant in all repetitions of the decision. Of course, the benefits and costs from cheating occur in the future and so must be discounted using the appropriate discount rate for the cheating firm. The present value of the benefits from cheating when the discount rate per period is r can be calculated as

$$PV_{\text{Benefits of cheating}} = \frac{B_1}{(1 + r)^1} + \frac{B_2}{(1 + r)^2} + \cdots + \frac{B_N}{(1 + r)^N}$$

where $B_i = \pi_{Cheat} - \pi_{Cooperate}$ for $i = 1, \ldots, N$. The cost of cheating in each period, after cheating is discovered and continuing for P periods, is the loss in profit caused by the retaliatory price cut that results in a noncooperative Nash

---

[11]The pattern of benefits and costs shown in Figure 13.5 assumes that the firm making the decision to cheat in period 1 can receive the cooperative profit payoff in period 1 if it makes the cooperative decision rather than the cheating decision. The pattern also assumes that there are no further costs for cheating after the punishment ends in period $(N + P)$. The figure also depicts equal benefits and costs of cheating in each time period. Other patterns of benefits and costs are certainly possible. Figure 13.5 provides a general approach to modeling the benefits and costs of cheating.

FIGURE 13.5

A Firm's Benefits and Costs of Cheating

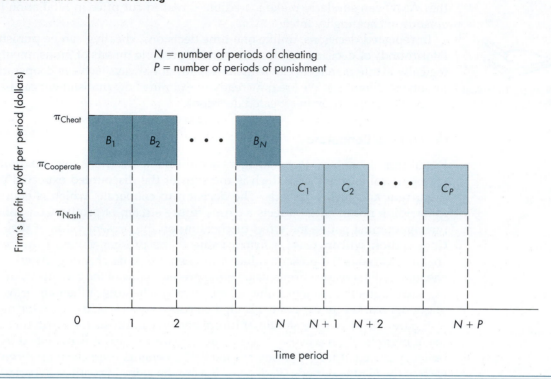

equilibrium: $\pi_{\text{Cooperate}} - \pi_{\text{Nash}}$. The costs of cheating, like the benefits from cheating, occur in the future and must be discounted. The present value of the costs of punishment for P periods (when the discount rate per period is r) can be calculated as

$$PV_{\text{Cost of cheating}} = \frac{C_1}{(1 + r)^{N+1}} + \frac{C_2}{(1 + r)^{N+2}} + \cdots + \frac{C_P}{(1 + r)^{N+P}}$$

where $C_j = \pi_{\text{Cooperate}} - \pi_{\text{Nash}}$ for $j = 1, \ldots, P$. We have now established the following principle.

Now try Technical
Problem 18.

Principle Cooperation (deciding not to cheat) maximizes the value of a firm when the present value of the costs of cheating is greater than the present value of the benefits from cheating. Cooperation is achieved in an oligopoly market when all firms decide not to cheat.

trigger strategies
Punishment strategies
that choose cooperative
actions until an episode
of cheating triggers a
period of punishment.

Trigger Strategies for Punishing Cheating

In repeated decisions, punishment itself becomes a strategy. We will now discuss a widely studied category of punishment strategies known in game theory as *trigger strategies*. Managers implement **trigger strategies** by initially choosing the cooperative action and continuing to choose the cooperative action in successive repetitions of the decision until a rival cheats. The act of cheating then "triggers" a punishment phase in the next repetition of the game that may last one or more repetitions, depending on the nature of the trigger scheme. The firm initiating the trigger strategy can announce openly to its rivals that it plans to follow a trigger strategy. Or, where attempts to facilitate cooperation might bring legal action, firms can secretly begin following a trigger strategy and hope that rivals will recognize what they are doing and choose to cooperate.

Two trigger strategies that have received much attention by game theorists are *tit-for-tat* and *grim strategies*. In a **tit-for-tat strategy,** cheating triggers punishment in the next decision period, and the punishment continues unless the cheating stops, which triggers a return to cooperation in the following decision period. In other words, if firm *B* cheated in the last decision period, firm *A* will cheat in this decision period. If firm *B* cooperated last time, then firm *A* will cooperate this time. Hence the name "tit-for-tat." Tit-for-tat is both simple to implement and simple for rivals to understand. A tit-for-tat strategy imposes a less severe punishment for cheating than a grim strategy. In a **grim strategy,** cheating triggers punishment in the next decision period, and the punishment continues forever, even if cheaters make cooperative decisions in subsequent periods. This is "grim" indeed!

Many experimental studies of repeated games have been undertaken to see how decision makers actually behave and also to determine which punishment strategies make cooperation most likely. In a famous "tournament" of strategies, Robert Axelrod at the University of Michigan invited game theorists to devise strategies for competition in repeated prisoners' dilemma games.[12] Numerous strategies were submitted, and computers were used to pit the strategies against each other in prisoners' dilemma decisions repeated hundreds of times. The strategies winning most of the time tended to be simple strategies rather than complicated or clever strategies. In a surprise to many game theorists, tit-for-tat emerged as the most profitable strategy because of its ability to initiate and sustain cooperation among oligopoly rivals. Other experimental studies and subsequent strategy tournaments have confirmed tit-for-tat to be the most profitable strategy to follow in repeated games. Eventually, game theorists, or perhaps oligopoly managers, may discover a better strategy for making repeated decisions, but for now, tit-for-tat is the winner.

Pricing Practices That Facilitate Cooperation

Cooperation usually increases profits, as well as the value of oligopoly firms; thus managers of firms in oligopoly markets frequently adopt tactics or methods of doing business that make cooperation among rivals more likely. Such tactics, called **facilitating practices** by antitrust officials, encourage cooperation either by reducing the benefits of cheating or by increasing the costs of cheating. And, sometimes, both of these things can be accomplished at

tit-for-tat strategy
A trigger strategy that punishes after an episode of cheating and returns to cooperation if cheating ends.

grim strategy
A trigger strategy that punishes forever after an episode of cheating.

facilitating practices
Generally lawful methods of encouraging cooperative pricing behavior.

---

[12]See Robert Axelrod, *The Evolution of Competition* (New York: Basic Books, 1984).

ILLUSTRATION 13.3

How to Avoid Price Wars and Stay Out of Jail Too

When a rival firm cuts its price, a manager's best strategic response, in many cases, is to retaliate with a price cut of its own. Successive repetitions of price cutting, frequently referred to as "price wars," can result in all firms doing worse than if they had not entered a price war. As we showed you in this chapter, if managers can find a way to cooperate in setting their prices, they can avoid getting into a low-price, low-profit situation and instead reach a higher-price, higher-profit situation. As the forces of globalization and deregulation of markets have made markets more competitive, price wars have become more common. Indeed, price wars are so common now that most managers will face a price war sometime in their careers.

Price wars leave oligopoly firms in situations like the noncooperative Nash cell D in the prisoners' dilemmas we have discussed in this chapter and the last chapter. Price wars can be avoided, just as cell D can be avoided, if firms can find ways to cooperate. As we have stressed several times, explicit arrangements to coordinate prices, called "collusion" and "price-fixing," are per se (categorically) illegal in the United States, and many other countries, especially in Europe, are outlawing price-fixing. Tacit collusion—agreement without explicit communication—is also illegal but is more difficult to discover and prove. As we mentioned in the text, penalties for price-fixing in the United States can be quite severe. In addition to facing steep fines, business executives can and do go to prison for the crime of price-fixing.

So there is the problem of price wars: Retaliatory price-cutting can lead to costly price wars, but attempts at setting prices cooperatively are generally illegal. What can managers do, that won't land them in jail for attempted price-fixing, to avoid being drawn into price wars? In a recent article in *Harvard Business Review*, Akshay Rao, Mark Bergen, and Scott Davis provide business executives with some practical advice on how to avoid price wars and, when they cannot be avoided, how to fight them successfully.[a] We will briefly discuss several of their tactics for avoiding price wars:

- Adopt a policy of price matching and advertise it so that your rivals believe your commitment to matching price cuts cannot (easily) be reversed. If rivals expect you to match price cuts, they are less likely to start a price war. And, if they expect you to match price hikes, they are more likely to expect you to cooperate by following their price increases.

- Make sure your competitors know you have low variable costs. Recall that firms only stop selling and shut down when price falls below average variable costs. Rivals will be wary of a price war if they believe you have low variable costs. In practice, it can be difficult to convince rivals that your variable costs are low, since rivals may believe you are providing them with false information about your costs to keep them from cutting price.

- Don't retaliate with a price cut of your own if you can maintain sales by increasing product or service quality. In those market segments where customers are particularly quality conscious, you may be able to hold on to customers, even though rivals' prices are lower, if consumers strongly demand quality products or services. When consumers view price as a measure of product quality, price-cutting may do permanent damage to a firm's reputation for high quality.

- Generally try to communicate to rivals that you prefer to compete in nonprice ways. Nonprice competition involves differentiating your product from rivals' products primarily through advertising and product quality.

These are a few of the practical (and legal) methods for avoiding price wars that are discussed in the article by Rao, Bergen, and Davis. While we agree with these authors that avoiding a price war is generally the most profitable policy, we must admit that, as consumers, we rather like price wars. Our advice to you, nonetheless, is to avoid price wars but don't go to jail trying!

[a]Akshay R. Rao, Mark E. Bergen, and Scott Davis, "How to Fight a Price War," *Harvard Business Review*, March–April 2000, pp. 107–16.

the same time. You should know about some of these practices because they are generally legal and they can increase the likelihood of achieving cooperation and earning higher profits.[13] While numerous business practices and tactics can assist or encourage cooperative behavior in oligopoly markets, we will limit our discussion here to four pricing practices that discourage or limit noncooperative price-cutting: price matching, sale-price guarantees, public pricing, and price leadership.

price matching
A commitment to match any rival's lower price.

Price matching From our discussion in the previous section, you know that any action a manager takes reducing the benefit of cheating will make cooperation more likely. Perhaps one of the most effective ways for reducing benefits of noncooperative price-cutting involves making a strategic commitment to *price matching*. A firm commits to a **price matching** strategy by publicly announcing, usually in an advertisement, that it will match any lower prices offered by its rivals. Price matching represents a strategic commitment in that legal costs and loss of goodwill would be substantial for any firm reneging on its public offer to match its rivals' lower prices. Thus, the benefit of cutting prices to steal rivals' customers largely vanishes when rivals force themselves to match immediately any other firm's price cuts.

sale-price guarantee
A firm's promise to give its buyers today any sale price it might offer during a stipulated future period.

Sale-price guarantees Another way oligopoly firms can discourage price-cutting behavior is for most, and better still, all rival firms to agree to give buyers *sale-price guarantees*. Your firm offers a **sale-price guarantee** by promising customers who buy an item from you today that they are entitled to receive any sale price your firm might offer for some stipulated future period, say, for 30 days after purchase. While this kind of insurance against lower future prices may increase current demand as some buyers decide to buy now rather than wait for a sale, the primary purpose of sale-price guarantees is to make it costly for firms to cut their prices. With a 30-day sale-price guarantee policy, for example, a manager who cuts price today not only loses revenue on today's sales but also loses revenue on *all* units sold for the past 30 days. Sale-price guarantees, then, discourage price-cutting by making the price cuts apply to more customers.

public pricing
Informing buyers about prices in a way that makes pricing information public knowledge.

Public pricing Noncooperative price-cutters expect to be discovered quickly, and so gain very little profit, when rival managers can monitor each other's pricing decisions easily and cheaply. For this reason, oligopoly managers frequently make pricing information available to their buyers using **public pricing** methods that give everyone access to their prices—not just potential buyers, but,

---

[13]While the facilitating practices discussed here are not prohibited under U.S. antitrust law, antitrust officials can, nonetheless, take legal action against firms engaged in any of these practices—or any other business practice for that matter—if they believe such practices "substantially lessen competition."

more importantly, rival sellers. To be effective, publicly available prices must be timely and authentic. Prices that are not up-to-date or that do not reflect actual transaction prices (i.e., list prices minus any negotiated discounts) offer little or no help for facilitating quick detection of noncooperative price cuts. As you can see in Figure 13.5, quick detection of a unilateral price-cut shortens the period during which a price-cutter benefits (N decreases in Figure 13.5), and early detection also speeds up delivery of retaliatory price cuts. Both of these effects reduce the likelihood that unilateral price cuts will increase the value of price-cutting firms.

Managers of oligopoly firms have found many simple, as well as ingenious, methods for making information about prices more openly available. Oligopoly managers, for example, may post their prices on the Internet, not so much as a convenience to buyers but to facilitate quick detection and punishment of unilateral price cuts. Oligopoly firms sometimes form trade associations or other similar types of organizations to monitor prices or even to publish member firms' prices in trade association publications or websites.

price leadership
A leader firm sets the industry profit-maximizing price and the follower firms cooperate by all setting the same price.

Price leadership   The final method we wish to mention for facilitating cooperative pricing involves behavior known as *price leadership*. **Price leadership** occurs when one oligopoly firm (the leader) sets its price at a level it believes will maximize total industry profit, and then the rest of the firms (the followers) cooperate by setting the same price. Once the price leader sets a price, all firms in the industry compete for sales through advertising and other types of marketing. The price remains constant until the price leader changes the price or one or more other firms break away. This arrangement does not require an explicit agreement among firms to follow the pricing behavior of the leader; the follower firms in the market just implicitly agree to the arrangement. For this reason, price leadership is not generally an unlawful means of achieving cooperative pricing.

Price leadership has been quite common in certain industries. It was characteristic of the steel industry some time ago. At times it has characterized the tire, oil, cigarette, and banking industries. Any firm in an oligopoly market can be the price leader. It is frequently the dominant firm in the market, while it may be simply the firm with a reputation for good judgment. There could exist a situation in which the most efficient—the least-cost—firm is the price leader, even though this firm is not the largest. In any case, the rival firms will follow the price leader only as long as they believe that the price leader's behavior accurately and promptly reflects changes in market conditions. We now turn our attention to the use of explicit price-fixing agreements to achieve cooperative pricing, which, in sharp contrast to price leadership, is always illegal.

Now try Technical Problem 19.

Explicit Price-Fixing Agreements and Cartels

While various facilitating practices can provide effective means of achieving cooperation, managers of oligopoly firms sometimes resort to explicit pricing agreements that seek to drive up prices by restricting competition. A group of

cartel
A group of firms or nations entering an explicit agreement to restrict competition for the purpose of driving up prices.

firms or nations entering such an agreement is called a price-fixing **cartel**. Cartel agreements may take the form of open collusion with members entering into contracts about price and other market variables, or the cartel may involve secret collusion among members. One of the most famous cartels is OPEC (the Organization of Petroleum Exporting Countries), an association of some of the world's major oil-producing nations. Numerous other cartels over the past century, often international in scope, have attempted to hike prices of agricultural products (such as rubber, tea, citric acid, lysine, cocoa, and coffee) and mineral resources (such as bauxite, tin, copper, uranium, and diamonds).[14] We now want to explain two reasons joining a cartel agreement to raise prices probably is not on this year's list of "Smartest Management Decisions."

We will begin with the clearest reason for avoiding cartels: Participating in cartels is illegal in most countries, and, if convicted, you will face personal fines and possibly prison time. All explicit agreements among industry rivals that actually do, or potentially could, lead to higher prices are illegal and actively prosecuted in the United States, Canada, Mexico, Germany, and the European Union. No manager or executive is above the law. Consider the sentence for Alfred Taubman, former chairman of Sotheby's art auction house, who was convicted in 2002 of conspiring with rival auction house Christie's International to fix sales commissions for art auctions. Federal Judge George Daniels sentenced the wealthy 78-year-old business tycoon—his personal wealth when incarcerated was estimated at $700 million—to serve one year and a day in federal prison. The judge also fined Taubman personally $7.5 million in addition to $186 million Taubman paid from his personal fortune to settle numerous civil lawsuits spawned by his criminal conviction. We could tell you quite a few more stories about pricing conspiracies, but, as you might guess, they all end painfully for convicted business executives.

Even if you think you can avoid getting caught conspiring to fix prices, you should know about another, even more compelling, reason to shun cartels: Historically, most cartels fail to raise prices much or for long. The tendency for cartels to fail can be explained using concepts developed in this chapter. As emphasized in our discussions of prisoners' dilemma situations, the opportunity for any one firm to increase its profit by unilaterally cutting price leads inevitably to a noncooperative Nash equilibrium with lower profits. The high prices desired by all firms in the industry are strategically unstable. Any one firm, if it is the only firm to do so, can cut its price and enjoy higher profit. When all firms do this, however, prices drop sharply, and every cartel member ends up making less profit.

Consider again in Table 13.5 the microprocessor pricing problem facing Intel and AMD. Suppose now both computer chip manufacturers reach a secret price-fixing agreement to set high prices for their computer chips. Cell A, then, is where

---

[14]For a fascinating and detailed study of international price-fixing cartels, see John M. Connor, *Global Price Fixing: Our Customers Are the Enemy* (Boston: Kluwer Academic Publishers, 2001).

the cartel conspires to operate. As you know from our previous discussions, cell A is not strategically stable. Either cartel member can, if it is the only firm doing so, cut its price and increase its own profit (see cells B and C) while reducing the profit of the other member. All cartel members have an incentive to cheat, so one or both of them will likely do so eventually. Once Intel and AMD discover each other's cheating behavior, they are likely to do what most cartels do: collapse. By abandoning all pretense of cooperation, widespread price-cutting breaks out, possibly even leading to a costly price war—a noncooperative pricing situation represented in cell D in Table 13.5.

Before we leave this discussion of cartel cheating, we should explain a bit more carefully why cartels face payoff tables structured like the one in Table 13.5, which forms the basis for believing cartels will fail. After all, the payoff matrix of Table 13.5 appears contrived to make Intel and AMD want to cheat. Why, exactly, do cartels face payoff structures that are strategically unstable? We can answer this question with the help of Figure 13.6, which illustrates why Intel is likely to cheat without resorting to specific numerical values for prices or quantities. Although Figure 13.6 shows why Intel wants to cheat, a similar figure also applies to AMD's incentive to cheat.

In Figure 13.6, which shows only Intel's pricing decisions, point A represents the situation when Intel and AMD are both pricing high in support of the cartel agreement (also cell A in Table 13.5). When both firms price high, Intel sells Q_A microprocessing chips. At this point, Intel believes that if it secretly cheats on the cartel agreement by cutting its price to P_{Low}, it can increase its sales tremendously as long as AMD does not detect the cheating and match Intel's

FIGURE 13.6
Intel's Incentive to Cheat

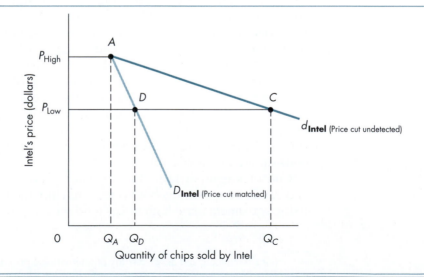

ILLUSTRATION 13.4

Does OPEC Cheating on Quotas Matter?

When the price of oil plunged from its July 2008 high of $147 per barrel, OPEC oil ministers began a series of reductions in the cartel's quota system aimed at preventing a complete meltdown of oil prices in the midst of the worst global recession in history. Crude oil prices fell below $40 before the slide subsided. Neil McMahon, a petroleum analyst at Sanford C. Bernstein, viewed the sharp drop in oil prices as evidence that "OPEC is turning into an increasingly irrelevant organization."[a] The commodity markets seemed to agree. In December 2008, after Saudi Oil Minister Ali al-Naimi announced new OPEC cuts in output of 2.2 million barrels per day, oil market traders were not convinced the promise of cuts was credible, and oil prices continued to fall.

OPEC began its production quota system in 1982. OPEC's central planning committee sets the maximum daily production rate for each member nation (i.e., a quota) in order to control, to some degree, the total global supply of crude oil and the world price of oil. Quotas are adjusted from time to time according to changes in the target price OPEC hopes to achieve and in response to changes in global demand and supply conditions. While it is unclear how OPEC leadership sets individual quotas, each nation's productive capacity seems to play an important role in allocating quotas across individual member nations. OPEC members who produce and sell more oil than allowed by their individual quotas are commonly referred to as "cheaters." OPEC's success as a cartel has always tracked its ability to control cheating by its members.

As we showed you in this chapter, cheating is a predictable outcome of strategic decision making by cartel members, whether they are managers of business firms or national oil ministers. Each country knows that if all members honor their individual quotas, total cartel revenue and profit will be higher than if widespread cheating causes a surge in oil production and decline in the world price of oil. However, a situation where all member countries comply with their quotas is strategically unstable because each nation knows that it can gain substantial sales and profit by secretly and unilaterally lowering its price (i.e., move to a cheating cell B or C in our examples of prisoners' dilemmas). All 12 OPEC members know that unilateral cheating can be profitable, and they expect their fellow cartel members will eventually try to cheat secretly. Furthermore, each oil minister knows that cutting price to sell more than quota is the best response if other oil ministers decide to cheat. Unless world oil demand is growing, the cooperating members will likely see a loss of sales as one or more other members "secretly" cheat and grab market share. Once a cooperating member believes it is losing substantial sales to cheating nations, history shows that nation will likely begin cheating as well.

The nearby table shows the individual quota targets for each OPEC nation and the percentage amount by which each nation, on average, has cheated on quotas over the period 1986–2004. These values for cheating were computed by Dibooglu and AlGudhea (2007) in their empirical study of OPEC cheating.[b] They measured cheating by using monthly production data for each country and computing for each country in each month the percentage difference between actual production and the level of production allowed by the quota system. A cursory look at the table confirms that nearly every member of OPEC has been, on average, a cheater. Only Indonesia was not, on average, a cheater, but the seemingly "cooperative" behavior was more likely caused by high domestic demand for crude oil relative to Indonesia's productive capacity. In 2008, Indonesia dropped out of OPEC because it had become a net importer of crude oil. According to these figures, it is interesting to note that Iran and Venezuela have been historically the smallest percentage cheaters in OPEC. These statistics, then, seem to support the contention that cheating is widespread in OPEC.

Dibooglu and AlGudhea applied rather sophisticated econometric methods to investigate whether the seemingly widespread cheating in the table actually undermined OPEC's ability to influence world crude oil prices through its quota system. One important issue had to be addressed: Did Saudi Arabia, the world's largest exporter of crude oil, act as an "enforcer" of the OPEC quota system by absorbing the overproduction of cheaters? If so, then widespread cheating by other nations could be offset by Saudi Arabia acting as

(Continued)

a "swing" producer by reducing its own production level enough to stabilize aggregate OPEC production. By taking on the role of swing producer, Saudi Arabia, or any other OPEC nation for that matter, could thereby impart credibility to OPEC's commitment to limit production to its (publicly announced) aggregate quota. This would "make quotas matter."

In an earlier examination of this matter, Griffin and Neilson (1994) found that Saudi Arabia generally tolerates a small amount of cheating by other OPEC members but will cut its production dramatically when it perceives there is "too much" cheating.[c] In other words, Saudi Arabia seems to follow a tit-for-tat strategy to punish member nations that cheat: "If you exceed your production quota by a large amount today, tomorrow we will cheat in a big way." When the level of cheating by other OPEC members is sufficiently egregious to trigger Saudi Arabia to punish other OPEC nations by pouring a large amount of Saudi crude onto world markets, crude prices fall sharply and painfully for all oil producers.

You might think that Saudi Arabia's threat of tit-for-tat punishment would prevent OPEC members from cheating, but, as the data in the table show, cheating is common and widespread. Perhaps the cheating nations do not view Saudi Arabia's threat as credible, since tit-for-tat dumping of Saudi crude oil hurts Saudi profitability during the punishment phase. Of course, the Saudi oil minister might rationally accept some short-term profit loss in order to create longer term cooperation by building a reputation as a tit-for-tat cheater. In both the Griffin/Neilson and Dibooglu/AlGudhea studies, the evidence suggests that Saudi Arabia has a relatively high trigger level for cheating. At low levels of cheating, "quotas matter" because Saudi Arabia plays the role of swing producer. At higher levels of cheating, Saudi Arabia has demonstrated a willingness to behave as a tit-for-tat cheater and then "quotas don't matter."

In all of this discussion of OPEC cheating, you should not lose sight of OPEC's serious limitations that have nothing to do with its ability to achieve cooperation and everything to do with the availability of substitutes for OPEC crude oil. Even when OPEC members cooperate completely with the quota system, there remains 60 percent of global oil supply that comes from non-OPEC exporters. Norway, Mexico, and Russia are large exporters who frequently undermine OPEC production cuts by opportunistically grabbing market share by expanding their exports. Perhaps the greatest threat to OPEC is long run in nature; high crude oil prices stimulate investment in alternative fuels such as natural gas, coal, nuclear, solar, and even wind.

OPEC Member	Quota[1] (Thousands of barrels per day)	Average percentage cheating (1986–2004)[2]
Algeria	853	3.0%
Angola	1,900	na[3]
Ecuador	520	na[3]
Indonesia[4]	1,385	−1.7
Iran	3,917	1.0
Iraq[5]	2,261	na
Kuwait	2,141	3.8
Libya	1,431	2.9
Nigeria	2,198	3.5
Qatar	692	5.0
Saudi Arabia	8,674	4.1
United Arab Emirates	2,444	17.6
Venezuela	2,333	1.9
OPEC (total)	30,749	3.4

[1]Quotas on October 31, 2000. *Source:* Energy Information Administration, U.S. Department of Energy.

[2]Percentage difference between actual production and quota, averaged over the period 1986 through 2004. See Dibooglu and AlGudhea, Table 1, p. 294.

[3]During the 1986–2004 period, averages are not calculated for three members: Angola and Ecuador were not members of OPEC quota in every year.

[4]Indonesia became a net importer of crude oil and left OPEC in 2008.

[5]Iraq is the only OPEC member with permission to opt out of the quota system given the weakened state of its oil sector due to war.

[a]See the article by Stanley Reed, "Does OPEC Still Matter?" *BusinessWeek,* January 5, 2009, p. 32.

[b]The empirical analysis discussed in this Illustration is from the study by Sel Dibooglu and Salim N. AlGudhea, "All Time Cheaters versus Cheaters in Distress: An Examination of Cheating and Oil Prices in OPEC," *Economic Systems* 31, 2007, pp. 292–310.

[c]See James Griffin and W. S. Neilson, "The 1985–86 Oil Price Collapse and Afterwards: What Does Game Theory Add?" *Economic Inquiry,* 2004, pp. 543–561.

price cut. Under these conditions, Intel believes its unmatched price cut will greatly increase its sales to Q_C (cell C in Table 13.5). In other words, Intel believes its price cut, if undetected by AMD, will move Intel down along a rather elastic demand from point *A* to point *C*. Of course, such price reductions are unlikely to go unnoticed for very long, because other members are likely to notice their own sales falling off.

Once AMD discovers Intel has been cheating on the cartel agreement to set high prices, AMD's best response is to lower its price as well, perhaps matching the amount of Intel's price cut. Notice, however, that when AMD matches Intel's price cut, Intel's demand is much less elastic since few, if any, AMD buyers will switch to Intel. Intel, then, ends up moving down along the less elastic demand segment in Figure 13.6 from point *A* to point *D*. At point *D*, both firms have abandoned their price fixing agreement and the cartel no longer works to increase profits for either firm. As you can see from this discussion, which does not rely on numerical payoff values, cartel members do indeed have incentives to cheat on price-fixing agreements, and they usually do.

Tacit Collusion

tacit collusion
Cooperation among rival firms that does not involve any explicit agreement.

A far less extreme form of cooperation than explicit price-fixing cartels arises when firms engage in **tacit collusion,** which refers to cooperative behavior that arises without any explicit communication. Recall that we mentioned this type of cooperation in our earlier discussion of price leadership, a pricing practice sometimes facilitating cooperation, which may arise without any explicit agreement to designate a price leader. There are many other types of tacit collusion that firms have tried. For instance, the producers in a market may restrict their sales to specific geographical regions or countries without meeting and explicitly designating marketing areas on a map. One firm's market area is understood from the ongoing relations it has had with its rivals. As opposed to forming a cartel to monopolize a market, tacit collusion is not categorically illegal. However, specific evidence of any attempt by rival firms to reach agreement would quickly tip the legal balance against accused participants.

Tacit collusion arises because all or most of the firms in an oligopoly market recognize their mutual interdependence and understand the consequences of noncooperation. The managers of these firms may wish to avoid the legal risks and penalties of getting caught making explicit agreements to cooperate (recall again the fate of Alfred Taubman). Or it may simply be too difficult to organize and coordinate behavior when there are numerous firms operating in the industry. In either case, tacit cooperation provides an alternative method of achieving cooperation, one that is generally less likely to result in charges of unlawful collusion. Tacit collusion might even be the end result of many repeated decisions in which oligopoly managers eventually learn that noncooperative decisions will be met with retaliatory noncooperative decisions from rivals, and everyone gives up cheating—at least until one of the firms hires a new manager!

13.4 STRATEGIC ENTRY DETERRENCE

Managers of firms in oligopoly markets sometimes use different types of strategic pricing and production behavior to prevent new rival firms from competing with them. **Strategic entry deterrence** occurs when an established firm (or firms) makes strategic moves designed to discourage or even prevent the entry of a new firm or firms into a market. Entry barriers arising from strategic behavior differ somewhat from the *structural* barriers to entry discussed previously in Chapter 12—economies of scale and scope, input barriers, government barriers, brand loyalty, consumer lock-in, and network externalities—as those barriers block entry of new firms by altering a market's underlying cost or revenue conditions so that a new firm cannot be profitable. Strategic entry deterrence is the result of actions taken by established firms to alter the *beliefs* potential entrants hold about the behavior of established firms—primarily pricing and output behavior—*after* they enter.

A firm selling in a particular market may be making positive economic profit. The firm's manager realizes that entry of new firms into the market will probably reduce, or possibly eliminate, its profit in the future. Sometimes the manager can take measures to reduce the probability of new firms entering. These actions are *strategic moves*—commitments, threats, or promises—designed to alter beliefs of potential entrants about the level of profits they are likely to earn should they decide to enter the market. Like all strategic moves, entry-deterring strategies only succeed if they are credible. This section discusses two types of strategic moves designed to manipulate the beliefs of potential entrants about the profitability of entering: lowering prices prior to entry of new firms (limit pricing) and increasing production capacity prior to entry of new firms.

Limit Pricing

Under certain circumstances, an oligopolist, or possibly a monopolist, may be able to make a credible commitment to charge a price lower than the profit-maximizing price to discourage new firms from entering the market. Such a strategic move is called **limit pricing.** To practice limit pricing, an established or incumbent firm must be able to make a credible commitment that it will continue to price below the profit-maximizing level even *after* new firms enter. If potential entrants think the incumbent is pricing low just to scare off new firms and the incumbent is likely to raise its price should new firms decide to enter anyway, then potential entrants see no credible commitment and will go ahead and enter.

We can best illustrate the use of limit pricing with an example. At the beginning of the year, Star Coffee is the only coffee shop in a fashionable San Francisco shopping mall. As a monopolist, it maximizes its profit by charging an average price of \$4 (P^*) for each cup of coffee it sells. (Coffee shops sell many different kinds of coffees in numerous sizes, so we must consider the *average* price of each cup sold.) Burned Bean, attracted by the economic profit earned by Star Coffee, wants to open its own shop in the mall and compete with Star.

FIGURE 13.7
**Limit Pricing:
Entry Deterred**

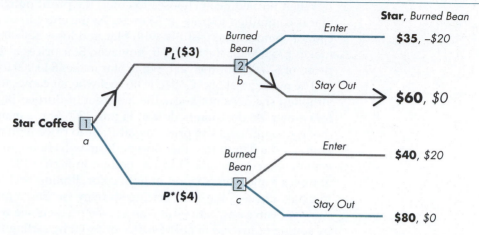

Payoffs measured in 1,000s of dollars of annual profits.

The manager at Star Coffee is aware of the potential new entrant and, as you would expect, she wants to discourage Burned Bean from entering. She is willing to consider lowering her average coffee price to $3 per cup ($P_L$) and commit to keeping it low for the rest of the year if she thinks this limit pricing strategy will prevent Burned Bean from entering the mall this year. To make a commitment to the low price, she cleverly asks the owners of the mall to make her sign an irreversible contract that requires Star Coffee to leave its coffee prices unchanged for the entire year, in effect fixing Star's prices at the level she chooses on January 1. She then tapes the signed contract to the front window of her shop for customers to see and, much more importantly, for the manager of Burned Bean to see. The manager of Bean Burned will make his decision to enter or to stay out of the mall after observing the contract on the door of the shop and after observing Star's coffee prices on January 1.

Figure 13.7 presents the sequential decision situation facing Star Coffee at the beginning of the year. On January 1 (decision node a), Star Coffee makes its pricing decision, and then Burned Bean makes a one-time decision either to enter or to stay out of the mall. Burned Bean's decision is represented by either node b or node c depending on the price Star Coffee commits to for the rest of the year: either profit-maximizing price, P^*, or limit price, P_L.

The payoffs shown in Figure 13.7 are the annual profits for the various combinations of decisions. The best outcome for Star, $80,000 of profit, happens when it sets its profit-maximizing price of $4 per cup and Burned Bean decides to stay out. Compare this with the outcome when Star implements the entry limit price of $3 per cup and Burned Bean decides to stay out: Star makes only $60,000 of profit at the lower price. In both situations for which Burned Bean chooses to stay out of the mall, Burned Bean makes no profit.

When Burned Bean chooses to enter, the profit outcomes depend on whether Star is committed to price at $3 or $4. At the entry limit price of $3, Burned Bean cannot compete successfully with Star and loses $20,000 for the year, while Star makes $35,000 for the year.[15] If, however, Star prices at $4, Burned Bean makes a profit of $20,000 for the year, while Star makes $40,000 for the year.

The manager at Star Coffee is no fool when it comes to strategic thinking. And, although she does not know the manager of Burned Bean, she assumes he is no fool either. At decision node a in Figure 13.7, Star's manager decides whether to make a commitment to price low at P_L or to price high at P^*. Using the roll-back method, she determines that Burned Bean will choose to stay out at decision node b and choose to enter at decision node c. In Figure 13.7, Burned Bean's decisions at nodes b and c are shaded in light color. Rolling back to decision node a, Star's manager chooses the limit pricing strategy (setting a price of $3) because, given Burned Bean's best actions at b and c, she predicts she will make $60,000 of profit by setting P_L instead of only $40,000 of profit by setting P^*.

Limit pricing succeeds in deterring entry in this example because Star's manager found a way to make a credible commitment to price at $3. Credibly committing to a limit price tends to be difficult in practice, however. Generally, incumbent firms do better after entry occurs by abandoning limit prices for Nash equilibrium prices, which are mutually best prices when the two firms make their pricing decisions simultaneously. In other words, when entry does occur, the best price for the established firm is found at the intersection of the two firms' best-response curves, and both firms earn more profit than if the incumbent continues at P_L. Thus, in the absence of an irreversible decision to price at P_L, the incumbent does best for itself, if entry occurs, by abandoning its limit price and setting a Nash equilibrium price instead. Suppose that, in this example, the best-response curves of Star Coffee and Burned Bean intersect at the Nash price P_N of $3.50.

To illustrate this argument, let us modify our coffee shop example by removing Star Coffee's ability to make an irreversible commitment to P_L. (Star Coffee discovers from its legal team that malls in California cannot legally control retail prices.) Now, without a credible commitment to maintain the price it chooses at decision node a, Star's initial pricing decision is reversible: Star can change its price after Burned Bean makes its entry decision. Figure 13.8 shows the new game tree now that Star cannot irreversibly choose its limit price of $3 per cup. Two additional decision nodes (d and e) represent Star's ability to change its price, which it would do in the event of entry by Burned Bean. Note also that, because Burned Bean spends several days contemplating its entry decision (nodes b and c), Star makes just a little less profit ($2,000 less to be precise) at P_N if it begins pricing at $3 instead of $4.

---

[15]If Burned Bean is to suffer a loss when the price of coffee is $3 while Star Coffee makes a profit at the same price, Star Coffee must have a cost advantage over Burned Bean, perhaps due to economies of scale or access to cheaper inputs or better technology. In general, limit pricing cannot succeed unless the incumbent firm has a cost advantage over potential new entrants.

FIGURE 13.8

Limit Pricing:
Entry Occurs

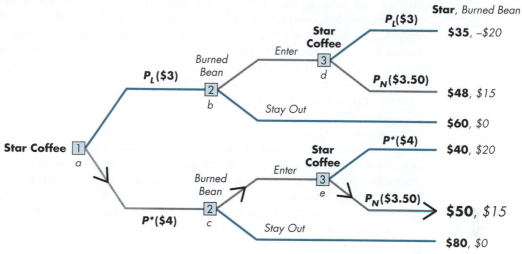

Payoffs measured in 1,000s of dollars of annual profits.

At decision node d, Star can either continue pricing at the limit price (P_L = $3) or raise its price to the more profitable Nash price (P_N = $3.50). Now, as we discussed previously, Burned Bean believes Star will abandon its limit price if Burned Bean enters because P_N is more profitable for Star than P_L. The limit price in this situation fails to deter entry. Burned Bean predicts Star will choose its best price, $P_{N'}$ when it enters, and thus Burned Bean makes the most profit by choosing to enter. Finishing the roll-back analysis, you can see that Star chooses to price at the profit-maximizing level, P^*, at the beginning of the year.

Many economists, game theorists, and government antitrust officials believe that limit pricing can seldom be practiced successfully because it is difficult for incumbents to make credible commitments to limit prices. No doubt you realize that our example of successful limit pricing utilized a rather unlikely, although not entirely farfetched, method of creating a credible commitment. Another method of making credible commitments (or credible threats and promises) is to create a reputation for yourself of being a "tough guy" or a "tough gal" who never reverses a decision (or backs down on threats or reneges on promises). Game theorists have suggested that developing an image of being irrational, or even crazy, may also serve to make strategic moves credible. Of course, we are not suggesting that craziness will advance your career as a manager, but rather that "crazy" people may be more clever than they appear.

Capacity Expansion as a Barrier to Entry

Under some circumstances, it is possible for an established firm to discourage entry of new firms by threatening to cut price to an unprofitable level should any new firm decide to enter its market. If the threat of a retaliatory price cut is to be credible, the threatened price cut must be the best decision for the established firm should a new firm decide to enter. In most cases, however, the best response to entry is for the established firm to accommodate the new firm's entry by reducing its own output so that price does not fall sharply after the new firm enters. This makes it difficult for established firms to issue credible threats that will successfully deter entry.

Sometimes, but not always, an established firm can make its threat of a retaliatory price cut in the event of entry credible by irreversibly increasing its plant capacity. When increasing production capacity results in lower marginal costs of production for an established firm, the established firm's best response to entry of a new firm may then be to increase its own level of production, which requires the established firm to cut its price to sell the extra output. If potential entrants believe the threatened price cut will make entry unprofitable *and* if they believe the capacity expansion cannot be reversed to accommodate their entry, then established firms may be able to utilize **capacity expansion as a barrier to entry**.

capacity expansion as a barrier to entry
Strategy in which an established firm irreversibly expands capacity to make credible its threat to decrease price if entry occurs.

We can use our previous example of Star Coffee to illustrate the nature of capacity expansion as a barrier to entry. Suppose that Star Coffee, the established coffee shop in the mall, is charging the monopoly price of $4 per cup and making $80,000 profit annually as the only coffee shop in the mall. Naturally, Star Coffee would like to deter Burned Bean from entering this profitable market. Suppose Star Coffee attempts to do this by threatening to lower its price from $4 to $3 per cup if Burned Bean enters. Can Star's threat to lower price deter Burned Bean from entering?

Consider Panel A in Figure 13.9, which shows the strategic decision-making situation when Burned Bean decides first whether to enter or stay out of the market, and then Star Coffee chooses its best price, either $3 or $4. As you can see from the payoffs in Panel A, Star's threat to charge $3 per cup is not credible: If Burned Bean enters, Star's best response is to charge $4 per cup and earn annual profit of $40,000.

As a way of making credible its threat to lower price if Burned Bean enters, the manager of Star Coffee decides to invest in greater capacity to serve coffee. Star's manager gets permission from the owners of the mall to remodel its store at its own expense. None of the remodeling costs will be paid for by the mall nor will Star be reimbursed for any of the remodeling costs should it decide to leave the mall. The remodeling project adds a sidewalk seating area in front of the store that increases seating capacity by 25 percent. Two additional brewing machines are also added to the store. This investment in greater capacity to serve coffee represents more seating and more brewing capacity than Star would find optimal if its monopoly were not being threatened. In fact, this extra capacity probably won't even be used if Burned Bean doesn't enter the market.

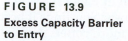

FIGURE 13.9

**Excess Capacity Barrier
to Entry**

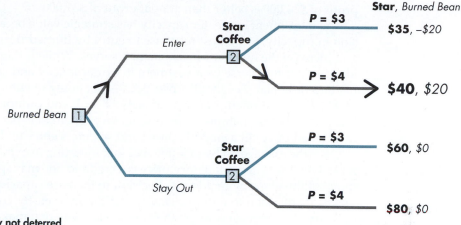

Panel A — Entry not deterred

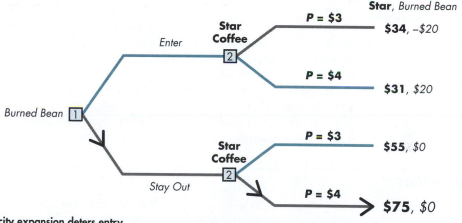

Panel B — Capacity expansion deters entry

Payoffs measured in 1,000s of dollars of annual profits.

We must emphasize, again, that the cost of the extra capacity must be sunk so that there is no chance for Star to reverse its commitment to the higher capacity that causes Star's marginal costs to fall. In this example, the costs of expanding capacity are largely sunk costs. While the cost of the two extra brewing machines is not a sunk cost, adding the sidewalk seating area is, of course, a sunk cost and this accounts for most of the cost of expanding capacity.

The profit payoffs after the investment in extra capacity are shown in Panel B of Figure 13.9. As you can see, Star makes lower profit in every outcome because it pays for more seating capacity and brewing capacity than in Panel A. Notice, however, that with the extra capacity and lower marginal costs, Star finds it best when Burned Bean enters to lower its price to $3 and sell more coffee: Annual profit of $34,000 is better than annual profit of $31,000.

The investment in greater capacity has strategic value because, with the expansion in capacity, Star's best response to entry by Burned Bean is to cut price to $3 and increase the number of customers it serves. While it might seem like a better idea for Star to reverse its investment in extra capacity and continue pricing at $4 per cup once Star sees that Burned Bean is not going to enter, Star cannot do this: Most of its investment in extra capacity is sunk and cannot be reversed. In fact, it is precisely this inability to reverse its investment in capacity that makes Star's threatened price cut a credible threat and so deters entry by Burned Bean.

Once the manager at Star Coffee sees that investing in extra production capacity makes its threat of a retaliatory price cut credible, the manager will seize the first move of the game by making its decision to increase capacity *before* Burned Bean makes its decision to enter or stay out of the market. By committing to expand capacity, Star effectively alters the payoffs in a way that makes credible the threat of lowering price in the event of entry. Thus Burned Bean will face the strategic situation shown in Panel B, and entry is deterred.

Once again, we must emphasize that, even though entry is deterred, Star is stuck with extra capacity that reduces the amount of profit it earns as a monopolist. Certainly holding idle capacity would add to a firm's costs, thereby reducing profits somewhat. However, compared with a limit pricing strategy, carrying idle capacity may be a less expensive (more profitable) way for a firm to deter entry. The choice would depend on the expected relative stream of profit from extra capacity compared with the stream from limit pricing. If demand is rather inelastic, a small increase in output would cause price to fall a great deal. In this case the required amount of idle capacity would be small, and capacity expansion may be a less costly way to block entry.

13.5 SUMMARY

■ Simultaneous decision games occur when managers must make their decisions without knowing the decisions of their rivals. A dominant strategy is a strategy that always provides the best outcome no matter what decisions rivals make. Dominant strategy equilibrium exists when all decision makers have dominant strategies and play them. A prisoners' dilemma arises when all rivals possess dominant strategies, and in dominant strategy equilibrium, they are all worse off than if they cooperated in making their decisions. Dominated strategies are strategies or decisions that are never the best strategy for any of the decisions rivals might make. Therefore, a dominated strategy would never be chosen and should be ignored or eliminated for decision-making purposes. If, after a first round of eliminating dominated

strategies, other strategies become dominated as a result of the first-round elimination, then successive elimination of dominated strategies should continue until no dominated strategies remain in the final payoff table. Nash equilibrium is a set of actions for which all managers are choosing their best actions given the actions they expect their rivals to choose. In Nash equilibrium, no single firm can unilaterally make a different decision and do better, a characteristic of Nash equilibrium called strategic stability. All dominant strategy equilibria are also Nash equilibria, but Nash equilibria can occur without either dominant or dominated strategies. Best-response curves are used to analyze simultaneous decisions when choices are continuous rather than discrete. A firm's best-response curve indicates the best decision to make (usually the profit-maximizing one) based on the decision the firm expects its rival will make. Nash equilibrium occurs at the price (or output) pair where the firms' best-response curves intersect. *(LO1)*

- Sequential decisions occur when one firm makes its decision first, and then a rival firm makes its decision. Game trees are used to analyze sequential decisions. Managers make best decisions for themselves by working backwards through the game tree using the roll-back method, which results in a unique path that is also a Nash decision path. If going first in a sequential decision game increases your payoff (relative to your payoff from going second), then a first-mover advantage exists. Alternatively, if going second increases your payoff (relative to your payoff from going first), then a second-mover advantage exists. Managers make strategic moves to achieve better outcomes for themselves. There are three types of strategic moves: commitments, threats, and promises. Only credible strategic moves matter; rivals ignore any commitments, threats, or promises that will not be carried out should the opportunity to do so arise. *(LO2)*

- In repeated games, when decisions are repeated over and over again by the same firms, managers get a chance to punish cheaters, and, through a credible threat of punishment, rival firms may be able to achieve the cooperative outcome in prisoners' dilemma situations. Cooperation increases a firm's value when the present value of the costs of cheating exceeds the present value of the benefits from cheating. A widely studied form of punishment strategy is the trigger strategy, in which managers initially choose the cooperative action and continue doing so in successive rounds of the game until a rival cheats. The act of cheating then "triggers" a punishment phase in the next repetition of the game that may last one or more repetitions. The two most commonly studied trigger strategies are tit-for-tat and grim strategies. Since cooperation usually increases profits, managers frequently adopt tactics known as facilitating practices to make cooperation more likely. Four such tactics are price matching, sale-price guarantees, public pricing, and price leadership. Cartels, which involve explicit collusive agreements among firms to drive up prices, are the most extreme form of cooperative oligopoly. Cartels find it extremely difficult to maintain cooperatively set cartel prices because cartel pricing schemes are usually strategically unstable. A far less extreme form of cooperation is tacit collusion, which occurs when oligopoly firms cooperate without an explicit agreement or any other facilitating practices. *(LO3)*

- Strategic entry deterrence occurs when an established firm makes a strategic move designed to discourage or even prevent the entry of a new firm or firms into a market. Two types of strategic moves designed to manipulate the beliefs of potential entrants about the profitability of entering are limit pricing and capacity expansion. Under limit pricing, an established firm tries to create a credible commitment to set its price sufficiently low to discourage rival firms from entering its market. Limit pricing is difficult in practice to accomplish because rival firms may believe the established firm will actually raise its price if the rival firm goes ahead with entry. The challenge in making limit pricing work is to successfully commit to a low price that will make entry unprofitable. Sometimes an established firm can make its threat of a price cut in the event of entry credible by irreversibly increasing its plant capacity. When increasing production capacity results in lower marginal costs of production for an established firm, the established firm's best response to entry of a new firm may then be to increase its own level of production, which requires the established firm to cut its price to sell the extra output. *(LO4)*

KEY TERMS

best-response curve	credible	game theory
capacity expansion as a barrier to entry	decision nodes	game tree
cartel	dominant strategy	grim strategy
cheating	dominant-strategy equilibrium	limit pricing
commitments	dominated strategies	Nash equilibrium
common knowledge	facilitating practices	oligopoly
cooperation	first-mover advantage	payoff table
	game	price leadership

price matching	second-mover advantage	successive elimination of
promises	sequential decisions	dominated strategies
public pricing	simultaneous decision games	tacit collusion
punishment for cheating	strategic behavior	threats
repeated decisions	strategic entry deterrence	tit-for-tat strategy
roll-back method	strategic moves	trigger strategies
sale-price guarantee	strategic stability	

TECHNICAL PROBLEMS

1. For each of the following statements concerning the role of strategic thinking in management decisions, explain whether the statement is true or false.

   a. "Managers of firms operating in perfectly competitive markets need to 'get into the heads' of rival managers to make more profitable decisions."

   b. "Strategic thinking by managers in oligopolistic industries promotes rational decision making, which will increase total industry profit."

   c. "Despite the interdependent nature of profits, oligopoly managers have the same goal as perfect competitors, monopolists, and monopolistic competitors."

2. Evaluate the following statement: "In simultaneous decision games, all players know the payoffs from making various decisions, but the players still do not have all the information they would like to have in order to decide which action to take."

3. In each of the following three payoff tables, two decision makers, Gates and Dell, must make simultaneous decisions to either cooperate or not cooperate with each other. Explain, for each payoff table, why it does or does not represent a prisoners' dilemma situation for Dell and Gates.

a.

		Gates	
		Don't cooperate	*Cooperate*
	Don't cooperate	**$75,** $75	**$600,** $50
Dell			
	Cooperate	**$100,** $300	**$400,** $400

b.

		Gates	
		Don't cooperate	*Cooperate*
	Don't cooperate	**$100,** $100	**$300,** $200
Dell			
	Cooperate	**$200,** $300	**$500,** $500

c.

		Gates	
		Don't cooperate	*Cooperate*
	Don't cooperate	**$100,** $100	**$600,** $50
Dell			
	Cooperate	**$50,** $600	**$500,** $500

4. Two firms, Small and Large, compete by price. Each can choose either a low price or a high price. The following payoff table shows the profit (in thousands of dollars) each firm would earn in each of the four possible decision situations:

		Large	
		Low price	High price
Small	Low price	$200, $500	$600, $600
	High price	$0, $1,500	$400, $1,000

  a. Is there a dominant strategy for Small? If so, what is it? Why?
  b. Is there a dominant strategy for Large? If so, what is it? Why?
  c. What is the likely pair of decisions? What payoff will each receive?
5. Verify the following statement: "The solution to the prisoners' dilemma in Table 13.2 is equivalent to the solution found by elimination of dominated strategies."
6. Find the solution to the following advertising decision game between Coke and Pepsi by using the method of successive elimination of dominated strategies.

		Pepsi's budget		
		Low	Medium	High
Coke's budget	Low	A $400, $400	B $320, $720	C $560, $600
	Medium	D $500, $300	E $450, $525	F $540, $500
	High	G $375, $420	H $300, $378	I $525, $750

Payoffs in millions of dollars of annual profit.

  a. Does Coke have a dominated strategy in the original payoff table? If so, what is it and why is it dominated? If not, why not?
  b. Does Pepsi have a dominated strategy in the original payoff table? If so, what is it and why is it dominated? If not, why not?
  c. After the first round of eliminating any dominated strategies that can be found in the original payoff table, describe the strategic situation facing Coke and Pepsi in the reduced payoff table.
  d. What is the likely outcome of this advertising decision problem?
  e. Pepsi's highest payoff occurs when Coke and Pepsi both choose high ad budgets. Explain why Pepsi will not likely choose a high ad budget.
7. Verify that each of the following decision pairs is a Nash equilibrium by explaining why each decision pair is strategically stable:
  a. Cell D of the prisoners' dilemma in Table 13.1.
  b. The decision pair for firms Large and Small in part c of Technical Problem 4.
  c. The decision pair for Coke and Pepsi in part d of Technical Problem 6.

8. Following the procedure illustrated in Panel A of Figure 13.1, show that when Arrow Airlines believes Bravo Airways is going to charge $200 per round-trip ticket, Arrow's best response is to charge $208.

9. Carefully explain why Arrow Airlines and Bravo Airways are not likely to choose the pair of prices at point *R* in Figure 13.2. Do not simply state that point *R* is not at the intersection of the best-response curves.

10. In Figure 13.2, point *C* makes both Arrow and Bravo more profitable. Getting to point *C* requires the airlines to cooperate: Arrow agrees to charge $230 per round-trip ticket and Bravo agrees to charge $235 per round-trip ticket.

    a. At these prices, how much profit does each airline earn? Does the higher price increase Arrow's profit? Does the higher price increase Bravo's profit?

    b. Suppose Arrow cheats by unilaterally lowering its price to $229, while Bravo honors the agreement and continues to charge $235. Calculate Arrow's profit when it cheats. Does cheating increase Arrow's profit?

    c. Suppose Bravo cheats by unilaterally lowering its price to $234, while Arrow honors the agreement and continues to charge $230. Calculate Bravo's profit when it cheats. Does cheating increase Bravo's profit?

11. Managers at Firm *A* and Firm *B* must make pricing decisions simultaneously. The following demand and long-run cost conditions are common knowledge to the managers

$$Q_A = 72 - 4P_A + 4P_B \quad \text{and} \quad LAC_A = LMC_A = 2$$

$$Q_B = 100 - 3P_B + 4P_A \quad \text{and} \quad LAC_B = LMC_B = 6.67$$

The accompanying figure shows Firm *B*'s best-response curve, BR_B. Only one point on Firm *A*'s best-response curve, point *G*, is shown in the figure.

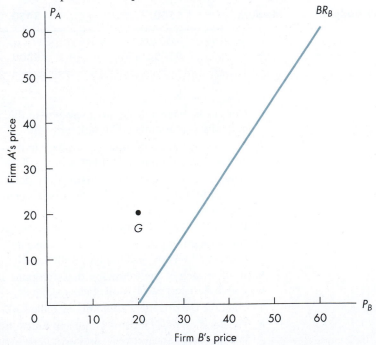

a. Find a second point on Firm *A*'s best-response curve by finding the best response when Firm *A* believes Firm *B* will set a price of $60. Plot this price pair on the graph, label it *H*, draw the best-response curve for Firm *A*, and label it BR_A.

b. What prices do you expect the managers of Firm *A* and *B* to set? Why? Label this point on the graph *N*.

c. Compute each firm's profit at point *N*.

d. Explain carefully why the pair of prices at point *H* in the figure is not likely to be chosen by the managers.

e. Suppose that the managers of the two firms decide to cooperate with each other by both agreeing to set prices P_A = $45 and P_B = $60. Label this point *C* in the figure. Compute each firm's profit at point *C*. Which firm(s) make(s) more profit at point *C* than at point *N*? Why didn't you give point *C* as your answer to part *b*?

12. Using the payoff table for Castle Pizza and Palace Pizza in Table 13.2, draw the game tree for a sequential decision situation in which Palace makes its pricing decision first.

    a. Find the equilibrium decision path using the roll-back method. Show the decision path on your game tree.

    b. Is the decision outcome in part *a* a Nash equilibrium? Explain why or why not.

13. In the technology choice game presented in Figure 13.4, draw the game tree when Sony makes its technology decision first. Find the outcome of the game using the roll-back method. Does Sony experience a first-mover advantage? Explain.

14. Consider again the sequential technology choice game in Technical Problem 13 in which Sony chooses its cell phone technology before Motorola. Motorola makes the most profit for itself if both firms choose analog technology for their cell phones. Motorola considers the following strategic moves:

    a. Motorola makes the following threat *before* Sony makes its decision: "If you (Sony) choose **Digital**, then we will choose *Analog*." Does this threat accomplish Motorola's objective of getting both firms to adopt analog technology? Explain.

    b. Motorola makes the following statement *before* Sony makes its decision: "If you (Sony) choose **Analog**, then we promise to choose *Analog*." Is this a strategic promise? Why or why not? Does the statement accomplish Motorola's objective of getting both firms to adopt analog technology? Explain.

15. Alpha and Beta, two oligopoly rivals in a duopoly market, choose prices of their products on the first day of the month. The following payoff table shows their monthly payoffs resulting from the pricing decisions they can make.

Alpha's price

		High	Low
Beta's price	**High**	A $200, $300	B $50, $350
	Low	C $300, $150	D $75, $200

Payoffs in thousands of dollars of profit per month.

a. Is the pricing decision facing Alpha and Beta a prisoners' dilemma? Why or why not?

b. What is the cooperative outcome? What is the noncooperative outcome?

    c. Which cell(s) represents cheating in the pricing decision? Explain.

    d. If Alpha and Beta make their pricing decision just one time, will they choose the cooperative outcome? Why or why not?

16. For the weekly decision by AMD and Intel to set the prices of their semiconductor chips, verify in Table 13.5 that AMD can credibly threaten to make a retaliatory price cut if Intel cheats.

17. In the pricing decision in Technical Problem 15, can Alpha make a credible threat to punish Beta with a retaliatory price cut? Can Beta make a credible threat of a retaliatory price cut?

18. Alpha and Beta in Technical Problem 15 repeat their pricing decision on the first day of every month. Suppose they have been cooperating for the past few months, but now the manager at Beta is trying to decide whether to cheat or to continue cooperating. Beta's manager believes Beta can get away with cheating for two months, but would be punished for the next two months after cheating. After punishment, Beta's manager expects the two firms would return to cooperation. Beta's manager uses a discount rate of 2 percent per month for computing present values.

    a. What is the monthly (undiscounted) gain to Beta from cheating? What is the present value of the benefit from cheating?

    b. What is the monthly (undiscounted) cost of punishment to Beta? What is the present value of the cost of cheating?

    c. Will Beta cooperate or cheat? Explain.

    d. Suppose Beta discounts future benefits and costs at a rate of 30 percent per week. Will Beta choose cooperation or cheating?

19. For each of the following events, explain whether Beta in the previous question would be more or less likely to cooperate.

    a. Beta expects to be able to cheat for more than two months before getting caught by Alpha.

    b. Alpha announces that it will match any price cut by Beta, and it will do so immediately following any price cut by Beta.

    c. Alpha hires a new CEO who has a reputation for relentlessly matching price cuts by rivals, even after rivals are ready to resume cooperative pricing.

    d. Alpha alters the design of its product to make it more desirable to some consumers than Beta's product.

APPLIED PROBLEMS

1. When McDonald's Corp. reduced the price of its Big Mac by 75 percent if customers also purchased french fries and a soft drink, *The Wall Street Journal* reported that the company was hoping the novel promotion would revive its U.S. sales growth. It didn't. Within two weeks sales had fallen. Using your knowledge of game theory, what do you think disrupted McDonald's plans?

2. The well-known nationally syndicated columnist David Broder reported the recent findings of two academic political scientists. These scholars found that voters are quite turned off by "negative campaigns" of politicians. Many people went as far as not voting because of this. Nevertheless, the political scientists noted it is futile to urge candidates to stay positive. The damage from staying positive is heaviest when the opponent is attacking. Explain the dilemma in terms of strategic behavior.

3. Dell Computer Corp., the world's largest personal-computer maker, is keenly aware of everything its rival PC manufacturers decide to do. Explain why Dell usually reacts more quickly and more substantially to pricing, product design, and advertising decisions made by Hewlett-Packard and Gateway than when these same types of decisions are made by Apple Computer.

4. Some states have had laws restricting the sale of most goods on Sunday. Consumers, by and large, oppose such laws because they find Sunday afternoon a convenient time to shop. Paradoxically, retail trade associations frequently support the laws. Discuss the reasons for merchants' supporting these laws.

5. Thomas Schelling, an expert on nuclear strategy and arms control, observed in his book *The Strategy of Conflict* (Cambridge, MA: Harvard University Press, 1960), "The power to constrain an adversary depends upon the power to bind oneself." Explain this statement using the concept of strategic commitment.

6. Many economists argue that more research, development, and innovation occur in the oligopolistic market structure than in any other. Why might this conclusion be true?

7. In the 2000 U.S. presidential contest, Al Gore was advised by his strategists to wait for George W. Bush to announce his vice-presidential running mate before making his own decision on a running mate. Under what circumstances would Gore be better off giving Bush a head start on putting together his presidential ticket? What kind of strategic situation is this?

8. When he retired as CEO of American Airlines, a position he held for 18 years, Robert Crandall was described in a *Newsweek* article (June 1, 1998) as "one tough [expletive]." Other nicknames Crandall garnered during his career included Fang, Bob the Butcher, and Wretched Robert. *Newsweek* noted that Crandall's "salty language and brass-knuckle, in-your-face" style of dealing with employees and rival airlines is now out of style in the executive suites of U.S. corporations. In strategic decision-making situations, why might Crandall's style of management have been advantageous to American Airlines?

9. The secretary-general of OPEC, Ali Rodriquez, stated that it would be easier for OPEC nations to make future supply adjustments to fix oil prices that are too high than it would be to rescue prices that are too low. Evaluate this statement.

10. A church signboard offers the following advice: "Live every day as if it were your last." Taken literally, could this advice encourage "bad" behavior? Explain.

11. In 1999 Mercedes-Benz USA adopted a new pricing policy, which it called NFP (negotiation-free process), that sought to eliminate price negotiations between customers and new-car dealers. An article in *The New York Times* (August 29, 1999) reported that a New Jersey Mercedes dealer who had his franchise revoked is suing Mercedes, claiming that he was fired for refusing to go along with Mercedes' no-haggling pricing policy. The New Jersey dealer said he thought the NFP policy was illegal. Why might Mercedes' NFP policy be illegal? Can you offer another reason why the New Jersey dealer might not have wished to follow a no-haggling policy?

12. Suppose the two rival office supply companies Office Depot and Staples both adopt price-matching policies. If consumers can find lower advertised prices on any items they sell, then Office Depot and Staples guarantee they will match the lower prices. Explain why this pricing policy may not be good news for consumers.

13. Recently one of the nation's largest consumer electronics retailers began a nationwide television advertising campaign kicking off its "Take It Home Today" program, which

is designed to encourage electronics consumers to buy today rather than continue postponing a purchase hoping for a lower price. For example, the "Take It Home Today" promotion guarantees buyers of new plasma TVs that they are entitled to get any sale price the company might offer for the next 30 days.

    a. Do you think such a policy will increase demand for electronic appliances? Explain.

    b. What other reason could explain why this program is offered? Would you expect the other large electronics stores to match this program with one of their own? Why or why not?

14. When Advanta Corp. decided that it wished to begin charging a fee to holders of its credit cards for periods during which the card is not used and for closing the account, it first "signaled" its intentions to hike fees by publicly announcing its plans in advance. The company notified its cardholders that it wouldn't begin charging the fees right away but would reserve the right to do so. One worried cardholder told *The Wall Street Journal*, "I hope the other credit card companies don't follow suit." Apparently, cardholders had good reason to worry, according to one credit card industry analyst: "Everyone is considering (raising fees), but everyone's afraid. The question is, who'll be daring and be second? If there's a second, then you'll see a flood of people doing it."

    a. If Advanta believes raising fees is a profitable move, then why would it delay implementing the higher fees, which could reduce the amount of profit generated by higher fees?

    b. Are rivals waiting for Advanta to implement its fee hikes before they do in order to secure a second-mover advantage? Explain. Is there any other reason rivals might wait to raise their prices?

    c. Could Advanta Corp. be trying to establish itself as the price leader in the consumer credit card industry?

15. Economists believe terrorists behave rationally: If country *A* (America) increases security efforts while country *B* (Britain) remains complacent, terrorists will focus their attacks on targets in the relatively less well-protected country *B*. Suppose the following payoff table shows the net benefits for the United States and Great Britain according to their decisions either to maintain their annual spending levels at the optimal levels (when both countries spend proportionately equal amounts) or to increase annual spending by 10 percent. The payoffs in the table measure net benefits (in dollars) from antiterrorism activities, that is, the value of property not destroyed and lives not lost due to reduced terrorism minus spending on antiterrorism.

		Britain's antiterrorism spending	
		$100 (per capita)	$110 (per capita)
America's antiterrorism spending	**$100 (per capita)**	A **$1,000**, *$1,000*	B $_____, $_____
	$110 (per capita)	C $_____, $_____	D **$800**, *$800*

Payoffs in millions of dollars of net benefit annually.

    a. Antiterrorism policy analysts believe allies in the war against terror face a prisoners' dilemma concerning how much each country chooses to spend on activities that reduce the incidence of terrorist attacks on their own nation's people and property.

In the payoff table, make up your own values for payoffs in cells B and C that will create a prisoners' dilemma situation.

b. "When all nations spend more and more preventing terrorist acts, they may actually all end up worse off for their efforts." Evaluate this statement using the payoff table you created in part *a*.

16. The two largest diner chains in Kansas compete for weekday breakfast customers. The two chains, Golden Inn and Village Diner, each offer weekday breakfast customers a "breakfast club" membership that entitles customers to a breakfast buffet between 6:00 A.M. and 8:30 A.M. Club memberships are sold as "passes" good for 20 weekday breakfast visits.

Golden Inn offers a modest but tasty buffet, while Village Diner provides a wider variety of breakfast items that are also said to be quite tasty. The demand functions for breakfast club memberships are

$$Q_G = 5{,}000 - 25P_G + 10P_V$$

$$Q_V = 4{,}200 - 24P_V + 15P_G$$

where Q_G and Q_V are the number of club memberships sold monthly and P_G and P_V are the prices of club memberships, both respectively, at Golden Inn and Village Diner chains. Both diners experience long-run constant costs of production, which are

$$LAC_G = LMC_G = \$50 \text{ per membership}$$

$$LAC_V = LMC_V = \$75 \text{ per membership}$$

The best-response curves for Golden Inn and Village Diner are, respectively,

$$P_G = BR_G(P_V) = 125 + 0.2P_V$$

$$P_V = BR_V(P_G) = 125 + 0.3125P_G$$

a. If Village Diner charges $200 for its breakfast club membership, find the demand, inverse demand, and marginal revenue functions for Golden Inn. What is the profit-maximizing price for Golden Inn given Village Diner charges a price of $200? Verify mathematically that this price can be obtained from the appropriate best-response curve given above.

b. Find the Nash equilibrium prices for the two diners. How many breakfast club memberships will each diner sell in Nash equilibrium? How much profit will each diner make?

c. How much profit would Golden Inn and Village Diner earn if they charged prices of $165 and $180, respectively? Compare these profits to the profits in Nash equilibrium (part *c*). Why would you *not* expect the managers of Golden Inn and Village Diner to choose prices of $165 and $180, respectively?

17. Samsung wants to prevent Whirlpool from entering the market for high-priced, front-load washing machines. Front-load washing machines clean clothes better and use less water than conventional top-load machines. Even though front-load machines are more costly to manufacture than top-loaders, Samsung is nonetheless earning economic profit as the only firm making front-loaders for upscale consumers. The following payoff table shows the annual profits (in millions of dollars)

for Samsung and Whirlpool for the pricing and entry decisions facing the two firms.

		Samsung	
		P = $500	P = $1,000
Whirlpool	**Stay out**	$0, $20	$0, $34
	Enter	−$5, $15	$17, $17

a. Can Samsung deter Whirlpool from entering the market for front-load washing machines by threatening to lower price to $500 if Whirlpool enters the market? Why or why not?

Suppose the manager of Samsung decides to make an investment in extra production capacity before Whirlpool makes its entry decision. The extra capacity raises Samsung's total costs of production but lowers its marginal costs of producing extra front-load machines. The payoff table after this investment in extra production capacity is shown here:

		Samsung	
		P = $500	P = $1,000
Whirlpool	**Stay out**	$0, $16	$0, $24
	Enter	−$6, $14	$12, $12

b. Can Samsung deter Whirlpool from entering the profitable market for front-load washing machines? What must be true about the investment in extra production capacity for the strategic move to be successful? Explain.

c. Construct the sequential game tree when Samsung makes the first move by deciding whether to invest in extra production capacity. Use the roll-back technique to find the Nash equilibrium path. How much profit does each firm earn? (*Hint:* The game tree will have three sequential decisions: Samsung decides first whether to invest in extra plant capacity, Whirlpool decides whether to enter, and Samsung makes its pricing decision.)

◻ **MATHEMATICAL APPENDIX**   **Derivation of Best-Response Curves for Continuous Simultaneous Decisions**

For simultaneous decisions in which managers choose actions or strategies that are continuous rather than discrete decision variables, best-response curve analysis can be employed to analyze and explain strategic decision making. In this appendix, we show how to derive the equations for best-response curves when two firms make simultaneous decisions. We examine first the situation in which the two managers choose *outputs* to achieve mutually best outcomes, and so the corresponding best-response curves give each firm's best output given its rival's output. Then we derive the best-response curves when managers choose their best *prices*, given the price they expect their rival to charge.

Best-Response Curves When Firms Choose Quantities

Assume two firms, 1 and 2, produce a homogeneous product, and the linear inverse demand for the product is

$$(1) \qquad P = a + bQ$$

$$= a + bq_1 + bq_2$$

where P is the price of the good, Q is total output of the good, q_1 is firm 1's output, q_2 is firm 2's output, and $Q = q_1 + q_2$. The price intercept a is positive, and the slope parameter for inverse demand, b, is negative.

Constant returns to scale characterize long-run costs, so costs are assumed to be constant and equal for both firms. Let c denote long-run marginal and average cost for both firms; thus each firm's total cost can be expressed as

$$(2) \qquad C_1(q_1) = cq_1 \quad \text{and} \quad C_2(q_2) = cq_2$$

To ensure that a positive quantity of the good is produced (i.e., marginal cost is below the vertical intercept of demand), c is restricted to be less than a ($c < a$). Common knowledge prevails: Both firms know market demand for the product, and they know their own cost and their rival's cost (and they both know they know).

The profit functions for the two firms are

$$(3a) \quad \pi_1 = Pq_1 - C_1(q_1) = [a + b(q_1 + q_2)]q_1 - cq_1$$

$$(3b) \quad \pi_2 = Pq_2 - C_2(q_2) = [a + b(q_1 + q_2)]q_2 - cq_2$$

Both firms choose their individual quantities to maximize their individual profits, taking the output of their rival as given. Profit maximization requires, respectively, for firm 1 and firm 2

$$(4a) \qquad \frac{\partial \pi_1}{\partial q_1} = a + 2bq_1 + bq_2 - c = 0$$

$$(4b) \qquad \frac{\partial \pi_2}{\partial q_2} = a + 2bq_2 + bq_1 - c = 0$$

The equations for best-response curves, which show the optimal output for a firm given the output of a rival firm, are obtained from each firm's first-order conditions for profit maximization. Solve equations (4a) and (4b) to get the following best-response functions for firms 1 and 2, respectively:

$$(5a) \qquad q_1 = BR_1(q_2) = \frac{c - a}{2b} - \frac{1}{2}q_2$$

$$(5b) \qquad q_2 = BR_2(q_1) = \frac{c - a}{2b} - \frac{1}{2}q_1$$

Firm 1's best-response function, $BR_1(q_2)$, gives the profit-maximizing level of output for firm 1, given the level of output produced by firm 2. Firm 2's best-response curve, $BR_2(q_1)$, gives firm 2's optimal output response to any given level of output produced by firm 1. For convenience in graphing the two firms' best-response functions, we find the inverse of firm 2's best-response function, which is $q_1 = BR_2^{-1}(q_2) = \frac{c - a}{b} - 2q_2$. Figure 13A.1 shows both firms' best-response curves.

Nash equilibrium occurs where the two best-response curves intersect: point N in Figure 13A.1. The Nash duopoly equilibrium can be found by substituting each best-response function into the other to obtain

$$(6) \qquad q_1^* = \frac{c - a}{3b} \quad \text{and} \quad q_2^* = \frac{c - a}{3b}$$

Thus total duopoly output is

$$(7) \qquad Q^*_{\text{Duopoly}} = q_1^* + q_2^* = \frac{2(c - a)}{3b}$$

and the duopoly price of the product is

$$(8) \qquad P^* = a + b(Q^*) = \frac{2(c + a)}{3}$$

For the demand and cost conditions set forth in equations (1) and (2), the output if the market is perfectly competitive is $Q_C = \frac{c - a}{b}$ and the output if the market is a monopoly is $Q_M = \frac{c - a}{2b}$. (Problem 1 in the Mathematical Exercises asks you to derive competitive output and monopoly output.) Thus competitive output is greater than *total* duopoly output, and total duopoly output is greater than monopoly output

$$(9) \qquad Q_C > Q_{\text{Duopoly}} > Q_M$$

Prices of the good, consequently, are related as follows:

$$(10) \qquad P_M < P_{\text{Duopoly}} < P_C$$

Best-Response Curves When Firms Choose Prices

Now we examine a simultaneous decision in which duopoly firms A and B, producing goods A and B, respectively, choose their prices rather than their outputs. Assume goods A and B are fairly close substitutes for each other. The linear demand functions for the two products are

$$(11a) \qquad Q_A = a + bP_A + cP_B$$

$$(11b) \qquad Q_B = d + eP_B + fP_A$$

where parameters a and d are positive, b and e are negative (by the law of demand), and c and f are positive (for substitutes).

FIGURE 13A.1

Best-Response Curves:
Firms Choose Quantities

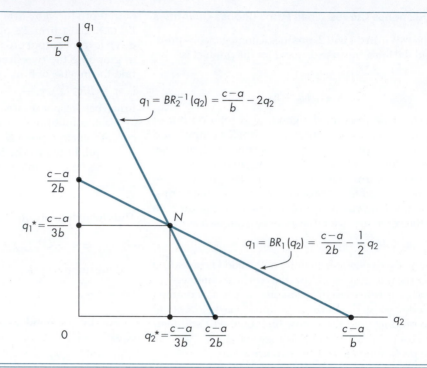

Again let constant returns to scale characterize long-run costs, so costs are assumed to be constant. In this example, however, we let costs differ between the two firms. Let c_A and c_B denote long-run marginal and average costs for firms A and B, respectively:

$$(12) \quad C_A(Q_A) = c_A Q_A \quad \text{and} \quad C_B(Q_B) = c_B Q_B$$

The profit functions for firms A and B are

$$(13a) \quad \pi_A = P_A Q_A - C_A(Q_A) = (P_A - c_A)(a + bP_A + cP_B)$$

$$(13b) \quad \pi_B = P_B Q_B - C_B(Q_B) = (P_B - c_B)(d + eP_B + fP_A)$$

Each firm's first-order condition for profit-maximization is

$$(14a) \quad \frac{\partial \pi_A}{\partial P_A} = a + 2bP_A + cP_B - bc_A = 0$$

$$(14b) \quad \frac{\partial \pi_B}{\partial P_B} = d + 2eP_B + fP_A - ec_B = 0$$

Solving equation (14a) for firm A's best-response curve:

$$(15a) \quad P_A = BR_A(P_B) = \frac{bc_A - a}{2b} - \frac{c}{2b}P_B$$

Solving equation (14b) for firm B's best-response curve:

$$(15b) \quad P_B = BR_B(P_A) = \frac{ec_B - d}{2e} - \frac{f}{2e}P_A$$

Firm A's best-response function, $BR_A(P_B)$, gives the profit-maximizing price for firm A, given the price firm A predicts firm B will set. Firm A's best-response function is shown in Figure 13A.2 as $BR_A(P_B)$. Firm B's best-response curve, $BR_B(P_A)$, gives firm B's optimal price response to any given price set by firm A. The inverse of firm B's best-response function, $P_A = BR_B^{-1}(P_B) = \frac{ec_B - d}{f} - \frac{2e}{f}P_B$ is shown in Figure 13A.2.

The intersection of the best-response functions is found by substituting each best-response function into the other best-response function to obtain the Nash equilibrium prices:

$$(16a) \quad P_A^N = \frac{2e(bc_A - a) + c(d - ec_B)}{4be - cf}$$

$$(16b) \quad P_B^N = \frac{2b(ec_B - d) + f(a - bc_A)}{4be - cf}$$

At point N in Figure 13A.2, where the two best-response functions cross, is the Nash equilibrium. Each firm is doing the best it can, given what the other is doing.

FIGURE 13A.2

Best-Response Curves:
Firms Choose Prices

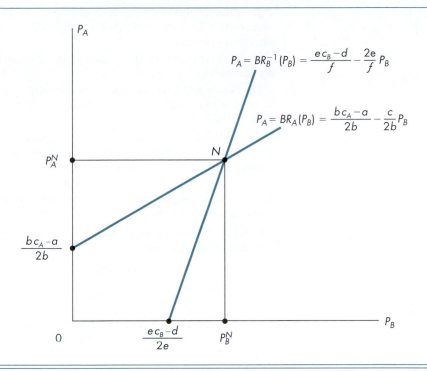

$$P_A = BR_B^{-1}(P_B) = \frac{ec_B - d}{f} - \frac{2e}{f}P_B$$

$$P_A = BR_A(P_B) = \frac{bc_A - a}{2b} - \frac{c}{2b}P_B$$

MATHEMATICAL EXERCISES

1. For the demand and cost conditions in equations (1) and (2), respectively, of the appendix, derive the output and prices under perfect competition and under monopoly and verify the output and price relations in equations (9) and (10), respectively.

2. Doctors Smith and Jones, two rival ophthalmologists, plan to enter the market for laser corrective eye surgery in a medium-size community in Illinois. Smith and Jones both utilize the same laser technology and face constant long-run costs of $1,000 per patient ($LMC = LAC = \$1,000$). For planning purposes, the doctors assume that all patients have both eyes corrected, so the $1,000 cost is for correcting both eyes of each patient. The doctors know about each other's plans to enter the market, and they both believe the (inverse) market demand for laser eye surgery is

$$P = 7,000 - 2Q$$

where $Q = q_s + q_J$ and q_s and q_J are the number of patients Drs. Smith and Jones, respectively, treat annually. Each of the doctors will choose the size of their clinic, and thus the number of patients they intend to treat each year, without knowledge of their rival's decision. Demand and cost conditions are common knowledge.

   a. Using calculus, derive the equations for the best-response curves.

   b. Sketch a graph of the two best-response curves. Be sure to label both axes and both response curves.

  c. If Dr. Smith expects Dr. Jones to treat 500 patients annually, what is Dr. Smith's best response? If Dr. Jones predicts Dr. Smith will treat 750 patients annually, what is Dr. Jones's best response?

  d. Find Nash equilibrium. How much profit does each doctor earn annually in Nash equilibrium?

  e. If Drs. Smith and Jones agree to serve annually only 750 patients *each* (1,500 patients in total in one year), how much annual profit does each doctor earn? Why don't they do this?

  f. If Drs. Smith and Jones merge into a single company forming a monopoly in the community, how many patients will they serve each year? What price will they charge? How much profit will they earn?

  g. Instead of the monopoly in part *f*, suppose perfect competition characterizes the market in the long run. How many patients will be treated? What price will they pay in a competitive market? How much profit will the doctors earn?

3. Two firms, *A* and *B*, produce goods *A* and *B*, respectively. The linear demands for the two goods are, respectively,

$$Q_A = 100 - 4P_A + 1.5P_B$$

$$Q_B = 120 - 2P_B + 0.5P_A$$

Production costs are constant but not equal:

$$LAC_A = LMC_A = \$2$$

$$LAC_B = LMC_B = \$3$$

  a. Using calculus, derive the equations for the best-response curves.

  b. Sketch a graph of the two best-response curves. Be sure to label both axes and both response curves.

  c. If firm *A* expects firm *B* to set its price at $20, what is firm *A*'s best response? If firm *B* predicts firm *A* will price good *A* at $36, what is firm *B*'s best response?

  d. What is the Nash equilibrium price and quantity for each firm?

  e. How much profit does each firm earn in Nash equilibrium?

  f. If firm *A* and firm *B* set prices of $22 and $35, respectively, how much profit does each firm earn? Why don't they choose these prices then?

14

Advanced Pricing Techniques

After reading this chapter, you will be able to:

14.1 Explain why uniform pricing does not generate the maximum possible total revenue and how price discrimination can generate more revenue.

14.2 Explain how to practice first-degree price discrimination to earn greater revenue and profit than charging a uniform price.

14.3 Explain how to practice second-degree price discrimination by using either two-part pricing or declining block pricing.

14.4 Explain how to practice third-degree price discrimination.

14.5 Determine the profit-maximizing prices when a firm sells multiple products related in consumption and explain how firms can profitably bundle two or more products to sell for a single price.

14.6 Understand why cost-plus pricing usually fails to maximize profit.

After completing the first four parts of this textbook, we can understand that you might be a bit apprehensive about tackling "advanced" topics in managerial economics. It is not uncommon for your semester of studying managerial economics to come to an end before you can cover all of the chapters in Part V. For this reason, you may only cover portions of these last three chapters. And, it is also possible that some of the topics in these chapters will show up in other business courses, such as finance, marketing, production management, and regulation of business enterprise.

This chapter examines a number of issues concerning pricing decisions for more complicated situations than we have so far encountered in this text. Specifically, until now we have considered only a rather simple firm. This firm has a single product that is sold in a single market at a single price set by equating marginal revenue to marginal cost. Although the simpler models provide great insight into a firm's decision process, this is frequently not the type of situation faced by real-world firms or corporations. In this chapter, we show how managers can deal with some of the real-world complexities that frequently arise in pricing decisions. As you will see, interesting and challenging complications arise when the firm charges different prices rather than a single, uniform price for every unit it sells, or produces multiple products that are related in consumption. These complexities create valuable opportunities for earning higher profits than would be earned by following the simpler pricing principles presented in previous chapters.

Managers of any kind of price-setting firm—a monopolist, monopolistic competitor, or an oligopolist—can utilize the pricing techniques described in this chapter to increase profit, as long as the necessary conditions are met to make a particular pricing technique suitable. The reason for implementing more complicated pricing methods is, of course, to increase profit. When properly executed, the techniques of price discrimination and multiproduct pricing will increase profit, often by a substantial amount.

As we will show you in this chapter, each of these more challenging pricing situations can be executed optimally by applying the concepts and principles set forth in Chapters 1 to 13 of this text. Our discussion of these pricing techniques will focus primarily on the fundamentals, as a complete examination of each of these techniques is beyond the scope of a single course in managerial economics. You may wish to take a course in industrial organization or advanced microeconomics to learn about more complex variations of the techniques presented in this chapter.

14.1 PRICE DISCRIMINATION: CAPTURING CONSUMER SURPLUS

Thus far we have examined firms that set just one price for their product. Sometimes firms charge more than one price for the very same product. For example, pharmacies may charge senior citizens lower drug prices than "regular" citizens, airlines frequently charge business travelers higher airfares than leisure travelers, and Walmart gives lower prices to buyers who choose to purchase large quantities. In other words, we have focused only on *uniform pricing*, which is the simplest form of pricing. **Uniform pricing** occurs when businesses charge the same price for every unit of the product they sell, no matter who the buyers happen to be or how much they choose to buy. In this section, we explain why firms wish to avoid uniform pricing whenever possible, and then we introduce price discrimination as a more profitable alternative to uniform pricing. As we will explain shortly, price discrimination is not always possible, and firms may be forced to charge the same price for all units they sell.

uniform pricing
Charging the same price for every unit of the product.

The Trouble with Uniform Pricing

The problem with uniform pricing concerns the consumer surplus generated when a firm charges the same price for all units it sells. Recall from Chapter 2 that consumer surplus is the area under demand and above market price over the range of output sold in the market. Charging the same price for every unit creates consumer surplus for every unit sold (except for the very last unit sold). Savvy

FIGURE 14.1
The Trouble with Uniform Pricing

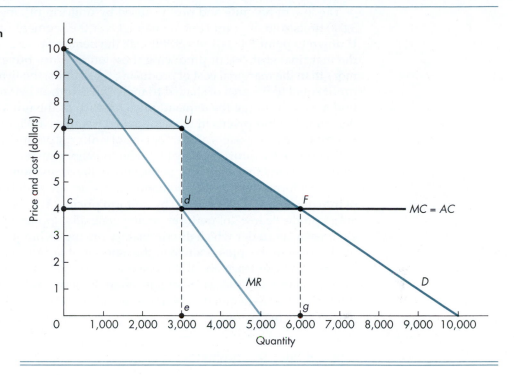

capturing consumer surplus
Devising pricing schemes to transform consumer surplus into economic profit.

marketing managers view the existence of any amount of consumer surplus as evidence of underpricing. They will then try to devise pricing schemes to take consumer surplus away from buyers, effectively transforming consumer surplus into profit for the firm. This process is called **capturing consumer surplus.**

Figure 14.1 illustrates the opportunity for price-setting firms to capture the consumer surplus generated by uniform pricing. Suppose a firm possessing market power faces the demand curve D and production costs are constant, so that marginal and average costs are both equal to $4 per unit for all output levels. If the firm practices uniform pricing, the manager maximizes profit by applying the $MR = MC$ rule, and charges $7 for each of the 3,000 units sold (point U). For the 3,000th unit sold, the uniform price of $7 is the maximum price a buyer will pay for this particular unit. However, for each of the other 2,999 units, consumers are willing to pay more than $7. As you learned in Chapter 2, buyers gain consumer surplus when they pay less for a product than the maximum amount they are willing to pay. The total consumer surplus generated by the uniform price of $7 is $4,500 ($= 0.5 \times 3,000 \times \$3$), which is the area of the triangle abU. If the firm could find a way to charge the demand price for every one of the 3,000 units sold, it could increase total revenue by $4,500 by taking all of the consumer surplus from buyers. As long as the process of capturing consumer surplus is costless, capturing consumer surplus adds $4,500 to the profit earned by producing and selling 3,000 units. The area abU is only part of the lost revenue and profit caused by uniform pricing.

The loss of revenue and profit caused by uniform pricing extends beyond the 3,000 units sold at point *U* on demand. Over the segment of demand from point *U* down to point *F* (3,001 to 5,999 units), the demand prices for these units exceed the marginal cost, $4, of producing these units. Since buyers are willing to pay more than the marginal cost of producing these units, the firm can earn additional profit equal to the area of shaded triangle *UdF*—but, as before, only if the firm can find a way to charge the demand price for each of the units between *U* and *F* on demand. The lost profits in the two shaded triangles in Figure 14.1 are sometimes referred to by marketers as the "curse" of uniform pricing. As we will show you in Section 14.2, capturing every bit of the consumer surplus in these two triangles, a practice called first-degree or perfect price discrimination, is practically impossible. Other forms of price discrimination, however, are widely used to capture some of the consumer surplus created by uniform pricing. We should mention here that, although the "curse" of uniform pricing generally applies in most cases, there are circumstances under which discriminatory pricing techniques may in fact increase total consumer surplus relative to the amount of surplus created under uniform pricing. You can learn about these special circumstances in advanced courses in microeconomics or industrial organization. We are now ready to discuss various types of price discrimination that can be used to capture the surplus created by uniform pricing.

Types of Price Discrimination

Economists and business firms have long recognized that when buyers can be separated into groups with different elasticities of demand, a firm can charge different prices for the same product and increase its profits above what could be earned if it charged a uniform price. In 1920, economist A. C. Pigou named this pricing practice **price discrimination,** decades before the word "discrimination" carried disparaging connotations. Most marketing managers and consultants avoid using the term "discrimination," instead calling this practice various other names, such as revenue management, yield management, or market segmentation. No matter what you call it, the objective of charging different prices for the same good or service is to capture consumer surplus, transforming it into profit for the firm.

price discrimination
Charging different prices for the same product for the purpose of capturing consumer surplus.

When a firm charges different prices across different units or different markets for the same product, the seller is price discriminating. There are two crucial points that must be carefully examined in the definition of price discrimination. First, *exactly* the same product must have different prices. If consumers perceive that goods are not identical, they will value the goods differently, creating separate demand curves and separate markets for the different goods. Obviously, a situation of "different prices for different goods" does not indicate the presence of price discrimination. Frequently, differences in timing or quality subtly create different products. For example, a lunchtime meal at Bern's Steakhouse is not the same product as a dinnertime meal at Bern's. Even if the lunch and dinner menus are identical, the dining experience differs. The purpose of a lunchtime meal may be to talk about business or take a quick nutritional break from work (with no wine service), while the purpose of an evening dinner may be to engage in relaxing social conversation with friends or family (with wine service). And, in many instances, quality differs between lunch and dinner dining experiences. Meal portions may be larger at dinner, and waiters may be more attentive during longer evening meals—tips are larger for evening meals! Obviously, lunch and dinner meals are different dining experiences, and thus different products. Second, for price discrimination to exist, costs must be the same for each market. If costs vary across markets, a profit-maximizing manager who follows the $MR = MC$ rule will, of course, charge different prices. This is not a case of price discrimination. Cost differences are frequently subtle and difficult to detect. A motel located near Busch Gardens offers 10 percent discounts for military families. According to the motel's owner/manager, military families are more reliable about checking in and out on time, and their children cause less trouble than children from nonmilitary families. Since costs differ between military and civilian families, the price difference is not a case of price discrimination.[1]

Sometimes the price differential between two separate markets is proportionately larger than the cost differential between the higher- and lower-priced markets. This situation is also a case of price discrimination, because the difference in prices cannot be fully explained by the difference in costs. To generalize the definition of price discrimination to cover this kind of price discrimination, economists say that price discrimination between two markets A and B exists when the price to marginal cost ratio (P/MC) differs between the two markets or buyers: $P_A/MC_A \neq P_B/MC_B$. In our motel pricing example, there is no price discrimination if the marginal cost of supplying motel rooms to military families is exactly 10 percent lower than the marginal cost of supplying civilian families. If providing rooms for military families is only 5 percent less costly, then the 10 percent price discount cannot be *fully* explained by cost differences, and thus the motel is practicing price discrimination.

Conditions for Profitable Price Discrimination

As you might expect, certain conditions are necessary for the firm to be *able* to price-discriminate profitably, otherwise price-setting firms would never engage in uniform pricing. First, a firm obviously must possess some market power. Since monopolists, monopolistic competitors, and oligopolists possess market power, they may be able to profitably price-discriminate, if they can meet the rest of the necessary conditions. Second, the firm must be able, in a cost-effective manner, to

---

[1]To be technically complete, we should mention that price discrimination also occurs if firms charge a *uniform* price when costs *differ* across buyers or across units sold. Profit-maximizing firms do not generally practice this type of price discrimination; it is usually undertaken by government agencies or government-regulated firms. For example, the U.S. Postal Service (USPS) charges all customers the same price to deliver a first-class letter, regardless of differences in the cost of supplying the service to different kinds of customers. Rural postal patrons, for example, are more costly to service than urban patrons, but all patrons pay the same price.

identify and separate submarkets. Submarkets must be separated to prevent resale of the product. If purchasers in the lower-price submarket are able to resell the product to buyers in the higher-price submarket, price discrimination will not exist for long. **Consumer arbitrage**—low-price buyers reselling goods in the high-price market—will soon restore a single, uniform price in the market. Goods and services that cannot be easily traded are more likely to experience discriminatory prices than those that can be easily transferred. For example, doctors, dentists, accountants, and lawyers are known to use "sliding scales" to charge higher prices to higher-income clients and lower prices to lower-income clients. Clearly, a patient paying a lower price for an appendectomy, a root canal, or a divorce settlement cannot resell these kinds of professional services to higher-price buyers. Finally, demand functions for the individual consumers or groups of consumers must differ. As we will demonstrate later, this statement can be made more specific to require that the price elasticities must be different. We have now established the following principle.

consumer arbitrage
When low-price buyers resell a product to buyers in a high-price market, which establishes a single, uniform price.

> **Principle** Price discrimination exists when the price to marginal cost ratio (P/MC) differs between markets: $P_A/MC_A \neq P_B/MC_B$. To practice price discrimination profitably, three conditions are necessary: (1) the firm must possess some degree of market power, (2) a cost-effective means of preventing resale between lower-price and higher-price buyers must be implemented, and (3) price elasticities must differ between individual buyers or groups of buyers.

The following sections describe the various types of price discrimination that can exist and set forth the theory explaining each type. We begin with an analysis of first-degree or perfect price discrimination, which allows the price-discriminating firm to capture all of the consumer surplus that is lost in uniform pricing. As mentioned previously, first-degree price discrimination is the most difficult type of price discrimination to practice. Second-degree price discrimination, which is something of an approximation to perfect price discrimination, can be implemented much more easily. We will discuss two particularly common forms of second-degree price discrimination: block pricing and two-part pricing. Third-degree price discrimination is the last type we will discuss. While generally less common than second-degree price discrimination, real-world examples of third-degree pricing are nonetheless easy to find and interesting to analyze.

Now try Technical Problem 1.

14.2 FIRST-DEGREE (OR PERFECT) PRICE DISCRIMINATION

first-degree price discrimination
Every unit is sold for the maximum price each consumer is willing to pay, which allows the firm to capture the entire consumer surplus.

Under **first-degree price discrimination,** the firm examines each individual's demand separately, and charges each consumer the maximum price he or she is willing to pay for every unit. Charging demand price (i.e., the maximum price) for every unit of the product effectively transforms every bit of consumer surplus into economic profit for the price-discriminating firm. While first-degree price discrimination is indeed "perfect" in the sense that it captures all consumer surplus, achieving this degree of pricing perfection is hardly ever possible. To know the maximum possible price for every unit sold, a firm must possess a tremendous amount of extremely accurate information about the demands of each and every consumer. Buyers, of course, will try to hide or misrepresent their true willingness to pay for a product.

Examples of successful first-degree price discrimination are rather hard to find. Perhaps the closest situation occurs at auction houses or on Internet auction sites. While auction methods vary, the fundamental purpose of auctions is generally to identify the buyer who values an auction item most and extract the highest payment possible from that buyer. To the extent that an auction is successful in these two tasks, consumer surplus is extracted from buyers and paid to sellers (and auctioneers). Examples of *attempted* perfect price discrimination can be found in most any market where price is negotiated on individual sales. Automobile salespeople, for example, try to size up each customer's willingness to pay by finding out how much income a potential buyer makes, whether the buyer currently owns an old or broken-down car, and so on. Experienced sports ticket scalpers can quickly and accurately estimate a buyer's willingness to pay for tickets. Scalpers look for indicators of affluence and strong team loyalty. A potential ticket buyer who arrives at a stadium decked out in the team's jersey and ball cap, wearing a 24-karat-gold University of Miami class ring, with the team mascot tattooed on his forearm, and acting eager to get seated before kickoff is certainly going to pay much more for his ticket than a buyer who avoids such obvious signals of high willingness to pay (i.e., high demand price).

To illustrate first-degree price discrimination, let's suppose the firm discussed in the previous section wishes to avoid the curse of uniform pricing by practicing perfect price discrimination. Figure 14.2 reproduces the demand and cost conditions for this firm. To keep matters simple, let's further suppose that each consumer buys just one unit of product. At a price of $7 (point U), for example, 3,000 consumers each buy one unit of the good. The firm knows that it faces precisely demand curve D and wishes to charge the demand price—the maximum price a buyer is willing to pay—for every unit it sells. When it sells every unit at its demand price, the firm's marginal revenue is no longer the curve labeled MR in Figure 14.1. Instead, marginal revenue under perfect price discrimination is the firm's demand curve D, because every unit sold adds P dollars to total revenue. Thus $D = MR$ in Figure 14.2. Since the equivalence of demand and marginal revenue is crucial for understanding perfect price discrimination, we must carefully examine this relation before we continue with our analysis.

Under perfect price discrimination, the 3,000th unit adds $7 (its demand price) to total revenue. However, under uniform pricing (see Figure 14.1), the 3,000th unit adds only $4 to total revenue, because increasing sales from 2,999 to 3,000 units requires the firm to cut price slightly below the demand price for the 2,999th unit. For this linear demand curve, the demand price for 2,999 units is $7.001 (= $10 - 0.001 \times 2,999$).[2] From the firm's point of view, the trouble with uniform pricing is now clear: selling the 3,000th unit requires cutting price by $0.001 (one-tenth of a penny) on *every* unit sold, not just the incremental unit. With a bit of

---

[2]You can confirm, based on Chapters 2 and 6, that the inverse demand equation for D in Figures 14.1 and 14.2 is $P = 10 - 0.001Q$.

FIGURE 14.2

First-Degree (Perfect) Price Discrimination: Capturing All Consumer Surplus

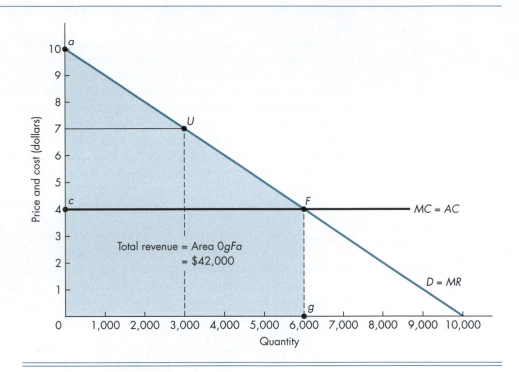

arithmetic, you can verify that the price cut required to sell the 3,000th unit reduces that unit's contribution to total revenue by approximately $3 (= 2,999 × $0.001). Thus, marginal revenue from selling the 3,000th unit is only $4 (= $7 − $3), which is distinctly less than its price, $7. Perfect price discrimination avoids this loss of revenue by selling every unit of the product at a different price.

To maximize profit under first-degree price discrimination, the firm will haggle over price to sell additional units until it reaches a total of 6,000 units, which is the output level for which $MR = MC$. Any units sold beyond the 6,000th unit can be sold only at prices below their marginal cost of production. At point F, the perfect-price-discriminating firm charges 6,000 different prices—consumers each buy just one unit—making it possible for the firm to collect total revenue equal to the area of the shaded trapezoid $0gFa$ in Figure 14.2. Total revenue for the perfectly discrim-inating firm is $42,000 [= 6,000 × ($10 + $4)/2]. The total cost of producing 6,000 units is $24,000 (= 6,000 × $4), and the firm earns $18,000 (= $42,000 − $24,000) of economic profit, which is the area of triangle acF in Figure 14.2.

First-degree price discrimination is clearly the goal of sellers who negotiate prices for each individual customer. However, perfect price discrimination is sel-dom actually achieved because, even if they can cheaply identify and separate lower- and higher-priced buyers, most firms do not know precisely the demand prices for every buyer of every unit sold. Second-degree price discrimination requires much less information about buyers' preferences.

ILLUSTRATION 14.1

Greyhound Ditches Uniform Pricing for Dynamic Pricing

Businesses engage in various methods of price discrimination because they can capture more consumer surplus and thus increase revenues and profit without making any changes in the underlying demand curve. The Greyhound bus company, for example, has decided to replace its uniform flat-rate pricing plan with a pricing system that was pioneered by mathematicians at American Airlines in the 1980s. The pricing technique is called "dynamic pricing" because the mathematical model varies the ticket prices for a trip on a bus or airline according to how demand conditions change over time.

Dynamic pricing is a complicated process that fundamentally tries to approximate first-degree price discrimination by varying the price of a ticket at every point in time—both points in time leading up to the point of departure and the time of departure itself. As Greyhound CEO Tim O'Toole explains, "No longer will a trip on

Greyhound cost the same on July 17 as the day after Thanksgiving." O'Toole should also have mentioned that ticket prices for travel on July 17 will vary over the time period leading up to the July 17th departure.

To give you an approximate idea about the substantial value from dropping simple uniform pricing for a price discrimination model such as dynamic pricing, *Bloomberg News* reports that Greyhound spent $40 million on the computers and software that are required to predict optimal time-varying ticket prices and to implement the resulting complex schedule of prices. Because uniform pricing is so much easier to administer than dynamic pricing, dynamic pricing must be richly rewarding in order to justify investing in the costly technology that the complicated pricing method requires. No airline has ever regretted its decision to ditch uniform pricing, and we are sure that Greyhound will never go back to uniform pricing either.

Source: Andrea Rothman, "Greyhound Taps Airline Pricing Models to Boost Profit," *Bloomberg.com*, May 20, 2013.

14.3 SECOND-DEGREE PRICE DISCRIMINATION METHODS

second-degree price discrimination
When a firm offers lower prices for larger quantities and lets buyers self-select the price they pay by choosing how much to buy.

When the same consumer buys more than one unit of a good or service at a time, the marginal value placed on consuming additional units declines as more units are consumed. **Second-degree price discrimination** takes advantage of this falling marginal valuation by reducing the average price as the amount purchased increases. For this reason, second-degree price discrimination only works for products and services for which consumers will buy multiple units during a given period. As an example of this, you may have noticed that Best Buy never offers quantity discounts on refrigerators but frequently offers "two for the price of one" deals on DVDs.

In first-degree price discrimination, the firm has complete information about every consumer's demand, which allows the firm to sort consumers according to willingness to pay and charge the maximum price for every unit sold. In third-degree price discrimination, which we will examine in the next section, the firm does not know every consumer's demand but does know the demands by *groups* of consumers and charges each group a different price. Second-degree price discrimination differs sharply from first- and third-degree price discrimination, because the firm possesses no information prior to the sale about individual or group demands. The second-degree price discriminator knows only that people who buy small amounts will have high *marginal* valuations and people who buy large amounts will have low marginal valuations. Accordingly, those who buy small amounts will be less price-sensitive than those who buy large amounts.

Under these circumstances, it makes sense to charge a higher price to smaller, less price-sensitive buyers with high marginal valuations and to charge a lower price to larger, more price-sensitive buyers with low marginal valuations. Unfortunately, when a customer walks into the store, a second-degree price discriminator does not know whether the buyer plans to purchase a little or a lot of product. Only when the customer makes a purchase and chooses to buy either a small amount or a large amount does the firm learn whether the buyer is, respectively, a relatively price-insensitive buyer (i.e., small quantity/high marginal valuation) or a relatively price-sensitive buyer (i.e., large quantity/low marginal valuation). Since the firm cannot determine prior to a sales transaction whether buyers possess high or low price sensitivities, the firm must offer all consumers the same price *schedule*. Even though the menu of prices is the same for all buyers, consumers self-select into different pricing categories through their own decisions about how much to buy: small buyers pay higher prices and large buyers pay lower prices. While implementation of second-degree price discrimination requires much less information about buyers than do other types of price discrimination, this reduced amount of information restricts the firm's ability to capture consumer surplus. As you will see, consumers get to keep some amount of consumer surplus under second-degree price discrimination, but less surplus than under uniform pricing.

Consider Home Depot's pricing decision for its interior wall paint. Home Depot knows that some buyers are only planning to paint one or two rooms of their homes. These smaller buyers, at the margin, will highly value an additional gallon of paint because they are buying so little. And, because they are buying so little paint, they are relatively insensitive to the price of paint. Home Depot also knows that other buyers are going to paint every room in their homes and will be purchasing many gallons of paint. These larger buyers will possess relatively low marginal valuations and will be much more sensitive to paint prices than smaller buyers. Obviously Home Depot employees cannot identify small and large buyers prior to the sales transaction, so they must offer all paint buyers the same pricing schedule—one that is designed to give larger buyers lower prices. In this way, Home Depot customers self-select themselves into lower- or higher-price groups.

There are many ways of designing pricing schedules to offer lower prices for larger quantities. We will now examine two of the most common ones: two-part pricing and declining block pricing. In both of these types of pricing, the firm designs a common pricing structure offered to all buyers and lets buyers self-select the price they will pay by choosing the amount of product to buy.

two-part pricing
A form of second-degree price discrimination that charges buyers a fixed access charge (A) to purchase as many units as they wish for a constant fee (f) per unit.

Two-Part Pricing

A **two-part pricing** plan creates average prices that decline with the amount purchased by a consumer. This declining price is accomplished by charging both a fixed access charge for the right to purchase as many units as desired and a constant usage fee for each unit purchased. Thus, the total expenditure (TE) for q units of a product is the sum of the fixed access charge (A) plus the usage charge, which is computed by multiplying the per-unit usage fee (f) times the number of units purchased (q)

$$TE = A + fq$$

The average price (or price per unit) is equal to the total expenditure divided by the number of units purchased

$$p = \frac{TE}{q} = \frac{A + fq}{q}$$

$$= \frac{A}{q} + f$$

The final expression for price shows clearly that product price falls as the consumer buys more of the good, because the fixed access fee is spread over more units of the good. The firm sets the values for the access charge and usage fee, and then buyers self-select the prices they will pay by choosing the quantities they wish to buy. Notice that all buyers face the same pricing menu or formula. Through the process of self-selection, however, those who buy larger amounts pay lower prices than those who choose to buy smaller amounts.

Finding the profit-maximizing values of A and f can be rather complex. To keep matters manageable, we will examine two of the easier situations for designing a two-part pricing plan. First, we will show you how to choose A and f when all consumers have identical demands for the product and the firm knows everything about consumer demand (i.e., knows the equation for demand). In this special case, as in the case of first-degree price discrimination, two-part pricing captures all of the consumer surplus. Second, we will show you how to extend the pricing plan to two different groups of identical buyers, and, again, the firm knows everything about consumer demand in each of the two groups (i.e., knows the equations for both demands). In this second case, a *single* or *common* two-part pricing menu applies to *both* groups of buyers, and, for this reason, the firm will not be able to capture the entire consumer surplus. This case allows for some difference among consumer demands, and so it more closely represents real-world applications of two-part pricing than the first case.

Before continuing, we should mention that more complicated pricing schemes arise when firms offer buyers *multiple* two-part pricing menus instead of a single plan that applies to all buyers. By letting consumers "subscribe" to their favorite one of the multiple pricing plans, firms can take advantage of buyer self-selection of price plans to target higher average prices at less elastic consumers and lower average prices at more elastic buyers. Cellular phone companies, for example, usually offer a variety of calling plans. In plan 1, buyers pay a high monthly charge for the right to purchase all the minutes they wish for a very low fee per minute (zero in some cases). The phone company also offers an alternative plan, plan 2, which allows buyers to pay a low monthly access charge (zero in some cases) coupled with a relatively high fee per minute. The phone company lets consumers choose the plan under which their bill will be computed. The choice of plans is yet another example of a self-selection process. The phone company devises values for the two plans— A_1, A_2, c_1, and c_2—so that it can tailor the two-part pricing structure for each

FIGURE 14.3

Inverse Demand Curve for Each of 100 Identical Senior Golfers:
$P_{SR} = 125 - 0.5Q_{SR}$

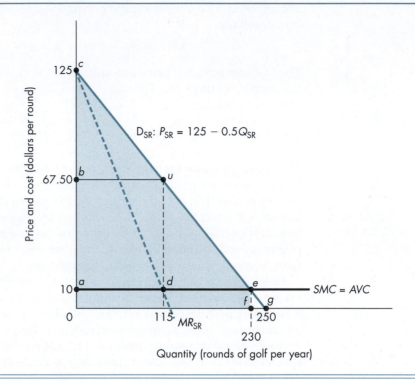

kind of buyer in a way that captures even more consumer surplus than using only a single two-part pricing schedule. Finding the optimal access charges and usage fees for multiple two-part pricing menus is rather complex, and, for this reason, we will not cover multiple two-part pricing plans in this text.[3]

All consumers are identical Let's first consider how to design a two-part pricing plan when all consumers have identical demands, and the firm knows this demand curve precisely. We can best explain this pricing practice with an example. Suppose you are the new manager of Northvale Golf Club, which is a private club catering exclusively to retired senior citizens who play golf most every day of the week. Northvale faces only limited competition from other golf clubs, because the nearest competing golf course is 25 miles away. The club's membership is composed of 100 seniors, all of whom possess *identical* demand curves for playing rounds of golf at Northvale. Based on marketing research done by an outside consulting firm, you know that the annual (inverse) demand equation for *each one* of the identical senior golfers is $P_{SR} = 125 - 0.5Q_{SR}$. Figure 14.3 shows this demand curve.

_____

[3]An excellent mathematical treatment of dual two-part pricing plans can be found in Dennis W. Carlton and Jeffrey M. Perloff, *Modern Industrial Organization*, 4th ed. (Pearson/Addison Wesley, 2005), pp. 344–349.

Like most golf clubs, Northvale Golf Club incurs both fixed and variable costs, and the fixed costs are much larger than the variable costs. The fixed costs of maintaining the golf course are outsourced to a company that specializes in golf course turf growth and maintenance. The turf company charges Northvale $800,000 annually. Other fixed costs, such as leasing 100 golf carts and other fixed "overhead" costs add another $200,000 to annual fixed costs. Thus, Northvale spends a total of $1 million annually on fixed costs, no matter how many rounds of golf are played each year. For each round of golf, variable costs include the cost of charging the golf cart's battery, a small amount of wear and tear on the course attributable to each round played, and a small amount of "administrative" labor expense. The average variable cost per round is constant and equal to $10 per round of golf. Because average variable cost is constant, marginal cost equals average variable cost, as shown in Figure 14.3 ($SMC = AVC = \$10$).

The owner recently fired Northvale's previous manager for making losses. The fired manager practiced uniform pricing by charging a price of $67.50 (i.e., a "green fee") for every round of golf. As shown in the figure, each one of the 100 identical senior members chooses to play 115 rounds of golf annually (point u) when facing a uniform price of $67.50 per round. Under the uniform pricing plan, annual total revenue is $776,250, which is the total amount spent on green fees by 100 golfers each spending $7,762.50 ($= \$67.50 \times 115$) annually. With 11,500 rounds played annually (115 rounds by each member), total variable cost is $115,000 ($= \$10 \times 11,500$). Under this uniform pricing plan, Northvale's previous manager incurred annual losses of $-$338,750 ($= \$776,250 - \$115,000 - \$1,000,000$). You naturally want to keep your new job, so you need to find a way to increase profit at the golf club. Increased advertising is unlikely to strongly stimulate demand—advertising can't create new golfers or motivate seniors to play much more than they already play—so you decide that your best hope for quickly increasing profit is to find a better pricing strategy.

After examining the demand and marginal revenue curves in Figure 14.3, you are able to see that the previous manager did, in fact, correctly implement uniform pricing at Northvale: the profit-maximizing *uniform* price is indeed $67.50 per round. However, having recently taken a course in managerial economics, you know that uniform pricing leaves a great deal of consumer surplus in your members' pockets. Because you know precisely the demand for every member, you realize that you can successfully practice perfect price discrimination. Unfortunately, first-degree price discrimination requires haggling over the green fee for every round of golf sold. Nonetheless, if you can stand all this haggling, you can collect the maximum fee golfers are willing to pay for each round played. Because the job pays you well, you decide to undertake the haggling to implement perfect price discrimination.

When you haggle over green fees to obtain the highest fee for every round played, you are aware that Northvale's marginal revenue curve (MR_{SR}) coincides with its demand curve (D_{SR}). You find it optimal to sell additional rounds until every player buys 230 rounds per year at point e (where $MR_{SR} = SMC$). By capturing the highest green fee for each round played, you can collect from each golfer $15,525 [$= 230 \times (\$125 + \$10)/2$], which is the area of the shaded trapezoid

0*cef* in Figure 14.3. With 100 identical golfers, annual total revenue is $1,552,500 (= $15,525 × 100). As shown in the figure, each of the 100 golfers plays 230 rounds annually for a total of 23,000 rounds annually. Because average variable cost is $10 per round, total variable cost is $230,000 (= $10 × 23,000). By practicing perfect price discrimination, you have increased Northvale's annual profit to $322,500 (= $1,552,500 − $230,000 − $1,000,000).

Although you expect the owner will be happy to see Northvale earning positive economic profit instead of losing money, you wish there was a way to avoid haggling with senior citizens over green fees for every one of the 23,000 rounds played. After some careful thinking, you realize that *exactly the same amount of profit* can be earned by optimally designing a two-part pricing plan. Furthermore, this two-part pricing plan will capture all consumer surplus without any haggling whatsoever over green fees! You set up a meeting with the owner of Northvale Golf Club to present your new pricing plan for approval.

You begin your meeting with the owner by explaining that, under your two-part pricing play, members will be allowed to play as many rounds of golf as they wish by paying a green fee (*f*) of $10 for each round played. However, to enjoy the privilege of paying such a "low" green fee, club members must also pay a "high" annual club membership charge (*A*) of $13,225 per year. Upon hearing your plan, the club owner threatens to fire you on the spot. Surely, he argues, nobody will pay an annual membership charge of $13,225 to play golf at Northvale. Fortunately, you are able to convince him that the pricing plan will work. On the back of an envelope, you sketch Figure 14.3 (good thing you learned how to draw graphs in economics!). Using this diagram, you carefully explain the concept of consumer surplus, and show the owner that when green fees are $10 per round, each golfer at Northvale enjoys annual consumer surplus of $13,225 (= 0.5 × 230 × $115)— the area of triangle *ace*. Thus seniors are just willing to pay the $13,225 annual membership charge to gain the privilege of paying a low green fee. This convinces the owner, and you get permission to implement the two-part plan.

Under your two-part pricing plan, annual total revenue is $1,552,500, which is the sum of total annual membership charges of $1,322,500 (= $13,225 × 100) and total green fees of $230,000 (= $10 × 230 × 100). It follows that annual profit will be $322,500 (= $1,552,500 − $230,000 − $1,000,000). Notice that this optimally designed two-part pricing plan generates the same total profit as perfect price discrimination. The optimal design involves setting the usage fee equal to marginal cost ($f^* = SMC$), and setting the access charge equal to one golfer's consumer surplus ($A^* = CS_i$).

We must emphasize here that, even though profit is exactly the same as under first-degree price discrimination, the two-part pricing plan is nonetheless a second-degree form of price discrimination. Instead of haggling over 23,000 green fees, every golfer faces the same pricing schedule: each golfer pays an annual membership charge of $13,225 and a "haggle-free" green fee of $10 for every round played. Under two-part pricing, as we explained previously, every golfer self-selects the average price he or she will pay for a round of golf by choosing the number of rounds to play. In this particular example, all golfers are assumed to be identical, so they all choose to play 230 rounds per year. This makes the average price per round $67.50 [= ($13,225 + $10 × 230)/230]. We can now summarize this discussion with the following principle.

Now try Technical
Problem 2.

Principle   When all consumers have identical demands for a product (and demand is precisely known), a manager can capture the entire consumer surplus through two-part pricing by setting the usage fee equal to marginal cost ($f^* = MC$) and setting the access charge equal to one of the identical buyers' consumer surplus ($A^* = CS_i$).

Two groups of identical consumers   Two-part pricing can also be utilized to price-discriminate when there are two or more *groups* of buyers and the buyers within each group possess identical demands (and the demands are known to the firm). While the procedure for finding the optimal values for f and A is a bit more complicated in this case, we can best illustrate the procedure by continuing our example of Northvale Golf Club, where you are the new club manager. Now you wish to find f^* and A^* when there are two groups of golfers, instead of one group of identical golfers.

Northvale's owner decides not to fire you because your decision to replace uniform green fees with a two-part pricing plan turned the club into a profitable enterprise. But now the owner expects you to further improve profits. One of the Northvale community residents, who is not retired and plays golf mostly on weekends, complains to you that the annual membership fee ($13,225) is too high for her to consider playing at Northvale Golf Club. Like the many other weekend golfers in the Northvale community, she drives some distance to play at a rival club. You now realize that Northvale has completely ignored a potential group of golfers who would play there if a more attractive pricing plan could be offered. To determine the profitability of trying to serve this group of golfers, you hire a marketing research firm to estimate the demand for golf at Northvale by nonretired, weekend players. The marketing experts estimate there are 100 such "weekend" golfers, all of whom possess *identical* demand curves. The marketing consultant determines that the (inverse) annual demand equation for each weekender is $P_{WK} = 120 - Q_{WK}$, which is shown as D_{WK} in Panel B of Figure 14.4.

You now can see why no weekenders are playing at Northvale. With green fees set at $10 per round, each weekender would choose to play 110 rounds of golf annually. At this rate of play, the most a weekend golfer would be willing to pay for an annual membership is $6,050 (= 0.5 × 110 × $110)—the area below D_{WK} above SMC up to 110 units. Because the current membership charge ($13,225) exceeds a weekend golfer's total consumer surplus, no weekend golfer joins the club.

To capture all consumer surplus from both groups, seniors and weekenders must pay *different* membership charges. Setting different membership charges will not work, however, because every golfer will claim to belong to the group receiving the lower membership charge. (You can't force applicants to truthfully reveal whether they are retired seniors or primarily weekend players.) For this reason, the membership charge must be the same for both groups. Not only must

FIGURE 14.4

Demand at Northvale Golf Club:
Seniors and Weekend Player Groups

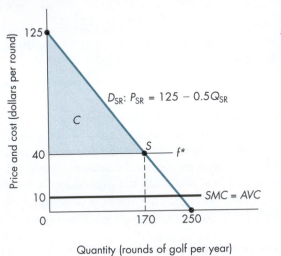

Panel A—One senior's demand

Panel B—One weekender's demand

the membership charge be equal for both groups, it cannot exceed the consumer surplus enjoyed by individual golfers in the group with the *lowest* consumer surplus—otherwise the low-consumer surplus golfers will not join.

To attract both groups of golfers to join the club, you set the membership charge for both groups equal to the consumer surplus of a weekend golfer. This will capture the entire consumer surplus of weekend golfers, while senior golfers keep a portion of their consumer surplus. It follows from this discussion that, for any particular green fee (f) and number of rounds played by a weekend golfer (Q_{WK}) facing that green fee, the annual membership charge (A) is

$$A = 0.5Q_{WK}(120 - f)$$

Now we turn to the task of finding the optimal green fee. To find the profit-maximizing green fee, you will need to know both the marginal revenue and marginal cost associated with changes in the green fee.

To find marginal revenue, you begin by expressing total revenue as the sum of membership charges and green fees

$$TR = [200(0.5Q_{WK}(120 - f))] + [f(100Q_{SR} + 100Q_{WK})]$$

The first term in the above expression shows the total revenue collected from 200 members paying a membership charge equal to the consumer surplus of a weekend golfer. The second term represents total green fees collected from 100 senior golfers playing Q_{SR} rounds annually and 100 weekend golfers playing Q_{WK} rounds annually. The addition to total revenue attributable to raising green fees by $1, MR_f, is equal to the sum of the effects of changing f on membership fees and changing f on green fees. After performing some rather tedious algebra, you discover that marginal revenue is a linear function of green fees

$$MR_f = N_{SR}(a_{SR} - a_{WK}) - [b_{WK}(N_{SR} - N_{WK}) - 2N_{SR}b_{SR}]f$$
$$= 100(250 - 120) - [(-1)(0) - 2(100)(-2)]f$$
$$= 13,000 - 400f$$

where N_{SR} and N_{WK} are the number of senior and weekend golfers, respectively, and demand parameters a_{SR}, a_{WK}, b_{SR}, and b_{WK} are taken from the two groups' demand equations[4]

$$Q_{SR} = a_{SR} + b_{SR}P_{SR} = 250 - 2P_{SR} \quad \text{and} \quad Q_{WK} = a_{WK} + b_{WK}P_{WK} = 120 - P_{WK}$$

To find the marginal cost of changing green fees, MC_f, you begin by expressing total variable costs as $AVC(N_{SR}Q_{SR} + N_{WK}Q_{WK})$. Then substituting the demand equations for Q_{SR} and Q_{WK} and recognizing that both seniors and weekenders pay the same green fee ($P_{SR} = P_{WK} = f$), you can relate total variable cost to the green fee as follows:

$$TVC = AVC[100(250 - 2f) + 100(120 - f)]$$

From this expression, it follows that MC_f—the addition to total variable cost attributable to raising green fees by $1 ($\Delta TVC/\Delta f$)—is constant and equal to $3,000

$$MC_f = c(N_{SR}b_{SR} + N_{WK}b_{WK})$$
$$= 10[100(-2) + 100(-1)]$$
$$= -3,000$$

We must stress the difference between SMC, which is $10, and MC_f, which is −$3,000. The addition to total cost attributable to playing one more round of golf is $10 per extra round played. The *increase* in total cost attributable to *lowering* the green fee by $1 is $3,000, because senior and weekend golfers together play 300 more rounds of golf, thereby adding $3,000 (= 300 × $10) to variable costs.

When marginal and variable costs are constant, as they are at Northvale, the profit-maximizing usage fee always exceeds the constant marginal cost (SMC) in the case of two or more groups of identical buyers. To show that f must exceed $10 in this example, suppose you initially set the green fee equal to marginal cost ($f = $10). Using the equation for MR_f presented above, it follows that the marginal revenue from raising the green fee by $1 is $9,000 (= 13,000 − 400 × 10). Thus, raising green fees by $1 causes profit to rise by $12,000 because total revenue rises

---

[4]See the mathematical appendix at the end of this chapter for a derivation of the mathematical solution for two-part pricing with two groups of identical buyers under conditions of constant costs. General mathematical solutions for nonlinear demand and cost structures can be quite complex, and we will not explore such cases in this book.

by $9,000 while total cost falls by $3,000. As the manager of Northvale, you will continue to raise green fees until $MR_f = MC_f$. Setting marginal revenue equal to marginal cost and solving for the profit-maximizing green fee, you find that $40 is the profit-maximizing green fee

$$MR_f = MC_f$$

$$13{,}000 - 400f^* = -3{,}000$$

$$f^* = \$40 = \frac{-16{,}000}{-400}$$

Points S and W in Figure 14.4 show the number of rounds played by each type of individual golfer, which can be computed as follows:

$$Q^*_{SR} = 170 = 250 - 2 \times 40 \quad \text{and} \quad Q^*_{WK} = 80 = 120 - 40$$

The optimal annual membership charge is equal to the consumer surplus for a weekend golfer who pays $40 per round. Thus you set the annual membership fee at $3,200 (= .5 × 80 × $80), which is the area of shaded triangle A^* in Panel B of Figure 14.4.

Now let's calculate the profit Northvale earns with the lower membership charge that attracts weekend players as well as retired seniors. The total number of rounds played annually drops from 34,000 rounds to 25,000 rounds (= 100 × 170 + 100 × 80). Annual profit at the club is $390,000

$$\text{Profit} = \text{Total membership charges} + \text{Total green fees} - TVC - TFC$$
$$= (200 \times \$3{,}200) + (25{,}000 \times \$40) - (25{,}000 \times \$10) - \$1{,}000{,}000$$
$$= \$390{,}000$$

Under the new two-part pricing plan, the golf club earns $67,500 (= $390,000 − $322,500) more profit than it earned when it set a high membership charge and low green fee, which ran off all of the weekend players.

In this example, Northvale Golf Club makes more profit by choosing to serve both types of buyers—seniors and weekender players—than by practicing perfect price discrimination by setting the highest possible access charge to capture all of (and only) the consumer surplus of the senior golfers. Sometimes, however, serving smaller groups of buyers or buyers with relatively low consumer surplus can result in lower profits. Thus you must always make sure that lowering the access charge to serve an additional group of buyers does in fact result in higher overall profits. This discussion establishes the following principle.

Now try Technical Problem 3.

Principle   When two groups of buyers have identical demand curves, a firm may find it profitable to charge each group identical access charges and usage fees. The optimal usage fee is the level for which $MR_f = MC_f$, and the optimal access charge is equal to the consumer surplus of a single buyer in the group possessing the lower consumer surplus. Serving two groups does not always increase profit, because serving a single group allows the firm to set a higher access charge and extract the entire consumer surplus from a single group.

Two-part pricing plans are not only valuable to businesses that wish to increase profits. As we will show you in Chapter 16, government regulatory agencies frequently employ access charges and usage fees to regulate public utilities, such as water, electricity, natural gas, cable, and local phone service. Learning how to design and implement two-part pricing schedules makes you valuable to both public utilities and state and federal regulatory agencies. Another form of two-part pricing used in both business and in regulating public utilities is declining block pricing, which we will briefly examine.

Declining Block Pricing

declining block pricing

Form of second-degree price discrimination that offers quantity discounts over successive blocks of quantities purchased.

Another common form of second-degree price discrimination is **declining block pricing,** which offers quantity discounts over successive discrete blocks of quantities purchased. Since the value of additional units of a product falls as a consumer buys more units, declining block pricing motivates individuals to buy more than they would buy when facing a single, uniform price. All consumers face the same pricing schedule, and those who buy more will reach lower-priced blocks of the product. Obviously, block pricing only makes sense when individuals buy more than one unit of the good or service per time period. In contrast to the constant usage fee (f) in two-part pricing plans, the marginal price in a declining block scheme is constant only within specified blocks of quantities sold. And, as the name implies, marginal prices drop as each block's threshold is passed.

Figure 14.5 illustrates how a declining five-block pricing plan can generate more profit than uniform pricing under identical demand and cost conditions. For this example, suppose many identical buyers possess individual demand curves like D in Figure 14.5. If the firm practices uniform pricing, the profit-maximizing price is $7 per unit and 30 units are purchased (point U), which is the output for which $MR = MC$. With a uniform price of $7, the firm earns profit of $90 [= ($7 − $4) × 30] from each one of the (identical) consumers that buys 30 units, and this profit is shown in the figure as the shaded area formed by the sum of rectangles $b + d + e$. Now let's see how $90 compares with the profit from a declining five-block pricing plan.

All buyers are presented with a common declining block pricing menu that determines the total expenditure by a consumer who buys q units of the good, $TE(q)$, according to the following five-block structure:

$$
\begin{aligned}
TE(q) &= 0 + \$9q & &\text{for } q \le 10 & &\text{(Block 1)} \\
&= \$90 + \$8(q - 10) & &\text{for } q \le 20 & &\text{(Block 2)} \\
&= \$170 + \$7(q - 20) & &\text{for } q \le 30 & &\text{(Block 3)} \\
&= \$240 + \$6(q - 30) & &\text{for } q \le 40 & &\text{(Block 4)} \\
&= \$300 + \$5(q - 40) & &\text{for } q > 40 & &\text{(Block 5)}
\end{aligned}
$$

For the first nine units purchased, the buyer's demand price (reservation price) exceeds the price charged for units in the first block ($9), so the buyer enjoys consumer surplus on those units. If the price remained $9 for all units, then the buyer would purchase only 10 units. But, for units 11 through 20, the price falls to $8.

FIGURE 14.5
Block Pricing with Five Blocks

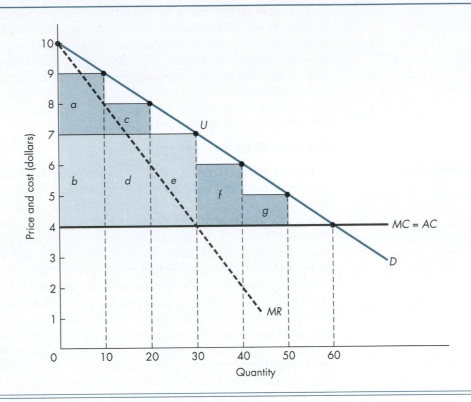

As you can see in the figure, the value of these units as measured by the demand curve is greater than $8, and the consumer will buy 10 more units. With successively lower prices in each block, the consumer continues buying more units until the value of the last unit purchased equals the lowest price in the last block of prices, $5. Thus each consumer chooses to purchase 50 units of the good. On the first block of 10 units purchased, the firm earns $50 of profit (areas $a + b$); on the second block of 10 units purchased, the firm earns $40 of profit (areas $c + d$); and so on through the fifth pricing block. Total profit is $150 for each customer. As you can see in Figure 14.5, the firm gains areas a, c, f, and g by implementing this block pricing plan rather than charging a uniform price of $7.

Now try Technical Problem 4.

14.4 THIRD-DEGREE PRICE DISCRIMINATION

third-degree price discrimination
Firm can identify and separate a market into two or more submarkets and charge a different price in each submarket.

The last type of price discrimination we will examine in this chapter is **third-degree price discrimination.** This technique can be applied when firms are able to *both* identify and separate two or more groups or submarkets of consumers. Each group or submarket is charged a different price for exactly the same product. In contrast to first-degree price discrimination, all buyers within each submarket pay the same price. Thus, a third-degree price discriminator does not haggle over prices in an effort to capture the entire consumer surplus, and so buyers in all of the submarkets end up keeping some of their consumer surplus. In contrast to second-degree price discrimination, third-degree price-discriminators do not rely on self-selection to create different prices. Because they can identify consumers in the various submarkets, they can successfully charge different prices to the different groups of buyers.

Movie theaters that charge adults higher ticket prices than children, pharmacies that charge senior citizens lower drug prices than nonseniors, and personal computer firms that charge students lower prices for PCs than other buyers are all examples of third-degree price discrimination. In each example, the price-discriminating firm can identify consumer types in ways that are practical, generally legal, and low cost. In many cases, consumer identification simply requires seeing a driver's license to verify age or checking a student ID to verify school enrollment. Once buyers are separated into different submarkets, the discriminating firm will charge the less elastic submarket a higher price than it charges the more elastic submarket. As we will explain shortly, when price elasticities differ across submarkets—as they must for successful discrimination—charging groups different prices increases profit compared to charging both submarkets the same uniform price. In other words, a movie theater earns more profit by (i) charging the less elastic adult submarket a relatively high ticket price and the more elastic children's submarket a relatively low ticket price than by (ii) charging all movie patrons the same ticket price.

Allocation of Sales in Two Markets to Maximize Revenue

To make the most profit, firms practicing third-degree price discrimination must decide how to optimally allocate total sales across different submarkets to generate the greatest amount of revenue (and consequently profit). To see how this is accomplished, let's assume there are only two submarkets, market 1 and market 2. Figure 14.6 shows the demand and marginal revenue curves for each submarket. Now let's further suppose the manager wishes for some reason to sell a total of 500 units in the two markets. How should this manager allocate sales between the two markets to maximize total revenue from the sale of 500 units?

Figure 14.6 shows two possible allocations of 500 units between markets 1 and 2. First, consider an *equal* allocation of 250 units in each market, as shown by points w and w' in the figure. When 250 units are sold in each market, you can see from Panels A and B that

$$MR_1 = \$10 < \$30 = MR_2$$

This allocation does not maximize total revenue because the manager can increase total revenue by decreasing the number of units sold in the lower-marginal-revenue market 1 and increasing the number of units sold in the higher-marginal-revenue market 2. Specifically, by selling one less unit in market 1, total revenue in market 1 falls by $10. To keep total sales at 500 units, the manager must sell one more unit in market 2, which increases total revenue by $30 in market 2. As you can now see, moving one unit from the low-marginal-revenue market 1 to the high-marginal-revenue market 2 causes total revenue to increase by $20 (= $30 − $10).

FIGURE 14.6

Allocating Sales Between Two Markets: The Equal Marginal Revenue Principle

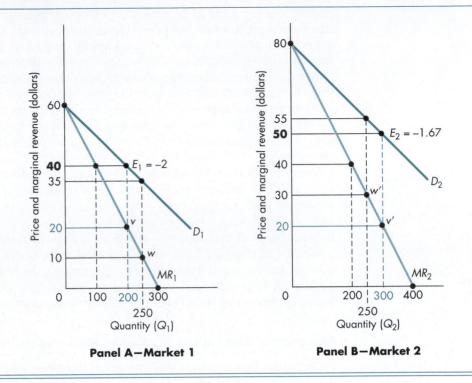

Panel A—Market 1

Panel B—Market 2

Now try Technical Problem 5.

To maximize total revenue from 500 units, the manager will continue moving units from the market where marginal revenue is lower to the market where marginal revenue is higher until marginal revenues are equal in both markets. Notice in Figure 14.6 that when Q_1 is 200 and Q_2 is 300 (points v and v'), marginal revenues are equal in both markets, and this allocation of 500 units maximizes the firm's total revenue. As you can see by examining the demand curves, the desired allocation of sales between markets 1 and 2 can be accomplished by charging a price of $40 to buyers in market 1 and charging a price of $50 to buyers in market 2.

We have now established that a manager maximizes total revenue from two submarkets when the total output is allocated across submarkets so that $MR_1 = MR_2$.[5] This establishes the following principle, which is sometimes called the *equal-marginal-revenue principle*:

---

[5]This condition should not be surprising because it is just another application of the principle of constrained optimization presented in Chapter 3. If a manager wants to maximize total revenue subject to the constraint that there is only a limited number of units to sell, the manager should allocate sales so that the marginal revenues (marginal benefits) per unit are equal in the two markets. The marginal cost of selling one unit in market 1 is the one unit not available for sale in market 2 ($MC_1 = MC_2 = 1$).

Principle A manager who wishes to maximize the total revenue from selling a given amount of output in two separate markets (1 and 2) should allocate sales between the two markets so that

$$MR_1 = MR_2$$

and the given amount of output is sold. This is known as the equal-marginal-revenue principle.

Although the marginal revenues in the two markets are equal, the prices charged are not. As we stated earlier, the higher price will be charged in the market with the less elastic demand; the lower price will be charged in the market having the more elastic demand. In the more elastic market, price could be raised only at the expense of a large decrease in sales. In the less elastic market, higher prices bring less reduction in sales.

This assertion can be demonstrated as follows: Let the prices in the two markets be P_1 and P_2. Likewise, let E_1 and E_2 denote the respective price elasticities. As shown in Chapter 6, marginal revenue can be expressed as

$$MR = P\left(1 + \frac{1}{E}\right)$$

Because managers will maximize revenue if they allocate output so that $MR_1 = MR_2$,

$$MR_1 = P_1\left(1 + \frac{1}{E_1}\right) = P_2\left(1 + \frac{1}{E_2}\right) = MR_2$$

Recall from Chapter 12 that firms with market power must price in the elastic region of demand to maximize profit. So MR_1 and MR_2 must both be positive, which implies that E_1 and E_2 must both be greater than 1 in absolute value (i.e., demand must be elastic in each market). Now suppose the lower price is charged in market 1 ($P_1 < P_2$) and the allocation of sales between markets satisfies the equal-marginal-revenue principle (i.e., $MR_1 = MR_2$). Then, by manipulating the equation above,

$$\frac{P_1}{P_2} = \frac{\left(1 + \frac{1}{E_2}\right)}{\left(1 + \frac{1}{E_1}\right)} < 1$$

Therefore, because $\left(1 + \frac{1}{E_2}\right) < \left(1 + \frac{1}{E_1}\right)$, it must be the case that $|1/E_2| > |1/E_1|$, so that

$$|E_1| > |E_2|$$

The market with the lower price must have the higher elasticity at that price. Therefore, if a firm engages in third-degree price discrimination, it will always charge the lower price in the market having the more elastic demand curve. Consider again the two markets, 1 and 2, in Figure 14.6. The lower price, $40, is charged in market 1, and the point elasticity of demand at this price is −2 [= $40/($40 − $60)]. In market 2, where the higher price, $50, is charged, the price elasticity is −1.67 [= $50/($50 − $80)]. As expected, demand is less elastic in market 2 where customers pay the higher price.

▣   **Principle**   A manager who price-discriminates in two separate markets, *A* and *B*, will maximize total revenue for a given level of output by charging the lower price in the more elastic market and the higher price in the less elastic market. If $|E_A| > |E_B|$, then $P_A < P_B$.

Profit Maximization with Third-Degree Price Discrimination

Thus far we have assumed that the price-discriminating firm wishes to allocate a *given level of output* among its markets to maximize the revenue from selling that output. Now we discuss how a manager determines the profit-maximizing level of *total* output. Once the total output is decided, the manager needs only to apply the equal-marginal-revenue principle to find the optimal allocation of sales among markets and the optimal prices to charge in the different markets.

As you probably expected, the manager maximizes profit by equating marginal revenue and marginal cost. The firm's marginal cost curve is no different from that of a nondiscriminating firm. The marginal cost for a third-degree price-discriminating firm is related to the *total* output in both markets ($Q_T = Q_1 + Q_2$) and does not depend on how that total output is allocated between the two markets—only total revenue depends on sales allocation. Therefore, we must derive the curve relating marginal revenue to total output Q_T, under the condition that output is allocated between markets according to the equal-marginal-revenue principle. This particular marginal revenue is called **total marginal revenue** (MR_T) because it gives the change in the combined total revenue in both markets (i.e., $TR_1 + TR_2$) when the price-discriminating firm increases total output (Q_T) and allocates the additional output to achieve equal marginal revenues in both markets. Total marginal revenue equals marginal cost ($MR_T = MC$) at the profit-maximizing level of total output.

Total marginal revenue is derived by horizontally summing the individual marginal revenue curves in each market. The process of horizontal summation can be accomplished either by graphical construction or by mathematical means. As you will see, horizontal summation enforces the equal-marginal-revenue principle in the process of deriving MR_T. We will now show you how to derive a total marginal revenue curve by graphical means, and then later in this section we will illustrate the algebraic method of finding the equation for MR_T.

total marginal revenue (MR_T)
The change in $TR_1 + TR_2$ attributable to an increase in Q_T when the extra output is allocated to maintain equal marginal revenues in both markets.

Profit-maximization: A graphical solution   For convenience, the marginal revenue curves MR_1 and MR_2 from Figure 14.6 are shown on the same graph in Panel A of Figure 14.7. (The corresponding demand curves are not shown because they are irrelevant for deriving the horizontal sum of MR_1 and MR_2.) Panel B in Figure 14.7 shows the total marginal revenue curve, MR_T, which is derived by summing Q_1 and Q_2 to get Q_T for a number of different values of marginal revenue—$80, $60, $40, $20, and zero

point *i*:	$MR_T = \$80$	for	$Q_T = 0 \quad = 0 + 0$
point *k*:	$MR_T = \$60$	for	$Q_T = 100 = 0 + 100$
point *l*:	$MR_T = \$40$	for	$Q_T = 300 = 100 + 200$

FIGURE 14.7

Constructing the Total Marginal Revenue Curve (MR_T):

Horizontal Summation

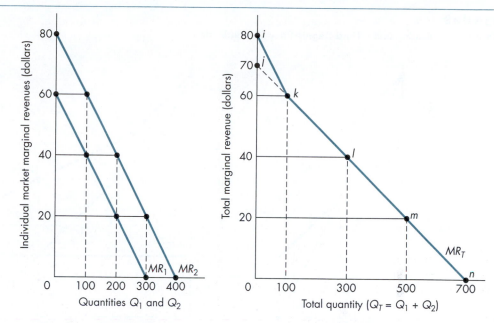

Panel A—MR in Markets 1 and 2

Panel B—Total Marginal Revenue Curve

point m: $MR_T = \$20$ for $Q_T = 500 = 200 + 300$

point n: $MR_T = \$0$ for $Q_T = 700 = 300 + 400$

For example, if the firm produces 300 units of total output, total marginal revenue is $40; this means the firm will maximize total revenue by selling 100 units in market 1 and 200 units in market 2. At 100 units of output (from Panel A), MR_1 equals $40. At 200 units of output (from Panel A), MR_2 also equals $40. Thus, it does not matter whether the 300th unit is the marginal unit sold in market 1 or in market 2; the firm's marginal revenue is $40 (as shown in Panel B at point l). Notice that this allocation of 300 total units is the only allocation that will equate the marginal revenues in the two markets. At every other total output in Panel B, the total marginal revenue is obtained in the same way.[6]

Now we can use MR_T to find the total output the firm should produce to maximize its profit. To see how this decision is made, consider Figure 14.8, which shows all the demand and marginal revenue relations. Suppose the firm

---

[6]When horizontally summing two *linear* marginal revenue curves, total marginal revenue will also be linear. For this reason, you can quickly construct a graph of MR_T by finding two points—points k and n in Figure 14.7, for example—and drawing a line through them. You must be careful, however, because the line you construct applies only to values of MR_T from zero up to the point where demand in the smaller market crosses the vertical axis. In Figure 14.7, MR_T kinks at point k, and coincides with MR_2 above $60.

FIGURE 14.8

Profit-Maximization under Third-Degree Price Discrimination

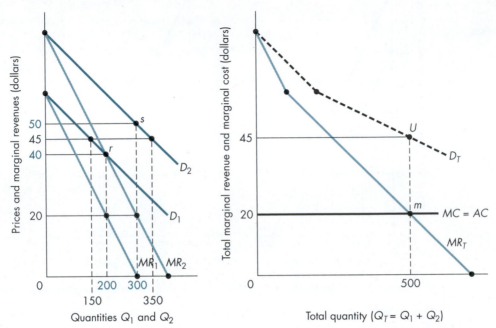

Panel A—Markets 1 and 2   **Panel B—Total Marginal Revenue and Marginal Cost**

faces constant marginal and average costs of production equal to $20 per unit, as shown in Panel B. Total output is determined by equating total marginal revenue with marginal cost, which occurs at 500 units (point m) and $MR_T = MC = \$20$. The 500 units are then allocated between the two markets 1 and 2 so that marginal revenue equals $20 in both markets. This allocation is accomplished by charging a price of $40 in market 1 (point r) and a price of $50 in market 2 (point s), which results in respective sales of 200 units and 300 units in markets 1 and 2.

By charging different prices in the separate markets, the firm collects total revenues of $8,000 (= \$40 \times 200$) in market 1 and $15,000 (= \$50 \times 300$) in market 2, for a combined total revenue of $23,000. Since the total cost of producing 500 units is $10,000 (= \$20 \times 500$), the price-discriminating firm's profit is $13,000.

To verify that charging two different prices generates more revenue and profit than charging the same (uniform) price to both groups of buyers, we will now calculate the total revenue the firm could collect if it instead charged all buyers the same price to sell 500 units.[7] The market demand when both submarkets 1

---

[7]Notice that the profit-maximizing output level when the firm chooses to charge all buyers a single price is also 500 units. This is true because MR_T in Panel B is also the firm's marginal revenue curve when the two market demand curves are horizontally summed to construct the total demand curve.

and 2 are grouped together as one single market is found by horizontally summing D_1 and D_2 to get the market demand curve, D_T, shown in Panel B. If the firm charged all customers a single price of \$45, it would sell 500 units and generate just \$22,500 (= \$45 × 500) in total revenue. The total cost of producing 500 units is the same as it was under price discrimination, \$10,000, so profit would drop to \$12,500. Thus the firm would experience a reduction in revenue and profit of \$500.

We can now summarize this discussion of pricing in two markets and extend our results to the general case of n separate markets:

Now try Technical Problem 6.

Principle A manager who wishes to sell output in n separate markets will maximize profit if the firm produces the level of total output and allocates that output among the n separate markets so that

$$MR_T = MR_1 = \cdots = MR_n = MC$$

The optimal prices to charge in each market are determined from the demand functions in each of the n markets.

Profit-maximization: An algebraic solution

Now we will show you an algebraic solution to the third-degree price discrimination problem presented graphically in Figure 14.8. The equations for the demand curves for these two markets are

$$\text{Mkt 1: } Q_1 = 600 - 10P_1 \quad \text{and} \quad \text{Mkt 2: } Q_2 = 800 - 10P_2$$

Solving for the inverse demand functions in the two markets,

$$\text{Mkt 1: } P_1 = 60 - 0.1Q_1 \quad \text{and} \quad \text{Mkt 2: } P_2 = 80 - 0.1Q_2$$

The marginal revenue functions associated with these inverse demand functions are

$$\text{Mkt 1: } MR_1 = 60 - 0.2Q_1 \quad \text{and} \quad \text{Mkt 2: } MR_2 = 80 - 0.2Q_2$$

To obtain the total marginal revenue function, $MR_T = f(Q_T)$, we first obtain the inverse marginal revenue functions for both markets in which the firm sells its product:

$$\text{Mkt 1: } Q_1 = 300 - 5MR_1 \quad \text{and} \quad \text{Mkt 2: } Q_2 = 400 - 5MR_2$$

For any given level of total output, $MR_1 = MR_2 = MR_T$; thus

$$\text{Mkt 1: } Q_1 = 300 - 5MR_T \quad \text{and} \quad \text{Mkt 2: } Q_2 = 400 - 5MR_T$$

Since $Q_T = Q_1 + Q_2$, the inverse of total marginal revenue is obtained by summing the two inverse marginal revenue curves to get

$$Q_T = Q_1 + Q_2 = 300 - 5MR_T + 400 - 5MR_T$$
$$= 700 - 10MR_T$$

ILLUSTRATION 14.2

Sometimes It's Hard to Price-Discriminate

In the theoretical discussion of third-degree price discrimination, we made two important points: (1) Firms must separate the submarkets according to demand elasticity, and (2) firms must be able to separate markets so as to keep buyers in the higher-price market from buying in the lower-price market (i.e., prevent consumer arbitrage). In some of the examples we used, it was relatively easy to separate the markets. For example, at movie theaters it is fairly simple, and relatively inexpensive, to prevent an adult from entering the theater with a lower-priced child's ticket. In other cases of price discrimination, it is rather difficult or costly to separate the markets. If it is impossible or expensive to separate markets, third-degree price discrimination will not be profitable, and the monopolist will either charge a single price to all customers or find a way to implement second-degree price discrimination.

One of the most frequently cited examples of a market in which separation is difficult is the airline market. It is no secret that airlines attempt to charge leisure fliers lower fares than business travelers. The story of such an attempt by Northwest Airlines illustrates the difficulty of separating markets.

The Wall Street Journal reported that Northwest Airlines would start offering a new discount fare that would cut down prices by 20 to 40 percent for people who were traveling in a group of two or more.

The Wall Street Journal noted that this change would be likely to stimulate family travel but would also eliminate the use of supersaver fares by business travelers. Previously, many business travelers purchased round-trip supersaver tickets when fares dropped below 50 percent, then threw away the return portion of the ticket or used it later. Northwest was planning to raise or do away with its other supersaver fares designed to attract leisure travelers. Most business travelers fly alone and would not be able to take advantage of the new, lower fares requiring groups of two or more. The Northwest executive also predicted that businesspeople would not abuse these tickets. Should the plan stick and spread, he said, it will allow airlines to maintain an attractive offering for the most price-sensitive travelers, while allowing the basic supersaver fares to continue rising along with business rates.

This reasoning was a bit optimistic on the part of the airline. *The Wall Street Journal* noted that groups of business travelers could work around the restrictions that currently applied to supersavers. One airline official expressed concern that travel agents would match travelers who did not know each other who were going to the same destination. Clearly there were many ways to defeat the airline's attempts to price-discriminate effectively.

But Northwest knew about the problems and tried to make the practice of cross-buying difficult. Travelers were required to book their flights together, check in together, and follow identical itineraries to qualify for the group discounts. The fares were nonrefundable, required a Saturday night stay, and had to be booked 14 days in advance—practices that business travelers typically would find difficult to accomplish. Of course, some of these restrictions designed to weed out business travelers could discourage many leisure travelers, the very people the new discounts were designed to attract. And obviously single leisure travelers would be left out.

As you can see, the problem of separating markets—preventing customers in the higher-price market from buying in the lower-price market—can be an extremely challenging task for the would-be price discriminator. For airlines, it would be much easier if passengers came with signs saying "business traveler" or "leisure traveler." As previously noted, in markets where separating the higher-price buyers from the lower-price buyers is too difficult or too expensive, third-degree price discrimination will not be profitable. Before resorting to uniform pricing, a firm that wishes to price-discriminate can try to implement one of the second-degree price-discrimination methods, because these methods rely on self-selection rather than market separation to charge different prices.

Source: Based on Brett Pulley, "Northwest Cuts Fares to Boost Leisure Travel," *The Wall Street Journal*, January 12, 1993.

Taking the inverse, we obtain the total marginal revenue function facing the price-discriminating firm

$$MR_T = 70 - 0.10Q_T$$

The firm's marginal cost function is

$$MC = 20$$

Equating estimated total marginal revenue and marginal cost,

$$MR_T = 70 - 0.10Q_T = 20 = MC$$

we then solve for Q_T to determine the profit-maximizing level of output is 500. To find the optimal allocation of 500 units between the two markets, sales levels must be chosen so that marginal revenues are equated across the two markets at a value of $20. The manager must solve the following two equations:

$$\text{Mkt 1: } 20 = 60 - 0.2Q_1 \quad \text{and} \quad \text{Mkt 2: } 20 = 80 - 0.2Q_2$$

Now try Technical Problems 7–8.

The solution is to sell 200 units in market 1 and 300 units in market 2. The price to charge in the two markets is found by substituting the optimal quantities into the demand equations in each of the markets. As we found in the graphical solution above, profit is maximized by selling the 200 units of output in market 1 at a price of $40 and the 300 units of output in market 2 at a price of $50.

14.5 PRICING PRACTICES FOR MULTIPRODUCT FIRMS

Many firms produce several different products, or at least several different models in their product lines. And, service firms frequently offer various levels or combinations of services: basic, premium, ultra, and so on. As you will recall from our discussion of economies of scope, many industries are composed primarily of multiproduct firms because cost-savings from multiproduct production can be substantial. We start this section by showing you how to make profit-maximizing pricing decisions if you are managing a firm that sells multiple products or services that are related in consumption—as either substitutes or complements.[8] As it turns out, you must incorporate the interrelations between the demand for each of the firm's products and the prices of the rest of the firm's products to find the profit-maximizing prices and quantities of multiple goods or services. Although this can be a computationally challenging process, we will show you that the fundamental principle of setting marginal revenue equal to marginal cost continues to provide the key to making optimal pricing decisions. Then we will examine a very common pricing tactic that involves bundling two or more individual products or services as a "package." We will explain why bundling can increase profit and what kinds of products and services can be profitably bundled.

---

[8]In this section, we will examine multiproduct pricing for goods that are related in *consumption*. However, goods may also be related in *production*. The rules making pricing decisions when goods are related in production are set forth in *Online Topic 3: Pricing Multiple Products Related in Production*.

Pricing Multiple Products Related in Consumption

Recall that the demand for a particular commodity depends not only on the price of the product itself but also on the prices of related commodities, incomes, tastes, and so on. For simplicity, we ignore the other factors and write one demand function as

$$Q_X = f(P_X, P_Y)$$

where Q_X is the quantity demanded of commodity X, P_X is the price of X, and P_Y is the price of a related commodity Y—either a substitute or complement.

In the discussion so far in the text, we have treated P_Y as if it were given to the firm. That is, we assumed P_Y to be a parameter determined outside the firm. Thus the firm would maximize its profits by selecting the appropriate level of production and price for X. If, however, the firm in question produces *both* commodities X and Y, the price of the related commodity Y is no longer beyond the control of the manager.

To maximize profit, the levels of output and prices for the related commodities must be determined *jointly*. For a two-product firm, the profit-maximizing conditions remain the same

$$MR_X = MC_X \quad \text{and} \quad MR_Y = MC_Y$$

However, the marginal revenue of X will depend on the quantities sold of both X and Y, as will the marginal revenue of Y. The interdependence of the two marginal revenues, MR_X and MR_Y, requires that the marginal conditions set forth earlier must be satisfied *simultaneously*. (Note that in this case the products are not related in production, so MC_X and MC_Y depend only on, respectively, the output of X and the output of Y.) When products are used together, consumers typically buy them together, and these kinds of goods are **complements in consumption.** A different situation, **substitutes in consumption**, arises when a firm sells multiple products that are substitutes. Then buyers would purchase only one of the firm's products. In both cases, marginal revenues are interdependent.

complements in consumption
Products that are used together and purchased together.

substitutes in consumption
Products are substitutes and buyers purchase only one of the firm's products.

> **Principle** When a firm produces two products, X and Y, that are related in consumption either as substitutes or complements, the manager of the multiple-product firm maximizes profit by producing and selling the amounts of X and Y for which
> $$MR_X = MC_X \quad \text{and} \quad MR_Y = MC_Y$$
> are *simultaneously* satisfied. The profit-maximizing prices, P_X and P_Y, are determined by substituting the optimal levels of X and Y into the demand functions and solving for P_X and P_Y.

To show how a manager would maximize profit under these circumstances, we will use another hypothetical example. In this example we will look at a firm that produces products that are substitutes in consumption, but exactly the same technique applies for products that are complements in consumption.

Consider Zicon Manufacturing, a firm that produces two types of automobile vacuum cleaners. One, which we denote as product X, plugs into the cigarette

ILLUSTRATION 14.3

Computer Printers and Replacement Cartridges: Pricing Multiple Products That Are Complements

When a firm sells two (or more) products that are related in consumption, as either substitutes or complements, the price of each good affects the demand for the other good. Therefore, a manager must account for this interdependence by choosing prices that result in equalization of marginal revenue and marginal cost for both goods *simultaneously*. While you may have found our discussion of this rule a bit tedious because of the messy algebra required to solve marginal conditions simultaneously, we want you to see that, messy or not, the rule can offer a manager a way to make sizable profits. Gillette, the manufacturer of razors and blades, understood this pricing relation and made a fortune nearly a half-century ago by setting a low price for razors to stimulate demand for its high-profit-margin blades.[a] Today, many multiproduct firms still can increase profits by making pricing decisions that account for product complementarities.

The Wall Street Journal recently reported that manufacturers of computer printers are enjoying exceptional profitability despite dramatically falling prices for computer printers.[b] Managers at companies such as Hewlett-Packard, Seiko-Epson, and Canon have exploited the multiproduct pricing rule for complements, discussed in this chapter, to make huge profits in the market for replacement printer cartridges—both inkjet cartridges and laser toner cartridges. Computer printers enjoy nearly the same popularity as personal computers: More than 100 million of them are in use worldwide. In the *Wall Street Journal* article John B. Jones, Jr., an analyst at Salomon Brothers, estimated that H-P, which has about half of the entire printer market, earned an astonishing $3.4 billion worldwide on sales of ink-jet and laser replacement cartridges.

The strategy for making the replacement cartridge market enormously profitable is a straightforward application of some of the tools developed in managerial economics. First, because the two goods, printers and replacement cartridges, are complements produced by the multiproduct firms, the printer firms lower prices on the printers and raise prices on replacement cartridges. *The Wall Street Journal* reported that the profit margin on printers is just 30 percent while the profit margin on replacement cartridges is a whopping 70 percent. One H-P official, commenting on the firm's pricing policy for replacement cartridges, was quoted as saying, "We just charge what the market will bear." Of course this is true of any firm with market power, but H-P has cleverly boosted "what the market will bear" by lowering prices of its printers, the complement good.

A second part of the strategy for exploiting profits in the printer–replacement cartridge business involves securing profits over the long run by slowing or blocking entry of rivals into the replacement cartridge market. The large printer manufacturers now design their printer cartridges so that they are not simply plastic boxes with ink or toner in them. Purposely, engineers design the cartridges to include some or all of the printer-head technology required to make the printer work. In so doing, the printer cartridge can be covered by patents to prevent other companies from producing "clone" replacement cartridges. Clearly, this second part of the strategy is just as important as the first part, at least if long-run profitability is the manager's objective.

It is interesting to note that H-P, Canon, and Seiko-Epson are all suing Nu-Kote Holding, a Dallas supplier of generic replacement cartridges, for patent infringement. Nu-Kote, in turn, is suing the three manufacturers for allegedly colluding to keep replacement cartridge prices artificially high. It seems to us that Nu-Kote would be smart to spend its litigation resources winning the patent infringement case and let any alleged pricing conspiracy continue to prop up prices of its product.

[a]King Gillette invented the disposable razor blade but did not make much profit selling it. He sold the patent and the name, and it was the new owner who devised the strategy of setting a low price for razors and a high price for the blades. Using this now widely used pricing strategy, the new owner of Gillette was enormously successful.

[b]Lee Gomez, "Industry Focus: Computer-Printer Price Drop Isn't Starving Makers," *The Wall Street Journal*, August 16, 1996.

lighter receptacle; the other, product Y, has rechargeable batteries. Assuming that there is no relation between the two products other than the apparent substitutability in consumption, the manager of Zicon wanted to determine the profit-maximizing levels of production and price for the two products.

Using the techniques described in Chapter 7, the demand functions for the two products were forecasted to be

$$Q_X = 80{,}000 - 8{,}000P_X + 6{,}000P_Y \quad \text{and} \quad Q_Y = 40{,}000 - 4{,}000P_Y + 4{,}000P_X$$

Solving these two forecasted demand functions simultaneously for P_X and P_Y, the manager obtained the following inverse demand functions in which each price is a function of both quantities[9]

$$P_X = 70 - 0.0005Q_X - 0.00075Q_Y \quad \text{and} \quad P_Y = 80 - 0.001Q_Y - 0.0005Q_X$$

The total revenue functions for each product are

$$TR_X = P_X Q_X = 70Q_X - 0.0005Q_X^2 - 0.00075Q_Y Q_X$$

and

$$TR_Y = P_Y Q_Y = 80Q_Y - 0.001Q_Y^2 - 0.0005Q_X Q_Y$$

The (grand) total revenue from both products is obtained by adding the revenues from both products: $TR = TR_X + TR_Y$. The associated marginal revenue functions for each product are[10]

$$MR_X = 70 - 0.001Q_X - 0.00125Q_Y \quad \text{and} \quad MR_Y = 80 - 0.002Q_Y - 0.00125Q_X$$

The production manager obtained estimates of the total cost functions

$$TC_X = 7.5Q_X + 0.00025Q_X^2 \quad \text{and} \quad TC_Y = 11Q_Y + 0.000125Q_Y^2$$

The marginal cost functions associated with these total costs are

$$MC_X = 7.5 + 0.0005Q_X \quad \text{and} \quad MC_Y = 11 + 0.00025Q_Y$$

---

[9]One way to solve these two equations simultaneously is to use the method of substitution. First, solve one demand function for P_X in terms of Q_X and P_Y and the other demand function for P_Y in terms of Q_Y and P_X. Then substitute the equation for P_Y into the equation for P_X, and vice versa. These two equations can then be solved for P_X and P_Y in terms of Q_X and Q_Y. The mathematical appendix at the end of this chapter shows how to use matrix algebra to find equations for linear inverse demand curves.

[10]As noted several times, the marginal revenue curve associated with a linear demand curve has the same intercept and is twice as steep as linear demand. In this case of interdependent demand curves, an additional term must be included in each marginal revenue function to reflect the effect of selling another unit of one good on the *price* of the other good. The intercepts for MR_X and MR_Y are, respectively, $(70 - 0.00075Q_Y)$ and $(80 - 0.0005Q_X)$. The additional terms reflecting the interdependence of MR_X and MR_Y are, respectively, $-0.0005Q_Y$ and $-0.00075Q_X$. Thus

$$MR_X = (70 - 0.00075Q_Y) - 2(0.0005)Q_X - 0.0005Q_Y = 70 - 0.001Q_X - 0.00125Q_Y$$

and

$$MR_Y = (80 - 0.005Q_X) - 2(0.001)Q_Y - 0.00075Q_X = 80 - 0.002Q_Y - 0.00125Q_X$$

The mathematical appendix at the end of this chapter provides the general algebraic solution for linear demands and marginal revenues for the case of two goods.

To determine the outputs of each product that will maximize profit, the manager of Zicon equated MR and MC for the two products

$$70 - 0.001Q_X - 0.00125Q_Y = 7.5 + 0.0005Q_X$$

$$80 - 0.002Q_Y - 0.00125Q_X = 11 + 0.00025Q_Y$$

Solving these equations simultaneously for Q_X and Q_Y (following the approach in footnote 8), the profit-maximizing outputs were found to be $Q_X^* = 30{,}000$ and $Q_Y^* = 14{,}000$. Using these outputs in the price functions, the manager of Zicon found that the profit-maximizing prices for X and Y were

$$P_X^* = 70 - 0.0005(30{,}000) - 0.00075(14{,}000) = \$44.50$$

and

$$P_Y^* = 80 - 0.001(14{,}000) - 0.0005(30{,}000) = \$51$$

The total revenue from selling the optimal amounts of X and Y was \$2,049,000, which was the sum of TR_X and TR_Y

$$TR_X + TR_Y = \$44.50(30{,}000) + \$51(14{,}000)$$

$$= \$2{,}049{,}000$$

The total cost of producing the optimal amounts of X and Y was \$628,500, which equals the sum of TC_X and TC_Y

$$TC_X + TC_Y = 7.5(30{,}000) + 0.00025(30{,}000)^2 + 11(14{,}000) + 0.000125(14{,}000)^2$$

$$= \$628{,}500$$

Now try Technical Problem 9.

The manager expected Zicon Manufacturing to earn profit of \$1,420,500 (= \$2,049,000 − \$628,500).

Bundling Multiple Products

bundling
Selling a bundle of two or more products at a single price.

One very common pricing practice employed by multiproduct firms involves **bundling** two or more products and selling the bundle of goods or services at a single price. For example, Disney World makes you buy one ticket for admission, which allows you to ride all of the rides, rather than separately selling individual tickets for each ride. Most computer manufacturers sell computer bundles that include the computer, some software, and a monitor. And, software companies offer "office suites," which are bundles of office programs that might include word processing, spreadsheet, database, and presentation tools. Bundling is not always profitable, however. Recently, some airlines decided to "unbundle" their flight and baggage services, charging separate fees for baggage service.

When a multiproduct firm only allows consumers to purchase their different products in a bundle, the practice is called, more precisely, *pure bundling*. Frequently, however, multiproduct firms offer several products in both a bundle and separately, a practice known as *mixed bundling*. With mixed bundling, then, consumers get to buy the bundle or instead purchase one or more of the products separately.[11] Both types of bundling can increase profit by capturing consumer surplus in a fashion similar to price discrimination. As it turns out, when price discrimination is possible, charging different prices to different buyers can generate even greater profit than bundling. However, price discrimination is not always possible, as we explained earlier in this chapter. Bundling, then, provides a way to capture greater consumer surplus when it is not possible to identify and separate consumers with high and low levels of willingness to pay and charge them different prices. For bundling to increase profit, certain conditions on demand must be met. We will explain these conditions shortly.

To illustrate the benefits of product bundling, let's consider an example: Crystal Channel Inc. is the local monopoly provider of digital cable television for a small community. Marketing analysis of the community served by Crystal Channel reveals two types of cable television viewers: family-oriented viewers and adult-oriented viewers. The family-oriented viewers are primarily interested in cable TV channels providing G- and PG-rated movies, educational programming, and some sports coverage, and also occasionally enjoy viewing some adult-oriented channels. The adult-oriented viewers are primarily interested in channels showing "films" with mature plots, news analysis programs, and comprehensive sports coverage, and also occasionally enjoy watching some family-oriented channels. The market study estimates there are 2,000 family-oriented viewers and 2,000 adult-oriented viewers in the local market for cable television. Unfortunately for Crystal Channel, the market study offers no means of identifying the type of viewer, which would then make price discrimination possible. (Note: You will see in Technical Problem 10 that when it is possible to identify and separate family- and adult-viewer types, price discrimination can generate more profit than bundling the family and adult channel packages.) To keep things as simple as possible, let's suppose Crystal Channel's total variable costs are zero, so that all of its costs are fixed costs. Consequently, the manager of Crystal Channel maximizes economic profit by maximizing total revenue.

Table 14.1 shows demand prices for each type of viewer. As you can see from the table, family-oriented viewers are willing to pay at most $100 per month for the family package of channels and at most $50 per month for the adult package of channels. Thus, for family-oriented viewers, the demand price for a bundle of both packages is equal to the sum of the two demand prices, $150 (= $100 + $50) per month.[12]

---

[11]In this text, we will limit our analysis of bundling to the case of *pure* bundling, because analysis of mixed bundling is a bit more complicated and would take more space than we wish to allocate to bundle pricing. You can find a complete treatment of pure and mixed bundling in Lynne Pepall, Daniel J. Richards, and George Norman, *Industrial Organization: Contemporary Theory and Practice*, third edition, Thomson/South-Western, 2005.

[12]We are assuming that the willingness to pay for family and adult packages are independent, which means the maximum willingness to pay for a bundle is computed by adding the two demand prices. When family and adult packages are either complements or substitutes for a viewer, then the demand price for the family and adult bundle will be, respectively, greater or less than the sum of the two demand prices. For example, if the two packages "overlap" or contain some of the same channels, then the demand price for the bundle of both packages would, of course, be *less* than the sum of the two demand prices for the family and adult packages.

	Number of viewer type	Type of viewer	Family package only	Adult package only	Family and adult bundle
TABLE 14.1 **Demand Prices for Family and Adult Channel Packages (Monthly Subscription Fees)**	2,000	Family-oriented	$100	$ 50	$150
	2,000	Adult-oriented	25	100	125

Adult-oriented subscribers are willing to pay at most $100 per month for the adult package of channels and at most $25 per month for the family package of channels. For adult-oriented subscribers, then, the demand price for a bundle of both packages is $125 (= $100 + $25) per month.

In order to increase profit through bundling multiple goods or services, the individual demands for the goods or services must satisfy two requirements. First, different consumer types must possess differing tastes for the multiple products, which has the effect of creating different demand prices across consumers for each of the multiple goods. You can see from Table 14.1 that family-oriented viewers and adult-oriented viewers do indeed possess different demand prices for family and adult channel packages. Second, the demand prices for the two products or services must be *negatively* (or oppositely) correlated with consumer types. In this example, the consumer type that *most* highly values one package must place the *lowest* value on the other package. In Table 14.1, you can see the required negative correlation between demand price and viewer type: Family-oriented viewers hold the highest demand price for the family package of channels ($100) and the lowest demand price for the adult package of channels ($50). Adult-oriented viewers hold the lowest demand price for the family package of channels ($25) and the highest demand price for the adult package of channels ($100).

The reason these two demand conditions make bundling profitable—when price discrimination cannot be implemented—is best explained by viewing bundling as a means of capturing consumer surplus. Recall from our discussion at the beginning of this chapter that the closer you can set the price of a good or service to its demand price, the greater will be the amount of consumer surplus that you can capture or transform into profit. When consumer tastes differ, demand prices will differ for the multiple goods. Bundling goods together reduces the (proportionate) variability in demand prices across buyers, and, in so doing, makes it possible to set price closer to the bundle's demand price for every consumer, thereby capturing more consumer surplus than separate prices can capture. As you can see in Table 14.1, it is not possible to set *one* price for either the family package or the adult package that will capture all consumer surplus because demand prices differ across consumer types. For the family package, the difference in demand prices is $75 (= $100 − $25), and for the adult package, the difference is $50 (= $100 − $50). Notice, however, that when the two packages are bundled, the difference in demand prices is reduced to just $25 (= $150 − $125). By simple arithmetic, bundling reduces the difference or variability in demand prices so that the price of the bundle can be set closer to the demand prices of the two consumer types than would be possible if *either* channel package is priced separately.

Crystal Channel must consider three tactics or options for setting prices for its two channel packages: (1) price each channel package at its highest demand price, (2) price each channel package at its lowest demand price, and (3) charge a single price for a bundle with both the family and adult channel packages. In the first option, Crystal Channel's manager sets the price of the family package at $100 per month and the price of the adult package at $100 per month, attracting 2,000 family-oriented viewers to subscribe to the family package and 2,000 adult-oriented viewers to subscribe to the adult package. The total revenue generated each month with this option is $400,000 (= $100 × 2,000 + $100 × 2,000). Alternatively, following the second pricing tactic, the manager sets the price of the family package at $25 per month and the price of the adult package at $50 per month, which attracts *all* 4,000 viewers to subscribe to *both* packages. The total revenue generated each month under the second option is $300,000 (= $25 × 4,000 + $50 × 4,000). So, in the absence of bundling, the manager of Crystal Channel clearly prefers the first pricing tactic when charging *separate* prices for each channel package.

Now consider a third option: Bundle the family and adult packages together and charge $125 for the bundle, attracting all 4,000 viewers to subscribe to the bundle. The bundling method of pricing the channel packages generates total revenue of $500,000 (= $125 × 4,000) each month, which beats the other two pricing options. As you can see from this example, bundling the two packages of channels reduces the variability in demand prices across consumer types, enabling Crystal Channel to transform the greatest possible consumer surplus into economic profit. We can now summarize our discussion of bundle pricing in the following principle:

Now try Technical
Problem 10.

Principle When price discrimination is not possible, bundling multiple goods and charging a single price for the bundle will be more profitable than charging individual prices for multiple goods as long as two conditions on product demands are met: (1) Consumers must have different demand prices for each of the goods in the bundle; and (2) The demand prices for the multiple products must be negatively correlated across consumer types.

14.6 COST-PLUS PRICING

It should be clear now that for firms with market power (i.e., price-setting firms), the pricing decision based on the equality of marginal revenue and marginal cost—the $MR = MC$ rule—yields the maximum profit for a firm. Why, then, do some firms use other techniques and rules of thumb to set the prices of their products? Surveys of managers report several reasons managers choose alternative pricing techniques. Some managers believe it is too difficult, or even impossible, for their firms to obtain reliable estimates of the demand and marginal cost functions. Other firms have long-established traditions of assigning responsibility for pricing (and production) decisions to senior executives with extensive industry experience. Their knowledge and feel for market conditions presumably give them the ability to make optimal pricing decisions using their judgment, perhaps coupled with one or more marketing rules of thumb.

One popular alternative technique for pricing is called *cost-plus pricing*. As we will explain carefully in this section, managers who use cost-plus pricing to set prices will fail to maximize profit. Illustration 14.4 discusses in more detail the reasons why this flawed pricing method remains strongly entrenched at some firms. Most sophisticated businesses today have abandoned cost-plus pricing and are now working to implement and improve their estimation and forecasting techniques to create more accurate knowledge about marginal revenue and marginal cost. We believe you should understand the flaws of cost-plus pricing because the allure of this simple technique might capture your fancy and because some senior executives still believe in cost-plus pricing. It may seem strange to you that we cover an antiquated and wrong pricing method in a chapter on "advanced" pricing techniques. While we are similarly troubled by spending valuable textbook space and class time covering this topic, we know that your firm cannot employ the advanced pricing techniques set forth in this chapter if senior executives continue to use this flawed technique.

cost-plus pricing
A method of determining price by setting price equal to average total cost plus a portion (*m*) of *ATC* as a markup.

Firms using **cost-plus pricing** determine their price by setting price equal to the projected average total cost (*ATC*) plus a percentage of this average total cost as a markup

$$P = ATC + (m \times ATC)$$

$$= (1 + m)ATC$$

where *m* is the markup on unit cost. Note that profit margin, which equals $P - ATC$ as we discussed in Section 11.3, can be calculated by multiplying the markup times average total cost: $P - ATC = m \times ATC$. For example, if the markup *m* is 0.2 and average total cost is $40, the percentage markup on average total cost is 20 percent, and price would be $48 (= 1.2 \times ATC). The profit margin, or profit per unit, is $8 (= 0.2 \times $40). As we stressed in our discussion of profit margin in Chapter 11, managers should ignore profit margin when making profit-maximizing decisions. We will return to this important point shortly.

Practical and Conceptual Shortcomings

The basic concept of cost-plus pricing is deceptively simple, and, as we mentioned previously, some managers choose to use the technique without recognizing or understanding its shortcomings. The problems with cost-plus pricing are both *practical* and *theoretical* in nature.

Practical problems using cost-plus pricing   Two important practical problems, which are frequently glossed over in marketing courses, complicate implementation of the cost-plus pricing formula. The first problem with using the formula involves choosing the value of average total cost (*ATC*), and the second problem concerns selecting the appropriate markup (*m*).

Since costs vary with the level of output produced, determining the value of *ATC* to multiply by $1 + m$ requires that a firm first specify the level of output that will be produced, which in turn determines the value of *ATC* for calculating price. Firms typically specify some standard or average level of production, based on the manager's *assumption* about how intensively the firm's fixed plant capacity will be utilized. However, without a consideration of prevailing demand conditions— a feature not incorporated in cost-plus pricing—the computed cost-plus price (absent extremely good fortune) will not equal the demand price for the output corresponding to the value of *ATC*. Consequently, the actual (or realized) profit margin will miss the target.

The nature of this critical problem is illustrated in Figure 14.9, which shows the firm's average total cost curve (*ATC*) and the prevailing demand and marginal revenue conditions facing the firm (*D* and *MR*), which are ignored when choosing *ATC*. Suppose the manager assumes the firm will operate at 5,000 units, which means that average total cost is expected to be $20 per unit (point *A*). Further suppose the firm historically employs a 50 percent markup on average total cost ($m = 0.5$), so the manager charges $30 (= $1.5 \times $20) per unit and expects a profit margin of $10 (= $30 − $20) per unit. If things were to go as planned, the firm would earn $50,000 (= $10 \times 5,000) of profit. However, because the price was

FIGURE 14.9

Practical Problems with Cost-Plus Pricing

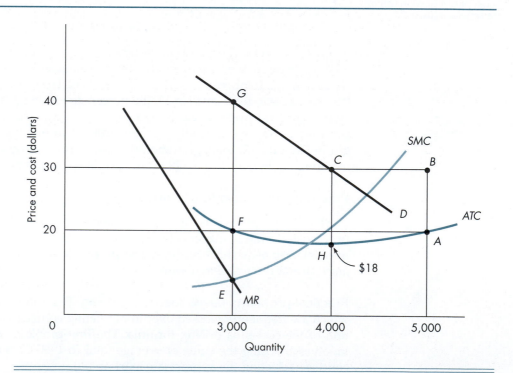

set without considering existing demand conditions (*D* and *MR* in Figure 14.9), there is no reason to believe 5,000 units can be sold for $30 apiece. Given actual demand *D*, only 4,000 units are sold at $30 (point C). While the manager might be pleasantly surprised by the higher than expected profit margin of $12 (= $30 − 18), the firm's actual profit is only $48,000 (= $12 × 4,000) instead of the expected $50,000.

Notwithstanding the difficulties involved in determining average cost, a potentially more troublesome problem is the selection of the markup. Recent studies suggest that firms select markups to achieve target profit margins that generate "fair" returns on invested capital. Of course, as we stressed in Chapter 1, owners do not want to earn just a "fair" profit: they want to earn the *maximum* profit possible, which maximizes the value of the firm. Profit margin (or average profit) plays no role in making profit-maximizing decisions (see the discussion in Section 11.3), so it is unlikely that following arbitrary rules or historical precedent to choose the markup will produce the maximum profit. For example, in Figure 14.9, a marketing expert using cost-plus methodology to reach point G must guess the required markup is precisely 1.0, after first guessing that the firm will produce exactly 3,000 units (to set *ATC* equal to $20). These two practical problems are actually closely related to the theoretical problems with cost-plus methodology.

Theoretical problems with cost-plus pricing Any method of pricing, whether it is cost-plus pricing or some other rule for setting price, will be generally unreliable for finding the profit-maximizing price and output if the technique is *not* mathematically equivalent to setting marginal revenue equal to marginal cost. In other words, a decision-making rule or technique that does not work in *theory* cannot generally provide optimal decisions in *practice*. Cost-plus pricing suffers from two conceptual problems that restrict the conditions under which cost-plus pricing is equivalent to the *MR* = *MC* rule.

As you know from Chapter 3, marginal cost must be used for making optimizing decisions. Since cost-plus pricing employs *average* rather than *marginal* cost, it does not generally give the profit-maximizing price.

Another conceptual problem arises because cost-plus pricing does not incorporate a consideration of prevailing demand conditions, which, as explained earlier, also creates practical problems for implementing the cost-plus technique. With the *MR* = *MC* pricing rule, demand conditions enter explicitly through the marginal revenue function, but cost-plus pricing does not utilize this information. While neglecting demand conditions does simplify the pricing decision, the lack of information about demand makes it impossible, except by sheer luck, to find the optimal or profit-maximizing price using the cost-plus pricing method.

The theoretical shortcomings alone make cost-plus pricing a poor choice for making pricing decisions. Add to the theoretical flaws the practical difficulties of implementing the technique, and you should now be convinced of at least one thing: Profit-maximizing firms do not employ cost-plus pricing methodology.

ILLUSTRATION 14.4

The "Untimely" Death of Cost-Plus Pricing

An "untimely" death usually means someone or something died too soon or prematurely. Even though costplus pricing is now officially dead in marketing textbooks—it died long ago in managerial economics textbooks—we believe the death of this flawed pricing technique came far too slowly. Until the early 1990s, this simple pricing technique enjoyed widespread acceptance by marketing managers, as well as by some marketing and economics faculty at business schools. Many businesses still cling to this technique (60 percent of U.S. manufacturers, according to one expert[a]) even though it is no longer held in high esteem in most business schools.

As an example of the slow death of cost-plus pricing, consider the following case. In 2001, when Donald Washkewicz took over as CEO at Parker Hannifin Corp., he discovered that the large industrial-parts manufacturer ($9.4 billion in revenue) was pricing over 800,000 different parts using a pricing scheme that seemed "crazy" to him.[b] As you might guess, Parker Hannifin was pricing its parts using cost-plus pricing. Managers calculated the cost of manufacturing and delivery for each part, then they added a "flat percentage on top" of 35 percent. Then Mr. Washkewicz experienced an "epiphany": prices should be determined by what a customer is willing to pay rather than its cost of production. A big part of the pricing problem at Parker Hannifin turned out to be the computer programs the company paid big bucks for in the 1990s primarily to calculate prices. Managers only had to type in all the cost details for each product, and then the software "cooked up" the price to charge. After Mr. Washkewicz hired marketing consultants to design a new pricing system that dumped old-fashioned cost-plus pricing and replaced it with pricing formulas based on demand-side data on willingness to pay, the company's prices increased anywhere from 3 percent to 60 percent on tens of thousands of its products. The result of killing cost-plus pricing: Profit increased from $130 million to $673 million and return on capital increased from 7 percent to 21 percent. As you can see, shareholders at Parker Hannifin lost a genuine fortune over the many years that managers "cooked up" prices based on a "healthy" 35 percent margin!

Ronald Baker, in his interesting new book *Pricing on Purpose: Creating and Capturing Value*,[c] offers his insight on the popularity of cost-plus pricing. In the chapter titled "Cost-Plus Pricing's Epitaph," Baker lists some of the reasons he has been given by "scores of business leaders" for using this flawed pricing technique. These "reasons" and "excuses" are insightful, so we will list some of them here, exactly as they are presented in Baker's book (2006, p. 88):

1. Although it may be a suboptimal way to maximize profitability, it is relatively easy to compute.

2. The method has served us well, why should we change?

3. Prices above a "fair" markup would attract competitors.

4. The Market Share Myth: Top line revenue growth is the pathway to profits, and higher prices would decrease volume.

5. Some executives think supernormal or windfall profits are immoral and unethical.

6. It helps stave off government regulations and antitrust litigation.

Each one of these statements is worth extended classroom discussion, and we hope that your instructor will have the time to discuss one or more of these in class. As Baker aptly puts it, doing something once is stupid, but "doing it twice is a philosophy."

We don't believe good managers are necessarily created by taking college courses in business—including this course—but taking a course in managerial economics or marketing should, at a bare minimum, kill any inclination you might have to add a "fair" markup to unit cost as a means of setting price. The death of cost-plus pricing is "untimely" only because it was so long in coming, and cost business owners so much lost profit.

[a]Thomas Nagle, a pricing consultant at the Monitor Group, quoted in Timothy Aeppel, "Changing the Formula: Seeking Perfect Prices, CEO Tears Up the Rules," *The Wall Street Journal*, March 27, 2007, p. A1.

[b]Aeppel, p. A1.

[c]Ronald J. Baker, *Pricing on Purpose: Creating and Capturing Value* (Hoboken, NJ: John Wiley & Sons, Inc., 2006).

14.7 SUMMARY

- Managers wish to avoid uniform pricing—the practice of charging the same price for every unit sold—because it creates too much consumer surplus. Marketing managers will try to devise pricing schemes to transform consumer surplus into profit for the firm. Price discrimination is the technique of charging different prices for the same product for the purpose of capturing consumer surplus and turning it into economic profit. Price discrimination between two separate markets A and B exists when the price-to-marginal cost ratio differs between products: $P_A/MC_A \neq P_B/MC_B$. To practice price discrimination profitably, three conditions are necessary: (1) the firm must possess market power, (2) a cost-effective means of preventing consumer arbitrage must be available, and (3) price elasticities must differ across markets. (LO1)

- Under first-degree price discrimination, the firm charges each consumer the maximum price he is willing to pay for every unit he purchases, and thus first-degree price discrimination captures all consumer surplus. First-degree price discrimination is very difficult to execute because it requires precise information about every buyer's demand, and sellers must negotiate different prices for every unit sold to every buyer. (LO2)

- Second-degree price discrimination takes advantage of falling marginal consumer valuation on successive units by reducing the average price as the amount purchased increases and lets buyers self-select the price they pay by choosing how much to buy. This chapter examines two such methods: two-part pricing and declining block pricing. Under two-part pricing, the firm charges buyers a fixed access charge, A, to buy any number of units for a constant usage fee, f, per unit. The total expenditure to purchase q units of the good, $TE(q)$, is $TE(q) = A + fq$. Average price is equal to $TE(q)$ divided by the number of units purchased: $p = TE(q)/q = (A/q) + f$, which reveals that p falls as q rises, giving the buyer a quantity discount. Determining the optimal values for A and f is a complex task. Declining block pricing offers quantity discounts over successive discrete blocks of quantities purchased. In so doing, declining block pricing motivates individuals to buy more than they would buy when facing a single, uniform price. (LO3)

- When a firm sells in two distinct markets, 1 and 2, it can practice third-degree price discrimination by allocating output or sales between the two markets such that $MR_1 = MR_2$. This maximizes the grand total revenue, $TR_1 + TR_2$, for the firm. The prices charged in each market result in the more elastic market getting the lower price and the less elastic market getting the higher price. (LO4)

- When a firm produces two products, X and Y, the firm maximizes profit by producing and selling output levels for which $MR_X = MC_X$ and $MR_Y = MC_Y$. When the products X and Y are related in consumption (as either substitutes or complements), MR_X is a function not only of Q_X but also of Q_Y, as is MR_Y. Consequently, the marginal conditions set forth above must be satisfied simultaneously. A common pricing practice used by multiproduct firms involves bundling two or more products and selling the bundle of goods or services at a single price. In order for bundling to be profitable, two conditions must be met. First, different consumer types must possess differing tastes for the multiple products, which has the effect of creating different demand prices across consumers for each of the multiple goods. Second, the demand prices for the two products must be *negatively* correlated with consumer types. (LO5)

- Firms using cost-plus pricing set their prices equal to the expected average total cost, ATC, plus a percentage of ATC as a markup, $P = (1 + m)ATC$, where m is the markup on unit cost. Managers who use cost-plus pricing to set prices will fail to maximize profit because cost-plus pricing faces a number of practical and theoretical problems. Two practical problems complicate the implementation of cost-plus pricing: (1) choosing the correct value for ATC depends on the level of output the firm ends up selling, because ATC varies with output, and (2) the markup on unit cost is usually arbitrarily set by management at whatever level the manager feels is "fair." Conceptually, cost-plus pricing is flawed because it employs average rather than marginal cost, which does not generally give the profit-maximizing price. Another conceptual problem arises because cost-plus pricing does not incorporate a consideration of prevailing demand conditions. (LO6)

KEY TERMS

bundling

capturing consumer surplus

complements in consumption

consumer arbitrage

cost-plus pricing

declining block pricing

first-degree price discrimination

price discrimination

second-degree price discrimination

substitutes in consumption

third-degree price discrimination

total marginal revenue (MR_T)

two-part pricing

uniform pricing

TECHNICAL PROBLEMS

1. Suppose the firm in Figure 14.1 sets a uniform price for its product.
   a. What is the maximum profit the firm can earn by setting a uniform price?
   b. What is the maximum profit the firm could earn if it sells 6,000 units and can charge the demand price for every unit?
   c. Compute the difference between the profits in parts *a* and *b*, and show that the difference is equal to the sum of the areas of the two shaded triangles in Figure 14.1.
   d. Explain why the difference in profit in part *c* can be interpreted as "captured" consumer surplus.

2. At Northvale Golf Club, the demand for rounds of golf by each one of the 100 identical senior golfer members is given by D_{SR} in Figure 14.3. Northvale's annual fixed costs are $500,000, and variable costs are constant and equal to $30 per round.
   a. If the manager of Northvale charges a uniform green fee to all senior golfers, the profit-maximizing green fee is $_____ per round. Under this uniform pricing plan, Northvale's annual total revenue is $_____ and total variable cost is $_____. Northvale's profit under uniform pricing is $_____ per year.
   b. If the manager instead decides to employ a two-part pricing plan, the profit-maximizing green fee is $_____ per round, and the annual membership charge is $_____. The two-part pricing plan results in total annual profit of $_____.
   c. Which pricing plan—uniform pricing or two-part pricing—generates more profit for Northvale's owner? Is this the pricing plan you expected to be more profitable? Why or why not?

3. Suppose Northvale Golf Club in Technical Problem 2 also has a second group of 100 identical golfers, weekend players, who wish to play at the club. The demand for rounds of golf by each one of the 100 identical weekend golfers is given by D_{WK} in Panel B of Figure 14.4. Assume the same cost structure as given in Technical Problem 2. The manager designs an optimal two-part pricing plan for these two groups of golfers.
   a. The optimal green fee to set for each round of golf is $_____.
   b. The optimal annual membership charge is $_____ for senior golfers and $_____ for weekend golfers.
   c. Under this two-part pricing plan, Northvale's annual profit is $_____.

4. In Figure 14.5, the declining five-block pricing plan can be expressed as a set of five successive, two-part pricing plans:

   Block 1: $A_1 =$ _____ and $f_1 =$ _____ .

   Block 2: $A_2 =$ _____ and $f_2 =$ _____ .

Block 3: $A_3 =$ _____ and $f_3 =$ _____.

Block 4: $A_4 =$ _____ and $f_4 =$ _____.

Block 5: $A_5 =$ _____ and $f_5 =$ _____.

5. Using Figure 14.6, verify that total revenue is higher at points v and v' than at points w and w' by calculating total revenue for both allocations of 500 units.

6. A hotel serves both business and vacation travelers and wishes to price-discriminate. The hotel manager can accurately identify and separate submarkets by looking for children when travelers check in to the hotel. If travelers have no children, they must pay the "business" price; if they have one or more children with them, they pay the "vacation" price. In the following figure, D_B is the demand by business travelers and D_V is the demand by vacation travelers. The hotel's marginal and average costs are constant and equal to $20 per unit.

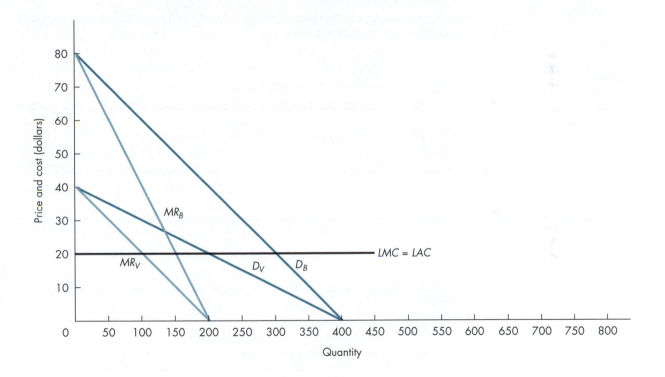

a. Construct the total marginal revenue curve in the figure and label it MR_T.

b. What is the profit-maximizing number of business travelers to serve? Vacationers?

c. What price should be charged to each type of traveler? How much revenue is collected from each type of traveler?

d. Calculate the price elasticities at the prices charged in each submarket. Do these price elasticities have the expected relative magnitudes? Explain.

e. How much profit does the price-discriminating hotel earn?

    f. If the hotel charged a uniform price to all travelers, what price would it be? How much revenue would the hotel collect? How much profit would it make?

    g. Is price discrimination more or less profitable than uniform pricing?

7. A manager faces two separate markets. The estimated demand functions for the two markets are

$$Q_A = 1{,}600 - 80P_A \quad \text{and} \quad Q_B = 2{,}400 - 100P_B$$

    a. Find the inverse marginal revenue functions.

    b. Find the total marginal revenue functions.

    c. Draw a graph of MR_A, MR_B, and MR_T. Check your algebraic derivation of total marginal revenue.

    d. If the manager has a total of 650 units to sell, how should the 650 units be allocated to maximize total revenue?

8. Suppose the manager in Technical Problem 7 decides to price-discriminate. The long-run marginal cost is estimated to be

$$LMC = 4.5 + 0.005Q$$

    a. How many units should the manager produce and sell?

    b. How should the manager allocate the profit-maximizing output between the two markets?

    c. What prices should the manager charge in the two markets?

    d. Measured at the prices found in part *c*, which market has the more elastic demand?

9. Look again at Zicon Manufacturing—a firm that produces products that are substitutes in consumption. Suppose that the production manager changed the estimates of the total and marginal cost functions to

$$TC_X = 27Q_X + 0.00025Q_X^2 \quad \text{and} \quad TC_Y = 20Q_Y + 0.000125Q_Y^2$$

$$MC_X = 27 + 0.0005Q_X \quad \text{and} \quad MC_Y = 20 + 0.00025Q_Y$$

    a. Calculate the new profit-maximizing levels of output and price for the two products.

    b. How much profit does Zicon earn?

10. Return to the bundle pricing problem facing Crystal Channel, Inc. In parts *a–c*, suppose the manager now knows not only the demand price information in Table 14.1, but also knows how to identify subscribers as either family-oriented or adult-oriented viewers.

    a. What prices should Crystal Channel Inc. charge family-oriented viewers for each of the two channel packages separately to maximize total revenue and profit? What prices should adult-oriented viewers be charged? How much total revenue can be generated each month under this pricing plan?

    b. Explain why the prices in part *a* represent price discrimination and identify the type of price discrimination.

    c. Does the total revenue generated under price discrimination in part *a* exceed the total revenue from charging $125 for the bundle containing both family and adult channel packages? Explain why or why not.

Now suppose demand prices for family-oriented viewers remain the same ($100 for the family package and $50 for the adult package), but the demand prices for adult-oriented viewers are $125 for the family package and $150 for the adult package. In parts *d–g*, Crystal Channel cannot identify consumer types and thus cannot price discriminate.

d. Are demand prices negatively correlated now? Explain why or why not.

e. What separate prices should Crystal Channel charge for the family and adult channel packages? How much total revenue will be earned each month?

f. What single price should Crystal Channel charge for the bundle containing both the family and adult channel packages? How much total revenue will be earned each month?

g. Compare the total revenues generated in parts *e* and *f*. Does bundling increase revenue? Why or why not?

APPLIED PROBLEMS

1. STIHL, Inc., manufactures gasoline-powered chain saws for professional, commercial, farm, and consumer markets. To "better serve" their customers, STIHL offers its chain saws in four different quality lines and associated price ranges: occasional use, mid-range, professional, and arborist. Under what circumstances could offering multiple qualities of a product be price discrimination? What form of price discrimination might this represent—first-, second-, or third-degree price discrimination? Explain why this practice could increase profit at STIHL.

2. Price discrimination sounds like a socially "bad" thing. Can you think of any reasons why price discrimination could be viewed as a socially "good" thing?

3. In the mid-1990s, long before September 11, 2001, airlines began requiring photo identification to check baggage and board flights, claiming their fervent commitment to secure and safe air travel. Do you think the airlines implemented this policy because they could foresee the coming terrorist threat to aviation? What might be a more plausible explanation for the airlines' early commitment to photo identification?

4. As markets for some products and services experience greater global competition, what is the likely consequence for the incidence of price discrimination? Do you think global competition fosters or impedes price discrimination? Can you give any examples from your own work experience?

5. "Declining block pricing is a crude form of perfect price discrimination." In what sense is this statement correct? In what important way is it wrong?

6. *The Financial Herald*, a weekly newspaper specializing in corporate financial news, is purchased by both businesspeople and students. A marketing research firm has estimated the two linear demand and marginal revenue functions shown in the following figure. MR_B is the estimated marginal revenue for the business readers, and MR_S is the estimated marginal revenue for the student readers. The production department at *The Financial Herald* estimates a linear marginal cost function for newspaper production, which also is graphed in the following figure. All quantities are in units of 1,000 per week.

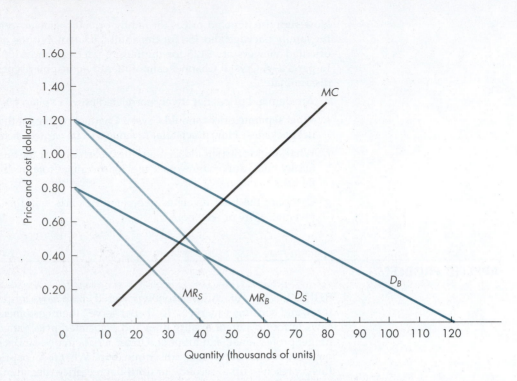

a. How many total copies should *The Financial Herald* print each week?

b. How many copies should be sold to business readers? How many copies should be sold to students?

c. What price should business readers be charged? What price should students be charged?

7. EZ Sharp Industries, Inc., manufactures the Keen Edge™ line of diamond-abrasive cutlery sharpeners for home use. EZ Sharp holds a patent on its unique design and can earn substantial economic profit if it prices its Keen Edge™ products wisely. EZ Sharp sells two models of its Keen Edge™ sharpeners: the Classic, which is the entry-level model, and the Professional, which has a sonic sensor that controls the speed of the sharpening wheels.

Short-run production of sharpeners is subject to constant costs: $AVC = SMC$ for both models. The constant costs of production at EZ Sharp Industries are estimated to be

$$\$20 = AVC_C = SMC_C$$
$$\$30 = AVC_P = SMC_P$$

where AVC_C and SMC_C are the constant costs for the Classic model and AVC_P and SMC_P are the constant costs for the Professional model. Total fixed costs each month are $10,000. The sole owner of EZ Sharp also manages the firm and makes all pricing decisions. The owner–manager believes in assuring himself a 200 percent profit margin by using the cost-plus pricing methodology to set prices for his two product lines. At these prices, EZ Sharp is selling 3,750 units of the Classic model per month and 2,000 units of the Professional model per month.

a. Using the cost-plus technique, compute the prices the owner-manager charges for the Classic and the Professional models, based on his required 200 percent profit margin.

b. How much profit is EZ Sharp earning each month using the cost-plus prices in part *a*?

The owner–manager is ready to sell the firm, but he knows the value of the firm will increase if he can increase the monthly profit somehow. He decides to hire Andrews Consulting to recommend ways for EZ Sharp to increase its profits. Andrews reports that production is efficient, but pricing can be improved. Andrews argues that the cost-plus pricing technique is not working well for EZ Sharp and presents a new pricing plan based on optimal pricing techniques (i.e., the $MR = MC$ rule).

To implement the $MR = MC$ methodology, Andrews undertakes a statistical study to estimate the demands for two Keen Edge™ products. The estimated demands are

$$Q_C = 6,000 - 75P_C + 25P_P$$

$$Q_P = 5,000 - 50P_P + 25P_C$$

where Q_C and Q_P are the monthly quantities demanded of Classic and Professional models, respectively, and P_C and P_P are the prices of the Classic and Professional models, respectively. Andrews Consulting solved the demand equations simultaneously to get the following inverse demand functions, which is why Anderson gets paid the "big bucks"

$$P_C = 136 - 0.016Q_C - 0.008Q_P$$

$$P_S = 168 - 0.008Q_C - 0.024Q_P$$

c. Find the two marginal revenue functions for the Classic and Professional model sharpeners.

d. Set each marginal revenue function in part *c* equal to the appropriate cost and solve for the profit-maximizing quantities.

e. Using the results from part *d*, what prices will Andrews Consulting recommend for each of the models?

f. When the owner–manager sees the prices recommended by Andrews Consulting, he brags about how close his simple cost-plus pricing method had come to their suggested prices. Compute the profit EZ Sharp can earn using the consultants' prices in part *d*. Is there any reason for the owner–manager to brag about his cost-plus pricing skills?

8. Although there is relatively little difference in the cost of producing hardcover and paperback books, these books sell for very different prices. Explain this pricing behavior.

9. *The Wall Street Journal* once reported on dating services, noting that the fees were $300 for men and $250 for women. The owner of the service said that the difference in fees was to compensate for inequalities in pay scales for men and women. Can you suggest any alternative reasons for this difference?

10. Berkley Golf & Tennis Club offers golf and tennis memberships. Marketing analysis of the local neighborhood served by Berkley Golf & Tennis Club shows that there are two types of families that might join the club: golf-oriented families, which are primarily interested in golf but enjoy playing some tennis, and tennis-oriented families, which are primarily interested in tennis but enjoy playing some golf. The study further estimates that there are 400 golf-oriented families and 300 tennis-oriented families in the neighborhood, and the estimated demand prices for golf and tennis memberships by family

type are given below. There is no way to identify family types for pricing purposes, and all costs are fixed so that maximizing total revenue is equivalent to maximizing profit.

Demand Prices for Golf and Tennis Memberships

Type of family	Golf membership only	Tennis membership only
Golf-oriented	$250	$100
Tennis-oriented	50	200

    a. If Berkley Golf & Tennis Club plans to offer golf and tennis memberships separately, what prices should be charged for each kind of membership if Berkley wishes to maximize profit? How much total revenue can be generated each month under this pricing plan?

    b. The manager of Berkley Golf & Tennis Club has just finished her MBA degree and has an idea that bundling golf and tennis memberships might increase profit for the club. Are the conditions right for bundle pricing to increase profit at Berkley Golf & Tennis?

    c. What is the optimal price to charge for a golf and tennis (bundled) membership? How much revenue will this produce for Berkley Golf & Tennis Club? Is bundling a profitable pricing tactic for the club?

11. Airlines practice price discrimination by charging leisure travelers and business travelers different prices. Different customers pay varying prices for essentially the same coach seat because some passengers qualify for discounts and others do not. Because the discounts are substantial in many cases, the customer who qualifies for a discount pays a significantly lower airfare.

    a. Which group of customers tends to pay the higher price: business travelers or leisure travelers?

    b. Why would business travelers generally have a different elasticity of demand for air travel than leisure travelers? Is the more elastic market paying the lower or higher price? Is this consistent with profit maximization?

Airlines rely on an assortment of restrictions that travelers must meet to qualify for the discounted fares. In effect, these restrictions roughly sort flyers into business travelers and leisure travelers.

    c. Explain how each of the following restrictions sometimes used by airlines tends to separate business and leisure travelers.

        (1) Advance purchase requirements, which require payment at least 14 days before departure.

        (2) Weekend stay requirements, which require travelers to stay over a Saturday night before returning.

        (3) Time-of-day restrictions, which disallow discounts for travel during peak times of the day.

    d. In each of these cases, which group of passengers effectively pays a higher price for air travel? Is this consistent with profit maximization?

12. A woman complained to "Dear Abby" that a laundry charged $1.25 each to launder and press her husband's shirts, but for her shirts—the same description, only

smaller—the laundry charged $3.50. When asked why, the owner said, "Women's blouses cost more." Abby suggested sending all the shirts in one bundle and enclosing a note saying, "There are no blouses here—these are all shirts."

a. Is the laundry practicing price discrimination, or is there really a $2.25 difference in cost?

b. Assuming the laundry is engaging in price discrimination, why do men pay the lower price and women the higher?

c. Could the laundry continue to separate markets if people followed Abby's advice? What about the policing costs associated with separating the markets?

13. A bar offers female patrons a lower price for a drink than male patrons. The bar will maximize profit by selling a total of 200 drinks (a night). At the current prices, male customers buy 150 drinks, while female customers buy 50 drinks. At this allocation between markets, the marginal revenue from the last drink sold to a male customer is $1.50, while the marginal revenue from the last drink sold to a female customer is $0.50.

a. What should the bar do about its pricing?

b. If the bar sells 151 drinks to males and 49 to females, what will be the increase (decrease) in total revenue?

□ **MATHEMATICAL APPENDIX**

Suppose a firm sells to two groups of identical consumers: L or "low" demand buyers and H or "high" demand buyers. The firm wishes to price-discriminate with a (single) two-part pricing plan, where the total expenditure for a consumer of either type L or H to buy q units of the product, $TE(q)$, is $TE(q) = A + fq$, where A denotes the fixed access charge, and f is the per-unit usage fee. The following linear demand equations give the demands for a single typical buyer of each type:

$$q_L = q_L(p_L) = a_L + b_L p_L \quad \text{and} \quad q_H = q_H(p_H) = a_H + b_H p_H$$

where $a_L, a_H > 0$ and $b_L, b_H < 0$. The price-intercepts for L and H demands are, respectively, $A_L = -a_L/b_L$ and $A_H = -a_H/b_H$. There are N_L identical buyers in group L, and N_H identical buyers in group H. For clarity of exposition, assume total consumer surplus for a single H buyer is greater than total consumer surplus for a single L buyer:

$$\frac{1}{2}a_H A_H > \frac{1}{2}a_L A_L.$$

The costs of production are characterized by constant marginal and average costs that are the same for both groups of consumers: $MC = AC = c$.

The common access charge for both types of buyers must equal the consumer surplus for a single buyer in the group with the smallest consumer surplus:

$$A = \frac{1}{2}q_L(f)(A_L - f)$$

Two-Part Pricing with Two Identical Groups of Buyers

Since all buyers pay the same usage fee, $p_L = p_H = f$, and total profit can be expressed as a function of usage fee f:

$$\pi(f) = TR(f) - TC(f)$$
$$= \{(N_L + N_H)A + f \cdot [N_L q_L(f) + N_H q_H(f)]\}$$
$$- \{c[N_L q_L(f) + N_H q_H(f)]\}$$

Marginal revenue and marginal cost associated with changes in f are, respectively, MR_f and MC_f:

$$MR_f = \frac{\Delta TR(f)}{\Delta f} = (N_L + N_H)\frac{\Delta A}{\Delta f} + [N_L q_L(f) + N_H q_H(f)]$$
$$+ f\left[N_L \frac{\Delta q_L(f)}{\Delta f} + N_H \frac{\Delta q_H(f)}{\Delta f}\right]$$
$$= N_H(a_H - a_L) - [b_L(N_H - N_L) - 2N_H b_H]f$$

and

$$MC_f = \frac{\Delta TC(f)}{\Delta f} = c\left[N_L \frac{\Delta q_L(f)}{\Delta f} + N_H \frac{\Delta q_H(f)}{\Delta f}\right]$$
$$= c(N_L b_L + N_H b_H)$$

Setting MR_f equal to MC_f and solving for f produces the optimal usage fee, f^*:

$$f^* = \frac{cb_L N_L + cb_H N_H - N_H(a_H - a_L)}{-b_L N_H + b_L N_L + 2b_H N_H}$$

To find A^*, substitute f^* into the expression for A:

$$A^* = \frac{1}{2}q_L(f^*)(A_L - f^*).$$

Third-Degree Price Discrimination in Multiple Submarkets

A third-degree price-discriminating manager maximizes profit at the level of output at which marginal revenue in each market equals marginal cost. The price in each market is given by the demand in that market.

Assume the firm sells its output in two markets. The demands in these markets are

$$P_1(Q_1), \quad \text{and} \quad P_2(Q_2)$$

Cost is a function of total output

$$C = C(Q_1 + Q_2) = C(Q)$$

The firm maximizes profit,

$$\pi = P_1(Q_1)Q_1 + P_2(Q_2)Q_2 - C(Q)$$

with respect to the levels of output sold in the two markets.

Thus the first-order conditions for profit maximization are

$$\frac{dP_1}{dQ_1}Q_1 + P_1 - \frac{dC}{dQ} = MR_1 - MC = 0$$

$$\frac{dP_2}{dQ_2}Q_2 + P_2 - \frac{dC}{dQ} = MR_2 - MC = 0$$

Thus profit maximization requires that the marginal revenues in the two markets be equal and equal to marginal cost. Once Q_1^* and Q_2^* are determined, P_1^* and P_2^* are given by the demand functions.

Multiproduct Firms: Finding Inverse Demands and Marginal Revenue Functions

For a firm producing two goods that are either substitutes or complements in consumption, let the demand functions be linear

$$Q_X = a + bP_X + cP_Y \quad \text{and} \quad Q_Y = d + eP_Y + fP_X$$

To facilitate simultaneously solving for P_X and P_Y, express the two demand equations as

$$bP_X + cP_Y = Q_X - a$$

$$fP_X + eP_Y = Q_Y - b$$

Now express the two-equation system in matrix form

$$\begin{pmatrix} b & c \\ f & e \end{pmatrix}\begin{pmatrix} P_X \\ P_Y \end{pmatrix} = \begin{pmatrix} Q_X - a \\ Q_Y - d \end{pmatrix}$$

The solution is found using the usual tools of matrix algebra

$$\begin{pmatrix} P_X \\ P_Y \end{pmatrix} = \begin{pmatrix} Q_X - a \\ Q_Y - d \end{pmatrix}\begin{pmatrix} b & c \\ f & e \end{pmatrix}^{-1}$$

$$= \begin{pmatrix} Q_X - a \\ Q_Y - d \end{pmatrix}\begin{vmatrix} \dfrac{e}{be - cf} & \dfrac{-c}{db - cf} \\ \dfrac{-f}{be - cf} & \dfrac{b}{be - cf} \end{vmatrix}$$

The inverse demand functions are

$$P_X = \frac{cd - ae}{be - cf} + \frac{e}{be - cf}Q_X + \frac{-c}{be - cf}Q_Y$$

$$P_Y = \frac{fa - bd}{be - cf} + \frac{-f}{be - cf}Q_X + \frac{b}{be - cf}Q_Y$$

The marginal revenue functions are derived by taking partial derivatives of total revenue with respect to Q_X to find MR_X and Q_Y to find MR_Y

$$TR = TR(Q_X, Q_Y) = P_X(Q_X, Q_Y)Q_X + P_Y(Q_X, Q_Y)Q_Y$$

$$= \frac{cd - ae}{be - cf}Q_X + \frac{e}{be - cf}Q_X^2 + \frac{-c}{be - cf}Q_YQ_X$$

$$+ \frac{fa - bd}{be - cf}Q_Y + \frac{-f}{be - cf}Q_XQ_Y + \frac{b}{be - cf}Q_Y^2$$

so

$$\frac{\partial TR}{\partial Q_X} = \frac{cd - ae}{be - cf} + \frac{2e}{be - cf}Q_X + \frac{-c - f}{be - cf}Q_Y$$

$$\frac{\partial TR}{\partial Q_X} = \frac{fa - bd}{be - cf} + \frac{-c - f}{be - cf}Q_X + \frac{2b}{be - cf}Q_Y$$

ONLINE APPENDIX 4: Pricing Multiple Products Related in Production

View this appendix via the Student Resources available through McGraw-Hill Connect®.

15

Decisions Under Risk and Uncertainty

After reading this chapter, you will be able to:

15.1 Explain the difference between decision making under risk and under uncertainty.

15.2 Compute the expected value, variance, standard deviation, and coefficient of variation of a probability distribution.

15.3 Employ the expected value rule, mean-variance rules, and the coefficient of variation rule to make decisions under risk.

15.4 Explain expected utility theory and apply it to decisions under risk.

15.5 Make decisions under uncertainty using the maximax rule, the maximin rule, the minimax regret rule, and the equal probability rule.

All the analysis of managerial decision making up to this point in the text has been developed under the assumption that the manager knows with certainty the marginal benefits and marginal costs associated with a decision. While managers do have considerable information about the outcome for many decisions, they must frequently make decisions in situations in which the outcome of a decision cannot be known in advance. A manager may decide, for example, to invest in a new production facility with the expectation that the new technology and equipment will reduce production costs. Even after studying hundreds of technical reports, a manager may still not know with certainty the cost savings of the new plant until the plant is built and operating. In other words, the outcome of the decision to build the new plant is random because the reduction in costs (the outcome) is not known with certainty at the time of the decision. Another risky decision involves choosing the profit-maximizing production level or the price to charge when the marginal benefit and marginal cost can take on a range of values with differing probabilities.

In this chapter we will present some basic rules that managers, and for that matter all decision makers, can and do use to help make decisions under conditions of risk and uncertainty. In the first section, we explain the difference between decision making under risk and decision making under uncertainty. The larger portion of this chapter is devoted to analyzing decisions under risk, rather than situations of uncertainty, because, as you will see, managers facing random benefits and costs are more often confronted with situations involving risk than uncertainty. As you will also see, the rules we present in this chapter for decision making under risk and uncertainty provide only guidelines for making decisions when outcomes are not certain, because no single rule for making such decisions is, or can be, universally employed by all managers at all times. Nevertheless, the rules presented give an overview of some of the helpful methods of analyzing risk and uncertainty.

Before plunging into our presentation of decision making under uncertainty and risk, we want to address a question that may be concerning you: Why do we devote such a large portion of this text to managerial decision making under certainty or complete information, knowing full well that a large proportion of managerial decisions are made with incomplete information—that is, under risk or uncertainty? There are two good reasons. First, the theory of optimization, weighing marginal benefits and marginal costs, as explained in Chapter 3 and applied throughout the text, provides the basic foundation for all decision making regardless of the amount of information available to a decision maker about the potential outcomes of various actions. To learn how to do something under less-than-ideal conditions, one must first learn how to do it under ideal conditions. Second, even though a decision maker does not have complete information about the marginal benefits and marginal costs of all levels of an activity or choice variable, the $MB = MC$ rule from Chapter 3 is the most productive approach to profit-maximization decisions under many, if not most, relevant circumstances.

15.1 DISTINCTIONS BETWEEN RISK AND UNCERTAINTY

risk
A decision-making condition under which a manager can list all outcomes and assign probabilities to each outcome.

When the outcome of a decision is not known with certainty, a manager faces a decision-making problem under either conditions of risk or conditions of uncertainty. A decision is made under **risk** when a manager can make a list of all possible outcomes associated with a decision and assign a probability of occurrence to each one of the outcomes. The process of assigning probabilities to outcomes sometimes involves rather sophisticated analysis based on the manager's extensive experience in similar situations or on other data. Probabilities assigned in this way are *objective probabilities*. In other circumstances, in which the manager has little experience with a particular decision situation and little or no relevant historical data, the probabilities assigned to the outcomes are derived in a subjective way and are called *subjective probabilities*. Subjective probabilities are based upon hunches, "gut feelings," or personal experiences rather than on scientific data.

An example of a decision made under risk might be the following: A manager decides to spend $1,000 on a magazine ad believing there are three possible outcomes for the ad: a 20 percent chance the ad will have only a small effect on sales, a 60 percent chance of a moderate effect, and a 20 percent chance of a very large effect. This decision is made under risk because the manager can list each potential outcome and determine the probability of each outcome occurring.

In contrast to risk, **uncertainty** exists when a decision maker cannot list all possible outcomes and/or cannot assign probabilities to the various outcomes. When faced with uncertainty, a manager would know only the different decision options available and the different possible *states of nature*. The states of nature are the future events or conditions that can influence the final outcome or payoff of a decision but cannot be controlled or affected by the manager. Even though both risk and uncertainty involve less-than-complete information, there is more information under risk than under uncertainty.

An example of a decision made under uncertainty would be, for a manager of a pharmaceutical company, the decision of whether to spend $3 million on the research and development of a new medication for high blood pressure. The payoff from the research and development spending will depend on whether the president's new health plan imposes price regulations on new drugs. The two states of nature facing the manager in this problem are (1) government does impose price regulations or (2) government does *not* impose price regulations. While the manager knows the payoff that will occur under either state of nature, the manager has no idea of the probability that price regulations will be imposed on drug companies. Under such conditions, a decision is made under uncertainty.

This important distinction between conditions of uncertainty and conditions of risk will be followed throughout this chapter. The decision rules employed by managers when outcomes are not certain differ under conditions of uncertainty and conditions of risk.

uncertainty
A decision-making condition under which a manager cannot list all possible outcomes and/or cannot assign probabilities to the various outcomes.

15.2 MEASURING RISK WITH PROBABILITY DISTRIBUTIONS

Before we can discuss rules for decision making under risk, we must first discuss how risk can be measured. The most direct method of measuring risk involves the characteristics of a probability distribution of outcomes associated with a particular decision. This section will describe these characteristics.

Probability Distributions

probability distribution
A table or graph showing all possible outcomes or payoffs of a decision and the probabilities that each outcome will occur.

A **probability distribution** is a table or graph showing all possible outcomes (payoffs) for a decision and the probability that each outcome will occur. The probabilities can take values between 0 and 1, or, alternatively, they can be expressed as percentages between 0 and 100 percent.[1] If *all possible* outcomes are assigned probabilities, the probabilities must sum to 1 (or 100 percent); that is, the probability that some other outcome will occur is 0 because there is no other possible outcome.

---

[1] If the probability of an outcome is 1 (or 100 percent), the outcome is certain to occur and no risk exists. If the probability of an outcome is 0, then that particular outcome will not occur and need not be considered in decision making.

To illustrate a probability distribution, we assume that the director of advertising at a large corporation believes the firm's current advertising campaign may result in any one of five possible outcomes for corporate sales. The probability distribution for this advertising campaign is as follows:

Outcome (sales)	Probability (percent)
47,500 units	10
50,000 units	20
52,500 units	30
55,000 units	25
57,500 units	15

Each outcome has a probability greater than 0 but less than 100 percent, and the sum of all probabilities is 100 percent (= 10 + 20 + 30 + 25 + 15). This probability distribution is represented graphically in Figure 15.1.

From a probability distribution (either in tabular or in graphical form), the riskiness of a decision is reflected by the variability of outcomes indicated by the different probabilities of occurrence. For decision-making purposes, managers often turn to mathematical properties of the probability distribution to facilitate a formal analysis of risk. The nature of risk can be summarized by examining the central tendency of the probability distribution, as measured by the expected value of the distribution, and by examining the dispersion of the distribution, as measured by the standard deviation and coefficient of variation. We discuss first the measure of central tendency of a probability distribution.

FIGURE 15.1

The Probability Distribution for Sales Following an Advertising Campaign

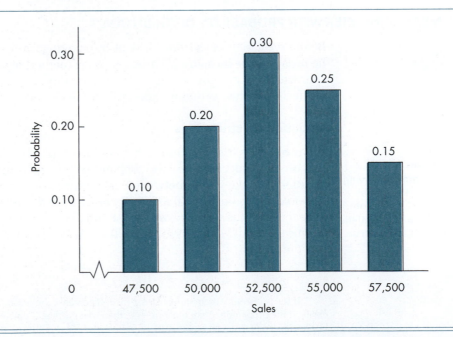

Expected Value of a Probability Distribution

expected value
The weighted average of the outcomes, with the probabilities of each outcome serving as the respective weights.

The **expected value** of a probability distribution of decision outcomes is the weighted average of the outcomes, with the probabilities of each outcome serving as the respective weights. The expected value of the various outcomes of a probability distribution is

$$E(X) = \text{Expected value of } X = \sum_{i=1}^{n} p_i X_i$$

where X_i is the ith outcome of a decision, p_i is the probability of the ith outcome, and n is the total number of possible outcomes in the probability distribution. Note that the computation of expected value requires the use of fractions or decimal values for the probabilities p_i, rather than percentages. The expected value of a probability distribution is often referred to as the **mean of the distribution**.

mean of the distribution
The expected value of the distribution.

The expected value of sales for the advertising campaign associated with the probability distribution shown in Figure 15.1 is

$$E(\text{sales}) = (0.10)(47{,}500) + (0.20)(50{,}000) + (0.30)(52{,}500)$$
$$+ (0.25)(55{,}000) + (0.15)(57{,}500)$$
$$= 4{,}750 + 10{,}000 + 15{,}750 + 13{,}750 + 8{,}625$$
$$= 52{,}875$$

While the amount of actual sales that occur as a result of the advertising campaign is a random variable possibly taking values of 47,500, 50,000, 52,500, 55,000, or 57,500 units, the expected level of sales is 52,875 units. If only one of the five levels of sales can occur, the level that actually occurs will not equal the expected value of 52,875, but expected value does indicate what the *average* value of the outcomes would be if the risky decision were to be repeated a large number of times.

Dispersion of a Probability Distribution

variance
The dispersion of a distribution about its mean.

As you may recall from your statistics classes, probability distributions are generally characterized not only by the expected value (mean) but also by the variance. The **variance** of a probability distribution measures the dispersion of the distribution about its mean. Figure 15.2 shows the probability distributions for the profit outcomes of two different decisions, A and B. Both decisions, as illustrated in Figure 15.2, have identical expected profit levels but different variances. The larger variance associated with making decision B is reflected by a larger dispersion (a wider spread of values around the mean). While distribution A is more compact (less spread out), A has a smaller variance.

The variance of a probability distribution of the outcomes of a given decision is frequently used to indicate the level or degree of risk associated with that decision. If the expected values of two distributions are the same, the distribution with the higher variance is associated with the riskier decision. Thus in Figure 15.2, decision B has more risk than decision A. Furthermore, variance is often used to

FIGURE 15.2

Two Probability Distributions with Identical Means but Different Variances

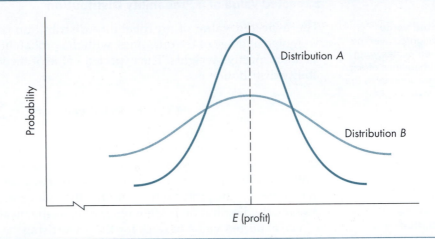

compare the riskiness of two decisions even though the expected values of the distributions differ.

Mathematically, the variance of a probability distribution of outcomes X_i, denoted by σ_x^2, is the probability-weighted sum of the squared deviations about the expected value of X

$$\text{Variance }(X) = \sigma_x^2 = \sum_{i=1}^{n} p_i[X_i - E(X)]^2$$

As an example, consider the two distributions illustrated in Figure 15.3. As is evident from the graphs and demonstrated in the following table, the two distributions have the same mean, 50. Their variances differ, however. Decision A has a smaller variance than decision B, and it is therefore less risky. The calculation of the expected values and variance for each distribution are shown here:

Profit (X_i)	Decision A			Decision B		
	Probability (p_i)	$p_i X_i$	$[X_i - E(X)]^2 p_i$	Probability (p_i)	$p_i X_i$	$[X_i - E(X)]^2 p_i$
30	0.05	1.5	20	0.10	3	40
40	0.20	8	20	0.25	10	25
50	0.50	25	0	0.30	15	0
60	0.20	12	20	0.25	15	25
70	0.05	3.5	20	0.10	7	40
		$E(X) = 50$	$\sigma_A^2 = 80$		$E(X) = 50$	$\sigma_B^2 = 130$

Since variance is a squared term, it is usually much larger than the mean. To avoid this scaling problem, the standard deviation of the probability distribution is more commonly used to measure dispersion. The **standard deviation** of a probability distribution, denoted by σ_x, is the square root of the variance:

$$\sigma_x = \sqrt{\text{Variance }(X)}$$

standard deviation
The square root of the variance.

FIGURE 15.3
Probability Distributions with Different Variances

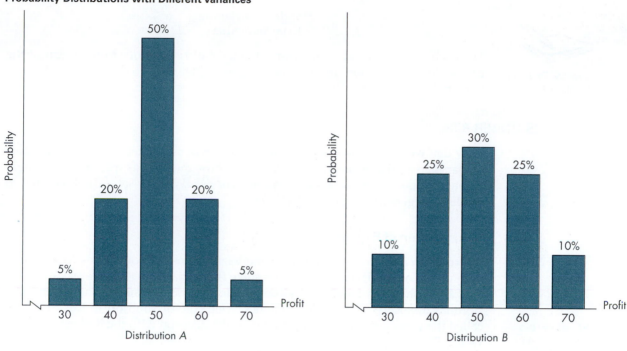

The standard deviations of the distributions illustrated in Figure 15.3 and in the preceding table are $\sigma_A = 8.94$ and $\sigma_B = 11.40$. As in the case of the variance of a probability distribution, the higher the standard deviation, the more risky the decision.

Managers can compare the riskiness of various decisions by comparing their standard deviations, as long as the expected values are of similar magnitudes. For example, if decisions C and D both have standard deviations of 52.5, the two decisions can be viewed as equally risky if their expected values are close to one another. If, however, the expected values of the distributions differ substantially in magnitude, it can be misleading to examine only the standard deviations. Suppose decision C has a mean outcome of $400 and decision D has a mean outcome of $5,000 but the standard deviations remain 52.5. The dispersion of outcomes for decision D is much smaller *relative to its mean value of $5,000* than is the dispersion of outcomes for decision C *relative to its mean value of $400*.

coefficient of variation
The standard deviation divided by the expected value of the probability distribution.

When the expected values of outcomes differ substantially, managers should measure the riskiness of a decision *relative* to its expected value. One such measure of relative risk is the coefficient of variation for the decision's distribution. The **coefficient of variation,** denoted by v, is the standard deviation divided by the expected value of the probability distribution of decision outcomes

$$v = \frac{\text{Standard deviation}}{\text{Expected value}} = \frac{\sigma}{E(X)}$$

Now try Technical
Problem 1.

The coefficient of variation measures the level of risk *relative* to the mean of the probability distribution. In the preceding example, the two coefficients of variation are $v_C = 52.5/400 = 0.131$ and $v_D = 52.5/5,000 = 0.0105$.

15.3 DECISIONS UNDER RISK

Now that we have shown how to measure the risk associated with making a particular managerial decision, we will discuss how these measures of risk can help managers make decisions under conditions of risk. We now set forth three rules to guide managers making risky decisions.

Maximization of Expected Value

expected value rule
Choosing the decision
with the highest
expected value.

Information about the likelihood of the various possible outcomes, while quite helpful in making decisions, does not solve the manager's decision-making problem. How should a manager choose among various decisions when each decision has a variety of possible outcomes? One rule or solution to this problem, called the **expected value rule,** is to choose the decision with the highest expected value. The expected value rule is easy to apply. Unfortunately, this rule uses information about only one characteristic of the distribution of outcomes, the mean. It fails to incorporate into the decision the riskiness (dispersion) associated with the probability distribution of outcomes. Therefore, the expected value rule is not particularly useful in situations where the level of risk differs very much across decisions—unless the decision maker does not care about the level of risk associated with a decision and is concerned only with expected value. (Such a decision maker is called *risk neutral,* a concept we will discuss later in this chapter.) Also, the expected value rule is only useful to a manager when the decisions have *different* expected values. Of course, if decisions happen to have identical expected values, the expected value rule offers no guidance for choosing between them, and, considering only the mean, the manager would be indifferent to a choice among them. The expected value rule *cannot* be applied when decisions have identical expected values and *should not* be applied when decisions have different levels of risk, except in the circumstance noted earlier: that is, when the decision maker is risk neutral.

To illustrate the expected value rule (and other rules to be discussed later), consider the owner and manager of Chicago Rotisserie Chicken, who wants to decide where to open one new restaurant. Figure 15.4 shows the probability distributions of possible weekly profits if the manager decides to locate the new restaurant in either Atlanta (Panel A), Boston (Panel B), or Cleveland (Panel C). The expected values, standard deviations, and coefficients of variation for each distribution are displayed in each panel.

FIGURE 15.4

Probability Distributions for Weekly Profit at Three Restaurant Locations

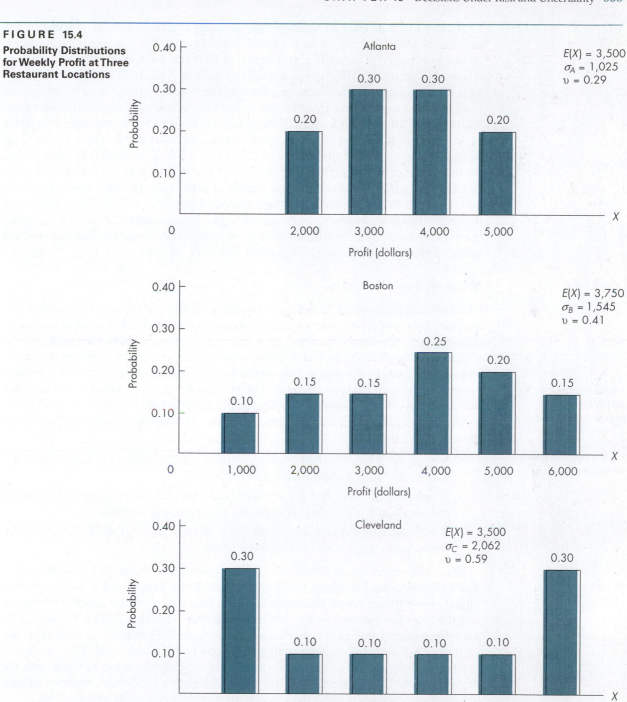

On the basis of past experience, the manager calculates that weekly profit in Atlanta will take one of four values: $3,000 or $4,000 per week each with a 30 percent chance of occurring, and $2,000 or $5,000 a week each with a 20 percent chance of occurring. The expected weekly profit in Atlanta is $3,500. If the manager decides to open a restaurant in Boston, the weekly profits may be any of six indicated values ranging from $1,000 to $6,000 weekly with the indicated probabilities and an expected value of $3,750. For Cleveland, the manager assigns a probability of 30 percent to weekly profits of $1,000 and $6,000 and a probability of 10 percent to each of the profits $2,000, $3,000, $4,000, and $5,000, with an expected value of $3,500 for the distribution. If the manager is not concerned with risk (is risk neutral) and follows the expected value rule, the new restaurant will be opened in Boston, with the highest expected profit of $3,750. Note that if the manager had been choosing between only the Atlanta and Cleveland locations, the expected value rule could not have been applied because each has an expected value of $3,500. In such cases some other rule may be used.

Mean–Variance Analysis

Managers who choose among risky alternatives using the expected value rule are, in effect, ignoring risk (dispersion) and focusing exclusively on the mean outcome. An alternative method of making decisions under risk uses both the mean *and* the variance of the probability distribution, which incorporates information about the level of risk into the decisions. This method of decision making, commonly known as **mean–variance analysis,** employs both the mean and the variance (or standard deviation) to make decisions according to the rules listed below.

mean–variance analysis
Method of decision making that employs both the mean and the variance to make decisions.

Given two risky decisions (designated *A* and *B*), the *mean–variance rules* for decisions under risk are

1. If decision *A* has a higher expected outcome *and* a lower variance than decision *B*, decision *A* should be made.
2. If both decisions *A* and *B* have identical *variances* (or standard deviations), the decision with the higher expected value should be made.
3. If both decisions *A* and *B* have identical *expected values,* the decision with the lower variance (standard deviation) should be made.

The mean–variance rules are based on the assumption that a decision maker prefers a higher expected return to a lower, other things equal, and a lower risk to a higher, other things equal. It therefore follows that the *higher* the expected outcome and the *lower* the variance (risk), the more desirable a decision will be. Under rule 1, a manager would always choose a particular decision if it has *both* a greater expected value *and* a lower variance than other decisions being considered. With the same level of risk, the second rule indicates managers should choose the decision with the higher expected value. Under rule 3, if the decisions have identical expected values, the manager chooses the less risky (lower standard deviation) decision.

Returning to the problem of Chicago Rotisserie Chicken, no location dominates both of the other locations in terms of any of the three rules of mean–variance analysis. Boston dominates Cleveland because it has both a higher expected value and a lower risk (rule 1). Atlanta also dominates Cleveland in terms of rule 3 because both locations have the same expected value ($3,500), but Atlanta has a lower standard deviation—less risk ($\sigma_A = 1,025 < 2,062 = \sigma_C$).

If the manager compares the Atlanta and Boston locations, the mean–variance rules cannot be applied. Boston has a higher weekly expected profit ($3,750 > $3,500), but Atlanta is less risky ($\sigma_A = 1,025 < 1,545 = \sigma_B$). Therefore, when making this choice, the manager must make a trade-off between risk and expected return, so the choice would depend on the manager's valuation of higher expected return versus lower risk. We will now set forth an additional decision rule that uses information on both the expected value and dispersion and can be used to make decisions involving trade-offs between expected return and risk.

Coefficient of Variation Analysis

As we noted in the discussion about measuring the riskiness of probability distributions, variance and standard deviation are measures of *absolute risk*. In contrast, the coefficient of variation [$\sigma/E(X)$] measures risk *relative* to the expected value of the distribution. The coefficient of variation, therefore, allows managers to make decisions based on relative risk instead of absolute risk. The **coefficient of variation rule** states: "When making decisions under risk, choose the decision with the smallest coefficient of variation [$\sigma/E(X)$]." This rule takes into account both the expected value and the standard deviation of the distribution. The lower the standard deviation and the higher the expected value, the smaller the coefficient of variation. Thus a desired movement in either characteristic of a probability distribution moves the coefficient of variation in the desired direction.

coefficient of variation rule
Decision-making rule that the decision to be chosen is the one with the smallest coefficient of variation.

We return once more to the decision facing the manager of Chicago Rotisserie Chicken. The coefficients of variation for each of the possible location decisions are

$$v_{\text{Atlanta}} = 1,025/3,500 = 0.29$$
$$v_{\text{Boston}} = 1,545/3,750 = 0.41$$
$$v_{\text{Cleveland}} = 2,062/3,500 = 0.59$$

The location with the smallest coefficient of variation is Atlanta, which has a coefficient of 0.29. Notice that the choice between locating in either Atlanta or Boston, which could not be made using mean–variance rules, is now resolved using the coefficient of variation to make the decision. Atlanta wins over Boston with the smaller coefficient of variation (0.29 < 0.41), while Cleveland comes in last.

Which Rule Is Best?

At this point, you may be wondering which one of the three rules for making decisions under risk is the "correct one." After all, the manager of Chicago Rotisserie Chicken either reached a different decision or reached no decision at all depending on which rule was used. Using the expected value rule, Boston was the choice. Using the coefficient of variation rule, Atlanta was chosen. According to mean–variance analysis, Cleveland was out, but the decision between Atlanta and Boston

ILLUSTRATION 15.1

Lowering Risk by Diversification

Although investors can't do much about the amount of risk associated with any specific project or investment, they do have some control over the amount of risk associated with their entire portfolio of investments. *The Wall Street Journal* advised: "The best strategy, investment advisors say, is to diversify by spreading your money among a wide variety of stocks, bonds, real estate, cash, and other holdings."

The Wall Street Journal pointed out that you will have to expect the value of your holdings to fluctuate with changes in the economy or market conditions. The returns should comfortably beat those from CDs, and the ups and downs should be a lot smaller than if you simply put all your money in the stock market. One investment adviser stated, "Diversified portfolios of stocks and bonds had much less risk while providing nearly as much return as an all-stock portfolio during the past 15, 20, and 25 years." During the period since 1968, stocks soared in five years but were losing investments in six years. Investors who put a third of their money in stocks, a third in Treasury bonds, and a third in "cash equivalent" investments would have lost money in only four years, with the largest annual loss being less than 5 percent. The annual compound return over the 25 years in that investment would have been 9 percent, compared with 10.56 percent in an all-stock portfolio, 8.26 percent in all bonds, and 9.89 percent in 60 percent stock and 40 percent bonds. But the more diversified investment would have been less risky.

The theoretical arguments in the *Wall Street Journal* article are based on portfolio theory. The core of portfolio theory is deceptively simple: As more securities are added to an investor's portfolio, the portfolio risk (the standard deviation of portfolio returns) declines. A particular security or investment is subject to two

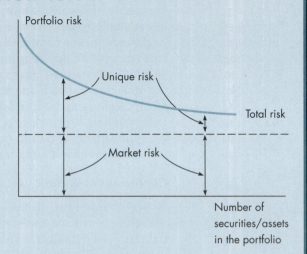

types of risk: market risk and unique risk. Market risk is the risk faced due to economywide changes, such as economic fluctuations and fluctuations in the market rate of interest. Unique risk is the risk associated with the particular security or investment, such as fluctuations in the sales of a particular firm or region relative to the entire economy.

As different securities are added to a portfolio, the unique risk associated with a specific security is diversified away. That is, as more securities are added, the entire portfolio is less subject to the unique risk associated with a given stock. As the number of securities or assets is increased, unique risk decreases and the total risk of the portfolio (the standard deviation) approaches the market risk.

Source: Based on Tom Herman, "The First Rollovers of Spring Bring Advice on Diversification," *The Wall Street Journal*, April 8, 1993.

could not be resolved using mean–variance analysis. If the decision rules do not all lead to the same conclusion, a manager must decide which rule to follow.

When a decision is to be made repeatedly, with identical probabilities each time, the expected value rule provides managers with the most reliable rule for maximizing (expected) profit. The average return of a given risky course of action repeated many times will approach the expected value of that action. Therefore, the average return of the course of action with the highest expected value will tend to be higher than the average return of any course of action with a lower expected value, when carried out a large number of times. Situations involving repeated decisions can arise, for example, when a manager must make the same risky decision once a month or even once every week. Or a manager at corporate headquarters may make a decision that directs activities of dozens, maybe even hundreds, of corporate offices in the country or around the world. When the risky decision is repeated many times, the manager at corporate headquarters believes strongly that each of the alternative decision choices will probably result in an average profit level that is equal to the expected value of profit, even though any one corporate office might experience either higher or lower returns. In practice, then, the expected value rule is justifiable when a decision will be repeated many times under identical circumstances.

When a manager makes a one-time decision under risk, there will not be any follow-up repetitions of the decision to "average out" a bad outcome (or a good outcome). Unfortunately, there is no best rule to follow when decisions are not repetitive. The rules we present for risky decision making should be used by managers to help *analyze* and *guide* the decision-making process. Ultimately, making decisions under risk (or uncertainty) is as much an art as it is a science.

The "art" of decision making under risk or uncertainty is closely associated with a decision maker's preferences with respect to risk taking. Managers can differ greatly in their willingness to take on risk in decision making. Some managers are quite cautious, while others may actually seek out high-risk situations. In the next section, we present a theory, not a rule, of decision making under risk that formally accounts for a manager's attitude toward risk. This theory, usually referred to as *expected utility theory*, postulates that managers make risky decisions with the objective of maximizing the expected *utility* of profit. The theory can, in some situations, provide a more powerful tool for making risky decisions than the rules presented in this section.

Now try Technical Problems 2–3.

15.4 EXPECTED UTILITY: A THEORY OF DECISION MAKING UNDER RISK

expected utility theory
A theory of decision making under risk that accounts for a manager's attitude toward risk.

As we just mentioned, managers differ in their willingness to undertake risky decisions. Some managers avoid risk as much as possible, while other managers actually prefer more risk to less risk in decision making. To allow for different attitudes toward risk taking in decision making, modern decision theory treats managers as deriving utility or satisfaction from the profits earned by their firms. Just as consumers derived utility from the consumption of goods in Chapter 5, in **expected utility theory,** managers are assumed to derive utility from earning profits. Expected utility theory postulates that managers make risky decisions in a way that maximizes the expected utility of the profit outcomes. While expected utility theory does provide a tool for decisions under risk, the primary purpose of the theory, and the reason for presenting this theory here, is to explain why managers make the decisions they do make when risk is involved. We want to stress that expected utility theory is an economic model of how managers *actually* make decisions under risk, rather than a rule dictating how managers *should* make decisions under risk.

Suppose a manager is faced with a decision to undertake a risky project or, more generally, must make a decision to take an action that may generate a range of possible profit outcomes, $\pi_1, \pi_2, \ldots, \pi_n$, that the manager believes will occur with probabilities $p_1, p_2, \ldots, p_n$, respectively. The **expected utility** of this risky decision is the sum of the probability-weighted utilities of each possible profit outcome

$$E[U(\pi)] = p_1 U(\pi_1) + p_2 U(\pi_2) + \cdots + p_n U(\pi_n)$$

expected utility
The sum of the probabilityweighted utilities of each possible profit outcome.

where $U(\pi)$ is a utility function for profit that measures the utility associated with a particular level of profit. Notice that expected *utility* of profit is different from the concept of expected *profit*, which is the sum of the probability-weighted profits. To understand expected utility theory, you must understand how the manager's attitude toward risk is reflected in the manager's utility function for profit. We now discuss the concept of a manager's utility of profit and show how to derive a utility function for profit. Then we demonstrate how managers could employ expected utility of profit to make decisions under risk.

A Manager's Utility Function for Profit

Since expected utility theory is based on the idea that managers enjoy utility or satisfaction from earning profit, the nature of the relation between a manager's utility and the level of profit earned plays a crucial role in explaining how managers make decisions under risk. As we now show, the manager's attitude toward risk is determined by the manager's *marginal utility of profit.*

It would be extremely unusual for a manager *not* to experience a higher level of total utility as profit increases. Thus the relation between an index of utility and the level of profit earned by a firm is assumed to be an upward-sloping curve. The amount by which total utility increases when the firm earns an additional dollar of profit is the **marginal utility of profit**

marginal utility of profit
The amount by which total utility increases with an additional dollar of profit earned by a firm.

$$MU_{profit} = \Delta U(\pi)/\Delta \pi$$

where $U(\pi)$ is the manager's utility function for profit. The utility function for profit gives an index value to measure the level of utility experienced when a given amount of profit is earned. Suppose, for example, the marginal utility of profit is 8. This means a $1 increase in profit earned by the firm causes the utility index of the manager to increase by eight units. Studies of attitudes toward risk have found most business decision makers experience *diminishing marginal utility of profit.* Even though additional dollars of profit increase the level of total satisfaction, the additional utility from extra dollars of profit typically falls for most managers.

The shape of the utility curve for profit plays a pivotal role in expected utility theory because the shape of $U(\pi)$ determines the manager's attitude toward risk, which determines which choices a manager makes. Attitudes toward risk may

risk averse
Term describing a decision maker who makes the less risky of two decisions that have the same expected value.

risk loving
Term describing a decision maker who makes the riskier of two decisions that have the same expected value.

risk neutral
Term describing a decision maker who ignores risk in decision making and considers only expected values of decisions.

be categorized as *risk averse, risk neutral,* or *risk loving.* People are said to be **risk averse** if, facing two risky decisions with equal expected profits, they choose the less risky decision. In contrast, someone choosing the more risky decision, when the expected profits are identical, is said to be **risk loving.** The third type of attitude toward risk arises for someone who is indifferent between risky situations when the expected profits are identical. In this last case, a manager ignores risk in decision making and is said to be **risk neutral.**

Figure 15.5 shows the shapes of the utility functions associated with the three types of risk preferences. Panel A illustrates a utility function for a risk-averse manager. The utility function for profit is upward-sloping, but its slope diminishes as profit rises, which corresponds to the case of diminishing marginal utility. When profit increases by $50,000 from point A to point B, the manager experiences an increase in utility of 10 units. When profit falls by $50,000 from point A to point C, utility falls by 15 units. A $50,000 loss of profit creates a larger reduction in utility than a $50,000 gain would add to utility. Consequently, risk-averse managers are more sensitive to a dollar of lost profit than to a dollar of gained profit and will place an emphasis in decision making on avoiding the risk of loss.

In Panel B, the marginal utility of profit is constant ($\Delta U/\Delta \pi = 15/50 = 0.3$), and the loss of $50,000 reduces utility by the same amount that a gain of $50,000 increases it. In this case, a manager places the same emphasis on avoiding losses as on seeking gains. Managers are risk neutral when their utility functions for profit are linear or, equivalently, when the marginal utility of profit is constant.

Panel C shows a utility function for a manager who makes risky decisions in a risk-loving way. The extra utility from a $50,000 increase in profit (20 units) is greater than the loss in utility suffered when profit falls by $50,000 (10 units). Consequently, a risk-loving decision maker places a greater weight on the potential for gain than on the potential for loss. We have now developed the following relation.

Now try Technical Problems 4–5.

> **Relation**   A manager's attitude toward risky decisions can be related to his or her marginal utility of profit. Someone who experiences diminishing (increasing) marginal utility for profit will be a risk-averse (risk-loving) decision maker. Someone whose marginal utility of profit is constant is risk neutral.

Deriving a Utility Function for Profit

As discussed earlier, when managers make decisions to maximize expected utility under risk, it is the utility function for profit that determines which decision a manager chooses. We now show the steps a manager can follow to derive his or her own utility function for profit, $U(\pi)$. Recall that the utility function does not directly measure utility but does provide a number, or index value, and that it is the magnitude of this index that reflects the desirability of a particular profit outcome.

The process of deriving a utility function for profit is conceptually straightforward. It does, however, involve a substantial amount of subjective evaluation. To illustrate the procedure, we return to the decision problem facing the manager of Chicago Rotisserie Chicken (CRC). Recall that CRC must decide where to locate

FIGURE 15.5
**A Manager's Attitude
toward Risk**

Panel A — Risk averse:
diminishing MU profit

Panel B — Risk neutral:
constant MU profit

Panel C — Risk loving:
increasing MU profit

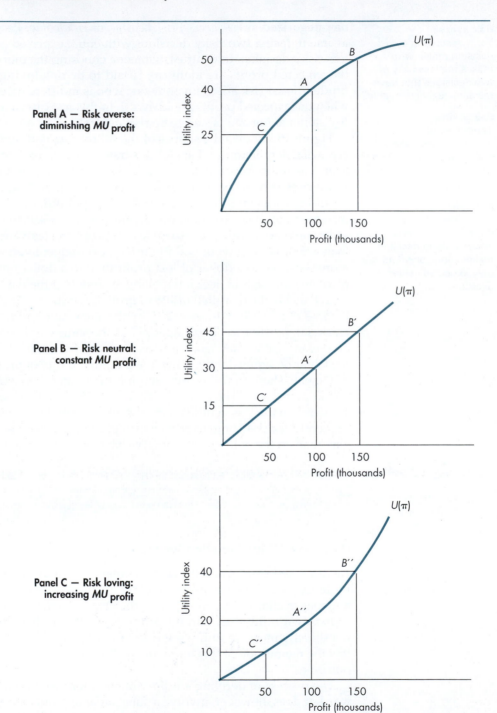

the next restaurant. The profit outcomes for the three locations range from $1,000 to $6,000 per week. Before the expected utilities of each location can be calculated, the manager must derive her utility function for profits covering the range $1,000 to $6,000.

The manager of CRC begins the process of deriving $U(\pi)$ by assigning minimum and maximum values that the index will be allowed to take. For the lower bound on the index, suppose the manager assigns a utility index value of 0—although any number, positive or negative, will do—to the lowest profit outcome of $1,000. For the upper bound, suppose a utility index value of 1 is assigned—any value greater than the value of the lower bound will do—to the highest profit outcome of $6,000. Again, we emphasize, choosing 0 and 1 for the upper and lower bounds is completely arbitrary, just as long as the upper bound is greater algebraically than the lower bound. For example, lower and upper bounds of -12 and 50 would also work just fine. Two points on the manager's utility function for profit are

$$U(\$1,000) = 0 \quad \text{and} \quad U(\$6,000) = 1$$

Next, a value of the utility index for each of the remaining possible profit outcomes between $1,000 and $6,000 must be determined. In this case, examining profit in increments of $1,000 is convenient. To find the value of the utility index for $5,000, the manager employs the following subjective analysis: The manager begins by considering two decision choices, A and B, where decision A involves receiving a profit of $5,000 with certainty and risky decision B involves receiving either a $6,000 profit with probability p or a $1,000 profit with probability $1 - p$. Decisions A and B are illustrated in Figure 15.6. Now the probability p that will make the manager indifferent between the two decisions A and B must be determined. This is a subjective determination, and any two managers likely will find different values of p depending on their individual preferences for risk.

Suppose the manager of Chicago Rotisserie Chicken decides $p = 0.95$ makes decisions A and B equally desirable. In effect, the manager is saying that the expected utility of decision A equals the expected utility of decision B. If the expected utilities of decisions A and B are equal, $E(U_A) = E(U_B)$

$$1 \times U(\$5,000) = 0.95 \times U(\$6,000) + 0.05 \times U(\$1,000)$$

FIGURE 15.6

Finding a Certainty Equivalent for a Risky Decision

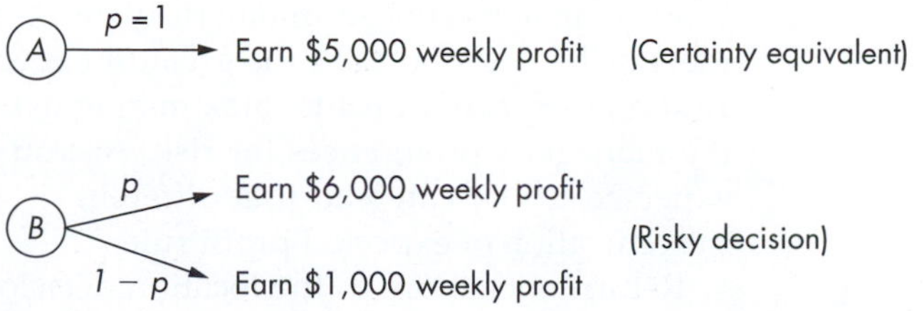

A — $p = 1$ → Earn $5,000 weekly profit   (Certainty equivalent)

B — p → Earn $6,000 weekly profit

$1 - p$ → Earn $1,000 weekly profit   (Risky decision)

Only $U(\$5,000)$ is unknown in this equation, so the manager can solve for the utility index for $5,000 of profit

$$U(\$5,000) = (0.95 \times 1) + (0.05 \times 0) = 0.95$$

certainty equivalent
The dollar amount that a manager would be just willing to trade for the opportunity to engage in a risky decision.

The utility index value of 0.95 is an indirect measure of the utility of $5,000 of profit. This procedure establishes another point on the utility function for profit. The sum of $5,000 is called the **certainty equivalent** of risky decision *B* because it is the dollar amount that the manager would be just willing to trade for the opportunity to engage in risky decision *B*. In other words, the manager is indifferent between having a profit of $5,000 for sure or making a risky decision having a 95 percent chance of earning $6,000 and a 5 percent chance of earning $1,000. The utility indexes for $4,000, $3,000, and $2,000 can be established in exactly the same way.

This procedure for finding a utility function for profit is called the *certainty equivalent method*. We now summarize the steps for finding a utility function for profit, $U(\pi)$, in a principle.

Principle To implement the certainty equivalent method of deriving a utility of profit function, the following steps can be employed:

1. Set the utility index equal to 1 for the highest possible profit (π_H) and 0 for the lowest possible profit (π_L).

2. Define a risky decision to have probability p_0 of profit outcome π_H and probability $(1 - p_0)$ of profit outcome π_L. For *each* possible profit outcome π_0 ($\pi_H < \pi_0 < \pi_L$), the manager determines subjectively the probability p_0 that gives that risky decision the same expected utility as receiving π_0 with certainty:

$$p_0 U(\pi_H) = (1 - p_0) U(\pi_L) = U(\pi_0)$$

The certain sum π_0 is called the certainty equivalent of the risky decision. Let the subjective probability p_0 serve as the utility index for measuring the level of satisfaction the manager enjoys when earning a profit of π_0.

Now try Technical Problem 6.

Figure 15.7 illustrates the utility function for profit for the manager of Chicago Rotisserie Chicken. The marginal utility of profit diminishes over the entire range of possible profit outcomes ($1,000 to $6,000), and so this manager is a risk-averse decision maker.

Maximization of Expected Utility

When managers choose among risky decisions in accordance with expected utility theory, the decision with the greatest expected utility is chosen. Unlike maximization of expected profits, maximizing expected utility takes into consideration the manager's preferences for risk. As you will see in this example, maximizing expected utility can lead to a different decision than the one reached using the maximization of expected profit rule.

Return once more to the location decision facing Chicago Rotisserie Chicken. The manager calculates the expected utilities of the three risky location decisions

FIGURE 15.7
A Manager's Utility Function for Profit

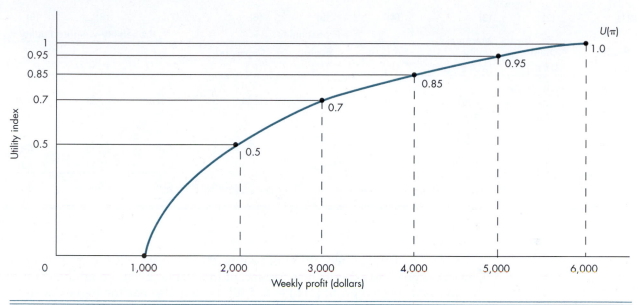

using her own utility function for profit shown in Figure 15.7. The expected utilities for the three cities are calculated as follows:

Atlanta $E(U_A)$ = $0U(\$1,000) + 0.2U(\$2,000) + 0.3U(\$3,000) + 0.3U(\$4,000)$
$+ 0.2U(\$5,000) + 0U(\$6,000)$

$= 0 + (0.2)(0.5) + (0.3)(0.7) + (0.3)(0.85) + (0.2)(0.95) + 0$

$= 0.755$

Boston $E(U_B)$ = $0.1U(\$1,000) + 0.15U(\$2,000) + 0.15U(\$3,000)$
$+ 0.25U(\$4,000) + 0.2U(\$5,000) + 0.15U(\$6,000)$

$= (0.1)(0) + (0.15)(0.50) + (0.15)(0.7) + (0.25)(0.85)$
$+ (0.2)(0.95) + (0.15)(1)$

$= 0.733$

Cleveland $E(U_C)$ = $0.3U(\$1,000) + 0.1U(\$2,000) + 0.1U(\$3,000) + 0.1U(\$4,000)$
$+ 0.1U(\$5,000) + 0.3U(\$6,000)$

$= (0.3)(0) + (0.1)(0.5) + (0.1)(0.7) + (0.1)(0.85) + (0.1)(0.95)$
$+ (0.3)(1.0)$

$= 0.600$

TABLE 15.1

Expected Utility of Profit: A Risk-Neutral Manager

(1)	(2)	(3)	(4)	(5)	(6)	(7)	(8)	(9)
		Marginal utility	Probabilities			Probability-weighted utility		
Profit (π)	Utility $[U(\pi)]$	$[\Delta U(\pi)/\Delta\pi]$	Atlanta (P_A)	Boston (P_B)	Cleveland (P_C)	$P_A \times U$	$P_B \times U$	$P_C \times U$
$1,000	0	—	0	0.1	0.3	0	0	0
$2,000	0.2	0.0002	0.2	0.15	0.1	0.04	0.03	0.02
$3,000	0.4	0.0002	0.3	0.15	0.1	0.12	0.06	0.04
$4,000	0.6	0.0002	0.3	0.25	0.1	0.18	0.15	0.06
$5,000	0.8	0.0002	0.2	0.2	0.1	0.16	0.16	0.08
$6,000	1.0	0.0002	0	0.15	0.3	0	0.15	0.3
						Expected utility = 0.50	0.55	0.50

To maximize the expected utility of profits, the manager of Chicago Rotisserie Chicken chooses to open its new restaurant in Atlanta. Even though Boston has the highest expected profit [$E(\pi) = \$3,750$], Boston also has the highest level of risk ($\sigma = 1,545$), and the risk-averse manager at CRC prefers to avoid the relatively high risk of locating the new restaurant in Boston. In this case of a risk-averse decision maker, the manager chooses the less risky Atlanta location over the more risky Cleveland location even though both locations have identical expected profit levels.

To show what a risk-neutral decision maker would do, we constructed a utility function for profit that exhibits constant marginal utility of profit, which, as we have explained, is the condition required for risk neutrality. This risk-neutral utility function is presented in columns 1 and 2 of Table 15.1. Marginal utility of profit, in column 3, is constant, as it must be for risk-neutral managers. From the table you can see that the expected utilities of profit for Atlanta, Boston, and Cleveland are 0.50, 0.55, and 0.50, respectively. For a risk-neutral decision maker, locating in Boston is the decision that maximizes expected utility. Recall that Boston also is the city with the maximum expected profit [$E(\pi) = \$3,750$]. This is not a coincidence. As we explained earlier, a risk-neutral decision maker ignores risk when making decisions and relies instead on expected profit to make decisions in risky situations. Under conditions of risk neutrality, a manager makes the same decision by maximizing either the expected value of profit, $E(\pi)$, or the expected utility of profit, $E[U(\pi)]$.[2]

Finally, consider how a manager who is risk loving decides on a location for CRC's new restaurant. In Table 15.2, columns 1 and 2 show a utility function for

---

[2]The appendix to this chapter demonstrates the equivalence for risk-neutral decision makers of maximizing expected profit and maximizing expected utility of profit.

TABLE 15.2
Expected Utility of Profit: A Risk-Loving Manager

(1)	(2)	(3)	(4)	(5)	(6)	(7)	(8)	(9)
		Marginal	Probabilities			Probability-weighted utility		
Profit (π)	Utility $[U(\pi)]$	utility $[\Delta U(\pi)/\Delta\pi]$	Atlanta (P_A)	Boston (P_B)	Cleveland (P_C)	$P_A \times U$	$P_B \times U$	$P_C \times U$
$1,000	0	—	0	0.1	0.3	0	0	0
$2,000	0.08	0.00008	0.2	0.15	0.1	0.016	0.012	0.008
$3,000	0.2	0.00012	0.3	0.15	0.1	0.06	0.03	0.02
$4,000	0.38	0.00018	0.3	0.25	0.1	0.114	0.095	0.038
$5,000	0.63	0.00025	0.2	0.2	0.1	0.126	0.126	0.036
$6,000	1.0	0.00037	0	0.15	0.3	0	0.15	0.3
					Expected utility =	0.32	0.41	0.43

Now try Technical Problems 7–8.

profit for which marginal utility of profit is increasing. Column 3 shows the marginal utility of profit, which, as it must for a risk-loving manager, increases as profit increases. The expected utilities of profit outcomes for Atlanta, Boston, and Cleveland are 0.32, 0.41, and 0.43, respectively. In the case of a risk-loving decision maker, Cleveland is the decision that maximizes expected utility. If Atlanta and Cleveland were the only two sites being considered, then the risk-loving manager would choose Cleveland over Atlanta, a decision that is consistent with the definition of risk loving. We now summarize our discussion in the following principle.

□ **Principle**   If a manager behaves according to expected utility theory, decisions are made to maximize the manager's expected utility of profits. Decisions made by maximizing expected utility of profit reflect the manager's risk-taking attitude and generally differ from decisions reached by decision rules that do not consider risk. In the case of a risk-neutral manager, the decisions are identical under either maximization of expected utility or maximization of expected profit.

15.5 DECISIONS UNDER UNCERTAINTY

Practically all economic theories about behavior in the absence of complete information deal with risk rather than uncertainty. Furthermore, decision science has little guidance to offer managers making decisions when they have no idea about the likelihood of various states of nature occurring. This should not be too surprising, given the nebulous nature of uncertainty. We will, however, present four rather simple decision rules that can help managers make decisions under uncertainty.

The Maximax Criterion

maximax rule
Decision-making guide that calls for identifying the best outcome for each possible decision and choosing the decision with the maximum payoff of all the best outcomes.

For managers who tend to have an optimistic outlook on life, the **maximax rule** provides a guide for making decisions when uncertainty prevails. Under the maximax rule, a manager identifies for each possible decision the best outcome that could

TABLE 15.3

The Payoff Matrix for Dura Plastic, Inc.

	States of nature		
Decisions	Recovery	Stagnation	Recession
Expand plant capacity by 20%	$5 million	−$1 million	−$3.0 million
Maintain same plant capacity	3 million	2 million	0.5 million
Reduce plant capacity by 20%	2 million	1 million	0.75 million

occur and then chooses the decision that would give the maximum payoff of all the best outcomes. Under this rule a manager ignores all possible outcomes except the best outcome from each decision.

To illustrate the application of this rule, suppose the management at Dura Plastic is considering changing the size (capacity) of its manufacturing plant. Management has narrowed the decision to three choices. The plant's capacity will be (1) expanded by 20 percent, (2) maintained at the current capacity, or (3) reduced by 20 percent. The outcome of this decision depends crucially on how the economy performs during the upcoming year. Thus the performance of the economy is the "state of nature" in this decision problem. Management envisions three possible states of nature occurring: (1) The economy enters a period of recovery, (2) economic stagnation sets in, or (3) the economy falls into a recession.

For each possible decision and state of nature, the managers determine the profit outcome, or payoff, shown in the *payoff matrix* in Table 15.3. A **payoff matrix** is a table with rows corresponding to the various decisions and columns corresponding to the various states of nature. Each cell in the payoff matrix in Table 15.3 gives the outcome (payoff) for each decision when a particular state of nature occurs. For example, if management chooses to expand the manufacturing plant by 20 percent and the economy enters a period of recovery, Dura Plastic is projected to earn profits of $5 million. Alternatively, if Dura Plastic expands plant capacity but the economy falls into a recession, it is projected that the company will lose $3 million. The managers do not know which state of nature will actually occur, or the probabilities of occurrence, so the decision to alter plant capacity is made under conditions of uncertainty. To apply the maximax rule to this decision, management first identifies the best possible outcome for each of the three decisions. The best payoffs are

payoff matrix
A table with rows corresponding to various decisions and columns corresponding to various states of nature, with each cell giving the outcome or payoff associated with that decision and state of nature.

$5 million for expanding plant size by 20 percent.

$3 million for maintaining plant size.

$2 million for reducing plant size by 20 percent.

Each best payoff occurs if the economy recovers. Under the maximax rule, management would decide to expand its plant.

While the maximax rule is simple to apply, it fails to consider "bad" outcomes in the decision-making process. The fact that two out of three states of nature result in losses when management decides to expand plant capacity, and neither of

ILLUSTRATION 15.2

Floating Power Plants Lower Risks and Energize Developing Nations

Two crucial industries in developing countries are agriculture and manufacturing. A third-world nation cannot emerge from poverty without achieving a significant ability to feed itself and to manufacture both durable goods for consumption and capital goods for production. Neither of these two crucial industries can develop without energy. Domestically generated electricity can provide a versatile source of energy capable of meeting many of the most fundamental energy demands of a developing country.

A serious roadblock to construction of electric power plants in developing countries has been the risk of default on the financing required to purchase power plants. With prices beginning in the hundreds of millions of dollars, investors are understandably reluctant to lend these enormous amounts when repossession of the asset is, for all practical purposes, impossible. Donald Smith, president of Smith Cogeneration, found a solution to the problem of default risk: Build floating power plants on huge barges that can be relocated in the event of a default.

The Wall Street Journal reported that Smith's idea of building power plants on barges spawned a niche industry that "could become a significant portion of the world's [electricity] generating capacity." Nations such as the Dominican Republic, Ghana, India, and Haiti have signed agreements with producers of floating power plants that would not have been financed without the risk reduction created by the mobility of a floating platform. Indeed, the *Wall Street Journal* estimated that the floating nature of the power plant not only makes financing possible but also probably "lower(s) the financing costs by two or three percentage points"—no small change on a half-a-billion-dollar loan.

This Illustration highlights the importance of risk in decision making. If financial institutions were managed by risk-loving managers, land-based power plants would likely be common in developing nations. Apparently, developing nations can expect to generate most of their electricity on barges anchored in their harbors—evidence that large financial lenders are indeed risk averse.

Source: Adapted from William M. Bulkley, "Building Power Plants That Can Float," *The Wall Street Journal*, May 22, 1996.

---

the other decisions would result in a loss, is overlooked when using the maximax criteria. Only managers with optimistic natures are likely to find the maximax rule to be a useful decision-making tool.

The Maximin Criterion

maximin rule
Decision-making guide that calls for identifying the worst outcome for each decision and choosing the decision with the maximum worst payoff.

For managers with a pessimistic outlook on business decisions, the *maximin rule* may be more suitable than the maximax rule. Under the **maximin rule,** the manager identifies the worst outcome for each decision and makes the decision associated with the maximum worst payoff. For Dura Plastic, the worst outcomes for each decision from Table 15.3 are

−$3 million for expanding plant size by 20 percent.

$0.5 million for maintaining plant size.

$0.75 million for reducing plant size by 20 percent.

Using the maximin criterion, Dura Plastic would choose to reduce plant capacity by 20 percent. The maximin rule is also simple to follow, but it fails to consider any of the "good" outcomes.

TABLE 15.4

Potential Regret Matrix for Dura Plastic, Inc.

	States of nature		
Decisions	Recovery	Stagnation	Recession
Expand plant capacity by 20%	$0 million	$3 million	$3.75 million
Maintain same plant capacity	2 million	0 million	0.25 million
Reduce plant capacity by 20%	3 million	1 million	0 million

The Minimax Regret Criterion

potential regret
For a given decision and state of nature, the improvement in payoff the manager could have experienced had the decision been the best one when that state of nature actually occurs.

Managers concerned about their decisions not turning out to be the best *once the state of nature is known* (i.e., after the uncertainty is resolved) may make their decisions by minimizing the potential regret that may occur. The **potential regret** associated with a particular decision and state of nature is the improvement in payoff the manager could have experienced had the decision been the best one when that state of nature actually occurred. To illustrate, we calculate from Table 15.3 the potential regret associated with Dura Plastic's decision to maintain the same level of plant capacity if an economic recovery occurs. The best possible payoff when recovery occurs is $5 million, the payoff for expanding plant capacity. If a recovery does indeed happen and management chooses to maintain the same level of plant capacity, the payoff is only $3 million, and the manager experiences a regret of $2 million (= $5 − $3 million).

Table 15.4 shows the potential regret for each combination of decision and state of nature. Note that every state of nature has a decision for which there is no potential regret. This occurs when the correct decision is made for that particular state of nature. To apply the **minimax regret rule,** which requires that managers make a decision with the minimum worst potential regret, management identifies the maximum possible potential regret for each decision from the matrix:

minimax regret rule
Decision-making guide that calls for determining the worst potential regret associated with each decision, then choosing the decision with the minimum worst potential regret.

$3.75 million for expanding plant size by 20 percent.
$2 million for maintaining plant size.
$3 million for reducing plant size by 20 percent.

Management chooses the decision with the lowest worst potential regret: maintain current plant capacity. For Dura Plastic, the minimax regret rule results in management's choosing to maintain the current plant capacity.

The Equal Probability Criterion

In situations of uncertainty, managers have no information about the probable state of nature that will occur and sometimes simply assume that each state of nature is equally likely to occur. In terms of the Dura Plastic decision, management assumes each state of nature has a one-third probability of occurring. When managers assume each state of nature has an equal likelihood of occurring, the decision can be made by considering the *average* payoff for each equally possible state of nature.

equal probability rule
Decision-making guide that calls for assuming each state of nature is equally likely to occur, computing the average payoff for each equally likely possible state of nature, and choosing the decision with the highest average payoff.

This approach to decision making is often referred to as the **equal probability rule.** To illustrate, the manager of Dura Plastic calculates the average payoff for each decision as follows:

$0.33 million [= (5 +(−1) + (−3))/3] for expanding plant size.

$1.83 million [= (3 + 2 + 0.5)/3] for maintaining plant size.

$1.25 million [= (2 + 1 + 0.75)/3] for reducing plant size.

Under the equal probability rule, the manager's decision is to maintain the current plant capacity since this decision has the maximum average return.

The four decision rules discussed here do not exhaust the possibilities for managers making decisions under uncertainty. We present these four rules primarily to give you a feel for decision making under uncertainty and to show the imprecise or "unscientific" nature of these rules. Recall that management could choose any of the courses of action depending upon which rule was chosen. These and other rules are meant only to be guidelines to decision making and are not substitutes for the experience and intuition of management.

Now try Technical Problem 9.

15.6 SUMMARY

- Decision making under conditions of risk or uncertainty occur when a manager must make a decision for which the outcome is not known with certainty. Under conditions of risk, the manager can make a list of all possible outcomes and assign probabilities to the various outcomes. The process of assigning probabilities to outcomes may involve either analysis of data on past outcomes or, if very little data exist, subjective probabilities may be used. Uncertainty exists when a decision maker cannot list all possible outcomes and/or cannot assign probabilities to the various outcomes. When faced with uncertainty, managers know only the different decision options available and the different possible states of nature. The states of nature are the future events or conditions that can influence the final outcome or payoff of a decision but cannot be controlled by the manager. (*LO1*)

- To measure the risk associated with a decision, managers can examine several statistical characteristics of the probability distribution of outcomes for the decision. The expected value or mean of a probability distribution is the weighted average of the outcomes, with the probabilities of each outcome serving as the respective weights. The expected value of a distribution does *not* give the actual value of the random outcome, but rather indicates the "average" value of the outcomes if the risky

decision were to be repeated a large number of times. The variance of a probability distribution measures the dispersion of the outcomes about the mean or expected outcome and is a measure of absolute risk. The higher (lower) the variance, the greater (lower) the risk associated with a probability distribution. The standard deviation is the square root of the variance. A measure of relative risk is appropriate when the expected values of outcomes differ substantially. The coefficient of variation, which is the ratio of the standard deviation divided by the expected value, is one measure of relative risk associated with a risky decision. (*LO2*)

- While decision rules do not eliminate the risk surrounding a decision, they do provide a method of systematically including the risk in the process of decision making. Three rules for making decisions under risk are presented in this chapter: the expected value rule, the mean-variance rules, and the coefficient of variation rule. Under the expected value rule, the manager should choose the decision with the highest expected value. Under the mean-variance rules, choosing between two risky decisions A and B is governed by a set of three rules: (1) If decision A has a higher expected outcome and a lower variance than decision B, decision A should be made, (2) if both decisions have identical variances, the decision with the higher expected value should be made, and (3) if both decisions have identical expected values, the decision with the lower variance should be made. Under the coefficient of variation rule, the manager should choose the decision with the smallest coefficient of variation. When these decision rules do not all lead to the same conclusion, a manager must decide which rule to follow. When a decision is made repeatedly, with identical probabilities each time, the expected value rule provides the most reliable rule for maximizing expected profit. When a manager makes a one-time decision under risk, without any follow-up repetitions of the decision, then there is no best rule to follow. Rules for risky decision making should be used to analyze and guide the decision-making process. Ultimately, making decisions under risk (or uncertainty) is as much an art as it is a science. (LO3)

■ Expected utility theory is a theory, not a rule, of decision making under risk that formally accounts for a manager's attitude toward risk, which postulates that managers make risky decisions with the objective of maximizing the expected utility of profit. The theory can, in some situations, provide a more powerful tool for making risky decisions than the rules presented in this chapter. Expected utility of a risky decision is the sum of the probability-weighted utilities of each possible profit outcome $E[U(\pi)] = p_1 U(\pi_1) + p_2 U(\pi_2) + \cdots + p_n U(\pi_n)$, where $U(\pi)$ is the manager's utility function for profit that measures the utility associated with a particular level of profit. People are said to be risk averse if, facing two risky decisions with equal expected profits, they choose the less risky decision. Someone who chooses the riskier of two decisions when the expected profits are the same is said to be risk loving. A risk-neutral person is indifferent about risky decisions that all have the same expected profit. A manager who experiences diminishing (increasing) marginal utility for profit will be a risk-averse (risk-loving) decision maker. If marginal utility of profit is constant, then the manager is risk neutral. Decisions made by maximizing expected utility of profit generally differ from decisions reached using rules that do not consider risk. In the case of risk-neutral managers, however, decisions are identical under either maximization of expected utility or maximization of profit. (LO4)

■ In the case of uncertainty, decision science can provide very little guidance to managers beyond offering them some simple decision rules to aid them in their analysis of uncertain situations. Four basic rules for decision making under uncertainty are presented in this chapter: the maximax rule, the maximin rule, the minimax regret rule, and the equal probability rule. To follow the maximax rule, managers identify the best outcome for each possible decision and choose the decision with the maximum payoff. Under the maximin rule, managers identify the worst outcome for each decision and choose the decision associated with the maximum worst payoff. To apply the minimax regret rule, managers first determine the worst potential regret associated with each decision, where the potential regret associated with any particular decision and state of nature is the improvement in payoff the manager could have experienced had the decision been the best one when that state of nature actually occurred. The manager then chooses the decision with the minimum worst potential regret. Under the equal probability rule, managers assume each state of nature is equally likely to occur, and compute the average payoff for each equally likely possible state of nature; then they choose the decision with the highest average payoff. (LO5)

KEY TERMS

certainty equivalent	marginal utility of profit	probability distribution
coefficient of variation	maximax rule	risk
coefficient of variation rule	maximin rule	risk averse
equal probability rule	mean of the distribution	risk loving
expected utility	mean-variance analysis	risk neutral
expected utility theory	minimax regret rule	standard deviation
expected value	payoff matrix	uncertainty
expected value rule	potential regret	variance

TECHNICAL PROBLEMS

1. Consider the following two probability distributions for sales:

Sales (thousands of units)	Distribution 1 probability (percent)	Distribution 2 probability (percent)
50	10	10
60	20	15
70	40	20
80	20	30
90	10	25

a. Graph the two distributions shown in the table. What are the expected sales for the two probability distributions?

b. Calculate the variance and standard deviation for both distributions. Which distribution is more risky?

c. Calculate the coefficient of variation for both distributions. Which distribution is more risky relative to its mean?

2. A firm is making its production plans for next quarter, but the manager of the firm does not know what the price of the product will be next month. He believes that there is a 40 percent probability the price will be $15 and a 60 percent probability the price will be $20. The manager must decide whether to produce 7,000 units or 8,000 units of output. The following table shows the four possible profit outcomes, depending on which output management chooses and which price actually occurs:

	Profit (loss) when price is	
	$15	$20
Option A: produce 7,100	−$3,750	+$31,770
Option B: produce 8,000	−8,000	+34,000

a. If the manager chooses the option with the higher expected profits, which output is chosen?

b. Which option is more risky?

c. What is the decision if the manager uses the mean–variance rules to decide between the two options?

d. What is the decision using the coefficient of variation rule?

3. Suppose in Technical Problem 2 that the price probabilities are reversed: The manager expects a price of $15 with a probability of 60 percent and a price of $20 with a probability of 40 percent. Answer all parts of Technical Problem 2 under the assumption of these reversed probabilities. What would the probabilities have to be to make the expected values of the two options equal?

4. A manager's utility function for profit is $U(\pi) = 20\pi$, where π is the dollar amount of profit. The manager is considering a risky decision with the four possible profit outcomes shown here. The manager makes the following subjective assessments about the probability of each profit outcome:

Probability	Profit outcome
0.05	−$10,000
0.45	−2,000
0.45	4,000
0.05	20,000

    a. Calculate the expected profit.

    b. Calculate the expected utility of profit.

    c. The marginal utility of an extra dollar of profit is _____.

    d. The manager is risk _____ because the marginal utility of profit is _____.

5. Suppose the manager of a firm has a utility function for profit of $U(\pi) = 20 \ln(\pi)$, where π is the dollar amount of profit. The manager is considering a risky project with the following profit payoffs and probabilities:

Probability	Profit outcome	Marginal utility of profit
0.05	$1,000	
0.15	2,000	_____
0.30	3,000	_____
0.50	4,000	_____

    a. Calculate the expected profit.

    b. Calculate the expected utility of profit.

    c. Fill in the blanks in the table showing the marginal utility of an additional $1,000 of profit.

    d. The manager is risk _____ because the marginal utility of profit is _____.

6. Derive your own utility function for profit for the range of profits shown in the following table:

Profit outcome	Utility index	Marginal utility of profit
$1,000	0.0	
2,000	_____	_____
3,000	_____	_____
3,200	_____	_____
4,000	1.0	_____

    a. Find the probability *p* that would make you indifferent between (1) accepting a risky project with probability *p* of making $4,000 and probability $1 - p$ of making a profit of $1,000 or (2) making a profit of $2,000 with certainty. Write this probability in the correct blank in the table.

    b. Repeat part *a* for $3,000 and $3,200.

    c. Compute the marginal utility of profit. (*Hint:* $MU_{profit} = \Delta$utility index$/\Delta$profit, and the denominator, Δprofit, is not constant in this table.)

    d. Does your utility index indicate that you have a risk-averse, risk-neutral, or risk-loving attitude toward risk? Explain.

7. Suppose the manager in Technical Problem 4 can avoid the risky decision in that problem by choosing instead to receive with certainty a sum of money exactly equal to the expected profit of the risky decision in Technical Problem 4.

   a. The utility of the expected profit is _____.

   b. Compare the utility of the expected profit with the expected utility of the risky decision (which you calculated in part b of Technical Problem 4). Which decision yields the greatest expected utility for the manager?

   c. Is your decision in part b consistent with the manager's attitude toward risk, as it is reflected by the utility function for profit? Explain.

8. The manager in Technical Problem 5 receives an offer from another party to buy the rights to the risky project described in that problem. This party offers the manager $3,200, which the manager believes will be paid with certainty.

   a. The utility of $3,200 is _____.

   b. Comparing the utility of $3,200 with the expected utility of the risky project (you calculated this for part b of Technical Problem 5), what should the manager do if the manager wishes to maximize expected utility of profit? Explain.

   c. Is your decision in part b consistent with the manager's attitude toward risk as it is reflected by the utility function for profit? Explain.

   d. Is the decision consistent with the mean–variance rules for decision making under risk? Explain.

9. Suppose the manager in Technical Problem 2 has absolutely no idea about the probabilities of the two prices occurring. Which option would the manager choose under each of the following rules?

   a. Maximax rule

   b. Maximin rule

   c. Minimax regret rule

   d. Equal probability rule

APPLIED PROBLEMS

1. Consider a firm that is deciding whether to operate plants only in the United States or also in either Mexico or Canada or both. Congress is currently discussing an overseas investment in new capital (OINC) tax credit for U.S. firms that operate plants outside the country. If Congress passes OINC this year, management expects to do well if it is operating plants in Mexico and Canada. If OINC does not pass this year and the firm does operate plants in Mexico and Canada, it will incur rather large losses. It is also possible that Congress will table OINC this year and wait until next year to vote on it. The profit payoff matrix is shown here:

	States of nature		
	OINC passes	OINC fails	OINC stalls
Operate plants in U.S. only	$10 million	−$1 million	$2 million
Operate plants in U.S. and Mexico	15 million	−4 million	1.5 million
Operate plants in U.S., Mexico, and Canada	20 million	−6 million	4 million

Assuming the managers of this firm have no idea about the likelihood of congressional action on OINC this year, what decision should the firm make using each of the following rules?

a. Maximax rule

b. Maximin rule

c. Minimax regret rule

d. Equal probability rule

2. Suppose your company's method of making decisions under risk is "making the best out of the worst possible outcome." What rule would you be forced to follow?

3. "A portfolio manager needs to pick winners—assets or securities with high expected returns and low risk." What is wrong with this statement?

4. Remox Corporation is a British firm that sells high-fashion sportswear in the United States. Congress is currently considering the imposition of a protective tariff on imported textiles. Remox is considering the possibility of moving 50 percent of its production to the United States to avoid the tariff. This would be accomplished by opening a plant in the United States. The following table lists the profit outcomes under various scenarios:

	Profit	
	No tariff	Tariff
Option A: Produce all output in Britain	$1,200,000	$ 800,000
Option B: Produce 50% in the United States	875,000	1,000,000

Remox hires a consulting firm to assess the probability that a tariff on imported textiles will in fact pass a congressional vote and not be vetoed by the president. The consultants forecast the following probabilities:

	Probability
Tariff will pass	30%
Tariff will fail	70%

a. Compute the expected profits for both options.

b. Based on the expected profit only, which option should Remox choose?

c. Compute the probabilities that would make Remox indifferent between options A and B using that rule.

d. Compute the standard deviations for options A and B facing Remox Corporation.

e. What decision would Remox make using the mean–variance rule?

f. What decision would Remox make using the coefficient of variation rule?

5. Using the information in Applied Problem 4, what decision would Remox make using each of the following rules if it had no idea of the probability of a tariff?

a. Maximax

b. Maximin

c. Minimax regret

d. Equal probability criterion

6. Return to Applied Problem 1 and suppose the managers of the firm decide on the following subjective probabilities of congressional action on OINC:

	Probability
OINC passes	40%
OINC fails	10%
OINC stalls	50%

a. Compute the expected profits for all three decisions.

b. Using the expected value rule, which option should the managers choose?

c. Compute the standard deviations for all three decisions. Using the mean–variance rule, does any one of the decisions dominate? If so, which one?

d. What decision would the firm make using the coefficient of variation rule?

⊡ **MATHEMATICAL APPENDIX**   **Decisions Under Risk**

The Equivalence of Maximizing Expected Profit and Maximizing Expected Utility of Profit

As discussed, but not demonstrated, in this chapter, maximizing expected profit $E(\pi)$ is equivalent to maximizing the expected utility of profit $E[U(\pi)]$ when the manager or decision maker is risk neutral. We now demonstrate this result for a simple case where profit can take only two values: π_A, with probability p, and π_B, with probability $(1 - p)$. Thus the expected profit in this case is

(1) $$E(\pi) = p\,\pi_A + (1 - p)\,\pi_B$$

Recall that the utility function for profit is linear for risk-neutral decision makers. Thus the utility function for profit $U(\pi)$ can be expressed as

(2) $$U(\pi) = a + b\pi$$

where $a \geq 0$ and $b > 0$. Using this expression for utility of profit, the *expected* utility of profit in the risky situation described above can be expressed as

(3) $$E[U(\pi)] = pU(\pi_A) + (1 - p)U(\pi_B)$$

Using the linear utility function for profit (2), expected utility in equation (3) can be expressed as a linear function of $E(\pi)$

(4) $$E[U(\pi)] = p[a + b\,\pi_A] + (1 - p)[a + b\,\pi_B]$$

$$= a + b[p\,\pi_A + (1 - p)\,\pi_B]$$

$$= a + bE(\pi)$$

From expression (4), it follows immediately that maximizing $E[U(\pi)]$ requires maximizing $E(\pi)$. Thus when the utility function for profit is linear—the decision maker is risk neutral—maximizing expected profit and maximizing expected *utility* of profit are equivalent.

16

Government Regulation of Business

After reading this chapter, you will be able to:

16.1 Define social economic efficiency and explain why well-functioning competitive markets achieve social economic efficiency without government regulation.

16.2 Explain the concept of market failure and explain why it provides an economic justification for government intervention in markets.

16.3 Identify deadweight loss associated with market power and discuss ways antitrust policy, second-best pricing, and two-part pricing can reduce the cost of market power.

16.4 Discuss pollution as a negative externality and show how government regulation can create incentives for firms to choose the optimal level of pollution.

16.5 Explain why common property resources and public goods are underproduced and how government can reduce market failure created by nonexcludability.

16.6 Discuss why imperfect information about product price and quality can lead to market failure.

Business executives cannot successfully maximize the value of their enterprises without developing strategies for dealing with the myriad rules and regulations that constrain the way businesses can operate. Domestic firms and multinational enterprises that do business in the United States, Canada, and the European Union face a comprehensive set of antitrust laws and policies designed to impose a set of "rules" on the way businesses compete with one another. The goal of antitrust laws is, simply put, the promotion of competition in the marketplace. As we will explain in this chapter, competitive markets can generate higher levels of social welfare than the imperfectly competitive market structures of monopoly, monopolistic competition, and oligopoly. Business activities that might lead to a high degree of market power, perhaps even monopoly, can provoke prosecution by antitrust authorities in numerous countries. Furthermore, any form of cooperation or collusion among firms for the purpose of raising prices or restricting competition will, if discovered, result in costly antitrust penalties and prison sentences for the executives involved.

Beyond these basic rules of competition, all governments at every level—national, state, and municipal—impose regulations on specific industries and firms designed to alter the way particular industries do business. Regulations imposed on the telecommunications industry differ from those that target the banking industry or the transportation sector. In many countries, public utilities that provide water, natural gas, waste disposal, electricity, telephone, or cable service are heavily regulated monopolies. The utility industries are purposely protected from competition because it is believed that monopoly can produce at lower cost than multiple competitors.

Public officials usually portray government intervention as a positive plan for making businesses work better from the viewpoint of society as a whole. As we will show you in this chapter, government intervention can indeed improve the social performance of business. The pursuit of profit, which maximizes the value of firms and the wealth of the owners, may not give rise to the price, quantity, mix of products, or product quality that creates the greatest well-being for everyone. Business executives can benefit from understanding the motives for, and consequences of, public policies aimed at business enterprise. Industry leaders cannot count on average citizens to use their voting power to mandate efficient government policy toward business. Business executives who understand the motives and goals of government policymakers may be able to influence government policy in ways that will be beneficial for producers and consumers. It is risky to rely on the good intentions of politicians and bureaucrats or the voting power of poorly informed citizens to establish a regulatory environment that promotes the well-being of business and society.

We begin this chapter with a careful examination of the desirable economic outcomes achieved by markets that operate under perfect competition. Perfect competition can lead to an equilibrium price and output that bring about social economic efficiency, which is just another way of saying no opportunity to improve social well-being has been wasted. Under some circumstances, however, competitive markets can fail to deliver the best possible price and quantity. And sometimes competition is replaced by other imperfectly competitive market organizations that cannot generally reach the point of social economic efficiency. We will analyze six situations—called market failures—that lead free markets to fall short of reaching social efficiency. In each case, we provide a brief explanation of what we believe are the better approaches for government policymakers and regulators to follow in their efforts to correct market failures.

No single chapter of any textbook can possibly hope to cover all of the important ideas and policy issues related to government policy toward business. We hope to give you a basic foundation of understanding and plant a seed of motivation for you to continue studying this important area for long-term business strategy. As we stated in the preface, our objective in writing this textbook is to help business students become architects of business strategy rather than simply middle managers plodding along the beaten path of others. This chapter is for future business *leaders* only.

16.1 MARKET COMPETITION AND SOCIAL ECONOMIC EFFICIENCY

social economic efficiency
When production and consumption are organized in a way that fulfills two efficiency conditions: productive efficiency and allocative efficiency.

As you learned in your first course in economics, every society must decide how best to use its scarce labor, capital, natural and environmental resources for production of goods and services. To get the most from society's scarce resources, production and consumption must be organized in ways that avoid inefficient use of resources and inefficient consumption of goods and services. In this chapter, we examine efficiency from the larger perspective of society as a whole, rather than a single firm as we did in Chapters 8 and 9. **Social economic efficiency** exists when the goods and services that society desires are produced and consumed with no waste from inefficiency in either production or consumption. To reach this goal, two efficiency conditions must be fulfilled: *productive efficiency* and *allocative efficiency*. We will examine both of these conditions shortly.

Under ideal circumstances, a perfectly competitive market reaches an equilibrium that is both productively efficient and allocatively efficient. Unfortunately, market conditions are not always ideal (or even approximately so), and perfectly competitive markets then fail to bring about social economic efficiency. In this chapter, we will discuss and analyze the six reasons why competitive markets can fail to perform in a socially efficient fashion. You will see that imperfectly competitive market structures—monopoly, monopolistic competition, and oligopoly—are never expected to achieve social economic efficiency because these market structures always lead to allocative inefficiency and, in some instances, may also fail to accomplish efficient production. The prospect that social economic efficiency can be reached through perfect competition is so compelling it serves as the foundation for antitrust policy in the United States, as well as competition policy in Canada, the European Union, and elsewhere around the world.

Efficiency Conditions for Society

productive efficiency
Industry output is produced at lowest possible total cost to society.

As stated above, two efficiency conditions must be met to avoid waste and thus ensure that society enjoys the greatest gain possible from its limited resources. Markets must operate with **productive efficiency** so that society gets the most output from its resources. Productive efficiency exists when suppliers produce goods and services at the lowest possible total cost to society. Should markets fail to achieve productive efficiency for any reason, then resources will be wasted, diminishing the amounts of goods and services that can be produced in every industry. Recall from our discussion in Chapter 9 that managers produce at the lowest possible total cost by choosing the combination of inputs on the firm's expansion path. Thus productive efficiency happens whenever managers operate along their firms' expansion paths in both the short-run and long-run periods.

allocative efficiency
Optimal levels of all goods are produced and sold to consumers who value them most.

Allocative efficiency, the second condition needed for social economic efficiency, requires businesses to supply the optimal amounts of all goods and services demanded by society, *and* these units must be rationed to individuals who place the highest value on consuming them. Because productive resources are scarce, the resources must be allocated to various industries in just the right amounts, otherwise too much or too little output gets produced. The optimal level of output is reached when the marginal benefit of another unit to consumers just equals the marginal cost to society of producing another unit. As you learned in Chapter 5, the price on the market demand gives the marginal benefit buyers place on consuming that extra unit of the good. Thus allocative efficiency requires production up to the point where the maximum price consumers are willing to pay for the last unit produced just equals its marginal cost of production. Because this is the point on demand where $P = MC$, economists frequently refer to this condition for efficiency as **marginal-cost-pricing**.

marginal-cost-pricing
Condition for allocative efficiency that price equals marginal cost.

Let's consider an example now. Suppose a market currently operates at the point on market demand where price is $100. At this output level, the value or marginal benefit of the last unit consumed is $100. At this output, suppose suppliers only need $60 worth of resources to make this last unit. Using the logic of marginal analysis, you can see that the current output level is too *little*, because an additional unit of output would add more total value ($MB = \$100$) than it adds to total cost ($MC = \$60$), thereby generating a net increase of $40 in social well-being. Now suppose that the market is operating at an output level for which consumers value the last unit at $35 and producers use $55 worth of scarce resources to make it. Now, too *much* output is produced, because it is inefficient to use $55 of resources to produce a good worth only $35 to consumers. Thus the optimal level of output is the unit for which demand price equals marginal cost.

Once society's scarce productive resources are allocated efficiently among competing industries, the resulting output must then be rationed or distributed to the individuals in society who get the most value from consuming them. This is exactly what happens when buyers engage in voluntary market exchange. At the current market price, consumers whose demand prices (i.e., marginal valuations) equal or exceed market price will choose to buy the good. Consumers whose valuations are less than the current price will not buy any of the good, leaving more for those who value consumption of the good more highly. This process by which prices serve to ration goods to their highest-valued users through voluntary exchange is generally referred to as the **rationing function of prices**. We now summarize the conditions required for social economic efficiency in a principle.

rationing function of prices
Process by which prices serve to ration goods to their highest-valued users through voluntary exchange.

Principle Social economic efficiency occurs when two efficiency conditions are met: (1) industry output is produced at the lowest possible total cost to society (productive efficiency), and (2) every industry produces the socially optimal amount of a good or service and these units are rationed or distributed to the individuals in society who value them most (allocative efficiency).

Social Economic Efficiency Under Perfect Competition

Now we will show you that markets in perfectly competitive equilibrium achieve both productive and allocative efficiency. In the next section of this chapter, however, we will present a number of important circumstances that can undermine the social efficiency of competitive markets.

FIGURE 16.1

Efficiency in Perfect Competition

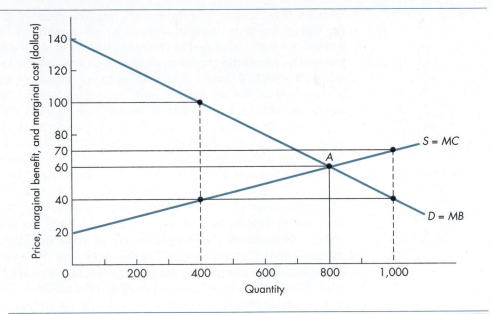

Figure 16.1 shows demand and supply curves for a perfectly competitive industry. These demand and supply curves are taken from Figure 2.11. Supply curve *S* represents either short-run or long-run industry supply. In competitive equilibrium, 800 units are bought and sold at the market-clearing price of $60 per unit (point *A*). We will now explain why the competitive equilibrium at point *A* is both productively efficient and allocatively efficient.

Productive efficiency under perfect competition As we explained, productive efficiency occurs when firms operate on their expansion paths, because input combinations on expansion paths—both short-run and long-run expansion paths—minimize the total cost of producing any particular level of output. Probably the most compelling reason to believe managers will actually operate on their expansion paths is rather simple, yet powerful: Economic profit cannot be maximized unless total cost is minimized *for the profit-maximizing output level.* Managers wishing to maximize profit and the value of their firms must operate on their expansion paths. This reasoning applies in both short- and long-run periods of production. In contrast to the short run, however, firms that fail to produce efficiently in the long run must exit the industry. These inefficient firms suffer losses at the long-run competitive equilibrium price—minimum long-run average cost—and will be forced either to produce efficiently or exit. As a further benefit of productive efficiency, consumers pay the lowest price possible for the good.

At point *A* in Figure 16.1, each firm in the industry produces its portion of total industry output by using the combination of inputs that minimizes its total cost of production. If S is a short-run industry supply curve, then the firms in the industry may earn positive, negative, or zero profit at the market price, $60. Alternatively, if S represents a long-run industry supply curve, then all firms earn zero economic profit and produce at their minimum average costs, $60. In either case, 800 units cannot be supplied at a lower total cost because all suppliers are producing on their expansion paths.

Allocative efficiency under perfect competition Recall that demand prices along a market demand curve are exactly equal to the marginal benefits buyers receive by consuming another unit of a good. For this reason, market demand, D, in Figure 16.1 is also labeled "MB." In Chapter 11, you learned that supply prices along both short-run and long-run industry supply curves equal the industry's marginal cost of producing additional units of output. Thus industry supply S is also labeled "MC."

Let's suppose the industry produces 400 units of output. At this level of output, buyers place a value of $100 on getting an additional unit to consume, while sellers require $40 worth of extra variable inputs to produce an additional unit. Since MB (= $100) exceeds MC (= $40), the 400th unit should be produced because it adds $60 to net benefit. This reasoning applies to every unit up to 800 units. Any output beyond 800 units, however, is too much output because MC exceeds MB beyond 800 units. For example, at 1,000 units, variable inputs worth $70 are used to produce the 1,000th unit of output, but the extra good is only worth $40 to consumers. Clearly, production and consumption beyond 800 units is inefficient.

Allocative efficiency in a perfectly competitive industry must occur at the equilibrium output level determined by the intersection of demand and supply. At the point of competitive equilibrium, demand price (MB) equals supply price (MC). In Figure 16.1, you can verify that the marginal benefit of the 800th unit is $60, which equals the marginal cost of the 800th unit. Competitive equilibrium always establishes the optimal level of output for society, as long as the demand curve correctly and fully measures marginal benefits of consumption and the supply curve correctly and fully measures marginal costs of production. As we will show you later in this chapter, demand and supply curves may not always correctly measure marginal benefits and costs. When this happens, competitive markets may produce either too much or too little output.

Finally, notice that the equilibrium price, $60, successfully rations 800 units of output to the consumers who value these goods most. Consumers with relatively low values, represented by the segment of demand below point A, do not voluntarily pay $60 to purchase output beyond the 800th unit because these units are worth less to them than the market price. These potential buyers *voluntarily* choose not to consume the good, leaving the 800 units for those buyers who place a value on the good of at least $60. Thus perfectly competitive markets achieve allocative efficiency because the optimal amount of the good is produced, and this amount is rationed or allocated to the highest-valued users.

Social economic efficiency and maximization of social surplus Chapter 2 introduced the concepts of consumer surplus and producer surplus, and defined social surplus as the sum of consumer and producer surpluses. We now wish to demonstrate that social surplus is maximized in competitive equilibrium. Consider again the 400th unit of output in Figure 16.1. The marginal value of this unit is $100. The buyer who purchases the 400th unit must pay the market price of $60 to get it, and so enjoys consumer surplus on this unit equal to $40 (= $100 − $60). The producer who supplies the 400th unit is willing to do so for a price as low as $40. The supplier of the 400th unit gains producer surplus equal to $20 (= $60 − $40). (Recall that the $20 producer surplus is economic rent if S in the figure represents long-run industry supply.) Thus, the consumption and production of the 400th unit generates $60 of net gain for society. By this reasoning, every unit for which demand price exceeds supply price contributes positively to society's total surplus. As you can see from the figure, production and consumption of all units between 0 and 800 must be undertaken to maximize social surplus.

For consumption and production levels greater than competitive equilibrium— beyond point A in the figure—social surplus will be smaller than at point A. Consider the 1,000th unit, for which demand price, $40, is less than supply price, $70. As we have previously explained, production and consumption of this unit are inefficient because $70 worth of scarce resources is transformed through production into a good worth only $40. Obviously, this would be wasteful for society. Fortunately, there is no price for this good that would stimulate buyers and sellers voluntarily to make such a wasteful transaction. Therefore, competitive market forces lead to the exact level of consumption and production that maximizes social surplus, and hence maximizes the value of this free market to society.

We must emphasize that, while competition maximizes social surplus, this does not imply that either consumer or producer surplus is maximized individually—it is the sum of the two that is maximized. Moving away from competitive equilibrium (point A) can result in one kind of surplus rising while the other surplus falls, but it must always reduce *total* social surplus. We can now summarize the results of this section in a principle.

Now try Technical Problems 1–3.

> **Principle** Markets in perfectly competitive equilibrium achieve social economic efficiency because, at the intersection of demand and supply curves, conditions for both productive efficiency and allocative efficiency are met. At the competitive market-clearing price, buyers and sellers engage in voluntary exchange that maximizes social surplus.

16.2 MARKET FAILURE AND THE CASE FOR GOVERNMENT INTERVENTION

Competitive markets can do a number of desirable things for society. Under perfect competition, producers supply the right amount of goods and services, charge the right price, and the right consumers get the goods produced. The "right" amount to produce is the allocatively efficient amount. All units of output are produced for which consumers value those units by more than society values the resources required to produce them. No units are produced that cost more to supply than they are worth to buyers. Competitive suppliers cannot control the price of the product, because there are many producers and the products they sell are virtually identical. Consequently, prices in competitive markets are determined by the impersonal forces of market demand and supply. In the long run, consumers get the very lowest price possible, consistent with firms remaining financially viable because market forces drive prices down to minimum long-run average cost. Even in the short run, however, market prices are determined by the cost structure of firms that operate on their short-run expansion paths, so costs are minimized given the fixed amount of productive capacity in the short run. Finally, voluntary exchange at the market-determined price insures that industry output is purchased by the consumers who place the highest value on consuming the goods and services.

market failure
When a market fails to reach an equilibrium that achieves social economic efficiency and thus fails to maximize social surplus.

Unfortunately, not all markets are competitive, and even competitive markets can sometimes fail to achieve maximum social surplus. **Market failure** occurs when a market fails to achieve social economic efficiency and, consequently, fails to maximize social surplus. The causes of market failure can stem from either productive or allocative shortcomings, or both. Six forms of market failure can undermine economic efficiency: Market power, natural monopoly, negative (and positive) externalities, common property resources, public goods, and information problems. We will briefly explore each of these market failures in this chapter and offer a short discussion of some of the most important policies government can adopt to improve matters.

In the absence of market failure, no efficiency argument can be made for government intervention in competitive markets. As long as competitive equilibrium works to maximize social surplus, any government intervention that moves the market away from competitive equilibrium will reduce social surplus. However, when market failure does create inefficiency, government intervention in the market can, at least theoretically, improve market performance. This motivation for government intervention to overcome market failure and increase social surplus supplies a *public interest rationale* for policymakers to justify government regulation of industry. Most politicians understand that "fixing a market failure" provides a politically attractive reason for intervening in the marketplace. For this reason, politicians frequently dress up their pet projects as solutions to "market failures"— real or imaginary.

government failure
Government intervention that reduces social surplus.

Market failure creates an important and genuine opportunity for government to improve market performance in ways that will add to social surplus. As history demonstrates more often than we wish, even the best-designed government policies fail to be effectively and successfully implemented. The reasons for **government failure**—government intervention that reduces social surplus— are not difficult to understand. The politics of special interest groups frequently generates government rules and regulations designed to promote the welfare of one group at the expense of the rest of society. And even the best intentions cannot guarantee successful implementation of policies because bureaucrats face challenges of their own. Government bureaucrats' best efforts can be partially

664 CHAPTER 16 Government Regulation of Business

thwarted or entirely compromised by incomplete or obsolete information about the industries they regulate. For example, the Environmental Protection Agency (EPA) cannot effectively regulate pollution emissions unless it knows and understands both the technology of producing goods and the technology of pollution control for dozens of pollutants and thousands of industries. Grappling with such an enormous amount of information and knowledge, which is constantly changing, makes it impossible for regulatory agents to always set pollution standards at the optimal level and perfectly enforce these standards. Of course, we should remind you that perfection is not usually optimal. Expecting zero episodes of government failure is not only unrealistic, but it is also not optimal since avoiding every instance of government failure would itself impose huge costs on society.

Many bureaucrats labor with little incentive to do the best job possible. Government agencies that implement cost-saving measures may find their budgets cut by Congress in the following fiscal year. In spite of the limitations facing government agents who administer and enforce government regulatory and antitrust policies, the pursuit of solutions to market failure problems constitutes one of the most valuable roles for government to play in any society. Business leaders who understand the strengths and weaknesses of various government policy options can play especially important roles in shaping rules and regulations under which their firms must operate. We will now examine the nature of market failure and discuss some of the more important and effective ways government can attempt to make markets generate greater social surplus.

16.3 MARKET POWER AND PUBLIC POLICY

The achievement of productive and allocative efficiency in perfectly competitive markets ensures that the market-determined prices and quantities will maximize social surplus. However, only perfectly competitive markets can meet the necessary condition for allocative efficiency—marginal-cost-pricing. As we have demonstrated in previous chapters, price will always exceed marginal cost under monopoly, monopolistic competition, and oligopoly, that is, under imperfect competition. The reason allocative efficiency is lost under imperfect competition can be directly attributed to the market power that all imperfectly competitive firms possess. Market power always leads to allocative inefficiency and lost social surplus. In this section, we will show you why market power reduces social surplus. We will also examine monopoly markets and briefly discuss the role of antitrust policy in promoting competition.

Market Power and Allocative Inefficiency

market power
Ability to raise price without losing all sales; possessed only by price-setting firms.

In Chapter 12 you learned that **market power** is something that competitive firms don't have—the power to raise product price without losing all sales. Firms with market power, however, do not sell standardized commodities in competition with many other firms. Firms with market power can set prices anywhere they wish along their downward-sloping demand curves. The value, of course, of possessing market power comes from the opportunity to raise price above costs and earn economic profit, something competitive firms cannot do. As explained in Chapter 12, all imperfect competitors possess some degree of market power. The problem with market power, from society's point of view, is the loss of allocative efficiency that comes about when imperfectly competitive firms set their prices to maximize profits.

For all firms with market power (not just pure monopolies), the marginal revenue curve lies below the firm's demand curve. For this reason, prices charged by firms with market power always exceed marginal revenue: $P > MR$. Since profit maximization requires producing at the output level for which $MR = MC$, it follows directly that firms with market power must price above marginal cost ($P > MC$) to maximize profit. As a consequence, all firms possessing market power fail to achieve allocative efficiency, and thus market power diminishes social surplus.

Any degree of market power reduces social surplus, but a high degree of market power may do so much damage to social surplus that a government remedy is warranted. When the degree of market power grows high enough, antitrust officials refer to it legally as **"monopoly power."** No clear legal threshold has been established by antitrust authorities to determine when "market power" crosses the line to become "monopoly power." Nevertheless, antitrust agencies aggressively seek to prevent firms from acquiring monopoly power and can severely punish firms that acquire or maintain monopoly power in illegal ways. Before we discuss antitrust policy toward monopoly practices, we must present the case against monopoly.

monopoly power
A poorly defined legal term used in antitrust law to refer to a high degree of market power.

Market Power and Deadweight Loss

The best way to understand the problem caused by market power is to compare an industry under two different equilibrium situations: perfect competition and pure monopoly. We will do this using the Louisiana white shrimp industry as our example. Initially, let's suppose the industry is perfectly competitive. Figure 16.2 shows market demand and supply conditions in the market for Louisiana white shrimp. Industry demand, D, is downward sloping and, as you know from Chapter 5, D also measures the marginal benefit to shrimp consumers. The long-run competitive industry supply curve for Louisiana shrimp, S_{LR}, is horizontal because the shrimp industry is a constant-cost industry. The flat supply curve indicates that long-run marginal and average costs are constant and equal to $100 per 10-pound basket ($LMC = LAC = \$100$).

The competitive, market-clearing price for 10-pound baskets of shrimp is $100, and the market quantity is 20,000 baskets per month. The competitive equilibrium at point C generates social surplus each month equal to $2 million (= $0.5 \times 20{,}000 \times \$200$). No greater amount of social surplus can be generated than under perfect competition at point C.

Now suppose that a consortium of investors form a company called Shrimp Depot, and they buy every one of the Louisiana shrimp suppliers, transforming the industry into a pure monopoly. As we will explain shortly, antitrust laws in the United States would certainly prevent such a consolidation, but let's compare the

FIGURE 16.2

The Louisiana White Shrimp Market

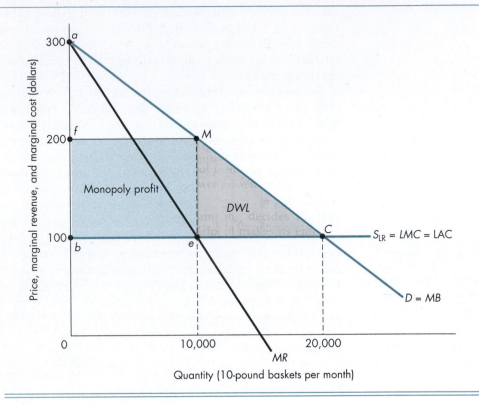

monopoly equilibrium (point *M*) to the competitive equilibrium (point *C*) anyway. Once Shrimp Depot owns all of the productive capacity, the competitive industry supply curve, S_{LR}, now represents the long-run marginal cost and average cost curve for the monopoly shrimp firm. Shrimp Depot possesses market power and finds its profit-maximizing production level by setting marginal revenue (*MR*) equal to marginal cost (*LMC*). As you can see in Figure 16.2, Shrimp Depot maximizes profit by producing 10,000 baskets of shrimp per month and charging a monopoly price of $200 per 10-pound basket.

Under monopoly, consumer surplus shrinks by $1.5 million, which is the area *fbCM*. A portion of this lost consumer surplus—the area of the red-shaded rectangle *fbeM* (= $1 million)—is transformed into producer surplus or monopoly profit in this example. Shrimp Depot makes $100 (= $P - LAC$ = $200 − $100) profit on each one of the 10,000 baskets of shrimp it sells, which amounts to $1 million of economic profit.

Allocative efficiency is lost under monopoly pricing since monopolists—and any other firm with market power—do not practice marginal-cost-pricing. At point *M*, the marginal benefit of the 10,000th basket of shrimp is $200, which exceeds its marginal cost of production, just $100. Because price exceeds marginal cost,

deadweight loss
Social surplus lost on units not produced when price diverges from marginal cost.

resources are underallocated to the shrimp industry, and too little (shrimp) is produced. As a result of this allocative inefficiency, social surplus falls by the amount of the gray-shaded triangle *eCM*. This lost surplus, which equals \$0.5 million ($= 0.5 \times 10,000 \times \$100$), is called **deadweight loss**, because the entire surplus lost on units not produced represents a complete loss of surplus to society. We must stress that deadweight loss, which is attributable to the lack of marginal-cost-pricing, arises not only in monopoly markets but also in markets with any degree of market power.

Promoting Competition through Antitrust Policy

To reduce the cost of market failure caused by market power, most industrialized nations rely on antitrust laws, as they are known in the United States. Canada and the European Union countries refer to their antitrust policies as *competition policies*. Because the purposes are quite similar, we will focus our rather brief discussion in this textbook on antitrust policy and enforcement in the United States. Antitrust laws seek to prohibit business practices and actions that reduce or restrain competition, based on the fundamental acceptance of competition as a powerful force for achieving large social surpluses and protecting consumers and competitors from firms with substantial market power. We can only take a brief look here at this fascinating area of law and policy. To gain an understanding of the theory and practice of antitrust policy, you must take at least one course in antitrust law.

Monopoly power, or a high degree of market power, can arise primarily in three ways: (1) actual or attempted monopolization, (2) price-fixing cartels, and (3) mergers among horizontal competitors. As you know from our discussion of limit pricing in Chapter 13, firms may engage in behavior designed specifically for the purpose of driving out existing rivals or deterring the entry of new rivals, thereby reducing competition, perhaps to the point of gaining a monopoly position. Firms may be found guilty of *actual* monopolization only if *both* of the following conditions are met: (1) the behavior is judged to be undertaken solely for the purpose of creating monopoly power, and (2) the firm successfully achieves a high degree of market power. Businesses can also be guilty of *attempted* monopolization if they engage in conduct intended to create a monopoly and there is a "dangerous probability of success."

When businesses are unable to drive out their rivals, or choose not to do so for fear of antitrust penalties, they may instead seek to reduce competition by colluding to raise prices. Recall that we discussed the nature of collusion and cartels in Chapter 13. Collusive price-setting is absolutely forbidden, and guilty parties incur substantial financial penalties and even jail time. Nonetheless, the enormous profit potential from successful price-fixing continues to attract plenty of practitioners. Fortunately, as we explained in Chapter 13, cooperation among rival firms can be very difficult to establish and maintain. Antitrust enforcement agents at the Department of Justice make no secret about their willingness to grant clemency from prosecution to the first cartel member to expose and plead guilty to a price-fixing deal. The prisoners' dilemma really works!

Horizontal merger policy represents the third important area of antitrust doctrine designed to prevent monopoly power from arising through the process of merger or acquisition of direct rival firms. Horizontal mergers or acquisitions happen when two or more firms that are head-to-head competitors—selling the same product in the same geographic markets—decide to join operations into a single firm. Such mergers can obviously lead to an increase in market power, although many horizontal mergers are too small to damage competition. Horizontal mergers can have beneficial effects on social surplus when the merged firm enjoys substantial economies of scale that could not be realized by separate production operations. Of course, consumers only benefit directly from such scale economies if the merged firm passes the cost saving along through reduced prices. Antitrust agencies require firms planning large mergers to notify antitrust authorities of their intentions prior to merging. Antitrust officials typically have 90 days after notification to study a proposed merger and to let the prospective merging firms know whether antitrust agencies intend to challenge the merger or to approve it. In most cases, businesses will abandon a merger if antitrust agencies plan to challenge the merger in court.

Antitrust policy and enforcement in the United States is the responsibility of the Department of Justice (DOJ) and the Federal Trade Commission (FTC).[1] While the language of the law itself is not particularly complex, the legal application can be tremendously complicated. Antitrust litigation can also impose heavy costs on businesses, whether they are defendants or plaintiffs. In 1993, American Airlines reportedly spent $25 million defending itself in a predatory pricing trial that took the jury less than one hour to decide the airline was *not* guilty.

Before leaving our examination of monopoly, we must consider a special kind of monopoly, called *natural monopoly*, which would be harmful to break up through the application of antitrust laws. We explain in the following section that natural monopoly arises when one firm can produce the amount of goods desired by society at a lower total cost than having two or more firms share in the production of industry output. As it turns out, antitrust remedies to break up a natural monopoly would increase total costs and create productive inefficiency. Natural monopoly requires other methods of government regulation to reach an efficient outcome that maximizes social surplus.

Natural Monopoly and Market Failure

natural monopoly
One firm can produce the entire industry output at lower total cost than can two or more firms.

Sometimes monopoly can have desirable consequences for society. One such occasion arises when a single firm can produce the total consumer demand for a product or service at a lower long-run total cost than if two or more firms produce the total industry output. This situation is called **natural monopoly**, and it causes market failure. In natural monopoly, productive efficiency requires a single monopoly

---

[1]Each of these agencies has its own website designed to inform and educate the public about antitrust law. See, for example, "Promoting Competition, Protecting Consumers: A Plain English Guide to Antitrust Laws" on the FTC website: www.ftc.gov.

producer, which, as you now know, results in allocative inefficiency and dead-weight loss to society. Many public utilities, such as electricity, water, natural gas, local telephone, and cable television, are commonly thought to be natural monopolies. If two or more local phone companies serve a community, then each phone company must string its own set of telephone wires. By having a single phone company, the community must pay for just one set of telephone lines. The same logic has been applied to other municipal services that require costly distribution infrastructure. One way to avoid the needless duplication of distribution lines is to give one company a monopoly franchise in return for the right to let public regulators set the price of service. We will examine some of the complexities of regulating price under natural monopoly shortly. First, we must explain more carefully the conditions on long-run cost that lead to natural monopoly.

subadditive
Costs are subadditive at $\overline{Q}$ if any division of this output among two or more firms is more costly than letting one firm produce it all. Natural monopoly means costs are subadditive.

Natural monopoly is another way of saying that long-run costs are *subadditive* at the level of output demanded by consumers. Long-run costs are **subadditive** at a particular output level $\overline{Q}$ if any division of $\overline{Q}$ among two or more firms is more costly than letting a monopoly produce all $\overline{Q}$ units. Thus the terms "natural monopoly" and "subadditive costs" mean exactly the same thing. One way for natural monopoly to develop is for long-run average cost to fall continuously, so that economies of scale extend to all output levels. With continuous economies of scale, cost subadditivity and natural monopoly exist at all levels of output. This can happen for public utilities when large quasi-fixed costs of distribution lines (pipelines, telephone lines, fiber-optic cable, electricity power lines, water lines, and sewage lines) are spread over more units of output.[2]

Figure 16.3 illustrates the nature of cost subadditivity for a water utility in a small town. The water plant and underground distribution lines cost $12 million and are quasi-fixed inputs because they are employed in a fixed amount for any positive level of output (recall the discussion of quasi-fixed inputs in Chapter 8). Municipal bonds are sold to pay for these inputs, and the debt payment on the bonds is $60,000 per month. The average quasi-fixed cost for the water plant and distribution lines, *AQFC*, declines continuously, as shown in Figure 16.3. (Note that water consumption is measured in 1,000-gallon units of consumption.) The long-run marginal cost of water is constant and equal to $2.50 per 1,000-gallon unit. Thus *LMC* is a flat line in Figure 16.3 equal to $2.50 for all output levels. Long-run average cost, *LAC*, is the sum of *AQFC* and *LMC*. *LAC* declines continuously as the $60,000 quasi-fixed cost is spread over more units of output, and *LAC* approaches *LMC* as water consumption gets very large. You can verify that costs are subadditive in this example by comparing the total cost if one firm produces 40,000 units, which is $160,000 (= $4 × 40,000), to the total cost if two equal-size

---

[2]Cost subadditivity also arises when long-run average cost is ∪-shaped. However, the range of output over which costs are subadditive for ∪-shaped *LAC* curves does not extend to all output levels, but rather subadditivity extends continuously from the first unit of output to some output beyond the minimum point on *LAC*. Thus with ∪-shaped *LAC*, the range of natural monopoly extends into, but never throughout, the region of diseconomies of scale.

FIGURE 16.3

Subaddtive Costs and Natural Monopoly

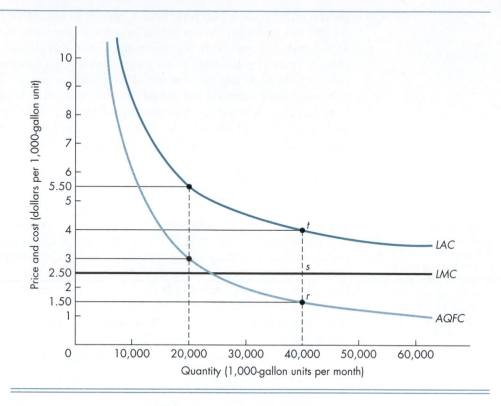

firms produce 20,000 units *each* to reach 40,000 units, which is $220,000 [= ($5.50 × 20,000) + ($5.50 × 20,000)]. When 40,000 units per month are demanded, monopoly water service saves the community $60,000 per month. With a monopoly water utility, the community pays for just one water plant and distribution network. With two water utilities, the community must pay for two water plants and two distribution networks. Incurring the quasi-fixed capital cost one time, instead of two or more times, and then spreading the cost over all of market demand creates large cost savings, and a natural monopoly arises.

Now try Technical Problem 5.

Regulating Price Under Natural Monopoly

When costs are subadditive at the level of output demanded by society, a monopoly produces the desired output at the lowest-possible total cost to society. A monopolist, however, maximizes profit by pricing above both marginal and average cost. Under monopoly, as we explained previously, consumers not only get too little output, they also can end up paying more than average cost for each unit purchased. Breaking up a natural monopoly is undesirable because increasing the number of firms in the industry drives up total cost and undermines productive efficiency. State regulators of public utilities—known as "public utility commissions" (PUCs) or "public service commissions" (PSCs)—face a challenging task in

FIGURE 16.4

Regulating Price Under Natural Monopoly

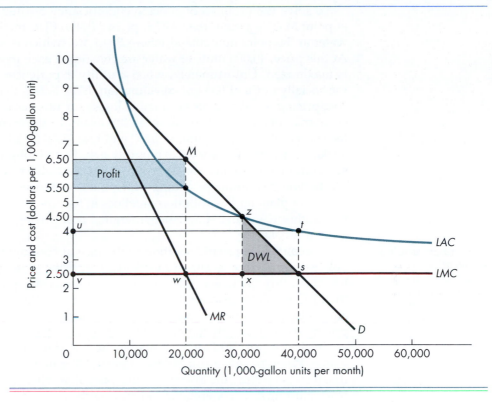

regulating the price that natural monopolies can charge. Regulators would like to force a pricing structure on natural monopolies that creates social economic efficiency. Under natural monopoly, as we will now show you, no one price can establish social economic efficiency.

We can best explain the pricing dilemma facing regulators by returning to the previous example of the water utility. Figure 16.4 reproduces the long-run average and marginal cost curves facing the water utility. Recall that *LAC* falls continuously as the quasi-fixed cost is spread over more units of water output. Clearly, then, regulators wish to maintain a monopoly in water service to fully exploit the cost subadditivity that extends over the entire range of water production, because economies of scale exist at all levels of output in this case. The city's demand for water and corresponding marginal revenue are shown in Figure 16.4 as *D* and *MR*, respectively. While utility regulators do not wish to encourage (or force) competition by increasing the number of water utilities, they also recognize that if the monopoly water utility is unregulated, it will operate at point *M* on demand, which maximizes the water utility's profit. When water price is $6.50 per 1,000-gallon unit, only 20,000 units are demanded, and the city faces a deadweight loss due to monopoly of $40,000, which is the area of the (unshaded) triangle *Mws* (= 0.5 × 20,000 × $4). At point *M*, the unregulated monopolist's economic profit is $20,000 per month [= 20,000 × ($6.50 − $5.50)].

To solve the problem of allocative inefficiency created by monopoly pricing at point M (P is greater than MC at point M), the PUC might set the legal price of water at the point on demand where $P = LMC$, which is $2.50 per unit (point s). At this price, 40,000 units of water are consumed each month and social surplus is maximized. Unfortunately, when a utility experiences economies of scale at the socially optimal level of consumption, LMC is less than LAC, and marginal-cost-pricing always creates economic losses for utilities operating in a region of economies of scale. As you can see in this example, the owners of the water utility face unit costs of $4 per unit (point t) and lose $1.50 (= $4 − $2.50) on each of the 40,000 units, creating a $60,000 monthly loss. Even though marginal-cost-pricing succeeds in maximizing social surplus, it is not a viable pricing scheme because no utility would continue providing water at a loss. Indeed, investors will not build the water plant and distribution pipelines in the first place if they believe regulatory authorities plan to implement marginal-cost-pricing in the face of continuous economies of scale.

second-best pricing
Setting price as close as possible to marginal cost, but just high enough to insure zero economic profit.

A **second-best pricing** solution in the face of continuously declining LAC involves setting price as close to marginal cost as possible, yet high enough to allow the utility to break even by earning zero economic profit. With this method, the PUC regulates price at the level that minimizes the loss of social surplus but allows investors to earn a normal rate of return. As it turns out, the second-best pricing solution simply requires setting price equal to LAC. In this example, $4.50 is the closest price to LMC that allows the water utility to remain economically viable. When paying a price of $4.50 per 1,000-gallon unit, buyers can be happy that they are paying the lowest possible price that will keep water-utility investors from shutting down operations and moving their capital to its best alternative use. The problem with average-cost pricing is that price exceeds marginal cost, resulting in a deadweight loss of $10,000 (= 0.5 × 10,000 × $2)—the area of the gray-shaded triangle zxs in Figure 16.4.

two-part pricing
Utility customers pay an access charge plus a usage fee for each unit purchased.

As long as economies of scale extend over the entire range of demand for utility services, no single, uniform pricing of output can achieve social efficiency and create financially viable firms. A pricing solution does exist that can satisfy social efficiency conditions and maximize social surplus: *two-part pricing* of utility services. A **two-part pricing** plan charges utility customers a fixed access charge plus a usage fee based on the number of units purchased. By wisely setting the access charge and usage fee, regulatory authorities can solve the utility pricing dilemma. The solution is to set the usage fee equal to marginal cost and set the access charge to spread the loss caused by marginal-cost-pricing across all utility customers. The total monthly water bill for Q units of water is computed as follows:

$$\text{Total bill for } Q \text{ units} = LMC \times Q + \frac{L}{N}$$

where L is the total loss generated by marginal-cost-pricing, and N is the number of households served by the utility. In this example, suppose the water utility in Figure 16.4 serves 4,000 households. The ideal two-part pricing plan is to set the usage fee at $2.50 per 1,000-gallon unit of water consumed and to set the monthly access charge for each household at $15 (= $60,000/4,000). The total monthly water bill for Q units of water is computed as follows:

$$\text{Total water bill for } Q \text{ units} = 2.50 \times Q + \frac{\$60,000}{4,000}$$
$$= 2.50Q + 15$$

Under this pricing plan, a household using 12,000 gallons of water per month ($Q = 12$) pays $45 (= $2.50 \times 12 + $15) per month for water. Notice that the allocatively efficient amount of water is consumed (40,000 units per month), and productive efficiency is achieved because economies of scale are fully exploited by letting one firm produce the entire industry demand.

We should not leave you with the impression that regulating natural monopoly is an easy matter. Many difficulties arise, and the brief treatment here serves only to introduce the fundamental nature of the problem. In a full course on regulation of natural monopoly, you will gain a more complete understanding of the financial complexities of rate-of-return regulation (a widely used average-cost-pricing practice), multiproduct cost subadditivity that can arise for multiproduct utilities, and incentive-compatible regulations designed to motivate utilities to invest in cost-saving technologies. Many economists have made lucrative careers for themselves by specializing in public utility regulation practices. Both utilities and regulatory agencies hire these experts.

Now try Technical Problem 6.

16.4 THE PROBLEM OF NEGATIVE EXTERNALITY

positive (negative) externalities
Occur when the actions of buyers or sellers create spillover or external benefits (costs) that spill over to other members of society.

Another important cause of market failure in competitive markets arises when the actions taken by market participants create either benefits or costs that spill over to other members of society. When these spillover effects are beneficial to society, economists call them **positive externalities.** Flu vaccination provides an example of a spillover or external benefit creating a positive externality. When one person at the office chooses to get a flu vaccine, everyone who works with that person benefits from a reduced probability of catching the flu at work. Alternatively, when spillover effects are costly to society, economists call them **negative externalities.** Pollution is a particularly important example of negative externality. If an upstream business chooses to dump polluted wastewater into a nearby river, parties downstream who use the river for recreational or productive purposes— swimmers, boaters, and fishing companies, for example—will bear the spillover or external cost of this pollution through reduced enjoyment and productivity of the river.

External or spillover benefits and costs undermine allocative efficiency because market participants, when making consumption and production decisions, rationally choose to ignore the benefits and costs of their actions that spill over to other parties. Consequently, competitive market prices do not include the social benefits or costs that spill over to other members of society. As you learned earlier in this chapter, equilibrium price must equal both marginal social benefit and marginal social cost to provide buyers and sellers with the correct incentive to make allocatively efficient decisions. In competitive markets experiencing either positive or negative externalities, the equilibrium price sends the wrong signal to buyers and sellers, causing them to consume and produce either too much or too little output. Since the wrong amount of output is produced, both types of externality create a deadweight loss reflecting the lost social surplus of allocative inefficiency. For many businesses, the externality of greatest consequence for their profits is the negative externality created by pollution since government environmental agencies usually attempt to impose remedies on business polluters. Thus we focus our analysis here on pollution generated by businesses in the process of making goods and services for society.

As we stated previously, managers rationally ignore spillover or external costs when making their profit-maximizing production decisions. Profit maximization only concerns *private costs* of production, that is, costs incurred by firm owners to use productive resources. Because external costs do not affect profits, managers will likely ignore these costs that spill over to others in society. External costs, nonetheless, are real costs borne by society for the production of goods and services. The social cost of production is the sum of the private cost incurred by producers and any external or spillover cost imposed on other members of society

$$\text{Social cost} = \text{Private cost} + \text{External cost}$$

Economists sometimes say that a negative externality drives a "wedge" between social and private costs of production

$$\text{Social cost} - \text{Private cost} = \text{External cost}$$

The larger the external costs of a negative externality, the greater the difference between social and private costs of production, and the greater will be the resulting deadweight loss.

Figure 16.5 shows why the "wedge" of negative externality makes allocative efficiency impossible to achieve in competitive markets. The demand curve for the competitively supplied good correctly measures the marginal social benefit of the good: $D = MSB$. The marginal private costs of production are given by the competitive supply curve: $S = MPC$. Competitive market equilibrium is established at the intersection of demand and supply (point C), where Q_C units are produced and consumed at price P_C. Production of this good by competitive suppliers creates an external cost that spills over to society. The marginal external cost, shown as MEC in Figure 16.5, increases with the level of output. At every output level, the marginal social cost curve is the vertical sum of the marginal private cost and marginal external cost: $MSC = MPC + MEC$. As you can see, in competitive equilibrium, too much output is produced because MSC exceeds MSB at point C. Allocative efficiency occurs at Q_E (point E), where MSC equals MSB. By producing the units from Q_E to Q_C, the competitive industry creates a deadweight loss on each unit that costs more to produce than it is worth to society. The area of the gray-shaded triangle DWL

FIGURE 16.5

**Negative Externality and
Allocative Inefficiency**

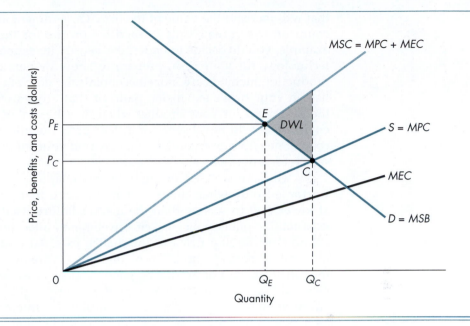

is the amount by which social surplus is reduced by overproducing and over-
consuming the good.

Perhaps you are now thinking that a "good" manager *should* consider all external costs that spill over to society to "do good for society." The issue of "doing
good for society" often surfaces in class discussions when we analyze the loss of
social surplus caused by pollution. As we will examine pollution externality in the
next section, perhaps now is a good time to stress how little economists have to
say about "doing good." As you know from your course in business ethics, any
debate about how managers should handle spillover costs to society raises complicated subjective and ethical issues concerning the appropriate level of social responsibility of business enterprises. Although ethical issues fall outside the realm
of objective (positive) economic analysis, we can offer you two *objective* reasons
to ignore external costs in decision making. First, managers who choose not to
ignore external costs will produce less output than would maximize profit, which,
of course, reduces profits and wealth of the firms' owners. If your firm operates in
a competitive industry, you will be forced to exit in the long run. You can safely
predict that other managers in your industry, wishing to survive in the long run,
will make profit-maximizing decisions.

A second important consideration concerns the possible legal consequences
for you if your shareholders believe your practice of including social costs in
decisions conflicts with your legal responsibilities to protect the value of the
firm. The legal standards that apply to this area of executive responsibility are
not clear, but we advise you, as we have throughout this book, to make decisions

that will increase the value of the firm. Government authorities certainly don't count on individual firms to sacrifice profits for the good of society. If, for example, you do decide to undertake a costly investment in "green" production technology for your firm, prepare to show owners of the firm that "green" production methods are indeed economically efficient (i.e., "green" production lies on your firm's expansion path) or that buyers will substantially increase their demand for your product when they hear about your sensitivity to the environment. In the absence of a clear profit justification for internalizing the costs of negative externalities, you may find yourself in legal trouble—while you search for a new job!

As we have stressed throughout this chapter, government intervention is warranted only when there is market failure that government policy can fix at lower cost to society than the market failure itself. In the case of negative externalities, public policymakers can eliminate allocative inefficiency by devising methods of forcing firms to internalize external costs they would otherwise rationally choose to ignore. Once external costs are internalized, firm owners face the full social cost of producing goods and services, and allocative efficiency is restored. Taxation and assignment of property rights provide two of the most effective methods government can employ for internalizing costs. In the next section, we will show how taxes can be used to restore allocative efficiency in the case of a negative externality caused by pollution. We will also show you how reassigning property rights can restore productive efficiency for common pool resources, which may suffer from negative externality problems. We can now summarize our discussion of negative externality in the following principle.

Now try Technical Problem 7.

> **Principle** A producer creates a negative externality by imposing an external cost on other members of society without making a compensating payment for the harm caused. Negative externality drives a wedge between social and private costs of production, which causes producers in competitive equilibrium to overproduce the good or service. The loss of allocative efficiency due to negative externality creates a deadweight loss to society.

Pollution: Market Failure and Regulation

Let's consider again the example we mentioned previously: An upstream competitive industry chooses to dump polluted wastewater into a nearby river. Parties downstream, who use the river for recreational or productive purposes—swimmers, boaters, and fishing companies, for example—are burdened by the external cost of this pollution through reduced enjoyment and productivity of the river. First we will analyze the market failure of this competitive industry caused by the pollution it creates. Then we will turn our attention to the role government environmental policymakers can play in solving the externality problem. We will show you how environmental economists identify the optimal level of pollution emissions and demonstrate that a properly set charge or tax on emissions can motivate profit-maximizing firms to reduce their pollution levels to the socially optimal level.

FIGURE 16.6

Pollution as a Negative Externality

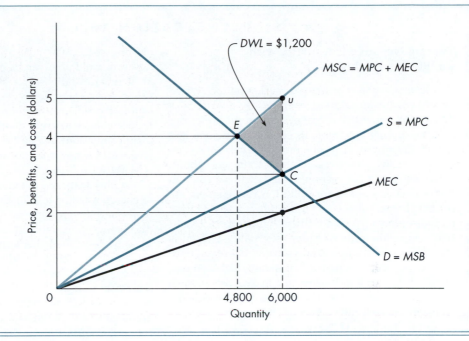

Allocative inefficiency and market failure In Figure 16.6, the marginal external cost (*MEC*) caused by the pollution externality is increasing as industry output rises. *MEC* for the 6,000th unit of output is $2. The marginal private cost (*MPC*) incurred by competitive firms to produce the 6,000th unit is $3. *MPC* represents the competitive industry supply curve, *S*, because suppliers ignore the external cost of pollution. Marginal social cost to produce the 6,000th unit is $5 (= $2 + $3). *MSC* is constructed by repeating the vertical summation at every output level.

As usual the competitive equilibrium price, $3, is found at the intersection of demand and industry supply (point *C* in the figure). Competitive suppliers behave inefficiently, because managers in this market increase production up to the point where price equals marginal *private* cost. Because the marginal *social* cost of the 6,000th unit is $5, industry output in competitive equilibrium exceeds the level that would maximize social surplus. Allocative efficiency happens when the industry produces 4,800 units at point *E* in Figure 16.6. The deadweight loss of social surplus caused by overproduction and overconsumption equals the area of the gray-shaded triangle *ECu*, which is $1,200 (= 0.5 × 1,200 × $2).

Regulators can restore allocative efficiency by taxing producers on their pollution emissions, causing them to internalize the external pollution costs. Environmental policymakers and enforcement authorities have employed numerous taxation methods with varying degrees of success. We will present one

ILLUSTRATION 16.1

Taming Negative Externality with Congestion Pricing

Traffic congestion represents a market failure caused by negative externalities generated by automobiles driving on crowded roadways. Even without congestion, driving a car creates exhaust emissions that pollute the air that everyone must breathe. This negative externality occurs regardless of traffic conditions. However, when congestion arises, each car stuck in traffic creates even more pollution (car engines are running longer) than when traffic flows freely. During periods of the day when traffic is light and no congestion occurs, the only negative externality created is the pollution cost imposed on society. However, once roadways become congested, not only the social cost of pollution rises but the time cost to each driver stuck in traffic rises as well. On a congested highway, each additional driver adds a small additional time cost to every other driver. This external cost on other motorists drives a wedge between private and social costs of using a roadway.

As we explained in our discussion of negative externalities, this spillover cost leads to allocative inefficiency in road use because all drivers ignore the external cost their cars impose on everyone else. Thus, motorists make road use decisions based on *private* costs that understate the true or full *social* cost of using a particular roadway at a particular time of day. If motorists incurred the full social cost of road use, they might choose to drive at a less congested time of day or even give up driving private cars and use public transportation. And, of course, if they also had to bear the full social cost of their auto emissions, they might well choose to drive a cleaner car or use public transportation.

Market failure created by traffic congestion provides an opportunity for government intervention to improve resource usage and social well-being. One way to improve traffic congestion is to build more public roadways and expand the number of lanes on existing roads. The cost of building new roads and expanding old ones can be exceedingly high in urban areas where land is scarce and expensive. (Of course, urban areas are typically the locations where congestion is a problem!) Furthermore, adding concrete to reduce congestion may worsen the problem of automobile emissions as more people will decide to drive when adding new roads or widening old ones reduces congestion.

Another way for government to improve matters is to charge a fee or toll for the privilege of driving on roads, and then to raise this toll to a level that will reduce congestion. Nobel laureate economist William Vickrey developed this approach, commonly called "congestion pricing," in the 1950s. Vickrey believed that charging drivers higher tolls during peak hours and lower tolls at off-peak hours would close the gap between the private and social costs of driving. By raising the toll at rush hour to reflect the higher marginal congestion costs, transportation officials seek to flatten out the "peaks" in demand each day by giving drivers an incentive to switch their time of travel from peak to off-peak periods.[a] This is precisely the technique that urban planners are experimenting with in Stockholm, Sweden.

According to a recent article in *The Wall Street Journal*, automobile traffic in Stockholm is such a nightmare, especially during morning and evening rush hours, that the city has undertaken an experimental test of "the world's most sophisticated traffic-management system." Traffic engineers and urban planners face a particularly difficult problem in Stockholm, because the metropolitan business district spans a number of small islands that are linked by several bridges. The drive into the city at the peak morning rush hour usually takes three times as long as it does during off-peak hours. The traffic control system charges drivers tolls that vary according to the time of day. To implement this complex pricing scheme, the Swedish government contracted with IBM Corporation to install transponder boxes that attach to windshields for the purpose of deducting tolls from bank accounts. IBM also installed laser detectors to read license tags, and a video camera network capable of tracking every car in Stockholm. During a six-month test period, the dynamic toll system successfully reduced peak-period travel time by one-third—without building or expanding a single new bridge or road. The figure below shows the structure of the congestion-pricing plan employed in Stockholm. *The Wall Street Journal* article also reported that during the trial period of the congestion-pricing system, exhaust emissions and carbon dioxide fell by 14 percent in the inner-city area of Stockholm. And "some of the biggest beneficiaries weren't the drivers, but cyclists and bus riders." Bus ridership rose by 9 percent during the trial period.

Now that the experiment is over, Stockholm government officials have scheduled a voter referendum to decide whether to continue using the congestion-pricing system. A poll of voters at this time finds 52 percent of the voters back the pricing plan. Because the purpose of government intervention is to remedy market failures for the public good, it must be encouraging to Stockholm officials to see their plan winning broad voter support. Indeed, urban and transportation planners in Bangkok, New York, Dublin, Prague, Copenhagen, and San Francisco are all considering the same sort of congestion-pricing plan for their inner-city roadways.

[a]Officials know that some commuters are neither willing nor able to change their drive times or to substitute public transportation for private cars, while others have much greater flexibility in making their commuting plans. Based on our discussion of price discrimination in Chapter 14, you can see that congestion pricing is a form of second-degree price discrimination—even though capturing consumer surplus is not the primary purpose of time-varying prices. Transportation officials, who set the congestion prices, know that commuters vary in their responsiveness to congestion tolls. Commuters will self-select the toll they pay: commuters who place a high value on peak-time travel will pay the higher congestion price and those who place a low value on peak-time travel will pay the lower, off-peak tolls.

Source: Adapted from Leila Abboud and Jenny Clevstrom, "Stockholm's Syndrome: Hostages to Traffic, Swedes Will Vote on High-Tech Plan to Untangle Snarls with Tolls," *The Wall Street Journal*, August 29, 2006, p. B1.

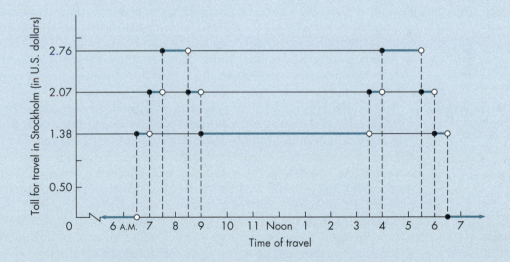

of the more widely used taxation methods here: *emissions taxes* (or *charges*). This method employs market incentives to encourage firms to choose the optimal level of emissions and control activity (called "pollution abatement"). To set the proper tax rate on pollution emissions, environmental authorities must first determine the socially optimal rate of emissions, which typically applies to a specific geographic area that regularly experiences "excessive" levels of pollution.

The optimal level of pollution (and abatement) Throughout this text, we have applied the reasoning of marginal analysis to solve a variety of optimization problems. Finding the socially optimal level of pollution provides one more opportunity to demonstrate the power of marginal analysis. To find the optimal pollution level, policymakers must be able to measure with a reasonable degree of accuracy the benefits and costs to society for different levels of pollution emissions. As you will see, finding the optimal level of emissions also determines the optimal level of effort for firms to expend reducing, preventing, or controlling pollution emissions from their production facilities. Such activity is called **pollution control** or **pollution abatement.**

pollution control (or abatement)
Costly efforts undertaken by firms to reduce or prevent emission of pollution from their production facilities.

The benefit accruing to society from reducing pollution is equal to the dollar value of damages from pollution avoided by pollution reduction or abatement. The measure of pollution damages to society includes all costs attributable to pollution, such as costs of illness to humans, value of lost productive and recreational use of environmental resources, cost to society of lost biological habitat, and so on. Measuring damages is a controversial "science" involving multidisciplinary analytical methods. You can learn more about this important area of research and methodology by taking a course in environmental economics or reading the textbook for that course. While the scientific and environmental cost data required to estimate accurately pollution damages are generally substantial and costly to obtain, the task must nonetheless be undertaken by government environmental agencies if they wish to make optimal policy decisions.

marginal damage (*MD*)
Additional damage incurred by society by discharging one more unit of pollution into the environment.

To find the optimal level of pollution, **marginal damage** caused by pollution must be estimated, that is, the addition to total damages attributable to discharging one more unit of pollution into the environment must be known. In Figure 16.7, the curve labeled "*MD*" shows marginal damage for various rates of pollution emission. As you can see by looking at *MD*, emissions cause no damage below a threshold level of 400 tons per year, after which each additional ton causes ever-greater marginal damage to society. The damage caused by the 600th ton discharged is $20. We can add marginal damages for all units discharged and obtain the **total damage** caused by any specific level of pollution emission. In this case, total damage caused by 600 tons of emissions is the area under *MD* from 400 units to 600 units, which is $2,000 (= 0.5 × 200 × $20). From this computation, it follows that the benefit to society of abating these 200 tons of pollution—reducing emissions from 600 to 400 tons—is the avoided damages of $2,000 per year. For this reason, the *MD* curve measures the marginal benefit of pollution control.

total damage
Dollar measure of all damages to society caused by pollution emissions.

FIGURE 16.7

**Finding the Optimal
Level of Pollution**

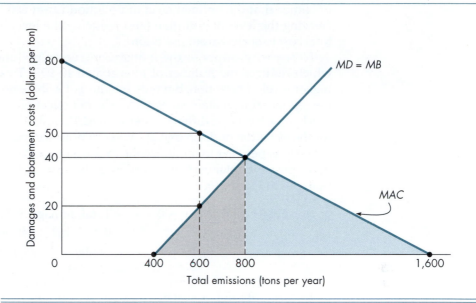

Reducing pollution emissions almost always requires an expenditure of resources on pollution control activities. Given that business owners are also members of society, their costs to abate pollution must be considered when policymakers determine the optimal level of pollution. The marginal cost of abatement, shown as *MAC* in Figure 16.7, gives the addition to total abatement cost of reducing emissions by one more ton per year. We must stress here that to interpret properly the *MAC* curve, you must recognize that abatement activity (the number of tons of pollution saved) *increases* by moving *leftward* along the *MAC* curve. The *MAC* curve intersects the emissions axis at the *uncontrolled* level of pollution, which is the amount of pollution that is discharged if producers make no effort at all to control pollution. In this example, the uncontrolled level of pollution is 1,600 tons per year. Because the cost of abating pollution usually starts off at a relatively low incremental cost and rises for higher levels of abatement effort, *MAC* rises as emissions fall (moving *leftward* from 1,600 tons per year to lower levels of emissions in Figure 16.7).

total abatement cost
Total cost of abating pollution; measured by the area under *MAC*.

Abating the 1,000th ton of pollution (resulting in 600 tons of emissions) requires producers to spend an additional $50 on abatement effort. The **total abatement cost** incurred by producers to abate 1,000 tons per year is the area under *MAC* from 1,600 tons *leftward* to 600 tons: $25,000 (= 0.5 × 1,000 × $50). At 600 tons of emissions (and 1,000 tons abated), the total cost to society for this level of annual pollution is the sum of total damage and abatement cost

$$\text{Total social cost of 600 tons} = \text{Total damage} + \text{Total abatement cost}$$
$$= \$2,000 + \$25,000$$
$$= \$27,000 \text{ per year}$$

Notice that the optimal level of pollution is not 600 tons per year because increasing the level of pollution (and reducing the level of abatement) reduces the total cost to society from pollution.

To see why, suppose the industry increases pollution to 601 tons per year, which reduces the number of tons abated to 999. Total damage rises with the higher level of pollution, but only by $20. Total abatement cost falls by $50 due to the reduction in abatement activity. The net effect on society of increasing pollution by one ton is the difference between MAC and MD, which is $30 (= $50 − $20) for the 601st ton of discharge. As you can now see, pollution should be increased to 800 tons per year to minimize the total cost to society from pollution. The minimum possible total cost of pollution is the sum of the areas of the two shaded triangles in Figure 16.7:

$$
\begin{aligned}
\text{Total social cost of 800 tons} &= \text{Total damage} + \text{Total abatement cost} \\
&= (0.5 \times 400 \times \$40) + (0.5 \times 800 \times \$40) \\
&= \$8{,}000 + \$16{,}000 \\
&= \$24{,}000
\end{aligned}
$$

To curb pollution to just 800 tons per year in this particular geographic region, environmental authorities may take a "command and control" approach. Let's suppose currently that no pollution control is happening, so 1,600 tons are discharged. Environmental authorities notify producers in the region that only 800 tons of discharge will be allowed henceforth. All producers may then be commanded to reduce pollution levels equally to accomplish a total reduction of 800 tons (= 1,600 − 800). The cost of compliance for the industry in this example is $16,000, the amount spent by the industry on pollution control efforts. Numerous policy shortcomings undermine the desirability of using this kind of direct command and control approach. Recently, environmental policymakers have turned to regulatory methods that create economic incentives for businesses to not only comply with emissions targets but to also go beyond compliance by investing in more pollution control assets and engaging in research and development to find new economically efficient means of controlling pollution. We limit our discussion to one of these methods: emission taxation.

emission taxes
Taxes levied on each ton of pollution discharged into the environment.

Optimal emission tax on pollution **Emission taxes** levied on each ton of pollutant discharged can create an effective economic incentive for firms to make pollution and abatement decisions efficiently. Figure 16.8 shows how an emission tax works using the same MD and MAC curves that led us to conclude that 800 tons of emissions per year are optimal, because this level of emissions minimizes society's total cost from pollution (including the cost of pollution abatement to reach 800 tons).

By setting the emission tax rate at $40 per ton, regulatory authorities create an incentive for firms in this industry to reduce pollution from the uncontrolled level of 1,600 tons per year to the optimal level, 800 tons per year. To see why this happens, suppose less abatement is undertaken, and the industry discharges

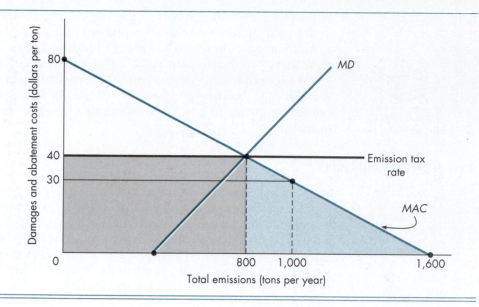

FIGURE 16.8

Optimal Emission Taxation

1,000 tons and abates 600 tons. At this level of pollution, firms can pay $40 to discharge legally one ton of pollutant or firms can spend $30 to abate the 1,000th ton of emissions. Obviously, the firm chooses to abate rather than pollute, and saves $10. In general, then, pollution abatement continues as long as *MAC* is less than the tax rate, $40 in this case. Firms will increase abatement effort and reduce emissions until the optimal level of pollution is reached at 800 tons of emissions. Notice that the industry will not reduce its pollution below 800 units, because then abatement becomes more costly than simply paying $40 to discharge the pollutant into the environment. So, by allowing firms legally to discharge all the pollutant they wish, as long as they pay $40 for every ton, regulators can motivate industry to pollute and abate at socially optimal levels, and collect $32,000 (= 800 × $40) in emission tax revenue from business in the process!

Emission taxation appeals to environmental authorities for several reasons. When authorities can estimate *MD* and *MAC* with reasonable accuracy, setting the efficient emission tax rate is a straightforward task. Once the tax rate is set optimally, regulatory authorities know that they can rely on the cost-minimizing behavior of business managers to choose the optimal levels of emissions and abatement. They also know that firms will have an incentive to invest in R&D for the purpose of finding less costly methods of abating pollution. A ton abated, after all, is a ton not taxed. Businesses may well prefer to have old-fashioned legal restrictions on the amount of pollution that can legally be dumped into the environment. A legal limit of 800 tons imposes only the cost of abatement, $16,000, on the industry, while businesses avoid paying $32,000 in emission fees.

Many other interesting issues concerning the regulation of pollution are covered in depth in courses on regulation and environmental economics. If you plan to work in an environmentally sensitive industry subject to a great deal of green regulation, you should plan to take at least one such course.

This concludes our discussion of externality as a source of market failure. We will now examine another form of market failure that arises when people cannot be forced to pay for consuming a good or service or using a natural resource.

Now try Technical
Problem 8.

16.5 NONEXCLUDABILITY

Suppliers of most goods and services can exclude people who do not pay the firm's price from consuming the firm's output. When access to a good or a scarce resource cannot be excluded, market failure may result. In this section, we examine two kinds of market failure caused by lack of excludability, which also possess some degree of the externality problem discussed in the previous section: *common property resources* and *public goods*. In the absence of any government intervention, common property resources are generally *over*exploited and public goods are *under*produced.

Common Property Resources

common property resources
Resources for which property rights are absent or poorly defined, which leads to overuse and underproduction.

Property rights to resources establish who owns them and who may rightfully use them. **Common property resources** are resources for which property rights are completely absent or so poorly defined that no one can effectively be excluded from accessing these resources.[3] Since everyone can use these resources and no one can be excluded, they will be overused and underproduced, which diminishes their contribution to social surplus. Some classic examples of overexploitation caused by nonexcludabilty are overhunting of whales, overhunting of bison, and overharvesting of ivory and forests.

The problem of open access to resources is very similar to the problem of negative externality. When a whaler takes his catch onboard, he establishes his property right to the whale under the "rule of capture" that applies to many nonexcludable resources. The whaler may well understand that leaving this whale to reproduce is necessary to insure a sustainable population of whales, but the whaler also knows that other whalers will take the whale if he does not. The whaler considers only his private share of the total social costs of harvesting the whale. In a fashion similar to the case of negative externality in the production of goods and services, nonexcludabilty drives a wedge between private and social cost of resource use, causing the resource to be overexploited.

---

[3] Economists define several types of resources that are plagued with problems of inefficient use stemming from lack of ownership: open-access resources, common pool resources, and common property resources. For our purposes, we will lump the three categories together as common property resources.

TABLE 16.1

Overexploitation of Common Property Resources

		BP's production rate	
		Fast	Slow
Shell's production rate	**Fast**	A **75,** *75*	B **175,** *50*
	Slow	C **50,** *175*	D **150,** *150*

Payoffs in millions of barrels of oil recovered.

You may also see here some similarity to strategic decision making in that one person's decision to take a resource depends on his belief about how others will decide to use the resource. Nonexcludability can create a prisoners' dilemma for resource exploitation. The gain to society from conservation is lost or severely undermined when weak property rights make "use it or lose it" a dominant strategy. We can best demonstrate this with a fictional example of a commonly owned underground pool of oil. Suppose the pool of oil flows under land owned by two companies, Shell and BP. Each company drills a well on its property into the common underground pool of oil. Geologists at both companies explain to managers that to get the maximum total number of barrels of oil, the oil must be pumped out of the ground slowly, so that pressure is maintained uniformly across the pool. Rapid pumping of the oil *by either company* will cause total yield to fall sharply. Unfortunately, property rights to the oil are poorly defined, and the "rule of capture" applies. Shell and BP share the right to pump the oil, but they only own the oil that comes out of their own company's well. This sets up a "use it or lose it" property rights situation.

Table 16.1 shows the payoffs according to the production rate each firm chooses. If both firms choose a "slow" (and equal) rate of production, the maximum total amount of oil that can be pumped from this field is 300 million barrels (approximately a 15-day supply for the United States), as given by cell D in the payoff table. Because the firms pump at equal rates in cell D, each firm gets 150 million barrels of oil. If either firm decides to pump "fast" while the other firm pumps "slow," the faster-pumping firm gets 175 million tons and the slower firm gets 50 million tons. Of course this diminishes the total amount of oil (225 million barrels is less than 300 million barrels). An even less desirable outcome results when both firms choose "fast" and each firm gets only 75 million barrels, for a total production from this pool of 150 million barrels.

Let's suppose each firm chooses its production rate simultaneously in a one-time decision, perhaps because all the oil is pumped out before either firm can reconsider its production decision. Using the techniques of solving games discussed in Chapter 13, you can see that both firms have dominant strategies: produce "fast." Each firm knows that the other firm can gain by cheating on any agreement they might make to both pump slowly. In cell B, Shell pumps at a fast rate while BP pumps at a slow rate, and Shell gets 25 million more barrels from the common pool than it would get if it cooperated with BP by pumping slowly. And, as Shell knows, BP has exactly the same incentive to cheat. Both firms see that they will both be better off if they cooperate by pumping slowly, but the prospect that the other will cheat makes pumping "fast" a dominant strategy. As in every prisoners' dilemma game, both parties play their dominant strategies (cell A) and both are worse off than if they had cooperated (cell D).

While the payoffs in this example are hypothetical, the problem certainly is not. By overpumping this pool, pressure falls, which creates numerous smaller pockets of oil that cannot be reached by any single well, and this effectively dooms recovery until drilling technology or crude prices advance sufficiently to make recovery economically feasible. To protect this mineral resource from this tragic outcome, government policymakers have several options. Government could take the property rights to the oil and assume the role of oil producer. Of course this option destroys the incentive for Shell or BP to search for oil in the first place. A second option is for government to regulate production by using government geologists to determine the efficient rate of production and then monitor Shell and BP to make sure neither firm exceeds this regulated rate of production. A third option is to fix the property rights problem that created the "use it or lose it" strategy in the first place. **Unitization** is a method of accomplishing this by defining property rights so that each owner of the oil pool possesses equal rights to the oil, regardless of who pumps it out of the ground. Government officials then simply monitor and enforce the unitized property rights. With unitized property rights, all owners will now wish to cooperate by producing at a rate that maximizes the total output (and value to society) of the oil pool.

Because property rights issues can be complicated to analyze, we cannot offer a simple policy recommendation that applies to all situations of market failure caused by nonexcludable access to resources. Improving property rights, however, can be a powerful tool for saving whales, elephants, bison, fish, forests, minerals, species, and the environment. Many environmentalists now believe that efficient assignment of property rights combined with market incentives can successfully replace many ineffective government regulations.

Public Goods

Public goods are characterized by two properties: they are nonexcludable and they are nondepletable. In the case of public goods, the problem of nonexcludabiltiy is called the **free-rider problem:** suppliers of a good cannot prevent nonpayers from consuming the good or service. If the free-rider problem is severe, firms cannot collect sufficient revenue to cover costs, and no firm will produce any of the afflicted good. A good is **nondepletable** (or nonrivalrous) in consumption if one person's consumption of the good causes no reduction in the amount or

---

unitization
Assigning equal property rights to a resource, regardless of which owner produces and sells the resource.

Now try Technical Problem 9.

public goods
Goods that are both non excludable and nondepletable.

free-rider problem
Inability of suppliers to prevent nonpayers from consuming their output.

nondepletable
One person's consumption of a good causes no reduction in the quantity or quality available to other members of society.

quality of the good available for consumption by other members of society. By this definition, most goods that are called public goods simply because government supplies them are not actually true public goods.

Either one of the two properties can, by itself, create a problem for the provision of public goods. Taken together, these two properties can completely eliminate the private provision of such goods, necessitating government provision of *pure* public goods. Goods that possess one or the other of these two properties, in varying degrees of severity, are not *pure* public goods and may be reasonably well supplied by profit-maximizing firms. It is best to view "pureness" of public goods as a matter of degree.

Perhaps the best example of a pure public good is national defense. Once national defense is provided for one citizen it cannot be withheld from any other citizen (nonexcludable). It is easy to be a free-rider of national defense. Furthermore, one citizen can consume national defense without depleting the amount available to any other citizen (nondepletable). No profit-maximizing firm will supply national defense because no one will voluntarily pay for a service if he can get it for free when someone else buys it. Examples of pure public goods are few in number. There are, however, many goods that exhibit varying shades of "public goodness."

Consider the enormously profitable computer software industry. Microsoft's current operating system software, Windows XP, can be reproduced at nearly zero marginal cost for any number of users who want it. For all practical purposes, computer software is nondepletable. When a good is nondepletable, the marginal cost of production is zero. And, when goods can be produced at zero *marginal* cost, social surplus for these unusual goods is maximized by giving the good away—that is, the socially optimal price is zero. When Microsoft charges a price greater than zero for its Windows XP software (currently $199 per copy), the market for this software is underserved in that price exceeds marginal cost. Deadweight loss is generated, because everyone who places a value on the software below $199 will choose not to buy it, even though the price he is willing to pay exceeds marginal cost. Of course, some of this deadweight loss is offset by software pirates who free-ride by making illegal copies to avoid paying Microsoft $199.

As you can see from the Microsoft example, many goods that are not pure public goods will be privately produced and do not require government provision. It would be foolish to have government provide computer software just to prevent free-riders from consuming this nondepletable good. As a general rule, only pure public goods need to be provided by government agencies because private firms will not supply them at all. We summarize our discussion of public goods in the following principle.

Now try Technical Problem 10.

Principle A pure public good is nonexcludable and nondepletable. The inability to exclude nonpayers creates a free-rider problem for the private provision of public goods. Even when private firms do supply public goods, a deadweight loss can be avoided only if the price of the public good is zero.

16.6 INFORMATION AND MARKET FAILURE[4]

Market failure may also occur because consumers do not possess perfect knowledge. Perfect knowledge includes knowledge by consumers about product prices and qualities, including the hazards associated with a product. Like all other activities we have studied, search for information is carried out to the point where the marginal benefit of more information equals the marginal cost of gathering it. Consumers choose the optimal level of search based on their individual valuations of benefit and their individual search costs. It is a rare consumer who finds it optimal to be perfectly informed. Even when consumers are optimally (but not perfectly) informed about product prices and qualities, market failure due to imperfect knowledge remains problematic. In this section, we will describe how lack of perfect knowledge may lead to prices greater than marginal cost and possibly too few or too many resources devoted to the production of some goods.

Imperfect Information about Prices

As we just mentioned, consumers will not gather every piece of information about prices and product characteristics as long as information is costly to obtain. We know already from a number of discussions in different contexts that the optimal amount of information for consumers occurs when the marginal benefit of its use is just equal to its marginal cost of collection. As long as marginal benefit is greater than marginal cost, more information will be gathered, but because marginal cost is positive, consumers will never collect information until marginal benefit is zero. This means that they will be unaware of higher-quality products or the lower prices some sellers charge for exactly the same product. Furthermore, the optimal level of information will not be the same across consumers. For some consumers the marginal cost of collecting information will be relatively high. Age, a handicap, high transportation costs, and the opportunity cost of a person's time all have an effect on the marginal cost of getting information. Marginal benefit will also be different across buyers.

The fact that consumers do not know everything about prices and product attributes creates an opportunity for product prices to vary from seller to seller. Recall that in the model of perfect competition with perfectly informed consumers, every seller charges the same price, because every seller's product is identical to every other seller's and consumers know this. In reality, as we are now arguing, consumers do not know the price that every seller is charging, even for homogeneous products. Consider even a particular product—like a 150-count box of white Kleenex tissue. Prices will vary from seller to seller, because all buyers will not go to the seller with the lowest price. The marginal cost of gathering information about the prices all sellers charge is simply too high relative to marginal benefit. Some sellers will, therefore, survive in the market charging relatively high prices, and consumers will not all be paying the same prices for the same goods.

---

[4]Portions of this discussion are adapted from S. C. Maurice and Owen R. Phillips, *Economic Analysis: Theory and Application*, 5th ed. (Homewood, IL: Richard D. Irwin, 1986).

In addition, firms will not be charging prices equal to marginal cost, because they know information is costly. As long as their prices are not outrageously high, customers will not find it optimal to continue searching for a lower-priced seller. The lack of information gives firms some degree of market power. As we demonstrated earlier in this chapter, market power creates market failure and deadweight loss. In this instance of imperfect information, market power arises not because of product differentiation, or even a lack of perfect substitutes. Market power emerges in competitive markets because imperfectly informed consumers do not possess knowledge of all producers and prices. Even though consumers are optimally informed, they are also (optimally) ignorant about the availability of substitutes. Their ignorance of substitutes creates market power for sellers of homogenous goods, something that did not happen in the model of perfect competition. Thus, imperfect information about sellers and prices can cause market failure in competitive markets.

Imperfect Information about Product Quality

Even when consumers have information, they may not be able to evaluate it correctly. Evaluating information about sellers and prices is not as challenging for consumers as successfully utilizing product quality information. Buyers are frequently unaware of undesirable side effects of chemicals in hair spray or new carpet. Foods may contain harmful substances that are listed on the label, yet the information means nothing to the shopper. And automobiles may have faulty designs that only an engineer can evaluate. We also know that producers sometimes provide false or misleading information to make consumers believe a product is better for the buyer than it actually is. Thus, possessing information does not guarantee that consumers will benefit from the information.

To illustrate the problem, suppose consumers of a product that is competitively supplied misjudge the quality of the product, either because the industry misinforms them or because they all mistakenly evaluate the quality information they possess. In Figure 16.9, market demand curve D is the demand when consumers evaluate product quality to be higher than the true level of product quality. Market equilibrium occurs at point C. Because the true quality is lower than the perceived quality, the marginal social benefit curve, MSB, lies below demand. The allocatively efficient level of consumption and production is found at point E where supply intersects MSB. Because the market price, P_C, does not equal marginal social benefit, a deadweight loss due to allocative inefficiency reduces social surplus by the area of the shaded triangle. Of course, if consumers underestimate the quality of a product, demand lies below MSB, and too little of the good is consumed.

The deadweight loss due to imperfect information about product prices and qualities opens the door for profit-seeking entrepreneurs to supply information services. Unfortunately, information is very much like a pure public good, so government provision of information about prices and product quality may be warranted if government agencies can provide information services at a lower cost than the deadweight loss consumers bear with their own individual search efforts.

FIGURE 16.9

Imperfect Information on Product Quality

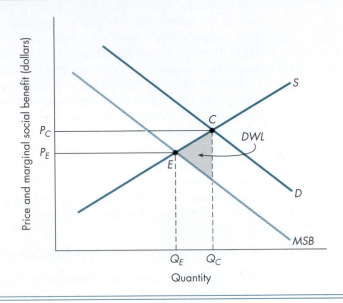

Information as a Public Good

Recall from our previous discussion that pure public goods are both nondepletable and nonexcludable. When one buyer consumes information about product quality, by reading an article in *Consumer Reports,* for example, that information remains fully available to other buyers in society. After the information is produced once, the marginal cost of providing additional consumers with product pricing and quality information is very close to zero. In the current digital age, it can be difficult for information suppliers to prevent nonpayers from receiving the information for free. It is certainly not impossible, however. Most city newspapers provide many of their news articles, sports scores, and weather forecasts online at no charge. By placing advertisements on their web pages, the newspapers can generate revenues from their Internet provision of information. A great deal of information now flows over the Internet, so the free-rider problem is apparently manageable.

In some cases, specific governmental bodies such as the Food and Drug Administration (FDA) and the Consumer Product Safety Commission (CPSC) may be necessary for the provision of information that is much costlier to produce than weather reports and sport scores. For instance, the CPSC annually inspects children's toys and alerts consumers to potentially dangerous features. In some cases, it may even set standards that eliminate the danger. Usually, the danger involved is reduced, but the cost is a more expensive product to consumers. For example, the Commission once determined that baby cribs were unsafe because infants could slip through the crib bars. It then set a maximum legal distance between the bars of cribs. Manufacturers as a group had to place bars closer together; this took more bars and cribs became more expensive.

ILLUSTRATION 16.2

Comparison Pricing in Health Care Off to a Slow Start

Consumers benefit from having better information about both prices and qualities because such information improves their ability to find the lowest price for the desired level of quality. However, as we explained in this chapter, obtaining information is costly and buyers will not usually find it optimal to gain complete knowledge about all prices and qualities. As a consequence of being imperfectly informed, consumers will make purchasing "mistakes," that is, with more and better information they would have made a different consumption decision. While it is usually too costly to eliminate all "mistakes," consumers should be willing to adopt new tools or methods for gathering information and comparing prices or qualities (or both)—especially when the new search tools can be employed for free or at a very low cost. Health care shoppers, however, have been slow to start using the many new search tools recently launched in the United States.

For the first time, consumers shopping for health care services are now gaining access to doctor and hospital prices for medical procedures, as well as software that makes comparison shopping across doctors and hospitals much easier. A number of major health care insurers—Aetna, Cigna, Humana, and UnitedHealth Group—are developing and expanding their online price search services to reveal rates negotiated with local physicians for various medical procedures and prices paid to local hospitals for health services. Several state governments are also getting into the information business by providing web-based services listing hospital fees. The primary purpose of these efforts to disseminate pricing information about health care services is to stimulate consumer search and competition among providers, thereby lowering costs to health insurers and state governments. Unfortunately, patients don't seem to be using these new information services. In a recent *Wall Street Journal* article

reporting on Aetna's experience with a new online pricing information program, almost all of the doctors in a survey done by Aetna said "their patients hadn't asked questions about their rates after the program was launched. . . . There really hasn't been any discussion (of prices)."

For all the effort and expense undertaken to create more transparent health care pricing, the usefulness of current pricing data still suffers from serious limitations. Currently, these web services cover a relatively small number of procedures—no more than 75 common medical services at any one website. And, in many instances, the price search software provides a range of prices, rather than specific prices, for each doctor or hospital. This creates uncertainty about the actual price patients will end up paying. None of the online price programs provides any information about service quality, so patients might worry that low price signals low service quality.

Perhaps the most important reason for the lackluster demand for pricing information can be attributed to the low insurance deductibles that many consumers still enjoy. Since they pay only a small fraction of the total doctor or hospital bill, patients don't have as much incentive to shop for low prices as they do when they are buying a new refrigerator for which they pay the entire price. According to Aetna, "as more consumers have plans with high deductibles, prices will become more important to them." We suspect Aetna is correct. However, until health care shoppers can access accurate information about a wide range of medical services by most of the suppliers in their local areas, market failure due to imperfect information will continue to keep health care prices higher than the competitive level.

Source: Adapted from Sarah Rubenstein, "Patients Get New Tools to Price Health Care," *The Wall Street Journal*, June 13, 2006, p. D1.

Such a change in product quality involves a trade-off to consumers. While standards usually relieve buyers of evaluating the hazards of products, they also make manufacturers conform to designs that restrict product variety or make products more expensive—and sometimes both of these things result. In the specific case of baby cribs, safety standards prevented consumers from buying less expensive cribs that were undoubtedly not as safe as those that conformed to the CPSC guidelines, but the *choice* was eliminated and the less expensive models may have suited some consumers' purposes and budgets.

Whether information problems justify government intervention is a controversial topic. Many economists argue that market failure stemming from information problems requires only additional information, not regulation. On the other hand, more is involved than simply acquiring a publication or reading a more informative description of a product. Once information is acquired, it must be studied, and if it is complicated or technically sophisticated, the costs associated with digesting the information can be high. Under these circumstances, many economists argue that safety and quality regulation are beneficial functions of government.

Now try Technical Problems 11–12.

16.7 SUMMARY

- Social economic efficiency occurs when two efficiency conditions are fulfilled: productive efficiency and allocative efficiency. Productive efficiency exists when suppliers produce goods and services at the lowest possible total cost to society. Allocative efficiency requires businesses to supply the optimal amounts of all goods and services demanded by society, and these units must be rationed to individuals who place the highest value on consuming them. The optimal level of output is reached when the marginal benefit of another unit to consumers equals the marginal cost to society of producing another unit, which is the point on demand where $P = MC$. Markets in perfectly competitive equilibrium achieve social economic efficiency because at the intersection of demand and supply curves, conditions for both productive efficiency and allocative efficiency are met. At the competitive market-clearing price, buyers and sellers engage in voluntary exchange that maximizes social surplus. *(LO1)*

- Market failure occurs when a market fails to achieve social economic efficiency and, consequently, fails to maximize social surplus. Six forms of market failure can undermine economic efficiency: monopoly power, natural monopoly, negative (and positive) externalities, common property resources, public goods, and information problems. Market failure creates an important and genuine opportunity for government to improve market performance in ways that can add to social surplus. However, absent market failure, no efficiency

argument can be made for government intervention in competitive markets. *(LO2)*

- The problem with market power is the loss of allocative efficiency. All firms that possess market power will maximize profit by pricing above marginal cost, $P^* > MC$, which results in less output than is socially optimal and an underallocation of resources to the industry. As a result of this allocative inefficiency, social surplus is lost on all the units not produced when price rises above marginal cost, and this lost surplus is called deadweight loss. Most industrialized nations rely on antitrust laws to reduce the social cost of market power. When the degree of market power grows high enough, antitrust officials refer to it legally as monopoly power. Monopoly power that would be targeted by antitrust agencies can arise in three ways: actual or attempted monopolization, price-fixing cartels, and mergers among horizontal competitors. Natural monopoly is a special kind of monopoly that would be harmful to break up through antitrust laws. Natural monopoly arises when a single firm can produce the total consumer demand for a product or service at a lower long-run total cost than if two or more firms produce the total industry output. Breaking up a natural monopoly is undesirable because increasing the number of firms in the industry drives up total cost and undermines productive efficiency. Government regulators typically allow natural monopolies to operate, but they regulate the prices natural monopolies charge and the profit they can earn. Regulators would like to force a pricing structure on natural monopolies that creates the social economic efficiency outcome under perfect competition. Under natural monopoly, no single price can establish social economic efficiency. Two-part pricing is a regulatory pricing solution that can maximize social surplus. *(LO3)*

■ An important cause of market failure arises when actions taken by market participants create benefits or costs that spillover to other members of society. When these spillover effects are beneficial to society, they are referred to as positive externalities, and when they are costly to society, they are called negative externalities. For many businesses, the externality of greatest consequence for their profits is the negative externality created by pollution, because government environmental agencies usually attempt to impose remedies on business polluters. Businesses create negative externalities by imposing external costs on other members of society without compensating the harmed parties. Negative externality drives a wedge between social and private costs of production, which causes producers in competitive equilibrium to overproduce the good or service. The loss of allocative efficiency due to negative externality creates a deadweight loss to society. Industrial pollution, which is one of the most significant negative externalities created by business, has become one of the most costly forms of government regulation for businesses. Without government regulation of pollution, businesses would certainly pollute beyond the optimal level. Pollution authorities have employed many kinds of regulatory tools to force businesses to control their pollution. Emission taxes, taxes levied on each ton of pollutant discharged, can create an effective economic incentive for firms to make pollution and abatement decisions efficiently. *(LO4)*

■ When access to a good or a scarce resource cannot be excluded, market failure usually results. Two kinds of market failure caused by lack of excludability are common property resources and public goods. Common property resources are resources for which property rights are completely absent or so poorly defined that no one can effectively be excluded from accessing them, and thus common property resources are generally overexploited and undersupplied. Improving and enforcing property rights is generally the best way to rescue common property resources from inefficient exploitation. A pure public good is nonexcludable and nondepletable. A good is nondepletable if one person's consumption of the good causes no reduction in the amount of the good available to other members of society. The inability to exclude nonpayers creates a free-rider problem for the private provision of public goods. Even when private firms do supply public goods, a deadweight loss can be avoided only if the price of the public good is zero. *(LO5)*

■ Market failure may also occur when consumers do not possess perfect knowledge. Perfect knowledge includes knowledge by consumers about product prices and qualities, including the hazards associated with a product. Market power emerges in competitive markets because imperfectly informed consumers do not possess complete knowledge of all producers and prices. Their incomplete knowledge about substitutes creates market power for sellers. Thus, imperfect information about sellers and prices can cause market failure even in competitive markets. Consumers may also overestimate or underestimate the quality of the goods and services they buy. If they overvalue (undervalue) quality, they will demand too much (little) product relative to the allocatively efficient amount. *(LO6)*

KEY TERMS

allocative efficiency

common property resources

deadweight loss

emission taxes

free-rider problem

government failure

marginal-cost-pricing

marginal damage (*MD*)

market failure

market power

monopoly power

natural monopoly

nondepletable

pollution control (or abatement)

positive (negative) externalities

productive efficiency

public goods

rationing function of prices

second-best pricing

social economic efficiency

subadditive

total abatement cost

total damage

two-part pricing

unitization

TECHNICAL PROBLEMS

1. The market for bagels in New York City is perfectly competitive. In New York City, the daily demand for bagels is $Q_d = 20{,}000 - 5{,}000P$, which is graphed as D in the figure below. The industry supply of bagels in NYC is $Q_s = -4{,}000 + 10{,}000P$, which is graphed as S in the figure.

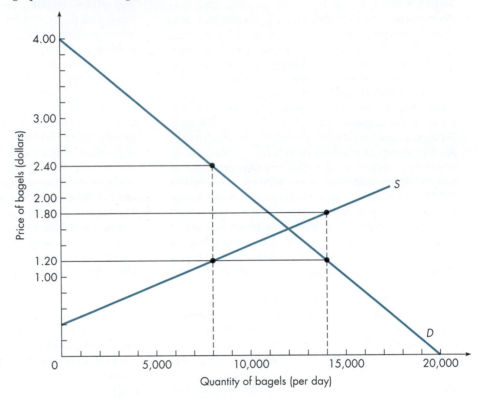

a. What is the market-clearing price of bagels in competitive equilibrium? How many bagels are bought and sold daily in NYC? (You can solve mathematically using the equations for demand and supply, or you can use the demand and supply lines in the figure, which are drawn precisely to scale.)

b. Explain why the NYC bagel market is expected to achieve productive efficiency in competitive equilibrium.

c. Suppose that NYC bagel businesses charged a price of $2.40 and sold 8,000 bagels per day. Explain carefully why society would benefit from an increase in bagel production.

d. Suppose that NYC bagel businesses produced 14,000 bagels per day and charged a price of $1.20. Explain carefully why society would benefit from a decrease in bagel production.

e. How does the market-clearing price found in part *a* serve to ration bagels to the consumers who place the highest value on them?

f. Does the NYC bagel market achieve social economic efficiency? Why?

2. Using the demand and supply conditions given in Technical Problem 1, answer the following questions concerning consumer, producer, and social surplus in the New York City bagel market.

   a. For the 8,000th bagel sold each day in NYC, compute the consumer surplus, producer surplus, and social surplus when the price of a bagel is $1.60.

   b. Compute total consumer, producer, and social surplus when 8,000 bagels per day are produced and consumed at a market price of $1.60.

   c. At the equilibrium price and quantity, compute social surplus. Is your computed value for social surplus in competitive equilibrium higher or lower than your computed value for social surplus at 8,000 bagels per day in part c? Is this what you expected? Explain.

3. Under the demand and supply conditions given in Technical Problem 1, suppose that the mayor of NYC asks the city council to impose a price ceiling on bagels sold in NYC. If the ceiling price is set at $1.20 per bagel, answer the following questions (and assume that bagels are somehow rationed to the highest-valued consumers):

   a. Does the ceiling price cause a surplus or shortage of bagels in NYC? What is the amount of the surplus or shortage?

   b. Calculate consumer surplus under the price ceiling. Are bagel consumers in NYC better off with the mayor's price ceiling on bagels? Explain carefully.

   c. Calculate producer surplus under the price ceiling. Are NYC bagel producers better off with the mayor's price ceiling on bagels? Explain carefully.

4. Use the figure below, which shows the linear demand and constant cost conditions facing a firm with a high barrier to entry, to answer the following questions:

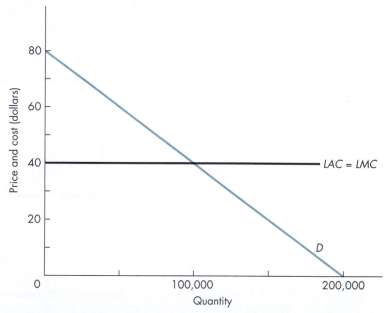

   a. The profit-maximizing price is $_____, and the firm will produce _____ units. The firm earns economic profit of $_____.

   b. Suppose antitrust officials find a way to remove the entry barrier to this market, and the market becomes perfectly competitive. Assuming that demand and cost conditions remain the same, what price and quantity will result? How much consumer surplus will buyers in this market gain?

c. How much deadweight loss is caused by the market power created by the high entry barrier?

5. Suppose a municipal water utility must pay $250,000 per month for its quasi-fixed capital inputs, the water treatment plant and distribution lines to homes. The figure below shows the cost structure of this utility for various levels of water service. Quantity of water consumption is measured in 1,000-gallon units per month. $AQFC$ is the average quasi-fixed cost curve, and LAC is long-run average cost. Long-run marginal cost, LMC, is constant and equal to $2 per 1,000-gallon unit. The inverse demand equation is $P = 26 - 0.00048Q_d$.

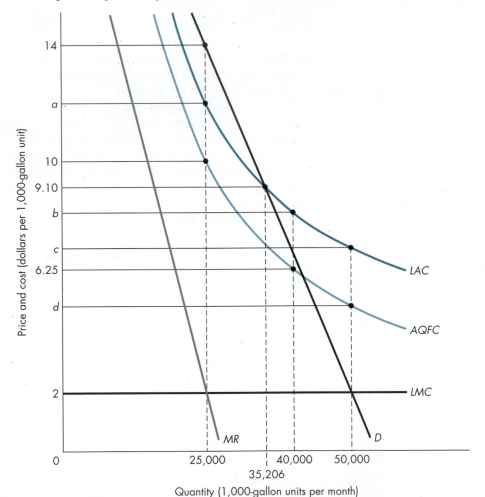

a. Find the value of costs in each of the blanks a through d in the figure.

b. When one firm produces 50,000 units of water service per month, the long-run total cost is $_____ per month.

c. If two equal-sized, but separate, water utilities provide the community with 50,000 units of water per month, the long-run total cost is $_____.

d. At 50,000 units per month, are costs subadditive for municipal water service?

e. Over what range of output, if any, are there economies of scale in municipal water service?

6. If the monopoly municipal water utility in Technical Problem 5 does not face any kind of government regulation of price or output:

a. The water utility will charge $_____ per 1,000-gallon unit, sell _____ units of water per month, and earn monthly profit of $_____.

b. The water market in this community will experience allocative inefficiency because there is a deadweight loss of $_____ per month.

c. To maximize social surplus, the price of water must be $_____, which results in monthly social surplus of $_____.

d. If the public service commission decides to impose the price on the water utility in part *c* that maximizes social surplus, the utility will earn _____ (profits, losses) equal to $_____. The utility will require a subsidy of $_____ to remain financially viable under this regulatory plan.

e. If the public service commission decides to employ second-best pricing, it will impose a water price equal to $_____ per 1,000-gallon unit, which results in a deadweight loss equal to $_____.

f. If the public service commission decides to design an optimal two-part pricing plan for the water utility, it will set the usage fee equal to $_____ per 1,000-gallon unit and set the monthly access charge for each of the 10,000 households equal to $_____ per month. The deadweight loss under this plan is $_____.

7. The firms in the competitive industry shown in the figure below generate a negative externality in the process of supplying the product. The marginal external cost imposed on society is given by the *MEC* curve, and the marginal private cost of production, *MPC*, is given by the industry supply curve, *S*. Industry demand, *D*, measures the marginal social benefits (*MSB*) of consuming this product, because there are no spillover costs or benefits caused by consuming this good.

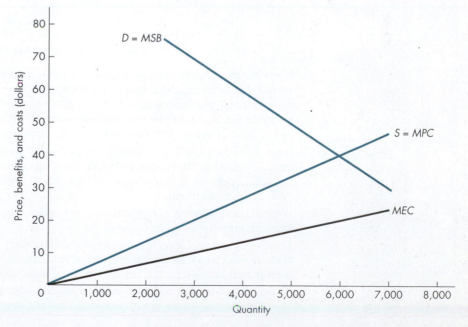

   a. For the 300,000th unit produced by this industry, the marginal external cost is $_____, the marginal private cost is $_____, and the marginal social cost is $_____.

   b. Construct the marginal social cost curve and label it *MSC*.

   c. In competitive equilibrium, the industry will produce _____ units. This level of output is _____ (productively, allocatively) inefficient because _____ is greater than _____.

   d. The competitive equilibrium results in a deadweight loss of $_____.

   e. The socially efficient level of output for this industry is _____ units, where marginal social benefit equals _____.

8. The figure below shows the marginal damage (*MD*) curve and the marginal abatement cost (*MAC*) curve facing an industry that discharges a pollutant into the environment.

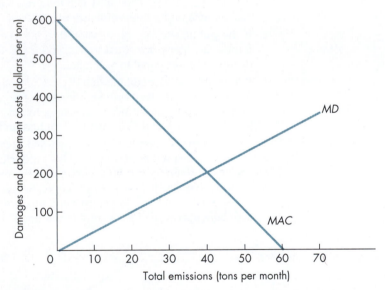

   a. If environment regulations do not restrict pollution by this industry, the industry would discharge _____ tons per month. At this level of emissions, total damage caused by pollution would be $_____ per month, and total abatement cost would be $_____ per month. Total social cost of pollution in this industry would be $_____ per month in the absence of any government restrictions on pollution.

   b. If environmental officials banned all pollution, forcing the industry to eliminate all pollution discharges, then total abatement cost for the industry would be $_____ per month, and total social cost of zero pollution in this industry would be $_____ per month.

   c. Why is zero pollution in this industry *not* optimal from society's point of view? Explain carefully using the figure above.

   d. The socially optimal level of emissions for this industry is _____ tons per month, which results in a total abatement cost of $_____ per month, and total damage from pollution of $_____ per month. Total social cost is $_____ per month.

   e. At the optimal level of pollution in part *d*, exactly what is maximized or minimized?

    f. What is the optimal level of abatement from society's point of view?

    g. If environmental authorities wished to control pollution in this industry by imposing an emission tax on pollution, the tax per ton of discharge should be set at $ _____ per ton. At this tax rate, the industry discharges _____ tons per month and pays a total tax bill of $ _____ per month. The industry abates _____ tons per month and incurs a total abatement cost of $ _____ per month.

9. What role do property rights play in creating common property resources? Why are common property resources subject to market failure due to nonexcludability?

10. *a.* What two properties characterize public goods?

    b. To avoid market failure, what price must be charged for public goods? Why?

11. How does imperfect information about product prices create market failure? Will too much or too little output be forthcoming in markets in which buyers do not know the prices charged by all sellers of the good?

12. In the figure below, consumers buy a good that is competitively supplied. Consumers are poorly informed about the quality of the good, and they believe the quality of the good is lower than the true quality of the good.

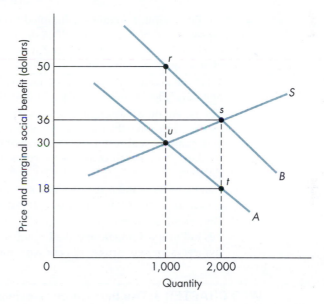

    a. Curve *A* in the figure represents _____ (demand, marginal social benefit) for the good in this market, and curve *B* represents _____ (demand, marginal social benefit) for the good.

    b. In competitive equilibrium, the price is $ _____ and _____ units are produced and consumed.

    c. Allocative inefficiency arises because, at the competitive output level, the marginal social benefit is $ _____, which is _____ (smaller, larger) than $ _____, the marginal social cost in competitive equilibrium.

    d. The deadweight loss caused by imperfect information about product quality is $ _____.

APPLIED PROBLEMS

1. Evaluate this statement: "The *only* time that a change in resource allocation clearly increases social welfare is when the change represents a 'win-win' situation."

2. What is wrong with this statement: "Whenever an industry fails to achieve allocative efficiency by producing too little output, a shortage arises."

3. How does a price ceiling undermine the rationing function of market-determined prices? How could rationing coupons insure that consumers with the highest values get the limited amount of a good supplied when government price ceilings create shortages?

4. Do you favor antigouging laws as a means of protecting consumers from high prices following natural disasters, such as Hurricane Katrina in New Orleans? If so, why? If not, why not?

5. Mirk Labs is a British pharmaceutical company that currently enjoys a patent monopoly in Europe, Canada, and the United States on Zatab (pronounced *zay-tab*), an allergy medication. The global demand for Zatab is

$$Q_d = 15.0 - 0.2P$$

where Q_d is annual quantity demanded (in millions of units) of Zatab, and P is the wholesale price of Zatab per unit. A decade ago, Mirk Labs incurred $60 million in research and development costs for Zatab. Current production costs for Zatab are constant and equal to $5 per unit.

   a. What wholesale price will Mirk Labs set? How much Zatab will it produce and sell annually? How much annual profit does the firm make on Zatab?

   b. The patent on Zatab expires next month, and dozens of pharmaceutical firms are prepared to enter the market with identical generic versions of Zatab. What price and quantity will result once the patent expires and competition emerges in this market? How much consumer surplus annually will allergy sufferers who take Zatab gain?

   c. Calculate the annual deadweight loss to society due to the drug firm's market power in Zatab. What exactly does this deadweight loss represent?

   d. Given your answer to part *c*, would it be helpful to society for competition authorities in Europe, Canada, and the United States to limit entry of generic drugs to just five years for new drugs? Why or why not?

WEB CHAPTER 1: The Investment Decision

View this web chapter via the Student Resources available through McGraw-Hill Connect®.

Statistical Tables

STUDENT'S t-DISTRIBUTION

The table on the next page provides critical values of the t-distribution at four levels of significance: 0.10, 0.05, 0.02, and 0.01. It should be noted that these values are based on a two-tailed test for significance: a test to determine if an estimated coefficient is significantly different from zero. For a discussion of one-tailed hypothesis tests, a topic not covered in this text, the reader is referred to William Mendenhall and Terry Sincich, *Statistics for Engineering and the Sciences*, 5th ed. (New York: Prentice Hall, 2006).

To illustrate the use of this table, consider a multiple regression that uses 30 observations to estimate three coefficients, a, b, and c. Therefore, there are $30 - 3 = 27$ degrees of freedom. If the level of significance is chosen to be 0.05 (the confidence level is $0.95 = 1 - 0.05$), the critical t-value for the test of significance is found in the table to be 2.052. If a lower level of significance (a higher confidence level) is required, a researcher can use the 0.01 level of significance (0.99 level of confidence) to obtain a critical value of 2.771. Conversely, if a higher significance level (lower level of confidence) is acceptable, the researcher can use the 0.10 significance level (0.90 confidence level) to obtain a critical value of 1.703.

THE F-DISTRIBUTION

The table on page 703 provides critical values of the F-distribution at the 0.05 and 0.01 levels of significance (or the 0.95 and 0.99 levels of confidence, respectively). To illustrate how the table is used, consider a multiple regression that uses 30 observations to estimate three coefficients; that is, $n = 30$ and $k = 3$. The appropriate F-statistic has $k - 1$ degrees of freedom for the numerator and $n - k$ degrees of freedom for the denominator. Thus, in the example, there are 2 and 27 degrees of freedom. From the table, the critical F-value corresponding to a 0.05 level of significance (or 0.95 level of confidence) is 3.35. If a 0.01 significance level is desired, the critical F-value is 5.49.

Critical *t*-Values

Degrees of freedom	Significance level			
	0.10	0.05	0.02	0.01
1	6.314	12.706	31.821	63.657
2	2.920	4.303	6.965	9.925
3	2.353	3.182	4.541	5.841
4	2.132	2.776	3.747	4.604
5	2.015	2.571	3.365	4.032
6	1.943	2.447	3.143	3.707
7	1.895	2.365	2.998	3.499
8	1.860	2.306	2.896	3.355
9	1.833	2.262	2.821	3.250
10	1.812	2.228	2.764	3.169
11	1.796	2.201	2.718	3.106
12	1.782	2.179	2.681	3.055
13	1.771	2.160	2.650	3.012
14	1.761	2.145	2.624	2.977
15	1.753	2.131	2.602	2.947
16	1.746	2.120	2.583	2.921
17	1.740	2.110	2.567	2.898
18	1.734	2.101	2.552	2.878
19	1.729	2.093	2.539	2.861
20	1.725	2.086	2.528	2.845
21	1.721	2.080	2.518	2.831
22	1.717	2.074	2.508	2.819
23	1.714	2.069	2.500	2.807
24	1.711	2.064	2.492	2.797
25	1.708	2.060	2.485	2.787
26	1.706	2.056	2.479	2.779
27	1.703	2.052	2.473	2.771
28	1.701	2.048	2.467	2.763
29	1.699	2.045	2.462	2.756
30	1.697	2.042	2.457	2.750
40	1.684	2.021	2.423	2.704
60	1.671	2.000	2.390	2.660
120	1.658	1.980	2.358	2.617
∞	1.645	1.960	2.326	2.576

Source: Adapted from R. J. Wonnacott and T. H. Wonnacott, *Econometrics,* 2nd ed. (New York: John Wiley & Sons, 1979).

Critical F-Values

Note: The values corresponding to a 0.05 significance level are printed in lightface type and the values corresponding to a 0.01 significance level are printed in boldface type.

Degrees of freedom for numerator $(k-1)$

Degrees of freedom fo denominator $(n-k)$	1	2	3	4	5	6	7	8	9	10	11	12	14	16	20	24	30	40	50	∞
1	161	200	216	225	230	234	237	239	241	242	243	244	245	246	248	249	250	251	252	254
	4052	**4999**	**5403**	**5625**	**5764**	**5859**	**5928**	**5981**	**6022**	**6056**	**6082**	**6106**	**6142**	**6169**	**6208**	**6234**	**6258**	**6286**	**6302**	**6366**
2	18.51	19.00	19.16	19.25	19.30	19.33	19.36	19.37	19.38	19.39	19.40	19.41	19.42	19.43	19.44	19.45	19.46	19.47	19.47	19.50
	98.49	**99.01**	**99.17**	**99.25**	**99.30**	**99.33**	**99.34**	**99.36**	**99.38**	**99.40**	**99.41**	**99.42**	**99.43**	**99.44**	**99.45**	**99.46**	**99.47**	**99.48**	**99.48**	**99.50**
3	10.13	9.55	9.28	9.12	9.01	8.94	8.88	8.84	8.81	8.78	8.76	8.74	8.71	8.69	8.66	8.64	8.62	8.60	8.58	8.53
	34.12	**30.81**	**29.46**	**28.71**	**28.24**	**27.91**	**27.67**	**27.49**	**27.34**	**27.23**	**27.13**	**27.05**	**26.92**	**26.83**	**26.69**	**26.60**	**26.50**	**26.41**	**26.30**	**26.12**
4	7.71	6.94	6.59	6.39	6.26	6.16	6.09	6.04	6.00	5.96	5.93	5.91	5.87	5.84	5.80	5.77	5.74	5.71	5.70	5.63
	21.20	**18.00**	**16.69**	**15.98**	**15.52**	**15.21**	**14.98**	**14.80**	**14.66**	**14.54**	**14.45**	**14.37**	**14.24**	**14.15**	**14.02**	**13.93**	**13.83**	**13.74**	**13.69**	**13.46**
5	6.61	5.79	5.41	5.19	5.05	4.95	4.88	4.82	4.78	4.74	4.70	4.68	4.64	4.60	4.56	4.53	4.50	4.46	4.44	4.36
	16.26	**13.27**	**12.06**	**11.39**	**10.97**	**10.67**	**10.45**	**10.27**	**10.15**	**10.05**	**9.96**	**9.89**	**9.77**	**9.68**	**9.55**	**9.47**	**9.38**	**9.29**	**9.24**	**9.02**
6	5.99	5.14	4.76	4.53	4.39	4.28	4.21	4.15	4.10	4.06	4.03	4.00	3.96	3.92	3.87	3.84	3.81	3.77	3.75	3.67
	13.74	**10.92**	**9.78**	**9.15**	**8.75**	**8.47**	**8.26**	**8.10**	**7.98**	**7.87**	**7.79**	**7.72**	**7.60**	**7.52**	**7.39**	**7.31**	**7.23**	**7.14**	**7.09**	**6.88**
7	5.59	4.74	4.35	4.12	3.97	3.87	3.79	3.73	3.68	3.63	3.60	3.57	3.52	3.49	3.44	3.41	3.38	3.34	3.32	3.23
	12.25	**9.55**	**8.45**	**7.85**	**7.46**	**7.19**	**7.00**	**6.84**	**6.71**	**6.62**	**6.54**	**6.47**	**6.35**	**6.27**	**6.15**	**6.07**	**5.98**	**5.90**	**5.85**	**5.65**
8	5.32	4.46	4.07	3.84	3.69	3.58	3.50	3.44	3.39	3.34	3.31	3.28	3.23	3.20	3.15	3.12	3.08	3.05	3.03	2.93
	11.26	**8.65**	**7.59**	**7.01**	**6.63**	**6.37**	**6.19**	**6.03**	**5.91**	**5.82**	**5.74**	**5.67**	**5.56**	**5.48**	**5.36**	**5.28**	**5.20**	**5.11**	**5.06**	**4.86**
9	5.12	4.26	3.86	3.63	3.48	3.37	3.29	3.23	3.18	3.13	3.10	3.07	3.02	2.98	2.93	2.90	2.86	2.82	2.80	2.71
	10.56	**8.02**	**6.99**	**6.42**	**6.06**	**5.80**	**5.62**	**5.47**	**5.35**	**5.26**	**5.18**	**5.11**	**5.00**	**4.92**	**4.80**	**4.73**	**4.64**	**4.56**	**4.51**	**4.31**
10	4.96	4.10	3.71	3.48	3.33	3.22	3.14	3.07	3.02	2.97	2.94	2.91	2.86	2.82	2.77	2.74	2.70	2.67	2.64	2.54
	10.04	**7.56**	**6.55**	**5.99**	**5.64**	**5.39**	**5.21**	**5.06**	**4.95**	**4.85**	**4.78**	**4.71**	**4.60**	**4.52**	**4.41**	**4.33**	**4.25**	**4.17**	**4.12**	**3.91**
11	4.84	3.98	3.59	3.36	3.20	3.09	3.01	2.95	2.90	2.86	2.82	2.79	2.74	2.70	2.65	2.61	2.57	2.53	2.50	2.40
	9.65	**7.20**	**6.22**	**5.67**	**5.32**	**5.07**	**4.88**	**4.74**	**4.63**	**4.54**	**4.46**	**4.40**	**4.29**	**4.21**	**4.10**	**4.02**	**3.94**	**3.86**	**3.80**	**3.60**
12	4.75	3.89	3.49	3.26	3.11	3.00	2.92	2.85	2.80	2.76	2.72	2.69	2.64	2.60	2.54	2.50	2.46	2.42	2.40	2.30
	9.33	**6.93**	**5.95**	**5.41**	**5.06**	**4.82**	**4.65**	**4.50**	**4.39**	**4.30**	**4.22**	**4.16**	**4.05**	**3.98**	**3.86**	**3.78**	**3.70**	**3.61**	**3.56**	**3.36**
13	4.67	3.80	3.41	3.18	3.02	2.92	2.84	2.77	2.72	2.67	2.63	2.60	2.55	2.51	2.46	2.42	2.38	2.34	2.32	2.21
	9.07	**6.70**	**5.74**	**5.20**	**4.86**	**4.62**	**4.44**	**4.30**	**4.19**	**4.10**	**4.02**	**3.96**	**3.85**	**3.78**	**3.67**	**3.59**	**3.51**	**3.42**	**3.37**	**3.16**
14	4.60	3.74	3.34	3.11	2.96	2.85	2.77	2.70	2.65	2.60	2.56	2.53	2.48	2.44	2.39	2.35	2.31	2.27	2.24	2.13
	8.86	**6.51**	**5.56**	**5.03**	**4.69**	**4.46**	**4.28**	**4.14**	**4.03**	**3.94**	**3.86**	**3.80**	**3.70**	**3.62**	**3.51**	**3.43**	**3.34**	**3.26**	**3.26**	**3.00**
15	4.54	3.68	3.29	3.06	2.90	2.79	2.70	2.64	2.59	2.55	2.51	2.48	2.43	2.39	2.33	2.29	2.25	2.21	2.18	2.07
	8.68	**6.36**	**5.42**	**4.89**	**4.56**	**4.32**	**4.14**	**4.00**	**3.89**	**3.80**	**3.73**	**3.67**	**3.56**	**3.48**	**3.36**	**3.29**	**3.20**	**3.12**	**3.07**	**2.87**
16	4.49	3.63	3.24	3.01	2.85	2.74	2.66	2.59	2.54	2.49	2.45	2.42	2.37	2.33	2.28	2.24	2.20	2.16	2.13	2.01
	8.53	**6.23**	**5.29**	**4.77**	**4.44**	**4.20**	**4.03**	**3.89**	**3.78**	**3.69**	**3.61**	**3.55**	**3.45**	**3.37**	**3.25**	**3.18**	**3.10**	**3.01**	**2.96**	**2.75**
17	4.45	3.59	3.20	2.96	2.81	2.70	2.62	2.55	2.50	2.45	2.41	2.38	2.33	2.29	2.23	2.19	2.15	2.11	2.08	1.96
	8.40	**6.11**	**5.18**	**4.67**	**4.34**	**4.10**	**3.93**	**3.79**	**3.68**	**3.59**	**3.52**	**3.45**	**3.35**	**3.27**	**3.16**	**3.08**	**3.00**	**2.92**	**2.86**	**2.65**

Critical F-Values (*continued*)

Degrees of freedom for numerator $(k - 1)$

Degrees of freedom for denominator $(n - k)$	1	2	3	4	5	6	7	8	9	10	11	12	14	16	20	24	30	40	50	∞
18 . . .	4.41	3.55	3.16	2.93	2.77	2.66	2.58	2.51	2.46	2.41	2.37	2.34	2.29	2.25	2.19	2.15	2.11	2.07	2.04	1.92
	8.28	**6.01**	**5.09**	**4.58**	**4.25**	**4.01**	**3.85**	**3.71**	**3.60**	**3.51**	**3.44**	**3.37**	**3.27**	**3.19**	**3.07**	**3.00**	**2.91**	**2.83**	**2.78**	**2.57**
19 . . .	4.38	3.52	3.13	2.90	2.74	2.63	2.55	2.48	2.43	2.38	2.34	2.31	2.26	2.21	2.15	2.11	2.07	2.02	2.00	1.88
	8.18	**5.93**	**5.01**	**4.50**	**4.17**	**3.94**	**3.77**	**3.63**	**3.52**	**3.43**	**3.36**	**3.30**	**3.19**	**3.12**	**3.00**	**2.92**	**2.84**	**2.76**	**2.70**	**2.49**
20 . . .	4.35	3.49	3.10	2.87	2.71	2.60	2.52	2.45	2.40	2.35	2.31	2.28	2.23	2.18	2.12	2.08	2.04	1.99	1.96	1.84
	8.10	**5.85**	**4.94**	**4.43**	**4.10**	**3.87**	**3.71**	**3.56**	**3.45**	**3.37**	**3.30**	**3.23**	**3.13**	**3.05**	**2.94**	**2.86**	**2.77**	**2.69**	**2.63**	**2.42**
21 . . .	4.32	3.47	3.07	2.84	2.68	2.57	2.49	2.42	2.37	2.32	2.28	2.25	2.20	2.15	2.09	2.05	2.00	1.96	1.93	1.81
	8.02	**5.78**	**4.87**	**4.37**	**4.04**	**3.81**	**3.65**	**3.51**	**3.40**	**3.31**	**3.24**	**3.17**	**3.07**	**2.99**	**2.88**	**2.80**	**2.72**	**2.63**	**2.58**	**2.36**
22 . . .	4.30	3.44	3.05	2.82	2.66	2.55	2.47	2.40	2.35	2.30	2.26	2.23	2.18	2.13	2.07	2.03	1.98	1.93	1.91	1.78
	7.94	**5.72**	**4.82**	**4.31**	**3.99**	**3.76**	**3.59**	**3.45**	**3.35**	**3.26**	**3.18**	**3.12**	**3.02**	**2.94**	**2.83**	**2.75**	**2.67**	**2.58**	**2.53**	**2.31**
23 . . .	4.28	3.42	3.03	2.80	2.64	2.53	2.45	2.38	2.32	2.28	2.24	2.20	2.14	2.10	2.04	2.00	1.96	1.91	1.88	1.76
	7.88	**5.66**	**4.76**	**4.26**	**3.94**	**3.71**	**3.54**	**3.41**	**3.30**	**3.21**	**3.14**	**3.07**	**2.97**	**2.89**	**2.78**	**2.70**	**2.62**	**2.53**	**2.48**	**2.26**
24 . . .	4.26	3.40	3.01	2.78	2.62	2.51	2.43	2.36	2.30	2.26	2.22	2.18	2.13	2.09	2.02	1.98	1.94	1.89	1.86	1.73
	7.82	**5.61**	**4.72**	**4.22**	**3.90**	**3.67**	**3.50**	**3.36**	**3.25**	**3.17**	**3.09**	**3.03**	**2.93**	**2.85**	**2.74**	**2.66**	**2.58**	**2.49**	**2.44**	**2.21**
25 . . .	4.24	3.38	2.99	2.76	2.60	2.49	2.41	2.34	2.28	2.24	2.20	2.16	2.11	2.06	2.00	1.96	1.92	1.87	1.84	1.71
	7.77	**5.57**	**4.68**	**4.18**	**3.86**	**3.63**	**3.46**	**3.32**	**3.21**	**3.13**	**3.05**	**2.99**	**2.89**	**2.81**	**2.70**	**2.62**	**2.54**	**2.45**	**2.40**	**2.17**
26 . . .	4.22	3.37	2.98	2.74	2.59	2.47	2.39	2.32	2.27	2.22	2.18	2.15	2.10	2.05	1.99	1.95	1.90	1.85	1.82	1.69
	7.72	**5.53**	**4.64**	**4.14**	**3.82**	**3.59**	**3.42**	**3.29**	**3.17**	**3.09**	**3.02**	**2.96**	**2.86**	**2.77**	**2.66**	**2.58**	**2.50**	**2.41**	**2.36**	**2.13**
27 . . .	4.21	3.35	2.96	2.73	2.57	2.46	2.37	2.30	2.25	2.20	2.16	2.13	2.08	2.03	1.97	1.93	1.88	1.84	1.81	1.67
	7.68	**5.49**	**4.60**	**4.11**	**3.79**	**3.56**	**3.39**	**3.26**	**3.14**	**3.06**	**2.98**	**2.93**	**2.83**	**2.74**	**2.63**	**2.55**	**2.47**	**2.38**	**2.33**	**2.10**
28 . . .	4.20	3.34	2.95	2.71	2.56	2.44	2.36	2.29	2.24	2.19	2.15	2.12	2.06	2.02	1.96	1.91	1.87	1.81	1.78	1.65
	7.64	**5.45**	**4.57**	**4.07**	**3.76**	**3.53**	**3.36**	**3.23**	**3.11**	**3.03**	**2.95**	**2.90**	**2.80**	**2.71**	**2.60**	**2.52**	**2.44**	**2.35**	**2.30**	**2.06**
29 . . .	4.18	3.33	2.93	2.70	2.54	2.43	2.35	2.28	2.22	2.18	2.14	2.10	2.05	2.00	1.94	1.90	1.85	1.80	1.77	1.64
	7.60	**5.42**	**4.54**	**4.04**	**3.73**	**3.50**	**3.33**	**3.20**	**3.08**	**3.00**	**2.92**	**2.87**	**2.77**	**2.68**	**2.57**	**2.49**	**2.41**	**2.32**	**2.27**	**2.03**
30 . . .	4.17	3.32	2.92	2.69	2.53	2.42	2.34	2.27	2.21	2.16	2.12	2.09	2.04	1.99	1.93	1.89	1.84	1.79	1.76	1.62
	7.56	**5.39**	**4.51**	**4.02**	**3.70**	**3.47**	**3.30**	**3.17**	**3.06**	**2.98**	**2.90**	**2.84**	**2.74**	**2.66**	**2.55**	**2.47**	**2.38**	**2.29**	**2.24**	**2.01**
40 . . .	4.08	3.23	2.84	2.61	2.45	2.34	2.25	2.18	2.12	2.08	2.04	2.00	1.95	1.90	1.84	1.79	1.74	1.69	1.66	1.51
	7.31	**5.18**	**4.31**	**3.83**	**3.51**	**3.29**	**3.12**	**2.99**	**2.88**	**2.80**	**2.73**	**2.66**	**2.56**	**2.49**	**2.37**	**2.29**	**2.20**	**2.11**	**2.05**	**1.81**
50 . . .	4.03	3.18	2.79	2.56	2.40	2.29	2.20	2.13	2.07	2.02	1.98	1.95	1.90	1.85	1.78	1.74	1.69	1.63	1.60	1.44
	7.17	**5.06**	**4.20**	**3.72**	**3.41**	**3.18**	**3.02**	**2.88**	**2.78**	**2.70**	**2.62**	**2.56**	**2.46**	**2.39**	**2.26**	**2.18**	**2.10**	**2.00**	**1.94**	**1.68**
60 . . .	4.00	3.15	2.76	2.52	2.37	2.25	2.17	2.10	2.04	1.99	1.95	1.92	1.86	1.81	1.75	1.70	1.65	1.59	1.56	1.39
	7.08	**4.98**	**4.13**	**3.65**	**3.34**	**3.12**	**2.95**	**2.82**	**2.72**	**2.63**	**2.56**	**2.50**	**2.40**	**2.32**	**2.20**	**2.12**	**2.03**	**1.93**	**1.87**	**1.60**
125 . . .	3.92	3.07	2.68	2.44	2.29	2.17	2.08	2.01	1.95	1.90	1.86	1.83	1.77	1.72	1.65	1.60	1.55	1.49	1.45	1.25
	6.84	**4.78**	**3.94**	**3.47**	**3.17**	**2.95**	**2.79**	**2.65**	**2.56**	**2.47**	**2.40**	**2.33**	**2.23**	**2.15**	**2.03**	**1.94**	**1.85**	**1.75**	**1.68**	**1.37**
∞ . . .	3.84	2.99	2.60	2.37	2.21	2.09	2.01	1.94	1.88	1.83	1.79	1.75	1.69	1.64	1.57	1.52	1.46	1.40	1.35	1.00
	6.64	**4.60**	**3.78**	**3.32**	**3.02**	**2.80**	**2.64**	**2.51**	**2.41**	**2.32**	**2.24**	**2.18**	**2.07**	**1.99**	**1.87**	**1.79**	**1.69**	**1.59**	**1.52**	**1.00**

Source: Adapted with permission from R. J. Wonnacott and T. H. Wonnacott, *Econometrics* (New York: John Wiley & Sons, 1970).

INDEX